W9-BXD-176

"A remarkable contribution to scholarship that is also a pedagogical treasure, *Women's Works* ... should be in every university and college library and open on the desks of everyone teaching courses on or including seventeenth-century English literature."

—Margaret Ferguson, Distinguished Professor of English, University of California at Davis, and 2014-15 President of the Modern Language Association

Your own review on Amazon.com, and your gift of *Women's Works* to other readers, will not only support our chosen charities but will also help to clear a place for the appreciation of women's history and early women's literature – in the classroom, the book club, and the family room. Thank you for your contribution.

WOMEN'S WORKS

Volume 3:
1603–1625

FIRST EDITION

Copyright © 2013, Wicked Good Books

First publication 2013.

Typeset in Times New Roman

Library of Congress Cataloging in Publication Data

Foster, Donald W., and Tobian Banton, eds.
  Women's Works
  Volume 3: 1603 - 1625

1. English Literature – 17th Century – Jacobean. 2. Women writers. 3. Women's history. 4. (Queen) Anna of Denmark. 5. Arbella Stuart (Seymour). 6. Cecilia Boulstred. 7. Lucy (Harington) Russell. 8. Elizabeth Brydges (Kennedy). 9. Anne Clifford (Sackville Herbert). 10. Margaret Cunningham (Hamilton Maxwell). 11. Elizabeth (Throckmorton) Dale. 12. Rachel Speght (Procter). 13. Ester Sowernam, pseud. 14. Witchcraft trials. 15. Margaret Fearnside (Fernseed). 16. Martha Scambler. 17. Elizabeth (Bessie) Clarkson. 18. Rose (Locke) Hickman (Throckmorton). 19. Dorothy (Kempe) Leigh. 20. Midwives. 21. Elizabeth (Knyvett) Clinton. 22. Elizabeth (Brook) Jocelin. 23. Elizabeth Melville (Colville). 24. Mary Oxlie (Reidhead). 25. Mary (Grey) Drayton. 26. Penelope Grey (Salter). 27. Anne (Grey) Masters. 28. Aemilia (Bassano) Lanyer. 29. Elizabeth (Tanfield) Cary. 30. Mary (Sidney) Wroth. 31. King James VI and I. (And others.)

Foster, Donald Wayne (1950–   ).
Banton, Tobian (1985-   ).

ISBN-10:   0988282062
ISBN-13:   978-0-9882820-6-3
Library of Congress Control Number: 2013935660

Wicked Good Books online address: www.wicked-good-books.com

*Dedicated in Memoriam
to my friend and collaborator,
Josephine Roberts*

WOMEN'S WORKS

Volume 3: 1603-1625

Edited by

Donald W. Foster

with Tobian Banton

WICKED GOOD BOOKS

NEW YORK

About the Imprint

Wicked Good Books, Inc., founded in 2012, is a registered not-for-profit cooperative, representing a consortium of scholars, artists, and writers. WGB is committed to book projects that significantly advance human knowledge, or that challenge received ideas about culture.

Submissions: Books intended either for the classroom or for scholarly reference are subject to the usual process of peer review, which may take up to six months. Books intended for the general market will be will be accepted from authors whose previous books have sold at least 10,000 copies; or by invitation.

Retail royalties from WGB titles support the educational foundation or charity of the author's choice.

Registered high school and college students with a family income of under $50,000 may apply for a free copy of any title in the WGB booklist.

Your book review on Amazon.com, and your gift of *Women's Works* to other readers, will not only support our charities but will help to make a place for the appreciation of women's history and early women's literature – in the classroom, the book club, and the family room.

Please visit WGB Inc. on the Web at wicked-good-books.com and "like" us on Facebook. Thank you for your contribution!

Every retail copy purchased of *Women's Works,* vol. 2, generates a donation to the Society for the Study of Early Modern Women

The Society for the Study of Early Modern Women

THE SSEMW is a network of scholars who meet annually, sponsor sessions at conferences, maintain a listserv and website, give awards for outstanding scholarship, and support one another's work in the field. SSEMW welcomes scholars and teachers from any discipline who study women and their contributions to the cultural, political, economic, or social spheres of the early modern period and whose interest in it includes attention to gender and representations of women.

Website: http://ssemw.org

• • •

Note for readers: Most of the poetry in this volume was first composed to be read aloud for an intimate audience. Various helps are therefore here supplied, so that extracts from *Women's Works* can be heard with pleasure, whether in the classroom or the family room. Spelling and punctuation have been normalized (without paraphrase or word-substitutions). Parallel translations are supplied for primary texts originally written in Scots dialect. Difficult words are glossed at the bottom of the page, not banished to a glossary at the rear. Accent marks are added to assist metrical fluency: an acute accent indicates a stressed syllable (*cóntent, contént*), while a grave (back-slashed) accent indicates an unstressed syllable (*blessèd, learnèd* [2 syllables.]; *blessed, learned* [1 syllable]). With a bit of rehearsal, there is no text in *Women's Works* that resists delivery by anyone with a high school education and a sense of play. (No musical settings are supplied for the song lyrics: readers may wish to invent their own.) All primary texts have been directly edited from the most authoritative manuscript or early printed text. Editorial interpolations, emendations and substantive variants are recorded in the Textual Notes (pp. 389-401) and signaled in the edited text by brackets or a degree symbol: [*interpolation*], *emendation°*.

Women's Works

Volume 3: 1603-1625

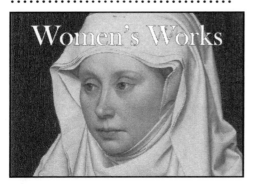

Women's Works

Panorama of London (1616) by Claes van Visscher

WELCOME to *Women's Works*, Volume Three

I will not say that women are better then men, but I will say,
men are not so wise as I would wish them to be…
—*Ester Sowernam* (1617), sig. D3r

QUEEN ELIZABETH died on March 24, 1603. King James died on March 17, 1625. In the interim, the people of a united Britain witnessed many romantic comedies and domestic tragedies, scripted by such wits as Shakespeare, Chapman, Jonson, Tourneur, Middleton, Webster, Fletcher, Beaumont, and Ford; whose comedies take as their central idea, "She is chaste: *I must have her*"; and in the tragedies, "She is not chaste: *she must die*." The true tragedies of the age, however, were experienced by women, daily, at all ranks of society. Among the unfortunate well-born: Arbella Stuart, Mary Wroth, Elizabeth Brydges, Margaret Cunningham, and Cecilia Boulstred (to name a few whose words and work are represented in Volume Three). At the bottom of the social pyramid, women led a hard-scrabble existence with no social safety net. Many even as children were put to hard labor, or prostitution. Dozens were put to death as adults for the crime of being poor, illiterate, angry, and superstitious. The "confessions" of hanged witches in particular provide a fascinating if pitiful glimpse into the daily lives of beggar-women in King James's Britain. Lacking property, social rank, and a significant male Other, elderly hags and unwed mothers wandered from manor to manor looking for work, or to beg a penny, a crust of bread, a pottle of milk; sometimes returning curses for cruelty or indifference – until someone's child took sick, or a dairy cow died, and then the local "witch" suddenly found herself before a hanging-judge, accused of killing by magic. Unfortunately, the most detailed record we have of their respective "confessions" is supplied by the very authorities who hanged the women, vetted their statements, and then authorized the trial-transcript for publication as a record of the defendants' depravity, thereby to reassure citizens that the State was ever-vigilant in rooting out clandestine terror cells comprised of penniless she-devils.

These threads of British culture were of course woven into the social fabric long before the succession of King James. But one reason that Jacobean women idealized "Elizabeth our late Soveraigne – not onely the glory of our Sexe, but a patterne for the best men to imitate" – was that, in the days of Queen Bess, one could sustain the illusion of the nation being cared for by a strong and capable mother, with liberty for many and justice for most. The House of Stuart brought changes to England, including peace with Spain, global exploration, and expanded trade. But most change, for most citizens, was for the worse. The nation's wealth became more tightly consolidated in the hands of the one percent who owned the Island's real estate – and who steadfastly resisted taxation, most especially for government-spending that would assist the poor. To raise revenue, King James sold "patents" and monopolies on the manufacture, the import and export, of virtually all traded goods, and for many services; which further enriched the few at the expense of the commonalty. The wealthiest lords and ladies entertained themselves at sporting events, at cards, or at dinner, waited on by troops of servants; traveled from one manor to the next, collecting rents from hard-pressed tenants; enclosed their lands so that the poor could no longer forage for food and firewood; and prepared their outfits, silks, and jewels for the next lavish Court masque. Meantime, poverty swelled, disease and crime increased. Hope for the future languished. With the death of the beloved and popular Prince Henry in 1612, national optimism presciently collapsed. [1]

The merchant class thrived well enough, thanks to increased trade, but in the latter years of James's reign, even the merchants fell on hard times. Violence at sea (firefights with competing Dutch and Portuguese trading companies, and with Barbary pirates) brought a declining return on investments, not infrequently a complete loss. Plus, the commonwealth was overtaken by a crushing economic depression that left most citizens without ready cash for such luxuries as tobacco or cinnamon – and in Scotland, no money even for food. What merchants' wives had to say of these developments is largely unrecorded: women of the virtuous middle class had no time for books other than the Bible, nor did much writing except in their household account books. The "middle" class is here represented by a few exceptional mothers who, before making their final exit, wrote books for their children, how-to manuals whereby to find "everlasting happiness without woe, want, or end" – but also, to set a maternal example, so that you will "remember to write a book unto *your* children, of the right and true way to happiness." [2]

---

[1] *Elizabeth…to imitate*] Ed. DWF from Ester Sowernam, *Ester Hath Hanged Haman* (1617), 21.

[2] *everlasting…happiness*] Ed. DWF from Dorothy Leigh, *The Mother's Blessing* (1616), 185, 16.

According to some contemporaneous reports, English-speaking ladies of the Jacobean period, although deprived of equal access to the printing press, nonetheless wrote freely to please themselves and their lovers; so much so, that in 1616 (at the height of the Swetnam controversy), clergyman Robert Anton threw up his hands in despair, fearing that his countrywomen were out of control, both as writers and as readers: [1]

> I much wonder [at] this lusty time—
> That women can both sing and sigh in rhyme,
> Weep and dissemble both, in bawdy meter,
> Laugh in luxurious pamphlets, like a creature
> Whose very breath some Ovid did create
> With provocations and a longing sate
> After some stirring meats. Wives covet books
> Not penned by artists, but the fruits of cooks
> Prescribing lusty dishes to enflame
> Their lusty fighting brood unto their game.
> Confections with infections of their kind
> Both rots° their body and corrupts the mind. […]

Rev. Anton may have constructed this dire report of female cultural depravity out of whole cloth, from his own paranoid imagination. At the very least, he was seeing something that we cannot: for what has actually come down to us from the Jacobean period – whether from a woman's pen, or in printed books that are known to have been read by women – is altogether chaste, modest, respectful, and dead-sober, containing no luxury for laughter from anyone.

What has survived is hit-or-miss, mostly a miss: Elizabeth Cary (for one) wrote at least three plays while young, plus many other "things for her private recreation, on several subjects and occasions, all in verse." In her later years, she penned biographies of "Saint Agnes the Martyr, Mary Magdalene, and Saint Elizabeth of Portugal"; plus a "paper of controversy" that "was thought the best thing she ever writ"; plus fresh translations of the Epistles of Seneca, the Meditations of Blosius, all or part of the *Replique* of Cardinal Jacques Davy du Perron; and of *Le mirroir du monde*, by Abraham Ortelius. What remains today of Cary's secular work is a rather dull prose history of the reign of Edward II; and one sad-funny play, *The Tragedy of Mariam*, which was printed in 1613 but "called in" soon afterward ("by her own procurement," though not, we believe, voluntarily); whereupon her dedication, bearing the Cary surname and subscribed "E.C.," was razored out or canceled. That was the end of Cary's publishing career until 1630 when – perhaps for a shilling or two to fend off hunger – she published, anonymously, Book One of her Perron. [2]

In 1621, Mary Sidney Wroth published her *Urania*, having high hopes for this, the first original novel in English by a woman author – and not by just any woman, but a Sidney. The volume also contains "Pamphilia to Amphilanthus," the first complete sonnet-sequence by a woman writing in English. The author of *Urania* is identified on the engraved title page as *"the right honorable, the Lady MARY WROATH: Daughter to the right Noble Robert* [Sidney] *Earle of Leicester. And Neece to the ever famous, and renowned Sʳ. Phillips Sidney, knight. And to yᵉ most exelēt Lady Mary* [Sidney,] *Countesse of Pembroke, late deceased."* Wroth dedicated the romance to her long-time best friend, Lady Susan (de Vere), first wife of Philip Herbert, earl of Montgomery, a favorite of King James; and Wroth was herself the partner of Lord Montgomery's elder brother, William Herbert, earl of Pembroke, a favorite of the Queen. These two sons of the "countess of Pembroke, late deceased," were two of the most powerful men in the kingdom. One might suppose, therefore, that her social connections would have insulated Wroth from censure; and indeed, the first critical notice was favorable: Henry Peacham praised Wroth, in print, as an author who "seemeth, by her late-published *Urania,* an inheritrix of the divine wit of her immortal uncle." But disaster ensued. As a *roman* à *clef* of the Jacobean Court, Wroth's novel painted an unflattering picture of the rich, powerful, and famous. Mary Wroth was accused of libel and denounced as a whore. [3]

---

[1] Ed. DWF from Robert Anton, "Venus," *The Philosophers Satyrs* (1616), lines 253-64;   *luxurious*] salacious.

[2] *things…in verse*] Cary, Anne, et al., *The Lady Falkland her Life* (see *Women's Works*, vol. 4, 203-13);   *called in*] *ibid.* In the Eton Library and Bodleian Library copies, cancelling the dedication also sacrificed the dramatis personae, printed on the verso of the same leaf. Cary's anonymous translation of Perron was printed at Douay in 1630.

[3] *seemeth…her immortal uncle*] Ed. DWF from Henry Peacham, *The Compleat Gentleman* (1622), 161-2.

In 1624 (long before Wroth died), Thomas Heywood mentions in passing "the ingenious Lady, the late composer of our extant *Urania*." He likens Wroth's extant *Urania* to the lost Works of Arbella Stuart, who "had a great facility in poetry, and was elaborately conversant amongst the Muses." But Arbella perished in 1615, in the Tower of London, for the offense of having married at age 35 without asking the King's permission; her poetry, which was never printed, perished as well. After *Urania*, neither did Mary Wroth publish another word, though she wrote at least 240,000.[1]

Women were not strictly forbidden to see their work through to the press. But the prevailing ideology did not provide much wiggle room concerning what kind of woman was permitted to take such liberties (chiefly, women of property). No less narrowly prescribed were the kinds of text deemed "appropriate to the sex" (chiefly, devotional meditations dedicated to children, or religious works translated from Latin, Spanish, French, German, or Italian). Mary Sidney Herbert's *Discourse of Life and Death* (1592), a translation of Philippe du Mornay, was reprinted in 1606, 1607, and 1608. Anne Lok's translation of Jean Taffin, *Of the Markes of the Children of God* (1590), was reprinted in 1608, 1609, and 1615. To these, Lady Elizabeth Russell added *A Way of Reconciliation of a Good and Learned Man; Touching the Trueth, Nature, and Substance of the Body and Blood of Christ in the Sacrament. Translated out of Latin by the Right Honorable Lady Elizabeth Russell, Dowager to the Right Honourable, the Lord Iohn Russell, Baron, and sonne and heire to Francis [Russell,] Earle of Bedford.*

Lady Elizabeth's copytext was written by Rev. John Ponet (1516-1656), an Anglican bishop who wrote to make peace between warring Christians. His *Diallacticon* was not otherwise available in print (even in Latin); and he had given his blessing to the book-project. Even so, Elizabeth Russell in 1605 was nervous, fearing it could damage her name to appear in print. "To seek the atonement of men is to be commended," she writes (in her Preface), "and it hath a sure promise of God: *Blessed be the peacemakers*. But I fear me, lest in greedily following the same, it happen to me which chanceth to them that part frays: while they seek others' safety, they bear the blows themselves. And I, while I study to make enemies friends, perhaps shall have small thanks." (Publish, and perish.) Russell dedicated the pamphlet to her daughter, with an apology: "Surely at the first I meant not to have set it abroad in print, but [for] myself only, to have some certainty to lean unto in a matter so full of controversy [...] but fearing lest after my death it should be printed according to the humors of other, and wrong of the dead (who in his lifetime *approved* my translation with his own allowance); therefore dreading, I say, wrong to *him* above any other respect, I have by anticipation prevented the worst." [2]

But if the women of Jacobean Britain generally wrote less, and fared worse, than women of previous generations, rebellion was in the air. Reform came initially from an unlikely catalyst. In 1615, Joseph Swetnam published *The Arraignment of Lewd, Idle, Froward, and Unconstant Women*, a compendium of chauvinist platitudes, bitterly expressed. Hugely controversial, Swetnam's diatribe had an unlooked-for benefit. By stripping the polite and pious veneer from off conventional gender discourse, Swetnam's *Arraignment* exposed the malice and insecurity that underlay a centuries-old system of masculine privilege. Joseph Swetnam was condemned or ridiculed in no fewer than six rebuttals. Whatever may have been said over the dinner table or in pillow-talk, no one in print came to the misogynist's defense. The prose polemics were further augmented by *Swetnam the Woman-Hater,* a comedy performed by Queen Anna's Men at the Red Bull Theater. In the penultimate scene, Swash the clown observes that Joseph Swetnam, as Misogynes,

> put his book i'the press, and published it,
> And made a thousand men and wives fall out,
> Till two or three good wenches, in mere spite,
> Laid their heads together, and railed him out of th'land. (sig. K1v)

In the play's Epilogue, the "Swetnam" character is hauled back onstage, wearing a *branks* (a scold's muzzle), being led by women who intend to have him arraigned, sentenced, and punished. His muzzle removed, Swetnam falls to his knees, promising womankind: "Here, forever, I put off this shape [of

---

[1] *the ingenious...Muses*] Ed. DWF from T. Heywood, "Of Poetesses," *Gynaikeion* (1624), 398; *240,000*] Wroth's lengthy draft of the *Second Part of Urania*, preserved today in the Newbury Library, was never completed.

[2] *Diallacticon*] Ponet's original Latin text, under the title *Diallacticon viri boni et literati, ... et sanguinis Christi in eucharistia,* etc. was eventually published in 1688; *To seek...the worst*] Ed. DWF from Elizabeth Russell, "The Author to the Reader," *Reconciliation* (1605), sig. A2v.

Misogynes,] / And with it, all my spleen and malice too, / And vow to let no time or act escape, / In which my service may be shown to you" (L1v).

Swetnam was not the only one who, presuming on masculine prerogative, skated too far upon cracking ice. King James made the same mistake. The entire economic system – whereby land, power, and revenue were concentrated in the hands of infinitely wealthy men – was by this time wearing thin. Those lords who owned the land, and who controled both production and trade, were sucking income from the labor of everyone beneath them, while inflating the cost of goods – "some by bribery, some by simony, others by perjury, and a multitude by usury; some stealing on the sea, others begging by land portions from every poor man, not caring if the whole commonwealth be impoverished" (Dorothy Leigh [1616]). The economy was a mess. Suffering of the masses was made worse by plague and smallpox in the cities, rising prices, food shortage, displaced families, and famine. Religion had become a cause of pain rather than peace. Promised the comforts of Christian faith by her minister, Rev. William Livingston, Bessie Clarkson replied, "If it were come, it would kith, it would bud forth. Oft and many a time have you said comfort was coming, but I cannot find it […] that cat that sits there is in better case nor I am. I shall beat down this carcase with beare-bread and water, but that doth not the turn."

Following the death of Queen Anna in 1619, King James presided over a melancholy Court and an angry commons. He was hated by his subjects; he despised them in return. He was in ill health. The Crown was deeply in debt, and still racking up enormous deficits. His plan to escape bankruptcy – a marriage between Prince Charles and the Roman Catholic Infanta of Spain – was both unpopular and improbable. Desperate for money and hoping to win support for "the Spanish match," James finally convened Parliament in January 1621, his first in seven years. But Britain was ready for change. Sir Edward Coke, Chief Justice and MP for the House of Commons, chaired a Committee of Grievances, a welcome move that unleashed a tidal wave of protest, most especially against monopolies sold by the Crown to restrict trade and profit the license-holder. The working poor and merchant class submitted their petitions against injustice faster than Parliament could read them: one petition, signed by "thousands of carpenters, smiths, plasterers, glaziers, painters, and other handicrafts men"; another in behalf of water-tankard bearers; another by brewers; another from wood-mongers; still others from the makers of felt, the makers of fustian, cloth-workers, hot-pressers, dyers, cutlers, clerks of the Custom House, wharf-keepers, and various other constituencies that had grown tired of legalized extortion. Among those who petitioned for relief or redress of grievance were many women, most of them widows who had been cheated of their jointure or property or had their children taken from them, and whose first appearance in the historical record was to join a groundswell of democratic protest against injustice.

As tensions rose between James and his Parliament, poets turned to satire, flyting the King, Buckingham, Bacon, and their crew, and complaining of a social system without either justice or compassion. Nearly everyone in England now agreed that Queen Elizabeth was a more effective sovereign than King James had been. In 1623 (while Charles was in Madrid wooing the Infanta), one unhappy poet placed in the hand of Elizabeth's effigy in Westminster Abbey a verse petition addressed to "Saint Elizabeth," begging her Majesty to look down from Heaven on her suffering commons; together with a second verse petition by the same anonymous poet, beseeching her Majesty to deliver it unto God, imploring Him to right England's wrongs. "Saint Elizabeth" became one of the most widely circulated political poems of the Seventeenth Century. It eventually reached print in 1642, as an indictment of Charles I, on the eve of the English Civil War.

Enraged that he should be criticized by satirical poetasters, King James wrote a verse reply to one such "libel" (as he called it), in which he figures himself as the deputy of God, having a divine right to rule unchallenged. A self-styled "Wiper-Away of the People's Tears," James threatened to silence dissent by putting his weepy critics to death. This foolish piece of royal poesy was answered with an unsigned verse epistle "by a Lady," advising the King to tamp down his rhetoric: "Condemn not, gracious King, our 'plaints and tears— / We are no 'babes' (the times us witness bears)." But James was not prepared to listen to his Parliament or his people, much less to a lady poet.

DWF

Anna of Denmark (1574 - 1619),
Queen of King James VI and I

> *La mia Grandezza dal Eccelso.*
> —Anna Dei Gratia Magnæ Britanniæ, Franciæ et Hyberniæ Regina [1]

A NNA, queen consort of Scotland from 1589, and of a united British Commonwealth from 1603, was the daughter of Frederick II of Denmark, a belligerent and philandering king who drank himself to death in 1588, the year of her engagement. Her mother was Sophie of Mecklenburg-Güstrow, a shrewd and learned woman who, as Regent of Schleswig-Holstein from 1590, governed the duchies with consummate skill and died in 1631, at age 74, the richest woman in Europe.

In 1580, Frederick offered Princess Anna's hand in marriage to James of Scotland, aged 14. Queen Elizabeth of England withheld her consent, which delayed negotiations; and King Frederick died in April 1588, before the prenuptials were signed, which delayed confirmation. But it all worked out. At age 13, in Denmark, Anna was united by proxy to James VI of Scotland, 22. Her dower included concession of the disputed Orkney and Shetland Islands, plus £150,000 (Scots) for the impecunious Scottish Crown.

Princess Anna sailed from Copenhagen in September 1589 aboard the *Danish Admiral*, with an escort of merchant ships that carried her trousseau. Westerly winds resisted their passage, trumped by a violent storm that nearly sank the fleet. Blown off-course, Anna's captain found harbor at Upsloe while ten of his twelve vessels limped back home. Word was sent to Scotland that the king's bride would be arriving late for the wedding, being forced to spend the winter in a small town of 8,000 on the coast of Norway.

Thomas Fowler – lawyer, diplomat, courtier, and a sometime retainer to the poet, Margaret Douglas, but best paid as an English spy in the household of King James – followed these developments closely. He had brokered the match between Mary Queen of Scots (James's mother), and Henry Stuart, Lord Darnley (Lady Margaret's son), which hadn't worked out: Mary's favorite courtier was murdered by her jealous husband (or at least, with his hearty approval); Mary's next favorite, Lord Bothwell, slew Darnley; and Queen Elizabeth beheaded Mary – an unhappy marriage, even by the standard of the British royals, who never set the bar very high.

None of that could be blamed on Thomas Fowler, he only arranged the match. But he hoped that King James would have better luck. England's Elizabeth was now aged 55 and single. Scotland's James VI was a leading contender to succeed her, as James I of England. All British Protestants wished him well.

The sticking point had been Scotland's demand for the disputed Islands, plus cash. In July 1589, Fowler wrote from Aberdeen to William Asheby (English ambassador in Edinburgh), to say that King James had at last struck a deal with Anna's brother, Christian IV:

for the cheffe of all is that the yonge ladi is so far in love with the Kinges majeste, as it were deathe to hir to have it broken of, and hathe made good proffe divers ways of hir affecyon, which his majeste is apt inowghe to require. [2]	for the chief of all is that the young lady is so far in love with the King's Majesty, as it were death to her to have it broken off! (and hath made good proof divers ways of her affection, which his Majesty is apt enough to requite).

Four centuries later, Fowler's rosy assessment found its way onto the World Wide Web, in garbled form: in their report on the courtship of King James, some 500 Web sites now mention Anna's "affection, which his Majesty is apt *in no way* to requite." Had the remark been written thus in 1588, it had proved an oracle. But the plain fact is that King James, at age 22, was quite keen to experience true love and a happily monogamous heterosexual marriage, which is something that he had read about, in books. Moreover, that his betrothed princess was now stranded in Norway gave him his first-ever opportunity to play the romantic hero. He did not disappoint. William Asheby writes: "The king's impatience for his love and lady hath so transported him in mind and body that he is about to commit himself, Leander-like, to the waves of the ocean." [3]

---

[1] *epigraph*] "My Greatness is from on High – Anna (by the Grace of God, of Great Britain, France, and Ireland) Queen": Anna's motto as queen of Great Britain.

[2] *for the cheffe...to require*] T. Fowler to W. Asheby (28 July 1589) *Calendar State Papers, Scottish Series*, vol. 10 (1936), p. 118; *apt enough to requite*] likely to love her as well as she loves him, when he meets her (so far, they had only seen one another's portrait in miniature and read the diplomatic correspondence.

[3] *The king's...ocean*] W. Asheby to Sir Francis Walsingham (23 Oct. 1589), ed. DWF from *S.P. Scot.*, *ibid.*, p. 568.

James knew of Anna's plight from her own pen, having received her letters of distress (in French), which she sent overland by Stephen Beale, a tireless Danish postman who journeyed from Upsloe to Kronberg to Calais; across the English Channel; and north to Edinburgh. Thomas Fowler, who was on hand when the King opened them, reports: "The letters of the young queen were tragical discourses, and pitiful, for she had been in extreme danger of drowning. King James has read them with tears, and with heavy, deep-drawn sighs." After reading those letters, nothing could dissuade the young King from sailing to Anna's rescue, in a Scottish vessel that was a poor match for the wintry blasts and deadly storms of the North Sea. [1]

This intrepid journey is rendered all the more remarkable when one considers the potential of an evil force at work: the tempest that took his bride to Norway, James believed, was raised by *witchcraft*; which was another thing that his Majesty had read about, in books. And what the witches did to Anna, they might well do, to him.

Embarking on 22 October, James reached Upsloe on 19 November, where he introduced himself to a surprised and grateful Danish princess. He consummated the marriage on the 23rd, then conducted Anna on a frosty pilgrimage across Norway and Sweden to Kronberg, where the newlyweds spent a jolly winter as guests of Anna's brother, a party boy. The royal couple arrived finally in Edinburgh in May, without money for wedding festivities or for the queen's coronation. (Anna's dowry was not yet arrived, in full) The royal Exchequer was so broke that James had to write to various lairds begging gifts and loans, not just of money but of cloth and flatware. From his boyhood friend the Earl of Mar, his Majesty asked to borrow a pair of silk stockings, as he owned none, and "Ye wad na that your King suld appear ane scrub, on sic an occasion!" [2]

Anna never got to meet Jane Kennedy, Lady Melville, the devoted friend who attended James's mother, Queen Mary, at her execution at Fotheringay. James appointed Lady Melville to be First Lady of the Queen's Bedchamber. Crossing to Leith, a ferry carrying Lady Melville was struck by another vessel. She drowned, together with two servants of Sir James Melville, who blamed the collision on witchcraft.

King James, a professed expert on witchcraft, put two and two together. He held that witches, mostly women, were a present and real danger to the Commonwealth, an opinion confirmed by the recent epidemic of sorcery in Denmark. The witches seemed to have him in their cross-hairs, and he was sincerely frightened. James ordered an investigation. A holistic healer named Agnes Sampson was arrested and brought to Holyrood Palace, where she was interrogated by the Privy Council, yet "stood stiffly in the denial of all that was laid to her charge." [3]

Scotland's royal couple in 1595, by Adrian Vanson (Courtesy of the National Galleries of Scotland)

---

[1] *The letters…sighs*] T. Fowler to W. Cecil (20 Oct. 1589), ed. DWF from H.M.C. Salisbury (Cecil)., *ibid.*, p. 438.

[2] *Ye…occasion*] You wouldn't want your king to look like a pot-scrubber on such an occasion. *Literary Gazette and Journal of the Belles Lettres* (1844): 395.

[3] *stood…her charge*] James Carmichael, *Newes from Scotland* (1592), A2v.

King James in a private interview determined that the defendant was indeed guilty: Agnes Sampson (as James told the Council afterward) possessed information knowable only to a witch, concerning what transpired between his royal self and his bride, Queen Anna, "at Upsloe in Norway the first night of their marriage." Yet Sampson would admit to nothing, even against the King's testimony, which was like calling the King a liar. [1]

James knew from the report of his prison wardens that accused witches could be proved guilty by inspecting their genitals ("the Devil doth generally mark them with a privy mark, by reason that [...] the Devil doth lick them with his tongue in some privy part of their body"). Agnes Sampson on the King's order was conveyed from Holyrood House to Edinburgh Castle, where she was stripped naked, shaved top and bottom, and tortured. The inquisitors fastened her to the wall of her cell by a witch's bridle. (This was an iron instrument thrust into the mouth having two sharp prongs pressed against the tongue, and two others against the cheeks.) She was kept without sleep, and thrown about with a rope pulled tight around her head – measures deemed too good for one who had commanded as many as 200 witches: "warn the rest of the sisters, to raise the wind this day, at eleven hours, to stay the queenès coming in Scotland"; and then, by magic, spied on King James and Queen Anna in their marriage bed. Still, "she would not confess anything – until the Devil's mark was found upon her privities." Tried on 16 January 1590/1, Agnes Sampson was garroted, then burned on the 27th. The cost to the Crown for her execution, including the scaffold and rope, came to six pounds, eight shillings, ten pence Scots. [2]

Sampson, it was learned, had peddled charms to ward off the pain of childbirth. Among her clients was Eupham McCallyum, tried for witchcraft on 9 June 1591, being indicted for "Consulting and seeking help at Anny Sampson, ane notorious witch, for relief of your pain in the time of the birth of your twa sons; and receiving frae her (to that effect) ane bored stane, to be laid under the bowster, put under your head; enchanted moulds and powder put in ane piece paper [...] the whilk, being practicèd by you, [...] your sickness was casten off you, unnaturally, in the birth of your first son [...] and in the birth of your last son." These remedies smacked not only of witchcraft but of blasphemous evasion of condign punishments set forth in Genesis 3:16 (Eve having sinned in the Garden, God said that all daughters of Eve must suffer the pain of childbirth as a necessary penalty: *i.e.*, no painkillers allowed). Lady McCallyum on these and sundry other charges was burned at the stake. The investigation eventually led to nine Master Witches (plus the Devil, "quha wes *with* thame, in likeness of ane black man," but he escaped custody). In 1597, King James published his manual, *Daemonologie,* to educate his citizens; and in the century that followed, more than three thousand accused Scottish witches were put to death; most of them women, most of them poor, uneducated, and defenseless. [3]

• • •

ANNA MADE CHANGES at Court, or tried. She found her husband's courtiers course and quarrelsome. She took a sharp dislike to the King's favorites, including Sir James Melville, and she irked the King by forming a close friendship with Beatrice Ruthven, whom James detested and whose entire clan he wished to exterminate. The queen learned English and Scots, and moved from palace to palace, to tidy up. She accommodated herself to a less opulent standard of living than she enjoyed in Denmark. But the King had at least one strange custom to which she would not yield: she would not have her firstborn taken from her to be raised by another.

In May 1593, Anna became pregnant. For her lying-in, she was transported to Stirling Castle, where the King himself grew up. Orphaned and crowned as an infant, James during his minority was raised by Scotland's Regent, John Erskine, 17th earl of Mar. King James and the 18th earl were virtual step-brothers. It was at Stirling Castle, on 19 February 1593/4, that Anna gave birth to her first child, a son. James directly gave the baby to the custody of John Erskine, earl of Mar, and to his mother, Dame Annabel Murray. What had worked so well for James was surely best for his infant son. The newborn prince was put to nurse, and Queen Anna was forcibly returned to Edinburgh Castle. James had little sympathy for his wife's protests.

Elizabeth, Queen of England, was named godmother. The christening was delayed until August, when Elizabeth finally sent the earl of Sussex to stand as her proxy for the baptism (with massy cups of gold and silver, which James melted for coining, and spent). The King named his son Henry Frederick, after Elizabeth's father (Henry VIII) and Anna's father (Frederick II). The baptism over, Anna was permitted to see Prince Henry only on supervised visits. Her fury at this arrangement, and the King's recalcitrance, put a strain on their marriage. Marshaling allies, Anna enlisted the support of Erskine's political enemies. The domestic quarrels soon spilled over into political brawls – for which the queen blamed the Earl of Mar, and the King blamed his wife.

---

[1] *at Upsloe...marriage*] Carmichael, *ibid.,* A4r.

[2] *the Devil...body* and *she would not...privities*] ed. DWF from Carmichael, *ibid.,* A2v-3r; *warn...Scotland*] Robert Pitcairn, *Criminal Trials in Scotland* (1833), 1.2.236; *twa*] two; *ane bored stane*] a stone with a hold bored through it; *bowster*] bolster, pillow; *whilk*] which; *sickness*] pain; *cost to the Crown*] Scottish Burgh Records Society, *Accounts of the Lord High Treasurer of Scotland* (1591).

[3] *Consulting...son*] Robert Chambers (1874), 1.217; *qua...thame*] was with them (Pitcairn, *ibid.*).

On 24 July 1595, following an attempt by Anna to kidnap Henry, James ordered tighter security; virtually eliminated his wife's access to the prince; and commanded Erskine not to surrender custody to the queen (or to any of her allies) for any reason whatever – not even in the event of the King's own death – until Prince Henry reached eighteen years of age. Anna that month had a miscarriage, which she blamed on the Earl of Mar.

A year later, Anna gave birth to the Princess Elizabeth (later queen of Bohemia); and in November 1600, to another son, Prince Charles (later King of Britain). But Anna could not rest content without Henry.

• • •

The Succession

JAMES VI of Scotland rode out of Edinburgh on 5 April 1603, with a great entourage. Destination: London, to be crowned James I of the British Commonwealth. The Earl of Mar accompanied the King, leaving Prince Henry in the custody of his wife, Lady Mary Erskine. Queen Anna, pregnant, was commanded to wait twenty days before leaving Scotland: the King needed time to appoint her English household and her new ladies in waiting. She was then to follow him to England. He would send her instructions, and transportation.

Elizabeth was buried 28 April. The next day, Lucy Russell, countess of Bedford, led a voluntary expedition to Scotland, to network with the new queen. She was accompanied by ladies Anne Harington (her mother); Dorothy Hastings, Elizabeth Hatton, and sundry others, all hoping for preferment.

The official embassage followed. On 2 May, the King dispatched to Berwick an envoy of six lords, accompanied by six ladies whom he had selected to attend the queen. On or about the same day, James sent Lord Mar back north to fetch Prince Henry from Stirling Castle. The earl would take the prince to Berwick, and there meet Queen Anna, with Lady Elizabeth and baby Charles. When all were gathered, they would set out together for London. But Anna without waiting put Lady Marr on notice: I will be coming for my son. [1]

Eight-year-old Prince Henry may have had the same idea. He wrote to his mother, asking to see her:

Prince Henry to his mother, Queen Anna (April 1603)°

Madame, and most honored Mother [...]

Seeing by his Majesty's departing, I will lose that benefit which I had by his frequent visitation, I must humbly request your Majesty to supply that in-lack by *your* presence (which I have more just cause to crave, that I have wanted it so long, to my great grief and displeasure); to the end that your majesty, by sight, may have (as I hope) the greater matter to love me; and I likewise may be encouraged to go forward in well-doing and to honor your majesty with a due reverence, as appertains to me, who is your majesty's most obedient and dutiful son,

Henry

• • •

That was all the encouragement Queen Anna needed. Needing money, she wrote to George Herriot (since 1597, court goldsmith and jeweler), asking to borrow £200. (This, her first extant letter, is in Scots: "Ane precept of the queen: I earnestlie dissyr youe present to send me tua hundrethe pundes with all expidition, because I maun hest me away presentlie.—Anna R."). Armed with Prince Henry's invitation, plus an armed escort of Scottish nobles (enemies of Lord Mar), Anna rode to Stirling Castle, to collect Henry from Mary Erskine before the earl her husband returned from London.

Lady Mar refused to open the gates to anyone but the queen (plus two attendants). Upon entering, Anna was shown the King's warrant, commanding that the prince must not be yielded up to his mother, on any condition whatever, except by a command from the King's own mouth. The queen refused to leave without him. [2]

The defiance of Lady Erskine, endorsed by the King himself, put the queen into such a rage that she had to be carried to the royal apartments at Stirling; where she remained, refusing to budge. Panicked lords of the Scottish Privy Council wrote to the King in London, seeking guidance. The lords came to reason with her, to no avail. The queen was now in such distress that she went into labor prematurely, in the home of her worst enemy, and on May 9th or 10th was delivered of a stillborn son. As Anna saw it, Lord Mar after having taken and kept her firstborn child, had now slain two others.

---

[1] *envoy*] James sent Robert Radclyffe and Theophilus Clinton (the earls of Sussex and Lincoln); William, Lord Compton; Sir Francis Norris (future earl of Berkshire); Sir George Carew; Sir John Buck; Elizabeth (Hastings) Somerset, countess of Worcester; Lady Frances (Howard) Fitzgerald, countess dowager of Kildare; Lady Anne Herbert, daughter to the earl of Pembroke; Lady Philadephia (Carey) Scrope; Lady Penelope (Devereux) Rich (wife to Robert Rich, mistress of Charles Blount); and Lady Audrey (Shelton) Walsingham.

[2] *Ane...presentlie*] *Literary Gazette, ibid.*: 394, as transcribed from Anna's holograph, MS then at Heriot's Hospital, current whereabouts unknown.

The archbishop of Glasgow was appointed by the Privy Council to carry this news to the King, together with letters of exculpation from the Privy Council, exonerating themselves and Lady Mar; and another from John Graham, Scottish Lord Chancellor, asking the King what to do: the queen would neither see the earl of Mar nor leave his castle without the prince. One dutiful lord made the mistake of suggesting to Anna that she was herself to blame for her disappointment: Although Anna had been brought up Lutheran, the Calvinist elders of the Kirk had found her dangerously tolerant of Roman Catholicism, and possibly a closet papist. Steaming mad, Anna wrote to James, reminding him that she was a woman of royal descent, a king's daughter, King James's wife, and Henry's mother; and she complained that his Majesty should prefer the earl of Mar to herself for the prince's care and education. That letter has not survived, only James's reply.

The King had to get Mar out of the way, and get Queen Anna to London, without a loss of face for either. He dispatched the duke of Lennox to Scotland, both to relieve Erskine and to reason with Anna. In his May 13th letter to the earl, James expressed his displeasure with the queen's "willfulness." He asked Mar to "give us up the names" of those who joined her "conspiracy" to abduct the prince, promising "due trial and condign punishment" for the would-be kidnappers. And he commanded Mar back to London, on the instant. [1]

Without waiting to hear from Mar, the King with the same post sent a letter to his wife: he denied having heard allegations from Mar that she was "upon any Papish or Spanish course"; Mar had said only that some of the lairds thought by force to have assisted the queen in abducting the heir apparent. Further to exonerate Mar, James stated that he had asked the earl to give up names (true); and that Mar graciously declined to do so, not wishing to implicate the queen (false, and false).

King James to Queen Anna (13 May 1603)°

My Heart,

Immediately before the receipt of your letter, I was purposed to have written unto you – and that, without any great occasion excepting for to free myself at your hands from the imputation of severeness. But now your letter has given more matter to write (although I take small delight to meddle in so unpleasant a process.) I wonder that nather your long knowledge of my nature, nor my late earnest purgation to you, can cure you of that rooted errour that any living dare speak or inform me in any ways to your prejudice – or yet, that ye can think they're *your* unfriends that are true servantès to *me*. I can say no more but protest upon the peril of my salvation and damnation that nather the earl of Mar, nor any flesh living, ever informed me that ye was on any Papish or Spanish course, or that ye had any other thouchts but a wrong-conceivèd opinion that he had more interest in your son [than you], or would not deliver him unto you. Nather does he farther charge the noblemen that was with you there, but that he was informed that some of them thoucht by force to have assisted you in the taking of my son out of his handès. (But as for any other papist or foreign practice, by God, he doth not so much as allege it.) Therefore, he says he will never presume to accuse them, since it may happen well to import *your* offense.

And therefore I say over again, leave these froward, womanly apprehensions! for I thank God I carry that love and respect unto you quhich by the Law of God and Nature I ought to do, to my wife and mother of my children – but *not* for that ye are "a king's dauchter": for quether ye waire a king's or a cook's dauchter, ye must be all alike to me, being once my wife. For the respect of your "honorable birth and descent," I married you. But the love and respect I now bear you is because that ye are my married wife, and so partaker of my honor as of my other fortunes. (I beseech you, excuse my rude plainness in this: for casting up your "birth" is a needless, *impertinent* argument to me!). God is my witness I ever preferred you to all my bairnès, much more than to any subject. [2]

But if you will ever give place to the reports of every flattering sycophant that will persuade you that *when I account well of an honest and wise servant for his true and faithful service to me*, that it is to compare or prefer him to *you*, then will nather you nor I be ever at rest, at peace. [...]

As for your dole made concerning it, it is utterly impertinent at this time. [...]

Praying God, my Heart, to preserve you and all the bairnès, [and] send me a blithe meeting – with you, and a couple of them.

Your awn,
James R.

---

[1] *willfulness...punishment*] Dalrymple, ed., *Memorials* (1762), 183-4.

[2] *bairnès*] bairns, children (MS *bairnis*).

Four years before, King James wrote *finis* to his *Basilikon Doron* ("Royal Gift"), addressed to his son, Prince Henry. In it, James counseled his son how to manage his life, his future wife, and, someday, the Scottish nation. The book is divided into three parts. The first describes those duties that a Christian king must yield to God. Part two discusses the responsibilities of office; and part three, proper conduct in daily life. Seven copies were printed in Edinburgh in 1599, one of which doubtless went to Queen Anna. James now authorized the book to be printed in London. Thousands of copies were sold, making it England's #1 best-seller.

His Majesty sums up in three precepts what's needed for a happy royal marriage:

King James, *Basilikon Doron* °

Keep specially three rules with your wife:

• First, suffer her never to meddle with the politic government of the Commonweal, but hold her at the economic rule of the house (and yet all to be subject to your direction).
• Keep carefully good and chaste company about her, for women are the frailest sex.
• And be never both angry, at once; but when ye see her in passion, ye should (with reason) danten yours. For both when ye are settled, ye are meetest to judge of her errors; and when she is come to herself, she may be best made to apprehend her offense and reverence your rebuke. [1]

• • •

Anna was not playing by the rules: she could not be persuaded to a truce, nor did she apprehend her offense, nor did she reverence the King's rebuke. When the duke of Lennox arrived bearing a letter and a jewel, plus the earl of Mar, the queen's wrath was rekindled, fueled by a week's bed-rest. Still without her eldest son, and having lost her baby, Queen Anna now so hated the earl of Mar that she refused to see him; refused to accept Henry from his hand; refused to depart from Stirling to Edinburgh, either with the prince or without him, if the earl of Mar travelled in the prince's company; and demanded reparations for the miscarriage. But Mar, by the King's commission, was forbidden to yield up his royal ward until they had arrived at Holyrood. Lennox wrote again to the King, who was now losing face in England on rumors that he could not rule his wife.

In the end, Anna won: Erskine bowed out, Lennox delivered up her son, and the queen proceeded to Berwick, a happy mother. But she did so at the cost of her reputation in the history books: few biographers have been able to pass over this episode without censuring the queen for willfulness or ill temper. Seen another way, however, Queen Anna's act of civil disobedience at Stirling Castle in the spring of 1603 was a moral triumph; chiefly regrettable in that, while saving one child, she lost another.

• • •

Unwilling to have his wife enter London looking as if she were newly arrived from the potato farm, James before leaving Scotland wrote to the Privy Council, sending for "such jewels and other furniture as you shall think to be meet for [Anna's] estate; and also coaches, horses, litters, and whatsoever else," together with the names of "some of the ladies of all degrees, who were about the late Queen," celebrities and others who could swell the ranks of Anna's royal progress southward. The Privy Council wrote back to say, respectfully, that it was illegal to send the Crown Jewels out of England. James asked again, requesting some of the late queen's less flashy accessories. Withholding the jewels, the Privy Council sent the requested transportation. Anna made her progress from Edinburgh to London wearing none of Elizabeth's jewelry. [2]

At Berwick, a new battle erupted. The King had already settled upon Sir George Carew to be the queen's Lord Chamberlain. Anna instead appointed Sir John Kennedy, a Scotsman. The King had sent the countesses of Worcester and Kildare to be her primary ladies in waiting. Queen Anna kept Jane Drummond, adding only Lucy Countess of Bedford – and appointed Lady Lucy's parents, Lord and Lady Harington, to be guardians of Princess Elizabeth. Those English candidates for office with whom she was unimpressed, Queen Anna assigned to posts that she knew were already reserved by the King for others; and in the meantime, she filled the vacant offices with her own appointees. The King, receiving this news, had an explosive fit of rage, uttering so many expletives in God's name that his astonished English Council feared a lightning strike. The King by letter reprimanded the Duke of Lennox, who had been charged with forming Anna's new household, and by him sent a message to his wife that "his Majesty took her continued perversity very heinously." Anna was commanded to cease and desist, and to begin her progress to London, at once, with the two older children. [3]

Anna deposited Baby Charles – as the King and queen called him until their dying day – with the laird of Fife, at Dunfermline. Accompanied by Henry and Elizabeth, and scores of would-be officers and attendants, Queen Anna departed from Berwick on June 2. Thousands of bystanders observed her progress, cheering her. But one wagon in the procession bore a tiny draped coffin, dead proof of the earl of Mar's villainy.

---

[1] *danten yours*] dampen your anger.

[2] *such jewels...Queen*] James to the Council (6 April 1603). Halliwell-Phillips, *Letters* (1848) 101; fr. Ashmole MS.

[3] *his Majesty...heinously*] Williams, *Anne of Denmark* (1970), 78.

The citizens and aldermen of York held a grand reception for the queen, June 11-15. Then it was on to Dingley, where the queen and her new first lady, Lucy Russell, and the rest of her company, were entertained by Sir Thomas Griffin. It was at Dingley that Queen Anna met Anne Russell, countess dowager of Warwick; Margaret Clifford (countess of Cumberland) and her daughter, Lady Anne; their cousin, Anne Vavasour; and Elizabeth Brydges; the last of whom fell instantly in love with Sir John Kennedy, to her own misfortune.

On 25 June, the queen came to Althorp (the seat of Lord Spencer, ancestor of the Princess Diana). There, she and her swelling retinue were entertained with *The Satyr*, a masque by Ben Jonson. Her majesty was much amused. In the decade to follow there would be many more masques presented for Anna's pleasure, each one more magnificent than the last.

After Althorp it was on to London. The King met the queen at Easton Neston, "with an infinite company of lords and ladies and other people, that the country could scarce lodge them." [1]

(The pillow talk of James and Anna that night is of course unrecorded; but one supposes that the late Agnes Sampson from her remote listening post got an earful.)

The royal procession arrived at Windsor on the last day of June. A great reception was held, to which all of the A-list socialites of England were invited, plus foreign dignitaries. Anne Clifford, then thirteen, was dazzled by the countesses and other ladies in attendance, "all of them most sumptuous in apparel, and exceeding rich and glorious in jewels, like the wearers." [2]

The European diplomats commenced their work of seeking intelligence. Ambassadors and visitors to England over the years were generally more impressed with Anna, than with James. A selection:

• • •

Maximilien de Béthune, Duke of Sully°

THE CHARACTER OF THIS PRINCESS was quite the reverse of her husband's: she was naturally bold and enterprising. She loved pomp and grandeur, tumult and intrigue. She was deeply engaged in all the civil factions, not only in Scotland (in relation to the Catholics, whom she supported, and had even first encouraged), but also in England – where the discontented (whose numbers were very inconsiderable) were not sorry to be supported by a princess destined to become their queen. […]

But [the King] was so weak as never to be able to resist, nor personally to contradict her [even] though she made no scruple publicly to show that she did not always conform to his sentiments.

He came to London long before her […] James wished she would not have departed from thence so soon (being persuaded that her presence would only be detrimental to affairs). He sent to acquaint her with his desire […] but she was very little affected by it. Instead of obeying, the queen prepared to quit Scotland after having (of her own accord and against the King's express desire) appointed herself a Great Chamberlain of her household. […]

[The queen] brought with her the body of the male child to which she had given birth in Scotland, because endeavors had been used to persuade the [English] public that his death was only feigned. She also brought with the Prince, her eldest son, whom she affected to govern absolutely […]

• • •

Zorzi Giustinian, Venetian Ambassador°

HIS MAJESTY is by nature placid, averse from cruelty, a lover of justice. He goes to chapel on Sundays and Tuesdays, the latter being observed by him in memory of his escape from a conspiracy of Scottish nobles in 1600. He loves quiet and repose, has no inclination to war, nay, is opposed to it – a fact that little pleases many of his subjects, though it pleases them still less that he leaves all government to his Council and will think of nothing but the chase. He does not caress the people nor make them that good cheer the late Queen did, whereby she won their loves: for the English adore their Sovereigns, and if the King passed through the same street a hundred times a day, the people would still run to see him. They like their King to show pleasure at their devotion, as the late Queen knew well how to do. But this King manifests no taste for them but rather contempt and dislike. The result is, he is despised and almost hated. In fact, his Majesty is more inclined to live retired with eight or ten of his favorites than openly, as is the custom of the country and the desire of the people.

The queen is very gracious, moderately good looking. She is a Lutheran. The King tried to make her a Protestant (others, a Catholic; to this she was and is much inclined, hence the rumor that she is one). She likes enjoyment and is very fond of dancing and of fêtes. She is intelligent and prudent, and knows the disorders of the government, in which she has no part, though many hold that (as the King is most de-

---

[1] *with an infinite company…lodge them*] Anne Clifford, Knole Diary (25 June 1603).

[2] *all…the wearers*] Quoted by Nichols, *Progresses, ibid.*, 1.195, from MS no longer extant.

voted to her) she might play as large a role as she wished. But she is young and averse to trouble: she sees that those who govern desire to be left alone, and so she professes indifference. All she ever does is to beg a favor for some one. She is full of kindness for those who support her, but on the other hand she is terrible, proud, unendurable, to those she dislikes. […]

Greatest and most eminent of all is Robert [Cecil], earl of Salisbury, first Secretary of State – whose authority is so absolute that *he* may truly be called "the King."

• • •

Guido Bentivoglio, nuncio to the Archduke °

THE KING OF ENGLAND […] eats and drinks much, and disregards all regimen. His chief exercise is hunting, for which he has so great a fondness that he consumes in it both the principal part of his time and (it may be said) himself also: for such continued and violent exercise must be rather pernicious than salutary. This is his first taste; his second is for books and literature, in which he professes to be greatly versed. […] Occupied by these two pursuits, the King of England lives remote and almost entirely estranged from the most important cares and concerns of the State […] more that of a theologian than a prince, a hunter than a king. […]

The queen, a sister of the King of Denmark, is praised as one of the handsomest princesses of her time. She shows a noble spirit, and is singularly graceful, courteous and affable. She delights beyond measure in admiration and praises of her beauty, in which she has the vanity to think that she has no equal. Hence she makes public exhibitions of herself in a thousand ways and with a thousand different inventions, and sometimes to so great an excess, that it has been doubted which went furthest, the king in the ostentation of his learning, or the queen in the display of her beauty. The queen is much attached to the free mode of life customary in England. And as she is very affable, she often puts it in practice with the ladies whom she admits to the greatest intimacy, visiting them by turns at their own houses, where she diverts herself with private amusements, laying aside all the dignity and majesty of a princess. She rails against the Italian jealousy of women, and has more than once said jestingly to the ambassadors of Italian princes, that their countrymen "ought to be banished from England, for fear of their introducing the fashion of jealousy." Her great passion is for balls and public entertainments, which she herself arranges, and which serve as a public theater on which to display her grace and beauty. She is fond of festivals after the mode of Italy, has a great taste for everything Italian, and understands the language very well.

• • •

From Windsor it was on to Hampton Court, but doubts were raised whether it were wise to enter the city. Already in June, the plague was hot and spreading. As a result, the public theaters were shut down, and the law courts adjourned for the summer; a month later, all public fairs were banned. Visitors were prohibited from approaching the royal Court to submit petitions, or for any reason whatever without an invitation. Even so, the contagion reached Windsor. Courtiers and officers who could not be accommodated inside the palace were lodged in tents outside, where (Anne Clifford reports) every day two or three perished of the plague.

Inside the palace, tempers were hot and quarrels brewing, chiefly between the Scottish and English lords, but also between the Essex and Ralegh factions. The lords whom Elizabeth imprisoned for their support of the 1601 Essex rising, James had pardoned; but the embers of resentment still simmered. On her first night at Windsor, Queen Anna was chatting politics (which she was forbidden to do) with the earl of Southampton, fresh out of prison. Anna expressed astonishment that so many great men did so little to defend themselves from dishonor. Southampton replied that if it were not for Elizabeth's censure, no private enemy would have dared oppose them. Taking offense, Thomas Lord Grey of Wilton said that they'd have been crushed by Ralegh's faction. Upon which, Lord Grey "had the '*Lie*!' warbled at him." The queen scolded the men and sent them to their lodgings. Hauled before the Council the next day, both men were sent to the Tower. The King and queen exchanged unhappy notes: James scolded Anna for causing the dispute. Anna demanded an apology from Lord Grey, who "offered me such a public scorn: for honor goes before life, I must ever think!" – and scolded King James for admitting to her presence such a rude man as Thomas Lord Grey of Wilton. [1]

The plague increased apace, the worst outbreak in forty years (close to three thousand fatalities every month in London alone; 6,400, in the first two weeks of September). Londoners blamed the epidemic on "the lewd and dissolute behavior of some base inhabitants" – "base inhabitants" being a euphemism for newly-arrived Scottish hordes. But many in England, more on the Continent, read the growing catastrophe as a sign that God disapproved of the English succession. If so, He was not alone. Much of the nation was soon grumbling as James and Anna embarked on a spending spree, plunging the English Crown into a sea of red ink, much of it in gifts of money and lands to Scottish lairds (to the fury of their English counterparts). The coronation – a private

---

[1] *had the Lie…at him*] Sir Dudley Carleton to Sir Thomas Parry (3 July 1603), ed. DWF from Anderson, *Balfour Letters* (1835), lii; *offered…think*] Anna to] James I (July 1603), ed. DWF from Maitland Club (1835), facs. 4.

event from which all but invited guests were excluded, for fear of the contagion – cost the Exchequer £20,591 in receipted expenses. And that was pocket change, to what lay ahead. Neither James nor Anna had any fiscal responsibility, or sense of limit. Plus, Anna raised doubts about her salvation: at the coronation, when it was her turn to be crowned queen consort, she declined the Anglican communion. It did not go unnoticed. [1]

Immediately after the ceremony, Anna retired with her ladies to Basing House, the seat of the Marquess of Winchester, fifty miles west of London. Here they remained until the King's arrival with his Court on August 17th. During their separation, Anna wrote James a note to say how much she missed him:

• • •

Anna Regina to King James (August 1603)°

My Heart,

I am glad that Haddington hath told me of your Majesty's good health, which I wish to continue. As for the blame you charge me with of "lazy" writing, I think it rather rests on yourself because *you* be as slow in writing as myself. [2]

I can write of no mirth – but of practice of *tilting*! of *riding*! of *drumming*! and of *music*! which is all – wherewith I am not a little pleased.

So wishing your Majesty perpetual happiness, I kiss your Majesty's hand, and rest—

Yours,
Anna R

• • •

A report reached the King concerning Charles Howard, Lord Admiral (the man credited with the defeat of the Spanish Armada in 1588). It was said that Lord Howard, 68, and a widower since January, was at Basing House with the Queen, partying with a much younger crowd and wooing Margaret Stuart, aged 13. Supposing Anna was amused, James wrote her to keep it secret. She wrote back to say that secrecy would not be possible:

Anna Regina to King James (August 1603)°

Sir,

Your Majesty's letter was welcome to me. I have been as glad of the fair weather as yourself. And the last part of your letter, you have guessed right that I would laugh – who would not laugh – both at the persons and the subject; but more, at so well a chosen Mercury between Mars and Venus! You know that women can hardly keep counsel, and I humbly desire your Majesty to tell me how it is possible that I should "keep this secret" that have already told it? (and *shall* tell it, to as many as I speak with!) If I were a poet, I would make a song of it, and sing it to the tune of "Three Fools, Well Met." So, kissing your hands, I rest yours,

Anna R

• • •

Meeting up at Basing on the 17th, James and Anna embarked on a royal progress through southern England. Their stops included Wilton House (Aug. 29-30), a home of William Herbert, earl of Pembroke, and of his mother, the poet Mary Sidney; Tottenham Park (Sept. 1-4), a home of the elderly first earl of Hertford and of his young bride, the poet Frances (Howard) Seymour; and Burford Priory (Sept. 9-11), home of Lawrence and Elizabeth Tanfield, parents of the future playwright, Elizabeth Cary. Then it was on to the much-decayed royal palace at Woodstock for a week, where the King and queen went hunting. The wildlife was less plentiful than James anticipated, in so wealthy a nation as England. Before the winter was out, he issued a proclamation ("By the King") that promised prison, exile, or death to any but landowners who hunted any deer, game, or wild fowl in "any forest, park, chase, or warren" whatsoever. (The country poor were still permitted to hunt rodents.) [3]

At Woodstock, while the King spent his days at the chase, the Privy Council conducted State business. On 16 September, a proclamation was issued ("By the King") announcing that overcrowded tenements in the city must be evacuated, and that any new tenements thrown up to house the poor would be torn down. On the 17th, a proclamation was issued ("By the King") against "Rogues, Vagabonds, Idle and Dissolute Persons." Noting that the poor and unemployed "have swarmed and abounded everywhere more frequently than in times past, which will grow to the great and imminent danger of the whole Realm" unless prevented "by the goodness of God Almighty, and [by] the due and timely execution of the said Law," offenders under this statute were to be whipped or exiled; repeat offenders, hanged (a law already on the books but not enforced hitherto). Also on the 17th: order was taken to proceed with indictments against Sir Walter Ralegh, Thomas Lord Grey of Wilton,

---

[1] *the lewd…inhabitants*] Nichols, *Progresses* (1828), *ibid.,* 1.228n.

[2] *Haddington*] John Ramsay, one of James's favorites; created viscount Haddington June 1606.

[3] *any forest,* etc.] The published Proclamation against hunting is dated 16 May 1603.

and others, who were suspected of a plot that would have put Arbella Stuart on the throne instead of King James; the Privy Council penciled in November dates for the traitors' trial and execution.

That same week at Woodstock, the King supplemented Queen Anna's income with an additional jointure of lands netting £5,000 annual revenue, the largest jointure ever granted to a queen consort of England. The extra funds would free Anna to engage in the masques and court entertainments, the architectural projects, and the fashion statements that were to become her chief contributions to British culture. (It would not be enough: in 1605, the queen spent £50,000, much of it on jewelry; to close the deficit, she was awarded many lucrative monopolies and patents, £3,000 in sugar duties alone, and more land, but it was never close to enough.)

The Councilors were soon discontented, at Woodstock: they complained of the accommodations, so different from the grandeur that accompanied Queen Elizabeth, even in the country. Of their September sojourn, Sir Robert Cecil writes: "The place is unwholesome, all the house standing upon springs. It is unsavory, for there is no savor but of cows and pigs. It is uneaseful: for only the King (and queen, with [her] Privy Chamber ladies), and some three or four of the Scottish Council, are lodged in the house. And neither the Chamberlain nor one English Councilor have a room." On 21 September, the Court returned to Basing House, where Lord Howard and Margaret Stuart were married. Fun was had by all. [1]

Queen Anna at this point in her marriage remained fond of the King, but courtiers and bishops observed in letters that nothing about the queen pleased his Majesty so well as her absence. In an undated note written during one of their many extended separations in the winter and spring of 1603/4, Anna promises to treat James well on his home-return. She suggests the pleasure of hawking, and of her own gentle touch:

Anna Regina to King James (November? 1603)°

My Heart,

    I crave pardon that I have not sooner answered your Majesty's letter. (You shall not fear the pain in my fingers – you shall find them well enough for you, when you come home!). I think it long to see my gyrfalcon fly, which I hope to see when I shall have the honor to kiss your Majesty's hands. [2]

Yours,
Anna R.

•••

In June 1604, Sir Thomas Somerset applied for the exclusive right to weigh coal brought to ships upon the rivers of Tyne and Wear. (Monopolies and patents, the King's chief fund-raising device, were selling fast: it took some ingenuity to think up something new to license.) Somerset's argument: "By this means the King will not be, as now, defrauded of custom by the shipmasters; who, by corrupting [bribing] the keelmen who bring the coals aboard, ship more chaldrons than they pay custom for, and than the coal-sellers receive money for." Writing in Somerset's behalf, Queen Anne took the opportunity to tell James she would like to see him again: [3]

Anna Regina to King James (June 1604)°

My Heart,

    I give you many thanks for the divers remembrances I have had from you since our parting. Whensoever your sport and other occasions will suffer you come hither, you shall be very welcome. I glad of so good appearance of my roes' offspring! Sir Thomas Somerset hath earnestly desired me to recommend a petition he is to prefer to you; which, if your Majesty find it reasonable, ye will please grant it, or at least refer it to the Council. So, desiring to be excused for thus troubling of you in time of your sport, I still continue—

Yours,
Anna R.

•••

The King evidently heeded Anna's summons: ten months after she rejoiced to see her roes giving birth, she did, too. (The King got her pregnant, then left London to go hunting at Royston.) But the royals' June 1604 *rapprochement* had another happy effect: later that summer, for one brief month – the only time in their thirty-year marriage – the King appointed Anna to represent the Crown in official business, as regal signatory to peace with Spain: the Treaty of London ended a costly and unproductive nineteen-year war. Negotiations were

---

[1] *The place…have a room*] R.Cecil to G.Talbot (Talbot Papers, vol. K, f.247; from Lodge, *Illustrations* (1828) 1.37.

[2] *By this means…money for*] H.M.C. Salisbury (Cecil), (misdated: "March 1605?"), vol. 17.

[3] *gyrfalcon*] a large arctic falcon of various colors; falconry (the hunting of wildfowl by trained falcons) was a costly and popular sport of the leisured class, the hunting season ranging from August to March.

held at Somerset House, the Queen's residence. The English delegation was headed by Robert Cecil, earl of Salisbury (Secretary of State); Thomas Sackville, earl of Dorset (Lord Treasurer); Henry Howard, earl of Northampton (Lord Warden of the Cinque Ports); and Charles Howard, earl of Nottingham (Lord High Admiral); and Charles Blount, earl of Devonshire (military commander). Anna was not involved, except as party host. Nor was much negotiation required: under the King's direction, England capitulated to virtually all of Spain's demands. But when it came to sign the unpopular Treaty, scheduled for 18/28 August, James went hunting, leaving town in July, deputing Anna to sign for him. [1]

The King on 4 August wrote to the lords on word that they were enjoying too well the nation's momentary return to female sovereignty; rather than obey the queen, as they did in Elizabeth's time, he suspected they were making love to his wife: "Ye and your fellows there are so proud now, that ye have gotten the guiding again of a feminine court, in the old fashion, as I know not how to deal with you!" Addressing the "wanton and wifeless" Robert Cecil, the King writes, "I cannot but be jealous of your greatness with my wife"; and of Northampton ("who is so lately fallen in acquaintance with my wife" and "whose face is so amiable it is able to entice"), "I am most of all suspicious." He was, of course, joking. [2]

On 7 April 1605, the queen was delivered of a baby girl, named Mary. The baptism was conducted with much pomp and State expense on May 5th. Lady Arbella Stuart (the king's cousin), and Duke Ulrik (the queen's brother, visiting from Denmark) stood as godmother and godfather. Sir Thomas Knyvett was appointed Mary's guardian. (Knyvett is the Privy Councilor who would become famous a few months later by his timely discovery of the Gunpowder Plot.) The wet-nurse, an artist's wife, was chosen from among many applicants. Before the newborn was delivered up to the Knyvetts, a shopping list was compiled, probably by Queen Anna, of the "necessaries to be provided for the child." These included "a carnation velvet cradle, fringed with silver fringe and lined with carnation satin; a double scarlet cloth to lay upon the cradle at night; a cradle cloth of carnation velvet with a train, laid with silver, and lined with taffeta to lay upon the cradle; two small mantles of unshorn velvet, lined with the same velvet; one large bearing cloth of carnation velvet, to be used when the child is brought forth of the chamber, lined with taffeta; one great head sheet of cambric for the cradle, containing two breadths, and three yards long, wrought all over with gold and colored silks and fringed with gold; six fine handkerchiefs of fine cambric, one to be edged with fair cut work, to lay over the child's face; six veils of lawn, edged with fair bone lace, to pin with the mantles; six gathered bibs of fine lawn with ruffles edged with bone lace; two bibs to wear under them, wrought with gold and colored silks." Estimated cost for the necessaries: £300 (today's rough equivalent: U.S. $250,000). [3]

That autumn, following the King of Denmark's visit, James and Anna cohabited once again, at Hampton Court, which is where the royals conceived their last child; after which, "though for complement, he visited Queen Anna, yet never lodged with her a night for many years [...] The queen, deprived of the nightly company of a husband, turned her delight to the prince, whom she respected above her other children." [4]

On 22 June 1606, a daughter was born, named Sophia after Anna's mother. The baby survived only a week. In September, two-year-old Mary contracted pneumonia; never thriving afterward, she died a year later, aged 3. Anna erected monuments in Westminster Abbey to her daughters' memory, and moved on. She was much praised for subduing her grief. But in 1612, after having lost her husband to Robert Carr, her eldest daughter to a Protestant marriage she opposed, and her best-beloved child, Prince Henry, to typhoid fever, Anna could no longer be consoled.

• • •

ANNA OF DENMARK is best remembered in scholarship for her sponsorship of lavish Court masques, four written by Ben Jonson, two by Samuel Daniel, with sets and costumes designed by Inigo Jones (who was also Anna's principal designer for her building projects). The ladies of Anna's Court typically danced and sang, sometimes had speaking roles. It has been fashionable lately to write of the Jacobean masque as an "important" cultural form, though *decadent* were the more apt term. Anna spent thousands of pounds on each of

---

[1] *Somerset House*] renamed "Denmark House" by Queen Anna, and renovated; the new gate alone, designed by Inigo Jones, cost £28,000 when the Crown was running a £140,000 annual deficit.

[2] King to Privy Council (5 Aug. 1603), A. Collins, *Letters and Memorials* (1746), 2.235; *joking*] Such banter was conventional guy-talk. In 1617, Lady Hatton, the wife of Sir Edward Coke, banished him from her marriage bed after he and James forced Frances her daughter, against her will, to marry John Villiers, elder brother of George, the King's favorite. The King hoped to make peace. His friend Gondomar (Spanish ambassador) quipped that it was no use, because (he said) "the Lady Hatton would not suffer the Lord Coke her husband to come into her fore-door, nor [the King] himself to her back door" Sir Edward Peyton, *Divine Catastrophe* (1652), 29.

[3] *necessaries...colored silks*] M.A.E. Green, *Lives* (1857), 90.

[4] Sir Edward Peyton, *ibid.*, 29, 13.

her masques, with no box-office return except in gratitude from the socialites and foreign dignitaries who were invited. Guests vied with one another in displaying their lavish silks and bling-bling jewelry, the one-night wardrobe of both men and women typically exceeding what dozens of tradesmen could earn in a year. The booze flowed freely. At Ben Jonson's *Masque of the Two Kings* – infamously performed at Theobalds on 24 July 1606 for King James and his brother-in-law Christian IV of Denmark, the women performers (not known to have included the queen) were so drunk they could not say their lines (one courtier being found in the morning dead in his own vomit); both Kings after passing out had to be carried to bed by courtiers.

Performed by the privileged class for its own amusement, the masques celebrated wealth and whiteness. On 6 January 1604/5, when Anna was six months pregnant with Mary, Ben Jonson's *Masque of Blackness* (commissioned by the queen) was performed in the Banqueting Hall of Whitehall Palace. Anna, who can be credited as patron with some creative input to each of her masques, wished the masquers to be disguised as black Africans; the ladies would appear in blackface and have their blackness "cleansed" by King James (as would appear in a sequel, the *Masque of Beauty*). Dudley Carleton reports:

"There was a great engine at the lower end of the room, which had motion. And in it were the images of sea-horses and other terrible fishes – which were ridden by *Moors* (the indecorum was, that there was all fish, and no *water!*) At the further end was a great shell in the form of a scallop, wherein were four seats. In the lowest sat the queen with my Lady Bedford. In the rest were placed my Ladies Suffolk, Derby, [Penelope] Rich, [Anne] Effingham, Anne Herbert, Susan Herbert, Elizabeth Howard, [Audrey] Walsingham, and [Frances] Bevill. Their appearance was rich, but too light and courtesan-like for such great ones: instead of vizards, their faces, and arms up to the elbows, were painted black (which was disguise sufficient, for they were hard to be known; but it became them nothing so well as their red and white – and you cannot imagine a more ugly sight than a troop of lean-cheeked Moors[…]

"The Spanish and Venetian ambassadors were both present and sat by the King, in State [...Spain's ambassador] was taken out to dance, and footed it like a lusty old gallant with his countrywoman. He [also] took out the queen (and forgot not to kiss her hand, though there was danger it would have left a mark on his lips!). The night's work was concluded with a banquet in the Great Chamber – which was so furiously assaulted that down went table and trestles before one bit was touched." [1]

Left: a 1609 sketch for a Naiad, made by Inigo Jones for Samuel Daniel's masque of *Tethys' Festival*, finally performed on 5 June 1610.

Right: 1609 miniature watercolor by Isaac Oliver of a woman wearing the Naiad costume in the Jones sketch (possibly Dorothy Boulstred, sister of Cecily).

Below: Somerset House (with additions commissioned by Anna, 1609-1619, designed by Inigo Jones), which she renamed Denmark House.

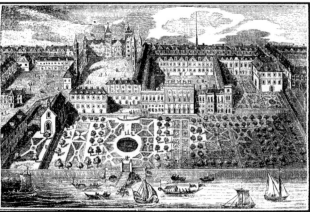

---

[1] *There was a great engine…touched*] D. Carleton to R Winwood (Jan. 1605/6); Winwood, *Memorials* (1725) 2.44.

[***Enter* George Villiers.**]

[**April 1614**.] "ABOUT THIS TIME the King cast his eye upon a young gentleman so rarely molded that [his Majesty] meant to make him a masterpiece: his name was George Villiers [...] The King, stricken with this new object, would not expose him to so much hazard as the malice of a jealous competitor, nor himself to so much censure as to be thought changeable. And taken (again!) with a sudden affection, therefore he instructs some of his confidants to bring [Villiers] in, by degrees – who intimated the King's pleasure to [his former favorite, Robert Carr, earl of Somerset] that [Villiers] should wait cupbearer-at-large (being at too great a distance of place to have any mark of favor for suspicion to be leveled at). And if the King had not received a new impression thus, the old character of Somerset could not so soon (as many men thought) have been blotted out° [...]" [1]

• • •

George Abbot, Archbishop of Canterbury, was by his own report chief among the royal confidants who promoted young Villiers to receive the King's favor. The Archbishop's idea was that Villiers – who at age 22 was one of the handsomest young men Abbot had ever seen – could drive a wedge between his Majesty (aged 49) and Robert Carr, earl of Somerset (27). To enlist support for this project, the Archbishop approached Queen Anna, who cautioned against it. As Abbot later told the story, "It was one of King James's maxims to take no favorite but what was recommended to him by his queen: [so] that, if she afterwards complained of this Dear One, he might answer, 'It is long of yourself, for you were the party that commended him unto me [...]'"

Queen Anna resisted the Archbishop's relentless urgings that she recommend Villiers. She cited her reason: "My Lord, you and the rest of your friends know not what you do. I know your Master better than you all. For if this young man be once brought in, the first persons that he will plague must be you that labor for him. Yea, I shall have my part also – the King will teach him to despise and hardly entreat us all, that he may seem to be beholden to none but himself." Eventually, Anna caved – and lived to regret it. In April, James in the queen's apartments borrowed a sword from 15-year-old Prince Charles; dubbed Villiers a knight of the Realm; and appointed him to be a Gentleman of the [King's] Bedchamber. Abbot reports the sequel:

(Noble Queen, how like a prophetess did you speak!) In the end, upon importunity, Queen Anne condescended thereunto – which was so stricken while the iron was hot that in the queen's bedchamber, the King knighted [Villiers] with the rapier which the prince did wear. And when the King gave order to swear him [a Gentleman] of the Bedchamber, Somerset (who was near) importuned the King with a message that [Villiers] might only be sworn a *groom* [as a servant who would help to dress the King]. But myself and others that were at the door sent to her majesty that she would perfect her work, and cause him to be sworn a Gentleman of the 'chamber [...] George went in with the King – but no sooner he *got loose* but he came forth unto me in the privy gallery and there [...] did beseech me that I would give him some lessons how he should carry himself... His countenance of thankfulness for a few days continued, but not long, either to me or any other of his well-wishers. (The Roman historian Tacitus hath somewhere a note, that "Benefits, while they may be *requited*, seem courtesies; but when they are so high that they cannot be repaid, they prove matters of hatred)°." [2]

• • •

In April, James made Villiers a Knight of the Garter and gave him lands worth £1500 per annum, then set out with Sir George for horse and greyhound races at Newmarket, and to hunt the hare and deer, at Thetford.

On 7 April 1616, King Christian of Denmark shipped to England twelve mares, all of which were thought to be pregnant, as a gift for his sister Anna; and on 1 July, he sent a riding horse for King James, one that Christian (who was a cowboy, at heart) had broken in by himself. In June, when the first horses arrived, Queen Anna sent word to King James, so that the Danish king could be thanked for his largesse. Anna that same month received word from Buckingham that he was keeping watchful care of his Majesty – for which Anna now thanked him, addressing Villiers (the King's beloved "Steenie"), as her "kind dog."

Anna took the opportunity to ask Buckingham for a favor: she wished to have her deer park at Byfield enclosed with paling, as the King had done surrounding his own land at Theobalds and elsewhere; thereby to prevent the deer from escaping and to keep peasants from trespassing on her land to gather food and firewood, or to graze their sheep, goats and dairy cows (a continual complaint of land-owners in the early Seventeenth Century, heard most often from those who, like both James and Anna, loved to shoot their deer without having to hunt very hard):

---

[1] Abbot, *Life and Reign* (1706), 698; *cupbearer-at-large*] *i.e.,* an unpensioned server (with a sly Ganymede joke that Carr was too dull to catch); *too great a distance of place*] too base socially for Carr to be jealous.

[2] Onslow, *Life of Archbishop Abbot* (1777) 25-6.

Anne Regina to Sir George Villiers (June 1616)°

My kind Dog,

   Your letter hath been acceptable to me. I rest already assured of your carefulness. You may tell your Master that the king of Denmark hath sent me twelve fair mares, and (as the bringer of them assures me) all great with foals! – which I intend to put into Byfield Park; where, being the other day a-hunting, I could find but very few deer, but great store of *other* cattle (as I shall tell your Master myself when I see him). I hope to meet you all at Woodstock at the time appointed; till when, I wish you all happiness and contentment. [1]

   I thank you for your pains taken in rememb'ring the King for the paling of me park. I will do you any service I can.

Anna R.
(To Sir George Villiers.)

• • •

Before the King left town, Anna had asked her "kind dog," in a semi-jocular way, to "lug the sow" (i.e., tug on the king's ear) whenever James behaved himself unseemly, which was more often than not. Buckingham, replying in August to the queen's note concerning horse and deer, wrote an unprintable jest of tugging on the sow until it was as long as a lug. Unhappy to be quoted thus, Anna dashed off two short notes for spin control, to clarify that she was not calling his Majesty a sow, nor did she mean "lug" in a bawdy sense: [2]

Anna Regina to King James (August 1616)°

My Heart,

   I am glad to hear of your Majesty's welfare. I am much bound to your Majesty, that desireth to know of my health (which is very well, I thank God); I am glad that our brother's horse does please you, and that my dog Steenie does well. For I did command him that he should make *your ear* hang like a sow's lug; and when he comes home, I will treat him better than any other dog.

So, kissing your Majesty's hands, I rest yours,
Anna R.

• • •

On August 1st, Villiers was elevated from knight to viscount. Anna was among the first to address him by his new title:

Anna Regina to George, Viscount Villiers (August 1616)°

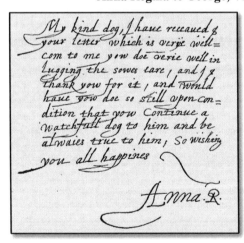

My kind dog, I haue receaued your letter, which is verie wellcom to me. yow doe verie well in lugging the sowes eare, and I thank yow for it, and would haue yow doe so still vpon condition that you continue a watchfull dog to him and be alwaies true to him, so wishing you all happines,

Anna R.

[*verso*] (To the Viscount Villiers)

• • •

In 1617, the King made his first visit to Scotland in fourteen years. On 6 January, before departure, he elevated Villiers to Earl of Buckingham. And on 15 March, James and his beloved Steenie left for Edinburgh. Anna with her ladies accompanied the King and his retinue part way, riding from London, to Theobald, to Ware. The queen then retired to Greenwich Palace, where she remained for the summer. This was not her idea: she had

---

[1] *paling*] enclosing with a fence;   *me*] my.

[2] *lug*] literally, the hanging earflaps of a bonnet (*OED* n.2), a term used often for pig's ears by way of resemblance; also, a long shaft or pole (*OED* n.1), not Anna's meaning; cf. *lug,* (v.) below, to tug or pull, esp. on the ear.

wished in the King's absence to serve as Queen Regent (as did Katherine Parr, during Henry VIII's French campaign of 1544). James would not permit it. He deputized instead Francis Bacon, Lord Verulam, who quickly alienated the Privy Council and his entire constituency.

The King was now as happy as he had ever been; Anna, less so. While on the road, James sent her a number of letters. Anna sent him only one perfunctory reply, in boilerplate language, to acknowledge that she had indeed received his messages; and to say that she loved him better than Buckingham ever would.

Anna Regina to King James (July 1617)°

Sir,

As nothing is more welcome to me than your letters (for which, I thank you), so can they bring me no better tidings than of your good health (of me, much desired); for I cease not to pray for the increase and continuance of your good, both of mind and body, and thereof rest assured. So, kissing your hands I remain:

She that will ever love you best,
Anna R.

• • •

On his home return, the King scheduled a layover in Woodstock for September 6-10. He summoned the Privy Council to meet him there. The King's intention may have been for Anna to accompany the Councilors – she had not seen him in almost six months – but she received no invitation. As the day drew near, the queen wrote to Buckingham, partly to inquire after the King's will, but also to suggest that she would rather not go. (By a slip of the pen, or perhaps in jest, Anna here addresses Villiers not as my kind, but as my "king" dog):

Anna Regina to George, Earl of Buckingham (September 1617)°

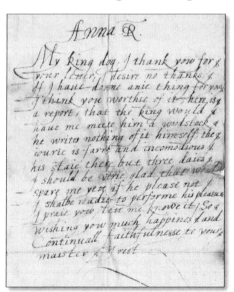

Anna R.

My king dog, I thank yow for
your letter. I desire no thanks.
If I have donne anie thing for yow,
I think you worthie of it. here is
a report, that the king would
haue me meete him a woodstock.
he writes nothing of it himself. the
iour[n]ie is farre and incomodious.
his staie there but three daies
I should be verie glad that would
spare me yett if he please not
I shalbe readie to performe his pleasure.
I praie yow, lett me know it. So,
wishing yow much happines and
Continuall faithfulnesse to your
maister, I rest—

[*verso*] (To the Earle of Buckingham)

• • •

King James returned from Scotland so smitten with George Villiers that he had little time for government responsibilities, and none for his wife. In a meeting with his Privy Council, he declared, "I, James, am neither a god nor an angel but a man like any other. Therefore I act like a man, and confess to loving those dear to me more than other men. You may be sure that I love the Earl of Buckingham more than anyone else, and more than you who are here assembled. I wish to speak in my own behalf, and not to have it thought to be a defect, for Jesus Christ did the same, and therefore I cannot be blamed. Christ had his John, and I have my George." [1]

Buckingham was promiscuously heterosexual, with an entourage of women whom he references in his letters with contempt as "the cunts." But it's clear from his correspondence that he also kept the King happy in bed. The Privy Councilors, who were better politicians than Christians, cared less about the bedroom than the Exchequer: Robert Cecil having died in 1612, there was no longer any effective check on the King's fiscal

---

[1] *I, James…have my George*] Gondomar to the Archduke Albert (2/12 Oct. 1617), Madrid Palace Lib.. Trans. Gardiner (1883), 3.98.

irresponsibility. His Majesty was fast giving away the store. He heaped upon Villiers (and his kindred) gifts of land, manors, government offices, lucrative monopolies and patents, jewels, even some of the Crown Jewels – while remaining oblivious to the failing economy, the escalating poverty of the Commons, and the rising animosity of the English peers.

On 1 January 1617/8, the King elevated Villiers to Marquess Buckingham. Queen Anna did not attend the ceremony, and ceased to appear at Court. By mid-January, gossip reported, "Her majesty is not well. They say she languisheth, whether with melancholy or sickness, or what-not; yet is she still at Whitehall, being scant able to remove." In March, wishing to avoid the drunken revels at Shrovetide, Anna was transported to Denmark House. In June she moved again, to her newly renovated palace at Oatlands. Before setting out, she sent a note to James, speaking offhand, as if for the first time, of her difficulty getting about: [1]

Anna to King James (June 1618)°

My Heart,

I desire your Majesty to pardon that I have not answered your Majesty sooner upon your letters – because I would know the truth of the park of Oatlands: As I understand, there is near forty *grossi beastiami* of divers kinds that devours my deer! – as I will tell your Majesty at meeting; and whereas your Majesty would have me to meet you at withal, I *am* content – but I fear some inconvenience in my legs, which I have not felt here. So kissing your Majesty's hands, I rest yours— *Anna R.*

• • •

As the summer wore on, Anna developed a persistent cough, and vomited blood. In the autumn, her physicians brought her to Hampton Court, where she only grew worse. One night, having blood in her lungs, she nearly suffocated. Understating the gravity of her symptoms but making light of them, Anna made it her last project to save the life of Sir Walter Ralegh. In 1603, Ralegh had been sentenced to die for his alleged support of a plot to place Arbella Stuart on the English throne instead of Scottish James. Ralegh's death sentence was then commuted to life in prison. Fifteen years later, to please the Spanish ambassador Gondomar, James gave command for Ralegh to be beheaded. Sir Walter, a noted scientist, had been assisting with the queen's medical care, from prison. In his verse-petition, "Address to Queen Anna," Ralegh begged her intervention for a request more urgent than the enclosure of a deer-park: he hoped she would rescue his neck from the chopping block. In what was to be her last letter, Anna went straight to the top: from her sickbed she wrote a letter to the Marquess Buckingham, urging him to intervene with his Majesty to save Ralegh's life:

Anna Regina to the Marquess Buckingham (Sept. 1618)°

My kind Dog,

If I have any power or credit with you, I pray you let me have a trial of it at this time in dealing sincerely and earnestly with the King that Sir Walter Ralegh's life may not be called in question. If you do it so that the success answer my expectation, assure yourself that I will take it extraordinarily kindly at your hands – and rest [as] one that wisheth you well, and desires you to continue still, as you have been, a true servant of your master. —*Anna R.*

• • •

IN THE OLD PALACE YARD at Westminster on 29 October 1618, Sir Walter Ralegh died, quite suddenly. His last words, as the executioner fidgeted, were "Strike, man, strike!" Queen Anna, less fortunate, outlived him by just four months, in constant pain. She died on 2 March 1618/9, unlamented by the King.

It is often said that after Queen Anna's death, James banished from Court all women except domestic servants. Not true. Anna's retinue was dismissed, but the King still welcomed the wives of his remaining favorites, including Lady Frances, duchess of Lennox and Richmond; Lucy Hay, countess of Carlisle; and Lady Anna, duchess of Hamilton – plus a multitude of women of the extended Villiers family ("the Kindred"). As a result, "King James (that naturally, in former times, *hated* women) had his lodgings replenished with them, and all of the Kindred [...] Here was a strange change [in] the King who formerly would not endure his queen and children in his lodgings: now you would have judged that none *but* women frequented them." [2]

Yet, for better or worse, the frivolity was gone. From the queen's death in 1619 until the King's death six years later, the royal palaces were relieved somewhat by all of the Kindred's children, but otherwise, the Court milieu was dreary; the lodgings, dirty and buggy; and morale, dismal. In his last years, James had only two goals: 1. more money (he had exhausted his resources); and 2. the marriage of Prince Charles with the Spanish Infanta (as a way to get more money). In both projects, King James found tactical support from an unlikely ally: his dead wife, Anna of Denmark. She had quite the jewelry collection.

---

[1] *Her majesty...remove*] J. Chamberlain to D. Carleton (10 Jan. 1617/18), Chamberlain, *Letters* (1939) 2.129.

[2] *King James...frequented them*] ed. DWF from A. Weldon, *The Court and Character of King James* (1650), 125.

Queen Anna's Jewels: A Mystery

QUEEN ANNA, since the time of her misery over Prince Henry's death, had been treated by Sir Theodore de Mayerne, a physician who diagnosed her in 1612 as suffering from an ulcerated leg, gout, and menstrual difficulties. By September 1618, Mayerne knew the queen was dying of dropsy and consumption: she had a rough road ahead. In January, with good intentions, he made her get out of bed to saw wood, to improve her circulation. Instead, the exertion nearly killed her. But Anna refused to write her will, denying the inevitable.

On 19 January, in the King's presence, Sir Edward Coke announced to fellow members of the Privy Council that the ailing queen "wished her debts paid out of her own revenues, without troubling the King; and her jewels, etc., to be annexed to the Crown." Anna was not present at the Council Table to contradict him. [1]

To ensure that nothing of the queen's considerable property was lost, order was taken on 25 February to conduct a thorough inventory of movables belonging to the richest woman in Britain. Her personal wealth was astounding: Anna's jewels were appraised at £400,000, her plate at £90,000. In addition to uncounted gowns and quantities of furniture, she possessed 124 whole pieces of cloth of gold and silver, "besides other silks and linen for quantity and quality beyond any prince in Europe." Also, cash: 80,000 Jacobus gold coins (about two thousand pounds Troy, or roughly U.S. $30 million in today's market). Most of that property was at Denmark House, secure in her private chambers. Not inventoried were her lands, palaces, tenements, monopolies, patents, and accounts payable, most of which would go to the King. [2]

While wasting away at Hampton Court, Anna was perhaps alarmed to hear that the Privy Council had descended like vultures, before her death, upon her private residence three miles away. She now made a nuncupatory will, spoken before witnesses. To her daughter, she bequeathed a great casket of her jewels, valued (depending on whom one believes) at £30,000, to be shipped to Lady Elizabeth in Heidelberg. One rich jewel, Anna reserved as a memento for her brother, Christian IV king of Denmark, her wished executor. After the discharge of her debts ("under £40,000"), and after provision was made for her servants (typically, a pension for life), she assigned all else to Prince Charles, to whom she had become devotedly attached. Of her husband the King (who already possessed an incontrovertible claim to her real estate), she made no mention. [3]

James had given little or no thought to Anna's will: all would he his, when she died. On hearing this unhappy news – of a witnessed, nuncupatory will from which he was himself excluded – the King was rattled into action. In February, still breathing, Anna received an unexpected visit from the Bishop of London and the Archbishop of Canterbury, urging upon her a written will. The queen was too ill, or too stubborn, to comply.

When Dr. Mayerne announced that the end was near, additional concerned guests converged on the queen's apartment at Hampton Court: in came the King's Privy Councilors.

At 2:00 a.m. on March 2nd, Anna Kroas, the queen's Danish maid alerted Prince Charles (who slept in the next room), that his mother could no longer see and was near the end; "most of the Council" entered as well, remaining at her bedside until 4:00 a.m., at which hour Anna of Denmark, 44, breathed her last.

Three days after her death, Sir Edward Coke announced that the queen had made her will (albeit, with an unexpected omission): "when she was within twenty-four hours of her end, she made her will in favor of the Prince, leaving a jewel to the King of Denmark, but nothing to Lady Elizabeth." Reported further: "it is not thought the King will consent" (*i.e.,* for Charles to inherit all). And indeed, his Majesty sent word from Newmarket that he claimed his wife's entire estate. Charles, in London, quickly deferred (it would be his shortly, anyway). Meanwhile, the queen's embalmed and lead-wrapped corpse was packed off to Denmark House, with lady-mourners and an armed watch appointed to guard her physical and material remains. [4]

During Anna's final illness (from 15 February), King James and Marquess Buckingham remained at Newmarket, attending horse and greyhound races. Informed of the queen's decline, the King promised to return to London by-and-by but he delayed his departure, complaining of gout in his legs. On news she had died, he decided to stay a while longer, since it was now too late. On March 19th, the King again stayed too long, in order to watch one last race. On the way to London, feeling ill, his Majesty was forced to put up for the night at a roadside inn at Whichfordbridge. By the time James returned home, his wife was three weeks dead.

There was no money for a State funeral. As an advance on expenses, his Majesty gave orders for some of Anna's plate to be melted into coin, and some of her lesser jewels to be pawned. A new inventory was now taken of the queen's movables – whereupon it was discovered that much had already moved: a trove containing £30,000 to £36,000 worth of jewels was missing and unaccounted for. "She was supposed likewise [to have] a great treasure of ready money; but not a penny found." [5]

---

[1] *19 January*] *S.P. Domestic James I* (1619-1623), p. 6.

[2] *inventory*] See B.L. MS Birch 4176. *S.P. Dom. James, ibid.,* p.18; Chamberlain, *ibid.,* 2.219, 224; Nichols, *ibid.,* 3.531n. The Jacobus or "Sovereign" was a gold coin first issued in 1603, current for 20s, later 24s.

[3] *will*] See *S.P. Dom., ibid.,* pp. 18, 27; and Chamberlain, *ibid.,* 2.219-20, 224.

[4] *when .... King will consent*] *S.P. Dom. ibid.,* 21, 25.

[5] *She was supposed...penny found*] B.L. MS Birch 4176;   *to have*] MS om.

The King was ill for much of April, remaining in London. Sufficiently recovered by April 17th, he retired to the country for some R&R with Buckingham. The royal entourage visited Royston and Ware, then stopped over until June at Theobalds Park, where the King hunted deer. With every slain buck, James opened the wound where he made the kill, to soak his feet and bathe his legs in warm deer-blood as a cure for the gout. But when he returned to London on June 5, the King came crisply dressed in a powder-blue suit with silver lace, with matching accessories that included a cap with blue and white feathers. He was met by foreign dignitaries dressed in black, still waiting to express their condolences to the King of Britain for the loss of Queen Anna.

The queen was now buried. She had lain in State at Denmark House for more a month; and then for another month. By May, the appointed lady mourners were arguing about whose turn it was to coffin-sit, and who would have precedency in the funeral procession. The theater companies complained of lost income, as they were not allowed to perform in London so long as the queen's body remained above-ground. And Buckingham was growing impatient to take occupation of Denmark House.

Well-liked for her gaiety but never well-loved, Anna by dying elicited small lamentation from the peers and none from the Commons. The royal funeral, which finally took place on 13 May, is described by John Chamberlain as "a drawling, tedious sight, more remarkable for number than for any singularity," "a poor show." "The number of lords and ladies was very great, yet [...] they came laggering all along, even tired with the length of the way and weight of their clothes, every lady having twelve yards of broad cloth about her (and the countesses, sixteen)." Following behind were "280 poor women, besides an army of mean fellows that were servants," paupers looking to receive alms. "It was full six o'clock at night before all the solemnity was done at church; where the hearse is to continue till the next term [...]" [1]

That same day, while Londoners watched the funeral parade trudge from Denmark House to Westminster Abbey, the late queen's movable property, including trunks of jewels, was brought under armed guard, in four wagons, from Denmark House to Greenwich.

There was plenty left over. As a gratuity to Buckingham for having nursed him through his April illness, the King gave the marquess one portion of Queen Anna's jewels (of unspecified value), plus an extra £1,000 per year in rental income, plus rent-free occupation of Denmark House (which would again be called Somerset House). The King could afford to be generous: by Anna's death, he was now spared the burden of her jointure (£24,000 year) and the cost of running her household (another £60,000 p.a.); and her clothing allowance; with augmented revenue that included £13,000 yearly from duties on imported sugar alone (one of Anna's grants, with reversion to the Crown; plus several others). This financial windfall came at a welcome time: by May 15 the exchequer was so low that certain of Anna's expendable jewels (with James's blessing, from Theobalds) were given to the English ambassadors, with instructions to market them abroad in lieu of their unpaid salary. [2]

The loss of Anna's jewels and gold was blamed on two servants of the late queen, "her Frenchman, Pierrot" (the queen's "creature and favorite," a suspected priest), and Anna Maria Kroas (a maid who had spent her entire adult life in Queen Anna's service). On 31 May, "by express commandment of the King," just before his return to London, the two suspects were arrested on suspicion of having embezzled £30,000 of the queen's £400,000 private jewelry collection (the missing gold coins seem not to have been mentioned). The villains were committed without indictment to the custody of Justice Doubleday (who doubled as Warden of the Mint); after which, both defendants disappear from the historical record and probably from the planet. Pierrot and Kroas were the two servants whom the queen most trusted throughout her final months. King James offered no reason why they would steal a vast trove of priceless jewelry (which they could neither sell nor pawn without being hanged) while leaving behind the gold and silver coins (which they could spend); nor why they remained in London two months later, to be taken by surprise and accused of grand larceny (and no jewels to be found in their possession). But the incarceration of the accused thieves rendered inaccessible their testimony concerning what the queen truly requested in her will and testament; with the added benefit of rendering moot the inconvenience of paying them a lifetime pension as surviving servants of the deceased. [3]

What most grieved the King was that the alleged theft prevented him from sending £30,000 in jewels across the Channel to his daughter, Lady Elizabeth, as per Anna's nuncupatory will.

On 26 June, £20,000 of Anna's extant jewelry was pawned in order to meet expenses for the King's summer progress through the counties with Buckingham. Overspending on that trip, as usual, and needing to finance the rest of his journey, James on July 2nd authorized the earl of Worcester to sell another £18,000 worth of Anna's jewels – an offering was that was snapped up on July 15th by the financier, Peter Vanlore; but he

---

[1] *a poor show…next term*] John Chamberlain, *ibid.*, 2.237. For other details of the funeral, see *S.P. Domestic James I* (1619-1623), 25-7, 37, 39-41, 43-5, 49, 75, 141, 335; and Nichols, *Progresses of James I* (1828), 3.538-46.

[2] *gratuity to Buckingham*] Chamberlain, *ibid.*, 2.224; *ambassadors…salary*] *S.P. Dom.*, *ibid.*, 46.

[3] *creature and favorite*] B.L. MS Birch 4176. See also Nichols, *ibid.*, 3.548-9; *S.P. Dom.*, *ibid.*, 49; Chamberlain, *ibid.*, 2.240.

bought only as much as he could resell for a quick profit. (Chamberlain reports: "the choice pearl and other rare jewels are not touched.") Among the rarest of the unsold items was a gold carcanet with ten knots of pearls, appraised at £40,000, venue unspecified, and affirmed to be the fairest of its kind ever seen in Christendom. [1]

Two months later, King James authorized the Chancellor of the Exchequer and Commissioners of the Treasury to fetch that £40,000 carcanet, and sell it: but it was not in the King's possession, or with any of Queen Anna's known jewelry: it was now in the Jewel House in the Tower of London, among the Crown Jewels; which may justly raise eyebrows, because its description matches that of the carcanet worn by Queen Jane Seymour (as in her famous 1536 portrait by Hans Holbein). Was King James – as alleged as early as 1614 – dispensing with the Crown Jewels of England?

A year later, by an order dated 4 August 1620, James authorized Sir Edward Coke to sell the rest of Anna's jewelry. The money was soon spent. In November, desperate for cash, the King summoned Parliament, his first in six years. His professed agenda: to raise money for a military expedition in support of Lady Elizabeth and her husband Frederick V, who had been booted from Prague by the hated Catholics. England's majority counted Lady Elizabeth a Protestant hero and clamored loudly for war; but the lords were generally unwilling to raise subsidies for the Crown; the King wished to avoid war, especially with Spain, but nonetheless demanded more subsidies. Nothing was accomplished.

In November 1621 – one month before he dissolved Parliament in rage – the King was pressed at last, by financial necessity, to dip into the jewels that Anna had intended for their daughter, Princess Elizabeth: these "secret" jewels, "found in Denmark House," had been placed in the custody of commissioners whom James appointed for the express purpose of keeping them secret; among them, Thomas Knyvett, the late queen's own privy councilor. The £30,000 trove for which Anna Kroas and Monsieur Pierrot went to prison was never actually stolen, nor did Lady Elizabeth ever learn otherwise. But the King now made a small concession. [2]

James had his portrait taken in miniature by Nicholas Hilliard. He authorized his new High Treasurer, Archbishop George Abbot, to remove from Queen Anna's "secret" collection, thirty-seven diamonds wherewith to garnish the frame, plus a pendant pearl. The King then sent his diamond-studded image as a gift to Lady Elizabeth, now living in exile in the Hague, as a gift.

That miniature of the King, encrusted with Queen Anna's purloined diamonds, still exists. It is the piece known as "the Lyte jewel," in the British Museum: an oval miniature with sixteen tiny table-cut diamonds in the frame, eight more in the monogram (I.R., for Jacobus Rex), plus thirteen more on the flip-up cover, for a total of thirty-seven.

Elizabeth could not say she never received her mother's jewels: she now had dozens of them; and she had them in a setting that she could not pawn without dishonoring her royal father. For James, it was win-win. From the same "secret" jewels, at the same time, the King removed ten choice pieces that he appropriated to himself and put to pawn. But that was still not enough. The very next day (10 November 1621), James authorized another raid on the Crown Jewels: the King's self-appointed Commissioners entered the Jewel House in the Tower and withdrew a collection of bejeweled gold carcanets. The precious stones were again removed and sold; and the gold again delivered to the Mint for coining.

Having dissolved Parliament for its refusal to raise revenue, and short of cash, King James could no longer stop himself from putting his hand in the candy bin: seven months later, on 28 June 1622, his Commissioners were back in the Tower, again removing Crown Jewels to be melted for coin or sold for ready cash, all of them at discount. But even the Crown Jewels of England could not last forever, at this rate. [3]

Made desperate by Parliament's tight-fisted opposition, the King chose to revive his fortunes by wedding Charles to the Roman Catholic Spanish Infanta, in hopes of securing a dowry of £600,000, a figure suggested by one of James's few remaining political allies, the Spanish ambassador, Count Gondomar. To elude the wrath of his subjects (most of whom were opposed to "the Spanish match"), James sent Buckingham and Charles to Spain incognito, traveling as "Thomas and John Smith." They sailed in February 1622/3, aboard a pinnace of (now Lord Admiral) George Villiers. To help Charles wow and woo the Infanta, James sent much of what was left in the Tower: the jewels for Charles and his Spanish Intended were carried aboard the *Adventure* (the same armed vessel that in 1611 apprehended a cross-dressed Arbella Stuart on her flight to France).

Estimates of what was sent to Spain for the Prince's courtship ranged as high as £800,000 in rare and irreplaceable jewels, some of them for the prince's wearing, some as gifts for the Infanta, others for Spanish lords who favored the match or who needed persuading. Others were given to the Spanish ambassador in England. Still more jewels were removed from the Tower on 16 April, more on 6 May 1623, and sent to Spain. Not all were disposed of: among the items sent to Spain was the world-famous Mirror of Portugal, a square 26-carat

---

[1] *26 June...15 July*] Chamberlain, *ibid.,* 2.249, 251; *S.P. Dom, ibid.,* 57, 62.

[2] *secret jewels*] *S.P. Dom, ibid.,* 171, 66.

[3] *10 November 1621*] *S.P. Dom, ibid.,* 308; *28 June 1622*] *ibid.,* 414.

diamond that Queen Elizabeth took from Dom Antonio in 1589: it was removed from the Tower on 13 March 1622/3, but Charles and Buckingham returned with it to England in September. And yet, there was grumbling, among those in the know, that the Crown Jewels of England were being passed out as gratuities to the very nation with whom the English people at the time wished to fight a war. [1]

So that his Councilors and their spouses did not complain too loudly, James gave them a share of the booty. One "old jewel" that was taken from the Tower and never returned holds special interest: it was given, not to the Spanish, but to a poet, Lady Frances (*née* Howard) Stuart – and not because she was a poet. Lady Frances was wife successively to two of James's favorite and most trusted Councilors: Edward Seymour, earl of Hertford (d. 1621), and Ludovic Stuart, Duke of Lennox and Richmond (d. 1624):

> *11 March 1622/3.* Warrant to [Sir Thomas Edmondes, Treasurer of the King's Household], to present, as His Majesty's gift, to the Duchess of Lennox, an old jewel in form of the letter H, set with seven diamonds and three pearls pendant, lately taken out of the Jewel House in the Tower. [2]

Twenty-six years later, Lady Frances (d. 1639) would mention that same "old jewel" in her last will and testament: it was, indeed, one of her most prized possessions (original spelling):

> […] to my Neece Elizabeth, the Lady Maltrevers, to use the H: with seven Diamondes and three pendant pearls which was Queene Katherine Howardes, which my godson Thomas must have also and not altered, as an heir loom to remaine to him and to the heires of the house of Arundell, forever. [3]

The pendant that James gave as a Lenten gift to the duchess of Lennox was one that Henry VIII presented in his 1540 lovesuit to young Katherine Howard (the jewel was a keeper, she was not: in 1542 Henry beheaded her).

It may surprise some readers that it was not flatly illegal for King James to have given away the nation's royal treasures, disbursing them as gifts to favorites who already owned too much, or as bribes to Spanish lords, to grease the wheels of his son's lovesuit. The Crown Jewels then belonged to the person who wore the Crown. In 1760, King George III gave most royal property, including the jewels, to the government, so that taxpayers forever after would be obliged to pay for their maintenance rather than the English Royals.

• • •

Sir Anthony Weldon tells a story of James's first year as King of Britain. There was great division between the Scots and English favorites, the Scots resenting English prejudice and their greater wealth, the English courtiers resenting the King's prior attachment to Scotsmen and his Majesty's tapping the Exchequer as if the treasury were a bottomless well from which to enrich his favorites: "And now do the English faction (seeing they could not sever the Scots from him) endeavor to raise a mutiny against the Scots that were his supporters, their agents divulging everywhere [that] 'The Scots would get all, and would beggar the Kingdom.' The Scots on the other side complain to the King they were so poor, they underwent the by-word of 'beggarly Scots.' — To which the King returned this answer (as he had a very ready wit): 'Content yourselves: I will shortly make the English as beggarly as you, and so end *that* controversy!' This is as true, as he truly performed it: for however he enriched many in particular (as Salisbury, Suffolk, Northampton, Worcester, Lake, etc.), yet he did beggar himself and the nation." [4]

 Archbishop George Abbot found "a convenient place" for Queen Anna, in a large vault in Henry VII's chapel. No monument was erected for her, not so much as a brass plaque. This was not an instance of gender- or nationalist bias: when King James died in 1625, he, too, was interred without a memorial. There was no money for it, and no affection.

The hearse that bore Anna of Denmark to Westminster Abbey was left standing beside the place of her interment until it was finally knocked to pieces a quarter-century later, during the English Civil War, and looted for firewood. Her surviving son, Charles I, was beheaded.

---

[1] *Mirror of Portugal*, etc.] *S.P. Dom, ibid.,* 506-7, 511-13, 519-28, 536, 558-9, 577;   *Pindar's diamonds*] *ibid.,* 503.

[2] *Warrant…to the Tower*] James I to Sir Thomas Edmondes (11 Mar. 1622/3). *S.P. Dom. James I (1619-1623),* 520.

[3] *to my Neece…forever*] Will of Frances (Howard) Stuart, duchess of Richmond and Lennox. P.R.O. PROB 11/181; Lady Frances notes in her will that James also gave her the "Lancaster and York" carcanet (a collar of red and white roses of diamonds and rubies, worn by Elizabeth of York as shown in a 16th Century portrait);   *heirloom to remain*] Edward Fitzalan-Howard, 18th Duke of Norfolk (b. 1956); and his heir apparent, Henry Fitzalan-Howard, Earl of Arundel and Surrey (b. 1987), are today the linear descendant of the house of Arundel.

[4] *And now…the nation*] Weldon, *ibid.,* sigs. E2v-3r;   *that*] for clarity; *1650 om.*

Arbella Stuart (Seymour) (1575 - 1615)

*I have binne long restrained from my liberty,
which is as much to be regarded as my life.*
—Arbella to the Lord Chief Justice (1611)

ARBELLA STUART was the granddaughter of the poet Margaret Douglas and a great-granddaughter of Henry VIII's older and wiser sibling, Margaret Tudor. At Elizabeth's death, Lady Arbella, then a 28-year-old prisoner in the home of her grandmother, stood second in line to the English throne. Citing the 1351 statute, *De Natis Ultra Mare,* England's birther faction considered Arbella to be *first* in line, arguing that the monarch must be someone born on English soil. Other supporters of Arbella's succession cited the 1585 Treason Act, which nullified the heritable rights of a traitor's offspring. James VI, King of Scotland, was born on 19 June 1566 in Edinburgh Castle. He was the son of Mary Stuart, beheaded in 1587 for high treason against Elizabeth; and of Henry Stuart, Lord Darnley, who was murdered in February 1566/7, probably by Bothwell his mother's lover, after Darnley murdered David Rizzio, his mother's former favorite. Lady Arbella, born in Derbyshire of virtuous English parents, never had a treasonable thought in her heart apart from her demand for personal liberty. But the nation preferred a man. [1]

Arbella Stuart never sought the English throne. James, King of Scotland, dreamed of almost nothing else. So badly did he wish to become King of England that James complied with Elizabeth's every firm suggestion, thereby to ensure her continuing favor and financial subsidies (£58,000, from 1586-1602). Securing the English Crown was the foundation of his foreign policy. In 1586, James signed the Treaty of Berwick. That, and Elizabeth's execution of his mother in 1587 (an act that James criticized, mildly, as a "strange procedure"), cleared away the obstacles to his succession – all but one. That single impediment was the rival claim of his young cousin, Arbella Stuart. To punish the child for her existence, James in 1580 annulled her hereditary titles, conferring them instead on his then-favorite, Esme Stewart.

When Arbella's parents were secretly wedded in 1574, Mary Queen of Scots was a prisoner at Tutbury Castle, in the custody of George Talbot (sixth Earl of Shrewsbury) and his wife, the legendary Bess of Hardwick. The ambitious countess arranged the elopement of Elizabeth Cavendish (her daughter by her first marriage) with Charles Stuart, grandson of Margaret Tudor, hoping that a child born of the match might succeed to the throne. Queen Elizabeth instead put the groom's mother in prison, and put Bess on notice that any child of this unwelcome marriage would be forever unwelcome at Court. Arbella lived for the next six years with her mother. Meanwhile, Grandmother Bess's marriage imploded.

As a child, Arbella wore a pendant in the shape of a heart, surmounted by a coronet and engraved with the half-prescient motto, "Pour parvenir j'endure": *To Achieve, I Endure.* Her father died in 1576, her mother in 1582. Arbella's vast hereditary lands were confiscated by Queen Elizabeth in 1578 and never returned; and her titles, by James, two years later. At age seven Arbella became a ward of her imperious grandmother, and was kept in isolation at Hardwick Hall. That same year, she was promised to Robert Dudley, earl of Leicester, for marriage to his son, Lord Denbigh, aged 3. The Queen forbade the match; shortly after, the boy died. King James then suggested a betrothal between Arbella and Esme Stewart so as to reward his favorite with a bride of royal descent, and to restore Arbella to her hereditary rights. On this news, Queen Elizabeth went ballistic. When she recovered, she suggested to King James that *he* might be permitted to wed Arbella; but at the same time her Majesty commanded Bess of Hardwick to bar all access to the girl. (In 1584, there were rumors that the Queen intended to give Arbella to her old boyfriend, the Duc d'Alençon; but he died, too.)

Arbella (Feb. 1577), aged 2, holding a doll and wearing her heart pendant, inscribed, *Pour parvenir j'endure*

The earliest extant letter by Lady Arbella is one she wrote at age twelve to her grandmother while visiting her Cavendish cousins:

---

[1] *succession*] Anne Stanley (granddaughter of Mary Tudor) had perhaps the best claim: both the Third Succession Act (1543) and the will of Henry VIII (1547) made her heir presumptive on the death of Elizabeth. By her first marriage to Grey Brydges (1607), Anne became the mother of five children; by her second marriage to Mervyn Tuchet (1624), she became a countess, a rape victim, and a sex slave of the earl's servants; she died in disgrace (1647).

Arbella Stuart to Elizabeth Talbot, Countess of Shrewsbury (8 Feb. 1587/8)°

Good Lady Grandmother,

I have sent your ladyship the ends of my hair (which were cut the sixth day of the moon on Saturday last); and with them, a pot of jelly which my servant made (I pray God you find it good!). My Aunt Cavendish was here on Monday last. She certified me of your ladyship's good health and disposition, which I pray God long to continue. I am in good health. My cousin Mary hath had three little fits of an ague, but she is now well and merry. This with my humble duty unto your ladyship and humble thanks for the token you sent me last, and craving your daily blessing, I humbly cease. [1]
From Fims, the 8th of February 1587[/8].

Your ladyship's humble and obedient child,
Arbella Steward [2]

• • •

The haircut was perhaps for Arbella's first visit to Whitehall to meet the Queen, which occurred shortly after: She was escorted by her uncle, Charles Cavendish, who reported to Lady Shrewsbury. "Her Majesty spake unto her – but not long, and examined her nothing touching her book[-learning]." At dinner, Lord Burghley "directed his speech to Sir Walter Ralegh, greatly in her commendation: as that she had 'the French, the Italian, played of instruments, danced, wrought needlework, and writ very fair'; 'wished she were fifteen years old,' and with that rounded Master Ralegh in the ear; who answered him, 'It would be a happy thing!'" (i.e., so that she could be taken to bed). "At supper [Cecil] made exceeding much of her [...] and since, he hath asked when she shall come again to Court." [3]

Arbella at thirteen was appointed a Maid of Honor, though not for long. Elizabeth caught her in the act of speaking, unchaperoned, with her Majesty's favorite, the earl of Essex. Arbella was sent home in disgrace. Grandmother Shrewsbury, though forced to receive her, never forgave Arbella for the disappointment.

Another disappointment: in 1589, James VI of Scotland married Denmark's Princess Anna, not waiting for Arbella to be his queen. Elizabeth I thereafter continually vexed James with teasing hints that Arbella would succeed her to the throne of England; while cajoling cooperation from her old friend, Bess of Hardwick, by inclining toward King James.

The countess of Shrewsbury, who wished more for her granddaughter than Arbella wished for herself, raised her to become Queen of England. Household servants were obliged to address her, from infancy, as "Your Highness." But for Arbella, a library was queendom enough: she became a great lover of books. (From the spring of 1589 through September 1592, she studied the classics under a university dropout who, on credible evidence, has been identified as the Walsingham spy and nascent playwright, Christopher Marlowe.)

Bess all this while was looking for a suitable king-consort for Elizabeth's heir apparent. From a spy in the Shrewsbury household (possibly Marlowe), Lord Burghley learned that Arbella's portrait had been taken in miniature, a conventional first step toward overtures of marriage. He wrote Lady Shrewsbury to warn her that Catholics in England and abroad were plotting to wed Arbella to a papist; and that they may try to abduct the maiden. The countess wrote back, assuring him that Arbella was well under wraps, and safe from popish plots: [4]

Bess Talbot, Dowager Countess of Shrewsbury, to William Cecil, Lord Burghley (21 Sept. 1592)°

My honorable good Lord,

I received your lordship's letter on Wednesday towards night, being the 20th of this September, by a servant of Mr. John Talbot's, of Ireland. My good lord, I was at the first much troubled to think that so wicked and mischievous practices should be devised to entrap my poor Arbelle and me! But I put my trust in the Almighty, and will use such diligent care as I doubt not but to prevent whatsoever shall be attempted by any wicked persons against the poor child. I am most bound to her Majesty that it pleased her to appoint your lordship to give me knowledge of this wicked practice, and I humbly thank your lordship for advertising it. If any such like be hereafter discovered, I beseech your lordship I may be forewarned!

---

[1] *Cousin Mary*] daughter of Mary and Gilbert Talbot; born the same year as Arbella;   *ague*] fever;   *token*] gift.

[2] *Fims*] uncertain place name;   *Steward*] (as per MS); as an adult Arbella always used the spelling, *Stuart*.

[3] *My Lady Arbelle...Court*] Ed. DWF from Costello (1844) 1.209-10; from a MS at Hardwick Hall;   *Cecil*] he *MS*.

[4] *miniature*] sold at auction by Christie's (5 June 2007) for £66,000: a Hilliard miniature of a young Arbella "in grey-embroidered lace dress with high-standing white lace collar, gold and drop-pearl pendant fastened at corsage, gold and pearl necklace, drop-pearl and gold earring adorned with black ribbon, gold and drop-pearl pendants and gauze scarf in her upswept and dressed fair hair; on blue ground within gold border" (Christie's sale 7469).

I will not have any unknown or suspected person to come to my house. Upon the least suspicion that may happen here, any way, I shall give advertisement to your lordship.

I have little resort to me (my house is furnished with sufficient company). Arbelle walks not late. At such time as she shall take the air, it shall be near the house and well attended on. She goeth not to anybody's house at all. I see her almost every hour in the day: she lieth in my bedchamber.

If I can be more precise than I have been, I will be. I am bound in nature to be careful for Arbelle. I find her loving and dutiful to me, nor more by me regarded than to accomplish her Majesty's pleasure and that which I think may be for *her* service. I would rather wish many deaths than to see this, or any such like wicked attempt, to prevail. [...]

Your lordship's, as I am bound,
E. Shrewsbury

• • •

Marriage schemes for Arbella, at home and abroad, continued apace. The names put forward included Henri IV, king of France; Alejandro, duke of Parma or his son Ranuccio; Sigismund, king of Poland; Charles de Bourbon, prince of Conde; Ulric, duke of Holstein; Charles, duke of Savoy; and the Pope's brother, a Cardinal, whom the Pope defrocked so that he could marry her.

Elizabeth's wish was for Arbella to remain a virgin for life, though not as a virgin queen. By the winter of 1602/3, when her Majesty was fading, though not fading fast, Lady Arbella lost patience with her grandmother's severity, enforced spinsterhood, and her close confinement in rural Derbyshire. Now 28, unmarried and therefore powerless, she moved to take charge of her own life. Looking about for a dynastic family that could guarantee her security under the new regime, Arbella leveled her aim at Edward Seymour, 16-year-old grandson to the first Earl of Hertford. She drafted a plan: a meeting must be arranged so that she and young Lord Edward could meet, thereby to consider the prospect of marriage. In a letter dispatched to Hertford without address or signature, Arbella advised the Seymours to begin with a casting call, retaining only such as could play their parts without discovery by her Argus-eyed grandmother. Young Lord Edward and his retinue should come to Hardwick Hall in disguise, and they should follow her script. Or else, Edward should come in his own person, but under pretense of wishing to sell more land to Lady Shrewsbury (she was a collector). Upon their arrival, the visitors should take scant notice of Arbella. And they must bring along sure confirmation of their identity: best would be some handwriting, or some other personal artifact, of Queen Jane Seymour (d. 1537), or of the Lady Jane Grey (beheaded 1554). Arbella's message, the stuff of romance novels, was carried (together with oral instructions) by John Dodderidge, referenced as Mr. Good:

Lady Arbella's Adventure: Instructions for the Earl of Hertford (December 1602)°

IF THEY COME *like themselves*, they shall be shut out at the gates; I, locked up; [and] my grandmother'll be the first shall advertise and complain to the Queen. If *disguised*, they must fully prove themselves to be no sycophants to me.

For the first, let them make some offer to sell land (and Master Hancock and Master Procter are good patterns to follow), so that they may have whom they will to tarry in the house and be welcome for a longer time than shall need (I desire this shall be some ancient, grave man). The younger may come (as his "son" or "nephew") and tarry or go away as we shall then think good.

For the second, I protest your witness, either by word or writing, shall fully satisfy me; but it will be counted discretion in you, and confirm their good opinion of me, if you require them to bring all the testimonies they can, as some picture or handwriting of Lady Jane Grey (whose hand I know; and she sent her sister a book at her death, which were the *very best* they could bring); or of the Lady Katherine [Grey], or of Queen Jane Seymour, or any of that family which we know they and none but they have.

And let some of the company be of my Uncle Henry's acquaintance. [Henry] yet must not come to the house (because of my Aunt Grace and his [own] servants), but [his acquaintance] shall meet him at some other place. *Their* care is no more but to come speedily and secretly to Mansfield (or some place near); and after, you (and such intelligence as you have in the house) will provide for the rest. You know none can better advise than John Good (whom I pray you acquaint with no more [information] but that it greatly concerns me, and he will, without inquisitiveness, do his best and perchance take them for northern rather than western men; and [secrecy] were the° best way, both to [Good] or anybody else. No mention of the earl of Hertford in any case, nor of that country, if they can! Cornish and Devonshire men (and generally, out of all parts of England) resort to Sir John Byron's; therefore, let them be wary. (The shortness of time will help them to keep counsel.)

• • •

At 3:00 p.m. on 30 December, the old Earl was interrupted by John Dodderidge, come from Hardwick Hall with an urgent message. Upon learning the purpose of the visit, Hertford recoiled. Arbella had made a fatal miscalculation: the earl, fearing the Queen's displeasure, locked up Dodderidge, and first thing in the morning set out with the prisoner and his papers to London, to cry treason before the Privy Council.

     Robert Cecil, Secretary of State, had staked his career on the succession of King James. On Hertford's news, fearing a conspiracy, Cecil in the Queen's name dispatched Sir Henry Brounker with armed guards to Hardwick Hall to interrogate Lady Shrewsbury and her scheming granddaughter.

     Under Brounker's interrogation, a furious Bess of Hardwick denied all knowledge of Arbella's plot. Arbella, always high-strung, fell to pieces but sufficiently kept her wits to plead her innocence: she was not plotting to seize the Crown but was only trying to draw attention to her unhappy plight at Grandma's house. Arbella slyly professed to be futilely in love with King James, who was now fourteen years married to Anna of Denmark. Brounker returned to London with a confession and a plea for mercy:

Lady Arbella to Queen Elizabeth (early Jan. 1602/3)°

To the Queen's most excellent Majesty:

     May it please your most excellent Majesty, Sir Henry Brounker hath charged me with many things in your Majesty's name, the most whereof I acknowledge to be true, and am heartily sorry that I have given your Majesty the least cause of offense. The particulars and the manner of handling I have (to avoid your Majesty trouble) delivered to Sir H. Brounker. I humbly prostrate myself at your Majesty's feet, craving pardon for what is past, and of your princely clemency to signify your Majesty's most gracious remission to me by your Highness's letter to my lady my grandmother, whose discomfort I shall be till then. The Almighty increase and forever continue your Majesty's divine virtues and prosperity, wherewith you [being] blessed, bless us all.

Your Majesty's most humble and dutiful handmaid,
Arbella Stuart

• • •

Arbella after Brounker's visit was locked in her room under guard, there to await the Queen's judgment. Uncertain what would become of her, she drafted an apology, blotted with her tears, in which she explained her behavior (though not very convincingly). Asking pardon, Arbella now preferred death to further confinement, whether at her grandmother's house or in an unromantic and arranged marriage:

Declaration of Arbella Stuart (2 March 1602/3)°

I TAKE Almighty God to witness, I am free from promise, contract, marriage, or intention to marry, and so mean to be whilst I live – and nothing whatsoever shall make me alter my long-settled determination but the continuance of these disgraces and miseries; and the peril of the King of Scots's life; and if her Majesty continue her hard opinion of me; and I continue in my lady my grandmother's hands: then, whatsoever befall, I have determined of a course which, if it please her Majesty to like of, will be for her Majesty's honor, and best to my liking. But yet so far from my liking is it to marry at all, that I take God to witness I should think myself a great deal happier of the sentence of *death*, than of her Majesty's choice. […] Please her Majesty to consider that I am debarred her presence, not suffered to confer with my friends, nor advertise her Majesty without acquainting my lady my Grandmother (which I neither have, nor *dare*, do), and that I have reason to doubt all my actions shall receive the hardest interpretation.[1] […]

     Being (in my opinion) forsaken of all the world, I have resolutely and with a settled determination grounded all my weak hopes and comfort upon this (I confess, doubtful) foundation (but the best I have left, now): *her Majesty's favor* […] which shaken, despair may drive me for mere fear to misliked courses and that I am resolved to end my life in tears and solitariness, or else to possess her Majesty's gracious opinion of my innocence and upright dealing (as I have deserved).

     Or else, to do worse (in my own opinion; and that, experience hath° taught me): there was no other way to draw down a messenger of such worth from her Majesty but by incurring some suspicion; and having no ground whereupon to work but this (and "this," being *love*); and, being bound in duty and conscience, to make all the means I could to defend myself from perishing. For if her Majesty's favor be withdrawn, I condemn death, torment, or whatsoever can be inflicted upon the most grievous offender […]

---

[1] *advertise*] alert, inform.

I protest my conscience doth not accuse me of any fault herein but a small, honest, necessary, and consequently most pardonable presumption; for which, I doubt not but to obtain pardon, in regard of the satisfaction and expiation I offer to make therefore; which I know will be acceptable to her Majesty and were sufficient penance for the greatest offense (as I take this is the *smallest* that ever was made):

~~First, I will never trouble her Majesty with any suit hereafter, but~~ [will] forget my long-desired land; and [will] confine myself to close prison for as little liberty as it shall please her Majesty in the severest rules of wisdom and policy to allot me; and [will] think it the highest favor I can possibly obtain – for I perceive daily more and more, to my increasing grief, I am (and ever hereafter shall be) more infortunate than I lately thought I could possibly have been.

Secondly, I will make a vow, if it shall so please her Highness to command (upon condition I may re-obtain her Majesty's favor and have my dear and due liberty): *I will never marry whilst I live, nor entertain thought, nor conceal any such or other matter whatsoever from her Majesty*; which I shall think worthy for her Majesty to incline her princely ear unto.

And if this be not sufficient reason to prove my dealing faultless (or at least *pardonable*!), or [if] this be not sufficient, I must confess myself void of sense and careless of anything in this world can happen to me (for my case cannot be made worse, any manner of way!). In her Majesty's hand it is to mend it and make me think myself as happy as I can be (and that will never be, absolutely, I perceive – such treacherous dealing have I found in this matter), and in God's [hands] to end my sorrows with death, which only can make me absolutely and eternally happy.

• • •

Lady Shrewsbury also wrote to the Queen, asking that Arbella be removed from her custody – which is what Arbella wished, though for a different reason. While waiting for a response from London, locked up and cut off from her imagined supporters, Arbella learned that her lovelorn and now terrified chaplain, Rev. John Starkey, had slit his own throat. Seeking comfort for that loss, she sent a servant to her study to collect her books; he was refused entry. That same day, Arbella received what she took for an unkind letter from Brounker, carried from London by Henry Holford, in which Brounker advised her to cease and desist her "idle conceits," since the more she wrote, the less it served her purpose. Distress boiling over into anger, Arbella dispatched another:

Lady Arbella to Sir Henry Brounker (7 March 1602/3)°

Sir Henry:

I sent my page this afternoon into my quondam study chamber – which he might not be suffered to enter, much less I to receive the comfort and good counsel of my dead counselors and comforters. [1]

If you think to make me weary of my life and to conclude it according to Mr. Starkey's tragical example, you are deceived. If you mean to shorten the time for your friends' sake, you are deceived in that too, for such means prevail not with me. If you think it her Majesty's pleasure her commandment should either be unjustly pretended or covertly and cunningly infringed, I hope it is not her Majesty's meaning [but] your delusive dealing. And sure I am, it is neither for her Majesty's honor nor your credit I should be thus dealt withal.

Your will be done. I recommend my innocent cause […] to God's holy protection, to whom only be ascribed all honor, praise, and glory, for now and for ever, amen. For "All men are liars." There is "no trust in man, whose breath is in his nostrils." And the day will come when "they that judge, shall be judged," and He that now keepeth their counsel and seemeth to "wink at iniquity," and suffer it to prosper "like the green bay tree," will root out deep-rooted pride and malice and make His righteousness "shine like the noonday." [2]

I was half a Puritan before, and Mr. Holford, who *is* one, whatsoever I be, hath shortened your letter, and will shorten the time more than you all, as he hath already driven me [from] my lady my grandmother's presence with *laughter* ([whom], upon just cause, you owe me good witness I cannot forbear). Farewell, good knight. [3]

Your poor friend,
Arbella Stuart

---

[1] *quondam*] former; *might not be suffered*] was not permitted; *dead counselors*] classical authors.

[2] *All men are liars*, etc.] Arbella paraphrases Psalm 116:1, Isa. 2:22; Matt. 7:1, Acts. 17:30, Psalm 37:35, Job 11:17.

[3] *Mr. Holford*] a retainer of the Talbots who was summoned to London to be interrogated; *forbear*] tolerate, endure.

Two days later, Arbella dispatched still another defiant epistle, this one more than seven thousand words long. Writing on Ash Wednesday, she reminds him that her beloved Essex was beheaded on Ash Wednesday, two years before. Her letter, though perfectly lucid, led to whispers at Court that Lady Arbella was now insane:

Lady Arbella to Sir Henry Brounker (9 March 1602/3)°

Sir:

As you were "a private person," I found all humanity and courtesy from you, and whilst I live, will thankfully acknowledge it [...But] you perceived some "truths" which I confessed not (as you promised some "favors," I found not). When it shall please her Majesty to afford me those ordinary rights which other subjects cannot be debarred of justly, I shall endeavor to receive them as thankfully now as if they had been in due time offered; though the best part of my time be past, wherein (my heart being not so seasoned with sorrow as it is) comfort should have been welcome, and better bestowed (because my heart was not then overworn with "just" unkindness; and sorrow hath been capable of joy, and thankfully glad of every small kindness or favor).

They are dead whom I loved. They have forsaken me in whom I trusted. I am dangerouworthy s to my guiltless friends – [who] in all respects (if it were not because they are my friends) [are] as her Highness's favorable countenance as they're unjustly (to my disgrace and their hurt) favored *enemies*. [1]

So that I must conclude: as "a private person," I would trust you as soon as any gentleman I know, upon so small acquaintance. But while her Majesty referreth the managing of every matter to those two councilors, [Sir John Stanhope and Sir Robert Cecil,] her Majesty shall be abused. For I am able to *prove* her Majesty is highly abused in this matter (and, I dare say, no more than *I* have [been]). And [I] will rather lose my life than utter one word more than I have done; nay, I will rather dishonor myself so much [as] to deny what I have affirmed, than commit my cause to *their* partial examination and relation. [2]

You delivered me at your first coming a most gracious message, wherein I apparently discerned the long diswonted beams of her Majesty's gracious inclination to me. *I* sincerely delivered the *truth* – and was rewarded with a most hard censure, and frustration of my most earnest and reasonable suits that I might attend on her Majesty (or be *from* my grandmother, at least!). [3]

But my wooden yoke was made of iron – and I can bear it, as long as I think good to convince them that impose it of [their] hardness of heart, and [shall] shake it off when I think good to take my Christian liberty [...] – which I do not doubt of, if it would please her Majesty to take that course which her royal inclination *would* take *to those of her own blood* – if it were not (to my great astonishment!) diverted from them, to these two *councilors' kindred*. [...] Are the *Stanhopes* and *Cecils* able to hinder or diminish the good reputation of a *Stuart*, her Majesty being judge?

Have I stained her Majesty's blood by unworthy or doubtful marriage? Have I claimed my land these eleven years, though I had her Majesty's promise I should have it? [...A]nd must I reveal the secrets of my heart, importing my soul, my life, all I hold dear in this world (in a shorter time than at your now first coming I told you I could), when it seems her Majesty careth not for knowing anything concerning me but to break my just desires?

Shall Mr. Holford be sent for by commission, and I not have commission to send for [witnesses] whom I will, and I not protest I have hard measure? [...A]nd for myself, I will rather spit my tongue in my examiner or torturer's face, than it shall be said, to the dishonor of her Majesty's abused authority and blood, an extorted truth came out of my lips. [...]

But I am "grown a woman" – and [if,] therefore (by her Majesty's own saying), [I] am not allowed the liberty of granting lawful favors to princely suitors, how then dare subjects justify their most justifiable affection? [...] How dare others visit me in distress, when the Earl of Essex – then in highest favor – durst steal a salutation in the Privy Chamber; where, however, it pleased her Majesty *I* should be disgraced in the Presence at Greenwich° and discouraged in the lobby at Whitehall°? [...]

But whither do my thoughts transport me now! Let me live like an owl in the wilderness, since my Pallas will not protect me with her shield. You saw what a despair the greatness of my enemies (and the hard measure I have received – and my fortune is not yet bettered) drove innocent, discreet, learned, and godly Mr. Starkey into. Will you be guilty of more blood? [...]

---

[1] *They are dead*] not just her parents or Starkey, but the executed Earl of Essex, with whom Arbella had fallen in love.

[2] *partial ... relation*] biased investigation and report.

[3] *diswonted*] unaccustomed.

For the passion of God, let me come to my trial in this my prison, instantly. […] Lay the axe to the root of the tree in time, and let me lose my head, which (for less cause and upon no ground but my friends' faults) her Majesty hath threatened to take (as I told you) whilst nobody will hinder it – and [which penalty] I shall joyfully and thankfully receive, as God receive my soul. […]

Why do you think I will not grant that ~~in your absence~~ [that] which you could not obtain whilst you were *here*? Admit I had been in love and would have declared his name, I assure you on my faith I would have delivered it you in writing […] (I would rather write than speak my mind in a love-matter, especially of my own); but I say this to convince your obstinate (and I think invincible) incredulity – [you] who judge of *love, charity, words, oaths, modesty, truth, vows, obedience, patience, silence*, according to certain prodigious examples and erroneous rules which the Prince of Darkness sets more usually and authentically before your eyes: […D]o not deceive yourself so much to think I either have, or will, confess my pure and innocent self "guilty" of *love* till you deserve that extraordinary trust. […] For why should I speak unless you will believe? How shall *I* believe any good will, till I see it? […] [1]

I have conquered my affection. I have cast away my hopes. I have forsaken all comfort. I have submitted my body and fortune to more subjection than could be commanded. I have disposed of my liberty. I have cut off all means of your attaining what you seek, till you seek it of me by such means as *I* tell you. What harm can all the world do me now? – even as much as it would do me *good* to follow *your* counsel – that is, none! […]

You present her Majesty with a misshapen, discolored piece of stuff, fitting none, nor fit for her Majesty to look upon […] so tossed up-and-down that it hath almost lost the gloss. […] The more you think to make, the more you mar. When all is done, I must take it [in] hand, and shape my own coat according to my cloth […] fit for me, and every way becoming of that virtue in me, whether it be a native property of that blood I come of, or an infective virtue of the Earl of Essex.

[Essex] could go neither-friend-nor-foe-knew-whither till he arrived amongst his unwitting enemies – from whom he ever returned with honor, and was received home with joy. […He] was punished for his unmannerly (but I think in any lover's opinion, pardonable) presumption of kissing that breast in his offensively wet riding-clothes with making those "mild, kind words of reprehension" – the last that ever his ear received out of his dear mistress's mouth. […A]nd were not I unthankfully forgetful if I should not *remember* my noble friend? —who graced me (by her Majesty's commandment: disgraced orphan, unfound ward, unproved prisoner, undeserved exile) in his greatest and happy fortunes, to the adventure of eclipsing part of her Majesty's favors [to] *him*, which were so dear, so welcome to him? Shall not I (I say), now I have lost all I can lose, or almost care to lose, […] spend thus much (or rather, thus little!) time, ink, and labor, without incurring the opinion of "writing much, to little purpose"? I do it not to be requited with your applause, for then I might utter more welcome matter in two words […] lest you return to that opinion I took so very unkindly at your hands, that the more I writ, "to the less purpose it was." […]

Being allowed no company to my liking, and finding this the best excuse to avoid the tedious conversation I am bound to, I think the time best spent in "tiring" you with the "idle conceits" of my travailing mind – till it make you ashamed to see into what a scribbling melancholy (which *is* a kind of "madness," and there are several kinds of it) you have brought me; and leave me (*if* you leave me!) till I be *my own woman* – and then your trouble and mine too will cease.

Misjudge me as you list: the panic is past already. Will you not use me as well as traitors are used, who am not guilty of thought, word, or deed, which, rightly interpreted, can be the least offensive to her Majesty? – and can be *racked*, to no greater [confession] than a service of silence? Had the Earl of Essex the favor to die unbound because he was a prince, and shall my hands be bound from helping myself in this distress, before I confess some fault? […]

How many vain words are spoken! – and who dare speak for *me*? How many wanton favors are earnestly and importunately begged – and who dare humbly, and even once and no more, remember her Majesty to cast her gracious eye upon me, at least with no less favor than I deserve? How many inquisitive questions are asked of me – and how little inquisitive are my friends and acquaintance what becomes of me! What fair words have I had of courtiers and councilors – and so, they are vanished into smoke.

Who is he (amongst you all) dare be sworn in his conscience I have [done] wrong? (and dare tell the Earl of Hertford he hath done it?).

And the two councilors? They wrong their estate to show such "respect" to ruined greatness, and [for] "wisdom" (and riches!) to let innocence be thus oppressed, and truth suppressed. […]

---

[1] *Admit I had been*] Supposing it were true that I am.

Neither will I first fly and then endure my punishment, but first endure my punishment. And then I trust her Majesty will give me leave to leave all my troubles behind me, and go into a better place than her Majesty hath provided for me, these twenty-seven years. […]

Declaring my mind to her Majesty more than I have done, I dare not. My words have been already too offensively taken, and too unjustly wrested by them that had least cause so to do. I am deaf to commandments, and dumb to authority. […]

Now I have spent this day in portraying my melancholy innocence in the undeceiving black-and-white you see, after my rude manner I must tell you true: I think it will not yet be your fortune to understand my meaning. […] I will not excuse my prolixity, neither is your wiser brevity so commended […] God forgive my excess and your defects in love and charity.

From Hardwick, this Ash Wednesday.
Your poor friend,
Arbella Stuart

• • •

The Lords of the Council to the Dowager Countess of Shrewsbury (14 March 1602/3)°

Minute to my Lady Shrewsbury, [sent] by Mr. Holford, concerning the Lady Arbella:

We are very sorry to find, by the strange style of Lady Arbella's letters, that she hath her thoughts no better quieted, especially considering her Majesty's own ready inclination – notwithstanding [Arbella's] first error in dealing with my Lord of Hertford – to have taken no other course with her than was expressed by our first. […] And next, whereas your ladyship complains that she is not removed from you, we must reply unto you (for the present) that her Majesty can in no sort be brought unto it; but rather wisheth that – seeing [Arbella] groweth so troublesome both to herself and to others – that you will deal as mildly with her in words as you can, howsoever she may offend you in this time of her passion (because that is the [ground] of her quarrel); and that, as much as may be, her sending up-and-down such strange letters may be forborne. […] These directions we have thought fit to give forth, first, because the dispersing of her letters abroad (of such strange subjects as she writes!) is inconvenient in many respects, and (in our opinion) disgraceful to herself. […]

[Her Majesty] hopeth that you will so fashion all things as the young lady may not mislike her habitation. […] From the Court, at Richmond.

• • •

With Queen Elizabeth now on her deathbed and Arbella Stuart a constant worry, Cecil sent her to gloomy Sheriff Hutton Castle in Yorkshire, on grounds that her behavior had destroyed the Queen's health and imperiled her Majesty's life. With Arbella out of the way, he next let it be bruited abroad (though it was untrue) that Arbella Stuart had converted to Roman Catholicism. And he terminated her pension of £200.

Soon after the Queen's death on March 24th, the Privy Council summoned Lady Arbella to appear as the official chief mourner at her Majesty's wake and funeral. Noting the irony but refusing the honor, Arbella replied that "Sith her access to the Queen in her lifetime might not be permitted, she would not after her death be brought so near her, as on a stage for public spectacle." Arbella was removed to Wrest House. [1]

Looking for better treatment from King James than she had received from the late Queen, Arbella wrote many times, asking that her pension be resumed. Much to Cecil's chagrin, James after his arrival in London granted Arbella her liberty plus £1,000 per year, plus an allowance of food for her household (benefits that Cecil took occasion to obstruct). James also appointed Arbella to be the official meat carver to Queen Anna.

The Bye Plot. In May, Catholic extremists spoke of kidnapping the King at Greenwich, in June. James of Scotland would be liberated to succeed Elizabeth only on a guarantee of religious toleration (plus a pardon for the kidnappers). Finding little support among recusant gentry for this goofball scheme, the "Bye Plot" was abandoned. But Cecil's relentless investigation turned up some forty named suspects who might have been involved, had the plan gone forward. Of these, he indicted seven for high treason.

The Bye inquiry led Cecil (through his alienated brother-in-law, George Brooke) to the so-called "Main Plot" of Henry Brooke Lord Cobham, whose alleged plan was to secure the succession of Arbella Stuart, with assistance from Spain. Lord Cobham evidently took some kind of initiative: Arbella had received a letter from him, which she had turned over to the Privy Council (the date and content of which were never disclosed). When arrested, Cobham on a charge of high treason imprisoned Sir Walter Ralegh and Thomas Lord Grey.

---

[1] *Sith…spectacle*] B.L. MS Sloane 718; Ellis, *Letters*, 3.59.

On 15 November at Winchester Castle, Cecil and Coke tried seven Bye conspirators. Six were condemned: William Watson and William Clark (priests); Griffin Markham, Anthony Copley, Bartholomew Brookesby, and George Brooke (Roman Catholic gentry). Sir Edward Parham was acquitted. Ralegh was tried on the 17th, lords Cobham and Grey on the 18th; all three were condemned. The case against Ralegh was comprised of hearsay accusations ascribed to Cobham (who did not appear); plus ad hominem vituperation from the prosecutor, Sir Edward Coke. (He also railed against Arbella, though she was known to be innocent). The failure of Cecil and Coke to supply credible evidence against Ralegh in particular fueled public skepticism:

Sir Anthony Weldon, from *The Court and Character of King James*°

[A] kind of treason brake forth, but what it was as no man could then tell; so, it is left – with so dark a comment that posterity will never understand the text or remember any such "treason." (It is true, some lost their lives, yet the world was never satisfied of the justice). [...] I shall as near as I can lead you to the discovery of this "treason," which consisted of Protestants, Puritans, Papists, and of an atheist – "a strange medley," you will say, "to meet in one and the same treason, and *keep counsel*!" – which surely they did, because *they knew* not of any! The Protestants were the Lord Cobham and George Brooke his brother (the one, very learned and wise; the other, a most silly lord); the Puritan: the Lord Grey of Wilton (a very hopeful gentleman, blasted in the very bud); the Papists: [William] Watson and [William] Clark (priests), and [Sir Edward] Parham (a gentleman); the atheist: Sir Walter Ralegh. [...] This "treason" was compounded of strange ingredients, and more strange, than true. It was *very* true most of these were discontented to see [Robert Cecil] their old friend, so high [as] to trample on them that before had been his chief supporters. [...] And [Cecil] in this had a double benefit: first, in ridding himself of such as he feared would have been thorns in his sides; secondly, by endearing himself to the King, by showing his diligence and vigilancy for his [Majesty's] safety. So that it might be said of him as of Caesar in another case, *Inveniam aut saciam*: "I will either find out a treason, or make one." [1]

• • •

The convicted conspirators received their sentence: "You shall be had from hence [...] to the place of execution; there to be hanged, and cut down alive; and your body shall be opened, your heart and bowels plucked out and your privy members cut off and thrown into the fire before your eyes; then your head to be stricken off from your body, and your body shall be divided into four quarters, to be disposed of at the King's pleasure. And God have mercy on your soul." [2]

Arbella says no more of this scandal than was appropriate for the eyes of anyone who might intercept and read her letters. But her preoccupation with courtliness – a theme of her correspondence that summer and fall – may reflect a certain discomfort with realpolitik. Released now from her isolation in Hardwick Hall, Arbella was being exposed for the first time to the violent incivilities on which the regime depended to maintain its grip on power:

Lady Arbella to her Uncle Gilbert Talbot, Earl of Shrewsbury (16 Sept. 1603)°

[...] If ever there were such a virtue as *courtesy* at the Court, I marvel what is become of it! for I protest I see little or none of it but in the Queen, who ever since her coming to Newbury hath spoken to the people as she passeth; and receiveth their prayers with thanks and thankful countenance, bare-faced, to the great contentment of native *and* foreign people – for I would not have you think the French Ambassador would leave that attractive virtue of our late Queen Elizabeth unremembered or uncommended when he saw it imitated by our most gracious queen [Anna], lest you should think we infect even our neighbors with incivility.

Lady Arbella, 20, with shooting star

From Woodstock the 16 of September.
Your lordship's niece,
Arbella Stuart

• • •

---

[1] *Cecil*] Q *Salisbury* (Cecil was not created earl of Salisbury until 1605).

[2] *You shall be had…on your soul*] Howell, ed., *State Trials James I* (1816), 2.31.

Arbella's courtesy made a deep impression upon the heart of Queen Anna's secretary, William Fowler, a Scotsman. Writing to her uncle Gilbert, Fowler praised "my Lady Arbella, who may be, to the first Seven, justly the Eighth Wonder of the World (if I durst, I would write more plainly)." Enclosing a sonnet in her praise, Fowler concedes, "I fear I am too saucy and overbold." In another letter, he laments that "My Lady Arbella spends her time in lecture, reading, hearing of service and preaching [...] She will not hear of marriage."[1]

Arbella paid scant attention to the queen's amorous secretary. Her letter of 6 October was posted from Winchester Castle, 150 miles west of London, in distant Hampshire. She does not say what took her there: Winchester was the venue that Cecil had chosen for the trial and execution of the accused traitors.

Preparations at the Castle began on 28 September for the arrival of the prisoners on 13 November. With the plague hot in London and a bloody spectacle to be seen in Hampshire, courtiers in October converged on Winchester. Queen Anna and her ladies entertained themselves the while with outdoor games remembered from childhood. The King and his favorites went hunting. But it was not for sport that Arbella was brought to Winchester: she was there to be interrogated concerning a foiled plot to make her Queen of England. She was then escorted back across the country, past London, to Fulston in Kent, where she sat out the trials (and remained there until Christmas festivities required her attendance in London). In her letters to her aunt and uncle during this period, Arbella makes no mention of the prisoners; but they cannot have been far from her mind. On December 5th, George Brooke was the first to die.

In her letter of December 8th, Arbella banters with her uncle Gilbert over a sexist witticism in his previous letter. Her thoughts return then to Hampshire: Nine "traitors" that night awaited execution, including Sir Walter Ralegh. Next morning six were to be hanged and dismembered on Winchester Castle green, the very ground on which Queen Anna and her ladies, in October, had played children's games late into the night:

Lady Arbella to Gilbert Talbot (8 Dec. 1603)°

[...] I pray you take not that *pro concesso* in general which is only proper to some monsters of our sex: I cannot deny so apparent a truth as that wickedness prevaileth with *some* of our sex (because I daily see some, even of the fairest amongst us, misled and willingly and wittingly ensnared by the Prince of Darkness). But yet ours shall still be the purer and more innocent kind. (There went ten thousand virgins to Heaven in one day! Look but in the almanac, and you shall find that glorious day!) And if you think there are some, "but not many," of us that may prove saints, I hope you are deceived. But "Not many *rich*, not many *noble*, shall enter into the kingdom of Heaven" – so that *riches* and *nobility* are hindrances from Heaven, as well as our "nature's infirmity." You would think me very full of divinity, or desirous to show that little I have (in both which, you should do me wrong if you knew what business I have at Court, and yet preach to you! – pardon me, it is not my function).

Now, a little more to the purpose. [...] The Spanish ambassador invited Mdme. de Beaumont (the French ambassador's lady) to dinner, requesting her to "bring some English ladies" with her. She brought my Lady [Lucy] Bedford, Lady [Penelope] Rich, Lady Susan [de Vere], and Lady Dorothy [Percy] with her, and great cheer they had. A fortnight after, he invited the Duke [of Lennox], the Earl of Mar, and divers of that nation, requesting them to "bring the Scottish ladies" – for he was desirous "to see some *natural* beauties." My Lady Anne Hay and my cousin, [Lady Jane] Drummond went. And after the sumptuous dinner, [they] were presented first with a pair of Spanish gloves apiece; and after, my cousin Drummond had a diamond ring of the value of two hundred crowns given her, and my Lady Anne a gold chain of Spanish work, near that value. [...]

Will you know how we spend our time on the queen's side? Whilst I was at Winchester, there were certain child-plays remembered by the fair ladies, *viz.*, "I Pray, my Lord, Give me a Course" (in your *park*); "Rise, Pig, and Go"; "One Penny, Follow Me," etc. And when I came to Court, they were as highly in request as ever cracking of nuts was. So I was by the Mistress of the Revels not only compelled to play at I knew not what (for till that day I never heard of a play called "Fire"), but even persuaded (by the princely example I saw) to play the child again. This exercise is most used from ten of the clock at night till two or three in the morning. But that day [on which] *I* made one, it began at twilight and ended at sup-pertime. There was an interlude, but not so ridiculous – as ridiculous as it *was* – as my letter; which here I conclude, with many prayers to the Almighty for your happiness. And so I humbly take my leave—

From Fulston, the 8th of December, 1603.
Your lordship's niece, *Arbella Stuart*

---

[1] *My lady Arbella...marriage*] W. Fowler to G. Talbot (11 Sept. 1603, 3 Oct. 1604), ed. DWF from Lodge, *Illustrations* (1791): 3.168-9, 236.

With the same post, Arbella wrote to her beloved Aunt. At the trials of Ralegh and Grey, Arbella though known to be innocent was roasted by Sir Edward Coke as a traitor. She tries to shrug it off and move on:

Lady Arbella to her Aunt Mary Talbot, Countess of Shrewsbury (8 Dec. 1603)°

Madame,

[…] When any great matter comes in question, rest secure, I beseech you, that I am not interested in it as an actor, howsoever the vanity of wicked men's vain designs have made my name pass through a gross and subtle lawyer's lips of late – to the exercise and increase [of] *my patience*, and not *their credit*. I trust I have not lost so much of your good opinion as your pleasant postscript would make one (that were suspicious of their assured friends, as *I* never was) believe. For if I should not prefer the reading of your kind and most welcome letters before *all* Court delights (admit I delighted as much in them as others do), it were a sign of extreme folly; and liking Court sports no better than I do (and than I think you think I do!), I know you cannot think me so transformed as to esteem anything *less* […] Wherefore, I beseech you, let me hear [you] often declare your love by the length of your letters. […]

For a New Year's gift for the Queen…I mean to give her Majesty two pair of silk stockings lined with plush and two pair of gloves lined, if London afford me not some daft toy I like better (whereof I cannot bethink me). […] I am making the King a purse. And for all the world else, I am unprovided: this time will manifest my poverty more than all the rest of the year. (But why should I be ashamed of it, when it is others' fault and not mine?) My quarter's "allowance" will not defray this one charge, I believe. […]

From Fulston, the 8th of December 1603.
Your ladyship's most affectionate niece to command,
Arbella Stuart

• • •

Activity at Winchester Castle the next day commenced with the ritual execution of Watson and Clark, the two priests. Clark, still alive when cut down, cried out when castrated and disemboweled. When it was over, the arms and legs of both men were hung on Winchester gates, their heads on the castle tower.

Execution of the other four Bye conspirators was deferred until the 10th. But when they were brought to the stage, each in turn was granted a last-minute reprieve. Cobham, Brooke, and Ralegh were returned to prison for a life sentence. The others were exiled to the Continent (Markham as a salaried spy for Robert Cecil, reporting on English Catholic émigrés).

Pleased to hear of the King's unexpected clemency, Arbella in her letter to the Talbots of 18 December closes with happy tidings: "I have reserved the best news for last, and that is the King's pardon of life to the non-executed traitors. I dare not begin to tell of the royal and wise manner of the King's proceeding therein, lest I should find no end of extolling him for it, till I had written out a pair of bad eyes." [1]

The next seven years were Arbella's happiest since before her mother's death. Although the King kept her dependent on his charity, declining to restore her confiscated lands and revenue, she was able to live in London, in her uncle Shrewsbury's house in Broad Street. Lacking the money and wardrobe necessary for continual attendance at Court, Arbella now had a measure of freedom and time to spend with her books.

In a letter to the Doge in May 1607, the Venetian ambassador commented on the progress of the renowned Lady Arbella, now 32 and still single:

Nicolo Molino, Venetian Ambassador, to the Doge and Senate (30 May 1607)°

The nearest relative the King has is Madame Arbella, descended from Margaret [Tudor], daughter of Henry VII (which makes her cousin to the King). She is twenty-eight, not very beautiful but highly accomplished: for besides being of most refined manners, she speaks fluently Latin, Italian, French, Spanish, reads Greek and Hebrew, and is always studying. She is not very rich, for the late Queen was jealous of everyone, and especially of those who had a claim on the throne, and so she took from her the larger part of her income, and the poor lady cannot live as magnificently nor reward her attendants as liberally as she would. The King professes to love her and to hold her in high esteem. She is allowed to come to Court. The King promised when he ascended the throne that he would restore her property, but he has not done so yet, saying that she shall have it all, and more, on her marriage; but so far the husband has not been found, and she remains without a mate and without estate.

---

[1] *I have…bad eyes*] A. Stuart to Gilbert Talbot (18 Dec. 1603), Talbot Papers MS 2, f. 211; ed. Steen, 197.

Whenever Arbella mentioned money or matrimony to the King or Lord Cecil, she was put off with excuses that the Crown had other, more necessary, expenses; which she accepted with as much patience as she could muster. In the meantime Arbella did what she could to bring good cheer and success to others:

Lady Arbella to Gilbert Talbot (17 June 1609)°

To the right honorable, my very good uncle, the Earl of Shrewsbury:

Because I know not that your lordship hath forsaken *one* recreation that you have liked heretofore, I presume to send you a few idle lines to read in your chair, after you have tired yourself, either with affairs or any sport that bringeth weariness; and (knowing you well-advertised of all occurrence in *serious* manner) I make it my end to make you merry, and show my desire to please you even in playing the fool: for no folly is greater, I trow, than to laugh when one smarteth. (But that, my *aunt's* divinity can tell you – Saint Lawrence, deriding his tormentors even upon the gridiron, bade them turn him on the *other* side, for that he lay on, was sufficiently broiled!) [1]

I should not know how to excuse myself from either insensibleness or contempt of injuries: I find if one rob a house and build a *church* with the money, the wronged party may go pipe in an ivy leaf for any redress, for *Money so well bestowed must not be taken from that holy work* (though the right owner go a-begging). Unto you it is given to understand parables or to command comment; but if *you* be of this opinion of the Scribes and Pharisees, I condemn your lordship (by your leave) for an *heretic*, by the authority of Pope Joan! – for there is a text sayeth, "You must not do evil that good may come thereof." [2]

But now, from doctrine to miracles: [...] I humbly pray your lordship to bestow two of the next good parsonages of yours, shall fall on me – not that I mean to convert them to my *own* benefit (for though I go rather for a good clerk than a worldly-wise woman, I aspire to no degree of "Pope Joan"), but [for] some good ends, whereof this bearer will tell your lordship one: My boldness shows how honorably I believe of your disposing of such livings. [3]

Your lordship's niece,
Arbella Stuart

• • •

Romance blossomed. In December, the King received word that Arbella Stuart had pledged herself in marriage to William Seymour, Lord Beauchamp. The intended groom was another grandson of the Earl of Hertford and a younger brother to the Edward Seymour whom Arbella had hoped to meet and marry in December 1602 (and who was no longer single). Arbella now stood fourth in line to the throne, after the three children of King James. Lord Beauchamp was sixth, after his brother Edward. Arbella therefore spent the 1609 Christmas holidays in prison. Writing to the King, she excused her engagement as an exigency of her "poverty." James boosted her annuity to £1,600 and released her from prison but forbade the marriage. On February 2nd, just days after she was permitted to walk, a defiant Arbella formally betrothed herself to Seymour. Summoned to appear before the Privy Council, Lord Beauchamp and Lady Arbella were compelled to swear, on pain of imprisonment, not to consummate their marriage without the King's consent. Their vow sworn, Arbella was taken again into the King's favor, but closely watched.

Despite the difference in their ages – she was 35, he was 22 (a commonplace, had the genders been reversed) – the newlyweds still loved one another. Risking prison, they secretly married at four a.m. on June 22nd. Their secret was not kept. On July 8th, the bride and groom were arrested. King James committed Seymour to the Tower of London and remanded Arbella to the custody of Sir Thomas Perry in Lambeth.

Arbella's first concern was for those who depended on her: from house arrest in Lambeth she begged clemency for her imprisoned servants. Her Aunt Mary did what she could to find places for those servants who were not arrested. Arbella's other requests – sent to King James, the Privy Council, Sir Robert Cecil, Queen Anna, Lady Jane Drummond, the Seymours, even to Sir Edward Coke – fell on deaf ears and had no effect. (Her beloved Uncle Gilbert, a politic member of the Privy Council, co-signed the harsh decrees against her.)

---

[1] *my aunt's divinity*] Mary Talbot was a Roman Catholic;   *Saint Lawrence*] a deacon of the 3rd century who, when tortured upon a great gridiron with coals beneath, is said to remarked cheerfully, "Flip me over, this side's done."

[2] *rob a house*] Arbella Stuart's suit to recover the lands confiscated by Elizabeth I was to this point unsuccessful, her income having been "well bestowed" elsewhere;   *pipe in an ivy leaf*] proverbial: to console oneself as best one can, after loss or failure;   *Pope Joan*] a legendary cross-dressing English woman who was said (by Protestants) to have become Pope, and gave birth while in office; *you must ... thereof*] a paraphrase of Romans 3:8.

[3] *clerk*] cleric, clergyman;   *bearer*] letter-carrier (who will tell you whom I have in mind for your next two appointments: Arbella wished to assist two clergymen seeking a benefice);   *livings*] a *living* or *benefice* was a position for a clergyman that came with a fixed income, the appointment to which was held by the lord of the manor.

Lady Arbella to the Privy Council (July 1610)°

To the Right Honorable the Lords of his Majesty's most Honorable Privy Council:

~~Right honorable and my very good Lords~~—

I am constrained to trouble you, rather than be guilty of the danger of life wherein Hugh Crompton and Edward Reeves, two of my servants, lately committed to the Marshalsea for my cause, remain. I am informed [that] divers [persons] near that prison, and in it, are lately dead; and divers others sick of contagious and deadly diseases; wherefore I humbly beseech your Honors to commiserate their distress, and consider that they are *servants*, and accountable for divers debts and reckonings, which, if they should die, would be a great prejudice to me and others. And therefore I humbly beseech you to move unto his Majesty my most humble suit, and theirs, that it will please his Majesty they may be removed to some other healthful air.

Arbella Seymour

Lady Arbella to King James (c. Oct. 1610)°

May it please your most excellent Majesty,

The unfortunate estate whereunto I am fallen by being deprived of your Majesty's presence (the greatest comfort to me on Earth), together with the opinion of me [that] is conceived of your Majesty's displeasure towards me, hath brought as great affliction to my mind as can be imagined.

Nevertheless, touching the offense for which I am now punished, I most humbly beseech your Majesty (in your most princely wisdom and judgment) to consider in what a miserable state I had been if I had taken any other course than I did: for my own conscience witnessing before God that I was then the wife of him that now I am, I could never have matched with any other man, but to have lived all the days of my life as an harlot, which your Majesty would have abhorred in any, especially in one who hath the honor (how otherwise unfortunate soever) to have any drop of your Majesty's blood in them.

But I will trouble your Majesty no longer, but (in all humility, attending your Majesty's good pleasure) for that liberty, the want whereof depriveth me of all health and all other worldly comfort. I will never forget to pray for your Majesty's most happy prosperity for ever in all things, and so remain—

Your Majesty's most faithful subject and servant,
Arbella Seymour

Lady Arbella to King James (c. Dec. 1610)°

I do most heartily lament my hard fortune that I should offend your Majesty [in] the least, especially in that whereby I have long desired to merit of your Majesty, as appeared before your Majesty was my Sovereign. And though your Majesty's neglect of me, and my love to this gentleman that is my husband, and my fortune, drew me to a contract before I acquainted your Majesty, I humbly beseech your Majesty to consider how impossible it was for me to imagine it could be offensive unto your Majesty, having few days before given me your royal *consent* to bestow myself on any subject of your Majesty's (which likewise your Majesty had done [before,] long since). Besides, never having been either prohibited any, or spoken to for any, in this land by your Majesty – these seven years that I have lived in your Majesty's house – I could not conceive that your Majesty regarded my marriage *at all*; whereas if your Majesty had vouchsafed to tell me your mind, and accept the freewill offering of my obedience, I could not have offended your Majesty – of whose gracious goodness I presume so much that if it were as convenient in a worldly respect as malice may make it seem to separate us whom God hath joined, your Majesty would not do evil that good might come thereof; nor make me, that have the honor to be so near your Majesty in blood, the first precedent that ever was (though our princes may have left some – as little imitable, for so good and gracious a King as your Majesty – [such] as David's dealing with Uriah). But I assure myself if it please your Majesty in your own wisdom to consider thoroughly of my cause, there will be no solid reason appear to debar me of justice and your princely favor, which I will endeavor to deserve whilst I breathe. And never ceasing to pray for your Majesty's felicity in all things, [I] continue – [1]

Your Majesty's
A. S.

---

[1] *David's dealing*] King David in 2 Samuel, desiring Bathsheba, causes her husband Uriah to be slain in battle.

Lady Arbella to her husband, William Seymour (n.d. 1610/1)°

Sir —

I am exceeding sorry to hear you have not been well. I pray you let me know truly how you do, and what was the cause of it (for I am not satisfied with the reason *Smith* gives for it!). But if it be a cold, I will impute it to some sympathy betwixt us, having myself gotten a swollen cheek at the same time with a cold. For God's sake, let not your grief of mind work upon your body. You may see, by me, what inconveniences it will bring one to. And no fortune, I assure you, daunts me so much as that weakness of body I find in myself, for *si nous vivons l'age d'un veau* (as Marot says), we may [yet] by God's grace be happier than we look for in being suffered to enjoy ourselves with his Majesty's favor. But if we be not able to live to it, I, for my part, shall think myself a pattern of misfortune in enjoying so great a blessing as you, so little a while. No separation but *that* deprives me of the comfort of you: for wheresoever you be, or in what state soever you are, it sufficeth me you are mine. [1]

"Rachel wept and would not be comforted, because her children were no more"; and that indeed is the remediless sorrow, and none else. And therefore God bless us from that, and I will hope well of the rest (though I see no apparent hope). But I am sure God's book mentioneth many of His children, in as great distress, that have done well after, even in this world. [2]

I assure you, nothing the State can do with me can trouble me so much as this news of your being ill doth. And you see: when I am troubled, I trouble you too, with tedious kindness – for so I think you will account so long a letter, yourself not having written to me for this good while, so much as how you do. But, sweet sir, I speak not this to trouble you with writing, but when you please.

Be well, and I shall account myself happy in being your faithful, loving wife,
Arbella

• • •

On word that Arbella Stuart had suffered a miscarriage at Lambeth, the King commanded that she be taken to the north of England, so that there could be no thought of a second legitimate pregnancy. Despairing now of a pardon, Arbella wrote to the Chief Justices, demanding a writ of habeas corpus and a speedy trial:

Lady Arbella to [Sir Thomas Fleming], Lord Chief Justice of England, and to Sir Edward Coke, [Lord Chief Justice of the Common Pleas] (n.d. Feb. 1610/1)°

My Lords,

Whereas I have been long restrained from my liberty (which is as much to be regarded as my life), and am appointed, as I understand, to be removed far from these courts of justice (where I ought to be examined, tried, and then condemned or cleared), to remote parts, whose courts I hold unfitted for the trial of my offense: this is to beseech your Lordships to inquire by an *Habeas Corpus* or other usual form of law, *What is my fault*? And if, upon examination by your lordships, I shall thereof be justly convicted, let me endure such punishment by your lordships; sentence as is due to such an offender. And if your lordships may not or will not of yourselves grant unto me the ordinary relief of a distressed subject, then I beseech you: become humble intercessors to his Majesty that I may receive such benefit of justice as both his Majesty by his oath (those of his blood not excepted) hath promised, and [that] the laws of this realm afford to all others. And though, unfortunate woman that I am, I should obtain neither, yet I beseech your lordships, retain me in your good opinion, and judge charitably till I be proved to have committed any offense, either against God or his Majesty, deserving so long restraint or separation from my lawful husband. So, praying for your lordships, I rest:

Your afflicted poor suppliant,
A. S.

The King sustained the order but permitted Arbella to be attended by her steward, Hugh Crompton (newly released from prison), and by Thomas Moundford (the King's own physician). On 16 March, the bishop of Durham arrived with armed guards to receive custody. He found the prisoner distraught, desperately ill, and her luggage half-packed. Too ill to ride, Arbella was carried on a litter. The expedition advanced just nineteen miles in five days. Reaching Barnet on the 21st, Arbella was insensible. Dr. Moundford determined that she risked death to proceed further. The King permitted an extended layover in a rented house at East Barnet.

---

[1] *si nous vivons l'age d'un veau*] if we live to the age of a calf; *that*] death.

[2] *Rachel wept*] Jer. 31:15, Mat. 2:17-18; James in 1618 pursued rumors that a living child had been born.

Taking advantage of this welcome delay, Mary Talbot sprang into action. Over the next month (and under her husband's nose), the countess of Shrewsbury smuggled £2,800, some jewels, and boy's clothing to her niece by way of Hugh Crompton. She enlisted allies, booked travel arrangements, paid bribes.

On 3 June 1611, Arbella Stewart walked to freedom dressed in baggy French breeches, a man's doublet, wig, black hat and cloak, and russet boots with red tops; at her side, a rapier.

Meanwhile, William Seymour disguised himself in the frock of a poor carter, with an unkempt wig and false beard, and walked from the Tower of London. His flight was made possible by sympathy and bribes, and by a white lie that his exit was for a brief conjugal visit, from which he would return voluntarily to the Tower later that same day.

It has never been learned what mishap or misinformation caused Lord Beauchamp to miss connections at the Blackwall Inn, where he was supposed to rendezvous with his sweet Arbella. He then missed the boat.

Without her husband but assisted by loyal servants, Arbella kept her appointment with the captain of a French vessel moored in the Thames near Gravesend. She waited there for William to join her.

The alarm being sounded by Seymour's own brother, the ever-paranoid King James fretted that Arbella was fled abroad to raise an army against him. A proclamation "By the King," printed on June 4th, denounced the fugitives for their "great and heinous offenses." Dozens of possible accomplices were arrested: servants, relatives, Dr. Moundford, London watermen. Gilbert Talbot was put under house arrest, his wife imprisoned. Seymour's valet, already in the Tower, was transferred to the dungeon. Houses were ransacked from London to Gravesend, and the European ports alerted. All British vessels were called upon to aid in the search.

Lord Beauchamp found passage across the Channel and reached Ostend. Arbella was less lucky: awaiting Seymour's arrival, she implored Captain Corvé to weigh anchor, a big mistake. The French vessel was spotted, pursued, and boarded. Arbella and her servants were taken into custody, at least two of them later tortured. The cash and jewels found in her luggage were confiscated by the King, to defray his expenses in apprehending her. Arbella was then committed to isolation in the Tower, where she remained for the rest of her life.

Mary Talbot confessed without remorse that she master-minded the escape. For this loyalty to Arbella, the countess spent most of the next twelve years in prison. As an inmate, she was informed by James's government that Arbella had betrayed her, accusing her of involvement in a Roman Catholic plot. That vicious lie, which Arbella was never given the opportunity to deny, is one that Mary Talbot is unlikely to have credited. But gullible historians have clucked their tongues over Arbella's treachery.

Cut off from her devoted servants, her truelove, and her imprisoned aunt, Arbella developed one last scheme whereby to achieve her freedom. On learning of Princess Elizabeth's 1613 marriage to the Elector Palatine, Arbella ordered four elegant new gowns – one of which cost £1,500 – so that she would look well at the Court wedding festivities. She needed only to receive an invitation. When King James saw her again, and on such a happy occasion, he might well restore her to favor, and eventually permit her husband to return from exile. But Arbella was not invited to the wedding. Her fashion-extravagance while still in prison was noted in Court gossip, with some amusement, as a sign that Lady Arbella had altogether lost touch with reality.

Over the next two years, Arbella succumbed to despair. If she was permitted to send or receive letters, they have not survived. It is said that she wrote much poetry, evidently discarded. In 1615, when she began her hunger strike, it was whispered at Court that she was insane – but that was said before, back when she was a prisoner at Hardwick Hall. Her symptoms of irrationality: a passion to love and be loved; a demand for self-determination; a right to challenge abusive authority; and "writing much, to little purpose."

Arbella Stuart died in prison on 25 September 1615. She passed without notice. At Court, James suffered no mention of his cousin's death (but quietly claimed all of her remaining property for the Crown, including gifts of jewelry she had given to fellow prisoner, Sir Walter Ralegh). Lady Arbella was interred in Westminster Abbey, by night, without a funeral, her coffin stashed atop that of James's mother, Mary Queen of Scots; and enclosed without a grave marker. That same month, a high-profile crime riveted the nation's attention: Sir Thomas Overbury death in 1613 was discovered to have been a murder, Arbella was soon forgotten – though not by everyone: Abraham Denderkin, a Dutch trader, complained to the Privy Council that he had supplied pearls to the value of £400, embroidered into a gown Arbella never wore that was still in the Tower and for which he had not been paid. A note was made of it, though to little purpose.

Arbella holding a watch and her lapdog, by Robt. Peake (National Portrait Gallery)

Cecilia Boulstred (1583-1609),

Maiden of the Bedchamber

Shee chang'd our world with hers.
—John Donne, *Elegie upon the Death of Mris Boulstred*

C ECILIA BOULSTRED (commonly known as *Cecily* or *Celia*) was the daughter of Edward and Cecily (Croke) Boulstred of Hedgerley Boulstred, in Buckinghamshire. The sixth of eleven children, Cecily was baptized at Beaconsfield on 12 February 1582/3. Nothing is known of her childhood. As a young adult, she became a noted wit in the court of James I. And in death, her body became a theme of court poets who competed for the literary matronage of Lucy Russell, countess of Bedford. [1]

In 1602, Ben Jonson's dearest friend, John Roe, courted Boulstred and received a pledge of her affection, possibly of marriage, but she ended the relationship. Shortly after the breakup, there circulated at court a verse epistle from John Roe addressed "To Mistress Boulstred." The poem though scurrilous is written as if it were a moral remonstrance, addressed by a concerned male friend to a woman of easy virtue. It is alleged that Boulstred solicited Roe for sex, which caused him to reject her as unfit for marriage. The poet, who values the pleasures of friendship above those of fornication, professes himself unwilling to suffer a lifetime of remorse and possible damnation for one hour's pleasure with a wanton courtesan:

An Elegy to Mistress Boulstred, 1602 °

Shall I go force an elegy? abuse
My wit, and break the hymen of my Muse
For one poor hour's love? Deserves it such,
Which serves not *me,* to do on *her* as much?
Or, if it *could,* I would that fortune shun! [2]
Who would be rich, to be so soon undone?
The beggar's best is, Wealth he doth not know
(And but to show it him *increaseth* woe). [3]
But "We two may enjoy an hour"? When never
It returns, who would have a loss for *ever*?
Nor can so short a love, if true, but bring
A half-hour's fear with the thought of losing.
Before it, all hours were hope; and all are
That shall come *after* it, years of despair.
This joy, brings this doubt: whether it were more
To have enjoyed it, or have died before? [4]
'Tis a lost Paradise, a fall from grace,
Which I think Adam felt more than his race;
Nor need those angels any other Hell:
It is enough for them, from Heaven they fell.

---

[1] *Edward*] Edward Sr. died c. 1599; his principal heir, Edward (1588-1659) married Margaret Astley, daughter to the chamberlain of Queen Anna's household.

[2] *Or, if*] And even if.

[3] *wealth he doth not know*] doesn't know what he's missing.

[4] *this joy...this doubt*] this joy of an hour's sexual pleasure ... this fear, that it were better to die innocent than to have illicit intercourse, and be damned.

Beside, *conquest* in love is all in all!   [1]
That, when I list, she under me may fall,
And for this, turn, both for delight and view?   [2]
~~I'll have a Succuba as good as you!~~

[25] But when these toys are past, and hot blood ends,
The best enjoying is, we still are friends.
Love can but be friendship's outside; their two
Beauties differ, as minds and bodies do.   [3]
Thus I this great good still would be to take
(Unless one hour, another happy make;   [4]
Or, that I might forget it instantly;
Or in that blest estate, that I might die).
But why do I thus travail in the skill
Of despised poetry? (and perchance spill
My fortune, or undo myself in sport
By having but that dangerous name in Court!)   [5]
 I'll leave. And since I do your poet prove,
 Keep you my lines as secret as my love.

The disclaimer that "we still are friends" is a rhetorical ploy in the interest of slander: Roe after having been jilted speaks as a pious and congenial narrator even as he smears pitch on Boulstred's reputation. That the poem is motivated by Roe's "love" for Cecily is transparently insincere ("I'll have a Succuba, as good as you"). Equally obvious: the poem was not kept "secret" – and it is beyond belief that Boulstred was herself the one who circulated the libel.

Less obvious: "To Mistress Boulstred" was not, in fact, penned by John Roe. The verse circulated in manuscript as an epistle from "J.R." to Boulstred. An attribution to Roe has never been challenged; but it was ghost-written by Ben Jonson, who years later quietly laid claim to it. Jonson often incorporated his earlier nondramatic verse into his new stageplays, which is precisely what he does with "To Mistress Boulstred," in *The New Inn* (1628/9):

Lovell. Who would be rich to be so soon undone?
The beggar's best is, wealth he doth not know:
(And but to show it him, inflames his want). /.../

Host. These, yet, are hours of hope.

Lovell.   But all hours following
Years of despair, ages of misery!
Nor can so short a happiness, but spring
A world of fear, with thought of losing it.
Better be never happy, than to feel
A little of it, and then lose it ever. /.../
If one hour could the other happy make,
I should attempt it. /.../ (2.6)

Lord Latimer.   He lies
With his own Succuba...   (4.3)

---

[1] *conquest is all*] besides which, it's no fun for the man if sex is freely offered and not won over her resistance.

[2] *when I list*] whenever I please; *under me may fall*] 1. as a conquest; 2. in the missionary position;   *turn*] favor; sexual encounter.

[3] *Beauties*] the beauty of *friendship*, and the beauty of heterosexual *love*, are as different as *mind* and *flesh*.

[4] *this great good*] i.e., non-sexual friendship.

[5] *dangerous name*] i.e., to be called a "poet"; cf. *Epicœne*: "It will get you the dangerous name of a Poet" (1.1).

Nine years younger than Jonson, two years younger than Boulstred, John Roe was born in 1581 at Higham Hill, Essex. In 1597, he matriculated at Queen's College, Oxford, but did not stay for a degree. The next few years took him to Russia and Ireland. In 1603, shortly after Boulstred sent him packing, Roe sold his inherited lands to his stepfather, Reginald Argall, for ready cash. With the proceeds, he bought himself a knighthood. (Ben Jonson describes Roe, his best friend, as "an infinite spender," which may be one reason that Jonson loved him so well, and why Boulstred had second thoughts.) [1]

On the accession of King James, Lucy Harington Russell, countess of Bedford, was appointed Lady of the Bedchamber to Queen Anna. Still single, Cecily and Dorothy Boulstred (whose mother was first cousin to Lady Lucy), rose with her, to serve as Maidens of the Queen's Bedchamber. The Boulstred sisters thereby leapt to prominence at Court while Sir John Roe was left in the cold.

Sir John in the company of Ben Jonson again crossed paths with Celia Boulstred on 8 January 1603/4, at a lavish Hampton Court production of Samuel Daniel's *Vision of the Twelve Goddesses.* Daniel's masque that night was performed by Queen Anna, Lucy Russell, Frances Howard Seymour, and nine other goddesses of the Jacobean court. Penelope Rich for the occasion is said to have worn jewelry worth £20,000; her extravagant ornamentation was exceeded only by the queen, who is said to have worn £100,000 in gems (adjusted for inflation: roughly £20 *million*). [2]

Before the evening was over, perhaps before the masque got started, Sir John Roe and Ben Jonson were expelled from the palace. Both men were escorted to the door by the Lord Chamberlain (Thomas Howard, earl of Suffolk), and threatened; a service that was performed by Suffolk at the behest of Jonson's own literary matron, Lucy Russell. The offense was evidently something that Ben Jonson said to, or about, Cecily Boulstred (she, at least, is the person whom Jonson later blamed for the incident).

Jonson resented having been "ushered" from Court (his word) or "thrust out" (Roe's phrase). Fifteen years later and still fuming, Jonson told William Drummond "that Sir John Roe loved him; and when they two were ushered by my Lord Suffolk from [the] masque, Roe wrote a moral epistle to him," with words of comfort and praise. Roe's verse letter "To Ben Jonson," dated January 1603/4, survives in multiple copies. In it, Roe counsels: "Forget we were thrust out! God threatens kings; kings, lords; as lords do us." Roe praises Jonson and discounts the Court: "The State and men's affairs are the best plays, / Next *yours.*"[3]

Roe digested the incident and moved on, but Jonson could not let it go. When he wrote the *New Inn* in 1628, the playwright not only adapted his 1604 lines "To Mistress Boulstred"; he revisited his embarrassment at Hampton Court, only to deny that it ever really bothered him:

Lovell. If a woman or child
Give me the lie, would I be angry? No,
Not if I were i' my wits, sure I should think it
No spice of a disgrace. …
If … I am kept out a masque, sometime thrust out,
Made wait a day, two, three, for a great word,
Which (when it comes forth) is all frown and forehead,
What *laughter* should this breed, rather than anger! (4.4)

Ben Jonson, by Isaac Oliver

---

[1] *infinite spender*] Drummond, 18.

[2] *goddesses*] The others were Katherine (Knyvett) Howard, countess of Suffolk; Elizabeth (Vere) Stanley, countess of Derby; Margaret (Stewart) Howard, countess of Nottingham; Penelope (Devereux) Rich, daughter of the countess dowager of Essex; Eliza (Cecil) Hatton, daughter of the earl and countess of Exeter; Audrey (Shelton) Walsingham, keeper of the Queen's robes; Susan Vere (soon, countess of Montgomery by her marriage to Philip Herbert); Dorothy Hastings (daughter of the earl and countess of Huntington); and Elizabeth (Howard) Knollys (daughter of the earl and countess of Suffolk). Audrey (Shelton) Walsingham, Keeper of the Queen's Robes, was the only one of the twelve performers who was not at least a countess or the unmarried daughter of a countess.

[3] *Sir John…epistle to him*] Drummond, 15;   *The State…next yours*] John Roe, "To Ben Jonson, 6 [*i.e.,* 8] Jan. 1603[/4]."

In May 1605, Sir John Roe left England to fight for the Protestant cause in the Low Countries (which is puzzling since Roe, like Jonson, was a Roman Catholic). On parting, he received a farewell gift, Casaubon's edition of Perseus, inscribed by Jonson to his best-proved friend, his "Amico Probatissimo." [1]

Wounded in battle, Roe returned home in 1606 to resume his role as Jonson's inseparable companion; and remained so until December 1608, when he died of the plague in the playwright's embrace (Jonson's unconfirmed report); whereupon Jonson underwrote the cost of Roe's funeral. In one of three affectionate epigrams on his deceased friend, Jonson is unashamed to say that he decked the coffin of John Roe with tears and verse; noting, however, that Sir John moved him to pursue only "glory, and not sin." [2]

In the decades that followed Roe's failed courtship, and the Hampton Court incident, and Roe's death, Ben Jonson had much to say about Celia Boulstred; beginning, perhaps, with the "Celia" poems:

Song: To Celia ° [3]	**Song to Celia** ° [4]	**Shall I not my Celia Bring?** ° [5]
Come, my Celia, let us prove,	Drink to me only with thine eyes,	Helen, did Homer never see [6]
While we can, the sports of love.	And I will pledge with mine;	Thy beauties, yet could write of thee?
Time will not be ours forever –	Or leave a kiss but in the cup	Did Sappho on her seven-tongued lute
He at length our good will sever.	And I'll not look for wine.	So speak (as yet, it is not mute!)
Spend not then his gifts in vain.	The thirst that from the soul doth rise	Of Phaos' form? Or doth the boy
Suns that set may rise again,	Doth ask a drink divine;	In whom Anacreon once did joy,
But if once we lose this light,	But might I of Jove's nectar sup,	Lie drawn to life in his soft verse,
'Tis with us perpetual night.	I would not change for thine. [7]	As he whom Maro did rehearse?
Why should we defer our joys?	I sent thee late a rosy wreath,	Was Lesbia sung by learn'd Catullus,
Fame and rumor are but toys.	Not so much honoring thee	Or Delia's Graces, by Tibullus?
Cannot we delude the eyes	As giving it a hope, that there	Doth Cynthia, in Propertius' song,
Of a few poor household spies,	It could not withered be.	Shine more than *she* the stars among?
Or his easier ears beguile,	But thou thereon didst only breathe	/... / And shall not I my Celia bring,
So removèd by our wile?	And sent'st it back to me;	Where men may *see* whom I do sing?
'Tis no sin love's fruit to steal–	Since when it grows, and smells, I swear,	Though I, in working of my song
But the sweet thefts to reveal.	Not of itself, but thee.	Come short of all this learnèd throng,
To be taken, to be seen,		Yet sure my tunes will be the best,
These have crimes accounted been.		So much my subject drowns the rest.

(1-12, 31-36)

Jonson's Celia poems may have been ghost-written for John Roe during his courtship of Boulstred; or written by Jonson in his own behalf after Roe's departure; or written as a mock; or penned in praise of a woman whose name was not Celia. But given Boulstred's prominence at Court as the only Celia in the Queen's retinue, and given Jonson's falling out with Lady Bedford and her Boulstred cousins, Jonson must have known that all three would poems be interpreted as tributes to Boulstred's sex appeal. He was not quick to publish them. The first appears in *Volpone* (pub. 1607); the second, in *The Forrest* (1616). The third was found with Jonson's papers after the poet's death – together with other previously unpublished verse addressed to other women under their real names (Mary Wroth, Venetia Digby, Jane Pawlett, et al.) – and published in *Underwood* (1641).

---

[1] *Amico Probatissimo*] "D: Joanni Rowe Amico Probatissimo Hun Amorem et Delicias suas Satiricorum doctissimum PERSIUM cum doctissimo commentario sacravit Ben: Jonsonius et L.M.D.D. [= *libens* merito dono dedit]. Nec prior est mihi parens amico" [*To John Rowe, his best-proved friend, Ben Jonson devotes this, his beloved and delight, Persius, of satirists the most learned, together with a most learned commentary; and gives the trifling prevsent as a gift: for me, a parent takes not rank before a friend*].

[2] *funeral*] £20, subsequently reimbursed, probably by Roe's brother (Drummond, 18); *glory, and not sin*] B. Jonson, "27. On Sir John Roe." *Workes* (1616), pp. 775-6.

[3] *Song*: *To Celia*] ed. DWF from B. Jonson, *Volpone* 3.7 (Q1 1607, F1 1616), and *The Forest* (1616), no. 5.

[4] *Song to Celia*] ed. DWF from B. Jonson, *The Forest* (1616), no.9; Jonson, it has been noted, cribbed this entire lyric from Philostratus.

[5] *Shall I not my Celia Bring?*] ed. DWF from B. Jonson, *Under-wood* (1641), no. 46.

[6] *never see*] *i.e.*, because Homer is reputed to have been blind.

[7] *might I*] even if I could; *change*] exchange the taste of your lips for the nectar of the gods.

In *Volpone,* the eponymous scoundrel sings "Come, my Celia," just moments before he attempts to rape her: this fictional Celia is the trophy wife of Corvino. Volpone's intended victim has received scant sympathy from Jonson scholars. C.G. Thayer, for one, describes the Celia of Jonson's *Volpone* as "an idiot, an eloquent Dame Pliant," "a humorless, prim, fatuous girl without a brain in her head and nothing but clichés in her mouth" (52, 62). There is no compelling reason to suppose that Corvino's bride represents Celia Boulstred, per se (for one thing, Jonson in 1607 was still hoping that Lucy Russell would resume her financial support). Nothing about Volpone or his retainers – a dwarf (Nano), a eunuch (Castrone), a hermaphrodite (Androgyno), and parasite (Mosca) – invites a reading of *Volpone* as one of Jonson's many stage-satires on public personages. But Jonson in *Volpone* clearly wished to showcase his most admired love-lyric; and if it helped to make peace with Celia Boulstred and her wealthy cousin Lady Bedford now that Roe was out of the picture, so much the better.

If it was Jonson's hope that *Volpone* would restore him to favor, he was disappointed. Lucy Russell now favored Samuel Daniel as her court poet. Jonson represents himself as unbothered, by that: "Though she have a better *verser* got / (Or "poet," in the court account), than I," he sneered, Samuel Daniel "doth *me*, though I not *him*, envíe"). Nor was Shakespeare's dramatic company – now, the King's Men – eager to attempt another Jonson play after the 1603 failure of *Sejanus*. Unbothered by Shakespeare-envy, Jonson in 1605 collaborated with George Chapman and John Marston on *Eastward Ho!* – a comedy written for the Children of the Revels at the Blackfriars playhouse; which, instead of restoring Jonson's credit at court, offended King James with its satire on the Scots and landed all three playwrights in prison. Condemned to have their ears and noses slit for the offense, Chapman, Marston, and Jonson were eventually pardoned; but not before Jonson's "olde Mother" had prepared "a lustie strong poison" for her son and for herself, had the shameful punishment been carried out. That, at least, is how Jonson told the story to William Drummond, many years later. [1]

The disgraces of longsuffering Ben Jonson were hardly permanent. He received a commission to write a court entertainment for May Day 1604, and a masque for the Christmas festivities of 1604/5. Released from prison in November 1605 following the *Eastward Ho* debacle, Jonson went on to produce some two dozen court masques in partnership with Inigo Jones, for which he was paid £40 each from the King's exchequer (royalties comparable to a year's wage for most London tradesmen).

Celia Boulstred, meanwhile, had responded warmly to a lovesuit from Sir Thomas Roe, who adored her with an ardor unmatched by his late cousin, Sir John. Thomas and Celia might indeed have married, were it not that Boulstred in 1609 became gravely ill. Physicians at first diagnosed her stomach trouble as "the mother," a.k.a. *wandering womb* – an imprecise medical diagnosis employed in the early modern period to cover ailments that were thought to attend upon feminine frailty. But no one, not even the doctors of the Medical College, could find a cure. By July, while in residence at Lucy Russell's palace at Twickenham Park, Cecily Boulstred was said to be slowly wasting away, unable to hold down even small amounts of food or liquid.

Hearing that Lady Lucy's vivacious cousin and best friend had fallen ill, John Donne – one of several poets who still enjoyed the countess of Bedford's generous support – requested and was granted a visit to Celia's bedside. Donne found the patient in good temper, her pulse vigorous, her "understanding and voice" no more remiss (in Donne's view) than usual. He concluded that her disease, though life-threatening, was hysterical. Writing the next day to his friend, Sir Henry Goodyere, Donne reports that Mistress Boulstred would not be not long for this world:

Samuel Daniel, frontispiece of his *Civil Wars* (1609)

<hr />

[1] *court poet*] It was to the countess of Bedford that Daniel dedicated the printed narrative of his *Vision of the Twelve Goddesses* (London, 1604); it is the longest epistle dedicatory in all of Jacobean drama; *Though she…envie*] ed. DWF from Jonson, "Epistle to Elizabeth [Sidney,] Countess Of Rutland," lines 69-70. *The Forrest*, in *Workes* (1616), 834; *olde mother…poyson*] Drummond, 26.

"I fear earnestly that Mistress Boulstred will not escape that sickness in which she labors at this time. I sent this morning to ask of her passage of this night; and the return is, that she is as I left her yesternight. And then – by the strength of her understanding and voice (proportionally to her fashion, which was ever remiss), by the evenness and life of her pulse, and by her temper – I could allow her long life, and impute all her sickness to her *mind*. But the history of her sickness makes me justly fear that she will scarce last so long as that you, when you receive this letter, may do her any good office in praying for her: for she hath not (for many days) received so much as a preserved barberry, but it returns; and all accompanied with a fever, the mother, and an extreme ill spleen." [1]

> The anonymous author of *A Closet for Ladies and Gentlewomen* (1608) urges homeopathic remedies to calm the *mother* when it rises: "Take aqua-composita, and beat bayberries in powder, and put it into the aqua-composita, and put a spoonful or two in a draught of beer or ale, and so drink it"; or else, "Take rosen and beat it very fine, and put into salad oil and white wine and drink it, and it will do you good" (166-7, 178-9).

When Ben Jonson heard of Boulstred's illness, he was less gracious than Donne. Celia had recently dared to "censure" his wit. No express criticism of Jonson survives from Boulstred's pen, nor is Jonson known to have published anything in the two years preceding that might have incurred her criticism; but Boulstred in the summer of 1609 had clearly heard about, and had evidently read in draft, Jonson's *Epicœne: the Silent Woman* (whose debut performance at Court was not till Christmas); and she had dared to give the play two thumbs down. Jonson's contempt for Cecily Boulstred from that moment forth took a dark turn toward character assassination, even as the young woman lay on her deathbed:

On the Court Pucell °

DOES THE COURT PUCELL then so censure me,
And thinks I dare not her? Let the world see:
What though her chamber be the very pit
Where fight the prime Cocks of the game, for wit? [2]
And that as any are strook, her breath creates
New in their stead, out of the candidates? [3]
What though with tribade lust she force a Muse
And in an Epicœne fury can write News [4]
Equal with that which for the best News goes – [5]

---

[1] *I fear…spleen*] John Donne to Sir Henry Goodyer (n.d., July 1609?).

[2] *Pucell*] from French *pucelle*, maiden; but in English slang, *prostitute* (from which is derived the modern slang terms *poozle* [from 1578; later conflated with *pussy, girl,* from the 1560s]). Jonson here puns also on *Cel* Boulstred's first name, and likens her to Joan de Pucelle, who in Elizabethan literature (as in Shakespeare's *1 Henry VI*) was typically depicted as deceitful and sexually promiscuous while parading as a virgin; *Cocks*] specifically, John Cock, one of the writers of courtly "News"; with bawdy innuendo concerning the prime cocks alleged to be thriving in Celia Boulstred's chamber and cockpit.

[3] *strook*] struck; *And that ... candidates*] as one is struck down (*i.e.* in the fight, but also perhaps by venereal disease), she continually beckons new candidates with each breath.

[4] *Epicœne*] In Greek grammar, an *epicene* noun is one that without changing its gender may denote either sex. Jonson (followed by others) adopts the term to denote neither *hermaphrodite* nor *androgyne* per se, but a *bisexual*. The playwright adapted this otherwise unprecedented use of "epicene" from *The Eagle and the Body* (1609), a sermon by Bishop William Barlow; who observes that the Jacobean "Court, a full Bodie [for] the fatnesse and marrow wherof, hath fetcht many Eagles from all corners" – "eagles of the *Epicene* gender, both Hees, & Shees" – who with their "Satyricall Invectives, both in Pulpits and Pamphlets," reduce the Court (or Church, or individual human) to "σκελετόν [skeleton], not σωμα [*soma,* body]; rather an Anatomie of Bones, then a Bodie of Substance" – so that they may cry with the prophet, "My leanness, my leanness!" (sig. B2). (Cf. Jonson's 1624 masque, *Neptune's Triumph,* where Jonson mocks "learned authors ... of the *Epicœne* gender, Hees, and Shees," a line copied directly from Barlow's 1609 text.) Barlow's *Eagle and the Body*, with its sexually indeterminate vultures feeding on the royal court, is the first recorded instance of Greek *epicene* being used metaphorically. In his caricature of Celia Boulstred's "Epicene fury," again in his figure of "Mistress Epicœne" (Master Morose's boy-bride), Jonson reverses Bishop Barlow's metaphor: he represents the eagle as the dominant male who snacks on bisexual prey.

[5] *tribade*] "A woman who engages in sexual activity with other women; a Lesbian" (*OED*); cf. Jonson's *Forest*, no. 10: "Venus…with thy *tribade* trine, invent new sports"; from Greek τρίβειν, to rub; *News*] Boulstred's *News of My Morning Work* (below) is her only exemplar of the "court news" genre to have survived.

As airy light, and as *like* "wit," as those?
What though she talk, and can at° once (with them)
Make state, religion, bawdry, all a theme?
And as lip-thirsty, in each word's expense,
Doth labor with the phrase more than the *sense*?
What though she ride two mile on holy days
To church, as others do to feasts and plays,
To show their 'tires, to view and to be viewed!   1
What though she be with velvet gowns endued
And spangled petticoats brought forth to th' eye
As new rewards of her old secrecy?
What though she hath won, on trust (as many do),
And that her "truster" *fears* her! Must I, too?
I never stood for any place: *my* wit
Thinks itself nought, though she should value it.   2

[25]   I am no statesman, and much less divine.   3
For bawdry? —'tis her language and not mine.
Farthest I am from the idolatry
To stuffs and laces. Those, my man can buy.
And "trust her" I would least, that hath forswore
In contract, *twice*. What, can she perjure more?   4
Indeed, her *dressing* some man might delight:
Her *face,* there's none can like, by candle-light;
(Not he, that should the *body* have, for case
To his poor instrument, now out of grace!).   5
        Shall I advise thee, *Pucell*? Steal away
From court, while yet thy fame hath some small day.
The *wits* will leave you, if they once perceive
You cling to *lords*; and *lords,* if you leave them
For *sermoneers*: of which, now one, now other,

[40]   They say you weekly invite, with fits o'th' mother,
And practice for a miracle. Take heed!
This age will lend no faith to Darrell's deed.   6
Of if it would, the Court is the *worst* place,
Both for the mothers and the babes of grace:
For there, the wicked in the chair of scorn
Will call't a "bastard," when a prophet's born.   7

---

1 *'tires*] attire, elegant outfit.

2 *stood for any place*] applied for a position at Court;   *though she should*] even if she *did* (value my wit).

3 *no statesman*] e.g., such as Sir Thomas Roe;   *much less divine*] 1. no god; 2. no clergyman, such as those who wait on Celia Boulstred's sickbed.

4 *in contract*] Jonson alleged that Boulstred has broken off two marital engagements (one to Sir John, the other to Sir Thomas Roe).

5 *some man*] Cf. *Epicœne* 5.4, where Lady Haughty's gentlewoman, Mistress Otter, remarks that a man has recently been tossed in a blanket at her house "for peeping in at the door";   *instrument*] penis;   *out of grace*] Sir Thomas Roe, whose 1608 betrothal Boulstred is alleged to have broken; but perhaps with a glance at Jonson's own "Celia" poems and fall from grace.

6 *Sermoneers*] both Lucy Russell and Celia Boulstred supported Puritan clergy, a few of whom had evidently been brought to Celia's bedside to pray for her recovery;   *Darrell*] John Darrell, Puritan exorcist and author of *A True Narration of the Strange and Grievous Vexation by the Devil*; Samuel Harsnet in 1603 exposed Rev. Darrell as a fraud who taught his accomplices to fake bewitchment and demon possession, thereby to secure convictions of suspected witches and to increase his own income as an exorcist.

7 *a bastard*] i.e., if Boulstred remains at court, she will abandon her tribade lovers for a man, and become pregnant; and yet any verse, witticism, or infant, coming from Boulstred, will be despised as illegitimate.

The venom in these lines is remarkable even for the always-irascible Ben Jonson. The poet's scattershot accusations – that Boulstred is promiscuous in her speech and behavior, pretentious in her learning, a terror, an oath-breaker, a clothes-horse, a painted doll, a bisexual, a hypocrite, a hypochondriac, a likely candidate for unwed motherhood, and the object of derision – cohere only as a deeply personal assault on a young woman's reputation.

For twenty-first century readers, Jonson's allegation that Celia Boulstred had a same-sex love interest, one that twice led to broken betrothals, is more likely to intrigue than to offend; but Jonson cannot have had much direct knowledge on the point of Boulstred's sexual activity, either way. Nor can his other insults be reconciled with the report of those closest to her that Boulstred was a pious young woman who remained a virgin to her death and a devout Puritan. But when a desirable and successful woman has censured a poet, and dumped his best male buddy (Sir John), and disappointed another (Sir Thomas), one convenient means to salve the injury to masculine narcissism is for the dejected troubadour to proclaim the woman a tribade Lesbian.

What is most surprising about Jonson's caricature of Boulstred as a lust-driven bisexual is the innuendo concerning the Court Pucell's significant other: courtiers and court-watchers could hardly have escaped making the inference that wealthy Lady Bedford – just a year older than Cel Boulstred and her constant companion – is the one who is alleged to have supplied Boulstred with an elegant wardrobe and other "new rewards of her old secrecy." Jonson with his bitter diatribe invites his readers to see the ladies Boulstred and Russell as painted signs of Lesbian vice in Queen Anna's own bedchamber, and he comes close to alleging that Cecily Boulstred is the countess of Bedford's salaried same-sex prostitute.

The countess of Bedford graciously performed in Jonson's 1605 *Masque of Blackness,* his 1608 *Masque of Beauty,* and others; but Jonson was never able to nestle himself back under the wing of her financial benefaction, and he had only himself to blame for that.

Jonson's denunciation of Cecily Boulstred was manifestly fueled by the poet's outrage over her literary criticism. That the Court Pucell is said to be possessed of "an Epicœne fury" suggests not only that Celia swings both ways in bed, but that she was too vocal in her response to Jonson's *Epicœne*, six months before its debut performance at Court. And if Jonson's play, in draft, was anything like the finished product, then she, and Lady Bedford, and Dorothy Boulstred, had good cause to be critical. *Epicœne* is a misogynistic comedy in which the noise-hating Master Morose weds Mistress Epicœne, a silent woman, only to discover in the fifth act that he has married a handsome cross-dressed boy. Morose's same-sex marriage is not, however, the primary object of the satire. In *Epicœne* Jonson targets the "collegiate" ladies at Court – three self-important, overdressed and well-painted women with intellectual pretensions: "Lady *CEnTAUR*" (a figure for *CE*lia *BUL*stred); "Doll" Mavis (Dorothy, who has "a worse face than she! you would not like this, by candle-light" [*Epicœne* 5.1; cf. "Pucell," 32]); and "Lady Haughty," president of the collegiates.

Having forfeited Lucy Russell's matronage by 1608, Jonson's payback came in the figure of the "grave and youthful matron," Lady Haughty: "no man can be admitted till she be ready, nowadays – till she has painted, and perfumed, and wash'd" (1.1). Not content with figuring Lady Bedford as Celia Boulstred's Lesbian paramour, Jonson also represents her as a failed mother: Married now for almost fifteen years, the countess of Bedford had given birth only once (in 1602, to a son who died within a few weeks of birth). Jonson in *Epicœne* alleges a cause for that seeming infertility: Mistress Haughty proudly confesses that she and the other collegiates, to keep their youthful figures, use abortifacient herbs: [1]

> *Morose.* And have you those excellent receipts, madam, to keep yourselves from bearing of children?
> *Haughty.* O yes, Morose. How should we maintain our youth and beauty else? Many births of a woman make her old, as many crops make the earth barren. (*Epicœne* 4.3) [2]

---

[1] *abortifacient herbs*] Jonson accuses Lady Bedford of birth-control aids that were commonly used throughout the Christian era and not criminalized until the early nineteenth century. Though condemned in patristic literature in the same breath and language with the sins of masturbation and non-horizontal marital sex, abortifacients were legal and freely available, and tolerated by Church authorities. The rare prosecution targeted suppliers, not the consumer.

[2] *receipts*] recipes.

Reminded by Haughty of the approach of age, and shielded from pregnancy by abortifacients, Doll (Dorothy) advocates youthful fornication, since the maiden who "excludes her lovers, may live to lie a forsaken beldame, in a frozen bed."

Mistress Centaur muses, "who will wait on us to coach, *then*? or write, or tell us the News, *then*? Make anagrams of our names, and invite us to the Cock-pit, and kiss our hands all the play-time, and draw their weapons for our honors?"

"Not one," replies Lady Haughty (4.3).

Jonson imagines a remorseful future for Centaur and Doll Mavis as decayed bachelorettes. But for the moment, all three collegiates are content to welcome, as a new member, Morose's androgynous bride, Mistress Epicœne: "We'll have her to the college," crows Haughty. And if "she have wit, she shall be one of us, shall she not, Centaur? We'll make her a collegiate!" (3.6).

Jonson's avatar, Master True-wit, characterizes the "collegiate" as a woman who must "know all the News, what was done at Salisbury, what at the Bath, what at Court, what in progress; or so she may censure poets and authors and styles, and compare 'em – Daniel with Spenser, Jonson with the t'other youth, and so forth; or be thought cunning in controversies, or the very knots of divinity; and have often in her mouth the state of the question […] in religion, to one; in state, to another; in bawdry, to a third" (2.2).

Sex-hungry Centaur is soon distracted by Morose's friend, Sir Dauphine, who said to be "as fine a gentleman of his inches, madam, as any is about the town." Doll Mavis praises Dauphine (a figure for Sir Thomas Roe) as a man who "profess[es] more neatness than a French hermaphrodite" and wears "purer linen" than herself. Centaur desires Dauphine as a man more handsome than others that "have their faces set in a brake […] I could love a man," she exclaims, "for such a *nose*! […] Good Morose, bring him to my chamber, first" (4.6). [1]

IT BECOMES a woman well at all times, and chiefly in her child-bearing, and after her delivery, to have a care, as much as she can possibly, of the preservation of her beauty; since there is nothing that sooner decays and spoileth it than the often-bearing of children. But as health is more precious and recommendable than beauty, and seeing that a woman with child may be troubled and oppressed with many accidents and infirmities during the nine months she bears her child, it will be therefore very necessary and profitable to seek out the means to free and deliver them thereof.... Oftentimes it happens to women that they cannot bear their burthen to the time prefixed by nature, which is the ninth month. This accident is called either a *shift* or *slipping away*; or else, *abortment* or (as our women call it) a *mischance*. The *shift* is reckoned from the first day the seed is retained in the womb till such time as it receiveth form and shape; in which time, if it chance to issue and flow forth, it is a *shift*. The *abortment* happeneth after the fortieth day, yea, even to the end of the ninth month. For the abortment is a violent expulsion or exclusion of the child already formed and endued with life, before the appointed time. But the sliding away, or shift, is a flowing or issuing of the seed, out of the womb, which is not yet either formed or endued with life....

Hippocrates is of opinion that women with child, in cases of necessity, may be purged from the fourth to the seventh month. But before and after those times he admits it not, nay, he forbids it directly; which, for all that, the physicians of our time observe not in cases of danger, because the medicines we use in these days (as rhubarb, manna, cassia, and tamarinds) are not so violent as those that were used by our ancients (which were hellebore, scammony, turbith, coloquintida, or the like).

—Jacques Guillemeau
Childbirth or, The Happy Delivery of Women.
Anon. trans. (1612), pp. 32, 69, 222.

The union of Morose with Mistress Epicœne, doomed from the start, comes unglued in Act 5: the promiscuous boy-bride is said to have had sex with Mr. Otter and with Mr. La-Foole as well as with Morose (whose marriage with Epicœne is now *"post copulam"* [5.3]); but Morose, like Gallimard in David Henry Hwang's *M. Butterfly,* has not yet discovered that his wife is a boy. "Not taking pleasure in your tongue, which is a woman's chiefest pleasure." Morose seeks a divorce (2.3). He does so on a false pretense of his own impotence (an argument cited to justify the 1540 divorce of Henry VIII from Anne of Cleves, and which would be cited again, by the wife, in the notorious 1613 divorce of Frances Howard from the 2nd earl of Essex). Avaricious Epicœne refuses his consent to the proposed annulment.

Haughty, Centaur, and Doll take pity on Epicœne. Just before the discovery of the boy-bride's concealed sex, the three collegiates threaten to toss Morose in a blanket for his impudence, and to thrust him from court, together with Daw and La-Foole (5.4):

---

[1] *purer linen*] cleaner underwear (*OED* linen, n.3); *brake*] bush; with bawdy innuendo.

Haughty.	Let 'em be cudgeled out of doors by our grooms!
Centaur.	I'll lend you my footman.
Doll.	We'll have our men blanket 'em i'the hall! […]
	I'll ha' the bridegroom blanketed, too!
Centaur.	Begin with him first!
Haughty.	Yes, by my troth.
Morose.	O, mankind generation!

Forced to "give satisfaction by asking [their] public forgiveness," Morose humbles himself before the female triumvir, a monstrous regimen of women:

> *Morose.* Ladies, I must crave all your pardons […] for a wrong I have done to your whole sex in marrying this fair and virtuous gentlewoman […] being guilty of an infirmity which, before I conferred with these learned men, I thought I might have concealed.

The concealed "infirmity" of Master Morose is his (pretended) impotence, his excuse for annulment.

The imperfectly concealed infirmity of Ben Jonson may that he fell in love, in 1600, with 19-year-old John Roe, now deceased; who fell in love with that poet-mocking, Lucy-loving, Puritan courtesan, Cecily Boulstred.

• • •

In the summer of 1609, while Jonson regaled his fellows at the Mermaid Inn with his libelous verses on Cel Boulstred, and perhaps with a draft of his new play, *Epicœne,* physicians at Lady Bedford's Twickenham manor labored to save Boulstred's life. A detailed narrative of her illness is supplied by Dr. Francis Anthony; who reports that he was summoned to Twickenham only after the combined expertise of the physicians in the College of Medicine despaired of success. Dr. Anthony that reports he was able to effect a cure with incremental doses of a pricey concoction called *Aurum Potabile* (Potable Gold).

An Apology or Defense of a Medicine called Aurum Potabile (1616)°

Part 2. Extreme Vomiting

MISTRESS CECILY BOULSTRED, a worthy gentlewoman and virgin, attending in near service our gracious Queen, in good favor and account, fell sick and had grievous passions; unto whom divers of the most famous physicians of the College [of Medicine] were called; who with great care and their utmost skill, sparing no cost (as was fitting in such a place) administered all kinds of conducing medicines, both cordials and other respectively, to the cause of her disease and passions: both such as be ready in the shops, as others by some singularity of art prepared. [1]

Her passions still continued, if not increased: continual vomiting and rejection of whatsoever she took – meat, drink, medicines – with swoonings, torture, torments of every part of her body, a miserable and pitiful spectacle, much lamented of many very honorable persons. She could not rest nor sleep, night or day; so that, sinking under the burden of this affliction, with the violence and continuance thereof, her strength utterly failed. She could not retain so much as one drop of any broth or other nourishment.

Her stomach, by conjecture of all physicians, was drawn together and shut up, without any power or faculty to perform the offices of nature. In this miserable estate, this distressed gentlewoman languished two whole months without any ease or relief by the use of any [of] the medicines given her by the advice of the said physicians – all things, tending to a more desperate and immedicable estate. Whereupon the mother of this gentlewoman demanded of these said doctors whether they had any hope to give help (or at leastwise, *ease*) to her daughter: "Else" (she said), she "would send for *Doctor Anthony.*"

Those doctors hereupon limited themselves to a certain time which they spent in their uttermost abilities to perform, to the intent I should *not* be called; to which purpose, they commanded an apothecary to attend in the chamber of the patient all the next day and night; and every third hour, to give her a cordial.

Then voluntarily they said to the mother, "Send for Doctor Anthony if you will, and God send him good success with your daughter."

Then I was sent for. And finding this gentlewoman in so desperate a case, left and given over by all the doctors of the College as not to be recovered (for besides the advice of these six, there had been public consultations in the College as is requisite in such-like cases, which seldom come in use), I desired God to bless my endeavors, and to continue His blessings in the administration of this, my happy medicine.

---

[1] *passions*] sufferings;   *conducing medicines*] serviceable;   *cordials*] stimulating or restorative medicines.

After a small time, upon due and mature consideration of all things, I gave her at the first, not a whole spoonful of my *Aurum Potabile,* as in other cases, but much less, scarce a quarter so much; which she cast up again with a vehement force and torture of her body. A little while after, I gave her as much more – which she cast up in the same manner as she did the first. Again I gave it the third time, some part of which she also cast up, but kept some, with a kind of strife or conflict between the medicine and the malady.

Then I advised that she should not further be troubled for a season, but to try if she could now take a little rest or sleep. So she disposed herself thereunto and slept soundly a whole hour; which divers of great account then present can witness. For she snored (that we all heard), which seemed strange to all, considering for a long time before, she had taken no rest.

When she waked, she said that she found herself somewhat better at ease. Then (which was the fourth time) I gave her half a spoonful, which she kept without any contending or trouble to her body. This gave me (and many worthy gentlewomen there present) great hope of a good recovery – wherein (God be praised!) we were not deceived. For in all the other administering of this medicine (orderly, as she was able to bear, increasing the quantity), her spirits were relieved! She daily recovered strength. All the passions, symptoms, and accidents of her diseases ceased. Her sickness fully left her, and she recovered perfect health!

Thus, with the use of this happy medicine, this gentlewoman was recovered, and cured of that dangerous disease wherein those other doctors had wearied themselves, and forsaken her – at which her friends wondered, mine rejoiced, and other malicious adversaries fretted (for which, God be praised!). If they will call these effects of "juggling" and of "a corrosive medicine," they will hardly find any "cordial" amongst all *their* dispensatories and magistral prescriptions: the cause, and effect, are essential relatives!

• • •

Dr. Anthony published his case study (in Latin and English) in 1616, seven years after he gave those doses of *Aurum Potabile* to Celia Boulstred. Extra copies of his title page were printed off for use as advertising bills. But in point of fact, Dr. Anthony's juggling was less miraculous than he remembers: within days of his first visit to the patient's bedside, Celia Boulstred was dead. The patient's brother-in-law, James Whitlocke, reports: "Cecil Boulstred, my wife's sister, gentlewoman to Queen Anna, ordinary of her bedchamber, died at Twick'n'am in Middlesex, the earl of Bedford's house, 4 August 1609." [1]

The local parish register indicates that she was buried on August 6th. The cause of death may have been a brain tumor (which can cause persistent, unexplained, vomiting without nausea); or gastric cancer.

Cecily Boulstred, though already ill when Jonson penned "The Court Pucell," lived long enough to read it. As Jonson a decade later told the story of his masterpiece, the paper on which it was written "was stolen out of his pocket by a gentleman," possibly George Garrard, "who drank him drowsy, and given Mistress Boulstred; which brought him great displeasure" (Drummond, 54). Jonson thereby suffered the "great displeasure," not only of Cel Boulstred but of his former benefactor, Lucy Russell.

On his 1618-19 tour of Scotland, Jonson happened to have his libel on Cecily Boulstred back where he wanted it: in his pocket. Visiting with William Drummond in Edinburgh over the Christmas holidays, the poet read "The Court Pucell" aloud for his host's amusement. That Drummond was unimpressed may be inferred from Jonson's self-justification immediately after: defending his "Pucell' as merely representative of universal lechery, Jonson told Drummond that "there was no abuses to write a satire of" – and in which he repeateth – "all the abuses in England and the world" (Drummond, 10).

Following the visit, Drummond expressed his censure in remarks not intended for publication. Ben Jonson, he wrote, "is a great lover and praiser of himself, a contemner and scorner of others; given rather to lose a friend than a jest; jealous of every word and action of those about him (especially after drink, which is one of the elements in which he liveth); a dissembler of ill parts which reign in him, a bragger of some good that he wanteth; thinketh nothing well but what either he himself, or some of his friends and countrymen, hath said or done. He is passionately kind and angry (careless either to gain, or keep); *vindictive* – but, if he be well answered, at himself' (Drummond, 56).

---

[1] *Cecil...1609*] Ed. DWF from Whitlocke, *Liber Famelicus,* 18; As a coincidental point of interest: on 13 August 1609 (a week after Boulstred's burial), Henry Cary, wife of Elizabeth Tanfield Cary, wrote Dr. Anthony from Barkhamsted, ordering fresh quantities of *aurum potabile*; with a glowing testimonial; Cary wrote again on 31 August to say that the drug since his last letter had healed a servant of paralysis, and his own infant daughter of the measles (Katherine Cary, then three months old). In 1616, Dr. Anthony reports that *aurum potabile* also healed Lucius, the Carys' eldest son, of the smallpox (1610, pp. 54-55; 1616, p. 87).

COURT POETS soon after the death of Cecily
Boulstred weighed in with their memorial tributes. Among them is an "Epitaphium" by Sir
Edward Herbert, a friend of Ben Jonson and of
Celia's forlorn lovers, Sir Thomas Roe and the
late Sir John Roe. In his Latin subtitle, which
the ladies could not read, Herbert insinuates
that Cecily Boulstred perished of an unquiet
conscience; and yet, the English text of Herbert's poem reconfigures the maiden's muti-
nous "powers" as religious "zeal." Herbert affirms that Boulstred during her starvation ("Her
fasts"), overcame excess; barred all access to
sin; withstood the long siege of Death; and finally surrendered the fortress of her virgin flesh
to the grave, even as her spirit found refuge in
Heaven:

Sir Edward Herbert, by Isaac Oliver

Epitaph. Caecil. Boulser °
quae post langue scentem morbum non sine
inquietudine spiritus & conscientiae obiit °   1

METHINKS Death like one laughing lies,
Showing his teeth, shutting his eyes,
Only thus to have found her here
He did with so much reason fear,
And she despise.   2

For barring all the gates of sin
Death's open ways to enter in,
She was with a strict siege beset,
To what by *force* he could not get,
By *time*, to win.

This mighty Warrior was deceivèd yet,
For what he *mutine* in her powers thought
Was but their *zeal*,
And what, by their excess, *might* have been wrought,
Her fasts did heal—   3

Till that her noble soul, by these, as wings,
Transcending the low pitch of earthly things,
As being relieved by God and set at large,
And grown, by this, worthy a higher charge,
   Triumphing over Death, to Heaven fled—
   And did not die, but left her *body* dead.

One-upping Sir Edward Herbert, John Donne composed two elegies in memory of Lady Bedford's
deceased favorite. In the first, "Death, I recant" (74 lines), Donne censures Death as an all-consuming
glutton who swallows the good with the wicked, a monster who has now audaciously swallowed down
Cecily Boulstred, though she was a maiden "proof 'gainst sins of youth," whose "virtues did outgo / Her

---

[1] *Epitaph…obiit*] "Epitaph on Cecily Boulstred who died young, languishing with an unquiet spirit and conscience."

[2] *found ... fear*] laughingly found here, dead, a woman who despised Death and whom Death once had cause to fear.

[3] *this mighty Warrior*] Death; *mutine*] a mutiny (What Death mistook for a rebellious spirit was in fact religious zeal); *their excess*] the excessive use of "her powers" (beauty, wit, etc.); *her fasts*] her illness starved her to death.

years." Seeking figurative compensation for the loss of that devoured feminine morsel, Donne invokes the specter of libels and gossip that might have dogged the heels such a good woman as Celia, had she lived on as a sociable virgin in the Jacobean court:

Elegy on Mistress Boulstred °
John Donne

> […] Had she perséver'd just, there would have been
> Some that would sin, mis-thinking *she* did sin:
> Such as would call her *friendship, love,* and fain [1]
> To *sociableness* a name profane;
> Or sin by *tempting,* or (not daring that)
> By *wishing,* though they never told her what […]

Politely disingenuous is the poet's speculation that Boulstred, had she survived, might have seen her sociability misrepresented as profane solicitation, her openness as promiscuity. Donne has in mind a particular instance: his reference is to that 1602 libel, in which a poet (thought to be John Roe) had accused a too-sociable Cecily Boulstred of having offered up illicit "love" in place of "friendship." Donne's elegy recuperates the reputation of his patron's deceased friend while excusing Roe's "To Mistress Boulstred" as a poem that arose from a simple misreading of her feminine nature. Donne's recuperative spin thereby ensures Lucy Bedford's favor without transgressing the buddy system.

John Donne
National Portrait Gallery

In a second elegy on Boulstred, "Language, thou art too narrow" (62 lines), Donne applies his hyperboles with a spatula, advising Death to take early retirement. Now that glutton Death has abducted Cel Boulstred, the sting of human mortality has vanquished the entire planet:

Elegy XI °
John Donne

> […] if we be thy conquest,
> Thou'ast lost thy end – for in *her*, perish all.
> Of if we live, we live but to rebel:
> They know her better now, that knew her well.
> If we should vapor out, and pine, and die
> (Since she first went), that were not misery.
> She changed our world, with hers. Now she is gone,
> Mirth and prosperity is oppression:
> For of all moral virtues, she was all
> The *Ethics* speak of "virtues cardinal."
> Her soul was Paradise: the Cherubin
> Set to keep it, was Grace, that kept out sin […]

With two elegies by John Donne to her credit, Cecily Boulstred might well have been permitted to rest in peace as the deceased epitome of all moral virtues. But Ben Jonson was not yet done with her.

On news of her decease, Donne's rival, Ben Jonson, hastily revised his verdict on Celia's character. In a poem titled, simply, "Epitaph," he praises Boulstred as the court's singular model of chastity. Perhaps Jonson regretted the extreme nastiness of his "Court Pucell." More certainly, the "Epitaph" that he wrote on the news of Boulstred's death represents a cynical move to recover his lost patronage and his standing at court now that Cecily Boulstred and her dramatic criticism no longer stood between him and the countess of Bedford:

---

[1] *fain*] ascribe (as presumption).

Epitaph °

Ben Jonson

STAY, view this stone. And if thou be'st not such,
Read here a little, that thou may'st know much:
It covers, first, a virgin; and then one
Who durst be that in Court, a virtue alone   [1]
To fill an epitaph. But she had more:
She might have claimed to have made the Graces, *four*;
Taught Pallas, language; Cynthia, modesty.
As fit to have increased the harmony
Of spheres, as light of stars: she was Earth's eye,
The sole religious house and votary,
Not bound by rites, but conscience. Wouldst thou all?
She was Sell Boulstred! – in which name I call
Up so much truth, as could I it pursue,
Might make the Fable of *Good Women,* true.

Informed by George Garrard that "greater wits have gone before" in their praise of Boulstred, Jonson sent him a copy of his "Epitaph" and forwarded a copy to the Countess of Bedford, possibly hoping that his epitaph would be chosen to grace Boulstred's tomb (it wasn't). But as if to clarify his intentions and to disambiguate his own eulogy, Jonson with his copy for Garrard included a cover note stating that the news of Celia's death has made him "a heavy man" (perhaps literally: Jonson in middle age grew obese, pushing almost 300 lbs.). Jonson remarks further to Garrard that he wishes he had seen Celia before she died – so that others, "that live, might have corrected some prejudices they have had injuriously of me." [2]

But if Jonson in his posthumous praise of Boulstred was seeking to repair his relations with a moneyed matron, he seems unable to resist, even here, the temptation to equivocate in his praise of Cecily Boulstred: her tombstone covers one that was "first, a virgin" (as what woman is *not*, chronologically speaking?); and she dared to be so at Court (where chastity, Jonson implies, is universal sham). "She might have claimed" to be gracious and witty. She might have claimed to teach modesty to Cynthia (Elizabeth I), and she might have claimed to have taught intelligible English to Pallas (Queen Anna). Jonson might, therefore, make credible Chaucer's "fable" of good women. But in the end, Jonson modestly excuses himself from that hypothetical challenge. He settles for calling up "so much truth" in Cecily's name: "Wouldst thou all? / She was *Sell* Boulstred" (spelled thus, both in Jonson's manuscript and printed text).

• • •

Celia Boulstred, Maiden of the Bedchamber: *News*

THE "NEWS" that Lady Centaur speaks of in *Epicœne* 4.3 refers to the literary game of writing moral or satirical news headlines, a genre that flourished at court c. 1605-1610. Extant examples include "News from Court" by Sir Thomas Overbury; "News from Sea," by William Strachey; "Country News" by Sir Thomas Roe; "News from the Very Country," by John Donne; "Answer to the Very Country News," by Lady Anne Southwell; and "News of my Morning Work," by Cel Boulstred.

Written probably in 1609, Boulstred's one surviving News article was destined to receive a second life, not in manuscript this time, but print, for the whole world to read. In his 1613 poem, *A Wife*, Sir Thomas Overbury had catalogued the feminine virtues that he deemed essential in marriage, none of which he could see manifest in Frances (Howard) Devereux, the vixen to whom his sometime friend, Robert Carr, had betrothed himself. Resenting the interference with her love-life, Lady Frances first contrived to have Overbury imprisoned in the Tower of London, where she poisoned him. In 1615, when it was discovered that Overbury's untimely death was in fact a murder, *Sir Thomas Overbury his Wife* became an instant bestseller, augmented by various courtly "News" items, previously unpublished; one of which was Cecily Boulstred's "News of my Morning Work":

---

[1] *Who durst be that in Court?*] Cf. John Roe: "Good wit never despair'd," at Court, or "Ah me!" said— / For never wench at court was ravishèd" (The witty wooer is never unrequited, nor is rape possible, at Court, a milieu in which no woman ever says "No" to sex – or at least, not if the price is right). J. Roe, "Love and Wit," lines 15-16.

[2] *a heavy man…injuriously of me*] B. Jonson to G. Garrard (Aug. 1609), Houghton Lib. MS JnB102, ed. DWF.

News of My Morning Work °

THAT to be *good*, the way is to be most alone—or the best accompanied.

That the way to Heaven is mistaken for the most melancholy walk.

That the most fear the world's opinion more than God's displeasure.

That a Court-friend seldom goes further than the first degree of charity.

That the Devil is the perfectest courtier.

That Innocency was first cousin to man; now Guiltiness hath the nearest alliance.

That Sleep is Death's ledger ambassador. [1]

That time can never be "spent": we pass by it and cannot return.

That none can be sure of more time than an instant.

That Sin makes work – for Repentance, or the Devil.

That Patience hath more power than Afflictions.

That everyone's memory is divided into two parts: the part losing all is the sea;
     the keeping part is land.

That Honesty in the court lives in persecution, like Protestants in Spain.

That Predestination and Constancy are alike uncertain to be judged of. [2]

That Reason makes Love the serving-man. [3]

That Virtue's favor is better than a King's favorite.

That being sick begins a suit to God; being well, possesseth it.

That health is the coach which carries to Heaven; sickness, the posthorse. [4]

That worldly delights, to one in extreme sickness, is like a high candle to a blind man.

That absence doth sharpen love, presence strengthens it; that the one brings fuel,
     the other blows it till it burns clear.

That love often breaks friendship, that ever increaseth love. [5]

That constancy of women, and love in men, is alike rare.

That Art is Truth's juggler.

That Falsehood plays a larger part in the world than Truth.

That blind Zeal and lame Knowledge are alike apt to ill.

That Fortune is humblest where most contemned. [6]

That no porter but Resolution keeps Fear out of minds.

That the face of Goodness without a body is the worst wickedness. [7]

That women's fortunes aspire but by other's powers.

That a man with a female wit is the worst hermaphrodite.

That a man not worthy being a friend, wrongs himself by being in acquaintance.

That the worst part of ignorance is making good and ill seem alike.

That all this is "news" only to fools.   —*Mistress B.*

Jonson's verbal fusillade may perhaps have been triggered by Boulstred's remark "That a man with a female wit is the worst hermaphrodite": Jonson had a career-long interest in hermaphroditism, a preoccupation which by 1609 was already exhibited in *Cynthia's Revels, Volpone,* and *Epicœne.* But "News of my Morning Work" was not Boulstred's only utterance before she died nor is Jonson the only poet whose plays may have met with Celia's criticism. In an epigram addressed to John Fletcher, Jonson laments that Fletcher's 1608/9 play, *The Faithful Shepherdess,* failed to please, having fallen victim to unnamed critics who sit in judgment upon "the life and death of plays," whether "knight, knight's man, /

---

[1] *ledger ambassador*] resident or ordinary ambassador.

[2] *Predestination and Constancy*] whether God has predestined your soul for Heaven or Hell, and whether or not your lover is faithful, are questions that leave room for anxious doubt.

[3] *That reason... Serving-man*] The reasonable person is not mastered by passion but makes love subject to reason.

[4] *posthorse*] postal horse; *health... sickness*] Spiritual health gets you to Heaven; sickness takes you there.

[5] *That love ... Love*] (Romantic) love has ruined many friendships; but friendship strengthens a love-relationship.

[6] *fortune ... contemned*] A turn of Fortune cannot harm one whose happiness does not depend on her favor.

[7] *face*] *appearance.*

Lady or Pucell that wears mask or fan, / Velvet or taffeta cap, ranked in the dark / With the shop's fore-men." [1]

That Jonson's resentment of Boulstred arose from a single sentence is doubtful; what angered him is that a pucell of the royal court, a maiden of the bedchamber close to Queen Anna and to Lady Bedford, could exercise the virtual powers of a Lord Chamberlain, presuming to applaud or hiss, to approve or damn, works of masculine genius by artists in need of Lucy Russell's matronage.

Cel Boulstred and her courtly "News" were now featured in one of the most widely read volumes of the seventeenth century. (By 1664, Overbury's *Wife* would pass through more editions than all of Jonson's plays and poems put together.) And despite Jonson's professed imperturbability, Boulstred's critical voice, if not that particular remark, fanned the embers of the playwright's malice. Within weeks of the posthumous 1614 publication of Boulstred's "News," Jonson took another swipe at the dead maiden's sexual reputation, this time in *Bartholomew Fair* (1614)*, in the figure of Alice of Turnbull, *alice* being an anagram of *Celia*, and Turnbull being another play on *Bull*stred: this time, the late Maiden of the Bedchamber is figured as a young prostitute who complains that "poor common whores can ha' no traffic, for the privy rich ones" (like Lady Bedford) who "lick the fat from us" (4.5).

In his conversations with William Drummond (Jan. 1618/9) – four years after Boulstred's "News" and Jonson's own *Bartholomew Fair* – we find the playwright still gloating over his poetical revenge on the court pucell, Cel Boulstred. A decade later he was still harping on the same string, this time in in *The New Inn*, a second play in which a morose protagonist competes with high-society strumpets for the love of a cross-dressed boy. The 1629 play does not invite viewers to see Jonson and Roe in the figures of Lovell and Frank, as the 1609 play does in the persons of Morose and his boy-bride. But the women of the Court are represented much as they were in *Epicœne*, and deliberately so: it is in *The New Inn* that Jonson recycles his 1602 libel, "An Elegy to Mistress Boulstred."

The doctrine that a poet who immortalizes a woman in verse has also the right to mortify her reputation was a catechism adopted by the "Sons of Ben" – a brotherhood of Cavalier poets who looked to Jonson as their chief mentor. Thomas Carew for one, after writing an elegy in praise of Jonson's *New Inn*, penned his own compendium of Celia poems in which he out-Jonson's Jonson's famous Celia lyrics. Carew's "Celia" (possibly Mary Villiers, daughter of the first duke of Buckingham) failed to give the poet what he wanted in exchange for his praise, whether sex or financial support; whereupon Carew reminded her, and his wider readership, that he might easily re-create his goddess as a pucell:

Ingrateful Beauty Threatened °

KNOW, CELIA, since thou art so proud,
'Twas I that gave thee thy renown:
Thou hadst in the forgotten crowd
Of common beauties lived unknown,
Had not my verse extolled thy name,
And with it imped the wings of Fame.

That "killing power" is none of thine:
I gave it to thy voice and eyes;
Thy sweets, thy graces, all are mine;
Thou art my star, shin'st in my skies.
Then dart not from thy borrowed sphere
Lightning on him that fixed thee there.

Tempt me with such affrights no more,
Lest what I made, I uncreate […]

Ben Jonson died in 1637. When his ungathered poems were collected for publication, his 1609 epitaph on Cecily Boulstred was not found; but the playwright had saved a copy of the Pucell libel, subsequently printed in *Underwood*. Jonson's "Court "Pucell" and the misattributed "Elegy to Mistress Boulstred" became the principal texts by which the notorious "Sell Bulstrode" has been known and remembered ever since.

---

[1] *life and death...foremen*] "To Mr. John Fletcher," ed. DWF from *Faithful Shepherdess*" (acted 1608, pub. 1609); *Velvet or taffeta cap*] 1. a cap of either velvet or taffeta; 2. velvet patches (to cover venereal sores) or a taffeta cap.

An effective antidote to Jonson's poison-pen comes neither from the equivocal "Epitaph," nor from John Donne nor from Edward Herbert, nor even from Lucy Russell, but from Sir Thomas Roe, who loved Cecily Boulstred and remembered her as the sum of human perfection.

In October 1614 (this was five years after Boulstred's death), the East India Company appointed Thomas Roe to be Britain's first ambassador to the court of the emperor Jangir in Mughal India. Knowing that he might never return but hoping to produce an heir, Roe on December 15th married Lady Eleanor Beeston, a nineteen-year-old widow of independent means. Seven weeks later, Roe embarked for the East, taking with him, as his most cherished possession, a miniature watercolor portrait of the late and well-beloved Cecily Boulstred.

Roe and his English entourage reached the anchorage off Surat on 18 September. There ensued a long overland trip north to Ajmir, during which Roe became gravely ill, arriving at Jahangir's palace in December, carried in a palkhi. In January 1616 Roe at last presented his credentials to the emperor, together with many gifts that included a lavish English coach. During his three-year sojourn in the East, Roe became Jahangir's drinking partner and favorite European. Roe's shrewd diplomacy marked the beginning of England's influence in the sub-continent.

On 2 September 1616, his birthday, Emperor Jahangir partied hardy, with feasting, drinking, dancing nautch girls, and processions of bejeweled elephants. About ten o'clock that night, with plenty of wine still remaining, his Majesty summoned the English ambassador from bed. Roe reports: "He had heard I had a picture which I had not showed him, [the emperor] desiring me to come to him, and bring it; and if I would not give it him, yet that he might see it and take copies for his wives. I rose and carried it with me."

Jahangir collected European art. In the hall of audience were now displayed portraits of King James and Queen Anna; of their daughter, Princess Elizabeth; Frances Howard, countess of Somerset; Sir Thomas Smythe, governor of the East-India Company; "a Citizen's wife of London"; and paintings of Christian saints. The one picture that Roe had not yet exhibited at the court of Ajmir was his private treasure: his water-color miniature of Cecilia Boulstred.

Thinking on his feet, Roe before leaving his quarters that night removed from the wall a French painting, oil on canvas, that had been brought from England. He carried both works of art to the palace.

"When I came, I found [his Majesty] sitting cross-legged on a little throne, all clad in diamonds, pearls, and rubies; before him, a table of gold; on it, about fifty pieces of gold plate set all with stone, some very great and extremely rich, some of less value, but all of them almost covered with small stones; his nobility about him in their best equipage, whom he commanded to drink frolicly (several wines standing by in great flagons).

"When I came near him, he asked for the picture. I showed him two. He seemed astonished at one of them – and demanded whose it was.

"I answered, a friend of mine that was dead. He asked me if I would give it him.

"I replied that I esteemed it more than anything I possessed, because it was the image of one that I loved dearly and could never recover; but that if his Majesty would pardon me my fancy and accept of the other, which was a French picture but excellent work, I would most willingly give it him.

"He sent me thanks, but that it was *that only* picture he desired, and loved as well as I; and that if I would give it him, he would better esteem of it than the richest jewel in his house. [...] He confessed he never saw so much art, so much beauty – and conjured me to tell him truly whether ever such a woman lived. I assured him there did one live, that this [picture] did resemble in all things but [her] perfection, and was now dead." [...] [1]

---

[1] *He sent me...now dead*] Ed. DWF from Roe (ed. 1899), 1.253-6. In the end, Jahangir "replied he would not take it – that he loved me the better for loving the remembrance of my friend, and knew what an injury it was to take it from me. By no means he would not keep it but only take copies (and with his own hand he would return it), and his wives should wear them. (For indeed, in that art of limning, his painters work miracles)." *Portrait*: identified woman, thought to be Cecilia Boulstred, dressed as Flora, goddess of flowers, c.1609, by Isaac Oliver.

Lady Lucy Russell (1581-1627),

Countess of Bedford

*Wear I an ower with yow I should give som reasons for divers things I have
donne, & may doe, which perhaps yow will not aprehend good grounds for; but
att this distance preserve mee in your opinion by an implicit fayth.*

—Letter to Dudley Carleton (1622), S.P. Dom., 14/139, f. 20r.

LUCY RUSSELL was the daughter of Anne (*née* Kelway), a cousin of Sir Philip and Lord Robert Sidney, and of Lady Mary Herbert, countess of Pembroke. Her father was Sir John Harington. a wealthy landowner of Burley (Rutlandshire), Stepney (Middlesex), and Combe Abbey (Warwickshire). Having parents sympathetic to women's education, Lucy was tutored from infancy in academic subjects. John Florio, in dedicating his *World of Words* to her in 1598, extols her fluency in Italian, French, and Spanish. John Dowland, dedicating his *Second Booke of Songes or Ayres* to her in 1600, praises her knowledge of music.

A beautiful child, and celebrated as a graceful dancer, Lucy Harington was courted by Edward Russell, third earl of Bedford, to whom she was married on 12 December 1594. She brought to the marriage a dowry of £3000 and the estate of Minster Lovell (which was more than her parents could afford, but it elevated their daughter to the rank of countess). Russell was then 22. She was 13.

Gracious, learned, and affable, the Russells were welcome at Court in the 1590s, a privilege that compelled them to spend beyond their means; which might not have mattered, were it not that Lord Edward became implicated in the 1601 Essex Rebellion: he rode into London with Devereux on 8 February, only to flee when he saw which way the wind was blowing. Bedford thereby saved his head, but Elizabeth banished him from Court and fined him £20,000. One wag wrote: "Bedford, he ran away / When we had lost the day. / Yet must his honor *pay,* / So it is assigned / If his fine-dancing dame / Do not their hard hearts tame / And say it is a shame, / Fools should be fined." Lucy's efforts to save her husband's estate were unavailing: Elizabeth reduced the penalty to £10,000 but that sum was still more than Bedford could muster (and more than most citizens could expect to gross in their entire lifetime). [1]

Shortly after Queen Elizabeth's death, a great host of English lords (including Lucy's father and uncle) made a mad dash for the north to meet the new King. Meanwhile the Privy Council appointed a coterie of English ladies to sail to Berwick, there to greet James's queen, Anna of Denmark. The Councilors chose delegates from among their own wives and daughters, and from among former attendants on Queen Elizabeth. Outflanking this official delegation was a welcoming party headed by Lucy Russell and her mother, Lady Anne Harington; who traveled overland and got there first. By the time the official greeting party arrived, Queen Anna had already made her choice: she appointed Lucy Russell First Lady of the Bedchamber. In May, the queen next appointed the poet, Lady Frances Seymour; but the elderly Earl of Hertford forbade his countess to accept the honor, and called her home; which left Lucy Russell unchallenged by any. Lady Lucy, 23, and Queen Anna, 30, became fast friends. [2]

Lucy Russell returned to Court life with gusto. She performed in all of Queen Anna's masques except Samuel Daniel's *Tethys' Festival* (in June 1610, when she was six months pregnant); and she became the single most important literary patron at Court, both in her own right and as gatekeeper to the queen. The countess extended her matronage to Ben Jonson (until he turned with venom on Cecily Boulstred), as well as to George Chapman, Samuel Daniel, John Davies, John Donne, John Dowland, Michael Drayton, John Florio, Sir Arthur Gorges, Inigo Jones, and Josuah Sylvester; and from 1609, to some dozen Puritan clergymen.

These and other panegyrists speak warmly of Lady Bedford's achievements, her virtue, her generosity. Ben Jonson when writing of women could be coarse and cynical, but even he (prior to the "Court Pucell" debacle) described the countess of Bedford as having "a learned, and a manly soul," which – coming from Jonson – was higher praise than if he were to have called her a goddess. He adds that she was "fair, and free, and wise, / Of greatest blood, and yet more good than great; / [...] courteous, facile, sweet, / Hating that solemn vice of great-

---

[1] *Bedford ... fined*] Ed. DWF from BL MS Harley 2127, f. 34r.

[2] *Lady Anne*] Queen Anna appointed the Haringtons as guardians of princess Elizabeth (b. 1596), with an annual pension of £1500 to cover their expenses, plus additional funds promised for tutors, servants, clothing, and a coach and horses. It wasn't enough: the honor nearly bankrupted the Haringtons; when Sir John died in 1613, the care of Princess Elizabeth had brought his estate to be encumbered with £40,000 in unpaid debts, which Lucy inherited.

ness, *pride*." None of these virtues are ones that Jonson himself possessed in great measure. But neither did Jonson's good opinion last. Lady Lucy's financial support earned Jonson's compliments as long as it lasted; after which, he mocked her in the figure of "Lady Haughty." [1]

Jonson was not the only poet who resented Lady Bedford's power, or who turned on her when the gratuities were not forthcoming. Her own cousin, Sir John Harington of Kelston, wrote snidely that the ladies of Anna's Court (unlike his own virtuous wife) "have learned the tongues, toys, tricks, of Rome, of Spain, of France. [...]

> These can corantoes and lavoltas dance,
> And though they foot it false, 'tis ne'er discerned.
> The virtues of these dames are so transcendent,
> Themselves are learned and their heroic spirit
> Can make disgrace an *honor,* sin a *merit.*
> All pens, all praisers, are on them dependent. [2]

That last complaint is the one that particularly infuriated Sir John: having been Queen Elizabeth I's beloved "saucy godson," he was no longer on high society's A-list; and Lucy, he fumed, was too busy dancing and receiving kudos from rival poets to provide her frustrated cousin with the recognition and advancement that he deserved under the new regime. But there were always more hungry poets hoping to be taken under Lady Lucy's wing than could be accommodated: the Countess of Bedford was the recipient of twenty-two printed book dedications between 1597 and 1621.

John Donne was fortunate in developing a personal relationship with Lucy Russell. Perhaps she recognized in Donne some sparks of extraordinary genius. In any case, while under her matronage from 1607 to 1615, Donne exchanged letters and verses with her and was often a guest at Twickenham, where the countess and her poet had spirited conversations about literature and religion. In one of his verse epistles to Lady Bedford, Donne writes, "Madame, / You have refined me [...] / For, as dark texts need notes, some must be / To usher virtue, and say: *This is she"* (1-2, 11-12).

In 1608-9 Donne became seriously ill with chronic neuritis. It was during this difficult time that he wrote his Holy Sonnets, including his famous apostrophe to Death:

Holy Sonnet 10
By John Donne

> DEATH be not proud, though some have callèd thee
> "Mighty" and "dreadful" – for thou art not so.
> For those whom thou *think'st* thou dost overthrow
> Die not, poor Death! – nor yet canst thou kill me.
> From rest and sleep (which but thy pictures be),
> Much pleasure: then from thee much more must flow!
> And soonest our best men with thee do go—
> Rest of their bones, and soul's delivery!
> Thou art slave to fate, chance, kings, and desperate men,
> And dost with poison, war, and sickness dwell.
> And poppy or charms can make us sleep as well,
> And better, than thy stroke. Why swell'st thou then?
> One short sleep past, we wake eternally,
> And death shall be no more: Death, thou shalt die. [3]

Throughout his illness, when able to write, Donne corresponded with Lucy Russell, who doubtless took some comfort in his Holy Sonnets during that summer of 1609 when her cousin and best friend died. Donne was among the last to visit Celia Boulstred as she lay on her deathbed, and he was the first to pen a eulogy in Boulstred's memory after she died – for which labor, he doubtless hoped to receive a gratuity. (Donne with his large family, dowry trouble, and his lack of gainful employment was always desperate for cash.) But in his elegy for Boulstred, Donne chose an unfortunate rhetorical strategy, recanting on his defiance and belittlement of Death in Holy Sonnets, in order now to refigure Death as an insatiable monster:

---

[1] *a learned...pride*] Ed. DWF from Ben Jonson, *Epigrammes* (London, 1616), no. 76.

[2] *These...dependent*] Ed. DWF from John Harington, "To his Wife, of Women's Virtues," *Epigrams,* Bk. 2, no. 66.

[3] *thou shalt die*] Cf. Thomas Adam, "The Proud" (1615): "Death stands at your doors. Be not proud, be not mad: *You* must die."

Elegy on Mistress Boulstred
By John Donne

DEATH I recant, and say, unsaid by me
What e'er hath slipped that might diminish thee.
Spiritual treason! atheism 'tis, to say,
That any can thy summons disobey.
Th' Earth's face is but thy table; there are set
Plants, cattle, men: dishes for Death to eat.
In a rude hunger now he millions draws
Into his bloody, or plaguy, or starvèd jaws.
Now he will seem to spare – and doth more waste,
Eating the best, first […]   [10]
How could I think thee nothing, that see now   [25]
In all, this All: Nothing else is, but thou […]

Together with his 74-line "Elegy on Mistress Boulstred," Donne composed an "Elegy to the Lady Bedford," a poem of consolation in which Donne acknowledges his patron's bereavement and celebrates her friendship with the deceased. Where the friendship of ladies Bedford and Boulstred had just been scorned by Ben Jonson as a debauchery of Lesbian "tribade lust," Donne celebrates their love as if it were a sacred same-sex marriage: Celia Boulstred's death is a loss such as a man suffers in the loss of a beloved wife:

Courtesy of the National Portrait Gallery

Elegy to the Lady Bedford
By John Donne

YOU that are she, and you that's double she:
In her dead face, half of your self shall see.
She was the other part – for so they do,
Which build them friendships, become one, of two—
So "two," that but themselves no third can fit.   [5]
Had you died first, a carcass she had been,
And we your rich tomb in her face had seen.
She (like the soul) is gone, and you here stay,
Not a live friend but th' other half, of clay.
And since you act that part – as men say, "Here   [15]
Lies such a prince" when but one part is there,
And do all honor and devotion due
Unto the whole – so we all reverence you;
For such a friendship who would not adore,
In you who are all, what "both" was before?   [20]
(Not "all" as if some *perishèd* by this,
But so, as *all,* in you. *contracted* is—
As of this *all,* though many parts decay,
The pure (which elemented them) shall stay
And, though diffused and spread in infinite,
Shall re-collect, and in one *all,* unite:
So, Madame, as her soul to Heaven is fled,
Her flesh rests in the earth, as in the bed,
Her virtues do (as to their proper sphere)
Return to dwell with you, of whom they were […] [30]

Lady Bedford did not respond to the flattery of Donne's "Elegy to the Lady Bedford." She replied instead to the cleverness of his "Elegy on Mistress Boulstred," where the poet dwells for thirty-six lines on Death's awesome power and infinite appetite before he so much as notes the passing of Celia Boulstred. "Death, I recant," gave Death too much credit, and Boulstred too little.

Correcting what one editor has called Donne's "frigid hyperboles," the Countess of Bedford advises Donne that he was right the first time: Death, to Lady Lucy's mind, is neither mighty nor dreadful. For Christians such as herself and Cecilia, Death has no reason to be proud. In her own "Elegy on Mistress Boulstred," Lady Lucy takes from Donne's sonnet a hook with which to rein in a clever poet who was given to overstatement:

Elegy on Mistress Boulstred

By Lucy Russell, Countess of Bedford

"DEATH, be not proud": thy hand gave not this blow.
Sin was her captive, whence thy power doth flow.
The executioner of wrath thou art,
But to destroy the just is not thy part.
Thy coming, *Terror, Anguish, Grief*, denounces;   1
Her happy state, *Courage, Ease, Joy* pronounces.
From out the crystal palace of her breast,
The (clearer) soul was called to endless rest
(Not by the thundering voice wherewith God threats,
But as with crownèd saints in heaven He treats),
And, waited on by angels, home was brought,
To joy that it through many dangers sought.   2
The key of mercy gently did unlock
The doors 'twixt Heaven and it when life did knock.
Nor boast, the fairest frame was made thy prey
Because to mortal eyes it did decay.   3
A better witness than thou art assures
That (though dissolved) it yet a space endures;
No dram thereof shall want, or loss sustain,
When her blest° soul inhabits it again.
Go then to people cursed before they were!   4
Their souls in triumph to thy conquest bear.
    Glory thou not thyself in these hot tears
Which our face (not for her, but our harm) wears,
The mourning livery given by Grace, not thee,   [25]
Which wills our souls in these streams washed should be;
And on our hearts (her memory's best tomb!),
In this her epitaph, doth write *thy* doom.
    Blind were those eyes saw not how bright did shine,
Through flesh's misty veil, those beams divine.
    Deaf were the ears not charmed with that sweet sound
Which did i'the Spirit's instructed voice abound.
    Of flint the conscience, did not yield and melt
At what, in her last act, it saw, heard,° felt.
    Weep not, nor grudge then, to have lost her sight
(Taught thus, our after-stay's° but a short night).
But by all souls not by corruption choked,
Let in high-raised notes that power be invoked,
Calm the rough seas by which she sails to rest
From sorrows here to a kingdom ever blest;
And teach this hymn of her with joy, and sing:
The grave no conquest gets, death hath no sting.   5

• • •

---

[1] *sin ... flow*] Your power comes from sin, yet she made a captive of sin;   *thy ... denounces*] Terror, etc., denounces thy coming;   *Her...pronounces*] Courage, etc., pronounce her happy state.

[2] *clearer*] *i.e.*, her soul was more pure even than her pure breast;   *not by ... treats*] not called by god in wrath, but entreated to come in that gentle voice reserved for the saints;   *to joy that*] to enjoy that which.

[3] *nor boast*] nor boast, Death, that;   *because*] do not boast simply because.

[4] *it*] Boulstred's "fairest frame";   *want*] be lacking;   *again*] in the resurrection of her body on Judgment Day; *were*] existed; were born.

[5] *hath no sting*] Citing I Corinthians 15:55: "O death, where is thy sting? O grave, where is thy victory?" This elegy, first printed in 1635, is Lucy Russell's only poem to have, though it's clear from Donne's letters that she wrote others.

Accepting correction, Donne started from scratch, writing a second elegy for Boulstred ("Language, thou art too narrow"), in which he celebrates the virtues of the deceased; transfers agency from Death to God; and laments the power of his own language to find the right words in which to express empathy in grief. In this second more personal elegy, Donne urges Lady Bedford to share her grief with others, lest the death of Cecilia break her heart: "We her sad-glad friends all bear a part / Of grief – for *all,* would waste a Stoic's heart" (61-2).

But Lucy Russell's troubles were just beginning. In 1610, the countess gave birth to a daughter, who survived only two hours. (Her first child, Francis, died in February 1602, living just three weeks.) Her final pregnancy, in 1611, ended in a miscarriage. November 6th, 1612, brought the death of Prince Henry, who had been like a younger brother to Lady Lucy. She took it hard: on 23 November, Richard Sackville, the husband of Anne Clifford, reports what sounds like an apoplexy: "My Lady Bedford last night, about one of the clock, was suddenly (and hath continued ever since) speechless – and is past all hope, though yet alive." [1]

When she recovered, Lucy Russell was a different person. Already sympathetic to the Puritan cause, she no longer took pleasure in the Court – to which she returned for the February 1613 wedding of Princess Elizabeth. John Chamberlain was among those who noted a difference: "she is somewhat reformed in her attire, and forbears painting (which, they say, makes her look somewhat strangely among so many vizards, which together with their frizzled, powdered hair, makes them look all alike, so that you can scant know one from another"). Elizabeth's marriage to the Elector Palatine, against Queen Anna's will, was another loss (Elizabeth said farewell to England, and to her mother and Lucy Russell, and departed to meet her fate in Bohemia). [2]

In July, the earl of Bedford fell from a horse, cracking his skull against a tree, which left him permanently crippled and with stammering speech. He was cared for thereafter by servants. (Lucy in her correspondence makes almost no mention of him; the Russells had been living mostly apart since 1603.) In August, Lucy's father died, leaving her 2/3 heir to an inheritance encumbered with £40,000 in unpaid debts, adding to her own. Sir John Harington in the meantime brought a costly Chancery suit against Lucy and her widowed mother. In February 1614, Lucy's brother died of smallpox. (Donne wrote "Obsequies" for him, addressed to the countess, hoping she would make good on her offer to pay his debts. Instead, she showed him to the door.)

In 1617, Lucy retired to Moor Park in Hertfordshire, where the Russells built a new house on land Elizabeth I granted to the 2nd Earl of Bedford in 1576. The Russells were now £50,000 in debt, but that did not slow down Lucy's spending; and as debts accumulated, the sorrows kept coming. On 2 March 1618/9, Queen Anna died. Three weeks later, Lady Lucy came down with a severe case of smallpox that left her disfigured, and blind in one eye. (Those who once praised her no longer saw any need. Edward Howard: "the smallpox hath seized on the Lady of Bedford and so seasoned her all over, that they say she is more full and foul than could be expected in so thin and bare a body.") And on 24 May 1620, the countess's mother, Lady Harington, died. [3]

At Moor Park, Lucy built a magnificent gardens and took up art collecting. In 1622, as Sir Nicholas Bacon lay on his deathbed, the countess wrote to his daughter-in-law, Lady Jane (Cornwallis) Bacon, asking to buy the old man's collection: "though I be but a late beginner," she wrote, "I have pretty store of choice pieces." She declared herself "a very diligent gatherer of all I can get of Holbein's, or any other excellent master's hand." She hoped to acquire Lord Bacon's collection of Holbeins before the earl of Arundel heard about them. Arundel, a great collector, had already "cozened" (tricked) her out of "some pictures promised me" from another source. Price, she said, was no object: "I had rather have them than jewels." [4]

The earl and countess of Bedford died within a few days of each other, at Moor Park, having spent their entire fortune and a good deal more. He died on 3 May 1627 and was buried at Chenies. Lady Lucy died on the 26th and was buried with her own family at Exton. None of her former poets paid tribute to her memory.

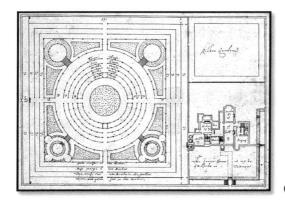

Below: Lady Lucy,
(Fitzwilliam Museum, Cambridge)

Left: Twickenham manor and gardens,
design by R. Smythson (1609)
(RIBA British Architectural Library)

---

[1] *My Lady...alive*] Richard Sackville to Sir Thos. Edmondes (23 Nov. 1612), ed. DWF from Williams (1849), 1.211.

[2] *She...another*] J. Chamberlain to D. Carleton (1 Aug. 1613), from *Chamberlain Letters* (1939), 1.470.

[3] *the smallpox...body*] E. Howard to D. Carleton (15 July 1619), ed. DWF from *S.P. James I,* 74/49.

[4] *though I...jewels*] Lady Jane Cornwallis, *Private Correspondence*, ed. DWF from Braybrooke (1842), 50-1.

ÆTATIS SVÆ . 14 2....
ANNO DNI . 1 5 8 9 2m....

Elizabeth Bruges daughter
to the Lord Giles Chandos

Elizabeth Brydges, [Lady Kennedy] (1575-1617), by Hieronimo Custodis (Courtesy of Woburn Abbey)
The orange blossom represents chastity; the butterfly, Elizabeth's soul; and the bird, loving constancy.

Elizabeth Brydges (Kennedy), (1575-1617),

Maid of Honor

> *I know you wilbe sory to heare, what grieues me to wryte of:*
> *Yt is spied out by Enuye that 1000 is againe fallen in Loue with*
> *his fairest B. Yt cannot chuse but come to 1500 Eares....*
> —Roland Whyte to Robert Cecil (11 Feb. 1597/8) [1]

ELIZABETH BRYDGES, born in 1575 in Sudeley Castle, was the daughter of Frances (*née* Clinton) and Giles Brydges, third Baron Chandos. She had two brothers, both of whom died as infants, and a sister, Katherine, born in 1583. As the daughter of a great property owner, Elizabeth "Bess" Brydges was courted from infancy by the parents of eligible bachelors; concerning which, a 1587 letter survives from Elizabeth's mother to John Manners, fourth earl of Rutland, regarding a proposed match between his son, Roger, aged 12, and her own daughter Elizabeth, 13. [2]

John's elder brother Edward (the late Baron Roos, Baron Manners, and third Earl of Rutland) had died in April 1587, naming John (Roger's father) as his principal heir. The younger brother thereby inherited the earldom of Rutland and barony of Manners, and all of Edward's lands and houses (including magnificent Belvoir Castle, which had been in the family for six hundred years). The barony de Roos, Lord Edward conferred upon his daughter and only child (Elizabeth Manners, not yet in her teens). And for that reason, Uncle John sued her. He wanted it all.

Without waiting for a judgment in his suit, earl Rutland in his son's behalf joined the company of suitors for the hand of Elizabeth Brydges, a young heiress-apparent (no brothers) who was likely to be snapped up soon by a rival if he did not move quickly.

Giles and Frances Brydges were of course thrilled to receive overtures from an earl, two steps up the social ladder. Roger Manners and Bess Brydges had met. They were not yet acquainted, but when the parents mentioned marriage, the girl (on her mother's testimony) voiced no objection. Lady Frances therefore dispatched her reply to the boy's father, offering to settle quickly.

Frances, Lady Chandos, to John Manners, 4th Earl of Rutland°

June 2 [1587], Sudeley.°

[...] My Lord and I do not doubt your plain dealing in this matter which touches us nearest of anything in the world; and therefore we are ready to inform you what revenue and portion will come to Bess: On these points, my lord says that if he have no son, he will assure Sudeley° to her after his and my decease; and that he will give her a lordship called Elton°, immediately upon her marriage, which will be worth £600 a year within eight years of the marriage. If my Lord have a son, she shall have £4,000 more, which will be charged upon Sudeley [rents].

When it was desired to know my young maid's liking, she answered that, for the little time she was in my lordship's° company, she saw nothing in him but what was worthy of commendation. As for the [other] suitors, I cannot deny these are of the best sort who are anxious to marry her.

(We have another daughter, of five years of age).

My lord is desirous to understand the young lord's estate and what jointure he will give – and if these offers are agreed to and liked, my lord would have the match concluded without delay.

Then came a glitch. In February 1588, earl John himself died, passing his titles and estate to Roger before the Manners-Brydges prenuptials were signed. Roger, fifth earl, bereaved of his uncle and his

---

[1] *1000*] Whyte's cipher for the Earl of Essex;   *1500*] Queen Elizabeth; *fairest B*] Elizabeth Brydges.

[2] *Sudeley Castle*] near Winchcombe, Gloucester; built in the 15th century on the site of an older fortress; burial place of Katherine Parr, the last of Henry VIII's six wives; gifted to John, first Baron Chandos after the execution of Lady Jane Grey and Thomas Seymour.

father, soon found his inheritance complicated by the demands of two Rutland wills, the jointures for two dowager countesses, costly litigation, and his own adolescent inexperience.   His father's marriage-plans for him fell through.

Roger Manners later married the poet, Elizabeth Sidney (the only surviving child of Sir Philip); and made her so miserable that, when he died in June 1612, it was rumored that she poisoned him (Two months later, when Lady Rutland also died, the rumor was that she had been poisoned by the Manners family in revenge, and in order to prevent her from marrying into the rival Howard clan.)

It was common practice among the well-to-do, when marketing a daughter either for marriage or for a position at court, to have her picture painted – at the very least, a water-color in miniature, placed in a locket; and for those who could afford it, a framed portrait in oils.   Giles and Frances hired Hieronimo Custodis for a large oil-on-canvas.   Elizabeth for the occasion wore a black brocade gown with puffed sleeves and a deep-vee waistline; the skirt supported by a French farthingale; an open-fronted cartwheel ruff (so as not to cover her lovely neck); and for accessories, a stone-encrusted caul, a necklace of interlaced white and black pearls, heavy gold chains, and half a dozen diamond-studded brooches.   More than one man who saw that picture, would find her an attractive catch.   Besides which, everyone agreed that she was quite pretty.

 Giles and Frances in 1589 may already have had a particular candidate in mind. Henry Wriothesley, earl of Southampton, was just two years older than Elizabeth, not yet wed, and the richest teenager in England (his father having died in 1581); and he may already have shown some interest: Pinned to Bess Brydges' hair on the right side (in the Custodis portrait) is a gold brooch, formed of a capital H overlaying a W, under a marble-sized pearl.   But whether it was Henry Wriothesley, some other H.W., or the painter's imagination that supplied the monogrammed brooch, the jewel while looking well in Elizabeth's hair did not lead to a marriage contract.

Lord Chandos died in February 1593/4, aged 46.   By will he provided both daughters with a generous dowry.   His land, including Sudeley Castle, he settled upon his wife Frances for life, with the future interest (the "remainder in fee") being assigned, not to his brother William, but to his own firstborn, Elizabeth.   His baronial title, he bequeathed upon William.

Elizabeth's uncle – now fourth Baron Chandos – was discontented to receive his brother's honorific title without the wealth to attend it.   Doubting the legality of Lord Giles' bequest of real estate in perpetuity to a daughter (rather than to himself, his younger brother), made no sense to William Brydges.   He therefore sued his sister-in-law and niece, claiming to have been defrauded of his brother's estate.   Lord William's logic was simple: he was a man, they were not.

The lawsuit made Elizabeth at age nineteen a less attractive mate for eligible noblemen who looked to expand their material wealth through a good marriage.   But that did not deter suitors altogether; it merely limited her marketabilty to long-term investors.

Following her husband's death, widow Frances with her daughters wintered in London, at Chandos Place (a city house in Lambeth Marsh); where, less than two weeks after Giles died, before he was even put in the ground, daughter Bess received a gentleman caller: Charles Lister, friend to the queen's godson Sir John Harington, came from Windsor Palace to Chandos Place, bearing gifts and affection for Elizabeth.

That interview was courteous but inconclusive.   Lady Frances had higher ambitions for her daughter than Charlie Lister.   She sought and soon obtained for Bess a position at court:

In July, Bridget Manners, 22, resigned her post as a maid of honor, making the excuse that she was needed at home to care for her ailing mother; when in fact, Bridget wished to get married (and did so, a month later, to Robert Tyrwhitt, without the queen's permission; a storm ensued). [1]

At Whitehall, the fresh face of Elizabeth Brydges caused a stir. One courtier, writing home to his father that July reports, "There is a very fine gentlewoman, very fair (and a very rich marriage!) of the Privy Chamber lately, within this fortnight: my lord Chandos' daughter. She is much eyed and pointed at." [2]

The queen's favorite, Robert Devereux, was among those who stared and pointed: he was sure that he had fallen in love with Brydges, at first sight – which is how Essex felt about virtually every wealthy and unconquered beauty. But he was also married (to Frances Walsingham, Sir Philip Sidney's widow).

---

[1] *Bridget Manners*] (1572-1604 [elder sister to Roger]); upon learning of the elopement, Queen Elizabeth gave to the newlywed Tyrwhitts a honeymoon in the Tower of London, in separate cells.

[2] *One courtier*] Philip Gawdy. Ed. DWF from H.M.C., *Seventh Report*, Part 1, p. 524.

Elizabeth Brydges was doubtless pleased with the attention that she received from the greatest man in the queendom, but she seems to have given Lord Essex only enough encouragement to keep him interested. And if that was her plan, it worked: he pursued her, with ardor.

Poor Charles Lister (or rather, *wealthy* Charles, but not for long) was utterly smitten with Mistress Brydges, and partly taken with thoughts of "a very rich marriage." Lister all this while gave Bess Brydges many gifts, and loaned her spending money. By way of reciprocation, he received some encouragement. The happiest day of his life must have been the day that Elizabeth Brydges said yes, she would marry him. Her father's permission was not required: the third Baron Chandos being dead, his daughter was a free agent – and Chandos had left her with a magnificent dowry, the entire package said to be worth £16,500. So far, so good.

But as the months and years dragged on, despite Charles's generosity and affection, Elizabeth declined to set a date. For one thing, she was having too much fun. Bess Brydges greatly overspent her stipend. She did not, at first, feel the pinch: when short of cash, she simply pawned another jewel, or else borrowed a few pounds sterling from her good friend, Mr. Lister, against her untouched dowry.

One April afternoon in 1597, Bess Brydges, together with Elizabeth and Anne Russell (her best friends and fellow maids of honor), slipped out of the palace without the Queen's permission. The plan was to watch the earl of Essex and other young men play ball, and to cheer them on. When her Majesty learned of this unauthorized day-trip (someone may have squealed), she had all three young ladies swinged soundly from the playing field and brought into her royal presence; where she scolded the Russell sisters but "used the Mistress Brydges with words and blows of anger." (As her Majesty's goddaughters, the Russell sisters could count on their special relationship with the Queen; but Bess Brydges had no such claim on the Queen's mercy.) Elizabeth then banished the three sport-loving women from her Coffer Chamber, exiling them for three days to the home of that dour Calvinist spinster, Dorothy Stafford. [1]

Writing of this scandal to Robert Sidney, Rowland Whyte quips, "you may conjecture whence these storms rise." [2]

For those who didn't guess: the storm arose from Essex's continued flirtation with Elizabeth Brydges, which infuriated Queen Elizabeth no less than it bothered Devereux's wife, Lady Essex.

In 1597, Essex, Ralegh, and Southampton sailed for the Azores on the "Islands Expedition" – with Queen Elizabeth's blessing, albeit on funds raised from private investors. Their mission: to attack the Azores; destroy the Spanish naval fleet; intercept the Spanish treasure fleet returning from the New World as it passed through the Azores; and return to England, laden with gold. Elizabeth Brydges was among those who subscribed – purchasing her shares for £150, on a loan from Charles Lister.

The expedition was a disaster. Contrary to the queen's express command, Lord Essex (who always thought he knew better) neglected to destroy the Spanish fleet before chasing the treasure fleet into bad weather. He came home empty-handed. The Spaniards had the last laugh, all the way to *el banco*.

In disgrace with the Queen for his failure at sea, Essex on his home-return turned for solace to Elizabeth Brydges, now 22 and still single. The flirtation though discreet did not escape notice. Writing in cipher to Robert Sidney, Rowland Whyte laments: "I know you will be sorry to hear what grieves me to write of: it is spied out by envy that 1000 [Essex] is again fallen in love with his fairest B[rydges]. It cannot choose but come to 1500 [Queen Elizabeth's] ears. Then he is undone, and all they that depend upon his favor." [3]

The tempest, when it hit, was not however brought by the Queen. It was raised by Charles Lister. Played for a chump one too many times, Bess's sugar-daddy grew as jealous of Robert Devereux as the Queen was of Bess Brydges. Unwilling and unable to keep throwing good money after bad, Lister demanded of his Love that she either marry him, or return his gifts and repay his loans.

Bess's three answers (not well thought out) were *No, no*, and *no*. Her impoverished fiancé straightaway filed executions for debt against Elizabeth Brydges, maid of honor; and filed a complaint with those higher up. Pretty Bess, maid of honor, was again the subject of Court gossip.

---

[1] *used...blows of anger*] R.Whyte to R. Sidney (13 April), ed. DWF from Sidney *Letters,* ed. Collins, 2.38; *Anne Russell*] (1578-1639), not the countess of Warwick, but the daughter of Elizabeth (*née* Cook) and John, Baron Russell; countess of Worcester by her 1600 marriage to Somerset; *Elizabeth Russell*] her elder sister (1575-1609), died single.

[2] *you may...storms rise*] *ibid.*

[3] *I know...favor*] Same to same (12 Feb. 1597/8), 2.90.

Without a settlement of her uncle's lawsuit against her father's estate, Elizabeth had no means to discharge her debts. Sobering up to her situation (and following what must have been a fierce quarrel with her mother), Bess approached her uncle with an offer: let him pay off her debts, and sign over, to *her*, the use of Sudeley Castle, with its manorial rents, for her lifetime; and she would yield all her title and interest to the rest of her father's estate. But Elizabeth was being naïve. Her widowed mother had inherited the lifetime use of Sudeley Castle, a right that could not legally be infringed upon. Uncle William did not bite. (Dudley Carleton reports: "he takes advantage of her disgrace, and hopes to possess it [all], shortly.") [1]

Charles Lister, meantime, pressed forward with his legal complaint against Elizabeth Brydges:

Affidavit of Charles Lister (before Sir Chas. Blount, Lord St. John, and three others)°

MISTRESS BRYDGES sent to me at Windsor, ten days after her father's death, to come to her at Lambeth Marsh; when she borrowed £100 of me, which I lent her (and numerous other sums at her request, amounting to £190), upon a contract made between us in marriage. I also sent her a purse and £50 in gold.

And within a fortnight after, I delivered her £10 in gold (in my Lady Stafford's chamber), when she asked for £10 more, which I gave her (in the chapel chamber); and paid her cousin, [Elizabeth] Cooke, £20. I also gave her a pearl chain which cost me £10, and redeemed a diamond of hers for £60 which was with Mr. Hardick in Paul's Churchyard. [2]

Then she desired me to lend her £150 to venture with my Lord of Essex, which I procured. As also, £10 for the physicians.

She then desired me to buy her some taffeta to make her a save-guard; also some lawn for ruffs, linen and other things, to the value of £30, which she also had. [3]

Then I gave her a silver basin and ewer, which cost me £30, and paid a bond for her to Sir Harry Gray of £200.

Then she asked me for a jewel. And I gave her a ruby and diamond which cost me £120, which she said should be the token between me and her, during our lives. Then she had of me, at sundry times, to the value of £20.

On 6 August last, Mr. Chune received [loan] of Mr. Campion, 2,000 marks for her; and I bound *myself and lands,* to pay the money within six months. This money was to redeem her diamonds which – as she promised Mr. Campion and me – should redeem my lands again, but she now keeps them in her own hands, and suffers *me* to pay the money, to my utter undoing, as I have already paid £1,150, and further stand bound with her in bonds to the value of £1,000, which she has taken up to her own use.

She had also delivered to her a suit of tapestry-hangings for her chamber. All these and other charges that I have been at with her, I have done upon her faithful promise of marriage; which, if she denies, I will that all these things shall be recovered of her, and be disposed of according to my will.

Charles Lister
11 December 1598

The apparent decision of the judges (no copy survives) was that the loans to Charles Lister must be repaid, pending settlement of the lawsuit. That gave Brydges some wiggle-room, as well as a disincentive to settle. The litigation stalled out.

The Russell sisters (Bess's cousins and best friends) were likewise having too much fun for their income. To continue the lifestyle to which they had grown accustomed, they would need husbands. But no maid of honor, not even the Queen's own goddaughter, could marry without asking permission of her Majesty; whose answer was always No. That impediment notwithstanding, Elizabeth Russell Sr. was working behind the scenes to find a match for her eldest. On 24 June 1597, on the heels of her daughters' three-day exile from Court, Lady Russell wrote to her nephew, Robert Cecil, Secretary of State, asking him to assist in clapping up a marriage between Elizabeth, now 22, and William Somerset, 22 (who was second and eldest living son to the fourth earl of Worcester):

---

[1] *he takes…shortly*] Carleton to Chamberlain (7 Aug. 1598), ed. DWF fr. *S.P. Dom. Elizabeth* (1598-1601), 78.

[2] *ten days after*] *i.e.*, on 3 March 1593/4.

[3] *save-guard*] an outer skirt worn by women to protect their clothing, especially when riding.

Elizabeth, Lady Russell to Robert Cecil, Viscount Cranborn (24 June 1597)° [1]

[…] This is all I have to trouble you with, but desire you in this (being of the Earl of Worcester's daily in Court), it will please you in your best opportunity to persuade the Earl so as my daughter Bess may ~~be wife to [William] Lord Harbart, his eldest son. Her virtue, birth, and place~~ – joined to the £100 of inheritance presently enjoyed, and the part in reversion of my Lady Gray, joined with £200 yearly after my death till £2,000 pounds be come out in ten years (to her own good, whether she be sole or married) – will be a sufficient portion for an Earl of so small revenue and so many children as the Earl of Worcester. It is the virtue and honor of the parents, joined with the young lord's best affections, that maketh me thus desirous. Else I seek it not.

24 June. Your loving Aunt,
Elizabeth Russell, dowager

Six months later, when William died and still no marriage contract, Lady Russell aimed for his brother: Henry Somerset, the next Lord Harbart new heir-apparent to the Earl of Worcester, was only a year younger than Elizabeth.

The two Russell sisters, meanwhile, continued to spend faster than they could borrow. In 1599, when their creditors ran out of patience, the Bess and Elizabeth sold to Robert Cecil their inherited interest in Russell House, an elegant mansion situated in St. Martin-in-the-Fields. (It was then being rented by the countess of Derby.) Forewarned by their mother that she would disown them if they ever parted with Russell House, the daughters did it anyway, to pay down their debt.

Following a great quarrel with her daughters, widow Russell wrote an icy letter to her nephew "Master Secretary," demanding that he cancel the sale, at whatever cost to herself:

Elizabeth, Lady Russell, to Robert Cecil, Viscount Cranborn (September 1599)°

Master Secretary,

I pray you pardon me: I cannot with my life frame my heart to be content to part with Russell House out of the name – whereby my dead husband's name shall be wronged and weeded up by the roots – but mean to sell all I am worth to give them what, of you, they should have. I know, "*perfecto odio odieris me*"; but I must bear the bitterest brunt thereof, as all the comfortable fruits that ever I received from my children. [2]

Yet as long as I offer no wrong nor do *you* no hurt therein (being so well provided of your father's house), and thinking this not worth more than *you* offer to *me* (not to be offended, to go without!), I must put my trust only in God to protect me, and bear what your coming malice may work me – since I can *not* bring my heart to be content to dishonor the dead, or not to give all due to my dead darling while I breathe. And therefore, desire you not to go about to take the remainder of the House out of the Crown.

Your honest, plain dealing Aunt.

—Wherein I may *else* pleasure you, I shall be most willing to do what I may – but I think that I go upon my last year. *Some* [year] will kill me, and therefore my kingdom is not of this world.

Elizabeth Russell, dowager
1599, September

Cecil kept the palace, but graciously allowed that it should still be called Russell House, not Cecil House. Lady Russell was not thereby placated.

Finding her elder daughter chiefly to blame for the sale, Elizabeth Russell Sr. disowned Elizabeth Jr., and substituted her younger daughter to become the bride of Henry Somerset (m. 1600); by which marriage Anne Russell eventually became Countess of Worcester. Bess Russell died unmarried in 1601, aged 26; at which time her mother, still offended, refused to memorialize Elizabeth among the other Russell family tombs in Westminster Abbey.

---

[1] *Elizabeth, Lady Russell*] (*née* Cook, 1528-1609), daughter of the humanist, Anthony Cook; widow of John, Lord Russell (d. 1584); sister-in-law of William Cecil, Lord Burghley, and maternal aunt to Robert Cecil; translator of John Ponet, *A Way of Reconciliation Touching the Lord's Supper* (1605).

[2] *perfecto odio odieris me*] I hate with a perfect hatred (from Psalms 139:22, "I hate them with perfect hatred: I count them mine enemies").

Anne therefore commissioned a monument: Elizabeth Russell is depicted sitting up (a first, for Westminster Abbey); upon a chair of osier (symbolizing rejected love); not dead, but asleep, with her chin resting upon her hand, and her foot upon a skull; with an inscription, in Latin, "She is not dead, but sleepeth: Sacred to the happy memory of Elizabeth Russell, her afflicted sister Anne has erected this monument." (Their mother doubtless took the skull-motif to represent her beloved husband, Lord Russell, being stomped on).

The next we hear of the Russells' cousin, Elizabeth Brydges, she is back on top of her game: In May 1601, George Whitton reports a marriage pending at court: Bess Brydges was about to tie the knot with Robert Cecil, Secretary of State (whose wife, Elizabeth *née*, Brooke had died in 1597), and take up residence in Russell House. By October, that gossip had evaporated. Enter the Frenchmen: when an envoy to Queen Elizabeth's Court arrived from Navarre, "the whole train were enamored" of Bess Brydges, the Queen's eldest maid of honor; chief among whom were the Governor of Bourbonnais and one Monsieur Sardigny, who became "rivals in love of Mistress Brydges." [1]

Elizabeth's litigious uncle died in the spring of 1602, with the lawsuit in abeyance and still unsettled. Grey Brydges, his son, resumed the fight with gusto. A conference was scheduled for 17 June, to negotiate a settlement to litigation that had now dragged on for eight years, and cost a fortune in legal fees.

The 11 June arbitration did not go as well as planned. When Elizabeth's attorney (her Clinton cousin, Sir Ambrose Willoughby) made a wisecrack that Grey Brydges thought insulting to himself and his father, he physically assaulted Willoughby, causing the man to be "hurt in the head and body." End of discussion. [2]

It's unclear whether Willoughby continued to represent Elizabeth Brydges after getting beat up. But progress was made: In October, Grey Brydges made a proffer: he would take Elizabeth to wife, thereby to unite their lands, revenue, and bodies in holy matrimony. The Archbishop of Canterbury for so good a cause as making peace between feuding families was empowered to grant a dispensation for marriage within the proscribed degrees of consanguinity – Grey and Elizabeth being first cousins – and he was willing to do so. Nor did Lady Frances have any objection; in fact, she insisted upon it. The talk at Court was that it was already a done deal. [3]

Elizabeth, however, refused: it was not her pugilistic male cousin that she wished to have and to hold, but her inheritance of Sudeley Castle; which she still believed should be hers, upon her mother's death, or sooner. Preferably, right now, her mother having already had a very long turn.

Grey's offer of marriage remained on the table, with a draft settlement, unsigned. The litigation continued, with mother and daughter no longer speaking to one another.

There was doubtless some talk of these matters when Anne Clifford, 13, and her mother Margaret, 43, traveled with Elizabeth Brydges in May 1603 to meet King James and Queen Anna on their royal progress from Scotland. Lady Margaret, countess dowager of Cumberland, hoped that daughter Anne would be chosen as a maid of honor. Elizabeth Brydges, who knew the ropes, could serve as her mentor.

Appointed a mourner for Elizabeth I, Brydges had duties lasting for nearly a month, from the queen's death on 24 March until her burial in Westminster Abbey on 28 April. She then joined the ladies Clifford for the trip north. They rode by horseback from London to North Hall (near Cambridge, a Clifford property), then south again to Theobalds Park. Here (in the same house in which James would die, twenty-two years later) they parted with the new king and his queen.

After two days of festivities, the royal progress pushed on toward London, the ranks of mounted aristocrats swelling to many dozens, and the roadside lined with thousands of well-wishers, cheering, banging drums, and lighting bonfires.

In the multi-volume history later compiled by Anne Clifford (in her diaries and "Life of Me"), Bess Brydges after May 1603 simply vanishes from the narrative. The reason: She was swept off her feet by Sir John Kennedy, a favorite of the queen. Anna in April had appointed Kennedy to be Chamberlain of her household – in defiance of the King, whose announced choice was Sir George Carew. James when he heard of it was so furious he swore that "if he should find that she do bring

---

[1] *rivals…Brydges*] G. Whitton to D. Carleton at the Hague (4 May 1601), ed. DWF from *S.P. Dom. Elizabeth, Addendum,* no. 282; unsigned to Dudley Carleton at Paris (24 Oct. 1601), *ibid.,* no. 284.

[2] *hurt…body*] J. Chamberlain to D. Carleton (17 June 1602), ed. DWF from Chamberlain, *Letters* (1939), 1.150.

[3] *done deal*] Same to same (15 Oct. 1602), *ibid.,* 1.166.

[Kennedy] hither to attend her in that place [of Queen's Chamberlain,] that he would break the staff of his chamberlainship across the man's head, and so dismiss him." [1]

Queen Anna on this word backed down; but Kennedy was struck instead by the beauty of Elizabeth Brydges, a maid of honor to the late queen. She was his own age (28) yet still single, with substantial rental income. Moreover, on the death of her mother, now aged 50, Elizabeth Brydges was set to inherit Sudeley Castle, Sudeley Park, the old Abbey of Winchcombe, plus demesnes, lands, rents, etc., across three English counties.

Kennedy asked her to marry him.

Perhaps, for Elizabeth, it was love at first sight; or perhaps she saw Sir John as a way to escape an unwanted marriage with her cousin. The engagement was brief, not more than a few weeks. They eloped. Frances Brydges on this news disowned Elizabeth, furious that her daughter and presumed heir, a distinguished socialite, a former love of Lord Essex, had inexplicably eloped with a jigging Scotsman, a fellow without much property, no visible livelihood, and nothing to commend him but apparent royal favor; this, too, after daughter Bess had just refused the hand of her own noble kinsman, Grey Brydges, a marriage that Frances had believed "would end all suits and quarrels." [2]

On hearing of Elizabeth's elopement, Grey Brydges vowed revenge. A forward-looking man, the 5th Baron Chandos prepared himself and his attorneys to wring every drop of blood from his cousin's feminine veins rather than allow one ha'penny-farthing of ancestral wealth to fall into the hands of cousin Bess's freckle-faced skirt-wearing bagpipe-blowing troubadour. Or words to that effect.

From here on, all critical decisions regarding the Chandos lawsuit were made behind closed doors. In February 1604, Baron Chandos received a personal letter from the King's Privy Council: having won the lands and castle of Giles and Frances Brydges but not their daughter, Chandos was advised to "deal kindly with her, for the sake of his Majesty's regard for Sir John." [3]

With the King and Lord Cecil involved, the dispute moved quickly: a month later, by direction of the Council, Brydges v. Brydges was referred to court-appointed "arbitrators," a board comprised of the nation's most powerful men: Sir John Popham, Lord Chief Justice of England; Sir Thomas Egerton, Lord High Chancellor; Charles Howard, Lord High Admiral; and the king's own representative, Sir Robert Cecil; the last of whom invited the plaintiff lord Chandos, and the two defendants, Frances Brydges and Elizabeth Kennedy, to meet with their lordships in London on 11 April 1604, for binding arbitration. A final resolution would be announced two days after.

Lady Frances was evidently in no mood to attend a conference in the same room with her adversary-nephew on one hand, and a selfish daughter on the other. She wrote to Lord Cecil, saying that she would certainly try to attend that April 11th meeting; and though doubtful that she could "obtain lodgings and counsel," in time, she would certainly "undertake to submit to your lordships' judgment on April 13th." As things fell out, Elizabeth's mother missed the meeting, "by reason of an extreme cold." She was represented by her attorney, Judge Lawrence Tanfield. [4]

The four arbitrators considered the competing claims: Lord Chandos demanded the real estate. Lady Frances, who already enjoyed guaranteed use of Sudeley Castle during her lifetime, demanded a guaranteed income until death, plus a dower for her daughter Katherine (aged 20 and not yet married). Sir John Kennedy, her son-in-law, though not strictly a party to the discussion, had expressed his need for a substantial cash settlement, in exchange for his wife's anticipated forfeiture of her rights in Sudeley. And Elizabeth Brydges desired for her father's will to remain in effect, so that she might pay off her debts without losing either the castle, the land, or her rental income.

The judges could not make everyone happy, but the arbitration was largely successful: everyone got what they wanted except Elizabeth:

Grey, fifth Baron Chandos, was judged to be the lawful male heir of Giles, third Baron; he would receive title to the lands, houses, rents, etc.

---

[1] *if…dismiss him*] Sir Thomas Edmonds to G. Talbot (15 June 1603), ed. DWF from Talbot Papers, vol. K, f.83.

[2] *would…quarrels*] J. Chamberlain to D. Carleton (21 Oct. 1600), ed. DWF fr. Chamberlain, *Letters* (1939), 1.111.

[3] *deal…Sir John*] James I to Grey Brydges (19 Feb. 1603/4, government copy), ed. DWF from *S.P. Dom. James I*, v. 6 (1603-4); Brydges was now in London to attend James's first Parliament.

[4] *obtain…cold*] F. Brydges to R. Cecil (1, 7, 11 April 1604), ed. DWF from H.M.C. *Salisbury* (*Cecil*), v. 16 (1604);   *Lawrence Tanfield*] the father of Elizabeth Cary; sixteen years later, when daughter Elizabeth spent part of her jointure from husband Lucius to meet expenses and her father learned of it, Tanfield disinherited her.

Sudeley Castle, where the Brydges sisters were born and raised, would remain in use by Lady Frances, rent-free, until her death. She would forfeit all rental income (which was now the nephew's responsibility to collect, from tenants); but she would receive from her nephew (from that same revenue) a comfortable pension of £12,000 yearly.

The two daughters would each receive a one-time lump-sum payment: Katherine, £6,000, as an endowment for her dowry; and Elizabeth, £18,000.

Sister Katherine with her award of £6,000 went on to become a countess by her marriage to Francis Russell, fourth earl of Bedford; with whom she enjoyed a happy life and raised eight children.

Elizabeth with her award of £18,000 proved less fortunate. The honeymoon was already over: and when the litigation ended, the domestic quarreling began. Sir John (having unpaid debts of his own) cared less about the deed to Sudeley Castle than about present acquisition of his wife's cash settlement. What he got instead, right away, was a loss of revenue. Contrary to her apparent expectation, Elizabeth forfeited the share of rental income she had been receiving heretofore from her father's real estate. Hard-pressed, she wrote to Lord Cecil, begging for his intervention with her stingy cousin, so that a portion of her prior revenue might be resumed:

Elizabeth, Lady Kennedy, to Robert Cecil, Viscount Cranborn (n.d., 1604)°

[…] Both out of your own noble disposition, and in memory of my kinswoman your wife, who happied me with her love, I must be a most humble lieger, that you will maintain the strength of such order for our possessions as you and the Lord Chief Justice allowed – whereby we may be "the possessors of such lands" whereof, till now, we received *the rents* it then afforded […] My cousin Chandos enjoyeth (by an order made also in the same kind for us) such lands as from our part [he] indirectly got – and since (by the agreed order) only [he] enjoyeth.

With another letter on the same subject, Elizabeth submitted to Lord Cecil a list of her remaining debts (one, a £600 loan from the financier, Sir Peter Vanlore). She humbly thanks Cecil for having "honored me with your good opinion (by which I have received much commodity in my injurious troubles so maliciously imposed upon me); which, and all other favors, I acknowledge with a grateful heart." [1]

But while honoring Elizabeth with his "good opinion," Cecil expressed no sympathy and lent no assistance. In his reply, he stated his understanding that Lord Chandos had fulfilled his obligations while Lady Kennedy was yet standing "upon things contrary to the agreement." [2]

For Elizabeth, ruin may have been waiting in the wings; but for Sir John, the fun was just beginning. The Kennedys in 1603 had purchased a mansion in Barn Elms, in the London borough of Richmond-upon-Thames. The purchase was funded with £300 that Sir John borrowed from his good friend, William Ferrers, a freeman of the London Mercers' Company, against his wife's anticipated settlement. A year later, the Kennedys bought a tenement in nearby Stoke Orchard, half of that purchase being funded with a £450 loan from their Barn Elms neighbor, Dr. William Paddy (a loan to which Sir Robert Cecil and Lord Henry Howard subscribed as Kennedy's feoffees in trust, being the owners of record while Kennedy had full use of the property as if it were his own). Meanwhile, Kennedy's drinking partner, William Beale, by September 1609 was in default on a loan of £463 that he owed to one John Atwood. Threatened with arrest, Beale (in collusion with Sir John) offered to Atwood the Stoke Orchard tenement, upon Atwood's discharge of Beale's debt and a payment of £460 to Kennedy (making him a £10 profit, on paper). Atwood agreed. Kennedy with his share could thereby pay off his loan to Dr. Paddy (but didn't). Kennedy promised also to be the feoffee in trust for Beale's transaction with Atwood, but then refused to sign. William Beale next signed a deed of "gift of all in his possession" (*i.e.*, nothing) to his friend, John Kennedy; who in return gave Beale refuge in his house at Barn Elms so that he could not be arrested for debt by Atwood's agents. Kennedy then told Atwood that the Stoke Orchard tenement would be foreclosed upon by lords Cecil and Howard, unless Atwood agreed to purchase other lands in Stoke Orchard for more than they were worth.

---

[1] *honored…heart*] E. Kennedy to R. Cecil ([March] 1604), ed. DWF from H.M.C. *Salisbury* (*Cecil*), Pt. 16, p.256.

[2] *good opinion…agreement*] R. Cecil and J. Popham to E. Kennedy ([c. May] 1604), ed. DWF, *ibid.*, p.444.

It's hard to see how this knavery could succeed as a scheme to discharge overdue loans; but at the time, Kennedy's friend Beale was at risk of being arrested for debt; besides which, they both were probably drunk. [1]

After the Atwood-Beale deal fell through, Kennedy reneged on the loan from Dr. Paddy. Lords Cecil and Howard, trustees of the property, then used the authority of their office to obtain from King James a succession of writs that protected Sir John against being prosecuted for debt by Paddy. The generous doctor, for his £450 loan to Kennedy (the equivalent of ten years income for a London journeyman in one of the trades), whistled in the wind for repayment. [2]

In February 1608/9, we find Ferrers and Kennedy teaming up to buy a messuage called "the Axe, with shops, cellars, etc., in St. Martin-in-the-Fields." Purchase price: £1,762; whereupon Ferrers and Kennedy clear-cut the forest, selling an astonishing 38,000 cords of wood in just three years. [3]

Elizabeth Brydges Kennedy subsequently testified that her husband all this while was committing infidelities, one of which was the marriage itself: Elizabeth learned that Sir John had a wife back in Scotland then living, whom he had abandoned. Elizabeth wished a divorce. Since that was not possible, she would seek an annulment, and let John return to his other wife, if she would have him.

Kennedy refused to consent: only over his dead body (or hers) would their marriage be ended. And since her £18,000 (or what was left of it) would belong to Sir John if she were to have a fatal accident, Lady Kennedy had cause to be nervous.

Elizabeth sought help from their neighbor, Sir William Paddy, who partly knew what Kennedy's unfortunate wife was up against. He kindly gave Elizabeth temporary refuge in his Barn Elms mansion – and for that act of kindness, he came within inches of losing something that he valued even more than £450: Sir John offered to cut off Dr. Paddy's English testicles.

On 3 September 1609, about midnight, Kennedy with a band of armed supporters launched a surprise attack on the Paddy residence, with intent to abduct Elizabeth Kennedy and to punish the meddling doctor.

Next morning, Sir Arthur Gorges wrote an urgent letter from his residence (at the west end of Chelsea), to Robert Cecil, Secretary of State, informing him of a scandal:

> This morning about the break of day there came to my gates the Lady Elizabeth Kennedy in very wretched manner, bare-legged in her petticoat and an old cloak, and her night gear, in great fright and starved for cold. She desired houseroom and fire of my wife her cousin in this extremity, being (as she said) driven out of her house by Sir John Kennedy, who with great violence brake in upon her; and she stole away in this haste at a back door, much terrified with his fury. Dr. Paddy came with her and hath left her with my wife […] [4]

Sir Arthur was perhaps unaware that Lady Kennedy that night had fled, not from her own residence, but from the home of Dr. Paddy.

Dudley Carleton, writing a month later to John Chamberlain, is amused to have heard, and passes along with extra seasoning, a version of the incident that he received from the Scotsman, Edward Wimark:

> You have heard I am sure of a great danger Sir William Paddy lately escaped at Barn Elms, where the house was assaulted by Sir John Kennedy by night with a band of furious Scots; who besides their warlike weapons came furnished (as Ned Wimark said) "with certain snippers and searing irons, purposing to have used him worse than a Jew, with much more ceremony than circumcision." Sir William, having the alarm given him, fled like a valiant knight out at a back door, leaving his breaches behind him, and the lady by his sweet side went tripping over the plains in her smock with her petticoat in her hand till they recovered the next castle. And now he walks London streets with three or four men in defense of his dimissaries. [5]

---

[1] *Beale*] See J. Atwood to R. Cecil (n.d., 1609), H.M.C. *Salisbury* (*Cecil*), vol. 24, Addenda, 1605-1668.

[2] *unpaid*] In 1626, after Kennedy's death and the coronation of King Charles, Paddy petitioned the House of Lords to reimburse him for his loss on that £450 loan in 1603, which King James by writ from the Privy Council had forbidden Paddy to collect. "Report" (24 March 1625/6), *Journal of the House of Lords*, vol. 3 (1620-1628).

[3] *Axe…years*] See Loseley House MS/349/52/1-11, MS/349/59/1.

[4] *This…wife*] Ed. DWF from transcript in Scharf (1877), p. 48. Summary in *S.P. Dom. James I*, 48/7.

[5] *dimissaries*] testicles; D. Carleton to J. Chamberlain (4 Oct. 1609), ed. DWF from *Carleton Letters* (1972) 113.

Knighted by King James at Windsor on 9 July 1603, Dr. Paddy at this time was a 54-year-old single parent with an adopted nine-year-old son; he had an honored position as personal physician, not only to King James, but to Lord Cecil; and he was newly appointed to the Privy Council. That he and Lady Kennedy were in bed together is most doubtful. (Indeed, if he was ever seriously tempted to have sex with the wife of a lunatic neighbor who still owed him £450, while making no secret where the reckless husband could find them, Dr. Paddy was a fool.) [1]

Elizabeth Kennedy met the very next week with Richard Bancroft, Archbishop of Canterbury at Lambeth Palace, where she told her sad story and begged him to annul the marriage. A wife could request annulment on four grounds: 1. prior contract to another; 2. an unfaithful husband; 3. wanton cruelty; 4. abandonment. Elizabeth alleged the first three. As for the fourth, the sooner Sir John abandoned her, the better: she would be better off, financially and in every other way, without him.

To decide a matter of holy matrimony that involved a well-connected Scots courtier, the Church deferred to the State. On 13 September, Bancroft dispatched a letter to Lord Cecil, seeking to be advised:

> Lady Kennedy has complained to me against her husband, charging him to have had a former wife living when he married her; with cruelty that has put her in fear of her life; and with divers adulteries. I attended upon his Majesty at St James's when he took notice of the suit begun between the parties, and [he] required me to deal justly. On the lady's complaint, Sir John promised me to entertain his counsel but has not been with me since. Pretending that divers [creditors] lie in wait to lay executions on him [for unpaid debts...] Sir John craved pardon for not° coming except I would send a protection.... which leads me to think that it were fit he had a [writ of] protection from his Majesty. [...] [2]

Whether or not the Archbishop knew that Robert Cecil was himself Kennedy's trustee for the contested Stoke Orchard tenement is unclear; but his information to Cecil was well received. On 30 September, the Privy Council granted to Kennedy a six-month writ of protection (several times renewed, over several years), so that Sir John could not be prosecuted for his unpaid debts.

In November, when Archbishop Bancroft expressed his unguarded sympathy for Lady Kennedy's plight and his approval of her wished annulment, King James himself objected; he then directly intervened over a period of three months to ensure that Lady Kennedy's request was denied. [3]

Having no escape from her marriage, Elizabeth again appealed to the charity, first, of her mother, then of her kin. But Bess had no claim on her mother's £12,000 pension (as Lady Frances coldly explained). And Lord Chandos, having fought a long and costly legal battle, intended to keep his award, every shilling of it.

He did not keep it for long. Grey Brydges upon coming into the estate "made such haste to spend it, that in four years, he sold fifteen fair manors of his own and worth £5,000 per annum, retaining only the [Sudeley] Castle manor" (which he could not sell till the death of Frances Brydges, dowager), plus the "park of Sudeley and the demesne lands of the Abbey of Winchcombe, out of which he sold £80 per annum of the best land (and it is like would fain have sold all the rest, if death had not prevented him)." [4]

The King's favor was like a Teflon coating: Sir John Kennedy thrived. In November 1610 we find him with his friend Ferrers again wheeling and dealing. Kennedy purchased a reversion (essentially, a lease, with the temporary rights of an owner) from Elizabeth Carey, Lady Hunsdon. By this deal Kennedy obtained control an enormous swath of land and buildings in county Kent, including the Carey mansions of Hadlow and Court Lodge. For Kennedy, it was an investment. His cost: £10,000.

---

[1] *Dr. Paddy*] Paddy's notion of honor did not, however, extend to confidentiality with his patients. During Elizabeth's reign, Paddy forwarded reports through Lord Cecil to James VI of Scotland, to inform on those lords and ladies who supported Arbella Stuart to succeed Queen Elizabeth. At Windsor on 9 July 1603, Paddy was knighted by the king, his reward for spying on his own clients; see D. Pady (1974).

[2] *Lady Kennedy..Majesty*] R. Bancroft to R. Cecil (13 Sept. 1609), H.M.C. *Salisbury* (*Cecil*), v. 21 (1609-1612).

[3] *King James...intervened*] See *S.P. Dom. James I,* vol. 49 (18, 27, 28 Nov. 1609), vol. 57 (21 Sept. 1609); H.M.C. *Salisbury* (*Cecil*), v. 21 (22 Jan. 1609/10).

[4] *made...him*] Baddeley, 141.

Sir John is known to have seen the inside of a prison only once, in June 1615, when he was committed to the Gate House overnight for having falsely accused an English gentleman of making "scandalous speeches against the Scots" (next day, he was pardoned). The last we hear of Kennedy while still living is from a Surrey man named Robert Blinckern, who "railed against the King as 'an unjust usurper,' and said he would be 'avenged on him for not doing justice to Sir John Kennedy'" (March 1622); for saying so, Blinckern was put in the stocks; but "he was in drink at the time" — wherefore, when Blinckern sobered up, he too was pardoned. [1]

Grey Brydges died in 1621; his aunt, Frances Brydges, died in September 1623. Sudeley Castle thus passed to Grey's son, George, then to William, in succession; both of whom died without a male heir: the barony of Chandos became extinct. And Grey's daughter (another Elizabeth) died childless.

The Kennedys after September 1609 lived apart. While her cousin Grey squandered her dead father's real estate and her estranged husband squandered her cash, Elizabeth Brydges survived on handouts. We last hear of her in October 1617. Writing to Sir Thomas Roe, George Carew (earl of Totnes) remarks in passing that "Lady Kennedy, my Lord Chandos' cousin-german, was lately surprised with a dead palsy; whereof in a few days (the seventh of this month), she died." [2]

John Chamberlain a day or two later fills in the blanks: "She lived (of late), and died, very poor — her maintenance being little or nothing." Her "strange convulsions," says Chamberlain, "made some suspect (more perhaps than there was cause) that she had done herself some wrong." [3]

Postscript. Lady Anne Clifford in her 1617 diary makes no mention of the unhappy end of her friend and kinswoman, Elizabeth Brydges. The tragedy cannot have escaped her notice; but it has escaped sympathetic commentary ever since. In historical works, Elizabeth Brydges, the daughter of 3rd Baron Chandos, the defendant in Brydges v. Brydges, has been the object of amused and largely inaccurate commentary. And genealogical reference works rarely supply more than a footnote, to distinguish her from Elizabeth Brydges her cousin; *i.e.*, the notorious daughter of her adversary in law, Grey Brydges, 5th Baron Chandos. That other Elizabeth Brydges was born the same year that the daughter of Giles and Frances died in Westminster, a poor beggar. And thereby hangs still another tragic tale of marriage, male issue, and masculine property rights.

Lord Chandos dying at Spa, Germany, on 21 August 1621, his body was returned to England and buried at Sudeley Castle. His title and lands passed to his eldest living son, George. Three years later, his landless widow Anne (b. Stanley) married Mervyn Tuchet, 2nd earl of Castlehaven; at whose home Elizabeth Brydges her daughter from age 12 was repeatedly raped by servants, under her stepfather's supervision, thereby to pleasure Lord Castlehaven's voyeurism and his express desire for a "lusty heir." The earl then wedded Elizabeth to his son (her 15-year-old stepbrother, James Tuchet); but with continued sexual abuse of the girl until age 17, when she was indicted for adultery, denounced as a whore, and turned out into the street, being refused hospitality even by her own grandmother. James Tuchet went on to inherit (after a brief sequestration) his father's title, lands, houses, and revenues. Elizabeth Brydges, his step-sister and wife, lived to age 55, dying at last in 1679, a penniless alcoholic. Within three months of her welcome death, the third earl of Castlehaven obtained a generous marriage settlement and married his long-time partner, Elizabeth Graves.

---

[1] *Gate House*] J. Chamberlain to D. Carleton (15 June 1615), *Letters,* 1.602; *Blinckern case*] Justices of Surrey to the Privy Council (15 Mar. 1621/2), *S.P. Dom. James I* [1619-1623], p.359; *Kennedy v. Vanlore*] Great Britain, *English Reports,* 1.510-11. For the real estate deals and Kennedy litigation see Loseley Manuscripts, LM/349/79, LM/114/1-2; LM/349/114/1-2; LM/349/135/1-4; and Malden, *V.C.H. Surrey* (1912), 4. Sir John's estate after his death later that year got tied up in lawsuits: Sir John's heir (his younger brother) sued Sir Peter Vanlore, a dispute that was not settled until 1634; see Kennedy *contra Dom.* Vanlore," *English Reports,* 1.510-11.

[2] *Lady Kennedy...died*] G. Carew to T. Roe (Oct. 1617), Carew, *Letters,* ed. Maclean (1860), 223; *dead palsy*] complete incapacity; paralysis or coma (not identical to Chamberlain's "strange convulsions").

[3] *strange...wrong*] Chamberlain to Carleton (18 Oct. 1617), ed. DWF from Chamberlain *Letters* (1939), 2.104-5.

Lady Anne Clifford (Sackville Herbert) (1590 - 1676),

Suo jure Baroness Clifford; Countess of Dorset; Countess of Pembroke and Montgomery

> *Preserve your loyalty,*
> *Defend your rights.*
> – Lady Anne's motto

ANNE CLIFFORD was born at Skipton Castle, in Yorkshire, the only surviving child of Margaret (Russell) Clifford, a commanding matriarch whom Aemilia Lanyer has lionized in *Salve Deus Rex Judæorum* as the epitome of female perfections. Anne's father, George Clifford, third Earl of Cumberland (1558 - 1605), was a buccaneer who with his 38-gun ship, *The Scourge of Malice,* terrorized the Spanish fleet in the Caribbean. At the time of his daughter's birth, the earl was away at sea upon one of the many voyages that he undertook (in Lady Anne's words) "for the service of Queen Elizabeth, for the good of England, and of his own person." He is said to have taken vast quantities of Spanish gold that the Spaniards first took from the American natives, and to have squandered it all on his passions for jousting, horse-racing, gambling, and adultery.

Lady Anne's mother was well-educated and intellectually active. She supported the performing arts, patronized the translation of Continental literature, and attracted dedications from poets and preachers who hoped to share in her largesse. An amateur scientist and alchemist, she had her own research laboratory. She invested in the East India Company. She supported experiments to smelt iron with coal. And she had more money than she could spend. But for all that, Margaret Russell came up one privilege short: she was unfortunate in her marriage, being wedded at age seventeen to George Clifford, the placket-chasing earl of Cumberland. Lady Margaret never complained, in public; but her domestic unhappiness, public knowledge, was pitied in print in verses by Samuel Daniel and Fulke Greville. An added stressor to the Cliffords' marriage was that their two sons – the only thing that George ever really wanted from his wife – both died as infants.

In 1600, after many quarrels over money and other women, Lady Margaret left Lord George, for good, at first moving in with her widowed sister, the countess of Warwick. She then moved her household (with her child, servants, and retinue) to Cookham, a manor that her brother rented for her use. Aemilia Lanyer, who was evidently employed as a music and singing tutor, depicts the Clifford household in those days as a women's paradise where the Countess of Cumberland, with her ladies in waiting and her hired retainers, freely discussed literature, religion, and women's rights.

"I was born a happy creature in mind, body, and fortune," reports Lady Anne, in her "Life of Me." As the only child of wealthy parents she had all the advantages of a princess. In Yale's Beinecke Library are preserved the account books of Lady Anne for the years 1600-1602, when she was 10-12 years old; in which are recorded her expenditures for books and tutoring, clothes, transportation, gifts, gratuities, alms, and gambling losses. She was waited upon by servants, with daily instruction in needlework, music, reading, writing, and arithmetic. Orators were paid to read aloud for her instruction and entertainment (a practice she continued throughout her adult life). She had a beloved governess (Anne Taylor), a dancing master ("Stephen"), and a lute instructor (the composer, John Jenkins). From her academic tutor, the poet Samuel Daniel, Lady Anne received something comparable to a university education, with training in French, Latin, rhetoric, classical and contemporary literature. Life was good.

In 1601, Anne's mother erected an obelisk in Hornsey church, Middlesex, to the memory of her kinsman, Sir Richard Cavendish; with an epitaph that was "promised and made by MARGARET, COUNTESS OF CUMBERLAND." The engraved poem is conventional tombstone stuff but worth note in that the countess praises Sir Richard for having those traits and accomplishments that she most admires: "derived from noble parentage, / Adorned with virtuous and heroic parts, / Most learnèd, bountiful, devout, and sage, / Graced with the Graces, Muses, and the Arts, / Dear to his prince, in English court admired, / Beloved of great and honorable peers, / Of all esteemed, embraced, and desired" – most of which virtues, Lady Margaret found lacking in her estranged husband but wished to cultivate in their eleven-year-old daughter. [1]

---

[1] *Richard Cavendish*] (a.k.a. Ca'ndish); in 1568/9, possibly as a planted spy, Cavendish carried letters from Thomas Howard, 4th duke of Norfolk, to Mary Queen of Scots, urging their marriage; on 16 Jan. 1571/2, at the duke's trial

Lady Anne admired and to a degree idealized her father, but she did not know him well. On those rare occasions when her parents came together, "their countenance did show the dislike they had of one another; yet he would speak to me (in a slight fashion) and give me his blessing." In the end, the earl and countess could hardly speak to one another, even in public, without quarreling. [1]

Lord George fired from the grave what might well have been the final shot: dying in 1605 without male issue, and preferring the bond of fraternity to the bonds of matrimony, Cumberland by his last will and testament bequeathed his baronial titles, together with all of his northern estates, to his younger brother, Sir Francis (and thence to his nephew, Henry); leaving his wife with nothing but her widow's jointure, an annuity guaranteed by her prenuptials. Uncle Frank scored the trifecta, inheriting the earldom of Cumberland, plus the Clifford real estate and all attendant revenue.

To Anne, the earl left £15,000 – at the time, a sizable fortune, a dowry suitable for marriage to an earl or duke. But from Anne's mother's point of view, £15,000 was chump change.

In a rigorous search of family and court records, Lady Margaret found what she needed to challenge the will: according to a deed executed as early as the reign of Edward II, the Clifford estates were entailed in perpetuity upon the eldest child lawfully begotten, irrespective of sex. The countess dowager resolved thereupon to obtain actual possession of those titles, lands, houses, and rents which belonged to her daughter, by right; and her late husband's will be damned, together with her husband.

Newly empowered and enriched as the fourth earl of Cumberland, Francis Clifford was no less determined to keep what was expressly bequeathed to him (and thence to his male issue). Thus began a whole new battleground in the Clifford gender Wars, fought now between the countess dowager of Cumberland and her daughter, versus the fourth earl of Cumberland and his son.

Having power of attorney as legal guardian of an underage ward, Lady Margaret filed two lawsuits in her daughter's behalf. The Earl Marshal's Court in 1606 quickly denied Anne's right to the baronial titles; but real estate law was less quickly adjudicated, especially when the plaintiff was a minor.

It has been said that Margaret Clifford in the Court of Wards "demolished Earl Francis's case" (*DNB*); but even so, the judges' decision supported Anne's claim only to the disputed Skipton properties (and to none of the Craven manors, which Anne also claimed). That partial victory notwithstanding, Anne's uncle retained possession of the entire bequest refused to yield. The litigation continued.

Lady Anne, 1620, unknown artist
Courtesy of Wikipedia Commons

Lady Anne, c. 1650, after Sir Peter Lely
Courtesy of the National Portrait Gallery

---

for treason, Cavendish testified against him; *promised and made by*] It is not certain that "made by" means "written by"; Clifford may only have commissioned the verses.

[1] *their countenance…blessing*] ed. DWF from Anne Clifford, "Life of Me" (Michaelmas, 1603).

In February 1609, Anne by her own free choice married Richard Sackville, earl of Dorset (a mistake). When Lady Margaret died in May 1616, Anne though forewarned by her mother permitted Richard to act in her behalf in the litigation (a second mistake). The earl her husband and the earl her uncle soon came to an agreement whereby Cumberland would receive free title to all of the real estate, in exchange for a substantial cash payment to Dorset – a settlement which, when presented to Anne, she refused to sign.

The battle was reconfigured: it was now Francis Clifford (who had the land) and Richard Sackville (who wanted the money) versus Anne Clifford Sackville, who wanted it all but who, for a very long time, received nothing but grief. Supported by King James, the agreement was forced upon her.

A chip off the maternal block, Lady Anne took her resistance a good deal further than her mother had done. Though sued and dispropertied by her uncle, though bullied by King James and her two husbands, though cheated by the law, ignored by King Charles, and robbed by Oliver Cromwell, the countess stood her ground and finally retook her lost empire, with profit. A survivor, she at last came into her inheritance by outliving all rival claimants to her father's and uncle's estates. She recorded her daily struggle, an ordeal lasting sixty years, in her own words, in the "Life of Me," her diaries, and the "Great Books"; here presented in extracts arranged chronologically, in a modern-spelling transcript by Tobian Banton.

Lady Anne at the marriage altar had roughly the same sorry luck as her mother, not once but twice. The earl of Dorset (Husband #1) and the earl of Pembroke and Montgomery (Husband #2) were no better behaved than her father had been. For more than forty years, Lady Anne fought bitterly – with an uncle and cousin who had got their mitts on her inheritance, and with two husbands who would not keep their mitts off other women. But the countess did not think of herself primarily as a wife, or even as a mother. In the voluminous story of her life as recorded in her diaries, Lady Anne mentions the two husbands infrequently, as a side show to the main event. And, yet, she had nice things to say about both of them, after they were dead.

> Those two lords of mine to whom I was afterwards (by the divine providence) married, were in their several kinds [as] worthy noblemen as any then were in the kingdom; yet was it my misfortune to have contradictions and crosses with them both – with my first lord, about the desire he had to make me sell my right in the lands of my ancient inheritance, for money (which I never did nor never would consent unto – insomuch as this matter was the cause of a long contention betwixt us; as also for his profuseness in consuming his estate – and some other *extravagancies* of his!); and with my second lord, because my youngest daughter, the Lady Isabella Sackville, would not be brought to marry one of his younger sons; and that I would not relinquish the interest I had in five thousand pounds (being part of her portion out of my lands in Craven). [1]
>
> Nor did there want divers malicious willers to blow and foment the coals of discontent betwixt us. So as in both [my husbands'] lifetimes, the marble pillars of Knole in Kent and Wilton in Wiltshire were to me oftentimes but the gay arbor of anguish – insomuch as a wise man that knew the insides of my fortune would often say that I lived in both these my lords' great families as the river of Roan or Rodamus runs through the Lake of Geneva, without mingling any part of its streams with that lake – for I gave myself wholly to retiredness (as much as I could, in both those great families), and made° good books and virtuous thoughts my companions (which can never deserve affliction (nor be daunted, when it unjustly happeneth!); and by a happy genius, I overcame all these troubles, the prayers of my blessed mother helping me therein. (*Life of Me*)°

The two human beings with whom Lady Anne had the closest relationship were her cousin, Frances Bourchier (d. 1612, unmarried), and her mother (d. 1616); after whose exeunt, the autobiography of Lady Anne Clifford Sackville Herbert becomes the epic drama of one woman and her land.

Lady Anne Clifford was not a pleasant person. Like the celebrated progenitors whose lives she memorialized for future generations to read and admire, she was a creature of privilege for whom the terms, *well-born* and *base-born,* signified innate merit. The class system seemed to Lady Anne to be as natural, as divinely providential, as gravity. Street beggars, hanged witches, and plague victims dying in tents were,

---

[1] *Isabella*] The earl, angry that Lady Anne would prefer Isabella's wishes over his own dynastic wisdom, thereupon banished both women from London, compelling them to live in one of his country houses in Wiltshire; the earl and countess no longer cohabited. In 1647, Isabella, 25, married the earl of Northampton, 25, a young lord of her own choosing.

from a Clifford's point of view, an unpleasant distraction from card games, court entertainments, and mansion-hopping. As a young teen, Anne and her mother, spurring forward on a hot day, could ride three horses to death with as little apparent concern as one today might abandon three overheated junkers in a race to New York City to see a Broadway show. As a mother writing her own life story, she almost never mentions either daughter by name, writing instead of "the child," and with little apparent affection. To others, Lady Anne could be obstinate, arrogant, voracious, and cruel. But never was it her ambition to be loveable. In her old age, having come at last into her own, the countess dowager of Dorset, Pembroke, and Montgomery was relentless in evicting or prosecuting penniless tenant farmers and leaseholders who, after the hardships of the Civil War, could not afford to pay. She is said to have expended £400 in legal fees prosecuting one of her poorest families for non-payment of a *chicken*, and was proud to have done so: it sent a message to tenants across the north of England that they had best give their new landlord her due: Lady Anne Clifford meant business. [1]

That said, Lady Anne understood gender discrimination. She recognized that real estate and inheritance law needed tweaking. From the dissolution of the monasteries under Henry VIII, until the massive land-grab conducted by Parliament during the English Civil War, most of Britain was owned by a very small percentage of its wealthiest citizens. The customary exclusion of women from heritable estates, and the general exclusion of younger sons, and intermarriage between the nation's wealthiest families,

ensured that a small and shrinking elite controled an ever-expanding share of the nation's real estate. Most city dwellers rented the homes they lived in; most farmers rented the use of the fields they tilled. This system not only kept most citizens dependent on the good will of their landlord, it kept most women, aristocratic women especially, dependent on the goodwill of their fathers and husbands. And because financial prosperity depended on land ownership, most of the very rich, most of their adult lives, were involved in one or more lawsuits concerning real estate. A woman who owned land was *always* a target – either for a marriage proposal, or a lawsuit. It would take a long and tedious search through the archives of the Public Record Office to find even one 17th Century woman of substantial property who was not, for that very reason, sued.

Seen in this light, Anne Clifford's "Life of Me" and her "Great Books" are a profile in courage, a mostly-true story of a hard-fought battle for women's property rights. When she died at age 86, Lady Anne was the richest woman in England, the seventeenth-century equivalent of a twenty-first century billionaire. Her story ends in triumph and conquest. But were it not for her own iron will, Anne Clifford might have been just another ordinary woman who, though well-born, perished in disgrace and poverty.

DWF

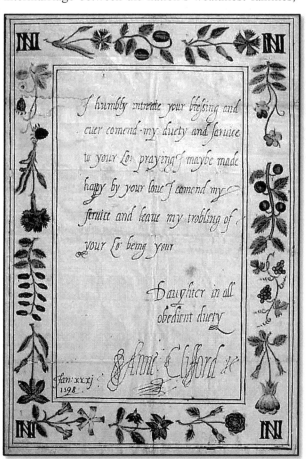

A hand-decorated letter from Lady Anne to her father, January 1598/9, shortly before her nineteenth birthday. Courtesy of Skipton Castle, Yorkshire

---

[1] *non-payment of a chicken*] See Sackville-West, *Knole and the Sackvilles* (1922), 74.

From **A True Memorial of the Life of Me** °

I WAS, through the merciful providence of God, begotten by my valiant father and conceived with child by my worthy mother the first day of May in 1589°, in the Lord Wharton's house in Channel Row in Westminster, hard by the river of Thames (as Psalm 139). Yet I was not born 'til the 30th day of January following, when my blessed mother brought me forth in one of my father's chief houses, called Skipton Castle, in Craven (Eccl. chap. 3); for she came down into the North from London with her two sons, being great with child with me, my father then being in great peril at sea in one of his voyages. For both a little before he begat me and a little after, it was ten thousand to one but that he had been cast away on the seas by tempests and contrary winds – yet it pleased God to preserve him, so as he lived to see my birth, and a good while after; for I was fifteen years and nine months old when he died. [1]

And some seven weeks before my mother was delivered of me, died her eldest son, the Lord Francis Clifford, in the said castle of Skipton; and the two-and-twentieth day of February after my birth was I christened by the name of Anne in the parish church at Skipton. [...]

I was but some ten weeks old when I came first up to London, yet did not I nor my mother return again into the North 'til after the death of my father, remaining both of us in the southern parts (as Northamptonshire, Hertfordshire, Kent, Berkshire, and Surrey, and in and about the court and city of London) all that time. When I was about a year and four months old, died my second brother Robert, then Lord Clifford, in North Hall in Hertfordshire, the four-and-twentieth of May in 1591°; and ever after that time I continued to be the only child to my parents, nor had they any other daughter but myself.

I was very happy in my first constitution, both in mind and body, both for internal and external endowments; for never was there child more equally resembling both father and mother than myself. The color of mine eyes were black like my father's,° and the form and aspect of them was quick and lively like my mother's; the hair of my head was brown and very thick, and so long that it reached to the calf of my legs when I stood upright – with a peak of hair on my forehead and a dimple in my chin like my father, full cheeks and round face like my mother, and an exquisite shape of body, resembling my father. But now time and age hath long since ended all those beauties, which are to be compared to the grass of the field (as Isaiah chap. 40, verse 6, 7, 8; I Peter, chap. 1, verse 24); for now (when I caused those memorables of myself to be written) I have passed the 63rd year of my age. [2]

And, though I say it, the perfections of my mind were much above those of my body. I had a strong and copious memory, a sound judgment and a discerning spirit, and so much of a strong imagination in me as that many times even my dreams and apprehensions beforehand proved to be true; so as old Mr. John Denham (a great astronomer that sometime lived in my father's house) would often say that I had much in me, in nature, to show that the sweet influences of the Pleiades and the bands of Orion (mentioned in the 38th chapter of Job, verse 31, 32, 33) were powerful both at my conception and nativity.

But happy births are many times attended on by cross fortunes in this world – which nevertheless I overcame, by the divine mercy of almighty God (Psalm 121); and from my childhood, by the bringing up of my said dear mother, I did, as it were, even suck the milk of goodness, which made my mind grow strong against the storms of Fortune – which few avoid that are greatly born and matched, if they attain to any number of years, unless they betake themselves to a private retiredness (which I could never do 'til after the death of both my two husbands). [...]

I must not forget to acknowledge that in my infancy and youth and a great part of my life I have escaped many dangers, both by fire and water, by passage in coaches and falls from horses, by burning fevers and excessive extremity of bleeding, many times to the great hazard of my life; all which (and many cunning devices of my enemies), I have escaped and passed through miraculously,

---

[1] *Channel Row*] Canon Row; *Psalm 139*] "Thou hast covered me in my mother's womb. I will praise thee; for I am fearfully and wonderfully made" (13-14); *Eccl. 3*] "To every thing there is a season, and a time to every purpose under the heaven: A time to be born, and a time to die" (1-2).

---

[2] *Isaiah...I Peter*] Henceforth, we omit quotation of Bible passages cited by Clifford; she clearly intended for her readers to look them up on their own.

and much the better by the prayers of my devout mother, who incessantly begged of God for my safety and preservation (James, chap. 5:6). […]

In my infancy and childhood, by the means of my said aunt of Warwick, I was much beloved by that renowned queen, Elizabeth, who died when I was about thirteen years and two months old. […] [1]

From **the Knole Diary**

IF QUEEN ELIZABETH HAD LIVED, she intended to have preferred me to be of the Privy Chamber – for at that time there was as much hope and expectation of me, both for my person and my fortunes, as of any other young lady whatsoever).

[*March 1603.*] A little after the Queen removed to Richmond, she began to grow sickly. My lady [mother] used to go often thither and carried me with her in the coach and using to wait in the coffee chamber and many times came home very late. About the 21st or 22nd of March my aunt of Warwick sent my mother word about six of the clock at night (she living then at Clerkenwell), that she should remove to Austin Friars (her house), for fear of some commotions; yet° God in his mercy did deliver us from it. [2]

Upon the 24th° Master Flocknall, my Aunt Warwick's man, brought us word from his lady that the Queen died about 2-3 o'clock in the morning. (This message was delivered to my mother and me in the same chamber where afterwards I was married.) [3]

About ten o'clock, King James was proclaimed in Cheapside by all the Council with great joy and triumph, which triumph I went to see and hear. (This peaceable coming-in of the King was unexpected of all sorts of people.) [4]

Within two or three days we returned to Clerkenwell again. A little after this, Queen Elizabeth's corpse came by night in a barge from Richmond to Whitehall (my mother and a great company of ladies attending it), where it continued a good while standing in the drawing chamber, where it was watched all night by several lords and ladies (my mother sitting up with it two or three nights, but my lady would not give me leave to watch, by reason I was held too young).

At this time we used very much to go to Whitehall, and walked much in the garden, which was much frequented by lords and ladies, my mother being full of several hopes (every man expecting mountains and finding molehills excepting Sir Robert° Cecil and the house of Howards, who hated my mother and did not much love my Aunt Warwick).

[*10 April.*] About this time my Lord Southampton was enlarged of his imprisonment out of the Tower. [5]

[*28 April.*] When the corpse of Queen Elizabeth had continued at Whitehall as long as the Council had thought fit, it was carried from thence with great solemnity to Westminster, the lords and ladies going on foot to attend it, my mother and my aunt of Warwick being mourners – but I was not allowed to be one because I was not high enough (which did much trouble me then), but yet I stood in the church at Westminster to see the solemnity performed.

[*May 1603.*] A little after this, my lady and a great deal of other company (as Mistress Elizabeth Brydges, Lady Newton, and her daughter Lady Finch) went down with my Aunt Warwick to North Hall, and from thence we all went to Tibbalds to see the King, who used my mother and aunt very graciously; but we all saw a great change between the fashion of the Court as it is now and of that in the Queen's, for we were all lousy by sitting in the chamber of Sir Thomas Erskine. [6]

---

[1] *Aunt Warwick*] Lady Anne (*née* Russell) Dudley, countess of Warwick, sister to the author's mother.

[2] *My lady*] Anne's mother, Margaret; *using to wait*] used to wait (on the Queen); *Austin Friars her*] the former Augustine Priory, now owned by Lady Warwick.

[3] *married*] in margin: *I was at Queen Elizabeth's funeral 13 years and 2 months old, and Master Richard Sackville was fourteen years old, he being then at Dorset House with his grandfather and that great family. At the death of this worthy queen, my mother and I lay at Austin Friar's in the same chamber where afterwards I was married.*

[4] *peaceable coming-in*] Many English aristocrats believed that Arbella Stuart should succeed Elizabeth I.

[5] *Lord Southampton*] Henry Wriothesley, sentenced to death, Feb. 1601, for his role in the Essex rebellion; sentence commuted to life imprisonment, by Cecil; pardoned and released ("enlarged") by King James on 10 April, before James departed for England.

[6] *Elizabeth Brydges*] *See* pp. 58-69; *Lady Newton*] Katherine, da. of Sir John Puckering, Lord Keeper, and wife of Adam Newton, dean of Durham; died in childbirth, April 1618; *Lady Finch*] Elizabeth (*b.* Heneage), wife of Sir Moyle Finch; said to have been the richest widow in England upon Finch's death in 1614; *North Hall*] in Hertfordshire, a Clifford property; *Tibbalds*] the house and park at Theobalds, Hertfordshire; *lousy*] infested with lice; *Erskine*] (1566-1639), first earl of Kellie, and captain of the yeomen of the guard 1603-1622, succeeding Sir Walter Ralegh.

As the King came out of Scotland, when he lay at York, there was a strife between my father and Lord Burghley° (who was then president), who should carry the sword; but it was adjudged on my father's side because it was an office by inheritance (and so is lineally descended on *me*). [1]

From Tibbalds the King went to Charter House where my Lord Thomas° Howard was created earl of Suffolk and my Lord Mountjoy earl of Devonshire; and [the King] restored my lords° of Southampton and Essex, who stood attainted. Likewise he created many barons. [...] And for knights, they were innumerable. [...]

About this time my Aunt Warwick went to meet [Anne] the Queen, having Mistress Brydges with her and my Aunt Vavasour. My mother and I should have gone with them, but that her horses (which she borrowed from Master Elmers), and old Master Hickley were not ready; yet [Mr. Meneril and] I went the same night and overtook my aunt at Tyttenhanger (my Lady Blount's house), where my mother came the next day to me about noon, my aunt being gone before. [2]

Then my mother and I went on our journey to overtake her (and killed three horses that day with extreme of heat!); and came to Wrest, my Lord of Kent's, where we found the doors shut and none in the house but one servant, who only had the keys of the hall; so that we were enforced to lie in the hall all night, 'til towards morning, at which time came a man and let us into the higher rooms, where we slept three or four hours. [3]

This morning we hasted away betimes and came that night to Rockingham Castle, where we overtook my Aunt Warwick and her company; where we continued a day or two with old Sir Edward Watson and his Lady. Then we went to my Lady Needham's (who once served my aunt of Warwick) and from thence to a sister of hers whose name I have forgotten. Thither came my Lady [Lucy Russell, countess] of Bedford who was then so great a woman with the Queen as everybody much respected her, she having attended the Queen from out of Scotland.

The next day we went to Master Griffin of Dingley's (which was the first time I ever saw the Queen and Prince Henry, where she kissed us all and used us kindly). Thither came also my Lady [Catherine Howard, countess] of Suffolk, my young Lady [Alice Spencer, countess of] Derby, and my Lady [Audrey] Walsingham (which three ladies were the great favorites of Sir Robert Cecil). That night we went along with the Queen's train, there being an infinite number of coaches; and, as I take it, my aunt and my mother and I lay at Sir Richard Knightley's, where Lady Elizabeth Knightley made exceeding much of us. [4]

The same night my mother and I and my cousin Anne Vavasour rid on horseback through Coventry, and went to a gentleman's house where the Lady Elizabeth her Grace lay, which was the first time I ever saw her (my Lady Kildare and the Lady Harington being her governesses). The same night we returned to Sir Richard Knightley's. [5]

[*25 June.*] The next day, as I take it, we went along with the Queen to Althorp, my Lord Spencer's house, where my mother and I saw my cousin Henry Clifford (my uncle's son), which was the first time we ever saw him.

From thence (the 29th being Monday), the Queen went to Hatton Fermers, where the King met her (where there were an infinite company of lords and ladies and other people, that the county could scarce lodge them!). [6]

From thence the court removed and were banqueted with great royalty by my father at Grafton, where the King and Queen were entertained with speeches and delicate presents. [...] (My mother was there but not held as mistress of the house by reason of the difference between my lord and her, which was grown to a great height.) [...]

From thence the court removed to Windsor, where the Feast of St. George was solemnized, though it should have been done before. There I stood with my Lady Elizabeth's Grace in the shrine of the great hall at Windsor, to see the King and all the knights set at dinner. Thither came the Archduke's ambassador, who was received by the King and Queen in the great hall (where there was such an infinite company of lords and ladies and so great a court, as I think I shall never see the like [again]).

---

[1] *Lord Burghley*] Thomas Cecil (1542-1643), president of the Council of the North.

[2] *the Queen*] Anna of Denmark;   *Aunt Vavasour*] Anne Vavasour, a maid of honor to Queen Elizabeth, longtime mistress to the elderly Sir Herbert Lee, married to Sir Richard Warburton c. 1604;   *Tyttenhanger*] St. Alban's, Hertfordshire, abbey granted at the Dissolution to Sir Thomas Pope, passing at his death to his widow, Elizabeth (Blount) Pope.

[3] *lord of Kent*] Sir Henry Grey, 6th earl of Kent.

[4] *great favorites*] Cecil is widely reported to have been sleeping with all three; and in two verse libels is said to have given them the pox.

[5] *Lady Elizabeth*] da. of King James and Queen Anna.

[6] *the 29th*] Ben Jonson's masque, *The Satyr,* was performed that night at Althorp.

From Windsor, the court removed to Hampton Court, where my mother and I lay at Hampton Court in one of the Round Towers; round about which were tents, where they died two or three in a day of the plague. [...]

[*July 1604.*] A little time afore this time, my mother and my aunt of Bath and my cousin Frances went to North Hall (my mother being extreme angry with me for riding before with Master Meneril); where my mother in her anger commanded that I should lie in a chamber alone – which I could not endure. But my cousin Frances got the key of my chamber and lay with me – which was the first time I loved her so very well. [1]

The next day Master Meneril as he went abroad fell down suddenly and died, so as most thought it was of the plague, which was then very rife. It put us all in great fear and amazement: for my aunt had then a suit to follow in court, and my mother to attend the King about the business between my father and her. [...]

Upon the 25th of July the King and Queen were crowned at Westminster, my father and my mother both attending them in their robes, [and] my aunt of Bath and my uncle Russell; which solemn sight my mother would not let me see because the plague was then so hot in London. Therefore I continued at Norbury, where my cousin did feed me with breakfasts and pear-pies and such things, [so] as shortly after I fell into the green sickness. [...] [2]

After the coronation the court returned to Hampton Court, where my mother fetched me from Norbury, and so we lay at a little house near Hampton Court about a fortnight (and my aunt of Bath lay in Huggin's lodgings); where my cousin Frances and I and Mary Carey did use to walk much, about the gardens and house, when the King and Queen were gone. [...] [3]

From Hampton Court my mother, my aunt of Bath, myself, and all our company went to Lancilwell° (Sir Francis Palmer's house); where we continued as long as the Court lay at Basingstoke; and I went often to the Queen and my Lady Arbella.

Now was my Lady Rich grown great with the Queen – insomuch as my Lady of Bedford was

something out with her, and when she came to Hampton Court was entertained but even indifferently (and yet continued to be of the Bedchamber).

One day the Queen went from Basingstoke and dined at Sir Henry Wallop's – where my lady, my aunt, and I had lain two or three nights before and did help to entertain her.

[*Oct. 1604*] As we rid from my Lady Wallop's to Lancilwell (riding late by reason of our stay at Basingstoke), we saw a strange comet in the night, like a canopy in the air, which was a thing observed all over England. [...]

[*Jan. 1604/5*] Now there was much talk of a Masque [of Blackness] which the Queen had at Winchester and how all the ladies about the Court had gotten such ill names that it was grown a scandalous place, and the Queen herself was much fallen from her former greatness and reputation she had in the world. [...]

Lady Anne Clifford at age 15
(from her "Great Picture," commissioned in 1646)
Courtesy of Skipton Castle

---

[1] *cousin Frances*] Frances Bourchier, daughter of the earl of Bath;   *aunt of Bath*] Elizabeth (Russell) Bourchier;   *my cousin Frances*] her daughter;   *green sickness*] chlorosis of the skin with indigestion, associated in the 16th-17th C. with adolescent women.

[2] *uncle Russell*] Edward Russell, earl of Bedford, husband of Lucy (Harington) Russell.

[3] *fortnight*] two weeks (from *fourteen nights*).

From **The Life of Me** (cont.)

THE FIRST OF SEPTEMBER in 1605° was the last time I ever saw my father in the air abroad [...] I took my leave of him on Greenwich Heath in Kent, as he brought me so far on my way towards Sutton in Kent, where my mother then lay. [...]

I had been (and stayed the space of a month) in the old house at Grafton in Northamptonshire, where my father then lived by reason of some unhappy unkindness towards my mother, and where he entertained King James and Queen Anna with magnificence; which was a time of great sorrow to my saint-like mother 'til I returned back again to her from my father, the first day of September (Psalm 90: 15, 16, 17).

The thirtieth day of October (being Thursday) 1605°, in the third year of the reign of King James, died my noble and brave father, George, Earl of Cumberland, in the Duchy House by the Savoy at London, near the River of Thames, when he was almost three months past forty-seven years old; my mother and I being present with him at his death (I being then just fifteen years and nine months old, the same day); where, a little before his death, he expressed with much affection to my mother and me [...] a great belief that he had, that his brother's son would die without issue male, and thereby all his lands would come to be mine (which accordingly befell about thirty-eight years after, for his brother's son, Henry, Earl of Cumberland, died without heirs male in the city of York the 11th of December 1643°).

My father – for the love he bore to his brother and the advancement of the heirs male of his house – by his last will and other conveyances which he had formerly sealed, did leave to his brother Francis (who succeeded him in the earldom of Cumberland) and to the heirs male of his body, all castles, lands and honors; with a proviso that they should all return to me, his only daughter and heir, if the heirs male failed (which they afterwards did. [...])

Presently after the death of my father, I being left his sole daughter and heir, his widow my dear mother, out of her affectionate care for my good, caused me to choose her my guardian; and then in my name she began to sue out a livery in the Court of Wards, for my right to all my father's lands, by way of prevention to hinder and interrupt the livery which my uncle of Cumberland intended to sue out in my name, without either my consent or my mother's – which caused great suits of law to arise between her and my said uncle, which in effect continued, for one cause or other, during her life; in which she showed a most brave spirit and never yielded to any opposition whatsoever. [...]

King James began to show himself extremely against my mother and me, in which course he still pursued, though his wife Queen Anne was ever inclining to our part and very gracious and favorable unto us; for in my youth I was much in the Court with her, and in masques attended her, though I never served her.

Now by reason of those great suits in law my mother and I were in a manner forced for our own good to go together from London down into Westmorland; and so we came into Appleby Castle the 22nd of July in 1607, to lie there for a while, it being the first time I came into that county or to any of my father's lands after his death. We lay also that summer for two or three nights in Brougham Castle in the chamber where my father was born (and wherein afterwards my mother died); and that was the first time I ever came into that castle. And about that time I lay for three or four nights in Naworth Castle in Cumberland, it being the first time I ever came into that country.

The 8th day of that October 1607 my dear mother and I went out of Appleby Castle on our journey towards London (it being the last time I was ever with her in the said castle, though I was after with her in Brougham Castle in the year 1616). And in our way through Craven, the 12th of October, my mother and I would have gone into the Castle of Skipton to have seen it, but were not permitted so to do, the doors thereof being shut against us by my uncle of Cumberland's officers in an uncivil and disdainful manner (to which castle I never came, after that time, 'til the 18th of July in 1649); [...] it being the last time my blessed mother ever lay in Craven or was in that country. And from thence she and I arrived safe at London the 23rd of that October at our house at Augustine Friars (where I was married about a year and four months after to my first lord, Richard, Earl of Dorset).

And the 18th day of April after our return in 1608, I being then a maid, was the great pleading in the Court of Wards concerning the lands of mine inheritance in Westmorland and Craven, which pleading is amongst the records of my mother's time when she was a widow.

• • •

From the accession of James until a year or two after her marriage, Lady Anne was often at court. She danced in masques with Queen Anna and her ladies, and filled speaking roles in a few; among them, Ben Jonson's Masque of Beauty, *a lavish affair performed at Whitehall on 10 Jan. 1607/8. The total cost to the Crown for that one social event came to £4,000, three percent of the Crown's total budget deficit that year. Lady Anne was the Nymph of the Air in* Tethys's Festival, *a masque written by her childhood tutor, Samuel Daniel, and performed at Whitehall on 5 June 1610.*

Jonson's Masque of Queens, *performed on 2 February 1608/9, included a lowbrow antimasque of "hags or witches." Acted by cross-dressed professional players, these "opposites to good fame" supplied "a spectacle of strangeness" only to be driven off in the end by the twelve good queens; one of whom was Anne Clifford, who performed the he role of Berenice, Queen of Egypt.*

Three weeks after, on 25 February, Lady Anne got married.

A sketch by Inigo Jones of his design for Anne Clifford's role as Berenice, Queen of Egypt, in Ben Jonson's 1608 *Masque of Queens*

The Course of Life of this Anne, Countess of Dorset, etc., while she was wife and widow to Richard Sackville, earl of Dorset

THE 25th DAY OF FEBRUARY 1609° (as the year begins on New Year's Day), I was married to my first lord, Lord Richard Sackville (then but "Lord Buckhurst"), in my mother's house and her own chamber in Augustine Friars, in London (which was part of a chapel [there] formerly), she being then present at my marriage. And within two days after I was married, died my said lord's father, Robert Sackville, Earl of Dorset, in little Dorset House in Salisbury Court, at London; by whose death my said lord and I came to be Earl and Countess of Dorset (Job 7:1, Ecclesiastes 3:1).[1]

And the 25th day of July, 1610° (a year and five months after my said first marriage), was my cousin-german Henry, Lord Clifford (only son of my uncle of Cumberland) married in Kensington, near London, to the Lady Frances Cecil, daughter to Robert, Earl of Salisbury (Lord High Treasurer of England and then the greatest man of power in the kingdom) – which marriage was purposely made, that (by that power and greatness of his) the lands of mine inheritance might be wrested and kept by strong hand from me – which notwithstanding came not to pass, by the providence of God, for the issue male which they had between them all died, and they left only one daughter behind them. […] [2]

About two years after I was married to my [first°] lord, he went to travel in France and the Low Countries for a year, upon a pre-engagement to his grandmother and others of his friends before he married me. He stayed beyond the seas about a year, and came to me at Knole the 8th of April in 1612, and lived twelve years after that. […] And in the time that I after lived his wife, I had by him five children, *viz.*, three sons and two daughters. The three sons all of them died young at Knole in Kent where they were born; but my first child, the Lady Margaret (who was born in Dorset House the 2nd of July in 1614) is now Countess of Thanet and mother of ten children.

• • •

In the spring of 1612, on his return from the Continent, Richard Sackville claimed power of attorney for his wife (with considerable resistance from his mother-in-law). Inserting himself into negotiations with Anne's uncle, he struck a compromise judgment: upon agreement by both sides, the Sackvilles could have the Skipton and West-

---

[1] *1609*] 1608 old style, until Conception Day (Mar. 25).

[2] *cousin-german*] first cousin.

morland estates, but not both. The earl of Dorset was fine with that; his wife was not.

Lady Anne, unwilling to yield her just claim to her legacy, refused to sign "the agreement." To enforce her compliance, Dorset enlisted all the powers at his disposal – Church, State, threats, blackmail, social isolation, and continual browbeating. Lady Anne remained adamant.

When my eldest daughter was near a year old, the 16th of June in 1615, was [held] the great trial for my lands in Craven, at the Common Pleas bar in Westminster Hall (as appears in the Records of my time when I was Countess of Dorset; but my first lord and my uncle of Cumberland and his son, being all three present, agreed together to put it to the arbitration of the four chief justices then in England; which though it never came to be effected because my mother and I absolutely refused to consent to it, yet it was the ground of that award which King James a little after did make, to my prejudice, for all the lands of mine inheritance (and the cause of many griefs, sorrows, and discontents; Psalms 40:15, 16, 17). And by reason of that intended arbitration of the four judges, I went to Brougham Castle in Westmorland, to my dear mother, to ask her consent therein; but she would never be brought to submit or agree to it, being a woman of a high and great spirit; in which denial, she directed for my good (as Psalms 32:8, Isaiah 30:21, 28; Isaiah 42:3)

• • •

Neither Lady Margaret nor Lady Anne fully trusted Sackville, fearing that he would sell out his wife's claim for cash. The two women conferred conspiratorially by correspondence. In her letter of 22 September 1615, Margaret counsels Anne to keep her head down in her husband's presence, but not to take her eyes off the prize:

Richard Sackville, by Wm Larkin (1613), detail
Courtesy of Kenwood House

"You writ wisely (and I fear too truly for the King and Queen, whom you might have had in a more favorable sort, but it was one of your lordship's and his friend's stratagems)." […]

• • •

Having written a letter of appeal to the judges, Margaret urged Anne to deliver it to them in person, "if my lord's tyranny lett it not."

"Well, it seems he hath not tasted of true spiritual comforts, that so much forgets that saying of the apostle, "He is worse than an infidel that provides not for his wife and family." Then he that hath not a heart to *defend their rights,* wants the true Spirit of God. […]) Lay all on me. And neither cross him in words but keep your resolutions with silence and what gentle persuasion you can, but alter not from your own wise course […]" [1]

• • •

Anne in the meantime had written to the Crackenthorps, who owned a share in her contested Brougham manor. Margaret learned Anne's letter in transit was "opened by chance": in it, Anne had boldly stated words to this effect: If my mother wishes me to come, I will *come, even if my lord tries to stop me. Margaret counsels Anne,*

Dear Heart, be very wary what you say – but most wary what you write: for they desire to have advantage, and to sever my lordship [Dorset] and you, as they lett me from my lord, [your father] – for you are too near me in resemblance, not of faces, but of fortunes; which God make better, and me thankful, that hath, and does, overcome. […] [2]

• • •

Anne wrote many unhappy letters to her mother in 1615. Divided in her loyalties to husband and mother, she urges Margaret to think well of Sackville. She defends him as a "very kind, loving, and dear father; and in everything will I commend him, saving in this business of my land, wherein I think some evil spirit works: for in this, he is as violent as is possible." In a letter of 20 January 1615/16, Anne writes in fear that if she deny to sign, it "will make such a breach between my lord and me as will not easily be mended; [but] I will do nothing without your ladyship's knowledge." [3]

---

[1] Margaret to Anne (22 Sept. 1615), ed. TB from Cumbria Record Office, MS WD/Hoth/Box 44.

[2] *Ibid.; lett*] obstructed.

[3] *very kind…knowledge*] Anne to Margaret, *ibid.,* ed. TB; *but*] *MS om.*

From **the Knole Diary**

[*January-February 1615/6.*] All the time I stayed in the country, I was sometimes merry and sometimes sad, as I heard news from London. […]

[*16 Feb.*] My cousin Russell came to me…and chid me and told me all of my faults and errors in this business. He made me weep bitterly. […] Upon the 17ᵗʰ being Saturday my Lord Archbishop of Canterbury, my Lord William Howard, my Lord Roos, my cousin Russell, my brother[-in-law, Edward] Sackville, and a great company of men of note were all in the gallery at Dorset House; where the Archbishop took me aside and talked with me privately one hour and half, and persuaded me, both by divine and human means, to set my hand to their° arguments. But my answer to his lordship was that I would do nothing 'til my lady [mother] and I had conferred together. Much persuasion was used by him and all the company, sometimes terrifying me and sometimes flattering me; but at length it was concluded that I should have leave to go to my mother and send an answer by the 22ⁿᵈ of March next, whether I will agree to the business or not; and to this prayer my lord of Canterbury and the rest of the lords have set their hands. […]

[*March 1615/6.*] Upon the 20ᵗʰ, in the morning, my Lord William Howard with his son, my cousin William Howard, and Mr. John Dudley, came hither to take the answer of my mother and myself: which was a direct *denial* to stand to the judges' award. […]

(Upon the 24ᵗʰ my Lady of Somerset was sent from Blackfriars by water, as prisoner to the Tower.) ¹

From **The Life of Me**

THE 2ⁿᵈ of that April 1616 I took my last leave of my dear and blessed mother with many tears and much sorrow to us both, some quarter of a mile from Brougham Castle in the open air; after which time she and I never saw one another; for then I went away out of Westmorland towards London and so to Knole House in Kent, whither I came the 11ᵗʰ day of that month to my first and then only child, the Lady Margaret, and her father, where I then lay 'til after my mother's death.

And the month following, the 24ᵗʰ day, that blessed mother of mine died, to my unspeakable grief, in that castle of hers of Brougham aforesaid in Westmorland, in the same chamber wherein my father was born (myself at the time of her death being at Knole House in Kent). And a little after her death I went down into Westmorland again, and was present at her burial in Appleby church the 11ᵗʰ of July following; the remembrance of whose sweet and excellent virtues hath been the chief companions of my thoughts ever since she departed out of this world.

• • •

Caught between a maternal rock and a hard place, Anne wrote to her mother, seeking peace and urging accommodation:

"Whatsoever you think of my lord, yet I have found him – *do* find him, and think, *shall* find him – the best and most worthiest man that ever breathed. Therefore, if it be possible, I beseech you have a better opinion of him. If you knew all I do, I am sure you would believe this that I writ. But I durst not impart my mind when I was with you, because I found you so bitter against him; or else I could have told you so many arguments of his goodness and worth, that you should have seen it plainly yourself." ²

• • •

From **The Knole Diary**

May 1616. Furious with Lady Anne for her non-compliance, Lord Sackville on 3 May threatened to evict her from Knole House in county Kent. To show he was serious, he commanded Lady Anne by letter to send their daughter Margaret to London, there to live with Sackville's married sister:

UPON THE 1ˢᵗ [of May,] Rivers came from London in the afternoon, and brought me word that I should neither live at Knole or Bolbroke. Upon the 2ⁿᵈ came Mr. Legg, and told divers of the servants that my lord would come down and see me once more – which would be the last time that I should see him again. […] His determination was that the child [Margaret] should live at Horsley, and not come hither any more – so as this was a very grievous and sorrowful day to me. […] ³

All this time, my lord was at London, where he had infinite and great resort coming to him. He went much abroad – to cocking, to bowling alleys, to plays, and horse races – and was commended by all the world. I stayed in the country, having many times a sorrowful and heavy heart, and being condemned by most folks because I would not consent to the agreement. So, as I may truly say, I am like an owl in the desert. […]

---

¹ *Lady of Somerset*] Frances (Howard) Carr, countess of Somerset, arraigned for the murder by poison of Sir Thomas Overbury.

² *Whatsoever…*] Anne to Margaret (26 April 1616), *ibid*.

³ *Mr. Legg*] Edward Legg, Lord Sackville's steward.

Upon the 24th (being Friday, between the hours of six and seven at night) died my dear mother at Brougham (in the same chamber where my father was born), thirteen years and two months after the death of Queen Elizabeth, and ten years and four months after the death of my father; I being 26 years and four months, and the child two years. [...That same day,] my Lady Somerset was arraigned and condemned at Westminster Hall (where she confessed her fault and asked the King's mercy, and was much pitied of all the beholders) [...] Upon the 25th my lord of Somerset was arraigned and condemned in the same place (and stood much upon his innocency).

Upon the 29th, Kendall came and brought me the heavy news of my mother's death, which I held as the greatest and most lamentable cross that could befall me. Also, he brought her will along with him, wherein she appointed her body should be buried in the parish church of *Alnwick*—which was a double grief to me when I considered her body should be carried away and not interred at Skipton (so as I took that as a sign that I should be disinherited of the inheritance of my forefathers) [...But] Mr. Jones brought me a letter from Mr. Woolrich, wherein it seemed that it was my mother's pleasure her body should be conveyed to what place *I* appointed; and which was some contentment to my aggrieved soul.

• • •

The death of Margaret Clifford left Lady Anne isolated, without emotional support, and often ill – though still resolute. Having reached an impasse, the earl of Dorset petitioned the King to intervene.

[*January 1616/7.*] I received a letter from my lord that I should come up to London the next day because I was to go before the King on Monday next. Upon the 17th, when I came up, my lord told me I must resolve to go to the King the next day [...]

Upon the 18th (being Saturday), I went presently after dinner to the Queen, to the drawing chamber; where my Lady Derby told the Queen how my business stood, and that I was to go to the King; so [Queen Anna] promised me she would do all in it she could. (The Queen gave me a warning not to trust my matters absolutely to the King, lest he should deceive me.)

When I had stayed but a little while there, I was sent for, out – my lord and I going through my Lord Buckingham's chamber, who brought us both into the King (being in the drawing chamber). He put out all that were there, and my lord and I kneeled by his chair-side; when he persuaded us both to peace, and to put the whole matter wholly into his hands – which my lord consented to; but I beseeched his Majesty to pardon me, for that I would never part with Westmorland while I lived, upon any condition whatsoever. Sometimes he used fair means and persuasions, and sometimes foul means; but I was resolved before, so as nothing would move me... at which the King grew into a great chafe (my Lord [William, Earl] of Pembroke, and the King's solicitor speaking much against me). [...]

At last, when they saw there was no remedy, my lord fearing the King would do me some public disgrace, [he] desired Sir John Digby to open the door, who went out with me and persuaded me much to yield to the King. My Lord Hay came out to me, to whom I told in brief how this business stood. Presently after, my lord came from the King – when it was resolved that if I would not come to an agreement, there should be an agreement made *without* me. [...]

This night, [19 January], the masque was danced at the court, but I would not stay to see it because I had seen it already...[1]

There was much ado at London about my business, insomuch that my lord, my uncle of Cumberland, my cousin Clifford, both the Chief Justices, and the counsel of both sides were divers times with the King about it; and then° the King hearing it go so directly for me, he said there was no law in England to keep me from the land.

There was during this time much cockfighting at the court, where my lord's cocks did fight against the King's. Although this business was somewhat chargeable to my lord, yet it brought him into great grace and favor with the King, so as [his Majesty] useth him very kindly and speaketh very often and better of him than [of] any other man. [...]

• • •

King James settled the dispute by assenting to the deal worked out by Cumberland and Sackville: Earl Francis and his male heirs would get most of the property, with £17,000 to be paid by Anne's uncle in compensation; but the King's ruling to be permanent and binding still required signatures.

---

[1] *masque*] Ben Jonson's *The Vision of Delight*, performed on Twelfth Night, 6 Jan. 1616/7 in the Banqueting House at Whitehall Palace, and repeated on the 19th.

[*February 1616/7.*] Legg came down and brought me word how that the King would make a composition, and take a course to put me from my right to the lands; so as if I did not consider of it speedily, it would be too late (and how bitterly the King stood against me) [...] My soul was much troubled and afflicted to see how things go; but my trust is still in God – and [I] compare things past with things present, and read over the *Chronicles*...

[*March 1616/7.*] The 14th being Friday, my uncle of Cumberland and my cousin Clifford came to Dorset House, where [my lord] and they signed and sealed the writings, and made a final conclusion of my business, and did what they could to cut me off from my right; but I referred my cause to God. [...]

[*April 1617.*] Upon the 5th my lord went up to my closet and saw how little money I had left, contrary to all they had told him. Sometimes I had fair words from him and sometimes foul – but I took all patiently and did strive to give him as much content and assurance of my love as I could possibly – yet I told him that I would *never* part with Westmorland upon any condition whatsoever. [...]

Upon the 16th, my lord and I had much talk about these businesses, he urging me still to go to London to sign and seal; but I told him that my promise was so far passed to my mother and to all the world that I would never do it, whatsoever became of me and mine. [...]

All this Lent, I ate flesh and observed no day but Good Friday. Upon the 26th [of April] I spent the evening in [needle-]working and going down to my lord's closet, where I sat and read much in the *Turkish History,* and Chaucer. [1]

Upon the 28th was the first time the child [Margaret] put on a pair of whalebone bodice. My lord went a-hunting the fox and hare. [...]

[*May 1617.*] Upon the 13th the child came to lie with me, which was the first time that ever she lay all night in a bed with me since she was born.

• • •

In May, Sackville sent Lady Anne a letter that he had canceled her jointure – her promised marriage portion in the event of his death.

By these proceedings I may see how much my lord is offended with me, and that my enemies have the upper hand of me. But I am resolved to take all patiently, casting all my care upon God. ([My lord's] footman told me that my cousin Russell and my Lady Bedford were agreed, and

my Lord Herbert and his lady, and that the next week they were to seal the writings and the agreement, which I [had] little expected [...]) [2]

I wrote a letter to my lord, to let him know how ill I took his cancelling of my jointure, but yet told him I was content to bear it, with patience, whatsoever he thought fit. [...]

[*June 1617.*] Whit Sunday we all went to church, but my eyes were so blubbered with weeping that I could scarce look up [...] My lord went up to London to christen Sir Thomas Howard's child, with the Prince (my lord being exceeding great with all them, and so with my brother[-in-law, Edward] Sackville – he hoping by their means to do me and my child a great deal of hurt. [3]

Upon the 30th: Still working and being extremely melancholy and sad to see things go so ill with me, and fearing my lord would give all his land way from the child.

• • •

The aftermath. *Richard Sackville and Francis Clifford both signed the royal letters patent: by payment of £17,000 – in three installments, all of which Dorset pocketed – Francis Clifford (and his heirs male and their assigns) thus gained free title to the disputed estates.*

But if the land battle was over, the domestic battles had just begun: Richard Sackville proceeded to squander Anne's legacy on gambling, horses, and women. The unhappy countess of Dorset thereafter always slept alone; the earl of Dorset, almost never. The couple rarely met, and quarreled always. Lady Anne looked elsewhere for companionship.

[*August 1617.*] I spent most of the time in playing Glecko, and hearing Moll Neville reading the *Arcadia.* Upon the 19th [...] I went to Penshurst on horseback, to my Lord Lisle; where I found Lady Dorothy Sidney, my Lady Manners (with whom I had much talk, and [with] my Lord Norris), she and I being very kind. There was Lady Wroth, who told me a great deal of news from beyond the sea. So we came home at night, my cousin Barbara Sidney bringing me a good part of the way. [4]

---

[1] *i.e.,* R. Knolles, *Generall Historie of the Turks* (1610).

[2] *Herbert*] William, earl of Pembroke (1580-1630); brother of Philip; *his lady*] Mary (*née* Talbot) Herbert (1594-1649); *Whit Sunday*] the Feast of the Holy Ghost, seven Sundays after Easter.

[3] *Whit Sunday*] the Feast of the Holy Ghost, seven Sundays after Easter.

[4] *Glecko*] *i.e. Gleek,* a three-person trick-taking card game; *the Arcadia*] a popular romance by Sir Philip

In November 1617, Lady Anne was again summoned to appear before King James, this time for a reconciliation.

I went to the court, where the Queen sent for me into her own bedchamber. And here I spake to the King. He used me very graciously, and bid me go to his attorney, who would inform him more of my desires. [...] (King James kissed me when I was with him, and that was the last time ever I was so near King James as to touch him.) [...]

The next day, my Lord Hay was married to my Lady Lucy Percy...

[*March 1618/9. The death of Queen Anna.*]

Upon the 2nd. The Queen died at Hampton Court between 2 and 3 in the morning. The King was then at Newmarket. Legg brought me the news of her death about four o'clock in the afternoon (I being in the bedchamber at Knole where I had the first news of my mother's death [in May 1616])....She died in the same room that Queen Jane, Harry the Eighth's wife, died in. [...]

The 5th. At night, about nine o' the clock, the Queen's bowels (all saving her heart) were buried privately in the Abbey at Westminster, in the place where the King's mother's tomb is. There was none came with it but three or four of her servants and gentleman-ushers which carried it, and a herald before it. The Dean of Westminster and about ten others were by. [...]

The 9th. The Queen's corpse was brought from Hampton Court to Denmark House by water in the night, in a barge, with many lords and ladies attending it. [...] (Most of the great ladies about the town put themselves in mourning and did watch the Queen's corpse at Denmark House, which lay there with much state.) [...]

[April] *the 19th.* [I] sat a good while there by the Queen's corpse; and then went into the privy galleries and showed my cousin Mary those fine, delicate things there. From thence I went to Bedford House and stayed with my lady of Bedford [...]

Friday the 23rd. I went to Blackfriars to see my Lady Cavendish [...] in that house where my Lady Somerset was brought to bed in her great troubles. Then I went to Denmark House and heard prayers there, and this night I watched all night by the Queen's corpse. There watched with me [...] divers other ladies and gentlewomen. [...][1]

The 28th. My lord and I, my cousin Sackville, and my Lady Windsor went [to the Tower] to see my Lady Somerset, where we saw her little child [...]

[*May*] The *2nd,* when I returned home, I found Mr. Hammon and his wife here. I told her that she had made so many scorns and jests of me, that for my part she was nothing welcome to me. [...]

The 13th I was one of the mourners at the Queen's funeral, and attended the corpse from Somerset House to the Abbey at Westminster. My lord also was one of the earls that mourned at this time. (I went all the way hand-in-hand with my Lady [Clinton, countess] of Lincoln.) After the sermon and all the ceremonies ended, my lord, myself, my Lord of Warwick and his Lady came home by barge. (Being come home, I went to my sister Beauchamp, to show her my mourning attire.) At this funeral, I met with my old Lady of Pembroke, and divers other of my acquaintance, with whom I had much talk. (That was the last time I saw my old Lady Pembroke.) [...][2]

The 14th [...] I went to see my Lady of Hertford in Channel Row, and spoke very earnestly to my Lord of Hertford in Wood's behalf, but I could not prevail; and his answer was that he would not pay any of his grandchildren's debts after his death. (This was the last time I saw my Lord of Hertford.)[3]

Sidney (1554-1586), revised and in 1593 published by his sister, Mary (Sidney) Herbert (dowager countess of Pembroke; mother of William and Philip Herbert), poet, *q.v., Women's Works,* vol. 2; *Penshurst*] the Sidney family seat in county Kent; *Lord Lisle*] (later, 2d earl of Leicester) Sir Robert Sidney (1563-1626), brother of Philip Sidney and Mary Herbert; *Dorothy Sidney*] (*née* Percy, 1598-1659), sister of Lucy (Percy) Hay and first wife of Robert, Lord Lisle, epistolary writer (*q.v.,* vol. 3); Lady Manners] Elizabeth (*née* Sidney) Manners, countess of Rutland, only surviving child of Sir Philip; poet ("Philomel"), *q.v.,* vol. 2; *Barbara Sidney*] (*née* Gamage, 1563-1621) first wife of Robert Sidney Sr., 1st earl of Leicester; *Lord Norris*] Francis Norris, Earl of Berkshire (1579-1622), estranged husband of Bridget de Vere, poet (*q.v.,* vol. 2); *Lady Wroth*] Mary (*née* Sidney, 1587-1653) Wroth, daughter of Robert and Barbara Sidney; author of *The Countess of Montgomery's Urania* (1621), *q.v.,* below.

---

[1] *Cavendish*] Elizabeth (*née* Bassett, 1601?-1643), mother of Cavendish and Elizabeth Egerton (*Women's Works,* vol. 4);   *great troubles*] while under house arrest, before her imprisonment, Frances (Howard) Carr gave birth to a daughter; the baby died soon after, probably in the Tower;   *Elizabeth Gray*] (*née* Talbot, 1582-1651), Countess of Kent.

[2] *Clinton*] Elizabeth (Knyvett) Clinton, widow of the 3rd Earl of Lincoln and author of *The Countess of Lincoln's Nursery, q.v.; Warwick*] Frances & Robert Rich (not earl till 1619); *Pembroke*] Mary (Sidney) Herbert, poet (*q.v., Women's Works,* vol. 2).

[3] *Hertford*] Frances (Prannell) Seymour, countess, poet, and essayist, *q.v. Women's Works,* vol. 2.

That night, my lord made a great supper to two or three of the Frenchmen that came over with the Ambassador. After supper, there was a play and then a banquet at which My Lady Penniston and a great many lords and ladies were. [...]

My lord and I intended to have gone home into the country and had sent the coach and horses; about then there came a sudden great shower, which stayed our going. My lord brought me to Westminster abbey, where I stayed to see the tombs, and the place where the Queen was buried in an angle in Henry VII's Chapel. [...]

About this time my Lady of Bedford had the smallpox, and had them in that extremity that she lost one of her eyes.

• • •

In 1620, Lady Anne established in Westminster Abbey a marble monument to the poet she most admired— [1]

EDMOND SPENCER THE PRINCE OF POETS IN HIS TYME WHOSE DIVINE SPIRRIT NEEDS NOE OTHIR WITNESSE THEN THE WORKS WHICH HE LEFT BEHINDE HIM.

The inscription is poignant, in that Anne likewise hoped that her books and architectural projects would bear a witness to her life. She bore three sons to Sackville: Thomas, in 1620; his younger brothers in 1621 and 1623, both of whom evidently died before christening. All three were delivered at Knole while their father resided at Great Dorset House in London, sharing his bed with Mrs. Penniston. By the spring of 1624, Thomas, too, was dead. [2]

From **The Life of Me** (July 1623-March 1624)

ON 10 July in 1623 did my said my lord, in Great Dorset House, he being then very sickly, make over to me my jointure of those lands in Sussex, part whereof I now enjoy, and part thereof I have assigned and made over to my two daughters. [...]

Though I was happy in many respects being his wife, yet was I most unhappy in having the malicious hatred of his brother, (then Sir) Edward Sackville, toward me; who afterwards came to be Earl of Dorset. [...] By the cunningness of his wit he was a great practisant against me, from the time I married his brother 'til his own death, which

happened not 'til the 17th of July 1652. For he outlived his brother twenty-eight years and almost four months [...] but I, whose destiny was guided by a merciful and divine providence, escaped the subtlety of all his practices and the evils he plotted against me (Psalms 35, 37, and 140; Ps. 3.10). [...]

Dorset died at Great Dorset House, at London, the 28th day of March, being Easter Sunday, in 1624, about twelve o'clock at noon [...] I was not with him when he died, being then very sick and ill myself, at Knole House in Kent, where I and my two daughters then lay. [...]

This first lord of mine was in his own nature of a just mind, of a sweet disposition, and very valiant in his own person. He had a great advantage in his breeding, by the wisdom and devotion of his grandfather, Thomas Sackville, Earl of Dorset, who was then held one of the wisest men of that time.

Dying without heirs male, Richard Sackville bequeathed his title and property to his younger brother; Anne received only her widow's jointure.

• • •

[*May 1624.*] In May (a little after my first lord's death at Knole House) I had the smallpox so extremely and violently that *I* was at death's door, and little hope of life in me; which infection I took of my eldest child, who had it there in great extremity some twelve days after her father was buried; which disease did so martyr my face, that it confirmed more and more my mind never to marry again (though the providence of God caused me after to alter that resolution).

Rising from her sickbed, Lady Anne counted her losses: her sons, long dead; her beauty taken by smallpox, and her husband taken, perhaps, by the Great Pox; her father's lands and rents taken by her uncle; her husband's lands and rents taken now by her brother-in-law. She and her daughters were no longer entitled to live either at Skipton (belonging to uncle Cumberland) or at Great Dorset House (belonging now to brother Sackville).

But with a jointure of £2000 yearly from the estate, the widow Sackville had (at long last) financial independence; whereupon she found frequent opportunity for payback. In her widowhood, Lady Anne supported the political opponents of her uncle Francis and cousin Henry, and underwrote legal counsel for tenants who opposed her Clifford kinsmen in the law courts. In 1628, she sued Cumberland herself, seeking rental income in her quondam manors of Craven and Westmorland; and this was just a warm-up.

---

[1] *monument*] Lady Anne's monument fell into decay and was replaced in 1778 by an exact copy.

[2] *Lady Penniston*] wife of Sir Thomas Penniston; she was Sackville's lover (known to Lady Anne), by whom he begot two daughters who received gifts from Lady Anne after her husband's death.

[…] I lived widow to this noble Richard Sackville, Earl of Dorset, about six years, two months (and four or five days over); most part of which time, I lived with my two daughters, either in Chenies House in Buckinghamshire (the chief seat of my mother's father and grandfather); or in Bolbroke House in Sussex (my chief jointure house); or at London (in several hired houses there, as in Tothill Street House in Westminster, and in St. Bartholomew's (in a house there which was anciently part of the priory); and besides, for a while I and my eldest daughter lay together in Woburn House in Bedfordshire (the August after her father's death, in which house died my grandmother of Bedford).

And just a year after the death of my first lord, died King James – I [was] then lying in Chenies House, Buckinghamshire, with both my daughters; from whence I and my two children removed to Bolbroke House in Sussex; there to live a good while – where I must not reckon it amongst the least of God's goodness and deliverances to me that on the sixth day of May in 1626°, after I had newly received my Lady Day rents (and had some money in the house before), I 'scaped miraculously by God's providence an attempt by my enemies to have robbed me (besides [escaping] the extreme fright it would have put me to, had it not been timely recovered and prevented by one who accidentally saw them enter in at the window). And it is thought to have been plotted by a great man, then mine extreme enemy. But God delivered me (Psalms 64, 124). [1]

In August 1628° were the first claims made by way of law and advice of counsel (after the awards before-mentioned) to maintain my right in the lands of my inheritance, in Craven and Westmorland. […]

• • •

In 1630, when Philip Herbert, earl of Montgomery, offered his hand in marriage, Lady Anne astonished many by saying yes. Lord Philip exhibited, in spades, all the vices of his social class (arrogance, profligacy, philandering) and none of the customary virtues (graciousness, learning, generosity, good manners). Though a sometime patron of playwrights, he was a sportsman not a reader. And he had a famously bellicose personality. But Lady Anne did not marry for love. Her ambitions for this second marriage were strictly dynastic. On the plus side of the ledger, Philip Herbert, Lord Chamberlain

to Charles I, was one of the kingdom's most powerful men. Fabulously rich, he was made more rich by the death of his elder brother William, earl of Pembroke, who died in 1630 without legitimate male issue.

ON THE 3rd DAY of June, after I had° continued a widow six years, two months (and five or six days over), was I married in Chenies Church in Buckinghamshire to my second husband, Philip Herbert, Earl of Pembroke and Montgomery, Lord Chamberlain of the King's Household and Knight of the Garter; he being then one of the greatest subjects in the kingdom. (My youngest daughter was present at this, my second marriage, but not my eldest.)

This second marriage of mine was wonderfully brought to pass by the providence of God for the crossing and disappointing, the envy, malice, and sinister practices of my enemies (Job 5:11-14). […]

And methinks it is remarkable that I should be the second time married in that church of Chenies – in the vault whereof lie interred my great-grandfather and grandfather of Bedford and their wives, ancestors to my blessed mother – as also her son, the Lord Robert Clifford; and her eldest sister, Anne, Countess Dowager of Warwick; and their niece, Lady Frances Bourchier, daughter to the Earl of Bath. […]

• • •

After the death of two sons by Herbert, both born prematurely, Lady Anne was past childbearing. The earl's thought thereafter was to expand the Herbert dynasty by betrothing his younger son to Anne's younger daughter: with Francis Clifford now an elderly widower, and Henry Clifford lacking male heirs, Lady Anne could look forward to recovery of her inheritance, by outliving him.

In December 1634 Lord and Lady Pembroke came to an agreement which ensured Anne's possession of the Westmorland lordships, giving Philip the use of Skipton for life; and Pembroke would raise £5000 towards the dower of Lady Anne's unmarried daughter Isabella.

But Isabella could not endure her stepbrother. Lady Anne sided with her daughter, unwilling to we her to a man she detested. Lady Anne then flatly refused to forfeit the £5000 that Herbert settled on Isabella when thinking she would marry his son. That's when the fireworks began. Herbert banished his wife and unmarried stepdaughter to a country house in Wiltshire; and when the Civil War broke out in 1642, removed her to Baynards Castle, where she sat out the war. But they saw one another only rarely, and never without quarreling. Anne was on her own.

---

[1] *great man*] Lady Anne suspected that her hated brother-in-law, Edward Sackville, was behind the attempted burglary.

Francis Clifford died in 1641. His son Henry died in 1643, and Henry's wife, a year later. Anne came thus into her inheritance thirty-eight years after her father's death – but she could not yet take possession. The war dragged on.

In 1649, after the Parliamentary victory and the beheading of King Charles, Lady Anne rode north to claim her estates; to evict her uncle's kinfolk or tenants who displeased her; and to collect rents.

In January came word from London that Pembroke was dead. This brought Lady Anne another jointure estate in Kent, worth £2000 a year to augment her newly acquired rental income from properties across the north of England.

Having seen the inability of Clifford women to reform unfaithful and quarrelsome husbands, Lady Anne resolved never to remarry ("I found by experience and retired life that saying to be true, Ecclesiastes 7.13 ["Consider the work of God: for who can make that straight, which He hath made crooked?"]); but having achieved wealth and independence, the countess dowager of Dorset, Montgomery, and Pembroke could afford to be gracious:

From the Kendal Diary

THIS SECOND LORD of mine was born a second son, the 10th of October in 1584°, in his father, Henry Herbert, Earl of Pembroke's house at Wilton in Wiltshire (which was once a nunnery). His mother was Mary Sidney°, daughter to Sir Henry Sidney and only sister to the renowned Sir Philip Sidney. He was no scholar at all to speak of, for he was not past three or four months at the University of Oxford, being taken away from thence by his friends presently after his father's death in Queen Elizabeth's time, at the latter end of her reign, to follow the court (as adjudging him fittest for that kind of life) when he was not passing fifteen or sixteen years old. Yet he was of a very quick apprehension, a sharp understanding, very crafty withal, and of a discerning spirit – but extremely choleric by nature, which was increased the more by the office of Lord Chamberlain to the King, which he held many years. [...]

[My second husband] was one of the greatest men of his time in England in all respects, and was generally throughout the realm very well beloved. He spent most of his time at Court, and was made Earl of Montgomery by King James, the 4th of May in 1605°, and Knight of the Garter

a little after – the year after he was married to his first wife (but she died before he came to be Earl of Pembroke; for his elder brother, Earl William, died but the tenth of April in 1630°, a little before I was married to [Philip]). [...]

A little after my second lord's death, *viz.*, on the 13th of February 1650°, I removed from Appleby Castle in Westmorland to my castle of Skipton in Craven...And that was the first time I came to Skipton where I was born. [...]

• • •

THE COUNTESS dowager of Dorset, of Pembroke and Montgomery, upon arriving in the north, found her estates in disrepair, her tenants rebellious and disinclined to pay their rents. Lady Anne (having some relish for the sport) hauled her tenants into court, one after the other, year after year, for nearly three decades. Delinquents were put into debtors' prison, or evicted from her land, or first one then the other. She demanded only her rights.

Serving as High Sheriff of Westmorland from 1653 to 1676 (a title that was hers, by hereditary right), Lady Anne Clifford exploited her authority in that office to defy court orders that she provide financial support for the East Grinstead almshouses that she and her first husband Dorset had founded. (In fairness: she also established a new almshouse at Appleby, and rebuilt another that had been founded by her mother, as noted upon stone inscriptions.)

With the proceeds from her rental income and two jointures, Lady Anne devoted the last three decades of her life to the restoration and profitability of her empire. Finding her castles in decay, she set about to rebuild them. Pendragon was mere rubble, having been destroyed by the Scots in 1341. Brough Castle had burnt down in 1521. Appleby, Barden Tower, and Brougham were damaged in the Civil War, and looted. Skipton, used as a royalist garrison during the war, was "slighted" by Parliament in 1648 – disroofed and substantially demolished. Lady Anne rebuilt and staffed every one of them. She also built or rebuilt seven churches on her lands.

Wishing to be remembered, Clifford placed upon every renovation or new structure a stone inscription of her own composition, bearing witness to her contribution. Many of those monuments survive. Her graver's editorial skills were not of the highest order:

THIS SKIPTON CASTLE WAS REPAYRED
BY THE LADY ANNE CLIFFORD, COVNTESSE
DOWAGER OF PEMBROOKEE, DORSETT, AND
MONTCOMERY, BARONESSE CLIFFORD, WEST
MERLAND, AND VESELE, LADY OF THE HONOR
OF SKIPTON IN CRAVEN, AND HIGH SHERIFF
ESSE BY INHERITANCE OF THE COVNTLE,
OF WESTMORLAND, IN THE YEARES 1657
AND 1658, AFTER THIS MAINE PART OF ITT HAI
LAYNE RVINOVS EVER SINCE DECEMBER 16
48, AND THE JANVARY FOLLOWINGE, WHEN
ITT WAS THEN PULD DOWNE AND DEMOL
ISHT, ALLMOST TO THE FOVNDACON, BY THE
COMMAND OF THE PARLIAMENT, THEN
SITTINGE AT WESTMINSTER, BECAVSE
ITT HAD BIN A GARRISON IN THE THEN
CIVILL WARRES IN ENGLAND. ISA. CHAP.
58, VER. 12. GODS NAME BE PRAISED.

Among her various memorials (including one at Chenies to her beloved cousin, Frances Bourchier), Lady Anne built a monument to her mother at Appleby Church, and erected "the Countess's Pillar" near Brougham, marking the spot of their last parting:

THIS PILLAR WAS ERECTED ANNO 1656
BY Yᵉ Rᵗ HONO^ble ANNE COUNTESS DOWAGER
OF PEMBROOK &c: DAUGHTER & SOLE HEIRE
OF Yᵉ Rᵗ HONO^ble GEORGE EARL OF CUMBER-
LAND, &c FOR A MEMORIAL OF HER LAST
PARTING IN THIS PLACE WITH HER GOOD &
PIOUS MOTHER, Yᵉ Rᵗ HONO^ble MARGARET,
COUNTESS DOWA^ger OF CUMBERLAND, Yᵉ 2ᵈ OF
APRIL 1616. IN MEMORY WHEREOF SHE ALSO
LEFT AN ANNUITY OF FOUR POUNDS TO BE
DISTRIBUTED TO Yᵉ POOR WITHIN THIS
PARRISH OF BROUGHAM EUERY 2ᵈ DAY OF
APRIL FOR EUER, UPON Yᵉ STONE TABLE HERE
HARD BY. LAUS DEO.

But if Lady Anne loved nothing better than stone and mortar, she also undertook to memorialize herself and her family on paper. To honor her father, she commissioned and personally dictated a volume of his noble exploits at sea (two copies, illustrated); plus a loving biography of her mother. She also funded a scribal record, in two volumes, of her mother's legal archive.

Lady Anne Clifford spent most of her last years reading, without family close by, but she was visited often by guests from London. She wore her hair short, smoked tobacco, collected her rents, and was well-attended by a host of obedient servants. Life was good.

Lady Anne Clifford died on 22 March 1676. She was buried April 14th burial at Appleby, in a vault of her own construction. Isabella predeceased her mother by fifteen years, leaving Margaret, Lady Thanet, sole heir to the Clifford estates. In poor health, Margaret did not attend her mother's funeral and died soon after.

The task of eulogizing Lady Anne was assigned to the bishop of Carlisle – a dour and severe clergyman with the unlikely name of Ned Rainbow. He rose to the occasion, with an hour-long sermon extolling Clifford's many virtues, never once mentioning the words, *chaste, silent, obedient*: "The countess "was absolutely mistress of herself, her resolutions, actions, and time." And though she was not a great writer, she was a great reader: Rainbow reports that Lady Anne in her old age would "frequently bring, out of the rich storehouse of her memory, things new and old – sentences, or sayings of remark; and with these, her walls, her bed, her hangings, and furniture must be adorned; causing her servants to write them in papers, and her maids to pin them up," so that "she or they, in the time of her dressing (or as occasion served) might remember, and make their descants on them": so that even her bedchamber "was dressed up with the flowers of a library." [1]

"Given to "much reading, and conversation with persons eminent for learning," she "early gained a knowledge, as of the best things, so an ability to discourse, in all commendable arts and sciences"; her conversation, "useful and grave but also pleasant and delightful. […] She could discourse with virtuosos, travelers, scholars, merchants, divines, statesmen, and with good housewives, in any kind [and] in all humane learning."

John Donne remembered Lady Anne as a scholar whose "penetrating wit soared up to pry into the highest mysteries," remarked that she "knew well how to discourse of all things, from predestination to slea-silk." [2]

Lady Anne Clifford wrote her last, brief journal entry from her bed in Brougham Castle, on 21 March 1676: "The 21st day. I went not out of the house nor out of my chamber on this day. Psalm 121—" (*i.e.*, "I will lift up mine eyes unto the hills, from whence cometh my help. My help cometh from the LORD, which made heaven and earth. He will not suffer thy foot to be moved").

The last words she was heard to speak:
"I thank God I am well."

TB

---

[1] *was absolutely…library*] Rainbow (1677), 38-40.

[2] *Given…learning*] *ibid.*, 53, 38-9; quoting Donne, 38.

Margaret Cunningham (Hamilton) (1587 – 1622?)

nothing was obtained but fair promises of my husband, y^t he
should do his duety to me in tyme coming q^{ch} he performed not.
—Margaret Hamilton (f. 2v)

MARGARET CUNNINGHAM, star-crossed wife, was the daughter of James Cunningham of Finlaystone (c. 1552-1630), the seventh (or by some accounts, the sixth) earl of Glencairn. Her father was a clan warlord who for many years took part in the Cunningham-Montgomery blood feud, a conflict between ancient clans, the true history of which makes Shakespeare's *Romeo and Juliet* look like two-hours' traffic in child's play.

Margaret's mother, Marion Campbell, countess of Glencairn, was the daughter of Sir Colin Campbell of Glenorchy; and a younger sister to that Lady Jean Campbell who slew herself for love on the same day that her leman sweete, John Kennedy, fifth earl of Cassilis, married bonnie Jean Fleming. Little else is known of Lady Marion except that she lent moral support and daily bread to Margaret during her troubled marriage; and that she died in 1610. [1]

In 1582, some five years before Margaret's birth, Glencairn participated in the Ruthven Raid, a political coup of Presbyterian nobles led by William Ruthven, first earl of Gowrie. (Glencairn's mother was a Ruthven.) King James VI of Scotland (later, James I of England) at age 16 was lured into Ruthven Castle; abducted; and kept under restraint for more than a year while the nobles established a fiercely Protestant regime.

When King James was liberated and restored to the throne, the earl of Glencairn renounced the interim government, reconciled himself to the king, and received a royal pardon. The Ruthvens were less fortunate: the first earl of Gowrie was attainted, forfeited all titles and honors, and in May 1584 was beheaded. His real estate holdings were bequeathed on the king's favorites (some lands were later restored to Gowrie's eldest son, James, the second earl; but he died too young to enjoy the favor).

The earl's second son, John, third earl of Gowrie, is the Ruthven who lends his name to "The Gowrie Conspiracy." John was a true Scotsman and ane hardie chip off ye olde blocke: eighteen years after his father's death, he sought vengeance for his father's execution. At age 22, John Ruthven (with his brother James, 19) perished in a rash attempt to murder King James in a turret of the Ruthvens' provincial hunting manor at Strathbraan, county Perth (a scandal glanced at, six years later, in Shakespeare's *Macbeth*). Gowrie lured James into his home, then upstairs to a locked chamber, to inspect a pot of gold that the Ruthvens said they had discovered. After some question concerning his Majesty's whereabouts, the king was heard calling from an upstairs window to John Erskine, earl of Mar: "I am murdered! Treason! My Lord Mar, help, help!" A swordfight ensued that left both Ruthven brothers dead; with letters and witchcraft talismans being found in Gowrie's pocket that proved his guilty plot to kidnap and murder the king.

That, at least, was the official narrative. According to another widely credited version, the Ruthven brothers were innocent victims. Gowrie, an immensely popular young lord, was a vocal opponent of the king's June taxation plan, which called on the estates to raise 100,000 crowns so that the king could raise an army. Plus, the king owed Ruthven unpaid loans to the tune of £48,000, money loaned to the crown by Gowrie's father while treasurer: the impatient son was demanding repayment of that debt, in order to discharge his own obligations. Plus, Ruthven was the son of the felon who had kidnapped and incarcerated the king, back in 1582. No one doubted that James heartily detested the third earl of Gowrie. So when the king and his retinue dropped in on the Ruthvens unexpectedly, during a hunting excursion, and the two young men tried to assassinate him only to be slain themselves, some skepticism arose concerning the royal narrative. Historians, considering equivocal evidence, have never reached a consensus concerning whose version contains the fewest outright lies.

---

[1] *Marion*] variously, "Margaret" or "Mariot."

In the catastrophic fall of the house of Ruthven, the Cunninghams lost a staunch ally in their ultra-Protestant and pro-English political sympathies. But James Cunningham, 7th earl of Glencairn, kept his head, and thrived: he was elected to Parliament and was subsequently appointed to the king's Privy Council. By his second marriage to Agnes (*née* Hay) Preston, he formed an alliance with James and Lucy Hay, court favorites of King James (later, of King Charles and Queen Henriette Marie). The earl of Glencairn acquired many honors, amassed great wealth, and died in 1630, an old man of fourscore years.

But until 1609 (when the king negotiated a peace), Montgomeries and Cunninghams continued to shed one another's blood, with gusto. In 1585, a Cunningham died in an attack on a Montgomery church; whereupon the earl of Glencairn and his brother John signed a pact with other kinsmen, vowing to protect whoever had the pluck to assassinate Hugh Montgomery, fourth earl of Eglinton. In April 1586, some thirty Cunninghams, Glencairn's brother among them, ambushed and slew Eglinton as he rode from his home, toward Sterling.

It was at about this time, at the height of the blood-feud, that Lady Marion, countess of Glencairn, gave birth to Margaret, our author.

More deaths ensued. Sir Robert Montgomery shot Alexander Cunningham of Montgreenan, at his own gate; in Paisley, he killed John Maxwell of Stainly, a Cunningham ally. In revenge, Patrick Maxwell of Newark shot William Montgomery and his eldest son. Alexander Cunningham of Aitket was also shot dead, while his wife (another Margaret Cunningham) fled for her life and became a recluse. John Cunningham of Clonbeith escaped but was pursued by the Montgomeries to a house in Hamilton. Found hiding in a chimney, Cunningham of Clonbeith was cut to pieces by John Pollock, a Montgomery ally. Etc.

Margaret's father from about 1585 distanced himself from the feud: he was not party to the ambush of Eglinton or to the killings that followed. When guilty kinsmen were apprehended, Glencairn was content for them to answer to the law.

James and Marion Cunningham had nine children – three boys, then six girls of whom Margaret was the eldest. All but one lived to adulthood, got married, had children. (Jean, the fourth daughter, died in 1597.)

Margaret had not yet recovered from the loss of her little sister when she lost her everything: In December, a contract was made between her father and Sir James Hamilton of Avondale. The two dads wished to make Glencairn's daughter, who was fast approaching puberty, the joyful bride of Hamilton's heir, James junior.

Finlaystone House, family seat of the Cunningham family (the earls of Glencairn), is a 15th century castle extended in 1760 and 1900. It is now the home of the chief of the Clan MacMillan. It was here that Margaret (Cunningham) Maxwell spent her childhood and much of her married life before her 1610 divorce from James Hamilton.

A month later, on 24 January, Margaret became the lawfully wedded wife of James Hamilton, the Master of Strathaven, heir apparent to Strathaven Castle and to the lands of Avondale, Libberton, and Crawford-John, in Lanarkshire. (He was the grandson of that Sir James Hamilton, who, having been the favorite of James V, was suddenly beheaded on a pretense, and is said to have returned in a series of visions to haunt the king, having in his hand a drawn sword.) [1]

In keeping with common practice, the marriage of Margaret Cunningham and Sir James Hamilton was deferred until after the bride's first period. For the first three years of wedded life, Margaret continued to reside with her parents at Finlaystone, "without receiving anything of [her°] husband's living"; during which time, her "good father" supplied her "abulziament and all things needful." Margaret throughout her subsequent married life would remember those days with nostalgia. [2]

In the autumn of 1600, James Hamilton paid a conjugal visit to Finlaystone, where the marriage was consummated. Margaret does not report how long the husband stayed on before returning home to Avondale; but by November, still living with her parents, she was pregnant. [3]

In February, Margaret packed her things, said goodbye to her parents and siblings and domestic servants, and rode to her new home at Avondale (43 miles to the east, with an overnight stay in Glasgow).

When she arrived at Strathaven Castle, the Hamilton family seat, Margaret was three months pregnant; but her husband was in no mood to have a wife underfoot in the family palace. Evidently with his father's consent, James kept his bride, for months, at a local inn – while refusing to pick up the tab.

Margaret Cunningham may not be a great writer, but she had a great spirit. She had within her a story that needed to be told and she told it to the judge; after which, her tale was largely forgotten. "A Part of the Life" was first published in 1827, by C.K. Sharpe, who at that time had two copies in his possession: one old, "now much torn and defaced"; the other was an 18th century copy owned by Sir Walter Scott, copied out by Sharpe and, presumably, returned to Sir Walter. Neither of those two manuscripts preserved can be identical to the author's holograph manuscript here transcribed by Emma Russell, and edited in normalized spelling.

We pick up the thread of Margaret's narrative in May 1601. She is now seven months pregnant with Hamilton's child, and has just been evicted from an Avondale inn, where, after a three-months' stay, "they would furnish me no longer because they gat evil payment."

From **A part of the life of lady Margaret Cunningham, daughter to the earl of Glencairn that she had with her first husband, the master of Avondale. The just and true account thereof as it was first written with her own hand.**

[...] SO THEN I WAS DESTITUTE,° and requested my good father and my good mother to deal with my husband, to give me some reasonable money to live upon – which I referred to themselves, how mickle. They dealt with him, but he continued careless. [4]

LONELY AND UNHAPPY, *ill-nourished and without ready cash, unwilling to bear her first child in a hostler's house, Margaret in the spring of 1601 returned to Finlaystone for her lying-in. On the fourth of July, she gave birth to a son and a few days later christened him* James.

Having given his daughter away in marriage, Glencairn (like Margaret herself) believed she should cohabit with her husband. The earl permitted his married daughter and his infant grandson to remain with him at Finlaystone until October; but he then sent her back "home" to Avondale.

On her return to Stra'ven Castle, Margaret was once more refused permission to dwell with her husband. Turned away, she and baby James took up lodging, again, at a local inn – with a promise of payment for food and shelter that was never forthcoming.

When evicted for non-payment, Margaret requested and received from her parents enough cash to rent a house in Avondale. They also gave her a one-time gift of grain – "eight bolls" (nearly fifty bushels). That parental largesse kept a roof over her head, and bread in her stomach, for six months; during which time Master Hamilton, with his servants, paid an occasional visit – "which was but at

---

[1] *Master*] in Scots usage, the heir apparent to the lands and titles of a living father.

[2] *abulziament*] clothing and accoutrements; Scots. for habiliament (*OED* n.1).

[3] *Avondale*] a parish of Lanarkshire, east of Glasgow.

[4] *how mickle*] (I let them decide) how much.

sometimes, for then he was under feed [as a gentleman retainer] with the earl of Mar." Margaret reports that she fed her husband, on those rare conjugal visits, with bread baked from her parents' grain. But James would not countenance her desire to co-habit. Impatient with his wife's desire to live together, deeply annoyed by her demands for sustenance and child support, Hamilton took comfort in the arms of a mistress. The newlyweds quarreled. Margaret became upset, then ill, then desperate: [1]

In May 1602 my husband conceived a great anger against me (he being in fancy with Jean Boyd); he would not come in the house I was in. I took sickness and lay bedfast,° six week. I requested my lady his mother to deal with him in my favors, but he would neither speak to me nor give whereupon to sustain° myself. So, being altogether destitute, I was forced to advertise my parents. My lady my mother° sent my sister, Mistress Anna, to Avondale to me, and desired me to come with her to Finlaystone. My sister dealt earnestly with my husband in my favors. He gave fair° words and made her many fair promises – but performed none of them. So in July 1602, I was compelled to ride with her in a very disordered estate, as my lord my father and my lady my mother can bear record – for my gown had never been renewed since my coming from them. So they furnished me with clothes; I remained with them till the next harvest. [2]

IN SEPTEMBER *John Hamilton, first marquess of Hamilton (Lanarkshire), having heard of Margaret's distress, invited his disorderly kinsman to his home for a conference ("tryst"); to which he also invited Margaret's parents, the earl and countess of Glencairn. James Cunningham was now better established, both financially and politically, than when his eldest daughter Margaret married. Lord Hamilton's design was to arrange a match between his son and heir (James Hamilton of eHamilton), and Glencairn's second daughter, Anne. But to make that happen, he would have to calm the scandal of Margaret's ill treatment by his kinsman, James Hamilton of Avondale. A wealthy and powerful man, Lord Hamilton's family seat was at Cadzow Castle – which today lies in ruins but was then a majestic palace overlooking the Avon Gorge. The tryst took place in October 1602:*

[M]y lord marquess of Hamilton caused my husband come to Finlaystone with his lordship. Which he did, at his lordship's request, and remained two or three nights, and was reconciled with me, and promised that he should send for me [to Avondale], to bring me home again to him. But the day° that he was to ride away with my lord marquess, my lord and my lady (my parents) accused him before my lord marquess (who was then his young chief – my lord, his lordship's father, being then alive) why he had used me so rigorously, without° cause? And because they spoke sharply to him before my lord his chief, his anger was renewed again toward me; he gave me all the wit, and would not let me come home° to him at that time. So [I] remained still with my lord my father till the next Martinmas.° Then, after many fair letters of request that I wrote to him, he suffered me to come home at the Martinmas. I° was boarded in ane hostler house fifteen weeks. [3]

Hamilton paid at least one visit to the Avondale inn to see his wife and infant son, for it was in February that Margaret became pregnant with his second child. He then dispatched her to Crawford-John, to collect his rents:

In March 1603, my husband caused me ride up to° Crawford-John, to save his means there – which I gart do, and remained there twenty days, boarded in ane hostler-house. Then I came to Avondale again and ate in my lady my good mother's house, eight weeks. [4]

---

[1] *forty marks*] about £20;   *bolls*] a *boll* is a measure of grain equal to six imperial bushels;   *under feed*] boarding with;   *earl of Mar*] John Erskine, a favorite of King James.

[2] *Susanna*] Glencairn's third daughter, m. 1603 to Alexander Lauder of Haltoun.

[3] *My lord marquess*] James, future husband of Margaret's sister Anne, not actually 2d marquess until the death of his father, John, 1st marquess of Hamilton, on 26 April 1604;   *the next Martinmas*] the feast of St. Martin, 11 November;   *chief*] i.e., acting as young chief of the clan during his father's old age;   *gave me all the wit*] as used elsewhere by Margaret, "all the knowledge or information";   i.e., my husband accused me of being complicit in the embarrassing lecture I received from her parents, at Lord Hamilton's place.

[4] *Crawford-John*] a hamlet 40 miles south of Avondale, Lanarkshire;   *which I gart do*] which I made happen;   *my mother's house*] i.e., my mother-in-law's house, Strathaven, Avondale;   it may be that James and his parents had separate dwellings on the Avondale lands.

Crawford-John was 25 miles southeast of Avondale, 55 miles southeast of Finlaystone. While Margaret was kept busy in that distant hamlet, collecting her husband's rents from tenant-farmers, she missed her sister's wedding. In April 1603 (some few days after the death of England's Queen Elizabeth), Anna Cunningham was married at Finlaystone to that other James Hamilton, age 14, a young lord of great expectations, in line to become 2nd marquess of Hamilton. Glencairn, too, by this time had become well-heeled. Anne brought to the marriage a dowry of 40,000 marks Scots (more than £22,000 sterling). If Margaret envied the good fortune of her younger sister, she does not say so.

[Second Pregnancy (February – October 1603)]

THEN MY HUSBAND caused me to ride *again* to° Crawford-John, where I remained eight weeks, very ill-furnished by ane hostler who was unable to furnish me without good payment.° He was informed by [John Hamilton,] the parson of Crawford-John that he would *never* get payment.° Therefore he would furnish me no longer – which I wrote oft-times to Avondale to my husband, but received no answer. So, having nothing there to live upon, I was forced to come to Avondale again.

Being great with bairn, I came to my lady (my good mother[-in-law]) and was with her ladyship three days. I showed her ladyship (and my husband also) that I wanted money to live upon. [1]

He would have had° me to go back again to Crawford-John – *again*, which I durst not do because of my hard estate there before.° […]

Outraged by his wife's refusal to return to Crawford-John, Hamilton evicted Margaret from Strathaven, and disclaimed any further responsibility for her. That was during the first or second week of August. Margaret was due to give birth in October.

I had not a house that I could remain in, to bear my bairn (for my lord Mar had the keys of the p'lace). So because I refused to go there [to Crawford-John], he would give me nothing°. Neither would he let me remain in Avondale, but discharged all the hostlers to give me "anything" – for *my own* payment. [2]

My lady (my good mother[-in-law]) sent to me the bailzie and said she would take no burden of me. So, being altogether destitute, I advertised my lady marquess° (my sister) of my estate; her ladyship sent for me gentlemen of her ladyship's own that conveyed me to the palace of Hamilton – where I remained a month – in which time, my lord marquess caused my young lord (his lordship's son, [Anne's husband]) write letters to my good father and my° husband, and appointed a day of meeting betwixt his lordship, my lord my father, and them – which day, they all met in the palace garden° and communed long concerning my estate. But nothing was obtained but fair promises of my husband, that he should do his duty to me, in time coming – which he performed not. So my estate being so hard, I being great with bairn, my lord my father pitying my estate, was content to take me home to his lordship while after my delivery. [3]

So after that tryst, I was very coldishly taken with by my husband. [4]

When I rode to Avondale, I remained there eight days and then returned to my lord my father to Finlaystone; where I remained till I was delivered of my second son°, John, the 12 of October 1603.

When I was delivered, I wrote to my husband to come to me. But he would not, but took voyage to France.° Within four days thereafter, he left his father and [John Hamilton,] the parson of Crawford-John, [as] intromitters with his living in his absence, and directed them to give me four hundred marks yearly during his absence, to sustain me and his bairns in meat and cloth. [5]

---

[1] *wanted*] lacked.

[2] *bairn*] child; *my lord Mar*] John Erskine (1585-1654), 19th (3rd) earl of Mar; *p'lace*] palace.

[3] *bailzie*] *Scots.* the bailiff (Lady Hamilton sent the sheriff to tell Margaret to leave Avondale).

[4] *my lord marquess*] John, first marquess; *my lady marquess*] sister Anne, who married on 30 January 1603 but was not actually a marquess until after Lord John's death on 26 April 1604; *my young lord*] Anne's husband James, who at this moment was still heir apparent; *while*] until; *tryst*] meeting at the palace of Hamilton.

[5] *left ... intromitters*] appointed these to men to be his agents in collecting rents from his property in and about Crawford-John; *four hundred marks*] a significant income, had she collected; skilled journeyman in London (in the

My lord my father […] that winter riding to Edinburgh, the parson came to his lordship – but his lordship [my father] would not speak to him because he had been ane instrument of my misery. Then the parson delivered to my lord my father's servants fourscore pounds of that portion which was directed to me; wherewith I bought some clothes, which were the first that ever I° received of my husband.

So I remained with my lord my father till my husband came out of France (which was the space of half ane year, that he remained in France). In April 1604 […] at his coming home, he came to Finlaystone to me and promised to behave himself more lovingly to me nor he had done in times past – which indeed he did, for the span of a quarter of ane year. For within a month after he came home, he took me home into Avondale, where I remained with him, very lovingly used by him. For he was reformed, and behaved himself both holily and civilly, so that he and I dwelt together very contentedly.° Howbeit, in meantime°, he had little of his living to the fore, for all he took with him to France, was *spent* – except a little quantity thereof. Wherewith he caused John Stodhart (his servant) buy provision to his house and contained himself very modestly and quietly the space of eight weeks. [1]

[Third Pregnancy (August 1604 – March 1605)]

BUT ALAS, he continued no longer in that estate. For then° he boarded himself, and me, and all his family, in his servant John Hamilton's house – in which time, he made filthy defection from God, and turned to all his° wonted iniquities, so that he was in a worse estate nor ever I kenned him before – and fra' once he neglected his duty towards God, he kept no duty to° me but became altogether unkind, cruel, and malicious – as appeared plainly by his behavior towards me, which was openly seen in all the° country to his great shame. [2]

Unable to win her husband's love, Margaret may have turned for comfort to her only companion: Abigail Hamilton was employed as Margaret's gentlewoman-in-waiting (which is the only luxury Lord James seems to have permitted). There were rumors, among the servants, that Margaret and Abigail Hamilton were closer than was generally approved of, by the Calvinists of Lanarkshire, Scotland.

There was an incident. Margaret provides few details. Evidently, Hamilton burst into his wife's chamber one night and discovered Margaret and Abigail naked in bed together. That in itself would not have been considered indecent or unusual. It was customary for persons of all social classes to sleep naked; the well-to-do, often, with a same-sex servant or attendant sleeping in a truckle-bed alongside. Nor was it a crime for two men, or two women, to "sleep together" in the literal sense. Both secular and ecclesiastical courts focused punitive attention on sexual acts that had a bearing on inheritance. The law was silent on cuddling by same-sex couples, so long as there was no penetration, no sodomy, no illegitimate offspring, and no forcible intercourse with a female below the age of 10 – rules that gave masculine privilege considerable wiggle-room. But James Hamilton despite his abusive behavior toward Margaret could tolerate no thought of a rival. That his wife was now pregnant with their third child made no difference in tempering his behavior that night:

He would not suffer my gentlewoman to remain with me – who was known to be a very godly and discreet woman, one of his own name (Abigail Hamilton, father's° sister to the laird of Stanhouse). He gave credit to misreports of her and me both – and truly, in the night, put both her and me forth of his house naked, and would not suffer us to put on our clothes; but said he should strike both our backs, in two, with a sword. [3]

---

trades) could earn up to a shilling a day (usually half that); while ten shillings had the purchasing power of about £41 GBP today. A mark was a unit of weight, not a coin; a mark of silver was equal to about 13 shillings. The promised income, compared to today's prices for food, shelter, and clothing, was in the neighborhood of £21,000 GBP.

[1] *nor he had done*] than ever he had done; *to the fore*] ready case (in advance of collection of rents).

[2] *worse … before*] in worse condition than I had ever known him before; *fra' once he*] after he once.

[3] *father's sister*] her husband's aunt Abigail, born 1565 at Stanhouse, Lanarkshire (date of death unknown); evidently employed by James Hamilton of Avondale to attend on Margaret.

So he and his two men, John Hamilton and William Murray, put us forth – the night being very foul, and I very sick – for I had lyen bedfast twenty days before; and being with bairn, I was unable° to go well in the night. He would not suffer his servant John Hamilton to help me to ane house, nor durst any in the town receive me. [1]

So I had no other relief but go to the minister's house, which was a great way off. Yet John Hamilton's wife and her sister, with great difficulty, *carried* me to the minister's house (in a very miserable estate, as the minister and his wife can bear record). I lay in the minister's three nights. Then I came to John Hamilton's and with great difficulty I got° a little chamber of his (my husband being boarded in John's)°. I ate there also the space of nine weeks, till John would furnish me no longer.

Then my husband boarded himself in another house but° would allow nothing ane me. So I remained desolate of any money of him. Then some informed him that if he took° all from me, I would obtain a living of him, by *law*. Therefore he sent to John Hamilton's wife and commanded her to furnish me half a mark's worth every day, and no more – which she did the space of eight days. But she left off her change and therefore would give me no more. [2]

So I continued desolate again the space of six weeks – all which time, I caused the minister (and sundry others) travail with him; also his father dealt with him in my favors°. But none could prevail with him, for he increased in cruelty against me.

In the mean time his father and he trysted sundry times with my lord my father. At the meetings, he ever promised that he should amend his behavior towards me, but he performed never his promises. He never amended nor yet gave his countenance (for all the requests could be made), till it pleased God to move his heart to agree with me voluntarily, about twenty days before the time of my delivery.

In February 1605 my husband was reconciled to me. Then he caused the hostler° (that furnished himself) give me a mark's worth every day, and he caused John Hamilton give me a better house nor I was in, then; where I remained, and was delivered of his oldest daughter° Jean, in March 1605. I remained furnished for a mark in the day, for the space of four months.

Just four months after her delivery, Hamilton judged his wife fit to resume earning her keep. A deal was struck whereby Hamilton leased his Strathaven mill ("miln") to Hugh Glen; who in turn made the earl of Glencairn his assign, with Margaret on hand to supervise the miln's two employees, and to collect receipts from tenant farmers who brought their grain ("ferm-corn") for grinding. The arrangement brought Margaret a dependable though small source of income – barely enough to nourish herself and her two sons (James, 5; John, 2), plus a nursing infant (Jean), and her "woman" (possibly, still, Abigail Hamilton).

[Fourth Pregnancy (February – November 1606)]

IN MARCH 1606 my good father[-in-law] deceased.

Then my husband took in his company (that ate daily° in his house) seven gentlemen, and his page, and the boys (by servants, men and women), that I behooved to have to serve them. I had nothing to sustain them all upon but the miln, and two hundred marks that he gave me before his father's death, and some of his duty-weeders. [3]

At the next Beltane he took on sundry sums of money (after the decease of his father). But I never received from him a penny thereof to the sustentation of his house, except three angels (and eight bolls of malt that he bought, to brew in beer and ale, to the burial of his father – whom he once purposed to bury honorably). [4]

So after the death of his father I held house to him the space of half ane year. [...]

---

[1] *unable to go well*] had a hard time walking;   *durst*] dared.

[2] *left off her change*] ran out of coins.

[3] *behooved to have to serve them*] I was forced to obtain and prepare food for them all, including the servants; *duty-weeders*] MS ducty weders (duty-collectors).

[4] *Beltane* (MS Beltoun, Gaelic *la bealltainn*) was celebrated on May 1;   *sustentation*] bearing of the expense; *angels*] gold coins;   *eight bolls of malt*] 48 imperial bushels of barley-grain, evidently purchased to make beer for his father's wake, which didn't happen.

Margaret's losses included the separation from her sister Anne. The Marquess and Marchioness of Hamilton followed King James to England, where they thrived. The king made James Hamilton (Margaret's brother-in-law) a gentleman of the bedchamber, a privy councilor, and steward of the royal household. He spent much of his time at court while Anne raised a family of at least eight children.

Anne had her father partly to thank for her husband's meteoric rise: Both as a member of the King's Privy Council and as a Parliamentarian, the earl of Glencairn had supported James's succession to Elizabeth's crown, and assisted in the planned union of Scotland with England. But no sooner was the King crowned and seated in London, than the Cunningham-Montgomery blood-feud erupted once more into violence, ending a two-year truce. On 1 July 1606, while the Scots Parliament was sitting in Perth, bloodshed reached the steps of the capital: the earl of Glencairn and Sir Alexander Seton (now master of Eglinton) passed one another on the High Street. Fighting broke out between their retinues. Glencairn escaped harm, but one of his men was slain.

It was also at about this time that Margaret's husband, James Hamilton of Avondale, killed a man. The victim must have been either a servant, or a duelist – Hamilton was spared the gallows, but suffered excommunication from the church as a homicide. ("Suffered" may be too strong a word; Hamilton seems to have taken in stride4r the news of his damnation.)

Glencairn's next feud, and Hamilton's next, was with one another although it was not, as might be expected, over Margaret and the children: the two men quarreled over a real estate deal gone bad. Alexander Burnett, laird of Leys and baron of Carstairs – a man ridiculed in Scots ballads as "The Rantin' Laddy" – was in sair need o' money. James Hamilton of Avondale had money but coveted a title. Burnett was willing to part with the baronetcy of Carstairs.

Carstairs at that time was a quiet village in South Lanarkshire; it has since acquired notoriety as the site of an excellent maximum-security psychiatric facility, home to some of Scotland's most violent sociopaths. But no such resource was available in 1606, when the earl of Glencairn filed letters of inhibition against the deal that his violent son-in-law had arranged with the philandering and bankrupt laird of Leys for the baronetcy of Carstairs.

Margaret says nothing of her father's motive for the interference, except that, for her, it did not work out. Hamilton quickly struck back. He was not then residing at Avondale, but Margaret was. Hamilton punished his wife for the sins of her meddling father:

[James my husband] was highly offended and sent the laird of Leys before him, to Avondale, commanding° me to go out of his house. For he would do no longer a duty to me, alleging that I had the wit° that my lord my father raised the letters [of inhibition]. So I was forced to come forth out of his house, and remained in a house of John Hamilton's, being great with bairn. [1]

When Burnett and his men arrived with a command that she pack her bags and leave, Margaret was eight months pregnant. She obeyed promptly. By the time her husband got home, Margaret had checked out with the three children, the clothes on her back, and pocket change. This time, Hamilton swore he would hear no talk of reconciliation:

He gart his page take the keys where the furniture of his house lay, and discharged him to send anything to me and my servants. Then he discharged the miller (who was placed° in my lord my father's name) to give me any of the profit of the miln: So I was destitute – while the laird of Dunrod° came by accident into Avondale. Unknown to me, he travailed with him [my husband] in my favor. At length, with great difficulty, he obtained a command to the miller to answer me as he did before. [2]

Then, on the first of November 1606, I was delivered of his second daughter, Christian – at which time I sent to him to come speak° with me; which he refused,° and came not till fifteen days after my delivery.

---

[1] *had the wit*] had the information (and did not tell him).

[2] *gart*] made, caused (*OED* gar v.);   *while*] until;   *answer me as he did before*] *i.e.,* Margaret through the laird of Sinrod's intervention was permitted by her husband to return to Crawford-John and resume authorized collection of receipts for grinding, from which she also fed her family and paid the two employees, in absence of other support from her husband and parents.

Margaret doubtless hoped that James would exhibit affection for a baby named Christian, after his deceased mother (Christian [Boyd] Hamilton); but it was not to be. Hamilton paid a visit to John Hamilton's rental unit, saw the baby but then skipped the christening service, saying that he must ride to Edinburgh, to "bring home his father's corpse to bury." By this time, the surplus malt that Hamilton had purchased for his father's wake was grown moldy – and not just the malt: His father, dead for nine months, still lay moldering in a coffin somewhere in Edinburgh, awaiting transport to Avondale to be interred.

[James] wrote to his honorable friends to meet him in Edinburgh […] but rode straightaway to Berwick. His servants, getting knowledge thereof, caused his Uncle Robert [Lindsay], and Master Robert Boyd [laird of Benheath, brother of James's mother], follow him to Berwick. There they found him and desired him to put some order to his adoes. [1]

"Uncle Robert" was the Rev. Robbie Lindsay, the new parson of Crawford-John. He was appointed by Margaret's husband James (who owned the patronage of the church) as a replacement for Rev. John Hamilton: in 1605 the previous minister of Crawford-John was sent to prison for a savage beating he gave to Alexander Lockhart, tutor of Wicketshaw (violence that included his amputation of the middle finger of Master Lockhart's left hand). [2]

With two uncles appointed to look after his family, his land, his cash receipts, and his father's corpse, and with a new parson installed at Crawford-John, James Hamilton departed once again for France, his pockets stuffed with inherited cash and his father still unburied. Fearing no violence while he was in Europe, Margaret resolved to put her own adoes in order, by suing her husband for cruelty and abandonment. She had threatened to do so, before. This time, she intended to follow through.

When King James's Privy Council of Scotland met in Edinburgh in January 1607, Margaret's best allies converged on the capital, including her brother-in-law, the marquess (who was up from London). Margaret mustered her courage and with sparse funds traveled to Edinburgh to see them; and before returning home took the extraordinary action of filing a lawsuit against her own husband. Her purpose was not to seek a divorce – she had no other man waiting in the wings who would take on the burden of a divorced woman with four children. What she sought was a "living," a portion of Hamilton's estate, with a guaranteed annuity:

Having nothing but the miln to me and my bairns, and servants, it not being sufficient to sustain us, I rode to Edinburgh – all my honorable friends and my husband's° both being there in January 1607. I rode to Edinburgh and showed° my estate to my lord marquess, my lord Abercorn, my lord my father, and the rest of my friends. My lord my father dealt with the parson° – who would show me no favor,° but bade me pursue° by the law, and what I obtained, should° have. In the meantime he impeded me in all he could, that I might obtain nothing. He did me all the *displeasure* he could: during all the time of my husband's absence, he gart me remain eight days in Edinburgh, where I spent ane hundred pound of expenses, and given to men of law. […] [3]

Someone – Margaret seems to have suspected the parson – sent word to James, in France, that his wife had taken him to court, in hopes of taking him to the cleaners; and advised him to return to Scotland post haste. On the rumor of her lord's imminent return, Margaret discontinued her costly lawsuit – but not before her friends and family opened negotiations with the two uncles in whom Hamilton had invested power of attorney – Robert Lindsay and Robert Boyd – both of whom could see, now, that Margaret was serious about litigation as a last resort. With Hamilton in France, and one of them (Boyd, the laird of Benheath) sympathetic to Margaret's plight, the uncles settled.

---

[1] *Berwick*] thus passing through Edinburgh and riding another 25 miles to the coastal village of Berwick;   *adoes*] activities, business (as in "much ado").

[2] *beating*] See Robert Pitcairn, *Ancient Criminal Trials in Scotland,* vol.2 (1833), p.474.

[3] *my lord marquess*] her sister's husband, James Hamilton;   *earl of Abercorn*] his kinsman, another James Hamilton;   *he gart me remain*] the hostile parson made her stay.

Hearing that my husband was to return shortly, I left my pursuit by law. My [brother-in-law,] lord marquess of Hamilton, dealt with the parson in my favor, and boasted him to let me have some part of my husband's living, to sustain me and his bairns upon. And by his lordship's earnest dealing, I obtained of the parson a security, subscribed by him and the laird of Benheath (who ever kithed himself a loving friend to me) of the sum of five hundred marks yearly during my husband's absence. [1]

I received, of the sum, two hundred and fifty marks. I bestowed ane hundred marks therefore on his miln, which was all broken and behooved to be bigged. [2]

Margaret was so thrilled, and so astonished, at the receipt of two hundred and fifty marks, that she took it as a sign of her husband's reformation, though he was still in France. In May, as work went forward on the renovation and expansion of the miln, Margaret dispatched a happy letter to husband James in La Rochelle, in which she "rejoiced no less nor the father of the prodigal son did, at the return of his child!" But her assurance of James's salvation was premature. On news of his wife's legal action, and of Boyd's disbursement of 250 marks on her discontinuance of that action, Hamilton returned home, in high rage.

My husband came home again out of France in June 1607. At his coming the parson was in Avondale. I was lying sick in the p'lace of Avondale.

My husband came not to me for the space of three days. The parson sued him that I had the rest of my silver to take up from the tenants, and bade him get (from me) the rentals that Benheath and he had subscrived to two tenants – who had, of their interest, to give me two hundred marks and fifty). [3]

So my husband sent to me and commanded me to send him the rentals, or else he would compel me. So I sent him the same; he took up the silver. Then I came to meet him and was but cauldrifely entertained by him. For he was of a very ungodly disposition, at his coming – which his outward behavior manifested to all that saw him; which moved me to fear to have society with him (remembering how unnaturally he had used me before, and seeing he had made so great defection from God, and delighted in abusing his body in all filthiness). I therefore absented myself° out of his chamber. [4]

I lay in another chamber for a short space. He inquired of me for which° cause I abstained from his company. I plainly showed him: in respect of his vigorous dealing against me oft-times before; and seeing he was, at the present, of so° perverse a disposition, I looked for no better, in time coming. Therefore I could not have society with him without great grief of conscience; also, I looked for nothing but that he would persecute me according to his wonted form, which was most heavy, fra' once he knew me to be with bairn. Therefore he would continue in persecuting me. I desired him not to accompany with me.° [5]

He then granted that he had neglected his duty to me and promised with great oaths and vows that he should in all time coming keep his body from adultery, and that he should use me most lovingly; and promised that he should allot° to me to sustain his house upon whatever my lord my father would bid him. [6]

To confirm all these promises, he desired me to give him a token, to put him in remembrance to keep them. I giving him credit, gave him a ring with a diamond in it – which he sware to wear in remembrance of his promises that he had made that day, so long as he had a hand.

---

[1] *boasted*] bullied, threatened (*OED* v.1);   *subscrived*] subscribed, contracted with (*OED* subscrive v.);   *kithed*] showed, manifest.

[2] *behooved to be bigged*] needed to be enlarged.

[3] *sued*] urged.

[4] *how unnaturally he had used me ... abusing his body in all filthiness*] Whatever actually happened in the Hamiltons' bedchamber, Margaret by employing this language invites her readers to believe that he forcibly sodomized her, "his wonted form" during her pregnancy, and to her own "great grief of conscience";   *cauldrifely*] icily (*Scots*).

[5] *fra' once*] from the time that.

[6] *allot*] allow.

[Fifth pregnancy (September 1607 - April 1608)]

SO HE WAS° RECONCILED. He rode to my lord my father and promised to his lordship that he should use his lordship's counsel and the laird of Benheath's. Then they appointed a tryst about the establishing his adoes. At that tryst, they ordained that I should have twenty marks and the profit of the miln to sustain him and his family.

—Which I got ill payment of. A part of it, I never got. Then, shortly thereafter, he forgot all his promises and entered in his byways, again committing iniquity, with greediness.

In September, Margaret suffered the loss of her mother-in-law, who had been an occasional though unreliable ally. Hamilton, in his grief, came together with Margaret at Avondale just long enough to get her pregnant. He then dispatched her to Libberton, north of Edinburgh, seventy miles from any acquaintance but her own children.

By the advice of his friends, he sent me to Libberton to dwell, and said he would also dwell with me. He caused me and the servants (and commanded me) to furnish his house, and 'hold an honest house to all that came.' He gave a precept° to David Meinzies, farmer in his means of Libberton, to answer me of his farm, which extended to 48 bolls of meal; 23 bolls, beare: [1]

I gart sell the beare, which gave but° £4-the-boll. Being desolate in *elding*, I gart *buy* (which was very dear, because they were not provided in due time). The rest of the beare was given for malt that we bought for ten marks the boll. As for the meal, I took up twenty bolls of meal. The rest of it was spended in horse-corn, taking five firlots of corn for a boll of meal. [2]

My husband made no residence with me. Notwithstanding, he gart me weekly provide his house for his coming. He gart a flesher in Lanark furnish beef and mutton weekly, promising to pay him every quarter – but paid him not. He remained the most part of the winter in Edinburgh, and sent his horse and boys to me to Libberton. He had five horses, which got two bolls and a half-boll of corn, every week – which spended me the farm-meal. I received about sixteen bolls of beare out of the town and barony of Libberton, which furnished the house in malt. As for all the rest of his farms in Libberton, he paid his mother's debts therewith. [3]

[A Fifth Child, and the last straw]

IN APRIL 1608 I was delivered of his third son, Thomas. I sent to Avondale to him, showing him my weak estate and earnestly desiring him to come to me, but he would not. I sent to him again, desiring him° to come baptize° his son and to give me some silver to buy necessaries to the house in the time of my lying-in°; for I was then evil provided, in respect the flesher in Lanark would furnish none, because he was not paid.

But he cared for nothing that° [which] I mistered. Neither came he to me till five weeks after I was delivered. Then he came to me and would have accompanied with me for his filthy pleasure; which [I] refused, for diverse respects – especially for his wicked life (at the present being excommunicate for slaughter, and also Jennet Campbell being with bairn to him, with many other heinous sins that he daily committed without any appearance of amendment); which terrified me, that I durst not accompany with him. [4]

Then I caused baptize his son quietly, he garing his brother, Master Thomas, present him to the minister. [5]

I remained thereafter in Libberton half a year – he never but once visiting me nor his bairns, nor caring for us.

---

[1] *Liberton*] a south suburb of Edinburgh, fifty miles from Avondale;   *precept*] instruction;   *answer me*] pay his rents to me;   *beare*] barley (*OED* n.2, the original England word for barley grain, a usage retained only in the north.

[2] *elding*] fuel; possibly, firelogs, more costly during cold weather;   *firlots*] a firlot was the fourth part of a boll.

[3] *flesher*] butcher (Hamilton ordered meat for his household on credit but never paid);   *which got...which spended*] Hamilton sent his horses down from Edinburgh to be fed, which used up the corn she had bought for other uses.

[4] *mistered*] lacked, required;   *accompany*] copulate.

[5] *garing*] making (Hamilton again skipped the christening, but made his brother be the presenter.

Then in August 1608 he (being in a great anger against me) wrote a letter to me, commanding me to remove out of his house within four days – which if I did not, he should come and force me to remove. Also, he wrote to his bailzie in Libberton, discharging° all his tenants in mains and barony to answer me, or° farm's meal or due service. [1]

I, being visited by the hand of God with sickness, sent to him the minister of Libberton, to show him my estate – desiring him to stay [my husband's] rigor till his meeting with my father and friends – which was appointed in Hamilton, within eight days. But he would not grant to the minister to stay. Then I requested the laird of Symingtown to deal with him, and he stayed his fury – till the tryst, at which meeting there was little done but a new tryst appointed that same day, month. [2]

In the meantime, he promised to my lord my father and my lady marquess (my sister) that he should write to his bailzie in Libberton to gar answer me° in all things needful, till the next tryst. But he kept not his promise. Within three days after the tryst, he ejected° a servant of my lord my father out of his miln in Stra'ven – my lord being assign to a tack of the miln that [my husband] set to Hugh Glen. [3]

The next tryst not being come, I [remain°] destitute at the present of any money to sustain me, my bairns, and family—

Remaining° in Libberton, the 29 of September 1608.

• • •

THE MOTHER of five children, homeless and penniless, her meager income from the millworks now cut off, Margaret aptly describes her condition, in September 1608, as "destitute." She must have returned with the children to Finlaystone, for we do not hear of her again until June 1610, when her mother died. Marion Cunningham had been Margaret's only remaining pillar of support.

At the very moment of her despair, the cavalry arrived in the person of Sir James Maxwell of Calderwood, a man who admired Margaret, possibly loved her, and proposed marriage to her, provided that her union with James Hamilton could be dissolved. Margaret said yes.

Reformed theology allowed divorce at common law, on grounds of adultery. The secular Commissary Court of Scotland, established in 1563 under James VI, had jurisdiction. By an Act of Parliament in 1573, legal grounds were extended to include desertion. Margaret Cunningham could make a case, on both counts, against James Hamilton. But divorce proceedings were initiated usually by the husband: most wives, by suing for divorce, stood to gain nothing but poverty and shame. Besides which, any case at law quickly ran up a legal tab that Margaret could not have afforded to pay.

One can only guess whether it was her father, or Sir James, who fronted the money for the court costs and attorneys' fees required to file a suit for divorce. But Margaret did it. "A Part of the Life of lady Margaret Cunningham, daughter to the earl of Glencairn" is not an autobiography *per se*. Margaret prepared the narrative as an affidavit to be submitted in evidence. She omits other significant aspects of her life (matters that were most dear to her heart, such as her relationship with her children), in order to state what was to the purpose: documentation of adultery and desertion by her husband, James Hamilton of Avondale and Crawford-John. The document names at least two other women made pregnant by Hamilton during his marriage to Margaret, and names witnesses who may be called in support of Margaret's complaint of physical abuse and desertion.

Possibly submitted as supporting evidence was a copy of Margaret's May 1607 letter to James Hamilton in France, preserved today with "A Part of the Life." Margaret's prose style here is that of a revival preacher, speaking to an acutely deaf audience (her absentee husband, who was then vacationing in La Rochelle, funded by inherited cash from his unburied father). Griselda-like, the long-suffering Margaret exhibits a sweet persona, and she lays it on thick. The value of such a document, in divorce proceedings, was its power to exhibit Margaret's good faith (in both senses: as a wife; as a devout Protestant); and her husband's bad behavior (he returned from France a month later, not as a penitent, but as her persecutor).

---

[1] *his bailzie*] his bailiff (as lord of the manor, Hamilton also controled the law);   *discharging all his tenants*] instructed them to withhold payment (until Hamilton found an agent other than his wife to receive the funds);   *or...or*] either...or.

[2] *same day, month*] a month later, on the same date.

[3] *answer me*] promised me that his bailzie would look after my financial needs.

The true copy of a letter that Lady Margaret Cunningham wrote to her husband, the Master of Avondale (from Stra'ven May 19ᵗʰ 1607):

The God° of all mercies and the Father of all consolation show unto you, more and more, the riches of His mercies in Christ Jesus our Lord, and grant you a lively faith to apprehend the same to your everlasting comfort. Amen.

My Dear Heart,

In the bowels of the Lord Jesus, in the midst of my manifold crosses and tribulations, I rejoiced for the hopes I have of your holy conversation – being somewhat informed by this messenger (your page) who [showed°] me your godly disposition, the time he was with you in England. Thereof,° I rejoice no less nor the father of the prodigal son did, at the return of his child! —praising the Lord who has the hearts of all creatures in His hand and can mollify them again when He thinks good, though that they were never so flinty or hard! All glory be to His holy name! [1]

For howbeit He suffer us to wander a while astray, yet such is His love° towards us (I mean His own chosen ones) that He° will not suffer us to perish, but like a loving and careful Shepherd brings° us home, upon His shoulder, to His fold – as it pleased our master and Savior to look back with His eye of compassion upon His apostle Peter, after his three-fold denial; so that [He] made him go forth of the porch and weep bitterly.

So, I trust, He hath of His free mercy drawn you forth of the company of the wicked here, who° oft-times hindered you of your good work (when it pleased God to give you any good motion) and was ever ready to spur you forward to evil. Blessed be His holy name, that He separated° you from them, to *His* glory, and *your* salvation! O [may] God, for Christ's sake, accomplish that good work which graciously He has begun in you – and° you, ane instrument to set forth His glory.

Now my Heart, seeing it hath pleased God of His great goodness to draw you out from among° the wicked and to give you a sight of your own misery, I beseech you, be thankful to His majesty and be instant in prayer, that it may please Him to continue His grace with you – and that He would remove all impediments that Satan (our old enemy!) lays before you to hinder the work of your salvation.

I am sure, wherever you be, you will get many letts, to stay you from God's service. For such is the malice of Satan with us, that he seeks continually our ruin. And when he sees that we have left *his* ways and are entered to walk in the *right* way, then is he most busy to devise inventions to draw us back – partly by° the enticements° of the wicked of the world, and partly by our own wild affections. [2]

But my Heart, heaven must be won by violence! Now, these are our enemies: the Devil, the World, and the Flesh, who stand in the way° to impede us. Fight we must, ere we win by them! But let us fight *manfully*, for we have a rich reward promised us if we continue to the end.

Therefore, my Heart, manfully° march forward, under the Lord's ensign! And strive against all impediments, not doubting but God in His mercies will grant you the victory and will crown you with that immortal crown of glory that He has promised to them that overcome.

I know I shall not need to bid you flee from idolatry (even that most detestable idolatry of the papists), for hope that the faith is so sure-grounded on that rock,° Christ Jesus, that all boisterous wind whatsoever shall not make it fail. Yet, my Heart, I will beseech you not to dwell among these idolaters! – for it is hard to handle pitch and not be defiled therewith. Evil company corrupts° good manners. [3]

Then, for Christ's sake, draw you to some part where God is truly served. For the society of the godly is exceedingly° sweet and profitable. And howbeit they be *strangers* to you, yet if they fear God, I know

---

[1] *In the bowels*] this odd phrase is borrowed from Paul the apostle ("For God is my record, how greatly I long after you all in the bowels of Jesus Christ" [Philippians. 1:8]; "Refresh my bowels in the Lord" [Philemon 1:20], et al.); *in England*] Margaret's sister and brother-in-law, the marquess and marchioness of Hamilton, had followed King James to London, where they met with great success until her brother-in-law's death at Whitehall, London, on 2 March 1625, three weeks before King James also died; Margaret's husband had evidently gone to Rochelle, France, in search of more money or pleasure than he was able to secure in provincial Lanarkshire; *nor*] than.

[2] *letts*] obstacles.

[3] *Papists…isolaters*] Roman Catholics; Margaret like her parents was a strong supporter of Reform theology. She was too good a Protestant, and had too sure a faith in the Apocalypse, to let pass this occasion of counseling her husband without also striking a rhetorical blow at the Papacy.

their company will be pleasanter to you, nor they were nearer of kin to you – for that Christian bond that is knit in Christ Jesus (our head) makes us His members to carry a greater love to others, nor any bond of flesh and blood can do – for it is knit with a surer knot, we being "all as members of one body" ([1 Cor. 12:12]). [1]

The Lord accompany you with His Spirit continually, and make you to grow in grace, more and more, to the setting-forth° His glory (to your salvation and to my comfort)! O how joyful news will it be to [me] when I hear that you grow in grace! Yea, more joyful than if you had obtained a kingdom and made me a queen! – for I know, *that* would perish (for says the Apostle, "The world shall perish with the lusts thereof" [Romans 6:12]) – but O, that glorious kingdom that the Lord has prepared for His elect! which shall endure forever! O [may] God make us enjoy the same, through the merits of His dear Son Jesus Christ, who shed His precious° blood to purchase that Kingdom unto us.

Oh, the love, the inestimable *love*, of our Lord and Savior! – who suffered death to give life to us° unworthy wretches that deserve no good thing at His hand.

Alas, we rebel continually against Him! Alas, for the wild defection of this land, in all estates, all are fallen away! "They have forsaken the Lord and provoked the Holy One of Israel to anger!" ([Isaiah 1:4]). His indignation is kindled over all this nation!

But alas, the devouring angel will get few mourners for the sins of the land. All are° fallen in such a senseless security as though all dangers were overpassed – but appearingly, there was never greater cause of *lamentation*, nor is in° this country *presently*. Truly, we have *all* cause to weep and mourn, night and day, for the abominations of this° land ([Ezek. 9:4]). The Lord's name is greatly dishonored among us, by all estates.

The candlestick of God's Word is like to be removed ([Rev. 2:5]). Christ is persecuted in His member grievously. The mouth of His faithful messengers are stopped, their message contemned, and themselves imprisoned and banished. [2]

"The joy of our heart," sayeth Jeremiah, "is gone. Our glory is fallen away. Our mirth is tuned to° mourning. The garland off our head° is fallen. Woe to us that ever we sinned" so sore! ([Lamentations 5:15-16]). Woe worth all abominations and wickedness, for [it] is our sin that hath made this desolation we might worthily lament and bewail our heavy estate and miserable condition! ([Jeremiah 44:22]). [3]

Yea, we might well accuse ourselves, and with Job curse these our troublous and° wicked last days of this world, were it not that we both see and believe (and find in God's sacred Word) that a *remnant* God hath in all ages reserved on whom He will show mercy ([Job 22:10]). (O Lord, make us members of that handful!)

Now, my Heart, in these dangerous days, let that be our city of refuge: let us strive in time while the time is, that tears will be accepted – that we may slacken the furious storms of the Lord's wrath, with unfeigned tears (both for your sins and mine, in particular – and for the sins of the whole land, in general).

For no question, the angel shall go through°, and mark the mourners for sin before the *destroying* angel come! And Christ has said that "They that mourn here shall have joy hereafter" ([Luke 6:25]).

(My Heart, I fear I fash you by my long letter, but in truth I do not conceal. And I fear I get not so-good occasion again shortly, of so trusty a bearer). [4]

I beseech you, my Heart, omit not to write to me the certainty of your estate, both in body and mind, for I long earnestly to know how the Lord deals with you. Therefore, be free with me and hide nothing from me of your estate, for it will do me much comfort and I° shall keep all as secret as you please to command me.

I beseech you, for Christ's sake, to resort where the Gospel is preached truly. Hear it diligently, for alas, our negligent° hearing in time past, I fear, make us to *famish* for that heavenly manna. (Because we loathed of it° then [when] we had it in abundance.)

---

[1] *nor*] than.

[2] *His member*] 1. the membership of His church; 2. in this context, a Freudian slip.

[3] *tuned*] "turned" may be the intended word, as per the Bible quotation.

[4] *fash you*] annoy you; *I do not conceal*] I'm being frank with you; *bearer*] letter-carrier.

If the Lord offer you the occasion to receive° that holy sacrament of His blessed body and blood, I beseech you, as you love your own salvation, abstain no longer but make a covenant with your sweet Savior – for the joy and comfort that ye° shall receive thereby cannot be expressed!

You shall receive from this bearer a book named *The Resolved Christian*. I hope the title of it belongs to you. The Lord, by His secret working of His blessed Spirit, work a happy resolution in your heart, and give the gift of perseverance – for they only obtain the reward that fight to the end! [1]

As to my estate I dare not, nor do not, conceal it from you – because I look for comfort and assistance at your hand. (For I hope the Lord has bestowed His graces° upon *you* in far greater measure nor upon *me*!) Therefore, I beseech you, hide not the Lord's talent, but put it to the profit, to your own comfort and the comfort of others°.

Since your passing of this country, I have had many strong and dangerous conflicts with my spiritual adversary – *all* which, were tedious to write. Particularly, let this far only suffice: I was thereby brought to a sight of my odious sins. My sleeping conscious wakened, I perceived my own frailty and fearful estate I stood in – which made me almost to *faint*, seeing the Lord's wrath kindled against me, for my sins.

But blessed be the name of my gracious and loving° Father! He has since that, to my great comfort, letten me taste of the sweetness of His mercies! For howbeit He hid His face for a moment in His anger, yet He will have everlasting° compassion. He delights not in the death of a sinner but rather that° he should convert, and live! Though our sins were as red° as scarlet, He has promised to make them as white as snow ([Isaiah 1:18]).

O the unspeakable love and mercies of the Lord! (which I delight to write of; but, fearing° to be fashous to you, I am forced to cease, till it please the Lord to offer us another occasion). [2]

You know my residence. Therefore, I beseech you, write to° me some comfortable lines as the Lord gives you the grace.

I am uncertain where you will remain, but by God's grace I shall not forget to be instant with the Lord in my private prayers, to prosper all your travels to His glory and your salvation. As oft as I recommend myself to God, I shall (God willing) remember you – as the Lord will give thee° grace. I beseech you also, have me in like remembrance – for the prayer of the faithful availeth much. Let us ever send up a song of praise to our good God.

The Lord grant a joyful meeting here, if it be His will – and also, in His heavenly Kingdom where we shall never be separate again, but reign with Him forever – through the worthy merits of Jesus Christ: to whom, with the Father and the Holy Spirit°, be all honor, praise, and glory, forever and ever. Amen.

your own to use in the Lord
for ever
Margaret Cuninghame

[P.S.] I have written to you the estate of all your° temporal affairs, as they are presently – which is not well, by appearance to the eyes of the world. Seek counsel of the Lord earnestly what is best to be done. "Cast your care upon him, for He careth for you ([1 Peter 5:7])." "Seek the Kingdom of heaven and the righteousness thereof, and all worldly things necessary shall be casten before you ([Luke 12:31])."

I hear that Mr. John Welsh minister of Ayr and some other of our banished° ministers are in the Rochelle. My Heart, I beseech you, haunt their company for I am sure you will get great comfort by them. [3]

Margaret Cunningham
Stra'ven May 19th 1607

---

[1] *this bearer*] the person carrying my letter to you; *The Resolved Christian*] a book by Gabriel Powell, pub. 1600, 1601, 1602, 1603, 1607.

[2] *fashous*] annoying.

[3] *John Walsh*] minister of Ayr, Scotland, who married a daughter of John Knox; a Covenanter committed to Presbyterian doctrine as the national religion; imprisoned by King James and exiled to France in 1606, where he continued to preach; *the Rochelle*] La Rochelle.

Margaret's epistle has as its postscript an inspirational poem of her own composition. In part:

Lines °

[…] A gracious God sounds to your soul: "Repent!"
And has begun to start you to that race.
Then linger not, go° forward! God is bent
To make your soul increase, and grow, in grace.
I shall° join hand with you, to serve the Lord.
Lift up your song! Praise Him with ane accord!   [1]
What greater wealth, than a contented mind?
What poverty so great, as want of grace?
What greater joy, than find Jehovah kind?
What greater grief, than see His angry face!
What greater wit, than run Christ Jesus' race?
What greater folly, than defection tell?
What greater gain, than godliness embrace?
What greater loss than change thee, Heaven – for Hell!

My Heart, I beseech you, accept of this informal "Lines" in good part. For I would willingly be a helper to the work of your salvation (for I am bound to do what in me lies to the furtherance of the same). But alas, it is little or nothing that I can do (which I hope ye will consider in respect of my weak sex); but I pray God that every one of us, according to that measure of grace the Lord hath given us, may bring our poor basket of stones to the strengthening of the walls of Jerusalem. Thereof°, by grace, we are all both citizens° and members.

finis

IN SUING for divorce after eight years of continuous misery and two years of separation, Margaret was unwilling to let her derelict husband get off scot-free. She also sued him for equity, filing a complaint with the king's Council for Scotland.

In common law up to the 17th century, in Scotland as in England, the wife was considered to be the husband's chattel, without separate legal existence apart from her "lord." She could neither enforce nor defend her interests in the courts unless her husband be joined with her as plaintiff or defendant. If her husband were the defendant (in any criminal or civil matter whatsoever), the wife could be examined at the investigative level but she could not testify under oath against him, not even if she were the victim, as in the case of physical abuse. In equity law, however, the separate entity between husband and wife had been recognized for centuries. The infusion of equity law into common law led to a gradual liberalization whereby a wife could sue her husband to enforce property rights, as for the collection of unpaid loans.

The Register of the Privy Council of Scotland for July 1610—her father was no longer a member – indicates that Margaret Cunningham lodged a complaint against her then "spouse," James Hamilton, for unpaid debts (which may have included an appeal for reimbursement of the £100 she invested in his Avondale miln). The outcome of that complaint is not stated. And divorce records of the Commissary Court do not survive. But it's clear from the sequel that Margaret obtained a measure of satisfaction, and that her divorce was granted: for on 8 September 1610, she was married (as his third wife) Sir James Maxwell of Caldwell, laird Calderwood.

By 1616, James Hamilton of Avondale was dead. He died intestate—no surprise—but his death triggered a twist in the plot that not even Margaret saw coming: her sister and brother-in-law, the Marquess and Marchioness Hamilton, now favorites of King James, acquired virtually all of James Hamilton's inherited lands of Avondale, Libberton, and Crawford-John: the demesnes, towns, manors, lands, and revenues. Hamilton's children by Margaret were left with no inheritance except for their mother's rights in the miln of Crawford-John. The details are murky and we have only Margaret's side of the story. Perhaps her ex died with an unpaid debt to his wealthier kinsman and namesake, and this was their way of collecting. But Margaret experienced it as a selfish land-grab that imperilled the future of her children.

---

[1] *ane accord*] in unison.

Happily, Sir James Maxwell of Calderwood proved a better husband than Sir James Hamilton of Avondale. Margaret reports of Maxwell that God "knit his heart and mine together in such entire affection that I think greater love was never betwixt two." [1]

Margaret gave birth to six children: Susanna; the twins, Alexander and Anna (Alexander died young); John, Margaret, and Katherine. These, in addition to Margaret's four surviving children by Hamilton, and Sir James's children by a prior marriage, made for a large and joyous household – until Sir James's death in 1622.

James Maxwell, Laird Calderwood, a man of modest income, made his son John his principal heir, leaving him property and a substantial inheritance of eight thousand five hundred marks. To John the younger, his son by Margaret, Sir James left but little; and to the four girls, nothing but his affection.

Fearing that her own death would leave the children destitute, Margaret reopened diplomatic relations with her old ally, sister Anna, who had since become one of Britain's wealthiest women. Ruthlessly acquisitive, the Marquess Hamilton had amassed a real estate empire extending from Kinneil in the east of Scotland to Arran in the west. Although Margaret saw her sister only rarely, Lady Anna was now living in Scotland to oversee of those Hamilton lands. (The marquess her brother-in-law remained in England, where he is said to have rivaled the amorous duke of Buckingham, for the uncounted multitude of his sexual conquests.)

On 2 October 1622, in failing health, Margaret sent to Lady Anna a last will and testament of her own composition, enclosing a cover-letter in which she reminds her more prosperous sister of the promise made to their father the earl of Glencairn – that her children by James Hamilton of Avondale would not go destitute. A resourceful mother, Margaret implores Anna to provide gainful employment for her three sons by that first marriage, Lord Hamilton's own kin. (Margaret had herself provided a dowry for Jean, the surviving Hamilton daughter, wedding him to her younger stepson, [Col.] John Maxwell.)

Having no property of her own, Margaret writes knowing that her five Maxwell children, in the event of her death, would be left without financial means but for 6000 marks entailed on her second husband's estate – a sum that her stepson Sir James of Calderwood was obliged to divide between them, for such needs as tutoring and dowries. Not really expecting Lady Anna to assist the Maxwell nephew and four nieces, Margaret asks only for posthumous assistance to prevent her stepson James from cheating her children of their small due.

Together with her last will and the cover letter, Margaret enclosed a sisterly gift – a writing tablet that she cherished because it had once belonged to their mother, the countess of Glencairn.

A letter written by lady Margaret Cunningham after the death of her second husband the Laird of Calderwood, unto my Lady Marquess of Hamilton her sister; with her last will sent to the said lady marquess enclosed therein [October 1622]:

Madam,

I have° thought good to put to ane point all my worldly affairs – that I may (with the more quietness of mind) meditate on the Kingdom of Heaven and my own salvation. I need not delate to your ladyship what my worldly state has been this long time. Your ladyship knows it well enough. It pleased the Lord to visit me with the cross of ane unloving husband first, who proved most unnatural to me and his poor children which I have borne to him; quhilk unloving dealing, he manifested to the world, in that he deprived them altogether of their birthright and left them destitute of any means to sustain them upon.

To discourse upon his unnaturality is not needful. Sin was the cause thereof, for he neglected his duty to God, forgot also quhat part he should have kept to me and to his children. But God (who is rich in mercy) I doubt not has called him to repentance before his departure out of this life; the hope whereof rejoices me greatly. For I long since heartily forgave him all the injuries ever he did to me – indeed, the desolate condition of these poor children is great grief to my heart and not without great cause. For when I look naturally to their estate I see nothing for them but misery in this life, without any appearance of ane out-gate; but yet, when I look with the eye of a lively faith to the providence of my loving God – who has so carefully oft-times provided for me, contrare to man's expectation –

[1] *knit…two*] Margaret Cunningham to Anna Cunningham (2 Oct. 1622), N.L.S. MS 906, f. 17v.

I cannot but be comforted, not doubting of His providence to my children. For He has promised to be our God and the God of our children, and He has abundance laid up in store for all that fear Him.

Therefore, I commit them heartily unto His blessed tuition so long as it pleased God to spare my days here. I discharged my duty to them in training them up in the true fear of God so far as in me lay; and now – seeing after my departure out of this vale of misery that mean portion quhilk I had [of] their father and which I bestowed upon them is now (among the rest) fallen to my Lord [Hamilton,] your ladyship's husband, and to your ladyship – therefore, I cannot but commit these poor children to his lordship and your ladyship as these who have greatest reason to be careful for them (for many respects, quhilk I need not repeat). Your ladyship knows how native they are to his lordship and your ladyship. But above all these respects, I humbly beseech his lordship and your ladyship that the fear of God may bind his lordship and your ladyship to have that care of them, [so] that they want not some reasonable money to live upon – calling to remembrance that it will be both sin and shame to his lordship to suffer them to live as beggars, seeing his lordship possesses all that portion by quhilk they should have lived. Thereof his lordship hath gotten an easy pennyworth: thereof his lordship has reason to be good unto my poor children, if his lordship would have God to give His blessing to his lordship in possessing that portion (for, except his lordship have it with the testimony of a good conscience, I know his lordship will once repent that ever he meddled with it!).

Therefore, Madam, not only for the care I have of my poor children but also for the Christian affection I have towards his lordship and your ladyship, I humbly beseech you both to give these desolate children no occasion to complain either before God or the world. For God hath promised to hear the cry of the oppressed! It hath pleased God to spare my days till the time of their infancy is almost past, so his lordship has not has not been burdened with them in holding them at schools, as his lordship promised to my father at Craigmiller when his lordship said "the stones in the walls of Craigmiller should bear witness and cry out" against him if he did not duty to these children. God, who made these words to proceed out of his lordship's own mouth, will challenge him if he break that promise!

I have done my endeavor to them and have never letten them be yet burdensome to his lordship. And by the merciful providence of God, I have provided my daughter [so] that she is not to trouble his lordship. Few would have thought but his lordship would have helped to have paid her tocher; but seeing (blessed be God!) I did the turn without his lordship's help, I would now beseech his lordship to be the better to my three sons who have no help but that quhilk it pleases his lordship to bestow upon them. [1]

[May the] Lord, who has the hearts of all in His hand, move his lordship's heart to enter in a godly consideration of the miserable estate of these young ones! If his lordship give liberally unto them, I am surely persuaded that God will recompense his lordship with the double and will give the greater blessing to all that his lordship hath.

If it please God to preserve the life of my eldest son and to bring him home from that dangerous estate he is in, I will beseech your ladyship (for God's sake), deal with my lordship your husband to give him some portion of heritage, that he may be the more able to serve his lordship. I hope in God his lordship will never have missing of it, that will do that boy good – and God, I am sure, will bless the rest the better in his lordship's hand.

Madam, I humbly beseech your ladyship, be ane good instrument to move his lordship to be good to these three lads! I look that your ladyship will be a mother to them in my stead. The confidence that I have of your ladyship's care and affection towards them assures me that your ladyship will not let them want.

My second son John hath a bit [of] land in Crawford-John, which I beseech your ladyship assist him in the peaceable bruiking thereof: it will help to be a life to him (with some more of lordship's support, as God moves his lordship's heart). [2]

As to my third son Thomas, now when he is young your ladyship would do well to put him to my Lord Arran your ladyship's son, to serve his lordship and let his lordship do to him as his lordship

---

[1] *tocher*] marriage portion, dowry paid by a bride's family (usually by her father) to the groom or his family.

[2] *bruiking*] use; *life*] living, income.

finds him worthy. I have little geir to leave them but what I have,° leave it to them (as your ladyship will find in a ticket). I have no more to leave them but my blessing, quhilk I heartily give them and commit them first to the tuition of God and next to my lordship marquess and your ladyship. [1]

Now, Madam, concerning my estate with my last dear husband (and loving), it pleased God in the time of his life to knit his heart and mine together in such entire affection that I think greater love was never betwixt two – quhilk now makes my grief the greater, for his removal (and makes me the better content to follow him – the Lord prepare me and make me ready!). The hard estate of his house impeded him that he could not be so beneficial to his children and mine as he would willingly have been, but I know he lacked not goodwill. He gave his son John about eight thousand five hundred marks of accidents, quhilk God did cast in his hand without hurt to his house; and that now is increased to the sum of more than nineteen thousand marks as your ladyship will see by the minutes of the writs thereof (I have left your ladyship a copy). His umquhile father haft left him tutors after my decease (as your ladyship will see by his testament). But I must beseech your ladyship to have a care that these tutors do a duty and that they make just count ilk year unto the honorable friends that they are bound unto in my husband's testament. [2]

I think it best that all my son John's writs be locked in a chest and two locks on it – and the one key given to the Laird Caprington to keep, and the other to Sir George Elphingstone (because all the obligations are unregistrate): the three tutors that are alive are William Maxwell in Cowglen; the Laird of Haliraigh; and James Lindsay. I hope they will all be faithful, yet I must beseech your ladyship to take the pains to cause-lay it on some man's land in the country, upon good security, so it will be surest and least trouble to the tutors. [3]

As to the rest of my children born to my last dear husband, they have a right of him of the ward of Milton which right I have left in your ladyship's hands, beseeching your ladyship to cause the tutors have a care that it be well-used and go to the fore unto them. Their [step-]brother, Sir James, should entertain them all five till he payeth one of them twelve hundred marks (which he is bound by his contract of marriage to pay within seven year after my father's decease). What movables will belong to them, I know not, but I beseech your lady to have a care of all – for my trust earthly is in your ladyship concerning all my poor children. (They have a right also of the plenishing of Crawford-John mains; quhilk right, I have left, with the right of the Milton, in your ladyship's hand.) [4]

God lend your ladyship many good and happy years, that your ladyship may bring up all your own sweet children and see them provided and that ladyship may also be a mother to my poor ones, who are both fatherless and motherless.

Your ladyship must cause the tutors [to] cause hold John Maxwell my son at the schools; and for the four lasses, I know my sister the Lady Hay will not want Susanna so long as it pleases God to spare her days; and for Anna, I would beseech your ladyship to take her to serve your ladyship's daughter, Lady Anna (and seeing her own geir will do her some good, she will not be over-expensive to your ladyship; but I would fain have her in your ladyship's company, which I know will do her more furtherance than *all* her geir!). And for the two youngest, Margaret and Katherine, I think their sister (my eldest daughter) will have a care of them, as she has reason (for I have been a loving mother unto her in prejudice of all the rest, but now I think it will turn to their well, seeing she may do them all good). I beseech God grant her His Holy Spirit, that she may discharge her duty to them all. God knows my care was ever great over that house I placed her into; and before I thought of her being in it, my chief care was to have it well (howbeit I was misreported of, but God, that knew my heart and secret affection to it, kithed it in His own time). [5]

---

[1] *Lord Arran*] James Hamilton Jr., who succeeded his father as 3rd Marquess Hamilton; *do to him*] recompense him in wages and benefits; *geir*] wealth, money; *ticket*] legal notice; *tuition*] protection, care.

[2] *accidents*] incidental revenue; *umquhile*] sometime; *make just count ilk year*] make a correct account each year (of their hours); *honorable friends*] my husband's executors.

[3] *writs*] witnessed and signed bequests (in this case, for tutors' wages); *unregistrate*] not recorded in court.

[4] *go to the fore*] paid as advance wages; *mains*] the home farm of an estate, cultivated for the proprietor.

[5] *kithed it*] made it manifest (that what I did was for the best).

All that ever I sought to any of my bairns (or got) was but accidents and not hurtful to the house. Neither have they anything that burdened the house (except only that six thousand marks that my good son should give my five children within seven years – quhilk is but a sober matter, among so many).

I have left a minute of sundry little things quhilk I beseech your ladyship to see done: for seeing God has removed my husband before me, there is now no one life so dear unto me as your ladyship, so that I can burden no other – beseeching your ladyship to excuse my presumption herein, for it proceeds from affection.

Now, Madam, not doubting of ladyship's care over all my poor children, I pray God grant your ladyship many happy years among your own children and a joyful departure into His heavenly Kingdom where we shall have (I hope!) a joyful meeting through the precious merits of Jesus Christ – into whose gracious protection, I heartily commit your ladyship, for now and ever.

Your ladyship's, to death—
Margaret Cunningham

Please your ladyship receive this tablet, which feckless token I beseech your ladyship to accept in good part as a sign of my hearty good will: it is the token that my mother left unto me; therefore, I loved it best. I have written also unto my lord marquess [Hamilton]; which letter, I must beseech your ladyship to present unto him and be a good instrument to move his lordship to accept it in good part.
Malsly, the 2nd of October 1622

• • •

TO UNDERSCORE the point that she was left with nothing, Margaret with her letter to her wealthy sister included "The Last Will of Lady Margaret Cunningham." In this succinct document, Margaret bequeaths her soul to God, and her body "to the earth whereof it came, not desiring it to be boweled but honestly accompanied with my friends to my dear husband his burial place." Having nothing else to give, she signed the will, dispatched it with her letter to Lady Anna, and died shortly after. Margaret was laid to rest beside Sir James Maxwell, in the parish kirk of Killbride.

Any accommodations made for Margaret's orphaned children are unrecorded; not much, evidently, if Margaret's prophecies were on target: The Marquess Hamilton had enjoyed a steady ascent to power and wealth, being appointed Privy Councilor (1613, Scotland; 1617, England); Gentleman of the Bedchamber (1621), and Lord Steward of the royal household (1624). But on 2 March 1624/5 at age 36, he suffered a violent seizure and died on the spot. Poison was suspected. Some court observers surmised that the Marquess was killed by a jealous husband; others, that he was slain by Scots Presbyterians, in revenge for Hamilton's betrayal of the Kirk (to please the King, Hamilton had enacted into law the Five Articles of Perth, designed to impose on Scotland the forms and ceremonies of Episcopalian worship). But if Hamilton's death was a homicide, King James had small opportunity to avenge it: three weeks later, the King too was dead, aged 58. Troubled in his last years by gout, suffering from painful arthritis and kidney stones, missing his teeth, and usually drunk, the King of Britain died on 27 March. The King's physicians blamed the duke of Buckingham. Villiers after quarreling with the King's medical team had acquired from one Dr. Remington a posset described by some as a white powder in red wine, and by others as a harmless recipe of hartshorn and marigold flowers, in milk and ale. The King drank it, with Buckingham at his bedside, but without the hoped-for relief: his majesty died in his bed shortly after, in a violent attack of diarrhea.

Soon after his accession to the throne, Charles I appointed Anna's eldest son, Lord James (1606-1649), third Marquess Hamilton, to be his principal Scottish advisor, with an annuity of £2500 sterling.

Remaining in Scotland, the resourceful Lady Anna his mother managed the Hamilton empire with intelligence and rigor. In her widowhood she learned to write, and to keep accounts (many of which have survived, in a bewildering mix of Arabic and Roman numerals and scrawled notations). For the next several years she rode continually from one estate to the next, ensuring that rents were paid, the livestock well fed, and her servants well employed. She supervised her own income-producing properties – a coalworks at Kinneil, fisheries, salt pans, farms and mills – as well as those of her eldest son, James Jr., the principal Hamilton heir. Her husband having purchased shares in the Somers Isles Company from the countess of Bedford, Lady Anna accrued additional income from the company's importation of Bermuda cedar. At her principal manors (Hamilton Palace and Kinneil House), she supervised building projects.

She hired the decorative artist, Valentine Jenkin, to embellish ceilings and walls. She re-stocked her deer parks, built elaborate gardens, and planted trees. In one letter thanking her kinsman Sir Colin Campbell of Glenorchy for fir seedlings, her ladyship writes: "Belive me, I think moir of them nor ye can imagin, for I love them moir nor I dou all the frout tris in the wordil. I have alrady ane four or fayf houndir of my awin planting that is pratti treis." [1]

Then came the Kirk o' Shotts Revival. On 30 June 1630, the dowager marchioness of Hamilton was one of an estimated 500 who were converted to Calvinist fundamentalism by the fiery two-and-a-half hour sermon of young John Livingston.

Though she may have done little to aid her impoverished sister, Lady Anna made up for it thereafter with her support of a circle of Calvinist reformers in Lanarkshire that included the unhappily married countess of Eglinton, the poet Elizabeth Melville; and their favorite evangelist, Master John. One of Lady Anna's letters to Livingston is perhaps worth quotation:

> To my assurit friend, Mr. Jhone Livingstone [from] Lady Marques Hamilton
> Mouch respeckit friend:
>
> I resevit yours. I am sorie that your maynd [*main* = strength, ability] geiveis you not to [do] that [which] I so harttily wishit; for, as I am trewe, I had no end in it but for Godis serveis, and the bettering of your fortoune: bot it apeiris the Lord hes soum udir serveis to you heir; bot, believe me, I sal steil weishe you happienes, and be
>
> Your effectionate frind,
> *ANNA CUNNYNGHAME* [2]

By 1637, Scotland was in turmoil. Following through with his royal father's ill-devised scheme for Christian unity, King Charles tried to impose upon Scotland the Anglican liturgy and the Book of Common Prayer. And when the plan met with resistance, the King threatened force, though without the funds to raise a convincing army. The Scots Presbyterians responded with a "New Covenant," affirming independence of the Scottish Kirk, or death. The Covenant in February 1638 was adopted and signed in Edinburgh, by a large gathering that included Anna Cunningham; with extra copies being distributed throughout the nation. Meantime, the Covenanters raised an army of their own.

In June 1638, James Hamilton, Anna's son, sailed for Scotland, commanding a royalist fleet to subdue the rebels. To meet her son, his mother led a troop of cavalry to the coast. Contemporary reports place her at the head of her battalion, "riding with two case-pistols at her saddle"; and with ensigns carrying flags whose symbol was a hand repelling a book, underwritten, "For God, the King, Religion, and the Covenant." Arriving at the Firth of Forth, Anna Cunningham is said to have dispatched word to her royalist son, anchored offshore, that "she would kill her sonne with her owne handes if he should offer to come a-laund in ane hostile way," and would personally shoot him between the eyes, with a gold bullet. [3]

It's doubtful that the marquess had a literal gold bullet in the chamber of her pistol (that was a rhetorical flourish: according to Scots folklore, it took a gold or silver bullet to kill a warlock). But her son got the message—"his mother, a violent spirited lady and a deep Presbytress [...] had no hard task to charm him." By and by, James Jr. received his mother's forgiveness. During the English Civil War, (now duke of Hamilton) James sent his eldest daughter to Scotland to live with his mother. In 1646 – having remained loyal to the crown as King Charles lost the First Bishops War, the Second Bishops War, the Civil War, and his head – the duke of Hamilton joined his mother and daughter in Scotland. [4]

Lady Anna Cunningham, dowager marchioness of Hamilton, died in September 1647. Asking to be buried "besayd my deir lord," she left most of her great wealth to her son James, noting with contentment that "the profit will be great, yif God send peace." [5]

---

[1] "I think more [well] of them nor ye can imagine—for I love them more nor I do all the fruit-trees in the world! I have already an four or five hundred of my own planting, that is pretty trees!" (from Breadalbane MS GD112/860b).

[2] *To...CUNNYNGHAME*] Transcription from a private manuscript, ed. Sharpe (1827), Preface, p. v.

[3] *riding...way*] ed. ER from James Gordon (1841) 249-50; cf. *Cal. S.P. Dom. Charles I* (18-30 June, 1639).

[4] *his mother...him*] ed. ER from Sir Philip Warwick, *Memoirs of the Reigne of King Charles I* (1813), 142.

[5] *besayd...peace*] ed. ER from Hamilton archives, RH98/29/3.

Of Husbands Beating Their Wives

Contrary are the furious and spiteful actions of many unkind husbands (heads too heady), whose favors are buffets, blows, strokes, and stripes; wherein they are worse than the venomous viper: for the viper for his mate's sake casteth out his poison. And wilt not thou, O husband, in respect of that near union which is betwixt thee and thy wife, lay aside thy fierceness and cruelty? Many wives, by reason of their husbands' fury, are in worse case than servants. For:

1. Such as will not give a blow to a servant, care not what load they lay upon their wives.

2. Where servants have but a time and term to be under the tyranny of such furious men, poor wives are tied to them all their life long.

3. Wives cannot have so good remedy by the help of law against cruel husbands, as servants may have against cruel masters.

4. Masters have not such opportunity to exercise their cruelty over servants as husbands over wives, who are to be continually at board and bed with their husbands.

5. The nearer wives are, and the dearer they ought to be to their husbands, the more grievous must strokes needs be when they are given by an husband's hand, than by a master's.

6. The less power and authority that an husband hath to strike his wife, than a master to strike a servant, the more heavy do his strokes seem to be, and the worse doth the case of a wife seem to be in that respect, than of a servant. Not unfitly therefore is such a man (if he may be thought a man rather than a beast) said to be like a father-queller and mother-queller.

—William Gouge, *Of Domesticall Duties* (1624), 389-90

Of Divorce

Notwithstanding whatsoever difficulties may arise between the husband and the wife, whether it be long, tedious, and incurable sickness of either party; whether natural and contrary humors that breed debate, wrangling, or strife about household affaires; whether it be any vice, as if the husband be a drunkard, or the wife a slothful, idle, or unthrifty housewife; whether either party forsake the truth and profession of religion, and do fall to idolatry or heresy: yet still the bond of marriage remaineth steadfast, and not to be dissolved. Neither may they be separated, even by their own mutual consent, for as the Holy Ghost hath pronounced: "That which God hath joined together, let no man put asunder."

Where Saint Paul speaking of the husband and wife, both believers, sayeth, "If the woman depart from her husband, let her remain unmarried, or be reconciled to her husband" (I Cor. 7:11), he therein meaneth NOT that it shall be lawful for the woman, because she cannot bear the troublesome nature of her husband, or to avoid strife and debate, to depart, and live as a widow; but only he showeth that when the husband upon such like occasion, shall put away, or cast off his wife, yet is not she at her liberty to marry another, but must remain unmarried, and labor to be reconciled. And therefore those women, which upon the hard dealing or troublesome disposition of their husbands, do forsake them, are greatly to be reproved, as thereby giving occasion of great mischief and trouble.

—Rev. Robert Cleaver and Rev. John Dodd, *A Godly Form of Household Government for the Ordering of Private Families, according to the Direction of God's Word* (1621), O4v-N1r

Of Civil and Canon Law

I have found [in the law] a certain kind of strictness and obdurity, against no condition more than against the estate of wives. For instance: It decrees a wife shall lose her dowry for giving a lascivious kiss. That a wife is legally bound to follow her husband wandering at his pleasure from city to city, be it from one land into another region, be it from her own country into banishment itself – especially if it be in pilgrimage unto the Holy Land. That the wife is only dignified by the husband, and not any ways the husband graced by the wife. That the husband's suspicion of his wife's lightness may be the wife's expulsion from her husband's company. Lastly, if a wife play the adulteress (a fault indeed deserving no excuse), her husband may then produce her into public judgment, deprive her of her promised dowry, and expose her to perpetual divorcement; but if the husband commit the like offense, though it were as open as the Sun and as odious as hate itself, yet the wife may not in public as much as open her mouth against it. (Infinite, such other.) Hard impositions, in my weak sense, for so weak a sex. And such also, as long since have been deplored by Syra in *The Comedian*:

> Alas, we women live in servile awe,
> But men enjoy a freedom of the law.
> For if a husband serve in Venus' pay,
> Apparently, the wife must nothing say.
> Yet if a wife chance steal her wantonness,
> The law is open for the man's redress.
> But were the laws equal, to both the same,
> We soon should see whom most deserveth blame.

If the adultery of a wife be a wrong unto the husband, why not the adultery of an husband an injury unto the wife? Or if suspicion only may discharge a man of his wife, who is more happy than the jealous husband?—who as often as his mind changes may therewithal change his wife! Or if all the lustre and glory of wedlock descend only from the husband unto the wife, and none reflects again from the wife unto the husband, it is hard to be conceived how there can be a true society, or a fit match. ...

Yet needs must I find some fault with interpreters of the law, who fit the square unto the timber, not the timber unto the square, working the law as a waxen nose hither and thither, as the tide and tempest of their brainsick fancy drives them. Which nowhere is more apparently seen than in the case we now have in hand: for in the whole body of either law (canon or civil), I have not yet found (neither, as I think hath any man else) set down in these or equivalent terms, or otherwise passed by any positive sentence or verdict, *That it is lawful for a husband to beat his wife*. But whatsoever is cited thence are either far-fetched conclusions or unfriendly sequels (which hang as well together, being touched in judicious trial, as the joints of a rotten carcase engibbeted, being tossed with a violent wind).   —William Heale, *An Apology for Women* (1609), 26-8

Writing for Women's Rights

WOMEN in early modern Britain had no right to representative government and had little recourse to the courts except through a father or husband. But the Jacobean period saw a steady increase in petitions from unmarried women to secular authorities. Most came from widows who had been cheated of their jointure, or land, or of money owed to the estate. Some petitions for aid succeeded; complaints against government officials, almost never. (If the King or a Councilor took offense at language in a petition, the petitioner could be imprisoned indefinitely without indictment or trial until she asked pardon and signed a release on the claims made therein.) Women, even these socially privileged women, had a startling range of grievances: [1]

• *To the Privy Council. From elderly Mme. Marie Courcelles*, former lady-in-waiting to Mary Queen of Scots (James I's mother), and instrumental in the queen's 1568 escape from Lochleven Castle. Petitioner requests that her bequest from the queen's will may at last be paid (now £340 in arrears); and that a pension from King James be increased from £20 to £30 per year (17 April 1604). Petition granted for the £30 p.a., but the bequest from the Queen's will, denied. Order taken, 29 May.

• *To Sir Robert Cecil, Secretary of State. From Mary Hills*, in behalf of a poor kinsman, asking a license that he may sell poultry for sick persons during the present Lent (12 Feb. 1604/5). Outcome unrecorded.

• *To the King. From Joan, widow of James Quarles*. Begs payment of £5,300 for corn supplied by her husband on contract for the Navy, during fifteen months scarcity in 1594-5. After her husband's death, though the debt was acknowledged by Elizabeth's government, she was referred from one party to another and never paid. Order taken for payment of £2,812, on condition she sign a release for the balance (27 May, 4 June 1605).

• *To the King. From Margaret Clifford*, countess dowager of Cumberland, in behalf of her daughter, Lady Anne. Requests that she be granted authority for the jail delivery and county court Quarter Sessions at Appleby Castle, an inherited right (May 1608). Denied, 29 May.

• *To Sir Robert Cecil. From Jane Shelley, widow*. Requests that she may be restored to possession of her house, Stondon Place, withheld from her by William Bird (due to unpaid fines levied against her as a recusant Catholic) (27 Oct. 1608); with documentation. *Action*: Order taken for her fines to be partly remitted; the lease of her sequestered house granted to Humphrey Clark of Falconhurst in reversion after her death.

---

[1] *Petitions*] Abstracts of manuscript petitions are gleaned from *S.P. Dom. James I*. Women's petitions represent less than one percent of those extant. A few are here omitted for lack of interest or undue complexity. But the selections are fully representative of the range of complaints and increasing frequency (and share) of petitions from women.

• *To the King. From Lady Arbella Stuart*. Requests a license to sell Irish hides, and asks a 31-year license to transport 40,000 hides yearly from Ireland (with a cut to for the Crown, and a rent of £50 per year). Reasons given in favor of the petition (608/9). *Action*: Leather being Ireland's only lucrative commodity (for which there was much competition), her petition was opposed, and denied. (Arbella in November was awarded a grant for 21 years, later revoked, to nominate the licensed sellers of wine, aqua vitae, or whiskey in Ireland.)

• *To the King. From Anne, wife of Sir Griffin Markham* (who was brought to the gallows in November 1603 to be beheaded, but then reprieved and banished for life, for his supposed involvement in a plot to put Arbella Stuart on the throne). Petitioner begs leave for her husband to return to England to sign leases of her jointure lands, thereby to relieve his debts (8 Sept. 1609). *Action*: Order taken, with stipulated restrictions.

• *To Sir Robert Cecil. From Eleanor, widow of John Denis* of Puckle-Church, Gloucestershire, that she may have custody of her son, her husband having died suddenly (n.d., 1608/1612). Outcome unrecorded.

• *To Sir Robert Cecil. From Winifred (née Stanley), widow of John Morris*, a Commissioner to the late Queen Elizabeth. Begs redress against executor John Watson, who deprives her children of their just inheritance (n.d., 1608/1612). Outcome unrecorded.

• *To the Council. From Lady Arbella Stuart*. Expresses sorrow for the King's displeasure with her marriage to William Seymour, and requests his Majesty's pardon (July 1610, with other requests following, 1610-1615; to the King, Queen, and Privy Council). Request denied.

• *To the justices of the King's Bench for Cornwall. From Anne Gubbin, widow*. Has resided in St. Laurence for 30 years, but having contracted leprosy, and having two children without paid jobs, all three must perish, without some charity. Requests 10 shillings a year; or else, for an order to place her in an almshouse, and her children to be given jobs (7 Oct. 1612). Order taken by Privy Council to pay Widow Gubbin 10 shillings yearly.

• *To Edward, Lord Zouch, Warden of the Cinque Ports*. From Agnes, widow of John Wenlock of Dover. Requests compensation from the moneys remaining at Dover Castle belonging to Samson Bate of London, who killed her husband.(6 Sept. 1615). Outcome unrecorded.

• *To Sir Edward Coke, Lord Chief Justice*. From Anne Turner, widow, imprisoned for the murder by poison of Sir Thomas Overbury Requests speedy trial or release from prison on bail, for the sake of her fatherless children. Hopes that her examinations have proved her innocent of the things of which she is maliciously accused (12 Oct. 1615). Speedy trial, 7 Nov. Hanged, 15 Nov. 1615.

• *To the Lords Commissioners. From Margaret Lady Monson*. Begs that her husband Sir Thomas, imprisoned on (false) allegations of involvement in the Sir Thomas Overbury homicide, may receive a visit from her, as also from the Bishop of Ely (c. April 1616).

• *To the Council. From Ellen, wife of John Hupper.* Requests that their shed in Long Acre, erected by her husband, now sick, may not be pulled down, as they will then be homeless and dependent on Poor Relief (June 1618). Outcome unrecorded.

• *To the King. From Lucy, wife of Sir John Molineaux.* Her husband (terminally ill) deals harshly with her and has sold his entire estate, worth £30,000, to Mr. Holt of Gray's Inn and to John Halsey, merchant of London, by their persuasion, much under its value. Requests that order be taken with the buyers for relief of herself and her six children (8 July 1618). *Action*: Order taken.

• *To the Council. From Lady Joan Whitbrook.* She requests an order that her husband, Sir John Whitbrook, a prisoner in the Fleet prison, may have his irons removed and that he may be lodged for his own safety in a private cell with his own clothing and a bed. She reminds the Council of an outstanding order for her husband's relief, which the Warden refused without further payments (July 1618). (The Warden responded with two letters to the Council stating that Whitbrook was faking his illness; had paid too little for a private cell; and was planning a prison break.) *Action*: Lady Whitbrook's petition was refused. Tragedy ensued. In October 1619, John Chamberlain reports that "Sir John Whitbrook was stabbed and killed in the Fleet by [Henry] Boughton, one of his fellow prisoners. The case is the harder, for that he had made means divers times to the warden or keeper, to be separated from such an unruly chamber-fellow, and could not obtain it.") [1]

• *To the Council. From Bridget Gray.* Requests that her grandson, John Throckmorton, prisoner in Newgate for felony theft, may escape an infamous death by hanging, it being his first offense, and Sir Thomas Smythe being ready to convey him beyond seas (19 July 1618); with confirmation from Smythe (11 July), and a certificate of the Mayor and Recorder of London that Throckmorton's crime was aiding in the theft of a hat worth six shillings, for which his accomplice, Robert Whisson, an old thief, was already tried and hanged (21-22 July). *Action*: Petition granted; Throckmorton, banished.

• *To the Council. From Joan, widow of Abraham Marleton* of Dover. Her garden produce is overrun by rabbits which come from the Castle grounds; requests that they may be killed (n.d. 1618). Outcome unrecorded.

---

[1] *Sir John...obtain it*] J. Chamberlain to D. Carleton (16 Oct. 1619), ed. DWF from Chamberlain, *Letters* (1939), 2.267. In 1621 (following a failed 1619 appeal to the Council), Catholic prisoners of conscience in the Fleet submitted a petition asking the House of Lords to investigate their complaints against prison warden Alexander Harris. They alleged that Harris charged excessive rates for lodging in the prison; taxed meat and firewood purchased privately by inmates; broke open prisoners' trunks, taking what little money they had; and subjected prisoners to brutality. Parliament was adjourned before any action was taken. (*See* "Alexander Harris," *Oxford DNB* and attendant documentation.)

• *To the Council. From Alice Carleton.* Requests relief for a poor couple who have suffered many hardships by sickness, and the death of their children (19 Dec. 1618). Outcome unrecorded.

• *To the Council. From Barbara Abercomby*, a laundry maid to the late Queen Anna. Requests three years' back wages, still unpaid (c. May 1619). Outcome unrecorded.

• *To the Council. From Amy Lady Blount.* Complaint against Lord Chancellor, Sir Francis Bacon (June? 1619). *Action taken*: Order in Council that Sec. Calvert, the Master of the Rolls, and Sir Edward Coke, Chief Justice, subpoena Lady Blount, to determine the writer of her petition against the Lord Chancellor (9 June 1619). At her examination before the Council on 12 June, Lady Blount stated that she gave directions for writing the petition but declined to name the scribe or confess who else might have seen it after it was drawn. No one encouraged her in her petition. Some told her it was "just, but full of danger"; she declined to say who they were. Petitioner was committed to prison. [2]

• *To the Council. From Amy (Tuchet), Lady Blount,* prisoner in the Fleet. Begs to be set at liberty, "as in justice" she should be, "having been in rigorous confinement since July 8, without conviction or accusation of crime." (May 1620). *Action*: Denied.

• *To the King. From Amy, Lady Blount.* Says she was ignorant that her imprisonment proceeded from his Majesty; thought it was only from the Council. Begs pardon (c. 10 May 1620). *Action*: Petition denied. Order in Council approving of the submissive terms of Lady Blount's reply to the King (as far as regards his Majesty and the Board), but commanding her to petition no more till she has acknowledged her offense against the Lord Chancellor (12 May 1620).

• *To the Council. From Amy, Lady Blount.* Asks that the charge against her of slandering the Lord Chancellor may either be withdrawn, or the grounds of it stated, in order that the proceedings against her "may carry at least a *show* of justice" (May? 1620). *Action*: Denied.

• *To the Council. From Amy, Lady Blount*, prisoner in the Marshalsea. Begs to be set at liberty, or for some course taken to acquit or convict her of the crime wherewith she is charged, as her health suffers by long and rigid restraint in the prison (Autumn? 1620).

• *To the Council. From Amy, Lady Blount*, prisoner. Begs release. Promises not again to trouble the King or Council concerning the Lord Chancellor; also, begs release of her servant, Richard Evans, who delivered the petition (8 Nov. 1620). Outcome unrecorded. (By May 1624, Lady Blount was released; at which time she petitioned the House of Commons concerning money owed her by William Holt of Gray's Inn.)

• *To the Council. From Anna Hayward*, a Roman Catholic imprisoned since January for refusing to attend

---

[2] *Amy Lady Blount*] sister of the Mervyn Tuchet earl of Castlehaven, and a poet (See *Women's Works*, vol. 4).

Anglican services in Haverford West, then for refusing the Oath of Allegiance and oath of Supremacy of the King over the Church. As a retainer of the Archduchess Isabella, born in Burgundy, and as a prisoner for conscience' sake, she begs release; her English husband has done what he can for her. (Feb. 1621/2). Order taken 21 March to inquire whether Hayward's wife is a denizen of the Realm; if so, she may be proceeded against for recusancy; if not, she may be released from prison.

• *To the Council. From Thomasine Powell*. Asks compensation from the East India Company or from the Hollanders, for the death of her son, who was abducted by the Hollanders at the Moluccas and starved to death in prison (1621). *Action*: wages, but no compensation.

• *To the Council. From Thomasine Powell and thirty other widows*. Petition for immediate relief and compensation for the death of their husbands, sons, and goods, taken at the Moluccas by the Hollanders. The States of Holland have given the Company satisfaction. But the compensation offered by the Company to the widows and widowed mothers is so small that they will be ruined (n.d. 1624). *Action*: Further aid denied.

• *To the Secretary of State. From Abigail, widow of William Phillips*, who was imprisoned without trial for having translated a French pamphlet at the request of stationer Nathaniel Newbury; and who became ill while died while in prison. Begs compensation from Newberry (n.d. 1623). *Outcome*: Petition denied.

• *To the Lord Treasurer. From Dame Margaret, widow of Sir Thomas Spencer* and a distressed mother. Begs wardship of her son, Sir William, who was forcibly taken from her and given to her brother-in-law (2 July 1623). *Action*: Petition granted, after a long delay.

• *To the King. From Ursula, widow of John Stokes*. Begs release from prison, having been falsely accused of murdering her husband, who drowned himself (23 Nov. 1623). Outcome unrecorded.

• *To the Secretary of State. From Lady Mary, widow* of Sir Robert Wroth. Begs another year's renewal of protection from imprisonment for unpaid debts (30 Jan. 1624). *Action*: Petition granted (many times renewed).

• *To the Council. From Bridget Kemp, widow* (arrested at Dover, by order of Sir Edward Dering, with her niece and servant, on charges of being a Roman Catholic). Incarcerated at her own expense and unable to pay, she begs to be freed from confinement (n.d., 1624). Outcome unrecorded.

• *To the Council. From Mary Overton*. Loaned £800 to the Muscovy Company which the merchants refuse to return without an express order from the Council. She requests that the order be issued. Outcome unrecorded.

• *To the Council. From Eleanor Thomas, widow*. Requests relief against John Poole, who by aid of her own attorney, Mr. Barrett, has unjustly seized her land and put her son-in-law, daughter, and servants, in Hereford jail (n.d., 1621/24).

• *To the Council. From Mary Lake, widow*. Regrets missing her appointment due to an accident; she still wishes to prove a pre-contract between a woman in Ireland and Mr. Domvill, who pretends to have married her daughter Bridget (n.d. 1621/4). Outcome unrecorded.

• *To the Council. From Lady Jane (Drummond) Kerr, countess of Roxburghe*. Requests exclusive license to assay all gold and silver intended for thread (in the bar, before it is manufactured); by granting of which, the King may discharge part of his unpaid debt to her (n.d. 1621/4); with reasons why the requested license differs from that of the earl of Holland, who held sole license to assay the thread after it is made. Outcome unrecorded.

• *To Edward Conway, Secretary of State. From Mary, Lady Leake*. Complains that her stepson, Sir Francis Leake Jr., has persuaded his senile father to convey to him the entire estate of Hawton for a rent of twelve cents, his father believing he was to be paid £15,000 for present possession. Lady Leake and her other son are thereby without land or income. Begs aid to regain the land, or at least to preserve her husband's personal estate (14 Sept. 1624). Outcome: Sir Francis dying in May 1626, Francis Jr. inherited the estate.

Printed petitions. *Many of the petitions submitted to the 1624 Parliament, including four by women, were formally prepared on a printing press*:

• *To the House of Commons. From Amy, Lady Blount*. William Holt of Gray's Inn, has been granted a writ of protection against collection of debts owed her; she asks that the protection be revoked, now that he has inherited the estate of Robert Holt, who died in 1624. Outcome unrecorded.

• *To the House of Commons. From Joane, widow of Samuel Thomas*. Married in 1574 with a £4000 dowry, she is now "a poor aged widow" with dependent grandchildren. In behalf of herself and all the widow jointuresses of the kingdom, begs a fair hearing against Bishop John Williams, Lord Keeper, who illegally ruled that the lands left her in jointure are liable for the debts of her eldest son, Sir Anthony Thomas. Her tenants were ordered to pay their rents not to her but to Thomas Powell, her son's creditor, or face imprisonment in the Fleet. Deprived of income, widow Thomas tried to arrest her tenants for debt, a strategy that backfired. When sufficient payment was not forthcoming, Powell with some forty men broke down widow Thomas's doors, took possession of her house and mill, evicted her, seized her goods, and imprisoned her servant (5 May 1624). Outcome unrecorded.

• *To the House of Commons. From Dame Grace Darcy, widow*. She complains that Bishop John Williams, Lord Keeper, illegally appointed Dr. Grant to a parsonage which belonged to her son. *Action*: Lady Darcie's printed petition was debated in the House of Commons on 7 May 1624 and settled in her favor.

• *To the House of Lords. From Elizabeth Lady Dale, widow*, regarding the theft of her late husband's goods and £20,000 by agents of the East India Company. Outcome: *See* next, "Elizabeth Dale" (pp. 114-20).

Elizabeth (Throckmorton) Dale (1569-1641)

> *[A]s for the mighty man, he had the earth, and the honourable man dwelt in it. Thou*
> *hast sent widowes away empty, and the armes of the fatherlesse have bene broken.*
> —Job 22:8-9, King James Version (1611)

E LIZABETH THROCKMORTON, the third of seven surviving children, was the daughter of Elizabeth (*née* Berkeley) and Sir Thomas Throckmorton, JP and sometime sheriff of Gloucestershire. Her father, a corrupt judge even by 16th century standards, served time in prison for graft when the complaints of bribery, extortion, quarreling, and jury-rigging became too egregious and persistent for the Star Chamber to excuse. A self-made man, Sir Thomas died in 1607, in possession of fourteen manors.

By the time Elizabeth wed, her four sisters were long married and her youngest brother, Sir William (twice widowed), was already on his third wife. Elizabeth's spinsterhood may not have been a matter of choice: in 1593, Throckmorton banished his wife from his home, together with his two unmarried daughters, Margaret (b. 1566) and Elizabeth. When Lady Elizabeth (their mother) petitioned the queen's Privy Council for relief, Throckmorton made the excuse that she was "a very obstinate recusant," having "done much harm by perverting some of her children and divers other of her family in matter of religion." The Council, examining Lady Elizabeth and her eldest daughter Margaret, found the allegation true, but nonetheless censured Throckmorton for his behavior. The Council obliged him to supply his wife and daughters with suitable housing in London (or within six miles) and a £100 annuity; but neglected to add: "plus a dowry for your unmarried daughters." Dowerless Margaret in 1601 married Barnabas Sanborn, a fellow Catholic. Elizabeth remained single. [1]

Sir William Throckmorton, Elizabeth's best-beloved sibling (and her father's heir), was one of the original subscribers to the Virginia Company. It was evidently through William that Elizabeth finally met her match in Sir Thomas Dale, a professional military man. When Sir William offered Sir Thomas a generous dowry, plus his sister Elizabeth, he accepted the proposal. Elizabeth, too, gave her consent.

Tom Dale began his career in 1588 as a mercenary soldier, fighting for the Dutch. In 1595 he was sent to Scotland, where he served in the retinue of the infant Prince Henry (and was knighted for that service by King James in 1606). Returning to Holland about 1603 as Captain of a company for the States General, Dale received favorable notice for imposing discipline on the rank and file. By recommendation of four great movers and shakers of the Virginia Company – Sir Robert Cecil and Lord Henry Wriothesley, and Dale's personal friends, Sir Thomas Gates and Sir Thomas West (Lord de la Warre) – Prince Henry in January 1610/1 nominated Dale to become the next High Marshal of the colony of Virginia. The fleet was already assembled, awaiting only on a suitable commander. Ralph Winwood, ambassador at the Hague, pulled strings, quickly and urgently, to secure from the States General a three-year leave of absence for their English captain.

Sir Thomas Dale arrived in England in the first week of February; received his commission; was introduced to 42-year year old Elizabeth Throckmorton and married her; trained his enlisted men; kissed his bride goodbye; waited for a favorable wind; and departed. On 27 March, he sailed from Land's End, in command of three ships and three carvels, carrying with him domestic animals and supplies; rusty armor from the Tower of London (for conversion to arrow-proof fortifications); plus guns and ammunition (wherewith to educate the unruly savages). His passenger list was comprised of men described by Dale as 300 "diseased and crazed bodies," recruited from "riotous, lazy, and infected places," men "full of mutiny and treasonable intendments."[2]

Arriving in Virginia on 10 May 1611, Sir Thomas was disappointed to observe that the established residents were no more virtuous than the newcomers he brought with him. Nor was Virginia the prosperous New World he had been given to expect: the colony was a lawless slum of ne'er-do-wells surviving on homemade ale, and on corn that was bartered or pillaged from the natives. Given a tour of the settlement by Captain Christopher Newport, Dale before the day was out grabbed Newport by the beard and threatened to hang him, for having endorsed Sir Thomas Smythe's rosily optimistic report in *A Brief Declaration of the Plantation of Virginia.*

---

[1] *petitioned the Queen's Privy Council*] See *Acts of the Privy Council*, vol. 24 (1592-3), pp. 279-81, 303, 346-7, 385.

[2] *diseased...intendments*] T. Dale to R. Cecil (17 Aug. 1611). Aspinall Papers. Cf. *S.P. Colonial, America*, 1.11.

Rolling up his sleeves, Sir Thomas began his reforms by transforming the colony into a work-or-death camp. Loiterers were whipped, rule-breakers tortured or shot. Upon learning that their Virginia passage was a one-way ticket with no home-return permitted or even possible, many of Dale's subjects thought to "flee, for relief, to the savage enemy; who, being taken again [by Dale], were put to sundry deaths." "Others attempting to run away in a barge and a shallop (all the boats that were then in the colony) and therein to adventure their lives for [a return to] their native country, being discovered and prevented, were shot to death, hanged, and broken upon the wheel." "Some for stealing to satisfy their hunger were hanged." "One, for stealing of two or three pints of oatmeal, had a bodkin thrust through his tongue and was tied with a chain to a tree until he starved. If a man through sickness had not been able to work, he had no allowance [of food] at all, and so consequently perished. Many through these extremities, being weary of life, digged holes in the earth and there hid themselves till they famished." [1]

So that everyone understood the new rules, Dale supervised the codification of the colony's theocratic statutes, gathering them into a volume of *Laws Divine, Moral, and Martial,* more commonly known as "Dale's Laws." All colonists were required to attend morning and evening worship, with a full day's work and military drills in between. To miss Anglican service once in a month cost you a day's food-ration; the second time, a whipping; the third offense, six months in the galleys, or hanging if the third miss was on a Sunday. The colonists neglected Dale's Laws only at their peril. No one ever got a fourth chance.

Having imposed discipline on the colony, Sir Thomas next set out to subdue the natives and expand his turf. The summer before Dale's arrival, Lord de la Warre had lopped the hand off a Paspahegh captive and sent him to Powhatan, the paramount chief, with a message: Return all English subjects and property, or your allied villages will be burned. From June to December 1611, Dale made good on that promise. In the spring of 1614, after a fresh series of raids on Indian villages along the Pamunkey River, and having captured and kept a daughter of Powhatan, Sir Thomas imposed the so-called "Peace of Pocahontas," by a treaty which lasted until 1622. The deal was cemented by the Christian baptism of Pocahontas and her marriage to Captain John Rolfe. To reinforce the bonds of amity (if not of holy matrimony), Dale next sought Chief Powhatan's youngest, age 11, for himself. In his missive to Powhatan, Dale noted "the exquisite perfection of your youngest daughter," "famous throughout all your territories" for her beauty. Pocahontas wished to see her again, said Dale, and so did he; for "if Fame hath not been prodigal" in exaggerating the child's virtues, Dale would himself make her his "nearest companion, wife, and bedfellow," a "bond of love" that would confirm a "natural union" between Christian Britain and the nation of Powhatan. As a token of his sincerity, Dale's messenger, Ralph Hamor, Secretary to the Colony of Virginia, presented his majesty with two large pieces of copper, five strings of white and blue beads, five wooden combs, ten fish-hooks, and a pair of knives. But the chief rejected Dale's lovesuit, saying that he considered it not "brotherly" for the English "to desire to bereave me of two of my children at once"; which is just as well, because Sir Thomas Dale was already married to an older woman, back home. [2]

Upon returning to London in 1614, Ralph Hamor published *A True Discourse of the Present State of Virginia.* Copies sold briskly. Had Dale ever disclosed that he was a married man, Hamor might have omitted the report of those unsuccessful marriage negotiations back in Virginia. Elizabeth Dale's mortification though unreported can be guessed at. She was, however, unable to argue the point: her husband did not come home with Hamor as promised, and he was now M.I.A. in Holland as well. On 19 August 1614, King James wrote to the States General, begging their pardon that Captain Thomas Dale had overstayed his leave; and requested an extension, "in order that he may complete the work so well begun." Sir Robert Cecil, the Earl of Southampton, and Sir James Hay also wrote in Dale's support. Permission was granted. [3]

His mission accomplished, Sir Thomas left Virginia in April 1616. His ship, the *Treasurer,* was full-fraught with tobacco, sassafras, pitch, potash, sturgeon, and caviar; plus Sir John Rolfe, his wife Pocahontas and their newborn, and ten other "salvaged" savages, mostly women. *The Treasurer* arrived at Plymouth (Devon) on June 3rd. The two-year extension having expired, Dale was again late to report for duty in Holland. His plans hit another snag upon his first conjugal visit in six years. The official version is that "his wife was sick, and he was afraid to lose her." A flurry of correspondence followed, with powerful allies supporting Dale's request for another six months' leave, which was granted; and which stretched to a year. [4]

---

[1] *Others...famished*] Ed. DWF from Brown, *First Republic* (1890), 172; and Tyler, ed., *Narratives* (1907), 422-3.

[2] *the exquisite...children at once*] Ed. DWF from Ralph Hamor, *A True Discourse of the Present Estate of Virginia and the successe of the affaires there till the 18 of Iune 1614* (1615), 40-1. Entered in the Stationers' Register on 20 October 1614, inspected by censors, and published after 25 March 1615.

[3] *in order...begun*] James I to the States General (19 Aug. 1614), ed. Brodhead, *Documents* (1856), 9.

[4] *his wife...lose her*] T. Dale to D. Carleton (n.d. 1616), *S.P. Colonial, East Indies*, vol. 3 (1870), p. xx.

While the Dales worked out their problems, King James wrote to the Hague: he asked that the States General not only pardon Dale's extended absence, but give the good captain £1,000 on his return to Holland (£100 salary for seven years, plus a bonus). Prince Maurice still hoped for England's military support for the Protestant cause on the Continent. Not daring to offend, the Hague complied with James's request. [1]

Sir Thomas returned to the Hague in February 1617/8 for a one-nighter; collected his £1,000 for a seven-year absence; deputized his friend, Sir Francis Willoughby (for a "consideration of money") to command his troops; and sailed away the same day, without notice. When Prince Maurice learned that his English Captain had already accepted another post with a salary of £480 per annum, as commander of a fleet for the British East India Company, he was furious. Dudley Carleton had to scramble to clean up the diplomatic mess.

Next came salt in the wound: Dale's secret assignment in South Asia was to *attack* the Dutch East India Company, whose viceroy, Jan Pieterszoon Coen, was interfering with English trade in the region.

20 February. Admiral Dale wrote a brief will, leaving all to his wife in the event of his death, and sailed for Indonesia aboard the *Sun*, his flagship, escorted by five other heavily-armed merchant ships. [2]

(Sir Thomas and his lady had parted as friends: he was not gone six months before she sent him a gift of fresh Virginia tobacco; and Sir Thomas from Batavia sent Elizabeth 500-weight of Asian silks, valued at £400, plus several dozen pieces of exquisite porcelain, to be split between his wife and his brother.)

The Admiral had some difficulty governing his crew, an "irregular and almost incorrigible scum of rascals." Other troubles mounted. The first near-catastrophe occurred off the Cape: Admiral Dale nearly drowned when a small skiff capsized. Reaching Indonesia, the *Sun* was wrecked on an island. Sir Thomas, luckier than some, escaped with his life. Redeeming himself on 23 December 1618, Sir Thomas (with his second ship, the *Moon*) attacked and captured Jan Coen's flagship, *de Zwaarte* (the Black Lion), without suffering English casualties. Coen in revenge burned an English trading settlement. Admiral Dale then lay siege to Jakarta. A major but indecisive sea-fight ensued on January 2nd. The fighting continued until summer between Dale and the Dutch, Dale and the Portuguese, Dale and the Chinese.

On 19 July 1619, Dale contracted a fever. He retired with his fleet to the Coromandel coast of India, where he died of dysentery at Masulipatam on 9 August.

At Michaelmas Quarter Court in 1619, Sir Edwin Sandys, treasurer and co-founder of the Virginia Company, eulogized Sir Thomas Dale as the giant who, "with great and constant severity *reclaimed*, almost miraculously, […] idle and disordered people and reduced them to labor and an honest fashion of life" (Brown, 225).

Elizabeth Dale's Story

At this point in the drama, Elizabeth Throckmorton Dale steps from the wings to play the heroine's part.

A colleague of Admiral Dale returning from India informed Elizabeth that her husband (before his illness) had intercepted a fleet of Chinese traders and relieved them of their ill-gotten goods. Besides a quantity of silks, Dale took from a single junk a staggering £20,000 in gold and silver; which he locked away in his cabin. But agents of the East India Company, when Dale died in August, boarded his ship, the *Moon*; broke into his cabin and storeroom; "and carried from thence all his money, goods, and estate there whatsoever." Elizabeth's source named the offenders – one of whom was Robert Owen, Dale's own servant; the other, Thomas Jones, a "factor" (agent) for the Company, came from the shore office and boarded the *Moon*, on orders from higher up.

When Lady Elizabeth reported this information and filed a complaint, she hit a brick wall. Not only did the Company deny having taken any property belonging to her husband, the Board of Directors refused to let Lady Dale review the *Moon*'s log, Admiral Dale's papers, or the Company's account books. [3]

Elizabeth Dale, plaintiff, submitted a petition to King James, stating her grievance. His Majesty referred the dispute to the Commissioners of the Navy; who, being sympathetic to Britain's most important and successful overseas trading concern, did nothing, on grounds that key witnesses were beyond seas.

31 January 1620/1. Having identified Widow Dale as a problem, the Board of the East India Company thought it best to send her a message – with an invoice: the silks she had received from her late husband, though a personal item, were transported from Indonesia to London on a Company vessel; she must therefore pay for shipping costs on 500 weight of silk from Indonesia to London.

October 1621. With the dispute still unsettled, Elizabeth learned that Robert Jones was returned home on the *Royal James*. Lady Dale possessed a sworn affidavit, by an eyewitness, that Jones had broken into her husband's cabin off the coast of India and stolen £20,000, £3,000 of which he received as his personal cut, none of which had been returned to her as the Admiral's sole heir and as sole executrix of the estate. She had

---

[1] *Note*: all details and quotations here below (except *A Brief of the Lady Dale's Petition* [London, 1624]) are edited from *Calendar of State Papers Colonial, East Indies*, vols. 3-6 (1617-1629), 8 (1630-24), and 9 (Addenda 1574-1674).

[2] *will*] For transcription of the wills of both Thomas and Elizabeth Dale, see Waters (1907), 2.748-9.

[3] *Board*] referenced as the "court" of the East India Company; here *Board*, to avoid confusion with the law courts.

Jones arrested. Elizabeth that same week (perhaps as a distraction) applied to the East India Company for payment of £100 of her husband's unpaid salary. An unsympathetic board of directors replied that "there was much to be charged upon Sir Thos. Dale, *viz*., certain reales-of-eight [silver coins] taken out of the fort at Jakarta by him; whereof the Dutch require restitution, *and* his arrears to the new [issue of] stock; besides other demands. The accounts," they told her, "shall be made up within fourteen days, when she shall receive what shall be due to her" (*i.e.*, another invoice will be computed, only bigger). Lady Dale, denying that her husband owed the East India Company tuppence, demanded to see account books in support of these allegations. The Company refused. [1]

Jones from prison applied to the Company for indemnification. He was "answered that the matter of arrest in no way concerned the Company." Jones then promised "to discover much matter whereof the Company may make good use" concerning factors for the Company who were trading privately in Southeast Asia. Noncommittal, the Board prepared interrogatories and took Jones's deposition, on a promise of £25 yearly wages for five years, and at the end of that time, if alive, £500 more, if he could presently discover those that do trade privately; from whose examination "it was conceived that this snowball gets bigger with rolling": "There is not a man free," said Jones, from private trading; Jones had "heard Spalding say he had more money than he knew what to *do* with." Jones believed that John Jourdain had lent Dale 2,000 reales, of Company money, after the wreck of the *Sun*; with which Dale purchased the silks he sent home to his wife. The Board informed Jones of Ball's statement that Dale had received *4,000* reales from Jourdain. Jones said, yes, that was quite possible: Dale on his deathbed was seen to have 2,000 reales, which he said came from "his wages." Questioned further, Jones said he was not present at Admiral Dale's attack on the Chinese traders, but confirmed that Dale had captured a small fleet and turned the junks over to agents Spalding, Ball, and Jourdain, together with some silks. Finding his deposition helpful, the Board gave Jones a £50 reward.

November 1621. While waiting for Dale v. Jones to be heard, Lady Dale sent a courteous note to Sir Thomas Smythe (now Governor of the East India Company), requesting a full and accurate statement of accounts between the Company and her husband. In the meantime she filed suit against her late husband's servant, Robert Owen, holding him accountable for her husband's clothing, personal articles, etc., worth £300, which vanished along with the Chinese loot. In their meetings of November 1, 2, 7, 14, and 16, the Board discussed Lady Dale's dogged persistence. The woman was like a pit bull. After much talk, the directors voted that no Company funds would be paid to Widow Dale, no matter how loudly she clamored, or to whom.

21-23 November. Elizabeth next sued a Company surgeon named William Wiley, a man with a record: he was prosecuted in 1617 for selling Company-owned pepper. Wiley nonetheless submitted a petition to the Board for indemnification in Dale v. Wiley. That request was denied.

30 January 1621/2. The Board resolved to indemnify Thomas Jones and Robert Owen, "for so much as concerns the Company." The vote was confirmed on 8 February: Jones and Owen could rest easy.

6-8 March 1621/2. The female contagion spread: Joan Viney, sister and executrix for Captain John Jourdain, asked that the Company provide reimbursement for her brother's funeral expenses. A trusted factor, Jourdain was ambushed and killed by Dutch traders on 16 July 1619, at Patani (three weeks before Thomas Dale died of fever in India). The Board voted "to forbear, lest it should lead to the discussion of other matters." (At Jourdain's death, 4,000 reales were taken from his *comptoire*, and never any account given of them.) [2]

15-17 May 1622. Searching for a legal precedent to use against Lady Dale, the Company found a red flag: the goods of any man dying at sea may "be sold at the mainmast"; "but no factor ashore ought to meddle therewith." The first premise was a plus; the second, problematic. Jones had boarded the *Moon* expressly to confiscate Admiral Dale's books and property, virtually none of which was auctioned at mainmast except a trunk of Virginia tobacco. The Board retained a "well-experienced advocate, for his advice."

---

[1] *stock*] shares in the company, "adventure" capital invested by privileged employees on expectation of a large return. An extract from the will of Captain John Jourdain is representative: "Bound on a voyage to the East Indies. I have made an agreement with the honorable [East India] Company to serve them five years to be their principal agent in the Indies, for which service they are to allow me £350 per annum. I have laid into their hands £1,200 [for shares in the Company], to be paid 3-for-1 at my return to England or 1.5-to-one if I die before my coming home. Also, of this £350 per annum for my wages I declare that they are to give £50 yearly unto my sister, [Joan] Viney, as long as I am wanting out of England. The house where my sister Viney dwelleth (which I bought of my cousin Ignatius Jourdain), cost £200; the writing thereof I leave with my sister Viney" (Waters [1907], 2.1071-2). The shares purchased by Thomas Dale having come to term, the Company alleged that Lady Dale had to purchase shares in the new issue; a demand overruled by Sir Edward Coke, Lord Chief Justice, in May 1624.

[2] *4,000 reales*] Company minutes of 16-18 March 1629 indicate that the 4,000 reales that Company agents took from the late Capt. Jourdain's chest were in fact Dale's repayment (from the Chinese reales) of the sum that the Company had said was loaned to Dale and never repaid. Having robbed the corpses of both men, the Company then defamed them, and cheated their female heirs.

22 May 1622. Lady Dale now disclosed the sworn deposition of Isaac Crowther, steward of the *Abigail*, in which Crowther stated that Thomas Jones, factor for the Company, abetted by Robert Owen, had broken into Admiral Dale's cabin and stolen £20,000, plus all goods, books, and other property of the deceased.

7 June 1622. Having learned the identity of Lady Dale's key witness, the Board suspended Crowther from paid employment until further notice. Next they hammered out a legal strategy. Adam Dent, manager at Patani, was summoned to appear before the Board; and presently accused of making "90 corge of pintadoes" (1,800 hand-decorated painted cloths) at Company expense, for his own private trading; which Denton denied. But on further questioning Denton confirmed that two of Dale's servants had removed 1,100 Spanish or Portuguese dollars from the Dutch fort at Jakarta (the Dutch, it would be argued, demanded restitution; for which Lady Dale was liable). More problematic: Denton, though aware that Admiral Dale had captured a number of Chinese junks off the coast of Patani, denied that Dale did so under his own instructions (or, for ought he knew, by any other manager's assignment). On the plus side, Denton had heard that Dale took only 5,000 Spanish dollars from the Chinese, not the £20,000 alleged in Crowther's sworn deposition.

18 June 1622. A judge for the Admiralty Court ruled that Jones and Owen were not liable for Lady Dale's alleged losses. Her suit against the Company, which remained with the Commissioners of the Navy, was of no pressing concern. Neither were Jones' and Owen's legal bills. Having never actually put in writing a promise of indemnification, the Board now declined to contribute to court costs or attorneys' fees. [1]

19-20 August 1623. More than three years after the initial referral, the Navy Commissioners prepared interrogatories for Lady Dale and the East India Company, causing a burst of activity. The Commission interviewed Lady Dale, and summoned representatives of Company to appear Friday next.

3 September 1623. Not wishing to deal with sworn depositions, or perhaps as a show of graciousness, the Company asked for a continuance – then suddenly offered to settle. The Board acknowledged to Lady Dale that Company agents had found a store of Virginia tobacco aboard the *Moon* that belonged to her husband; which the Company at his death sold for £16. Lady Dale was therefore offered £16, on condition she sign a release for her other claims, and every of them.

10 October 1623. The Board ordered their accountant, Edward Seagar, Purser General, "to perfect his books."

31 October 1623. Sir Thomas Smythe, Governor of the East India Company, graciously "offered on behalf of the Commissioners to examine witnesses, also on the part of the Company." The Commissioners, to their credit, declined his volunteered assistance and proceeded with subpoenas.

4 November 1623. Lady Dale turned up the heat: she threatened to publish the story told her by eyewitnesses. The Board members of the East India Company were not easily upset, but this threat jiggled them. Sir Thomas Dale was viewed by many as a hero. It would not do to have his widow printing stories that his cabin was burglarized at his death, and £20,000 taken – booty that he had taken on the high seas, on his own initiative and at his own risk, from pagans.

Smythe drafted a preemptive statement, countering the allegations: Astonished "at the unreasonable pretenses of Lady Dale," the board and officers of the East India Company were now "sorry they had done her any courtesy in letting her have the silk that came home on her husband's account. [...] She reports her husband 'took £20,000 out of a Chinese junk.' But if it *were* taken, it belonged to those that employed him! Also, that 'he carried an estate in money' – but the contrary appeared at his going, for he was so ill provided of money, he was forced to borrow £100 of the Company. And if he had not accepted when he did, the Company resolved not to have employed him at all, their ships being ready to depart without him. Nay, more [...We] were so little desirous he should go, that [we] offered him £100 to *stay*, but an honorable lord, his friend, pressed him to go."

More cause for alarm: the Board learned that Dale had other witnesses besides Crowther. [2]

The Company's replies to the Commission's interrogatories were returned to the Navy on November 10th. On the 11th, the Board in consultation with its counsel prepared its own set of interrogatories for Lady Dale's witnesses, whom Governor Smythe now cursed as "a company of idle fellows," none of whom henceforth would ever be employed by the East India Company. He directed the Board to stay on script.

14 December 1623. The Board received word from the Dutch merchants in Jakarta that, contrary to what Denton had told them, Sir Thomas Dale took away nothing from their fort that was not given to him as a gift, including a chest of silver plate which the Dutch gave him hoping that he would give their traders and merchant vessels better treatment.

2 January 1623/4. The defendant for more than four years had demanded, without success, that the Company open its books. Elizabeth's brother, Sir William Throckmorton of the Virginia Company, at last

---

[1] *Board's promise*] Thomas Jones uttered "some tart words" when the Company reneged on its promise to pay his legal bills in Dale v. Jones; and was therefore denied future employment with the Company; he applied repeatedly over the next eleven years but was refused.

[2] *We...we*] They...they in *Cal. S.P. Colonial East Indies*, vol. 4 (1622-1634), 174.

came to Smythe, pleading cooperation: since the King had referred the complaint to a Commission, said Throckmorton, it was the Company's duty "not to decline that course but to attend the issue thereof." No luck.

23 January 1623/4. A Mr. Hopkins came forward, alleging that Admiral Dale died owing him £600, but he was willing to settle for Lady Dale's stock in the Company. The Board told Hopkins to take the proverbial long walk off a short pier, noting that the Company had its own claim on Lady Dale's shares.

February-March. Whether Elizabeth's next move was courage or folly is a tough call: she took her complaint to a stationer's shop, and had it printed. She then submitted copies to the House of Lords, humbly requesting action. (This was the first time in history when a printed petition by a female subject was presented to the House of Lords. Three other printed petitions the same year – by widows Grace Darcy and Joane Thomas, and one by Lady Amy Blount – were submitted to the House of Commons. Since the MPs for the Commons were largely controled by the Merchants, Lady Dale went over their heads.)

26 March 1624. Having received a subpoena to appear before the House of Lords, Sir Thomas Smythe distributed the summons and irritably directed Board members "to have in readiness what has been required from the Parliament, on Tuesday come se'nnight."

April 1624. The printed petition of Lady Dale was exhibited in Parliament on 2 April and read aloud – at which point the Company requested and received an adjournment until Monday next, in order to retain "the help of some expert lawyers." On the 7th, representatives of the Company appeared for the continuance "but could not be heard." Then, on the 14th, good news: Lady Dale's petition would not be heard by the Upper House: the Lords had referred the matter to Sir Edward Coke's Committee of Grievances, in the House of Commons. Sir Thomas Smythe and Sir Maurice Abbot, meeting with Coke on April 16th, complained bitterly that Lady Dale "did by her counsel press foully against the Company; and that which stuck most against the factors was the testimony of Crowther." Coke nonetheless urged Smythe and Abbot, even if "the Company were no way faulty, yet to give *something* to Lady Dale"; which they refused to do.

Coke adjourned the inquest. Later that afternoon, at a meeting of the Board, Sir Edwin Sandys moved that the Company attend no more meetings about Lady Dale's matter unless subpoenaed. The motion passed.

14 May. Subpoenaed to appear once again before the Committee on Grievances of the House of Commons, Governor Smythe warned his fellow officers that "some motion would be made for a compromise, and the Company pressed to [offer] something by the friends of the Lady [Dale] ([she] being allied to sundry gentlemen of quality in that House). Resolving not to cooperate, the Board authorized Abbot and two other officers to appear as summoned, but without counsel – and there (cynically but shrewdly), to answer all interrogatories with a line borrowed from Sir William Throckmorton: "that his Majesty having granted a Commission to hear the business, the Company thought it their duty not to waive that course."

21-28 May. At the next hearing, when Abbot and Smythe refused to answer questions, they were subjected (by Abbot's report) to "coarse usage, and not without some words of reproach and scandal" from Sir Edward Coke; "whereto they made such answer as was fit for their defense." Worse, the Company was ordered to appear the next day before the Lords' Committee for Petitions in the Upper House; at which interview the Company was further criticized, not only for its treatment of Lady Dale, but for having gone another three years (since the last Parliament) without having paid compensation to a number of widows and mothers whose husbands and sons in the Company's service were captured by the Dutch and starved to death in a Molucca prison. (The Company having paid back wages in 1621, the Board insisted its obligations were fulfilled.) One appellant after another came forward to complain of abuse or neglect. But Smythe and Abbot played their cards well, and carried the day. On 28 May, a jubilant Governor Smythe reported to the Board that the business of Lady Dale had been returned without prejudice to the Navy Commissioners (who could be counted on to do nothing); "wherein if she were unjustly dealt withal, she shall be at liberty to complain to the *Parliament*" – which would never happen, for "An honorable Lord, finding the [printed] petition of Lady Dale to be *scandalous*, took a resolution to move […] that 'If any scandalous petition shall be exhibited and not proved, the party so exhibiting shall be subject to exemplary punishment!'" (*i.e.*, prison), which the offended Lord "conceived to be a ready way to deliver the House of much unnecessary trouble." Smythe and Abbot had dutifully "maintained the reputation of the Company against the scandalous informations exhibited against them by Lady Dale," and were duly applauded by the Board.

On 30 June 1624, the East India Company paid Elizabeth Dale, widow the sum of £15 for a parcel of tobacco sold at auction after her husband's death, "more than by any right she could claim" (Sir Thomas Smythe). The woman could go whistle in the wind for the £20,000 which company agents took from his cabin. The Board issued a resolution in September that "if nothing be done, it is merely the fault of Lady Dale." *Nothing* is indeed what happened: in December, the Commissioners of the Navy summoned Lady Dale to appear before them and did "their best to persuade an end, as friends," without further compensation.

A Brief of the Lady Dale's Petition to the Parliament (1624)

SHOWING,

That Sir THOMAS DALE her husband, being employed in the year 1617 by the East India Company as Chief Commander of their fleet into the East Indies, and there dying (in the year 1619), left° a great estate there in money and other things (in his Ship called the *Moon*, then floating at sea) to the value of £20,000; all which after his death belonged to the Petitioner as sole executrix of his last will, made before his going in that voyage.

Shortly after his death, one Thomas Jones, a factor for the Company there, and Robert Owen, a servant of the said Sir Thomas, by confederacy with George Ball, William Methald, and Augustine Spaulding, factors likewise for the said Company – according to the usual customs of those factors in case of any man's death there, by a forehand private direction from the Governors, Treasurers, and Committees of that Company to seize upon all his goods for the use of the Company and so to swallow up all his estate – got aboard the said ship in the absence both of the Master and Purser of the same, and there unlawfully brake into Sir Thomas's cabin and storeroom, and took and carried from thence all his money, goods, and estate there whatsoever, together with divers written books and memorials of the particulars of his estate there; which books and memorials they have suppressed and concealed, and have shared all the said estate between themselves; and the said Governors, Treasurers and Committees of the said Company giving no part thereof, nor the sight of the said books and memorials to the Petitioner ever sithence.

The said Governors, Treasurers and Committees not herewith content, have since practiced to defeat the Petitioner of all her estate at home (lying all in their hands) being a matter of £2,000 or near thereabouts, adventured by her said husband in both the joint stocks of that Company, besides the profits thereof and some other moneys owing by the Company to her husband; causing an officer of theirs to charge her for that purpose with supposed debts of her husband's to the Company, to the value of £2,600 pounds; which upon examination of another of their officers in her cause, hath been since confessed by him, upon oath, to be an unjust charge, and excused as a "mistake"° by the Company.

That the Petitioner hath sought remedy for the former of these wrongs (done in the Indies) by a suit in the Admiralty Court against the said Jones and Owen, being the principal actors of the said wrongs and spoil there; where – notwithstanding that good proof was made, as well of their said unlawful fact as of divers particulars of the said estate (to a great value) so unlawfully taken away by them, besides a much greater estate concealed by their taking and suppressing of the said books and memorials, yet through the greatness and potency of the said Governors, Treasurers and Committees bearing those fellows out in that suit against the Petitioner – she could not there obtain recompense of the said wrongs, according to her proof made thereof.

So the said Governors, Treasurers and Committees, and those others before-mentioned, detaining from the Petitioner all she hath; and the said Governors, Treasurers and Committees not only denying to yield her any part of her means in their hands, either for the righting of herself by suit or for her necessary maintenance, but refusing also very scornfully as much as to treat with her (or her friends for her) of justice and equity, especially because the depositions already taken in her cause will not avail her in any other ordinary Court; and her witnesses (of the wrongs done her beyond seas) being sea-faring men, are not to be produced at all times to serve her turn, some of them (who have been examined already in her cause) being since gone again to sea; humbly therefore prayeth this honorable Court to take her cause into their considerations; to call the parties above-mentioned (or such of them as are near at hand) to appear forthwith before them, commanding them to bring the said books and memorials into the Court; and upon view thereof, together with such proofs as are already made in the cause, without further trouble or other examinations, to take such order for her relief and satisfaction for the said several wrongs, as their wisdoms shall find agreeable to justice and equity.

[*Elizabeth, Lady Dale*]

•••

Suffering heavy losses in 1626 (among them, Admiral Dale's old ship, *The Moon,* which sank with £55,000 worth of pepper), the East India Company made new rules for venture-capital (Dec. 1626); at which time Lady Dale was certified by the Board as a "delinquent" investor, for having sued the Company. She thereby forfeited her rights in her husband's 1618 shares, a £2,000 investment. Lady Dale sued (Chancery Court, Jan. 1626/7). The Company solicited the Lord Keeper (4 April) to bar depositions taken for the Navy Commission; then moved (31 Oct.) for the complaint to be dismissed, with Lady Dale being held liable for the Company's court costs. As of April 1629, the Chancery suit was still undecided. Meantime, the Board appealed first to King James, then to King Charles for aid, saying to Charles: "If his Majesty do not effectually curb the insolence of the Dutch, the [East India] Company can promise to themselves nothing but loss and destruction of their estates […] Since Sir Thomas Dale's going out, there hath been no good returns" (30 May 1627).

Elizabeth Dale's last will and testament is dated 4 July 1640 (prob. 2 Dec.). She died without collecting one reale of that £20,000 that her husband took from the Chinese. All was not lost: Lady Dale died possessed of more than one thousand acres of prime Virginia real estate that Sir Thomas took from the Powhatans.

Elizabeth Arnold (fl. 1616)

I am no couer for a puppet play,
I haue no cerusse in mine Iuory boxe,
In dressing me I spend not all the day,
I neuer learnd to phrizle spangled locks.
        —"Sonet," in R. Brathwaite, *The Golden Fleece* (1611, sig. G8r)

THE OVERBURY MURDER, when discovered in 1615, produced a flood of news-related pamphlets; one of which darkly intimates that the poisoned knight would still be alive, were it not for the bewitching lipstick, rouge, powder, and face-paint that can turn lords into lechers, and courtesans into killers. The tract is titled, *A Discourse against Painting and Tincturing of Women. Wherein the Abominable Sinnes of Murther and Poysoning, Pride and Ambition, Adultery and Witchcraft are Set Foorth & Discovered. Whereunto is Added The Picture of a Picture; or, The Character of a Painted Woman.* The author and editor, Thomas Tuke (1580 - 1657), issues a warning: Let all men abhor golden locks, rosy cheeks, and a fair complexion unless *very* certain that the effect has not been achieved with artificial beauty aids. Reverend Tuke, a widower, had remarried only a few months prior, taking as his second wife the daughter of William Stampe of Berkshire, a maiden who (it may be presumed) did not wear cosmetics; or at least, not after she married Pastor Tom. But face-paint, for Thomas Tuke, was not merely personal; rather, it was an issue of national and eternal security: he fears that women's cosmetics in a modern society contribute to all of the seven deadly sins and to most of the more ordinary ones.

A frequent pamphleteer and self-promoter, Rev. Tuke supplemented his meager income as a vicar by publishing translations, plus many of his own original sin-thumping sermons (twenty-three titles, 1607-1625, several of which were twice printed). Most of his books begin with a laudatory epistle dedicatory, addressed to one or more B-list patrons from whom Tuke expected to receive a handsome gratuity. A fierce anti-papist with a long C.V., he never plainly states whether the Church of Rome (that "mother of fornications"), or Woman generally, represents the greatest single danger to Christian manhood; but he is fond of neither.

A Discourse against Painting is addressed to the general public. Hoping to capitalize on widespread interest in a high-profile homicide, Tuke models his 1615 discourse on *Sir Thomas Overbury His Wife* (a best-seller). Overbury in his 1612 poem ("A Wife") had described, for the edification of his friend Robert Carr, the qualities of the ideal Christian spouse; for which service, Overbury was poisoned with fruit tarts prepared for him by that less-than-ideal exemplar of womanhood, Frances Howard Devereux. Many times reprinted, Overbury's *Wife* owed much of its enduring popularity to the additions: these included prefatory poems and satirical "News" headlines contributed by the social circle of the late Sir Thomas; augmented further by witty Theophrastan "Characters," a popular genre throughout the Stuart period.

Having composed his own Theophrastan "Picture of a Picture; or, The Character of a Painted Woman," Rev. Tuke had thoughts of expanding his readership. Toward that end, he invited his circle of acquaintance to contribute prefatory verses to his next publication, which was to be a denunciation of women's face-paint. Many of those who were asked took pleasure in the assignment – perhaps more pleasure than Tuke intended. The twelve contributors to Tom Tuke's front matter (preachers, attorneys, scholars) include Thomas Farnaby (the editor of Perseus and Juvenal) and John Owen (the well-known epigrammatic wit); most of whom (without any hint of sincerity) equate cosmetics with female sexual prostitution. Conspiratorially, they underscore the point by riffing on a Latin word not often spoken in polite dinner conversation, though it was one of five innocent and available Latin words for face-paint: *fucus* (n.) can signify both *rouge* and *dye,* and *disguise* or *sham.*

The Latin titles of all this textual foreplay serve as an Explicit Content advisory for the *fucus, fucum, fuco, fucorum* in the verse that follows, to wit: "Infucatas," by John Jeffery; "Infucatas," by John Owen; "In fucum," by Robert Hall; "De fucaiis," by Robert Felton; "De fuco" and "Ad fucatam," by Edward Tillman; and another "De fuco" by Farnaby.

To this all-male chorus, the title-page author contributes just eight lines of verse, under the modest title, "Again" – a poem whereby Tuke reins in the exuberance of his colleagues. Pastor Tom observes that the very word, *fucus,* should counsel modest women not to touch the stuff, and virtuous men, not to be tempted thereby.

> *Fucus* is paint, and *fucus* is deceit,
> And *fucus* they use, that do mean to cheat.
> Me thinks the very name, should stir up shame,
> And make it hateful, to each modest dame. [...] (sig. A4v)

(Rev. Tuke's meter is lumpy but the lyrics might do well even today, in performance by a Christian rap-star.)

More material was yet needed for the volume. Overbury's *Wife* had been augmented with prose contributions by Anne Southwell and Cecilia Boulstred. Following suit, Tuke's *Discourse* includes an argument "Against the Painting of Women [...] translated out of Spanish by Mistress Elizabeth Arnold."

Of Elizabeth Arnold nothing is known. There were at the time at least five adults of this name dwelling in London, four of whom lived within fourteen city blocks of Rev. Tuke's church of St. Giles in the Fields (near the London mansion of Lucy Russell, countess of Bedford). One of those five women was probably the same Elizabeth Arnold who in July 1614 had a gold ring stolen from off her finger by a cutpurse named Thomas Sherfield, only a few doors down from the Chancery Lane bookshop of Thomas Tuke's publisher, Richard Bolton. (On 30 June 1614, Mr. Bolton entered Tuke's *Christian's Looking-Glass* into the London Stationers' Register; it is therefore pleasant to suppose that M^ris. Arnold lost her gold ring while on her way to his bookshop, to purchase a copy of Pastor Tom's *Looking-Glass*.) [1]

The contribution by Arnold, which appears immediately after the glib misogyny of the prefatory verses, regrettably adds to it, being a literal translation of an "Invective" by Andres de Laguna; but Arnold's "Argument against the Painting of Women" is nonetheless one of the few English texts of the period to warn consumers against the physical, rather than just the moral, danger of toxic beauty aids.

Ceruse gave one's face a fashionable pallor, over which vermilion (*fucus*) was applied to rouge the cheeks. A lead-based powder, ceruse not only whitened the face, but over time destroyed it: the hydroxide and carbonate in ceruse reacted with the skin's natural moisture to form acids that slowly ate away the skin, first turning it gray, then causing it to peel. Users applied the poison directly to their skin (sometimes, as they grew older, with a spatula, to repair the craters). Meanwhile, the hydrate-lead in ceruse invaded the entire body. Daily use over an extended period caused hair loss and tooth decay, and eventual death.

Ceruse and vermilion were used by men as well as by women, most frequently by professional actors and male prostitutes, but also by male courtiers. ("I never saw that you did painting need / And therefore to your fair no painting set," writes Shakespeare to his stylish boyfriend, in Sonnet 83). Nor were cosmetics merely for sex appeal: smallpox, which raged throughout the Elizabethan and Jacobean periods, left the face badly scarred, sometimes hideous. Syphilitic sores, which stubbornly resisted more organic treatments, likewise responded to skin creams whose active ingredient was mercury ("quicksilver").

Thomas Tuke's "Discourse against Painting and Tincturing of Women," which follows Arnold's article in the original publication, is a 21,000-word diatribe in four parts: "Of Painting of the Face"; "Of Pride and Ambition"; "Of Adultery"; "Of Witchcraft." Rev. Tuke models these upon the *Essays* (1605) of Sir Francis Bacon, whose patronage Tuke sought and eventually obtained. Less urbane than Bacon, Tuke bitterly condemns popery, face-paint, and pride. Popery, face-paint, and adultery. Popery, face-paint, and witchcraft. Along the way, in a towering moral rage, Tuke lets slip with remarks that he could not have uttered during the reign of Elizabeth, for fear of having his ears trimmed (England's late queen was a great and habitual consumer of ceruse, and not just for special occasions, but daily; some say it's what killed her, at age 70.) Tuke's bitter "Discourse" is here omitted. So, too, together his "Picture of a Picture; or, The Character of a Painted Woman," which was the *raison d'etre* for the entire publication and probably the cleverest thing that Thomas Tuke ever wrote – though somewhat less clever, say, than the essay of John Donne "That Women Ought to Paint." Donne argues glibly, "If her face be painted upon a board or a wall, thou wilt love it; and the board, and the wall. Canst thou loathe it then, when it smiles, speaks, and kisses, because *it* is painted? [...] If in kissing or breathing upon her, the painting fall off, thou art angry. Wilt thou be so too, if it stick on? Thou didst love her: if thou beginn'st to hate her then, it is because she is *not* painted." [2]

---

[1] *gold ring*] See Sess. Roll 533/79, 86. G.D.R. 2/27d. *Sessions of the Peace* (*1614*), ed. Le Hardy (1936).

[2] *That Women Ought to Paint*] ed. DWF from Donne, *Juvenilia* (1633), B1r-2r.

The Invective of Doctor Andreas de Laguna, a Spaniard and Physician to Pope Julius III, "Against the Painting of Women," in his *Annotations upon Dioscorides*, 51.5. chap. 62

Translated out of Spanish by Mistress Elizabeth Arnold

THE CERUSE, or white lead, wherewith women use to paint themselves was, without doubt, brought in use by the Devil, the capital enemy of nature, therewith to transform human creatures – of fair, making them ugly, enormious and abominable. For certainly it is not to be believed that any simple women, without a great inducement and instigation of the Devil, would ever leave their natural and graceful countenances, to seek others that are suppositions and counterfeits, and should go up and down whited and sized-over with paintings laid one upon another in such sort that a man might easily cut off a curd or cheesecake from either of their cheeks. Amongst which unhappy creatures, there are many who have so betarred their faces with these mixtures and slubber-sauces, that they have made their faces of a thousand colors; that is to say, some as yellow as the marigold, others a dark green, others blunket color, others as of a deep red, dyed in the wool. [1]

O desperate madness, O hellish invention, O devilish custom! Can there be any greater dotage or sottishness in the world than for a woman, in contempt of Nature (who like a kind mother giveth to every creature whatsoever is necessary to it, in its kind), to cover her natural face and that pure complexion which she hath received, with stench of plasters and cataplasms? [2]

What shall God say to such in the Last Judgment, when they shall appear thus masked before Him with these anti-faces? "Friends, I know you not! Neither do I hold you for My creatures, for these are not the faces that I formed." Thus the use of this ceruse (besides the rotting of the teeth and the unsavory breath which it causeth), being ministered in paintings, doth turn fair creatures into infernal Furies. Wherefore let all gentlewomen and honorable matrons that make price of their honesty and beauty leave these base arts to the common strumpets, of whom they are fittest to be used, that by that filthiness they may be known and noted. [3]

Yet do I not altogether mislike that honest women should wash themselves, and seek to make their faces smooth, but that they should use the barley water, or the water of lupines, or the juice of lemons, and infinite other things which Dioscorides prescribes as cleanly and delicate to clear the face, and not go continually with rank smells of ointments and plasters about them. [4]

Howbeit that you may not think that this unhappy trade and practice of painting is altogether new and of late brought into the world, I will recount unto you a story, which Galen allegeth in that little book of his, which he entituleth, *An Exhortation to Good Arts.* Phryne, a famous harlot of Athens, being present at a great feast or banquet where every one of the guests might by turns command what he pleased to the rest there invited, she seeing many women there that were painted with ceruse, enjoined that they should execute her command very severely, which was that they should bring a bowl full of warm water, and that they should all wash their faces therein – which was done without gainsaying, for that was the law of the feast. Whereupon the faces of all the women there present appeared foully deformed and stained over, the painting running down their cheeks to their utter shame and confusion, and the horror of all that stood by, to whom they seemed and appeared as horrible monsters. Only Phryne appeared much more beautiful and fair than before; for albeit her life were not free from blame, yet was her beauty and comely grace pure, natural, and without artifice.

European cosmetics box and utensils, 17th C (Nat'l Palace Mus., Taipei)

"But God be thanked," sayeth [Dr. Andreas de Laguna], "our ladies of Spain are so fair of themselves, that they have no need of anything to clear their complexions, but only a little orpin, and soliman, or mercury sublimate." [5]

---

[1] *enormious*] monstrous;   *sized-over*] covered with size, a glutinous base used in cosmetics, paint, and glue; *betarred*] with a pun on *bettered*; Q *betard*;   *blunket color*] light blue.

[2] *cataplasms*] poultices made of herbs and milk.

[3] *make price*] value.

[4] *barley water*] a drink made by the decoction of pearl barley;   *water of lupines*] lupinin, a glucoside obtained from the seeds of *Lupinus albus.*

[5] *orpin*] orpiment; trisulfide of arsenic;   *soliman*] *i.e.*, calomel, the protochloride of mercury.

Now, that you may know that he *flouteth* his countrywomen, hear what [de Laguna] sayeth of this soliman in his annotation upon the 69th chapter [of Dioscorides]: "The excellency of this mercury sublimate," sayeth he, "is such that the women who often paint themselves with it, though they be very young, they presently turn old, with withered and wrinkled faces like an ape; and before age come upon them, they tremble, poor wretches, as if they were sick of the staggers, reeling, and full of quicksilver, for so are they. For the soliman and quicksilver differ only in this, that the soliman is the more corrosive and biting – insomuch that, being applied to the face, it is true that it eateth out the spots and stains of the face, but so that withal it drieth up and consumeth the flesh that is underneath; so that, of force, the poor skin shrinketh – as they speak of the famous *pantofle* of an ancient squire called Petro Capata, which, being often besmeared over to make it black and to give it luster, it shrunk and wrinkled and became too short for his foot. [1]

This harm and inconvenience, although it be great, yet it might well be dissembled if others greater than this did not accompany it; such as are a stinking breath, the blackness and corruption of the teeth, which this soliman engendereth. For if quicksilver alone – applied only to the soles of the feet, once or twice, and that in a final quantity – doth mar and destroy the teeth, what can be expected from the soliman, which is without comparison more powerful and perinative, and is applied more often, and in greater quantity, to the very lips and cheeks? So that the infamous inconveniencies which result from this mercury sublimate might be somewhat the more tolerable, if they did stick and stay only in them who use it and did not descend to their offspring. For this infamy is like to original sin, and goes from generation to generation: whenas the child born of them, before it be able to go, doth shed his teeth one after another, as being corrupted and rotten – not through his fault, but by reason of the viciousness and taint of the mother that painted herself; who, if she loathe and abhor to hear this, let her forbear to do the other. [2]

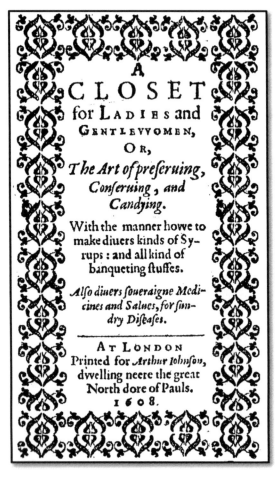

A
C L O S E T
for L A D I E S and
G E N T L E V V O M E N,
O R,
The Art of preſeruing,
Conſeruing, and
Candying.

With the manner howe to
make diuers kinds of Sy‐
rups : and all kind of
banqueting ſtuffes.

Alſo diuers ſoueraigne Medi‐
cines and Salues, for ſun‐
dry Diſeaſes.

A T L O N D O N
Printed for *Arthur Iohnſon,*
dwelling neere the great
North dore of Pauls.
1 6 0 8.

The anonymous (possibly female) author of a popular Jacobean cookbook urges homeopathic cosmetics. "*To Anoint the Face and to Make it White*: Take fresh bacon grease, and the whites of eggs, and stamp them together, and a little powder of bays; and anoint your face therewith, and it will make it white. *For a Fair Face, Proved Another Way*: Take plantain and white vinegar, and still them together, and wash your face therewith fifteen days, morning and evening; and after this, drink a draught of vinegar in the morning, once in three days. *To Make the Face White*, and *Fair*: Take rosemary, and boil it in white wine, and wash thy face therewith, and you shall be fair; then take oregano, and stamp it, and take the juice thereof, and put it all together, and wash thy face therewith." And for teens, "*Against red pimples of the face*: Take an ounce of camphire; as much, of brimstone, beaten; myrrh, frankincense, of each, four drams; of rose water, a pound; put all these in a glass, and set it in the sun ten days and then lay it on the places. *Another*: Take the distilled water of ash-tree, tamarinds (oft eaten), wine of strawberries, laid upon the face. *Another*: Take the distilled water of mullein and a little camphire, mixed together, and laid to the face" (162-3). Or else, "Take bayberries and pluck off the husks and make fine powder thereof, and temper it with honey, and anoint thy face therewith six times, and it will help you."

—*A Closet for Ladies and Gentlewomen* (1608), 188-9.

---

[1] *quicksilver*] mercury in liquid form; *pantofle*] slipper.

[2] *perinative*] unnatural (unexampled in the *OED*); *final quantity*] limited amount; *to go*] to walk.

Rachel Speght (Procter) (1598 – c.1660)

> *The Bayter of Women hath blasphemed God,*
> Ergo, *he ought to die the death.*
> —R. Speght, *A Mouzell for Melastomus* (1616), p. 34

RACHEL SPEGHT at age nineteen became the first English woman ever to a publish an argument for women's rights. About her mother, virtually nothing is known, not even her name. Her father, James Speght, was rector of St. Mary Magdalene in Milk Street, London; from 1611, he was rector also of St. Clement in Eastcheap. These two "livings" – which came to £120 yearly, plus another £20 "from the church stock" of St. Mary's – enabled Rev. Speght to raise his children amidst plenty, and to invest in real estate in and around Deptford, where he later retired. [1]

[margin: claim to fame]

The high point of James Speght's career came on 6 January 1609/10, when he was invited to preach to the Lord Mayor and Aldermen of London. For that occasion he delivered "The Day-Spring of Comfort," which sounds rather like the name of a good mattress but was nothing of the sort: in his text of 11,000 words, Speght for two hours thundered down the wrath of God upon Roman Catholicism ("idolatrous masses"), Jesuits ("the limbs of Antichrist"), and infidels ("unbelieving Jews"). He denounced both the City of London ("each corner evaporating the stink of filthy whoredoms and adultery") and its suburbs ("her filthiness is in her skirts"). As a daring climax, Speght scolded the Mayor and Aldermen for their religious tolerance ("a grievous fault, and defect of duty"), and demanded that the "magistrates put life into penal laws" by putting Roman Catholics in prison. Pastor Jamey was never invited back. [2]

[margin: surprising]

Rachel Speght, aged twelve at the time, may already have been living elsewhere than under her father's roof. It was common practice among the English gentry to board pre-pubescent daughters in the home of a wealthier neighbor, there to receive tutoring in academic subjects, to acquire genteel manners, and to remain out of the way as the parents shopped around for an advantageous marriage. Rachel was perhaps placed in the London home of Thomas Moundford, a prominent member of Speght's Milk Street congregation (and second in wealth only to Sir Baptist Hicks). Dr. Moundford was a well-respected physician, six times president of the Royal College. His wife Mary (*née* Hill) was Rachel's godmother; she was the obvious choice to supervise the maiden's education.

[margin: sending your daughter to learn in another's house]

In her *Muzzle for Melastomus* (1616), Rachel Speght regrets her "defective" knowledge and "little smattering of learning." In *Mortality's Memorandum* (1621), she partly explains: an "occurrence" (prior to the Swetnam controversy) compelled her to abandon her studies and return home to Milk Street: "I therefore to that place returned again / From whence I came," she laments, "and where I must remain." [3]

The occasion: her father had fallen victim to a "grievous and long-languishing malady." [4]

In September 1615, Dr. Moundford's expert medical care and Rachel's daily attendance at last gave Pastor Speght "some strength," enough to return to the pulpit. To celebrate his recovery, he dusted off his *Day-Spring of Comfort* and published it, dedicating the book to Sir Baptist Hicks. [5]

Dr. Moundford all this while had been treating the unfortunate Arbella Stuart, imprisoned in the Tower of London for the offense of having married a man of her own choosing. After Arbella began her hunger strike, Moundford could do little to save her. Arbella Stuart died on 25 September 1615.

[margin: hunger strike of death]

Shortly after these events, and adding to Rachel's growing impatience with the prevailing gender ideology, came the publication of Joseph Swetnam's famous diatribe against women: *The Arraignment of Lewd, Idle, Froward, and Unconstant Women* (1615) is a pithy digest of every argument ever advanced why men should despise and avoid the other half of the human race. Swetnam's book made *querelle des femmes* a topic of dinner conversation all across Britain: he "put his book i'the press, and published it, and made a thousand men and wives fall out" – and not just married couples, but fathers and daughters. [6]

[margin: divided the sexes]

---

[1] *mother*] Rachel's mother may be the "Alyce Cawell" (Cowell) who married "Jeames Spade" 23 Jan. 1596 in London (International Genealogical Index); for Rachel's biography, see H. Speight (2002), and Keene (1987), 24-6.

[2] *idolatrous masses…defect of duty*] James Speght, *Day-Spring* (1615), pp. 12, 21, 28, 62, 61.

[3] *defective…remain*] R. Speght, "To the Reader" (F1r), *"*Dream" (234-240), *Muzzle* (1621).

[4] *grievous…malady*] R. Speght, *Mortality's Memorandum* (1621), B4r.

[5] *Day-Spring*] Entered in the Stationers' Register on 29 October 1614; *some strength*] sig. 4v.

[6] *put his book…wives fall out*] *Swetnam the Woman-Hater* (1620), sig. K1v.

Still living at home, but with a father who was able now to fend for himself, Rachel set out to write a rebuttal to Swetnam, in two parts ("A Muzzle for Melastomus" and "Certain Queries to the Baiter of Women"). She had this work printed under her own name, under the imprint of Thomas Archer – the same publicity-loving London stationer who published *The Arraignment of Women*.

Speght makes some unwelcome concessions. She credits the myth of an originary father from whose rib woman took her first birth. She concedes that woman brought sin, disease, and death into what had been a perfect world. She takes for granted that man, not woman, is "the most excellent creature under the canopy of heaven," and she accepts that every woman must have, for her "head," a virtuous man. Ester Sowernam, in her own, more secular reply, to Swetnam, faults Speght, "a minister's daughter," for "the slenderness of her reply" (a remark that left Speght still bristling in 1621); but from within the confines of her biblical world view, Rachel Speght is remarkably inventive: she uses her rhetorical brush to whitewash the Bible's patriarchalism, and extracts from the Good Book great cause for her readers to reject, or at least to temper, the gender bias that not only made Swetnam's book possible, but made it a best-seller. Figuring Swetnam as a black-mouthed dog, Speght mocks *The Arraignment of Women* as "a deformed object," "a pestiferous obtrectation," "a wry-necked pot," "a tailor's cushion that is botched together of shreds [...] altogether without method, irregular, without grammatical concordance, and a promiscuous mingle-mangle." The "absurdities therein contained are so many," writes Speght, "that to answer them severally, were as frivolous a work as to make a trap for a flea." She nonetheless goes on to present a reasoned rebuttal, answering Swetnam's smugness with her own inventive readings of Scripture; and she underscores Swetnam's grammatical and rhetorical lapses with her own snarkily inventive spelling: "If it bee true, *asse* you affirme, [...] such a monster in nature *asse* yourself [...] And where-*asse* you say [...] *Asse* you not onely in this place, but also in others have done" ("To the Reader," sig. F1).

Speght's rebuttal was followed by others: Daniel Tuvill, *Asylum Veneris; or A Sanctuary for Ladies* (1616); William Goddard, *A Satirical Dialogue* (1616); Ester Sowernam, pseud., *Ester Hath Hanged Haman* (1617); Constantia Munda, pseud., *The Worming of a Mad Dog* (1617); Christopher Newstead, *An Apology for Women: or, Womens Defense* (1620). These were followed by *Swetnam, the Woman-Hater, Arraigned by Women*, a remarkably sympathetic comedy, performed by Queen Anna's Men in 1618-19 and published in 1620. But where each of the many rebuttals to Swetnam was printed only once, *The Arraignment* outsold them all; copies of which survive from editions dated 1615, 1617, 1622, 1628, 1629, 1634, 1637, 1645, 1660, 1667, 1682, 1792, 1707, 1714, 1720, and 1733. But Mad Dog Swetnam can hardly be said to have had the last laugh. Finding himself placed in the position of the feminine, shamefaced, silenced and marginalized, Swetnam for his next book-project fought to repair his injured narcissism with *The School of the Noble and Worthy Science of Defense* – a fencing manual. The author complains bitterly of readers who "will never commend nor allow any other man's manhood," and concludes his discourse with a threat: if any critic dare speak against this second book, Swetnam shall "answer them not only with words, but with weapons" (*School*, 195-7).

In June 1620, in Deptford, Mrs. Speght died suddenly. Six months later, as a tribute to her mother, Speght published a volume of poetry: *Mortalities Memorandum, with A Dream Prefixed*. Dedicated by Rachel to her godmother, Mary Moundford, the "Memorandum" is a conventional Christian meditation on the brevity of life and the necessity of eternal salvation. More interesting, and included here, is the prefixed "Dream," in which Speght revisits her role in the Swetnam debate; professes to have foreseen her mother's death in a vision; and defends the education of women.

On 18 January 1620/1, Speght registered her *Memorandum* to be printed. On that same day, her father registered a new will and testament, one that provided his children with only token bequests of books and cash; and those, only on condition that Rachel and her siblings refrain from suing Elizabeth Smith, a widow sixteen years his junior whom Rev. James Speght named as his executrix and principal heir. [1]

Three weeks later, on February 12th, James Speght and Elizabeth Smith were married. And on August 6th, Rachel Speght, 24, married William Procter, 29. That Rachel had her father's blessing is doubtful: the ceremony was held at St. Mary Woolchurch, not at one of Rev. Speght's two churches.

Rev. Will Procter was, however, as staunchly pious as his Puritan father-in-law. *The Watchman, Warning* (1625), Procter's only publication, is a 55-page rant in which Rachel's husband, the eponymous Watchman, warns his readers of God's wrath against "The follies of the times": "Most men, but especially *women*, are more painful and curious in tricking their bodies than in preparing their hearts for the

---

[1] *will*] To Rachel, Speght bequeathed the *Workes* of the Puritan divine, Richard Greenham (though Rachel was not, like her father, a Puritan), and a copy of *Maison Rustique; or, The Country Farm*. The second marriage evidently gave James Speght a new lease on life: he died in 1637, at which time Rachel doubtless received the promised books.

services of the Lord. Many dainty dames are wont to waste many hours in painting and signifying of their bodies, but they cannot afford one half-hour to read, meditate, and pray." Feeling perhaps the pinch of temptation, Procter condemns "brazen-faced strumpets" who "entice men as they pass in the open streets." But he condemns as well men who "spend all (or the greater part of their most precious time) in feasting delicately, in drinking immoderately, in singing profanely, in dancing wantonly, and such-like sinful mirth and jollity" (*Watchman,* 29, 7, 14).

Thanks, perhaps, to Rachel's temporizing influence, Will Procter in middle age loosened his collar. But he may also have relaxed his exacting standards of Christian virtue: from 1641 until his eviction as rector of Stradishall three years later, Procter was the object of bitter complaints by residents of his parish. Certain self-described "godly" Christians complained to Parliament that the minister of Stradishall was a "ceremonialist," one who resisted demolition of the altar-rails despised by Puritans, and retained kneeling for prayer. At the parsonage (it was alleged) "servants worked on appointed fast days, and Procter did his hedging on the sabbath. There were cards and other games played in the house, 'night after night,' and the ale flowed freely." Rev. Procter was himself "an 'alehouse haunter' who got drunk, he swore, and listened to bawdy tales." Procter once requested and received, but then refused to pay, for "five loads of muck" – yet he prosecuted parishioners who owed him money or who trespassed on his land; and he is said to have dismissed, as "the worst of all sorts of people, " the Puritans in his flock who criticized him. These allegations culminated in a lengthy indictment (1644). Will Procter was fired from his benefice, his living sequestered, and his family evicted from the parsonage. Rev. John Pindar, a certifiable Puritan, was appointed in Procter's place.[1]

ceremonialist tendencies

Rachel's reply to the allegations against her husband have escaped record; but she evidently made her voice heard, often enough: Parliament, in its campaign to purge the Church of old school clergy, generally awarded the evicted dependents a pension amounting to one fifth of the rectory's income. Rachel Procter received the customary settlement for herself and her children, but only on her good behavior, conditions which included "Mrs. Procter removing out of the said town and residing three miles from thence, and avoiding all occasions of raising or fomenting any faction in the said parish against Mr. Pindar." The Procters thereafter operated a school. At the Restoration, Will Procter was restored to his living but died shortly after, in the spring of 1661. Rachel, not mentioned in his will, evidently died first.[2]

severance package

Woodcut from *Swetnam the Woman-Hater, Arraigned by Women,* performed by the Queen's Men

---

[1] *Complained to Parliament*] quotations and details are from Helen Speight (2002), 458-9.

[2] *Ibid.*

To all virtuous Ladies honorable or worshipful, and to all other of Hevah's sex fearing God and leaving their just reputation, grace and peace through Christ, to eternal glory:

IT WAS the simile of that wise and learned Lactantius, that if fire, though but with a small spark kindled, be not at the first quenched, it may work great mischief and damage. So likewise may the scandals and defamations of the malevolent in time prove pernicious if they be not nipped in the head at their first appearance. The consideration of this (right honorable and worshipful ladies) hath incited me (though young, and the unworthiest of thousands) to encounter with a furious enemy to our sex; lest, if his unjust imputations should continue without answer, he might insult and account himself a *victor*; and by such a conceit deal as historiographers report the viper to do – who in the wintertime doth vomit forth her poison and in the springtime sucketh the same up again, which becometh twice as deadly as the former; and this our pestiferous enemy, by thinking to provide a more deadly poison for women than already he hath foamed forth may evaporate (by an addition unto his former illiterate pamphlet entituled *The Arraignment of Women*) a more contagious obtrectation than he hath already done – and indeed, hath threatened to do.

Secondly, if it should have had free passage without any answer at all (seeing that *tacere* is *quasi consentire*) the vulgar ignorant might have believed his diabolical infamies to be infallible truths, not to be infringed; whereas now they may plainly perceive them to be but the scum of heathenish brains, or a building raised without a foundation (at least from sacred Scripture) which the wind of God's truth must needs cast down to the ground. [1]

A third reason why I have adventured to fling this stone at vaunting Goliah is, to comfort the minds of all Hevah's sex, both rich and poor, learned and unlearned, with this antidote: that if the fear of God reside in their hearts, maugre all adversaries, they are highly esteemed and accounted of in the eyes of their gracious Redeemer, so that they need not fear the darts of envy or obtrectators. For shame and disgrace (sayeth Aristotle) is the end of them that shoot such poisoned shafts. Worthy therefore of imitation is that example of Seneca, who when he was told that a certain man did exclaim and rail against him, made this mild answer, "Some dogs bark more upon custom than curstness"; and some speak evil of others, not that the defamed deserve it, but because through custom and corruption of their hearts they cannot speak well of any. This I allege as a paradigmatical pattern for all women noble and ignoble to follow, that they be not enflamed with choler against this our enraged adversary, but patiently consider of him according to the portraiture which he hath drawn of himself, his writings being the very emblem of a monster.

This my brief apology (right honorable and worshipful) did I enterprise, not as thinking myself more fit than others to undertake such a task, but as one who (not perceiving any of our sex to enter the lists of encountering with this our grand enemy among men, I being out of all fear because armed with the truth), [...] did no whit dread to combat with our said malevolent adversary. And if in so doing I shall be censured by the judicious to have the victory, and shall have given content unto the wronged, I have both hit the mark whereat I aimed and obtained that prize which I desired. But if Zoilus shall adjudge me presumptuous in dedicating this my chirograph unto personages of so high rank (both because of my insufficiency in literature and tenderness in years), I thus apologize for myself, that seeing the Baiter of Women hath opened his mouth against noble as well as ignoble, against the rich as well as the poor, therefore meet it is that they should be joint spectators of this encounter; and withal in regard of my imperfection both in learning and age, I need so much the more to impetrate patronage from some of power to shield me from the biting wrongs of Momus, who oftentimes setteth a rankling tooth into the sides of Truth. Wherefore I (being of Decius's mind, who deemed himself safe under the shield of Caesar) have presumed to shelter myself under the wings of you (honorable personages) against the persecuting heat of this fiery and furious dragon; desiring that you would be pleased not to look so much *ad opus*, as *ad animum*. [2]

And so, not doubting of the favorable acceptance and censure of all virtuously affected, I rest
Your Honors and Worships humbly at commandment,

Rachel Speght

---

[1] *tacere ... quasi consentire*] Under Roman law, silence when accused was considered tacit consent.

[2] *Zoilus*] a Cynic philosopher and common figure for a carping critic; *chirograph*] a public instrument in writing; *Momus*] in Greek myth, the god of blame and mockery; *ad opus...ad aninum*] at (my) work... at (his) animus.

A Muzzle for Melastomus, the Cynical Baiter of and Foul-Mouthed Barker against Hevah's Sex:[1]
Or, An Apologetical Answer to that Irreligious and Illiterate Pamphlet Made by Jo[seph]
Sw[etnam] and by him entituled, **The Arraignment of Women**

by Rachel Speght

SEDUCER OF THE VULGAR sort of men,
Was Satan crept into thy filthy pen,
E nflaming thee with such infernal smoke,
T hat (if thou had'st thy will) should women choke?
N efarious fiends thy sense herein deluded,
A nd from thee all humanity excluded,
Monster of men (worthy no other name),
    For that thou did'st assay our sex to shame!

    RA. SP.

Not unto the veriest idiot that ever set pen to paper, but to the cynical Baiter of women, or meta-morphosed Misogynes, Joseph Swetnam:

FROM STANDING WATER (which soon putrifies) can no good fish be expected, for it produceth no other creatures but those that are venomous or noisome – as snakes, adders, and such-like. Semblably, no better stream can we look should issue from your idle corrupt brain, than that whereto *the ruff of your fury* (to use your own words) hath moved you to open the sluice; in which excrement of your roving° cogitations, you have used such irregularities touching concordance, and observed so disordered a method, as I doubt not to tell you that a very accidence scholar would have quite put you down, in both! You appear herein not unlike that painter who, seriously endeavoring to portray Cupid's bow, forgot the string: for you – being greedy to botch up your mingle-mangle invective against women – have not therein observed, in many places, so much as *grammar* sense. But the emptiest barrel makes the loudest sound; and so we will account of you.[2]

Many propositions have you framed, which (as you think) make much against women. But if one would make a logical assumption, the conclusion would be flat against your *own* sex. Your dealing wants so much discretion that I doubt whether to bestow so good a name as "the Dunce" upon you (but minority bids me keep within my bounds; and therefore I only say unto you, that your corrupt heart and railing tongue hath made you a fit scribe – for the Devil).[3]

In that you have termed your virulent foam the *Bear-baiting of Women*, you have plainly displayed your own disposition to be cynical, in that there appears no other dog or bull to bait them but yourself. Good had it been for you to have put on that muzzle which Saint James would have all Christians to wear: "Speak not evil one of another" (James 4:11); and then had you not seemed so like the serpent Porphirus as now you do – which, though full of deadly poison, yet being toothless hurteth none so much as himself. For you – having gone beyond the limits not of humanity alone but of Christianity – have done greater harm unto your own soul than unto women, as may plainly appear: First, in dishonoring of God by palpable blasphemy, wresting and perverting every place of Scripture that you have alleged; which by the testimony of Saint Peter is to the destruction of them that so do (1 Pet. 3:16). Secondly, it appears by your disparaging of, and opprobrious speeches against, that excellent work of God's hands which in His great love He perfected for the comfort of man. Thirdly and lastly, by this your hodge-podge of heathenish sentences, similes, and examples, you have set forth yourself in your right colors, unto the view of the world; and I doubt not but the judicious will account of you according to your demerit. As for the vulgar sort, which have no more learning than you have showed in your book, it is likely they will applaud you for your pains.

---

[1] *Hevah*] Eve.

[2] *very accidence scholar*] mere grammar-school boy; *concordance*] coherence; *botch up*] cobble together.

[3] *minority*] the fact that I'm not yet of age.

As for your bugbear (or "advice") unto women, that whatsoever they do think of your work, they should conceal it, lest in finding fault, they bewray their galled backs to the world (in which you allude to that proverb, "Rub a galled horse, and he will kick"): unto it, I answer by way of apology, that though every galled horse, being touched, doth kick; yet every one that kicks, is not galled: so that you might as well have said that "Because burnt folks dread the fire, therefore none fear fire but those that are burnt," as made that illiterate conclusion which you have absurdly inferred.

[margin note: Your metaphors suck]

In your title-leaf you arraign none but "Lewd, Idle, Froward and Unconstant Women"; but in the sequel (through defect of memory as it seemeth), forgetting that you had made a distinction of good from bad, condemning all in general, you advise men to beware of, and not to match, with any of these six sorts of women, *viz*: "good and bad, fair and foul, rich and poor." But this doctrine of devils, Saint Paul (foreseeing [it] would be broached in the latter times) gives warning of (1 Tim. 4:3).

There also you *promise* a commendation of "wise, virtuous, and honest" women; when, as in the subsequent, the worst words and filthiest epithets that you can devise, you bestow on them in general, excepting *no* sort of women. Herein may you be likened unto a man which upon the door of a scurvy house sets this superscription: "HERE IS A VERY FAIR HOUSE TO BE LET"; whereas, the door being opened, it is no better than a dog-hole and dark dungeon. *[margin note: I love this]*

Further, if your own words be true – that you wrote with your hand but not with your heart – then are you an hypocrite in print; but it is rather to be thought that your pen was the bewrayer of the abundance of your mind, and that this was but a little mortar to daub up again' the wall which you intended to break down.

The revenge of your railing work we leave to Him who hath appropriated vengeance unto Himself; whose pen-man hath included "railers" in the catalogue of them that shall *not* inherit God's kingdom, and [leave] yourself unto the mercy of that just Judge who is able to save and to destroy.

Your undeserved friend,
RACHEL SPEGHT

Of Woman's Excellency (with the causes of her creation and of the sympathy which ought to be in man and wife each toward other).

[...] THE WORK OF CREATION being finished, this approbation thereof was given by God himself, that "All was very good"; if *all*, then *woman* – who (excepting man) is the most excellent creature under the canopy of heaven. But if it be objected by any—

First, that woman, though created good, yet by giving ear to Satan's temptations brought death and misery upon all her posterity (Gen. 1:31°);

Secondly, that "Adam was not deceived," but that "the woman was deceived, and was in the transgression" (I Tim. 2:14);

Thirdly, that Saint Paul sayeth, "It were good for a man not to touch a woman" (I Cor. 7:1);

Fourthly (and lastly), that of Solomon, who seems to speak against all of our sex: "I have found one man of a thousand, but a woman among them all have I not found" (Ecc. 7:28°; whereof, in its° due place). [1]

—To the first of these objections, I answer that Satan first assailed the woman because "Where the hedge is lowest, most easy it is to get over"; and she, being the weaker vessel, was with more facility to be seduced (like as a crystal glass sooner receives a crack than a strong stone pot). Yet we shall find the offense of Adam and Eve almost to parallel: for as an ambitious desire of being made like unto God was the motive which caused her to eat, so likewise was it his; as may plainly appear by that *ironia*°, "Behold, man is become as one of us" (Gen. 3:22). Not that he was so indeed, but hereby his desire – to attain a greater perfection than God had given him – was reproved. Woman sinned, it is true, by her infidelity – in not believing the word of God but giving credit to Satan's fair promises that she should not die (Gen. 3:4) – but so did the man, too. And if Adam had not approved of that deed which Eve had done and been willing to tread the steps which she had gone, he (being her head) would have reproved her, and have made the commandment a bit to restrain *him* from breaking his Maker's injunction. [2]

---

[1] *Ecc. 7:30*] *i.e.*, Ecc. 7:28.

[2] *ironia*] ironical remark.

[*The stronger vessel.*] For if a man burn his hand in the fire, the bellows that blowed the fire are not to be blamed, but himself rather, for not being careful to avoid the danger; yet if the bellows had not blowed, the fire had not burnt. No more is woman simply to be condemned for man's transgression; for by the free will which (before his fall) he enjoyed, he might have avoided (and been free from being burnt or singed with) that fire which was kindled by Satan and blown by Eve. It therefore served not his turn a whit afterwards to say, "The woman which Thou gavest me, gave me of the tree, and I did eat" (Gen. 3:12); for a penalty was inflicted upon him as well as on the woman – the punishment of *her* transgression being particular to her own sex and to none but the female kind; but for the sin of *man*, the whole earth was cursed (Gen. 3:17). And he, being better able than the woman to have resisted temptation (because the stronger vessel), was first called to account, to show that "To whom much is given, of them much is required," and that he who was the sovereign of all creatures visible should have yielded greatest obedience to God.

[*Shame comes from Adam.*] True it is (as is already confessed) that woman first sinned, yet find we no mention of spiritual nakedness till man had sinned. Then it is said, "Their eyes were opened" – the eyes of their mind and conscience – "and then perceived they themselves naked" (Gen. 3:7); that is, not only bereft of that integrity which they originally had, but felt the rebellion and disobedience of their members in the disordered motions of their now-corrupt nature; which made them for shame to cover their nakedness. Then, and not afore, is it said that they saw it – as if sin were imperfect and unable to bring a deprivation of a blessing received, or death on all mankind, till man (in whom lay the active power of generation) had transgressed. The offense therefore of Adam and Eve is by Saint Austin thus distinguished: "The man sinned against God and himself; the woman against God, herself, and her husband." Yet (in her giving of the fruit to eat) had she no malicious intent towards him, but did therein show a desire to make her husband partaker of that happiness which she thought, by their eating, they should both have enjoyed. This – her giving Adam of that sauce wherewith Satan had served her (whose sourness, afore he had eaten, she did not perceive) – was that which made her sin to exceed his. Wherefore – that she might not of him who ought to honor her be abhorred (I Pet. 3:7) – the first promise that was made in paradise, God makes to woman: that by her seed should the serpent's head be broken; whereupon Adam calls her *Hevah* ("life"; Gen. 3:15); that, as the woman had been an *occasion* of his sin, so should woman bring forth the *Savior* from sin; which was in the fullness of time accomplished (Gal. 4:4); by which was manifested that he is a Savior of believing women no less than of men; that, so the blame of sin may not be imputed to his *creature* (which is good), but to the *will* by which Eve sinned. And yet (by Christ's assuming the shape of man) was it declared that his mercy was equivalent to both sexes; so that, by Hevah's° blessed seed (as Saint Paul affirms), it is brought to pass that male and female are "all one in Christ Jesus" (Gal. 3:28).

[*Adam's fault.*] To the second objection, I answer that the apostle doth not hereby exempt man from sin, but only giveth to understand that the woman was the primary transgressor, and not the man. But that man was not at all deceived was far from his meaning – for he afterward expressly sayeth that "As in Adam all die, so in Christ shall all be made alive" (I Cor. 15:22).

[*St. Paul's change of heart.*] For the third objection – "It is good for a man not to touch a woman" – the apostle makes it not a positive prohibition, but speaks it only because of the Corinths' "present necessity" (who were then persecuted by the enemies of the church; I Cor. 7); for which cause and no other he sayeth, "Art thou loosed from a wife? Seek not a wife" – meaning, whilst the time of these perturbations should continue in their heat. But "If thou art bound, seek not to be loosed." "If thou marriest, thou sinnest not" (only increasest thy care). "For the married careth for the things of this world." "And I wish that you were without care [...] that ye might cleave fast unto the Lord without separation." "For the time remaineth, that they which have wives be as though they had none" (for the persecutors shall deprive you of them, either by imprisonment, banishment, or death); so that manifest it is that the apostle doth not hereby forbid marriage but only adviseth the Corinths to forbear a while till God in mercy should curb the fury of their adversaries. For (as Eusebius writeth) Paul was afterward married himself, the which is very probable, being that interrogatively he sayeth, "Have we not power to lead about a wife (being a sister) as well as the rest of the apostles, and as the brethren of the Lord, and Cephas?" (I Cor. 9:5).[1]

---

[1] *I Cor. 7*] the biblical quotations are a pastiche of I Cor. 7: 1, 26, 27b, 27a, 28a, 33, 32, 35, 29; *being a sister*] i.e., a spiritual sister, a Christian wife; *brethren ... Cephas*] the brothers of Jesus and St. Peter.

[*Solomon's fault.*] The fourth and last objection is that of Solomon: "I have found one man among a thousand, but a woman among them all have I not found" (Ecc. 7:28°); for answer of which, if we look into the story of his life, we shall find therein a commentary upon this enigmatical sentence included: for it is there said that Solomon had seven hundred wives and three hundred concubines, which number, connexed, make one thousand (I Kings 11:3). These women turning his heart away from being perfect with the Lord his God, sufficient cause had he to say that among the said thousand women found he not one upright. He sayeth not that among a thousand women never *any* man found one worthy of commendation, but speaks in the first person singularly, "*I* have not found," meaning in his own experience; for this assertion is to be holden a part of the confession of his former follies, and no otherwise (his repentance being the intended drift of Ecclesiastes).

[*The excellency of women.*] Thus having (by God's assistance) removed those stones whereat some have stumbled, others broken their shins, I will proceed toward the period of my intended task, which is to decipher the excellency of women. [...] The material cause or matter whereof woman was made was of a refined mold, if I may so speak: for man was created of the dust of the earth (Gen. 2:7), but woman was made of a part of man after that he was a living soul. Yet was she not produced from Adam's foot, to be his too-low inferior; nor from his head, to be his superior; but from his side, near his heart, to be his *equal* – that where he is "lord," she may be "lady." And therefore sayeth God concerning man and woman jointly, "Let *them* rule over the fish of the sea and over the fouls of the heaven and over every beast that moveth upon the earth" (Gen. 1:26). This, being rightly considered, doth teach men to make such account of their wives as Adam did of Eve: "This is bone of my bone, and flesh of my flesh" (Gen. 2:23); as also, that they neither do or wish any more hurt unto them than unto their own bodies – for men ought to love their wives as themselves, because "he that loves his wife loves himself" (Eph. 5:28); and never man hated his own flesh (which the woman is) unless a monster in nature. [...]

[*Sympathy between man and woman.*] The final cause or end for which woman was made was to glorify God, and to be a collateral companion for man to glorify *God*, in using her body and all the parts, powers, and faculties thereof, as instruments of his honor – as with her voice, to sound forth his praises, like Miriam and the rest of her company (Exod. 15:20); with her tongue, not to utter words of strife but to give good counsel unto her husband, the which he must not despite – for Abraham was bidden to give ear to Sarah his wife (Gen. 21:12). Pilate was willed by his wife not to have any hand in the condemning of Christ; and a sin it was in him that he list'ned not to her (Mat. 27:19). Leah and Rachel counseled Jacob to do according to the word of the Lord (Gen. 31:16), and the Shunamite put her husband in mind of harboring the prophet Elisha (2 Kings 4:9). Her hands should be open (according to her ability) in contributing towards God's service and distressed servants, like to that poor widow which cast two mites into the treasury; and as Mary Magdalene, Susanna, and Joanna the wife of Herod's steward, with many other, which of their substance ministered unto Christ (Luke 8). Her heart should be a receptacle for God's Word, like Mary, that treasured up the sayings of Christ in her heart (Luke 2°:51). Her feet should be swift in going to seek the Lord in his sanctuary, as Mary Magdalena made haste to seek Christ at his sepulcher (John 20:1). Finally, no power external or internal ought woman to keep idle, but to employ it in some service of God, to the glory of her Creator and comfort of her own soul.

[*Division of household labor.*] The other end for which woman was made was to be a companion and *helper* for man; and if she must be an *helper*, and *but* an helper, then are those husbands to be blamed which lay the whole burthen of domestical affairs and maintenance on the shoulders of their wives. For as yoke-fellows they are to sustain part of each other's cares, griefs, and calamities; but, as if two oxen be put in one yoke, the one being bigger than the other, the greater bears most weight, so the husband (being the stronger vessel) is to bear a greater burthen than his wife; and therefore the Lord said to Adam, "In the sweat of thy face shalt thou eat thy bread, till thou return to the dust" (Gen. 3:19). And Saint Paul sayeth that "he that provideth not for his household is worse than an infidel" (I Tim. 5:8). Nature hath taught senseless creatures to help one another – as the male pigeon, when his hen is weary with sitting on her eggs and comes off from them, supplies her place (that in her absence they may receive no harm) until such time as she is fully refreshed.[1]

Of small birds the cock always helps his hen to build her nest; and while she sits upon her eggs, he flies abroad to get meat for her who cannot then provide any for herself. The crowing cock'rel helps his hen to defend her chickens from peril, and will endanger himself to save her and them from harm. Seeing then that these unreasonable creatures by the instinct of nature bear such affection each to other (that without

---

[1] *senseless*] lacking the human power of reason (as later, *unreasonable*).

any grudge they willingly, according to their kind, help one another), I may reason, *à minore ad majus*, that much more should man and woman, which are reasonable creatures, be helpers each to other in all things lawful, they having the Law of God to guide them, his Word to be a lanthorn unto their feet and a light unto their paths – by which they are excited to a far more mutual participation of each other's burthen than other creatures; so that neither the wife may say to her husband, nor the husband unto his wife, "I have no need of thee" (I Cor. 12:21), no more than the members of the body may so say each to other (between whom, there is such a sympathy that if one member suffer, all suffer with it).[1]

Therefore, though God bade Abraham forsake his country and kindred, yet He bade him not forsake his wife, who (being flesh of his flesh and bone of his bone) was to be copartner with him of whatsoever did betide him, whether joy or sorrow. Wherefore Solomon sayeth, "Woe to him that is alone" (Ecc. 4:10); for when thoughts of discomfort, troubles of this world, and fear of dangers do possess him, he wants a companion to lift him up from the pit of perplexity, into which he is fallen (Ecc. 4:10); for "a good wife," sayeth Plautus, "is the wealth of the mind and the welfare of the heart" – and therefore a meet associate for her husband. And "woman," sayeth Paul, "is the glory of the man" (I Cor. 11:7).

Marriage is a *merri-age*, and this word's paradise, where there is mutual love. […] Thus, if men would remember the duties they are to perform in being heads, some would not stand a-tiptoe as they do, thinking themselves lords and rulers, and account every omission of performing whatsoever they command, whether lawful or not, to be matter of great disparagement, and indignity done them; whereas they should consider that women are enjoined to submit themselves unto their husbands no other-ways than "as to the Lord" (Eph. 5); so that from hence, for man, there ariseth a lesson not to be forgotten: that as the Lord commandeth nothing to be done but that which is right and good, no more must the husband; for if a wife fulfill the evil command of her husband, she obeys him as a tempter, as Sapphira did Ananias (Acts 5:2).

[*Moral discrimination.*] But lest I should seem too partial in praising women so much as I have (though no more than warrant from Scripture doth allow) I add to the premises that I say not, "all women are virtuous," for then they should be more excellent than men – sith of Adam's sons there was Cain as well as Abel, and of Noah's, Cham as well as Sem; so that of men as of women there are two sorts, namely, good and bad, which in Matthew the five-and-twenty chapter, are comprehended under the name of *sheep* and *goats*. And if women were not sinful, then should they not need a Savior. But the Virgin Mary, a pattern of piety, "rejoiced in God her *Savior*" (Luke 1:47); ergo, she was a sinner. In the Revelation, the Church is called the "spouse of Christ"; and in Zachariah, "Wickedness" is called a woman (Zach. 5:7) – to show that of women there are both godly and ungodly. For Christ would not purge his floor if there were not chaff among the wheat, nor should gold need to be 'fined if among it there were no dross. But far be it from anyone to condemn the righteous with the wicked, or good women with the bad, as the baiter of women doth (Gen. 18:25). For though there are some scabbed sheep in a flock, we must not therefore conclude all the rest to be mangy. And though some men, through excess, abuse God's creatures, we must not imagine that all men are gluttons; the which, we may with as good reason do, as condemn all women in general for the offenses of some particulars. Of the good sort is it that I have in this book spoken, and so would I that all that read it should so understand me; for if otherwise I had done, I should have incurred that "woe" which, by the prophet Isaiah, is pronounced against them that "speak well of evil" (Isa. 5:20), and should have "justified the wicked," which thing "is abhominable to the Lord" (Prov. 17:15). […]

The Preface unto the Subsequent

JUDGE of this lion by his paw: for if the forefoot be monstrous, doubtless the whole body is correspondent thereto. The porch indeed is foul, but he that views the sequel, as I have done, shall find a laystall of heathenish assertions, similes, and examples, illiterate composition, irreligious invectives, and (which is worst) impious blasphemies therein included – filthy rubbish, more fit to be heaped up by a pagan than one that beareth the name of a Christian.[2]

But lest it should not only be thought, but also said, that I find fault where none is; or that I do ill to mislike the work and not make the author therewith acquainted – that if he please, he may answer for himself – I think it not amiss to propose some few queries unto the Baiter of women, which I have abstracted out of his "infamous book," as himself confesseth it to be in his Epistle to Women [sig. A3v].

---

[1] *lanthorn*] lantern; Ps. 119:105.

[2] *laystall*] a place where garbage and dung is laid.

Certain Queries to the Baiter of women, with confutation of some part of his diabolical discipline

IF your *assertion* – that "A woman is better lost than found, better forsaken than taken" (page 5, line 4) – be to be credited, methinks, Great pity it is, that afore you were born, there was none so wise as to counsel your father not to meddle with a woman – that he might have escaped those troubles which you affirm that all married men are cumbered with (p. 2, line 20); as also that he might not have begotten such a monster in nature *ass* yourself, who (like the priest which forgot he was parish clerk) defame and exclaim against women as though yourself had never had a mother, or you never been a child. [...]

[margin, handwritten: If only you'd never been born]

You "count it wonderful to see the mad feats of *women*, for she will now be merry, then sad" (p. 11, line 8); but methinks it is far more wonder-*fool* to have one that adventures to make his writing as public as an innkeeper's sign, which hangs to the view of all passengers, to want grammatical concordance in his said writing and join together *women*, plural, and *she*, singular, *as*s you not only in this place, but also in others have done. [...]

"Men I say may live without women, but women cannot live without men" (p. 14, line 18). If any *religious* author had thus affirmed, I should have wondered that unto Satan's suggestions he had so much subjected himself as to cross the Almighty's providence and care for man's good; who positively said, "It is not good for man to be alone" (Gen. 2. 18). But being that the sole testimony hereof in is your own *dico* ["I say"], I marvel no whit at the error, but heartily wish that unto *all* the untruths you have uttered in your infamous book you had subscribed your *dico*, that *none* of them might be adjudged truths. [...]

You counsel all men to "shun idleness" (p. 34, line 19); and yet the first words of your "Epistle to Women" are these: "musing with myself, being idle." Herein you appear not unlike unto a fencer which teacheth another how to defend himself from enemy's blows, and suffers himself to be stricken without resistance: for you warn others to eschew that dangerous vice wherewith (by your own confession) your self is stained. [...]

[margin, handwritten: this juxtaposes well w/ his later book on fencing]

"If God had not made women only to be a plague to man, He would never have called them 'necessary evils'" (p. 31, line 15). Albeit I have not read Seaton or Ramus, nor so much as seen (though heard of) Aristotle's *Organon*°, yet by that I have seen and read in compass of my apprehension, I will adventure to frame an argument or two, to show what danger (for this your blasphemy) you are in: [1]

The Reward according to Law Divine due unto the Baiter of women

TO FASTEN a lie upon God is blasphemy. But the Baiter of women fastens a lie upon God: *ergo*, the Baiter is a blasphemer. The Proposition, I trow, none will gainsay. The assumption, I thus prove: Whosoever affirms God to have called women "necessary evils," fastens a lie upon God. For from the beginning of Genesis to the end of the Revelation is no such instance to be found – but the Baiter affirms God so to have called women. *Ergo*, the Baiter fastens a lie upon God.

[margin, handwritten: Baiter = blasphemer. No evidence to this misogynistic claim]

Whosoever blasphemeth God, ought by His Law, to die. The Baiter of women hath blasphemed God. *Ergo*, he ought to die the death. The Proposition is upon record: Leviticus 24:14-16: ["Let all that heard him lay their hands upon his head, and let all the congregation stone him. And thou shalt speak unto the children of Israel, saying, 'Whosoever curseth his God shall bear his sin.' And he that blasphemeth the name of the Lord, he shall surely be put to death, and all the congregation shall certainly stone him: as well the stranger as he that is born in the land, when he blasphemeth the name of the Lord, shall be put to death."] [...]

Wishing unto every such Misogynes, a Tyburn tiffany (for curation of his swollen neck, which only through a cynical inclination will not endure the yoke of lawful matrimony), I bid farewell. [2]

> **F** ret, fume, or frump at me who will – I care not.
> **I** will thrust forth thy sting to hurt, and spare not!
> **N** ow that the task I undertook is ended,
> **I** dread not any harm to me intended,
> **S** ith justly none therein I have offended.

[margin, handwritten: Acrostic poems are the best way to end a writing]

---

[1] *Seaton or Ramus*] John Seaton (1498-1567), whose *Dialectica* (1572), and Petrus Ramus (1515-1572), whose *Dialecticae Partitiones* (1547), were influential works of logic and rhetoric in the English universities.

[2] *Tyburn tiffany*] a hangman's noose made of finest silk.

Mortality's Memorandum

I KNOW these populous times afford plenty of forward writers and critical readers. My self hath made the number of the one too many, by one; and having been touched with the censures of the other (by occasion of my *muzzling Melastomus*), I am now, as by a strong motive induced (for my rights' sake) to produce and divulge this offspring of my endeavor, to prove them further (futurely) who have (formerly) deprived me of my due, imposing *my* abortive upon the father (of me – but *not*, of *it*!). Their variety of verdicts have verified the adagy, *Quot homines, tot sententiae* ["There are as many opinions, as there are men"]; and doth confirm that apothegm which doth affirm *censure* to be inevitable to a public act. [...] Yet ere I leave, give me leave to put you in mind of Paul's precept: *Be not weary of well-doing, for in due time you shall reap, if you faint not.* [Epistle Dedicatory, A2v-3r].

Part 1: The Dream

WHEN 'splendent *Sol*, which riseth in the east,
Returning thence took harbor in the west;
When *Phoebus* laid her head in *Titan*'s lap,
And creatures sensitive made haste to rest;
When sky, which erst looked like to azure-blue,
Left color bright and put on sable hue: 1

Then did *Morpheus* close my drowsy eyes
And stood as porter at my senses' door,
Diurnal cares excluding from my mind,
Including rest (the salve for labor's sore).
Night's greatest part in quiet sleep I spent.
But nothing in this world is permanent –   2

For ere *Aurora* spread her glittering beams
Or did with robes of light herself invest,
My mental quiet *Sleep* did interdict
By entertaining a nocturnal guest—
A Dream, which did my mind and sense possess,
With more than I by pen can well express.   3

At the appointment of supernal *Power*,
By instrumental means methought I came
Into a place most pleasant to the eye,
Which for the beauty some did "Cosmos" name,
Where stranger-like on everything I gazed,
But, wanting wisdom, was as one amazed.   4

Upon a sudden, as I gazing stood,   [25]
Thought came to me, and asked me of my state,
Inquiring what I was and what I would,
And why I seemed as one disconsolate;
To whose demand, I thus again replied,
"I as a stranger in this place abide.   5

"The haven of my voyage is remote;
I have not yet attained my journey's end.
Yet know I not, nor can I give a guess,
How short a time I in this place shall spend;
For that high power which sent me to this place
Doth only know the period of my race.

"The reason of my sadness at this time
Is 'cause I feel myself not very well.
Untó you I shall much obligèd be,
If for my grief a remedy you'll tell."
Quoth she, "If you your malady will show,
My best advice I'll willingly bestow.

"My grief," quoth I, "is callèd *ignorance*,
Which makes me differ little from a brute:
For animals are led by nature's lore;
Their seeming science is but custom's fruit.   6
When they are hurt, they have a sense of pain
But want the sense to cure themselves again.

"And ever since this grief did me oppress,
Instinct of nature is my chiefest guide;   [50]
I feel disease, yet know not what I ail,
I find a sore, but can no salve provide;
I hungry am, yet cannot seek for food,
Because I know not what is bad or good.

"And sometimes when I seek the golden mean,
My weakness makes me fail of mine intent,   7
That suddenly I fall into extremes.
Nor can I see, a mischief to prevent,
But feel the pain when I the peril find,
Because my malady doth make me blind.

---

1 *Phoebus*] Speght makes Phoebus-Sol a woman; not a mistake for *Phoebe* (the Moon): she (the Sun) goes to bed at nightfall; *Titan*] Ocean, a Titan god of Greek mythology; *sensitive*] sentient; *sable*] black.

2 *Morpheus*] the god of sleep; *Including*] bringing (including rest, excluding all anxiety).

3 *Aurora*] goddess of the dawn; *Sleep did interdict*] Morpheus interrupted sleep with a dream).

4 *supernal*] heavenly; *wanting*] lacking.

---

5 *Thought*] personified (cf. l. 41, *she*); *would*] desired.

6 *Their seeming... fruit*] Their apparent "knowledge" of the world is merely the result of habit or instinct.

7 *the golden mean*] a "happy medium", the course of balance that runs between extremes.

"What is without the compass of my brain,
My sickness makes me say, 'It cannot be;
What I conceive not, cannot come to pass'—
Because for it I can no reason see.
I measure all men's feet by mine own shoe,
And count all well, which I appoint or do.

"The pestilent effects of my disease
Exceed report, their number is so great.
The evils which, through it, I do incur
Are more than I am able to repeat.
Wherefore, good Thought, I sue to thee again,
To tell me how my cure I may obtain."

Quoth she, "I wish I could prescribe your help.
Your state I pity much and do bewail.
But, for my part, though I am much employed, [75]
Yet in my judgment I do often fail.
And therefore I'll commend unto your trial
Experience; of whom, take no denial,

"For she can best direct you what is meet
To work your cure and satisfy your mind."
I thanked her for her love, and took my leave,
Demanding where I might Experience find.
She told me if I did abroad inquire,
'Twas likely *Age* could answer my desire.

I sought, I found. She asked me what I would.
Quoth I, "Your best direction I implore,
For I am troubled with an irksome grief";
Which, when I named, quoth she, "Declare no more—
For I can tell as much as you can say,
And for your cure I'll help you what I may.

"The only medicine for your malady,
By which (and nothing else) your help is wrought,
Is *knowledge*, of the which there is two sorts:
The one is good, the other bad and naught.
The former sort by labor is attained;
The latter may without much toil be gained. [1]

"But 'tis the good which must effect your cure."
I prayed her then that she would further show
Where I might have it. "That I will," quoth she.
"In *Erudition*'s garden it doth grow,   [100]
And in compassion of your woeful case,
Industry shall conduct you to the place." [2]

Dissuasion, hearing her assign my help
And seeing that consent I did detect,
Did many remoras to me propose,
As dullness, and my memory's defect,
The difficulty of attaining lore,
My time, and sex, with many others more;   [3]

Which when I heard, my mind was much perplexed,
And as a horse new-come into the field
Who with a harquebus at first doth start,
So did this shot make me recoil and yield.
But of my fear when some did notice take
In my behalf, they this reply did make: [4]

First quoth *Desire*, "Dissuasion, hold thy peace!
These oppositions come not from above."
Quoth *Truth*, "They cannot spring from reason's root,
And therefore now thou shalt no victor prove."
"No," quoth *Industry*, "be assurèd this:
Her friends shall make thee of thy purpose miss—

"For with my sickle I will cut away
All obstacles that in her way can grow,
And by the issue of her own attempt,
I'll make thee '*Labor omnia vincet*' know."
Quoth *Truth*, "And sith her sex thou dost object, [125]
Thy folly I by reason will detect: [5]

"Both man and woman of three parts consist,
Which Paul doth *body*, *soul*, and *spirit* call:
And from the soul three faculties arise,
The *mind*, the *will*, the *power*; then wherefore shall
A woman have her intellect in vain,
Or not endeavor knowledge to attain?

"The talent God doth give must be employed;
His own with 'vantage he must have again.
All parts and faculties were made for use;
The God of knowledge nothing gave in vain.
'Twas Mary's choice our Savior did approve,
Because that she the better part did love.   [6]

"Cleobulina and Demophila,
With Telesilla, as historians tell
Whose fame doth live, though they have long been dead,
Did all of them in poetry excel.
A Roman matron that Cornelia hight
An eloquent and learnèd style did write.   [7]

---

[1] *knowledge*] here figured as a medicinal herb to salve and cure to the sore of ignorance.

[2] Speght's 1621 text includes Bible citations as marginal notations, here omitted: 1 Thes. 5:23 (at line 128); Luke 19:23 (134), 1 Sam. 2:3 (136); Luke 10:42 (138), Col. 3:10 (205), Prov. 19:2 (210), John 17:3 (222); Prov. 19:2 (210), John 17:3 (222).

[3] *detect*] show, make evident; *again at 125*; *remoras*] hindrances; *lore*] learning.

[4] *harquebus*] a matchlock gun; *doth start*] is startled.

[5] *Labor omnia vincet*] "Labor conquers all"; *sith*] since.

[6] *'vantage*] interest, profit; *the better part*] learning, rather than housework.

[7] *Cleobulina*] Cleobula, daughter of Cleobulus, one of

"Hypatia in astronomy had skill;
Aspasia was in rhetoric so expert
As that Duke Pericles of her did learn;
Areta did devote herself to art,
And by consent (which shows she was no fool)
She did succeed her father in his school.   2 [150]

"And many others here I could produce,
Who were in science counted excellent;
But these examples which I have rehearsed,
To show thy error are sufficient."
Thus having said, she turned her speech to me,
That in my purpose I might constant be.

"My friend," quoth she, "regard not vulgar talk;
For dunghill cocks at precious stones will spurn,
And swine-like natures prize not crystal streams—
Contemnèd mire and mud will serve their turn.
Good purpose seldom oppositions want;
But constant minds Dissuasion cannot daunt.

"Shall every blast disturb the sailor's peace,
Or boughs and bushes, travelers affright?
True valor doth not start at every noise;
Small combats must instruct for greater fight.
Disdain to be with every dart dismayed;
'Tis childish to be suddenly afraid.

"If thou didst know the pleasure of the place
Where knowledge grows, and where thou may'st it gain,
Or rather knew the virtue of the plant,
Thou wouldst not grudge at any cost or pain
Thou canst bestow, to purchase for thy cure
This plant, by which of help thou shalt be sure.

"Let not Dissuasion alter thy intent –   [175]
'Tis sin to nip good motions in the head.
Take courage, and be constant in thy course,
Though irksome be the path which thou must tread.
Sick folks drink bitter medicines to be well;
And to enjoy the nut, men crack the shell."

When Truth had ended what she meant to say,
Desire did move me to obey her will;
Whereto consenting, I did soon proceed
Her counsel (and my purpose) to fulfill—
And by the help of Industry, my friend,
I quickly did attain my journey's end.

Where, being come, *Instruction*'s pleasant air
Refreshed my senses, which were almost dead;
And fragrant flowers of sage and fruitful plants
Did send sweet savors up into my head;
And taste of science, appetite did move,
To augment theòry of things above.

There did the harmony of those sweet birds
(Which higher soar with contemplation's wings
Than barely, with a superficial view,
Denote the value of created things)
Yield such delight as made me to implore
That I might reap this pleasure more and more.

And as I walked, wandering with Desire
To gather that for which I thither came   [200]
(Which, by the help of Industry, I found),
I met my old acquaintance, Truth by name,
Whom I requested briefly to declare
The virtue of that plant I found so rare.   3

Quoth she, "By it, God's image man doth bear.
Without it, he is but a human shape,
Worse than the Devil (for he knoweth much).
Without it, who can any ill escape?
By virtue of it, evils are withstood.
The mind without it is not counted good.

"Who wanteth knowledge is a Scripture-fool.   4
Against the ignorant the prophets pray,
And Hósay threatens judgment unto those
Whom want of knowledge made to run astray.   5
Without it, thou no practic' good canst show
More than by hap (as blind men hit a crow).   6

the Seven Sages of Greece; celebrated for her skill in riddles; *Demophila*] Speght may be swelling the ranks with a poet of her own invention; *Telesilla*] celebrated lyric poet and heroine of Argos (fl. ca. 510 BCE). She led a band of her countrywomen in the war against Sparta; a statue of her was erected at Argos in the temple of Aphrodite; *Cornelia*] (fl. 2d century CE) mother of the Gracchi; following the murder of her second son, Gaius, Cornelia retired to Miseum, where she studied Greek and Latin literature and came to be celebrated for her own elegant writing style; *hight*] was called.

1 *Hypatia*] mathematician; held the chair of Platonic philosophy at Alexandria; murdered in 415 by a Christian mob; *Aspasia*] (470?-410 BCE) famed consort of Pericles; held an esteemed place in the intellectual life of Athens; *Pericles*] (ca. 495-429 BCE) Athenian statesman, orator, and military commander.

2 *Areta*] wife of Alcinous (king of the Phaecians) and protector of Odysseus.

3 *that plant*] knowledge.

4 *wanteth*] lacks.

5 *Hosay*] see Hosea 4:1-6.

6 *practic'*] practical.

"True knowledge is the window of the soul
Through which her objects she doth speculate.
It is the mother of faith, hope, and love—
Without it, who can virtue estimate?
By it, in grace thou shalt desire to grow;
'Tis life eternal, God and Christ to know.

"Great Alexander made so great account
Of knowledge that he oftentimes would say
That he to Aristotle was more bound   [225]
For knowledge (upon which death could not prey)
Than to his father Philip for his life
(Which was uncertain, irksome, full of strife)."

This true report put edge unto Desire,
Who did incite me to increase my store,
And told me 'twas a "lawful avarice,"
To covet knowledge daily more and more.
This counsel I did willingly obey,
Till some occurrence callèd me away

And made me rest content with that I had
(Which was but little, as effect doth show),
And quenchèd hope for gaining any more—
For I my time must other-ways bestow.
I therefore to that place returned again
From whence I came, and where I must remain.

But by the way I saw a full-fed beast,
Which roarèd like some monster or a devil,
And on Eve's sex he foamèd filthy froth,
As if that he had had the falling evil;
To whom I went, to free them from mishaps,
And with a *Muzzle* sought to bind his chaps.   1

But, as it seems, my mood outran my might,
Which when a self-conceited creature saw,
She passed her censure on my weak exploit,
And gave the beast a harder bone to gnaw: [250]
Haman she hangs. 'Tis past, he cannot shun it!
For Esther, in the preterit tense, hath done it!   2

—And yet her enterprise had some defect.
The monster surely was not hangèd quite,
For, as the child of Prudence did conceive,
His throat not stopped, he still had power to bite.
She therefore gave to Cerberus a sop
Which is of force his beastly breath to stop.   3

But yet if he do swallow down that bit,
She other-ways hath bound him to the peace,
And like an artist takes away the cause,
That the effect, by consequence, may cease:
This frantic dog, whose rage did women wrong,
Hath Constance wormed, to make him hold his tongue.   4

Thus leaving them, I passèd on my way—
But ere that I had little further gone,
I saw a fierce insatiable foe,
Depopulating countries, sparing none.
Without respect of age, sex, or degree,
It did devour, and could not daunted be.

Some feared this foe, some loved it as a friend;
For though none could the force of it withstand,
Yet some by it were sent to Tophet's flames,
But others led to heavenly Canaan land.
On some it seizèd with a gentle power,   [275]
And others furiously it did devour.   5

The name of this impartial foe was *Death*,
Whose rigor (whilst I furiously did view)
Upon a sudden, ere I was aware,
With piercing° dart my mother dear it slew;
Which, when I saw, it made me so to weep,
That tears and sobs did rouse me from my sleep.

But when I waked, I found my dream was true:
For Death had ta'en my mother's breath away
(Though of her life, it could not her bereave,
Sith she in glory lives with Christ for aye—
Which makes me glad, and thankful for her bliss,
Though still bewail her absence, whom I miss).

A sudden sorrow pierceth to the quick;
Speedy encounters, fortitude doth try;
Unarmèd men receive the deepest wound
(Expected perils, time doth lenify):   6
Her sudden loss hath cut my feeble heart
So deep that daily I endure the smart.

The root is killed. How can the boughs but fade?
But sith that Death this cruel deed hath done,
I'll blaze the nature of this mortal foe,
And show how it to tyrannize begun.
The sequel, then, with judgment view aright:
The profit may, and will, the pains requite.   [300]

Esto Memor Mortis   7

---

1 *beast*] Joseph Swetnam;   *the falling evil*] epilepsy;
them] women;   *chaps*] jaws.

2 *Haman ... done it*] Sowernam prematurely (using past
tense) boasts she "hath hanged" the misogynist.

3 *the child of Prudence*]   John Stephens ("Constantia
Munda," pseud., daughter of "Prudentia") whose *Sop
for Cerberus* (1617), the most aggressive of the replies
to Swetnam;   *Cerberus*] three-headed dog that guards
the gate of Hades;   *sop*] treat thrown to a dog to quiet
it (and in this case, to choke it).

4 *wormed*] extracted a small piece of the dog's tongue,
a custom thought to remedy canine diseases.

5 *Tophet's flames*] (see Jer. 19:4) a place near Gehenna,
outside Jerusalem, where human sacrifices were made
and which was taken by Christians to be a name for
Hell;   *Canaan land*] the promised land, Heaven.

6 *lenify*] mitigate.

7 *Esto memor mortis*] "Thou shalt be mindful of death."

Ester Sowernam (1588-1673)

*forbeare to charge women with faults which come
from the contagion of Masculine serpents.*

—*Ester hath Hang'd Haman*, p. 48

ESTER SOWERNAM's pamphlet, *Ester Hath Hang'd Haman* (1615), is the most scholarly of the six prose replies to Joseph Swetnam's vitriolic *Arraignment of Women* (1615). The author quotes or cites Homer, Semonides of Amorgos, Sophocles, Euripides, Plato, Diogenes, Aristotle, Menander, Plautus, Cicero, Lucillius, Ovid, Lucian, Galen, Juvenal, and Julian the Apostate, and supplies her own original translations. Quoting from the Bible exclusively from a Latin edition, she again supplies her own English rendering. She knows Greek and Roman mythology, philosophy, medicine, poetry and drama, and British history from the Saxons through Elizabeth I. Some of her classical citations are incorrect, but that makes her performance all the more impressive, for it is clear that Sowernam cites her authorities from memory, not just cribbing them from a secondary source.

The patronymic pseudonym, "Sower-nam[e]," announces the author's opposition to "Swe[e]tnam[e]," while the Christian name Ester evokes the biblical story of a heroine who saved her people from the monstrous injustice of Haman. In the printed quarto of 1617, *Ester* and *Hester, Sowernam* and *Sowrenam*, appear interchangably and may be printshop spellings: one suspects that the author intended a fully alliterative title, a popular convention: "Hester Hath Hanged Haman." But the question inevitably arises: who *is* she? Sowernam drops a number of hints. But unlike "Constantia Munda" (author of *The Worming of a Mad Dog*), she does not deliberately give up her identity – a reticence that may point to sincerity of purpose even if, unlike Rachel Speght, she is unwilling to identify herself.

Sowernam's extensive learning and fluent Latin point us toward an aristocrat. So, too, the reported dinner table conversation with guests, and the mention of a gentleman who returned to his library or visited the London bookshops to fetch forth a copy of Rachel Speght's book and delivered it to her the next day, so that our author could read it for herself.

Apart from the congratulatory front matter in *Muzzle for Melastomus* (1617), Sowernam was the first reader to comment in print on Speght's achievement; but she offers only faint praise for an unnamed "minister's daughter" and expresses disappointment in "the slenderness of her answer." Sowernam openly rejects the system of masculine privilege where Speght accepts it as the ordained will of God. Where Speght acknowledges her "little smattering of learning," and takes the Bible as her principal source, Sowernam flaunts her superior education and breadth of reading. And where Speght rejoices that she is at least a better grammarian than Swetnam, Sowernam shows that the man is downright ignorant. Speght doubtless appreciated having a second to her motion; but she did not appreciate the tone of Sowernam's condescension, and commented upon it in *Mortality's Memorandum* (1621).

It has been everywhere taken for granted in literary scholarship that "Ester Sowernam" is the pseudonym of a woman writer. One might counter that inference with the observation that higher learning, in the early modern era, was a jealously guarded male prerogative; and that no Jacobean woman, in print or in private correspondence, exhibits such advanced scholarship as Ester Sowernam. (Some readers doubted even the learning exhibited by Rachel Speght, and on that account unfairly assigned her book to her father.) But it begs the question to cite her knowledge as *a priori* evidence that Sowernam is a man: for if girls were tutored in Latin and as young adults had both the leisure and the library resources to read as much and as widely as university scholars, what might their writing look like, if not like this?

In the contemporaneous play, *Swetnam the Woman-Hater,* Swash the clown mentions "two or three good wenches" who, "in mere spite" (a pun on Speight) "Laid their heads together and railed" the misogynist out of England. So Swash, at least, and perhaps the theater audience, found it perfectly credible that Rachel Speght, "Ester Sowernam," and/or "Constantia Munda" were indeed real women.

In 1589, Robert Greene writing as "Jane Anger" published *Her Protection for Women.* In 1640, John Taylor writing as "Mary Tattlewell" and "Joan Hit-him-home" published *The Women's Sharp Revenge.* Both tracts are obvious (indeed, smug) exercises in ventriloquism. Is it possible, then, that a seventeenth-century woman, if given an equal education, could "write like a man"? That question invites still others: Was it possible, even for a man with a university education, to "write like a woman"? Where does "gender" reside – in the author, in the text, or in our own interpretive constructions?" And what difference does it make?

Ester Hath Hang'd Haman; or
An Answer to a Lewd Pamphlet Entituled *The Arraignment of Women*

—With the arraignment of lewd, idle, froward, and unconstant men and husbands. Divided into two parts: the first proveth the dignity and worthiness of women, out of divine testimonies; the second showing the estimation of the fœminine sex in ancient and pagan times; all which is acknowledged by men themselves in their daily actions. Written by Ester Sowernam, neither maid, wife, nor widow, yet really all and therefore experienced to defend all.

John 8.7: "He that is without sin among you, let him first cast a stone at her."

Neque enim lex iusticior ulla [est]°
Quam necis artificem arte perire sua. [1]

To All Right Honorable, Noble, and Worthy Ladies, Gentlewomen,
and Others, Virtuously Disposed, of the Fœminine Sex:

RIGHT HONORABLE, and all others of our sex, upon my repair to London this last Michaelmas term, being at supper amongst friends where the number of each sex were equal, as nothing is more usual for table-talk, there fell out a discourse concerning women, some defending, others objecting against our sex – upon which occasion, there happened a mention of a pamphlet entituled *The Arraignment of Women,* which I was desirous to see. The next day a gentleman brought me the book, which when I had superficially run over, I found the discourse as far off from performing what the title promised, as I found it scandalous and blasphemous; for where the author pretended to write against "lewd, idle, and unconstant women," he doth most impudently rage and rail generally against all the whole sex of women.[2]

Whereupon I, in defense of our sex, began an answer to that shameful pamphlet – in which, after I had spent some small time, word was brought me that an apology for women was already undertaken (and ready for the press) by a minister's daughter. Upon this news I stayed my pen, being as glad to be eased of my intended labor as I did expect some fitting performance of what was undertaken. At last the maiden's book was brought me; which, when I had likewise run over, I did observe that whereas the maid doth many times excuse her tenderness of years, I found it to be true in the slenderness of her answer. For she, undertaking to defend women, doth rather charge and condemn women (as in the ensuing discourse shall appear). So that whereas I expected to be eased of what I began, I do now find myself double charged – as well to make reply to the one as to add supply to the other. [3]

[margin: Speight not enough]

In this my apology, right honorable, right worshipful, and all others of our sex, I do in the first part of it plainly and resolutely deliver the worthiness and worth of women, both in respect of their creation as in the work of redemption. Next I do show in examples out of both the Testaments what blessed and happy choice hath been made of women as gracious instruments to derive God's blessings and benefits to mankind.

In my second part I do deliver of what estimate women have been valued in all ancient and modern times, which I prove by authorities, customs, and daily experiences. Lastly, I do answer all material objections which have or can be alleged against our sex; in which also I do arraign such kind of men which correspond the humor and disposition of the author – lewd, idle, furious and beastly-disposed persons.

This being performed, I doubt not but such as heretofore have been so forward and lavish against women will hereafter pull in their horns and have as little desire, and less cause, so scandalously and slanderously to write against us than formerly they have.

The ends for which I undertook this enterprise are these: First, to set out the glory of almighty God in so blessed a work of his creation. Secondly, to encourage all noble, honorable, and worthy women to express, in their course of life and actions, that they are the same creatures which they were designed to be

---

[1] *Neque ... sua*] "There is no law more just than to make perish the creators of death by their own creation"; adapted from Ovid, *Ars.* 1.655-6.

[2] *Michaelmas*] the autumn term of the English business year, commencing 29 September; *run over*] perused (it).

[3] *apology...by a minister's daughter*] Rachel Speght's *Muzzle for Melastomus,* registered for publication Nov. 1616.

[margin note: we were made perfect by God]

by their creator and by their redeemer; and to parallel those women whose virtuous examples are collected briefly out of the Old and New Testament. Lastly, I write for the shame and confusion of such as degenerate from womanhood and disappoint the ends of creation and redemption.

There can be no greater encouragement to true nobility than to know and stand upon the honor of nobility, nor any greater confusion and shame than for nobility to dismount and abase itself to ignoble and degenerate courses.

You are women: in creation, noble; in redemption, gracious; in use, most blessed. Be not forgetful of yourselves nor unthankful to that Author from whom you receive all.

To All Worthy and Hopeful Young Youths of Great Britain,
but respectively to the best-disposed and worthy apprentices of London:

Hopeful and gallant youths of Great Britain (and this so famous a city):

There hath been lately published a pamphlet entitled *The Arraignment of Lewd, Idle, Froward, and Inconstant Women*. This patched and misshapen hotch-potch is so directed, that if Socrates did laugh but once to see an ass eat thistles, he would surely laugh twice to see an idle Frantic direct his misshapen labors to giddy-headed young men. He would say, as he did when the ass did eat thistles, "Like lips, like lettuce." So a frantic writer doth aptly choose giddy savories. [1]

The author of the *Arraignment* and myself in our labors do altogether disagree. He raileth without cause. I defend upon direct proof. He sayeth women are the worst of all creatures. I prove them blessed above all creatures. He writeth that men should abhor them for their bad conditions. I prove that men should honor them for their best dispositions. He sayeth women are the cause of men's overthrow. I prove, if there be any offense in a woman, men were the beginners. Now, in that it is far more womanlike to maintain a right than it is man-like to offer a wrong, I conceived that I could not err in my choice if I did direct a labor well-intended to worthy young youths, which are well disposed.

[margin note: Beautiful fiery comparisons]

When you have passed your minority, or served your apprenticeships under the government of others, when you begin the world for yourselves, the chiefest thing you look for is a good wife. The world is a large field, and it is full of brambles, briars, and weeds. If there be any more tormenting, more scratting, or more poisonable weeds than other, the author hath collected them in his loathsome pamphlet and doth utter them to his giddy company. Now myself presuming upon your worthy and honest dispositions, I have entered into the Garden of Paradise, and there have gathered the choicest flowers which that garden may afford. And those I offer to you.

If you believe our adversary, no woman is good, howsoever she be used. If you consider what I have written, no woman is bad, except she be abused.

If you believe him, that women are so bad creatures, what a dangerous and miserable life is marriage! If you examine my proofs to know directly what women are, you shall then find there is no delight more exceeding than to be joined in marriage with a paradisian creature – who, as she cometh out of the Garden, so shall you find her a flower of delight, answerable to the country from whence she cometh.

---

[1] *Like lips, like lettuce*] Sowernam has Socrates laughing at the thistle-munching ass, though the anecdote is from Lucillius, in reference is to Crassus. Cf. Sir Thomas Brown, *Pseudodoxia Epidemica*, 7.xvi (1646), 424: "The Relation of *Lucillius*, and now become common, concerning *Crassus* [...] that he never laughed but once in all his life, and that was at an ass eating thistles"; Thomas Jackson, *Third Book of Commentaries* (1614), p. 233: "I knew him for another Heraclitus, or Crassus Agelastus, who never laughed in all his life save once, when he saw an ass feed on thistles. Surely he must have an ass's lips that can taste, and a swine's belly that can digest, this great clerk's divinity. Stephen Jerome, *Seven Helps* (1614), ascribes the laughter to Cato; *Like lips, like lettuce*] a conventional gloss on the Crassus anecdote. The ass's hard lips are insensible to the pain: Helkiah Crooke, *Mikrokosmographia* (1615), chap. 14, p. 755: "The ass can mumble a thistle as well as a man can eat lettuce, whence the proverb is, *Similes habent Labra a Lactucas*, Like lettuce, like lips" cf. Thomas Campion, *Art of English Poesy* (1602), chap. 2 p.6 "like lips, like lettuce"; Ray's *Proverbs* (1678), p. 168, on usage: "*Like* lips, like lettuce ... A thistle is a salad fit for an ass's mouth. We use [this proverb] when we would signify that things happen to people which are suitable to them, or which they deserve: as when a dull scholar happens to a stupid or ignorant master." The proverb suggests also that the beast who chews on what is nasty hurts only himself. Cf. George Chapman, "To the Reader," *The Iliads of Homer* (1611), sig. A2v. And though ye dream ye feast in Paradise, / Yet Reason's daylight, shows ye at your meat, asses at thistles, bleeding as ye eat"; *savories*] cooking herbs.

There can be no love betwixt man and wife, but where there is a respective estimate one towards the other. How could you *love*? Nay, how would you *loath* such a monster to whom Joseph Swetnam pointeth! Whereas, in view of what I have described, how can you but regardfully love, with the uttermost strain of affection, so incomparable a jewel! [1]

Some will perhaps say, I am a woman and therefore write more for women than they do deserve. To whom I answer: if they misdoubt of what I speak, let them impeach my credit in any one particular. In that which I write, Eve *was* a good woman before she met with the *serpent*. Her daughters are good virgins, if they meet with good tutors.

[margin: Rebuttal]

You, my worthy youths, are the hope of man-hood! The principal point of *manhood*, is to defend and what more man-like defense than to defend the just reputation of a woman? I know that you, the apprentices of this city, are as forward to maintain the good, as you are vehement to put down the bad.

[margin: Appeals to the apprentices' manhood]

That which is worst, I leave to our adversary; but what is excellently best, that I commend to you: Do you find the gold. I here deliver you the jewel, a rich stock to begin the world withal (if you be good husbands, to use it for your best advantage).

Let not the title of this book in some point distaste you, in that "men" are arraigned, for you are quit by non-age. None are here arraigned but such old fornicators as came with full mouth and open cry to Jesus, and brought a woman to him, taken in adultery; who when our Savior stooped down and wrote on the ground, they all fled away. Joseph Swetnam sayeth, "A man may find pearls in dust" (p. 47). But if they who fled had seen any *pearls*, they would rather have stayed to have had share than to fly and to leave the woman alone. They found some foul reckoning against themselves in our Savior's writing (as they shall do who are here arraigned). And if they dare do like as our Savior bade the woman's accusers – "He that is without sin throw the first stone at her" – so let them rail against women who never tempted any woman to be bad. [2]

Yet this is an hard case. If a man rail against a woman, and known no lewdness by any, he shall prove himself a compound fool! If he rail at women who, in his own experienced trial, hath *made°* bad, he shall show himself a decompounded K (I do not mean, *knight*). The best way is: *He that knoweth none bad, let him speak well of all.* He who hath made more bad than he ever intended to make good, let him hold his peace, lest he shame himself. [3]

[margin: Great saying]

Farewell.

Ester Sowernam

Chapter 1. An Answer to the First Chapter of the *Arraignment of Women*:

IF THE AUTHOR of this *"Arraignment"* had performed his discourse either answerable to the title or the arguments of the chapters, he had been so far off from being answered by me, that I should have *commended* so good a labor which is employed to give vice just reproof, and virtue honorable report. But at the very first entrance of his discourse, in the very first page, he discovereth himself neither to have truth in his promise, nor religious performance.

If in this answer I do use more vehement speeches than may seem to correspond the natural disposition of a woman; yet all judicious readers shall confess that I use more mildness than the cause I have in hand provoketh me unto. I am not only provoked by this author to defend women, but I am more violently urged to defend divine Majesty in the work of his creation. In which respect I say with Saint Jerome, *"Meam iniuriam patienter sustinui; impietatem contra deum ferre non potui."* For as Saint Chrysostom sayeth, *"iniurias Dei dissimulare impium est."* [4]

[margin: Defending God's creations]

---

[1] *respective*] respectful.

[2] *quit by non-age*] excused in that you are still boys, and not yet "men"; *Jesus ... fled away*] The anecdote appears in Gospel of John, chap. 8.

[3] *K*] she is calling Swetnam a *Knave* (scoundrel).

[4] *Meam...potui*] "I have endured my own injury with patience, but I could not bear an impiety against God"; citation in margin: *Epist. ad Ciprianum* [St. Jerome's Epistle to Ciprian]; quoted from Dionysius Cartusianus, *Epistolarum* (Paris, 1540); *iniurias ... est.*] "It is impious to hide wrongs against God"; citation in margin: *Sup. Math.* [St. John Chrysostom's *Homilies on the Gospel of Matthew*]; source unidentified.

If either Julian the apostate° or Lucian the atheist should undertake the like work, could the [one] devise to write more blasphemously, or the other to scoff and flout at the divine creation of woman more profanely, than this irreligious author doth? [1]

Homer doth report in his *Iliads* that there was at the siege of Troy a Grecian called Thersites, whose wit was so blockish, he was not worthy to speak; yet his disposition was so precipitate, he could not hold his tongue. Joseph Swetnam in all record of histories cannot be so likely paralleled as with this Thersites. What his composition of body is I know not, but for his disposition otherwise, in this pamphlet I know he is as monstrous as the work is misshapen, which shall plainly appear in the examination of the first page only.

The argument of the first chapter is "to show to what use women were made"; it also showeth "That most of them degenerate from the use they were framed unto," etc.

Now, to show to what use woman was made, he beginneth thus: "At the first beginning a woman was made to be an helper to man: and so they are indeed, for they help to consume and spend," etc. This is all the use, and all the end, which the author setteth down in all his discourse for the creation of woman. Mark a ridiculous jest in this: spending and consuming of that which man painfully getteth, is by this author the use for which women were made. And yet (sayeth he in the argument) "most of them degenerate from the use they were framed unto." Woman was made to spend and consume at the first; but women do degenerate from this use. *Ergo*, Midas doth contradict himself. Beside this egregious folly, he runneth into horrible blasphemy. Was the end of God's creation in woman to spend and consume? Is *helper* to be taken in that sense, to help to spend, etc.? Is spending and consuming *helping*?[2]

He runneth on and sayeth, "They were made of a rib; and that, their froward and crooked nature doth declare, for a rib is a crooked thing," etc.

Woman was made of a crooked rib, so she is crooked of conditions. Joseph Swetnam was made (as from Adam) of clay and dust, so he is of a dirty and muddy disposition: the inferences are both alike in either. Woman is no more crooked in respect of the one but he is blasphemous in respect of the other. Did woman receive her soul and disposition from the *rib*? Or, as it is said in Genesis, "*God* did breathe in them the spirit of life"? Admit that this author's doctrine be true (that "woman receiveth her froward and crooked disposition from the rib"); woman may then conclude upon that axiom in philosophy, *Quicquid efficit tale, illud est magis tale* ("That which giveth quality to a thing, doth more abound in that quality") – as fire which heateth, is itself more hot; the sun which giveth light, is of itself more light. So, if woman received her crookedness from the rib, and consequently from the man, how doth man excel in crookedness, who hath more of those crooked ribs! See how this vain, furious, and idle author furnisheth woman with an argument against himself, and others of his sex!

The author, having desperately begun, doth more rashly and impudently run on in blasphemy, which he doth evidently show in the inference upon his former speeches; and therefore (sayeth he) "Ever since, they have been a *woe* unto *man*, and follow the [line] of the first leader." Now let the Christian reader please to consider how dishonestly this author dealeth, who undertaking a particular, prosecuteth (and persecuteth) a general – under the cloak and color of "lewd, idle, and froward women," to rage and rail against all women in general.

Now – having examined what collections Joseph Swetnam hath wrested out of Scriptures to dishonor and abuse all women – I am resolved, before I answer further particulars made by him against our sex, to collect and note out of Scriptures, first, what incomparable and most excellent prerogatives God hath bestowed upon women, in honor of them and their creation; secondly, what choice God hath made of women, in using them as instruments to work his most gracious and glorious designs, for the general benefit of mankind, both during the law of nature and of Moses; thirdly, what excellent and divine graces have been bestowed upon our sex, in the law of grace and the work of redemption; with a conclusion, that to manifest the worthiness of women, they have been chosen to perform and publish the most happy and joyful benefits which ever came to mankind.

---

[1] *Julian the apostate*] Flavius Claudius Julianus (331-363); emperor of Rome for eighteen months (361-363), and the last to champion paganism;   *Lucian the atheist*] Greek sophist and satirist (c. 125- c. 190).

[2] *Midas*] *i.e.*, the ass.

Chapter 2. What incomparable and excellent prerogatives God hath bestowed upon women, in their first creation:

IN THIS ENSUING CHAPTER I determine briefly to observe (not curiously to discourse at large) the singular benefits and graces bestowed upon women: in regard of which, it is first to be considered that the almighty God, in the world's frame, in his divine wisdom designed to himself a main end to which he ordained all the works of his creation – in which he (being a most excellent workmaster) did so create his works that every succeeding work was ever more excellent than what was formerly created. He wrought by degrees, providing in all for that which was and should be the end. [1]

It appeareth – by that sovereignty which God gave to Adam over all the creatures of sea and land – that man was the end of God's creation; whereupon it doth necessarily (without all exception) follow that Adam, being the last work, is therefore the most excellent work of creation. Yet Adam was not so absolutely perfect but that, in the sight of God, he wanted an helper; whereupon God created the woman, his last work, as to supply and make absolute that imperfect building which was unperfected in man (as all divines do hold) till the happy creation of the woman. Now of what estimate that creature is and ought to be – which is the last work, upon whom the Almighty set up his last rest, whom he made to add perfection to the end of all creation – I leave rather to be acknowledged by others, than resolved by myself.

It is furthermore to be considered – as the maid in her *Muzzle for Melastomus* hath observed – that God intended to honor woman in a more excellent degree, in that He created her out of a subject refined, as out of a quintessence. For the rib is in substance, more solid; in place, as most near (so in estimate most dear) to man's heart – which doth presage that, as she was made for an helper, so to be an helper to stay; to settle all joy, all contents, all delights, to and in man's heart, as hereafter shall be showed. [2]

That delight, solace, and pleasure, which shall come to man by woman, is prognosticated by that place wherein woman was created; for she was framed in Paradise, a place of all delight and pleasure. Every element hath his creatures; every creature doth correspond the temper and the inclination of that element wherein it hath and took his first and principal *esse*, or being; so that woman neither can nor may degenerate in her disposition from that natural inclination of the place in which she was first framed. She is a paradisian, that is, a delightful creature, born in so delightful a country. [3]

When woman was created, God brought her unto Adam, and then did solemnize that most auspicious marriage betwixt them, with the greatest majesty and magnificence that Heaven or Earth might afford. God was the Father which gave so rich a jewel; God was the priest which tied so inseparable a knot; God was the steward which provided all the pleasures, all the dainties, all the blessings, which His divine wisdom might afford, in so delightful a place. The woman was married to Adam, as with a most sure and inseparable band, so with a most affectionate and dutiful love: Adam was enjoined to receive his wife (as is noted in the Bible printed 1595). [4]

There is no love (always excepting the transcending love) which is so highly honored, so graciously rewarded, so straightly commanded, or which being broken, is so severely punished, as the love and duty which children owe to their parents; yet this love (albeit never so respective) is dispensed withal in respect of that love which a man is bound to bear for his wife: "For this cause," sayeth Adam (as from the mouth of God), "shall a man leave father and mother, and cleave only to his wife." This word *cleave* is uttered in the Hebrew with a more significant emphasy than any other language may express; such a cleaving and joining together, which admitteth no separation. It may be necessarily observed that the gift of the woman was most singularly excellent, which was to be accepted and entertained with so inestimable a love and made inseparable by giving and taking the ring of love, which should be endless. [5]

---

[1] *in the world's frame*] when framing the world.

[2] *quintessence*] purest or most perfect form of any substance.

[3] *his ... his*] its ... its; *esse*] essence, Latin for "to be."

[4] *band*] bond; *Adam ... wife*] The reference is not actually to Adam and Eve, but to Joseph and Mary: "Joseph, being raised from sleepe, did as the Angel of the Lord inioyned him, and tooke his wife" (Matthew 1:24, Geneva Bible); *Bible printed 1595*] a politic equivocation: both the Calvinist Geneva Bible and the High Church Bishops Bible were printed in 1595; Sowernam quotes from neither, supplying her own rendering from a Latin Bible.

[5] *albeit ... respective*] no matter how respectful; *emphasy*] emphasis.

Now, the woman taking view of the garden, she was assaulted with a serpent of the masculine gender; who maliciously envying the happiness in which man was at this time, like a mischievous politician, he practiced – by supplanting of the woman – to turn him out of all; for which end he most craftily and cunningly attempteth the woman, and telleth her that therefore they were forbidden to eat of the fruit which grew in the middest of the garden: that in eating, they [should be] like unto God; whereupon the woman accepted, tasted, and gave to her husband. In accepting the serpent's offer, there was no sin; for there was no sin till the fruit was eaten.

[margin note: splitting hairs]

Now – albeit I have undertaken the defense of women and may in that respect be favored in taking all advantages I may to defend my sex – there are many pregnant places in the Scripture which might be alleged to extenuate the sin of the woman in respect of the sin of Adam. It is said (Ecclesiastes 25), "Sin had his *beginning* in woman"; ergo, his *fullness* in man.

Saint Paul sayeth (Romans 5), "By one man's sin, death came into the world" – without mention of the woman. The same Saint Paul writeth to the Corinthians, to whom he affirmeth that "All die in Adam" ([*1 Cor. 15:22*]) – in which the fullness and effects of sin are charged upon Adam alone (not but that woman had her part in the tragedy, but not in so high a degree as the man). When Adam had eaten, and sin was now in fullness, he beginneth to multiply sin upon sin. First he flyeth from the sight of God; next, being called to account, he excuseth his sin and doth expostulate (as it were) with almighty God, and telleth him that "Woman, which *thou* gavest me, gave me, and I did eat" – as who should say, if thou hadst not given the cause, I had not been guilty of the effect; making (herein) *God* the author of his fall! Now what is become of that "love" which Adam was bound to bear towards his wife? He chargeth *her* with all the burden! So he may discharge himself, he careth little how he clog her.[1]

[margin note: passing all blame]

God having examined the offenders, and having heard the uttermost they could allege for themselves, He pronounceth sentence of death upon them – as a punishment in justice due and deserved. Justice He administered to Adam. Albeit the woman doth taste of justice, yet mercy is reserved for her; and of all the works of mercy which mankind may hope for, the greatest, the most blessed, and the most joyful, is promised to woman. Woman supplanted by tasting of fruit; she is punished in bringing forth her own fruit. Yet what by fruit she lost, by fruit she shall recover. What more gracious a gift could the Almighty promise to woman, than to bring forth the fruit in which "all nations shall be blessed" ([Gal. 3:8])? So that, as woman was a means to lose Paradise, she is, by this, made a means to recover Heaven. Adam could not upbraid her for so great a loss, but he was to honor her more for a greater recovery.

All the punishments inflicted upon women are encountered with most gracious blessings and benefits. She hath not so great cause of dolor in one respect, as she hath infinite cause of joy in another: She is commanded to obey her husband: the cause is, the more to increase her glory. "Obedience is better than sacrifice" (I Sam. [15°:22]); for nothing is more acceptable before God than to obey. Women are much bound to God to have so acceptable a virtue enjoined them for their *penance*! Amongst the curses and punishments heaped upon the serpent, what greater joy could she hear, or what greater honor could be done unto her, than to hear from the voice of God these words: "I will put enmity betwixt the woman and thee, betwixt thy seed and her seed" ([Gen. 3:15]) and that her seed should break the serpent's head? This must perforce be an exceeding joy for the woman, to hear and to be assured that her fruit should revenge her wrong.

After the fall, and after they were all arraigned and censured (and that now Adam saw his wife's dowry and what blessings God hath bestowed upon her), he being now a bondslave to death and Hell, struck° dead in regard of himself, yet he comforts himself, he taketh heart from grace, he engageth his hope upon that promise which was made to the woman. Out of this most comfortable and blessed hope, he now calleth his wife by a name in whose effects not only he, but all mankind should most blessedly share: He calleth her *Eve*, which is, "the mother of the living"; which is suitable, as well in respect of the promise made to her and her seed as in respect of those employments for which, in her creation, she and all women are designed – to be helpers, comforters, joys, and delights. And in true use and government they ever have been and ever will be – as hereafter shall be showed, maugre the shameful, blasphemous

---

[1] *as who should say*] as if to say; *clog*] encumber.

and profane speech of Joseph Swetnam (page 31, beginning line 15), as followeth: "If God had not made them only to be a plague to a man, He would never have called them *necessary evils*." [1]

Out of what Scripture, out of what record, can he prove these impious and impudent speeches? They are only feigned and framed out of his own idle, giddy, furious, and frantic imaginations. If he had cited Euripides for his author, he had had some color, for that profane poet in *Medea* useth these speeches: "*Quod si Deorum aliquis mulierem formavit, opificem se malorum sciat, maximum et hominibus inimicum*" ("If any of the gods framed woman, let him know he was the worker of that which is naught, and what is most hurtful to men"). Thus a pagan writeth, profanely; but for a *Christian* to say that God calleth women "necessary evils" is most intolerable, and shameful to be written and published. [2]

Chapter 3. What choice God hath made of women to be instruments to derive His benefits to mankind:

ABRAHAM, being in danger, was blessed and preserved in respect of Sara (Gen. 20)

Rebecca, by God's providence, was the means to bring the blessing of Isaac to fall upon Jacob (Gen. 17).

The Egyptian midwives were a means to preserve the male children of the Israelites from the murther intended by Pharaoh (Exod. 1).

Moses was preserved by the daughter of Pharaoh (Exod. 2).

The messengers sent by duke Joshua to view the land of promise were harbored and freed from danger by a woman (Josh. 2:6).

When the children of Israel had been twenty years oppressed by Jabin, king of Canaan, Deborah and Isabel, two women – the one won the battle, the other slew the general (Judges 4).

When Abimilech had murthered seventy of his brethren, he was punished and slain by a woman at the siege of Thebes (Judges 9).

Michal adventured the hazard of her father's displeasure to preserve her husband David (I Kg. 19). [3]

Abigail by incomparable wisdom withheld David from shedding of innocent blood (I Kg. 25). [4]

The city of Abdela, being in danger, was preserved by a wise woman of that city (2 Kg. 20). [5]

In the great famine of Samaria, the widow of Sarepta was chosen to preserve Elias, and Elias to preserve her (3 Kg. 17). [6]

The like provision did the woman, a Sunamite, make for Elizeus, and Elizeus for the woman (4 Kg. 4). [7]

When the blood-royal of Judah had been all murthered, Joash (afterwards king) was preserved by a woman (4 Kg. 11). [8]

What was that noble adventure so blessedly performed by Judith, in cutting off the head of Holofernes! (Judith [13]).

With what wisdom did queen Esther preserve her people, and caused their enemies to be hanged! (Esther [7-9]).

What a chaste mirror was Susanna, who rather hazarded her life than offend against God! (Susanna [22-44]).

Never was greater magnanimity showed by a woman than by that mother which saw her seven children tormented most cruelly – yet she encouraged them to the death (2 Macchabees 7). [9]

---

[1] *maugre*] despite.

[2] *Quod...inimicum*] the actual source appears to be Nik. Selnecker, *Theophania* (Wittenberg, 1560): "*Si Deum aliquis mulierem formavit, Se opificem malorum maximorum credat esse, inimicum hominibus.*"; *naught*] wicked.

[3] *1 Kg. 19*] *i.e.*, 1 Sam. 19:11-17. (The Latin Bible presents 1-2 Book of Samuel and 1-2 Book of Kings as 1-4 Book of Kings.)

[4] *1 Kg. 25*] *i.e.*, 1 Sam. 25.

[5] *Abdela*] Abela; *2 Kg. 20*] *i.e.*, 2 Sam. 20:13-22.

[6] *Sarepta*] Zarephath; *3 Kg. 17*] *i.e.*, I Kg. 17:8-16.

[7] *4 Kg. 4*] *i.e.*, 2 Kg. 4:1-37; *Elizeus*] Elisha.

[8] *4 Kg. 11*] *i.e.*, 2 Kg. 11:2.

[9] *to the death*] until their death.

What excellent blessings and graces have been bestowed upon women in the law of grace:

THE FIRST which cometh in this place to be mentioned, is that blessed mother and mirror of all womanhood, the virgin Mary, who was magnified in the birth of Jesus, glorified by angels, chosen by the Almighty to bear in her womb the Savior of mankind.

With what a faithful salutation did Elizabeth, Saint John Baptist's° mother, entertain the Virgin upon her repair unto her! (Luke 1).

Anna the old prophetess did miraculously demonstrate our Savior (Luke 2). The woman which had the issue of blood (Matthew 9:19-22°); the woman of Canaan (John 4); the Samaritan woman; Martha (the 11 of John) – all these and sundry others are saved, healed, and have their sins forgiven, in respect of their true and lively faith. [1]

What faith, what zeal, what devotion did Mary Magdalene show toward Jesus! – in prostrating herself at the feet of Jesus, anointing them with precious ointment, washing them with tears, and drying them with the hair of her head (Luke 7).

With what bounty and devotion did the Marys, the wife of Herod's steward, did Joanna, with other women, contribute of their goods to Jesus! (Luke 8).

How charitable was that poor widow whose two mites our Savior valued at a greater estimate than any gift of any other whatsoever! (Luke 21°).

In all dangers, troubles, and extremities which fell to our Savior, when all men fled from him, living or dead, women never forsook him (Luke 23).

I should be over-tedious to repeat every example of most zealous, faithful, and devout women, which I might in the New Testament, whose faith and devotion was censured by our Savior to be without compare. [2]

I will conclude for women that they have been chosen, both to set out God's glory and for the benefit of all mankind, in more glorious and gracious employments than men have been.

The first promise of a messias to come was made to a woman. [3]

The birth and bearing of that promised messias was performed by a woman.

The triumphant resurrection, with the conquest over death and hell, was first published and proclaimed by a woman.

I might hereunto add those wives, widows, and virgins, which flourished in the primitive church, and all succeeding ages sithence, who in all virtues have excelled, and honored both their sex in general and themselves in particular, who in their martyrdoms, in their confession of Jesus, and in all Christian and divine virtues, have in no respect been inferior unto men. [4]   *Church mothers*

Thus, out of the second and third chapters of Genesis and out of the Old and New Testaments, I have observed, in proof of the worthiness of our sex, first, that woman was the last work of creation (I *dare* not say "the *best*"); she was created out of the chosen and best-refined substance; she was created in a more worthy country; she was married by a most holy Priest; she was given by a most gracious Father; her husband was enjoined to a most inseparable and affectionate care over her. The first promise of salvation was made to a woman. There is inseparable hatred and enmity put betwixt the woman and the serpent. Her first name, Eva, doth presage the nature and disposition of all women, not only in respect of their bearing, but further for the life and delight of heart and soul to all mankind. I have further showed the most gracious, blessed, and rarest benefits in all respects bestowed upon women – all, plainly and directly, out of Scriptures. All which doth demonstrate the blasphemous impudency of the author of the *Arraignment*, who would or durst write so basely and shamefully, in so general a manner, against our so worthy and honored a sex.

---

[1] *demonstrate*] identify.

[2] *censured*] deemed.

[3] *messias*] messiah, savior.

[4] *sithence*] since.

To the Courteous and Friendly Reader:

GENTLE READER, in my first part I have (what I might) strictly observed a religious regard, not to intermingle anything unfitting the gravity of so respective an argument. Now that I am come to this second part, I am determined to solace myself with a little liberty. What advantages I did forbear to take in the former, I mean to make use of in this second. Joseph Swetnam hath been long unanswered – which had been performed sooner, if I had heard of his book before this last term, or if the report of the maiden's answer had not stayed me. I have not so amply and absolutely discharged myself in this apology as I would have done, if either my leisure had been such as I could have wished, or at the time more favorable, that I might have stayed. What my repair into the country enforceth me to leave rather begun than finished, I mean (by God's grace) to make perfect the next term. In the meantime, gentle reader, I bid thee kindly farewell. [1]

Ester Sowernam

Chapter 4. At what estimate women were valued in ancient and former times:

PLATO, in his books *De Legibus*, estimateth of "women, which do equal men in all respects. Only in body they are weaker, but in wit and disposition of mind nothing inferior, if not superior." Whereupon he doth in his so absolute a commonwealth admit them to government of kingdoms and commonweals, if they be either born thereunto by nature or seated in government by election. [2]

It is apparent that, in the prime of antiquity, women were valued at highest estimate, in that all those most inestimable and incomparable benefits which might either honor or preserve mankind are all generally attributed to the invention of women – as may appear in these few examples following:

When *meum* and *tuum*, mine and thine, when right and wrong, were decided by wars and their weapons then were the furniture of nature – as fists, teeth, stones, stakes, or what came next to hand – a lady of an heroical disposition, called Bellona, did first invent a more manlike and honorable weapon for war (which was the sword, with other armor correspondent); for which, she was at first (and so ever since) honored as the goddess of war.

When, at the first, the finest manchet and best bread in use was of acorns, by the singular and practical wit of a lady called Ceres, the sowing of corn (and tillage) was invented. [3]

The invention of the seven liberal sciences, of all arts, of all learning, hath been generally with one consent ascribed to the invention of Jupiter's daughters, the nine Muses (whose mother was a royal lady, Mnemosyne°). [4]

Carment is a lady first invented letters, and the use of them by reading and writing. The royal and most delightful exercise of hunting was first found out and practiced by Diana, who thereupon is celebrated for the goddess of hunting. [5]

The three Graces, which add a decorum and yield favor to persons, actions, and speeches, are three ladies – Aglaia, Thalia, and Euphrosyne. [6]

The heroical exercises of Olympus were first found and put in practice by Palaestra, a woman. [7]

The whole world being divided into three parts in more ancient times, every division to this day keepeth the name in honor of a woman. [8]

---

[1] *what I might*] as much as possible; *respective*] respectful.

[2] *De Legibus*] Sowernam references the Latin trans. by Marsilio Ficino (Lyons: 1588), but the citation is mistaken; she may be thinking of Plato's *Republic*, 5.455.D-E: "the gifts of nature are equally diffused in both sexes; all the pursuits of men are the pursuits of women as well, and in all of them women is only a lesser man" (DWF).

[3] *manchet*] cake of bread.

[4] *Mnemosyne*] goddess of memory and by Zeus mother of the Muses.

[5] *Carment*] Carmenta (a.k.a. Carmentis), ancient Italian goddess of prophecy; *celebrated for*] celebrated as.

[6] *the three Graces*] Aglaia, "brightness"; Thalia, "bloom"; and Euphrosyne, "joyfulness."

[7] *Palaestra*] a feminine noun meaning *gymnasium*; as a woman's name, the goddess of wrestling.

[8] *three parts*] In Greek and Roman mythology, Earth, (Greek *Ge* or *Gaea*; Roman *Tellus*), is female while Sky and Ocean (*Ouranos/Caelus* and *Oceanus/Neptunus*, respectively), are both male. The author is perhaps thinking of Aphrodite as goddess of the sea and of Urania as the Muse of astronomy, or perhaps she is simply reconstructing the myth.

The fœminine sex is exceedingly honored by poets in their writings. They have gods as well for good things as for bad, but they have no women-goddesses but in things which are especially good. They have Bacchus for a drunken god, but no drunken goddess. They have Priapus the lustful god of gardens, but no garden-goddesses (except of late, in the garden-alleys!). They will object here unto me Venus. She indeed is the goddess of love, but it is her blind son which is the god of lust. Poor lady, she hath but her jointure in the manor of love. Cupid is lord of all the rest; he hath the royalty. She may not strike a deer but she must employ her son, that saucy boy. [1]

For pride, they held it so far from women that they found out Nemesis or Rhamnusia, to punish and revenge pride – but none to infect with pride. [2]

They have Pluto, the god of Hell, but no proper goddess of Hell, but Proserpina (whom Pluto *forcibly* took from Mount Aetna, and carried her away and made her queen of Hell; yet she doth not remain in Hell but one half of the year, by a decree from Jupiter). [3]

If I should recite and set down all the honorable records and monuments for and of women, I might write more books than I have yet written lines. I will leave and pass over the famous testimonies of foreign kingdoms and commonwealths in honor of our sex; and I will only mention some few examples of our own country and kingdom, which have been incomparably benefited and honored by women:

Amongst the old Britains, our first ancestors, the valiant Boadicea – that defended the liberty of her country against the strength of the Romans when they were at the greatest, and made them feel that a woman could conquer them who had conquered almost all the men of the then-known world. [4]

The devout Helen – who (besides that she was the mother of that religious and great Constantine who first seated Christian religion in the imperial throne, and in that respect may be styled the mother of religion) is still more honored for her singular piety and charity towards him (and his members) who died for us upon the cross than for her care and industry in finding out the wood of that cross on which he died. [5]

In the time of the Danes, chaste Emma – whose innocency carried her naked feet over the fire-hot plowshares unfelt; with the Saxons' queen Elfgive, the holy widow, and the king's daughter Edith, a virgin saint (both greater conquerors than Alexander the Great that men so much boast of, who could not conquer himself!). [6]

Since the Normans, the heroical virtues of Eleanor, wife to Edward the first – who, when her husband in the Holy Land was wounded with a poisoned arrow of which there was no hope of recovery from the chirurgeons, she sucked the poison into her own body to free him; together curing that mortal wound, and making her own fame immortal – so that I think this one act of hers may equal all the acts that her great husband did in those wars besides. [7]

Phillip, wife to Edward the third – no less to be honored for being the mother of so many brave children, than of so many good deeds (which worthily got her the title of "Good"). [8]

---

[1] *Priapus*] son of Dionysus and Aphrodite; god of reproductive power, later regarded as a god of lechery and obscenity; *jointure*] property set aside for a woman in her widowhood but controled by the male owner during his lifetime; *deer*] deer; dear.

[2] *Nemesis or Rhamnusia*] Greek goddess of retributive justice, worshiped at Rhamnus; *none ... ride*] i.e., no woman goddess who will cause pride.

[3] *but Prosperpina*] except Prosperpine; *yet she*] yet even she.

[4] *Boadicea*] Boudicca, a celebrated warrior-queen of ancient Britain. After the death of her husband (King Prasutagus, d. 61 CE), the Romans seized her territory and raped two of her daughters. Boudicca raised an insurrection. When finally routed by Suetonius Paulinus, she poisoned herself.

[5] *Helen*] St. Helena (c. 248 – 328 CE), mother of Constantine the Great (who established Christianity in 325 CE as the religion of Rome). She caused churches to be erected on the alleged sites of Christ's nativity and ascension, and was posthumously credited (from the latter fourth century onward) with having discovered the true cross of Jesus during her pilgrimage to the Holy Land.

[6] *Emma*] (d. 1052) daughter of Richard II, duke of Normandy; wife of Ethelred, king of England; and mother of Edward the Confessor; *Elfgive*] St. Elfgiva (d. 971), queen of Edmund the Magnificent (r. 940-45); widely celebrated for her tireless charity; *Edith*] St. Edith of Wilton (d. 984, often confused with St. Edith of Polesworth), daughter of King Edgar son of Edmund. When her body was exhumed in 987, her thumb was reportedly found to be incorrupt; whereupon her thumb was exhibited long afterward for veneration by pilgrims.

[7] *Eleanor*] Eleanor of Castile (d. 1290) went with Edward I in 1270 on his crusade, where she reportedly saved him from death as noted above; *chirurgeons*] surgeons.

[8] *Phillip*] daughter of the count of Hainault; as queen of Edward III she bore seven sons and five daughters.

Margaret the Wise, wife to Henry the sixth – who, if her husband's fortune, valor, and foresight had been answerable to hers, had left the crown of England to their own son and not to a stranger. [1]

The other Margaret (of Richmond), mother to Henry the seventh – from whose breasts he may seem to have derived as well his virtues as his life, in respect of her heroical prudence and piety (whereof, besides other monuments, both the universities are still witnesses!). [2]

Besides this, it was by the blessed means of Elizabeth, wife to Henry the seventh, that the bloody wars betwixt the houses of York and Lancaster were ended, and the red rose and the white united, etc. [3]

It was by the means of the most renowned queen (the happy mother of our dread sovereign) that the two kingdoms, once mortal foes, are now so blessedly conjoined. [4]

And that I may name no more (since in one only were comprised *all* the qualities and endowments that could make a person eminent) Elizabeth our late sovereign – not only the glory of our sex, but a pattern for the best men to imitate; of whom I will say no more but that while she lived, she was the mirror of the world (so then known to be, and so still remembered, and ever will be!).

[margin note: someone for all sexes to imitate]

Daily experience, and the common course of nature, doth tell us that women were by men in those times highly valued, and in worth by men themselves preferred and held better than themselves. I will not say that women are better than men, but I will say men are not so wise as I would wish them to be, to woo us in such fashion as they do except *they* should hold and account of us as their betters. [5]

What travail, what charge, what study do not men undertake to gain our goodwill, love, and liking! What vehement suits do they make unto us! With what solemn vows and protestations do they solicit us! They write, they speak, they send, to make known what entire affection they bear unto us – that they are so deeply engaged in love, except we do compassion them with our love and favor, they are men utterly cast away! One he will starve himself, another will hang, another drown, another stab, another will exile himself from kin'red and country, except they may obtain our loves! What? Will they say that we are baser than themselves? Then they wrong themselves exceedingly to prefer such vehement suits to creatures inferior to themselves. [6]

[margin note: If women are so base, why do men try so hard to have them?]

Suitors do ever in their suits confess a more-worthiness in the persons to whom they sue. These kind of suits are from nature, which cannot deceive them. Nature doth tell them what women are – and custom doth approve what nature doth direct. Aristotle sayeth, *Omnia appetunt bonum* ("Every thing by nature doth seek after that which is good"). Nature then doth carry men with violence to seek and sue after women. They will answer, and seek to elude this maxim with a distinction, that "*bonum*" is duplex, "*aut verum aut apparens*" – that *goodness* (or the thing which is good) is either *truly* good, or but *apparently* good; so, they may say, women are but apparently good. But the heathen orator and the divine philosopher too affirm: if we follow the true direction of nature we shall never be deceived. Nature in her vehement motions is not deceived with apparent shows. "It is natural," they will say, "for the male to follow the female." So it is as "natural" for the female to be *better* than the male – as appeareth to be true in observation of hawks: The sparhawk is of more esteem than the musket; the goshawk more excellent than the tercel; so in falcons, the females do excel. The like, men are bound to acknowledge [of] women (the rather in respect of their own credit and honor). To what obsequious duty and service do men bind themselves, to obtain a favor from their devoted mistress! which, if he may obtain, he thinketh himself to be much honored, and puts [it] in place of most noted view, that the world may take note; he weareth in his

---

[1] *Margaret the Wise*] Margaret of Anjou (1430-82), married to Henry VI in 1445; mother of Edward, Prince of Wales (1453-71; slain at Tewkesbury by the Yorkists). Margaret was an ardent champion of her husband's and son's right to the English crown.

[2] *Margaret of Richmond*] Margaret Beaufort (1443-1509), who in 1485 aided her son Henry to gain the crown. Margaret founded professorships of divinity at the universities of Oxford and Cambridge; completed the foundation of Christ's College, Cambridge; and left her wealth for the founding of St. John's College.

[3] *Elizabeth*] Elizabeth of York (1465-1503), eldest surviving child of Edward IV following the murder of her two brothers; for Elizabeth's own epithalamion on her marriage to King Henry, see Vol. 1.   *the bloody ... Lancaster*] the Wars of the Roses, a series of civil wars during the reigns of Henry VI, Edward IV, and Richard III, which ended with the marriage of Henry VII to Elizabeth of York.

[4] *mother of ... sovereign*] Mary Queen of Scots, mother of James I;   *the two kingdoms*] England and Scotland, united in 1603. For the life and writings of Margaret of Anjou, Margaret Beaufort, and Elizabeth of York, see *Women's Works,* vol. 1 (900-1550); and for Mary Queen of Scots, *Women's Works,* vol. 2 (1550-1603).

[5] *unless they should hold*] unless men themselves hold.

[6] *except.. them*] unless we show them compassion;   *prefer*] put forward, proffer.

hat, or on his breast, or upon his arm, the glove, the scarf, or ring of his mistress. If these were not relics from saintly creatures, men would not sacrifice so much devotion unto them. [1]

Amongst divers causes which proceed from nature and custom why men are so earnest suitors to women, I have observed one which by practice is daily confessed: Plato sayeth that "Honesty is of that worthiness that men are greatly enflamed with the love of it; and as they do admire it, so they study how to obtain it." It is apparent, young men which are unmarried and called bachelors, they may have a dis-position (or may serve an apprenticeship) to honesty, but they are never free-men, nor ever called "hon-est men," till they be married – for that is the portion which they get by their wives. When they are once married, they are forthwith placed in the rank of "honest men." If question be asked, what is such a man? it is presently resolved, "He is an honest man" – and the reason presently added, "for he hath a wife." She is the sure sign and seal of honesty. It is usual amongst old and grave fathers, if they have a son given to spending and company-keeping, who is of a wild and riotous disposition, such a father shall presently be counseled, "Help your son to a good wife, marry him, marry him! That is the only way to bring him to good order, to tame him, to bring him to be an honest man." The ancient fathers do herein acknowledge a greater worthiness in women than in men: the hope which they have of an untowardly son, to reclaim him, is all engaged upon the woman.

In no one thing men do acknowledge a more excellent perfection than in the estimate of the offenses which a woman doth commit: The worthiness of the person doth make the sin more markable. What an hateful thing it is to see a woman overcome with drink! – when as in men it is noted for a sign of good fellowship. And whosoever doth observe it, for one woman which doth make a custom of drunkenness, you shall find an hundred men. It is abhorred in women, and therefore they avoid it. It is laughed at and made but as a jest amongst men, and therefore so many do practice it. Likewise, if a man abuse a maid and get her with child, no matter is made of it, but as a trick of youth; but it is made so heinous an of-fense in the maid, that she is disparaged and utterly undone by it. So in all offenses: those which men commit are made light and as nothing, slighted over; but those which women do commit, those are made grievous and shameful. And not without just cause – for where God hath put hatred betwixt the woman and the serpent, it is a foul shame in a woman to curry° favor with the devil, to stain her womanhood with any of his damnable qualities (that she will shake hands where God hath planted hate!). [2]

Joseph Swetnam in his pamphlet aggravateth the offenses of women in the highest degree, "not only exceeding, but drawing men into all mischief." [3]

If I do grant that women, degenerating from the true end of womanhood, prove the greatest offenders, yet in granting that I do thereby prove that women in their creation are the most excellent creatures, for [through] corruption *boni pessima* ("the best thing corrupted proveth the worst") – as for example, the most glorious creature in Heaven is by his fall the most damnèd devil in Hell. All the elements in their purity are most precious, in their infection and abuse most dangerous. So the like in women: in their most excellent purity of nature, what creature more gracious? but in their fall from God and all goodness, what creature more mischievous! which the Devil knowing, he doth more assault woman than man, because his gain is greater by the fall of one woman than of twenty men. Let there be a fair maid, wife, or woman, in country, town, or city, she shall want no resort of serpents, nor any variety of tempter. Let there be, in like sort, a beautiful or personable man, he may sit long enough before a woman will solicit him. For where the devil hath good acquaintance, he is sure of entertainment there, without resistance. The serpent at first tempted woman. He dare assault her no more in that shape; now he employeth men to supply his part – and so they do. For as the serpent began with Eve to delight her taste, so do his instru-ments draw to wine and banqueting. The next, the serpent enticed her by pride, and told her she should be like to God; so do his instruments: first they will extol her beauty, what a paragon she is in their eyes; next, they will promise her such maintenance, as the best woman in the parish or country shall not have better. What care they, if they make a thousand oaths, and commit ten thousand perjuries, so they may deceive a woman? When they have done all, and gotten their purpose, then they discover all the woman's shame – and employ such an author as this (to whose *Arraignment* I do make haste) to rail upon her and the whole sex. [4]

---

[1] *sparhawk ... musket*] the female and male of the sparrowhawk;   *goshawk*] a fierce hawk of which the female was used in falconry;   *tercel*] the male of any kind of hawk, but especially the peregrine, and smaller than the goshawk;

[2] *men do*] i.e., do men;   *markable*] noteworthy.

[3] *aggravateth*] exaggerates.

[4] *his instruments*] i.e., men, as Satan's instruments.

Chap. 5. The Arraignment of Joseph Swetnam, who was the author of the *Arraignment of Women*
—and under his person, the arraignment of all idle, frantic, froward, and lewd men

JOSEPH SWETNAM having written his rash, idle, furious, and shameful discourse against women, it was at last delivered into my hands. Presently I did acquaint some of our sex with the accident, with whom I did advise what course we should take with him. It was concluded that (his unworthiness being much like of that to Thersites, whom I have formerly mentioned) we would not answer him with Achilles' fist or Stafford law, neither pluck him in pieces as the Thracian women did Orpheus, for his intemperate railing against women; but as he had arraigned women at the bar of fame and report, we resolved at the same bar where he did us the wrong, to arraign him, that thereby we might defend our assured right. And withal (respecting ourselves) we resolved to favor him so far in his trial that the world might take notice there was no partial or indirect dealing, but that he had as much favor as he could desire, and far more than he did or could deserve. [1]

So that we brought him before two judgesses, *Reason* and *Experience*, who being both in place, no man can suspect them with any indirect proceedings; for albeit Reason of itself may be blinded by passion, yet when she is joined with Experience, she is known to be absolute and without compare. As for Experience, she is known of herself to be admirable excellent in her courses. She knoweth how to use every man in her practice: she will whip the fool to learn him more wit; she will punish the knave to practice more honesty; she will curb in the prodigal, and teach him to be wary; she will trip up the heels of such as are rash and giddy, and bid them hereafter look before they leap. To be short, there is not in all the world, for all estates, degrees, qualities, and conditions of men, so singular a mistress or so fit to be a judgess as she. Only one property she hath above all the rest: no man cometh before her but she maketh him ashamed, and she will call and prove almost every man a fool, especially such who are wise in their own conceits. [2]

For his jury, albeit we knew them to be of his dearest and nearest inward familiar friends – in whose company he was ever, and did spend upon them all that he could get, or devise to get – yet we did challenge no one of them, but were well pleased that his five *Senses* and the seven deadly *Sins* should stand for his jury.

The party which did give evidence against him, we knew to be a sure card, and one which would not fail in proof of anything, and such proof which should be without all exception: *Conscience* is a sure witness.

So all things being accordingly provided, the prisoner was brought to the bar, where he was called and bid hold up his hand, which he did (but a false hand, God he knows). His indictment was read, which was this which followeth.

Chapter 6. Joseph Swetnam his indictment:

JOSEPH SWETNAM, thou art indicted by the name of Joseph Swetnam of Bedlammore, in the county of Onopoly; for that thou the twentieth day of December, in the year [1615], didst most wickedly, blasphemous, falsely, and scandalously publish a lewd pamphlet, entitled 'The Arraignment of Women'; in which, albeit thou didst honestly pretend to arraign lewd, idle, froward and unconstant women, yet contrary to thy pretended promise thou didst rashly and maliciously rail and rage against all women, generally writing and publishing most blasphemously that women by their Creator were made for "helpers" – for "helpers," thou sayest, "to spend and consume that which man painfully getteth." [3]

Furthermore, thou dost write that "Being made of a rib, which was crooked, they are therefore crooked and forward in conditions," and that "Woman was no sooner made but her heart was set upon mischief"; which thou dost derive to all the sex generally, in these words: "And therefore, ever since, they have been a 'woe' unto 'man,' and follow the line of their first leader."

Further than all this, thou dost affirm an impudent lie upon almighty God, in saying that God calleth them "necessary evils," and that "therefore they were created to be a plague unto man." Thou writest also that "Women are proud, lascivious, froward, curst, unconstant, idle, impudent, shameless," and that

---

[1] *Stafford law*] a cudgel (from a pun on *staff*ered).

[2] *such... conceits*] those who think themselves wise.

[3] *Bedlammore*] fictional name (from *Bedlam*, the popular name for the St. Mary of Bethlehem Hospital, England's ancient asylum for the insane, founded in 1247; *Onopoly*] author's marginal gloss: *pamphlet-maker*.

"They deck and dress themselves to tempt and allure men to lewdness" – with much and many more foul, intemperate, and scandalous speeches, etc.

When Joseph Swetnam was asked what he said to his indictment, "guilty," or "not guilty," he pleaded the general issue, "not guilty."

Being asked how he would be tried, he stood mute – for Conscience did so confront him that he knew upon trial there was no way but one; whereupon he thought it much better to put himself upon our mercy than to hazard the trial of his own jury.

Whereupon we did consider: if we should have urged him to be pressed, the disadvantage had been ours. For then his favorites would have said (as some *did* say) that Joseph Swetnam did not stand mute as misdoubting the proof of what he had written; but (seeing the judgesses, the jury, the accuser, and all others, most of them of the fœminine gender) he suspelled the question by us being made general, that "They would rather condemn him to please a general, although in particular respect of himself he knew they would favor him"; and besides, that he held it "a strange course that the self and the same persons should be judges and accusers." Whereupon we resolved to grant him longer time to advise with himself whether he would put himself to trial, or upon better deliberation to recall his errors. [1]

But that the world might be satisfied in respect of the wrongs done unto us, and to maintain our honorable reputation, it was concluded that myself should deliver before the judges, to all the assembly, speeches to these effects following.

Chapter 7. The answer to all objections which are material, made against women

Right honorable and worshipful, and you of all degrees:

It hath ever been a common custom amongst idle and humorous poets, pamphleteers, and rhymers, out of passionate discontents (or having little otherwise to employ themselves about) to write some bitter satire-pamphlet or rhyme against women; in which argument, he who could devise anything more bitterly or spitefully against our sex, hath never wanted the liking, allowance, and applause of giddy-headed people. Amongst the rabble of scurrile writers, this prisoner now present hath acted his part – whom albeit women could more willingly let pass than bring him to trial, and (as ever heretofore) rather contemn such authors than deign them any answer – yet seeing his book so commonly bought up (which argueth a general applause), we are therefore enforced to make answer in defense of ourselves, who are by such an author so extremely wronged in public view. [2]

You all see he will not put himself upon trial. If we should let it so pass, our silence might implead us for guilty; so would his pamphlet be received with a greater current and credit than formerly it hath been. So that as well in respect of our sex as for a general satisfaction to the world, I will take this course with our prisoner: I will at this present examine all the objections which are most material which our adversary hath vomited out against woman, and not only what he hath objected but what other authors of more import than Joseph Swetnam have charged upon women. Alas (silly man!) he objecteth nothing but what he hath stolen out of English writers, as *Euphues*, *The Palace of Pleasure*, with the like, which are as easily answered as vainly objected. He never read the vehement and professed enemies against our sex as, for Grecians, Euripides, Menander, Semonides, Sophocles, with the like; amongst Latin writers, Juvenal, Plautus, etc.

But of all that ever I read, I did never observe such general scurrility° in any as in this adversary, which you shall find I will make as manifest as the sun to shine at midday.

It is the main end that our adversary aimeth at in all his discourse to prove and say that women are bad. If he should offer this upon particulars, no one would deny it – but to lavish generally against all women, who can endure it? You might, Mr. Swetnam, with some show of honesty have said *some* women are bad, both by custom and company; but you cannot avoid the brand both of blasphemy and dishonesty to say of women generally they are all naught, both in their creation and by nature, and to ground your inferences upon Scriptures.

I let pass your objections in your first page because they are formerly answered; only whereas you say, "Woman was no sooner made, but her heart was set upon mischief," if you had then said, "She had no sooner eaten of the fruit, but her heart was set upon mischief," you had had some color for your

---

[1] *pressed*] when accused persons refused to confess or to testify against themselves, they were sometimes tortured by having weights loaded upon their chest; *suspelled*] anticipated, suspected (not in *OED*).

[2] *scurrile*] scurrilous, crude in language; *contemn*] condemn.

speeches – not in respect of the woman's disposition, but in consideration both of her first tutor and her second instructor. For whereas Scripture doth say woman was supplanted by a *serpent*, Joseph Swetnam doth say, "she was supplanted by the devil – which appeared to her in the shape of a beautiful young man." Men are much beholding to this author, who will seem to insinuate that the devil would in so friendly and familiar a manner put on the shape of *man* when he first began to practice mischief. (The devil might make bold of them whom he knew in time would prove his familiar friends!) Hereupon it may be imagined [how] it cometh to pass that painters and picture-makers, when they would represent the devil, they set him out in the deformed shape of a *man*, because under that shape he began first to act the part of a devil—

[margin: well-done reversal]

And I doubt he never changed his suit sithence. Here it is to be observed, that [that] which is worst is expressed by the shape of a man, but what is the most glorious creature is represented in the beauty of a woman, as angels. [1]

Woman at the first might easily learn *mischief*. Where or how should she learn *goodness*? Her first schoolmaster was abundant in mischief, and her first husband did exceed in bad examples. First, by his example he taught her how to fly from God; next, how to excuse her sin; then, how to cample and contest with God, and to say as Adam did, *Thou* art the cause ("for the woman, whom *Thou* gavest me, was the cause I did eat"). What Adam did at the first, bad husbands practice with their wives ever sithence (I mean in bad examples). It was no good example in Adam, who having received his wife from the gift of God, and [being] bound to her in so inseparable a bond of love, that forthwith he being taken tardy would presently accuse his wife and put her in all the danger; but the woman was more bound to an upright Judge than to a loving husband. It would not serve Adam's turn to charge her thereby to free himself. It was an hard and strange course, that he who should have been her defender is now become her greatest accuser! I may here say with Saint Paul, "by one man's sin, Death," etc. – so, by the contagion of original sin in Adam, all men are infected with his diseases. And look what examples he gave his wife at the first, the like examples and practices do all men show to women ever sithence. (Let me speak freely, for I will speak nothing but truly, neither shall my words exceed my proof.) [2]

In your first and second page, you allege David and Solomon for exclaiming bitterly against women, and that Solomon sayeth, "Women (like as wine) do make men drunk with their devices." What of all this, Joseph Swetnam? A man which hath reason will never object that unto his adversary which (when it cometh to examination) will disadvantage himself. Your *meaning* is in the disgrace of women, to exalt men – but is this any commendation to men, that they have been, and are, overreached by women? Can you glory of their holiness, whom by women prove sinful? or in their wisdom, whom women make fools? or in their strength, whom women overcome? Can you excuse that fall which is given by the weaker, or color that foil which is taken from women? Is holiness, wisdom, and strength so slightly seated in your masculine gender as to be stained, blemished, and subdued by women?

[margin: fragile men]

But now, I pray you, let us examine how these virtues, in men so potent, came (by women) to be so impotent. Do you mean, in comparative degree, that women are *more* holy, *more* wise, *more* strong, than men? If you should grant this, you had small cause to write against them. But you will not admit this. What is or are the causes, then, why men are so overtaken by women? You set down the causes in your fourth page. There you say, "They are dangerous for men to deal with, for their faces are lures, their beauties baits, their looks are nets, and their words are charms, and all to bring men to ruin."

Incidit in Scyllam qui vult vitare Charybdim! – whilst he seeketh to avoid one mischief, he falleth into another. It were more credit for men to yield our sex to be more holy, wise, and strong than to excuse themselves by the reasons alleged; for by this, men are proved to have as little *wit* as they are charged to exceed in *wickedness*! Are external and dumb shows such potent baits, nets, lures, charms – to bring men to ruin? Why, wild asses, dotterels, and woodcocks are not so easily entangled and taken! Are men so idle, vain, and weak as you seem to make them? Let me now see how you can free these men from dishonest minds, who are overtaken thus with beauty, etc. How can beauty hurt? How can it be a cause of man's ruin, of itself? What, do women forcibly draw? Why, men are more strong! Are they so eloquent to persuade? Why, men are too wise! Are they mischievous to entice? Men are more holy! How, then,

---

[1] *doubt*] suspect that; *sithence*] since.

[2] *to cample*] to talk back; to quarrel with a superior; a marginal note in the 1595 Geneva Bible states, "His wickednesse and lacke of true repentance appeareth in this, that he burdeneth God with his fault, because he had giuen him a wife"; *"by one man's sin"*] "by one man sin entered into the world, and death by sin; and so death passed upon all men" (Romans 5:12, AV).

are women causes to bring men to ruin? Direct causes they cannot be in any respect. If they be causes, they are but accidental causes – a cause, as philosophers say, *causa sine qua non* – a remote cause, which cause is seldom alleged for cause but where want of wit would say somewhat and a guilty conscience would excuse itself by anything.° Philosophers say *Nemo læditur nisi a se ipso* ("No man is hurt but the cause is in himself"). [1]

The prodigal person amongst the Grecians is called *asotos* (as a "destroyer," an undoer of himself). When an heart fraughted with sin doth prodigally lavish out a lascivious look out of a wanton eye; when it doth surfeit upon the sight, who is *asotos*? Who is guilty of his lascivious disease but himself? *Volenti non fit iniuria* ("He who is wounded with his own consent hath small cause to complain of another's wrong"). Might not a man as easily and more honestly (when he seeth a fair woman which doth make the best use that she can to set out her beauty) rather glorify God in so beautiful a work than infect his soul with so lascivious a thought? And for the woman (who, having a jewel given her from so dear a Friend), is she not to be commended rather – that in the estimate which she showeth she will, as carefully and as curiously as she may, set out what she hath received from almighty God – than to be censured that she doth it to allure wanton and lascivious looks? The difference is in the minds! Things which are called *adiaphora* ("things indifferent"), whose qualities have their name from the uses, are commonly so censured (and so used) as the mind is inclined which doth pass his verdict. A man and a woman talk in the fields together: an honest mind will imagine of their talk answerable to his own disposition, whereas an evil-disposed mind will censure according to his lewd inclination. When men complain of beauty, and say that "Women's dressings and attire are provocations to wantonness, and baits to allure men," it is a direct means to know of what disposition they are. It is a shame for men, in censuring of women, to condemn themselves. But a common inn cannot be without a common sign: it is a common sign to know a lecher by [his] complaining upon the cause and occasion of his surfeit. Who had known his disease but by his own complaint?

It is extreme folly to complain of another when the root of all resteth within himself. Purge an infected heart and turn away a lascivious eye, and then neither their dressings, nor their beauty can any ways hurt you. Do not men exceed in apparel, and therein set themselves out to the view? Shall women betray themselves and make it known that they are either so bad in their disposition, or so wanton in their thoughts, or so weak in their government, as to complain that they are tempted and allured by men? Should women make themselves more vain than youngest children, to fall in love with babies? Women are so far off from being in any sort provoked to love upon the view of men's apparel and setting-forth [of] themselves, that no one thing can more draw them *from* love, than their vanity in apparel. Women make difference betwixt colors and conditions, betwixt a fair show and a foul substance. It shows a levity in man to furnish himself more with trim colors than manlike qualities. Besides that, how can we love at whom we laugh? We see him gallant it at the court one day, and brave it in the Counter° the next day. We see him wear that on his back one week which we hear is in the broker's shop the next. Furthermore, we see divers wear apparel and colors made of a *lordship* – lined with farms and granges, embroidered with all the plate, gold, and wealth, their friends and fathers left them. Are these motives to love or to laughter? Will, or *dare*, a woman trust to their love for one month who will turn her [off] the next? This is the surfeit which women take by brave apparel: they rather suspect his worth, than wish his love who doth most exceed in bravery. [2]

So, Mr. Swetnam, do you (and all yours) forbear to censure of the dressings and attires of women for any such lewd intent as you imagine. Bad minds are discovered by bad thoughts and hearts. Do not say and rail at women to be the cause of men's overthrow when the original root and cause is in yourselves. If you be so affected that you cannot look but you must forthwith be infected, I do marvel, Joseph Swetnam, you set down no remedies for that "torment of love," as you call it. You bid men "shun and avoid it," but those be common and ordinary rules and instructions (yet not so ordinary as able to restrain the extraordinary humors of *your* giddy company!). I will do you and your friends a kindness if you be so scorched with the flames of love: Diogenes did long since discover the sovereign salve for such a wound.

---

[1] *Incidit in ... Charybdim*] He who wishes to avoid Charybdis, falls victim to Scylla;   *dotterels*] a species of plover noted for the ease with which it is captured;   *which cause ... say somewhat*] a cause that is seldom used as a defense except by lack-brain fools who must nevertheless say something.

[2] *brave it in the Counter*] show it off in debtor's prison;   *divers wear...of a lordship*] i.e., many noblemen sell off their inheritance for the sake of a flashy wardrobe;   *brave..bravery*] elegance...finery;   *surfeit... Take*] i.e. women interpret men's brave apparel as surfeit or excess.

The receipt is no great charge; yourself may be the apothecary. It is comprehended in three words. First, try with *Chronos*; next, with *Limos*. If both these fail, the third is sure: *Brokhos*.° This was Diogenes' antidote against that venomous infection. There *are* more milder remedies which you may put in practice. If your hearts be so fleshly or your eyes so tender that you dare trust neither of them, then trust to your reason to turn your eyes away – or trust to your heels as Joseph did, to carry all away.[1]

After you have railed against women, you bring in a fable of a contention° betwixt the wind and the sun, and you apply the moral to women – when as it hath a far other relation; for it ever hath been applied to men, to instruct them in the government of woman. For I pray you, who is to govern, or who are to be governed? (You should seem to come from the Sauromatians, whose wives were their masters!) But I will set you down both the fable and the moral as it was written in English verse long sithence: [2]

> The sun and wind at variance did fall,
> Whose force was greatest in the open field.
> A traveler they choose to deal withal:
> Who makes him first unto their force to yield
> > To cast off cloak (they that agreement make),
> > The honor of the victory must take.
>
> The wind began and did increase each blast
> With raging beat upon the silly man;
> The more it blew, the more he graspèd fast
> And kept his cloak, let wind do what it can.
> > When all in vain the wind his worst had done,
> > It ceased, and left a trial to the sun.
>
> The sun begins his beams for to display,
> And by degrees in heat for to increase;
> The traveler, then warm, doth make a stay,
> And by degrees his cloak he doth release,
> > At length is forced both coat and cloak to yield—
> > So gives the sun the honor of the field.
>
> Who by extremes doth seek to work his will
> (By raging humors thinking so to gain),
> May, like the wind, augment his tempest still,
> But at the length he finds his fury vain.
> > For all he gets by playing frantic parts,
> > He hard'neth more the mild and gentle hearts:
>
[25]
> Like as all plants, when at the first they spring,
> Are tender and soft-barked on every side;
> But as they grow, continual storms do bring
> Those are more hard which northern blasts abide;
> > What's toward the southern, tenderer we find,
> > And that more hard which feels the northern wind.
>
> Nature his course most carefully doth bend,
> From violence to seek itself to arm;
> Where raging blasts the trees would break and rend,
> There Nature strives to keep her plants from harm;
> > Where violence is unto nature strange,
> > Continual custom there doth nature change. [3]

---

[1] *Diogenes*] Athenian philosopher (c. 400 - c. 325 BCE), founder of the Cynics;   *receipt*] recipe; *Chronos...Limos...Brokhos*] (Κρόνος...λιμός...βρόχος) time, hunger, a noose;   *Joseph*] see Gen. 39.

[2] *Sauromatians*] the Sarmatæ, a people of eastern Scythia whom Herodotus reports were ruled by women (IV. 21, 17);   *the fable and the moral*] There were several English versions of the fables in print by 1617, but nothing like this version appears elsewhere; it is surely Sowernam's own.

[3] *Nature*] one's biological nature;   *his*] its;   *nature*] as mother Nature.

> So 'tis with women, who by nature mild,
> If they on froward crabbèd husbands light,
> Continual rage by custom makes them wild,
> For crooked natures alter gentle quite.
> > Men evermore shall this, in trial, find:
> > Like to her usage, so is woman's mind. [1]

> As of themselves, let men of others judge:
> What man will yield to be compelled by rage?
> At crabbedness and curstness hearts do grudge,
> And to resist, themselves they more engage.
> > Forbear the wind! Shine with the sun awhile—
> > Though she be angry, she will forthwith smile.

This is the true application of the moral. As for that crookedness and frowardness with which you charge women, look from whence they have it, for of themselves and their own disposition it doth not proceed – which is proved directly by your own testimony. For in your 45th page, line 15, you say, "A young woman of tender years is flexible, obedient, and subject to do anything, according to the will and pleasure of her husband." How cometh it, then, that this gentle and mild disposition is afterwards altered? Yourself doth give the true reason, for you give a great charge not to marry a widow. But why? Because (say you *in the same page*) "A widow is framed to the conditions of another man." Why then, if a woman have froward conditions, they be none of her own, she was *framed* to them! Is not our adversary ashamed of himself, to rail against women for those faults which do all come from men? Doth not he most grievously charge men to learn their wives bad and corrupt behavior? for he sayeth plainly, "Thou must unlearn a widow, and make her forget and forgo her former corrupt and disordered behavior." Thou must "unlearn her"; *ergo*, what fault she hath, she learned. Her corruptness cometh not from her own disposition, but from her husband's destruction. Is it not a wonder, that your pamphlets are so dispersed? Are they not wise men to cast away time and money upon a book which cutteth their own throats? 'Tis pity but that men should reward you for your writing, if it be but as the Roman Sertorius did the idle poet – he gave him a reward, but not for his writing, but because he should never write more! As for women, they laugh that men have no more able a champion. This author cometh to bait women, or (as he foolishly sayeth) the "bear-baiting of women," and he bringeth but a mongrel cur, who doth his kind to brawl and bark, but cannot bite. [2]

The mild and flexible disposition of a woman is in philosophy proved in the composition of her body, for it is a maxim, *Mores animi sequntur°temperaturam corporis* ("the disposition of the mind is answerable to the temper of the body"). A woman in the temperature of her body is tender, soft, and beautiful; so doth her disposition in mind correspond accordingly: she is mild, yielding, and virtuous. What disposition accidentally happeneth unto her is by the contagion of a froward husband – as Joseph Swetnam affirmeth. [3]

And experience proveth. It is a shame for a man to complain of a froward woman – in many respects, all concerning himself. It is a shame he hath no more government over "the weaker vessel." It is a shame he hath hardened her tender sides and gentle heart with his boist'rous and northern blasts. It is a shame for a man to publish and proclaim household secrets – which is a common practice among men, especially drunkards, lechers, and prodigal spendthrifts. These when they come home drunk or are called in question for their riotous misdemeanors, they presently show themselves the right children of Adam: they will excuse themselves by their wives, and say that their [wives'] unquietness and frowardness at home is the cause that they run abroad – an excuse more fitter for a beast than a man. If thou wert a man, thou wouldst take away the cause which urgeth a woman to grief and discontent, and not by *thy* frowardness increase her distemperature. Forbear thy drinking, thy luxurious riot, thy gaming and spending, and thou shalt have thy wife give thee as little cause at home, as thou givest her great cause of disquiet

---

[1] *usage*] treatment.

[2] *to learn their wives*] *i.e.*, to teach their wives (standard usage in 17th c.); *but that men should reward*] if men did not reward; *if it be but*] even if only; *but because*] but so that; *Sertorius*] an error for Sulla the Dictator; see Cicero, *Pro Achaia poeta* 10.25; *have no more able a*] lack a more competent.

[3] *Mores…corporis*] from Galen, *De atra bile*.

abroad. Men which are *men*, if they chance to be matched with froward wives (either of their own making or others' marring), they would make a benefit of the discommodity – either try his skill to make her mild, or exercise his patience to endure her curstness. For all crosses are inflicted either for punishment of sins or for exercise of virtues.

But humorous men will sooner mar a thousand women, than out of a hundred make one good. And this shall appear in the imputation which our adversary chargeth upon our sex, to be lascivious, wanton, and lustful. He sayeth, "Women tempt, allure, and provoke men." How rare a thing is it for women to prostitute and offer themselves! How common a practice is it for men to seek and solicit women to lewdness! What charge do they spare? What travail do they bestow! What vows, oaths and protestations do they spend, to make them dishonest! They hire panders, they write letters, they seal them with damnations and execrations, to assure them of love, when the end proves but lust. [Men] know the flexible disposition of women; and the sooner to overreach them, some will pretend they are so plunged in love that except they obtain their desire they will seem to drown,° hang, stab, poison, or banish themselves from friends and country. What motives are these to tender dispositions? Some will pretend marriage, another offer continual maintenance. But when they have obtained their purpose, what shall a woman find? Just that which is her everlasting shame and grief: she hath made herself the unhappy subject to a lustful body, and the shameful stall of a lascivious tongue. Men may with foul shame charge *women* with this sin! – which [she] had never committed if she had not trusted, nor had ever trusted if she had not been deceived with vows, oaths, and protestations. To bring a woman to offend in *one* sin, how many damnable sins do *they* commit? I appeal to their own consciences. The lewd disposition of sundry men doth appear in this. If a woman or maid will yield unto lewdness, what shall they want? But if they would live in honesty, what help shall they have? How much will [men] make of the lewd! How base account of the honest! How many pounds will [men] spend in bawdy houses! But when will they bestow a penny upon an honest maid or woman, except it be to corrupt them? [1]

Our adversary bringeth many examples of men which have been overthrown by women. It is answered before: the fault is their own. But I would have him, or anyone living, to show any woman that offended in this sin of lust, but that she was first solicited by a man:

"Helen was the cause of Troy's burning"; first, Paris did solicit her. Next, how many knaves and fools of the male kind had Troy, which to maintain whoredom would bring their city to confusion!

When you bring in examples of "lewd women," and of men which have been stained by women, you show yourself both frantic, and a profane irreligious fool, to mention *Judith* for cutting off Holofernes' head, in that rank! [2]

You challenge women for "untamed and unbridled tongues"; there was never woman was ever noted for so shameless, so brutish, so beastly a scold as you prove yourself in this base and odious pamphlet. You blaspheme God, you rail at his creation, you abuse and slander his creatures (and what immodest or impudent scurrility is it which you do *not* express in this lewd and lying pamphlet?).

Hitherto I have so answered all your objections against women that, as I have not defended the wickedness of any, so I have set down the true state of the question. As Eve did not offend without the temptation of a serpent, so women do seldom offend but it is by provocation of men. Let not your impudency, nor your consorts' dishonesty, charge our sex hereafter with those sins of which you yourselves were the first procurers. I have in my discourse touched you and all yours to the quick; I have taxed you with bitter speeches. You will, perhaps, say *I* am a railing scold. In this objection, Joseph Swetnam, I will teach you both wit and honesty. The difference between a railing scold and an honest accuser is this: the first rageth upon passionate fury, without bringing cause or proof; the other bringeth direct proof for what she allegeth. You charge women with clamorous words, and bring no proof. I charge you with blasphemy, with impudency, scurrility, foolery, and the like. I show just and direct proof for what I say. It is not my desire to speak so much; it is your desert to provoke me upon just cause so far. It is no railing to call a crow black, or a wolf a ravener, or a drunkard a beast. The report of the truth is never to be blamed; the deserver of such a report, deserveth the shame.

Now, for this time, to draw to an end, let me ask according to the question of Cassian, *Cui bono?* What have you gotten by publishing your pamphlet? Good, I know you can get none. You have, per-

---

[1] *panders*] go-betweens;   *flexible*] responsive or tractable;   *stall*] market-stall (in that the man will afterward advertise his conquest);   *want*] lack;   *make of*] praise and extol.

[2] *Judith ... Holofernes' head*] In the apocryphal book of Judith, the title character delivers Israel by decapitating the Assyrian general, Holofernes, in his own tent.

haps, pleased the humors of some giddy, idle-conceited persons. But you have dyed yourself in the colors of shame, lying, slandering, blasphemy, ignorance, and the like. [1]

The shortness of time and the weight of business call me away, and urge me to leave off thus abruptly, but assure yourself where I leave now, I will by God's grace supply the next term, to your small content. You have exceeded in your fury against widows, whose defense you shall hear of at the time aforesaid. In the mean space, recollect your wits. Write out of deliberation, not out of fury. Write out of advice, not out of idleness. Forbear to charge women with faults which come from the contagion of masculine serpents.

Have good motives you cunt

finis

The next reply to Swetnam (published shortly after Sowernam's) was titled *The Worming of a Mad Dog: A Sop for Cerberus, the Jailor of Hell*, "By Constantia Munda." The pseudonym is that of the satirist, John Stephens, who makes no effort to conceal his identity. But neither does Stephens make any serious effort to refute Swetnam's misogynist rant. As declared on the title page, *The Worming of a Mad Dog* is "No Refutation, but a Sharp Redargution [*reproof* or *rebuke*] of the Baiter of Women." Stephens takes Joseph Swetnam apart piece by piece, in thirty-five pages of biting and relentless mockery, mostly *ad hominem*.

Whereas "Constantia Munda" bullies Swetnam, "Ester Sowernam" reasons with him. The author's voice sounds authentic. The editors of *Women's Works*, when first undertaking Volume Three, set out to show that *Ester Hath Hanged Haman* may been written by one of England's learned aristocratic women; among whom, one in particular seemed quite likely: Frances Seymour, countess of Hertford.

• Sowernam reports having come to London from the country in Michaelmas Term 1616; so, too, did Lady Hertford and her husband—and they spent the winter of 1616/7 in London.

• Joseph Swetnam condemns "unmarried wantons" for having "made yourselves neither maidens, widows, nor wives" (27); Sowernam, tongue-in-cheek, proclaims herself on the title page "neither maid, wife, nor widow, yet really all, and therefore experienced to defend all." Possibly a self-conscious jest: the countess of Hertford in 1617 was no longer a maiden or widow though she lived as one from 1601-1625, during her unhappy second marriage as wife to the elderly Edward Seymour.

• Sowernam writes in chapter three that a man in love "will starve himself, another will hang, another drown, another stab, another will exile himself from kin'red and country, except they may obtain our loves." In one of the text's few unnecessary repetitions, she states again in chapter 7 that men in love "will pretend they are so plunged in love that except they obtain their desire, they will seem to drown, hang, stab, poison, or banish themselves." In December 1601, Sir George Rodney, in love with Frances Seymour, not only threatened to stab himself for love, he actually did it (*Women's Works,* vol. 2).

• The countess of Hertford was well educated, an accomplished poet, and a wit. She spoke up clearly and often in defense of women's rights. And her "Elegia" to Sir George Rodney is the single most compelling indictment of masculine love-discourse to have survived from the early modern period. She seemed a promising candidate.

We are therefore disappointed to report (albeit with conviction), that *Ester Hath Hanged Haman* was written by Richard Brathwait. The vocabulary, coined words, the classical quotations and allusions, the English, Latin, Greek, and Italian source-texts, the original Biblical translations from Latin, including self-repetitions, are a seamless match for Brathwait's prose and verse. Even the grammar and syntax exhibit Brathwait's writing habits and turn of phrase. Perhaps Brathwait was motivated by love or chivalry: on 4 May 1617 he married Frances Lawson of Durham, a marriage that produced nine children, lasted sixteen years, and broke Brathwait's heart when Frances died. He was a good man, a thoughtful polemicist, and an accomplished poet and wit. Still, we considered pulling *Ester Hath Hanged Haman* from *Women's Works* upon learning that it was written by an impostor. And yet, many, perhaps most, of her contemporaries took Ester Sowernam for a woman; and her pamphlet significantly helped to dismantle the ideology of male superiority. Our verdict, in the end, was to save Ester's neck; because if Sowernam is right, and Swetnam, wrong, and if Sowernam's tract helped to move forward the cause of women's rights, then indeed (in the words of Foucault), *What matter who's speaking*?

---

[1] *Cassian*] John Cassian (360-435 CE), monk and theologian who stressed moral effort as a means to obtain grace; *Cui bono*] "For whose benefit?" (originally a standard legal query).

Witchcraft Act of 1604 (1 Jas. 1, c.12), ed. DWF

An Act against Conjuration, Witchcraft, and Dealing with Evil and Wicked Spirits

BE IT ENACTED by the King our Sovereign Lord, the Lords Spiritual and Temporal and the Commons in this present Parliament assembled, and by the authority of the same, that the Statute made in the fifth year of the reign of our late sovereign Lady of the most famous and happy memory, Queen Elizabeth, entituled *An Act against Conjurations, Enchantments, and Witchcrafts*, be – from the Feast of St. Michael the Archangel next coming, for and concerning all offenses to be committed after the same Feast – utterly repealed.

AND FOR THE BETTER RESTRAINING OF SAID OFFENSES, and more severe punishing the same, be it further enacted by the authority aforesaid: That if any person or persons after the said Feast of Saint Michael the Archangel next coming, shall use, practice, or exercise any invocation or conjuration of any evil and wicked spirit, or shall consult, covenant with, entertain, employ, feed, or reward any evil and wicked spirit to or for any intent or purpose; or take any dead man, woman, or child out of his, her, or their grave or any other place where the dead body resteth, or the skin, bone, or any other part of any dead person, to be employed or used in any manner of witchcraft, sorcery, charm, or enchantment; or shall use, practice, or exercise any witchcraft, sorcery, charm, or enchantment whereby any person shall be killed, destroyed, wasted, consumed, pined, or lamed in his or her body, or any part thereof; then, that every such offender or offenders, their aiders, abettors, and counselors, being of the said offenses duly and lawfully convicted and attainted, shall suffer pains of death as a felon or felons, and shall lose the privilege and benefit of clergy and sanctuary.

AND FURTHER, to the intent that all manner of practice, use, or exercise of declaring by witchcraft, enchantment, charm, or sorcery should be from henceforth utterly avoided abolished and taken away:

BE IT ENACTED by the authority of this present Parliament, that if any person or persons shall (from and after the said Feast of Saint Michael the Archangel next coming, take upon him or them, by witchcraft, enchantment, charm, or sorcery, to tell or declare in what place any treasure of gold or silver should or had in the earth or other secret places, or where goods or things lost or stolen should be found or become; or to the intent to provoke any person to unlawful love, or whereby any cattle or goods of any per-

son shall be destroyed, wasted, or impaired, or to hurt or destroy any person in his body, although the same be not effected and done; that then: All and every such person or persons so offending, and being thereof lawfully convicted, shall for the said offense suffer imprisonment by the space of one whole year, without bail or mainprise, and once, in every quarter of the said year, shall in some market town, upon the market day, or at such time as any fair shall be kept there, stand openly upon the pillory by the space of six hours; and there shall openly confess his or her error and offense.

And if any person or persons being once convicted of the same offenses as is aforesaid, do eftsoons perpetrate and commit the like offense, that then: Every such offender, being of the said offenses the second time lawfully and duly convicted and attainted (as is aforesaid) shall suffer pains of death as a felon or felons, and shall lose the benefit and privilege of clergy and sanctuary; saving to the wife (of such person as shall offend in anything, contrary to this act) her title of dower; and also, to the heir and successor of every such person, his or their titles of inheritance, succession, and other rights, as though no such attainder of the ancestor or predecessor had been made; provided always that if the offender in any cases aforesaid shall happen to be a peer of this realm, then his trial therein is to be had by his peers (as it is used in cases of felony or treason) and not otherwise.

Beggar Women (1622), A.L. Richter after Jacques Callot

The Witches of Pendle Forest (fl. 1610-1612)

*[P]ersons which chiefly practise Witch-craft are such as are in great
~~miserie and pouertie~~, for such the Deuil allures to follow him.*
—Thomas Potts, ~~Court Recorder~~ (sig. O3r)

*And the Devill then further commaunded this Examinate to call him by
the name of* Fancie; *and when she wanted any thing, or would be
revenged of any, call on* Fancie, *and he would be ready.*
—from "The Confession of Anne Whittle" (sig. D3)

ELIZABETH SOUTHERNS, an elderly blind beggar known throughout the hamlets of Pendle Forest as "Old Dembdike," lived for many years as a squatter or tenant in the country between Blacko and Newchurch. With her widowed daughter Elizabeth Device and three grandchildren, Southerns dwelt in a "firehouse" (a thatched cottage with a wood-burning fireplace), at "Malkin Tower" – which, despite its grand name, was not an ancient fortification but a sarcasm: from the 13th through the 19th century, *malkin* was the usual word used to denote a low-class country slut. John Device having died in 1601, his wife Elizabeth and their children (Alison, James, and Jennet) survived on day-labor and itinerant begging. A fourth child born to Elizabeth as a widow, by one Sellar, evidently died as an infant.

Early in *Anno Domini* 1612, the Device family came home to find their cottage had been robbed, their grain for making bread and pottage stolen, and their linen clothing; which on their meager income was an irreparable loss.

The following Sunday, Alison Device spotted Bessie Chaddock of West Close, Higham, wearing a ribboned coif (a close-fitting women's cap) that was among the missing goods. The Devices complained to the Greave of the Forest, who referred the matter to Roger Nowell of Read Hall, the local magistrate.

Nowell summoned Chaddock to appear before him at Read on 13 March; at which meeting, Alison Device stated that she "and her mother had their firehouse broken, and all or the most part of their linen clothes, and half a peck of cut oatmeal, and a quantity of meal, *gone*. All which, was worth twenty shillings or above. And upon a Sunday then next after, she did take a band and a coif, parcel of the goods, upon the daughter of Anne Whittle, and claimed them."[1]

Judge Nowell committed Bessie to prison, to await trial at the next Quarter Sessions; but not before Bessie got off an accusation that Alison Device and her grandmother were notorious witches – an allegation that set in motion the tragic machinery that would destroy Alison's family, and Bessie's too.

When the hearing adjourned, Nowell detained Alison to ask her a few questions about witchcraft, a subject in which he had a keen interest. Alison gave Nowell an earful concerning the activities of Bessie Chaddock's mother, Anne Whittle (alias "old Chattox"): Alison said that Whittle every year had extorted from her late father a dole of grain, for protection from her black arts; and when he declined to pay in 1601, old Chattox killed him, by witchcraft. About five years later, said Alison, Hugh Moore of Pendle accused Whittle of bewitching his cattle; whereupon she cursed poor Hugh, causing him to fall sick and die. A little after that, Whittle cursed a cow of the Nutters, causing it to die because young John Nutter, son of Whittle's landlord, had maliciously kicked over her can of milk.

There was more. Two years ago, Alison and her friend Anne Nutter of Pendle had made the mistake of laughing at Whittle; whereupon the old woman snarled, "I will be meet with the one of you." Anne Nutter the next day fell sick, and two weeks after, died. Later that same year (1610), John Moore, a Higham neighbor, accused Whittle of bewitching his ale, causing it to spoil; whereupon Whittle made a clay image of a child, "thought to be a picture of the said Moore's child," which she stuck with pins. One of the Moore children shortly afterward fell sick, languished for half a year, and died. Bessie's sister, Anne Redfern, Whittle's elder daughter, was a witch, too.

With Bessie Chaddock in prison for theft and likely to hang for it, her friends circulated their own anthology of storied deaths, featuring Witch Alison, the granddaughter of the wicked hag, Dembdike.

---

[1] *13 March*] Potts swaps the dates of Alison's depositions of March 13 ("xiij," C1r) and 30 ("thirtieth," C4r); this mistake, though corrected in the trial report (E4r), has since caused general confusion in the commentary. And by a misplaced phrase about her father's death ("about eleuen yeares agoe…about eleuen yeares since, C4r-v), Potts's text mistakenly dates the Malkin Tower burglary in 1601 when in fact it had occurred shortly before the 13 March hearing at Read Hall; *take … upon*] caught her with a parcel (part) of the stolen goods; *and…claimed them*] ed. DWF from Potts, *Discoverie* (1613), sig. E4r.

On 18 March, five days after the hearing at Read Hall, Alison on her begging circuit was headed for Trawden, east of Colne, when she met John Law, an old peddler of Halifax. Alison asked him to give her a few pins. Law had doubtless heard what witches do with pins besides hold their clothing together: he refused even to open his pack, to exhibit his goods. Whereupon Alison cursed him.

The terrified peddler walked two hundred yards and collapsed from an apoplexy. He was carried to an alehouse another two hundred yards distant. Following behind, Alison looked in on him, alarmed by her own powers. She needed no convincing: it was her curse that had caused the man's sudden stroke.

Abraham Law hurried from his home in Yorkshire to be with his father, who was unable to speak, and paralyzed on his left side. When the old man had sufficiently recovered, he stated the facts of his bewitchment: in a dispute over pins, Alison Device, the teen Witch of Malkin Tower, had cursed him.

Law searched out the young woman. When he found her he brought her to see what she had done to his father – at which meeting, a remorseful Alison Device fell to her knees, confessed her fault, and sobbingly begged John Law's pardon for having injured him.

That confession sealed the question of Alison's guilt – but when Abraham demanded that the wicked girl reverse the curse, and heal his father, she begged off, saying that she didn't know how.

Armed with a confession from the whore's own mouth, an angry Abraham Law rode to Read Hall, told his story to Judge Nowell, and demanded justice; to whose ears, this news of a proved bewitchment was sweet music. Like King James, Nowell believed that Britain was infested with witches, a cancer on the commonwealth that must be rooted out. And as a local magistrate looking for advancement, he guessed that this case could be his lucky break. Nowell summoned Alison Device to stand before him a second time at Read Hall.

If hearsay evidence can be admitted – answers spoken by Alison, paraphrased by Nowell, excerpted by Potts, vetted by the hanging judge, and printed a year later by William Stansby to be sold in the London bookshop of John Barnes – then Alison in her March 30th interview with Judge Nowell gave up the store, confessing her guilt. There was nothing natural about the paralysis of John Law, peddler of Halifax. He was attacked Alison Device's black Devil-dog, at her express command: "Lame him!"

Alison evidently let it slip that Elizabeth Southerns was a witch as well. By way of illustration, she said that her blind grandmother once charmed a quarter-pound of butter from a can of skim milk, without churning and without getting out of bed; that she possibly cursed to death a cow belonging to John Nutter of Bull-Hole Farm that she had been asked to heal; and possibly bewitched to death the infant daughter of Richard Baldwin of Colne-Weethead (Elena was buried at Colne on 8 September 1610).

On April 2nd, Judge Nowell summoned the four accused witches – Old Dembdike and Alison Device of Malkin Tower, and Anne Whittle and Anne Redfern of West Close, to appear before him, in Fence, at Ashlar House (today, a tourist site). This inquiry was the equivalent of a grand jury. Putting first things first, Nowell reached back eighteen years to inquire about the death of Robert Nutter Jr., grandson of the Whittles' landlord. The young man died in 1595 believing he was bewitched by Anne Whittle and Anne Redfern. Each of the four women had her own version of the story, and each had someone to blame.

Others came forward. The Nutter kin who testified were agreed that Whittle and Redfern had caused Robert's death. Whittle, however, blamed Jane Boothman and Loomshaw's wife of Burnley (who could not be questioned because both women had just died). James Robinson said that Anne Whittle alias Chattox had also bewitched his ale. It was a bad day for Whittle and Redfern. But when the inquiry was over, Judge Nowell sent all four women to the Lancaster jail (to dark underground cells in the Well Tower of Lancaster Castle). He then sent Richard Shuttleworth, gent., to the Whittles' cottage in West Close, with instructions to gather up all of the clothing found there, and to take it to Bessie Chaddock, also in jail (perhaps to let the prisoners sort out whose linens were whose; or perhaps for trial evidence).

April 10-12 was Easter weekend. On Friday, Elizabeth Device hosted a picnic at Malkin Tower so that family and friends could discuss what to do. The main dish that Good Friday afternoon was roast mutton, supplied by her son James, who stole a sheep from John Robinson of Barley.

Learning of this Good Friday event, Judge Nowell realized he was on to something important, dark, and big.

James and Jennet Device were brought to him for questioning, from whom Nowell elicited the names of almost everyone who attended the Malkin Tower event – one man, two boys (including James) and eighteen women, a gender-imbalance that was *prima facie* evidence for witchcraft.

On 27 April, Roger Nowell with Nicholas Bannester interrogated Alison's younger brother all day long, who confirmed Judge Nowell's darkest suspicions: gathered at the Device residence on Good Friday were "all the most dangerous, wicked, and damnable witches in the County, far and near" (C3r);

the purpose of whose enclave was to hatch the most heinous terror-plot Britain had seen since the Gunpowder Treason of 1605, when Guy Fawkes and English Jesuits would have blown up the Parliament building, had the plot not been discovered in the nick of time by Sir Thomas Knyvett. On 28 April, Nowell dispatched an urgent terror-warning to King James and to the Assize judges of the Northern Circuit: there had been discovered in Pendle Forest a conspiracy of witches whose plan was to murder Thomas Covell, the Governor of Lancaster prison; and then, with massive quantities of dynamite, to blow up Lancaster Castle.

By May 1 Nowell committed seven more witches to Covell's custody: Elizabeth Device and James her son; Katherine Hewitt and Alice Grey (of Colne), and Jane Bulcock and her son John (of Moss End); plus Alice Nutter (of Crowtrees, Burnley). An eighth she-devil, Jennet Preston, was arrested at her home in Yorkshire and held at York. Meanwhile, JP Nicholas Bannester indicted Margaret Pearson of Padiham for the bewitchment of a horse (not her first arrest); and JP Sir Thomas Gerard arrested Isabel Robey of Windle. In nearby Samlesbury, JP Robert Holden arrested seven more alleged offenders, including three (Jane Southworth, Jennet Bierley, and Ellen Bierley) who were said by 14-year-old Grace Sowerbutts to be blood-sucking baby-killers who could change themselves into the shape of dogs and who "danced, every one of them, with one of the black things" that "did abuse their bodies" (L2v).

The Assize courts, which tried most homicides, convened no more than four times a year. Lancaster's next Assize was in August, with Sir James Altham and Sir Edward Bromley presiding. By the time the JPs arrived, eighteen accused witches awaited trial. (Old Dembdike died in custody. Jennet Preston was executed by Altham and Bromley, in York, on 29 July.) Ten of the accused Lancashire witches were hanged. Three of seven Samlesbury witches were acquitted upon discovery that the allegations were invented by "popish plotters"; whereupon charges against the remaining five Samlesbury defendants were dismissed.

Information about the Pendle witch trials is provided by the Court Recorder, Thomas Potts. His 188-page text – commissioned, vetted, and authorized by the presiding justice, Sir Edward Bromley – was registered for publication on 7 November 1612 and published some months later as *The Wonderful Discoverie of Witches in the Countie of Lancaster.* "Thus at one time," says Potts, "may you behold witches of all sorts, from many places," in a Protestant commonwealth which "abound[s] as much in witches of divers kinds, as seminaries, Jesuits, and papists" (T2r). Drawing on depositions both from the magistrate's inquisition and the trial record, Potts supplies one of our most detailed and authoritative accounts of the British justice system at work, as the regime undertook to root out the burdensome poor by criminalizing poverty. Potts's *Discovery* proved influential: by 1645, Puritan witch-finders, paid by local communities to clean up the neighborhood, passed through town after town, sweeping up as many as one hundred women at a time, most of whom were unmarried, poor, and expendable.

Dedicating his work to Sir Thomas Knyvett (the same Thomas Knyvett who in 1605 discovered the Gunpowder Treason), Potts discloses a secret threat from cells of godless female terrorists, living in poverty and anger, and in league with Satan against the commonweal. He condemns the accused witches of Lancashire (including those who were found innocent); celebrates the destruction of those were condemned; eulogizes the judges who hanged them; and applauds the triumph of good over evil. But a close reading of *The Wonderful Discovery* discloses evil elsewhere than in the place we are instructed to look for it. In the words of Judge Bromley (speaking without reflection to nine women and one boy when putting them to

Detail fr. John Speed, map of Lancashire (1610)

death): "the more you labor to acquit yourselves, the more evident and apparent you make your offenses to the world" (*finis,* sig. Z3v).

A word about the text: *A Wonderful Discoverie* is here systematically redacted: the depositions, disorganized in the 1613 text, are rearranged chronologically; the drumbeat repetition of "the said" or "aforesaid" in Potts's text has been quietly deleted; and the third-person attribution ("this examinate sayeth") is here replaced by a first-person speaking position. These emendations do not restore a reliable account in the defendants' own words (the "confessions" of illiterate defendants represent their answers to questions, presented as voluntary statements); but the intervention at least clears away vague antecedents and facilitates reading aloud.

Dramatis personae

With the allegations ("nixed": shorthand for killed by witchcraft)

Sir James Altham, of Markshal. JP for the Northern Assize Circuit with Judge Bromley.

James Anderton, Clayton Magistrate (May 19th inquest).

Richard Baldwin, of Clayton, magistrate (May 19th).

Nicholas Baldwin, schoolmaster of Colne (d. 1610). Nixed for saving Thomas Redfern from Whittle's co-conspirators.

Richard Baldwin of Weethead-Colne. Miller. Father of ten children. Refused to pay Elizabeth Device for her labor; later accused Old Dembdike and Elizabeth Device of nixing his youngest child, Elena, buried 8 Sept. 1610.

Nicholas Bannester, of Altham, esq., JP. With Roger Nowell on 27 April investigated the Good Friday feast.

Jennet Booth of Padiham, wife of James, mother of Margery. Accused Margaret Pearson of keeping a toad.

Jane Boothman, of Burley. Conspired with Loomshaw's wife to nix Robert Nutter (d. 1595).

Sir Edward Bromley, of Shifnall, Salop., JP for the Northern Assize Circuit with Judge Altham.

Jane Bulcock of Moss-End, Newchurch. Wife of Christopher. Attended the Good Friday feast. Accused of bewitching Jennet Dean, insane. Hanged 20 August.

John Bulcock. Accused with his mother of bewitching Jennet Dean. Hanged 20 August.

Elizabeth ("Bessie") Chaddock. A. Whittle's daughter, whose burglary precipitated the witchcraft inquisition.

Thomas Covell, Coroner; Governor of Lancaster prison (19 May, examined of A. Whittle and James Device).

Anne Crunkshey, of Marchden (*i.e.,* Cronkshaw of Marsden). Attended the Good Friday feast. Not indicted.

Margaret (Nutter) Crook. Accused A. Whittle and A. Redfern of nixing her brother, Robert Nutter (d. 1595).

Elizabeth Device (c.1567-1612), of Malkin Tower, Pendle. Daughter of E. Southerns. Mother of Alison, James, and Jennet; keeper of a spirit named Ball. Hanged 20 August.

John Device, of Pendle, her husband, died 1601. Paid protection, in grain, to Anne Whittle. Alison Device alleges that Whittle nixed him for not paying, the last year.

Alison Device (1596?-1612). Daughter of Elizabeth. Bewitched John Law with paralysis. Hanged 20 August.

James Device (1600?-1612), son of Elizabeth. Kept a "spirit" named Dandy, a brown dog. Condemned for nixing Anne Towneley and John Duckworth. Testified against his mother and others. Hanged 20 August.

Jennet Device (1603-1636), daughter of Elizabeth. Key witness. Indicted as a witch, March 1633/4, died in prison.

John Duckworth, of the Laund. Nixed by James Device for reneging on the promised gift of an old shirt. Son of the John Duckworth beheaded at Halifax, 1586.

Anne Foulds. Nixed by Katherine Hewitt and Alice Gray. Buried at Colne 4 July 1607.

Alice Gray, of Colne. Attended the Good Friday feast. Accused of nixing Anne Foulds. Acquitted.

Richard "Blaze" Hargreaves of Higham (d. 1609). Nixed by Jas. Device.

Elizabeth Hargreaves, wife of Christopher Hargreaves of Thorneyholm. Attended on Good Friday. Not indicted.

Henry Hargreaves, Constable of Pendle Forest. m.1, Jennet Fearnside (1598); m.2 Elizabeth Law (1603).

Jennet Hargreaves, wife of Hugh Hargreaves of Barley. Attended the Good Friday feast. Not indicted.

John Hargreaves of Goldshaw (d. 1609). Nixed by James Device.

Grace Hay, of Padiham. Attended the Good Friday feast. Indicted and acquitted.

Katherine Hewitt, wife of next. Attended the Good Friday feast. Nixed Anne Foulds. Hanged 20 August.

John Hewitt a.k.a. Mold-heels, of Waterside-Colne. Katherine's husband. Son of Nicholas Hewitt, hanged 1587.

Christopher Holgate, of Rossendale. Son of Dembdike, b.1565?; m.1 Isabel Robinson 1590; m.2 Elizabeth —.

Christopher Jacks, of Thorneyholme. At the Friday feast.

John Law, of Halifax, peddler. Bewitched by Alison Device.

Abraham Law, of Halifax, cloth-dyer. His son.

Thomas Lister Sr., of Westby (d. 1607). Nixed by witchcraft of Jennet Preston, at whose touch his corpse bled afresh.

Thomas Lister Jr., of Westby (d. 1619). Stalked Jennet Preston as a witch; perjured himself, motive unclear.

Loomshaw's wife, of Burnley. Conspired with Jane Boothman to nix Robert Nutter in 1595.

Henry Mitton, of Roughlee. Nixed by Dembdike.

Hugh Moore, of Pendle. Nixed by Anne Whittle after she nixed one or more of his cows.

John Moore, gent., of Higham. Accused Anne Whittle of bewitching his ale. Alison Device alleges that Whittle also nixed Moore's son, by clay image.

Roger Nowell, esq., of Read Hall, Whalley magistrate.

Alice Nutter of Crowtrees, Roughlee (c.1542-1612). Widow of Richard (mother of Miles). Clearly framed. Hanged 20 August.

Anthony Nutter of Goldshaw. Dembdike-Device ally.

Anne Nutter His daughter, a friend of Alison Device. Nixed by Whittle for having laughed at her.

Christopher Nutter of Greenhead. The Whittles' landlord. Nixed by Anne Whittle and her daughter Anne Redfern.

John Nutter Sr. of Bull-Hole Farm. Asked Dembdike to cure a sick cow that she is said to have nixed instead.

John Nutter Jr. of Bull-Hole Farm. Bessie Whittle having begged some milk and taken it to her mother, John Nutter Jr. came and kicked over the can. On the morrow, one of his father's cows was nixed by Anne Whittle, in revenge.

Robert Nutter, the younger (d. 1595). Son of Christopher, Grandson of Robert Nutter the elder. Nixed by Anne Whittle and Anne Redfern.

Margaret Pearson, of Padiham. (Previously tried and acquitted.) Bewitched a horse. Sentenced to stand in the pillory six hours a day for four market days.

Thomas Potts, of London. Court clerk for Judge Bromley, and editor of *The Wonderful Discoverie.*

Jennet Preston, of Gisburn (then in Yorkshire). Nixed Thomas Lister Sr. of Westby Hall. Hanged 29 July, at York.

Anne Redfern. Daughter of Anne Whittle, third wife of Thomas Redfern (n. 11 Jan. 1604/5). Made clay images ("pictures") of her enemies. Hanged 20 August.

Thomas Redfern of Higham. Died 1612.

Isabel Robey of Windle. Accused by Peter Chaddock of causing sickness. Hanged 20 August.

James Robinson Sr., of Barley. Accused Anne Whittle and Anne Redfern of nixing Robert Nutter (d. 1595) and of bewitching his brew (about 1606).

James Robinson, his son. Nixed by Elizabeth Device.

John Robinson, his son. Nixed by Elizabeth Device.

William Sands, mayor of Lancaster (May 19th).

Elizabeth Southerns alias **"Old Dembdike"** (c. 1535-1612), of Malkin Tower. Blind. Acquainted with a devil-boy named Tibb. Died in custody before trial.

Anne Towneley, of Carr Hall. Nixed by clay image for having accused James Device and his mother of stealing.

Anne "Chattox" Whittle (c.1535-1612), nearly blind. Kept a spirit named Fancy. Mother of Elizabeth Chaddock and Anne Redfern. Hanged 20 August.

From *The Wonderful Discovery of Witches in the County of Lancaster; with the Arraignment and Trial of Nineteen Notorious Witches, at the Assizes and General Jail-Delivery holden at the Castle of Lancaster upon Monday, the 17th of August last, 1612: A particular declaration of the most barbarous and damnable practices, murthers, wicked and devilish conspiracies, practiced and executed by the most dangerous and malicious witch, Elizabeth Southerns alias Dembdike, of the Forest of Pendle in the county of Lancaster, widow, who died in the Castle at Lancaster before she came to receive her trial. Published and set forth by commandment of his Majesty's Justices of Assize in those parts.*

By Thomas Potts, esq., Court Recorder

The Examination of ALISON DEVICE, daughter of Elizabeth Device, of the Forest of Pendle, in the county of Lancaster, spinster; taken at Read in the said county of Lancaster, [Friday,] the [13][th] day of March, before Roger Nowell, esq., [J.P.] ° [1]

THIS EXAMINATE *sayeth that*:

"[M]y father, called John Device, being afraid that Anne Chattox should do him or his goods any hurt by witchcraft, did covenant with Anne, that if she would hurt neither of [us], she should yearly have one aghen-dole of meal; which meal was yearly paid until the year which [my] father died in, which was about eleven years since – [my] father upon his then-deathbed taking it that Anne Whittle alias Chattox did bewitch him to death, because the meal was not paid the last year." [2]

And she this examinate further sayeth that:

"About six or seven years ago, Chattox did fall out with one Hugh Moore of Pendle […] about certain cattle of Moore's, which Moore did charge Chattox to have bewitched; for which, Chattox did curse and worry Moore, and said she would be revenged of Moore; whereupon Moore presently fell sick and languished about half a year, and then died; which Moore, upon his deathbed, said that Chattox had bewitched him to death." [3]

And she this examinate further sayeth that:

"About six years ago, a daughter of Anne Chattox, called Elizabeth, having been at the house of John Nutter of the Bull-Hole [Farm] to beg or get a dish full of milk […] brought [it] to her mother), who was [dwelling] about a field's breadth of Nutter's house; which her mother Anne Chattox took and put into a can, and did churn the same with two sticks across (in the same field); whereupon John Nutter's son […] misliking her doings, put the can and milk over with his foot. And the morning next after, a cow of John Nutter's fell sick, and so languished three or four days, and then died."

And she also sayeth that:

"About two years agone, [I] being in the house of Anthony Nutter of Pendle, and being then in company with Anne Nutter" (daughter of Anthony), "Anne Whittle alias Chattox came into Anthony Nutter's house. And seeing [me] and Anne Nutter laughing, and saying that [we] laughed at *her*, […] 'Well-said, then!' says Anne Chattox. 'I will be met with the one of you.' And upon the next day after, […] Anne Nutter fell sick and, within three weeks after, died. […]

"About two years ago, [I] heard that Anne Whittle alias Chattox was suspected for bewitching the drink of John Moore of Higham, gentleman. And not long after, [I] heard Chattox say that she 'would meet with John Moore, or his' – whereupon a child of John Moore's, called John, fell sick and languished about half a year, and then died; during which languishing, [I] saw Chattox sitting in her own garden, and a picture of clay like unto a child in her apron; which [I] espying, Anne Chattox would have hid with her apron. And [I] declaring the same to [my] mother, [my] mother thought it was the picture of John Moore's child."

On Wednesday next, Alison had her deadly encounter with John Law; whose son Abraham, a Yorkshire cloth-dyer, was sent for. When the peddler had sufficiently recovered his speech, he explained that he was bewitched by Alison Device of Malkin Tower. Forced to confront her stricken victim on Sunday the 29th, Alison begged his forgiveness, and received it. But the very next day she found herself standing before Judge Nowell on a capital charge of witchcraft.

Abraham Law was first to testify. (According to the usual practice, Alison as the defendant would not have been permitted to hear her accuser's deposition, prior to trial).

---

[1] *spinster*] though Alison was indeed single, the term her is literal, denoting her trade as a woman able to spin flax and wool in exchange for food or wages.

[2] *aghen-dole*] a kneading-dole, or the quantity of meal, etc., usually taken for kneading at one time.

[3] *worry*] vex, harass.

The Examination of ABRAHAM LAW, of Hal-lifax, in the county of York, cloth-dyer, taken upon oath [Monday] the 30ᵗʰ day of March 1612 °

ABRAHAM LAW [...] *being sworn and examined sayeth that*:

"Upon Saturday last save one, being the one-and-twentieth day of this instant March, [I] was sent for, by a letter that came from [my] father [...] who then lay in Colne speechless, and had the left side lamed (all save his eye). And when [I] came to [my] father, [he] had something recovered his speech, and did complain that he was pricked with knives, elsins, and sickles; and that the same hurt was done unto him at Colne-Field, presently after that Alison Device had offered to buy some pins of him, and she had no money to pay for them withal. But as [my] father told [me], he *gave* her some pins. [...]" [1]

"[I] heard [my] father say that the hurt he had in his lameness was done unto him by Alison Device, by *witchcraft*, and [...] that Alison Device did lie upon him and trouble him. And [I] seeing [my] father so tormented with Alison and with one other old woman, whom [my] Father did not know as it seemed, [I] made search after Alison; and having found her, brought her to [my] father yesterday (being the nine-and-twentieth of this instant March). [My] father in the hearing of [myself] and divers others did charge Alison to have bewitched him; which Alison confessing did ask [my] father forgiveness, upon her knees for the same; whereupon [my] father accordingly did forgive her."

Nowell next interrogated Alison Device. Insofar as his report of that interview is accurate, she made some damning admissions. (This portion of Alison's March 30ᵗʰ examination was read aloud at her trial on August 19ᵗʰ):

The Examination of ALISON DEVICE, of the Forest of Pendle, in the county of Lancaster, spin-ster; taken at Read in the said county of Lancas-ter, the [30ᵗʰ] day of March °

The Confession of Alison Device (30 March)

"[My] grandmother [...] did sundry times, in going or walking together as [we] went begging, persuade and advise [me] to let a devil or familiar appear unto [me]; and [...] let him suck at some part of [me], and [I] might have and do what [I] would. And so, not long after these persuasions [...] walking towards the Rough-Lee, in a close of one John Robinson's,

there appeared unto [me] a thing like unto a black dog, speaking unto [me] and desiring [me] to give him [my] soul, and he would give [me] power to do anything [I] would: whereupon [I] being therewithal enticed, and setting [myself] down, the black dog did with his mouth (as [I] then thought) suck at [my] breast a little below [my] paps, which place did remain blue half a year next after. [2]

"[The] black dog did not appear to [me] until the 18ᵗʰ day of March last; at which time [I] met with a peddler on the highway, called Colne-Field, near unto Colne: and [I] demanded of the peddler to buy some pins of him; but the peddler sturdily answered [me] that he would not loose his pack; and so [I] part[ed] with him.

"Presently, there appeared to [me] the black dog which appeared unto [me] as before; which black dog spake unto [me] in English, saying, 'What wouldst thou have me to do unto yonder man?'

"—To whom [I] said, 'What *canst* thou do at him?'

"And the dog answered again, 'I can lame him!'

"Whereupon [I] answered and said to the black dog, 'Lame him!'

"And before the peddler was gone forty rods further, he fell down lame. And [I] then went after the peddler, and in a house about the distance aforesaid, he was lying lame. And so [I] went begging in Trawden Forest that day, and came home at night. And about five days next after, the black dog did appear to [me] as [I] was going a-begging in a close near the New-Church in Pendle. And [it] spake again to [me], saying, 'Stay and speak with me!' But [I] would not – sithence which time, [I] never saw him." [3]

Nowell also elicited from Alison some damaging allegations concerning her grandmother (this portion was not read at trial, Old Dembdike by that time having already perished in the Lancaster prison):

She further sayeth that:

"One John Nutter" (of the Bull-Hole [Farm] in Pendle) "had a cow which was sick, and requested [my] grandmother to amend the cow. And [my] grandmother said she would. And so [my] grandmother, about ten of the clock in the night, desired [me] to lead her forth; which [I] did, [she] being then blind. And [my] grandmother did remain about half an hour forth, and [my] sister did fetch her in again. But what she did when she was so forth, [I] cannot tell. But the next morning [I] heard that the cow was dead. [...]

---

[1] *elsins*] (Northern dialect) cobbler's awls.

[2] *close*] outhouse.

[3] *forty rods*] about 200 meters.

"About two years agone, [I] having gotten a piggin full of blue-milk by begging, brought it into the house of [my] grandmother; where ([I] going forth presently and staying about half an hour) there was ~~butter, to the quantity of a quartern of a pound, in the~~ milk – and the quantity of the milk still remaining! And [my] grandmother had no butter in the house when I went forth – during which time, Grandmother still lay in her bed." [1]

And further this examinate sayeth that:

"Richard Baldwin of Weethead" (within the Forest of Pendle) "about two years ago, fell out with [my] grandmother, and so [he] would not let her come upon his land. And about four or five days then next after, [my] grandmother did request [me] to lead her forth about ten of the clock in the night; which [I] accordingly did. And she stayed forth then about an hour. And [my] sister fetched her in again. And [I] heard the next morning that [Elena,] a woman-child of Richard Baldwin's was fallen sick, [which] did languish afterwards by the space of a year or thereabouts, and died.

"[I] heard my grandmother say presently after her falling out with Baldwin, she would pray for Baldwin, both still and loud. And [I] heard her curse Baldwin, sundry times."

Waiting outside during Nowell's interrogation of Alison Device were her mother and brother. Judge Nowell did not waste the opportunity. When finished with Alison he called for James to come inside, to answer a few questions; during which interview, James Device disclosed to the Judge's satisfaction that his sister's behavior toward John Law had precedent. To injure another with her potent speech, and then to make a show of remorse, was (on this report) standard practice for Alison Device:

The Examination of JAMES DEVICE, brother to ALISON DEVICE, taken upon oath before Roger Nowell Esquire, aforesaid, the thirtieth day of March, 1612 °

JAMES DEVICE *of the Forest of Pendle, in the county of Lancaster, laborer, sworn and examined, sayeth that*: "About Saint Peter's Day last, one Henry Bulcock came to the house [...] and said that Alison [...] had bewitched a child of his; and desired her that she would go with him to his house; which accordingly she did. And thereupon [...] Alison fell down on her knees and asked Bulcock forgiveness, and con-

fessed to him that she *had* bewitched the child! (as [I] heard [my] sister confess unto [me])." [2]

Elizabeth Device was next to be called. Nowell asked her if it were true that her elderly mother, Elizabeth Southerns, had a devil's mark upon her body, Device is said to have replied that her mother "hath had a place on her left side, by the space of forty years." That is the full length of her reported answer, and the only excerpt recorded from the entire interview – from which it seems clear enough that Device tried to protect her mother from suspicion. But Nowell was now hot on the trail of an elderly female rat that he intended to catch and kill.

The Judge dismissed the Devices without indictment but their ordeal was not yet over. He next issued a warrant for Elizabeth Southerns to appear before him in three days time, on 2 April, at Ashlar House, in Fence, the home of James Wilsey; together with Elizabeth Device, Anne Whittle, and Anne Redfern; with a general call to anyone having information concerning local witchcraft, in particular with respect to the death of cows or children of the Nutter, Baldwin, or Moore families.

In her first interview with Judge Nowell, Elizabeth Southerns accused Anne Whittle and her Redfern daughter – but is said also to have admitted to Nowell that her soul belonged to the Devil.

The Examination of ELIZABETH SOUTHERNS alias OLD DEMBDIKE, taken at the Fence in the forest of Pendle in the county of Lancaster, the 2nd day of April [1612] °

THIS EXAMINATE *sayeth upon her examination that*:

"About half a year before Robert Nutter died [in 1595, ... I] went to the house of Thomas Redfern, which was about midsummer...And there, within three yards of the east end of the house, [I] saw Anne Whittle alias Chattox, and Anne Redfern" (wife of Thomas Redfern and daughter of Anne Whittle alias Chattox), "the one on the one side of the ditch, and the other on the other, and two pictures of clay or marl lying by them. And the third picture, Anne Whittle alias Chattox was making. And Anne Redfern, her daughter, wrought her clay or marl to make the third picture withal. [...] [3]

"[I] passing by them, the spirit called Tibb (in the shape of a black cat) appeared unto [me] and said, 'Turn back again, and do as they do.'

"To whom [I] said: 'What are they doing?'

---

[1] *piggin*] a small wooden milking-pail with one stave longer than the rest to serve as a handle;   *blue milk*] milk that is low in butter fat, and hence has a bluish tinge; skimmed milk.

[2] *Saint Peter's Day...confess*] (sig. 2v). This allegation, dated 30 Mar., is repeated in identical language in James Device's reported deposition of 27 April (sig. C2r).

[3] *pictures*] clay image or model;   *marl*] a mixture of clay and lime, otherwise used as fertilizer.

"Whereunto the spirit said, 'They are making three pictures.'

"Whereupon [I] asked whose pictures they were.

"Whereunto the spirit said, 'They are the pictures of Christopher Nutter, Robert Nutter, and Marie, wife of Robert Nutter.'

"But [I] denying to go back to help them make the pictures, the spirit seeming to be angry therefore shoved or pushed [me] into the ditch, and so shed the milk which [I] had in a can or kit. And so thereupon, the spirit at that time vanished out of [my] sight. But presently after that, the spirit appeared to [me] again in the shape of a hare, and so went with [me] about a quarter of a mile, but said nothing to [me,] nor [I] to it. [...] [1]

"About twenty years past, as [I] was coming homeward from begging, there met [me] near unto a stonepit in Goldshaw, in the Forest of Pendle, a spirit or devil in the shape of a boy, the one half of his coat black, and the other brown; who bade [me] stay, saying to [me] that if [I] would give him [my] soul, [I] should have anything that [I] would request. Whereupon [I] demanded his name, and the spirit answered his name was Tibb."

(And so this examinate, in hope of such gain as was promised by the said devil or Tibb, was contented to give her soul to the said spirit.)

"And for the space of five or six years next after, the spirit or devil appeared at sundry times unto [me] about daylight-gate, always bidding [me] stay and asking [me] what [I] would have or do. To whom [I] replied, "Nay, nothing!" – for [I] said [I] wanted nothing yet. [2]

"And so, about the end of the six years, upon a sabbath day in the morning, [I] having a little child upon [my] knee and [I] being in a slumber, the spirit appeared unto [me] in the likeness of a brown dog, forcing himself to [my] knee, to get blood under [my] left arm; and [I] being without any apparel saving [my] smock, the devil did get blood under [my] left arm.

"[I], awaking, said, 'Jesus, save [my] child!' – but [I] had no power, nor could not say, 'Jesus save [my] *self*!' – whereupon the brown dog vanished out of [my] sight – after which, [I] was almost stark mad for the space of eight weeks. [...]

And upon her examination, she further confesseth:

"A little before Christmas last, [my] daughter having been to help Richard Baldwin's folks at the mill, [my] daughter did bid [me] go to Baldwin's house and ask him something for her helping of his folks. [...]

"Baldwin said to [me] and [to my granddaughter] Alison Device, who at that time led [me,] being blind: 'Get out of my ground, whores and witches! I will burn the one of you and hang the other!'

"To whom [I] answered, 'I care not for thee! Hang thyself!.' [...]

"Going over the next hedge, [...] Tibb appeared unto [me] and said, 'Revenge thee of him!'

"To whom [I] said again [...] 'Revenge *thee*, either of him, or his!' And so the spirit vanished out of [my] sight, and [I] never saw him since." [...]

One item of business remained: a devil's teat "was to be seen at this examinate's examination." Before dismissing her, Nowell required Old Dembdike to expose her left side and evidently found what he was searching for. He then committed Elizabeth Southerns to the prison in Lancaster Castle. She died soon after while in custody and never came to trial.

[*Thomas Potts, Court Recorder*:] I pray you give me leave, with your patience and favor, before I proceed to the indictment, arraignment, and trial of such as were prisoners in the Castle, to lay open the life and death of this damnable and malicious witch of so long continuance: "Old Dembdike," of whom our whole business hath such dependence, that without the particular declaration and record of her evidence, with the circumstances, we shall never bring anything to good perfection: for from this sink of villainy and mischief have all the rest proceeded. [...]

She was a very old woman, about the age of fourscore years, and had been a witch for fifty years. She dwelt in the Forest of Pendle, a vast place, fit for her profession. What she committed in her time, no man knows. Thus lived she securely for many years, brought up her own children, instructed her grandchildren, and took great care and pains to bring them up to be witches. She was a general agent for the Devil in all these parts. No man escaped her or her furies, that ever gave them any occasion of offense or denied them anything they stood need of. And certain it is, no man near them was secure or free from danger. [...]

But God, who had in His divine providence provided to cut them off and root them out of the Commonwealth, so disposed above that the justices of those parts – understanding, by a general charm and muttering; the great and universal resort to Malkin Tower; the common opinion, with the report of these suspected people; the complaint of the King's subjects for the loss of their children, friends, goods, and cattle (as there could not be so great fire without some smoke) – sent for some [officials] of the country and took great pains to inquire after [these suspected persons,] their proceedings and courses of life.

---

[1] *kit*] a wooden tub or pail used for carrying milk, butter, fish, etc.

[2] *daylight-gate*] dawn.

In the end, Roger Nowell, esquire, one of his Majesty's justices in these parts – a very religious, honest gentleman, painful in the service of his country; whose fame for this great service to his country shall live after him – took upon him to enter into the particular examination of these suspected persons; and (to the honor of God and the great comfort of all his country!) made such a discovery of them in order, as the like hath not been heard of – which, for your better satisfaction, I have here placed in order against her as they are upon record amongst the Records of the Crown at Lancaster; certified by Master Nowell and others.

If Elizabeth Southerns confessed to having sold her soul to the Devil, others came forward to confirm her testimony that it was Anne Whittle and her daughter Anne Redfern who killed Robert Nutter by witchcraft, back in 1595.

Among those who pointed the finger at Whittle was Margaret (Nutter) Crook, who said that her brother Robert on his deathbed "did a hundred times at the least say that Anne Redfern and her associates had bewitched him to death." John Nutter likewise took Old Dembdike's part against Whittle and her Redfern daughter. (Nutter seems not to have known that Whittle stood accused of killing his niece, for laughing at her; and her rival, Dembdike of having killed one of his cows, to revenge a can of milk.)

The Examination of JOHN NUTTER, of Higham Booth, in the Forest of Pendle, in the County of Lancaster, yeoman, against Anne Redfern, taken [2 April] °

THIS EXAMINATE, *sworn and examined upon his oath, sayeth that*:

"In or about Christmas, some eighteen or nineteen years ago, […] coming from Burnley with Christopher Nutter and Robert Nutter, [my] father and brother, [I] heard [my] brother then say unto [my] father these words, or to this effect: 'Father, I am sure I am bewitched by the Chaddocks – Anne Chattox and Anne Redfern her daughter. I pray you, cause them to be laid in Lancaster Castle.' Whereunto [my] father answered, 'Thou art a foolish lad! It is not so, it is thy miscarriage.' Then [my] brother weeping, said. 'Nay, I am sure that I am bewitched by them, and if ever I come again' (for he was ready to go to Sir Richard Shuttleworth's, then his master), 'I will procure them to be laid where they shall be glad to bite lice in two with their teeth!'"

Next to testify was James Robinson, who took the part of Southerns and Device against Whittle and Redfern (which may have been premature: before the investigation was complete, Elizabeth Device and her brown dog, Ball, would stand accused of killing the brothers, James and John Robinson, who criticized

Elizabeth for giving birth to Master Sellar's bastard. The deceased Robinson brothers were cousins to the James Robinson who testified against Whittle and Chattox, Dembdike's rivals.)

The examination and evidence of JAMES ROBINSON, taken the day and year aforesaid before Roger Nowell, esquire, aforesaid, against Anne Whittle alias Chattox, prisoner at the Bar °

THE SAID EXAMINATE *sayeth that*:

"Anne Whittle alias Chattox, and Anne Redfern her daughter, are commonly reputed and reported to be witches. […] About some eighteen years ago, [I] dwelled with one Robert Nutter the elder, of Pendle. […] Young Robert Nutter, who dwelled with his grandfather in the summertime, he fell sick. And in his sickness he did several times complain that he had harm by them. And [I] asking him what he meant by that word, 'them,' he said that he verily thought that Anne Whittle alias Chattox and Redfern's wife had bewitched him.

"And Robert Nutter, shortly after – being to go with his then-master, called Sir Richard Shuttleworth, into Wales – [I] heard him say (before his then going), unto Thomas Redfern, that if ever he came again, he would get his father to put Redfern out of his house, or he himself would pull it down; to whom Redfern replied, saying, 'When you come back again, you will be in a better mind.' But [Nutter] never came back again, but died before Candlemas in Cheshire, as he was coming homeward. […]

"About six years ago, Anne Whittle alias Chattox was hired by [my] wife to card wool. […] Upon a Friday and Saturday she came and carded wool with [my] wife, and so the Monday then next after she came likewise to card. And [my] wife having newly tunned drink into stands which stood by, Anne Whittle [was seen] taking a dish or cup, and drawing drink several times. And so, never after that time, for some eight or nine weeks, [could we] have any drink but spoiled!"

[*Thomas Potts, Court Recorder*:] Since the voluntary confession and examination of a witch doth exceed all other evidence, I spare to trouble you with a multitude of examinations or depositions of any other witnesses, by reason this bloody fact, for the murder of Robert Nutter (upon so small an occasion, as to threaten to take away his own land from such as were not worthy to inhabit or dwell upon it!), is now made (by that which you have already heard) so apparent, as no indifferent man will question it or rest unsatisfied.

I shall now proceed to set forth unto you the rest of her actions remaining upon Record. And how dangerous it was for any man to live near these° people, to give them any occasion of offense, I leave it to your good consideration!

[*Thomas Potts, Court Recorder*:] Hereupon Anne Whittle alias Chattox, [Redfern's] mother, was brought forth to be examined.

Anne Whittle's version: Robert Nutter's mother hatched the plot so that she'd not lose the land to her son on her husband's death. Whittle and Redfern, with Jane Boothman and Loomshaw's wife, agreed to bewitch Robert; but Redfern, by persuasion of her husband, withdrew; whereupon a schoolmaster was called in to protect Thomas Redfern from the others' curse.

Later, Anne Redfern refusing his sexual advance, Robert Nutter threatened to throw her family off his land. Instead, Robert died young; which the Nutters blamed on Anne Redfern. and her mother (The schoolmaster, Jane Boothman, and Loomshaw's wife could not be questioned: all three were recently dead.)

The Voluntary Confession and Examination of ANNE WHITTLE alias Chattox, taken at the Fence in the Forest of Pendle, in the county of Lancaster, the 2ⁿᵈ day of April °

ANNE WHITTLE *alias* CHATTOX *upon her examination, voluntarily confesseth, and sayeth that*:

"About fourteen or fifteen years ago, a thing like a Christian man for four years together did sundry times come to [me], and requested [me] to give him [my] soul. And in the end [I] was contented to give him [my] soul, [I] being then in [my] own house in the Forest of Pendle – whereupon the Devil, then in the shape of a man, said to [me], 'Thou shalt want nothing, and be revenged of whom thou list.' […]

"And then the Devil further commanded [me] to call him by the name of *Fancy*, and when [I] wanted anything, or would be revenged of any, call on Fancy, and he would be ready. […]

"[Fancy] did appear unto [me] not long after, in man's likeness, and would have had [me] to have consent that he might hurt the wife of Richard Baldwin of Pendle. But [I] would not then consent unto him. […He] would then have bitten [me] by the arm—and so vanished away, for that time. […]"

And this examinate further sayeth that:

"Robert Nutter did desire [my] daughter" (one Redfern's wife) "to have his pleasure of [her], [Nutter] being then in Redfern's house; but [she] denied [him]; whereupon Robert, seeming to be greatly displeased therewith, in a great anger took his horse and went away, saying in a great rage that if ever the ground came to him, [she] should never dwell upon his land – whereupon [I] called Fancy to [me]; who came to [me] in a parcel of ground called the Laund, asking [me] what [I] would have him to do. And [I] bade him go revenge her of Robert Nutter. After which, [Robert] lived about a quarter of a year and then died. […]

"Elizabeth Nutter, wife to old Robert Nutter, did request [me] – and Loomshaw's wife of Burley, and one Jane Boothman of the same" (who are now both dead; which time of request was before that [young] Robert Nutter desired the company of Redfern's wife) – "to get young Robert Nutter's death, if [we] could (all being together at that time); to that end, that if Robert were dead, then the women ([our] cousins) might have the land. "By [Elizabeth Nutter's] persuasion, [we] all consented unto it.

"After which time, [my] son-in-law, Thomas Redfern, did persuade [me] not to kill or hurt Robert Nutter; for which persuasion Loomshaw's wife had like to have killed *Redfern*, but that one Master Baldwin (the late schoolmaster at Colne) did by his learning stay Loomshaw's wife, and therefore had a capon from Redfern. […Methinks] Loomshaw's wife and Jane Boothman did what they could to kill Robert Nutter" (as well as this examinate did)." [1]

Asked whether she ever cursed the family or goods of John Moore, Whittle replied, "[I] was sent for by the wife of John Moore, to help [amend] drink that was forspoken or bewitched; at which time [I] used this prayer for the amending of it, *viz*.,

A Charm °

Three bitters hast thou bitten,
The heart, ill eye, ill tongue:
Three bitters° shall be thy boot,
Father, Son, and Holy Ghost, a' God's name. [2]
Five paternosters, five avès, and a creed,
In worship of five wounds of our Lord.

"After which time that [I] had used these prayers and amended her drink, Moore's wife did chide [me], and was grieved at [me]. And thereupon [I] called for [my] devil, Fancy, and bade him go bite a brown cow of Moore's by the head, and make the cow go mad. And the Devil then, in the likeness of a brown dog, went to the cow and bit her; which cow went mad accordingly, and died within six weeks next after, or thereabouts. […]

"Perceiving Anthony Nutter of Pendle to favor Elizabeth Southerns alias Dembdike, [I] called Fancy to [me] (who appeared like a man) and bade him go kill a cow of Anthony's; which the Devil did, and that cow died also. […]

"In summer last save one, the Devil, or Fancy, came upon [me] in the nighttime, and at divers and sundry times, in the likeness of a bear, gaping as though he would have wearied [me]. And the last time of all [I] saw him was upon Thursday last year but one, next before Midsummer Day, in the evening, like a bear, and [I] would not then speak unto him, for the which the Devil pulled [me] down.

---

[1] *capon*] a rooster castrated (for more tender meat), payment for Baldwin's assistance.

[2] *bitters*] 1. bitter food or experience; 2. *biters*; *boot*] profit, payback.

"The Devil, or Fancy, hath taken most of [my] sight away from me." […]

• • •

[Thomas Potts, Court Recorder:] [She] confessed the making of the pictures of clay, and in the end cried out very heartily to God to forgive her sins, and upon her knees entreated for this Redfern, her daughter.

Here this worthy justice, Master Nowell, out of these particular examinations (or rather accusations), finding matter to proceed – and having now before him old Dembdike, old Chattox, Alison Device, and [Anne] Redfern (both old and young, *Reos confitentes, et accusantes invicem*) – about the second of April last past, [he] committed and sent them away to the Castle at Lancaster, there to remain until the coming of the King's Majesty's justices of Assize, then to receive their trial.[1]

But here they had not stayed a week, when their children and friends (being abroad at liberty) labored a special meeting – at Malkin Tower in the Forest of Pendle, upon Good Friday, within a week after they were committed – of all the most dangerous, wicked, and damnable witches in the county, far and near. Upon Good Friday they met, according to solemn appointment; [and] solemnized this great festival day according to their former order, with great cheer, merry company, and much conference.

• • •

[The Arrest of Jennet Preston]

Among those said to have attended the Good Friday picnic at Malkin Tower on 10 April 1612 was Jennet Preston of Gisburn, Yorkshire, a woman who after spending weeks in prison had just been tried at York and acquitted, on 6 April, of killing an infant of one Dodgson, by witchcraft; a charge brought against her by Thomas Lister Jr.

Married to William Preston of Gisburn, Jennet (née Balderston) worked as a servant in the home of Thomas Lister Senior of Westby Hall; who died suddenly on or about 1 February 1606/7. Lister, 37, was then in Bracewell parish to celebrate the wedding of his son and principal heir, Thomas Jr., 17, to Jane Heber, 14. Before returning home, Lister Sr. became mysteriously ill; and before dying he is said to have cried out, "Help me, help me! Jennet Preston lays heavy upon me, Preston's wife lays heavy upon me! Help me, help me," and so departed. Thomas Jr. (to whom we are indebted for the quotation) affirmed that this was not a confession of adultery but proof of murder by witchcraft (Y2r).[2]

Perhaps because Preston was named to receive a bequest, Lister Jr. was relentless in his efforts to see the poor woman hanged. Five years after his father's death, and still having no indictment, Lister alleged that Jennet Preston had bewitched and killed the Dodgsons' child. Preston (on this sworn statement of a gentleman) stood trial at the York Assize on 6 April 1612; with his son-in-law, Thomas Heber, JP, serving as prosecutor. But the evidence presented against her was so thin that she was acquitted.

What happened next (the official story) is that Jennet Preston following her acquittal "rode in haste to the Great Meeting at Malkin Tower, and there prayed aid for the murther of Master Thomas Lister" (sig. Y3r).

In the third week of April, a knock came on the door of the Preston residence in Gisburn. Thomas Heber, Yorkshire magistrate and prosecutor, together with Henry Hargreaves (Constable of Pendle Forest) had come to arrest her, again, on a charge of witchcraft; this time, for the attempted murder of Thomas Lister Jr. The evidence against her: Hargreaves had obtained a statement from Anne Whittle alias Chattox, prisoner in Lancaster, who had named Jennet Preston of Gisburn as a guest "at the said feast upon the said Good Friday, and that she was an ill woman, and had done Master Lister of Westby great hurt" (Y4v). Whittle did not herself attend the Good Friday event, being in prison. But to prove that she was correct, Hargreaves had in hand twelve-year-old James Device (son of Elizabeth), who "having had full view of her," said Yes, "she was the selfsame woman which came amongst the witches on the last Good Friday, for their aid for the killing of Master Lister" (Y4r). Heber committed Jennet Preston to the York prison, to await trial in July.

Before or after his trip to Gisburn with James Device, Hargreaves supervised the boy in a dig on the west side of his mother's firehouse at Malkin Tower. Their shovels discovered a buried clay image and four teeth. Hargreaves then took James and the unearthed items to Ashlar House in Fence, where the boy was interrogated by Roger Nowell and Nicholas Bannester. He cooperated fully.

Nowell is said to have learned from James Device that the hapless peasants gathered at Malkin Tower on 10 April not only agreed to help Jennet Preston kill Thomas Lister: the same wicked crew on Good Friday hatched a plot to murder Thomas Covell, the jailer at Lancaster Castle; and then to blow up the Castle with massive quantities of dynamite. (The similarity between Thomas Knyvett's discovery of the 1605 Gunpowder Plot on the one hand, and Roger Nowell's discovery of the Lancaster gunpowder plot of 1612, would not go unnoticed by King James.)

• • •

---

[1] *Reos…invicem*] the criminals confessing and accusing one another.

[2] *Preston*] See Clayton (2007) for the extant records of Jennet Preston and other defendants.

[The Good Friday Conspiracy] °

[*Thomas Potts*:] This [conspiracy] was not so secret but some notice of it came to Master Nowell; and by his great pains taken in the examination of Jennet Device, all their practices are now made known: Their purpose to kill Master Covell and blow up the Castle is prevented! All their murders, witchcrafts, enchantments, charms, and sorceries are discovered! And even in the midst of their consultations, they are all confounded and arrested by God's justice; brought before Master Nowell and Master Bannester upon their voluntary confessions, examinations, and other evidence accused; and so (by them) committed to the Castle; so as now both old and young have taken up their lodgings with Master Covell until the next Assizes, expecting their trial and deliverance, according to the laws provided for such-like. [...] [1]

But because I have charged [Elizabeth Device] to be the principal agent to procure a solemn meeting at Malkin Tower of the Grand Witches, to consult of some speedy course for the deliverance of her mother (old Dembdike), her daughter, and other witches at Lancaster; [plus] the speedy execution of Master Covell (who little suspected or deserved any such practice or villainy against him), the blowing-up of the Castle, with divers other wicked and devilish practices and murthers, I shall make it apparent unto you, by the particular examinations and evidence of [Elizabeth's] own children, such as were present at the time of their [Good Friday] consultation, together with her own examination and confession amongst the Records of the Crown at Lancaster, as hereafter followeth.

The Examination and Evidence of JENNET DEVICE, daughter of Elizabeth Device, late wife of John Device, of the Forest of Pendle, in the county of Lancaster, against Elizabeth Device, her mother [27 April 1612] °

JENNIFER DEVICE *sayeth that*:

"Upon Good Friday last there was about twenty persons, whereof only two were men [...] at [my] grandmother's house" (called Malkin Tower), "about twelve of the clock; all which persons, my mother told [me] were witches, and that they came to give a name to Alison Device's spirit or familiar" (sister to this examinate, and now prisoner at Lancaster).

"[They] had to their dinners beef, bacon, and roasted mutton; which mutton (as [my] brother said) was of a wether of Christopher Swyer's° of Barley; which wether was brought in the night before [...] by James Device, [my] brother, and in [my] sight, killed and eaten."

The Examination of JAMES DEVICE, son of Elizabeth Device, of the Forest of Pendle, laborer, taken the seven-and-twentieth day of April [...] before Roger Nowell and Nicholas Bannester °

JAMES DEVICE [...] *sayeth that*:

"Twelve years ago, Anne Chattox, at a burial at the New-Church in Pendle, did take three scalps of people which had been buried and then cast out of a grave...and took eight teeth out of the scalps, whereof she kept four to herself and gave other four to Dembdike, [my] grandmother; which four teeth – now showed to me – are the four teeth that Chattox gave to [my] grandmother as [...] have ever since been kept, until now found by Henry Hargreaves and [me] at the west end of [my] grandmother's house, and there buried in the earth; and a picture of clay there likewise found by [us], about half-a-yard over in the earth, where the teeth lay; which picture, so found, was almost withered away – and was the picture of Anne, Anthony Nutter's daughter, as [my] grandmother told [me]. [...] [2]

"About three years ago, [I] being in [my] grandmother's house with [my] mother, there came a thing in shape of a brown dog, which [my] mother called Ball, who [...] bade her make a picture of clay like unto John Robinson alias Swyer; and dry it hard, and then crumble it, by little and little; and as the picture should crumble or mull away, so should John Robinson alias Swyer his body decay and wear away. And within two or three days after, the picture shall so all be wasted and mulled away; so then John Robinson should die presently.

"Upon the agreement betwixt the dog and [my] mother, the dog suddenly vanished out of [my] sight. And the next day, [I] saw [my] mother take clay at the west end of her house, and make a picture of it after Robinson, and brought into her house, and dried in some two days. And about two days after the drying thereof, [my] mother fell on crumbling the picture of clay, every day some, for some three weeks together; and within two days after all was crumbled or mulled away, John Robinson died. [...]

"Upon Shear Thursday was two years, [my] grandmother Elizabeth Southerns alias Dembdike did bid [me] go to the church to receive the Communion (the next day after being Good Friday); and then, not to eat the bread the minister gave [me], but to bring it and deliver it to such a thing as should meet [me] in [my] way homewards.

"Notwithstanding her persuasions, [I] did eat the bread. And so in [my] coming homeward, some forty rods off the church, there met [me] a thing in the shape of a hare, who spoke unto [me] and asked [me]

---

[1] *taken up their lodgings*] i.e., *in jail; a witticism.*

[2] *scalps*] the head or skull exclusive of the lower jaw; *Anne Nutter*] Alison is said to have said that her friend Anne Nutter was slain by Anne "Chattox" Whittle.

whether [I] had brought the bread that [my] grand-mother had bidden [me], or no? Whereupon I an-swered I had not. And thereupon the thing threatened to pull [me] in pieces, and so [I] thereupon marked [myself] to God. And so the thing vanished out of [my] sight. And within some four days after that, there appeared in [my] sight, hard by the New-Church in Pendle, a thing like unto a brown dog, who asked [me] to give him [my] soul, and [I] should be revenged of any whom [I] would; whereunto [I] an-swered, that [my] soul was not [mine] to give, but was [my] Savior Jesus Christ's."

(But as much as was in him this examinant to give, he was contented he should have it.)

"And within two or three days after, [I] went to the Carr Hall; and upon some speeches betwixt Mistress Towneley and [me] – she charging [me] and [my] mother to have stolen some turves of hers, bade [me] 'Pack the doors!' – and withal, as [I] went forth of the door, Mistress Towneley gave [me] a knock between the shoulders. And about a day or two after that, there appeared unto [me], in [my] way, a thing like unto a black dog, who put [me] in mind of Mistress Towneley's falling out with [me]; who bade [me] make a picture of clay like unto Mistress Towneley: and [said] that [I] with the help of [my] spirit (who then ever after bid [me] to call it *Dandy*) would kill or destroy Mistress Towneley. [1]

"And so the dog vanished out of [my] sight. And the next morning after, [I] took clay and made a picture of Mistress Towneley, and dried it the same night by the fire. And within a day after, [I] began to crumble the picture, every day some, for the space of a week; and within two days after all was crumbled away, Mistress Towneley died.

"About two years ago, [I] saw three pictures of clay, of half-a-yard long, at the end of Redfern's house. [Thomas] Redfern had one of the pictures in his hand, Marie his daughter had another in her hand, and Redfern's wife, now prisoner at Lancaster, had another picture in her hand, which picture she (Red-fern's wife) was then crumbling. But whose pictures they were, [I] cannot tell. And at [my] returning back again, some ten rods off them, there appeared unto [me] a thing like a hare, which spit fire at me.

"[I] heard [my] grandmother say about a year ago that my mother" (called Elizabeth Device) "and oth-ers had killed one Henry Mitton of the Rough-Lee by witchcraft. The reason wherefore he was so killed, was for that [my] grandmother, Old Dembdike, had asked Mitton a penny; and he denying her thereof, thereupon she procured his death. [...]

"In Lent last, one John Duckworth of the Laund promised [me] an old shirt. And within a fortnight after, [I] went to Duckworth's house and demanded the old shirt; but Duckworth denied me thereof. And going out of the house, the spirit Dandy appeared

unto [me] and said, 'Thou didst touch Duckworth?' Whereunto [I] answered [I] did not touch him. 'Yes,' said the spirit again, thou didst touch him, and there-fore I have power of him!' Whereupon [I] joined with the spirit and then wished the spirit to kill Duck-worth. And within one week then next after, Duck-worth died. [...] [2]

"About a month ago, as [I] was coming towards [my] mother's house, and at day-gate of the same night, [I] met a brown dog coming from [my] grand-mother's house, about ten rods distant...and about two or three nights after, [I] heard a voice of a great number of children shrieking and crying pitifully, about daylight-gate – and likewise, about ten rods' distant of [my] grandmother's house.

"And about five nights then next following, pres-ently after daylight, within twenty rods of the [...] house, [I] heard a foul yelling like unto a great num-ber of cats. But what they were, [I] cannot tell. [...]

"About three nights after that, about midnight of the same, there came a thing and lay upon [me] very heavily about an hour, and went then from [me] out of [my] chamber-window – colored black, and about the bigness of a hare or cat....

"Upon Shear Thursday last, in the evening, [I] stole a wether from John Robinson of Barley and brought it to [my] grandmother's house" (Old Demb-dike), "and there killed it. [...] The day following being Good Friday, about twelve of the clock in the daytime, there dined in [my] mother's house a number of persons, whereof three were men with [myself], and the rest women. They met there for three causes following, as [my] mother told [me]: The first was for the naming of the spirit which Alison Device (now prisoner at Lancaster) had; but [they] did not name him, because she was not there. The second cause was for the delivery of [my] grandmother, [my] sister Alison, [and] Anne Chattox and her daughter Redfern [by] killing the jailer at Lancaster; and before the next Assizes to blow up the Castle there, to the end [they] might by that means make an escape and get away; all which, [I] then heard them confer of. [3]

"And the third cause was for that there was a woman dwelling in Gisburn parish, [Jennet Preston,] who came into [my] grandmother's house, who there came and craved assistance of the rest of them that were then there, for the killing of Master Lister of Westby, because (as she then said) he had borne malice unto her, and had thought to have put her away at the last Assizes at York, but could not. And [I] heard the woman say that her power was not strong enough to do it herself, being now less than before-time it had been [...] Preston's wife promised to make them a great feast. And if they had occasion to meet in the mean time, then should warning be

---

[1] *turves*] slabs of peat used as fuel.

[2] *John Duckworth of Laund*] buried 8 May 1608.

[3] *wether*] a castrated ram.

given, that they all should meet upon Romley's Moor." […]

"I heard them all give their consents to put Master Thomas Lister of Westby to death. And after Master Lister should be made away by witchcraft, then all the witches gave their consents to join all together to hank Master Leonard Lister, when he should come to dwell at the Cowgill, and so put *him* to death. […]

"Preston's wife had a spirit with her, like unto a white foal with a black spot in the forehead…and when she got on horseback,…presently vanished out of [my] sight." [1]

The Examination of ELIZABETH DEVICE °

On 27 April at Ashlar House, Nowell and Bannester also interrogated Elizabeth Device about the Good Friday luncheon, most of which interview was omitted from the record, perhaps because she denied any wrong-doing. But the one fragment ascribed to her was by itself enough to warrant hanging.

ELIZABETH DEVICE, mother of James, being examined, confesseth and sayeth that (at the third time), her spirit (the spirit Ball) appeared to her in the shape of a brown dog, at or in her mother's house in Pendle Forest. About four years ago, the spirit bid this examinate make a picture of clay after John Robinson alias Swyer; which this examinate did make accordingly, at the west end of her mother's house, and dried the same picture with the fire, and crumbled all the same picture away within a week or thereabouts. And about a week after the picture was crumbled or mulled away, Robinson died.

The reason wherefore she (this examinate) did so bewitch Robinson to death was for that Robinson had chidden and becalled this examinate for having a bastard child with one Sellar. And this examinate further sayeth and confesseth that she did bewitch James Robinson to death, as in Jennet Device her examination is confessed. And further she sayeth and confesseth that she with the wife of Richard Nutter, and [with Dembdike,] this examinate's mother, joined all together, and did bewitch Henry Mitton to death. [2]

Between the three Devices, the authorities came up with twelve guests present at the Good Friday feast: Jennet Hargreaves of Burley (wife of Hugh); Christopher Holgate (illegitimate son of Dembdike) and his wife Elizabeth; Richard Miles's wife of Roughlee; Jane Bulcock of Moss End (wife of Christopher) and her son John; Alice Cronkshaw of Marsden, Alice Gray and Katherine Hewitt of Colne, and Jennet Preston of Gisburn (Yorkshire); added later, Grace Hay of Padiham; added much later, Alice Nutter of Crowtrees, mother of Miles Nutter of Roughlee.

To the other alleged murders were now added a few more: Elizabeth Device was charged with the witchcraft-murder of Henry Mitton of Roughlee; and of the brothers, John and James Robinson of Barley. (John Robinson was named executor to the Sept. 1609 will of Elizabeth Hargreaves of Watermeetings but did not live long enough to perform the service, dying himself shortly after). James Device was charged with the deaths of Henry Hargreaves' kinsmen, Richard "Blaze" Hargreaves of Higham and Burnley and of John Hargreaves of Goldshaw, who also died in 1609, when James was just nine years old and newly introduced to the profession.

Having got what they needed from Constable Hargreaves, Judge Nowell committed Elizabeth and James Device both to Lancaster Castle to join the other prisoners, taking nine-year-old Jennet under his own custody. In the months following, the little girl supplied him with a mountain of fresh evidence.

Additional interrogations followed on May 5th and 19th. James Device, not yet 13 and naïve, doubtless made his April 27th confession trusting to the usual false "promise of favor." But after three weeks in prison to reflect on his situation, James when brought before the Lord Mayor tried to mitigate his guilt:

The Voluntary Confession and Declaration of JAMES DEVICE, prisoner in the Castle at Lancaster, before William Sands, Mayor of Lancaster; James Anderton, esquire, one of his Majesty's Justices of Peace within the County of Lancaster. And Thomas Covell, gentleman, one of his Majesty's Coroners [19 May 1612] °

JAMES DEVICE, *prisoner in the Castle at Lancaster, sayeth that*:

"[My] spirit Dandy, being very earnest with [me] to give him [my] soul, [I] answered [I] would give him that part thereof that was [my] own to give. And thereupon the spirit said he was above Christ Jesus, and therefore [I] must absolutely give him [my] soul; and, that done, he would give [me] power to revenge [myself] against any whom [I] disliked. […]

"The spirit did appear unto [me] after, sundry times, in the likeness of a dog, and at every time most earnestly persuaded [me] to give him [my] soul absolutely. [I] answered as before, that [I] would give him [my] own part and no further. […]

"The last time that the spirit was with [me] which was the Tuesday next before [my] apprehension, when as he could not prevail with [me] to have [my] soul absolutely granted unto him, the spirit departed from [me], then giving a most fearful cry and yell, and withal caused a great flash of fire to show about [me]. Which said spirit did never after trouble [me]."

William Sands, [Mayor of Lancaster]
James Anderton, [Magistrate of Clayton]
Thomas Covell, Coroner, [Governor of the prison]

---

[1] *hank*] garotte with a rope.

[2] *becalled me*] called me names (whore, witch);

Sands, Anderton, and Covell also examined Anne Whittle one last time, evidently promising favor if she would name others. First augmenting the allegations against old Dembdike, Whittle went on to accuse Margaret Pearson of Padiham, alleging that Pearson bewitched to death Robert Childer's daughter (d. 1594) and his wife Isabel (d. 1602). These are crimes for which Pearson had already been accused, twice tried, and twice acquitted; to which Anne Whittle now added a fourth and fifth offense: Pearson had bewitched and killed a horse in John Dodgson's locked barn, and had sold her soul to the Devil:

The Confession and Examination of ANNE WHITTLE alias Chattox, being prisoner at Lancaster; taken the 19th day of May °

ANNE WHITTLE *alias* CHATTOX *sayeth that*:

"About fourteen years past, [I] entered, through the wicked persuasions and counsel of Elizabeth Southerns alias Dembdike, [...the] profession of witchcraft. Soon after which, the Devil appeared unto [me] in the likeness of a man, about midnight, at the house of Dembdike. And thereupon, Dembdike and [I] went forth of the house unto him; whereupon the wicked spirit moved [me] that [I] would become his subject and give [my] soul unto him – the which, at first, [I] refused to assent unto. But after, by the great persuasions made by Dembdike, [I] yielded to be at his commandment and appointment – whereupon the wicked spirit then said unto [me] that he must have one part of [my] body for him to suck upon; the which [I] denied then to grant unto him – but withal [I] asked him what part of [my] body he would have, for that use. He said he would have a place of [my] right side near to [my] ribs for him to suck upon; whereunto [I] assented. [...]

"At the same time, there was a thing in the likeness of a spotted bitch, that came with the spirit unto Dembdike, which then did speak unto her in [my] hearing, and said that she should have gold, silver, and worldly wealth, at her will. And at the same time [...] there was victuals, *viz.*, flesh, butter, cheese, bread, and drink, and [he] bid [us] eat enough. And after [our] eating, the devil called Fancy, and the other spirit calling himself Tibb, carried the remnant away. [...] Although [we] did eat, [we] were never the fuller nor better for the same. [...] At [our] banquet, the spirits gave [us] light to see what [we] did, although [we] neither had fire nor candlelight. [... T]hey were both she-spirits, and devils."

And being further examined how many sundry persons have been bewitched to death, and by whom they were so bewitched, she sayeth that one Robert Nutter, late of the Greenhead in Pendle, was bewitched by this examinate, Dembdike, and widow Loomshaw (late of Burnley, now deceased). And she further sayeth that Dembdike showed her that she had bewitched to death Richard Ashton, son of Richard Ashton of Downham, esquire [...and] that the wife of one Pearson of Padiham is a very evil woman, and confessed to this examinate that she is a witch, and hath a spirit which came to her the first time in likeness of a man, and cloven-footed, and that she [...] hath done very much harm to one Dodgson's goods, who came in at a loophole into Dodgson's stable, and she and her spirit together did sit upon his horse or mare until the horse or mare died. And likewise, that [...] she bewitched unto death one Childer's wife and her daughter. [...] [1]

Margaret Pearson was arrested and committed to the prison while the authorities searched for a corroborating witness. Their efforts at last paid off on 9 August, only a week before the Assize judges arrived: Jennet Booth came forward to testify that she had seen a spirit or familiar hop forth from Margaret Pearson's fireplace, in the shape of a toad:

The Examination of JENNET BOOTH, of Padiham in the county of Lancaster, the 9th day of August 1612; before Nicholas Bannister, esquire, one of his Majesty's justices of Peace in the county of Lancaster °

JENNET, *the wife of James Booth, of Padiham, upon her oath sayeth that*:

"[I] was carding [wool] in Pearson's house, having a little child with [me], and willed Margery to give [me] a little milk to make [my] child a little meat; who fetched [me] some and put it in a pan. [2]

"Meaning to set it on the fire, [I] found the fire very ill; and taking up a stick that lay by [me, I] brake it in three or four pieces, and laid upon the coals to kindle the same; then set the pan and milk on the fire. And when the milk was boiled to [my] content, [I] took the pan (wherein the milk was) off the fire – and withal, under the bottom of the same, there came a toad, or a thing very like a toad; and to [my] thinking [it] came out of the fire [...whereupon] Margery did carry the toad out of the house in a pair of tongs."

(But what she Margery did therewith, this examinate knoweth not.)

In the meantime, on 12 July, Sir Thomas Gerard, JP, gathered evidentiary statements from four respectable citizens of Windle, alleging that Isabel Robey had afflicted them with ailments ranging from muscle pain to unquenchable thirst. Robey was an elderly widow who had fallen on hard times and was reduced to begging; which caused tension in the home of her grown goddaughter, the wife of Peter Chaddock of Windle; not least, because Isabel from the first had disapproved of her goddaughter's marriage to the brute. Peter complained to Judge Gerard that his godmother was, quite literally, a pain in the neck.

---

[1] *loophole*] a narrow opening or spy-hole; *Richard Ashton*] bapt. 10 Feb. 1604/5, death unk.; mother Mary Holt kin to Nicholas Bannester and John Hargreave.

[2] *carding*] carding wool; *meat*] something to eat.

The Examination of PETER CHADDOCK of Windle, in the county of Lancaster. Taken at Windle, the 12 day of July 1612 [...] Before Sir Thomas Gerard, knight and baronet, one of his Majesty's justices of the peace °

THE EXAMINATE *upon his oath sayeth that*:

"Before [my] marriage [I] heard say that Isabel Robey was not pleased that [I] should marry [my] now wife; whereupon [I] called Isabel *Witch*, and said that [I] did not care for her. Then within two days next after, [I] was sore pained in [my] bones: And [I] having occasion to meet Master John Hawarden at Peasley Cross, [I] wished one Thomas Lyon to go thither with [me], which [we] both did so. But as [we] came homewards, [we] *both* were in evil case! But within a short time after, [I] and Thomas Lyon were both very well amended. [...]

"About four years last past, [my] now wife was angry with Isabel, she then being in [my] house. And [my] wife thereupon went out of the house. And presently after that, Isabel went likewise out of the house – not well pleased, as [I] then did think. And presently after, upon the same day, [I] with [my] wife working in the hay, a pain and a starkness fell into [my] neck [...] which grieved [me] very sore; whereupon [I] sent to one James, a glover which then dwelt in Windle, and desired him to pray for [me]. And within four or five days next after, [I] did mend very well. Nevertheless, [I] during the same time was very sore pained, and so thirsty withal, and hot within [my] body, that [I] would have given anything [I] had to have slaked [my] thirst – having drink enough in the house and yet could not drink until the time that James the glover came to [me]. And [I] then said before Glover, 'I would to God that I could drink!' Whereupon the glover said to [me,] 'Take that drink, and in the name of the Father, the Son, and the Holy Ghost, drink it, saying, *The Devil and witches are not able to prevail against God and his Word.* Whereupon [I] then took the glass of drink, and did drink it all, and afterwards mended very well, and so did continue in good health until our Lady Day in Lent was twelvemonth or thereabouts."

—Since which time, this examinate sayeth that he hath been sore pained with "great warch in his bones and all his limbs," and so yet continueth. And this examinate further sayeth that his warch and pain came to him rather by means of Isabel Robey than otherwise, as he verily thinketh. [1]

As corroborating witnesses, Peter Chaddock brought along three neighbors:

The Examination of MARGARET LYON, wife of Thomas Lyon the younger, of Windle: Taken before Sir Thomas Gerard [...] against Isabel Robey°

MARGARET LYON *upon her oath sayeth that*:

"Upon a time Isabel Robey came into [my] house and said that Peter Chaddock should never mend until he had asked her forgiveness, and that, she knew, he would never do. Whereupon [I] said, 'How do you know that? for he is a true Christian, and he would ask all the world forgiveness.'

"Then Isabel said, 'That is all one, for he will never ask me forgiveness; therefore he shall never mend.' [...]

"[I] being in the house of Peter Chaddock, the wife of Peter, who is goddaughter of Isabel – and hath in times past used her company much – did affirm that Peter was now satisfied that Isabel Robey was no witch (by sending to one Halseworths, which they call a *wiseman*).

"And the wife of Peter then said, 'To abide upon it, I think that my husband *will* never mend until he have asked her forgiveness, choose him whether he will be angry or pleased, for this is my opinion.'

"To which he answered, when he did need to ask her forgiveness, he would; but he thought he did not need, for anything he knew. And yet [...] Peter Chaddock had very often told [me] that he was very afraid that Isabel had done him much hurt; and that he being fearful to meet her, he hath turned back at such time as he did meet her alone – which Isabel hath since then affirmed to be true, saying, that he (Peter) did turn again when he met her in the lane."

The Examination of JANE WILKINSON, wife of Francis Wilkinson, of Windle. Taken before Sir Thomas Gerard, Knight and Baronet, the day and place aforesaid. Against Isabel Robey °

THE EXAMINATE *upon her oath sayeth that*:

"Upon a time, Isabel Robey asked [me] milk, and [I] denied to give her any. And afterwards [I] met Isabel, whereupon [I] waxed afraid of her – and was then presently sick, and so pained that[I] could not stand. And the next day after, [I] going to Warrington was suddenly pinched on [my] thigh – as [me]thought, with four fingers and a thumb, twice together. And thereupon [I] was sick, insomuch as [I] could not get home but on horseback, yet soon after [I] did mend." [2]

---

[1] *warch*] pain.

[2] *mend*] the repeated statements about mending or recovery reflect Gerard's line of questioning, which differed from that of Roger Nowell; while also showing how answers to questions became transposed into voluntary statements but in the examiner's own words.

The Examination of MARGARET PARR, wife of Hugh Parr of Windle. Taken before Sir Thomas Gerard [...] against Isabel Robey °

THE EXAMINATE *upon her oath sayeth that*:

"Upon a time, a time, Isabel Robey came to [my] house, and [I] asked her how Peter Chaddock did. And Isabel answered she knew not, for she went not to see. And then [I] asked her how Jane Wilkinson did, for that she had been lately sick and suspected to have been bewitched. Then Isabel said twice together, "I have bewitched her, too." And then [I] said that [I] trusted [I] could bless [my]self from all witches, and defied them. And then Isabel said twice together, 'Would you defy *me*?" And afterwards, Isabel went away, not well pleased."

Judge Gerard arrested Isabel Robey and sent her to Lancaster, together with the four sworn depositions proving that she was a witch.

[The Hanging of Jennet Preston] °

The arrival of the Justices of the Peace in Lancaster was now less than a month away. Sir Edward Bromley and Sir James Altham, judges for the Northern Circuit, and their recorder, Thomas Potts, were in York. Among the defendants tried and hanged at York in the last week of July was Jennet Preston, of Gisburn-in-Craven.

Jennet was tried, not for killing Thomas Jr., who was alive and well, but for the death of Thomas Sr., five years before. Lister Jr. was again the main witness, and his father-in-law, Thomas Heber, was again the prosecutor. This time, Lister came supplied with incontestable proof of the defendant's guilt: in February 1606/7 (he said), Preston "being brought to Master Lister [Sr.] after he was dead and laid out to be wound up in his winding-sheet, the said Jennet Preston coming to touch the dead corpse, [it] bled fresh blood presently, in the presence of all that were there present."

Thomas Lister Jr. was not alone in stating that Jennet's touch caused the shrouded corpse to bleed. Corroborating testimony was offered by Lister's servant, Anne Robinson.

Thomas Potts in The Wonderful Discovery *adds his legal opinion that the bleeding-corpse test "hath ever been held a great argument to induce a jury to hold him guilty that shall be accused of murther, and hath seldom, or never, failed in the trial"* (Potts, T2v-3r).

This compelling evidence was supplemented by the examination of James Device, read aloud by the prosecutor, in which the youth was said to have seen Jennet Preston on Good Friday at a witches' meeting convened to kill Thomas Lister Jr.

Preston was condemned at the York Assize on July 27th and put to death on the 29th, on the Knavesmire gallows (current site of the York Racetrack), Jennet still protesting her innocence.

Their work completed in Yorkshire, Judges Altham and Bromley, and Recorder Thomas Potts, rode next to Lancaster. Now awaiting trial in the Castle prison were at least eighteen witches: the five surviving Pendle witches (three adults, two children), plus five others who were said to have attended the Good Friday picnic (Alice Gray, Katherine Hewitt, Jane Bulcock and her son John), and Alice Nutter; plus two women accused of malicious mischief short of homicide (Margaret Pearson and Isabel Robey); plus the seven accused witches of Samlesbury (Jennet and Ellen Bierley, Jane Southworth, John Ramsden, Elizabeth Astley, Alice Gray, Isabel Sidegraves, and Lawrence Hay, here omitted).

The Assize judges arriving at Lancaster on Sunday, August 16, preparations were made to commence trial on Monday morning.

The prisoners could do nothing but wait: as commoners, they had no right to seek legal counsel, or to receive disclosure of the evidence against them, or to call witnesses in their own defense. They would be allowed to enter their plea: Guilty, *or* Not Guilty.

• • •

Lancaster Castle, Europe's oldest and longest-working prison, in use from 1196 to 2011.

[The Trial at Assize (16-19 August 1612)] °

Thomas Potts, court recorder

UPON SUNDAY in the afternoon, my honorable lords the judges of Assize came from Kendall to Lancaster; whereupon Master Covell presented unto their lordships a calendar containing the names of the prisoners committed to his charge, which were to receive their trial at the Assizes (out of which, we are only to deal with the proceedings against witches) […] The next day being Monday, the seventeenth of August, were the Assizes holden in the Castle of Lancaster. […]

Here you may not expect the exact order of the Assizes, with the proclamations and other solemnities belonging to so great a Court of Justice, but [only] the proceedings against the witches, who are now upon their [jail-]deliverance here [presented] in order as they came to the Bar, with the particular points of evidence against them – which is the labor and work we now intend, by God's grace, to perform as we may to your general contentment. Whereupon, the first of all these, Anne Whittle alias Chattox, was brought to the Bar; against whom, we are now ready to proceed.

[Monday, 17 August]

The Arraignment and Trial of ANNE WHITTLE alias CHATTOX, of the Forest of Pendle, in the county of Lancaster, widow, about the age of four-score years or thereabouts °

This ANNE WHITTLE alias CHATTOX was a very old, withered, spent, and decrepit creature, her sight almost gone – a dangerous witch of very long continuance, always opposite to Old Dembdike: for whom the one favored, the other hated deadly. (And how they envy and accuse one another, in their examinations may appear!) In her witchcraft always more ready to do mischief to men's goods than themselves, her lips ever chattering and talking (but no man knew what), she lived in the Forest of Pendle amongst this wicked company of dangerous witches. […]

This odious witch was branded with a preposterous mark in nature even from her birth: which was her left eye standing lower than the other, the one looking down, the other looking up – so strangely deformed, as the best that were present in that honorable assembly and great audience did affirm they had not often seen the like. […]

Yet in her examination and confession, she dealt always very plainly and truly; for upon a special occasion (being oftentimes examined in an open court), she was never found to vary, but always to agree in one and the selfsame thing. I place her in order next to that wicked fire-brand of mischief, old Dembdike, because from these two sprung all the rest in order and were the children and friends of these two notorious witches.

Many things in the discovery of them shall be very worthy your observation, as the times and occasions to execute their mischief; and this, in general: the spirit could never hurt till they gave consent. And – but that it is my charge to set forth a particular declaration of the evidence against them, upon their arraignment and trial (with their devilish practices, consultations, meetings, and murders committed by them in such sort as they were given in evidence against them; for the which, I shall have matter upon record) – I could make a large commentary of them. But it is my humble duty to observe the charge and commandment of these my honorable good lords, the judges of Assize, and not to exceed the limits of my commission. Wherefore I shall now bring this ancient witch to the due course of her trial, in order, *viz*.:

Indictment [of ANNE WHITTLE] °

This ANNE WHITTLE alias CHATTOX of the Forest of Pendle in the county of Lancaster, widow, being indicted for that she feloniously had practiced, used, and exercised divers wicked and devilish arts called *witchcrafts, enchantments, charms,* and *sorceries,* in and upon one Robert Nutter of Greenhead, in the Forest of Pendle, in the county of Lancashire; and by force of the same witchcraft, feloniously Robert Nutter had killed, *contra pacem,* etc., [and] being at the Bar, was arraigned. [1]

To this indictment, upon her arraignment, she pleaded *Not guilty*; and for the trial of her life, put herself upon God and her country.

Whereupon my Lord Bromley commanded [Sir Cuthbert Halsall,] Master Sheriff of the county of Lancaster, in open court, to return a jury of worthy, sufficient gentlemen of understanding, to pass between our sovereign lord the King's Majesty, and her and others, the prisoners, upon their lives and deaths […] Which being done, and the prisoner at the Bar ready to receive her trial, Master Nowell (being the best-instructed of any man of all the particular points of evidence against her and her fellows, having taken great pains in the proceedings against her and her fellows), humbly prayed [that] her own voluntary confession and examination (taken before him when she was apprehended and committed to the Castle of Lancaster for witchcraft) might openly be published against her. […]

Judge Bromley directed Nowell to read the "Voluntary Confession and Examination of Anne Whittle" (*Nowell's third-person paraphrase of answers ascribed to Whittle during her interrogation of 2 April, at Ashlar House*). *That done, Nowell next read aloud the "evidence" he obtained from Alison Device,*

---

[1] *contra pacem*] against the peace (conventional legal phrasing for an indictment).

James Device, Elizabeth Southerns alias Dembdike, and James Robinson); all of whom affirmed that Whittle by witchcraft had killed Robert Nutter Jr.

[*Thomas Potts, Court Recorder*:] In the end, being openly charged with all this in open court, with weeping tears [Anne Whittle] humbly acknowledged them to be true, and cried out unto God for mercy and forgiveness of her sins, and humbly prayed my lord [Bromley] to be merciful unto Anne Redfern her daughter, of whose life and condition you shall hear more, upon her arraignment and trial; whereupon [Whittle] being taken away, Elizabeth Device comes now to receive her trial being the next in order, of whom you shall hear at large.

[Tuesday, 18 August 1612]

The Arraignment and Trial of ELIZABETH DEVICE [...] widow, for witchcraft; upon Tuesday the 18ᵗʰ of August, at the Assizes and general jail-delivery holden at Lancaster °

[*Thomas Potts*:] Elizabeth Device! O barbarous and inhuman monster, beyond example! so far from sensible understanding of thy own misery, as to bring thy own natural children into mischief and bondage, and thyself to be a witness upon the gallows, to see thy own children, by thy devilish instructions hatched up in villainy and witchcraft, to suffer with thee, even in the beginning of their time, a shameful and untimely death. Too much (so it be true) cannot be said or written of her.

This ELIZABETH DEVICE was the daughter of Elizabeth Southerns (old Dembdike), a malicious, wicked, and dangerous witch for fifty years as appeareth by record (and how much longer, the Devil and she knew best, with whom she made her covenant). It is very certain that amongst all these witches there was not a more dangerous and devilish witch to execute mischief [than Elizabeth Device], having old Dembdike her mother to assist her; [with] James Device and Alison Device, her own natural children, all provided with spirits, upon any occasion of offense, *ready* to assist her. [...]

Upon her examination – although Master Nowell was very circumspect and exceeding careful in dealing with her – yet she would confess nothing until it pleased God to raise up a young maid, Jennet Device, her own daughter, about the age of nine years (a witness unexpected) to discover all their practices, meetings, consultations, murthers, charms, and villainies: Such, and in such sort, as I may justly say of them, as a reverend and learned judge of this kingdom speaketh of the greatest treason that ever was in this kingdom: *Quis haec posteris sic narrare poterit,*

ut facta non ficta esse videantur (that when these things shall be related to posterity, they will be reputed matters feigned, not done). [...] [1]

This Elizabeth Device [...] labored not a little to procure a solemn meeting at Malkin Tower of the Grand Witches [...] to consult of some speedy course for the deliverance of their friends, the witches at Lancaster, and for the putting in execution of some other devilish practices of murther and mischief – as [...] shall hereafter in every particular point appear at large against her.

Indictment [of ELIZABETH DEVICE] °

The first indictment. This ELIZABETH DEVICE, late the wife of John Device of the Forest of Pendle, in the county of Lancaster, widow, being indicted for that she feloniously had practiced, used, and exercised divers wicked and devilish arts called *witchcrafts, enchantments, charms,* and *sorceries,* in and upon one John Robinson alias Swyer; and by force of the same feloniously the said John Robinson alias Swyer had killed, *contra pace,* &c., being at the Bar, was arraigned.

Second indictment. The said ELIZABETH DEVICE was the second time indicted, in the same manner and form, for the death of James Robinson, by witchcraft, *contra pacem,* &c.

Third indictment. The said ELIZABETH DEVICE was the third time with others (*viz.,* Alice Nutter and Elizabeth Southerns alias Old Dembdike her grandmother), indicted, in the same manner and form, for the death of Henry Mitton, *contra pacem,* &c.

To these three several indictments upon her arraignment, she pleaded *Not guilty;* and for the trial of her life, put herself upon God and her country. So as now the gentlemen of the Jury of Life and Death stand charged to find whether she be guilty of them, or any of them.

Whereupon there was openly read, and given in evidence against her, for the King's Majesty, her own voluntary confession and examination when she was apprehended, taken, and committed to the Castle of Lancaster by Master Nowell and Master Bannester, two of his Majesty's justices of peace in the same county [...]

Nowell read aloud the statements ascribed to Elizabeth Device taken from the 27 April examination, the day she was committed to prison. He then read statements allegedly made by Jennet and James that same day. Next, for a climactic moment of courtroom theater, Nowell called to the Bar nine-year-old Jennet Device.

---

[1] *greatest treason*] Sir Edward Coke, attorney general, speaking of the 1605 Gunpowder Treason, a plot so outrageous it would seem to future generations like a fiction.

The defendant had not been told that her youngest child, from whom she had been separated by prison walls for the past four months, was suborned by the prosecution to testify against her. Elizabeth became hysterical.

[*Thomas Potts, Court Recorder*:] The said JENNET DEVICE, being a young maid about the age of nine years, and commanded to stand up to give evidence against her mother, prisoner at the Bar, her mother (according to her accustomed manner, outrageously cursing) cried out against the child in such fearful manner as all the Court did not a little wonder at her; and so amazed the child, as with weeping tears she cried out unto my lord the judge, and told him she was not able to speak in the presence of her mother.

No entreaty, promise of favor, or other respect, could put [Elizabeth Device] to silence, [she] thinking by this her outrageous cursing and threatening of the child, to enforce her to deny that which [Jennet] had formerly confessed against her mother before Master Nowell; [also] forswearing and denying her *own* voluntary confession! (which you have heard), given in evidence against her at large.

And so – for want of further evidence to escape that which the justice of the law had provided as a condign punishment for the innocent blood she had spilt, and [for] her wicked and devilish course of life – in the end, when no means would serve, his lordship [Judge Bromley] commanded the prisoner to be taken away, and the maid to be set upon the table in the presence of the whole Court; who delivered her evidence in that honorable assembly, to the gentlemen of the Jury of Life and Death, as followeth, *viz.*

The Examination and Evidence of JENNET DEVICE […] against her Mother, Elizabeth Device, prisoner at the Bar °

JENNET DEVICE (daughter of Elizabeth Device, late wife of John Device, of the Forest of Pendle aforesaid, widow) confesseth and sayeth that her mother is a witch. […] This she knoweth to be true for that she hath seen her spirit sundry times come unto her mother in her own house, called Malkin Tower, in the likeness of a brown dog, which she called Ball. And at one time amongst others, the said Ball did ask this examinate's mother what she would have him to do. And [her] mother answered that she would have the said Ball to help her to kill John Robinson of Barley, alias Swyer; by help of which Ball, Swyer was killed by witchcraft accordingly. […]

And further, this examinate confesseth that about a year after, [her] mother called for Ball; who appeared as aforesaid, asking [her] mother what she would have done; who said that she would have him to kill James Robinson alias Swyer of Barlow, brother to the said John; whereunto Ball answered he would do it; and about three weeks after, the said James died.

And this examinate also sayeth that one other time she was present when her mother did call for Ball, who appeared in manner as aforesaid and asked [her] mother what she would have him to do; whereunto [her] mother then said she would have him to kill one Mitton of the Rough-Lee; whereupon Ball said he would do it, and so vanished away. And about three weeks after, the said Mitton likewise died.

Just six years old when the Robinson brothers died, Jennet was fuzzy on dates; but Thomas Potts confirms that it nonetheless made a favorable impression upon the Court, to see a little girl testify with such courage and conviction against her own evil mother.

When Jennet stood down, her mother was brought back in, to hear the verdict: Guilty, on all counts.

• • •

[*Thomas Potts, Court Recorder*:] The next in order was her son James Device, whom [Elizabeth Device] and her mother, Old Dembdike, brought to act his part in this woeful tragedy.

The Arraignment and Trial of JAMES DEVICE, son of Elizabeth Device, of the Forest of Pendle, within the county of Lancaster aforesaid, laborer, for witchcraft; upon Tuesday the 18th of August °

[*Thomas Potts, court recorder*:] This wicked and miserable wretch, whether by practice or means to bring himself to some untimely death and thereby to avoid his trial by his country, and just judgment of the Law; or ashamed to be openly charged with so many devilish practices and so much innocent blood as he had spilt; or by reason of his imprisonment so long time before his trial (which was with more favor, commiseration, and relief than he deserved), I know not: but being brought forth to the Bar to receive his trial (before this worthy judge, and so honorable and worshipful an assembly of justices for this service) was so insensible, weak, and unable in all things, as he could neither speak, hear, or stand, but was holden up when he was brought to the place of his arraignment, to receive his trial.

[The Indictment of JAMES DEVICE] °

This JAMES DEVICE of the Forest of Pendle, being brought to the Bar, was there according to the form, order, and course, indicted and arraigned for that he feloniously had practiced, used, and exercised divers wicked and devilish arts called *witchcrafts, enchantments, charms,* and *sorceries,* in and upon one Anne Towneley, wife of Henry Towneley of the Carr, in the county of Lancaster, gentleman, and her by force of the same, feloniously had killed, *contra pacem,* &c.

The said JAMES DEVICE was the second time indicted and arraigned, in the same manner and form, for the death of John Duckworth by witchcraft, *contra pacem,* &c.

To these two several indictments upon his arraignment, he pleaded *Not guilty*, and for the trial of his life put himself upon God and his country. So as now the gentlemen of the Jury of Life and Death stand charged to find whether he be guilty of these, or either of them; whereupon Master Nowell humbly prayed Master Towneley might be called, who attended to prosecute and give evidence against [James Device] for the King's Majesty; and that the particular examinations taken before him and others might be openly published and read in Court, in the hearing of the prisoner.

But because it were infinite to bring him to his particular trial for every offense which he hath committed in his time and every practice wherein he hath had his hand, I shall proceed in order with the evidence remaining upon record against him, amongst the Records of the Crown; both how and in what sort he came to be a witch; and show you what apparent proof there is to charge him with the death of these two several persons; for the which he now standeth upon his trial for all the rest of his devilish practices, incantations, murders, charms, sorceries, meetings to consult with witches to execute mischief.

Take them as they are against him, upon record: Enough, I doubt not. For these, with the course of his life, will serve his turn to deliver you from the danger of him that never took felicity in any things but in revenge, blood, and mischief, [facts] crying out unto God for vengeance; which hath now at the length brought him to the place where he stands to receive his trial – with more honor, favor, and respect, than such a monster in nature doth deserve. And I doubt not, but in due time by the justice of the Law, to an untimely and shameful death.

"The Examination and Confession of James Device" was read aloud. Next, his sister Jennet was again called to the Bar. She confirmed that her brother's devil-spirit, Dandy, in the shape of a black dog, had slain Anne Towneley of Carr Hall (buried 4 March 1611/12).

[*Thomas Potts, Recorder:*] Herein do but observe the wonderful work of God, to raise up a young infant, the very sister of the prisoner, Jennet Device to discover, justify, and prove these things against him at the time of his arraignment and trial [...] Which examinate, although she were but very young, yet it was wonderful to the Court, in so great a presence and audience, with what modesty, government, and understanding she delivered this evidence against the prisoner at the Bar, being her own natural brother; which he himself could not deny but there acknowledged in every particular to be just and true.

But behold a little further [...] there is yet *more* blood to be laid unto his charge! For although he were but young and in the beginning of his time, yet was he careful to observe his instructions from Old Dembdike his grandmother and Elizabeth Device his mother: insomuch that no time should pass since his first entrance into that damnable art and exercise of witchcrafts, enchantments, harms and sorceries, without mischief or murder. [...] He was again indicted and arraigned for the murder of these two, *viz.,*

[Third and Fourth Indictments of JAMES DEVICE]

The said JAMES DEVICE, the third time indicted and arraigned for the death of John Hargreaves of Goldshaw-Booth...[and] fourth time indicted for the death of Blaze Hargreaves of Higham, [...] by witchcraft as aforesaid [...] to this indictment, upon his arraignment, he pleaded thereunto *Not guilty*; and for the trial of his life, put himself upon God and the country, &c.

The Examination and Evidence of Jennet Device °

Hereupon Jennet Device (produced, sworn, and examined, as a witness on his Majesty's behalf against the said James Device) was examined in open Court. [...]

Jennet told the Court how her brother, "a witch for the space of three years," coached his spirit Dandy the devil-dog to kill Blaze Hargreaves of Higham, and John Hargreaves of Goodshaw, both of whom died, though she did not know when. (Both men died in 1609.)

—all which things, when he heard his sister upon her oath affirm, knowing them in his conscience to be just and true, [James] slenderly *denied* them! – and thereupon insisted [...whereupon] Master Nowell humbly prayed his own examination, taken and certified, might openly be read.

Nowell read from his report of James's April 27th examination; after which, he read from the report of the boy's May 19th interview with Anderton, Sands, and Covell concerning the boy's negotiations with the dog Dandy (for ownership of his soul) – none of which made mention of Henry or John Hargreaves, but this was sufficient evidence to persuade the Court that James Device was guilty on all four counts.

[*Thomas Potts, Recorder:*] Jennet Device his sister, in the very end of her examination against James Device, confesseth and sayeth that her mother taught her two prayers, the one to get drink, which was this, *viz., "Crucifixus hoc signum vitam eternam.* Amen" ["The crucifix is the sign of eternal life"]. And she further sayeth that her brother James Device, the prisoner at the Bar, hath confessed to her (this examinate) that he by this prayer hath gotten drink – and that within an hour after the saying the prayer, drink hath come into the house after a very strange manner. And the other prayer (James Device affirmed) would cure one bewitched; which she recited as followeth. [...]

Charm °

Upon Good Friday,
I will fast while I may
Until I hear them knell
Our Lord's own bell
[Mess afore the Rood]
With his twelve Apostles good.   1
What hath he in his hand?
Ligh in leath wand!   2
[What in th' other hath he?]
Heaven's door key!
[Open, open, heaven-door,]
Stick, stick, hell-door.
Let chrizum child
Go to it mother mild.   3
"What is [yond]
That casts a light so farrandly?   4
Mine own dear son
That's nailèd to the tree!
He is nailèd sair   5
By the heart and hand.   6
O holy bairn,
Well is that man
That *Friday* spell can
His child to learn."
A cross of red, and another of blude   [25]
As good Lord was [nail'd] to th' rood.   7
Gabriel laid him down to sleep
Upon the ground of holy weep.
Good Lord came walking by:
"Sleep'st thou, wak'st thou, Gabrelíe?"
"No, Lord, I am stead with stick and stake   8
That I can neither sleep nor wake."
"Rise up, Gabriel, and go with me.
The stick nor the stake
Shall ne'er dere thee."   9

Sweet Jesus our Lord, Amen.
James Device

[*Thomas Potts, Court Recorder*:] What can be said more of this painful steward that was so careful to provide mutton against this feast and solemn meeting at Malkin Tower, of this° hellish and devilish band of witches? […] I have been very sparing to charge him with anything but with sufficient matter of record and evidence, able to satisfy the consciences of the gentlemen of the Jury of Life and Death; to whose good consideration I leave him, with the perpetual badge and brand of as dangerous and malicious a witch as ever lived in these parts of Lancashire, of his time, and spotted with as much innocent blood, as ever any witch of his years.

After all these proceedings, by direction of his lordship, were their several examinations (subscribed by every one of [the defendants] in particular), showed unto them at the time of their trial and acknowledged by them to be true, delivered to the gentlemen of the Jury of Life and Death, for the better satisfaction of their consciences: after due consideration of which several examinations, confessions, and voluntary declarations, as well of themselves as of their children, friends and confederates, the gentlemen delivered up their verdict against the prisoners, as followeth (*viz.*, "The Verdict of Life and Death"); who found Anne Whittle alias Chattox, Elizabeth Device, and James Device, guilty of the several murthers by witchcraft contained in the indictments against them, and every of them. [10]

The last accused witch to be tried on Tuesday was Anne Redfern, Whittle's widowed daughter. Redfern was indicted for having conspired with her guilty mother in the death of Robert Nutter, eighteen years before. The "evidence" against both women was more or less identical, except for Whittle's testimony that Anne withdrew from the plot, by her husband's good persuasion.

Late in the evening, Anne Redfern was found Not guilty *in the witchcraft death of Robert Nutter.*

On Wednesday morning, the first order of business was to try the Samlesbury witches (omitted here though narrated at length by Thomas Potts in his Wonderful Discovery). *A devout Protestant, Roger Nowell immediately disclosed that the Samlesbury indictments were a papist plot, and that the chief witness, Grace Sowerbutts, was a Roman Catholic liar: Grace's uncle, Christopher Southworth, alias Thompson, a Jesuit priest, had coached her to slander innocent Anglicans. Three defendants were acquitted. The other four were dismissed without standing trial.*

After lunch, the court re-convened. Roger Nowell now brought a second indictment against Anne Redfern, this time for the 1595/6 witchcraft-murder of Christopher Nutter, Robert Nutter's father.

---

[1] *Mess…Rood*] Last Supper…Cross (Q, *Lord in his messe*).

[2] *Ligh*] lieth, is held; *leath wand*] leather switch for urging horses or livestock.

[3] *chrizum*] Christian; *it*] its.

[4] *farrandly*] beautifully, becomingly.

[5] *sair*] most painfully.

[6] *bairn*] child; Q "*bairnpan*," possibly for *brainpan* (skull), but *bairn* provides a rhyme for *learn* (pron. *larn*).

[7] *Gabriel*] archangel named in the Bible.

[8] *stead*] stayed.

[9] *dere*] trouble, vex.

---

[10] *acknowledged by them to be true*] though unable to read or write, they had subscribed their marks to Nowell's record of their examinations.

[Wednesday, 19 August 1612]

The Arraignment and Trial of ANNE REDFERN, daughter of Anne Whittle alias Chattox, of the Forest of Pendle, in the county of Lancaster, for witchcraft; upon Wednesday the 19th of August °

[*Thomas Potts, Court Recorder*:] Upon Tuesday night (although you hear little of her at the arraignment and trial of old Chattox, her mother) yet was [Anne Redfern] arraigned for the murther of Robert Nutter […] By the favor and merciful consideration of the jury, the evidence being not very pregnant against her, she was acquitted, and found *Not guilty*.

[But] such was her condition and course of life, as had she lived, she would have been very dangerous. […] The innocent blood yet unsatisfied and crying out unto GOD for satisfaction and revenge, the cry of His people (to deliver them from the danger of such horrible and bloody executioners, and from her wicked and damnable practices) hath now again brought her to a second trial, where you shall hear what we have upon record against her.

[The Indictment of ANNE REDFERN] °

[*Thomas Potts*:] This ANNE REDFERN, prisoner in the Castle at Lancaster, being brought to the Bar before the Great Seat of Justice, was there (according to the former order and course) indicted and arraigned, for that she feloniously had practiced, exercised, and used her devilish and wicked arts, called *witchcrafts, enchantments, charms*, and *sorceries*, in and upon one Christopher Nutter, and him (the said Christopher Nutter) by force of the same witchcrafts, feloniously did kill and murther, *contra formam statuti &c. et contra pacem &c.*

Upon her arraignment to this indictment, she pleaded *Not guilty*; and for the trial of her life put herself upon GOD and the country. So as now the gentlemen of the Jury of Life and Death stand charged with her as with others.

Presenting the evidence against Redfern, Nowell read aloud from the April 2nd confession of Elizabeth Southerns, deceased, who was said to have seen Redfern making clay images (in 1594/5, prior to the death of either Nutter), one of which Dembdike believed was of Christopher Nutter. He then read from the examinations of Margaret Nutter Crook and John Nutter, who had said their father died of witchcraft, but did not know by whom. Corroborating testimony was supplied by James Device who, though born five years after the victim's death, observed clay images at the Redfern residence in 1610, not far from a fire-spitting rabbit. Those images, though not said to be of Christopher Nutter, nonetheless confirmed a

pattern of behavior. This time, Anne Redfern was found guilty as charged, and sentenced to hang.

[*Thomas Potts*:] All men that knew [Anne Redfern] affirmed she was more dangerous than her mother: for she made all or most of the pictures of clay that were made or found at any time. Wherefore I leave her to make good use of the little time she hath, to repent in! – but no means could move her to repentance, for as she lived, so she died.

• • •

The next case to be heard was one that certain of the gentry were keenly awaiting. Alice Nutter of Burnley, although she was the widow of a landowner, was accused of dining (and killing) with the penniless beggars of Malkin Tower.

The Arraignment and Trial of ALICE NUTTER, of the Forest of Pendle, in the county of Lancaster, for witchcraft; upon Wednesday the 19th of August, at the Assizes and general jail delivery, holden at Lancaster before Sir Edward Bromley °

[*Thomas Potts, Court Recorder*:] The two degrees of persons which chiefly practice witchcraft are such as are in great misery and poverty: for such the Devil allures to follow him by promising great riches and worldly commodity. Others, though rich, yet burn in a desperate desire of revenge. He allures them by promises, to get their turn satisfied to their heart's contentment (as in the whole proceedings against old Chattox, the examinations of old Dembdike and her children, there was not one of them but have declared the like, when the Devil first assaulted them).

But to attempt *this* woman in that sort, the Devil had small means! For it is certain she was a rich woman; [she] had a great estate and children of good hope. In the common opinion of the world, [she was] of good temper, free from envy or malice. Yet, whether by the means of the rest of the witches or some unfortunate occasion she was drawn to fall to this wicked course of life, I know not. But hither she is now come to receive her trial, both for murder and many other vild and damnable practices.

Great was the care and pains of his lordship to make trial of the innocency of this woman, as shall appear unto you upon the examination of Jennet Device, in open Court, at the time of her arraignment and trial; by an extraordinary means of trial, to mark her out from the rest.

It is very certain she was of the Grand Council at Malkin Tower upon Good Friday, and was there present – which was a very great argument to condemn her.

[The Indictment of ALICE NUTTER] °

This ALICE NUTTER, prisoner in the Castle at Lancaster, being brought to the Bar before the Great Seat of Justice, was there according to the former order and course indicted and arraigned, for that she feloniously had practiced, exercised, and used her devilish and wicked arts, called *witchcrafts, enchantments, charms* and *sorceries*, in and upon Henry Mitton; and him (the said Henry Mitton), by force of the same witchcrafts, feloniously did kill and murther, *contra formam statuti, &c., et contra pacem, &c.*

Upon her arraignment to this indictment she pleaded *Not guilty*; and for the trial of her life, put herself upon GOD and the country. So as now the gentlemen of the Jury of Life and Death stand charged with her, as with others.

The prosecutor, Roger Nowell, introduced into evidence, first, a quotation from the 27 April "Examination of JAMES DEVICE," taken before Roger Nowell and Nicholas Bannester: "The said examinate [James Device] sayeth, upon his oath, that he heard his grandmother say about a year ago that his mother, called Elizabeth Device, and his grandmother, and the wife of Richard Nutter of the Rough-Lee aforesaid, had killed one Henry Mitton, of the Rough-Lee, by witchcraft." [1]

Nowell followed with a statement he ascribed to Elizabeth Device from 27 April, confirming that Alice Nutter conspired with Dembdike, Elizabeth, and her dog, to bewitch Henry Mitton.

James Device is said to have known the motive: "The reason wherefore he was so killed, was for that this examinate's said grandmother had asked Mitton a penny; and he denying her thereof, thereupon she procured his death." Nowell made no effort to explain why Alice Nutter, a widow of the gentry living on a comfortable jointure, would join a conspiracy to murder Henry Mitton after the man denied a penny to old Dembdike.

Next came the theatre: A lineup of women was brought to stand before the Bar, one of whom was Widow Nutter. It was announced to the Court that Jennet Device knew the names of only six of her mother's Good Friday guests, not including Alice Nutter. Jennet was then brought in and asked if she saw anyone who was present that day at Malkin Tower. She confidently pointed to Alice, and even named where Mrs. Nutter sat at the dinner table.

[*Thomas Potts*:] This could be no forged or false accusation, but the very act of GOD to discover her […] and to this, [Alice Nutter] could give no answer. But nothing would serve: for old Dembdike, old Chattox, and others, had charged her with innocent blood, which cries out for revenge, and will be satisfied. And therefore almighty GOD, in his justice, hath cut her off. [2]

And here I leave her, until she come to her execution, where you shall hear she died very impenitent; insomuch as her own children were never able to move her to confess any particular offense, or declare anything, even *in articulo mortis*; which was a very fearful thing to all that were present, who knew she was guilty.

• • •

That Nutter, a 70-year-old widow, insisted on her innocence – "even in articulo mortis,*" at the moment of death, on penalty of eternal damnation – makes it all the more remarkable that none of her grown children came to her defense, but instead demanded that she confess.*

That Alice Nutter was known to be a Roman Catholic may be one reason that her accusers were so contented to see her hang. But there were other, more material, counts against Widow Nutter, motives that Potts does not name.

Alice Nutter was not "rich" by London standards, nor still living in luxury at Roughlee Hall. When her eldest son Miles inherited Roughlee at her husband's death, he had the right to evict his mother from the property, and he appears to have done so: at the time of the indictment, Miles occupied his father's manor while Alice Nutter dwelt in a modest house at Crowtrees. But her widow's jointure still had to be paid out from the estate, a constant drain on Miles Nutter's wealth until his mother died or remarried ("Like to a step-dame or a dowager / Long withering out a young man revenue," quoth Shakespeare); and yet, Alice in her seventies was still robust and single. And even if the younger Nutters were cash-strapped and wishing to sell land, their mother's dower gave her veto-power on the sale of their deceased father's real estate; a dilemma that drove many an heir to dreams of matricide.

That Alice Nutter's grown children insisted that she confess is cited by Potts as a sign of their piety. More probably, they wanted her dead without inviting suspicion that their mother was the victim of a plot by her own estranged children, and without disclosing that nine-year-old Jennet Device was coached.

---

[1] *the wife of Richard Nutter*] this phrase is inserted by Nowell for "others" as earlier introduced into evidence against Elizabeth Device; where James's deposition reads: "he heard his grandmother say about a year ago that his mother, called Elizabeth Device, and his grandmother, and others [*sic*], had killed one Henry Mitton of the Rough-Lee aforesaid, by Witchcraft."

---

[2] *old Dembdike, old Chattox*] more bad faith: nowhere in the records presented by Potts do Southern or Whittle mention Alice Nutter.

Following the 1601 Act for the Relief of the Poor, elderly or handicapped women such as Dembdike and Chattox were resented by the respectable middle class for their claim on parish revenue; if harassment could not force such parasites from the community, a charge of witchcraft could remove them from the planet altogether, and the courts were only too happy to assist. But Alice Nutter, a woman of substance, most likely died for her legal claim to a continuing share of her husband's estate.

Unique among the defendants, Alice Nutter was literate. Prosecutor Nowell nowhere suggests that she had a spirit or devil-dog. Nor was he able to produce a signed "Examination and Confession" in which Nutter acknowledged her guilt (as Nowell did for all other Pendle defendants, who were obliged to endorse his work with their mark, without being able to read what they were signing). That Alice Nutter dined with the Malkin Tower crowd, on Good Friday or any other day, is doubtful. That she conspired in the murder of Henry Mitton for denying a penny to Dembdike is preposterous. But the Jury of Life and Death having heard the allegations rendered its verdict: Guilty.

• • •

The Arraignment and Trial of KATHERINE HEWITT wife of John Hewitt alias "Mold-Heels," of Colne, clothier °

Katherine Hewitt, who attended the Good Friday picnic, was charged with collaboration in "a damnable course for the deliverance of [her] friends at Lancaster, as to kill the jailer and blow up the Castle"; to which the prosecutor added statements ascribed to James Device and Elizabeth Device that Katherine Hewitt and Anne Gray, also of Colne, had confessed to killing an infant of Anne Foulds, by witchcraft; after which (said James), Katherine Hewitt mounted a horse and "vanished," together with Jennet Preston on her white foal (as stated in the examinations of 27 April, sig. P3r-4v).

Jennet Device, who was said not to know Katherine Hewitt, was then called to the Bar. As before with Alice Nutter, Jennet picked the defendant out of a lineup, proving Hewitt's guilt.

Anne Redfern, Alice Nutter, and Katherine Hewitt were found guilty on all counts and taken away.

The court adjourned for lunch.

• • •

In the afternoon session, Jane Bulcock and her son John were tried. As with the elderly wife of John "Mold-Heels" Hewitt, the Bulcocks were charged in the alleged plot to kill Thomas Covell and blow up Lancaster Castle; after which they, too, mounted on

spirits and vanished from sight; to which was added a charge that mother and son, by witchcraft, had caused Jennet Dean to go insane (an allegation not found among Nowell's various "examinations").

Jane Bulcock and her son professed ignorance of any Good Friday plot and denied driving Jennet Dean crazy. Prosecutor Nowell again brought in Jennet Device, who picked the Bulcocks from out of a courtroom lineup, as before. The Jury of Life and Death rendered its verdict: Guilty.

• • •

Next up was Alison Device, daughter of one condemned witch and granddaughter to another. Roger Nowell called Alison Device to the Bar.

The Arraignment and Trial of ALISON DEVICE, daughter of Elizabeth Device, within the Forest of Pendle, in the county of Lancaster aforesaid, for witchcraft [on the body of John Law, peddler] °

[Thomas Potts, Court Recorder:] Behold, above all the rest, this lamentable spectacle of a poor distressed peddler, how miserably he was tormented, and what punishment he endured for a small offense, by the wicked and damnable practice of this odious witch, [Alison Device!] first instructed therein by old Dembdike her grandmother, and by her mother brought up in this detestable course of life; wherein I pray you, observe but the manner and course of it in order, even to the last period at her execution for this horrible fact, able to terrify and astonish any man living.[1]

[The Indictment of ALISON DEVICE] °

This ALISON DEVICE, prisoner in the Castle of Lancaster, being brought to the Bar before the Great Seat of Justice, was there (according to the former order and course) indicted and arraigned; for that she feloniously had practiced, exercised, and used her devilish and wicked arts, called *witchcrafts, enchantments, charms,* and *sorceries,* in and upon one John Law, a petty chapman, and him had lamed so that his body wasted and consumed, &c., *Contra fomam statuti, etc.* […]

Upon the arraignment, the poor peddler (by name, John Law) being in the Castle about the Moot-hall, attending to be called (not well able to go or stand, being led thither by his poor son, Abraham Law); my lord [Sir Thomas] Gerard moved the Court to call the poor peddler, who was there ready and had attended all the Assizes, to give evidence for the King's Majesty against Alison Device, prisoner at the Bar, even now upon her trial.

The prisoner being at the Bar (and now beholding the peddler – deformed by her witchcraft and transformed beyond the course of Nature – appeared to

---

[1] *fact*] crime, violent deed.

give evidence against her), having not yet pleaded to her indictment, [she] saw it was in vain to deny it or [to] stand upon her justification. She humbly upon her knees at the Bar with weeping tears, prayed the Court to hear her [...] and there on her knees, she humbly asked forgiveness for her offense.

As the defendant remained on her knees weeping, Nowell read extracts from the March 30th "Examination of Alison Device."

My Lord Bromley and all the whole Court not a little [wondered] (as they had good cause!) at this liberal and voluntary confession of the witch (which is not ordinary with people of their condition and quality). And (beholding also the poor distressed peddler standing by) [they] commanded him upon his oath to declare the manner how and in what sort he was handled; how he came to be lame, and so to be deformed; who deposed upon his oath, as followeth:

The Evidence of JOHN LAW, petty chapman, upon his oath, against Alison Device, prisoner at the Bar ° [1]

He deposeth and sayeth that:

"About the 18th of March last past, [I] being a peddler, went with [my] pack of wares at [my] back through Colne-Field where unluckily [I] met with Alison Device, now prisoner at the Bar, who was very earnest with [me] for pins. But [I] would give her none – whereupon she seemed to be very angry. And when [I] was past her, [I] fell down lame, in great extremity. And afterwards, by means, [I] got into an ale-house in Colne, near unto the place where [I] was first bewitched. And as [I] lay there in great pain, not able to stir either hand or foot, [I] saw a great black dog stand by [me], with very fearful fiery eyes, great teeth, and a terrible countenance, looking [me] in the face; whereat [I] was very sore afraid. And immediately after came in Alison Device, who stayed not long there, but looked on [me] and went away.

"After which time, [I] was tormented both day and night with Alison Device; and so [have] continued lame, not able to travel or take pains ever since that time."

With weeping tears, in great passion, [John Law] turned to the prisoner. In the hearing of all the Court he said to her, "This, thou knowest to be too true!"

And thereupon she humbly acknowledged the same, and cried out to God to forgive her. And upon her knees with weeping tears, [she] humbly prayed [John Law] to forgive her that wicked offense, which he very freely and voluntarily did.

Hereupon Master Nowell standing up, humbly prayed the favor of the Court, in respect this fact of witchcraft was more eminent and apparent than the rest, that for the better satisfaction of the audience, the examination of Abraham Law might be read in court— [*Permission granted, and read aloud by Nowell*] —which examination in open Court, upon his oath, [Abraham Law] justified to be true; whereupon it was there affirmed to the Court that this John Law the peddler, before his unfortunate meeting with this witch, was a very able, sufficient, stout man of body, and a goodly man of stature. But by this devilish art of witchcraft, his head is drawn awry, his eyes and face deformed, his speech not well to be understood, his thighs and legs stark lame – his arms lame (especially the left side), his hands lame and turned out of their course, his body able to endure no travel; and thus remaineth at this present time.

The prisoner being examined by the Court whether she could help the poor peddler to his former strength and health, she answered she could not. [...]

These things being thus openly published against her, and she knowing herself to be guilty of every particular, [she] humbly acknowledged the indictment against her to be true, and that she was guilty of the offense therein contained, and that she had justly deserved death (for that, and many other such-like!); whereupon she was carried away until she should come to the Bar to receive her judgment of death.

The Arraignment and Trial of MARGARET PEARSON [...and] ISABEL ROBEY °

Margaret Pearson of Padiham, accused of having bewitched Mr. Dodgson's horse, was tried and found guilty. She was sentenced to stand for six hours, on four successive market days, at Clitheroe, Padiham, Whalley, and Lancaster, with a printed paper upon her head stating her crime; followed by a year in prison (which was usually fatal and appears to have been so in Pearson's case).

Isabel Robey of Windle, the last to be tried, was convicted of afflicting her goddaughter's husband with cramps. She was sentenced to death.

[*Thomas Potts, Court Recorder:*] Here then is the last that came to act her part in this lamentable and woeful tragedy, wherein his Majesty hath lost so many subjects; mothers, their children; fathers, their friends and kinsfolks – the like whereof hath not been set forth, in any age! What hath the King's Majesty written and published in his *Daemonology* by way of premonition and prevention, which hath not here (by the first or last) been executed, put in practice, or discovered? (sig. T2r).

Potts's one regret was that "Many more, which being bound over to appear at the last Assizes, are since that time fled, to save themselves" (sig. R2r).

---

[1] *petty chapman*] itinerant peddler of portable wares.

The Verdict of Life and Death

HERE THE GENTLEMEN of the last Jury of Life and Death having taken great pains, the time being far spent, and the number of the prisoners great, returned into the Court to deliver up their verdict against them, as followeth. *viz.*, Master Covell was commanded by the Court in the afternoon to bring forth all the prisoners that stood convicted, to receive their judgment of life and death. For his lordship [Sir Edward Bromley] now intended to proceed to a final dispatch of the Pleas of the Crown […] (sig. V1r-v).

When the convicted felons were convened before the Bar, Judge Bromley delivered a solemn and pointed sermon in which he lamented the "offenses and bloody practices" of those condemned to die; whose sins "cried out unto the Lord against you, and solicited for satisfaction and revenge." He concludes:

"I pronounce the judgment of the Court against you, by the King's authority, which is: You shall all go from hence to the Castle, from whence you came; from thence you shall be carried to the place of execution for this county, where your bodies shall be hanged until you be dead. And God have mercy upon your souls. For your comfort in this world I shall commend a learned and worthy preacher to instruct you, and prepare you for another world" (sig. V4).

• • •

In May 1612, shortly before Edward Bromley and James Altham commenced their summer tour of Assize, Thomas Adams published The Gallant's Burden. *This was a Saint Paul's Cathedral sermon in which Rev. Adams fretted over the growing menace of whoredom (which no one doubted) and witchcraft (of which many were skeptical): "if the destroying power were not controled, manacled, mastered," wrote Adams, "how stand we undevoured?" He presented a challenge: "Let the Devil speak, to shame and convince the atheist […] to know there* is *a witch"* (16).

The ensuing Assize for the Northern Circuit took Judges Bromley and Altham to York, Durham, Newcastle, Carlisle, Appleby, and Lancaster, with hangings at every stop. Returning to London, they had cause to hope for applause and gratitude, not only from the pulpit but from the King. Assisted by Roger Nowell, Henry Hargreaves, Thomas Lister, and other gentlemen, the evidence presented at Lancaster effectively proved true what King James had said of witches in his book of Daemonology:

• The Devil obliges himself to them by forms. […T]o some of the baser sort of them, he obliges himself to appear at their calling upon him by such a proper name which he shows unto them, either in likeness of a dog, a cat, an ape, or suchlike other beast (p. 19).

• There are twenty women given to that craft where there is one man […F]or as that sex is frailer than man is, so is it easier to be entrapped in these gross snares of the Devil (as was over-well proved to be true by the Serpent's deceiving of Eva at the beginning, which makes him the homelier with that sex) […] (43-4)

• He teacheth [them] how to make pictures of wax or clay, that by the roasting thereof, the persons that they bear the name of may be continually melted or dried away by continual sickness (44).

• The witches may transport themselves to places far distant […] carried by the force of the spirit which is their conductor, either above the earth or above the sea swiftly, to the place where they are to meet (38).

• They ought to be put to death according to the Law of God, the civil and imperial law, and municipal law of all Christian nations (77).

It had been a successful tour. Seven Protestants falsely accused of witchcraft by a Roman Catholic teenager had been exonerated at Lancaster, yet Bromley and Altham had nonetheless set a new record for the number of witches hanged during a single circuit.

But ingratitude was stirring in and about Gisburn, Yorkshire: the husband, family, and friends of Jennet Preston refused to believe that she was a witch or in any way deserving of death. They resented it that their loved one had been condemned and hanged by the Court of Sir Edward Bromley on no better evidence than the unproved allegations of a wealthy landowner who had been libeling and tormenting Jennet Preston for five years.

Sir Edward had been hoping for a promotion: he wished to be appointed Justice of the Peace for the coveted Midland Circuit. The unrest in Yorkshire spelled trouble. It was to contain the damage that Bromley commissioned Thomas Potts to write not one book, but two. Appended to The Wonderful Discovery of Witches, *is a second volume with its own title page – The Arraignment and Trial of Jennet Preston of Gisburn. This anxious supplement sets forth the allegations against Preston, and eulogizes Judge Bromley for having hanged her. The trial evidence – the 1607 murder of Lister Sr. by Jennet Preston (as proved by a bleeding corpse), her 1611 murder of Dodgson's child (for which she was "mercifully" found innocent); her intended murder of Thomas Lister Jr.; and her participation in the plot to blow up Lancaster Castle – is duly set forth in order, as presented to the York Assize on 27 July 1612 by the Prosecutor, Master Thomas Heber.*

An unsigned prologue, written by Potts, Altham, or Bromley, puts the trial record in perspective for London readers while condemning Preston's husband and family for having slandered their social superiors:

From
The Arraignment and Trial of JENNET PRESTON of Gisburn-in-Craven, in the County of York °

As by this late *Wonderful Discovery of Witches in the County of Lancaster* may appear – wherein I find such 'apparent matter to satisfy the world – how dangerous and malicious a witch this Jennet Preston was! How unfit to live, having once so great mercy extended to her and again to revive her practices, and return to her former course of life! ... I think it necessary not to let the memory of her life and death die with her, but to place her next to her fellows and to set forth the "Arraignment, Trial, and Conviction of [Jennet Preston]," with her offenses for which she was condemned and executed. And although she died for her offense [on 29 July,] before the rest, I yet can afford her no better place than in the end of this book. [...]

You that were husband to this Jennet Preston, her friends, and kinsfolks – who have not been sparing to devise so scandalous a slander out of the malice of your hearts as that she was maliciously prosecuted by Master Lister and others, her life unjustly taken away by practice; and that (even at the gallows where she died *impenitent* and void of all fear or grace!) "she died an innocent woman" – because she would *confess* nothing! You, I say, may not hold it strange! – though at this time, being not only moved in conscience, but *directed*...to report of her – I suffer you not to wander any further, but with this short discourse [I] oppose your idle conceits, [...] imputations, and slander laid upon the justice of the land. [...]

That this Jennet Preston was for many years well thought of and esteemed by Master Lister (who afterwards *died* for it!); had free access to his house, kind respect and entertainment; nothing denied her [that] she stood in need of. Which of you that dwelleth near them in Craven but can and will witness it? — which might have encouraged a woman of any good condition to have run a better course.

The favors° and goodness of this gentleman (Master [Thomas] Lister [Jr.,] now living) [...] are so palpable and evident to all men, as no man can deny them. These were sufficient motives to have persuaded her from the murder of so good a friend [as his father]. But such was her execrable ingratitude, as even this grace and goodness was the cause of his miserable and untimely death! And even in the beginning of his greatest favors extended to her, began she to work this mischief. [...]

I heartily desire you, my loving friends and countrymen (for whose particular instructions this is added to the former, of *The Wonderful Discovery of Witches in the County of Lancaster*, and for whose particular satisfaction this is published): Awake in time, and suffer not yourselves to be thus assaulted!

Consider how barbarously this gentleman [Thomas Lister] hath been dealt withal. And especially you that hereafter shall pass upon any Juries of Life and Death: let not your connivance (or rather foolish pity!) spare such as these, to execute farther mischief. Remember that she was no sooner set at liberty, but she plotted the ruin and overthrow of this gentleman and his whole family.

"Expect not" – as this reverend and learned Judge, [Sir Edward Bromley] sayeth – "such apparent proof against them, as against others: since all their works are the works of *darkness*. And unless it please almighty God to raise witnesses to accuse them, who is able to *condemn* them?"

Forget not the blood that cries out unto God for "Revenge!" – bring it not upon your own heads.

Neither do I urge this any farther than with this: that I would always entreat you to remember that it is as great a crime (as Salomon sayeth, Proverbs 17) to condemn the innocent, as to let the guilty escape free.

Look not upon things strangely alleged [by the husband and friends of Jennet Preston], but judiciously consider what is justly proved. [...]

Take example by this gentleman to prosecute these hellish furies to their end! Labor to root them out of the commonwealth, for the common good of your country! [...]

And for this great deliverance, let us all pray to GOD Almighty, that the memory of these worthy judges may be blessed to all posterities.

finis

Sir Edward Bromley, who commissioned both The Wonderful Discovery *and* The Arraignment and Trial of Jennet Preston, *kindly vetted Potts's manuscript before the book went to press. Finding the work satisfactory, he supplied two letters of endorsement, one of them co-signed by Judge Altham:*

[To the General Reader:] °

UPON the arraignment and trial of these witches at the last Assizes and general jail-delivery holden at Lancaster, we found such apparent matters against them that we thought it necessary to publish them to the world – and thereupon imposed the labor of this work upon this gentleman by reason of his place, being a clerk at that time in court, employed in the arraignment and trial of them.

James Altham
Edward Bromley

AFTER he had taken great pains to finish it, I took upon me to revise and correct it, that nothing might pass but matter of fact, apparent against them by record. It is very little he hath inserted – and that, *necessary*, to show what their offenses were, what people, and of what condition they were. The whole proceedings and evidence against them, I find upon examination carefully set forth and truly reported, and judge the work fit and worthy to be published.

Edward Bromley

As a final touch, Potts dedicated The Wonderful Discovery *to Thomas Knyvett, famous for his role in having discovered the 1605 Gunpowder Treason:*

To the right honorable, Thomas, Lord Knyvett, [and] the Lady Elizabeth Knyvett his wife °

Right Honorable, […]

Here is nothing of my own act worthy to be commended to your honors. It is the work of those reverend magistrates, his Majesty's Justices of Assizes in the North parts. […]

Here shall you behold the justice of this land, truly administered, *proemium* and *poenam*, mercy and judgment, freely and indifferently bestowed and inflicted (and above all things to be remembered: the excellent care of these judges in the trial of offenders).

It hath pleased them out of their respect to me to impose this work upon me, and according to my understanding, I have taken pains to finish and (now confirmed by their judgment) to publish the same, for the benefit of my country, that the example of these convicted upon their own examinations, confessions, and evidence at the Bar, may work good in others – rather by withholding them *from*, than emboldening them *to*, the achieving such desperate acts as these or the like. These are some part of the fruits of my time spent in the service of my country.

From my lodging in Chancery Lane,
the 16th of November 1612.
Your Honor's humbly devoted servant,
Thomas Potts

• • •

IN 1615, THOMAS POTTS was awarded the keepership of Skalme Park, to breed and train King James's beloved hunting dogs. Sir Edward Bromley in 1616 was at last promoted to the Midland Circuit, a position he held until his death in 1626.

The State's key witness in the 1612 trials was less fortunate: in 1633, Jennet Device was arrested as a witch. The trouble began on All Saints Day. Nine-year-old Edmund Robinson (alias "Ned of the Roughs") was gathering plums when he was approached by two stray greyhounds. He beat them – whereupon the black dog turned into a neighbor woman named Frances Dickenson; and the brown one, into a boy. Mrs. Dickenson then changed the devil-boy into a white horse, mounted him, and rode to a barn at Hoarstones, a quarter-mile off. There Ned peeped through a loop-hole and discovered a convention of sixty women, six of whom pulled on ropes that magically produced butter, milk, cheese, and smoking meat, raining down into basins placed beneath the ropes. Ned recognized eighteen of the witches – one of whom was 30-year-old Jennet Device. (Also named was James Loind's wife, a neighbor whom Ned once saw fly directly up father's chimney.)

Accompanied by his father and an evangelical magistrate, Ned Robinson went from church to church, where he identified other closeted witches. Twenty were indicted, three of whom died in prison before coming to trial. The other seventeen were convicted at the Lancaster Assizes of 24 March 1633/4. Jennet Device was tried and condemned for the witchcraft-death of Isabel Nutter (a woman buried at Colne on 11 February 1627/8).

Made nervous by vocal skeptics, the judge respited execution. He sent Ned and his father, and four of the seventeen convicted witches, to London, there to be examined by King Charles and his Privy Council. Under interrogation, Ned admitted to having fabricated his allegations. As a result of this wonderful discovery, the prisoners were spared hanging – but denied parole. Four were eventually pardoned. The others died, one by one, in Lancaster Castle. (A record dated 22 August 1636 lists Jennet Device as one of the prisoners then living.)

In 2012, as the 400th anniversary of the Pendle hangings drew near, a Burnley brewer mounted a campaign for the women to be pardoned, a move opposed by the local tourist industry. Petitions were signed and submitted to Parliament and to Queen Elizabeth II, who declined to act. But at Roughlee, at least, citizens erected a statue in memory of Alice Nutter. Of those put to death on 20 August 1612 for crimes against humanity, only Alice Nutter was said to be a gentlewoman, a person of quality.

The Flowers of Belvoir Castle (d. 1619)

> [M]*other put it into hot water, & then taking it out, rubd it on*
> *Rutterkin, bidding him flye, and go; wherevpon Rutterkin whined and*
> *cryed Mew: whereupon shee said, that Rutterkin had no power…*
>
> —From The Examination of Phillip Flower, 4 Feb. 1618/9, sig. F4r

M ARGARET AND PHILLIP FLOWER when begging with their mother often stopped at "Beaver" (Belvoir) Castle, the family seat of Roger Manners, fifth earl of Rutland. In June 1612, the earl died, leaving his Castle, lands, and titles to his brother. His widow, the countess dowager Elizabeth, moved out. Francis Manners, 6th earl, moved in, taking possession that autumn. When the three Flower women next came begging for alms at the Castle gate, the earl's wife, Lady Cecilia, offered them employment: Margaret was appointed a residential maid in charge of the laundry and the poultry-house. Joan and Phillip worked as day-laborers in and about the Castle, returning at night to their own cottage.

Not everyone smiled on the rising fortunes of the three Flower women. Joane was an irritable woman who (foolishly) bragged of expertise in black magic, and was denounced by her wealthier neighbors as a witch. Phillip by night was known to entertain a fellow named Thomas Simpson, and (though she loved him) was denounced by her neighbors as a whore. Margaret was a young woman whom "nobody loved but the earl's household" – but one of those lovers was a gentleman related to the earl on his mother's side, living at Belvoir: Thomas Vavasour, gent. (b. 1595) loved Margaret Flower as opportunity served, and she was okay with that. The Flowers never had it so good.

Observing that Margaret frequently left the Castle to visit her mother's cottage, neighbors gossiped that she must be stealing from the Manners family, and bringing the loot home to Joane and Phillip.

The countess was duly warned that Joane Flower kept three devils, in the form of a cat, a rodent, and an owl; that she was "a monstrous malicious woman" with a foul mouth ("and for anything they saw by her, a plain atheist"). But the countess, who saw no evidence of wrong-doing, discounted the gossip.

When Margaret was employed at Belvoir for about a year, she was "abandoned" by Thomas Vavasour. Soon afterward, the countess fired her. Lady Rutland gave Margaret a fairly generous severance package: a bolster, a mattress, and forty shillings; and she invited her to continue working as a day-laborer; but Margaret was no longer welcome to sleep and board at the Castle.

Returning home angry, Margaret consulted with her mother. Together, they plotted their revenge. Lord Francis had a daughter, Katherine, by his first marriage to Frances (*née* Knyvett) Bevill (d. 1605); and two sons, Henry and Francis, by his second wife, Cecilia (m. 1608). From Joane's point of view, it was tit-for-tat: the Rutlands had harmed her children: she would now undertake to harm theirs. On her mother's command, Margaret stole a right-hand glove belonging to Henry Manners, aged three. Her mother steeped it in a broth of blood and hot water; rubbed it on the belly of Rutterkin her cat, and pricked it with a pin. The child became sick and eventually died. Joane Flower happily took credit for the Rutlands' misfortune, and bragged about it to her friend, Joane Willimot.

A year or two later, Margaret brought to her mother a glove of baby Francis that she found upon a dunghill while working at Belvoir. Joane Flower did as before. She then buried the glove outside her cottage, predicting that as it rotted in the ground, so too would the liver of the Manners' surviving son.

While waiting for the curse to take effect, Joane Flower paid a visit to the Castle, to lodge a complaint with earl of Rutland against one Master Peake; but the earl sided with the defendant. Exasperated, Joane launched another assault: using cotton-stuffing from the Manners' mattress and a pair of gloves that Margaret had received as a gift from Thomas Vavasour, she cursed the earl and countess with infertility ("the lord and the lady should have more children, but it would be long").

On her mother's commandment, Margaret next stole "a piece of a handkerchief" belonging to Katherine Manners. Joane took the cloth and did as before. But when she rubbed the handkerchief on Rutterkin's tummy, the cat cried "mew": for it had no power to hurt the girl.

Not until his second son died did Lord and Lady Manners realize that their family was bewitched. In March 1619 the Flowers were arrested. Other arrests followed: Anne Baker, Joane Willimot, and Ellen Green, elderly beggars, were likewise suspected of dabbling in the black arts. To ensure that justice was done, Lord Rutland served as the women's accuser, interrogator, judge, and jury, in his capacity as a Justice of the Peace.

Anne Baker was a familiar figure in villages north of the Castle, where she begged for food in return for doing chores. Crazy, possibly schizophrenic, she heard voices, beheld strange visions, and spoke with her white dog as if he were a person. Baker said that her dog was a "good spirit," and that neither she nor it ever harmed anyone. Others – Anne Stannidge, for one, doubted that. When her infant became ill, Stannidge suspected witchcraft. To identify the doer of it, she burnt fingernail and hair clippings taken from the child (a divining method approved by the clergy). Not long afterward, Anne Baker came to the door, begging; which confirmed that Baker was the one. Hoping for pity, Mrs. Stannidge let the old witch hold her baby, but the infant later died.

Anne Baker.   *Ioane Willimot.*   *Ellen Greene.*

William Fairbarn of Bottesford was more direct: when his son Thomas became ill, Fairbarn confronted Baker, called her "witch" and beat her bloody; whereupon his son's health improved.

Others came forward to accuse Anne Baker, including Matthew Hough (whose wife Elizabeth had died); Anthony and Joane Gill (whose infant had died); and Henry Milles (who suffered cramps or sleeplessness); thereby bringing Baker's alleged body count to at least four.

Joane Willimot of Goodby was a local "wise woman." She is represented in the 1619 woodcut as an elderly cripple supported by crutches, and with a pet owl upon her shoulder. Willimot in her deposition said that she knew how to tell if a sick child were bewitched ("forspoken"); and that she had a "good spirit" who appeared to her in various shapes (most recently in the figure of a woman, but mumbling, so that she could not understand what was said); but never, said Willimot, had she dabbled in witchcraft.

Ellen Green of Stathern, however, testified that Joane Willimot was the one who first introduced her to the Devil; from whom Green had received two familiars, a kitten named Puss and a mole named Hiff-Hiff. Green proudly stated to the court that Puss and Hiff-Hiff had bewitched at least four people to death, villains who deserved it for having abused her with the names of *witch, jade,* and *whore.*

Joane Flower died in custody before trial by gagging on bread, "as they say," at the very moment she dared God to kill her if she were guilty. Margaret and Phillip were tried by the earl of Rutland, his brother George, and a priest; found guilty; and put to death at Lincoln. The fate of the three older witches (and of their devilish household pets), is unrecorded.

A note about the text. Our main source for the alleged crimes of the Leicestershire witches – *The Wonderful Discouerie of the VVitchcrafts of Margaret and Phillip Flower, daughters of Ioan Flower* (1619) – was written by Rev. Henry Goodcole, chaplain of London's Ludgate prison. Working from depositions, Rev. Goodcole makes a muddle of the text. His syntax is a tangle of verbs without subjects, and of pronouns having vague or impossible antecedents: "Being examined concerning a Childe of Anne Stannidge, which shee was suspected to haue bewitched to death; saith, the said Anne Stannidge did deliuer her childe into her hands, and that shee did lay it vpon her skirt, but did no harme vnto it" (sig. D4v-E1r). Goodcole's intended sense: *Anne Stannidge suspected that her deceased child was bewitched to death by Anne Baker. Being examined, Baker sayeth that she received the child from Anne Stannidge and held it in her lap but did no harm to it.* Goodcole continues (same paragraph): "confesseth that she was angry with her and said she might haue giuen her of her better bread, for she had gone too often on her errands, but more she saith not" (i.e., *Anne Baker admits that she was angry with Elizabeth Hough, and said that Hough might have given her some better bread – for Baker had gone too often on Hough's errands; but more, Anne Baker sayeth not*). Faced with such a mess, the editor of *Women's Works* has made emendations to clarify the sense (in square brackets [thus], to signal editorial intervention); and restored the first person to the depositions. These remedies in a twice-mediated text are applied without any presumption that the redaction thereby restores the original speaker's authentic voice.

As with Thomas Potts's text of the proceedings against the Pendle witches, the drumbeat repetition of "the said" and "aforesaid" is here quietly deleted; and the frequent third-person attribution to "this examinate" is here replaced by personal pronouns. For purists, Goodcole's original text without emendation is available online from Early English Books.

The Wonderful Discovery of the Witchcrafts of Margaret and Phillip Flower, Daughters of Joan Flower, near Belvoir Castle: executed at Lincoln, March 11, 1618[/9]

By Rev. Henry Goodcole, chaplain of Ludgate Prison

AFTER the right honorable Sir Francis Manners succeeded his brother in the earldom of Rutland (and so not only took possession of Belvoir Castle, but of all other his demesnes, lordships, towns, manors, lands, and revenues appropriate to the same earldom), he proceeded so honorably in the course of his life, as neither displacing tenants, discharging servants, denying the access of the poor, welcoming of strangers, and performing all the duties of a noble lord; [so] that he fastened, as it were, unto himself, the love and good opinion of the country – wherein he walked the more cheerfully and remarkable, because his honorable countess marched arm-in-arm with him in the same race; so that Belvoir Castle was a continual palace of entertainment, and a daily receptacle for all sorts, both rich and poor, especially such ancient people as neighbored the same. [1]

Amongst whom one Joane Flower, with her daughters Margaret and Phillip, were not only relieved at the first from thence but quickly entertained as charwomen, and Margaret admitted as a continual dweller in the castle, looking both to the poultry abroad and the wash-house within doors – in which life they continued with equal correspondency till something was discovered to the noble lady which concerned the misdemeanor of these women. [...] [2]

First, that Joane Flower (the mother) was a monstrous malicious woman, full of oaths, curses, and imprecations irreligious, and for anything they saw by her, a plain atheist.[3]

Besides, of late days her very countenance was estranged: her eyes were fiery and hollow, her speech fell and envious, her demeanor strange and exotic, and her conversation sequestered – so that the whole course of her life gave great suspicion that she was a notorious witch. (Yea, some of her neighbors dared to affirm that she dealt with familiar spirits, and terrified them all with curses and threatening of revenge if there were never so little cause of displeasure and unkindness.) [4]

Concerning Margaret: that she often resorted from the Castle to her mother, bringing such provision as they thought was unbefitting for a servant to purloin, and coming at such unseasonable hours that [the neighbors] could not but conjecture some mischief between them and that their extraordinary riot and expenses tended both to rob the Lady [Rutland], and to maintain certain deboised and base company which frequented this Joane Flower's house (the mother); and especially, her youngest daughter. [5]

Concerning Phillip: that she was lewdly transported with the love of one Thomas Simpson, who presumed to say that she had bewitched him, for he had no power to leave her, and was (as he supposed) marvelously altered both in mind and body, since her acquainted company.

These complaints began many years before either their conviction or public apprehension. Notwithstanding – such was the honor of this earl and his lady; such was the cunning of this monstrous woman in observation towards them; such was the subtlety of the Devil to bring his purposes to pass; such was the pleasure of God to make trial of His servants; and such was the effect of a damnable woman's wit and malicious envy – that all things were carried away in the smooth channel of liking and good entertainment on every side, until the earl by degrees conceived some mislike against [Margaret Flower]; and so, peradventure, estranged himself from that familiarity and accustomed conferences he was wont to have with her.

—Until one Peake° offered her some wrong, against whom she complained but found that my lord did not affect her clamors and malicious information.

—Until one Master Vavasour abandoned her company, as either suspicious of her lewd life, or distasted with his own misliking of such base and poor creatures (whom nobody loved but the earl's household). [6]

---

[1] *demesnes*] possessed real estate; *ancient*] elderly.

[2] *relieved ... from thence*] received charity from Belvoir; *charwomen*] women hired by the day to do odd jobs of household work; *correspondency*] agreement, concord; *discovered*] disclosed; *countess*] not Frances (*née* Knyvett) Manners (d. 1608) but the earl's second wife, Cecilia (*née* Tufton).

[3] *imprecations irreligious*] curses.

[4] *fell*] cruel; *conversation sequestered*] behavior was solitary.

[5] *deboised*] early form of *debauched*; corrupt, depraved.

[6] *affect her clamors*] sympathize with her complaints; *Vavasour*] Thomas, son of William and Anne (Manners) Vavasour of Hazelwood.

—Until the countess, misconceiving of [Joane's] daughter Margaret, and discovering some indecencies both in her life and neglect of her business, discharged her from lying any more in the Castle (yet gave her 40 shilling, a bolster, and a mattress of wool, commanding her to go home).

—[And] until the slackness of her repairing to the Castle as she was wont, did turn [Margaret's] love and liking toward this honorable earl and his family into hate and rancor. [1]

Whereupon, despited to be so neglected and exprobrated by her neighbors for her daughter's casting out of doors (and other conceived displeasures), [Joane Flower] grew past all shame and womanhood, and many times cursed them all that were the cause of this discontentment; and made her, so, loathsome to her former familiar friends and beneficial acquaintance. [...] [2]

At last, as malice increased in these damnable women, [Lord Rutland's] family felt the smart of their revenge and inficious disposition. For his eldest son, Henry Lord Roos, sickened very strangely, and after a while died. [Francis Jr.,] his next-named Lord Roos, accordingly was severely tormented by [the Flowers], and most barbarously and inhumanely tortured by a strange sickness. Not long after, the Lady Katherine was set upon by their dangerous and devilish practices, and many times in great danger of life, through extreme maladies and unusual fits. [...] [3]

Thus were [the Flowers] apprehended about Christmas [1618] (and carried to Lincoln jail after due examination before sufficient justices of the peace and discreet magistrates, who wondered at their audacious wickedness).

But Joane Flower (the mother) before conviction, (as they say) "called for bread and butter, and wished it might never go through her if she were guilty" of that whereupon she was examined; so mumbling it in her mouth, [she] never spake more words after, but fell down and died as she was carried to Lincoln jail, with a horrible ex-cruciation of soul and body, and was buried at Ancaster.

When the earl heard of their apprehension, he hasted down with his brother Sir George, sometimes examining them himself and sometimes sending them to others. At last, [he] left them to the trial of law, before the judges of Assizes at Lincoln. And so they were convicted of murther and executed accordingly, about the 11th of March, to the terror of all the beholders, and example of such dissolute and abominable creatures. [4]

And because you shall have both cause to glorify God for this discovery, and occasion to apprehend the strangeness of their lives and [the] truth of their proceedings, I thought it both meet and convenient to lay open their own examinations and evidences against one another – with such apparent circumstances as do not only show the cause of their mislike and distasting against the earl and his family but the manner of their proceedings and revenges, with other particulars belonging to the true and plain discovery of their villainy and witchcraft. [...]

The examination of ANNE BAKER of Bottesford in the county of Leicester, spinster; taken March 1st, 1618[/19], by the right honorable Francis, earl of Rutland, [and] Sir George Manners, knight, [...] and Samuel Fleming, doctor of divinity, [...] his Majesty's Justices of the Peace. [...]

SHE SAYETH THAT "There are four colors of planets: black, yellow, green, and blue," and that "Black is always death"; and that she saw the blue planet strike Thomas Fairbarn (the eldest son unto William Fairbarn of Bottesford aforesaid), by the pinfold there. Within the which time, William Fairbarn did beat her and break her head (whereupon Thomas Fairbarn did mend). [5]

And being asked, "Who did send that planet?" [she] answered, "It was not I."

Further she sayeth that she saw a hand appear unto her, and that she heard a voice in the air said unto her, "Anne Baker, save thyself! For tomorrow thou and thy master must be slain!" And the next day her master and she were in a cart together and suddenly she saw a flash of fire, and said her prayers, and the fire went away.

---

[1] *40 shilling*] nominal equivalent of £164 GBP; *bolster*] a long stuffed pillow or cushion; *slackness...wont*] being reduced to occasional day labor.

[2] *despited*] condemned;   *exprobated*] reproached; *so*] for that reason.

[3] *inficious*] lying, untruthful;   *Lady Katherine*] (1600-1649), daughter of Francis, 6th earl, by his first wife, Frances (*née* Knyvett); 1620 m. George Villiers, 2nd Duke of Buckingham.

---

[4] *Assizes of Lincoln*] sessions of criminal court for the county of Lincolnshire.

[5] *pinfold*] a pen or enclosure for livestock;   *Thomas Fairbarn*] christened at Bottesford 22 Jan. 1596.

And shortly after, a crow came and picked upon her clothes: and she said her prayers again, and bade the crow go to whom he was sent, and the crow went unto her master, and did beat him to death. And she with her prayers recovered him to life, but he was sick a fortnight after; and sayeth that if she had not had more knowledge than her master, both he and she and all the cattle had been slain. [1]

Being examined concerning a child of Anne Stannidge (which [Anne Baker] was suspected to have bewitched to death), sayeth, [...] "Anne Stannidge did deliver her child into [my] hands, and [I] did lay it upon [my] skirt but did no harm unto it."

[...] The mother of the child [chargeth] that upon the burning of the hair and the paring of the nails of the child, Anne Baker came in and set her[self] down, and for one hour's space could speak nothing.

[Baker] confesseth she came into the house of Anne Stannidge in great pain, but did not know of the burning of the hair and nails of the child; but said she was so sick that she did not know whither she went.

Being charged that she bewitched Elizabeth Hough (the wife of William Hough) to death, for that [Elizabeth Hough] angered her in giving her alms of her second bread, confesseth, "[I] *was* angry with her! [...] She might have given [me] of her better bread, for [I have] gone too often on [Hough's] errands." [...]

[She further] confesseth, "[I] came to Joane Gill's house, her child being sick. [...] She entreated [me] to look on the child, and to tell her whether it was forspoken or not and [I] said it was forspoken, but when the child died [I] cannot tell."[2]

And being asked concerning Nortley carrying of his child home unto his own house, where the said Anne Baker was:

"[I] asked him, 'Who gave the child that loaf?'"

"He told [me,] 'Anthony Gill.'"

"—to whom [I] said, 'He might have had a child of his own, if he would have sought in time for it.'" [...]

Being blamed by Henry Milles in this sort: "'A fire set on you! I have had two or three ill nights' – to whom [I] made answer, 'you should have let me alone, then.'" [...]

Anne Baker, March 2nd, 1618, confessed before Samuel Fleming, doctor of divinity, that "About three years ago, [I] went into Northamptonshire. [...] At [my] coming back again, one Peak's wife, and Denise, his wife of Belvoir, told [me] that my young lord Henry was dead – and that 'there was a glove of the lord buried in the ground; and, as that glove did rot and waste, so did the liver of the lord rot and waste.'"

Further she said (March 3rd 1618, before Sir George Manners, knight, and Samuel Fleming, doctor of divinity) that she hath a spirit which hath the shape of a white dog, which she calleth her "good spirit."

Samuel Fleming, testis

The Examination of JOANE WILLIMOT, taken the 28th of February [...] before Alexander Amcotts, esq., one of his Majesty's Justices of the Peace

THIS EXAMINATE SAYETH THAT:

"Joane Flower told [me] that my lord of Rutland had 'dealt badly' with her, and that they had put away her daughter; and that, although she could not have her will of my lord himself, yet she had spied my lord's son and had 'stricken him to the heart.'" (And she sayeth that 'my lord's son was stricken with a white spirit'; and that she can cure some that send unto her; and that some reward her for her pains, and of some, she taketh nothing...) She further sayeth that "Upon Friday night last, [my] spirit came to [me] and told [me] that there was a bad woman at Deeping who had given her soul to the Devil. [...My] spirit did then appear unto [me] in a more ugly form than it had formerly done. [...] It urged [me] much to 'give it something although it were but a piece of [my] girdle'; and told [me] that it had taken great pains for [me]. But [I] would give it nothing, and told it that [I] had sent it to no place but only to see how my Lord Roos did, and [my] spirit told [me] that he should do well."

The examination of JOANE WILLIMOT, taken the 2nd day of March [...]

THIS EXAMINATE SAYETH THAT she hath a spirit which she calleth "Pretty," which was given unto her by William Berry (of Langholme in Rutlandshire), whom she served three years. [...] Her master, when he gave it unto her, willed her to open her mouth and he would blow into her a fairy which should do her good. [...] She opened her mouth, and he did blow into her mouth. [...] Presently after his blowing, there came out of her

---

[1] *crow ... beat him*] The crow (bird) is imagined to have beaten its master like a crow (iron crowbar).

[2] *forspoken*] bewitched.

mouth a spirit, which stood upon the ground in the shape and form of a woman – which spirit did ask of her, her soul; which she then promised unto it, being willed thereunto by her master. […]

"[I] never hurt anybody, but did help divers that sent for [me], which were stricken or forspoken; and [my] spirit came weekly to [me], and would tell [me] of divers persons that were stricken and forspoken. […] The use which [I] had of the spirit was to know how those did which [I] had undertaken to amend […I] did help them by certain prayers which [I] used, and not by [my] own spirit. Neither did [I] employ [my] spirit in anything, but only to bring word how those did which [I] had undertaken to cure. […]

And she further sayeth, "[My] spirit came unto [me] this last night (as [I] thought) in the form of a woman, mumbling, but [I] could not understand what it said."

And being asked whether she were not in a dream or slumber when she thought she saw it, she said no, and that she was "as waking as at this present."

Alexander Amcotts
Thomas Robinson, test.

The examination of JOANE WILLIMOT of Goodby in the county of Leicester, widow, taken the 17th of March 1618[/9], by Sir Henry Hastings, knight, and Samuel Fleming, doctor of divinity, two of his Majesty's justices of the peace. […]

SHE SAYETH THAT she told one Cook's wife of Stathern in the said county, laborer, that "John Patchet might have had his child alive, if he would have sought forth for it in time, an' if it were not death-stricken in her ways"; and that "Patchet's wife had an evil thing within her, which should make an end of her" (and that, she knew by her girdle). [1]

She sayeth further, that Gamaliel Greet of Waltham in the said county, shepherd, "had a spirit like a white mouse put into him, in his swearing"; and that "if he did look upon anything with an intent to hurt, it should be hurt"; and, that he had "a mark on his left arm, which was cut away"; and that her own spirit did tell her all this before it went from her. […]

Further she sayeth: "Joane Flower, Margaret Flower, and [I] did meet (about a week before Joane Flower's apprehension), in Blackborough

Hill, and went from thence home to Joane Flower's house. And there [I] saw two spirits, one like a rat, and the other like an owl. (And one of them did suck under [Joane Willimot's] right ear, as [me]thought.) And Joane told [me] that her spirits did say that she should neither be hanged nor burnt […] Further, […] Joane Flower did take up some earth and spat upon it, and did work it with her finger, and put it up into her purse – and said though she could not hurt the Lord [Rutland] himself, yet she had sped his son which is dead."

Henry Hastings
Samuel Fleming

The examination of ELLEN GREEN of Stathern in the county of Leicester, taken the 17th of March 1618[/9] […]

SHE SAYETH THAT:

"Joane Willimot of Goodby came about six years since to [me] in the Wolds, and persuaded [me] to forsake God, and betake [me] to the Devil; and she would give [me] two spirits – to which [I] gave [my] consent. And thereupon Joane Willimot called two spirits, one in the likeness of a kitlin, and the other of a moldiwarp. The first, Willimot called Puss, the other, Hiff-hiff. And they presently came to her. And she departing left them with [me], and they leapt on [my] shoulder, and the kitlin sucked under [my] right ear on [my] neck, and the moldiwarp on the left side in the like place. [2]

"After they had sucked [me, I] sent the kitlin to a baker of that town, whose name [I remember] not, who had called [me] "Witch" and stricken [me], and [I] bade [my] spirit go and bewitch him to death. The moldiwarp [I] then bade go to Anne Dawse of the same town and bewitch her to death, because she had called [me] *witch, whore, jade*, etc.; and within one fortnight after, they both died. [3]

"And further, [I] sent both [my] spirits to Stonesby, to one Willison a husbandman, and Robert Williman, a husbandman's son, and bade the kitlin go to Willison and bewitch him to death, and the moldiwarp to the other, and bewitch him to death, which they did; and within ten days they died."

(These four were bewitched while this examinate dwelt at Waltham aforesaid.)

---

[1] *his child*] Edward, son of John Patchet of Stathern, was christened 28 and died 30 Oct. 1617.

[2] *kitlin*] kitten; *moldiwarp*] mole (*OED* mouldwarp n.).

[3] *six years since ... Anne Dawse*] Anne Dawse of nearby Knossington was buried 25 April 1612.

"About three years since, [I] removed thence to Stathern, where [I now dwell.] Upon a difference between Willimot and the wife of John Patchet" (of Stathern, yeoman), [Willimot called me] to go and touch John Patchet's wife and her child, which [I] did, touching John Patchet's wife in her bed, and the child in the grace-wife's arms. And then [I] sent [my] spirits to bewitch them to death, which they did; and so the woman lay languishing by the space of a month and more, for then she died. The child died the next day after [I] touched it. […]

"Joane Willimot had a spirit sucking on her, under the left flank, in the likeness of a little white dog, which [I saw] sucking in barley-harvest last, being then at the house of Joane Willimot.

"And for [myself, I] gave [my] soul to the Devil to have these spirits at [my] command; for a confirmation whereof, [I] suffered them to suck [me] always as aforesaid, about the change and full of the moon."

Henry Hastings
Samuel Fleming

The examination of PHILLIP FLOWER, sister of Margaret Flower and daughter of Joane Flower; before Sir William Pelham, and Master Butler, justices of the peace, February 4th 1618[/9]. Which was brought in at the Assizes as evidence against her sister Margaret:

SHE SAYETH THAT:

"[My] mother and [my] sister maliced the earl of Rutland, his countess, and their children, because [my] sister Margaret was put out of the lady's service of laundry, and exempted from other services about the house. Whereupon [my] sister, by the commandment of [my] mother, brought from the castle the right-hand glove of the lord Henry Roos, which she delivered to [my] mother; who presently rubbed it on the back of her spirit Rutterkin, and then put it into hot boiling water. Afterward she pricked it often, and buried it in the yard, wishing the Lord Roos might never thrive. And so [my] sister Margaret continued with [my] mother, where [I] often saw the cat Rutterkin leap on her shoulder, and suck her neck. […] [I] heard [my] mother often curse the earl and his Lady; and thereupon would boil feathers and blood together, using many devilish speeches and strange gestures.

The examination of MARGARET FLOWER, sister of Phillip Flower, etc., about the 22nd of January 1618[/9].

SHE SAYETH AND CONFESSETH THAT:

"About four years since, the countess growing into some mislike with [me] gave [me] forty shillings, a bolster, and a mattress, and bade [me] lie at home, and come no more to dwell at the Castle; which [I] not only took in ill part but grudged at it […] swearing in [my] heart to be revenged. […]

[My] mother bade [me] go again into the Castle of Belvoir, and bring down the glove or some other thing of Henry, Lord Roos. And [I] asked, 'what to do?' [My] mother replied, 'to hurt my lord Roos'; whereupon [I] brought down a glove, and delivered the same to [my] mother, who stroked Rutterkin her cat with it, after it was dipped in hot water, and so pricked it often. After which, Henry lord Roos fell sick within a week, and was much tormented. […]

"Finding a glove about two or three years since of Francis, Lord Roos on a dunghill, [I] delivered it to [my] mother, who put it into hot water; and after took it out and rubbed it on Rutterkin the cat, and bade him, 'Go upwards!' And after [my] mother buried it in the yard and said, 'A mischief light on him! – but he will mend again.' […]

"After this, [my] mother complained to the earl against one Peak, who had offered her some wrong, wherein she conceived that the earl took not her part, as she expected; which dislike, with the rest, exasperated her displeasure against him. And so she watched an opportunity to be revenged; whereupon she took wool out of the said mattress, and a pair of gloves which were given [me] by Master Vavasour, and put them into warm water, mingling them with some blood and stirring it together. Then she took the wool and gloves out of the water, and rubbed them on the belly of Rutterkin her cat, saying the lord and the lady should have more children, but it would be long. […]

"By [my] mother's commandment, [I] brought to her a piece of a handkerchief of the lady Katherine (the earl's daughter). And [my] mother put it into hot water; and then, taking it out, rubbed it on Rutterkin, bidding him fly, and go; whereupon Rutterkin whined and cried *mew* […] Rutterkin had no power over the lady Katherine to hurt her."

The examination of PHILLIP FLOWER, the 25th of February 1618[/9], before Francis, earl of Rutland; Francis lord Willoughby of Eresby; Sir George Manners; and Sir William Pelham:

SHE CONFESSETH AND SAYETH THAT she hath a spirit sucking on her in the form of a white rat, which keepeth her left breast, and hath so done for three or four years. And concerning the agreement betwixt her spirit and herself, she confesseth and sayeth that when it came first unto her, she gave her soul to it, and it promised to do her good, and cause Thomas Simpson to love her if she would suffer it to suck her, which she agreed unto. And so, the last time it sucked was on Tuesday at night, the 23rd of February.

The examination of MARGARET FLOWER, at the same time:

SHE CONFESSETH THAT she hath two familiar spirits sucking on her: the one white, the other black-spotted. The white sucked under her left breast; and the black-spotted, within the inward parts of her secrets. When she first entertained them, she promised them her soul, and they covenanted to do all things which she commanded them, etc.

She further sayeth that "About the 30th of January, last past, being Saturday, four devils appeared unto [me] in Lincoln jail, at eleven or twelve o'clock at midnight. The one stood at [my] bed's feet, with a black head like an ape, and spake unto [me]; but what, [I] cannot well remember – at which, [I] was very angry because he would speak no plainer, or let [me] understand his meaning. The other three were Rutterkin, Little Robin, and Spirit. But [I] never mistrusted them, nor suspected [my]self, till then.

• • •

These examinations and some others were taken and charily preserved for the contriving of sufficient evidences against them. And when the judges of Assizes came down to Lincoln about the first week of March – being Sir Henry Hobart, Lord Chief Justice of the Common Pleas, and Sir Edward Bromley, one of the Barons of the Exchequer – [the examinations] were presented unto them, who not only wondered at the wickedness of these persons, but were amazed at their practices and horrible contracts with the Devil to damn their own souls. [1]

And although the right honorable earl had sufficient grief for the loss of his children, yet no doubt it was the greater to consider the manner, and how it pleased God to inflict on him such a fashion of visitation. Besides, as it amazed the hearers to understand the particulars and the circumstances of this devilish contract, so was it as wonderful to see their desperate impenitency, and horrible distraction, according to the rest of that sort – exclaiming against the Devil for deluding them and now breaking promise with them, when they stood in most need of his help.

Notwithstanding all these aggravations, such was the unparalleled magnanimity, wisdom, and patience of this generous nobleman, that he urged nothing against them more than their own confessions; and so quietly left them to judicial trial, desiring of God mercy for their souls, and of men, charity to censure them in their condemnation.

BUT GOD IS NOT MOCKED, and so gave them over to judgment. Nor man so reformed [them,] but for the earl's sake, [the Justices] cursed them to that place which they themselves long before had bargained for.

What now remains, gentle Reader, but for thee to make use of so wonderful a story and remarkable an accident – out of which, to draw to a conclusion, thou mayest collect these particulars: First, that God is the supreme commander of all things, and permitteth wonderful actions in the world, for the trial of the godly, the punishment of the wicked, and His own glory; of which man shall never attain to know the reason or occasion. Secondly, that the Devil is the mere servant and agent of God.

Yet "Let not a witch live" (sayeth God) and "Let them die" (sayeth the Law of England) "that have conversation with spirits, and presume to blaspheme the name of God with spells and incantation." O then, you sons of men, take warning by these examples, and either divert your steps from the broad way of destruction, and irrecoverable gulf of damnation, or with Joshua's counsel to Achan, "Bless God for the discovery of wickedness," and take thy death patiently, as the prevention of thy future judgment and saving innocents from punishment who otherwise may be suspected without a cause.

• • •

Francis Manners, sixth Earl of Rutland, died without male issue in 1632. His elaborate marble tomb at St. Mary's Bottesford bears a lengthy inscription recalling the villainy of the Flower women in its mention of his two sons, Henry and Francis: "BOTH W:[CH] DYED IN THEIR INFANCY BY WICKED PRACTISE & SORCERYE."

---

[1] *charily*] carefully.

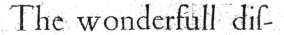

Entered in the London Stationers' Register on 27 April 1621, just eight days after Elizabeth Sawyer's execution and "published by authority," *The Wonderfull Discoverie*, by Rev. Henry Goodcole, chaplain of Newgate Prison, presents the true script of Sawyer's villainy:

"In Dialogue manner are here expressed the persons that she murthered, and the cattell that she destroyed by the helpe of the Diuell. In this manner was I inforced to speake vnto her, because she might vnderstand me and giue vnto me answere according to my demands, for she was a very ignorant woman…"

"And thus much of the meanes that brought her to her deserued death and destruction, I will addresse to informe you of her preparation to death, which is alone pertinent to my function, and declare vnto you her Confession verbatim, out of her owne mouth deliuered to me, the Tuseday after her conuiction, though with great labour it was extorted from her, and the same Confession I read vnto her at the place of her execution, and there shee confessed to all people that were there, the same to be most true" (B4r, C1v).

Taking Goodcole's pamphlet as a narrative source, Dekker, Ford and Rowley represent Sawyer as a woman more sinned against than sinning. In *The Witch of Edmonton* (1621), Sawyer's reputed victim, Agnes Radcliffe, enters mad, speaks gibberish, and exits, pursued by Tom the Devil-Dog. She then beats out her own brains offstage. Sawyer is blamed for her death, and for having "bewitched Gammer Washbowl's sow to cast her pigs a day before she would have farried."

Cuddy Banks, an invented character, is a good-natured clown who gets pranked by Tom the Devil-Dog but cannot be corrupted by him.

Though performed as early as December 1621 *The Witch of Edmonton* was not published until 1658, when the death of Oliver Cromwell brought relief from Puritan extremism.

ELIZABETH SAWYER (d. 1621)

The Witch of Edmonton

> *Sawy.* if every poor old VVoman be trod on thus by slaves, revil'd, kick'd,
> beaten, as I am daily, she to be reveng'd had need turn VVitch. [...] Men in
> gay clothes, whose Backs are laden with Titles and Honours, are within far
> more crooked then I am; and if I be a VVitch, more VVitch-like.
>
> —T. Dekker, et al., *The Witch of Edmonton, a Known True Story*

ELIZABETH SAWYER fit the profile: elderly and destitute, bent over with arthritis, dependent on charity and receiving none, she went from door to door seeking a handout for the sale of her homemade brooms. Meanwhile, God-fearing Edmonton dairy farmers sometimes lost a cow to disease, for no good reason. Children in the custody of a wet-nurse sometimes languished or died. And when she was accused of mischief or when rudely handled, the old hag could curse like a sailor. For all of these reasons, Elizabeth Sawyer was despised by homeowners as a parasite and a nuisance, and denounced by many as a notorious witch.

By means of the Thatch Test, probably also by the Scratch Test, her Edmonton neighbors confirmed, "frequently," that Sawyer was guilty: for the first test, you pulled thatch from the suspect's cottage when she was not at home; set the dried grass on fire; and waited. If the person of interest made an appearance soon after, she was a witch. The Scratch Test was most useful when a suspected bewitchment was already in progress: you jumped the suspect in the street; scratched or poked her with a nail, a fingernail, or a needle, so as to draw a drop or two of blood "above the breath" (usually, on the face); and if the afflicted citizen, child, or livestock then mended, the suspect was a witch. (The leading witch-hunters of the seventeenth century concede that these tests may need to be performed repeatedly, since the Devil will often produce a false negative, to protect his own.) [1]

In the autumn of 1620, Agnes Radcliffe, a neighbor, became lunatic after striking Bess Sawyer's pig for having licked a block of soap in her yard. Four days later, Radcliffe is said to have died, either by "foaming at the mouth" or by "braining herself." Before perishing, Radcliffe is said to have stated "confidently" that the Witch of Edmonton "was the occasion of her death." Sawyer was duly arrested and imprisoned, to await trial at the next Assize.

The defendant was tried and found guilty of murder, under the 1604 Witchcraft Statute. Executions after trial usually followed within two days (Sundays excepted). Literate convicts by reading their "neck verses," typically a Latin Psalm, were excused the gallows, for a first offense (but branded on the thumb for future reference, as when the playwright Ben Jonson was reprieved in 1598 after having killed Gabriel Spencer). But never was a woman granted of Benefit of Clergy; besides which, the 1604 Witchcraft Statute expressly forbade granting Benefit of Clergy to anyone found guilty of witchcraft. Nor was Sawyer literate, nor did she have any right to appeal the court's decision. Her doom was sealed.

Sawyer was then taken to Newgate, London's most horrific prison, a facility chiefly for violent felons. Upon admission, inmates whether male or female were stripped naked, provided with rags, and treated as well as their keepers or fellow-prisoners saw fit. Sir John Birkenhead, writing with perverse jocularity of a fictional case, describes business as usual:

> Then she was led to Newgate Jail,
> Where she was naked stripped;
> They whipped her 'till the cord did fail,
> As dogs used to be whipped. [...]
> Some say she was a Scottish girl,
> Or else, at least, a witch,
> But she was born in Colchester.
> (Was ever such a *bitch*?) [2]

---

[1] See Rev. W. Perkins (1610): "Besides these, in other countries they have a further proof, justified by some that be learned. The party is taken and bound hand and foot, and cast crossways into the water. If she sink, she is counted innocent and escapeth [hanging]; if she fleet [*i.e.*, float] on the water and sink not, she is taken for a witch, convicted, and accordingly punished" (1610), 206). The Swimming Test was used for the trial of Mary Sutton (pub. 1615).

[2] *Then...bitch*] John Birkenhead, *The Four-Legg'd Elder* (1647), lines 69-72.

The floors were covered in human waste. Sleep was disrupted by cursing, fights, and the howls of the insane. Men and women were housed together. Rape though commonplace went unpunished since most of the inmates were to die soon anyway. The prisoners received no food except from visitors and generally went to the gallows hungry.

Two necessary items of business yet remained, following a convicted felon's delivery to Newgate: 1. spiritual counsel in the prison chapel, and 2. a signed confession of guilt (an "X" or some other symbol on the bottom line, after the confession was agreed upon and read aloud to the penitent felon). The confession was again read aloud from the scaffold, to the crowd in attendance on hanging day.

But Elizabeth Sawyer, even after her trial, stubbornly said she was innocent. Her denial, a familiar tactic of condemned criminals, delayed her death but not for long. The keepers at Newgate were authorized to do whatever was necessary to extort a confession from those who were condemned to die but who pretended still to be innocent. Favored methods included whipping and pressing.

Sawyer was tried and condemned on 14 April 1621. Three days later, a confession of guilt was finally "extorted" from her (sig. B4r), and signed with Sawyer's mark in the presence of multiple witnesses, who co-signed. Her crimes being confirmed from her own mouth, Sawyer was hanged on the 19th.

Executions were conducted outdoors, staged as religious ceremonies for the public good. These rituals of justice sometimes lasted all day, depending on the number of persons convicted at the Assize. (At Tyburn, offenders could be turned off three at a time.) Sawyer's execution having been delayed for a few days, she may have died alone. She was clearly the star attraction. Henry Goodcole, chaplain of Newgate and Sawyer's "continual visitor" in the days preceding her death, reports his disgust with "base and false ballads, which were sung at the time of our returning from the Witch's execution" – "ridiculous fictions of her bewitching corn on the ground, of a ferret and an owl daily sporting before her, of the bewitched woman braining herself, of the spirits attending in the prison" (A2r, A3v).

It was those last two allegations – that Agnes Radcliffe died by suicide, and that the Witch of Edmonton was attended by evil spirits even in prison, that most rankled Rev. Goodcole: the courts had just proved Radcliffe's death was a murder by witchcraft, and it was Goodcole himself, not evil spirits or ferrets, who attended on Sawyer in Newgate; yet here were spurious narratives and confessions in verse, already on sale, being peddled to onlookers at her 19 April execution. Goodcole regrets that "such lewd ballad-mongers should be suffered to creep into the printers' presses and people's ears" (A3v).

Those ephemeral ballads, hot off the press on hanging day, are remembered in *Cures for the Itch* (1626), a book of characters in which Henry Parrot ridicules "The Ballad-Maker": "No massacre or murder comes to him amiss, but brings sufficient matter for invention – wherein he shows himself so nimble, that if any witch be by chance condemned, he'll have a ballad out in print before such time as she goes to Tyburn; wherein all her confession and the manner of her death shall be described by way of *prophecy* – witness the famous witch of Edmonton, condemned at Newgate about four years past" (A2v-3r).

Those half-penny ballads of the Witch of Edmonton and her owl and ferret soon perished. Elizabeth Sawyer's name and fate would thereafter have escaped notice in the historical record but for two competing publications: the first was Henry Goodcole's corrective master-narrative, *The Wonderful Discovery of Elizabeth Sawyer, a Witch, Late of Edmonton*. The other is *The Witch of Edmonton*, by Thomas Dekker, William Rowley, and John Ford, a stage-play that made Sawyer famous throughout England. Rev. Goodcole professes to supply the Truth: "I meddle here with nothing but matter of *fact*, and to that end produce the testimony of the living and the dead, which I hope shall be authentical for the confirmation of this narration" (A3r). For Goodcole and his readers, Sawyer's bad life and violent end present a lesson in divine and civil justice, illustrating how "God did wonderfully overtake her in her own wickedness, to make her tongue to be the means of her own destruction" (B1r).

Henry Goodcole worked on assignment. Most of his pamphlets, 1618-1637, report on cases where the condemned criminal stubbornly professed innocence, or where the public doubted that justice was done; his task, always, was to set the record straight. In *A Wonderful Discovery of the Witchcrafts of Margaret and Phillip Flower* (1619), Goodcole justified the execution of the Flowers of Belvoir Castle. He was then serving as chaplain at Ludgate, earning only six pounds thirteen shillings four pence a year. His vigorous defense of the JPs received favorable notice. In July 1620, he was appointed chaplain of Newgate Prison, at twice the salary. Not long after his counseling of Elizabeth Sawyer, and his report on her death and execution, Goodcole received another £10 raise. Here, then, is *A Wonderful Discovery of Elizabeth Sawyer,* the story of an old woman and her unruly speech; containing a "wonderful warning to many, whose tongues are too frequent in these abominable sins."

DWF

A True Declaration of the Manner of Proceeding against ELIZABETH SAWYER late of Edmonton, spinster; and the evidence of her conviction. [1]

By Rev. Henry Goodcole, chaplain of Newgate Prison

A GREAT and long suspicion was held of this person to be a witch. And the eye of Mr. Arthur Robinson (a worthy Justice of Peace, who dwelleth at Totnam, near to her) was watchful over her and her ways; and that, not without just cause [...] seeing the death of nurse-children and cattle, strangely and suddenly to happen. [2]

And to find out who should be the author of this mischief, an old ridiculous custom was used, which was to pluck the thatch of her house, and to burn it; and it being so burned, the author of such mischief should presently then come. And it was observed (and affirmed to the Court) that Elizabeth Sawyer would presently frequent the house of them that burned the thatch which they plucked off her house, and [would] come without any sending for.

This trial, though it was slight and ridiculous, yet it settled a resolution in those whom it concerned: to find out, by all means they could endeavor, her long and close-carried witchery, to explain it to the world; and [...] to pay in the end such a worker-of-iniquity her wages and that which she had deserved: namely, shame and death. [...] [3]

The Devil (that had so long deluded her!) did not come as she said [he would do,] to show the least help of his unto her, to deliver her – but being descried in his ways and works, immediately he fled, leaving her to shift and answer for herself, with public and private marks on her body as followeth:

1. Her face was most pale and ghost-like, without any blood at all, and her countenance was still dejected to the ground.

2. Her body was crooked and deformed (even bending together, which so happened but a little before her apprehension).

3. That tongue – which, by cursing, swearing, blaspheming, and imprecating (as afterward she confessed was the occasioning cause of the Devil's access unto her, even at that time, and to claim her thereby as his own) – by it, *discovered* her lying, swearing, and blaspheming (as also, evident proofs produced against her, to stop her mouth with Truth's authority): at which hearing, she was not able to speak a sensible or ready word for her defense, but sends out, in the hearing of the judge, jury, and all good people that stood by, many most fearful *imprecations* [...] the which, the righteous Judge of Heaven (whom she thus invocated to judge then, and discern her cause) did reveal.

Thus God did wonderfully overtake her in her own wickedness, to make her tongue to be the means of her own destruction, which had destroyed man. [...] By her swearing and cursing blended, it thus far made against her, that both judge and jury (all of them) grew more and more suspicious of her, and not without great cause: for none that had the fear of God, or any the least motion of God's grace left in them, would [...] presume so impudently, with execrations and false oaths, to affront justice.

• • •

On Saturday, being the 14th day of April, *anno domini* 1621, this Elizabeth Sawyer late of Edmonton in the County of Middlesex, spinster, was arraigned and indicted three several times at Justice Hall in the Old Bailey in London, in the parish of Saint Sepulchers, in the ward of Farrington Without. Which indictments were, *viz*.: [4]

• That she (the said Elizabeth Sawyer) – not having the fear of God before her eyes, but moved and seduced by the Devil – by diabolical help, did out of her malicious heart (because her neighbors where she dwelt would not buy brooms of her) would therefore thus revenge herself on them in this manner: namely, witch to death their nurse-children and cattle. (*But for brevity's sake, I here omit forms of law and informations.*)

• She was also indicted, for that she (the said Elizabeth Sawyer) by diabolical help, and out of her malice aforethought, did witch unto death Agnes Radcliffe, a neighbor of hers, dwelling in the town of Edmonton where she did likewise dwell. And the cause that urged her thereunto was because that [Agnes] Radcliffe did strike a sow of hers in her sight, for licking up a little soap where she had laid it. And for that, Elizabeth Sawyer [...] threatened Agnes Radcliffe that "it should be a

---

[1] *spinster*] a woman who earned wages by spinning flax and wool into thread.

[2] *nurse-children*] babies in the care of a wet-nurse.

[3] *This trial*] this witch-test, of the burned thatch.

[4] *spinster*] a woman who works spinning wool or flax into thread; *Farringdon Without*] a ward in the City of London (outside the west city wall); *Old Bailey*] the central criminal court, on Bailey Street.

dear blow" unto her; which accordingly fell out, and suddenly: for that evening, Agnes Radcliffe fell very sick and was extraordinarily vexed, and in a most strange manner in her sickness was tormented.

Oath whereof, was by this Agnes Radcliffe's husband given to the court (the time when she fell sick, and the time when she died, which was within four days after she fell sick). And [he] further then related that, in the time of her sickness, his wife Agnes Radcliffe lay foaming at the mouth and was extraordinarily distempered; which many of his neighbors seeing (as well as himself) bred suspicion in them that some mischief was done against her – and by none else, but alone by this Elizabeth Sawyer, it was done! Concerning whom, the said Agnes Ratcliff, lying on her deathbed, these words confidently spake: namely, that if she did die at that time, she would verily take it on her death, that Elizabeth Sawyer her neighbor (whose sow with a washing-beetle she had stricken, and so for that cause [Sawyer's] malice being great) was the occasion of her death. [1]

To prove her innocence, [Sawyer] put herself to the trial of God and the country – and what care was taken both by the honorable Bench and jury, the judicious standers-by can witness (and *God* knows, who will reward it!): The jury hearing this evidence given upon oath by the husband of the above-named Agnes Radcliffe (and his wife's speeches […], namely, that if she died… Elizabeth Sawyer was the cause […]), this made some impression in their minds, and caused due and mature deliberation. Not trusting their own judgments what to do, […] the foreman of the jury asked of Master Heneage Finch, Recorder, his direction and advice; to whom he Christian-like thus replied, namely, "Do in it as God shall put in your hearts."

Master Arthur Robinson (a worshipful Justice of Peace dwelling at Totnam) had often and divers times, upon the complaints of the neighbors against this Elizabeth Sawyer, laboriously and carefully examined her – and still his suspicion was strengthened against her, that doubtless she *was* a witch. An information was given unto him by some of her neighbors that this Elizabeth Sawyer had a private and strange mark on her body by which their suspicion was confirmed against her.

And he, sitting in the court at that time of her trial, […sent] for women to search her presently, before the jury did go forth to bring in the verdict concerning Elizabeth Sawyer, whether that she was guilty or no; to which motion of his, they most willingly condescended.

The Bench commanded officers appointed for those purposes to fetch in three women to search the body of Elizabeth Sawyer, to see if they could find any such unwonted mark as they were informed of. One of the women's names was Margaret Weaver, that keeps the Sessions House for the City of London, a widow of an honest reputation. And two other grave matrons, brought in by the Officer out of the street, passing by there by chance, were joined with her in this search of the person named.

[Elizabeth Sawyer], fearing and perceiving she should by that search of theirs be then discovered, behaved herself most sluttishly and loathsomely towards them, intending thereby to prevent their search of her (which my pen would forbear to write these things for modesty's sake, but I would not vary in what was delivered to the Bench, expressly and openly spoken). [2]

Yet nevertheless, niceness [the three women] laid aside, and according to the request of the Court, and to that trust reposed in them by the Bench, they all three severally searched her; and made severally their answer unto the Court, being sworn thereunto to deliver the truth. And they all three said that they – a little above the fundament of Elizabeth Sawyer (the prisoner there indicted before the Bench, for a witch) – found a thing like a teat, the bigness of the little finger and the length of half-a-finger, which was branched at the top like a teat, and seemed as though one had sucked it, and that the bottom thereof was blue and the top of it was red. [3]

This view of theirs, and answer that she had such a thing about her (which boldly, [Sawyer] *denied*) gave some insight to the jury of her: who, upon their consciences, returned the said Elizabeth Sawyer to be guilty, by diabolical help, of the death of Agnes Radcliffe only; and acquitted her of the other two indictments.

And thus much of the means that brought [Elizabeth Sawyer] to her deserved death and destruction, I will address to inform you of her pre-

---

[1] *a dear blow*] *i.e.*, Radcliffe would pay dearly for striking Sawyer's pig;   *washing-beetle*] a wooden bat used to beat clothes in the process of washing.

[2] *sluttishly*] dirtily, carelessly.

[3] *fundament*] anus; the three woman searching Sawyer's body evidently discovered a thrombosed hemorrhoid; which the Court inferred was a witch's teat, sucked by the Devil.

paration to death, which is alone pertinent to my function, and declare unto you her confession verbatim, out of her own mouth delivered to me, the Tuesday after her conviction – though with great labor it was extorted from her – and the same confession I read unto her at the place of her execution. And there she confessed to all people that were there the same to be most true, which I shall here relate. […] [1]

A true relation of the confession of Elizabeth Sawyer, spinster, after her conviction of witchery, taken on Tuesday the 17th day of April, anno 1621, in the jail of Newgate where she was prisoner, then in the presence and hearing of divers persons, whose names to verify the same are here subscribed to this ensuing confession, made unto me, Henry Goodcole, minister of the Word of God, ordinary and visitor for the jail of Newgate. [2]

In dialogue-manner are here expressed the persons that she murthered, and the cattle that she destroyed, by the help of the Devil. (In this manner was I enforced to speak unto her, because she might [thereby] understand me and give unto me answer according to my demands: for she was a very ignorant woman.)

Q. By what means came you to have acquaintance with the Devil? and when was the first time that you saw him? and how did you know that it was the Devil?

A. The first time that the Devil came unto me was when I was cursing, swearing and blaspheming. He then rushed in upon me. And never before that time did I see him, or he me: and when he (namely the Devil), came to me, the first words that he spake unto me were these: "Oh! have I now found you cursing, swearing, and blaspheming? Now you are mine!" [3]

(*A wonderful warning to many whose tongues are too frequent in these abhominable sins […] to put their tongues to a more holy language than the accursed language of Hell. The tongue of man is the glory of man, and it was ordained to glorify God. But worse than brute beasts they are, who have a tongue as well as men, that therewith they at once both bless and curse.*)

Q. What said you to the Devil when he came unto you and spake unto you? Were you not afraid of him? If you did fear him, what said the Devil then unto you?

A. I was in a very great fear when I saw the Devil, but he did bid me not to fear him at all, for he would do me no hurt at all, but would do for me whatsoever I should require of him. And, as he promised unto me, he always did such mischiefs as I did bid him to do, both on the bodies of Christians and beasts. If I did bid him vex them to death, as oftentimes I did so bid him, it was then presently by him so done.

Q. Whether would the Devil bring unto you word or no, what he had done for you, at your command? And if he did bring you word, how long would it be, before he would come unto you again, to tell you?

A. He would always bring unto me word what he had done for me, within the space of a week. He never failed me at that time; and would likewise do it to creatures and beasts two manner of ways, which was by scratching or pinching of them.

Q. Of what Christians and beasts? And how many were the number that you were the cause of their death? And what moved you to prosecute them to the death?

A. I have been by the help of the Devil, the means of many Christians' and beasts' death. The cause that moved me to do it was malice and envy. For if anybody had angered me in any manner, I would be so revenged of them, and of their cattle; and do now further confess that I was the cause of those two nurse-children's death, for the which I was now indicted and acquitted by the jury.

Q. Whether did you procure the death of Agnes Radcliffe, for which you were found guilty by the jury?

A. No, I did not by my means procure against her the least hurt. [4]

---

[1] *function*] i.e., position as chaplain of Newgate prison.

[2] *ordinary*] chaplain with official jurisdiction over the spiritual instruction of the prisoners.

[3] *Note in margin*: A gentleman by name Mr. Maddox standing by (and hearing of her say the word, *blaspheming*, did ask of her, three or four times, whether the Devil said, "Have I found you blaspheming?" And she confidently said, "Ay."

[4] *No*] Rev. Goodcole's interview as reported convicts Sawyer for the murders of which she was found innocent, and exonerates her of the murder for which was found guilty; Goodcole thereby establishes that God's justice against witches is accomplished even when the jury makes mistakes.

Q. How long is it since the Devil and you had acquaintance together? And how often times in the week would he come and see you, and you company with him?

A. It is eight years since our first acquaintance. And three times in the week, the Devil would come and see me (after such his acquaintance gotten of me). And he would come sometimes in the morning, and sometimes in the evening.

Q. In what shape would the Devil come unto you?

A. Always in the shape of a dog, and of two colors, sometimes of black and sometimes of white.

Q. What talk had the Devil and you together when that he appeared to you? And what did he ask of you? And what did you desire of him?

A. He asked of me, when he came unto me, how I did, and what he should do for me; and demanded of me my soul and body, threatening then to tear me in pieces if that I did not grant unto him my soul and my body which he asked of me.

Q. What did you after such, the Devil's asking of you to have your soul and body, and after this his threatening of you? Did you for fear grant unto the Devil his desire?

A. Yes, I granted for fear unto the Devil his request of my soul and body; and to seal this my promise made unto him, I then gave him leave to suck of my blood, the which he asked of me.

Q. In what place of your body did the Devil suck of your blood? And whether did he himself choose the place, or did you yourself appoint him the place? Tell the truth, I charge you, as you° will answer unto the almighty God! And tell the reason, if that you can, why he would suck your blood. [1]

A. The place where the Devil sucked my blood was a little above my fundament, and that place chosen by himself. And in that place, by continual drawing, there is a thing in the form of a teat, at which the Devil would suck me. And I asked the Devil why he would suck my blood, and he said it was to nourish him. [...] [2]

Q. Whether did you pull up your coats, or no, when the Devil came to suck you?

A. No I did not. But the Devil would put his head under my coats, and I did willingly suffer him to do what he would.

Q. How long would the time be that the Devil would continue sucking of you? And whether did you endure any pain, the time that he was sucking of you?

A. He would be sucking of me the continuance of a quarter of an hour, and when he sucked me, I then felt no pain at all.

Q. What was the meaning that the Devil, when he came unto you, "would sometimes speak, and sometimes bark"? [3]

A. It is thus: when the Devil *spake* to me, then he was ready to do for me what I would bid him to do. And when he came *barking* to me, he then had done the mischief that I did bid him to do for me.

Q. By what name did you call the Devil? And what promises did he make to you?

A. I did call the Devil by the name of *Tom*, and he promised to do for me whatsoever I should require of him.

Q. What were those two ferrets that you were feeding on a form, with white bread and milk, when divers children came and saw you feeding of them? [4]

A. I never did any such thing.

Q. What was the white thing that did run through the thatch of your house? Was it a spirit or Devil?

A. So far as I know, it was nothing else but a white ferret.

---

[1] *Note in margin:* I demanded this question of her to confirm the women's search of her, concerting that she had such a mark about her, which they upon their oaths informed the Court that truth it was, she had such a mark.

[2] *Note in margin:* This I asked of her very earnestly, and she thus answered me, without studying for an answer.

[3] *Note in margin:* I asked this question because she said that the Devil did not always speak to her.

[4] *a form*] a wooden bench;   *Note in margin:* I asked this of her because that some children of a good bigness and reasonable understanding informed the Court that they had divers times seen her feed two white ferrets with white bread and milk.

Q. Did anybody else know but yourself alone of the Devil's coming unto you? and of your practices? Speak the truth, and tell the reason why you did not reveal it to your husband or to some other friend! [1]

A. I did not tell anybody thereof, that the Devil came unto me, neither I durst not. For the Devil charged me that I should not, and said that if I did tell it to anybody, at his next coming to me, he then would tear me in pieces.

Q. Did the Devil at any time find you praying when he came unto you? And did not the Devil forbid you to pray to Jesus Christ, but to him alone? And did not he bid you pray to him the Devil, as he taught you? [2]

A. [...] Yes, he found me once praying, and he asked of me to whom I prayed. And I answered him, to Jesus Christ. And he charged me then to pray no more to Jesus Christ, but to him the Devil, and he (the Devil) taught me this prayer, *"Sanctificetur Nomen Tuum.* Amen." [3]

Q. Were you ever taught these Latin words before, by any person else? Or did you ever hear it before of anybody? Or can you say any more of it?

A. No, I was not taught it by anybody else but by the Devil alone. Neither do I understand the meaning of these words, nor can speak any more Latin words.

Q. Did the Devil ask of you, the next time he came unto you, whether that you used to pray unto him in that manner as he taught you?

A. Yes, at his next coming to me he asked of me, if that I did pray unto him as he had taught me; and I answered him again, that sometimes I did, and sometimes I did not, and the Devil then thus threatened me: It is not good for me to mock him.

Q. How long is it since you saw the Devil last?

A. It is three weeks since I saw the Devil.

Q. Did the Devil never come unto you since you were in prison? [...] Speak the truth, as you will answer unto almighty God. [4]

A. The Devil never came unto me since I was in prison. Nor, I thank God, I have no motion of him in my mind since I came to prison. Neither do I now fear him at all.

Q. How came your eye to be put out? [5]

A. With a stick which one of my children had in the hand. That night my mother did die it was done – for I was stooping by the bedside, and I by chance did hit my eye on the sharp end of the stick.

Q. Did you ever handle the Devil when he came unto you? [6]

A. Yes, I did stroke him on the back. And then he would beckon to me and wag his tail as being therewith contented.

Q. Would the Devil come unto you all in one bigness?

A. No, when he came unto me in the black shape, he then was biggest, and in the white, the least. And when that I was praying, he then would come unto me in the white color.

Q. Why did you at your trial forswear all this, that you now do confess?

A. I did it thereby hoping to avoid shame.

Q. Is all this truth which you have spoken here unto me, and that I have now written?

---

[1] *Note in margin*: "I asked this question of her because her husband testified to the Bench he saw such a white thing run through the thatch of the house; and that he catched at it but could not get it; and he thought it was a white ferret."

[2] *Note in margin*: Upon my general suspicion I asked of her this question.

[3] *sanctificetur Nomen Tuum*] Hallowed be thy name (from the Lord's prayer). *Note in margin*: "I do here relate the self-same words upon this question propounded unto her, *What prayer the Devil taught her to pray.*"; cf. misspelled Latin in woodcut.

[4] *Note in margin*: "I asked this question because it was rumored that the Devil came to her since her conviction (and shamelessly printed and openly sung in a ballad, to which many give too much credit)." Sawyer's ascribed reply indicates that Rev. Goodcole's prison ministry was more successful than indicated in the street ballad, and more powerful than the workings of the Devil.

[5] *Note in margin*: The reason why I asked this was because her father's and mother's eye, one of theirs was out.

[6] *Note in margin*: I asked of her this question because some might think this was a visible delusion of her sight only.

A. Yes, it is all truth, as I shall make answer unto almighty God.

Q. What moves you now to make this confession? Did any urge you to it, or bid you do it? Is it for any hope of life you do it?

A. No, I do it to clear my conscience, and now having done it, I am the more quiet and the better prepared, and willing thereby to suffer death, for I have no hope at all of my life (although I must confess, I *would* live longer, if I might!).

A Relation what she said at the place of execution, which was at Tyburn on Thursday, the 19th day of April, 1621.

All this being by her thus freely confessed (after her conviction) in the jail of Newgate, on Tuesday, the 17th day of April, I acquainted Master Recorder of London therewith; who thus directed me to take that (her confession) with me to the place of execution, and to read it to her; and to ask of her whether that was truth which she had delivered to me in the prison on Tuesday last, concerning what she said.

   And how she died, I will relate unto you: "Elizabeth Sawyer, you are now come unto the place of execution. Is that all true which you confessed unto me on Tuesday last, when that you were in prison? I have it here, and will now read it unto you, as you spake it then unto me out of your own mouth. And if it be true, confess it now to God, and to all the people that are here present."

A. This confession which is now read unto me by Master Henry Goodcole, minister, with my own mouth I spake it to him on Tuesday last at Newgate. And I here do acknowledge, to all the people that are here present, that it is all truth; desiring you all to pray unto almighty God to forgive me my grievous sins.

Q. By what means hope you now to be saved?

A. By Jesus Christ alone.

Q. Will you now pray unto almighty God to forgive unto you all your misdeeds?

A. Ay, with all my heart and mind.

This was confirmed, in the hearing of many hundreds at her last breath, what formerly she in prison confessed to me (and at that time spake more heartily, than the day before of her execution); on whose body, Law was justly inflicted– but mercy in God's power reserved to bestow, when and where He pleaseth.

• • •

My labor thus ended concerning her, to testify and avouch (to the world and all opposers hereof) this to be true, those that were present with me in the prison that heard her confession, I have desired here their testimonies, which is as followeth:

WE WHOSE NAMES are here subscribed do thereby testify that Elizabeth Sawyer – late of Edmonton in the county of Middlesex, spinster; did in our hearings confess on Tuesday the 17th of April in the jail of Newgate, to Master Henry Goodcole, minister of the Word of God, the repeated foul crimes, and confirmed it at her death the 19th of April following to be true. And if we be thereunto required, will be ready to make faith of the truth thereof, namely that this was her confession being alive, and a little before her death. [1]

Conclusion

Dear Christians,

   Lay this to heart, namely, the cause and first time that the Devil came unto her: then, even then when she was cursing, swearing, and blaspheming! The Devil rageth, and malice reigneth in the hearts of many. O let it not do so! – for here you may see the fruits thereof, that it is a plain way to bring you to the Devil; nay – that it brings the Devil to *you*! For it seemed that when she so fearfully did swear, her oaths did so conjure him, that he must leave then his mansion-place and come at this wretch's command and will, which was by her imprecations. Stand on your guard and watch with sobriety to resist him (the Devil your adversary, who waiteth on you continually, to subvert you); that so, *you*, that do detest her abominable words and ways, may never taste of the cup nor wages of shame and destruction of which she did in this life. From which and from whose power, Lord Jesus save and defend thy little flock. Amen.

---

[1] *We whose names are here subscribed*] The promised endorsements are omitted from Goodcole's printed text.

Witch Discourse, from the pulpit...

Alexander Roberts, *A Treatise of Witchcraft* (1616)

The First Proposition.   It is a query (though need-less!) whether there be *any witches*:

For they have some proctors who plead a nullity in this case; persuade themselves (and would induce others to be of the same mind) that there be no witches at all, but a sort of melancholic, aged, and ignorant women, deluded in their imagination; and [women who] acknowledge such things to be effected by them which are unpossible, unlikely, and they never did; and therefore magistrates who inflict any punishment upon them, be unmerciful and cruel butchers. Yet by the way (and their good leave, who take upon them this apology), not all who are con-vented upon these unlawful actions are strucken¨ in years, but some even in the flower of their youth be nuzzled up in the same, and *convicted* to be practicers thereof; neither be they overflowed with a black mel-ancholic humor, dazzling the fantasy, but have their understandings clear and wits as quick as other...

The Second Proposition: *Who those be, and of what quality, that are thus ensnared of the Devil, and un-dermined by his frauds*:

More women in a far different proportion prove witches than men, by a hundred to one; therefore the Law of God noteth that [their] sex as more *subject* to that sin (Exodus 22:18). It is a common speech amongst the Jewish Rabbins, "Many women, many witches!" (and it should seem that this was a generally received opinion, for so it is noted by Pliny, Quintil-ian, and others). Neither doth this proceed (as some have thought) from their frailty and imbecility, for in many of them there is stronger resolution to undergo any torment than can be found in man...

First, they are by nature credulous, wanting expe-rience, and therefore more easily deceived.

Secondly, they harbor in their breast a curious and inquisitive desire to know such things as be not fitting and convenient...

Thirdly, their complexion is softer, and from hence more easily receive the impressions offered by the Devil; ... so consenting to the suggestions of evil spirits, [they] become notoriously wicked, so that there is no mischief above that of a woman (Eccles. 25:13. &c.).

Fourthly, in them is a greater facility to fall, and therefore the Devil at the first took that advantage, and set upon Eve in Adam's absence (Gen. 3:3).

Fifthly, this sex, when it conceiveth wrath or ha-tred against any, is unplacable, possessed with un-satiable desire of revenge, and transported with appe-tite to right (as they think) the wrongs offered unto them...

Sixthly, they are of a slippery tongue, and full of words: and therefore if they know any such wicked practices, are not able to hold them.

...and the stage

The Witch of Edmonton, a play by Thomas Dekker, John Ford, and William Rowley; performed eight months after Elizabeth Sawyer's execution (1621)

Sawyer.
And why on me? why should the envious world
Throw all their scandalous malice upon me?
'Cause I am poor, deformed and ignorant,
And (like a bow) buckled and bent together
By some more strong in mischiefs than myself!
Must I, for that, be made a common sink
For all the filth and rubbish of men's tongues
To fall and run into? Some call me "witch"—
And (being ignorant of myself) they go
About to teach me how to *be* one: urging
That my "bad tongue" (by their bad usage, made so)
Forspeaks their cattle, doth bewitch their corn,
Themselves, their servants, and their babes at nurse.
This, they enforce upon me—and in part,
Make me to credit it...
                    A witch? who is not?
Hold not that universal name in scorn then!
What are your painted things in princes' Courts,
Upon whose eyelids Lust sits blowing fires
To burn men's souls in sensual hot desires,
Upon whose naked paps a lecher's thought
Acts sin in fouler shapes than can be wrought....
These, by enchantments, can whole lordships change
To trunks of rich attire; turn plows and teams
To Flanders mares and coaches, and huge trains
Of servitors, to a French butterfly;
Their husbands' wares, whole standing shops of wares,
To sumptuous tables, gardens of stolen sin—
In one year wasting what scarce twenty win.
Are not these witches?...
                    Why then on me,
(Or any lean old beldame)? Reverence once
Had wont to wait on age. Now an old woman
Ill-favored, grown with years, if she be poor
Must be called "bawd" or "witch." Such, so abus'd,
Are the *coarse* witches: t'other are the *fine*,
Spun for the Devil's own wearing....
Dare any swear I ever tempted maiden,
With golden hooks flung at her chastity,
To come and lose her honor? (and being lost,
To pay not a denier for't?) Some slaves have done it![1]
Men-witches can (without the fangs of law
Drawing once one drop of blood) put counterfeit pieces
Away for true gold....
I am torn in pieces by a pack of curs
Clapped all upon me...
                    I am dried up
With cursing and with madness—
What would you have? Cannot a poor old woman
Have your leave to die without vexation?

[1] *denier*] (DEN-i-er) tenth party of a penny

Elizabeth Jennings (1609-1680)

No bodie knowes what ails mee within.

—Elizabeth Jennings (1622), B.L. MS Add. 36674, f.135

IN ISLEWORTH, Middlesex, in January 1622, Elizabeth Jennings accused four local women of having bewitched her. Elizabeth, then aged twelve, was terrified by the recent death of two siblings. During or after their illness and death, Elizabeth's mother, the Lady Jennings, had quarreled with a well-known London apothecary named Stephens Higgins, possibly over medicines that had failed to produce the desired effect in treating the sick children.[1]

One day, while this quarrel was still smoldering, a poor woman attempted to beg a pin of Elizabeth Jennings. Terrified, the girl ran screaming into the house. She fell sick, refused to eat, and languished week after week with a variety of hysterical symptoms. Various physicians were called in, but to no avail.

In one of her trances, Elizabeth announced that she had been bewitched by four women, chiefly Margaret "Countess" Russell, a poor local woman so nicknamed after her namesake, Margaret Russell, countess of Cumberland. Elizabeth feared that Countess was responsible for the deaths of the other Jennings children. (Countess was possibly the same woman who had attempted to beg a pin.) Elizabeth also accused Jane Flower and Katharine Stubbs. Flower, a local woman, bore no evident relationship with the three Leicestershire witches, Joan, Margaret, and Phillip Flower, who perished in 1619; nor was this Katherine Stubbs the same woman whose famous deathbed battle with the devil is recorded in *A Crystal Glass for Christian Women* (1591, many times reprinted). In accusing women who bore the names, respectively, of an executed witch, a famously potent spirit, and of a wealthy and infamously strong-minded aristocrat, Elizabeth Jennings seems to have intuited that their names alone carried a potent and fearsome notoriety. As her fourth oppressor, Elizabeth named "Nan Wood," about whom nothing else is known, but whose name suggests madness (*OED* wood, ad.). It seems clear that Elizabeth, fearful for her life following the death of her siblings, fretted over the supernatural power of women who bore extraordinary names.

Following Elizabeth's accusation, Countess was arrested and imprisoned. But while Elizabeth blamed Countess, Countess seems to have suspected that the girl remained ill due to a bad prescription from Higgins the apothecary.[2]

When interviewed, Countess reported an opinion—evidently her own opinion, though not clearly expressed—that a quarrel "betwixt two houses" was at the root of Elizabeth's illness.

A sad comedy of errors followed. The court recorder's vague pronoun reference caused Rev. Goodcole, chaplain of Newgate prison and our narrator, to believe that Countess had quoted either his wife (Anne) or sister-in-law (Frances Aston), concerning a "controversy betwixt two houses," alleging a quarrel between the Jennings family and Higgins the apothecary. And perhaps she did. But Countess, Mrs. Goodcole, and Mrs. Aston all subsequently denied having said any such thing. The upshot of the court recorder's vague pronoun reference is that the justices came to believe that Countess had been lying to them.

After having labored for Elizabeth's recovery, Countess now found that she was herself a prime suspect. Her evident guilt was doubly confirmed, first by Elizabeth's express accusation, then by Elizabeth's sudden recovery upon word that Countess was now in prison.

---

[1] *Lady Jennings*] Lady Alice (*née* Spencer), of Hertfordshire and Middlesex, wife of Sir John Jennings the younger (John Sr. was knighted on 11 May 1603 but died a lunatic in October 1609 and was buried on the Savoy Palace grounds); Lady Alice is said to have given birth to twenty-two children by Sir John (d. 1642).

[2] *Higgins*] Stephen Higgins, a charter member of the Society of Apothecaries (1617); practiced at the Savoy Palace, 1609-1640; from 1619-1621, Higgins had a long and bitter quarrel, first with Mr. Darnley, a colleague, then with the Company itself; he is described in the Society's Minute Book as "an obstinate, contentious, and troublesome person" Barret (1905), 2, 9, 14, 18, 37-40, 56.

The Bewitchment of Elizabeth Jennings

Recorded by John Latch (1622)

ELIZABETH, the daughter of the Lady Jennings, a child now thirteen years of age, being in Thistleworth [in Isleworth, Middlesex], shortly after she was frighted with the sight of an old woman (who suddenly appeared to her at the door and demanded a pin of her) was taken with an infirmity in her throat about the 13th of January [1622 n.s.], refusing ever after all manner of flesh-meat. The 15th of February she complained to be exceeding sick, and from that present time lost she the use of both her legs. The 19th day at night she was taken with extreme fits of panting and sighing, and began to talk idly and grow very ill, insomuch that her parents, fearing her death, sent presently to London for Doctor Fox, who brought her (being very sick) to London with him, where she continued languishing, complaining of aches in divers parts of her body and often weeping extremely.

About the end of February, every night after midnight, she had a great fit of sighing and groaning, expressing divers pains in her knees, arms, head, and heart, very suddenly removing from one of these parts to another, and at last being settled in the head and heart. She would then lie continually sighing and groaning, four hours at the least, as if death were at hand.

The 17th of March at night she had an exceeding great fit of strange convulsions, no part of her body being free, which lasted the greatest part of the night; after which fit, her understanding was very much weakened and her memory of all things past quite lost. And shortly after, all her right side was benumbed, and her right arm lost all motion and sense as if it had been taken with a dead palsy. And after this, these fits of convulsions never failed coming once or twice in twenty-four hours (but only for four or five days, about [a] fortnight before her recovery); and in her fits her dead arm was as violently moved as any other part of her body. During this time many things were applied by the physicians for her help, but all in vain, the medicines rather producing contrary effects. [1]

On Easter eve the 20th of April, after her fit in the afternoon, she began to stammer in her speech and could not pronounce divers words.

After her fit on Easter day she lay speechless for divers hours – but towards night, spake again – but on Monday she became altogether speechless, her strange fits still continuing in their violent manner twice in twenty-four hours.

Upon Tuesday the physicians, finding her estate desperate, had a consultation and resolved of three courses for remedy: 1. to give her a vomit; 2. to let her blood; 3. to bathe her in oil. On Wednesday she had the vomit accordingly, which wrought neither amendment nor alteration. But the intention of letting blood being discovered to Countess (who divers times came to the house), she with much earnestness desired it might not be so, saying the doctors would kill her thereby as they had done [the earl of] Exeter's child. [2]

On Thursday in the midst of her accustomed fit at six o'clock in the morning (having been four days speechless), she spake only these words: "Well I thank you" and (after a good space of time) "How dost thou do, Countess?" and (not long after) "How dost thou do, Jane?" – and after, remained speechless as before. This day she was let blood, and in her fit in the afternoon she lay still (being drawn), [and] spake these words following, distinctly and with an audible voice, staying an equal distance of time betwixt each sentence: [3]

"Jane Flower. [4]
"Katharine Stubbs.
"Countess.
"Nan Wood.
"These have bewitched all my mother's children.
"East, west, north and south, all these lie.
"All these are damnable witches.
"Set up a great sprig of rosemary in the middle of the house.
"I have sent this child to speak to show all these witches.

---

[1] *dead palsy*] paralysis.

[2] *a vomit*] an emetic; emetics, blood-letting, and laxatives were often administered to the ill in an effort to purge the body of harmful material.

[3] *being drawn*] after having had her blood drawn.

[4] *Jane Flower*] possibly Jane Flower of Stepney, buried 7 Aug. 1645, the daughter of Nicholas and Isabel Flower.

"Put Countess in prison, this child will be well.

"If she had been long ago, all th'other had been alive.

"Them she bewitched by a catstick. [1]

"Till then, I shall lie in great pain.

"Till then, by fits I shall be in great extremity. [2]

"They died in great misery.

"A hundred more have been hanged in the West Country.

"The guts and garbage and all that was within them was drawn nine several ways. [3]

"No man could tell without.

"They had power over all them to bewitch them to death but me.

"And me in great misery, but to live.

"Nobody knows what ails me within.

"When she is in prison, then I shall be well, never till then by fits.

"She came first of all that ever my mother saw her in the kitchen. [4]

"And Nan Arpe was there." [5]

All these words were spoken and presently written 25th of April, 1622, in the presence of John Latch, the writer; William Giddings, surgeon; Mistress Katharine Percy; Mistress Faith Saxton; Agnes Faulkner, a servant. These persons came after she had begun to speak: the Lady Jennings; Mistress Elizabeth Arpe; Mistress Anne Bradborne; Katharine Brown, a servant. And no sooner was the fit ended but she remained speechless and in her palsy as before.

That evening, her parents (having set down the words aforesaid by her spoken) resorted to Sir William Slingsby, the next justice, to advise what to do; and they found the means to bring Countess to him to be examined (she not knowing their intent), whose examination following:

---

[1] *catstick*] a stick used in the children's games tip-cat and trap-ball.

[2] *by fits*] with fits of illness.

[3] *guts and garbage*] Felons were typically hanged before a large public audience, then publicly disemboweled. The gutted corpses were then sometimes quartered (limbs chopped off), and the mangled remains left on display for a time as a lesson to others who might be tempted to break the law. The spectacle of public executions appears to have made a lasting impression on young Elizabeth Jennings.

[4] *She*] Countess.

[5] *Nan Arpe*] This may be Anne Harpe of Stepney, who wedded John Whitcombe on 4 Oct. 1615.

The examination of Margaret Russell alias "Countess," taken before Sir William Slingsby, knight, one of the justices of the peace in the county of Middlesex, 25th of April:

MARGARET RUSSELL alias Countess, accused for bewitching Elizabeth, daughter of the Lady Jennings, being examined, confesseth that yesterday she went to Mistress Dromondby in Black-and-White Court in the Old Bailey, and told her that the Lady Jennings had a daughter strangely sick; whereupon she, [the] said Dromondby, wished her to go to inquire at Clerkenwell for a minister's wife [Mrs. Goodcole,] that could help people that were sick; but she must not ask for a "witch" or a "cunning woman," but for one that is a "physician woman."

And there [at the Goodcoles'] this examinate found her and a woman [Frances Aston] sitting with her, and told her in what case the child was. And she [Mrs. Goodcole] said she would come this day but she ought her no service, and said she had been there before, and left receipts there, but the child did not take them. And she said further that there was two children that the Lady Jennings had by this husband that were bewitched and dead, for there was controversy between two houses, and that as long as they dwelt there they could not prosper, and that there should be no blessing in that house by this man. And being demanded [*i.e.,* in this present examination?] what she meant by the 'difference betwixt two houses,' she answered it was betwixt the house of God and the house of the world; but being urged to express it better, she said we knew it well enough — it was the difference betwixt Higgins the apothecary (the next neighbor) and the Lady Jennings. [6]

And she further confesseth that above a month ago she went to Mistress Saxey in Gunpowder Alley who was forspoken herself and that had a book that could help all that were forspoken; and that she would come and show her the book and help her (under God); and [she] further said to this examinate that none but a seminary priest could cure her. [7]

Sir William Slingsby, having thus examined her and finding much inconstancy in her answers, made a warrant for her commitment; by virtue whereof she was conveyed away, [and] about twelve o'clock that night delivered into Newgate [Prison].

---

[6] *ought her*] owed her;   *receipts*] recipes; medical prescriptions, to be made from herbs, etc.

[7] *forspoken*] bewitched.

On Friday the 26th of April, between ten and eleven o'clock in the forenoon (at which time Countess was brought out of the jail to speak [with] the minister and his wife and others at a private house), the child had another very dangerous fit of convulsions, which Doctor Fox beholding, said it nearly touched her life.

—In which fit she began to speak again, as followeth: "The height of my disease is witchcraft." And after a good space she spake again thus: "They have no power to witch me to death, but only to put me to pain." And anon after, with a smiling countenance, she said, "One is in prison, th'other is hanged." And presently after, "It is ceased, it is ceased." And presently her fit went off, her speech returned, and her palsy arm recovered motion and sense – and ever since hath been, and is, perfect in her understanding and memory, and of very good health in all respects, and eateth her meat as well as ever she did before she fell sick. These words were spoken, and she thus recovered, in the presence of Sir Thomas Fowler, knight; Doctor Fox, the minister; William Power, esq.; the Lady Jennings; Mistress Katharine Percy; Katharine Brown [and] Agnes Faulkner, servants.

The second examination of Margaret Russell alias Countess, taken before Sir Thomas Fowler and Sir William Slingsby, knights, and Doctor Bates, justices of the peace in the county of Middlesex the 26th of April:

That Mistress Goodcole the minister's wife did not [say] as in her [Countess's] former examination is set down (but that it was a woman that sat by her working, who was her sister).

But she confesseth that this morning, about ten or eleven o'clock, she was brought out of Newgate to the house of James the clerk, where we did now examine her, to speak with Master Goodcole and his wife and with Mistress Dromondby. And she further confesseth that when Mistress Gargrave lay at Master Higgins' house when my Lady Jennings' first child was sick, that she was then there with her; and that a maidservant of the Lady Jennings came thither to wash a mop, of whom Mistress Higgins did inquire how they did, and she answered "Not well"; to whom Mistress Higgins replied that they [the Jennings] had much wronged them, and that "it would come home by them and theirs."

The examination of Frances Aston, Anne Goodcole, and Henry Goodcole, taken before Sir William Slingsby, one of the justices of the peace in the county of Middlesex, 27th of April:

FRANCES ASTON, the wife of Thomas Aston dwelling in Clerkenwell, examined, confesseth that yesterday about nine o'clock, her sister Goodcole sent for her and showed her a note in writing, the which her brother Master Goodcole did read unto her: the which did contain that there was a woman in Newgate committed for a witch who had named a woman in Clerkenwell with whom she had lately been. And presently Master Goodcole, his wife, and this examinate and Robert Duffield (a cutler who married one of their sisters), went to Master James his house in the Old Bailey, who is clerk of Newgate, and being there they sent for Master James, at whose coming Master Goodcole and his wife desired to have Countess the prisoner brought unto them, which was betwixt ten and eleven o'clock – where this examinate did first ask her whether she were acquainted with her sister or no, and what reason she had to make a speech of her as was in the note – and she [*i.e.,* Countess] answered she had said no such thing. And in like manner Master Goodcole did question her, to whom she made the like answer (but did weep and cry). But she [*i.e.,* Mrs. Goodcole] utterly denieth that either she or her sister did speak anything concerning the Lady Jennings' children that were "bewitched and dead," or of any "controversy betwixt two houses."

ANNE GOODCOLE, wife of Master Henry Goodcole, minister, dwelling at Clerkenwell, confesseth that on Thursday Countess came to her and asked her if she were a physician woman. And she said she had medicines that did sometimes help children in sickness. And that Countess told her there was a lady's child in the Strand in great extremity, whom she thought was bewitched, and therefore desired her help. To whom this examinate replied that she had been there with my Lady Fowler and had left a medicine there, but that the child had not taken it. But she utterly denieth that she or her sister did either speak anything or know anything either of the death or bewitching of the Lady Jennings' other children that were dead, or of any "controversy betwixt two houses." And that Countess told her she was sent to her from a woman in the Strand that she had done good unto, and from the child's grandmother, and prayed her at the last that she should come when she heard further from her.

And [she] further sayeth that yesterday in the morning there came a man to speak with her husband ([Rev. Goodcole,] who was in bed with her), but she knew him not, being a black man about forty years old, like a citizen, who did desire him to do some business for him sometime the next week. [1]

After he was gone, her husband did rise and went abroad, but did return about ten o'clock to her sister's house, Mistress Duffield's, and sent for this examinate and her sister to go with him to Master James his house before eleven o'clock; whose maid fetched him thither as soon as they came. Master Goodcole and his wife desired him to bring Countess unto them. And then they did inquire of her [*i.e.,* Countess] whether she knew this examinate [*i.e.,* Mrs. Goodcole]. She [*i.e.,* Countess] answered that she never saw her nor knew her but the day before, as is confessed. And she also confesseth that her brother Robert Duffield went with them. Which done, James carried the prisoner to the jail and they [*i.e.,* the Goodcoles] returned to Master Duffield's again, and there dined together.

MASTER HENRY GOODCOLE, being the Ordinary in Newgate, examined, sayeth that about seven o'clock he did rise and went abroad with Master Edmondes, a minister, and about eight or nine o'clock went to Newgate to visit the prisoners, according to his custom; where he heard by Wells the jailer that there was a warrant which did concern his wife; which warrant he did desire to have of James – and did presently carry it to show his wife, to his sister's house, Mistress Duffield'[s] (to which place he sent for her). And when she and his other sister (Aston) were come thither, they and Master Duffield went presently to James his house (after he had read the warrant unto her); and being there, he desired James to send for Countess – who they asked if she knew Mistress Goodcole; but she denied that ever she saw her before Thursday in the afternoon (concerning the business confessed about the helping of the Lady Jennings' child). [2]

Henry Goodcole

finis

Elizabeth was not wholly cured. Despite short-term improvement, Elizabeth's bouts with hysteria continued for months afterward. Lady Jennings on 30 July 1622 hired Dr. Napier to examine her daughter. Napier in his notebook for that date records Elizabeth's birth (20 April 1609, in the Strand), and took notes, as it appears, directly from the formal inquest, with additional comments being supplied by the Lady Jennings. After examining Elizabeth, Napier concluded that the girl was not bewitched but suffering from the *mother* ("epileptica matricis" and "morbus matricis"). On 29 Oct 1627, in Stepney, Middlesex, Elizabeth was wedded to Christopher Davies. She died as a widow, age 71, being buried Stepney on 4 Jan. 1680.

The fate of Countess is unrecorded. She evidently died in prison, prior to the next Assize at which she was to have been indicted and tried for witchcraft.

Newgate Prison as it looked in the 17th Century, where Henry Goodcole served as chaplain to accused felons.

---

[1] *black man*] in early modern English, a black-haired man; here, the Rev. Edmondes.

[2] *Ordinary*] the chaplain of Newgate prison, whose duty it was to prepare prisoners for their execution.

Margaret Fearnside (c. 1575 – 1608),

London prostitute

[T]o iustifie my selfe were sinne, since no flesh can appeare pure in thy sight…
—from "The Confession and Repentance of Margaret Fernseed"

MARGARET FEARNSIDE was a London bawd put to death in 1608 for the murder of her husband, a crime that she did not commit. Margaret was not a lucky person. She is said to have been "a prostitute whore" since puberty ("the age of aptness") – which our reporter mentions as a sign of her own vile inclination from childhood and not as an instance of the culture's pervasive sexual exploitation of minors. Her maiden name is unknown. In 1593 she wedded Anthony Fearnside, 20, a London tailor originally from Yorkshire. The Fearnsides had one child, Marie (born January 1593/4). Margaret may have been some years older than Anthony, and she may already have been pregnant when they married; after which, the couple lived four miles apart and seem never to have cohabited apart from Anthony's occasional conjugal visits to Margaret's house.

In the autumn of 1607, a man's body was found in Peckham Field, near Lambeth Palace south of London. His throat had been cut. The apparent weapon was in his hand but his death was no suicide: the swollen corpse (which observers said was certainly not there the day before) was already infested with maggots (which in hot weather might have taken only two days, but would certainly not happen overnight). Nor was robbery the motive: the victim had gold rings upon his fingers, and forty shillings in his purse (a substantial sum in an era when a single half-penny would buy you twelve ounces of wheat bread or one-third gallon of beer). A search of his pockets identified the dead man as Anthony Fearnside, a journeyman tailor whose shop was in Carter Lane (two miles east of his residence) near St. Paul's Cathedral, an upscale shopping district; and whose Duck Lane residence was in the Soho district. Fearnside had evidently been killed in the city; hidden for a day or two; then loaded onto a cart, transported by night across London Bridge and through Southwark, and dumped in Peckham Field; but if the offender hoped the crime would escape prosecution, he ought to have checked Fearnside's pockets.

Upon learning that the victim's wife of fifteen years kept an unlicensed brothel at Irongate near the Tower of London, the authorities fetched Margaret and brought her to view the body. She turned up her nose and made a sour face when she smelled him, but shed no tears. Had she known that she was the prime suspect, Margaret might have made a greater show of sorrow; but her indifference to Anthony's death further convinced the authorities of her guilt.

A child who worked for Margaret turned State's evidence, reporting under interrogation that the Fearnsides often quarreled, and that Margaret had a lover who had suddenly left town. (His identity and whereabouts are points that seem to have aroused no curiosity in the prosecutor, Assize judge, or news reporter: but with the obvious suspect having vanished, someone had to be punished; and Margaret Fearnside, a known sex worker, was the bird in hand.)

Public executions were a routine matter throughout the sixteenth and seventeenth centuries, for crimes ranging vagrancy or the theft of bread, to high treason. During the reign of Henry VIII, at least 57,000 were put to death, mostly paupers. Under Elizabeth's regime an estimated forty thousand were executed; another twenty thousand during the briefer reign of King James. The accused generally remained in prison without bail until the next Assize. If found guilty by the judge and jury (which was usually the case), execution followed within 1-3 days, depending on how many others were condemned at the same Sessions, and how many citizens came to watch. Each hanging or burning took about an hour, from the invocation to the benediction. [1]

The State counted it essential to extract a confession from anyone sentenced to death, which was then typically read to the audience, at the execution. When a convicted offender flatly denied his guilt even after trial, a confession could be legally obtained by torture, most commonly by pressing; or by threats of punitive action to be taken upon his children or next of kin. Rarely did a condemned felon still maintain innocence from the gallows, and never with success. But when it happened, a published pamphlet often followed soon after, typically a news sheet that presented a lurid, much embellished account of the convicted felon's wickedness; and lavish praise of the Assize judges for having put the villain to death.

---

[1] *57,000*] Holinshed's *Chronicles* puts the total at 72,000: "Henrie the eight, executing his laws verie seuerelie against such idle persons, I meane great theeues, pettie theeues and roges, did hang vp threescore and twelue thousand of them in his time" (1587): 1.186.

Had there been printed a news-sheet for every execution, crime literature would have outweighed all religious, scholarly, and literary works put together. The true-crime stories that found their way into print served, almost always, as State propaganda. All printed notice of homicides was subject to censorship; many such pamphlets were printed under the express authority of the hanging judge, sometimes with line edits. Some tracts were issued in response to public demand (as with the high-profile Overbury murder); or else, to silence public skepticism concerning the guilt of those who were hanged (as in witchcraft news-sheets); and sometimes (when the wheels of justice turned horribly awry) to rewrite the narrative altogether, as with *The Crying Murther of Mr. Trat* (1620), a bizarre case in which four poor people of county Somerset, three men, one woman, were executed not only for a murder that they did not commit, but for a murder that did not take place – the actual killer, Rev. Trat (the supposed victim), having exchanged places with an Irish Catholic whom he killed in a fit of rage and then dismembered.

Following the Anthony Fearnside homicide, the reporter's task was to justify the execution of Margaret when there was no scrap of evidence that she participated in the death of her husband, or even knew about it till after the fact. The title-page allegation that Margaret "once before attempted to poison him with broth" is a transparent lie, a conventional embellishment intended by the reporter to persuade readers of premeditated murder by a hardened sociopath. The allegation that Fearnside's wife "sold all his goods" after his death is suspect as well (not even the corpse had been robbed, much less Fearnside's shop or residence; nor could much have been sold from Margaret's house between the time of the homicide and the moment of her arrest).

Even the reported conversations are suspect – as when Anthony Fearnside on a conjugal visit to his wife's residence hears a bargeman cough in the next room, and is amazed to discover "strangers lodged in his house." Only moments later, the reporter has him advising those same strangers to leave, informing them that the house is a brothel belonging to his wife. The reporter's gestures toward objectivity (she was "a woman well-spoken, of fair deliverance, and good persuasion") are a sham: every word put into Margaret's mouth is given a sinister twist, even her profession of innocence. When Margaret Fearnside from the gallows faces down threats of eternal damnation – still denying her guilt in the matter of Anthony's death while confessing to other sins – the reporter interprets her protest as the visible sign of her devilish soul, a sinful obstinacy even in the hour of her death, as might well be expected from a prostitute-whore and a husband-killer.

But if Margaret Fearnside was condemned for a violent crime that she did not commit, she nonetheless speaks with conviction with respect to the London sex trade. How this "more-than-bestial" female first came to prostitution – whether it was by her own free choice, or whether she was forced into it as a child – is impossible to say on the available evidence, but her confession provides an authoritative first-person account of how the system worked. Prostitution did not have to be a full-time career. Ordinary housewives, whether from loneliness or sexual desire or financial need, could visit an "ill house," return home an hour later with pocket change, and her husband none the wiser unless she was so unlucky as to contract an infection. But what an otherwise "honest" woman might view as a one-time fling could be a fatal trap: if she neglected to conceal her identity on such visits, the married woman by one assignation made herself a target for blackmail. Fearnside confesses to having preyed also upon guileless maidens arriving from the counties to seek employment in London (who for their first time could fetch as much as £10). Once entrapped, escape was difficult, marriage was beyond hoping for, and syphilis inevitable. A hardy few, like Margaret herself, went on to become bawds even after losing their looks; others became two-penny prostitutes who walked the streets and found their clients among the working poor. Life expectancy was short.

Margaret Fearnside was not a good woman. But to describe her confession, in conventional scholarese, as "an important text," may imply that her life was not; which is the mistake that was made by those who killed her.

THE
Araignement & bur-
ning of *Margaret Ferne-seede*,
for the Murther of her late Husband
Anthony Ferne-seede, found deade in Peckham Field neere Lambeth, hauing once before attempted to poyson him with broth,
being executed in S. Georges-field the
last of Februarie.
1 6 0 8

LONDON
Printed for *Henry Gosson*, and are to be solde at the Signe
of the Sunne in Pater-noster-rowe.
1 6 0 8

The Arraignment and Burning of Margaret Fernseed, for the Murther of her Late Husband, found dead in Peckham Field near Lambeth (having before attempted to poison him with broth); being executed in St. George's Field the last of February 1608[/9]).

MARGARET FERNSEED – a woman that even from her time of knowledge ("if the general report of the world," according to the old adage, "may be taken for an oracle") – was given to all the looseness and lewdness of life which either unlawful lust or abhominable prostitution could violently cast upon her, with the greatest infamy; yea, and with such a public and inrespective unchastity, that neither being chaste nor caute, she regarded not either into what ear the loathsomeness of her life was sounded, or into what bed of lust her lascivious body was transported. [1]

In this more-than-bestial lasciviousness, having consumed the first part of her youth, finding both the corruption of her blood to check the former heat of her lust, and the too-general ugliness of her prostitution to breed a loath in her ordinary customers, being then confirmed in some more strength of years, [she] took a house near unto the Iron Gate of the Tower; where she kept a most abhominable and vild brothelhouse, poisoning many young women with that slime wherewith her own body long before was filthily bebotched.

From this house at the Iron Gate she was married unto one Anthony Fernseed, a tailor dwelling in Duck Lane, but keeping a shop upon Addle Hill, near Carter Lane. This Anthony was amongst his neighbors reputed to both sober and of very good conversation.

Now it happened that some few months ago, in the fields of Peckham near London, there was found a man slain, having his throat cut, a knife in his hand, gold rings upon his fingers, and forty shillings in money in his purse; his wounds, of so long continuance that [the body] was not only corrupted, but there was also maggots or such-like filthy worms engendered therein – which gave testimony to the beholders that he had not slain himself in that place; as well because the place was free from such a spectacle the day before, as also that such corruption could not proceed from a present slaughter.

Again, what [was] the person slain, no man knew, both because his phys'nomy was altered in his death, and because his acquaintance was little or none in those parts about Peckham. [2]

In the end, searching his pockets and other parts of his apparel, amongst other notes and reckonings, they found an indenture wherein a certain youth which did serve him was bound unto him. This indenture gave them knowledge both of his name and of the place of his dwelling; whereupon certain discreet persons of Peckham sent to London, to Duck Lane, and inquired for the house of one Anthony Fernseed.

[They] delivered to his wife the disaster and mischance which had befallen her husband – which her hardened heart received not as a message of sorrow; neither did the grudging of an afflicted countenance gall her remembrance. But as if it had been the report of some ordinary or vulgar news, she embraced it with an inrespective neglect and carelessness – and demanded instantly (before the message would tell her how he died) whether his throat were cut or that he had cut his own throat (as either knowing or prophesying how he died). Yet, to observe a customary fashion, or (as the proverb is, "to carry a candle before the Devil"), she prepares herself and her servant, in all haste, to go to Peckham to behold her husband.

And in the way as she went, it was her chance to meet with one of her husband's ancient acquaintance, who (feeling that in charity, which she ought to have felt in nature) began to complain [of] her misfortune: telling her she had "lost a most honest and good husband."

She whom the Devil now would not suffer to dissemble (though his greatest art be in dissimulation) told him *her* fear was, she "should not hear so well of him!"

He, wondering at her ungodly carelessness, let her pass, when presently she met another of her acquaintance, who with like charity to the former began to pity her griefs (though grief was never further from her heart) and to wish her those comforts which are fit for affliction. But she as careless as before gave him (by the neglect of her words) true testimony how far sorrow was from her heart; which, when he noted, he said, "Why Mistress Fernseed, is the loss of a good husband so slightly to be regarded? For mine own part, had such a mischance fallen to my fortune, I should ere this have wept out mine eyes with true sorrow!"

But she quickly made him answer, "Tut, sir, mine eyes are ill already, and I must now preserve them to mend my clothes, not to mourn for a husband!"

After that, in her going, the wind blowing the dust in her face, she takes her scarf and wiped her eyes, and said she should "scarce know her husband, when she saw him." These courtesan-like speeches made her acquaintance leave her, and wished her more grace.

So she and her boy came where the body was, where – more for awe of the magistrate than any terror she felt – she made many sour faces; but the dryness of her brain would suffer no moisture to descend into her eyes.

---

[1] *caute*] cautelous, cautious.

[2] *phys'nomy*] physiognomy; form of the body.

Many questions were asked her, to which she answered with such constancy that no suspicion could be grounded against her.

Then was her boy taken and examined, who delivered the abhomination of her life – and that since her marriage with his master, she had lived in all disquietness, rage, and distemperature, often threatening his life and contriving plots for his destruction; that she had ever since her marriage, in most public and notorious manner, maintained a young man with whom (in his view) she had often committed adultery; that the same young man since his master's loss was fled, he knew not wither; and that his mistress had even then, before the message of his master's death, sold all his goods (as he supposed) to fly also after him whom she loved.

All these speeches were not only seconded, but almost approved by some of her neighbors, which lived near unto her; insomuch that she was the second time taken into a more strict examination; wherein albeit she could not deny any of her general affections, yet touching the death of her husband? that, she forswore and renounced the fact or practice thereof to be hers! ([and] with such a shameless constancy that she struck amazement into all that heard her).

In the end, by authority of Justice, she was committed to the White Lion in Southwark; during the time of which imprisonment till her time of trial, thinking to outface truth with boldness and sin with impudence, she continued out all her examinations (taken before several justices) in her former denials.

And whereas the rod of imprisonment laid upon others is received as a gentle correction whereby to look into themselves, it was to her rather the bellows of indignation than a temperer to patience; rather a kind of frenzy than a cooler of fury; and rather a provoker to evil than a persuader to goodness. For she was seldom found to be in charity with any of her fellow prisoners, nor at any time in quiet with herself; rather a provoker than an appeaser of dissensions; given to much swearing; scarce praying but continually scolding – so that she was as hateful to all them that dwelt with her (in that, her last home, the prison) as she was to people of honest conversation (having deserved the name of a *bawd*) while she lived abroad.

In this uncivil order spending her hours, the time of trial coming on (when such offenders were to appear before the earthly judge, to give account of their lives past) amongst many others, this Margaret Fernseed was one. And at the Assizes last, according to the order of law, she was indicted and arraigned – the purpose of which indictment was to have practiced the murther of her late husband Anthony Fernseed, who (as before[said]) was found dead in Peckham field near Lambeth. [1]

To the indictment she pleaded *Not guilty*, putting her cause to God and the country – which were a credible jury paneled, and had made their personal appearance for that purpose. Then were these several witnesses produced against her: namely, of the incontinentness of her life past; her attempt to poison her husband before this murther, as also to prepare broth for him and put powder in it; her slight regard of him in his life; and her careless sorrow for him after death; with other circumstances, as the flight of the fellow whom she had lived long in adultery withal; her present sale of her goods upon her husband's murther (as it may be justly thought, with purpose to fly after him); on which lawful evidence, she was convicted and after judgment given her, to be burned. And from thence she was conveyed back to the White Lion till the time appointed for her execution.

The Confession and Repentance of Margaret Fernseed, after her condemnation; in the White Lion

To prepare the reader for this confession of hers, know that I was credibly satisfied, that when the heat of her fury was past (to which she was much subject unto), she [was] a woman well-spoken, of fair deliverance, and good persuasion; and so, to her confession:

"To excuse myself, O Lord, before Thee – who knows the conspiracies of our thoughts even to the utmost of our actions, however so private or publicly committed – were folly! or to justify myself were sin, since no flesh can appear pure in Thy sight. I here therefore, with prostrate knees and dejected eyes, as unworthy to look up unto Thy divine Majesty, with a contrite heart and penitent soul, also here voluntarily confess: I am the greatest of sinners, which have deserved Thy wrath and indignation." […]

In this good manner she proceeded and withal satisfied all that came and desired to have private conference with her of the whole course of her life: that in her youth, even from the age of aptness, she had been a prostitute whore. But growing into disabled years, to please the loose desires of such customers, she after turned bawd, a course of life more hateful in tempting and seducing youth than the other in committing sin. The one makes but spoil and ruin of herself; and the other, of a multitude. "For," quoth she, "I myself have had ten several women retaining to my house for that purpose. Some were men's wives, which repaired thither both by appointment and at convenient hours, when their husbands might least suspect to have knowledge of their absence; and these women did I first tempt to their fall – some, by persuading them they were not beloved of their hus-

---

[1] *to have practiced*] to review, investigate.

bands, especially if I could at any time have note of any breach or discontent between them; others, that their husbands maintained them not sufficiently to express their beauty and according to their own deserts.

"Of these, then having brought my purpose to effect, and that I knew they had offended, I made this booty: that they were as fearful to offend *me* (as their husbands should have knowledge of their offenses); and these allowed me a weekly pension for coming to my house, and durst not at all times but find opportunity to come, whensoever myself (or such loose friends, whom either they had been familiar withal or now desired to be acquainted with them) should send for any of them.

"To supply my house and make spoil of young maids who were sent out of the country by their friends, therewith hoping° to advance themselves, I went weekly to the carriers; where, if the maid liked me, I so wrought with the carrier that she seldom left me till I had brought her to be as bad as I purposed; which effected, every one of them I compelled to give me ten shillings a week out of their gettings— having, as I said, seldom less than ten whose bodies and souls I kept in this bondage.

"Besides, I confess I was a continual receiver of thefts° stolen. But in all this, as it was badly got, so was it worse consumed, for nothing of it did prosper with me; whereby […] I acknowledge I have deserved death, and in the highest degree. But for this which I am condemned, Heaven that knoweth best the secrets of our hearts, knows I am *innocent*."

• • •

But who knows not that in evil there is a like impudence to *deny* as there is a forwardness to *act*? – in which we will leave her whom the Law hath found guilty; and having thus truly related her own confession, we proceed to the manner of execution.

First only [this], touching the evidence of two sailors, given to the jury at her arraignment (among other circumstances that was availablest to condemn her, this was one and the chiefest): During the time while she kept a bad house about the Iron Gate by Towerditch, there happened a couple of bargemen to come to revel at her house with such guests as she kept to entertain loose customers. And having spent the whole day in large riot and much expense, the night being late, for that time they made their lodging there. They being a-bed, it happened that night (which was seldom), [that] her husband came to make his lodging there also; and being chambered with his wife, but a wall between where these bargemen lay, [the bargemen] could expressly hear [the Fernseeds] – every word that passed between them – the effect of which was the [husband's] reproving of

her for her bad life [and] his persuading her to amendment; which she, not willing to listen unto, fell a-scolding at him, and so left both his bed and chamber.

Some time passing, at last Master Fernseed heard these bargemen cough; and wondering to have strangers lodged in his house (for it was not common, to his knowledge) arose out of his bed and demanded of them what they were.

Who asked of him also, wherefore he questioned them.

"Mary," quoth he, "for if you be honest men, and have a care either of your bodies or souls, avoid this house as you would do poison, lest it be the undoing of you all!"

They seeing him of a comely personage, and that his words tended to some purpose, demanded of him what he was that gave them such wholesome counsel.

"I am," quoth he, "the master of this house, if I had my right. But I am barred of the possession and command thereof by a devilish woman, who makes a stews of it, to exercise her sinful practices." So, with some other admonishment, [he] left the room.

When these bargemen told Mistress Fernseed what they had heard of her husband, she° replied, "Hang him, slave and villain! I will before God be revenged of him – nay, ere long, by one means or other, so work that I will be rid of him." Which, making good in the judgment of the judge to gather with her life and practices, she as aforesaid was condemned.

• • •

On Monday being the last of February, she had notice given her that in the afternoon she must suffer death; and a preacher [was] commended unto her to instruct her for her soul's health; who labored much with her for the confession of the fact – which she still obstinately denied, but made great show of repentance for her life past; so that, about two of the clock in the afternoon, she was stripped of her ordinary wearing apparel, and upon her own smock put a kirtle of canvas, pitched clean through; over which she did wear a white sheet, and so was by the keeper delivered to the shrieve (one each hand, a woman leading her, and the preacher going before her). Being come to the place of execution, both before and after her fastening to the stake, with godly exhortations [he] admonished her. that now, in that *minute*, she would confess that fact for which she was now ready to suffer; which she denying, the reeds were planted about, unto which fire being given, she was presently dead. [1]

finis

---

[1] *fact*] violent crime;   *canvas pitched clean through*] hempen cloth soaked in tar to facilitate burning; *shrieve*] sheriff.

Martha Scambler (1614-1614),

Monster by kind

> *Wo worth the traines which still are laid*
> *Whereby we woemen are betraid!*
> —Margaret Scambler's Repentance, 7-8

DEEDS AGAINST NATURE *and Monsters by Kind* (1614), an anonymous news report, features two cases of poor women whose sexual encounters outside wedlock resulted in four deaths, including their own. The author writes from the worldview of merchant-class Calvinism, which held that all men and women deserve to suffer poverty in this life and Hell in the next, as a penalty for sin. Only by the grace of God (and their own hard work) do the Lord's chosen few achieve prosperity. From evangelical Protestant pulpits, charity to the poor was vigorously discouraged. (To give alms to beggars is to provide the graceless poor with spending money for alcohol and sex, when God's good ought to be invested, thereby to produce more wealth, as in Christ's parable of the talents.)

The first reported "monster by kind" in *Deeds against Nature* was a deformed beggar named John Arthur, a man crippled from birth, having incomplete limbs, who survived to adulthood on the alms given him by decent but gullible citizens. Like "others of his base fraternity," he was a "graceless wretch" who bore the visible signs of God's displeasure in his grotesque body. "The Cripple" is said to have partnered with a penniless slut: they begged together, spent their alms on alcohol together; and when drunk, "heated with lust, fell into familiarity." The Cripple "so lusted after his begging companion that he obtained the daily use of her body," continually committing, in "fields and highways," "that sin of lust and shame," performing "such beastly offenses" that God himself was disgusted, angry "that a deformed lump of flesh and no perfect creature should thus abuse the seed of generation." When the Cripple grew tired of his recreation and "began to cast her off," his female "associate" pressed him to marry her; whereupon he strangled her with her own girdle as she slept, and was duly arrested.

The second report tells of "a lascivious young damsel named Martha Scambler," who "made away the fruit of her own womb, that the world might not see the seed of her own shame." But God in His Providence disclosed her secret homicide. She, too, was arrested.

It is reported that the Cripple and Martha Scambler, with "divers others, were executed at Tyburn the 21st of July 1614." Appended to the two news reports are "sorrowful ditties of these two aforesaid persons, made by themselves in Newgate, the night before their execution."

The Martha Scambler case is of special interest to women's history. Developing simultaneously with the witchcraft hysteria of the seventeenth century was a growing conviction, by God-fearing middle-class Christians, that the latrines of England were being stuffed with the murdered babies of unmarried beggars and heartless prostitutes who were not subject to the rigors of sexual segregation practiced by respectable families. No evidence has ever emerged that infanticide was a common occurrence. The social stigma of pregnancy outside wedlock, and the usually disastrous consequences for the unmarried maiden, were strong disincentives to premarital sex. Among those who had opportunity to indulge, oral sex and petting to climax were commonly practiced diversions to avoid pregnancy (as attested by countless literary jests and confirmed by court records). Abortifacients were freely available and used by women of all classes, including the herbal equivalent of a morning-after pill (with more powerful "medicines" for advanced pregnancy). When all else failed and an "illegitimate" human was born, the baby was typically cared for by the mother, usually without financial support from the father, and without hope of future inheritance. Despite all of that, in London and Middlesex for the years 1558-1593, there were just seven indictments for infanticide.

Nevertheless, it became 'common knowledge' in the Jacobean period that hundreds, perhaps thousands, of unmarried women were concealing their pregnancy, delivering healthy babies, and killing them. Moral outrage found expression, not in a campaign to save the hypothetical infants (who were destined to become beneficiaries of the hated Poor Tax), but to find the infanticidal mothers and put them to death; which was infuriatingly difficult because the pregnancies and attendant corpses, among the unpropertied masses, evaded discovery and prosecution.

Martha Scambler is described as a young woman who lodged with a kinsman in a house in London's Bishopsgate parish. Finding herself pregnant (the father is not named), she tried but failed with the usual abortifacient herbs to terminate her pregnancy. Craftily concealing her condition even from other residents in the same house, she came to full term. And because she was unusually robust, she was able to deliver a healthy infant, unassisted, without crying out, and without anyone's knowledge. She then strangled the babe and dropped it into the toilet – a close-stool whose latrine hole was connected by a tunnel to the house next door. Within a few days, Scambler was convinced that her crime would go undiscovered. But God in His providence made use of a waggish lad, who for a prank took a "cur-dog" and dropped him down the toilet of the neighboring house; whose goodman, for the next three days, could neither stand nor sit without a yelping dog making a racket, down there. When the starving dog was finally rescued, the slain baby was discovered.

What's most remarkable about *Deeds against Nature and Monsters by Kind* is that, despite its gloss of historicity, neither of its featured stories is reliably true. Two forms of crime reporting existed side by side in the Jacobean era. The first, represented by such pamphlets *The Arraignment and Burning of Margaret Fernseed*, reported actual cases, and were authorized for publication in order to control the public narrative when the court's verdict had been impugned. Official reporting was typically assigned to such trusted allies of Justice as Rev. Henry Goodcole, chaplain of Newgate Prison, or court recorders such as Thomas Potts. Alongside these official and sanctioned narratives were printed many lurid tales of violent crime, usually featuring a secret felony discovered and solved through God's miraculous intervention. Hack writers who began with an actual felony were obliged to bury the facts beneath an avalanche of fiction, or else fabricate the entire bloody narrative. A well-known but not well-researched instance: *The Most Cruel and Bloody Murder committed by an Innkeeper's Wife, called Annis Dell, and her Son, George Dell, foure yeeres since on the bodie of a childe called Anthony Iames in Bishops Hatfield in the countie of Hartford, and now most miraculously reuealed by the sister of the said Anthony, who at the time of the murther had her tongue cut out, and foure yeeres remayned dumme and speechlesse, and now perfectly speaketh, reuealing the murther, hauing no tongue to be seen* (London, 1606). Another: *A Most Rare, Strange, and Wonderfull Accident, which by Gods Just judgement was brought to passe, not farre from Rithin in Wales, and showne upon three most wicked persons, who had secretly and cunningly murdered a young gentleman named David Williams, that by no meanes it could be knowne, and how in the end it was revenged by a childe of five yeeres old, which was in his mothers wombe, and unborne when the deed was done* (London, 1620). Scholarly commentary on these and similar pamphlets has proved remarkably gullible, taking the printed reports as fundamentally true while seeking to rationalize the miracles and to account for the narrative inconsistencies.

The story of Martha Scambler contains many red flags: no name is supplied for the author, the judges, or for any witness save the accused. No allegation is supported with a quotation or summary of court depositions. The story depends on obvious improbabilities, as when Martha is somehow able to conceal not only her pregnancy, but her labor and her delivery of a live infant, undetected by those living in the same house; or the dog who gets pranked next door at the very moment when a secret infanticide awaits discovery in a shared latrine-hole; or the goodman who for three days does nothing to rescue the dog in his toilet though its barking drives the neighbors nuts. The author's grim *deus ex machina* – a scapegoated friend of man who spends three days and three nights in the vault before being raised, thereby to dispense with sin – owes a debt to Christian soteriology; and the narrative strategy illustrates homiletic conventions that developed from the Parables of Jesus in the New Testament, where a story's truth-value resides in its moral lesson rather than in its historicity.

If Martha Scambler was ever a real human being, in *Deeds against Nature* she becomes "a creature more savage than a she-wolf," a monster by kind. But no other record survives of her existence. Even the name is suspect. The word, *scambler* or *scamler* (meaning social parasite), enters the English language in the early sixteenth century but is rarely found as a surname before the seventeenth century (in London parish records, not before 1631); while *Martha* means "mistress" or "lady," a fact known to every clergyman. The name of the offender, "Martha Scambler," conveniently serves to denote the type of woman whom the reporter wishes to shame and whom God intends to punish: "Mistress Parasite," the shameless unwed female who fornicates, gets pregnant, and when abortifacients fail gives birth in a latrine, strangles the child, and hides her sin in a privy – until God makes her "deeds of darkness clear as day, that the world may behold His high-working powers, and that no malefactor […] escape unpunished."

The story of Martha's secret crime, and discovery, and burning, published as a news story, nevertheless served as a particular written confirmation of Puritan fears that infanticide was occurring all around them, in poor neighborhoods; while providing a cautionary tale to other maids who might think of following Martha Scambler's bad, if imaginary, example. [1]

Nowhere is the anonymous author's bad faith more evident than in "Martha Scambler's Repentance," a poem that is said to have been composed by our notorious she-wolf on the eve of her execution. By ascribing to the accused a first-person narrative in her own words, with a date assigned to her burning, the reporter produces evidence that Martha Scambler really did exist; while the poem attributed to her confirms that everything we have just read about her is accurate. (As Shakespeare's Mopsa remarks in *The Winter's Tale*, "I love a ballad in print, a' life! – for then we are sure they are true" [4.4.260-1).

Deeds against Nature and Monsters by Kind contributed to public outcry and, eventually, to legislation. Bills dealing with infanticide had been discussed in the Parliaments of 1606-7 and 1610, without action being taken. But in 1624, ten years after the Martha Scambler story was published, King James's fourth Parliament finally passed a law to end the holocaust:

An Act to Prevent the Destroying and Murthering of Bastard Children (21 James I, 1624)°

WHEREAS many lewd women that have been delivered of bastard children, to avoid their shame and to escape punishment, do secretly bury or conceal the death of their children; and after, if the child be found dead, the said women do allege that the said child was born dead;

Whereas it falleth out sometimes (although hardly it is to be proved) that the said child or children were murthered by the said women their lewd mothers, or by their assent or procurement:

For the preventing therefore of this great mischief, be it enacted by the authority of this present Parliament, that if any woman (after one month next ensuing the end of this session of Parliament) be delivered of any issue of her body male or female, which being born alive, should by the laws of this realm be a bastard, and that she endeavor privately, either by drowning or secret burying thereof, as that it may not come to light, whether it were born alive or not, but be concealed, in every such case the mother so offending shall suffer death as in case of murther, except such mother can make proof by one witness at the least, that the child (whose death was by her so intended to be concealed) was born dead.

• • •

Under the terms of this statute, even a miscarried fetus was presumed to have been born alive, and the mother was presumed guilty of having killed it unless she could produce eyewitness testimony that the infant never acquired breath (*pneuma,* spirit). Because the women who suffered miscarriage far outnumbered those who murdered breathing infants, the law fell heavily upon unmarried women who – having been observed to be pregnant – could not thereafter exhibit a living infant. The unwed mother was thereby obliged, on fear of her life, to avoid miscarriage; and at full term to have a midwife present. The terror of being prosecuted for a miscarriage thus created the very conditions that the law sought to punish: attempted concealment of pregnancy out of wedlock until the fetus came to full term and a midwife was summoned. Women had good cause to be frightened: Far more women were prosecuted under the Infanticide Statute than were indicted as witches, with prosecutions peaking during the Puritan Interregnum. In 1803, the law was finally repealed. [2]

---

[1] Following publication of *Deeds against Nature,* life may have imitated art, persuading one unwed mother that the latrine was a safe place to dispose of an inconvenience (a crime unlikely to be discovered, short of a miracle). Only a few months later, the Aldgate records mention "Elizabeth Asher, the reputed daughter of Thomas Asher in Woolsack Alley in Houndsditch (the mother, named Joan Tagge, servant to Thomas Newton, a broker in Houndsditch); who, like a murderous strumpet, cast her said child into a privy. But by God's good grace it was heard to cry by the neighbors, and saved alive, and christened the tenth day of May anno. 1615. She [Elizabeth Asher] was taken afterward and arraigned, but escaped death. The poor infant died within a fortnight after." Ed. from T.R. Forbes, *Aldgate* (1971), 151.

[2] *the law*] James Sharpe, *Crime in Seventeenth Century England: A County Study* (1983), p. 191, reports that 83 women were indicted for infanticide, 1620-1680, in Essex alone, and at least 31 put to death. *Women's Works,* vol. 4, features the true story of Anne Green, whose miscarriage in a latrine caused her to be tried and hanged under the Infanticide Statute, only to be revived from her supposed death moments before her cadaver was to be dissected at Oxford University (December 1650).

From **Deeds against Nature and Monsters by Kind**

WE are to place in our discourse another cat-erpillar of Nature, a creature more savage than a she-wolf, more unnatural than either bird or beast: for every creature hath a tender feeling of love to their young except some few murtherous-minded strumpets – "women" I cannot call them, for a woman esteems the fruit of her own womb the precious and dearest jewel of the world. And for the cherishing of the same [she] will, as it were, spend her life's purest blood; where contrariwise,° the harlot, delighting in shame and sin, makes no conscience to be the butcher of her own seed (nay, the image of God created in her own body!), and now and then in the conception makes spoil of the bed of creation before it can receive true form.

Therefore an example likewise cast your eyes upon this other monster of Nature, which was a las-civious, lewd, and close strumpet, a harlot lodging privately near Bishopsgate in Bedlam – at a kins-man's house of hers, which little suspected this her unwomanly carriage. But shame, long raked up in the ashes of secrecy, though close-smoking, will at last break forth into open flame. So this graceless wanton, spending her youth in lascivious pleasures (as many a one doth in and about this city) happed to prove with child, and – having no husband to cover this her act of shame, and withal fearing the disgrace of the world – by a devilish practice sought to con-sume it in her body before the birth. But not pre-vailing (as God would have it), she was forced by Nature to deliver it alive to the world, and so was made the unhappy mother of a man-child ("un-happy" I may name her, for her own hand made her unhappy!).

To our purpose: her lusty body, strong nature, and fear of shame brought an easiness to her deliv-ery and required in her agony no help of a midwife (which among women seemeth a thing very strange); for not so much as the least child in the house where she lodged had knowledge of her labor, nor hardly was she thought to be with child, so closely demeaned she herself But the Devil, we see, adds force unto wickedness and puts a kind of strength to Nature in that kind; otherwise had she been discovered in the childbirth.

Consider this: the child being born with shame (and she by it made a scandal to her acquaintance) renewed the remembrance of her past sins and pre-sented present shame unto her grieved thoughts. [These] troubled cogitations, by the persuasions of the Devil, put her in mind violently to make it away and to give it death before the body had well recovered life; whereupon taking the poor tender babe as it were new dropped from the mother's womb and (not like a mother, but a monster) threw it down into a loathsome privy-house, therein to give it an undecent grave and (as she thought) thereby make to herself a riddance of a further infamy.

But God is just and will reward shame where it is deserved. And such unnatural deeds, let them be acted in deserts, in the caverns of the Earth where never light of day nor Sun shines, yet will they be discovered and brought to the world's eye. So hap-pened it with this harlot: When all fear of suspicion was passed, she safely delivered the child in the privy, smothered; and in the world no notice taken thereof, yet in the end was it thus most strangely discovered:

The tunnel of the aforesaid vault or privy as-cended up into the next neighbor's house (as in many places they do); where by chance (as God had ordained) dwelled an untoward lad that, in taking delight in knavish pastimes, took a cur dog then us-ing the house, and carelessly threw it down the tun-nel into the vault where the murthered infant lay; and taking no regard thereof, suffered the dog to remain there starving and crying for food the space of three days and nights; during which, the yelping of the dog much disquieted the neighbors, and so troubled the dwellers thereabouts that they could not sleep a-nights for the noise; but especially the goodman of the house, who (grieved to see a dumb beast so starved, and for want of food, to perish) like a kind-natured man caused the privy to be opened and the poor cur taken up – which proved by God's justice the only discoverer of the foresaid fact. For in taking up the dog, they were woeful witnesses of the sweet babe lying all besmeared with the filth of that loathsome place; the sight whereof caused no small amazement, especially to the goodman of the house.

[He] with a diligent care (as his duty was both to God and his country), and that all such inhumane deeds might be brought to light, made it known to the magistrates. [They] likewise with Christian care caused a certain number of substantial women to make a search of suspected persons and of such who were like to be the murthered infant's mother or murtherer; amongst many other loose livers and common harlots (of which number, those by-places have too many, the more is the pity!).

This aforesaid murtheress came to the touch; where, upon examination, she confessed the child to be born with life and herself not worth of life. And so pleading guilty, she was brought to her trial and for the same arraigned and condemned by the bench of Assize in the Old Bailey the 18 and 19 of July last (1614); and hath suffered death at Tyburn the 21 following, as an example that God (either by beasts of the field, fowls of the air, fishes in the seas, worms in the ground, or things bearing neither sense nor life) will by one means or other make deeds of darkness clear as day, that the world may behold His high-working powers, and that no malefactor can escape unpunished though his deeds be as secret as the work of Hell, beyond the thought of human imagination.

Convert us from sin, great God of Israel! So shall we never be endangered with the like persuasion – which God in His mercy grant. Amen.

Martha Scambler's Repentance

POOR I, the poorest now on Earth,
May well accuse my cause of birth:
Not being born, I ne'er had known
This guilt that hath me overthrown.
Woe worth the cause of sin and shame
Which stains my credit and good name!
Woe worth the trains which still are laid   1
Whereby we women are betrayed!
When I was won to folly's will
And took delight in doing ill,
No thought I had of pleasures past
But still my youth did vainly waste
Till, at the length, my womb did breed
A substance of unlawful seed—
Which I supposed a shame to be
(God knows!) unto my friends and me.
And to prevent the world's disgrace,
I sought to find a secret place
My shameful burthened womb to ease
(That way, which did my God displease).
O, when my hour of labor came
To bring to light this fruit of shame,
No midwife's help at all I sought
But soon my own delivery wrought.
The babe being born and in my arms   [25]

I should have kept it from all harms,
But like a bear or wolf in wood
I wished it smothered up in blood.
Where at strange motions, without fear,
From Hell to me presented were
And bade me bury it in a vault
(For none alive did know my fault).
And so my credit and good name
Should take no spot of black defame
And I as pure and chaste should be
From such a crime as any She,
My soul then (blinded by the Devil)
Bid me consent unto this evil
Where I full soon thereto agreed:
To act a more-than woman's deed.
The loathsome Jakes received my child   2
Which all misdoubts and fear exiled—
For being tumbled down therein,
There well might end my shame and sin.
But God this deed more dark than night
In wondrous sort did bring to light,
For by a dog the child was found
As it was thrown therein to drownd.
Three days and nights with yelping cry
It troubled much the dwellers by   [50]
Which caused them to release him thence—
And so found out this vile offense
For which I surely now must taste
Reward for my offenses past
And die for that accursèd crime
That makes me monster of my time.
Both maids and men, both young and old,
Let not good lives with shame be sold,
But bear true virtues to your grave
That honest burials you may have.

finis

Woodcut from *The Apprehension, Arraignment, and Execution of Elizabeth Abbot, for a Cruel and Horrible Murther* (1608).

Reworked woodcut depicting the execution of Martha Scambler, from *Deeds against Nature and Monsters by Kind* (1614).

---

1 *trains*] guile, tricks, lies (*OED* n.1)

2 *so*] so that; *Jakes*] slang for latrine.

From *A World of Wonders*

LET US NOW CONSIDER HOW … preachers declaiming thus in general against the wickedness of their times, do in particular also reprove and censure men for all sorts of vices. And (that I may proceed in order) I will begin with that which (as Juvenal would make us believe) is of all other vices the most ancient – and so much the more ancient, by how much the Silver Age is more ancient than the Iron Age: "What is this vice?" may some say.

Surely, whoredom! (otherwise called "carnality," "sensuality," or "lechery").

[T]hey complain much of murthers and manslaughters. And their manner is (in speaking of the sins of their time), to range whoredom, theft, and murther in the first rank. And [preachers] seem to be grieved to the very soul that they are not punished.… But there are other "murthers," for which they weep water and snot: as those which women commit in causing an abortion; and "which is worse, for that priests," as Maillard sayeth, "persuade them that in so doing, they commit no mortal sin" (f. 74, col. 2).…

[Gabriel] Barletta also crieth out against this sin (f. 262, col. 2): "*O quot luxuriae, O quot Sodomiae, O quot fornicationes, clamant latrinae, latibula ubi sunt pueri suffocati!*" [O what lust! O what Sodomy! O what fornications! What a claim for the latrine, the vault where children are stifled!"

Pontanus also allegeth an example of this "currish cruelty," affirming it to be more usual with nuns than with others.…(But it is now high time we should hear how these preachers say *churchmen* their lessons…)

Of Murthers Committed at this Day

AS FOR WOMEN which have murthered their children, I persuade myself there are but few to be found which murther them after they are once grown in years. Howbeit, many there are, as well of those which kill their newborn babes as of those who execute their cruelty upon them in the womb before they see the light of the Sun… Now there are two main reasons of this wicked practice. Some do it for fear they should be known to have played the wantons and lost their virginity; or, to speak somewhat more generally, for fear of being disclosed to have had to do where they ought not, be they married women or widows; others, for fear of abridging and shortening their youth… I have further heard of certain gentlewomen, and myself have known some, who made no bones to wear poitrels or stiff stomachers, endangering thereby the life of their child; and, to the end they might not lose the credit of having a fine slender body, made no conscience to destroy that which should have been as dear unto them as their own lives: I speak of such housewives as "miscarried" in the carriage.

As for those murthering Medeas who made away their newborn babes by casting them into ponds, privies, etc., nunneries within these few years would have furnished us with store of examples, as well as of those which "murther them in the womb".… Moreover, in that they see sundry nuns leave their nunneries (I mean their brothel-houses) and beds, and betake themselves to the marriage bed (where they live orderly and well), it makes them look a little better to their consciences (before they go about such murthers). Yet it cannot be denied but that this wicked murthering of poor innocents extendeth itself beyond the cloisters, not only to marriageable maids who are under the mother's wing or in the government of their kinsfolks (even to such as are worshipfully and nobly descended), but to widows also.…

Maidservants, of all other, are oftenest taken tardy with this fault, and they only (poor souls!) are called *coram* before the magistrate… For I have often seen such at Paris hanged for this crime, and none but such. And I remember I once saw an anatomy in the physic schools of a maid that was hanged for casting her child into a privy.…

True it is indeed, our *ladies* at this day need not to take so cruel a course, considering they have so many *prophylactica* to keep their bellies from tympanizing.

—Henri Estienne, *A World of Wonders,* anon. trans. (London, 1607): 155-7.

---

[1] *poitrels*] literally, body armor; slang for a stiff stomacher.

[2] *taken tardy*] caught by surprise; *called coram*] called to account; *anatomy in the physic schools*] dissection, in medical school, of a cadaver; *tympanizing*] swelling up.

Bessie Clarkson (1603-1625)

"What availeth words when there is nothing within?"
– Bessie Clarkson

ELIZABETH "BESSIE" CLARKSON, a housewife in the parish church of Lanark, Scotland, attended the local worship service every Sunday with her husband and children, listened carefully, and meditated upon the lessons in Scripture. Bessie is said to have trusted and obeyed the Word of God: she cherished, as a key to salvation, the words of her minister, the Rev. William Livingston. Like most Scottish clergymen of the period, Rev. Livingston held to a vigorously Calvinist view of the world. Week after week, he explained to his congregation that all humanity deserves eternal damnation. By God's grace (but through no merit of their own) selected sinners will be saved from Hell in order to dwell eternally with the Lord in Heaven. These chosen ones were destined, even before the creation of the world, to receive God's forgiveness for their sins, according to God's inscrutable and undeserved grace: no man marked for redemption will be damned, however wicked he may seem to earthly eyes, nor can any woman marked for damnation be saved, no matter how virtuous. From Rev. Livingston's Calvinistic point of view, one could hardly even presume to call oneself a "Christian," except by faith, for no one can be sure of salvation except insofar as one feels the grace of God within, this being an indication of the Lord's forgiveness.

Taking Rev. Livingston at his word, Bessie Clarkson became worried, and finally convinced, that she was not among God's elect – for she could not feel the inner assurance that God was said to give to those who are destined for Heaven. Bessie eventually confessed to her minister that she was beyond hope of God's grace. This startling disclosure led to a series of interviews between Clarkson and Livingston in which the minister attempted to persuade Bessie of her spiritual election. Bessie was not easily persuaded. Soon, the elders of the local church, and indeed the entire community, were enlisted in an evangelical crusade to help their beloved neighbor Bessie Clarkson to find divine assurance of her salvation.

Early on in these interviews, it occurred to Rev. Livingston that he had been chosen by God to record the spiritual conflict of this remarkable woman – even as Philip Stubbs, more than three decades earlier, had recorded the now-famous spiritual conflict of Katherine Stubbs. Rev. Livingston reports that he "found the words of this deare defunct of greater worth than that they should fall to the ground, and not to be gathered. So at last, as I visited°, I wrote." […] In recording his interviews with Bessie, Rev. Livingston looked forward to that blessed day when she could proclaim her ultimate victory over Satan, even as Katherine Stubbs had done from her deathbed so many years before.

While in the midst of this spiritual crisis, Bessie inadvertently found herself in a novel situation: almost overnight, she had become a local celebrity, the focus of an entire community. With that insight, her spiritual crisis deepened. Half astonished that she had been made "such a spectacle to the world by all others," Bessie at one point asked of her audience, "Heard you, read you, knew you ever one like me?" They had not.

As her audience grew larger and more attentive, Bessie became more insistent that her soul could not be redeemed. Her apostasy was in part a loss of faith in language. Unable to read or write, and unable to trust the reading of others, Bessie announced to the good people of Lanark that her unbelief had drawn down "all the ill of the word," indeed, the ill of words themselves. She began speaking in hyperboles, borrowing familiar phrases from Rev. Livingston's sermons whereby to illustrate her own irremediable damnation, and troping on his words with pun after pun, as if to expose the emptiness of words without referents. "[Y]ou book me," she observed, "and carries my name in many arts, but I cannot mend it."

DWF

The Conflict in Conscience of Bessie Clarkson

Minister. "Bessie, how are you?"

Bessie. "I find the wrath of an angry God, of a crabbèd God; and all the wrath that you preached, which come on me now. I find Him daily coming against me."

Min. "Bessie, God will for good ends let His own dear children taste of His anger and wrestle with His wrath in this world, that they be not casten up in a dead sleep of fleshly security, and so perish in that great wrath that is to be revealed. [...T]he calm after the tempest may be the sweeter when it comes, and God's glory the greater, and more manifest in that dealing – in casting down and plunging in the Hell, and heaving again to the Heavens. And this sort of dealing drives atheism best out of the heart."

Bes. "I am not a devil to contemn God, and I cannot get faith to believe in God."

Min. "It is a degree of faith to find the want of faith: it is a step to a greater growth."

When I was about to comfort her, she said, "Will ye speak to me as ye should – and say, 'Thou wretched, sinful, and wicked woman!' – and not tell me sweet words?"

I answered her, "No, Bessie, I must not measure you as ye do yourself by your own sense, but to teach you to hope above hope, and say with Job, 'Lord, if thou will slay me I will trust in thee!'" [1]

Bes. "O there was grace there, but there is a great dissension betwixt God and me. I am cast away! O, that this wakening had come twenty years since! – but now my time is lost. Many come to word and sacrament that knows not what they are doing. The morn when God's people come to hear you, I cannot come. I am cast aside."

Min. "It is yet the acceptable time wherein the Lord may be found. He is yet on the throne of grace. Give no place to such suggestions of Satan and distrustful cogitations, arising of your corruption, and where ye cannot come to the Word." [...]

When I pressed to persuade her that God in His own time would ease her and speak peace to her: "I cannot find that," said she.

Min. "Albeit ye feel it not, pray that the Lord would 'Remember mercy in wrath,' as [sayeth]° the prophet"° (Habbakuk 3.2).

"Mercy in wrath!" said she. "O, that is a strange word! O for *absolution*! O for a drop to cool my tormented soul! O that I could win a step nearer Him!"

Min. "'Blessed are they that hunger and thirst, for they shall be satisfied.' It is the Lord who is our sufficiency, who works the will and the deed; it is He who wakens those desires in you, and He will work the work." [2]

When I said the Lord dealt with her as He doth, to humble her: "To humble me!" said she. "And that I am – that cat that sits there is in better case nor I am. I shall beat down this carcase with bear-bread and water, but that doth not the turn." [3]

When her servant-woman said, "You were a good body," and began to commend her: "Cease," said she, "I am but a dog, and worse nor a dog. God's wrath is on me, for my invisible sins, and if I were away, there would be none but Christians on the earth. I know Christ would go betwixt me and all my sins but one. I will not lain it, nor hide it: it is despair." [4]

Min. "You are very sensible of your unbelief, and God will make you also sensible of a lively faith ere° all be done: 'For a little while hath He forsaken you,' as He sayeth (Isa. 54.7-10);° but with great compassion will He gather you. For a moment, in His anger, hath He hid His face from you, for a little season, but with everlasting mercy will He have compassion on you" (*ibid.*, 10-11: "O thou afflicted and tossed with tempest!" etc.).

Bes. "Is it God that doth this to me? Can God spoil Himself? I had faith and prayer! Now they are reft, couped and spoiled. Can God do it? Will God rob Himself? Will He take away the matter of His own glory? I am ashamed to look any man in the face! I have lost the favor of God and man. O for a drop of grace! O for as much faith as a grain of mustard seed!" [5]

Min. "Bessie, it is the Lord who deals with you, but not to rob your faith, which is His gift; and, once given, cometh never under revocation." [...]

And when I showed her that we walk by faith and not by feeling,° and must not measure ourselves, nor God's goodness and love, by our sense, she answereth: "If faith do it not, I have done with it!"

---

[1] *if*] even if; "*Lord ... thee*"] Job 13:15.

[2] *Blessed ... satisfied*] Mat. 5.6.

[3] *bear-bread*] barley-bread; *that...turn*] that is insufficient.

[4] *lain*] conceal.

[5] *couped*] overturned.

When one beside spake to her of God's favor and presence, she said, "God! If I were as sure of it as you are! I have feet," said she, "hands, eyes, knees. I can do anything but one: I cannot believe. Well were the soul that ever it was ordained, that had faith! O, the great want of faith and love to God in these days! It was never less, and they will find out one day what it is, to want it! One thing holds me from God: it is unbelief. God's hand is sore on me. I would fain believe. Pray, pray, pray," said she, "—ye that have faith."

[...] When I told her of God's dealing with His own by diverse sorts of trouble in mind, body, and estate, she answereth, "No trouble, to the trouble in *mind*! I care not," said she, "for legs, arms, eyes, and all the rest, if I could get comfort in the blood of Jesus. I would not care [if]° my carcase lay lame, leper, sick, sore, so that my mind were pacified and at one with God. I care not for all Satan's assaults if he were even standing there, so that I could find God with me and not against me." [1]

"Wait on," said I. "The Lord will come."

She answereth, "He cometh daily – in wrath."

"But He will come in mercy," said I, "in His own time."

She answereth, "Ever since this bred in me, you said that – but I can never find it. Would I willingly lose my soul if I could get faith? Well is the soul that ever it was ordained of God, that gets the comforts of the Holy Ghost."

Min. "Would you not, Bessie, be one of His?"

"Wally, Wally," said she. "To be one of His, to have one drop of grace from His finger-end! Who would *not* be one of His?" [...] [2]

And after I had prayed for her, and pressed by some passages of scripture to comfort her, she said, "It is heavy to my heart to hear those sweet admonitions and prayers, and to get no part of them in my soul, and not to find Him whom you seek." She sayeth again, "Whither shall I turn? Whither shall I go? What shall I do? Whither shall I run to seek God, to grip Him? I cannot get grips fastened on Him. Dear minister," said she, "tell me what sin hath procured this, that I am such a spectacle to the world by all others! Heard you, read you, knew you ever one like me? [...] I think if I ever had had faith I could not have lost it."

I answered, "You have not lost it. You *desire* – which God reputes for faith, and hath the same promise of satisfaction which faith hath made unto it."

She answereth, "I would be burnt quick to be sure of salvation. I live without faith. I live, and worship not God. I can find no comfort from God nor man. My life is miserable and comfortless. [...] I am the most miserable and wretched creature in the world, for my sins are hid to myself, and known to God!"

[...] After I had prayed, she said, "If your prayers have a good ground and be according to God's will, it's the better: it will be the better heard."

"But that it is," said I. "I have a warrant to mourn with them that mourn, and to pity and pray for all that are in trouble, chiefly of my own flock."

"Your warrant were the better," said she, "if I were one of Christ's flock. Happy were that soul that were one of those."

"But ye *are* one of these," said I.

"Ye have aye said that," said she, "but I can never find it." [3]

"You will find it," said I, "in the Lord's time. Tarry His leisure – He will come with comfort."

"Tarry, must I?" said she. "Where shall I flee or flit! He cometh, ay, in due time – but He cometh to me in wrath!" [4]

When I remembered her again of Job, who said, "if thou wilt slay me, I will believe in thee," she answereth, "Where will ye get the like of *Job*? No, not amongst you all that are ministers! Faithful was he, but I have none. No salvation for *me*."

Then, to try her, I said, "Will ye sell me your part of it, your title, right, and kindness? What shall I give you for it? If you have none, you may the better cheap quit it, and I will give you for it."

She answereth, "Why scorn ye me, a siely poor woman, and ye a wise man? I would buy and not sell! If I had ten thousand millions of gold – if I had a thousand worlds – if it were to be bought for money, I would give you all for it." [5]

Min. "I said not this to scorn you Bessie, but to draw out your desire by this demand – as it doth! – whereby it is easy to discern that ye have a sure title to that salvation, albeit it seem tint to your sense."

---

[1] *No trouble to*] There is no trouble comparable to; *so that*] so long as.

[2] *Wally*] Unless William Livingston was known to his parishioners as "Wally," this is either a typographical error or a deliberate obfuscation to conceal Livingston's identity.

[3] *aye*] always.

[4] *ay*] yes; truly.

[5] *siely*] simple, unsophisticated.

Bes. "I have no pleasure in anything, neither in husband nor child. I can do nothing but sin. My life is all sin. An' it were to peel the bark of a kale castock and eat, I sin in the doing of it. Why live I then? I cannot die," said she; "I cannot live. They will bury a carcase [when]° they bury me, a carcase of sin: yea, sin itself." [1]

When I sparred at her if she desired mercy, she answered, "O that His desire to *me* were as great as mine to *Him*! O for a look of love!" [2]

"Cry and pray," said I, "for the Lord hath said, 'seek and ye shall find. Knock and it shall be opened unto you.'"

"My prayer," said she, "is repelled. My cry is not respected. It doth no good. I cannot have faith, except God give it. None hath any grace but from Him. Happy are they that can bless Him and call on His name."

Min. "And happy are they, Bessie, that counts them happy, and would with all their hearts be of that number, as ye would.

Bes. "That stone in the wall hath as great appetite to any bodily comfort of meat, drink, clothes, or such like as I have, for I cannot get the comforts of the Holy Spirit."

When I prayed for that consolation to her, that solid comfort which is stronger nor tentation, tribulation, or death itself, she said, "Why wear ye your prayers on such a vile wretch? God hath counted the number, and gathered them – and I am one moe." [3]

"I will not believe you," said I. "Bessie, albeit you believe the suggestions of Satan in your false heart, it is otherwise in the accompt of God. And I will pray for you, that it may be revealed to you – and pray ye with me."

And after I had prayed, she said, "Sayings will not do it! You do your part, but if God work not, and He give not, I cannot have comfort. Can any have grace till God give it? Can that stone believe? [...] There is no friend to that soul that is under God's seed! I am under God's seed: and my husband, children, nor no other are friends to me. Nay, not myself is a friend to myself! As for my corpse, I care not [if] it were casten up to the Heaven and kept on iron graps, so my soul had peace."

Min. "Bessie, many hath peace with themselves that hath none with God, as secure sinners sleeping in sin, and crying 'peace.' And some hath peace with God that hath none with themselves. And as many have not the grace and faith which they think they have, so some have the grace and faith which they think they have not."

Bes. "I care not [for] my own damnation, if God be glorified. What reck of me if He get His own glory?" [4]

Min. "Bessie, assure yourself these are not the wishes and words of a castaway. An' God's glory be dear to you, you and your salvation are dear to Him." [5]

When I sparred if she took meat to refresh her body, she answered, "No, all craves that, both faithful *and* unfaithful – albeit the unfaithful be *unworthy* of it, for they cannot glorify that God who gives it."

When I desired her to pray, she answered, "I have no warrant, and hath many letts." [6]

"Will you say," said I, "'God, be merciful to me for Jesus' sake'?"

She said, "God be merciful to me for thy *own* sake – for Christ hath not redeemed all."

"Bessie," said I, "ye must seek in the name of Jesus, whom the Father hath sealed, in whom alone He is reconciled with us, and for whose sake He giveth grace and mercy. Lay your compt you will never come to the Father but by him [...] Bessie, do ye not pray when ye are alone?" [7]

She answered, "I will not commend myself."

When one parting with her said, "God be with you, Bessie," she answered, "God forbid He were with you as He is with me! O there is a great change coming, a fearful alteration, a cup of wrath coming! We are conceived and born in sin, and what shall be the end of sin? [...] I know if the Devil were chained there beside me, he cannot without God's permission hurt an hair of mine head; but God being angry with me, He turns him louse and all his instruments against me." [8]

Min. "Bessie, the Lord loosed him upon Job – but so many links only, that he won to his goods, children, body, but not to his life, far less to his soul. The Lord will not give the soul of His turtle to the beast. The good shepherd hath you in His

---

[1] *and it were ... castock*] even if it were only to peel the bark of a cabbage stalk.

[2] *sparred*] made a rhetorical thrust.

[3] *nor tentation*] than temptation; *one moe*] one more; one extra, left behind.

[4] *What reck of*] What consideration should be given to.

[5] *And God's*] If God's.

[6] *letts*] obstacles.

[7] *Lay your compt*] You may wager all that; *you ... him*] John 14:6.

[8] *louse*] loose.

hand, and none shall pluck you out of it, whatever be your fears, doubtings, or apprehensions under your trial and present desertion." [1]

When some standing by spake to her, she says, "Take all that to yourself, that ye say to me. Ye have no borrows, no assurance, more nor I – and knows not but ye may come in the like case!" [2]

[…] I coming to her says, "Bessie, have ye gotten any comfort yet?"

She answered, When God sends it, I will get it."

"But seek ye it not?" said I.

She answereth, "What availeth words when there is nothing within?"

When I was blessing the Lord, she doubled the word, and said, "Blessed be He, blessed be He! O that I could glorify Him! O that I could get grips fastened on Him!" [3]

"I see, Bessie," said I, "albeit you pray not, yet you praise and bless God."

"I cannot," said she, "*bless* Him. He is blessed in Him*self*; and I never heard Him blasphemed, but I was grieved at it. I had rather have heard the evil spirit named ten times nor Him once blasphemed. Fie on them that cannot bless, and yet will blaspheme Him."

When I earnestly prayed for her, she said, "Why take ye pains on such a vile wretched creature?"

"I would, Bessie," said I, "have God glorifying Himself, in saving a lost soul, and magnifying His mercy on you who is miserable."

"Ay," said she, "that is right good! God grant it, God grant it. O, there is little faith in the earth! – and love is grown cold…I had the *will* of prayer, but who hath the *spirit* of prayer? God knows, well is the soul that is in Christ – but they that are founded on that old father Adam, fearful is their estate."

[…] When I was posing her with some questions about her inward estate, she said, "Why examine ye me so sore? Ye use a sharp examination, and yet *ye* will not be my judge."

"Bessie," said I, "I would know your constitution, that I may the better know how to deal with you! I am about to instruct and comfort you, to use the means and beg a blessing from God upon them – and I have seen, when ye were better content, that I conferred with you and prayed for you."

She answered, "It is a token that I get small comfort by them. […] It were," said she, "a great comfort to me if I were persuaded of it; but I cannot be quit of infidelity and despair. Well is the soul that ever it came in the world, that can be freed of unbelief, and gets grace to believe. Lord, banish the Devil, and I shall believe!"

And some gentlemen and others being with me, she directs her speech to them, saying, "Ye gentlemen, and simple, and all, let my casting-back be your forward-coming. Well are ye that can believe and pray, but I have none. I have no wit in the world, either to bless God or benefit myself. Many thousands get grace and faith, and I would as fain have it as any of them." [4]

Min. "Bessie, God measureth His own by their unfeigned desire, and what you would be in an hearty affection, that you are in the accompt of God, and that secret seed of grace – which in this exercise, under the ashes of your corruption, lieth hidden and dead, as it were, like seed in the ground, or hot coals under ashes – shall hereafter in the mercy of God bud and break forth: for it may be discerned already in these divine desires, in your estimation of the blessedness of those that believe and affection to be in that number. […] Bessie, is there any comfort come yet?" [5]

She answereth, "If it were come, it would kith, it would bud forth. Oft and many a time have you said comfort was coming, but I cannot find it. Alas! I am an outlaw to God, I weep in the night when I should sleep, I mourn when others are merry. I am bound when they are free. I have a longsome lair, a fearful and sore lair here. When others go up and down, to and fro, I am a wonder to the world, and I am worthy to be so." [6]

Min. "[…] We have, Bessie, brought you a drink of wine to comfort your spirit."

"Wine!" said she. "The worst water in the well is over-good for me. I will have no wine. Why should I have the benefit when it is neither blessed to me, neither can I bless Him that gives it? I care not for outward bodily comforts, since I cannot get the inward and spiritual."°

Min. "[…] But say, 'Jesus, intercede for me.'"

"I will not blaspheme Him," said she, "nor be a liar. I am a liar great enough already, for to me to speak the words with my mouth without faith in my heart, what is that but to take His name in vain?"

---

[1] *turtle*] turtledove.

[2] *borrows*] guarantees (as for the payment of a debt); *and knows not but*] and ye know not but that.

[3] *grips*] (*alt. form*, gripe) my grip.

[4] *simple*] ordinary (*i.e.*, unpropertied or unlearned); *fain*] gladly, earnestly.

[5] *accompt*] reckoning;   *affection to be*] desire to be.

[6] *kith*] show itself;   *longsome lair*] long-lasting bed or grave.

Min. "Shall I pray for you, Bessie?"

"What good," said she, "can I get by your prayers, except I had a heart to pray for myself? I have many things to seek, if I could get faith to believe, and relief to my spirit, and what matter of saws then? When I see that I saw not, then shall I do that I did not. These three year I had not a faithful desire; indeed, I thought it came all from your own mouth, all the in-lack of my prayers." [1]

Min. "Howso, Bessie? What heard you me say?"

"That prayers availed not," said she.

Min. "I have oft complained of our prayers, as I had just cause, and that God might be angry against them (Psalm 81:9) and might repel them if He dealt in justice with us – but this was not to make us leave off prayers, but to repent and pray more fervently! But the time hath been when you delighted in prayer," said I.

She answered, "I found comfort then in prayer. I had no comfort *but* in prayer. I had many calamities, and whom-to should I seek but to God? And oft went I to Him with a grievèd heart. Had one God, what reck of all the world! What reck who be against them if He be with them? But if a soul be under God's seed, what availeth friends, kin, jewels, and all the world? Oh and alas for ever, that I should want that blessing of His favor, which He bestows on so many! Alas, I have gotten the poor man's answer: *You will not be served.*" [2]

Min. "Take not that answer, Bessie° […] I know God in His own time will give you comfort."

Bessie. "The knowledge is yours," said she, "but the sorrow is mine. Well is the soul that getteth the Holy Spirit, to seek grace and mercy at His hands. Well is the soul that getteth the benefit and the blessing with it – but fie on them that counts° the 'fore' afore the glory, the fore of the earth before the glory of Heaven. It is no *fore* to them but a *fear*ful curse. [3]

"Alas, I have long to live, and a wretched life. I weary up, and I weary down. Sighs help not, sobs help not, groans help not, and prayer is faint. It is a fearful calamity, to have woe here and woe hereafter, to have Hell here and Hell hereafter forever. The matter is the less, they that gets a light life, a lightsome life, that they get woe here

after – and a lightsome life is the faith that many hath – but it is most woeful and doleful, to have woe here, and woe hereafter forever. I will tell you my testament: I have been in Hell these many years, and I look never for another Heaven. O wretch that I am! Alas for ever! There's° a great fly coming, a fearful cup, and I will get my share of it – and it is nothing I feel here, to that that I fear forever." [4]

Min. "Bessie, the Lord corrects you here, that you perish not with the world for ever. He woundeth and He will heal again, albeit you can neither think it nor feel it, nor hope for it. Yet in His name I will assure you in His own time He will ease you and speak peace to you."

"I cannot," said she, "find you a good speyman." [5]

Min. "Yet if ever, Bessie, I spake truth, you *will* find it! I promise you, in the name of the Lord."

She answered, "The Lord's lieutenant will be loath to lie. Well is His lieutenant." [6]

"Whom call you," said I, "his lieutenant?"

"You," said she, "and such as you. Ye are 'tenants – and not masters. […] What reck of words," said she, "since I cannot get mends to my inward parts?" [7]

"I am sure," said I, "if you should go to Hell, Bessie, you would go to Hell with love to God."

She answered, "What reck of my love to Him, since He hath none to me? If He had love to me, all were well." [8]

Min. "But He loves you, Bessie, before you love Him – for your love is the effect of His, and they whom He loveth can never perish."

"His *own*," said she, "shall never perish."

Min. "But you are one of those, Bessie, and hath right to His promise."

She answered, "How shall I believe you who believeth not Him who hath all power and is truth itself? I would fain seek God, but I feel many stops and letts, and my prayers are dung back. If any had had four and twenty hours, yea, a touch of that, under which I have lain these three years, they would think their case fearful, and would give a world (if they had it) for a blink of His reconciled face. But my calamity will make others

---

[1] *saws*] sayings; with ensuing pun on *see* and *saw*, and perhaps also on *sauce* (suggested by the wine); *that … that*] that which … that which.

[2] *Had one God*] If one had God.

[3] *fore*] prelude (*playing on* afore, before, fearful).

[4] *fly*] plague.

[5] *cannot … speyman*] cannot think that you are a skilled fortune-teller.

[6] *lieutenant*] designated representative.

[7] *'tenants*] lieutenants (as *mere* substitutes); with pun on *tenants* as *lessees*; *mends*] a remedy.

[8] *want*] lack.

run and cry for mercy. My grief and displeasure is your joy and gladness." [1]

Min. "How so, Bessie? We take no pleasure in your grief!"

She answered, "The Christian that is sealed, seeing me, will fly to mercy like a bird – but I want wings."

After I had prayed for her, she says, "If God would give me a heart to give you thanks for your good prayer, I would give it; and if I had a motion in the right way of salvation, O as I should run and fly to Him like a bird!"

"God be blessed!" said I. "I see some forerunning tokens of His coming with comfort."

She answered, "They are but sober and small tokens."

"Your words," said I, "smell sometimes of the spirit of grace and faith, and sometimes of the flesh, infidelity, and infirmity – for the prayers of the saints are oft like a fire, which at the first hath smoke and reek, without light or heat, but breaketh out ere all be done in a clear light and comfortable heat, as may be seen in sundry of David's psalms; where he beginneth with heavy plaints, and endeth in heavenly praises and prayers ere all be done."

At another time I sparred if any comfort was yet come. She answered, dolor was come, but no comfort: "You are troubled with me in pulpit, and out of pulpit, and in coming unto me day after day. Will you make you quit of this cumber?" [2]

"Bessie," said I, "I think no cumber of it. It is the duty of my calling, and would God you got comfort by it! But how shall I free myself of it?"

She answered, "Cause – cut me off!" [3]

"And wherefore," said I, "would you have me, or any, taking your blood on us, and sin on our souls?"

"Nay, no sin," said she, "for there is just cause."

"What cause?" said I. "What have you done deserving death?"

"Is not unbelief," said she, "the greatest sin in the world? And I am guilty of it!"

"We have," said I, "no warrant for that. [...] You are a sufferer in this against your will. You are spiritually oppressed, and groans to God under the bondage."

Then she uttereth these words: "O that I could get that fountain of faith – astern of it! O as grace would grow! O for a blessed blink of the favorable face of the Father of the faithful! O to win to that holy fountain! I know He is ready to give, if I were ready to receive and seek. Glory pertaineth to Him, and glorified shall He be."

Min. "I pray you, Bessie, seek on, and glorify Him by encalling on His name. Pray Him in Jesus' name to be merciful to you and help your unbelief."

"I can," said she, "*name* Jesus, but He will not be pleased with words, except I had a warrant of faith in my heart to seek by."

Min. "Yet will you say the words? I think there is none but you, but they will do this much for me."

"Many speaks them," said she, "with little faith. But I dare not, that I draw not down His punishments."

Min.° "[...] But continue, and let me hear you and be a witness to it. Do this for my pleasure."

"It were my *own* pleasure and good," said she, "if I could do it *rightly* – it were my own weal – but God hath a work to work with me, that you never saw the like of it.° O that I could welcome His send, how bitter soever, and reverence the sender! What recks of me, if He get His own glory? But alas, I have many wants, many woes, many wans, wan-grace, wan-chance, no weals. I am sorely shaken. A sore shake of wrath is come on my soul." [4]

Min. "He shakes you, Bessie, to make you sure."

"If it were so," said she, "I would seek to Him."°

"[...] Blessed be God for it!" said I. "Seek on, and I will pledge my soul for yours, that you shall be safe."

"Seek must I," said she, "and seek shall I, though He should ding me back to the bottom of the sea. And charge the whole family that they do the like, as you do me – for come weal, come woe, they will get a share of it."

"I will," said I, "for they have to concur with you."

The next time that I visited her, and demanded how she did, she answered, "The life of the body is not like to go out, and comfort is not like to come into the soul."

"Yet wait, Bessie, in hope, and give not over. It will come."

---

[1] *dung back*] dinged (knocked or thumped) back to me.

[2] *cumber*] encumbrance.

[3] *Cause ... off*] Free yourself of me, with just cause, by killing me.

[4] *his send*] what he sends;   *wans ... weals*] blows or bruises, lack of grace, ill fortune, no blessings;   *sore*] severe;   *shake*] damaging blow (*OED* sb. 6).

"I know," said she, "your tales and tidings, but cannot find them true. Alas that ever I came in the world! I am not booked, I am not baptized, I am not written in the book of life, I am not baptized with the right baptism, I cannot find the fruit of it." [1]

"Bessie," said I, "I am sorry that I find you not as I left you. Continued you not calling on God in Christ's name, as you promised?"

She answered, "I was the *worse* of the words that you caused me to say! I am ever since a thousandfold more troubled than before."

"Bessie, the words have not the wit. It's Satan that rageth before he be cast out. [...] Wherefore hearken not, Bessie, to Satan's suggestions, that your heart be not bound up, that you pray not."

"That is," said she, "a true tale! Satan binds up my heart!"

"But pray," said I, "*against* it. Say the Lord's prayer."

"I can," said she, "say the words, but I have no warrant to pray it. I cannot call Him 'Father.' He is the father of the faithful alone, but that privilege of children is not given me. I cannot find a warrant that I am His. Alas, that ever I was the cursed ground whereon the ill seed was sown. [...] I am not," said she, "worthy that He should give me any grace or mercy. [...] I cannot," said she, "speak the word can please you – no, not them that came out of my bowels. How then can it please the Lord? Mine own mind and Satan lets me not believe, and my unbelief draweth down all the ill of the word. And you book me, and carries my name in many arts, but I cannot mend it." [2]

Min. "Bessie, nothing to your prejudice carry I your name – for why should not the saints know of your estate?"

Bes. "I pray you, tell me," said she, "how the people think of me, whether are they blithe or woe?" [3]

Min. "I will assure you, Bessie, God's people mourns with you, and bears a part of your burthen. As for myself I have five children sick of the fever. God, who knows my heart, is my witness that I would not so fain have them raised up in their bodies, as you comforted in spirit."

Bes. "You know your reward," said she.

Min. "I look not to that. I seek mercy."

Bes. "But," said she, "if I had spiritual grace and could, I would give you a reward. Will ever that day dawn that God will draw me, a wandering sheep, home to Himself?"

Min. "Bessie, in God's mercy I am assured of it."

Bes. "The God," said she, "who made Heaven and earth, who hath all power, grant it in mercy. Well is them forever finds His favor, but woe is them that feels His seed! Had I hope, it would mitigate my sorrow. [...] Happy," said she, "are they who suffer for Christ's sake, for righteousness' sake. They will be comforted, now and then. But they that suffer for sin, without sense of His favor, comfortless is their condition. Will one go through the earth, up and down, to and fro – where will they find a wearied wight, till they come to me? And you that hear me, with the pith of prayer that I can, I ask of God that ye never know the way that I am in. It is lack of faith that is my loss. Want of faith is my wrack. I lie under fearful weights, and wanteth faith to get the remission of them. I am fallen without° a resurrection. My judge is my party: I have no claim to His mercy. I have no ground of faith to fasten grips on Him. I find not a spark of light, and I find no fruit of your prayers, albeit I hear them. No Christian should come near me. [...] Shall I seek hot water under cold ice? I have not come in the precise and blessed hour of grace. I am come behind – and where[fore] will you will me to pray? Wherefore serves the prayer that glorifieth not God?" [4]

Min. "Bessie, it is yet the acceptable time, and He who is found of them that seek Him not will much more reveal Himself to them who seeketh. And as for prayer, by it you greatly glorify God [...] and we have not only His command to pray, but also His promise to be heard."

Bes. "Then all break His command, and chiefly I, and so will be seen on the whole swack." [5]

After this, when I had read some comfortable places to her and prayed for her, she cried out and doubled it oft: "O blessed are they that have that spirit of prayer! O blessed are they!"

---

[1] *booked*] registered; *book of life*] the heavenly register of those who are to be saved (*see* Rev. 20:12-15).

[2] *you book me*] you put my words in your book; *and carries ... arts*] something like, "and you turn me into literature"; *mend it*] remedy my unbelief.

[3] *blithe or woe*] merry or woeful.

---

[4] *wight*] creature, person; *party*] part; *My judge ... party*] My lot is to know God only as judge (?).

[5] *swack*] (= swatch) a "tally" or "tail" fixed to cloth sent to dye, of which the owner kept the other part (but *swack* can also signify a whack or heavy blow).

Rev. Livingston, as Lanark's representative to the provincial assembly, left the village for a trip to Glasgow in April 1625, when word arrived of the death of King James. Bessie was by now a local celebrity, but "greatly extenuate and worn – what by heavy sickness on her body, what by this longsome and fearful exercise in her soul" (41). Prior to his departure, Livingston assured his flock that God's comfort would yet kith and bud forth to Bessie Clarkson. But in the minister's absence, Bessie's condition worsened. A number of the church elders gathered about her bedside, to stand watch over Bessie's soul and to await the promised resolution of her conflict in conscience. They knew what to expect by the famous example of Katherine Stubbs, who from her deathbed had fought a battle of words with the Devil, and won. The "Most Wonderful Conflict" of Katherine Stubbs, recorded by Rev. Philip Stubbs and published in his Crystal Glass for Christian Women (1591) *was known throughout the British Isles. Rev. Stubbs's tract had provided the inspiration and model for Rev. Livingston in recording Bessie's own most amazing conflict.*

When Rev. Livingston returned from Glasgow, he learned that Bessie Clarkson was dead. Sadly, there had been no vocal sparring betwixt the devil and her soul. Her three-and-a-half year struggle with Satan had ended quietly. Livingston set aside his manuscript, deciding that "the words of this dear defunct" should not, after all, be "put out to the view of the world" as he had originally intended (sig. A2).

Five years later, however, someone obtained a copy of Livingston's record of Bessie Clarkson's struggle and published it. Bessie was thus "booked" by an Edinburgh stationer without the minister's consent, from a corrupt copytext in which many of Bessie's speeches were assigned to

Rev. Livingston, and vice versa. This was an unforeseen embarrassment. It was as if the spirit of Bessie had returned to haunt her minister's text. Livingston therefore prepared a corrected version for the stationer, which was published in 1632 as The Conflict in Conscience of a Dear Christian. *Livingston, with an earnest wish "that you who reads it may make a profitable use of it," added a postscript to explain the final circumstances of her end, lest Bessie's silent death be misunderstood as a disappointing denouement (41-2):*

Death on a suddainty dealt with her heart, that her words and speech failed her. But in presence of diverse witness, her hands and eyes were heaved to the heavens. And so, giving that sign of victory, she rendered her spirit. And although it pleased not our gracious God (who in His great wisdom worketh after diverse sorts with His own) to let us hear, out of her own mouth, of the glorious victory and unspeakable joys that He had given her inwardly in her soul, yet I am sure there is none that is illuminate from above and taught to discern spiritually that will any way doubt of her blessed deliverance (albeit no *outward* sign had been seen). Yea, it was a wonderful mercy that God so long, under such horrors, held her own hand out of herself. Which at last with her eyes she lifted up to the heavens, when her speech could not express her inward feeling of an unspeakable joy and victorious faith.

Only herein we have our warning to be wise in time, and to get oil into our lamps and not to please ourselves with tomb lamps and with a bare show of an outward profession, but labor to have a lively and effectual faith in the deep of our souls. For a conceit or opinion will seem sufficient till we be put at, which will not do our turn nor stand us in stead in the fiery trial.

The ruins of St. Kentigern's Church, Lanark, where Bessie Clarkson lost her faith listening to the sermons of Rev. Wm. Livingston

Rose (Locke) Hickman Throckmorton (1526 - 1613) [1]

*I, now being aboue 84 years old and looking continually when the Lord will
call me forth of this lyfe, haue thought good to set down the same in writing
and so leaue it to my children, to moue them to continue y[t] thankfullnes…*

–British Library MS Add. 43827A, f. 6

ROSE LOCKE (as she spelled it) was the twelfth of nineteen children
born to William Lok of London and Wiltshire (Rose was his third
child by his second wife, Katherine Cook). As a prominent member of the
Mercers' Company and a prosperous merchant-adventurer, Lok was often
gone from home, on voyages that were sometimes lengthened by his other
job as a spy for the English government. In 1526 (the year of Rose's
birth), Lok for his service to the State received a profitable license to
import cloth of gold and silver, silks, and jewels, much of which was
earmarked for King Henry and his Court. He exported English beer and
traded in leather goods. His trips to the Mediterranean indicate that he may
have imported wine. Business was good. By the time he died in 1550,
Henry Lok had acquired, besides his London mansion on Bow Lane, two
commercial buildings in Cheapside (one at the sign of the Lock, another at
the Bell, with shops and appurtenances), plus dozens of rental units.

Writing many years later, Rose's youngest brother Michael remembers the thrill of growing up as the
son of an English merchant, at the dawn of a new age of global exploration and international commerce:

My late father, Sir William Lok, Knight, alderman of London, kept me at schools of grammar in
England until I was eight years old (which was A.D. 1545). And he being sworn servant to King
Henry the Eighth, and his mercer, and also his agent beyond the seas in divers affairs, he then sent me
overseas to Flanders and France, to learn those languages and to know the world. Since which time I
have continued these thirty-two years in travail of body (and study of mind), following my vocation in
the trade of merchandise [...] through almost all the countries of Christianity.° [2]

Formal education, and travel, and adventure, were for boys. With her brothers at boarding school and her
father often in Flanders or at sea, Rose grew up in a mostly female household on Bow Lane, summering
in Wiltshire. Her mother (a Protestant no less devout than Lok's first wife, Alice) read to Rose and her
sisters from the vernacular Bible, and from Reformist literature that William smuggled into England.
(This was at a time when Henry VIII still subscribed to Roman Catholic doctrine in all matters save
supremacy of the Pope, and divorce.)

Rose was just seven years old when her father had a moment of glory that is still celebrated by many
of his descendants: in 1533 at Dunkirk, William Lok boldly pulled down the papal bull excommunicating
Henry VIII for his marriage to Anne Boleyn. For this daring act Lok was appointed a gentleman usher of
the Chamber, with an annuity of £110 per annum; and he received honorable mention in Holinshed's
Chronicles of England.

When Lok returned from the great Mart at Antwerp in September 1537, finding the plague hot in
London and his wife pregnant, he removed his family to Martin Abbey in Surrey, to keep them safe. By
this time, five of his sons by Alice were dead, plus two sons and two daughters by his second marriage.
But Katherine while in childbed contracted the plague at the abbey, and died there on 14 October. Rose
was then eleven years old.

---

[1] *Note*] For many biographical details many biographical details of Rose Hickman and her circle, the editors of
Women's Works are indebted to Maria Dowling and Joy Shakespeare (1982).

[2] *travail*] 1. labor; 2. travel.

William Lok remarried in 1540, to Eleanor Marsh. In November 1543 Rose married as well, to Anthony Hickman, the business partner of her eldest brother, Thomas. She was 17, he was 33. Anthony had houses in London and Essex, his own trading vessel, and a shared horror of Roman Catholicism. The marriage would last thirty years and produce eight children.

Lok's third wife died the same year in which John Lascelles and Anne Askew were burned at the stake as Protestant heretics. But on 28 January 1547/8 – by auspicious coincidence, the same day on which Henry VIII died – Lok remarried. His fourth and last wife was Elizabeth Meredith.

Better times lay ahead, briefly. On 3 March 1548/9, Lok was created Sheriff of London and knighted by Edward VI. He expanded his political influence, his trading fleet, and his wealth. So too did Thomas Lok and Anthony Hickman. In Rose's words, "It pleased God to bless and prosper well their adventures."

Edmund Lok (the sixth son by Alice Spencer), is said to have "died for the love of Sir Brian Tuck's daughter" in 1545. Sir William Lok dying in 1550, he split his extensive real estate holdings between his five surviving sons (Thomas and Matthew; John, Henry, and Michael), reserving an annuity for his widow, and a dowry for Elizabeth, the youngest. He makes no mention in his will of Rose, his other surviving daughter, perhaps because he considered the marriage of daughters a final transaction between men, with no strings attached. But the Hickmans were doing well enough financially without a bequest from Sir William. If Rose resented her father's will, she makes no mention of it.

In the first year of Mary's reign, Thomas Lok and Anthony Hickman were arrested and charged with heresy: the Hickmans' London residence had been identified as a gathering place for Reformists, and the Lok-Hickman trading concern as a source for the smuggling and distribution of Protestant literature. For several months Lok and Hickman remained incarcerated in the Fleet, in separate cells, unsure whether they would be burned at the stake. Dutch traders appealed to England for their release, and a sympathetic bishop of Winchester put in a good word for them. When Rose greased the wheels of justice with bribes of sugar and velvet to William Cecil, Lord High Treasurer, the two men were finally set free. But the terror of those days confirmed Rose's belief that papists were cruel, and the Pope, evil.

Liberated from prison, Anthony and Thomas organized a new sea venture. On 11 October 1554, they sailed for West Africa with three trading vessels, the *Eremite,* the *Bartholomew,* and the *John Evangelist.* One of the three ships was piloted by John Lok. Anchoring off the Guinea coast on 26 January and staying until 22 April 1555, the Hickman-Lok expedition returned to England laden with more than four hundred pounds of 22-carat gold, thirty-six butts of African grains, about 250 elephant tusks, and the complete skull of an elephant, which had not been seen before in England. John Lok returned with five African slaves he obtained in Guinea, the first purchase in a history of shame. [1]

Between her husband's release from prison and his departure for Guinea, Rose became pregnant. While he was away, she retired with the children to a country home in Oxfordshire. By the time he returned, she had given birth. But the persecution of Protestants had since escalated. Hickman therefore crossed the Channel, rented a house in Antwerp, and sent for his family. Rose invited her unmarried younger sister, Elizabeth, to come along; also, her sister-in-law (Mary, Thomas's wife) and children. When Mary Lok could not be persuaded, Rose and Elizabeth left without her. Shortly after, Thomas Lok and all but one of his eight children died, which Rose took as a sign of God's judgment on Mary Lok, who preferred worldly goods to religious freedom.

Antwerp was then one of the wealthiest cities in Europe, a major port, and a haven for political refugees. Safe and happy in an émigré community of English Protestants, the Hickmans remained there until the death of Mary. On the accession of Elizabeth I, the family returned to England, and prospered.

Following Anthony's death in 1573, Rose married Simon Throckmorton, who died on 1585; after which, she remained a widow. But as the last survivor of William Lok's nineteen children, she sat down in 1610, at age 84, to write her favorite stories. Rose's last tale is of her son William, an adventurer like his father and brothers, who traveled to Russia, to the court of Ivan the Terrible.

On 21 November 1613 – with "Certain Old Stories" now recorded for posterity – Rose Locke Hickman, aged 86, at last hoisted anchor, and set sail to meet her Maker.

---

[1] *John Lok*] Rose's next younger sibling. Hakluyt (*Voyages,* 1598-1600), excerpts Lok's journals of the trips to Jerusalem and Guinea. Of Rose's five brothers who outlived their father, Matthew died in 1552, Thomas in 1556 (step-brothers). John died in France, shortly after his African voyage. Michael became famous as a trader and traveler. He invested heavily in Martin Frobisher's first voyage to the Northwest, the first of many bad investments that broke him. Brother Henry (married to the translator Anne Prowse Lok) also joined the Mercer's Company, and failed: he drops from view in 1608, when he was imprisoned for the second time as an insolvent debtor. Elizabeth married twice, first to a mercer, secondly to a bishop, and died in 1581, the mother of fifteen children.

The two extant manuscripts of *Certain Old Stories* have been transcribed and collated, and are here presented in a modern-spelling text, by Tobian Banton.

Certain Old Stories recorded by an aged Gentlewoman

To be perused by her children and posterity,
Written by her with her hand in the 85th year of her age
and about the year *anno domini* 1610

By Rose Throckmorton

Of My Father

IN HOLINSHED's *Chronicle* I find this story: "In the 25th year of King Henry the Eighth, being the year of our Lord 1534, at the suit of the lady Catherine, dowager, a curse was sent from the Pope which cursed both the King and the realm. This curse was set up in the town of Dunkirk in Flanders (for the bringer thereof durst not nearer approach), where it was taken down by William Locke of London, mercer."

Now I, his daughter, Rose Throckmorton (widow, late wife, of Simon Throckmorton esq., and first the wife of Anthony Hickman, a merchant of London), reading this of my father, have thought good to leave to my children this addition to it: that for that act the King gave him £100 a year and made him a gentleman of his Privy Chamber, and he was the King's mercer, and his Majesty vouchsafed to dine at his house. Moreover, he was knighted, although he was never mayor, but only sheriff, of London (and so was never any Londoner before him).[1]

I remember I have heard my father say that when he was a young merchant and used to go beyond sea, Queen Anne Boleyn (that was mother to our late Queen Elizabeth) caused him to get her the gospels and epistles written in parchment, in French, together with the psalms.

"At the suit of the Lady Catherine [of Aragon], dowager, a curse was sent from the Pope, which accursed both the king and the realm. This curse was set up in the town of Dunkirk in Flanders (for the bringer thereof durst no nearer approach); where it was taken down by one William Lock, a mercer of London. Because it was known that the lady Catherine dowager had procured this curse of the Pope, all the order of her court was broken; for the duke of Suffolk being sent to her (as then lying at Bugden beside Huntingdon), according to that he had in commandment, discharged a great sort of her household servants; and yet left a convenient number to serve her like a princess, which were sworn to serve her not as queen, but as "princess dowager." Such as took that oath she utterly refused, and would none of their service, so that she remained with the less number of servants about her" (Raphael Holinshed, *Chronicles of England, Scotland, and Ireland*, vol. 1 (1577): 1561; normalized text ed. DWF)

The anecdote noted by Rose is not her father's only mention in Holinshed's *Chronicles*. William Locke, sheriff of London, was present at the arrest of Edward Seymour (duke of Somerset, Lord Protector during the minority of Edward VI). Having ruled as virtual dictator, Somerset alienated the ruling elite and much of the commons. His sudden fall in October 1549 – made possible by an alliance between Somerset's enemies on the Council with the aldermen of London – came as a mighty thunderclap. On 11 October, "the Lords of the Council came to Windsor to the King, and the next day they brought from thence the Lord Protector, and the other that were there stayed, and conveyed them through the city of London (with as much wonderment as might be!) unto the Tower, where they remained prisoners. Touching the manner of the duke's coming to the Tower from Windsor, I find that it was on the fourteenth of October in the afternoon, at which time he was brought on horseback through Holborn, in at Newgate, and so to the Tower of London; accompanied with diverse lords and gentlemen, with three hundred horse: the Lord Mayor; Sir Rafe Warren [mayor, 1536, 1544]; Sir John Gresham, Master Recorder [mayor 1547]; Sir William Locke [sheriff, 1549], and both the sheriffs [the other being Sir John Alife]; and other knights, sitting on their horses against Soper Lane; with all the officers, with halberds; and from Holborn Bridge to the Tower, certain aldermen or their deputies on horseback in every street, with a number of householders standing with bills [pikes] as he passed. Shortly after, the lords resorted to the Tower; and there, charged the Protector with sundry articles...."

(R. Holinshed, *Chronicles of England, Scotland, and Ireland*, vol. 3 (1586), p. 1059; normalized text ed. DWF)

---

[1] *sheriff*] William Locke, sheriff of London in 1549 (*temp.* Edward VI), was grandson of John Lock, sheriff of London in 1462 (*temp.* Edward IV).

Of My Mother

MY MOTHER in the days of King Henry the Eighth came to some light of the Gospel by means of some English books sent privately to her by my father's factor from beyond sea. Whereupon she used to call me with my two sisters into her chamber to read to us out of the same good books – very privately, for fear of trouble because those good books were then accepted "heretical." And a merchant named Pakington who used to bring English Bibles from beyond sea was slain with a gun, as he went in the street. Therefore my mother charged us to say nothing of her reading to us, for fear of trouble. [1]

Then there was a plague in London, and my father and mother removed seven miles off, into the country where she was delivered of a child, fell sick, and died. In time of her sickness she fell asleep; and being awaked she smiled, saying that she saw God the Father and Christ at His right hand, stretching forth His hands to receive her – and so died comfortably in the faith.

(Actual size)
Courtesy of the Pierpont Library and Museum

Anne Boleyn's psalter, in the French translation of Lefèvre d'Étaples, is a parchment volume produced in Rouen, France, c. 1529, and bound in white satin, in London, c. 1530, embroidered in white silks. On the front cover is an image of the pelican feeding her young from her own bleeding breast ("The Pelican in her Piety"); with flowers on the rear. Illuminated by the Master of the Ango Hours, the volume was a special order for Anne Boleyn when she was still a maid of honor to Catherine of Aragon. The shield shown here (verso) is the Rochford badge of the black lion, the symbol of Queen Anne's father, Thomas Boleyn (1477-1539), first Earl of Wiltshire.

Other volumes have survived that once belonged to Anne Boleyn, including two hand-illuminated Books of Hours. From the 13th century through the Reformation, it was de rigueur for wealthy and educated ladies to own a personal prayer book, containing (typically) meditations, a calendar of church festivals, psalms, favorite saints, and services for the dead. A volume of this sort was called a "Book of Hours," from the short services to the Virgin Mary that were read at eight fixed hours during the day. In the collection at Hever Castle is a Book of Hours produced at Bruges c. 1450, a half-century before her birth, but bearing her poignant century inscription, "La temps viendra, Je Anne Boleyn" (The time will come. I, Anne Boleyn).

---

[1] *factor*] agent.

How my husband and I spent our time in the reign of Queen Mary

AS IN TOKEN of my most bounden duty and thankfulness to the Almighty, I do use often in the daytime but especially in the night, as I lie waking in my bed, to meditate on His most merciful deliverances which He hath given to my good husband Master Anthony Hickman and me in the days of Queen Mary when the cruel papists persecuted the people of God. So I, now being above 84 years old and looking continually when the Lord will call me forth of this life, have thought good to set down the same in writing and so leave it to my children, to move them to continue that thankfulness to almighty God which I, their old mother, cannot acknowledge too much nor too often, to His glory and praise, and to stand fast in that faith and service of God, unto which their father and mother did stand so firmly, and manifest such zeal and affection as in this little treatise appeareth.

My husband before he did marry me was found to be worth £1000 by his books of accompt that were examined by my father's appointment and he being a great dealer in the trade of a merchant venturer was in the same joint-partner with my eldest brother, and they together had some ships of their own and did make divers voyages into far countries, some of which voyages were of such note and fame as they are specially recorded by Mr. Richard Hakluyt in his second printed volume of English voyages, to the south and southeast parts of the world. And I do well remember one goodly ship they builded at their own charges, which they named the Mary Rose, being the names of us their wives, for my brother's wife's name was Mary, and mine, Rose. This ship Queen Elizabeth afterwards had and went in Calais voyage 1596.

It pleased God to bless and prosper well their adventures and though thereby their riches did increase yet they did not set their hearts upon them. They had learned not to trust in uncertain riches but in the living Lord who giveth abundantly all things to be enjoyed for they were not unmindful to use and employ their substance to the glory of God and good of His Church; as they daily manifested by giving entertainment to Bishop Hooper, Master Foxe, Master Knox, and divers other godly preachers of which some did aft'wards suffer martyrdom in Queen Mary's days; who if they were living on earth as undoubtedly they are in Heaven, would not forget to declare what kind usage and bounty they have found at the hands of my good husband for the Gospel of Christ's sake.

When Queen Mary came to the crown, the idolatrous mass was set up, with public profession of popery throughout this realm, and cruel persecution of those good Christians that in a good conscience refused to yield themselves to that idolatry. At which time we did receive into our house in the city of London divers godly and well-disposed Christians that were desirous to shelter themselves from the cruel persecution of those times. And we and they did table together in a chamber, keeping the doors close-shut for fear of the promoters, as we read in Gospel the disciples of Christ did, for fear of the Jews. And

---

An exporter of cloth, Robert Pakington (c. 1489-1536) was a prominent member of the Mercers Company of London. From 1523 he represented his colleagues as a lobbyist to Parliament. He was himself elected to Parliament in 1533, again in 1536. Stridently anti-clerical, the Mercers objected to the Bishops' peremptory fines for such offenses as cursing, and for heavy taxation on such necessaries as the probating of testaments. An outspoken advocate of the Reform movement, Pakington when elected to Parliament "talked somewhat against the covetousness and cruelties of the clergy" (Edward Hall, *Union of the Two Noble and Illustre Famelies*, ff. 231v–232r). Favored by Thomas Cromwell, the bishops saw Pakington as a dangerous enemy.

On 13 November 1536, Pakington rose early to attend morning Mass at the Mercers Chapel of St. Thomas of Acre. While crossing Cheapside, he was gunned down in the street – a rare event in an era when premeditated murders, though frequent, were generally conducted behind closed doors. The shooter vanished. Pakington's supporters demanded a rigorous investigation that never materialized. His death was not greatly lamented by the higher powers: Pakington's zeal for reform had raised the ire of both king and clergy. It was widely believed in London that the murder was a contract hit, arranged by the bishops. Holinshed (1570) reports that the assassin was a felon hanged at Banbury for another offense, who confessed on the gallows to the Pakington murder, though previously he "was never had in anie suspicion thereof" (Holinshed, 1570, p.). According to John Foxe (*Actes and Monuments of the Christian Church*, ed. 1563), the Dean of St. Paul's Cathedral, John Incent, arranged the shooting, finally repenting of the contract to his confessor, from his deathbed in 1545.

On Queen Mary's accession, the High Commissioners cynically charged Rev. Robert Singleton with supposed offenses against the Crown and Church, and included among the allegations that Singleton was guilty of Pakington's death. No one supposed that the accused – a Cromwell protégé, former Chaplain to Anne Boleyn, and a leading Protestant – had anything to do with the Pakington murder; but Singleton on 7 March 1544 was executed for treason, at Tyburn.

thus we kept our house in London in the beginning of Queen Mary's days. But then there came forth a very strict proclamation, enjoining all to come to church and receive the sacrament after the popish fashion. After which proclamation we durst no longer keep our house, but my husband used means to convey away the preachers and other good Christians that were in our house, beyond sea, giving them money to supply their wants.

And one of those men was named Reniger being then a proper young gentleman that went to Louvaine to study divinity and afterwards became doctor of divinity and died some few years since, being one of the masters of the close at Lincoln. This man had £5 in gold of my husband at his going away which at his return he thankfully repaid; and whilst he lived he was ready to acknowledge the kindness that he received from my husband. [1]

Then my good husband was accused to the High Commissioners for the conveying away and relieving those good Christians whom the High Commissioners called "the Queen's enemies," and for not conforming himself to popery according to the Queen's Injunctions. And for the same, my husband and my brother (who was also accused with him) were committed to close prison in the Fleet. And during the time of their imprisonment they could not be suffered to have any private conference together, neither could any other be suffered to have any conference with either of them. But they were kept in several rooms in the prison, and were often severally examined, and when either of them was examined the commissioners would endeavor to make him believe that the other had confessed as much as they would have drawn from him, and thereupon they would advise him to confess as his brother had done before him. But nevertheless there was not much gotten forth of their own confessions by that means, although indeed there was a collection of 40 marks a week duly collected and exhibited by my husband and brother with some other well-disposed merchants to the relief of the distressed ministry, about which my husband and brother were sore charged in their examinations.

The original *Mary Rose*, flagship of King Henry's navy, was the most famous vessel of the Tudor period. Built in 1509-11, during the first year of Henry's reign, the warship was named after Mary Tudor, sister to the king, and the Tudor rose, his emblem. In 1545, the England and French navies fought the Battle of Solent, during which the Mary Rose, overloaded with a crew of 700, capsized and sank, killing all but 35 of her crew. On October 11, 1982, with funds from the Mary Rose Trust, the wreck was lifted from the sea and may be visited today at the Portsmouth Historic Dockyard.

Anthony Hickman's *Mary Rose* may be the ship of this name built in 1555-56, a galleon later refitted for the English navy, and condemned in 1618, with its timbers recycled as a wharf for the Chatham dockyard.

---

[1] *Reniger*] Michael Reniger (1530-1609), refuge in Zurich during Mary's reign, chancellor of Lincoln 1566.

And at the same time there was also in the Fleet the jury that acquitted Sir Nicholas Throckmorton upon his arraignment of high treason, who because they chose rather to discharge their consciences by finding him not guilty (than to please the commissioners and judges that sat upon his trial by finding him guilty, contrary to their consciences) were committed to the Fleet, but so as they had the liberty of the prison. And these jurymen (being all merchants of London) had compassion upon the distress of my husband and brother: for these jurymen having the liberty that was wanting to my husband and brother in the prison, would come under the chamber window where my brother was, and under the chamber window where my husband was, and talk aloud one to another to th' end that my husband and brother might hear them, what they heard touching any of the matters for which my husband and brother were questioned; and so by that means gave them light of many things before their examinations. [1]

Nicholas Throckmorton

Afterwards by great means that was made for them, they were removed from the Fleet to the house of the marquess of Winchester, who then was Lord Treasurer but were also kept there in several rooms as close prisoners not being suffered to come together but by stealth, when the marquess was at dinner or gone abroad – then they procured to themselves liberty to come together, by giving gratuities to the gentlemen that attended about the house.

And whilst they were thus detained prisoners, there came to the court the lord of Barrow in the Low Countries, who became a great suitor for their enlargements in regard of the want that his country had of their trading and merchandise. And partly by his means, and partly by the Lord Treasurer's favor (which we purchased with chests of sugar and pieces of velvet to the value of £200 or thereabouts) they were (after long imprisonment) set at liberty.

Afterwards my husband (to drive away the wicked days) went to Antwerp, where he had a fair house which he rented for £40 a year; and I being with child went into Oxfordshire to a gentleman's house that was a lodge and stood far off from any church or town (the name thereof was Chilswell); and there I was delivered. And from thence I sent to Oxford to the bishops (who were then and there in prison and did afterwards suffer martyrdom there), to be advised by them whether I might suffer my child to be baptized after the popish manner; who answered me that the sacrament of *baptism* as it was used by the papists, was the least corrupted, and therefore I might. But therewithal they said that I might have been gone out of England before that time, if I had done well; and so my child was there baptized by a popish priest. But because I would avoid the popish stuff as much as I could, I did not put salt into the handkerchief that was to be delivered to the priest at the baptism, but put sugar in it instead of salt. Afterwards I prepared to go to Antwerp, to my husband's house there, and although my husband had two fair houses in England, the one in London, the other in Essex at Romford, both of them well furnished with household stuff, yet I accounted all nothing in comparison to liberty of conscience for the profession of Christ.

So I conveyed my household stuff into certain friends' houses carrying none with me but a large featherbed which I laid in the bottom of the old hulk wherein we went to Antwerp. (I may well call it an "old hulk," for the master of it said that if it pleased God to speed us well in that voyage, it should never go to sea again.) We were five days and nights upon the seas in stormy and tempestuous weather.

I might here tell that my brother Thomas Locke (who was partner with my husband) would have gone with us, but that he could not get his wife's goodwill to go out of England; whereupon I would say to her: "Sister, you stay here for covetousness and love of your husband's lands and goods. But I fear the Lord's hand will be upon you for it." And indeed so it came to pass: for he being constrained for fear of further trouble to fashion himself outwardly to the popish religion in some sort, was so grieved in mind thereat, that he died shortly after, with seven of his children. [2]

---

[1] *jurymen*] The jurymen in prison with Simon Throckmorton and his brother were there because they had found Nicholas Throckmorton and James Crofts innocent of treason; whereupon the defendants and jury were all confined to punishment, Throckmorton and Crofts (for more than a year) and released after paying heavy fines; the jury for having disappointed the government's expectation of a guilty verdict.

[2] *shortly after*] will proved 11 Dec. 1556; children: William, Rowland, Thomas, Matthew; John and Mary, deceased, and one child not yet born at the time of his death. By 1560, Thomas and all but one child were dead.

The reason why we did think ourselves safer in Antwerp than in England was not for any more liberty of the Gospel given there, but because there were not parish churches but only [a] cathedral; wherein, though the popish service was used, yet it could not be easily known who came to church and who not. But there was a chapel for the English merchants and thereunto all of them were compellable to go upon solemn feast days to wait upon their governor. And the night before that day my good husband would lie mourning in his bed and could not sleep for grief to think he was on the morrow to go with the governor to that idolatrous service. But the governor though he was a papist yet he was no persecutor nor cruel papist, for he was contented to bear with my husband so far as he might without being seen to do it, and would say to him that though he did bark yet he did not bite.

Whiles I was in Antwerp I had another child and had great care to keep it from the baptism of the papists; for in hatred that the inhabitants there do bear to the Anabaptists, the magistrates used to enter at midnight into houses where any children were suspected to be kept unbaptized; and if he found any such, he used to put them in a sack and cast them into the water and so drown them. From which cruelty, to save my child, I did as followeth: *viz.*, whereas it is the custom there to hang at the street's door where a woman lyeth in, a little piece of lawn, it was so that our house opened into two streets; therefore I hanged forth a piece of lawn upon either side our door, to the end that the neighbors on either side might suppose that it went out at the *other* door to be baptized. And it so pleased God that there was a secret congregation of Protestants, unto which congregation by the help of some godly women there I procured my child to be secretly carried, and there to be baptized by a Protestant minister, I not knowing godfather nor godmother.

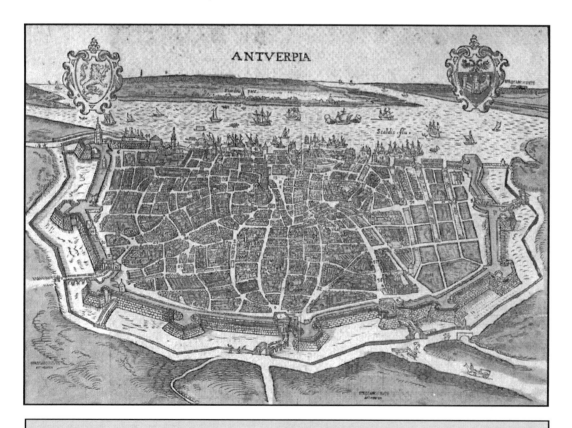

ANTVERPIA

At its height in the Sixteen Century – the city's "Golden Age" – Antwerp accounted for nearly 40% of world trade. Tolerant of religious and cultural diversity, the city flourished as a center of banking, industry, book-publishing, and the arts. Religious riots in 1566, and the Dutch war of independence against King Philip of Spain (1572 ff.) brought about Antwerp's decline.

And thus I continued in Antwerp till the death of Queen Mary, which was not a little joyful to me to hear of; for during the time of her tyrannous reign I had often prayed earnestly to God to take either her or me forth of the world. In all which time I never was present at any of the popish masses, or any other of their idolatrous service. [For in all her time we were not only afflicted for our consciences, but also greatly hindered in our traffics and trading, by the grievous oppressions done unto us by such as were in authority under her. For when our ships were laden and victualled and ready to set forward upon a great voyage, we were compelled to unlade and our ships were taken to serve the Queen in her wars. But by the coming of Queen Elizabeth we were restored to that happiness which we had formerly enjoyed in King Edward's days.] [1]

For all which blessings and deliverances sent to me from my good God I most humbly beseech his Majesty that I and mine may never forget to be thankful, not seeking our own vainglory thereby, but giving all praise and glory to His goodness who so graciously preserved, blessed, and delivered me.

Deliverances sent to Sir William Hickman from his childhood observed by the said old gentlewoman, his mother

FIRST, he being child of five or six years, went to bed in the sight of me his mother and of others then about him, in perfect health; and when I awaked forth of my first sleep I heard him groaning pitifully; and laying my hand on his mouth I perceived that his teeth were set in his head so fast together that my husband could not open them to pour in some *rosa solis* into his mouth before he broke two of them out; and his body so wrought that two of our men could not hold it still, neither yet could we then perceive but that he waxed worse and worse. Whereupon some of our good friends and neighbors, being called up to come to our house, we fell to prayer together for him – thinking that he had here but a short time to live, for we could not perceive him alive but only by a little easy drawing of his breath, which we could scarce feel. So my husband cast his napkin on his face. And no means serving, we desired the will of the Lord to be done. Then he fell asleep for two or three hours. Afterwards he awaked, looked up and saw nothing. So then we gave him drink and he slept again and recovered. We then imagined that the meat which he did eat at supper before, caused that working of his stomach when he could not cast it up nor avoid it. And thus in mercy God delivered him.

Afterwards, about twelve years old, he fell into the water and was in great danger of drowning. But by his catching some hold on the land, he escaped.

Afterwards, being with some of his fellow scholars, he fell down from a housetop, to which he being over-venturous had climbed up. Yet he was not slain by the fall.

Afterwards, being about eighteen or nineteen years old, one Mr. Randall (a good friend of his father's) was to go as Lord Ambassador from our late Queen Elizabeth to the Emperor of Russice. With whom my husband sent him to wait upon his lordship into that country that thereby he might see some fashions in the world. Thus by the way going in boats in a river in that country, they happened to land some of them for their pleasure to walk on foot a while. And it so fell out that they all returned to their boats saving only my son who (upon some occasion) was left alone behind the rest of the gentlemen on the land. So not missing him, they set forward. And after some time passed in sailing it came into my Lord Ambassador's mind to ask for Hickman; to whom answer was made that he was in some of the boats by. And so he made no more inquiry for that time. But going on and it drawing near night, my lord (having some special care of him as of the son of his loving friend) inquired again, and commanded to make search where Hickman was; and not finding him, he caused a trumpet to be sounded for him and a light beacon to be set up (as the manner is, in such cases); if peradventure by that means he might either hear or see them and so come to them. [2]

---

[1] *For…days*] This passage, omitted from our copytext, is supplied by the C text; we are grateful for to Maria Dowling and Joy Shakespeare, both for noting the variant, and for their accurate transcription, from which this paragraph has been edited.

[2] *Mr. Randall*] Sir Thomas Randolph (a.k.a. Randall, 1523-1590), Elizabeth's diplomatic agent to Russia and Scotland; *Russice*] Russia.

Now all this while, he was traveling by land after them, all along the seacoast; and had gone on foot about fifteen miles in the desert, not meeting any but an old man by the way, with whom he could have no society of speech (neither of them understanding of other), Yet he made use of this stranger by making signs to him to conduct him. And so by the direction and guidance of this strange man, he passed on, being now and then in great difficulty to get over creeks that came in his way; yet prayed God to deliver him and it pleased His goodness so to do. Thus at length, before night, he came within sight of the boats and was received into one of them and so escaped danger we know not how great. For if he had lyen all night in the wilderness, it was as likely that he should have been devoured of some wild beast (whereof that country yieldeth plenty), as otherwise that he should escape their teeth. Thus God saved him and brought him to the company where he would be.

And now drawing towards Moscow (the chief city of Muscovy and seat of the Emperor), they were to leave the water and travel by land (for want of water to carry their vessels). Thus then there were hired for them [in°] that country mares whose trotting was so hard with shaking that all saving only my son had blood shaked out of the ends of their vents and avoided it – some at the nose, some at the ears, and a third sort at the fundament. [1]

So my Lord Ambassador returned, and being come home would say to my husband, "Mr. Hickman, you have a son that you may send to what country you will. He will endure all hardness! We were thus-and-thus handled by riding on the hard-trotting mares of the country. Only he endures them without any harm."

finis

• • •

In 1637, twenty-four years after the author's death, a grateful relative or descendent of Rose Locke Hickman appended to her "Certain Old Stories" an anonymous "Epitaph upon the Death of this Old Gentlewoman":

> GOD gave unto this matron in her days,
> As pledges firm of His affliction* dear,   * *affection* is evidently intended
> Such happy blessings as the psalmist says
> They shall receive, as serve the Lord in fear. [...]
> Now, having fought a good and Christian fight
> Against the spiritual common enemy,
> And exercised herself both day and night
> In oracles divine continually,
> And kept the sacred faith with constancy,
> Even in the midst of persecution's rage,
> Expressed by worthy works of piety
> From time to time, as well in youth as age,
>   She finished her course and doth possess,
>   In heavenly bliss, the crown of righteousness.   T.B.

Sir Thomas Randolph, young William Hickman, and their colleagues landed on the White Sea coast on 23 July 1568; traveled southeast on the Mezen River, and completed their journey by land, finally arriving in Moscow on 15 October—whereupon the English embassage was obliged to wait another four months before receiving an audience with Ivan IV, Czar of Muscovy. Elizabeth desired increased trade. Ivan the Terrible wished a promise of asylum in England, if a coup was threatened (which Elizabeth was willing to consider); and a joint military invasion of Poland (no chance). The cost of the mission (£1,527) was underwritten by English merchants. Randolph returned in 1569 with a satisfactory grant, which led to the formation of the Muscovy Company. Ivan, however, was disappointed, complaining that the English ambassador's "talke was of bowrishnes and affaires of marchaunts... [O]f our princelie affaires, he made them of none effect" (G. Tolstoy, *The first forty years of the intercourse between England and Russia, 1553–1593* [1875], pp. 110, 114).

Ivan the Terrible

---

[1] *avoided*] voided, discharged blood.

Dorothy (Kempe) Leigh (1561-1613)

> *Can a Mother forget the child of her wombe? [...] Is it possible that shee which hath carried her child within her, so neere her hart, and brought it forth into this world with so much bitter paine, so many grones and cries, can forget it? [...] will shee not blesse it euery time it suckes on her brests, when shee feeleth the bloud come from her heart to nourish it? Will shee not instruct it in the youth, and admonish it in the age, and pray for it continually? [...] Therefore let no man blame a mother, though she something exceede in writing to her children, since euery man knowes that the loue of a mother to her children is hardly contained within the bounds of reason. Neither must you, my sonnes, when you come to bee of iudgement, blame me for writing to you, since Nature telleth me, that I cannot long bee here to speake vnto you, and this my mind will continue long after mee, in writing...*
> —*The Mothers Blessing* (1616), pp.11-12

DOROTHY LEIGH was the wife (and, by 1616, the widow) of Ralph Leigh, a Cheshire gentleman who served under Robert Devereux, earl of Essex, in the Cadiz expedition; about whom, almost nothing else is known. The Leighs had three sons, at least one of whom (George) fulfilled his mother's dream by becoming a Christian minister.

Dorothy Leigh's *Blessing* was written long before her book came to the press. She first undertook the project intending it for no other audience than her own young children. By the time her work was finished, she envisioned a national readership. Fearing her ambition would be censured even by other women ("who, I fear, will blush at my boldness"), Leigh defends her work as a duty promised to her deceased husband. In seeking approval for her work, she therefore aims high, dedicating her completed manuscript – as a scribal copy, in advance of publication – to Princess Elizabeth, the daughter of King James and Queen Anna. Leigh does not expressly seek a gratuity for the gift of *The Mother's Blessing*: she requests only that the princess might permit her "name to be seen in it," when published – a request that was evidently granted; without which *nihil obstat*, the book might never have been printed.

Leigh's original presentation copy must have been completed shortly before or after Elizabeth's marriage, on 14 February 1612/13, to Frederick, elector palatine of the Rhine. On 26 April 1613, Elizabeth and her husband left England for the continent – by which time, it may be presumed, Leigh had received the blessing of Britain's princess. But printed publication of *The Mother's Blessing* was delayed – being interrupted, in part, by the death of Ralph Leigh. (He may be one of the two Ralph Leighs who were buried at Grappenhall, Cheshire, in 1614-15, one on 14 August 1614, the other on 11 July 1615).

By the time Dorothy wrote a second letter of dedication for *A Mothers Blessing* – this one for the print edition, addressed to her three sons – she was recently widowed, and ill. She lamented her "going out of the world," just as her fatherless sons were "coming in" (not as newborns, but as adolescents on the threshold of adult responsibility). Leigh never saw her book in print: she died before *The Mother's Blessing* reached the press. The book may have been ushered into print by one of her sons, which is clearly what Leigh desired.

Entered into the Stationers' Register on 26 February 1615/16 and printed shortly after, *The Mothers Blessing* became a best-seller. Reprinted more than twenty times in the seventeenth century, Leigh's book was still well regarded in 1665, when Anne Clifford, countess of Pembroke, Dorset, and Montgomery, gave copies of *The Mother's Blessing* to the boys in her household (probably the 1563 edition). Additional reprints appeared in 1667, 1674, 1685, 1718, and 1729.

The extracts here reprinted in a modern-spelling text are not representative of the whole. Well over half of the text is devoted to advice about prayer. Selections from the original duodecimo of 270 pages has been guided by those topics that may be of greatest interest to modern readers, and to students of 17th century British culture. Dorothy Leigh would doubtless find the selection unsatisfactory – but she would not be displeased to know that readers, male and female, young and old, would still be receiving her *Blessing* four centuries after her death.

DWF

The Mother's Blessing

Or, The Godly Counsel of a Gentlewoman, not long since deceased, left behind her for her children

(containing many good exhortations and godly admonitions, profitable for all parents to leave as a legacy to their children, but especially for those who by reason of their young years stand most in need of instruction)

By Mistress DOROTHY LEIGH

Proverbs 1.8: *My son, hear the instruction of thy father, and forsake not the law of thy mother.*

**TO THE HIGH and excellent Princess, the Lady ELIZABETH her Grace,
daughter to the high and mighty King of Great Britain
and wife to the illustrious prince, the Count Palatine of the Rhine,
D. L. wisheth all grace and prosperity, here, and glory in the world to come.**

Most worthy and renowned Princess,

    I being troubled and wearied with fear, lest my children should not find the right way to Heaven, thought with myself that I could do no less for them than every man will do for his friend: which was, to write them the right way (that I had truly observed out of the written Word of God); lest, for want of warning, they might fall where I stumbled; and then I should think myself in the fault, who knew there were such downfalls in the world, that they could hardly climb the hill to Heaven without help, and yet had not told them thereof. Wherefore I writ them the right and ready way to Heaven, well warranted by the Scriptures of the Old and New Testament, which is the true Word of God; and told them how many false paths they should find; how they should find them; and what care they should have to shun them; if they took a false way, what a trouble they should have in turning again, what danger if they went on; and of many doubts which the world would make, without a cause; and how silent it would be, in danger.

    Thus when I had writ unto them of these things, I was at much peace, quiet and contentment.

    But as no contentment in the world continueth long, so suddenly there arose a new care in my mind, how this scroll should be *kept* for my children: for they were too young to receive it; myself, too old to keep it; men, too wise to direct it to; the world, too wicked to endure it. Then in great grief I looked up to Heaven, from whence I knew cometh all comfort. And looking up, I saw a most angelical throne of princely peers and peerless princes – prepared for Heaven, and yet by the appointment of God were here to comfort us on the Earth. Then I perceived that this throne was the joy of England! Then I considered that the highest blood had the lowest mind; then I saw *humility,* looking downward, while the sweet slips of her virtue grew upward; then, even then, princely lady, I beheld your mild and courteous countenance! – which showed your heart was bent to do good to all. Wherefore, without fear, and with much faith, I adventured to make your Grace the protectress of this my book; knowing that if you would but suffer your name to be seen in it, wisdom would allow it, and all the wicked wind in the world could not blow it away.

    The Lord multiply His graces more and more on you, and vouchsafe unto you a numerous posterity, in whom your Grace may receive much joy and comfort; and God's Church and true religion, continual defense and propagation.

Your Grace's, in all humble and observant duty,

D. L.

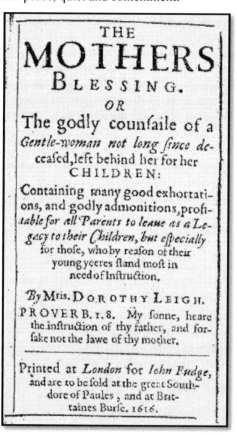

THE
MOTHERS
BLESSING.
OR
The godly counsaile of a
Gentle-woman not long since deceased, left behind her for her
CHILDREN:

Containing many good exhortations, and godly admonitions, profitable for all Parents to leave as a Legacy to their Children, but especially for those, who by reason of their young yeeres stand most in need of Instruction.

By Mris. DOROTHY LEIGH.

PROVERB. 1. 8. My sonne, heare the instruction of thy father, and forsake not the lawe of thy mother.

Printed at London for Iohn Budge, and are to be sold at the great Southdore of Paules, and at Brittaines Burse. 1616.

From **The Mother's Blessing**

To my Beloved Sons,
GEORGE, JOHN, and WILLIAM LEIGH,
all things pertaining to life and godliness

My Children,

God having taken your father out of this vale of tears to His everlasting mercy in Christ – myself not only knowing what a care he had in his lifetime that you should be brought up godlily; but also at his death being charged in his will, by the love and duty which I bare him, to see you well instructed and brought up in knowledge – I could not choose but seek (according as I was, by duty, bound) to fulfill his will in all things; desiring no greater comfort in the world than to see you grow in godliness; that so, you might meet your father in Heaven (where I am sure he is, myself being a witness of his faith in Christ).

And seeing myself going out of the world, and you but coming in, I know not how to perform this duty so well as to leave you these few lines (which will show you as well the great desire your father had, both of your spiritual and temporal good, as the care I had to fulfill his will in this, knowing it was the last duty I should perform unto him). But when I had written these things unto you and had (as I thought) something fulfilled your father's request, yet I could not see to what purpose it should tend, unless it were sent abroad to you: for should it be left with the eldest, it is likely the youngest should have but little part in it.

Wherefore, setting aside all fear, I have adventured to show my imperfections to the view of the world, not regarding what censure shall, for this, be laid upon me; so that herein I may show myself a loving mother, and a dutiful wife. And thus I leave you to the protection of Him that made you; and rest, till death—

Your fearful, faithful, and careful mother,
D. L.

Counsel to My Children

MY SONS, the readers of this book,
I do you not entreat
To bear with each misplacèd word:
For why? my pain's as great
To write this little book to you
(The world may think, "Indeed!")
As it will be at any time
For you, the same to read.
But this, I much and oft desire
That you would do for me:

To gather honey of each flower
As doth the laborous bee. [...]
Then gather well and lose no time:
Take heed, now you do see,
Lest you be unprovided found
As was the *idle* bee.

D.L.

1. *The* occasion *of writing this book was the consideration of the care of parents for their children*: My Children, when I did truly weigh, rightly consider, and perfectly see the great care, labor, travail, and continual study which parents take to enrich their children – some wearying their bodies with labor, some breaking their sleeps with care, some sparing from their own bellies, and many hazarding their souls; some by bribery, some by simony, others by perjury, and a multitude by usury; some stealing on the sea, others begging by land portions from every poor man, not caring if the whole commonwealth be impoverished, so their children be enriched (for themselves, they can be content with meat, drink, and cloth, so that their children, by their means, may be made rich); always abusing this portion of Scripture: "He that provideth not for his own family is worse than an infidel" (1 Tim. 5.8); ever seeking for the temporal things of this world, and forgetting those things which be eternal – when I considered these things, I say, I thought good (being not desirous to enrich you with transitory goods) to exhort and desire you to follow the counsel of Christ: "First, seek the kingdom of God and His righteousness, and then all these things shall be administered unto you" (Mat. 6:33).

2. *The first* cause *of writing is a motherly affection*. But lest you should marvel, my children, why I do not, according to the usual custom of women, exhort you by word and admonitions (rather than by writing, a thing so unusual among us) – and especially in such a time, when there be so many godly books in the world that they mold in some men's studies, while their masters are marred because they will not meditate upon them (as many men's garments, moths eat in their chests, while their Christian brethren quake with cold in the street for want of covering); know therefore, that it was the motherly affection that I bear unto you all, which made me now (as it often hath done heretofore) forget my self, in regard of you. Neither care I what you, or any, shall think of me, if among many words I may write but one sentence which may make you labor for the spiritual food of the soul [...]

4. The second cause is to stir them up to write. The second cause, my sons, why I write unto you (for you may think that, had I had but one cause, I would not have changed the usual order of women) is needful to be known and may do much good: For where I saw the great mercy of God toward you in making you *men*, and placing you amongst the wise, where you may learn the true-written Word of God (which is the pathway to all happiness, and which will bring you to the chief city, New Jerusalem), and the seven liberal sciences (whereby you shall have at least a superficial sight in all things); I thought it fit to give you good example, and, by writing, to entreat *you* – that when it shall please God to give both virtue and grace with your learning, He having made you men, that *you* may write (and speak the Word of God without offending any); that then you would remember to write a book unto *your* children, of the right and true way to happiness, which may remain with them and theirs for ever.

5. The third cause is to move women to be careful of their children. The third is, to encourage women (who, I fear, will blush at my boldness) not to be ashamed to show their infirmities, but to give men the first and chief place. Yet let us labor to come in the second; and because we must needs confess that sin entered by us into our posterity, let us show how careful we are to seek to Christ to cast it *out* of us and our posterity, and how fearful we are that our sin should sink any of them to the lowest part of the earth; wherefore let us call upon them to follow Christ, who will carry them to the height of Heaven.

6. The fourth cause is, to arm them against poverty. The fourth cause is to desire you that you will never fear poverty, but always know it is the state of the children of God to be poor in the world. Christ sayeth, "Ye shall have the poor with you always" (John 12:8). It may be he hath appointed you or yours to be of this poor number: do not strive against Christ. "It is as hard," sayeth He, "for a rich man to enter into Heaven, as for a camel to go through the eye of a needle" (Mat. 19:24). Saint James sayeth, "Woe be to you that are rich" (Jam 5:1). St. Paul sayeth, "The desire of money is the root of all evil" (1. Tim. 6. 10); which, if it be true (as it is not to be doubted of), and you fear poverty, then doth it necessarily follow that you will desire the root of all evil, which is money; and so become good for nothing. The fear of poverty maketh men run into a thousand sins, which nothing else could draw them to. For many, fearing the cold storms of poverty (which

never last long), run on to the hot fire of Hell (which never hath an end). This matter requireth many words, for it is hard to persuade the nature of man from the fear of poverty; wherefore I will speak more of that afterwards. Only I now say: Fear not to be poor with Lazarus, but fear a thousand times to be rich with Dives. [1]

7. The fifth cause is, not to fear death. [...Y]ou can by no means shun it; you must needs endure it. And therefore it is meet that you should be always prepared for it, and never fear it. [...]

8. The sixth cause is, to persuade them to teach their children. The sixth reason is, to entreat and desire you, and in some sort to *command* you, that all your children, be they males or females, may in their youth learn to read the Bible in their own mother tongue [...] I am further also to entreat you, that all your children may be taught to read beginning at four years old or before, and let them learn till ten (in which time they are not able to do any good in the Commonwealth but to learn how to serve God, their king, and country, by *reading*. [...]

9. The seventh cause is, that they should give their children good names. The seventh cause is, to entreat you, that though I do not live to be a witness to the baptizing of any of your children, yet you would give me leave to give names to them *all*; for though I do not think any holiness to be *in* the name (but know that God hath His, in every place, and of every name), yet I see in the Bible it was observed by God Himself to give *choice* names to His children, which had some good signification.

[*On virginity, seduction, and rape.*] Whoso is truly chaste is free from idleness and from all vain delights, full of humility and all good Christian virtues. Whoso is chaste, is not given to pride in apparel nor any vanity, but is always either reading, meditating, or practicing some good thing which she hath learned in the Scripture. But she which is unchaste, is given to be idle. Or, if she do anything, it is for a vain glory, and for the praise of men, more than for any humble, loving and obedient heart that she beareth unto God and His Word, who said: "Six days thou shalt labor" (Exod. 20:9); and so left no time for idleness, pride, or vanity – for in none of these is there any holiness.

The unchaste woman is proud, and always decking herself with vanity; and delights to hear the vain words of men – in which there is not only

---

[1] *Dives*] rich man; Luke 16:19-31.

vanity, but also so much wickedness; that the vain words of men, and women's vainness in hearing them, hath brought many women to much sorrow and vexation (as woeful experience hath, and will, make many of them confess).

But some will say, "Had they only lent an ear to their *words*, they had done well enough!" – To answer which, I would have everyone know that one sin begetteth another. The vain words of the man, and the idle cares of the woman, beget unchaste thoughts oftentimes in the one, which may bring forth much wickedness in them both. Man said once, "The woman which Thou gavest me, beguiled me, and I did eat" (Gen.3. 12). But we women may now say, that men le in wait everywhere to deceive us, as the elders did to deceive Susanna. Wherefore let us be (as she was) chaste, watchful, and wary, keeping company with maids.

Once Judas betrayed his master with a kiss, and repented it. But now men, like Judas, betray their mistresses with a kiss and repent it not – but laugh and rejoice, that they have brought sin and shame to her that trusted them – the only way to avoid all which, is to be chaste with Susanna and, being women, to embrace that virtue which, being placed in a woman, is most commendable.

An unchaste woman destroyeth both the body and the soul of him she seemeth most to love; and it is almost impossible to set down the mischiefs, which have come through unchaste women! Salomon sayeth that "Her steps lead to Hell" (Prov. 2.18). Wherefore, bring up your daughters as Susanna's parents brought up her: teach them the Law of the Lord continually, and always persuade them to embrace this virtue of chastity; […] to whom, for this cause, God hath given a cold and temperate disposition, and bound them with these words: "Thy desire shall be subject to thy husband" (Gen. 3.6), as if God in mercy to women should say, "You of your selves shall have no desires, *only* they shall be subject to your *husbands*" – which hath been verified in heathen women so as it is almost incredible to be believed: for many of them, before they would be defiled, have been careless of their lives and so have endured all those torments that men would devise to inflict upon them, rather than they would lose the name of a *modest maid* or a *chaste matron*. Yea, and so far they have been from consenting to any immodesty, that if at any time they have been ravished, they have either made away themselves, or at least have separated themselves from company, not thinking themselves worthy of any society after they have once been deflowered, though against their wills.

Wherefore, the woman that is infected with the sin of uncleanness is worse than a beast: because it desireth but for nature; and she, to satisfy her corrupt lusts. Some of the Fathers have written that it is not enough for a woman to be chaste, but even so to behave herself that no man may think or deem her to be unchaste. We read that in the primitive Church, when there were wars between the Christians and the pagans, if at any time the pagans had gotten the victory, that then they would seek to deflower the virgins; to the which sin, before the Christians would yield, they would continually lay violent hands upon themselves; insomuch that the doctors of the Church were oftentimes constrained to make divers sermons and orations to them, to dissuade them from that cruelty (which they inflicted upon themselves rather than they would suffer themselves to be deflowered; such a disgrace did they think it, to have but one spot of uncleanness […]

Especially above all other moral virtues, let women be persuaded, by this discourse, to embrace chastity – without which, we are mere beasts, and no women.

12. *Choice of wives.* Now for your wives, the Lord direct you; for I cannot tell you what is best to be done. […] Love not the ungodly. Marry with none, except you love her. And be not changeable in your love. Let nothing, after you have made your choice, remove your love from her. For it is an ungodly and very foolish thing of a man to mislike his own choice, especially since God hath given a man much choice among the godly; and it was a great cause that moved God to command His [own] to marry with the godly, that there might be a continual agreement between them.

13. *It is great folly for a man to mislike his own choice.* Methinks I never saw a man show a more senseless simplicity than in misliking his own choice, when God hath given a man almost a world of women to choose him a wife in! If a man hath not wit enough to choose him one whom he can love to the end, yet methinks he should have discretion to cover his own folly; but if he want discretion, me thinks he should have *policy* (which never fails a man!) to dissemble his own simplicity in this case. If he want wit, discretion *and* policy, he is unfit to marry *any* woman.

Do not a woman that wrong, as to take her from her friends that love her, and after a while to begin to hate her. If she *have* no friends, yet thou knowest not but that she may have a *husband* that may love her. If thou canst not love her to the end, leave her to him that can. Methinks my son could not offend me in anything, if he served God, except he chose a wife that he could not love to the end [...]

14. *How to deal with servants.* Yet one thing I am to desire you to do at my request, and for my sake: and though it be some trouble to you to perform it, yet I assure myself you will do it: If God shall at any time give you or any of you a servant or servants, you shall ask them if they can read. If they cannot, you shall at my request teach them, or cause them to be taught, till they can read the Ten Commandments of almighty God. And then you shall persuade them to practice by themselves, and to spend all their idle time in reading, that so they may come the better to know the will of God written in his Word. Remember, your servants are God's servants as well as yours: [...] and then remember they are your brethren. Use them well, and be as ready to do them good as to have their service. Be not chiding for every trifle, for that will hinder good living and nothing enrich you.

41. *Prodigality set out.* Some think that the prodigal man taketh too little care for the world; but I say he is a wicked man, and taketh too *much* care for the world [...] He is a wasteful man: he will spend wastefully for the vainglory of the world (which some say they care not for). He leaveth those things which God hath given him and his family without care. Yea, he is a covetous man: for he will borrow of others, and spend it wastefully, and never pay it again. He breaketh the commandment which sayeth, "Owe nothing to any man but this, that you love one another" (Rom. 13.8); for the Holy Ghost sayeth, "The ungodly borroweth, and payeth not again, but the merciful man is liberal, and lendeth" (Psa. 37.21). Some will say, they *would* pay, if they had it. But indeed, they will *not* have it because they will not obey God, and live as He hath appointed them. They are proud, and will spend so far beyond their calling that they have nothing to lend to the poor children of God, because they spend either upon the wicked, or in excess when there is no need, or upon those that have as little or less need than themselves. "Such a person is worse than an infidel because he provideth not for his own household" (1 Tim. 5.8). [...] And yet there be some so ignorant that they will say, "The prodigal man beareth a noble mind" – but he bears a *wicked* mind, and they know not what a noble mind is, that say so. Our peers and princes are called "noble" men because they bear noble minds; that is, they are virtuous and temperate and

discreet, governing the Commonwealth according to their calling: regarding the virtuous, and keeping under the vicious, holding in the prodigal (who would run away with a whole kingdom, if they might have it).   Nay, no kingdom is able to satisfy prodigal persons, for their disobedient humor will never be satisfied.

44. *The honorable calling of ministers, stained by worldliness.* I must needs say, I have been very desirous, and have often begged of God, that some of you might be preachers (yea, and *all* of you and yours, if it might please His divine Majesty to bestow such graces upon you as were meet for so high a calling). But God knows I never desired it because you should *get* anything in the world. [...] But if it please God that any of you hereafter should be a preacher, *and* love the world, I cannot express the grief it would be to me, even so long as I were in the world. If any of you should ask me, if it were "not as evil in another man, as in a preacher?" I answer, No: for it is a very dangerous and indeed a damnable estate, to love the world. I know what I say (I do not say, "to be covetous," or "desire to be rich, whereby one is moved to use *unlawful* means to get goods: but I say, to love *lawful* goods which God hath given thee, and to neglect the service of God about them, if it be but in *thinking* of them, and to be at any time more loath to lose thy lawful goods than to go to law to the hurt of thy brother whom Christ died for, it is a wicked sin in any man.

To set a rent or price, of any of thy lawful goods or lands, more than thou in such a case wouldst be willing to give, it is a wicked sin. To let or sell anything to any man, for sinister respects, that thou dost not think to be the true and faithful servant of God, if thou mayest let it well to those that *are*, is a sin. But to let a farm to any that thou doest not think to be the true servant of God, but because he is richer, or is better able to pay thee, or will give thee more for it, is a great sin. [...] He hath left his goods with thee, bids thee to deal well with His servants, and let them good pennyworths; and "Deal not with His enemies, neither make any marriage with them" (2. Cor. 6.14); yet thou for a little money wilt buy and sell, marry and give in marriage with them, yea thinkest, because thou findest them more rich in the world, they are better for thee to deal withal; and yet they are the utter enemies of thy Lord, and will be ready at His coming to bid Him battle, and strike at Him with His own sword.

• • •

Of Midwives

DAILY EXPERIENCE doth show us that many women are delivered without the help of the midwife. Notwithstanding, antiquity telleth us that there have been midwives even from the beginning; yea, that divers of that sex have practiced physic.... Necessity (the mistress of arts) hath constrained women to learn and practice physic, one with another: for finding themselves afflicted and troubled with divers dis-eases in their natural parts (and being destitute of all remedies, for want whereof, many perished and died miserably), they durst not discover and lay open their infirmities to any but themselves....

Among those that have practiced physic, there were some that have applied themselves most to the delivering of women; and for a difference from others, they were commonly called "cunning women" (or else caused themselves to be so called, for women are of this disposition, that they desire to excel men or at least to *seem* to go beyond them). Wherefore it may easily be perceived, that there hath been some women that have practiced *physic*, and others that were employed in the *delivery of women*. And these last took upon them three things:

The first office was to make the match and to join the husband with the wife, and likewise to judge whether they were fit and capable, or else unable and unsufficient to have issue and beget children (which is very difficult to be knowen, and at this day there is no woman so cunning who is able to tell it).

The second office was to be present at the delivery of women, and birth of children; whether it were in giving of some medicines or else by using her handiwork: which work was committed to none, but those that had *had* children; because (as Plato sayeth) "One cannot be so apt and skillful in exercising a work not known, as they which have had the perfect knowledge and experience thereof...

The third office was to know and tell whether a woman was with child or no....

But since that time (beside the three former offices) another office of midwife they have taken upon them: authority to judge of the virginity of maids. Nevertheless all the famous universities of Italy have rejected and condemned the opinion of such midwives, who say they can judge thereof. And Master Cuiacius hath done the like for the French, saying, that "It is very difficult, yea impossible, to know whether a maid be a virgin or no"; and that this power "was never given unto midwives by the Civil Law, to judge thereof.

What Manner of Woman, a Midwife ought to be

MANY THINGS are requisite and needful in a midwife... First, concerning her person: she must be of an indifferent age, neither too young nor too old; well composed of body, not being subject to any diseases, nor mis-shapen or deformed in any part thereof; neat in her apparel and person; especially having little hands and not thick, clean, and her nails pared very near and even. Neither must she wear rings upon her fingers nor bracelets upon her arms when she is about her business. She must be pleasant, merry, of good discourse, strong, painful and accustomed to labor, that she may be able (if need be) to watch two or three nights by the woman.

Concerning her behavior: she must be mild, gentle, courteous, patient, sober, chaste, not quarrelsome; nor choleric, neither proud or covetous, nor a blabber or reporter of anything she shall either hear or see in secret, in the house or person of her she hath delivered. For as Terence sayeth, "It is not fit to commit her into the hands of a drunken or rash woman, that is in travail of her first child."

As for her mind, she must be wise, discreet, able to make use sometime of fair and flattering speeches: as Plato reporteth midwives were wont to do in times past, which was done to no other end but only to busy and beguile the poor apprehensive woman. And it is a commendable deceit, allowed also in a chirurgeon when it is done for the patient's good. For as the same Terence sayeth: "Deceit doth serve oftentimes for a good medicine in extreme diseases."

Now above all things, the said midwife ought to know that Nature, the handmaid of this great God, hath given to everything a beginning, increase, state, perfection, and declining, which He doth manifestly and chiefly show (sayeth Galen) in the birth of a child, when the mother brings him into the world. For Nature surpasseth all, and in that she doth, is wiser than either art, or the midwife (whosoever she be), yea, than the best or most cunning workman that may be found ([*De Naturalibus Facultatibus*, 3.3]). For it is she that hath set down the day of the child's conformation and the hour of his birth. And certainly, it is a thing worthy of consideration to see how in a little space, yea, even in the twinkling of an eye, the neck of the womb (which all the time of the nine months was so perfectly and exactly closed and shut that the point of a needle could not enter therein), how (I say) in an instant it is dilated and enlarged, to give passage and way for the child; the which "cannot be comprehended" (as the same Galen sayeth) "but only wondered at, and admired." The same author in his fifteenth book, *de Usu Partium* [15.7], desirous to show the providence of Nature, sayeth that "The faults of Nature are very rare," and that "she worketh always and in such order and measure, that of a thousand births, there is scarce one found that is amiss" . Wherefore neither the midwife, nor any of the woman's kinsfolks or assistants, ought to do anything rashly, but suffer Nature to work (helping her notwithstanding in that which shall be needful).

—Jacques Guillemeau, *Childbirth or, The Happy Delivery of Women*. Anon. trans. (1612), pp. 32, 69, 222.

Elizabeth (Knyvett) Clinton (1575 - 1638),
Countess of Lincoln

> [B]ee not accessary to that disorder of causing a poorer woman to
> banish her owne infant, for the entertaining of a richer womans
> child, as it were, bidding her vnloue her owne to loue yours.
> — *Nurserie*, sig. D2r.

E LIZABETH CLINTON was the seventh child of Elizabeth (*née* Stumpe) and Sir Henry Knyvett of Charlton, Wiltshire. On 21 September 1584 she was married to Thomas Fiennes de Clinton, the only son of Edward, earl of Lincoln. She was then nine years old. Thomas was thirteen. Consummation of the marriage evidently took place on, or shortly after, Elizabeth's twelfth birthday (which was the legal age under canon law, even if the bride had not yet had her first period). By 1595 Elizabeth Clinton, age 20, had already given birth to seven children: Henry, Thomas, Catherine, Lucy, Elizabeth, Dorcas, and Anne. Eleven more would follow.

In August 1597, Queen Elizabeth's Privy Council, noting the young couple's penniless state and Elizabeth's recent brush with death, wrote to the Earl of Lincoln, directing him on displeasure of the Queen to provide some financial aid to his son and his wife and their many children, reminding the Earl "what it is for young folks to want," and imploring him to provide "some convenient house where the young lord and lady may live with their children." [1]

Edward Clinton dying in 1616, Thomas succeeded as third earl of Lincoln, inheriting the family castle at Tattershall, Lincolnshire; but he died three years later, leaving his widow with a large family (nine surviving children, still at home). Theophilus, 19, succeeded to the estate. Elizabeth and the other eight children removed to Sempringham. Two more died shortly afterward.

Whatever other hardships she may have suffered in her marriage of 34 years, Elizabeth Clinton in keeping with the expectations of her social class never stooped to nursing her own children. Typically, the aristocratic mother nursed her newborn for a few days, then yielded the infant to the care of a hired surrogate, a woman whose baby had died, or who nursed her own and the consigned child simultaneously. The infant often lived with the wet-nurse, not with the mother, until fully weaned.

Many merchant-class Puritan ministers openly condemned this aristocratic practice as unnatural; among whom was Rev. William Gouge, London's most strident and well-known Calvinist preacher. People from all over England came to London to hear England's "Arch Puritan" thunder down God's wrath against sin and the well-to-do. He also published. In his treatise, *Of Domestical Duties* (entered 1620, printed 1622), Gouge condemns wealthy mothers who, "when no necessity requireth, put forth their children to be nursed by others." He names their several excuses:

1. Some do it for ease and quiet, because they cannot endure to have their sleep broken, or to hear their child wrangle and cry.
2. Others do it for "niceness," because they are loath to open their breasts, or to soil their clothes.
3. Others upon pride, conceiting that their beauty would be impaired, and they look old too soon.
4. Others upon gain, because they can have a child cheaper nursed abroad than at home (where at least they must hire a maid the more).
5. Others, upon pleasure, that they might more freely ride abroad, and meet their gossips.
6. Others, upon other by-respects – all which do argue much self-love, little love to their child, and little respect to God. They can be counted but half-mothers: for *nursing* a child is as much as bearing and bringing it forth. (517-8)

While condemning aristocratic women who pay for the service, Gouge also condemns the working-class providers, representing the typical wet-nurse as careless or incompetent:

> Children as are nursed by their mothers prosper best. Mothers are most tender over them, and cannot endure to let them lie, crying out, without taking them up and stilling them – as nurses will let them cry and cry again, if they be about any business of their own. For who are commonly chosen to be nurses? even poor country women which have much work to do, and little help! – and so are forced to let the child lie and cry many times, till it burst again.

---

[1] *what…children*] Privy Council to Lord Clinton (Aug. 1597), ed. DWF from H.M.C. *Cecil Papers*, v.7 (1899), p. 375.

Children nursed by their mothers are for the most part more cleanly and neatly brought up, freer from diseases. Not so many die [and] I am sure not so many, through negligence, cast away.

The number of nurse-children that die every year is very great. It hath been observed, in many country villages, that the most part that from time to time die there, are *nurse-children*. Are not mothers that might have nursed their own children (if they would) accessory to the death of those that are cast away by the nurse's negligence?

On these and other like reasons, heathen women, and very savages, have in all ages been moved to nurse their own children. And some heathen philosophers have urged and pressed the necessity of this duty. Never was it more neglected than among those that bear the name of Christians! Let mothers know – of what rank or degree so ever they be, that (out of the case of necessity) *they have no warrant to put forth their children to others to nurse.* We read not in all the Scripture of any holy women that ever did it. (512-3)

Rev. Gouge will admit no excuse. He lists a dozen objections, and counters them:

Objection. Mothers that are of great wealth and high place cannot endure the pain of nursing, nor take the pains in handling young children as they must be handled.

Answer. The greatest that be, must set themselves to do that duty which God *requireth* at their hands, though it be with pain. […]

Objection. Many husbands will not suffer their wives to nurse their children themselves.

Answer. Because it is a bounden duty, wives must use all the means they can, by themselves or others, to persuade their husbands to let them perform it. They must take heed that they make not this a pretext to cover their own sloth, and loathness to this duty. They may not make themselves accessory to their husband's fault by providing a nurse and sending the child away themselves. (If their husbands will stand upon their authority, and be persuaded by no means to the contrary, they must be mere patients in suffering the child to be taken away…) (515-6)

Rev. Gouge's book followed on the success of Robert Cleaver's *A Godly Form of Household Government for the Ordering of Private Families* (1621), in which Rev. Cleaver warns aristocratic mothers that their babes imbibe the nurse-mother's bad nature together with her milk; and he closes with a sarcasm:

The children's bodies be commonly so affected as the milk is which they receive. Now if the nurse be of an evil complexion, as she is affected in her body or in her mind, or hath some hidden disease, the child sucking of her breast must needs take part with her. And if that be true which the learned do say, that "The temperature of the mind follows the constitution of the body," needs must it be, that if the nurse be of a naughty nature, the child must take thereafter. […]

Such women as be oppressed with infirmities, diseases, want of milk, or other just and lawful causes are to be dispensed withal. But whose breasts have this perpetual drought? Forsooth, it is like the gout: No beggars may have it, but citizens or gentlewomen! In the ninth of Hosea, verse 14, dry breasts are named for a curse. What a lamentable hap have gentlewomen, to light upon this curse more than others! Sure, if their breasts be dry as they say they are, they should fast and pray together, that this curse might be removed from them. (116)

Persuaded that Christian women who hire a wet-nurse offend both God and Rev. Gouge, Clinton performed her penance: in *The Countess of Lincoln's Nursery,* published some weeks or months after Cleaver's *Godly Form* and Gouge's *Domestical Duties,* she publicly expressed shame for having neglected her duty as a mother. Dedicating the book to her only daughter-in-law, Lady Bridget (the wife of Theophilus), the countess urges her not to follow that same wicked course. But even when setting aside her aristocratic resistance to breast-feeding, Clinton could not escape the assumptions of her class concerning who's better than whom, or whose right it is to legislate proper motherhood.

Neither could her son. In 1625, Theophilus sued his mother in Chancery to gain custody of his three surviving brothers, Charles, Knyvett, and James. In 1630, the two surviving daughters, Anne and Arabella, and one son, Charles, emigrated to Massachusetts with Thomas Dudley, former steward to Theophilus. Arabella (for whom the ship was named) died in route. Charles returned to England and drops from view. Elizabeth Clinton, countess dowager of Lincoln, having given birth to eighteen children by one husband, is thought to have died alone, about 1630.

The Countess of Lincoln's Nursery

by Elizabeth Clinton

BECAUSE it hath pleased God to bless me with many children, and so caused me to observe many things falling out to mothers and to their children, I thought good to open my mind concerning a special matter, belonging to all child-bearing women seriously to consider of – and, to manifest my mind to the better, even to write of this matter (so far as God will please to direct me). In sum, the matter I mean is the duty of *nursing*, due by mothers to their own children: in setting down whereof, I will first show that every woman ought to nurse her own child; and, secondly, I will endeavor to answer such objections as are used to be cast out against this duty, to disgrace the same.

The first point is easily performed, for it is the express ordinance of God that mothers should nurse their own children; and (being His ordinance) they are bound to it in conscience. This should stop the mouths of all repliers, for God is "most wise" (Isa. 31:2), and therefore must needs know what is fittest and best for us to do; and, to

Artemisia Gentileschi, Mother and Child (1609)
Courtesy of Spada Gallery, Rome

prevent all foolish fears or shifts, we are given to understand that he is also "all-sufficient" (Gen. 17:1), and therefore infinitely able to bless His own ordinance and to afford us means in ourselves (as continual experience confirmeth) toward the observance thereof.

If this (as it ought) be granted, then how venterous are those women that dare venter to do otherwise, and so to refuse (and, by refusing, to despise) that order which the most wise and almighty God hath appointed – and instead thereof, to choose their own pleasures? O what peace can there be to these women's consciences? – unless, through the darkness of their understanding, they judge it no disobedience (and then they will drive me to prove that this nursing and nourishing of their own children in their bosoms is God's ordinance). They are very willful, or very ignorant, if they make a question of it, for it is proved sufficiently to be their duty, both by God's Word and also by His works. [1]

By His word it is proved, first, by examples – namely, the example of Eve. For who suckled her sons Cain, Abel, Seth, etc., but herself? – which she did not only of mere necessity (because yet no other woman was created), but especially because she was their mother, and so saw it was her duty; and because she had a true natural affection which moved her to do it gladly. Next, the example of Sarah, the wife of Abraham: for she both gave her son Isaac suck (as doing the duty commanded of God) and also took great comfort and delight therein (as in a duty well pleasing to herself); whence she spake of it as of an action worthy to be named in her holy rejoicing (Gen. 21:7). Now if Sarah, so great a princess, did nurse her own child, why should any of us neglect to do the like, except (which God forbid!) we think scorn to follow her whose daughters it is our glory to be – and which we be, only upon this condition, that we imitate her well-doing (I Pet. 3:6). Let us look therefore to our worthy pattern, noting withal that she put herself to this work when she was very old, and so might the better have excused herself than we younger women can – being also more

---

[1] *venterous ... venter*] venturous ... venture.

able to hire and keep a nurse than any of us! But why is she not followed by most in the practice of this duty? Even because they want her virtue and piety! This want is the common hindrance to this point of the woman's obedience; for this want makes them want love to God's precepts, want love to his doctrine, and (like step-mothers) want due love to their own children. [...] [1]

To proceed, take notice of one example more: that is, of the blessed Virgin. As her womb bare our blessed Savior, so her paps gave him suck. Now who shall deny the own mother's suckling of their own children to be their duty, since every godly matron hath walked in these steps before them? – Eve, the mother of all the living; Sarah, the mother of all the faithful; [...] Mary, blessed among women, and called blessed of all ages; and who can say but that the rest of holy women mentioned in the holy Scriptures did the like (since, no doubt, that speech of that noble dame, saying, "Who would have said to Abraham that Sarah should have given children suck!" was taken from the ordinary custom of mothers in those less-corrupted times [Gen. 21:7])? [...]

Now, another work of God proving this point is the work of His provision for every kind to be apt and able to nourish their own fruit. There is no beast that feeds their young with milk but the Lord even from the first ground of the order of nature – "Grow and multiply" – hath provided it with milk to suckle their own young; which every beast takes so naturally unto, as if another beast come towards their young to offer the office of a dam unto it, they show, according to their fashion, a plain dislike of it! As if Nature did speak in them, and say, "It is contrary to God's order in Nature," commanding each kind to increase and multiply in their own bodies and by their own breasts, not to bring forth by one dam and to bring up by another. But it is his ordinance that every kind should both bring forth, and also nurse, its own fruit. [2]

Much more should this work of God prevail to persuade women made (as man) in the image of God (and [who°] therefore should be ashamed to be put to school to learn good nature of the unreasonable creature). In us also, as we know by ex-perience, God provideth milk in our breasts the time of our children's birth; and this He hath done ever since it was said to us also, "Increase and multiply"; so that this work of His provision showeth that He tieth us likewise to nourish the children of our own womb – with our own breasts, even by the order of Nature. Yea, it showeth that He so careth for and regardeth little children, even from the womb, that He would have them nursed by those that in all reason will look to them with the kindest affection, namely their mothers. And in giving them milk for it, He doth plainly tell them that He requires it. [3]

Oh consider, how comes our milk? Is it not by the direct providence of God? Why provides He it, but for the child? The mothers then that refuse to nurse their own children, do they not despise God's providence? Do they not deny God's will? Do they not (as it were) say, "I see, O God, by the means thou hast put into me, that Thou wouldst have me nurse the child Thou hast given me, but I will not do so much for Thee." Oh impious and impudent unthankfulness! yea, monstrous unnaturalness, both to their own natural fruit born so near their breasts and fed in their own wombs, and yet may not be suffered to suck their own milk!

And this unthankfulness and unnaturalness is oftener the sin of the higher and the richer sort than of the meaner and poorer (except some nice and proud idle dames who will imitate their betters till they make their poor husbands beggars!). And this is one hurt which the better rank do by their ill example egg and embolden the lower ones to follow them, to their loss. Were it not better for us greater persons to keep God's ordinance, and to show the meaner their duty in our good example? (I am sure we have more helps to perform it, and have fewer probable reasons to allege against it, than women that live by hard labor and painful toil!) If such mothers as refuse this office of love and of Nature to their children should hereafter be refused, despised, and neglected of those their children, were they not justly requited according to their own unkind dealing? [4]

---

[1] *want*] lack.

[2] *dam*] female parent.

[3] *unreasonable*] unreasoning; *be put...creature*] to have to learn what is good in the eyes of God by the example of mere animals; *against the time of*] in preparation for.

[4] *the meaner*] those women who are less privileged.

(I might say more in handling this first point of my promise. But I leave the larger and learnèder discourse hereof unto men of art and learning. Only I speak of so much as I read, and know in my own experience; which, if any of my sex and condition do receive good by, I am glad. If they scorn it, they shall have the reward of scorners. *I* write in modesty, and can reap no disgrace by *their* immodest folly.) [...]

It is objected that [nursing] is troublesome, that it is noisome to one's clothes, that it makes one look old, etc. All such reasons are uncomely, and unchristian to be objected (and therefore unworthy to be answered). They argue unmotherly affection, idleness, desire to have liberty to gad from home, pride, foolish fineness, lust, wantonness, and the like evils. Ask Sarah, Hannah, the blessed Virgin, and any modest loving mother, what trouble they accounted it to give their little ones suck. Behold most nursing mothers, and they be as clean and sweet in their clothes, and carry their age and hold their beauty, as well as those that suckle not. And most likely are they so to do! – because, keeping God's ordinance, they are sure of God's blessing; and it hath been observed in some women that they grow more beautiful, and better favored, by very nursing their own children.

But there are some women that object "fear," saying that they are so weak and so tender that they are afraid to venter to give their children suck, lest they endanger their health thereby. Of these, I demand: why then they did venter to marry and so to bear children? And if they say they could not choose, and that they thought not that marriage would impair their health, I answer that for the same reasons they should set themselves to nurse their own children – because they should not choose but do what God would have them to do. And they should believe that this work will be for their health also, seeing it is ordinary with the Lord to give good stomach, health, and strength to almost all mothers that take this pains with their children. [...] [1]

Now if any reading these lines return against me that it may be I myself have given my own children suck, and therefore am bolder and more busy to meddle in urging this point (to the end to

insult over and to make them to be blamed that have not done it), I answer that whether I have or have not performed this my bounden duty, I will not deny to tell my own practice: I know and acknowledge that I *should* have done it. And, having not done it, it was not for want of will in myself, but partly I was overruled by another's authority, and partly deceived by some ill counsel, and partly I had not so well considered of my duty in this motherly office – as since I did, when it was too late for me to put it in execution. Wherefore, being pricked in heart for my undutifulness, this way I study to redeem my peace: first by repentance towards God, humbly and often craving His pardon for this my offense; secondly, by studying how to show double love to my children, to make them amends for neglect of this part of love to them when they should have hung on my breasts and have been nourished in mine own bosom; thirdly, by doing my endeavor to prevent many Christian mothers from sinning in the same kind against our most loving and gracious God.

And for this cause I add unto my performed promise this short exhortation: namely, I beseech all godly women to remember how we elder ones are commanded to instruct the younger to love their children. Now, therefore, love them – so as to do this office to them when they are born (more gladly for love's sake than a stranger, who bore them not, shall do for lucre's sake). Also, I pray you to set no more so light by God's blessing in your own breasts, which the Holy Spirit ranketh with other excellent blessings. [2]

If it be unlawful to trample under feet a cluster of grapes in which a little wine is found, then how unlawful is it to destroy and dry up those breasts in which your own child, and perhaps one of God's very elect (to whom, to be a nursing father is a king's honor, and to whom, to be a nursing mother is a queen's honor), might find food of sincere milk, even from God's immediate providence, until it were fitter for stronger meat? I do know that the Lord may deny some women either to have any milk in their breasts at all, or to have any passage for their milk, or to have any health, or to have a right mind; and so they may be letted from this duty by want, by sickness, by lunacy,

---

[1] *object "fear"*] claim to be afraid.

[2] *lucre's sake*] for the sake of money (as a hired wet-nurse);   *to set ... blessing in*] no more to place so little value on the blessing of.

etc. But I speak not to these. I speak to you whose consciences witness against you, that you cannot justly allege any of those impediments. [1]

Do you submit yourselves to the pain and trouble of this ordinance of God? Trust not other women (whom wages hires to do it) better than yourselves (whom God and nature ties to do it). I have found (by grievous experience!) such dissembling in nurses – pretending sufficiency of milk when indeed they had too much scarcity; pretending willingness, towardness, wakefulness, when indeed they have been most willful, most froward, and most slothful – as I fear the death of one or two of my little babes came by the default of their nurses. Of all those which I had for eighteen children, I had but two [nurses] which were thoroughly willing and careful.

Divers have had their children miscarry in the nurse's hands – and are such mothers (if it were by the nurse's carelessness) guiltless? I know not how they should, since they will shut them out of the arms of nature, and leave them to the will of a stranger! – yea, to one that will seem to estrange herself from her own child, to give suck to the nurse-child! (This she may feign to do upon a covetous composition, but she frets at it in her mind if she has any natural affection.) [2]

Therefore, be no longer at the trouble and at the care to hire others to do your own work. Be not so unnatural, to thrust away your own children. Be not so hardy as to venter a tender babe to a less tender heart. Be not accessory to that disorder of causing a poorer woman to banish her own infant for the entertaining of a richer woman's child – as it were, bidding her unlove her own, to love yours! We have followed Eve in transgression; let us follow her in obedience. When God laid the sorrows of conception, of breeding, of bringing forth, and of bringing up her children upon her (and so upon us in her loins), did she reply any word against it? Not a word! So, I pray you all – mine own daughters, and others that are still child-bearing – reply not against the duty of suckling them when God hath sent you them.

Indeed, I see some – if the weather be wet or cold, if the way be foul, if the church be far off – I see they are so coy, so nice, so lukewarm, they will not take pains for their own souls. Alas, no marvel if these will not be at trouble and pain to nourish their children's bodies. [3]

But fear God: be diligent to serve Him, approve all His ordinances, seek to please Him; account it no trouble or pain to do anything that hath the promise of His blessing; and then you will, no doubt, do this good, laudable, natural, loving duty to your children.

If yet you be not satisfied, inquire not of such as refuse to do this – consult not with your own conceit; advise not with flatterers – but ask counsel of sincere and faithful preachers.

If you be satisfied, then take this with you, to make you do it cheerfully: think always that, having the child at your breast and having it in your arms, you have God's blessing there – for children are God's blessings. Think again how your babe crying for your breast, sucking heartily the milk out of it, and growing by it, is the Lord's own instruction – every hour and every day that you are suckling it instructing you, to show that *you* are *His* new-born babes (by your earnest desire after His word and the sincere doctrine thereof, and by your daily growing in grace and goodness thereby); so shall you reap pleasure and profit.

Again, you may consider that when your child is at your breast, it is a fit occasion to move your heart to pray for a blessing upon that work, and to give thanks for your child and for ability and freedom unto that which a mother would have done, and could not; who have tried and ventured their health, and taken much pains, and yet have not obtained their desire. But they that are fitted every way for this commendable act have certainly great cause to be thankful. And I much desire that God may have glory and praise for every good work, and you much comfort, that do seek to honor God in all things. Amen.

(1622)

---

[1] *letted*] hindered.

[2] *Divers*] Many (mothers);   *miscarry*] die.

---

[3] *they will not ... souls*] i.e., by attending church.

Mother's Milk in Medical Discourse

[W]omãs mylke is the chiefe and principall reliefe for such as be feble & weke, yea beynge broughte to deathes doore, they are therby restored ageyne vnto helthe. And the phisitions say: That the heat of a womans breastes and pappes, layde and ioyned to the breastis of feble olde men, consumed a way by age, styrreth vp, encreaseth, and conserueth in them lyuely heate. (Clapham, 1542)

DECLARE UNTO ME a daily diet, whereby I may live in health." Thus begins chapter five of *Approved Directions for Health* (1612), by William Vaughan, M.D. The doctor replies with nine daily steps to wholeness: 1. morning stretches; 2. a rubdown; 3. a bowel movement; 4. seasonable clothing; 5. hair-grooming; 6. clean teeth; 7. washed face, eyes, ears, hands, feet; and 8. morning prayers. For those who are unwell, Vaughan adds that "woman's milk – with which there is no comparison, as being the most agreeable to the sympathy of our natures" – will remedy complaints ranging from insomnia and depression, to poor vision, to consumption (tuberculosis) (44, 77-8). For a sleep aid, Vaughan directs his readers to "Take a little camphor, and mingle it with some woman's milk, and anoint your temples therewith" (59). For those who are "dim of sight," he prescribes a detailed recipe of vervain, betony, fennel, white wine, tutia [*zinc oxide*], sugar-candy, aloes hepatic, and camphor; all which, dissolved into breast milk, must be applied directly to the eyes (145-7).

Dr. Vaughan's confidence in breast-milk, recommended in print from the earliest days of movable type, receives only a qualified endorsement from Tobias Venner, M.D. (1620): "Cow's milk for sound and healthful bodies is best," he writes, "for it is fattest and thickest, and consequently of most nourishment. Next unto it (for grossness) is sheep's milk. But for bodies that are with long sickness extenuated, or are in a consumption, woman's milk is best because it is most familiar unto man's body, and even of like nature" (90).

Throughout the seventeenth century, human milk was used to treat virtually every kind of ailment, whether in children or adults. *A Closet for Ladies and Gentlewomen; or, The Art of Preserving, Conserving, and Candying* (1608), by an anonymous (possibly female) author, contains chiefly recipes for culinary treats, but also includes some common homeopathic medicines, several of which take breast milk as the active ingredient:

For the heat in the kidneys: Take house-leek and plantain, and not wash them, but wipe them, with a cloth; and beat them and strain them. And put to the juice thereof, red rose water and wine vinegar, and woman's milk. And take the herbs and put them into cloths, and tie the cloths with thread like a couple of balls. And you must (when you do use it) have one to do it for you in the morning when you are in your bed. And the party must take the balls, and dip them in this liquor, and so bathe your kidneys. And as soon as one of the balls is hot with doing of them, take the other. And so use it an hour, every morning (74-5).

A medicine for sore eyes: Take a little ground ivy (and strain it) and woman's milk together (and let it be somewhat green of the ivy), and then drop a drop or two into the eyes (153).

For a pearl [*cataract*] in the eye: Take red fennel, and the leaves and roots of white daisies (use them without any liquor), and put together three spoonfuls of either of them. Then take one good spoonful of clarified honey, and two or three spoonfuls of woman's milk, and drop this into your eye, three or four times a day. And if there be any sight in the eye, this will cure it (155-6).

A medicine for them that are deaf (so that they have heard before): Take juice of betony; woman's milk (that hath a man-child), mingle them together, and dip a piece of black wool into it, and put a piece of it into your ear for the space of ten or eleven days or more (163).

A medicine for a burn: Take oil of roses and woman's milk, and put it into the open place, and it will heal it (180).

An alternative treatment for severe burns is supplied by Daniel Widdowes (1621), who recommends lettuce boiled in breast-milk (p. 45). Edmund Gardiner (1611) further recommends breast-milk to anoint sore nostrils (p.33). And Gervase Markham (1616) writes that women's milk, when mixed with the flowers of celandine, "dryeth up the scars and ulcers" and "healeth the ringworms and itch of the head, and the falling [out] of the hair of little children" (198).

Breast milk was used to treat virtually all eye and vision problems, from dryness, to conjunctivitis, to glaucoma. More than two dozen ophthalmological prescriptions were published during the Jacobean period alone, many of which call for a mixture of breast-milk mingled with rose-water or egg-whites or sodden apples. The strangest prescriptions may be those of the naturalist Edward Topsell (1607): "There is an excellent remedy for the overspreading of the eyes [*glaucoma*], or to cure the disease in them called 'the pin and the web,' or to help them which are altogether blind, which is this: to take the blood of a mouse, the gall of a cock, and some part or quantity of woman's milk; and to take of each of them alike, and then to mingle or mix them together; and (being well wrought or kneaded until it come to an ointment) to rub or spread it upon the eyes; and this will in very short space help them unto their sight: for it hath been tried, and hath helped many" (516). For cataracts: "parings of an ass's hoof, scraped and mingled with breast milk," "cureth the scars and webs of the eyes" (27). The gall of a sheep, "distilled with a woman's milk, doth also most certainly heal their ears which are broken within and full of mattery corruption" (645); and "if there be any rupture in the ear, then use therewith a woman's milk or warm oil of roses; likewise, against the cankers in the gums" (254). Taken internally, "woman's milk or ass's milk wherein a flint-stone hath been sodden" can heal stomach ailments (83); and a calf's thighbone, when ground to powder and "drunk in woman's milk, cureth all filthy running ulcers" (90-1).

James I's accession to the English throne was ushered in with a plague epidemic. Of 38,244 reported London deaths recorded in 1603, bubonic plague accounted for 30,578 fatalities. (More than thirteen percent of the city's population died in a single year.) In *Present Remedies against the Plague* (1603), "by a learned physician," mother's milk is recommended as a sedative: "To procure sleep to the sick persons that are diseased either with the plague or the hot fever, take of a woman's breast-milk a good quantity. Put thereunto, of the like quantity of aqua-vitae. Stir them well together. And moisten therewith the temples of the patient and his nosthrils. Lay it on with some feather, or some fine thin rag" (sig. B4r).

Thomas Bretnor, M.M., in his 1618 revision of Angelo Sala's *Opiologia,* reports that opium is another excellent analgesic, but most especially when it is fortified with breast-milk: opium "appeaseth all aches or pains, helpeth digestion, stayeth all coughs" even when "taken crude and raw"; but when taken "with saffron and woman's milk, it is singular in *gouts*," a painful arthritic condition that made the last years of both King James and Queen Anna most miserable (2-3).

Breast milk was believed further to help with ailments of the head and heart. Robert Chester (1611) states that green mad-stone, mingled with the milk of a woman who has given birth to a son, "remedieth the wit-assailing frenzy, and purgeth the sad mind of melancholy" (105-6). Robert Burton in *The Anatomy of Melancholy* (1621) similarly recommends a compress of women's milk for relief from depression or insomnia (478). And Dr. Timothy Bright (1615) writes that "vitriol also, dissolved in woman's milk," is "very effectual to purge the head, in the jaundice" (47).

Edward Topsell comes close to recommending breast-milk as a daily staple ("woman's milk is best for the nourishment of man because it is not too fat"); with only this caveat: "Galen sayeth if it be eaten without honey, water, and salt, it curdleth in the belly of a man like a cheese and strangleth him; and being so used, it purgeth the belly," causing him to vomit (237).

Most extant recipes, if not prescribed by highly trained physicians, represent traditional homeopathic treatments. Robert Burton, in recommending breast-milk frontlets (medicated bandages), remarks that "*Frontlets* are well-known to every good wife: rosewater and vinegar with a little woman's milk, and nutmegs grated upon a rosecake, applied to both temples" (478).

The medical efficacy of breast-milk was universally accepted; skepticism, virtually non-existent. And the applications were almost limitless, although the supply was not. Edward Topsell (without lending his personal endorsement) suggests that breast-milk may be healthful even for dogs: "Some again say that if a dog taste of a woman's milk which she giveth (by the birth of a boy), he will never fall mad" (186). George Turberville, in his *Book of Falconry* (1611), prescribes breast-milk remedies for diseased falcons and hawks. And Gervase Markham recommends breast-milk for various ailments of horses and chickens (1610, 235; 1616, 43, 69).

This valorization of woman's milk is all the more remarkable given a persistent superstition concerning menstrual blood. Male horror of women's menses, underscored by the Bible's strict prohibitions, gave rise to a doctrine that menstrual blood was the most potent toxin on Earth, able to kill any plant or animal life that came into contact with it (female flesh alone, being immune to its fatal poison). Warnings about the deadly power of menstrual blood, memorably detailed in Pliny's *Historia Naturalis*, were repeated throughout the sixteenth century and widely credited. A mother's milk was believed by early modern physicians to come from blood as well: but where the "corrupt" blood in a woman's body traveled to her uterus to be expelled, her better blood was refined by the body into milk, and passed from the liver to the breast (even as the good blood in man was transformed into semen).

Mother's milk was not just a way to feed babies, it was a marketable commodity that the poor produced and the rich hoarded. But it was commonly assigned value and virtue only in accord with the "noble" or "base" blood that produced it. When James I visited Oxford on 29 August 1605, he was accompanied by his personal physician, Dr. William Paddy, who challenged university scholars in public debate. Paddy argued the King's position against two popular beliefs: that "The morals of nurses are imbibed by infants with the milk," and that "Smoking tobacco is favorable to health." Paddy's view (that wet-nursing was not a moral issue) carried the day until the mid-nineteenth century, when the practice of surrogate nursing succumbed to popular fears that the poor abandoned their own children  on doorsteps in order to earn nurse others, for a wage; that surrogate nursing placed the child in physical and moral peril; and that nurse-children had a higher mortality rate. In the twentieth century – as the female breast was increasingly fetishized as an erotic object – the obscene lactating breast was banished to the private nursery or replaced by cow's milk administered from a bottle.

DWF

Elizabeth (Brook) Jocelin (1596-1622)

I may perhaps bee wondred at for writing in this kinde, considering there are so many excellent bookes, whose least note is worth all my meditations. I confesse it, and thus excuse my selfe. I write not to the world, but to mine own childe, who it may be, will more profit by a few weake instructions comming from a dead mother (who cannot euery day praise or reproue it as it deserues) than by farre better from much more learned. These things considered, neither the true knowledge of mine owne weaknesse, nor the feare this may come to the worlds eie, and bring scorne vpon my grave, can stay my hand...

– "To her Unborn Child" (sigs. C2v-3r)

ELIZABETH JOCELIN was the only child of Jane Chaderton (1583-1601), by her husband, Sir Richard Brook (knighted in Ireland; died 1632). Sir Peter Leycester (a seventeenth-century antiquary) reports that "through some dislike after marriage, Sir Richard and Jane his wife lived asunder." Jane Brook died in 1602. Leycester notes that Sir Richard's first marriage produced only "a daughter, married to one Jocelin of Cambridgeshire, who had all her mother's lands." (By his second wife, Katherine Neville, Brook had five sons, and lands to boot.) [1]

Just six years old when her mother died, Elizabeth was raised by her widowed grandfather, William Chaderton, Bishop of Chester and Lincoln, Master of Queen's College (Cambridge), and a professor of divinity: "by and under whom she was from her tender years carefully nurtured," with tutoring "in languages, history, and some arts," but "principally in studies of piety" (Goad, sig. a1v).

By her grandfather's death in 1608, Elizabeth Brook became a wealthy orphan, aged twelve. Her ensuing marriage (probably arranged prior to Bishop Chaderton's death) was to William Sandys of Histon, a nephew of the Bishop of Worcester. The marriage, which ended with Sandys's death in April 1615, may never have been consummated. The couple had no children.

A year and some few days later, Elizabeth married Tyrell Jocelin (1592/3-1656), an affectionate husband of her own choosing. The marriage on Elizabeth's testimony was both happy and blest.

A difficult first pregnancy in her seventh year of marriage prompted Elizabeth to ponder her death, a subject that her husband Tyrell could not endure to hear spoken of. But Elizabeth secretly purchased a winding sheet for her corpse, just in case; and she undertook to write a tract of religious instruction for their unborn child. Having received from her own mother a legacy of real estate and rental income, and having been raised in a bishop's palace, Elizabeth had always enjoyed material comforts a-plenty; but she wished her own legacy to be one of spirituality. Addressing her infant as if from the grave, the expectant mother prays that her infant, if a son, will go into the ministry; if a daughter, that she will study the Bible, embroidery, and housewifery. A strict sabbatarian with a painful (and doubtless over-developed) estimate of her own sinful condition, Jocelin trusts that her child of either gender will follow prayerfully in her footsteps, with "shame and sorrow" for sin, and a contrite heart.

On 12 October 1622, Elizabeth Jocelin gave birth to a daughter (named Theodora, after Tyrrel's mother). The baby came through the delivery just fine. But Elizabeth developed a puerperal infection and died nine days later.

The *Mother's Legacy* was found in a desk drawer – an unfinished manuscript of some 10,000 words – together with a cover letter from Elizabeth to her husband, in which she expressed her affection for him, defended her writing-project, and stated her hopes for their child. Tyrell Jocelin was so moved by the discovery of his wife's secret writing project that he wished to see it through to the press. He therefore enlisted the aid of Rev. Thomas Goad, chaplain to the Archbishop of Canterbury. Unwilling to leave well enough alone, Goad revised and completed Elizabeth's manuscript, finally publishing the work in 1624, with a *nihil obstat*, augmented by his own 1,200-word "Approbation."

Presenting himself as an ecclesiastical referee of the manuscript and as a judge of Jocelin's character, Rev. Goad extols those traits that he considers exemplary: Forsaken by her father and bereaved of her mother, Elizabeth as a child dutifully observed her mother's dying injunction, which was that she show "all obedience and reverence to her father, Sir Richard Brook, and to her reverend Grandfather." Although she once loved to study classical literature and foreign languages, Elizabeth never let her learning be known to others ("Of all which knowledge she was very sparing in her discourses, as pos-

---

[1] *a daughter...lands*] Leycester (1673), 327.

sessing it rather to hide, than to boast of"). The deceased had an extraordinary memory, "enabling her upon the first rehearsal to repeat above forty lines in English or Latin"; but her gift was made "more happy by her employment of it in carrying away an entire sermon." As a married woman, Elizabeth abandoned her study of all subjects but religion, in order to deliver "unspotted love" to her husband, "who enjoyed her about the space of six years and a half." And though she may have done some writing, "Her prose is "chaste and modest, like the author." "In the whole course of her pen," crows Rev. Goad, I observe her piety and humility: these her lines scarce showing one spark of the elementary fire of her secular learning: this, her candle, being rather lighted from the lamp of the sanctuary" (Goad, A5v-7v).

That Elizabeth Jocelin fully internalized the churchman's values receives confirmation from the author herself. In 1616, Daniel Tuvill, in his *Asylum Veneris; or A Sanctuary for Ladies*, had written in favor of women's secular education, condemning those chauvinists who make fun of learned women as frail ships with too much sail. Jocelin cites Tuvill only to disagree with him. She advises her unborn daughter: "good housewifery, writing, and good works: other learning a woman needs not. Though I admire it in those whom God hath blessed with discretion, [...] sometimes women have greater portions of learning than wisdom, which is of no better use to them than a mainsail to a flyboat, which runs in under water" (Jocelyn, B3v-Br4).

What Rev. Goad most admires about Elizabeth Jocelin is that "The course of her life was a perpetual meditation of *Death*, amounting almost to a prophetical sense of her dissolution, even then when she had not finished the twenty-seventh year of her age, nor was oppressed by any disease or danger other than the common lot of childbirth. [...L]ooking Death in the face, privately in her closet between God and her, she wrote these pious meditations; whereof herself strangely speaketh to her own bowels in this manner: "It may seem strange to thee to receive these lines from a mother that died when thou wert born" (8v-9v).

Dying on October 31st, Elizabeth Brook Jocelin left "unto the world a sweet perfume of good name; and to her only child (besides a competent inheritance), this manual being a deputed mother, for instruction; and for solace, a twin-like sister, issuing from the same parent, and seeing the light about the same time," a *Mother's Legacy,* thus approved: "*Sic approbavit.* Thomas Goad" (sig. 10r-v).

LEARNING, in the breast of a woman, is likened by their stoical adversaries to "a sword in the hands of a madman, which he knoweth not how to rule as reason shall inform him, but as the motions and violent fits of his distemperature shall enforce him." "It doth not ballast their judgments, but only addeth more sail to their ambition"; and like the weapon of Goliath, serveth but as "an instrument to give the fatal period to their honor's overthrow." And surely this fond imagination hath purchased a free inheritance to itself in the bosoms of some undiscreter parents, who hereupon will by no means endure that their daughters should be acquainted with any kind of literature at all. The pen must be forbidden them as the Tree of Good and Evil, and upon their blessing, [their daughter] must not handle it: [the pen] is a pandar to a virgin chastity and betrayeth it by venting forth those amorous passions that are incident to hotter bloods; which otherwise, like fire raked up in embers, would peradventure in a little space be utterly consumed. But if this be their fear, let them likewise bar [maidens] the use of their needle: with this, did Philomela fairly character those foul indignities which had been offered her by Tereus...

To converse with the dead – and this is to converse with books – hath been still accounted the readiest way to moralize our harsher natures, and to wean them from all inbred Barbarism to more humane and civil conversation... But if those prohibitions proceed from a providence in [parents] to prevent a curious desire of searching further into the cabinets of Minerva than is fitting (an error incident to capricious and working wits, such as *they* would have women's for the most part to be), let them show me what men are free from the like weakness.

But *Scientia inflat*: Knowledge puffeth up, and "There is nothing," say our opposites, "more swelling and imperious, than a woman that seeth she hath the superiority and start of her husband in *anything*"... As if [women] should conform themselves to men's weaknesses, and pattern out their own abilities by [men's] defects! He that is deprived of his bodily sight is content to be led, though by a child; and shall he that is blind in his understanding disdain to be directed by her who (by the ordinance of God and the rules of sacred wedlock) is allotted him a fellow-helper in all his businesses?

The husband and the wife are the eyes of a family; if the right one be so bleared that it cannot well discern, the guiding of the household must of necessity be left unto the left, or on the sudden all will go to wrack. And surely, I see no reason but *the hen may be permitted to crow, where the cock can do nothing but cackle*; so that learning, we see, is an ornament and a decency most expedient for women, were it for no other respect than to supply, as occasion may require, the defects that are in men. And truly, some of them, by seconding a natural propension in themselves to letters, with an industrious pursuit have attained to so high a perfection in them, that men considering how imperiously they challenge a preheminence over them herein, have had just cause to blush at their own ignorance.

—Daniel Tuvill, *Asylum Veneris; or A Sanctuary for Ladies, justly protecting them, their virtues, and sufficiencies from the foul aspersions and forged imputations of traducing spirits* (1616).

Epistle to Tourell Jocelin. From *A Mother's Legacy to her Unborn Child*

To my truly loving, and most dearly loved husband, Tourell Jocelin:

MINE OWN DEAR LOVE, I no sooner conceived an hope that I should be made a mother by thee, but with it entered the consideration of a mother's duty; and shortly after followed the apprehension of danger that might prevent me from executing that care I so exceedingly desired – I mean, in religious training our child. And in truth, death, appearing in this shape, was doubly terrible unto me: first, in respect of the painfulness of that kind of death; and, next, of the loss my little one should have, in wanting me. But I thank God these fears were cured with the remembrance that all things work together for the best to those that love God, and [with] a certain assurance that He will give me patience according to my pain.

Yet still I thought there was some good office I might do for my child more than only to bring it forth. Though it should please God to take me, when I considered our frailty, our apt inclination to sin, the Devil's subtlety, and the world's deceitfulness – against these, how much desired I to admonish it! But still it came into my mind that death might deprive me of time if I should neglect the present.

I knew not what to do: I thought of writing, but then mine own weakness appeared so manifestly that I was ashamed, and durst not undertake it. But when I could find no other means to express my motherly zeal, I encouraged myself with these reasons:

First, that I wrote to a child, and though I were but a woman, yet to a child's judgment what I understood might serve for a foundation to a better learning.

Again, I considered it was to my own, and in private sort, and my love to my own might excuse my errors.

And lastly but chiefly, I comforted myself that my *intent* was good, and that I was well assured God is the prosperer of good purposes.

Thus resolved, I writ this ensuing letter to our little one, to whom I could not find a fitter hand to convey it than thine own, which may'st with authority see the performance of this my little *Legacy*, of which my child is executor.

And, Dear Love, as thou must be the overseer, for God's sake, when [our child] shall fail in duty to God or to the world, let not thy indulgence wink at such folly, but severely correct it. And that thy trouble may be little when it comes to years, take the more care when it is young: first, in providing it a nurse: O make choice, not so much for her complexion, as for her mild and honest disposition!

Likewise if the child be to remain long abroad after weaning, as near as may be, choose a house where it may not learn to swear or speak scurrilous words. (I know I may be thought too scrupulous in this: but I am sure thou shalt find it a hard matter to break a child of that [which] it learns so young. It will be a great while ere [our child] will be thought old enough to be beaten for evil words; and by that time, it will be so perfect in imperfections, that blows will not mend it. And when some charitable body reproves or corrects [our child] for these faults, let nobody pity it with the loss of the mother.)

Next, good Sweetheart, keep [our child] not from school, but let it learn betimes. If it be a son, I doubt not but thou wilt dedicate it to the Lord as his minister, if He will please of His mercy to give him grace and capacity for that great work.

If it be a daughter, I hope my mother Brook (if thou desirest her) will take it among hers, and let them all learn one lesson. I desire her bringing up may be learning the Bible (as my sister's do), good housewifery, writing, and good works. Other learning a woman needs not. Though I admire it in those whom God hath blest with discretion, yet I desired not much in my own, having seen that sometimes women have greater portions of learning than wisdom; which is of no better use to them than a mainsail to a fly-boat, which runs in under water. But where learning and wisdom meet in a virtuous-disposed woman, she is the fittest closet for all goodness. She is like a well-balanced ship that may bear all her sail.

She is – indeed, I should but shame my *self*, if I should go about to praise her more! But, my Dear, though she have all this in her, she will hardly make a poor man's wife. Yet I leave it to thy will. If thou desirest a learnèd daughter, I pray God give her a wise and religious heart, that she may use it to His glory, thy comfort, and her own salvation.

But howsoever thou disposest of her education, I pray thee labor by all means to teach her true humility. Though I much desire it may be as humble if it be a son as a daughter, yet in a daughter I more fear that vice, *pride* (being now rather accounted a virtue in our sex worthy praise, than a vice fit for reproof). Many parents read lectures of [pride] to their children, how *necessary* it is! – and they have principles that must not be disputed against. As first: "Look how much you esteem yourself, others will esteem of you." Again: "What you give to others, you derogate from yourself." (And many more of these kinds.) I have heard men accounted wise that have maintained this kind of pride under the name of generous "knowing" or "understanding" themselves. But I am sure that he that truly knows himself shall know so much evil by himself, that he shall have small reason to think himself better than another man. Dearest, I am so fearful to bring thee a proud high-minded child, that, though I know thy care will need no spur, yet I cannot but desire thee to double thy watchfulness over this vice. [Pride] is such a crafty insinuating devil, it will enter little children in the likeness of wit, with which their parents are delighted – and that is sweet nourishment to it.

I pray thee, Dear Heart, delight not to have a bold child: modesty and humility are the sweetest groundworks of all virtue. Let not thy servants give it any other title than the Christen name, till it have discretion to understand how to respect others. And I pray thee, be not profuse in the expense of clothes upon it. Methinks it is a vain delight in parents to bestow that cost upon one child which would serve two or three. If they have not children enow of their own to employ so much cost upon, *Pauper ubique iacet.* (There wants not poor at every door.) Thus, Dear, thou see'st my belief: if thou canst teach thy little one humility, it must needs make thee a glad father. [1]

But I know thou wonderest by this time what the cause should be that (we two continually unclasping our hearts one to the other) I should reserve this to *writing*. When thou thinkest thus, Dear, remember how grievous it was to thee but to hear me say, "I may die," and thou wilt confess this would have been an unpleasant discourse to thee – and thou knowest I never durst displease thee willingly, so much I love thee! All I now desire is that the unexpectedness of it make it not more grievous to thee. But I know thou art a Christian, and therefore will not doubt of thy patience. And though I thus write to thee, as heartily desiring to be religiously prepared to die, yet, my Dear, I despair not of life; nay, I hope and daily pray for it, if so God will be pleased.

Nor shall I think this labor lost, though I do live: for I will make it my own looking-glass wherein to see when I am too severe, when too remiss; and in my child's fault through this glass to discern mine own errors. And I hope God will so give me His grace that I shall more skillfully *act,* than *apprehend,* a mother's duty.

My Dear, thou knowest me so well, I shall not need to tell thee I have written honest thoughts in a disordered fashion, not observing method. For thou knowest how short I am of learning and natural endowments to take such a course in writing. Or if that strong affection of thine have hid my weakness from thy sight, I now profess seriously my own ignorance (and though I did not, this following treatise would bewray it!). But I send it only to the eyes of a most loving husband, and of a child exceedingly beloved, to whom I hope it will not be altogether unprofitable.

Thus humbly desiring God to give thee all comfort in this life and happiness in the life to come, I leave thee and thine to His most gracious protection.

Thine inviolable,
Eliza. Jocelin

---

[1] *Pauper ubique iacet*] The poor lie everywhere.

Women's Rites: Tradition and Change

Maydens all, be rul'd by mee
Doe not belieue their flatterye,
While you Liue, Liue euer free,...

—from "Love Lamenting" (c. 1619)

The Lullaby. In the Middle Ages and throughout the Tudor period, the English *lullay,* or lullaby, was a much-loved and often-praised form of women's cultural activity. During the Jacobean period that centuries-old tradition all but evaporates from the paper trail. From 1603-1625 only three new lullays appeared in print, plus a reprint of the lullaby sung by fairies in *A Midsummer Night's Dream* (performed in 1594; first published in 1600; reprinted in the Shakespeare First Folio, 1623). Of the three new lullabies, the first was scored by Francis Pilkington, who transgenders the tradition. His lullaby (1605) is not sung by a mother to her babe, but features a lutenist and four male voices, serenading nymphs to a golden sleep and sweet dreams: [1]

NYMPHS, *let golden sleep*
Charm your star-brighter eyes,
Whiles my lute the watch doth keep
With pleasing sympathies,
Lulla lullaby, lulla lullaby.
Sleep sweetly, sleep sweetly,
Let nothing affright ye,
In calm contentments lie.
Lulla lullaby, lulla lullaby.

Dream, fair virgins, of delight
And best Elysian groves:
Whiles the wand'ring shades of night
Resemble your true loves:
Lulla lullaby, lulla lullaby
Your kisses, your blisses,
Send them by your wishes,
Though they be not nigh.

Thus, dear damsels, I do give
Good night and so am gone.
With your heart's desires long live
Still joy and never moan.
Lulla lullaby, lulla lullaby
Hath pleased you and eased you,
And sweet slumber seized you,
And now to bed I hie.

Rest, sweet nymphs, let golden sleep
Charm your star-brighter eyes,
Whiles my lute the watch doth keep
With pleasant sympathies,
Lulla lullaby, lullaby, lullaby.
Sleep sweetly, sleep sweetly,
Let nothing affright ye,
In calm contentments lie.
Lulla lullaby, lullaby, lullaby.

A second printed lullaby, comprised of a single stanza, was scored by Thomas Ravenscroft in 1614 as a round for three singers of indeterminate gender, addressing a woodland nymph who may be pregnant: [2]

OAKEN LEAVES *in the merry wood so wild,*
When will you grow green-a?
Fairest maid, an' thou be with child,
Lullaby may'st thou sing-a,
Lulla lullaby, lulla-lulla, lullaby,
Lullaby may'st thou sing-a.

The third and last, scored by Martin Peerson for four male voices (1620), speaks for the Madonna, pledging her breast and obedience to her sovereign Son in a fantasy not unlike Shel Silverstein's modern classic, *The Giving Tree:* [3]

UPON MY LAP *my sovereign sits,*
And sucks upon my breast,
Meantime his love maintains my life,
And gives my sense her rest.
Sing lulla, lullaby, sing lulla,
Lullaby, my little, little boy,
Sing lulla, lullaby, sing lulla,
Lullaby, mine only joy.

When thou hast taken thy repast,
Repose, my babe, on me:
So may thy mother and thy nurse,
Thy cradle also be.
Sing lullaby, my little boy.
Sing lullaby, mine only joy.

---

[1] *NYMPHS*] Pilkington (1605), Canto 6.

[2] *OAKEN LEAVES*] Ravenscroft (1614), no. 6.

[3] *UPON MY LAP*] Peerson (1620), no. 12.

I grieve that duty doth not work
All what my wishing would:
Because I would not be to thee
But in the best I should.
Sing lullaby, my little boy.
Sing lullaby mine only joy.

Yet as I am, and as I may,
I must and will be thine:
Though all too little for thy self,
Vouchsafing to be mine.
Sing lullaby, my little boy.
Sing lullaby, mine only joy.

After 1603, one can still find a sermon or two in which mention is made of angels singing lullabies to restless children of God; but the *lullaby* otherwise becomes a synonym for *siren song*, soothing music against which Christian men must stop their ears or forfeit their masculine *vertú*. There were doubtless many reasons for this sea-change, one of which was the English nation's growing revulsion for Roman Catholicism: the *lullaby* was a cultural form associated with veneration of the Madonna, sentiment that was transferred in some measure to queens Mary and Elizabeth. After Elizabeth's death, Protestant writers and preachers, both Scots and English, exhibit near-unanimous discomfort with anything that smacks of mother-worship.

For Rev. Thomas Tuke, a *Lullaby* is what the Devil "singeth usually to the witch till she come to the stake, and to the carnal man till he come to his grave – and so, rocks them fast asleep in the cradle of sensual security (*The True Trial and Turning of a Sinner*, 1607).

Thomas Walkington condemns preachers who make "the pulpit a cage to sing *placentia* in, to sing a *lullaby* to Solomon's sinful sluggard, who lies snorting fast asleep upon the downy bed of iniquity and security" (*Salomons Sweete Harpe*, 1608). [1]

William Est, in his 1617 translation of Willibald Pirckheimer, condemns those women who wear face-paint and wear blonde periwigs, "nets of the Devil to ensnare unstable souls," like "little *lullabies*" (*The Praise of the Gout*, 1617).

In the anonymous *History of Morindos* (1609), the courtesans of the Spanish King are said to be "feeders of his lust. For every day in the year he had a several concubine, all young, beautiful, and lovely. Nature framed their bodies fair, though sin made their souls black (for both art and riches endeavored to delight his insatiate desires). Earth's chiefest pleasures were at his command.

And all the *lullabies* of content rocked him in the cradle of security. Thus careless of Heaven's wrath, he more honored the Devil than he loved God."

Robert Chester, in his critique of British society, frets that old-fashioned nursery lullabies are being displaced by birth control. He writes disapprovingly of a popular Jacobean abortifacient, a recipe composed of cyclamen and a syrup of birthroot worts: "Women grown with child," he laments, "carry this same sowbread / Or plant it in their gardens," knowing "'Twill kill the issue they about them bring, / When mother, *lullaby* with joy should sing. / Yet wanton, scaping maids perhaps will taste / this unkind herb, and snatch it up in haste" (*The Anuals of Great Britain*, 1611).

John Davies a year later represents the Earth itself as a loathsome mother, a witch whose lullabies tempt world-hungry men to drop their guns to be nursed by the whore of Babylon:

For, ah, this witch (the world) with pleasing charms
So lullabies our sense in soft delights,
That though we be upon our guard, in arms,
Yet we are taken in our appetites
And made to serve the Devil…
                    (*The Muses Sacrifice*, 1612)

Addressing the infantile fool who gives ear to flattering adulation, John Andrews warns that men of virtue, "scorning by thy pitch to be defiled / Or by thy sweet-tuned *lullabies* beguiled, / Do loathe to view thy vild deformity" (*The Anatomie of Baseness*, 1615).

Barnabe Rich similarly cites the mother's lullaby as a figure for the soothing delights of a permissive and sinful society: "Let us have him that can sing lullaby to folly, that can smooth up sin and wink at any manner of wickedness" (*My Ladies Looking Glasse*, 1616).

Thomas Adams condemns the miser who prefers his barns to his bairns: the greedy man "dreams his belly full, and now his pipes go: he sings requiem, and *lullabies* his spirit in the cradle of his barn" (*The Happines of the Church*, 1619).

For Robert Aylett, the *lullaby* is a call to lethargy:

Oh, this is Satan's subt'lest lullaby,
Our souls with stupid laziness to charm,
And then of spiritual arms and weapons to disarm …
                    (*Thrifts Equipage*, 1622)

Thomas Scott likewise pities the unarmed man who can be "rocked asleep in desperate security with a *lullaby* of peace and safety." Comfortable in "the sluggard's cradle," and "shutting his eyes

---

[1] *placentia*] pleasantly.

Blissful ignorance

against the knowledge of danger, he cares not who kills him" (*The Belgicke Pismire*, 1622).

To value the lullaby, even to speak with affection of the lullaby, is to fall under the spell of the mother's dangerous voice, which invites infantilization of the adult male, and a fatal passivity.

Under King Charles and throughout the Puritan Interregnum, contempt for the lullaby becomes even more virulent. Thomas Beard attributes "the great overflow of vice in this age" to "the false and deceitful *lullaby* of effeminate pleasures." One representative anti-papist tract represents Christianity as "a sucking babe" which, "smiling to the mother's *lullaby*, / Hangs on her melting breast, and whilst it takes / The honey flowing from those milky lakes," the old whore of Rome snatches the child from her bosom and cruelly dashes out its brains, splattering the rocks with "the tender softness of that infant matter."[1]

JESUS

John Reading (a preacher, not an anthropologist) writes of "African mothers' *lullabies* who (as we noted) use to still their weeping babes which they offered to Moloch, with songs and kisses, that they might not cast a crying sacrifice into those flames."[2]

This discourse is the more astonishing when set beside the many dozens of idealized references to the lullaby in the Elizabethan period. But if *lullaby* in the seventeenth century became a dirty word, and lullabies largely omitted from the written record as a result, women clearly did not stop singing, revising, or passing along traditional lyrics.

from print to verbal tradition

That the traditional woman's lyric survived in the nursery if not in print is partly indicated by a single surviving Jacobean exemplar, copied in 1606 into the commonplace book of Thomas Chaffyn of Mere, Wiltshire – a lyric which, though sentimental, is as poignant as any lullaby composed before or since:

[Lulla by Lully]

My little sweet darling, my comfort and joy,
　Sing lulla by lully,
In beauty excelling the princes of Troy,
　Sing lulla by lully,
Now suck, child, and sleep, thy mother's sweet boy,
　Sing lulla by lully,
The gods bless and keep thee from cruel annoy,
　Sing lully, lully, lully,
　Sweet baby, lully, lully,
　Sweet baby, lully, lully,

---

[1] Beard, *The Theatre of Gods Judgments* (1642), 3; ABCDE, pseud., *Novembris monstrum* (1641), 5.

[2] Reading, *A Guide to the Holy City* (1651), 439.

Thy father, sweet infant, from mother is gone,
　Sing lully, lully, lully,
And she in the woods here with thee left alone,
　Sing lulla by lully,
To thee little infant why do I make moan,
　Sing lully, lully, lully,
Sith thou canst not help me to sigh nor to groan?
　Sing lully, lully, lully,
　Sweet baby, lully by lully,
　Sweet child, lully, lully.

It is perhaps no coincidence that this last example of a dying form, with its appeal to the gods and its evocation of fallen Troy, marks a turning-away from the dominant religious discourse that had turned with venom on the form itself.

good explanation

• • •

Lover's Laments. Another genre of music popular throughout the medieval and Tudor periods is that of the woman's lament – a rich tradition of song exampled in *Woman's Works*, volume one. The speaker typically sorrows for an absent lover or husband, or grieves for her own lamentable condition. Sometimes, she mourns a partner slain in war or lost at sea. More often she has been forsaken by her lover for another woman, or abandoned by him after he has raped her, or seduced her and gotten her pregnant.

This isn't nearly as wholesome as a lullaby

Women's laments typically take one of three musical forms, the most frequent of which is the cautionary tale: the singer, narrating her sexual experience, advises young women to remain virgins until married. (Most surviving medieval exemplars were written by clerics who did a poor job of ventriloquizing a woman's voice.) Nearly as common are masculinist satires on the form, in which a fallen woman is made the object of ridicule, or of the singer's own sexual fantasy. Least common in the written record are lyrics that speak with clarity and sympathy of a woman's place in a man's world; the surpassing examples of which are Elizabeth Sidney's "He is Gone" and "I Know Not What."

the singer

Many extant songs from the Jacobean period admonish young women to preserve their chastity and to distrust the oaths of male suitors; but few were written for a woman's voice, and few of those appear to have been of woman's composition. "Love Lamenting" is exceptional in that it claims a Pyrrhic victory for female agency. Unlike most songs in this vein, men are here blamed for woman's grief while maids are urged to "live ever free," rather than submit themselves to masculine deceit.

Love Lamenting (c. 1619)

Shall I weep or shall I sing?
I know not best which fits mourning.
If I weep I ease my brain;
If I sing I sweeten pain.
> *Weeping I'll sing, and singing weep,*
> *Because that men no faith can keep.*

They have still deceitful parts
To rob poor ladies of their hearts.
When we love, they tyrants grow,
Glorying in our overthrow—
> *Wherefore I'll sing, and singing, weep,*
> *Because that men no faith can keep.*

Maidens all, be ruled by me:
Do not believe their flattery.
While you live, live ever free,
Lest that this your ditty be:
> *"Weeping I'll sing, and singing, weep,*
> *Because that men no faith can keep."*

The lyric did not go unnoticed. Despite or perhaps because of its biting critique of masculine psychology (stanza 2) and its call for women's independence (stanza 3), "Love Lamenting" became a well-known song, as is attested by the numerous manuscript copies that have survived from the early and mid seventeenth century.

In 1620, Richard Johnson, a hack writer and noted plagiarist, capitalized on the popularity of "Love Lamenting," published his own new version, and "to a delicate new tune." Johnson captions his text, "The Maiden's Complaint of her Love's Inconstancy, / Showing it forth in every degree, / She being left as one forlorn, / With sorrows she herself t' adorn, / And seems for to lament and mourn." Drawn out to eighteen stanzas, "the Maiden's Complaint" bears a refrain: it "makes me sigh and sob and weep / To see false men no faith can keep."

The narrator confesses to have lost not only her heart but also her virginity: "He did me with his arms embrace, / He kissed me on't, and swore that he / Would never have no one but me." As a predictable result, "The jewel's lost, the thief is fled, / And I lie wounded in my bed." Moreover, as a gullible woman, Jonson's singer has created for herself an unavoidable legacy of shame: "If to repent I should begin, / They'll say 'twas I that let him in." What the pathetic and giddy girl seeks now, and cannot get, is to have her lover back again: "I love where I have cause to hate, / Such is my foolish fickle state, / My time I spend in grief and woe, / Which sure will be mine overthrow." Since she cannot have him, she advises everyone, male and female, to avoid the bad luck of sexual desire: "What hap hath any he or she, /

That can but live at liberty / And not be troubled as I am."

Having no hope of redemption, Johnson's woebegone maiden is reduced to speechless misery: "My body's faint and I am weak, / My tongue is tied, I cannot speak." The weeping singer and singing weeper of the original lyric is thus reduced by Johnson to a sop of blubbering femininity, "sobbing, sighing, and weeping," no singer, just a sinner, having no future but death: "My days are short, my life's not long, I cannot well declare my song. / Yet in some part, I here do show / That you the cause hereof may know" (*i.e.,* premarital sex), "Wherefore I sigh and sob and weep, / To see that men no faith can keep."

While exploiting the popularity of "The Maiden's Complaint," Richard Johnson's redaction moves to contain the subversive potential of "Love Lamenting." Other poems and song-lyrics of the Jacobean period, though written as if for a woman's voice, are frankly hostile to the "fallen" woman who speaks (not infrequently, a ventriloquized offender, such as the countess of Essex or Anne Turner or Martha Scambler). But throughout the Jacobean period, in pseudo-women's verse – whether gynophobic or moral or satirical or merely jocular – one finds evidence of growing unrest among women, a resistance to their assigned subordination and lack of personal agency.

Fine examples are supplied by the composer Robert Jones. In *A Musicall Dreame* (1609), Jones creates a setting for Thomas Campion's "Though your strangeness frets my heart" (which was evidently written as a reply to Anne Vavasor's "Though I seem strange"); together with witty love-lyrics from the pen of Elizabeth Sidney (a poet recognized even by the misogynist Ben Jonson to be one of the great talents of his generation. In the same volume, Jones included a number of spiritual songs, at least two of them by Lady Anne Southwell (see *Women's Works,* volume 4).

In *The Muses Gardin for Delights*, Jones set to music another anonymous woman's lyric, "Cantus XV," here titled the "Song of the Marrying Maiden." Whether it was penned by a male or female poet cannot be determined. That it was written by a fourteen-year-old girl is doubtful. The father, who intends to marry his daughter to an older man, presumably to suit his own dynastic objectives, has no tolerance for romance. The reluctant mother wishes to keep her daughter from marriage until she is older. And the maid, who at fourteen has reached sexual maturity, will not be restrained. She, too, is a stereotype of the age. As the speaker, she may represent only the projection of a male poet. But whoever wrote it, this plucky lyric – which was set to music by Jones so that it might be sung – articulates a cry of resistance that would be heard with increasing frequency and clarity in the seventeenth century: a demand from women (including the daughters of aristocrats, who usually had the least freedom) that they must be permitted to marry for love, to men of their own choosing.

XV. [Song of the Marrying Maiden]

My father fain would have me take
A man that hath a beard.
My mother, she cries, "Out, alack!"
And makes me much [afeared.]

Forsooth, I am "not old enough."
Now surely this is goodly stuff!
Faith, let my mother marry me,
Or let some young man bury me. Wow

For I have lived these fourteen years—
My mother knows it well.
What need she then to cast such fears?
Can anybody tell?—

As though young women do not know
That custom will not let them woo!
I would be glad if I might choose—
But I were mad if I refuse.

My mother bids me "go to school"
And "learn to do some good."
'Twere well if she would let the fool
Come home and suck a dug!—

As if my father knew not yet
That maidens are for young men fit!
Give me my mind, and let me wed—
Or you shall quickly find me dead.

How soon my mother hath forgot   [25]
That ever she was young,
(And how that she denièd not
But sung another song!)

I must not speak what I do think;
When I am dry, I may not drink
(Though her desire be now grown old,
She must have fire, when she is cold!).

You see the mother loves the son,
The father loves the maid.
What would she have me be – a nun?
I will not be denayed!

I will not live thus idle still.
My mother shall not have her will.
My father speaketh like a man:
I will be married, do what she can!

But that daughters could more freely sing of personal agency than exercise it in real life is poignantly illustrated in Mary Wroth's *Urania*:

ONE DAY my Father called me to him, telling me what a match he had made for me, and (not doubting of my liking) showed much comfort which he had conceived of it; and so went on with joy, as if the marriage had been straight to be consummated.

I was truly a little amazed withal – till he, finding I made no answer, pulling me to him, told me he hoped my silence proceeded from no other ground than bashfulness, since he assured himself I would not gainsay what he commanded, or so much as dislike what he intended to do with me; wherefore he would have me join my dutiful agreement to his choice and order my love to go along with his pleasure: "for young maids' eyes should like only where their father liked, and love where he did appoint."

This gave me sight to my greater mischief, wherefore I kneeled down. Words I had few to speak, only with tears I besought him to remember his promise, which was never to force me, against my will, to marry any.

"Will?" said he. "Why, your *will* ought to be no other than *obedience*! And in that, you should be rather willful in obeying than question what I appoint. If not, take this and be assured of it: that if you like not as I like, and wed where I will you, you shall never from me receive least favor, but be accounted a stranger and a lost child."

These words ran into my soul like poison through my veins, chilling it. […] [1]

Mary Sidney in 1604 reluctantly yielded to her parents' will, married Robert Wroth, and regretted it for the rest of her life. Other Jacobean women chose their own mates, in defiance of their father and social convention (in some cases, defying the King himself). Elizabeth Southwell eloped with Robert Dudley. Penelope Rich secretly married her long-time lover, Charles Blount. Arbella Stuart eloped with William Seymour. Lucy Percy married James Hay. Elizabeth Norris, a ward of the King, eloped with Edward Wray. These and many other such marriages, arranged by the lovers rather than by the bride's father, tended toward tragedy rather than comedy. But that they happened at all indicates a slowly swelling chorus of resistance from British women who, in matters of the heart, were prepared to sing: "I will not be denayed."

---

[1] *One day...chilling it*] Ed. DWF from *Urania* (1621), p. 207.

Elizabeth Melville (Colville) (1578? – 1640?),

Lady Culross

Tak the pen in your hand, and seik a blissing...
—Elizabeth Melville to John Livingston

ELIZABETH MELVILLE, poet, was the daughter of Christian Boswell and James Melville, of Halhill, Scotland. Her father was a diplomat whose career began in 1549 with his appointment as a fourteen-year-old page to Mary, Queen of Scots, in France. By age twenty-nine – when he was dispatched to the court of Elizabeth I to defend Queen Mary's proposed union with Lord Darnley – James Melville was a seasoned statesman. Weathering the storm after Darnley's murder and Mary's disgrace, Melville won the confidence of James VI, and for his service to the crown was knighted in 1590, at the coronation of the queen consort, Anna of Denmark. When King James succeeded to the English throne following the death of Elizabeth I, Melville, now 68, retired to Halhill, an estate he had acquired as the adopted heir of the reformer, Henry Balnaves. He spent the last years of his life writing his autobiography – *Memoirs of His Own Life*, 420 pages – in which he makes no mention of his children. [1]

Elizabeth's first literary notice appears shortly after her marriage. In 1599, the protestant minister Alexander Hume issued a pamphlet of original *Hymns, or, Sacred Songs*, which he dedicated with affection to the faithful and virtuous poet, Elizabeth Melville of Comrie. His epistle dedicatory merits quotation in full, for it illuminates both Elizabeth's character and Rev. Hume's Calvinist construction of feminine virtue:

TO THE FAITHFUL AND VERTUOUS Lady, Elizabeth Melville, Ladie Comrie, grace, mercy, and peace, from God the Father, and from our Lord Jesus Christ.

WHEN I READ *that epistle written by the Apostle John unto "an elect lady (beloved in the Lord Jesus)," I call to mind the godly and elect ladies in this our age, which within this country are known unto me; of the which number, I count you to be one: even a lady chosen of God to be one of His saints, and the godly daughter of a faithful father (for the children of God have their own marks). Therefore, when I first perceived the spiritual conference, the grave behavior, the fervent zeal, and the great sense of natural corruption with the strang resistance of the same that was in you, I think them as infallible signs of sanctification. (Let no man suspect me of flattery, for I speak not after the flesh.) Neither fear I, Sister, that this my commendation puff you up (for where the spirit of Jesus dwells, there is humility); but rather, that thereby ye shall be stirred up and encouraged to persevere and grow in godliness.* [2]

It is a rare thing to see a lady, a tender youth, sad, solitaire, and sanctified, oft sighing and weeping through the conscience of sin. Would to God that all the ladies of this land, especially they of the greatest rank, were of the like modest and godly disposition! For the most part of them we see to delight mair in covetousness, and in oppression of the pure, for the entertainment of their pride; or else, to spend their days in chambering, wantonness, decking of their bodies in delicate feeding, and in satisfying their lusts (nor to have ane incorrupt and holy heart, with a meek and quiet spirit, arraying themselves in comely apparel with shamefastness and modesty, and with good works, as the Apostles of Jesus Christ hath commanded them, 1 Timothy 2.9, 1 Peter 3.3). Let such women remember that [one] day they shall appear and give account before the judgment seat of Christ, and shall receive a reward in their bodies according to their works. I would wish them to have this weighty saying of the Apostle ever recent in memory, as a dicton: "She that lives in pleasure is dead while she liveth" (1 Tim. 5:6). But ye live more in murmuring and in pain! – therefore, ye shall rejoice eternally.

---

[1] *children*] The Melvilles had four children. Elizabeth may have been the eldest (though her brother James, Jr., an elder son, inherited Halhill on their father's death in 1617). Younger brother Robert entered the ministry as an assistant pastor at Culross. Sister Margaret married Andrew Balfour of Montquhany. And Elizabeth married Sir John Colville of Comrie, who received ecclesiastical revenue under his inherited title as "the Commendator of Culross."

[2] *strang*] strong.

Now to come to the point: Having composed in my youth a few songs in verse to the glory of God – seeing the custom of men is to dedicate their works to their favorites and patrons – shall it not be lawful to me also, after the manner of men, to present unto you (a faithful and beloved lady) a part of my little labours? And sa meikle the rather, because I know ye delight in poesy yourself! – and, as I unfeignedly confess, excels any of your sex in that art that ever I heard, within this nation. I have seen your compositions – so copious! so pregnant! so spiritual! – that I doubt not but it is the gift of God in you.

Finally, because so little a work as this is, requires a short epistle, I take my leave, not doubting but my good meaning shall be favourably accepted. Continue (good Lady and Sister) in that godly course which ye have begun. Let nothing be done upon ostentation. Love your husband. Have a modest care of your family. And let your chief care be casten upon the Lord Jesus, who will recompense us at his coming. To God therefore – the Father, and our Lord Jesus Christ – be all praise for ever. Amen.

At Logie, the 16 of February 1598[/9].
Your brother in the Lord Jesus, Minister of the Evangel,
Alexander Hume

Much of Melville's verse was presumed lost until 2002, when Jamie Reid Baxter discovered and edited for publication some two dozen poems by Melville that circulated in manuscript. These include sequences of spiritual sonnets, and an adaptation of "Come live with me and be my love" in which Melville transfigures Christopher Marlowe's "passionate shepherd" as the Good Shepherd Jesus, calling out to sinners. Evidently written in the 1590s when Melville was still young, the verses found by Baxter provide a poignant illustration of a young Scots writer attempting to negotiate the irreconcilable conventions of literary aspiration, feminine virtue, and Calvinist shame. The tone of Melville's early work ranges from embarrassing self-contempt ("The sensual sow in filth I far exceed […]") to an ambitious invocation for Jehovah, her Muse, to "Direct my pen" ("That I a triple talent may restore").

Melville's Scottish texts are here presented in the original spelling (on the left) but with normalized punctuation,, and with a parallel English text on the right.

A note on pronunciation. *Quh—* (as in *quhat, quhy, quhair, quhen*) represents a strongly aspirated *h—*. Scots *r-* is trilled when appearing as the first letter of a word or syllable; *–ch* (*licht, thocht*) is gutteral, as in *loch* (not as in English *lock* or *latch*). Scots vowels tend to be longer than in English. Words such as *even, heavens,* and *over* are often elided (*e'en, h'ens, o'er*) even when spelled out in the text.

Invocation

by Elizabeth Melville

O great Iehovah michtie, King of Kingis,
Thrie persounis joyned in one and one in thrie—
O loving lord, that onlie livis and ringis
Ovir hevin above below ovir land and sea—
O that is and was and ay sall be,
That nevir did begin nor ȝit sall end,
Quhois dwelling place is in the hevinis so hie
Quhois majestie no hairt can comprehend—
Sum succour to Thy simple servand send
Mak haist to help me with thy holie Spirit—
Direct my pen and lat me not offend
In writting of thy worthie word so sweit:
    Bot grant thy giftis may still grow more and more,
    That I ane tripill talent may restore.

Invocation

trans. DWF

O great Jehovah mighty, King of kingès,
Three persons joined in one and one in three—
O loving Lord, that only lives and reignès
O'er Heaven above, below, o'er land and sea—
O that is and was and aye shall be,
That never did begin nor yet shall end,
Whose dwelling place is in the heavens so high,
Whose majesty no heart can comprehend—
Some succor to Thy simple servant send,
Make haste to help me with Thy holy Spirit—
Direct my pen and let me not offend
In writing of Thy worthy Word so sweet:
    But grant Thy gifts may still grow more and more,
    That I a triple talent may restore. [1]

---

[1] *triple talent*] three talents of gold (an ancient unit of weight). In Jesus' parable of the talents, the good slave invests talents received from his Master and earns a profit while the bad slave who returns the Master's principal without a profit is condemned to Hell.

Sonnet 3.

The sensuall sow in filth I far exceid,
Quhois nature is to wallow in the myre:
It hurts hir not bot doth hir eass and feid,
Quilk is the end of all sche can desyre.
Bot I, alace, quho heicher sould aspyre,In lothsum
lusts my lyf hes long mispent;
Quhairof I fynd ay greif to be the hyre,
Yit to the myre my nature still is bent.   [1]
O then, quhat caus haue I for to lament
My bypast lyfe and humblie for to pray
Unto the Lord, his wraith for to relent,
That with Chrysts blude my blotts be wascht away
  Then I auow and promeis by godis grace
  To turne bak bot fordward hold my race.   [2]

Sonnet 4.

In brittil bark of fraill fant feble flesch
My sillie saul with contrair winds is tost.   [3]
Calms, me corrupt. In storms, I frett and fasch.   [4]
In rest, I roust. In trubell, all seims lost.
No hold I haue nor beild quhairof to bost.   [5]
My skill is small, the schalds and rocks ar ryfe.
The storme of sin still dryues on liward cost.   [6]
No anker serues bot *hope*, to saue my lyue.
Alace, my sins have raisd this storme and stryfe
Quhilk none can swage bot Jesus Chryst alone.
He can (and will, at neid) these storms reproue
Thocht he delay till the thrid watche be gone
  Cum, Jesus! Say, "Tak courage, it is I."
  Tho first I fear, yit will I death defy.

From **Love's Lament for Christ's Absence**

What marvell though I make my moane, my moane?
My mourning muse cannot be still.
What marvell though I sigh and groane, and
groane?
I long for to lament my fill,
For love, alace, I must lament:
This mynde of myne is mal-content
And cannot hold her peace.
Alace, I lack both life and light—
My lord hath tane a long goodnight.
How should my sorrow cease?
Drop downe, my eyes, and never tyre
Untill I have myne heart's desyre.

Sonnet 3.

The sensual sow in filth I far exceed,
Whose nature is to wallow in the mire:
It hurts her not, but doth her ease, and feed,
Which is the end of all she can desire.
But I, alack, who higher should aspire,
In loathsome lusts my life have long misspent;
Whereof I find aye grief to be the hire,
Yet to the mire my nature still is bent.   [1]
O then, what cause have I for to lament
My by-past life! – and humbly for to pray
Unto the Lord, His wrath for to relent,
That with Christ's blood my blots be washed away.
  Then I avow and promise by God's grace
  To turn back – but forward hold my race.   [2]

Sonnet 4.

In brittle bark of frail faint feeble flesh
My siely soul with contrare winds is tossed.   [3]
Calms, me corrupt. In storms, I fret and fash.   [4]
In rest, I rust. In trouble, all seems lost.
No hold I have nor beild whereof to boast.   [5]
My skill is small, the shoals and rocks are rife.
The storm of sin still drives on leeward coast.   [6]
No anchor serves but *hope*, to save my life.
Alas, my sins have raised this storm and strife
Which none can 'suage but Jesus Christ alone.
He can (and will, at need) these storms reprove
Though he delay till the third watch be gone.
  Come, Jesus! Say, "Take courage, it is I."
  Though first I fear, yet will I death defy.

What marvel though I make my moan?
My mourning Muse cannot be still.
What marvel though I sigh and groan?
I long for to lament my fill,
For love, alas, I must lament:
This mind of mine is malcontent
And cannot hold her peace.
Alas, I lack both life and light—
My Lord hath ta'en a long goodnight.
How should my sorrow cease?
Drop down, my eyes, and never tire
Until I have mine heart's desire.

---

[1] *fynd ay / find aye*] always find; *hire*] payment.

[2] *turn back*] repent.

[3] *bark*] boat (the feeble body); *siely*] simple.

[4] *fash*] become troubled or vexed.

[5] *hold*] cargo-hold; fig., refuge; *beild*] courage.

[6] *leeward*] on the side turned away from the wind.

Melville is best known (somewhat inaccurately) as the author of *A Godly Dream*. Her original text, in Scots dialect, was first issued under the title, *Ane Godlie Dreame, compylit in Scottish Meter be M.M., Gentlewoman in Culros* (Edinburgh, 1603). (The title page attribution to "M.M." coyly denotes "Mistress Melville.") An allegorical narrative in 55 stanzas, *Ane Godlie Dreame* appeared at a critical moment in British history, when England was soon to be ruled by the king of Scotland. A year later, Melville's Edinburgh publisher, Robert Charteris, issued an Anglicized version, "by Eliz. Melvill, Ladie Culros yonger, at the request of a friend." The English version was several times reprinted in the Seventeenth Century (always in Scotland) and sold in London bookshops. The 1603 Scots and 1604 English versions are here presented in a parallel text for the first time, in normalized orthography, both of which invite reading aloud as a dramatic performance. [1]

Melville's *Dream* takes as its epigraph a Latin text of Matthew 7:13: "Enter ye in at the strait gate: for wide is the gate, and broad is the way, that leadeth to destruction." The narrative features just two speaking characters: Jesus Christ, and the poet. Melville's female narrator seeks to eschew a course of life that Shakespeare's Scottish Porter describes, in jest, as "the primrose way to the everlasting bonfire." For Melville, Hell is a literal "lake of fire and brimstone" (Rev. 19-20), a spectacle that terrifies—

> I looked down and saw a pit most black,
> Most full of smoke, and flaming fire most fell.
> That ugly sight made me to flee aback;
> I feared to hear so many shout and yell!   (257-60) [2]

Jesus urges her over the din to "play the man – thou need'st not tremble so. / For I shall help, and hold thee by the hand" (274-5). But neither can the narrator be carried: Heaven is reached, and a fall into the pit of Hell avoided, only with rigorous spiritual exercise. The "strait gate" of Protestant conversion is just a starting-gate, a point of entrance for a long and often frightening pilgrimage "Through thorns and briars, and many dangers moe" (151). The way is vexed at every turn by hazards that the Lord takes in stride but which cause the poet a world of hurt:

> I held Him fast as He did give command,
> And through that 'trance together then we went;
> Where, in the midst, great pricks of iron did stand
> Wherewith my feet was all betorn and rent.
> "Take courage now," said He, "and be content
> To suffer this – the pleasure comes at last."   (225-30)

By the *Dream*'s end, "death and Hell have lost their cruel sting" and "The serpent's head hath [been] stoutly trampèd down" (433-8). Waking from her dream with a heart of joy, the poet conveys to her readers, male and female, the same advice she received from Jesus: "Though "pricks of iron do prick you wondrous sore / (As noisome lusts that seek your soul to slay)," "Prepare yourselves, be valiant men of war, / And thrust with force out through the narrow way," into spiritual rebirth (389-92, 465-6).

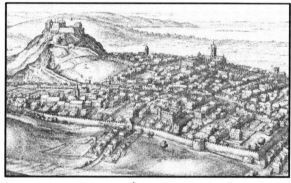

Edinburgh in the 17th Century (Wenzel Hollar)

---

[1] *be*] by.

[2] *fell*] cruel.

Ane Godly Dream (1603)

UPON ANE DAY, as I did mourne full soir
With sindrie things quhairwith my saull was greifit,
My greif increasit, and grew moir and mair.
My comfort fled and could not be releifit.
With heavines my heart was sa mischeifit,
I loathit my lyfe, I could not eit nor drink;
I micht not speik, nor luik to nane that leifit,
Bot musit alone, and divers things did think.   1

The wretchit warld did sa molest my mynde—
I thocht upon this fals and Iron age
And how our harts war sa to vice inclynde
—That Sathan seimit maist feirfullie to rage.
Nathing in earth my sorrow could asswage.
I felt my sin maist stranglie to incres;
I greifit my Spreit that wont to be my pledge;
My saull was drownit into maist deip distress.   2

All merynes did aggravate my paine,
And earthlie joyes did still incres my wo.
In companie I na wayes could remaine,
Bot fled resort, and so alone did go.
My sillie saull was tossit to and fro
With sindrie thochts, quhilk troublit me full soir.
I preisit to pray but sichs overset me so,
I could do nocht bot sich, and say no moir.   3

The twinkling teares aboundantlie ran down: [25]
My heart was easit quhen I had mournit my fill;
Than I began my lamentatioun,
And said, "O Lord! how lang is it thy will
That thy puir Sancts sall be afflictit still?
Alace, how lang sall subtill Sathan rage?
Mak haist, O Lord, thy promeis to fulfill!
Mak haist to end our painefull pilgramage.

"Thy sillie Sancts ar tossit to and fro,
Awaik,° O Lord! quhy sleipest Thou sa lang?
We have na strenth agains our cruell fo.
In sichs and sobbs now chaingit is our sang;
The warld prevails, our enemies ar strang.
The wickit rage, bot we ar puir and waik.
O shaw thy self! With speìd revenge our wrang,
Mak short their days, even for thy chosen's sake.

"Lord Jesus, cum, and saif thine awin Elect,
For Sathan seìks our simpill sauls to slay.
The wickit warld dois stranglie us infect,
Most monsterous sinnes increasses day be day.
Our luif growes cald, our zeill is worne away,
Our faith is faillit, and we ar lyke to fall.
The Lyon roares to catch us as his pray—
Mak haist, O Lord, befoir we perish all!

A Godly Dream (1604)

UPON A DAY, as I did mourn full sore
For sundry things wherewith° my soul was grievèd,
My grief increased, and grew more and more.
I comfort fled and could not be relievèd.
With heaviness my heart was so mischievèd,
I loathed my life, I could not eat nor drink;
I might not speak, nor look to none that livèd,
But mused alone, and divers things did think.   1

This wretched world did so molest my mind—
I thought upon this false and iron age
And how our hearts were so to vice inclined
—That Satan seemed most fearfully to rage.
Nothing in earth my sorrow could assuage.
I felt my sin most strongly to increase;
I grieved the spirit that wont to be my pledge;
My soul was plunged into most deep distress.   2

All merriness did aggravate my pain,
And earthly joys did still increase my woe.
In company I no ways could remain,
But fled resort, and so alone did go.
My siely soul was tossèd to and fro
With sundry thoughts, which troubled me full sore.
I pressed to pray but sighs o'erset° me so,
I could do nought but groan, and say no more.   3

The twinkling tears abundantly ran down:
My heart was eased when I had mourned my fill;
Then I began my lamentatìon,
And said, "O Lord! how long is it Thy will
That Thy poor saints shall be afflicted still?
Alas, how long shall subtle Satan rage?
Make haste, O Lord, Thy promise to fulfill!
Make haste to end our painful pilgrimage.

"Thy siely saints are tossèd to and fro,
Awake, O Lord! why sleepest Thou so long?
We have no strength against our cruel foe.
In sighs and sobs now changèd is our song;
The world prevails, our enemies are strong.
The wicked rage, but we are poor and weak.
O show Thyself! With speed revenge our wrong,
Make short these days, even for Thy chosen's sake.

"Lord Jesus, come, and save Thine own elect,
For Satan seeks our simple souls to slay.
The wicked world doth strongly us infect,
Most monstrous sins increases day by day.
Our love grows cold, our zeal is worn away,
Our faith is failed, and we are like to fall.
The lion roars to catch us for his prey—
Make haste, O Lord, before we perish all!

---

1 *might*] could.

2 *wont*] was wont; was accustomed.

---

3 *sich / groan*] sigh.

"Thir ar the dayes that thou sa lang foretald
Sould cum befoir this wretchit warld sould ende; [50]
Now vice abounds and charitie growes cald,
And evin thine owne most stronglie dois offend.
The Devill prevaillis. His forces he dois bend,
Gif it could be, to wraik thy children deir.
Bot we ar thine! thairfoir, sum succour send,
Resave our saullis. Wee irk to wander heir. [1]

"Quhat can wee do? Wee cloggit ar with sin.
In filthie vyce our senseles saules ar drownit.
Thocht wee resolve, wee nevir can begin
To mend our lyfes, bot sin dois still abound.
Quhen will thou cum? Quhen sall thy trumpet sound?
Quhen sall we see that grit and glorious day?
O save us, Lord, out of this pit profound,
And reif us from this loathsum lump of clay! [2]

"Thou knawis our hearts; thou sies our hail desire.
Our secret thochts, thay ar not hid fra thee.
Thocht wee offend, thou knawis we strangelie tire
To beir this wecht. Our spreit wald faine be free.
Allace, O Lord, quhat pleasour can it be
To leif in sin, that sair dois presse us downe?
Oh, give us wings that wee aloft may flie—
And end the fecht, that wee may weir the crowne!" [3]

Befoir the Lord, quhen I had thus complainit,
My mynde grew calme; my heart was at great rest.
Thocht I was faint, from fuid yit I refrainit [75]
And went to bed, becaus I thocht it best.
With heavines my spreit was sa opprest
I fell on sleip; and sa, againe (me thocht),
I maid my mone, and than my greif increst,
And from the Lord, with teares, I succour socht:

"Lord Jesus, cum," said I, "and end my greif.
My spreit is vexit – the captive wald be frie!
All vice abounds – O send us sum releif!
I loath to live; I wishe desolvit to be.
My spreit dois lang, and thristeth efter thee
As thristie ground requyris ane shoure of raine;
My heart is dry as fruitles, barren tree.
I feill my selfe – how can I heir remaine?"

With siches and sobs as I did so lament,
Into my dreame I thocht thair did appeir
Ane sicht maist sweit, quhilk maid me weill content:
Ane Angell bricht, with visage schyning cleir,
With luifing luiks, and with ane smyling cheir.
He askit me, "Quhy art thou thus sa sad?
Quhy grones thou so? quhat dois thou, dwyning heir
With cairfull cryes, in this thy bailfull bed? [4]

"These are the days that Thou so long foretold
Should come before this wretched world should end;
Now vice abounds and charity grows cold,
And e'en Thine own most strongly do offend.
The Devil prevails. His forces he doth bend,
If it could be, to wreak thy children dear.
But we are Thine! therefore, some succor send,
Receive our souls. We weary, wand'ring here. [1]

"What can we do? We cloggèd are with sin.
In filthy vice our senseless souls are drowned.
Though we resolve, we never can begin
To mend our lives, but sin doth still abound.
When wilt Thou come? When shall thy trumpet sound?
When shall we see that great and glorious day?
O save us, Lord, out of this pit profound,
And reave us from this loathsome lump of clay! [2]

"Thou know'st our hearts; Thou seest our whole desire.
Our secret thoughts, they are not hid from Thee.
Though we offend, Thou know'st we strangely tire
To bear this weight. Our spirit would fain be free.
Alas, O Lord, what pleasure can it be
To live in sin, that sore doth press us down?
O give us wings that we aloft may flee—
And end the fight, that we may wear the crown!" [3]

Before the Lord, when I had thus complained,
My mind grew calm; my heart was then at rest.
Though I was faint, from food yet I refrained
And went to bed, because I thought it best.
With heaviness my spirit was so oppressed
I fell on sleep; and so, again (methought),
I made my moan, and then my grief increased,
And from the Lord, with tears, I succor sought:

"Lord Jesus, come," said I, "and end our grief.
My spirit is vexed – the captive would be free!
All vice abounds – O send us some relief!
I loathe to live. I wish dissolved to be.
My spirit doth long, and thirsteth after Thee
As thirsty ground requires a shower of rain.
My heart is dry as fruitless, barren tree.
I fail myself – how can I here remain?"

With sighs and sobs as I did so lament,
Into my dream I thought there did appear
A sight most sweet, which made me well content:
An angel bright, with visage shining clear,
With loving looks, and with a smiling cheer.
He askèd me, "Why art thou thus so sad?
Why groan'st thou so? What dost thou, dwining here
With careful cries, in this thy baleful bed? [4]

----

[1] *wraik / wreak*] wrack or rack;   *irk / weary*] suffer.

[2] *reave...clay*] take us fr. our loathsome flesh; let us die.

[3] *flee*] fly.

[4] *dwyning*] dwindling, wasting away.

"I heir thy sichs, I see thy twinkling teares.
Thou seimes to be in sum perplexitie.
Quhat meanes thy mones? Quhat is the thing thou feares?
Quhom wald thou have? In quhat place wald you be?
Fainte not sa fast in thy adversitie,   [101]
Mourne not sa sair (sen mourning may not mend).
Lift up thy heart, declair thy greif to mee—
Perchance thy paine brings pleasure in the end."

I sicht againe, and said, "Allace for wo!
My greif is greit, I can it not declair.
Into this earth I wander to and fro,
Ane pilgrim puir, consumit with siching sair.
My sinnes (allace!) increases mair and mair.
I loath my lyfe. I irk to wander heir.
I long for Heaven – my heritage is thair.
I long to live with my Redimer deir."

"Is this the caus?" said he. "Ryse up anone
And follow mee, and I sall be thy gyde.
And from thy sichs leif off thy heavie mone;
Refraine from teares, and cuist thy cair asyde.
Trust in my strenth, and in my word confyde,
And thou sall have thy heavie heart's desyre.
Ryse up with speid, I may not lang abyde.
Greit diligence this matter dois requyre."   1

My Saull rejoysit to heir his words sa sweit.
I luikit up and saw His face maist fair;
His countenance revivit my wearie Spreit.
Incontinent I cuist asyde my cair.
With humbill heart, I prayit him to declair,   [125]
Quhat was his name? he answerit me againe,
"I am thy God for quhom thou sicht sa sair.
I now am cummit; thy teares ar not in vaine.   2

"I am the way, I am the treuth and lyfe.
I am thy spous that brings thee store of grace.
[I am thy Lord, that sone sall end thy stryfe.]
I am thy luif quhom thou wald faine imbrace.
I am thy joy, I am thy rest and peace.
Ryse up anone and follow efter mee!
I sall thee leid into thy dwelling place,
The Land of rest, thou langs sa sair to see."

With joyfull heart I thankit him againe.
"Reddie am I," said I, "and weil content
To follow thee, for heir I leive in paine.
O wretch unworth! My dayes ar vainlie spent.
Nocht ane is just, bot all ar fearcelie bent
To rin to vyce, I have na force to stand;
My sinnes increase, quhilk maks me sair lament.
Mak haist, O Lord! I lang to sie that Land."

"I hear thy sighs, I see thy twinkling tears.
Thou seem'st to be in some perplexity.
What mean thy moans? What is the thing thou fears?
Whom would thou have? In what place would thou be?
Faint not so fast in thy adversity,
Mourn not so sore (since mourning may not mend).
Lift up thy heart, declare thy grief to me—
Perchance thy pain brings pleasure in the end."

I sighed again, and said, "Alas for woe!
My grief is great, I can it not declare.
Into this earth I wander to and fro,
A pilgrim poor, consumed with sighing sore.
My sins (alas!) increases more and more.
I loathe my life. I weary, wand'ring here.
I long for Heaven – my heritage is there.
I long to live with my redeemer dear."

"Is this the cause?" said He. "Rise up anon
And follow Me, and I shall be thy guide.
And from thy sighs leave off thy heavy moan;
Refrain from tears, and cast thy care aside.
Trust in My strength, and in My word confide,
And thou shalt have thy heavy heart's desire.
Rise up with speed, I may not long abide.
Great diligence this matter doth require."   1

My soul rejoiced to hear His words so sweet.
I lookèd up and saw His face most fair;
His countenance revived my weary sprite.
Incontinent I cast° aside my care.
With humble heart, I prayed Him to declare,
What was His name? He answered me again,
"I am thy God for whom thou sighs so sair.
I now am come°; thy tears are not in vain.   2

"I am the way, I am the truth and life.
I am thy spouse that brings thee store of grace.
I am thy Lord, that soon shall end thy strife.
I am thy love whom thou wouldst fain embrace.
I am thy joy, I am thy rest and peace.
Rise up anon and follow after me!
I shall thee lead unto thy dwelling place,
The land of rest, thou long'st so sore to see."

With joyful heart I thanked Him again.
"Ready am I," said I, "and well content
To follow Thee, for here I live in pain.
O wretch unworth! My days are vainly spent.
Not one is just, but all are fiercely bent
To run to vice, I have no force to stand;
My sins increase, which makes me sore lament.
Make haste, O Lord! I long to see that land."

---

1 *cuist*] cast.

---

2 *spreit* (*sprite*)] spirit;   *incontinent*] straightaway;
sicht (1606 *sighs*)] sighed;   *sair*] sore, painfully.

"Thy haist is greit," he answerit me againe.
"Thou thinks thee *thair*, thou art transportit so!
That pleasant place most purchaist be with paine.
The way is strait, and thou hes far to go!
Art thou content to wander to and fro
Throw greit deserts, throw water, and throw fire, [150]
Throw thornes and breirs, and monie dangers mo?
Quhat says thou now? Thy febill flesh will tyre."

"Allace!" said I, "howbeit my flesh be waik,
My spreit is strang and willing for to flie.
O leif mee nocht, bot for Thy mercies saik
Performe thy word, or els for duill I die!
I feir no paine, sence I sould walk with thee.
The way is lang, yit bring me throw at last."
"Thou answeirs weill. I am content," said hee,
"To be thy guyde – bot sie thou grip me fast." 1

Than up I rais and maid na mair delay.
My febill arme about his arme I cast.
He went befoir and still did guyde the way.
Thocht I was waik, my spreit did follow fast.
Throw moss and myres, throw ditches deip wee past,
Throw pricking thornes, throw water & throw fyre,
Throw dreidfull dennes quhilk maid my heart agast.
(Hee buir mee up quhen I begouth to tyre.)

Sumtyme wee clam on craigie Montanes hie,
And sumtymes staid on uglie brayes of sand;
They war sa stay that wonder was to sie,
Bot quhen I feirit, hee held mee be the hand.
Throw thick and thin, throw sea and eik be land,
Throw greit deserts wee wanderit on our way.
Quhen I was waik and had no force to stand, [175]
Yit with ane luik hee did refresh mee ay. 2

Throw waters greit wee war compellit to weyd,
Quhilk war sa deip that I was lyke to drowne.
Sumtyme I sank, bot yit my gracious gyde
Did draw me out half deid, and in ane sowne. 3
In wods maist wyld, and far fra anie towne,
Wee thristit throw. The breirs together stak;
I was sa waik thair strenth did ding me downe,
That I was forcit for feir to flie aback.

"Curage," said hee, "thou art midgait and mair.
Thou may not tyre, nor turne aback againe.
Hald fast thy grip – on mee cast all thy cair.
Assay thy strenth – thou sall not fecht in vaine.
I tauld thee first that thou sould suffer paine.
The neirer heaven, the harder is the way.
Lift up thy heart, and let thy hope remaine.
Sence I am guyde, thou sall not go astray."

"Thy haste is great," He answered me again.
"Thou think'st thee *there*, thou art transported so!
That pleasant place must purchased be with pain.
The way is strait, and thou hast far to go!
Art thou content to wander to and fro
Through great deserts, through water, and through fire,
Through thorns and briars, and many dangers moe?
What sayst thou now? Thy feeble flesh will tire."

"Alas!" said I, "although my flesh be weak,
My spirit is strong and willing for to fly.
O leave me not, but for Thy mercy's sake
Perform Thy word, or else for dole I die!
I fear no pain, since I should walk with Thee.
The way is long, yet bring me through at last."
"Thou answer'st well. I am content," said He,
"To be thy guide – but see thou grip me fast." 1

Then up I rose and made no more delay.
My feeble arms about His neck I cast.
He went before and still did guide the way.
Though I was weak my spirit did follow fast.
Through moss and mire, through ditches deep we passed,
Through pricking thorns, through water and through fire,
Through dreadful dens which made my heart aghast.
(He bare me up when I began to tire.)

Sometime we clamb on craggy mountains high,
And sometimes stayed on ugly brayes of sand;
They were so stey that wonder was to see,
But when I feared, He held me by the hand.
Through thick and thin, through sea and eke through land,
Through great deserts we wandered on our way.
When I was weak, and had no strength to stand,
Yet with a look He did refresh me aye. 2

Through waters great we were compelled to wade,
Which was so deep that I was like to drown.
Sometime I sank, but yet my gracious guide
Did draw me up half dead, and in a swoun. 3
In woods most wild, and far from any town,
We thirsted through. The briars together stack;
I was so weak their strength did beat me down,
That I was forced for fear to flee aback.

"Courage," said He, "thou art mid-way and more.
Thou may not tire, nor turn aback again.
Hold fast thy grip – on me cast all thy care.
Assay thy strength – thou shall not fight in vain.
I told thee first that thou should suffer pain.
The nearer Heaven, the harder is the way.
Lift up thy heart, and let thy hope remain.
Since I am guide, thou shalt not go astray."

---

1 *duil / dole*] sorrow.

2 *clam / clamb*] climbed; *brayes*] dikes; *stay / stey*]
steep; *wonder was*] it was wondrous, awesome.

3 *sowne / swoun*] swoon; *stak / stack*] stuck.

Fordwart wee past on narrow brigs of trie
Over waters greit, that hiddeouslie did roir.
Thair lay belaw, that feirfull was to sie,
Maist uglie beists, that gaipit to devoir.
My heid grew licht, and troublit wonderous soir;
My heart did feir, my feit began to slyde.
Bot quhan I cryit, hee heard mee ever moir
And held mee up. (O blissit be my guyde!) [200]

Wearie I was, and thocht to sit at rest,
Bot hee said, "Na, thou may not sit nor stand!
Hald on thy course, and thou sall find it best,
Gif thou desyris to sie that pleasant Land."
Thocht I was waik, I rais at his command
And held him fast. At lenth he leit mee sie
That pleasant place, quhilk semit to be at hand.
"Tak curage now, for thou art neir," said hee.

I luikit up unto that Castell fair,
Glistring lyke gold, and schyning silver bricht.
The staitlie towres did mount above the air.
Thay blindit mee, thay cuist sa greit ane licht.
My heart was glaid to sie that joyfull sicht;
My voyage than I thocht was not in vaine.
I him besocht to guyde mee thair aricht,
With manie vowes never to tyre againe.

"Thocht thou be neir, the way is wonderous hard,"
Said hee againe. "Thairfoir thou mon be stout.
Fainte not for feir, for cowarts ar debard,
That hes na heart to go thair voyage out.
Pluck up thy heart, and grip mee fast about.
Out throw yon trance together wee man go.
The yet is law, remember for to lout.
Gif this war past, wee have not manie mo." [1]

I held him fast as hee did gif command, [225]
And throw that trance together than wee went;
Quhair. in the middis, grit pricks of Iron did stand,
Quhairwith my feit was all betorne and rent.
"Tak curage now," said hee, "and be content
To suffer this – the pleasour comes at last."
I answerit nocht, bot ran incontinent
Out over them all, and so the paine was past.

Quhen this was done, my heart did dance for joy.
I was sa neir, I thocht my voyage endit.
I ran befoir and socht not his convoy,
Nor speirit the way, becaus I thocht I kend it.
On statelie steps maist stoutlie I ascendit;
Without his help I thocht to enter thair.
Hee followit fast, and was richt sair offendit,
And hastelie did draw mee down the stair. [2]

Fordward we passed on narrow brigs of tree
O'er° waters great, that hideously did roar.
There lay below, that fearful was to see,
Most ugly beasts, that gapèd to devour.
My head grew light, and troubled wondrous sore;
My heart did fear, my feet began to slide.
But when I cried, He heard me evermore
And held me up. (O blessed be my guide!)

Weary I was, and thought to sit at rest,
But He said, "No, thou may not sit nor stand!
Hold on thy course, and thou shalt find it best,
If thou desirest to see that pleasant land."
Though I was weak, I rose at His command
And held Him fast. At length He let me see
That pleasant place, that seemed to be at hand.
"Take courage now, for thou art near," said He.

I lookèd up unto that Castle fair,
Glist'ring like gold, and shining silver-bright.
The stately towers did mount above the air.
They blinded me, they cast° so great a light.
My heart was glad to see that joyful sight;
My voyage then I thought was not in vain.
I Him besought to guide me there aright,
With many vows never to tire again.

"Though thou be near, the way is wondrous hard,"
Said He again. "Therefore thou must be stout.
Faint not for fear, for cowards are debarred,
That have no heart to go their voyage out.
Pluck up thy heart, and grip me fast about.
Out through this 'trance together we must go.
The way is low, remember for to lout.
If this were passed, we have not many moe." [1]

I held Him fast as He did give command,
And through the 'trance together then we went;
Where, in the midst, great pricks of iron did stand,
Wherewith my feet was all betorn and rent.
"Take courage now," said He, "and be content
To suffer this – the pleasure comes at last."
I answered not, but ran incontinent
Out over the fire, and so the pain was past.

When this was done, my heart did dance for joy.
I was so near, I thought my voyage ended.
I ran before and sought not His convoy,
Nor asked the way, because I thought I kenned it.
On stately steps most stoutly I ascended;
Without His help I thought to enter there.
He followed fast, and was right sore offended,
And hastily did draw me down the stair. [2]

---

[1] *'trance*] 1. entrance; 2. dream-vision;   *yet is law*] gate
is narrow (mistranslated 1604); *lout*] bow down, duck.

[2] *convoy*] escort or guidance;   *speirit* (1606 *asked*)]
searched out;   *kenned*] knew, perceived.

"Quhat haist!" said hee. "Quwhy ran thou so befoir?
Without my help thinks thou to clim sa hie?
Cum down againe! Thou yit mon suffer moir
Gif thou desyres that dwelling place to sie.
This staitlie stair, it is not maid for thee.
Hald thow that course, thow sall be thrust aback."
"Allace!" said I, "lang wandring weiriet mee,
Quhilk maid mee rin, the neirest way to tak."

Than hee began to comfort mee againe,   [249]
And said, "My freind, thou mon not enter thair:
Lift up thy heart, thou yit must suffer paine.
The last assault, perforce, it mon be **sair**.   1
This godlie way, althocht it seime sa fair,
It is to hie – thou cannot clim sa stay.
Bot luik belaw, beneath that staitlie stair,
And thou sall sie ane uther kynde of way."

I luikit down and saw ane pit most black,
Most full of smuke, and flaming fyre most fell.
That uglie sicht maid mee to flie aback;
I feirit to heir so manie shout and yell!
I him besocht that hee the treuth wald tell:
"Is this," said I, "the papists' purging place,
Quhair they affirme that sillie saulles do dwell,
To purge thair sin, befoir thay rest in peace?"   2

"The braine of man maist warlie did invent
That Purging place," He answerit me againe.
"For grediness, together thay consent
To say that saulles in torment mon remaine
Till gold and gudes releif them of thair paine.
O spytfull spreits that did the same begin!
O blindit beists! Your thochts ar all in vaine.
My blude alone did saif thy saull from sin."   3

"This Pit is Hell, quhairthrow thou now mon go,
Thair is the way that leids thee to the land.
Now play the man – thou neids not trimbill so,
For I sall help, and hald thee be the hand."   [275]
"Allace!" said I, "I have na force to stand.
For feir I faint to sie that uglie sicht!
How can I cum amongst that bailfull band?
Oh help mee now – I have na force nor micht!

"Oft have I heard, that thay that enters thair,
In this greit golfe, sall never cum againe."
"Curage!" said hee, "have I not bocht thee deir?
My precious blude – it was nocht shed in vaine.
I saw this place, my saull did taist this paine,
Or euer I went into my father's gloir.
Throw mon thou go, bot thou sall not remaine,
Thou neids not feir, for I sall go befoir."   4

"What haste!" said He. "Why ran thou so before?
Without my help think'st thou to climb so high?
Come down again! Thou yet must suffer more
If thou desirest that dwelling-place to see.
This stately stair, it was not made for thee.
Hold thou that course, thou shalt be thrust aback."
"Alas!" said I, "long-wand'ring wearied me,
Which made me run, the nearest way to take."

Then He began to comfort me again,
And said, "My friend, thou must not enter there:
Lift up thy heart, thou yet must suffer pain.
The last assault, perforce, it must be sair.   1
This goodly way, although it seems so fair,
It is too high – thou cannot climb so stey.
But look below, beneath that stately stair,
And thou shalt see another kind of way."

I lookèd down and saw a pit most black,
Most full of smoke, and flaming fire most fell.
That ugly sight made me to flee aback;
I feared to hear so many shout and yell!
I Him besought that He the truth would tell:
"Is this," said I, "the papists' purging place,
Where they affirm that siely souls do dwell,
To purge their sin, before they rest in peace?"   2

"The brain of man most warily did invent
That purging place," He answered me again.
"For greediness, together they consent
To say that souls in torments must remain
While gold and goods relieve them of their pain.
O spiteful spirits that did the same begin!
O blinded beasts! Your thoughts are all in vain.
My blood alone doth cleanse the soul from sin."   3

"This pit is Hell, wherethrough thou now must go,
There is the way that leads thee to thy land.
Now play the man – thou need'st not tremble so,
For I shall help, and hold thee by the hand."
"Alas!" said I, "I have no force to stand.
For fear I faint to see that ugly sight!
How can I come amongst that baleful band?
O help me now – I have no force nor might!

"Oft have I heard, that they that enters here,
In this great gulf, shall never come again."
"Courage!" said He, "have I not bought thee dear?
My precious blood – it was not shed in vain.
I saw this place, My soul did taste this pain,
Ere e'er° I went into my Father's glore.
Through must thou go, but thou shalt not remain,
Thou need'st not fear, for I shall go before."   4

---

1 *sair*] sore, difficult.

2 *fell*] fierce;   *papists' purging place*] purgatory.

3 *maist warily / most warily*] with great cunning;   *did saif thy / doth cleanse the*] saved your.

4 *Or ever / Ere e'er*] Before ever;   *gloir (glore)*] glory.

"I am content to do thy haill command,"
Said I againe, and did him fast imbrace.
Then lovinglie he held mee be the hand,
And in wee went into that feirfull place.
"Hald fast thy grip," said hee. "In anie cace,
Let mee not slip, quhat ever thou sall sie.
Dreid not the deith, bot stoutlie forwart preis,
For Deith nor Hell sall never vanquish thee."   1

His words sa sweit did cheir my heavie hairt;
Incontinent I cuist my cair asyde.
"Curage!" said hee, "play not ane cowart's pairt.
Thocht thou be waik, yit in my strenth confyde."
I thocht me blist to have sa gude ane guyde;   [301]
Thocht I was waik, I knew that he was strang.
Under his wings I thocht mee for to hyde
Gif anie thair sould preis to do mee wrang.

Into that Pit, quhen I did enter in,
I saw ane sicht quhilk maid my heart agast:
Puir damnit saulls, tormentit sair for sin,
In flaming fyre war frying wonder fast,
And uglie spreits. And as I through° them past,
My heart grew faint and I begouth to tyre.
Or I was war, ane gripit mee at last,
And held me heich above ane flaming fyre!   2

The fyre was greit. The heit did peirs me sair.
My faith grew waik. My grip was wonderous smal.
I trimbellit fast. My feir grew mair and mair.
My hands did shaik that I him held withall;
At length, thay lousit – than I° begouth to fall,
I cryit, "O Lord!" and caucht Him fast againe.
"Lord Jesus cum, and red mee out of thrall."
"Curage!" said he, "now thou art past the paine." 3

With this greit feir, I stackerit and awoke,
Crying, "O Lord, Lord Jesus, cum againe."
Bot efter this no kynde of rest I tuke.
I preisit to sleip, bot that was all in vaine.
I wald have dreamit of pleasour after paine   [325]
Becaus I knaw I sall it finde at last.
God grant my guyde may still with mee remaine!
It is to cum that I beleifit was past.   4

This is ane dreame, and yit I thocht it best
To wryte the same, and keip it still in mynde,
Becaus I knew thair was na earthlie rest
Preparit for us that hes our hearts inclynde
To seik the Lord. We mon be purgde and fynde.
Our dros is greit – the fyre mon try us sair –
Bot yit our God is mercifull and kynde.
Hee sall remaine and help us ever mair.   5

"I am content to do thy whole command,"
Said I again, and did Him fast embrace.
Then lovingly He held me by the hand,
And in we went into that fearful place.
"Hold fast thy grip," said He. "In any case,
Let me not slip, whatever thou shalt see.
Dread not the death, but stoutly forward press,
For death nor Hell shall never vanquish thee."   1

His words so sweet did cheer my heavy heart;
Incontinent I cast° my care aside.
"Courage!" said He, "play not a coward's part.
Though thou be weak, yet in My strength confide."
I thought° me blest to have so good a guide;
Though I was weak, I knew that He was strong.
Under His wings I thought me for to hide
If any there should press to do me wrong.

Into that pit, when I did enter in,
I saw a sight which made my heart aghast:
Poor damnèd souls, tormented sore for sin,
In flaming fire were frying wonder fast,
And ugly spirits. And as we through° them passed,
My heart grew faint and I began to tire.
Ere I was 'ware, one grippèd me at last,
And held me high above a flaming fire!   2

Th' fire was great. The heat did pierce me sore.
My faith grew weak. My grip was wondrous small.
I trembled fast. My fear grew more and more.
My hands did shake that I Him held withal;
At length, they loosed! – then I began to fall,
And cried, "O Lord!" and caught Him fast again.
"Lord Jesus come, and rid me out of thrall!"
"Courage!" said He, "now thou art past the pain." 3

With this great fear, I started and awoke,
Crying aloud, "Lord Jesus, come again."
But after this no kind of rest I took.
I pressed to sleep, but it was all in vain.
I would have dreamed of pleasure after pain
Because I know I shall it find at last.
God grant my guide may still with me remain!
It is to come that I believed was passed.   4

This is a dream, and yet I thought it best
To write the same, and keep it still in mind,
Because I knew there was no earthly rest
Prepared for us that hath our hearts inclined
To seek the Lord. We must be purged and 'fined.
Our dross is great – the fire must try us sore –
But yet our God is merciful and kind.
He shall remain and help us evermore.   5

---

1 *Let me not slip*] Do not let go of me.

2 *wonder*] wondrous.

3 *that*] with which;   *thrall*] bondage.

4 *stacherit / started*]] lurched;   *It… passed*] That
which I dreamed had happened will indeed take place.

5 *fynde / 'fined*] refined.

The way to heaven I sie is wonderous hard.
My Dreame declairs that we have far to go.
Wee mon be stout, for cowards ar debarde.
Our flesh on force mon suffer paine and wo.
Thir grivelie gaits and many dangers mo
Awaits for us. Wee cannot leive in rest.
Bot let us learne (sence wee ar wairnit so)
To cleave to Christ, for He can help us best.

O sillie saulls with paines sa sair opprest,
That love the Lord and lang for Heaven sa hie,
Chainge not your mynde, for ye have chosen the best.
Prepair your selves, for troblit mon ye be.
Faint not for feir in your adversitie—
Althoch that ye lang luiking be for life.   [350]
Suffer ane quhile and ye sall shortly see
The land of rest, quhen endit is your strife.   1

In wilderness ye mon be tryit aquhile,
Yit fordwart preis and never flie aback.
Lyke pilgrimes puir, and strangers in exyle,
Throw fair and foull your journay ye mon tak.
The Devill, the warld, and all that thay can mak,
Will send thair force to stop yow in your way.
Your flesh will faint and sumtyme will grow slak,
Yit clim to Christ and hee sall help yow ay.

The thornie cairs of this deceitfull lyfe
Will rent your heart and mak your saull to bleid.
Your flesh and spreit will be at deidlie stryfe.
Your cruell fo will hald yow still in dreid
And draw yow down; yit ryse againe with speid,
And thocht ye fall, yit ly not loytring still,
Bot call on Christ to help yow in your neid,
Quha will nocht faill his promeis to fulfill.   2

In floudes of wo quhen ye ar lyke to drowne,
Yit clim to Christ and grip him wonder fast;
And thocht ye sink and in the deip fall downe,
Yit cry aloud and hee will heir at last.
Dreid nocht the death, nor be not sair agast.
Thocht all the eirth against yow sould conspyre,
Christ is your guyde, and quhen your paine is past
Ye sall have joy above your heart's desyre.   [376]

Thocht in this earth ye sall exaltit be,
Feir salbe left to humbill yow withall—
For gif ye clim on tops of Montaines hie,
The heicher up, the nearer is your fall.
Your honie sweit sall mixit be with gall;
Your short delyte sall end with paine and greif.
Yit trust in God, for His assistance call,
And he sall help and send yow sum releif.

---

1 *Althoch ... life*] that you be long[-time] looking for life; cf. *It ... life* (1604).

2 *rent*] rend, tear.

Thocht waters greit do compas yow about,
Thocht Tirannes threat°, thocht Lyouns rage & roir,
Defy them all! – and feir not to win out.
Your guyde is neir to help yow ever moir.
Thocht prick of Iron do prick yow wondrous soir
(As noysum lusts that seik your saull to slay),
Yit cry on Christ and hee sall go befoir:
The neirer Heaven, the harder is the way.   1

Rin out your race! ye mon not faint nor tyre,
Nor sit, nor stand, nor turne aback againe.
Gif ye desyre to have your heart's desyre,
Preis fordwart still althocht it be with paine.
Na rest for yow sa lang as ye remaine
Ane pilgrim puir into thy loathsum lyfe.
Fecht on your faucht – it sall not be in vaine.
Your riche rewarde is worth ane gritter stryfe. [400]

Gif, efter teires, ye leif ane quhyle in joy
And get ane taist of that Eternal gloir,
Be nocht secure, nor slip nocht your convoy,
For gif ye do ye sall repent it soir.
He knawes the way, and he mon go befoir.
Clim ye alane? Ye sall nocht mis ane fall!
Your humblit flesh, it mon be troublit moir
Gif ye forget upon your guyde to call.

Gif Christ be gaine – althocht ye seime to flie
With golden wings above the firmament—
Come down againe. Ye sall nocht better be.
That pryde of yours ye sall right sair repent!
Then hald him fast, with humbill heart ay bent
To follow him, althocht throw Hell and Death.
Hee went befoir. His saull was torne and rent.
For your deserts hee felt his father's wraith.

Thocht in the end ye suffer torments fell,
Cleave° fast to him that felt the same befoir.
The way to Heaven mon be throw Death and Hell;
The last assault will troubill yow full soir.
The Lyoun than maist cruellie will roir;
His tyme is short, his forces hee will bend.
The gritter stryfe, the gritter is your gloir.
Your paine is short – your joy sall never end.   2

Rejoyce in God! Let nocht your curage faill,   [425]
Ye chosin Sancts that ar afflictit heir.
Thocht Sathan rage, hee never sall prevaill.
Fecht to the end, and stoutlie perseveir.
Your God is trew, your blude is to him deir.
Feir nocht the way, sence Christ is your convoy.
Quhen Clouds ar past, the weather will grow cleir.
Ye saw in teares, bot ye sal reap in joy.

Though waters great do compass you about,
Though tyrants threat, though lions rage and roar,
Defy them all! – and fear not to win out.
Your guide is near to help you evermore.
Though pricks of iron do prick you wondrous sore
(As noisome lusts that seek your soul to slay),
Yet cry on Christ and He shall go before:
The nearer Heaven, the harder is the way.   1

Run out your race! Ye must not faint nor tire,
Nor sit, nor stand, nor turn aback again.
If ye intend to have your heart's desire,
Press forward still although it be with pain.
No rest for you so long as ye remain
As pilgrim poor into this loathsome life.
Fight out your fight – it shall not be in vain.
Your rich reward is worth a greater strife.

If, after tears, ye live a while in joy
And get a taste of that eternal glore,
Be not secure, nor slip not your convoy,
For if ye do ye shall repent it sore.
He knows the way, and He must go before.
Climb you alone? Ye shall not miss a fall!
Your filthy flesh, it must be troubled more
If ye forget upon your guide to call.

If Christ be gone – although ye seem to flee
With golden wings above the firmament—
Come down again. Ye shall not better be.
That pride of yours ye shall right sore repent!
Then hold Him fast, with humble heart aye bent
To follow Him, although through Hell and death.
He went before. His soul was torn and rent.
For your deserts He felt His Father's wrath.

Though in the end ye suffer torments fell,
Cleave fast to Him that felt the same before.
The way to Heaven must be through death and Hell;
The last assault will trouble you full sore.
The lion then most cruelly will roar;
His time is short, His forces He will bend.
The greater strife, the greater is your glore.
Your pain is short – your joy shall never end.   2

Rejoice in God! Let not your courage fail,
Ye chosen saints that are afflicted here.
Though Satan rage, he never shall prevail.
Fight to the end, and stoutly persevere.
Your God is true, your blood is to Him dear.
Fear not the way, since Christ is your convoy.
When clouds are past, the weather will grow clear.
Ye sow in tears, but ye shall reap in joy.

---

1 *noisome*] noxious, harmful.

2 *The lion*] Satan (1 Peter 5:8).

Baith deith and hell hes lost thair cruell sting,
Your Captaine Christ hes maid them all to yeild;
Lift up your hearts, and praises to him sing,
Triumph for joy, your enemies ar keilde!
The Lord of Hostis, that is your strenth and sheild,
The Serpent's heid hes stoutlie trampit downe.
Trust in His strenth, pass fordwart in the feild,
Overcum in fecht, and ye sall weare the Crowne.

The King of kings, gif he be on our syde,
Wee neid nocht feir quha dar agains us stand.
Into the feild may wee not baldlie byde
Quhen hee sall help us with his michtie hand
Quha sits above° and reules baith sea and land?
Quha with his breath doth mak the hilles to shaik?
The hostes of Heaven ar armit at his command,
To fecht the field, quhen wee appear maist waik!

Pluck up your heart – ye ar nocht left alone!
The Lambe of God sall leid yow in the way;   [450]
The Lord of Hostes, that rings on royall Throne,
Against your foes your Baner will display.
The Angels bricht sall stand in gude array
To hald yow up. Ye neid not feir to fall.
Your enemies sall flie and be your pray.
Ye sall triumphe – and thay sall perish all.

The joy of Heaven is worth ane moment's paine.
Tak curage than, lift up your hearts on hie!
To judge the eirth quhen Christ sall cum againe,
Above the cloudes ȝe sall exaltit be:
Ane Crowne of joy and trew felicitie
Await for you, quhen finishit is your fecht.
Suffer ane quhyle, and ye sall shortlie sie
Ane gloir maist grit, and infinite of wecht.

Prepair your selfes, be valiant men of weir,
And thrust with force out throw the narrow way.
Hald on thy course and shrink not back for feir.
Christ is your guyde; ye sall not go astray.
The tyme is neare – be sober, watch and pray.
Hee sies your teares, and he hes laid in stoir   [470]
Ane riche rewarde, quhilk in that joyfull day
Ye sall resave, and ring for ever moir.

Now to the King that creat all of nocht,   ¹
And Lord of Lords that reules baith Land and sie,
That saifit our saullis and with His blude us bocht,
And vanquisht Death, triumphant on the trie;   ²
Unto the greit and glorious Trinitie
That saifis the puir and dois His awin defend
Be laud and gloir, honour and Majestie,
Power and praise. Amen, Warld without end.

Both death and Hell hath lost their cruel sting,
Your captain Christ hath made them all to yield;
Lift up your hearts, and praises to Him sing,
Triumph for joy, your enemies are killed!
The Lord of hosts, that is your strength and shield,
The serpent's head hath stoutly trampèd down.
Trust in His strength, pass forward in the field,
O'ercome° in fight, and ye shall wear the crown.

The King of kings, if He be on our side,
We need not fear who dare against us stand.
Into the field may we not boldly bide
When He shall help us with His mighty hand
Who sits above and rules both sea and land?
Who with His breath doth make the hills to shake?
The hosts of Heaven are armed at His command,
To fight the field, when we appear most weak!

Pluck up your heart – ye are not left alone!
The Lamb of God shall lead you in the way;
The Lord of hosts, that reigns on royal throne,
Against your foes His banner will display.
The angels bright shall stand in good array
To hold you up. Ye need not fear to fall.
Your enemies shall flee and be your prey.
Ye shall triumph – and they shall perish all.

The joy of Heaven is worth a moment's pain.
Take courage then, lift up your hearts on high!
To judge the earth when Christ shall come again,
Above the clouds ye shall exalted be:
The crown of joy and true felicity
Await for you, when finished is your fight.
Suffer a while, and ye shall shortly see
A glore most great, and infinite of weight.

Prepare yourselves, be valiant men of war,
And thrust with force out through the narrow way.
Hold on thy course and shrink not back for fear.
Christ is your guide; ye shall not go astray.
The time is near – be sober, watch and pray.
He sees your tears, and He hath laid in store
A rich reward, which in that joyful day
Ye shall receive, and reign forevermore.

Now to the King that create all of nought,   ¹
The Lord of lords that rules both land and sea,
That saved our souls and with His blood us bought,
And vanquished death, triumphing on the tree;   ²
Unto the great and glorious Trinity
That saves the poor and doth His own defend
Be laud and glore, honor and majesty,
Power and praise. Amen, world without end.

---

¹ *creat / create*] created..

² *tree*] Cross.

• • •

Although Elizabeth Melville continued to write poetry, little else survives of her work from the Jacobean period. Readers of *Women's Works* will therefore kindly pardon the editor for reaching beyond the stated *terminus ad quem* for Volume Three, to reproduce a selection of the poet's extant correspondence, a series of extraordinary letters written to Rev. John Livingston from 1626 to 1631.

After graduating Master of Arts in July 1621 from Glasgow College, John Livingston, 18, returned to Lanark, there to live with his widowed father, Rev. William Livingston, a staunch Calvinist who was on the bishops' watch-list as a Presbyterian rabble-rouser. While at university, Livingston had studied to become a medical physician; but on his home-return, his thoughts turned to religion. On 2 January 1625, he preached his first sermon, from his father's pulpit, which was well received. For the next two years young Livingston preached often in Lanark and in the village kirks roundabout. Called to the ministry (as he believed) by the Spirit of God, he soon applied for ordination in the Kirk of Scotland, with promised financial support from the countess of Wigton, the countess of Eglinton, and others; but he was continually thwarted by the bishops, James Law of Glasgow in particular, who considered him an untutored exegete, a youngster of dubious theology, a rebel who encouraged the laity not to kneel when receiving communion and therefore an even greater firebrand than his father. This opposition of the bishops only strengthened Livingston's commitment to a Presbyterian form of church government; and it greatly augmented his popularity throughout Lanarkshire, where Episcopalians were viewed with nearly the same disdain as Roman Catholics ("papists"). [1]

During these formative years in the younger Livingston's ministry, a group of reformers gathered often to study the Bible in the Lanark parsonage – among them, Elizabeth Melville, the famous author of *Ane Godlie Dreame,* whose family seat was fifty miles to the north. Lady Culross on her visits to Lanark grew deeply fond of the charismatic young evangelist. That John Livingston was born in 1603, the same year in which she conceived and published her *Godlie Dreame,* seemed to confirm a spiritual bond between them; and she loved nothing better than to hear his passionate sermons. Melville may indeed have felt a stronger affection for John Livingston than for the men of her own family: she rarely mentions her sons with approval, and never with a word of praise. In a letter of 19 June 1631, addressed to Livingston in Ireland, Melville notes that she "forgot" her son Samuel was also there, in the service of Sir Robert Ker; and she asks Livingston to convey a message. Of her husband, John Colville, we hear nothing at all in Melville's extant correspondence. But her affection for young Livingston was unbounded, if unreciprocated.

As Livingston's ministry expanded and his reputation grew, he was kept on the road for weeks at a time. Melville resented his absence. In a series of admonitory letters, she addressed him always as "My very worthy and dear brother" – but scolded him as if he were an inattentive son ignoring his mother.

Lady Culross to John Livingston (n.d.)° [2]

My wery worthy and deir brother,

I am glad that ye have bein so well exercised this while, that ye could neither spend a hour's riding (being within three miles!), nor yet a quarter of ane hour's writing upon me. Ye promised otherwise quhen we parted – for ye knew how earnest I wes to hear of your sister's case, also quhat course ye wes mindet to tak. Bot I will help you to mak ane excuse: it appeirs that ye have judgèt me by yourself: *out of sicht, out of thoucht!* Tho' it wes so with you, yet it wes not so with me. If ye had ta'en journey in haste, as I apprehendet, I would have digested all; bot staying so long, and wisiting other friends, I think ye micht have spent a hour or two upon *me*, among the rest! [3]

When I apprehendet that ye wes neir the end of your journey, they told me that ye wes preaching in *Dunfermling!* – quhilk I could not believe at the first, considering quhat charge ye gat, for that is a moir publict place than any that ye have been in; but quhen I gat certain word, I thocht ye had ran a hazard. [4]

---

[1] *William Livingston*] editor of *The Conflict in Conscience of Bessie Clarkson, q.v.*

[2] *n.d.*] for dating on internal evidence, see ed. Tweedie (1845); Livingston began to preach in 1625.

[3] *sister*] Livingston had seven sisters; it's unclear which one is intended here, or what her "case" involved.

[4] *Dunfermling*] Dunfermling is just ten miles from Culross, yet Livingston had neglected to contact Melville; *had ran a hazard*] were pushing your luck (by preaching openly, in a town the size of Dunfermling, having been charged by the bishops to cease and desist).

Since it is so, I wish it may do guid to others and no hurt to you nor the rest, nor to that business ye have in hand.

If ye had not seen Mr. Robert Colville, I would have heard no word at *all* from you!

Bot I will quarrel you no moir, for I neither can or will threap kindness upon creatures. Althocht ye forget me, I hope ye will not forget your self, nor that cause ye have in hand. Your stay is against my heart. Bot if that business be als well done without you, and ye als well excercised at hame, I am content. I hope ye are earnest with God, and will do as He directs. [1]

As for that exercise of *humiliatioun*, I would knaw quhat liberty ye had for yourself for *that* cause – and if ye gat any *heart*, to remember me and my bands. [2]

As for me, I found never so strong impediments without. And within? I wished from my heart als sensible a *shower* of grace upon *you* all, as *I* felt a great *droughth*. (Thocht I wes as Gideoun's "dry flesh," yet if there be a dew upon the rest, I sall press to be content, and bliss the Lord if any[one] hes gotten guid, thocht *I* sould want the sense of it for a while.) It is the Lord with quhom we have ado, who gives and taks, casts doun and raiseth up, kills and revives, as pleases his Majesty. Let Him have regard to His owen glory, and to the salvatioun and sanctificatioun of our sauls, and do with me and mine quhat He thinks best.

My task is still augmented and tripled – and yet, I fear worse. Sin in me and mine is my greatest cross. I would, if it were the Lord's will, choose afflictioun rather than iniquity! (Lord, tak us away in mercy, or we be a blot to that professioun!. […])

I desiret you to tell my Lady Eglintoun that she sall be freed of that lash quhen it pleases her (bot I think ye have forgot – at least, ye write nothing of that, to me); bot it touches me neir, and holds me in some fear, since ye spak to me. Neither can I get rest in that particular till she be *out* of that company! If my Lady could find out either some aweful man, or, if that can[not] be, some guid, aweful wife to tak her of her hand, it would greatly ease my mind. If not, desire her to send her[self] to John Gillon's house, and I sall bring her hame, because I am but mending a old house. […] I have no moir to say, bot wishes she may get better. [3]

I have no time. An' Monday comes, I think I sall hear from you. In the mean time, I hope ye will remember me to God – if He give you a heart. As for writing or wisitatioun, let them not hinder better exercises. Now watch and pray (never moir need), and praise also (great cause!).   Strive against sluggishness—

Bid me do as I say! Lord work that in us, quhilk He requires! His grace be with you!

In haste,
Yours in C.
E. Melville

[P.S.] I wrote Tuesday from Cumbernauld. If my foolish kindness mak you moir unkind, I sall mend that as I may. […] I have written at length to Master David [Dickson], having moir time than I expected. His letter will inform you moir particularly of my estate, for I wes in haste quhen I wrote to you, and angry also, not without cause. Excuse as ye please. Neither will I forgive you, till ye confess your fault and mak amends. This letter will show you quhat need I have of help. Be the moir earnest for me, and quhen ye may spare a little painès to write, seik it from God, and write as He directs, bot ye will not go by *your* diet! [4]

• • •

---

[1] *threap .. creatures*] heap kindness upon mere mortals.

[2] *As for that ... my bands*] but I'd still like to know what license you had to humiliate me by neither visiting me nor writing me, and whether you have thought of my feelings and or a sense of your spiritual bond to me.

[3] *Lady Eglintoun*] Lady Anne Livingston (1588-1632), Maid of Honor to Queen Anna of Denmark; countess of Eglinton by her 1612 marriage to Alexander [Seton *later* Montgomery], 6th Earl of Eglinton; and one of John Livingston's financial supporters from 1625 until her death in 1632. Lord and Lady Eglinton from 1624 were involved in a bitter and protracted domestic dispute over the earl's alleged confiscation of lady Anne's property, and her alleged jealousy over his interest in Helena Livingston;   *aweful*] awe-inspiring, powerful (Lady Eglintoun complained she could not "labor" her cause in the courts, for lack of powerful allies).

[4] *diet*] habit, behavior.

Lady Culross to John Livingston (n.d.)°

My deirly belovet brother in the Lord Jesus,

I have na leisure to write, only this few lines, desiring you to be earnest with God in this matter […] I knaw ye will come this way, and give us either ane guid nicht, or *Welcome hame!* (as pleases Him). […]
~~O watch and pray! Beware to grieve that blissèd Sprite, and come here on Monday so soon as ye may,~~ that ye be not over-late as ye [were] last….Remember me earnestly – never moir need! This heart is like a gissnet wessel – all rins out! (Lord lay up for me, that cannot lay up for myself!). […] I think ye sall scarce read this. I have no moir time. The Lord be with you, again. [1]

Your loving sister in Christ,
E. Melville

[P.S.] This is a proof of your pen. [2]

• • •

As he preached from town to town, Livingston attracted an ever larger and more enthusiastic flock. His sermons moved hearers to thunder out alleluias and to weep aloud for sin – religious "ecstasies" that troubled the bishops. He was often invited to preach in the hamlet of Shotts, in North Lanarkshire; and when his schedule permitted, he was always pleased to do so because "In that place I used to find moir liberty in preaching than elsewhere" – less resistance from Anglican conformists, and less surveillance by Episcopal spies. [3]

On the weekend of 19-20 June 1630, Livingston was invited to speak once again at the Shotts kirk, for a weekend retreat that came to be known, in after-years, as the "Kirk o' Shotts Revival." Melville dispatched a letter to Livingston, urging him to participate:

Lady Culross to John Livingston (17 June 1630)°

My wery worthy and deir brother,

My heart wes amongst you this last Sabboth, bot it pleaset God to hold me back (soir against my will; justly, I confess, yet I hope, in mercy). I mind by His grace to come over the morn and to be at that banket if it will please Him to send a calm, within and without. Pray for a blissing, I beseech you – never sich need! I hope ye will be there. I beseech you, disappoint me not now, bot mak amends for the fault ye made to us all. We looked certainly for you! We could never hear quhat wes your stay…. Ye will come, I hope. As for your text, I hope ye will say out that quhilk ye left. [4]

Come, in the name of God, and do as He directs you. He will furnish you, according to our need. ….The communioun is not far from us here, bot I long to come there if the Lord will permit. […] The Lord conwey you, or else ye can do nothing. Pray earnestly for a blessing. (I hear that my tutor will be there!) Lord be amongst us, and give us all that whereof we stand in greatest need. His grace be with you till meeting, and for ever. In post-haste,

Your loving sister in Christ ever,
E. Melville

• • •

On Saturday, hundreds of people converged on Shotts for a "Day of Humiliatioun," with calls for repentance, followed by a potluck banquet. On Sunday, holy communion was served, Presbyterian style, without the sin of kneeling; followed by more sermons, group Bible study, and private reflection.

That night, although he was slated to deliver the keynote address on Monday (his 27th birthday), Livingston with Lady Culross and a number of others stayed up till dawn, "in conference and prayer," in a large room that was to have served as Melville's sleeping quarters.

---

[1] *gissnet wessel*] cracked vessel; *rins out*] runs out, leaks.

[2] *a proof ... pen*] a test, to see if you will write to me.

[3] *In that place…elsewhere*] John Livingston, *Memorable Characteristics* (ed. 1845), 1.138.

[4] *mind*] intend; *banket*] banquet (spiritual feast); *say out .. left*] continue preaching from the text where you left off in that last sermon.

After breakfast, before it was time to go to sermon, "all going apart for their private devotioun, [Melville] went into the bed and drew the curtains, that she might set herself to prayer." Her maid remained close by (J. Livingston, 346).

Livingston wandered off alone in the fields, to ponder his sermon. He was nervous. The crowd had now grown to more than one thousand, a new record: and "There came such a misgiving of spirit upon me, considering my unworthiness and weakness, and the multitude and expectatioun of the people, that I was consulting with myself to have stolen away somewhere, and declined that day's preaching" (138).

Lady Culross, meanwhile, continued in silent prayer, in bed, though with a great deal of audible anguish. "William Ridge of Adderny coming into the room, and hearing her have great motioun upon her (although she spake not out), he *desired* her to speak out, saying that there was none in the room but him and her woman (as, at that time, there *was* no other). She did so. And the door being opened, the room filled full. She continued in prayer, with wonderful assistance, for large three hours' time" (346).

The Presbyterians in those early days did not permit women to preach in assembly, but there was no rule against dozens of faithful Christians eavesdropping on the prayers of a pious woman as she spoke aloud to God behind the curtains of a canopy-bed; nor was Livingston inclined to interrupt these proceedings, to begin his sermon.

Shortly before noon, Elizabeth Melville was heard to say, "In Jesus name, Amen." The audience adjourned for lunch.

That afternoon, John Livingston delivered a sermon on Ezekiel chapter 36, verses 25-26, that some followers credited with altering the course of Scottish history. The congregation gathered in the graveyard outside the kirk – this being the only place that could accommodate seating for one thousand people. Inspired in part by the religious exercise of Lady Culross, Livingston was now refueled, fired up, and ready to preach: "I had about one hour and ane half," he reports, "upon the points I had meditated." To deliver his message, Livingston stood on a tombstone. As he spoke, hundreds raised their arms heavenward, with tears streaming down their cheeks. But when his ninety minutes had ended and he offered "to close with some words of exhortatioun," a miracle intervened: John Livingston was himself overtaken with a fresh infusion of the Spirit (138). [1]

For another hour, with renewed fervor, Livingston preached "in ane strain of exhortatioun and warning, with such liberty and melting of heart as I never had the like in public all my life" (138-9). He later said it was the greatest sermon he ever delivered and regretted only that he was unable to reconstruct it from his notes. Others agreed. Rev. Robert Fleming in his *Fulfilling of the Scripture,* reports that Livingston's sermon of 21 June 1630 brought an "extraordinary appearance of God, and down-pouring of the Spirit with a strange unusual motioun on the hearers," insomuch that five hundred of those who attended had "a discernible change wrought upon them, of whom most proved lively Christians, afterwards" (355). From that day forth, Elizabeth Melville's youthful correspondent came to be introduced in Presbyterian pulpits as "the worthy famous Master John Livingston."

In August, Livingston was at last called to the ministry – on condition that he leave the country. Invited by Lord Claneboy to a benefice in Killinchy, Ireland, Livingston accepted. Ordained in haste by the elderly bishop of Raphoe, and without taking leave of Lady Culross, the Reverend John Livingston packed his books and bags and shipped for Ireland, there to serve as a Scots missionary to Irish Roman Catholics and English Episcopalians.

Elizabeth Melville disapproved of Livingston's sudden departure for a land of papists – she had hoped to see him appointed to a benefice in Scotland. And she was dismayed, though not greatly surprised, when he neglected to write. Melville bore those indignities with patience.

Seven lonely months passed. In March 1631, Rev. Livingston finally returned to Scotland for a visit. Melville rejoiced at the news. But after three weeks had expired with no word from him, Lady Culross on Conception Day dispatched a letter, to express her fierce displeasure.

---

[1] *Ezekiel 36:25-26*] "Then will I sprinkle clean water upon you, and ye shall be clean: from all your filthiness, and from all your idols, will I cleanse you. A new heart also will I give you, and a new spirit will I put within you: and I will take away the stony heart out of your flesh, and I will give you an heart of flesh" (AV). An iconoclast, Livingston inveighed against the "idol-worship" of venerating images of Jesus, Mary, and the saints.

Lady Culross to John Livingston (25 March 1631)°

My worthy and deir brother,

I could not have *thoucht* that ye would have forgot us so long (yet would be loath to forget *you*!). To tell you the truth, it troublet me that ye neither come to take guid nicht, nor yet would write ane excuse, nor send any word sinsen. If we had bein bound with natural bands, it would have bein great incivility, if not unkindness; bot I see *spiritual* bands is not in request! [1]

I hear that ye are come to this country three weeks since, and we have heard no word from you, quhilk I can not believe. If it be so, the first fault is evil-mendet. Howsoever, I must strive to be content with the Lord's will. Though all sould change, yet He remains unchangeable, who can (quhen it pleases Him) supply all wants. [2]

A long time efter ye parted from us, they made me believe that ye wes not away bot would stay till winter wes past, quhilk made me digest all. Bot quhen I heard the contrair, it grievet me moir than before, because I had some hope that if ye had not bein in sich *haste*, God would have providet a place for you in *this* land! Bot your post-haste marred all, and troublet me at the first, moir than enouch.

Bot I have gotten greater matters to digest, sinsen.

And yet, I will never excuse your fault till ye come to excuse your *self*.

I confess it is no time for me to quarrel now, quhen God is quarreling us and hes ta'en away our deir pastour, who hes preached the Word of God among us almost forty yeirs, plainly and powerfully – a soir stroke to this congregatioun, and chiefly to me, to quhom he wes not only a pastour and a brother, bot (under God) a husband and a father to my children. Nixt his owen family, I have the greatest loss.

Your sudden woyage hes troublet me moir sinsen than ever, and many of this congregatioun who would have preferred you to others, and would have uset all means possible if ye had bein in this land. Bot now I fear the charm be spilt. Yet, ye cannot go out of my mind, nor out of the mind of some others quhilk wishes you here with our hearts to supply that place, and prayès for it (if it be the Lord's will) – thoucht by appeirance, there is no possibility of it, for I think they have agreet with another.

Yet if God have a work, He can bring it about, and work contrair to all means, for there is nothing too hard for Him. If ye knew quhat need we have, ye would not rest till ye came to us. Many longs for you […] I beseik you, haste you to come wisit us, and delay not. If any sponk of that old kindness remain, I knaw ye will be als earnest to come, as we are to desire. It is a work of charity now, quhilk ye owe to all Christians, chiefly to us to quhom ye are bound (if love can bind you to any). Be earnest with God and do as He directs, and pray for us earnestly. Never so great need as now—do as we would, to you. [3]

I will say no moir till meeting – quhilk I look for, shortly. In the meantime (if ever ye remembret me), double your prayers now, for my task is doublet and tripled. Lord, that pitied yet pure people under that cruel bondage, pity me! – and grant a right use of all, with help and relief, in His time. Lord bring you here, with a blissing. His grace be with you till meeting, and for ever. In haste,

Yours ever in C.
The 25 of March
E. Melville

• • •

In June, Livingston returned to his ministry in Ireland. Melville tried to see him before he shipped, and was again disappointed.

---

[1] *sinsen*] since then;   *bands*] bonds, ties of blood or kinship.

[2] *the first fault*] your departure to Ireland, last August, without saying goodbye;   *evil-mendet*] poorly mended.

[3] *sponk*] spark or trace.

Lady Culross to John Livingston (17 June 1631)°

My wery worthy and deir brother,

Ye sall wit that I came to Airth a little efter ye went away. And hearing that ye wes in Kinnaird, I posted efter you – bot ye wes gone. And I did quwhat I could, to follow you, but could not get horse (neither a boy to send, till the morning). [1]

Since ye cracked tryst from Wednesday till Friday, ye might have borne with me for a few hours! Ye trysted to meet the horse by ten hours, bot if ye be remembred, I *told* you that I could not come so soon! Bot ye said they sould stay upon me in Airth, quhilk I looked for. Bot I see ye have bein holden by your diet, quhilk has disappointed me. Althocht I had come, I would not have ta'en *your* horse (and I could get na other here); therefore it fell out well, for your horse's sair back. […] [2]

If there be any horse to spare, I desire two to be sent this Saturday, by 8 or 9 hours: ane for myself (with any woman's saddle), and another for a gentleman who is with me. So, hoping ye will do this, I rest, desiring you to pray for a blissing to all our meetings, in publict and private. His grace be with you till then, and ever.

In haste,
Yours in Christ,
E. Melville
Friday, the 17 of June.

[P.S.] I durst not bring over horse. I wes in some fear to come myself, because the wind wes somequhat great, and the tide against us; but I took the hazard of my promise and wes in fear that my lady's horse sould stay over-long upon me. I could not bring a saddle. We wes forced to go moir than a mile on foot, quhilk made me wery weary. Bot your kind aunt helped me with a horse to Kinnaird – bot I could get nane to come there. [3]

• • •

Having returned to Ireland, Livingston on August 24 had a close brush with death by fire, but the Lord was pleased to deliver him: "I lay in ane high room of ane John Stewart's house, in Ballemeroon. The room was strawed with ane great deal of dried sea-bent. I used never, after I fell asleep, to awaken till the morning; yet that night, about one o'clock, all the house being fast asleep, I awakened peaceably and thought it had been day; and for ane little space, keeped my eyes shut and neither heard any noise nor felt any smell.

"With ane while, I opened my eyes – and saw the bent, burning within two ells of the bed where I lay! – for ane great fire in the room below, the nicht before (making ready the meat of the reapers) had fired the mantle-tree of the chimney, the end whereof came to the room where I lay.

"The fire was between me and the door of the chamber! I rose, and took with me my breeches, my Bible, and my watch – giving my books and anything else I had for *gone*, and got out of the door, and called up those of the house. […]

"If I had sleeped ane quarter of ane hour longer, the fire had seized on the roof of the house, covered only with straw, and so not only house and guids, but our lives had been consumed" (Livingston, 145). [4]

Despite this heavenly intervention, Livingston only a few weeks later found himself out of a job. Bishop Robert Echlin deposed both Livingston and his friend, Robert Baird, on allegations of "unconformity" in theology, and for "stirring up the people to ecstasies and enthusiasms" (145). Knowing he would need support from his friends back home, Livingston eventually wrote a letter to Lady Culross.

Melville upon receiving his sad news from her protégé replied with a letter of consolation and encouragement.

---

[1] *Ye sall wit*] You shall know;   *Airth*] a village just eight miles west of Culross;   *Kinnaird*] 50 miles north.

[2] *cracked tryst*] broke trust;   *ten hours*] ten o'clock;   *stay upon*] wait for;   *holden by your diet*] behaving as usual;   *Althocht*] although (Even if);   *fell out weill…back*] lucky for your horse's sore back (a sarcasm).

[3] *nane to come there*] I could find no one to escort me (it being unsafe for women to travel alone).

[4] *sea-bent*] a coarse wiry grass that grows upon the moorlands and was used to strew the floors of houses.

Lady Culross to John Livingston (10 December 1631)°

My wery worthy and deir brother,

~~I receivet your letter, and hes no time to answer you as I would.~~

I thank the Lord, who upholds you in all your trials and tefntatiouns. It is guid for you to be holden in exercise. Otherwise, I would suspect that all were not well with you. God is faithful (as ye find by experience) and will not try you above your strength. [1]

Courage, deir brother! All is in love. All works together for the best. Ye must be hewen and hammered down, and dressed and prepared, before ye be a LIVING STONE fit for His building. And if He be mindet to mak you meet to help to repair the ruins of His house, ye must look for other manner of strokes than ye have felt. Ye must feel your owen waikness, that ye may be humbled and cast doun before Him, that so ye may pity pure waik ones that are borne doun with infirmities. And quhen ye are laid low, and wile in your owen eyes, then will He raise you up, and refresh you with some blinks of His faworable countenance, that ye may be able to comfort others with these consolatiouns wherewith ye have bein comforted by Him. This ye knaw by some experience, blissed be God. [2]

And as strength and grace increases, look for stronger trials – fechtings without, and fears within! the Devil and his instruments, against you! and your Lord, hiding His face! Deeply, almost overwhelmed with troubles and terrors, and yet out of all this misery, He is working some gracious work of mercy for the glory of His great name, the salvatioun and sanctificatioun of your owen saul, and for the comfort of His distressed children – there, or here, or both, as pleases Him. [3]

Up your heart, then! And prepare for the battle! Put on the whole armour of God. Thoucht ye be waik, ye have a strong Captain, whose power is made perfit in waikness, and whose grace is sufficient for you. Quhat ye want in yourself, ye have in Him, who is given to you of God to be your wisdom, richteousness, sanctificatioun and redemptioun, your treasure and treasurer, who keeps all in store. The stock and the anwil is in His owen hand, and He drops doun, drop and drop, as ye have need. And quhen ye want long, ye sall get double profit – and at length, the hale sum, so that ye sall be rich for ever. [4]

Since He hes put His work in your waik hands, look not for long ease, here. Ye must feel the weicht of that worthy calling, and be holden under with the sense of your owen waikness, that He may kith His strength in due time – a waik man, and a strong God, who will not fail nor forsak you, bot will furnish strength, and gifts, and grace, according to that employment that He puts in your hands. [5]

The pain is bot for a moment; the pleasure, everlasting. The battle is bot short. Your Captain fechts for you – therefore the victory is certain, and the reward, glorious. A croun and a kingdom is worth the fechting for! Blessed be His name who fechts all our battles and works all our works for us. Since all is in Christ, and He ours, quhat would we have moir, but thankful hearts? and grace to honour Him in life and death who is our advantage in life and death, who guides with His counsel, and will bring us to His glory?

To Him be all honour, power, and praise, for now and for ever, amen!

Now I have reft this time from my sleip, I have no time to show you my [own] estate: cross upon cross! The end of ane, is bot the beginning of another – bot guiltiness in me and mine is my greatest cross. Many times like to faint and fall doun, bot my Lord puts under His hand, sustains and upholds me with His secret strength, and oftimes most near quhen He seems to be farthest off, and sometimes [He] seasons bitterness with some sweitness.

No creature hes moir cause to complain quhen I look to myself; [nor] none so unworthy [as I], so great cause to rejoice and be thankful for, quhen I look to *His* crosses and comforts (for that quhilk He hes done, is doing, and will do; and for the least persuasioun of His unchangeable love; for taking sich pains to ding me out of myself, out of all creatures and means under the sun – and many times seems to ding

---

[1] *holden in exercise*] constant in religious discipline.

[2] *waikness…waik*] weakness…weak;   *wile*] vile (humbly conscious of your own sinful condition).

[3] *fechtings without*] fightings outside yourself.

[4] *hale sum*] whole sum (of God's reward).

[5] *kith*] make abundant.

me from Himself!). Bot quhen He puts back, by *appeirance*, yet He is drawing forward. Quhen He strikes with ane hand, He sustains with the other. The greatery misery I find in my self, the greater mercy in Him (and the greater mercy, the greater guiltiness, quhen it is abuset). Then, quhen sin and misery abounds, there grace and mercy *super*-abounds.

So I am in a labourinth – how sall I win out? Only this is my comfort: that mercy sall prewail. Our sins are finite – bot His grace, infinite. Our guiltiness, great – bot His guidness is greater, and exceeds. The rage and malice of our enemy is cruel yet it is boundet – bot the love of Jesus passeth bounds, is incomprehensible, overcomes all things. And to conclude, our misery will end shortly, bot His mercy endures for ever.

Quhen I begin, I cannot end: it is some comfort to me that they get liberty to pray for me. My great tentatioun now is that I fear my *prayers* be turned into sin: I find and sees the clean contrair in me and mine; at least, some of them.

Samuel is going to the college in Saint Andrews, to a worthy master there, bot I fear him deadly. (I depend not on creatures!) Pray earnestly for a blessing – he quhom ye knaw is like to overturn all, and hes broken all bands, Lord pity him! There wes some beginning of order, bot all is wrong again, for the death of his brother maks him to tak liberty – so I have double loss. [1]

And sweit Marie Preston is with God. Sweit wes her end, bot a sair stroke, to me! Nane except her husband and children will have moir missing of her.

I have abuset many benefits and right bitter strokes, yet can mak right use of nothing. Lord help and work that quhilk He requires, and tak the glory to Himself.

Ye write that ye are like to have no settling there. If God have a work ado with you there, He can change hearts. If here, He can and will open a door, thoucht never so fast closet. Ye say my watch is "oft wrong, goes sometime too slow and sometime too swift." Ye say *ye* are "oft too slow but cannot be like the watch in rinning too swiftly." I fear quhen ye went first to Ireland ye *did* run too swiftly; therefore ye are like to be driven back again till ye be better temperet. Bot God hes a work in all, for His glory and your guid. Therefore cast yourself upon Him. He knawès quhat is most meet. Wink, and let the Lord work. Submit to His will, and He sall do better than ye can think, and direct you to do the best, and crown His work with mercy and compassioun. As for your suffering, I know ye had bitter tentatiouns in it; and yet I doubt not bot ye had answerable comforts—sour, seasoned with sweit! Be humblet quhen ye look to your part, bot be thankful quhen ye look to the Lord's part. Bliss His name for that quhilk He hes done to you, and for you, and by you, and press to walk before Him, answerable in some measure to His fatherly care, blessed providence, and loving kindness, whereof ye have had so many sweit experiences.

O watch and pray, that ye fall not in tentatioun! Seik early, and ye sall find better than gold, pearls, and precious stones. The gold is better won early than late: if ye mak a use of winning a penny quhen ye sould rest, and sleip quhen ye sould rise early to your work, the winning of that penny may lose you a pound. Therefore, sleip in time, and awake in time, and fall to work in due season, and ye sall find by experience the truth of His precious promises. Therefore strive against sluggishness, I charge you. It is bot a custom. Work early, and ye sall win enouch to mak you rich. Ye knaw the proverb, *Sanat, dicat, sanctificat.* "Try a month," as ye said once, "and ye sall find some gain that will stir you up to seik Him early, quhom your saul would love." Suppone that he hes trysted you to meet *Him*! Read the Proverbs, and ye sall find that He calls you instantly and earnestly to seik Him early – and ye sall find. [2]

Bid me do as I say! Alas, I fear I have tint the tide – bot yet, I would mint to it again. Lord, help and draw us with the cords of love, and mak guid that new covenant, and do all things for us quhen we can do nothing, and accept our waik endeavors in the merit of him in quhom He is well pleaset.

Now I have forgot myself – I fear I lose my sleip and the gold also. Therefore, send me something, with the first sure bearer, to recompense the loss: write something on some guid subject. The last werses of the 40 of Isaiah, that ye taucht in Culross, or upon the Song of Zachary, or anything ye please. Seik somequhat from Him that hes aboundance. Tak the pen in your hand, and seik a blissing – and set to, and God will furnish, ye will find. If ye will not, I will write no moir to you (quhilk will be no small loss!). Be not sweir, I beseik you. [3]

---

[1] *fear him deadly*] fear his salvation;   *death of his brother*] James, the middle son, about whom almost nothing is known and who evidently died at about this time.

[2] *Sanat, dicat, sanctificat*] (Early to bed, early to rise makes one) healthy, wealthy, and holy;   *Suppone*] suppose.

[3] *tint*] missed;   *mint to it*] attempt it;   *in the merit of him*] for Jesus' sake;   *bearer*] letter-carrier;   *sweir*] lazy.

Now lauch at my shortness! [1]

Help me and mine – earnestly, with prayer and praises – never sich need! Forget not our Saturday of humiliatioun, nor our Sabboth of thanksgiving, as the Lord will assist. Commend me heartily to all our deir friends there. Chiefly, remember my love to Mr. Robert Blair, and to his kind wife. (If I had time, I would press to overcome unkindness with kindness.) Remember me heartily to Mr. Robert Cunningham, to Mr. Josiah Welsh, to Mr. George Dunbar, to Mr. Edward Bryce, and to all the rest of the pastours, and all their guid wives, and to all the Lord's conwerts there – to pastour and people. Blessed be God for that gracious work there! Lord increase the number, and increase and cherish His owen grace! Forget [not] Mr. John Livingston with John Simple, and Hugh Graham, and all the rest. [2]

Pray all for me earnestly, never sich need.

Lord, pour out the sprite of prayer and praises, and let us never forget that quhilk we sould prefer to our [own] particulars. The powerful presence and blessed Sprite of Jesus Christ be with you all, and comfort and encourage you, as He knaws your need. Now, I leave you in His arms.

Yours ever in Christ,
E. Melville
At midnicht, the 10 of December.

[P.S.] Receive thir blotted lines, written on your name, in post-haste. Bear with the blots, I have no time to write them over. All your deir acquaintance remembers you, and desires earnestly to be rememberet of you. God's blessing be with you again I am efter a great journey. I write from Halhill. 10 Dec. 1631. [3]

• • •

John Livingston, by Frans Hals
Courtesy Wikipedia Commons

Rev. John Livingston may have been a poor correspondent, but after the death of Lady Melville he recorded a tribute to her memory: "Of all that ever I saw," he wrote, "she was most unwearied in religious exercises. And the more she attained access to God therein, she hungered the more" (Livingston, 346).

After being deposed from his benefice in Ireland, Livingston spent much of the next thirty years as an itinerant evangelist, traversing Ireland and Scotland, spreading the Presbyterian Gospel and his fervor for the Kirk's independence from Anglican interference. In 1635, he again outraged the bishops and was excommunicated. Continuing his ministry underground, John Livingston lived to see the bishops run out of Scotand, and "the people universally entered into the Covenant of God for reformation of religion" (160). At the Restoration of the monarchy, refusing to take an oath of allegiance to King Charles, John Livingston was banished from Britain and in 1663 emigrated to Rotterdam, where he died on 9 May 1672.

Lady Culross's son Alexander (d. 1666), like his father and grandfather, became an ordained minister of the Scottish Church. He went on to serve as a professor of theology, first at the University of Sedan, then at the New College of St. Andrews. The younger son, though an aspiring poet, made good on his mother's dim assessment of his spirituality: Samuel Colville raised such hell at college that the masters of St. Andrews, in a report to the Presbytery, report having been "much offended with his levity, unsettledness of spirit, and his disorderly carriage toward his reverend brother [Alexander], presenting railing libels against him, for which he hath been diverse times gravely rebuked." [4]

During the Puritan Interregnum, the prodigal younger brother sojourned in France, where he poked fun at Presbyterians and pursued a lifestyle distinctly free of religious exercise. At the Restoration, Samuel returned to Scotland, whereupon he wrote *The Whig's Supplication; Or, the Scots Hudibras: A Mock Poem* (pub. 1681); a work that the Rev. Matthew Leishman subsequently condemned as a "mass of ribaldry and indecency," penned by "the ungodly son of a pious mother." In an "Author's Apology" pre-

---

[1] *lauch at my shortness*] laugh at my (promised) brevity.

[2] *conwerts there*] Irish converts from Roman Catholicism to Scottish Presbyterianism.

[3] *thir*] these.

[4] *much offended...rebuked*] ed. DWF from Abbotsford Club, *Ecclesiastical Records*, vol. 7 (1837): 66-7.

fixed to *The Whig's Supplication*, Samuel Colville sums up his biography by quoting lines penned by his drinking buddy, John Cockburn: [1]

> Samuel was sent to France,
> To learn to sing and dance
> And play upon a fiddle.
> Now he's a man of great esteem:
> (His mother 'got him in a dream,
> At Culross, on a griddle.) [2]

Elizabeth Melville – without notable success, but with unflagging zeal – labored to reform the Kirk, and kirkmen, and her son Samuel, until about 1640. By the time Samuel Colville achieved his notoriety as a poet, his dear mother was long gone and her dream vision of 1603 largely forgotten. Her death is unreported. Nor has there survived any record of her burial. But if Melville's passing is well adumbrated in *Ane Godlie Dreame,* the poet doubtless made her final departure from this wretchit warld with ane heart full of courage, speaking truth to power. One imagines that her ensuing pilgrimage to Heaven was a journey packed with adventure, with Jesus at her side, through flood, through thorn and briar, past "uglie beists that gaipit to devoir," o'er craggy mountains high, and high above the flames of Hell – to a land of everlasting gloir in which a woman can speak without being silenced, and may take up the pen and seek a blissing not only from Heaven, but from a responsive readership. O nevir sich great neid, as nou!

Culross today

---

[1] Leishman (ed. 2008), 23.

[2] John Cockburn, untitled. Normalized text ed. DWF from Samuel Colvil (Colville), "The Authors Appology to the Reader," sig. prelim. A5r.

Mary Oxlie (Reidhead) (fl. 1616),

"Parthenius"

Perfection in a Womans work is rare;
From an untroubled mind should verses flow...
– Mary Oxlie to William Drummond

WILLIAM DRUMMOND, the Scots poet, in 1616 published his *Poems: Amorous, Funerall, Divine, Pastorall.* The volume is comprised largely of amorous sonnets, one section being addressed a living mistress, his "Northern Phoenix"; and the other, to a mistress who is figured as recently dead (quite possibly the same woman). Prefixed to Drummond's work is a single commendatory poem, "To the Author," by a young woman who signs herself "Parthenius" (a male name meaning "maiden-like"). Parthenius flirts with Drummond, praising him for the seductive quality of his pastoral verse but without committing herself to his spell. She figures Drummond as Apollo, and his female auditor (evidently, herself) as the Daphne who refused his embrace; but she professes to grow pitiful, and goes so far as to proffer "the grace / A garland for [his] locks to interlace" – in the form a commendatory sonnet.

At about the same time, perhaps at the same sitting – though Drummond did not include it in his first edition – Parthenius wrote a longer poem "To William Drummond." Parthenius there elaborates on her relationship to Drummond, stating that her "rustic Muse" is less bright than his ("Then do not sparks with your bright suns compare – / Perfection in a woman's work is rare.") She again figures herself as "tree-turn'd Daphne," having rejected Apollo's suit, but "from her boughs would gladly spare / To frame a garland for [his] hair."

Drummond's editors in 1711, on thin evidence, identified the dead mistress of Drummond's *Poems* as Mary Cunningham of Barns, Scotland, a young woman who died on 23 July 1616 and whose family had ties to Drummond's. But whoever the poet's Northern Phoenix may have been, his "Parthenius" was not Mary Cunningham, but rather Mary Oxlie, a young woman of Morpeth, Northumberland – the same Mary Oxlie who wrote a much admired poem, "To William Drummond," first published in 1656 (in a posthumous edition of Drummond's works).

If both Mary Cunningham and Mary Oxlie were love interests, then Drummond was disappointed in love not once, but twice, within weeks of publishing his *Poems.* On 26 November 1616, Mary Oxlie married Edward Reidhead of Morpeth.

How Drummond might have known either woman remains a mystery – Hawthornden is 85 miles from Barns, and 90 miles from Morpeth. Perhaps Drummond and Oxlie had kinship relations; or perhaps he and Edward Reidhead were school chums at the University of Edinburgh (then known as the College of Edinburgh). Whatever the circumstance, Mary Oxlie in both of her poems to Drummond addresses him in a tone of guarded intimacy, conferring praise that she seems to offer as compensation to a gifted poet though a jilted lover.

William Drummond, 1612
Scotland's National Galleries

DWF

To the Author

WHILE thou dost praise the roses, lilies, gold
Which in a dangling tress and face appear,
Still stands the sun in skies, thy songs to hear;
A silence sweet each whispering wind doth hold;
Sleep in Pasithea's lap his eyes doth fold;
The sword falls from the god of the fifth sphere;
The herds to feed, the birds to sing, forbear;
Each plant breathes love, each flood and fountain cold.[1]
And hence it is that that once-nymph, now tree,
Who did th'Amphrisian shepherd's sighs disdain
And scorned his lays, moved by a sweeter vein,
Is become pitiful, and follows thee,
   Thee loves, and vaunteth she hath the grace
   A garland for thy locks to interlace.   2

Parthenius

To William Drummond of Hawthornden

I NEVER rested on the Muses' bed,
Nor dipped my quill in the Thessalian fountain. 3
My rustic muse was rudely fosterèd
And flies too low to reach the double mountain. 4
Then do not sparks with your bright suns compare–
Perfection in a woman's work is rare.
From an untroubled mind should verses flow;
My discontents makes mine too muddy show. 5
And hoarse encumbrances of household care,
Where these remain, the Muses ne'er repair.
If thou dost extol her hair,
Or her ivory forehead fair,
Or those stars whose bright reflection
Thralls thy heart in sweet subjection; 6
Or when to display thou seeks
The snow-mixed roses on her cheeks,
Or those rubies soft and sweet,
Over those pretty rows that meet

The Chian painter (as ashamed)
Hides his picture, so far-famed; 7
And the queen he carved it by,
With a blush her face doth dye,
Since those lines do limn a creature
That so far surpassed her feature. 8
When thou show'st how fairest Flora [25]
Pranked with pride the banks of Ora,
So thy verse her streams doth honor,
Strangers grow enamored on her! 9
All the swans that swim in Po
Would their native brooks forgo
And (as loathing Phoebus' beams)
Long to bathe in cooler streams. 10
Tree-turned Daphne would be seen
In her groves to flourish green,
And her boughs would gladly spare
To frame a garland for thy hair,
That fairest nymphs with finest fingers
May thee crown the best of singers. 11
But when thy muse, dissolved in show'rs,
Wails that peerless prince of ours,
Cropped by too untimely fate,
Her mourning doth exasperate
Senseless things, to see thee moan—
Stones do weep and trees do groan. 12
Birds in air, fishes in flood,
Beasts in field forsake their food.
The nymphs, forgoing all their bowers,
Tear their chaplets decked with flowers. 13
Sol himself with misty vapor
Hides from earth his glorious taper [50]
And (as moved to hear thee plain)
Shows his grief in show'rs of rain. 14

---

[7] *rows*] i.e., of teeth; *Chian painter*] Homer (said to have been a native of Scio, an island in the Aegean); *as*] as if; *his picture*] Homer's *Hymn to Venus.*

[8] *limn*] illuminate or portray.

[9] *Flora*] the goddess of flowers; *Pranked*] decorated; *Ora*] the river Ore, in Fife, ran near Drummond's home and is celebrated in his verse.

[10] *Po*] a river of northern Italy; *Phoebus'*] the sun's.

[11] *Daphne*] a nymph who was changed into a laurel tree as she fled Apollo's amorous pursuit; *garland*] laurel wreath.

[12] *prince of ours*] Prince Henry, the heir apparent, whose death in 1612 was lamented in Drummond's *Tears on the Death of Moeliades,* Drummond's first published work.

[13] *chaplets*] wreaths or garlands worn on the head.

[14] *Sol*] the Sun; *plain*] (as a verb) lament; (as an adverb, re: *plainly moved to hear thee*).

---

[1] *Sleep*] Morpheus, the god of sleep; *Pasithea*] the Greek goddess of rest; *god of the fifth sphere*] on the geocentric Ptolemaic system, the planet Mars (god of war).

[2] *that once nymph, now tree*] Daphne, who flying from Apollo's desire was changed into a tree; *Amphrisian shepherd*] Apollo, disguised as a shepherd.

[3] *Thessalian fountain*] in some ancient sources, Thessaly is identified as the home of the Muses.

[4] *double mountain*] Parnassus, sometimes described as having twin peaks, one sacred to Apollo, the other sacred to Dionysus.

[5] *makes*] make [*sic*].

[6] *her hair*] i.e., of Auristella (the unidentified woman celebrated in Drummond's sonnets).

The Grey Sisters (fl. 1615)

Disdaine this seruile Yoke of base Subiection...
—Mary Grey Drayton

ELIZABETH GREY, wife of James Martin, was the second daughter of Mary (*née* Dade)
Richard Grey, a barrister of the Inner Temple. When she died in 1614, at the age of 24,
her three sisters joined hands to memorialize her in print: Sister Mary was married to William
Drayton, a cousin of Michael Drayton the poet); Penelope (b. 1591) was the future wife of
Thomas Salter; Anne (b. 1595), was the wife of William Masters of Lichfield. Their sisterly
tribute – *A Memoriall of M*ris*. Elizabeth Martin, late deceased* – was published with *A Letter of
Mr. Casaubon* (1615), a volume anonymously edited by Elizabeth's husband, James.

Mary (Grey) Drayton (1585-1643) of Atherston, Warwickshire

On the Decease of My Incomparable Sister, Mistress Elizabeth Martin

TO THE DEAR memory of the most dear,
I set apart this ink, more sad than tears.
These are the cypress branches that I bear,
The mourning habit that my sad soul wears,
This the impresa that my sorrow bears.[1]
  If this not feelingly define my smart,
  'Tis not defect of woe but want of skillful art.

Within the center of my troubled soul
A monument unto thy name I'll build,
And there with tear-filled characters enroll
Those bright perfections that thy life did gild,
The grace-full good that all thy actions filled.
  There shall my love thy sad loss memorize[2]
  When all the world shall cease to mind thy obsequies.

Then deign to take of the obscurest hand
These well-deservèd attributes of praise.
I know thy trophies not the higher stand
Because my hand desired thy name to raise.
Fair angelized soul, these humble lays
  And worthless numbers give thy light no luster,
  But show those shapeless woes that in my bosom muster.

Mary

---

[1] *impresa*] heraldic emblem.

[2] *thy ... memorize*] memorialize the sad loss of thee.

A FUNERAL PYRAMID

to
the dear
memory of
the most dear

Ευθανασία   I consecrate this   Αθανασία

threne, these fune-
ral tears.   These are
the cypress branches that
I bear, the mourning habit
that my sad soul wears, this
the impresa that my sorrow bears.
If this not feelingly define my smart,
'tis not defect of woe but want of skillful art. Within the center of my troubled
soul, a monument unto thy name I'll build;
and   there with tear - filled characters enroll
those bright perfections that thy life did gild, the
graceful good that all thy actions filled. There shall my
love thy sad loss memorize when all the world shall cease
to mind thy obsequies. Then deign to take of the obscurest
hand these well-deservèd attributes of praise. I know thy trophies
not the higher stand because my hand desired thy name to raise. Fair
angelized soul, these humble lays and worthless numbers give
thy light no luster, but show those shapeless woes that in my bosom muster.

Erected to the honor of that rare-virtuous gentlewoman (now in glory) Mistress ELIZABETH GREY –
daughter to Richard Grey, Esquire, and sometime wife to J. M., Master of Arts – by her sister, Mistress
Mary Drayton, allied to the prince of English poesy, Michael Drayton, Esquire. Interred at Atherston,
where she departed this life, calling on the Lord Jesus to the last, anno 1614. Ætat. 24.

Mary Grey Drayton's poem "To the Soul" may be read as a tribute to the soul of her deceased sister (as was perhaps
principally intended), or to her own memorial verse as the idea or abstract of that perfection. In line 1, "art" may thus
be read as either a verb or noun. "Hateful passion" (line 15) may refer to sexual passion of the deceased (which is
banished unto "hell") or to the poet's own affection and blinding grief for the sister's absent body. Elizabeth's soul is
thereby urged not to mourn the loss of the world even as the poet urges herself not to grieve for the corporeal
Elizabeth but to strive rather for a poetics of affirmation than for a poetics of loss.

To the Soul

PERFECTION'S fair idea, that art crowned
With more rich attributes of excellence
Than all the wonders of this spacious round,
Of more regard, of higher consequence,
Above them all thou hast preeminence,
　　In thy most powerful Maker's arms embraced,
　　And with his own endowments amply graced.

Just, holy, righteous, innocent, and wise,
Such is the soul, Jehovah's sole belov'd.
These are the lusters of her sphery eyes
That her to Him unparalleled approved.
Angels, at this amazed, stand unmoved
　　To see the glories that do her endow
　　As Heaven itself to abject earth should bow.

Then banish hateful passion unto hell,
That veils with Cupid's scarf the clearest sight
And doth true judgment from His throne expel,
Circling with shades heaven's love-deserving light,
Making obscurity than day more bright.
　　Disdain this servile yoke of base subjection,
　　For drossy earth deserves not thy affection.

Heaven's brightest abstract, canst thou condescend
These mundane vanities to meditate?
Why dost thou not thy best devotions bend
Thy mighty Maker's power to contemplate?
To him thy love and service consecrate,
　　Whose ever-grateful truth knows no defect,
　　But gives for love a more than dear respect.

---

[1] Ευθανασία Αθανασία] good death ... deathlessness;   *threne*] threnody, funeral song.

[2] *sphery*] star-like, heavenly; *unparalleled approved*] proved without earthly comparison; *unmoved*] motion-
less; perhaps also unfeeling (those who will not condescend to credit the glories of Elizabeth's "abject earth."

Penelope Grey (Salter) (b. 1591), of Wrockwardine, Shropshire

PENELOPE GREY's "Parodia," like sister Mary's "To the Soul," invites a double reading as a meditation on Elizabeth's death and as a commentary on the poet's own doubtful attempt to construct a timeless memorial in which a sister's name may forever dwell. Penelope's title, "Parodia," is self-deprecating, implying that her verse tribute is but a poor imitation of Elizabeth's soul. Yet the "place" in which Elizabeth now reigns "emparadised," and the "palace" in which she dwells, are at once the radiant heaven of Christian belief and the illuminating words of the poetic text. If the "wight" of the close refers principally to the departed sister as a creature of God, it glances also at the paper on which her life is now preserved, the white of the dirge-singing Swan, and thus, self-referentially, to the poetic text: "my words [are] but light," yet "light" is, after all, "the palace where she dwells." However, the final couplet contains a doubt that "impotent words" may be the *only* palace wherein the lost soul can dwell, thus deconstructing its own affirmation of a heaven after death. There is a sense in which every "heavenly sight," whether as the spectacle of a Biblical paradise or as the vision of a poet, is only a matter of strong feigning.

Parodia

SO DOWN the silver streams of Eridan,
On either side banked with a lily-wall,
Whiter than both, rides the triumphant swan
And sings his dirge and prophesies his fall,
Diving into his wat'ry funeral—
As she whose gold-beamed fame shall never date,
Forewarned in sleep, did pre-divine her fate.   [1]

So fairest Phosphor, the bright morning star,
But newly washed in the green element,
Before the drowsy night is half aware,
Shooting his flaming locks with dew besprent,
Springs lively up into the Orient,
As globes of wingèd angels, swift as thought,
Eliza's soul to her dear Savior brought.   [2]

Why spend we tears (that never can be spent)
On her that vale of tears no more shall see?
Why send we sighs (that never can be sent)
To her that died to live, and would not be,
To be there where she *would*? Here bury we
This heavenly earth. O, let it softly sleep.   [3]
Let's not for her, but for our own sins weep.

---

[1] *So*] Even as;   *Eridan*] the Eridanus, in Ovid, a river of northern Europe; later identified with the Po river in Italy; *As*] so;   *she*] Elizabeth Martin, the poet's sister.

[2] *Phosphor*] Venus (the planet, here identified as masculine);   *green element*] sea;   *besprent*] besprinkled.

[3] *spent*] used up;   *On her.. shall see*] On her who no more shall see...*vale*] the world-full, "this earthly life of tears";   *died to live*] died here in order to live eternally.

[25]

Had I a voice of steel to tune my song,
Were every verse as smoothly filed as glass,
And every member turnèd to a tongue,
And every tongue were made of sounding brass,
Yet all that skill, and all that strength, alas,
Should it presume to gild, were misadvised,
The place where now she reigns, emparadised.   1

Impotent words, weak sides, that strive in vain,
In vain t' emblazon that so-heavenly sight,
So heavenly sight as none can greater feign,
Feign what he can that seems of greatest might.
Might any yet compare with Infinite?
Infinite sure those joys, my words but light.
Light is the palace where she dwells. O blessed wight!   2

"Blessed are the dead that die in the Lord."

Penelope Grey

Anne Grey Masters (b. 1595), of Lichfield, Warwickshire

ANNE MASTERS, of the three sisters who survived Elizabeth Martin, seems the least con-
flicted with respect to the elegiac enterprise. Anne's epitaph is presented as a heartfelt
but unnecessary sacrifice, presented to a saint whose transcendence over death depends rather
on the unpoetical but happy "annals of eternity" – the "Lamb's Book of Life," in which are recorded the souls of those marked for eternal salvation (Rev. 17:8, 20:12-15).

Triple Portrait (of unidentified sisters),
Lucas de Heere, c. 1570
Courtesy of the Milwaukee Art Museum

To Her Soul-Loved Sister, Mistress E. M.

THOUGH marble, nor the proudest monument,
Can splendor add to thy star-crownèd fame
(That now triumph'st above the firmament,
Where glorious lights all mortal sparks out-flame),
Yet deign, sweet saint, t'accept these lines of mine
Which here I offer at thy sacred shrine: 3

EPITAPH

WHO, LIVING, was her sex's anadem,
Heaven's fair idea, nature's rarer gem,
Needs not the luster of divinest praise
Though golden statues kings to her should raise,
Since that her name is regist'red on high
In th' happy annals of eternity.   4

Anne Grey

---

1 *should ... misadvised*] were misadvised should it presume to gild.

2 *light*] insignificant; but cf. change to *light* as divinity;   *wight*] creature.

3 *Though*] Though neither.

4 *Who*] She who;   *anadem*] crown-garland;   *Though*] even if.

Aemilia (Bassano) Lanyer (1569 -1645)

Then let us haue our Libertie againe,
And challendge to your selues no Sou'raigntie...

—from *Salve Deus Rex Judaeorum*

AEMILIA LANYER, the second of two daughters, was born in London to Margaret Johnson, the common-law wife of Baptist Bassano. Her father, the son of a Jewish emigré from Venice, was employed as a musician in the Elizabethan court. When Aemilia was just seven years old, her father died, leaving his family in difficult financial straits. Aemilia was evidently taken in by Lady Susan Grey (widow of Lord Reynold, earl of Kent, who had died in 1573): she is reported by her physician, Dr. Simon Forman, to have been brought up in the county of Kent; and in dedicatory verses written many years later, Aemilia describes Lady Susan as "the Mistress of my youth, / The noble guide of my ungoverned days." Those days ended with the countess dowager's marriage in 1581 to Sir John Wingfield of Stenigot, Lincoln, a marriage that took Lady Susan to the Netherlands and left Aemilia in search of a patron. [1]

Little else can be inferred concerning the poet's childhood. As a teenager, possibly out of financial need following the death of her mother in 1587, Aemilia became mistress to Henry Carey, Lord Hunsdon (1526-1596). Although forty-three years her senior, Lord Hunsdon "loved her well and kept her and did maintain her long." A man of extraordinary wealth, he cheerfully decked out his young companion "in great pomp" so that she was able to go "very brave," dressed in elegant silks and costly jewelry. Undoubtedly, as Lord Hunsdon's consort, Aemilia would have frequently attended courtly entertainments; for Hunsdon was Queen Elizabeth's Lord Chamberlain after 1585, a senior officer whose duties included the scheduling and supervision of court festivities. Coming from a family of professional musicians, Aemilia herself may have sung or played for Queen Elizabeth. In any case, she is said to have been "favored much" by her Majesty. [2]

On 18 October 1592 Aemilia was married to Captain Alfonso Lanyer, a court musician. This was a marriage of convenience – principally, to the convenience of Lord Hunsdon. Aemilia was then carrying his child. A few months after the wedding, Aemilia Bassano Lanyer gave birth to a son, whom she named Henry, after his biological father, Henry Carey. (As an adult, Henry Lanyer followed the career of his maternal grandfather Bassano and stepfather Lanyer, finding employment as a flautist, from 1629 in the royal court.) [3]

Aemilia Lanyer? (Wikipedia Commons)

The relationship of Lord Hunsdon with Aemilia Bassano prior to 1592 (when Shakespeare was just beginning his dramatic career), led A. L. Rowse in 1973 to announce that he had positively identified the dark mistress referenced in Shakespeare's sonnets. Lord Hunsdon served as the licensing patron to Shakespeare's dramatic company (the Lord Chamberlain's Men) from about June 1594 until his death on 22 July 1596. On this evidence Rowse concluded that the Lord Chamberlain of England and William Shakespeare the player must, then, have shared the same mistress. By way of proof, Rowse characterizes Aemilia as sexually promiscuous, and states as fact a presumption that she must have had a dark complexion, since she had an Italian father. But as there are several thousand dark-complected Englishwoman whom Shakespeare may have met during his lifetime, Rowse's hypothesis carries little conviction. If Aemilia Bassano Lanyer is to be remembered, it will be for her own poetry and not as a supposed object of Shakespeare's Sonnets or sexual desire.

---

[1] *Bassano*] also called Bassana and Bassany in various 16th-century documents;   *the Mistress...days*] ed. DWF from Lanyer, "To the Lady Susan," lines 1-2, *Salve* (1611).

[2] *loved her...favored much*] Ed. DWF from Forman casebooks, Bodleian MS Ashmole 226, f. 110v, 201r; cf. additional visits and notes, 13 May 1597-7 Jan. 1599/1600, MS Ashm. 226, ff. 93v, 95v, 122v, 206r, 207v, 214v, 222v, 256v; MS Ashm. 236, f. 5r.

[3] *marriage of convenience*] Forman reports that Aemilia "was for collour maried to a minstrell" (MS Ashm. 226, f. 95v); Rowse mistakes this for an indication of Lanyer's complexion; but the phrase "for color" is Elizabethan idiom meaning "for the sake of appearances": Hunsdon arranged her marriage to Alfonso Lanyer while keeping Aemilia as his mistress, providing the husband with a stipend (a common practice in the 16th and 17th centuries); her child by Lord Hunsdon was then counted as Alfonso's.

In giving Aemilia's hand to Captain Alphonso Lanyer, Lord Hunsdon allowed his young mistress to keep the gifts of clothing, money, and jewels that he had lavished upon her during their years together. Aemilia also brought to her match with Lanyer a marriage portion of £100 that was left to her by her father's will in 1576. She therefore came quite "welthy to him that maried her"; but Alphonso Lanyer, whether from sheer prodigality or from sexual jealousy, wasted no time in squandering his wife's property – and when the money was gone, Lanyer left Aemilia to shift for herself. [1]

Henry Carey

Lord Hunsdon died in the summer of 1596. Not long afterward, Alphonso Lanyer decided to seek his fortune by joining the 1597 Island expedition, a campaign that was led by the earl of Essex. (It may be that Lanyer was also on board for the failed Cadiz expedition in 1596.) In the frugal reign of Queen Elizabeth I, the military typically paid its own way. If soldiers and their commanders were to recover their expenses in the defense of queen and country, it was to be at the cost of the enemy. But by 1597, military service had become a famously bad career move, which presented problems in recruitment. Essex therefore sweetened the package with intimations of knighthood as a reward for those men who served most heroically. Alphonso Lanyer took the bait. All or most of his provisions for the expedition were, however, funded by his wife's remaining property, leaving her not just penniless, but in debt.

A few months after Lord Hunsdon's death, while Alphonso was away at sea, Aemilia Lanyer turned for advice to Simon Forman, London's best-known physician and astrologer. Much of what we know about Lanyer's biography comes from Dr. Forman's casebooks, now preserved in the Bodleian Library. Aemilia consulted with Forman repeatedly from 13 May to 20 September 1597, chiefly to inquire about health matters, but also about questions of money. She repeatedly asked the doctor to cast her horoscope, to see whether she might yet recover her past good fortune, whether by the knighting of Alphonso or by a second marriage to a lord. Since divorce was not an option, Lanyer asked hopefully whether her husband might not perish of the "suet" (the sweating sickness, one of the most feared and deadly diseases of the Tudor and Stuart periods). Forman divined that both she and Alphonso would become ill but that Aemilia would be "first in despair of it." [2]

Simon Forman

The good doctor provided Aemilia with marital and financial forecasts, most of which later proved incorrect. But his own notebooks indicate that Forman viewed his 28-year-old client principally as a sexual conquest. From female clients who could not otherwise afford his services, Forman regularly extorted intercourse; and cash-strapped Aemilia Lanyer, 28, looked to be a promising candidate. After one early consultation, Dr. Forman recorded the memo that Aemilia's "husband hath Delt hardly wt her and spent and consumed her goods, and she is now very n[e]edy and in debt an[d] it seames for lucrese sake wilbe a good fellowe, for necesity doth compel." In other words, out of financial necessity, for the sake of "lucre," she will submit to my advances – but Forman's orthography, "for lucrese sake," suggests that somewhere in the back of his mind he was ready to play the role of Tarquinius Sextus, in the Rape of Lucrece. [3]

When Forman tried most aggressively to make his move on Lanyer, she was not fully cooperative. On a September night in 1597, five months after their first interview, Lanyer allowed Forman to stay with her and to fondle "all parts of her body," but she would not consent to intercourse. Miffed that the woman would not "halek" (the doctor's code-word for copulation), Forman in his journal scrawled an angry note about this encounter, an entry in which he speaks of himself in the third person. He and Aemilia are said to have been made "frendes again afterward but he never obteyned his purpose & she was a hore and delt evil with him after." [4]

---

[1] *gifts*] See Forman's casebooks, MS Ashmole 226, f. 110v. *Father's will*] P.C.C. will of Baptist Bassano, Public Record Office Prob. 11/58, f. 153; *welthy...her*] MS Ashmole 226, ff. 110v, 201.

[2] *suet*] MS Ashmole 226, f. 110. Recent commentators have mistaken Forman's "suet" for *suit*, confusing Aemilia's inquiry after the health of her husband with a query after his advancement.

[3] *husband...lucrese sake*] MS Ashmole 226, f. 201r.

[4] *a hore*] MS Ashmole 226, f. 222v. Such language, in the parlance of rejected suitors, usually meant just the reverse: "Alas, she wasn't the whore that I took her to be, and the woman has even dared to protest my behavior."

Alphonso Lanyer's return home led in December 1598 to the birth of a daughter, Odillya. This was the couple's only child to have come to term, the others having been lost through "mani fals conceptions." Odillya lived only ten months before she, too, passed away. On 6 September 1599, Odillya Lanyer was laid to rest beside Aemilia's parents in the churchyard of St. Botolph's Bishopsgate. [1]

In January, Aemilia sent once again to Simon Forman. This was apparently her first contact with the doctor since his night of unconsummated lust in 1597. The topic of Lanyer's query is not recorded, nor whether Forman cast her horoscope. After January 1600, she disappears permanently from his casebooks. [2]

Aemilia found new employment at Cookham, under the matronage of Margaret Clifford, countess of Cumberland. Lanyer, a music tutor, doubtless worked shoulder to shoulder with fellow poet Samuel Daniel, instructor in the classics, in providing a private education for Lady Anne, aged 10. Tutoring children (Lady Anne Clifford not excepted) was a labor that Daniel detested; but Aemilia Lanyer recalls the time spent with Lady Anne as among her warmest memories. In "The Description of Cookham" Lanyer represents the household of Margaret Clifford as a women's lyceum "Where many a learned book was read and scanned." The household was charged with intrigue and fired with discussion of women's rights. (After the death of Lady Margaret's philandering husband in 1605, the Clifford women spent much of their time and energy pursuing litigation to recover, for Lady Anne, the vast properties that her father, George Clifford, had bequeathed instead to his brother, in a will made eleven days before his death.)

Aemilia's happy days with the Clifford women ended in February 1609, when Lady Anne was married to Richard Sackville, earl of Dorset. The manor at Cookham was evacuated by the Clifford women, after which Lanyer was again thrown upon her own resources. She hit upon a plan to compose a verse narrative relating the trial and crucifixion of Jesus Christ. "The Passion of Christ" was to be a poem written by a woman, for women, amplifying the role of various women characters in the gospel records. Central to Lanyer's text is "Eve's Apology for Women," a framed narrative in which the Eve of Genesis is defended by the wife of Pontius Pilate (who in Lanyer's version seems also to be named Eve). In sermons and misogynistic tracts of the period, Eve was typically figured as the root of all evil, the "Woe" unto "man" signified by "Woman." In Lanyer's version, women are all that stand between men and total enslavement to spiritual blindness. Adam is responsible for the Fall. Eve's disobedience to God may be excused by her desire for knowledge; indeed, her only shortcomings were those of too little information about the forbidden fruit and too much love for an undeserving husband.

The work was published in 1611 under the title *Salve Deus Rex Judaeorum* ("Hail, God, King of the Jews"). Lanyer's text closes with a note "To the Doubtful Reader" in which the poet justifies her title and topic as a divine calling:

To the Doubtful Reader

Gentle Reader,

If thou desire to be resolved why I give this title, *Salve Deus Rex Judaeorum,* know for certain that it was delivered unto me in sleep many years before I had any intent to write in this manner – and was quite out of my memory until I had written "The Passion of Christ," when immediately it came into my remembrance what I had dreamed long before; and thinking it a significant token that I was appointed to perform this work, I gave the very same words I received in sleep as the fittest title I could devise for this book.

The multiple dedications of Lanyer's *Salve* include epistles addressed to Susan Bertie, countess dowager of Kent; Margaret Clifford, countess dowager of Cumberland; and Anne Clifford (now Sackville), countess of Dorset – three women who had played a significant role in Lanyer's biography. Also included are dedications to Queen Anna; Princess Elizabeth Stuart; Lady Arbella Stuart; Mary Herbert, countess dowager of Pembroke; Lucy Russell, countess of Bedford; and Lady Katherine (Knyvett) Howard, countess of Suffolk. In these poems, as also in her "Description of Cookham" and in the main text of *Salve,* Lanyer deals unabashedly in the conventions of praise, often to the embarrassment of modern readers. But Lanyer has no monopoly on sycophancy. No hyperbole in *Salve* lacks its match, equally egregious, in the verse of the canonical male poets. Recent critics sympathetic to Lanyer's project have excused her sometimes shameless compliments as a literary representation of ideal womanhood. But to be honest, the form had far more to do with cash considerations than with neo-platonic idealism. The excess in Lanyer's praise poetry stems from a class-consciousness that we do not share and arises from the humiliation of financial dependency.

Salve Deus Rex Judaeorum was entered in the London Stationers' register on 2 October 1610, at least six months before its eventual publication and nearly two years after Lanyer's separation from the Cliffords.

---

[1] *mani fals conceptions*] MS Ashmole 226, f. 110v.

[2] *January*] 7 Jan. 1599/1600 (5:00 p.m.), MS Ashmole 236, f. 5.

Despite her continuing pension from Lord Hunsdon, there is no doubt that Lanyer hoped with her *Salve* to acquire new patronage, and in so doing she appealed exclusively to women. But evidently none of the noblewomen addressed by Lanyer shared her noble vision of a women's literature funded by women, or gave her more than a one-time gratuity. After printing her *Salve*, Lanyer never again sought publication as a means to financial security, nor ever, so far as we know, wrote another line of poetry.

Alphonso Lanyer died in 1613, two years after Aemilia's *Salve* was printed. In his will, the captain made partial amends for having wasted his wife's money: he bequeathed to Aemilia his most valuable income-producing property, a royal patent for weighing hay and straw coming into the city of London, granted to him by King James in 1604 for a period of twenty years. But this licensed monopoly was to become the subject of costly, protracted, and futile litigation. In 1616, the poet's brother-in-law, Innocent Lanyer, persuaded Aemilia "to surrender her right therein that he might obtain a new grant and allow [Aemilia] half the profits." Innocent then petitioned the king for renewal, obtaining a new patent for twenty-one years from November 1616. But having acquired Aemilia's rights, Innocent thereafter paid Aemilia only eight pounds a year from a patent that generated upwards one hundred pounds a year. Thus defrauded, Aemilia filed suit to recover her inheritance, without success. From Innocent the patent passed to Clement Lanyer, who in 1635 petitioned the king for another renewal. Aemilia upon hearing this news promptly petitioned King Charles for half the profits from Clement's patent. In March 1635 King Charles awarded a new grant of twenty-one years to Clement Lanyer, upon condition that he pay Aemilia twenty pounds annually, and after her decease, ten pounds to her two grandchildren during the continuance of the grant. Clement neglected to pay even this, which led to further litigation. [1]

Endlessly resourceful, the poet in 1617 founded a school, most probably for instruction in music, in the parish of St. Giles-in-the-Field, which was then a semi-rural but upscale neighborhood. Lanyer entrusted the lease agreement to her landlord, an attorney named Edward Smith, who subsequently cheated her. Of the three structures that Smith had available to let, Aemilia rented only the farmhouse, which she repaired at her own expense, while declining to rent the stables and hayloft. When Smith two years later found a tenant who would give him more rent and also take the stables and hayloft, he used the terms of the contract to evict her, without so much as reimbursement for repairs. The school was closed in 1619 or 1620, again resulting in a lawsuit, the outcome of which is unrecorded. [2]

Lanyer's old age was spent in relative obscurity. Her son Henry Lanyer died in 1633, leaving a wife, two small children, and bills to be paid. Aemilia in her last years evidently lived with her daughter-in-law, Joyce, in the London parish of St. James, Clerkenwell, helping with the care and support of Joyce Lanyer's two children, Henry Jr., and Mary. In 1635, as litigation continued over the hay-and-straw patent, Lanyer petitioned King Charles for assistance, describing herself as living "in great misery and having two grandchildren to provide for." But the family cannot have been destitute, for Aemilia retained until her death the annuity of forty pounds that had been bequeathed to her by her first partner, Lord Hunsdon. ("Great misery" was a phrase often heard in petitions to the King and his Privy Council.) Money was tight, but Aemilia stood on principle to the bitter end: after more than twenty years later of legal wrangling, her suit ended in defeat with her dignified refusal to accept £5, for two quarters of the year, from a patent that usually generated upwards of £100 annual income. [3]

On 3 April 1645, Aemilia Lanyer was buried by her son in the churchyard of St. James, Clerkenwell. She was 76 years old.

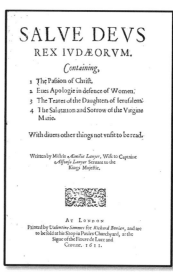

DWF

---

[1] *Innocent Lanyer*] a court musician who, in partnership with the composer Alphonso Ferrabosco and others, also earned money from a patent to dredge the Thames, a service which earned him tolls (charged to boats of transport), and profits from selling the dredged sand and gravel;   *litigation*] See *Cal. S.P. Dom. James I*, vol. 8 (1603-1610), p. 146 (23 Aug 23 1604); v. 9 (1611-1618), 210 (23 Nov. 1613) and 407 (22 Nov. 1616); *S.P. Dom. Chas I*, v. 7 (1634-1635), 516-7 (19 Feb. 1635), 564 (7 March 1635); v. 9 (1637), 115-6; vol. 10 (1637-8), 472. The particulars of the case and its settlement are misreported by Woods.   A generally accurate account is given in A. L. Rowse (1974), 116-7.

[2] *lawsuit*] For the details of this dispute, see Woods, pp. xxvii-xxix, and P.R.O. Chancery Case C2/James I L11/64.

[3] *Cal. S.P. Dom. Charles I*, vol. 7 (1634-1635), p. 516 (19 Feb. 1635).

From *Salve Deus Rex Judaeorum*

To the Virtuous Reader

OFTEN have I heard that it is the property of some women, not only to emulate the virtues and perfections of the rest, but also, by all their powers of ill-speaking, to eclipse the brightness of their deservèd fame. Now, contrary to their custom (which men, I hope unjustly, lay to their charge), I have written this small volume, or little book, for the general use of all virtuous ladies and gentlewomen of this kingdom; and in commendation of some particular persons of our own sex, such as, for the most part, are so well known to myself and others that (I dare undertake) Fame dares not to call any better.

And this have I done, to make known to the world that all women deserve not to be blamed, though some, forgetting they are women themselves and in danger to be condemned by the words of their own mouths, fall into so great an error as to speak unadvisedly against the rest of their sex; which, if it be true, I am persuaded they can show their own imperfection in nothing more; and therefore could wish (for their own ease, modesties, and credit) they would refer such points of folly to be practiced by evil-disposed men; who – forgetting they were born of women, nourished of women, and that if it were not by the means of women, they would be quite extinguished out of the world, and a final end of them all – do like vipers deface the wombs wherein they were bred, only to give way and utterance to their want of discretion and goodness.

Such as these were they that dishonored Christ His apostles and prophets, putting them to shameful deaths. Therefore we are not to regard any imputations that they undeservedly lay upon us (no otherwise, than to make use of them to our own benefits, as spurs to virtue, making us fly all occasions that may color their unjust speeches to pass current) – especially considering that they have tempted even the patience of God Himself, who gave power to wise and virtuous women to bring down their pride and arrogancy: as was cruel Cesarus by the discreet counsel of noble Deborah, judge and prophetess of Israel; and resolution of Jael, wife of Heber the Kenite; wicked Haman, by the divine prayers and prudent proceedings of beautiful Hester; blasphemous Holofernes, by the invincible courage, rare wisdom, and confident carriage of Judith; and the unjust judges, by the innocency of chaste Susanna (with infinite others, which for brevity's sake° I will omit). As also in respect it pleased our Lord and Savior Jesus Christ (without the assistance of man, being free from original and all other sins from the time of His conception till the hour of His death) to be begotten of a woman, born of a woman, nourished of a woman, obedient to a woman; and that He healed women, pardoned women, comforted women; yea, even when He was in His greatest agony and bloody sweat, going to be crucified, and also in the last hour of His death, took care to dispose of a woman; after His resurrection, appeared first to a woman, sent a woman to declare His most glorious resurrection to the rest of His disciples. [1]

Many other examples I could allege of diverse faithful and virtuous women, who have in all ages not only been confessors, but also endured most cruel martyrdom for their faith in Jesus Christ; all which is sufficient to enforce all good Christians and honorable-minded men to speak reverently of our sex, and especially of all virtuous and good women. To the modest censures of both which, I refer these my imperfect endeavors, knowing that according to their own excellent dispositions they will rather cherish, nourish, and increase the least spark of virtue where they find it, by their favorable and best interpretations, than quench it by wrong constructions. To whom I wish all increase of virtue, and desire their best opinions. [2]

---

[1] *Christ His*] Christ's; *Cesarus*] *i.e.*, Sisera, captain of the Canaanite host in the book of Judges, who is defeated in battle by Deborah and Barak, and slain by Jael, who lulls him to sleep and then drives a tent stake through his head (Judges 4:1-5:30); *Hester*] Esther; for her triumph over Haman, see Est. 8:1-9:32; *Holofernes*] in the apocryphal book of Judith, the captain of the Assyrian host; he is decapitated by Judith, who thereby delivers Israel; *carriage*] behavior; *the unjust judges*] in the apocryphal chap. 13 of Daniel, Susanna is slandered by two of the elders and condemned to die; but she is miraculously delivered, and her accusers are slain; *dispose of a woman*] In the gospel of John, Jesus from the cross asks a disciple to take care of his mother, Mary (Jn. 19:25-27); *sent*] and sent (*See* Mat. 28:8-10).

[2] *censures*] judgments.

To the Queen's Most Excellent Majesty

RENOWNÈD empress and great Britain's queen,
Most gracious mother of succeeding kings,
Vouchsafe to view that which is seldom seen:
A woman's writing of divinest things.
    Read it, fair queen, though it defective be;
    Your excellence can grace both it and me.

. . . .

Behold, great queen, fair Eve's apology,
Which I have writ in honor of your sex
(And do refer unto your Majesty   [75]
To judge if it agree not with the text—
    And if it do, why are poor women blamed,
    Or by more faulty men so much defamed?)   [1]

. . . .

And pardon me, fair queen, though I presume
To do that which so many better can –
Not that I learning to myself assume
Or that I would compare with any man;
    But as they are scholars, and by art do write,
    So Nature yields my soul a sad delight.   [150]

And since all arts at first from Nature came
(That goodly creature, mother of perfection,
Whom Jove's almighty hand at first did frame,
Taking both her and hers in His protection),
    Why should not she now grace my barren muse
    (And in a woman all defects excuse)?

So, peerless princess, humbly I desire
That your great wisdom would vouchsafe t'omit
All faults, and pardon if my spirits retire,
Leaving to aim at what they cannot hit:
    To write your worth (which no pen can express)
    Were but t'eclipse your fame and make it less. [2]

[1] *text*] Christian Scripture.

[2] *omit*] overlook; *leaving to aim*] no longer aiming.

[3] *Lady Elizabeth's Grace*] Princess Elizabeth (1596-1662), daughter of King James and Queen Anna.

[4] *phoenix*] Queen Elizabeth I.

[5] *Vouchsafe you*] Please extend your.

[5] *Penbrooke*] Mary (Sidney) Herbert, countess of Pembroke (1561-1621); sister to Sir Philip Sidney and posthumous editor and reviser of his literary works; literary patron and a poet (see *Women's Works,* vol. 2).

To the Lady Elizabeth's Grace   [3]

MOST GRACIOUS lady, fair Elizabeth—
Whose name and virtues puts us still in mind
Of her of whom we are deprived by death,
The phoenix of her age, whose worth did bind   [4]
All worthy minds, so long as they have breath,
    In links of admiration, love and zeal,
    To that dear mother of our commonweal—

Even you, fair princess, next our famous queen
I do invite unto this wholesome feast;
Whose goodly wisdom, though your years be green,
By such good works may daily be increased.
Though your fair eyes far better books have seen,
    Yet (being the first fruits of a woman's wit),
    Vouchsafe you favor in accepting it.   [5]

The Author's Dream: to the Lady Mary,   [5]
the Countess Dowager of Penbrooke

METHOUGHT I passed through the Idalian groves
And asked the Graces if they could direct
Me to a lady whom Minerva chose,
To live with her in height of all respect.   [6]

Yet, looking back into my thoughts again,
The eye of reason did behold her there,
Fast tied unto them in a golden chain.   [7]
They stood, but she was set in honor's chair.

[6] *Idalian groves*] forests of Cyprus sacred to Aphrodite; *Graces*] the three sister goddesses (Aglaia, Thalia, and Euphrosune) who grant charm and beauty to mortals; *Minerva*] Roman goddess of wisdom, invention, and the arts, identified with Greek Pallas Athena.

[7] *her*] Mary Sidney Herbert, lady honored by Minerva (queen Anna).

And nine fair virgins sat upon the ground
With harps and viols in their lily hands,
Whose harmony had all my senses drowned
But that before mine eyes an object stands

Whose beauty shined like Titan's clearest rays. [1]
She blew a brazen trumpet, which did sound
Through all the world that worthy lady's praise;
And by eternal fame I saw her crown'd.

. . . .

For to this lady now I will repair,
Presenting her the fruits of idle hours;
Though many books she writes that are more rare,
Yet there is honey in the meanest flowers

Which is both wholesome and delights the taste. [2]
Though sugar be more finer, higher prized,
Yet is the painful bee no whit disgraced,
Nor her fair wax or honey more despised. [200] [3]

And though that learnèd damsel and the rest
Have in a higher style her trophy framed,
Yet these unlearnèd lines, being my best,
Of her great wisdom can no whit be blamed.

And therefore first, I here present my dream,
And next, invite her Honor to my feast;
For my clear reason sees her by that stream
Where her rare virtues daily are increased.

So, craving pardon for this bold attempt,
I here present my mirror to her view
Whose noble virtues cannot be exempt;
My glass, being steel, declares them to be true. [4]

And, Madame, if you will vouchsafe that grace
To grace those flowers that springs from virtue's ground
(Though your fair mind on worthier works is placed,
On works that are more deep, and more profound. [5]

Yet is it no disparagement to you
To see your Savior in a shepherd's weed,
Unworthily presented in your view,
Whose worthiness will grace each line you read),

Receive Him here by my unworthy hand,
And read His paths of fair humility;
Who though our sins in number pass the sand,
They all are purged by His divinity.

• • •

To Lady Margaret Clifford, Countess Dowager of Cumberland [6]

An invective against outward beauty unaccustomed with virtue

That outward beauty which the world commends [185]
Is not the subject I will write upon,
Whose date, expired, that tyrant Time soon ends;
Those gaudy colors soon are spent and gone.
But those fair virtues which on thee attends
Are always fresh; they never are but one.
    They make thy beauty fairer to behold
    Than was that queen's for whom proud Troy was sold. [7]

As for those matchless colors, red and white,
Or perfit features in a fading face,
Or due proportion pleasing to the sight,
All these do draw but dangers and disgrace.
A mind enriched with virtue shines more bright,
Adds everlasting beauty, gives true grace,
    Frames an immortal goddess on the earth,
    Who though she dies, yet fame gives her new birth.

That pride of nature which adorns the fair,
Like blazing comets to allure all eyes,
Is but the thread that weaves their web of care,
Who glories most, where most their danger lies;
For greatest perils do attend the fair,
When men do seek, attempt, plot and devise,
    How they may overthrow the chastest dame,
    Whose beauty is the white whereat they aim. [8]

'Twas beauty bred in Troy the ten years' strife,
And carried Helen from her lawful lord.
'Twas beauty made chaste Lucrece lose her life,
For which proud Tarquin's fact was so abhorred;
Beauty, the cause Antonius wronged his wife,
Which could not be decided but by sword:
    Great Cleopatra's beauty and defects
    Did work Octavia's wrongs, and his neglects. [9]

---

[1] *virgins*] the nine Muses of Greek mythology;   *viols*]
large stringed instruments, played with a curved bow;
had drowned / But that] would have drowned, except
that;   *Titan's*] the sun's.

[2] *more rare*] more valuable than these verses of mine;
meanest] most common.

[3] *painful*] laborious, pains-taking.

[4] *glass ... steel*] steel, unlike primitive glass mirrors,
produced no distortion in the reflected image.

[5] *Madame*] Herbert (here addressed directly).

---

[6] *Countess of Cumberland*] Margaret Clifford (d. 1616),
Lanyer's patron, to whom the *Salve* is formally
addressed; mother of Anne Clifford Herbert.

[7] *Whose*] beauty's;   *expired*] when expired;   *thee*]
Margaret Clifford; *attends*] attend; *that queen's*] In
Helen's beauty, which leads to the Trojan War.

[8] *white*] fair complexion; white breast of a deer as the
hunter's target.

[9] *bred*] that bred; *her lawful lord*] her husband, King

What fruit did yield that fair forbidden tree,
But blood, dishonor, infamy, and shame?
(Poor blinded queen, couldst thou no better see
But to entertain disgrace instead of fame?
Do these designs with majesty agree:
To stain thy blood and blot thy royal name?
　　That heart that gave consent unto this ill,
　　Did give consent that thou thyself shouldst kill!) [1]

Of Rosamond

Fair Rosamund, the wonder of her time,   [225]
Had been much fairer, had she not been fair.
Beauty betrayed her thoughts aloft to climb,
To build strong castles in uncertain air,
Where th' infection of a wanton crime
Did work her fall. First poison, then despair,
　　With double death did kill her perjured soul,
　　When heavenly justice did her sin control.   [2]

Of Matilda

Holy Matilda in a hapless hour
Was born to sorrow and to discontent,
Beauty the cause that turned her sweet to sour,
While chastity sought folly to prevent.
Lustful King John refused, did use his power
By fire and sword to compass his content:
　　But friend's disgrace, nor father's banishment,
　　Nor death itself, could purchase her consent. [3]

Menelaus;   *Lucrece*] the virtuous wife of Collatinus
(Collatine), legendary heroine of Rome who after being
raped by Tarquin slays herself rather than bear ascribed
guilt; story told in Shakespeare's *Rape of Lucrece*
(1594);   *fact*] crime; the rape of Lucrece;   *Tarquin*]
Tarquinius Sextus, legendary early Roman, driven from
Rome by enraged citizens;   *cause*] reason that;
Antonius]   Mark Antony, who for love of Cleopatra
forsook his wives Fulvia and Octavia;   *Octavia*] (d. 11
BCE) sister of Octavius (emperor Augustus); married for
political reasons to Mark Antony, who abandoned her
for Cleopatra.

[1] *What fruit...tree*] what fruit did the tree of adultery
yield? (referencing the forbidden Tree of Knowledge in
Eden).

[2] *Rosamund*] Rosamond the Fair (d. 1176), concubine
of Henry II of England;   *wanton crime*] Higden, monk
of Chester who reports (c. 1350) that Rosamond (d.
1177) was poisoned by jealous Queen Eleanor; story
told also in Samuel Daniel's *Complaint of Rosamond*
(1592).

[3] *Matilda*] Matilda de Briouse, whom King John starved
to death in prison together with her son, William the
younger, to punish her husband, a recalcitrant baron;
Lanyer refers here to the romanticized version of the
story, in which Matilda is the subject of King John's
amorous advances; story told in Michael Drayton's
Matilda (1594).

Here beauty, in the height of all perfection,
Crowned this fair creature's everlasting fame,
Whose noble mind did scorn the base subjection
Of fears, or favors, to impair her name.
By heavenly grace, she had such true direction, [245]
To die with honor, not to live in shame;
　　And drink that poison with a cheerful heart,
　　That could all heavenly grace to her impart.

Salve Deus Rex Judaeorum

A preamble of the Author, before the Passion

These high deserts invites my lowly muse
To write of Him, and pardon crave of thee.
For time so spent, I need make no excuse,
Knowing it doth with thy fair mind agree
So well, as thou no labor wilt refuse
That to thy holy love may pleasing be.
　　His death and passion I desire to write,
　　And thee to read – the blessed soul's delight.

But, my dear Muse, now whither wouldst thou fly
Above the pitch of thy appointed strain?
With Icarus thou seekest now to try,   [275]
Not waxen wings, but thy poor barren brain,
Which, far too weak, these siely lines descry;
Yet cannot this thy forward mind restrain,
　　But thy poor infant verse must soar aloft,
　　Not fearing threat'ning dangers, happening oft.   [4]

Think when the eye of wisdom shall discover
Thy weakling muse to fly (that scarce could creep)
And in the air above the clouds to hover
(When better 'twere mewed up and fast asleep!);
They'll think, with Phaeton, thou canst ne'er° recover,
But, helpless (with that poor young lad), to weep
　　The little world of thy weak wit on fire,
　　Where thou wilt perish in thine own desire.   [5]

But yet the weaker thou dost seem to be
In sex or sense, the more His glory shines
That doth infuse such powerful grace in thee,
To show thy love in these few humble lines.
The widow's mite with this may well agree,
Her little all more worth than golden mines,
　　Being more dearer to our loving Lord   [295]
　　Than all the wealth that kingdoms could afford [...] [6]

---

[4] *Icarus ... waxen wings*] Icarus made wings out of wax
in order to escape the Minotaur, but he flew too close to
the sun and the wings melted;   *siely*] unsophisticated;
descry] descries;   *forward*] presumptuous.

[5] *mewed up*]   confined;   *Phaeton*] tried to drive
Apollo's chariot, the sun, but lost control and was
thrown by Zeus into a river so as not to set the world
afire.

[6] *mite*] alluding to Jesus' parable of the poor widow
who gave all she had (*see* Mark 12:41-44);   *agree*]
concord.

Lanyer in Salve Deus Rex Judaeorum *relates her story of the Crucifixion, celebrating Jesus' female disciples. She represents women as having uncanny wisdom, compassion, and spiritual insight – the dearth of which, in the male figures, has led to Jesus' suffering and death. One of Lanyer's central characters is the wife of Pontius Pilate, a woman noted in the Gospel of Matthew: during the trial, the Roman governor receives from his wife a warning not to become implicated in Jesus' death:* "When the morning was come, all the chief priests and elders of the people took counsel against Jesus to put him to death. And when they had bound him, they led him away, and delivered him to Pontius Pilate the governor. [...] [And] when Pilate was set down on the judgment seat, his wife sent unto him, saying, 'Have thou nothing to do with that just man, for I have suffered many things this day in a dream because of him.'" *The governor offers some feeble resistance, offering to release either Jesus, who is innocent, or Barabbas, a convicted felon – but his audience cries out for Barabbas to be freed and for Jesus to be crucified. The governor quickly capitulates:* "When Pilate saw that he could prevail nothing, but that rather a tumult was made, he took water, and washed his hands before the multitude, saying, I am innocent of the blood of this just person: see ye to it'" (Mat. 27:1-2, 19, 24). *In Lanyer's version, Pilate is typical of a masculine impulse to shirk moral responsibility. Women, vilified ever since Adam for the sins of men, are defended by Pilate's wife in a lengthy apology that situates both Jesus, as a Son of God, and Eve, as the mother of humanity, as parallel victims of male injustice.*

[An Apology for Women]

Now Pontius Pilate is to judge the cause
Of faultless Jesus, who before him stands;
Who neither hath offended prince nor laws,
Although he now be brought in woeful bands.   [1]
O, noble governor, make thou yet a pause!
Do not in innocent blood imbrue thy hands,   [750]
   But hear the words of thy most worthy wife,
   Who sends to thee, to beg her Savior's life:

"Let barb'rous cruelty far depart from thee,
And in true justice take affliction's part.
Open thine eyes, that thou the truth may'st see!
Do not the thing that goes against thy heart.
Condemn not Him that must thy Savior be,
But view His holy life, His good desert.
   Let not us women glory in men's fall
   Who had power given to over-rule us all.   [2]

---

[1] *bands*] bonds.

[2] *Let not ... us all*] Let not women gain glory by the fall of man (in this case, by the fall of Pilate himself).

Eve's Apology

Till now your indiscretion sets us free
And makes our former fault much less appear:
Our mother Eve, who tasted of the tree,
Giving to Adam what she held most dear,
Was simply *good*, and had no power to see—
The after-coming harm did not appear.
   The subtle serpent that our sex betrayed,
   Before our fall so sure a plot had laid   [3]

That undiscerning ignorance perceived
No guile or craft that was by him intended;
For had she known of what we were bereaved,
To his request she had not condescended—
But she, poor soul, by cunning was deceived.
No hurt therein her harmless heart intended:
   For she alleged God's word; which he denies   [775]
   That they should die, but even as gods, be wise.   [4]

But surely Adam cannot be excused!
Her fault, though great, yet he was most to blame.
What weakness offered, strength might have refused.
Being lord of all, the greater was his shame.   *Adam should be*
Although the serpent's craft had her abused,   *blamed*
God's holy word ought° all his actions frame,
   For he was lord and king of all the earth,
   Before poor Eve had either life or breath.

Who, being framed by God's eternal hand
(The perfect'st man that ever breathed on earth),
And from God's mouth received that strait command
(The breach whereof he knew was present death),
Yea, having power to rule both sea and land,
Yet, with one apple won, to lose that breath
   Which God had breathèd in his beauteous face,
   Bringing us all in danger and disgrace—

And then, to lay the fault on patience' back,   [5]
That we, poor women, must endure it all!
We know right well he did discretion lack,
Being not persuaded thereunto at all.
If Eve did err, it was for knowledge' sake;
The fruit being *fair* persuaded *him* to fall.
   No subtle serpent's falsehood did betray him.
   If he would eat it, who had power to stay him?   [800]   *She couldn't stop Adam*

Not Eve, whose fault was only too much love,
Which made her give this present to her dear,
That what she tasted, he likewise might prove,
Whereby his knowledge might become more clear.
He never sought her weakness to reprove
With those sharp words which he of God did hear.
   Yet men will boast of knowledge, which he took
   From Eve's fair hand as from a learnèd book.   [6]

---

[3] *your indiscretion*] of Pilate; and of all men;   *that ... betrayed*] that betrayed our sex.

[4] *undiscerning ignorance*] Eve's unwitting ignorance.

[5] *patience' back*] the back of patient women.

[6] *he*] man.

If any evil did in her remain,
Being made of him, he was the ground of all.
If one of many worlds could lay a stain
Upon our sex, and work so great a fall
To wretched man by Satan's subtle train,
What will so foul a fault amongst you all?
   Her weakness did the serpent's words obey—
   But you, in malice, God's dear Son betray!

Whom, if unjustly you condemn to die,
Her sin was small to what you do commit.
All mortal sins that do for vengeance cry
Are not to be comparèd unto it.
If many worlds would altogether try
By all their sins the wrath of God to get,
   This sin of yours surmounts them all, as far
   As doth the sun another little star.

Then let us have our liberty again,   [825]
And challenge to yourselves no sov'reignty.
You came not in the world without our pain—
Make that a bar against your cruelty!
Your fault being greater, why should you disdain
Our being your equals, free from tyranny?
   If one weak woman simply did offend,
   This sin of yours hath no excuse, nor end!"   1

—To which (poor souls) we never gave consent.
Witness: thy wife, O Pilate, speaks for all;
Who did but dream, and yet a message sent
That thou shouldst have nothing to do at all
With that just man; which, if thy heart relent,
Why wilt thou be a reprobate with Saul,
   To seek the death of Him that is so good,
   For thy soul's health to shed His dearest blood?   2

Yea, so thou may'st these sinful people please,
Thou art content, against all truth and right,
To seal this act, that may procure thine ease
With blood and wrong, with tyranny and might.
The multitude thou seekest to appease,
By base dejection of this heavenly light,
   Demanding which of these that thou shouldst loose:
   Whether the thief, or Christ, king of the Jews.   3

Base Barabbas the thief they all desire,
And thou, more base than he, perform'st their will! [850]
Yet when thy thoughts back to themselves retire,
Thou art unwilling to commit this ill.
O that thou couldst unto such grace aspire
That thy polluted lips might never kill
   That honor which right judgment ever graceth,
   To purchase shame (which all true worth defaceth)!

Art thou a judge, and asketh what to do
With one in whom no fault there can be found?
The death of Christ wilt thou consent unto,
Finding no cause, no reason, nor no ground?
Shall He be scourged, and crucifièd too?
And must His miseries by thy means abound?
   Yet (not ashamed to ask what He hath done
   When thine own conscience seeks this sin to shun)

Three times thou ask'st, 'What evil hath He done?'—
And say'st, thou find'st in Him no cause of death.
Yet wilt thou chasten God's beloved Son
Although to thee no word of ill He sayeth?
For "Wrath must end what malice hath begun,"
And thou "must yield," to stop His guiltless breath!
   This rude tumultuous rout doth press so sore
   That thou condemnest Him thou shouldst adore.   4

Yet, Pilate, this can yield thee no content
To exercise thine own authority,
But unto Herod He must needs be sent,   [875]
To reconcile thyself by tyranny.
Was this the greatest good in justice meant,
When thou perceiv'st no fault in Him to be?
   If thou must make thy peace by virtue's fall,
   Much better 'twere not to be friends at all.

Yet neither thy stern brow, nor His great place,
Can draw an answer from the holy one:
His false accusers, nor His great disgrace,
Nor Herod's scoffs – to Him, they are all one.
He neither cares, nor fears His own ill case,
Though being despised and mocked of every one.
   King Herod's gladness gives him little ease;
   Neither his anger seeks he to appease.   5

Yet this is strange, that base impiety
Should yield those robes of honor which were due:
Pure white, to show His great integrity,
His innocency, that all the world might view;
Perfection's height in lowest penury,
Such glorious poverty as they never knew:
   Purple and scarlet well might him beseem
   Whose precious blood must all the world redeem!

And that imperial crown of thorns He wore,
Was much more precious than the diadem
Of any king that ever lived before
Or since His time. Their honor's but a dream   [900]
To His eternal glory, being so poor
To make a purchase of that heavenly realm
   Where God with all His angels lives in peace.
   (No griefs, nor sorrows, but all joys increase!)   6

---

1 *challenge to*] claim for;   *Lines 833 ff. appear to be spoken by the narrator (1611 Q has no quot. marks)*.

2 *Saul*] King Saul, who sought to kill David (*see* 1 Samuel 18.6-24.22);   *soul's health*] personal well-being (ironic).

3 *dejection*] abasement.

4 *Wrath ... begun*] a common proverb, here ascribed to Pilate as his excuse for capitulating to the crowd;   *lines 869-870*] ironic restatement of Pilate's self-defense.

5 *are all one*] make no difference;   *his ... he*] Herod's ... Jesus.

6 *so*] too.

Those royal robes, which they in scorn did give
To make Him odious to the common sort,
Yield light of grace to those whose souls shall live
Within the harbor of this heavenly port;
Much do they joy, and much more do they grieve,
His death, their life, should make His foes such sport;
  With sharpest thorns to prick His blessèd face,
  Our joyful sorrow, and His greater grace.   [1]

Three fears at once possessèd Pilate's heart:
The first, Christ's innocency, which so plain appears;
The next, that He which now must feel this smart
Is God's dear Son, for anything he hears;
But that which proved the deepest wounding dart,
Is people's threat'nings, which he so much fears
  That he to Caesar could not be a friend,
  Unless he sent sweet Jesus to His end.   [2]

Now, Pilate, thou art proved a painted wall,
A golden sepulcher with rotten bones,
From right to wrong, from equity to fall!
If none upbraid thee, yet the very stones
Will rise against thee, and in question call   [925]
His blood, His tears, His sighs, His bitter groans.
  All these will witness at the latter day,
  When water cannot wash thy sin away.

Canst thou be innocent, that 'gainst all right
Wilt yield to what thy conscience doth withstand?
Being a man of knowledge, power, and might,
To let the wicked carry such a hand?
Before thy face to blindfold heaven's bright light,
And thou to yield to what they did demand?
  Washing thy hands thy conscience cannot clear,
  But to all worlds this stain must needs appear.

"For lo, the guilty doth accuse the just,
And faulty judge condemns the innocent;
And willful Jews, to exercise their lust,
With whips and taunts against their Lord are bent.
He – basely usèd, blasphemed, scorned, and cursed—
Our heavenly King to death (for us) they sent:
  Reproaches, slanders, spittings in His face,
  Spite doing all her worst in His disgrace."

And now this long-expected hour draws near
When blessèd saints with angels do condole:
His holy march, soft pace, and heavy cheer,
In humble sort, to yield His glorious soul,
By His deserts, the foulest sins to clear
And in th'eternal book of heaven to enroll   [950]
  A satisfaction, till the general doom,
  Of all sins past and all that are to come.

They that had seen this pitiful procession,
From Pilate's palace to Mount Calvary,
Might think He answered for some great transgression,
Being in odious sort condemned to die.
He plainly showed that His own profession
Was virtue, patience, grace, love, piety;
  ~~And how by suffering He could conquer more~~
  Than all the kings that ever lived before.

First went the crier, with open mouth proclaiming
The heavy sentence of "Iniquity!"
The hangman next (by his base office claiming
His right in Hell, where sinners never die),
Carrying the nails; the people, still blaspheming
Their Maker, using all impiety;
  The thieves attending Him on either side,
  The sergeants watching – while the women cried […]

Comparing the beauty of Jesus' life to the beauty of women, Lanyer relates how the "blessed daughters of Jerusalem" pitied Jesus while "spiteful men with torments did oppress / Th' afflicted body of this innocent dove." When Jesus arises from the tomb, he therefore reveals himself first to the women who lamented his death, appearing to them his in full glory:

Christ Risen, by Rubens
(1616) Galleria Palatina

A Brief Description of his Beauty
(upon the Canticles)   [3]

This is that bridegroom that appears so fair,   [1305]
So sweet, so lovely in His spouse's sight,
That unto snow we may His face compare;
His cheeks, like scarlet; and His eyes so bright
As purest doves, that in the rivers are
Washèd with milk, to give the more delight;
  His head is likened to the finest gold;
  His curled locks, so beauteous to behold,   [4]

Black as a raven in her blackest hue;
His lips, like scarlet threads, yet much more sweet
Than is the sweetest honey-dropping dew
Or honeycombs where all the bees do meet.
Yea, He is constant, and His words are true.
His cheeks are beds of spices, flowers sweet;
  His lips like lilies, dropping down pure myrrh—
  Whose love, before all worlds, we do prefer.   [1320]

---

[1] *grieve*] grieve that; *With … grace*] that these injuries should produce salvation and grace.

[2] *for anything he hears*] despite anything that Pilate hears otherwise.

---

[3] *upon the Canticles*] in imitation of the Old Testament "Canticles" (also known as the Song of Solomon).

[4] *that bridegroom*] Christ; *his spouse's*] the Church's.

In her closing lines, Lanyer again addresses Lady Margaret Clifford, praising the countess dowager of Cumberland as a successor to Christ – indeed, depicting her as a woman whose compassion and god-like qualities nearly surpass those of Christ:

To My Lady of Cumberland

Ah, give me leave, good Lady, now to leave
This task of beauty which I took in hand!
I cannot wade so deep; I may deceive
Myself before I can attain the land.
Therefore, good Madame, in your heart I leave [1325]
His perfect picture, where it still shall stand,
  Deeply engravèd in that holy shrine,
  Environèd with love and thoughts divine.¹

There may you see Him as a God in glory
And as a man in miserable case.
There may you read His true and perfect story;
His bleeding body there you may embrace,
And kiss His dying cheeks with tears of sorrow.
With joyful grief, you may entreat for grace,
  And all your prayers and your alms-deeds
  May bring to stop His cruel wounds that bleeds.²

Oft times hath He made trial of your love,
And in your faith hath took no small delight.
By crosses and afflictions He doth prove,
Yet still your heart remaineth firm and right,
Your love so strong as nothing can remove,
Your thoughts being placed on Him both day and night.
  Your constant soul doth lodge between her breasts
  This sweet of sweets, in which all glory rests.³

Sometime H'appears to thee in shepherd's weed
And so presents Himself before thine eyes,
A good old man that goes his flock to feed.
Thy color changes, and thy heart doth rise.
Thou call'st, He comes. Thou find'st 'tis he indeed.
Thy soul conceives that He is truly wise, [1350]
  Nay more, desires that He may be the book
  Whereon thine eyes continually may look.⁴

Sometime imprisoned, naked, poor, and bare,
Full of diseases, impotent, and lame,
Blind, deaf, and dumb, He comes unto his fair,
To see if yet she will remain the same;
Nay, sick and wounded, now thou dost prepare
To cherish Him in thy dear lover's name.
  Yea, thou bestow'st all pains, all cost, all care,
  That may relieve Him, and His health repair.⁵

These works of mercy are so sweet, so dear
To Him that is the Lord of life and love,
That all thy prayèrs He vouchsafes to hear,
And sends His Holy Spirit from above.
Thy eyes are op'ned, and thou seest so clear,
No worldly thing can thy fair mind remove.
  Thy faith, thy prayèrs, and His special grace
  Doth open heaven, where thou behold'st His face.

These are those keys Saint Peter did possess,
Which, with a spiritual power, are given to thee
To heal the souls of those that do transgress,
By thy fair virtues; which, if once they see,
Unto the like they do their minds address.
Such as thou art, such they desire to be.
  If they be blind, thou giv'st to them their sight; [1375]
  If deaf or lame, they hear and go upright.

Yea, if possessed with any evil spirits,
Such power thy fair examples have obtained
To cast them out, applying Christ's pure merits
By which they are bound, and of all hurt restrained.
If strangely taken, wanting sense or wits,
Thy faith (applied unto their souls so pained)
  Healeth all griefs and makes them grow so strong
  As no defects can hang upon them long.⁶

Then, being thus rich, no riches dost respect,
Nor dost thou care for any outward show;
The proud, that do fair virtue's rules neglect,
Desiring place, thou sittest° them below.
All wealth and honor thou dost quite reject
If thou perceiv'st that once it proves a foe
  To virtue, learning, and the powers divine.
  Thou may'st convert (but never wilt incline⁷

To) foul disorder or licentiousness,
But in thy modest veil dost sweetly cover
The stains of other sins, to make themselves –
That by this means thou may'st in time recover
Those weak lost sheep that did so long transgress,
Presenting them unto thy dearest lover;
  That when He brings them back into His fold,
  In their conversion then He may behold [1400]⁸

Thy beauty, shining brighter than the sun;
Thine honor, more than ever monarch gained;
Thy wealth, exceeding His that kingdoms won;
Thy love unto His spouse; thy faith unfeigned;
Thy constancy in what thou hast begun,
Till thou His heavenly kingdom have obtained,
  Respecting worldly wealth to be but dross,
  Which, if abused, doth prove the owner's loss.⁹

---

¹ *good Lady*] Margaret Clifford (the addressee).

² *alms-deeds*] charitable gifts; *bleeds*] bleed.

³ *crosses*] frustrations; *prove*] make trial; *her*] your soul's; *sweet of sweets*] your heart/love for him.

⁴ *weed*] garb.

⁵ *his fair*] his beloved.

---

⁶ *to*] as to; *By which*] to those spirits by which; *strangely taken*] mentally deranged.

⁷ *Desiring ... below*] See Luke 14.7-11.

⁸ *to make*] to correct; *presenting*] and present.

⁹ *spouse*] the Church.

Great Cleopatra's love to Antony°
Can no way be comparèd unto thine.
She left her love in his extremity,
When greatest need should cause her to combine
Her force with his, to get the victory.
Her love was earthly, and thy love divine.
  Her love was only to support her pride;
  Humility thy love and thee doth guide.

That glorious part of death, which last she played
T'appease the ghost of her deceasèd love,
Had never needed, if she could have stayed
When his extremes made trial and did prove
Her leaden love unconstant (and afraid
Their wicked wars the wrath of God might move,
  To take revenge for chaste Octavia's wrongs
  Because she enjoys what unto her belongs). [1]

No, Cleopatra, though thou wert as fair   [1425]
As any creature in Antonius' eyes;
Yea, though thou wert as rich, as wise, as rare,
As any pen could write, or wit devise;
Yet with this lady canst thou not compare,
Whose inward virtues all thy worth denies. [2]
  Yet thou° a black Egyptian dost appear:
  Thou false, she true and to her love more dear.

She sacrificeth to her dearest love
With flowers of faith and garlands of good deeds;
She flies not from him when afflictions prove;
She bears his cross and stops his wounds that bleeds;[3]
She loves and lives chaste as the turtle dove;
She attends upon him, and his flock she feeds;
  Yea, for one touch of death which thou didst try,
  A thousand deaths she every day doth die.

Her virtuous life exceeds thy worthy death.   [4]
Yea, she hath richer ornaments of state,
Shining more glorious than in dying breath
Thou didst, when either pride or cruel fate
Did work thee to prevent a double death
To stay the malice, scorn, and cruel hate
  Of Rome, that joyed to see thy pride pulled down,
  Whose beauty wrought the hazard of her crown.

Good Madame, though your modesty be such   [5]
Not to acknowledge what we know and find   [1450]
And that you think these praises overmuch
Which do express the beauty of your mind,
Yet pardon me (although I give a touch
Unto their eyes that else would be so blind
  As not to see thy store, and their own wants),
  From whose fair seeds of virtue spring these plants.

And know, when first into this world I came,
This charge was given me by th' eternal powers:
Th' everlasting trophy of thy fame,
To build and deck it with the sweetest flowers
That virtue yields. Then, Madame, do not blame
Me when I show the world but what is yours
  And deck you with that crown which is your due,,
  That of heaven's beauty earth may take a view.

Though famous women elder times have known
Whose glorious actions did appear so bright
That powerful men by them were overthrown
And all their armies overcome in fight—
The Scythian women by their power alone
Put King Daríus unto shameful flight;
  All Asia yielded to their conquering hand;
  Great Alexander could not their power withstand, [6]

Whose worth, though writ in lines of blood and fire,
Is not to be comparèd unto thine
– Their power was small to overcome desire   [1475]
Or to direct their ways by virtue's line.
Were they alive, they would thy life admire,
And unto thee their honors would resign.
  For thou a greater conquest dost obtain
  Than they who have so many thousands slain.

Wise Deborah that judgèd Israel,
Nor valiant Judith, cannot equal thee.
Unto the first, God did His will reveal,
And gave her power to set His people free;
Yea, Judith had the power likewise to quell°
Proud Holofernes, that the just might see
  What small defense vain pride and greatness hath
  Against the weapons of God's word and faith. [7]

But thou far greater war dost still maintain
Against that many-headed monster, sin,
Whose mortal string hath many thousand slain,
And every day fresh combats do begin;
Yet cannot all his venom lay one stain
Upon thy soul – thou dost the conquest win!
  Though all the world he daily doth devour,
  Yet over thee he never could get power.

For that one worthy deed by Deb'rah done
Thou hast performèd many in thy time.
For that one conquest that fair Judith won
(By which she did the steps of honor climb),   [1500]
Thou hast the conquest of all conquests won
When to thy conscience hell can lay no crime.
  For that one head that Judith bare away,
  Thou tak'st from sin a hundred heads a day.

[1] *did prove*] i.e., had not proved;   *she...her*] Cleopatra ... Octavia.

[2] *this lady*] Margaret Clifford, the ideal woman.

[3] *bleeds*] bleed.

[4] *her ... thy*] Clifford's...Cleopatra's;   *worthy*] deserved

[5] *Good Madame*] not Cleopatra but Margaret Clifford.

[6] *elder*] former;   *Scythian women*] In the apocryphal book of 1 Esdras, chaps. 3-4, Scythian women are said to be stronger than Darius, king of Persia; Darius was defeated militarily by Alexander the Great in 331 CE.

[7] *Deborah...Judith*] See the book of Judges, chaps. 4-5, and the apocryphal book of Judith;   *quell*] (kĕll) kill.

Though virtuous Esther fasted three days' space
And spent her time in prayèrs all that while
(That by God's power she might obtain such grace
That she and hers might not become a spoil
To wicked Haman, in whose crabbèd face
Was seen the map of malice, envy, guile);
  Her glorious garments though she put apart
  (So to present a pure and single heart   1

To God, in sack-cloth, ashes, and with tears),
Yet must fair Esther needs give place to thee,
Who hath continued days, weeks, months, and years,
In God's true service, yet thy heart being free°
From doubt of death or any other fears.
Fasting from sin, thou pray'st thine eyes may see
  Him that hath full possession of thine heart,
  From whose sweet love thy soul can never part.   2

His love, not fear, makes thee to fast and pray.
No kinsman's counsel needs thee to advise.
The sack-cloth thou dost wear both night and day,
Is worldly troubles, which thy rest denies;
The ashes are the vanities that play   [1525]
Over thy head and steal before thine eyes;
  Which thou shak'st off when mourning time is past,
  That royal robes thou may'st put on at last.   3

Joachim's wife – that fair and constant dame
Who rather chose a cruel death to die
Than yield to those two elders void of shame,
When both at once her chastity did try;
Whose innocency bare away the blame
Until th' Almighty Lord had heard her cry
  And raised the spirit of a child to speak,
  Making the powerful judgèd of the weak—   4

Although her virtue do deserve to be
Writ by that hand that never purchased blame,
In holy Writ where all the world may see
Her perfit life and ever-honored name,
Yet was she not to be compared to thee,
Whose many virtues do increase thy fame.
  For she opposed against old doting lust,
  Who with life's danger she did fear to trust;

But your chaste breast, guarded with strength of mind,
Hates the embracements of unchaste desires.
You, loving God, live in yourself confined
From unpure love; your purest thoughts retires,
Your perfit sight could never be so blind   [1550]
To entertain the old or young desires
  Of idle lovers which the world presents,
  Whose base abuses worthy minds prevents.

Even as the constant laurel, always green,
No parching heat of summer can deface,
Nor pinching winter ever yet was seen
Whose nipping frosts° could wither or disgrace:
So you, dear Lady, still remain as queen,
Subduing all affections that are base,
  Unalterable by the change of times,
  Not following, but lamenting, others' crimes.

No fear of death or dread of open shame
Hinders your perfect heart to give consent,
Nor loathsome age (whom time could never tame
From ill designs whereto their youth was bent),
But love of God, care to preserve your fame,
And spend that precious time that God hath sent
  In all good exercises of the mind,
  Whereto your noble nature is inclined.

That Ethiopian queen did gain great fame,
Who from the southern world did come to see
Great Solomon; the glory of whose name
Had spread itself o'er all the earth, to be
So great that all the princes thither came,
To be spectators of his royalty:
  And this fair queen of Sheba came from far,   [1575]
  To reverence this new-appearing star.   5

From th' utmost part of all the earth she came,
To hear the wisdom of this worthy king,
To try if wonder did agree with fame.
And many fair rich presents did she bring,
Yea, many strange hard questions did she frame,
All which were answered by this famous king.
  Nothing was hid that in her heart did rest,
  And all to prove this king so highly blest.

Here majesty with majesty did meet—
Wisdom to wisdom yielded true content—
One beauty did another beauty greet—
Bounty to bounty never could repent—
Here all distaste is trodden under feet.
No loss of time, where time was so well spent
  In virtuous exercises of the mind!—
  In which this queen did much contentment find.

Spirits affect where they do sympathize.   6
Wisdom desires wisdom to embrace.
Virtue covets her like, and doth devise
How she her friends may entertain with grace.
Beauty sometime is pleased to feed her eyes
With viewing beauty in another's face.
  Both good and bad in this point do agree,
  That each desireth with his like to be.   [1600]

---

1 *Hester*] Esther;   *Haman*] *see* Esther 4.1-17.

2 *doubt of*] anxiety about.

3 *which*] all which;   *royal*] i.e., heavenly.

4 *Joachim's wife*] Susanna.

---

5 *Ethiopian queen...Great Solomon*] *See* 1 Kings 10:1-13.

6 *Spirits ... sympathize*] Kindred spirits have affection for one another.

And this desire did work a strange effect,
To draw a queen forth of her native land,
Not yielding to the niceness and respect
Of womankind. She passed both sea and land;   1
All fear of dangers she did quite neglect,
Only to see, to hear, and understand
  That beauty, wisdom, majesty, and glory,
  That in her heart impressed his perfect story.

Yet this fair map of majesty and might
Was but a figure of thy dearest love,
Born t' express that true and heavenly light
That doth all other joys imperfect prove.   2
If this fair earthly star did shine so bright,
What doth that glorious Son that is above
  Who wears th' imperial crown of heaven and earth,
  And made all Christians blessèd in his birth?

If that small spark could yield so great a fire
As to enflame the hearts of many kings
To come to see, to hear, and to admire
His wisdom, tending but to worldly things,   [1620]
Then much more reason have we to desire
That heavenly wisdom which salvation brings—
  The Son of righteousness, that gives true joys
  When all they sought for were but earthly toys. 3

. . . .

To the Lady Dowager of Cumberland

Pure-thoughted lady, blessed be thy choice
Of this almighty, everlasting king,
In thee His saints and angels do rejoice
And to their heav'nly Lord do daily sing
Thy perfect praises in their loudest voice;
And all their harps and golden vials bring
  Full of sweet odors, even thy holy prayers,
  Unto that spotless Lamb that all repairs.   [1680]

. . . .

Lo, Madam, here you take a view of those   [1825]
Whose worthy steps you do desire to tread,
Decked in those colors which our Savior chose,
The purest colors both of white and red;
Their freshest beauties would I fain disclose,
By which our Savior most was honorèd—
  But my weak muse desireth now to rest,
  Folding up all their beauties in your breast,

Whose excellence hath raised my sprites to write
Of what my thoughts could hardly apprehend;
Your rarest virtues did my soul delight,
Great lady of my heart: I must commend
You, that appear so fair in all men's sight.
On your deserts my muses do attend—
  You are the arctic star that guides my hand,
  All what I am, I rest at your command.   [1840]

---

1 *niceness and respect*] delicacy and inclination.

2 *figure*] image, prefiguration.

3 *they*] "kings" (l. 1618) coming to hear Solomon.

Ben Jonson's "To Penshurst" is often cited as the first example in English of the country-house poem, a tradition that finds its classical models in Horace, Martial, and Vergil; but Jonson was anticipated, at least in print, by Aemilia Lanyer's "Cookham." The manor of Cookham (near Maidenhead) was owned by the English crown, but leased to Lady Margaret's brother, William Russell of Thornhaugh. In her diary, the Lady Anne Clifford records a visit to Cookham in 1603, where her uncle's family was then lodged. The residence of Margaret and Anne Clifford is thought to have begun not long afterward, during the estrangement of Lady Margaret from her husband, the earl of Cumberland (who died in 1605). No external record exists of Lanyer's sojourn at the Cookham estate. She appears, however, to have been employed by the Clifford family for a period extending over some months or years.

Lanyer depicts Cookham as an idyllic place in which a few lucky women were able for a time to pursue their intellectual interests, to commune with nature and with one another, without interference from the workaday world. At the center of that paradise stands Lady Margaret, countess of Cumberland, whom the poet figures as its presiding goddess.

The Description of Cookham

FAREWELL, sweet Cookham, where I first obtained
Grace from that Grace where perfit grace remained;
And where the Muses gave their full consent
I should have power the virtuous to conten—
Where princely Pallas° willed me to indite
The sacred story of the soul's delight.   4
Farewell, sweet place (where virtue then did rest,
And all delights did harbor in her breast):
Never shall my sad eyes again behold
Those pleasures which my thoughts did then unfold:
Yet you, great lady, mistress of that place
(From whose desires did spring this work of grace),
Vouchsafe to think upon those pleasures past
As fleeting worldly joys that could not last,
Or as dim shadows of celestial pleasures
(Which are desired above all earthly treasures).   5
Oh how, methought, against you thither came,
Each part did seem some new delight to frame!
The house received all ornaments to grace it
And would endure no foulness to deface it.   6
The walks put on their summer liveries,

---

4 *Pallas*] Pallas Athena, or Minerva, goddess of wisdom and the arts (here, Margaret Clifford; with a pun on *palace* (Q *Palace*); *indite*] to compose (as inspired); *sacred story*] her *Salve Deus Rex Judaeorum*, here said to have been inspired or commissioned by Lady Margaret as Pallas Athena.

5 *great lady*] Margaret Clifford; *Vouchsafe*] grant.

6 *against*] whenever.

And all things else did hold like similes.   [1]
The trees with leaves, with fruits, with flowers clad,
Embraced each other, seeming to be glad,   [25]
Turning themselves to beauteous canopies,
To shade the bright sun from your brighter eyes;
The crystal streams, with silver spangles graced
While by the glorious sun they were embraced;
The little birds in chirping notes did sing,
To entertain both you and that sweet spring.
And Philomela, with her sundry lays,
Both you and that delightful place did praise.   [2]
Oh how, methought, each plant, each flower, each tree
Set forth their beauties then to welcome thee!
The very hills right humbly did descend
When you to tread upon them did intend.
And as you set your feet, they still did rise,
Glad that they could receive so rich a prize.
The gentle winds did take delight to be
Among those woods that were so graced by thee,
And in sad murmur uttered pleasing sound,
That pleasure in that place might more abound.   [3]
The swelling banks delivered all their pride
When such a phoenix once they had espied.
Each arbor, bank, each seat, each stately tree,
Thought themselves honored in supporting thee.
The pretty birds would oft come to attend thee,
Yet fly away for fear they should offend thee.
The little creatures in the burrow by
Would come abroad to sport them in your eye; [50] [4]
Yet, fearful of the bow in your fair hand,
Would run away when you did make a stand.
Now let me come unto that stately tree
Wherein such goodly prospects you did see—
That oak that did in height his fellows pass
As much as lofty trees low-growing grass;
Much like a comely cedar, straight and tall,
Whose beauteous stature far exceeded all.
How often did you visit this fair tree
Which, seeming joyful in receiving thee,
Would like a palm tree spread his arms abroad,
Desirous that you there should make abode;
Whose fair green leaves, much like a comely veil,
Defended Phoebus when he would assail;   [5]
Whose pleasing boughs did yield a cool fresh air,
Joying his happiness when you were there;
Where, being seated, you might plainly see
Hills, vales, and woods (as if on bended knee
They had appeared, your honor to salute

Or to prefer some strange unlooked-for suit),
All interlaced with brooks and crystal springs,
A prospect fit to please the eyes of kings!   [6]
And thirteen shires appeared all in your sight
(Europe could not afford much more delight—
What was there then but gave you all content?); [75]
While you the time in meditation spent
Of their Creator's power, which there you saw,
In all His creatures, held a perfit law;
And in their beauties did you plain descry
His beauty, wisdom, grace, love, majesty.
In these sweet woods how often did you walk,
With Christ and His apostles there to talk;
Placing His Holy Writ in some fair tree,
To meditate what you therein did see.
With Moses you did mount His holy hill,
To know His pleasure and perform His will.
With lovely David you did often sing
His holy hymns to Heaven's eternal King.   [7]
And in sweet music did your soul delight,
To sound His praises, morning, noon, and night.
With blessed Joseph you did often feed
Your pinèd brethren when they stood in need.   [8]
And that sweet lady sprung from Clifford's race—
Of noble Bedford's blood, fair stem° of grace,
To honorable Dorset now espoused,
In whose fair breast true virtue then was housed— [9]
Oh, what delight did my weak spirits find
In those pure parts of her well-framèd mind!
And yet it grieves me that I cannot be
Near unto her, whose virtues did agree   [100]
With those fair ornaments of outward beauty
Which did enforce, from all, both love and duty.
Unconstant Fortune, thou art most to blame,
Who casts us down into so low a frame,
Where our great friends we cannot daily see,
So great a difference is there in degree.
Many are placèd in those orbs of state,
Partners in honor (so ordained by fate),
Nearer in show, yet farther off in love
(In which the lowest always are above).   [10]
But whither am I carried in conceit,
My wit too weak to conster of the great?   [11]
Why not! Although we are but born of earth,
We may behold the heavens.° Despising death,
And loving heaven that is so far above,
May in the end vouchsafe us entire love.

---

[1] *liveries*] uniforms.

[2] *Philomela*] the nightingale.

[3] *sad*] solemn, pensive.

[4] *them*] themselves.

[5] *defended Phoebus*] defended (from) the sun.

[6] *prefer*] offer, advance.

[7] *with lovely David*] as author of the Psalms;

[8] *Joseph*] Jacob's youngest son, who feeds his brothers in Gen. chap. 47; *pinèd*] famished.

[9] *that sweet lady*] Anne Clifford, Lady Margaret's only child, who likewise writes of her mother's piety; in the Appleby Castle portrait commissioned by Anne, her mother holds a book of Psalms in her right hand.

[10] *Parters*] division-makers.

[11] *wit*] my wit being; *conster of*] construe; interpret.

Therefore, sweet memory, do thou retain
Those pleasures past, which will not turn again:
Remember beauteous Dorset's former sports, [1]
So far from being touched by ill reports;
Wherein my self did always bear a part
While reverend love presented my true heart.
Those recreations let me bear in mind,
Which her sweet youth and noble thoughts did find
(Whereof deprived, I evermore must grieve,   [125]
Hating blind fortune, careless to relieve).
And you, sweet Cookham, whom these ladies leave,
I now must tell the grief you did conceive
At their departure, when they went away,
How everything retained a sad dismay—
Nay, long before, when once an inkling came,
Methought each thing did unto sorrow frame.
The trees, that were so glorious in our view,
Forsook both flowers and fruit when once they knew
Of your depart. Their very leaves did wither,
Changing their colors as they grew together.
But when they saw this had no power to stay you,
They often wept (though, speechless, could not pray you),
Letting their tears in your fair bosoms fall,
As if they said, "Why will ye leave us all?"
This being vain, they cast their leaves away,
Hoping that pity would have made you stay.
Their frozen tops, like age's hoary hairs,
Shows their disasters, languishing in fears.
A swarthy rivelled rine all overspread
Their dying bodies, half alive, half dead. [2]
But your occasions called you so away
That nothing there had power to make you stay.
Yet did I see a noble, grateful mind,
Requiting each according to their kind,   [150]
Forgetting not to turn and take your leave
Of these sad creatures, powerless to receive
Your favor, when with grief you did depart,
Placing their former pleasures in your heart; [3]
Giving great charge to noble memory,
There to preserve their love continually—
But specially the love of that fair tree
That first and last you did vouchsafe to see,
In which it pleased you oft to take the air
With noble Dorset, then a virgin fair; [4]
Where many a learned book was read and scanned;
To this fair tree, taking me by the hand,
You did repeat the pleasures which had passed,
Seeming to grieve they could no longer last.

And with a chaste, yet loving, kiss took leave
(Of which sweet kiss I did it soon bereave,
Scorning a senseless creature should possess
So rare a favor, so great happiness; [5]
No other kiss it could receive from me,
For fear to give back what it took of thee.
So I (ingrateful creature!) did deceive it
Of that which you vouchsafed, in love, to leave it. [6]
And though it oft had given me much content,
Yet this great wrong I never could repent:
But, of the happiest, made it most forlorn,   [175]
To show that nothing's free from fortune's scorn;
While all the rest with this most beauteous tree,
Made their sad consort sorrow's harmony. [7]
The flowers, that on the banks and walks did grow,
Crept in the ground; the grass did weep for woe;
The winds and waters seemed to chide together
Because you went away, they knew° not whither;
And those sweet brooks, that ran so fair and clear,
With grief and trouble wrinkled did appear.
Those pretty birds that wonted were to sing,
Now neither sing, nor chirp, nor use their wing,
But with their tender feet on some bare spray,
Warble forth sorrow and their own dismay.
Fair Philomela leaves her mournful ditty,
Drowned in dead sleep, yet can procure no pity.
Each arbor, bank, each seat, each stately tree,
Looks bare and desolate now for want of thee,
Turning green tresses into frosty gray
While in cold grief they wither all away.
The sun grew weak, his beams no comfort gave,
While all green things did make the earth their grave.
Each briar, each bramble, when you went away,
Caught fast your clothes, thinking to make you stay.
Delightful Echo, wonted to reply
To our last words, did now for sorrow die.   [200] [8]
The house cast off each garment that might grace it,
Putting on dust and cobwebs to deface it.
All desolation then there did appear
When you were going, whom they held so dear.
This last farewell to Cookham here I give:
When I am dead thy name in this may live,
Wherein I have performed her noble hest
Whose virtues lodge in my unworthy breast,
And ever shall, so long as life remains,
Tying my heart to her by those rich chains.

finis

---

[1] *Dorset*] Anne Clifford, married to Richard Sackville, earl of Dorset on 25 February 1609.

[2] *rivelled rine*] *rind* as either bark (*OED* sb. 1) or hoarfrost (*OED* sb. 3); *rivelled* as *furrowed* or *withered* (hence, the trees seemed to languish of disease as the women left Cookham and winter advanced).

[3] *grateful mind*] Margaret Clifford, as mistress of Cookham.

[4] *noble Dorset*] Lady Anne, prior to her marriage.

[5] *kiss*] to the tree; *senseless*] insensible.

[6] *it*] the oak tree.

[7] *consort*] company.

[8] *Echo*] a nymph whose love for Narcissus, unrequited, caused her to pine away until only her voice remained.

Elizabeth Tanfield Cary (1585? - 1639)

Lady Falkland

> *Ile be the custome-breaker: and beginne*
> *To shew my Sexe the way to freedomes doore…*
> —*Tragedy of Mariam,* 1.4

ELIZABETH CARY was born in Burford, Oxfordshire, the only child of Elizabeth (Symonds) and Sir Lawrence Tanfield, a prominent attorney and hanging judge. Her remarkable biography is recorded in *The Lady Falkland, her Life, by One of her Daughters,* a text featured in *Women's Works,* volume 4; but a few salient details will be helpful here as well. At age 17, though not for love, Elizabeth was married to Henry Cary (later, Viscount Falkland): her father offered Cary £2000 up front, another £2000 after two years of marriage, and his entire estate, after his death. Cary accepted. The marriage got off to a rocky start. Bookish and built like a fireplug, Elizabeth was openly disdained by her husband, who banked the cash and left for the Lowlands. A long separation ensued, followed by grudging acceptance and eleven children (several of whom died young), and a sojourn in Ireland. The couple separated following Elizabeth's announced conversion to Roman Catholicism and her refusal to recant. Disowned by her husband as also by her widowed mother, the poet's last years were consumed by beggary, ill health, and malnutrition; and buoyed only by a passion to convert her children. Lord Falkland died in 1633; after which, Elizabeth gained legal custody of her daughters and kidnapped her younger sons, conveying them to France. (All four of her daughters eventually became Benedictine nuns.) She died alone in 1639.

Addicted to reading from childhood, Cary wrote and translated many works of secular, devotional, and hagiographic literature, the bulk of which has perished. Early in her marriage she wrote at least three secular plays, a "Sicilian tragedy" and a "Life of Tamburlaine" (not extant), plus her best-known work, *The Tragedy of Mariam, Fair Queen of Jewry,* which was published in 1613 but soon recalled (perhaps to appease the wrath of her embarrassed husband or parents). A few lucky copies escaped the flames.

Cary never had the lavish silks, flashy jewelry, or prestige to participate in Queen Anna's masques, but until 1606 she was a welcome guest at the Court (again, briefly, after 1625); and she took much pleasure in the entertainment. On 1 November 1604, Cary may have seen Shakespeare's *Othello* performed at Whitehall Palace (which would account for the many verbal similarities that have been noted between the two scripts). But her principal narrative source for *Mariam* was Thomas Lodge's 1602 translation of *The Wars of the Jews* and *The Antiquities of the Jews,* by Josephus. Cary follows the historical record closely, with no major departures from its broad outline, and invents only a few minor characters.

The historical Mariamne was the last of the Hasmoneans (the Jewish royal dynasty). In 41 she was married to Herod (79-4 BCE, known today as Herod the Great), king of Palestine (under Rome) from 39 BCE until his death. In 29, Herod was summoned to Rome to answer for the drowning of High Priest Aristobulos, Mariam's brother. During his absence it was rumored that Octavian (Caesar Augustus) had put Herod to death – when in fact Herod forsook his old friend Marc Antony, allied himself with Octavian, and soon returned to Palestine more powerful than ever. Returning home, he tried Mariam for adultery and put her to death.

Having prepped her audience to expect a homicidal tyrant, Cary finally introduces Herod in Act 4 as a goofy Romeo, belting out lover's conceits in praise of a wife who would have been dead by now, had his decrees been obeyed. Enter Pheroras – a brother prince who has married his true-love, Graphina, rather than a child-bride of the tyrant's choosing. Herod explodes into anger, interrupting his fit for just two seconds to say, "Mariam! Where is she?"; then directly adds to the body count by commanding the instant death, not of Pheroras, but of his brother-in-law Constabarus and the sons of Baba, the emblems of faithful friendship. In his final speech in the same short scene, Herod promises to recompense Salome for her villainy, but in a telling slip miscalls her "gentle Mariam."

With deft economy, Cary thus articulates the nature of Judaea's patriarch: he is a king who exercises power without rationality or justice. Give this cruel knucklehead another ten minutes, and he is likely to put even Mariam to death – which is exactly what happens, without trial, without evidence, and without

Effigy of Elizabeth Cary in the Burford Church

any offense having been committed – also, without remedy but for Herod's hallucinatory fancy that he can restore Mariam to life. When Nuntio cannot suppress a smile, the king interprets his grin as an expression of joy, signalling Mariam's escape; when in fact Nuntio smiles because the awesome patriarch has become ridiculous, a babbling idiot.

But if *Mariam*'s Herod with his buffoonish ranting out-Herods the Herod of Tudor mystery plays, he is not the only character at whom Cary's script pokes fun. Swaggering Silleus (Monty-Python-like) demands, after getting stabbed, to fight again; only to get stabbed again, that's twice in two minutes. Antipater aspires to become a homicidal villain. Dominated by his mother, he speaks once, falls silent, and does nothing. The Chorus, meanwhile, utters a litany of moral platitudes, blandly advising Mariam to escape Herod's violence by means of her chastity, silence, and obedience.

Mariam is more than a glib satire on patriarchs and machismo: Cary presents a fictional society, based on prerogative rather than merit, in which even the matriarchs are corrupted. Alexandra, the mother from Hell, is a selfish materialist who boasts of having offered her own children as sex-toys in exchange for her own political advantage – and is disappointed that Antony declined. Alexandra's character owes something to the notorious Lady Elizabeth Symonds Tanfield; speaking of whom, the playwright's eldest daughter recalls: "her mother was never kind to her." Even as a married adult, Cary was obliged to remain on her knees in her mother's presence, often "for more than an hour together; though she was but an ill kneeler and a worse riser." A real-life Alexandra, Lady Tanfield was kind to no one: resented by the locals for her grasping ways and relentless litigation, she made herself the most feared woman in Oxfordshire and is said by the locals, even today, to haunt the countryside round about Burford. [1]

Doris, the woman who loved Herod first, is the new queen's bitter rival. She addresses Mariam with the same haughty scorn that Elizabeth Cary as a young bride received from her mother-in-law and domestic jailer, Lady Katherine Cary.

The Tragedy Mariam does not easily support readings that take it for a *drame à clef* featuring Herod as Henry the cruel husband, and Mariam as a figure for Elizabeth Cary the longsuffering heroine. Never sure of what she wants or how to get it, Mariam begins the play fearing that she talks too much ("How oft have I with public voice run on [...]"); and by the end of her first, public, long-running speech (78 lines), her audience is thinking, "How *true*." Five acts later, when accused of attempted murder, Mariam says nothing at all in her own defense. She then dies offstage, unseen and speechless. The queen at her death (we are told) said nothing, but only "smiled – a dutiful, though scornful smile." And yet, when his wife is gone, what Herod misses most about Mariam is neither her graceful figure and ivory bosom, nor her ruby lips, nor her star-like eyes, but her intelligence ("world-amazing wit"), and her voice ("Each word she said / Shall be the food whereon my heart is fed.").

Elizabeth Cary's own voice and values are diffused across the dramatis personae. Graphina – an invented character whose name suggests both *picture* and *writer* – is loved by Pheroras as his equal and dearest companion. Unlike Herod, Pheroras loves to hear his lover speak ("For silence is a sign of discontent"); but there is no place in Herod's world for romantic love, or for a companionate marriage such as Graphina and Pheroras had looked to find in Herod's absence.

Among the female characters, only Salomé claims the right to choose, the right to disobey, the right to divorce, the right to speak her mind. Cary punishes her for that independence, representing Herod's sister as a female devil, a second Jezebel, shameless, deceitful, and worthless. But the playwright, while writing *Mariam* and scapegoating Salomé, was herself trapped in a loveless marriage to an autocratic and abusive husband, and had no recourse to divorce: Cary may have been of the devil's party without knowing it.

Readers of *The Tragedy of Mariam* are invited by the author, throughout her script, to imagine the action taking place, not in Palestine in the first century BCE, but as a live performance: the 1613 quarto includes stage directions marking entrances and exits for the actors, and a few staging notes. Additional directions are here supplied [in brackets], to facilitate a lively delivery, whether in the classroom or in the family room, or on stage. *Mariam* may be a closet tragedy never intended for the public theaters, but it rewards reading aloud. With some trimming of the longer speeches, an inventive director, playful actors, and a musical chorus, one might even venture a full-scale production – not because of *The Tragedy of Mariam* happens to be the first original play in English by a woman playwright, but rather because Elizabeth Cary's *Mariam*, even in our own cultural moment, can speak truth to power.   DWF

---

[1] "The Lady Falkland her Life," *Women's Works,* vol. 4, p. 205. The hated Tanfields claimed even a portion of the Sunday offering plate; whose evil spirits as recently as the 19th century were warded off by the local poor with a ritual of pouring water on the bridge. Tingle (1989), 2.

The Tragedy of Mariam, the Fair Queen of Jewry
The Argument [1]

HEROD, the son of Antipater, an Idumean, having crept (by the favor of the Romans) into the Jewish monarchy, married Mariam, the [grand]daughter° of Hyrcanus (the rightful king and priest). And for her (besides her high blood, being of singular beauty) [Herod°] repudiated Doris, his former wife, by whom he had children. [2]

This Mariam had a brother called Aristobolus; and next him and Hyrcanus his grandfather, Herod in his wife's right had the best title. Therefore to remove them, [Herod°] charged the first with treason and put him to death, and drowned the second under color of sport. [3]

Alexandra, daughter to the one and mother to the other, accused [Herod°] for their deaths before Antony. So when he was forced to go answer this accusation at Rome, [Herod°] left the custody of his wife to Josephus° (his uncle that had married [Herod's°] sister Sálomé). And out of a violent affection (unwilling any should enjoy [Mariam°] after him), [Herod°] gave strict and private commandment that, if he were slain, she should be put to death. […]

[Herod°] returned with much honor, yet found his wife extremely discontented, to whom Josephus° had (meaning it for the best, to prove Herod loved her) revealed his charge.

So, by Salomé's accusation, [Herod°] put Josephus to death, but was reconciled to Mariam (who still bare the death of her friends exceeding hardly). [4]

In this mean time, Herod was again necessarily to revisit Rome, for Caesar, having overthrown Antony his great friend, was likely to make an alteration of [Herod's°] fortune. [5]

In his absence, news came to Jerusalem that Caesar had put [Herod°] to death. Their willingness it should be so, together with the likelihood, gave this rumor so good credit as Sohemus, that had succeeded Josephus' charge, succeeded him likewise in revealing it. So at Herod's return, which was speedy and unexpected, he found Mariam so far from joy that she showed apparent signs of sorrow. He still desiring to win her to a better humor, she – being very unable to conceal her passion – fell to upbraiding him with her brother's death. As they were thus debating, came in a fellow with a cup of wine, who (hired by Salomé) said first it was a love-potion, which Mariam desired to deliver to the king; but afterwards he affirmed that it was a poison, and that Sohemus had told [Mariam°] somewhat which procured the vehement hate in her. [6]

The king, hearing this, more moved with jealousy of Sohemus than with this intent of poison, sent her away; and presently after, by the instigation of Salomé, [Mariam°] was beheaded; which rashness was afterward punished in him with an intolerable and almost frantic passion for her death.

Mariamne, Queen of the Hebrews: detail from *De mulieribus claris*, by Giovanni Boccaccio (BnF 599, f.73)

---

[1] *Argument*] (*i.e.,* plot). Careless errors of fact in The Argument and Dramatis Personae may indicate that Cary wrote these for the 1613 publication, years after *Mariam* was first completed (1605/9).

[2] *Herod*] Herod the Great (ruled 39-4 BCE); *Antipater*] Antipater II (d. 43 BCE); *Mariam*] Mariamne (c. 49-29 BCE), second wife of Herod the Great (m. 32 BCE); *granddaughter*] daughrer [*sic*] Q; *Hyrcanus*] Hyrcanus II (ruled 63-40 BCE, d. 30 BCE); *Doris*] Doris of Judea, a.k.a. Sara, said to be the last of King David's line.

[3] *Alexandra*] Alexandra the Maccabe (died c. 28 BCE), daughter of Hyrcanus II, mother of Aristobolus; opposed her son-in-law Herod; after Mariam's execution tried to seize power but was unsuccessful and was herself executed; *the first*] *i.e.,* the second, Hyrcanus (executed 30 BCE); *the second*] *i.e.,* the first, Aristobolus (drowned 35 BCE); *under color of*] in pretended sport, a supposed accident; *Antony*] Marc Antony (83-30 BCE); who in 37 installed his ally Herod as puppet-king of Judaea.

[4] *bare ... hardly*] bore the death of her relatives with much difficulty.

[5] *Caesar*] Caesar Augustus (Octavian); *was likely*] Caesar was likely to depose or kill Herod.

[6] *came*] there came; *somewhat which procured*] something that produced (namely, that Herod had ordered Mariam to be killed if he should die, which provoked her to poison Herod upon his return. Salome falsely incriminates Mariam with a supposed plot to kill the king her husband).

**To Diana's earthly deputess, and my worthy
sister, from Mistress Elizabeth Cary** [1]

WHEN cheerful Phoebus his full course hath run,
His sister's fainter beams our hearts doth cheer. [2]
So your fair brother is to me the Sun,
And you his sister as my Moon appear. [3]
You are my next belov'd, my second friend—
For when my Phoebus' absence makes it night,
Whilst to th' Antípodés his beams do bend,
From you, my Phoebe, shines my second light. [4]
He like to Sol, clear-sighted, constant, free;
You Luna-like, unspotted, chaste, divine. [5]
He shone on Sicily. You destined be
T'illumine the now-obscured Palestine. [6]
    My first was consecrated to Apollo
    My second to Diana now shall follow. [7]
                  —E. C.

The names of the Speakers:

HEROD	*King of Judea*
DORIS	*his first wife*
MARIAM	*his second wife*
SÁLOMÉ	*Herod's sister*
ANTIPÁTER	*his son by [Doris]*
ALEXANDRA	*Mariam's mother*
SILLÉUS	*Prince of Arabia*
CONSTABÁRUS,	*husband to Salomé*
PHERORAS,	*Herod's brother*
GRAPHINA,	*his love*
BABA'S° FIRST SON	
BABA'S° SECOND SON	
ÁNANELL	*the high priest*
SOHÉMUS	*a counselor to Herod*
NUNTIO	*[messenger]*
BUTLER°	*another messenger*
CHORUS	*a company of Jews*

[SERVANT *of Silleus*, ATTENDANTS *on Herod*,
SOLDIER *of Herod*, GUARD]

---

[1] *sister*] Elizabeth (b. Bland) Cary, the playwright's sister-in-law and wife of Philip Cary.

[2] *Phoebus*] the Sun (Phoebus Apollo), Henry Cary

[3] *brother*] your brother Henry, my husband.

[4] *Antípodés*] opposite side of the earth;   *Phoebus ...
Phoebe*] Sun (my husband, Sir Henry Cary) ... Moon (my sister-in-law, Elizabeth Cary).

[5] *Luna-like*] like the Moon.

[6] *He ... Sicily*] Cary's first play, a Sicilian tragedy (not extant), was dedicated to Henry Cary ("Apollo").

[7] *E. C.*] the author, Elizabeth Tanfield Cary.

The Tragedy of Mariam

ACT 1, SCENE 1

[*Enter*] MARIAM, *sola*, [*in black.*] [8]

Mariam.
How oft have I with public voice run on,
To censure Rome's last hero for deceit
Because he wept when Pompey's life was gone—
Yet, when he lived, he thought his name too great. [9]
    [*Speaking as if to Caesar.*]
But now I do recant, and, Roman lord,
Excuse too rash a judgment in a woman!
My sex pleads pardon. Pardon then afford!
Mistaking is, with us, but too too common.
Now do I find (by self-experience taught),
One object yields both grief and joy.
    [*To herself.*]
You wept indeed when on his worth you thought,
But joyed that slaughter did your foe destroy. [10]
So at his death your eyes true drops did rain
Whom, dead, you did not wish alive again.
When Herod lived (that now is done to death),
Oft have I wished that I from him were free;
Oft have I wished that he might lose his breath;
Oft have I wished his carcass dead to see.
Then rage and scorn had put my love to flight—
That love which once on him was firmly set.
Hate hid his true affection from my sight
And kept my heart from paying him his debt—
And blame me not, for Herod's jealousy
Had power even constancy itself to change: [11]
For he, by barring me from liberty, [25]
To *shun* my ranging, *taught* me first to range. [12]
But yet too chaste a scholar was my heart
To learn to love another than my lord.
To leave his love, my lesson's former part,
I quickly learned; the other, I abhorred. [13]
    [*Tearfully.*]
But now his death to memory doth call
The tender love that he to Mariam bare,
And mine to him. This makes those rivers fall
    [*Suddenly angry.*]
Which, by another thought, unmoist'ned are. [14]

---

[8] *sola*] alone.

[9] *last hero*] Julius Caesar;   *he ... he ... his*] Pompey ... Caesar ... Pompey's.

[10] *you ... his*] Caesar, Pompey.

[11] *power...change*] power to change even constancy itself.

[12] *shun*] prevent   *ranging*] inconstancy.

[13] *the other*] to love another.

[14] *rivers*] streams of tears;   *another thought*] the following thought.

For Aristobolus – the loveliest° youth
That ever did in angel's shape appear—
The cruel Herod was not moved to ruth!   1
Then why grieves Mariam *Herod's* death to hear?
Why joy I not the tongue no more shall speak
That yielded forth my brother's latest doom?   2
Both youth and beauty might thy fury break,
And both, in him, did ill befit a tomb.   3

    [Speaking as if to Hyrcanus.]
  And worthy Grandsire! Ill did he requite
His high ascent (alone by thee procured),
Except he murd'red thee to free the sprite
Which still he thought on earth too long immured. 4

    How happy was it that Sohemus' mind°
Was moved to pity my distressed estate!
Might Herod's life a *trusty* servant find,
My death to his had been unseparate!   [50] 5
These thoughts have power his death to make me bear,
Nay, more, to wish the news may firmly hold!
– Yet cannot this repulse some falling tear
That will, against my will, some grief unfold—
And more I owe him for his love to me,
"The deepest love that ever yet was seen."

    Yet had I rather much a milkmaid be
Than be the monarch-of-Judea's queen!   6
It was for "nought but love" he wished *his* end
Might to *my* death but the vaunt-courier prove.   7
But I had rather still be foe, than friend
To him that saves for hate, and kills for love.

    [Sudden self-reproach.]
Hard-hearted Mariam! At thy discontent
What floods of tears have drenched his manly face!
How canst thou then so faintly now lament
Thy truest lover's death, a death's disgrace?

    [Tears.]
Ay, now, mine eyes, you do begin to right
The wrongs of your admirer and my lord.°
Long since you should have put your smiles to flight;

Ill doth a widowed eye with *joy* accord.
Why now, methinks the love I bare him then,
When virgin freedom left me unrestrained,
Doth to my heart begin to creep again—

    [Enter ALEXANDRA.]
[Aside.] My passion now is far from being feigned,
But tears, fly back, and hide you in your banks! [75]
You must not be to Alexandra seen,
For if my moan be spied, but little thanks
Shall Mariam have from that incensèd queen.

ACT 1, SCENE 2

MARIAM, ALEXANDRA.

Alexandra, [*cheerful*].
What means these tears? My Mariam doth mistake—
The news we heard did tell the tyrant's *end*!
What, weep'st thou for thy brother's murth'rer's° sake? 8
Will ever wight a tear for Herod spend?   9
My curse pursue his breathless trunk and spirit!
Base Edomite, the damnèd Esau's heir!—   10
Must he, ere Jacob's child, the crown inherit?
Must he, vile wretch, be set in David's chair?
No! David's soul, within the bosom placed
Of our forefather Abram, was ashamed
To see his seat with such a toad disgraced—
That seat that hath by Judah's race been famed°!

    [Speaking as if to Herod.]
Thou fatal enemy to royal blood,
Did not the murther of my boy suffice
To stop thy cruel mouth, that gaping stood?   11
But must thou dim the mild Hyrcanus' eyes,
My gracious father?—

    [To Mariam.] —whose too-ready hand
Did lift this Idumean from the dust!—
And he, ungrateful caitiff, did withstand
The man that did in him most friendly trust.)   12
What kingdom's right could cruel Herod claim?
Was he not Esau's issue, heir of Hell?
Then what succession can he have, but *shame*?

---

1 *ruth*] compassion, pity.

2 *the tongue*] that Herod's tongue (presumed silent now by the report of his death); *latest*] ultimate, final.

3 *youth and beauty*] that is, of Aristobolus, and obliquely Mariam's own youth and beauty; *might ... break*] should have broken Herod's fury.

4 *worthy grandsire ... he*] Hyrcanus ... Herod; *sprite*] spirit; *immured*] imprisoned (on Earth).

5 *Might ... find*] Had ... found; *my death to his*] my death and Herod's.

6 *more I owe him*] I owe him the more grief; *monarch of Judea's*] Herod's.

7 *wished*] that he wished; *vaunt-courier*] herald; thus, "It was supposedly all for love that his death should be the precursor to my own execution.

---

8 *murth'rer's*] murderer's.

9 *wight*] earthly creature.

10 *Edomite*] According to biblical genealogy, the Israelites were descended from Jacob, the Edomites or Idumaeans from Jacob's brother, Esau. The historical Edomites were forced into the southern half of Judea, in and about Hebron, a region that the Greeks called Idumea. Though Herod was an Idumaean, his first wife, Doris, was of the lineage of David.

11 *Thou fatal enemy*] spoken as if to Herod's ghost.

12 *withstand*] stand opposed to.

Did not his ancestor his birthright sell?
O yes, he doth from Edom's name derive   [25]
His *cruel nature* – which with blood is fed,
That made him me of sire and son deprive;
He ever thirsts for blood, and blood is red.   1
~~Weep'st thou because his "love" to thee was bent,~~
And read'st thou "love" in crimson characters?   2
Slew he thy friends to work *thy* heart's content?
No, *hate* may justly call that action hers.
He gave the sacred priesthood, "for thy sake,"
To Aristobolus – yet doomed him dead
Before his back the ephod warm could make
And ere the miter settled on his head!   3
Oh, had he given my boy no less than right,
The double oil should to his forehead bring
A double honor, shining doubly bright—
His birth anointed him both priest and king.
And say my father and my son he slew
To royalize, by right, *your* prince-born breath—
Was "*love*" the cause? Can Mariam deem it true–
That Herod° gave commandment for her death?
I know, by fits he showed some *signs* of love,
And yet *not* love, but raging *lunacy*;
And this – his hate to thee – may justly prove
That sure he hates Hyrcanus' family.
Who knows if he (unconstant wavering lord)
His love to Doris had renewed again;   [50]
And that he might his bed to her afford,
Perchance he wished that Mariam might be slain.

Mariam°.
Doris? Alas, her time of love was passed!
Those coals were raked in embers – long ago –
Of° Mariam's love; and she was now disgraced,
Nor did I glory in her overthrow.
He not a whit his firstborn son esteemed,
Because as well as his he was not mine.   4
My children only for his own he deemed;
These boys that did descend from royal line,
These did he style his "heirs to David's throne."
My Alexander – if he live – shall sit
In the majestic seat of Solomon!
To will it so, did Herod think it fit.

Alexandra.
Why, who can claim *from* Alexander's brood
That gold-adornèd, lion-guarded chair!
Was Alexander not of David's blood,
And was not Mariam Alexander's heir?
What more than *right* could Herod then bestow,
And who will think except for more than right?
He did not "raise" them, for they were not low,
But born to wear the crown in his despite.   5
Then send those tears away that are not sent
To thee by Reason, but by Passion's power.
Thine eyes to cheer, thy cheeks to smiles, be bent–   [75]
And entertain with joy this happy hour!
Felicity – if, when she comes, she find
A mourning habit and a cheerless look—
Will think she is not welcome to thy mind,
And so perchance her lodging will not brook.   6
Oh, keep her whilst thou hast her! If she go,
She will not easily return again.
Full many a year have I endured in woe,
Yet still have sued her presence to obtain!
    And did not I to her as presents send
A table (that best art did beautify)
Of two – to whom Heaven did best feature lend—
To woo her love by winning Antony?   7
For when a prince's favor we do crave,
We first their minions' loves do seek to win;
So I, that sought Felicity to have,
Did with her minion Antony begin.
With double sleight I sought to captivate
The warlike lover! – but I did not right;   8
For if my gift had borne but half the rate,
The Roman had been overtaken quite.
But now he farèd like a hungry guest
That to some plenteous festival is gone—
Now this, now that, he deems to eat were best;
Such choice doth make him let them all alone!   [100]
The boy's large forehead first did fairest seem;
Then glanced his eye upon my Mariam's cheek,
And that without comparison did deem.   9

---

1 *red*] punning on name of Esau (Edom), which according to biblical etymology meant "red." *See* Gen. 25:25.

2 *in crimson characters*] characters [*i.e.* words] written in blood; also recalls the bloodied "characters" of Aristobolus and Hyrcanus.

3 *ephod*] priestly vestment;   *miter*] ceremonial headdress.

4 *his*] Herod's;   *he*] Antipater, the historical Herod's only child by his first wife Doris, both of whom Herod banished in order to wed Mariam.

5 *them*] Mariam's children;   *in his despite*] whether or not Herod liked it.

6 *she*] felicity (personified in lines 77-92 as a new guest to Mariam's life, to be welcomed).

7 *table*] painting;   *To woo her love*] to court "Felicity," or happiness, by seeking the favor of Antony, the "minion" (favorite) of goddess Felicity;   *And ... Antony* (lines 85-88)] Josephus relates that the historical Alexandra (as counseled by Dellius) sent pictures of her two children to Antony, whereby to entice him to restore the priesthood to Aristobolus (Josephus, *Antiq.* 15.2.5-6.)

8 *double sleight*] a double trick or temptation (by offering up both my children as sex partners, but it backfired because they were both so beautiful Antony couldn't decide which one he wanted most.

9 *boy's large forehead*] of her son Aristobolus.

What was in either, that° he most did seek°;
And, thus distracted, either's beauty's might
Within the other's excellence was drowned.   1
Too much delight did bare him from delight—
For either's love the other's did confound—
Where, if thy portraiture had only gone,
His life from Herod, Antony had taken.   2
He would have lovèd thee, and thee alone,
And left the brown Egyptian clean forsaken;
And Cleopatra then to seek had been
So firm a lover of her wanèd face.   3
Then great Antonius' fall we had not seen
By her that fled, to have him hold the chase.
Then Mariam, in a Roman's chariot set,
In place of Cleopatra might have shown:
A mart of beauties in her visage met,
And passed° in this, that they were all her own. 4

Mariam.
Not to be empress of aspiring Rome
Would Mariam like to Cleopatra live!
With purest body will I press my tomb
And wish no favors Antony could give.

Alexandra.
Let us retire us, that we may resolve   [125]
How now to deal in this reversèd state.
Great are th' affairs that we must now revolve,
And great affairs must not be taken late.

ACT 1, SCENE 3

MARIAM, ALEXANDRA, [*and enter*] SALOMÉ.

Salomé.
More plotting yet? Why, now you have the thing
For which so oft you spent your suppliant breath–
And Mariam hopes to have another king.
Her eyes do sparkle *joy* for Herod's death!

Alexandra.
If she desired another king to have,
She might before she came in Herod's bed
Have had her wish. More kings than one did crave
For leave to set a crown upon her head.

I think with more than reason she laments
That she is freed from such a sad annoy!   5
Who is't will weep to part from discontent°?
And if she joy, she did° not causeless joy.

Salomé.
You durst not thus have given your tongue the rein
If noble Herod still remained in life.
Your daughter's betters far, I dare maintain,
Might have rejoiced to be my brother's wife.

Mariam.
My betters far? Base woman, 'tis untrue!
You scarce have ever my superiors *seen*—
For Mariam's servants were as good as you,
Before she came to be Judea's queen.

Salomé.
Now stirs the tongue that is so quickly moved—
But more than once your choler have I borne.   6
Your fumish words are sooner said than proved,
And Salomé's reply is only scorn.

Mariam.
Scorn those that are for thy companions held.   [25]
Though I thy brother's face had never seen,
My birth thy baser birth so far excelled,
I had to both of you the princess been.
Thou party Jew and party Edomite!   7
Thou mongrel, issued from rejected race!
Thy ancestors against the heavens did fight,
And thou like them wilt heavenly birth disgrace.

Salomé.
Still twit you me with nothing but my birth?
What odds betwixt your ancestors and mine?
Both born of Adam, both were made of earth,
And both did come from holy Abram's° line.

Mariam.
I favor thee when nothing else I say.
With thy black acts I'll not pollute my breath—
Else to thy charge I might full justly lay
A shameful life, besides a husband's death.

Salomé.
'Tis true indeed, I did the plots reveal
That passed betwixt your favorites and *you*.
I meant not I a traitor to conceal.
Thus Salomé *your* minion, Joseph, slew.   8

---

1 *beauty's might*] strength of beauty.

2 *bare*] or, *bear* (bare *Q 1613*); 17th-C usage of *bare* includes *bear* (carry away), *strip* (bare), and *obstruct* (bar);   *only gone*] i.e., if just Mariam's picture had been sent. Since Mariam was already married to Herod, Antony sent instead for Aristobolus. Josephus reports that Herod intervened by writing back that the Jews would revolt if Aristobolus were sent out of the country.

3 *then to seek had been*] would then have had to seek.

4 *And passed ... own*] and Mariam's market of beauties surpassed Cleopatra's in that Mariam's beauties were unaided by cosmetics.

5 *annoy*] annoyance, trouble.

6 *choler*] wrath.

7 *both of you*] Salome and Herod;   *party*] partly.

8 *Thus*] by revealing Josephus's "traitorous" breech of secrecy.

Mariam.

Heaven, dost thou mean this infamy to smother?
Let sland'red Mariam ope thy closèd ear!
Self-guilt hath ever been suspicion's° mother,
And therefore I this speech with patience bear.
No, had not Salomé's unsteadfast heart
In Joseph's° stead her Constabarus placed,   [50]
To free herself she had not used the art
To slander hapless Mariam for unchaste.

Alexandra.

Come, Mariam, let us go. It is no boot
To let the head contend against the foot.   1
     [*Exit* MARIAM, ALEXANDRA.]

ACT 1, SCENE 4

SALOMÉ, *sola.*

Salomé.

Lives Salomé to get so base a style
As "foot" to the proud Mariam? Herod's spirit,
In happy time for *her,* endured exile!
For did he live, she should not miss her merit.   2
But he is dead, and though he were my brother,
His death such store of cinders cannot cast
My coals of love to quench; for though they smother
The flames awhile, yet will they out at last.   3
Oh blest Arabia, in best climate placed,
I by the fruit will censure of the tree:
'Tis not in vain thy happy name thou hast
If all Arabians like Silleus be.   4
Had not my fate been too too contrary
When I on Constabarus first did gaze,
Silleus had been object to mine eye—
Whose looks and personage must all eyes° amaze.
But now, ill-fated Salomé, thy tongue
To Constabarus by itself is tied;
And now, except I do the 'Ebrew wrong,
I cannot be the fair Arabian bride.   5
     What childish letts are these? Why stand I now
On honorable points? 'Tis long ago
Since shame was written on my tainted brow,
And certain 'tis that shame is honor's foe.   6
Had I upon my reputation stood,   [25]

Had I affected an unspotted life,
Josephus' veins had still been stuffed with blood,
And I to him had lived a sober wife.
Then had I never cast an eye of love
On Constabarus' now-detested face!   7
Then had I kept my thoughts without remove
And blushed at motion of the least disgrace.
But shame is gone and honor wiped away,
And Impudency on my forehead sits.
She bids me work my will without delay—
And for my will, I will employ my wits.   8
He loves, I love. What then can be the cause
Keeps me from° being the Arabian's wife?
It is the principles of Moses' laws!
For Constabarus still remains in life.
If he to me did bear as earnest hate
As I to him, for him there were an ease:
A separating bill might free his fate
From such a yoke that did so much displease.   9
Why should such privilege to men° be given?
Or, given to them, why barred from women then?
Are men than we in greater grace with heaven?
Or cannot women hate as well as men?
I'll be the custom-breaker and begin
To show my sex the way to freedom's door –   [50]
And with an offering will I purge my sin.
The law was made for none but who are poor.
If Herod had lived, I might to him accuse
My present lord. But for the future's sake,
Then would I tell the king he did refuse
The sons of Baba in his power to take.   10
But now I must divorce him from my bed,
That my Silleus may possess his room.   11
Had I not begged his life, he had been dead.
I curse my tongue, the hind'rer of his doom!
But then my wand'ring heart to him was fast,
Nor did I dream of change.
     [*Enter* SILLEUS.]   Silleus said
He would be here – and see, he comes at last.
Had I not named him, longer had he stayed.   12

---

1 *boot*] profit.

2 *Herod's ... exile*] It is good timing for Mariam that Herod's spirit has suffered its exile (death); *merit*] punishment, just deserts.

3 *out*] come out, rekindle.

4 *censure of*] judge; *Silleus*] prince of Arabia, chief minister to King Obodas.

5 *except*] unless.

6 *letts*] hindrances; *shame*] blushing, figured as a text of shame.

7 *had I never*] never would I have.

8 *She*] Impudence (here personified).

9 *separating bill*] renunciation, bill of divorce (See Deut. 24:1, which extends to men the privilege of so divorcing their wives).

10 *he*] Constabarus.

11 *now I must*] because I cannot now have him put to death by accusing him of treason against Herod.

12 *Had I ... stayed*] Salomé suggests that whenever she mentions his name, Silleus comes running (but cf. the old proverb, "Speak of the devil and he will appear").

ACT 1, SCENE 5

SALOMÉ, SILLEUS.

Silleus.

Well found, fair Salomé, Judea's pride!
Hath thy innated wisdom found the way
To make Silleus deem him deified,
By gaining *thee*, a more-than-precious prey?   1

Salomé.

I have devised the best I can devise—
A more imperfect means was never found,
But what cares Salomé? It doth suffice,
If our endeavors with their end be crowned!
In this our land we have an ancient use,
Permitted first by our lawgiver's head:
Who hates his wife, though for no just abuse,
May with a bill divorce her from his bed.   2
But in this custom women are not free—
Yet I for once will wrest it. Blame not thou
The ill I do, since what I do's for thee.
Though others blame, Silleus should allow.

Silleus.

Thinks Salomé Silleus hath a tongue
To censure her fair actions? Let my blood
Bedash my proper brow! For such a wrong,
The being *yours*, can make even vices good.   3
Arabia, joy, prepare thy earth with green,
Thou never happy wert indeed till now!
Now shall thy ground be trod by beauty's queen.
Her foot is destined to depress thy brow.
Thou shalt, fair Salomé, command as much   [25]
As if the royal ornament were thine:
The weakness of Arabia's king is such,
The kingdom is not his so much as mine.
My mouth is our Obodas' oracle,
Who thinks not aught but what Silleus will.°   4
And thou, rare creature, Asia's miracle,
Shalt be to me as it: Obodas' still.   5

Salomé.

'Tis not for glory I thy love accept.
Judea yields me honors, worthy store!   6
Had not affection in my bosom crept,

My native country should my life deplore.   7
Were not Silleus he with whom° I go,
I would not change my Palestine for Rome;
Much less would I, a glorious state to show,
Go far to purchase an Arabian tomb.

Silleus.

Far be it from Silleus so to think!
I know it is thy gratitude requites
The love that is in me and shall not shrink
Till death do sever me from earth's delights.   8
    [*Enter* CONSTABARUS.]

Salomé.

But whist! Methinks the wolf is in our talk.   9
Be gone, Silleus! Who doth here arrive?
'Tis Constabarus that doth hither walk.
I'll find a quarrel, him from me to drive.

Silleus.

Farewell – but were it not for thy command,
In his despite Silleus here would stand.   [50]
    [*Exit* SILLEUS.]

ACT 1, SCENE 6

SALOMÉ, CONSTABARUS.

Constabarus.

Oh Salomé, how much you wrong your name,
Your race, your country, and your husband most!
A stranger's private conference is shame.
I blush for you that have your blushing lost.
Oft have I found, and found you to my grief,
Consorted with this base Arabian here.
Heaven knows that you have been my comfort chief;
Then do not now my greater plague appear.
Now, by the stately carvèd edifice
That on Mount Zion makes so fair a show,
And by the altar fit for sacrifice –   10
I love thee more than thou thyself dost know.
Oft with a silent sorrow have I heard
How ill Judea's mouth doth censure thee;
And, did I not thine honor much regard,
Thou shouldst not be exhorted thus, for me.   11
Didst thou but know the worth of honest fame,
How much a virtuous woman is esteemed,

---

1 *innated*] innate;   *him*] himself.

2 *first lawgiver*] Moses;   *Who hates*] whoever hates.

3 *Bedash*] splatter over;   *The*] It (idiomatic).

4 *Obodas*] the king of Arabia; see Josephus, *Antiq.*
13.13.5;   *not ... will*] only as Silleus wishes him to
think.

5 *Obodas' still*] The power that I have over King
Obodas shall be yours, making you the oracle that I
have been.

6 *honors, worthy store*] a worthy supply of honors.

7 *My ... deplore*] my whole life I would deplore having
lost my native country.

8 *shall*] that shall; can be read as either Silleus' love or
Salome's supposed gratitude that "shall not shrink."

9 *whist*] silence;   *in*] in on;   *the wolf ... talk*] keen
ears are eavesdropping (proverbial); with unconscious
irony concerning a wolfish speaker.

10 *edifice*] the Hebrew temple on Mt. Zion in Jerusalem.

11 *for me*] concerning me.

Thou wouldst like Hell eschew deservèd shame
And seek to be both chaste and chastely deemed.
Our wisest prince did say, and true he said,
"A virtuous woman crowns her husband's head."[1]

Salomé.
Did I, for this, uprear thy low estate?
Did I for this requital beg thy life
That thou hadst forfeited? Hapless fate,°   [25]
To be to such a thankless wretch the wife!
This hand of mine hath lifted up thy head,
Which many a day ago had fall'n full low
Because the sons of Baba are not dead.
To me thou dost both life and fortune owe.

Constabarus.
You have my patience often exercised.
Use makes° my choler keep within the banks.   2
Yet boast no more, but be by me advised.
A benefit, upbraided, forfeits thanks.   3
I prithee, Salomé, dismiss this mood;
Thou dost not know how ill it fits thy place.
My words were all intended for thy good,
To raise thine honor and to stop disgrace.

Salomé, [*with feigned outrage.*]
"To stop disgrace"? Take thou no care for me.
Nay, do thy worst, thy worst I set not by.
No shame of mine is like to light on thee.   4
Thy love and admonitions I defy.
Thou shalt no hour longer call me wife!
Thy jealousy procures my hate so deep
That I from thee do mean to free my life,
By a divorcing bill, before I sleep.

Constabarus.
Are Hebrew women now transformed to men?   5
Why do you not as well our battles fight
And wear our armor? Suffer this, and then
Let all the world be topsy-turvèd quite!   [50]
Let fishes graze, beasts swim°, and birds descend;
Let fire burn downwards whilst the earth aspires;
Let winter's heat and summer's cold offend;
Let thistles grow on vines and grapes on briers;
Set us to spin or sow, or at the best
Make us wood-hewers, water-bearing° wights;
For sacred service let us take no rest—
Use us as Joshua did the Gib'onites.   6

Salomé.
Hold on your talk till it be time to end.
For me, I am resolved it shall be so.
Though I be first that to this course do bend,
I shall not be the last, full well I know.

Constabarus.
Why then, be witness, Heaven, the judge of sins.
Be witness, spirits that eschew the dark.
Be witness, angels; witness, cherubins,
Whose semblance sits upon the holy ark.
Be witness, earth; be witness, Palestine;
Be witness, David's city, if my heart
Did ever merit such an act of thine
Or if the fault be mine that makes us part.
Since mildest Moses, friend unto the Lord,
Did work his wonders in the land of Ham
And slew the first-born babes without a sword
(In sign whereof we eat the holy lamb),
Till now that fourteen hundred years are past—   [75]
Since first the Law with us hath been in force,
You are the first, and will, I hope, be last,
That ever sought her husband to divorce.   7

Salomé.
I mean not to be led by precedent.
My will shall be to me in stead of law.   8

Constabarus.
I fear me much, you will too late repent
That you have ever lived so void of awe.
This is Silleus' love that makes you thus
Reverse all order. You must next be his.
But if my thoughts aright the cause discuss,
In winning you he gains no lasting bliss.
Í was Silleus and (not long ago)
Josephus then was Constabarus now.
When you became my friend, you proved his foe—
As now for him you break to me your vow°.   9

Salomé.
If once I loved you, greater is your debt.
For certain 'tis that you deserved it not—
And undeservèd love we soon forget,
And therefore that to me can be no blot.
But now, fare ill, my once-belovèd Lord—
Yet never more belov'd than now abhorred.
    [*Exit* SALOMÉ.]

---

[1] *crowns*] See Prov. 12:4.

[2] *Use... banks*] Being used to this, my temper is kept in check.

[3] *A benefit...thanks*] One cannot be thankful for a favor that brings reproach.

[4] *set not by*] count for nothing; *like*] likely.

[5] *transformed to men*] (only men could issue a divorce).

[6] *Set... wights*] Let men do women's work (sowing also suggests sewing), or worse: let men be slaves; *Joshua ... Gib'onites*] See Josh. 9-10.

[7] *Ham*] Egypt (in biblical geography, north Africa is inhabited by the descendants of Ham, grandson to Noah); *Law*] the Talmud.

[8] *My will...law*] My desires shall serve as my only law.

[9] *his*] Josephus's; *him*] Silleus.

Constabarus.
Yet Constabarus biddeth thee fare well.
Farewell, light creature. Heaven forgive thy sin!
My prophesying spirit doth foretell
Thy wavering thoughts do yet but new begin. [100]
    Yet I have better scaped than Joseph did—
But if our Herod's death had been delayed,
The valiant youths that I so long have hid
Had been by her, and I for them, betrayed.
Therefore in happy hour did Caesar give
The fatal blow to wanton Antony.
For had he lived, our Herod then should live;
But great Antonius' death made Herod die.
Had he enjoyed his breath, not I alone
Had been in danger of a deadly fall,
But Mariam had the way of peril gone,
Though by the tyrant most belov'd of all.
The sweet-faced Mariam, as free from guilt
As Heaven from spots! Yet had her lord come back,
Her purest blood had been unjustly spilt—
And Salomé it was would work her wrack.
Though all Judea yield her innocent,
She often hath been near to punishment.   1
    [*Exit* CONSTABARUS.]

Chorus.
Those minds that wholly dote upon delight
(Except they only joy in inward good),
Still hope at last to hop upon the right,
And so from sand they leap in loathsome mud
    (Fond wretches), seeking what they cannot find;2
    For no content attends a wavering mind.
If wealth they do desire, and wealth attain,   [125]
Then wondrous fain would they to honor leap.   3
If° mean degree they do in honor gain,
They would but wish a little higher step.
    Thus step to step, and wealth to wealth they add—
    Yet cannot all their plenty make them glad.
Yet oft we see that some in humble state
Are cheerful°, pleasant, happy, and content,
When those indeed that are of high estate°
With vain additions do their thoughts torment.
    Th'one would to his mind his fortune bind,
    Th'other° *to* his fortune frames his mind.
To wish variety is sign of grief—
For if you like your state as now it is,
Why should an alteration bring relief?
Nay, change would then be feared as loss of bliss.
    That man is only happy in his fate
    That is delighted in a settled state.

---

1 *her*] Mariam.

2 *fond*] foolish.

3 *wondrous fain*] incredibly eager.

Still Mariam wished she from her lord were free,
For expectation of variety.
Yet, now she sees her wishes prosperous be,
She grieves, because her lord so soon did die.
    Who can those vast imaginations feed
    Where, in a property, contempt doth breed? 4
Were Herod now perchance to live again,
She would again as much be grieved at that.   [150]
All that she may, she ever doth disdain.
Her wishes guide her to she knows not what.
    And sad must be their looks, their honor sour,
    That care for nothing being in their power.

ACT 2, SCENE 1

[*Enter*] PHERORAS and GRAPHINA.

Pheroras.
'Tis true, Graphina — the time draws nigh
Wherein the holy priest, with hallowed right,
The happy long-desirèd knot shall tie,
Pheroras and Graphina to unite.
How oft have I with lifted hands implored
This blessèd hour – till now implored in vain—
Which hath my wishèd liberty restored
And made my subject self my own again.
Thy love, fair maid, upon mine eye doth sit—
Whose nature hot doth dry the moisture all
Which were in nature, and in reason fit,
For my monarchal° brother's death to fall.   5
Had Herod lived, he would have plucked my hand
From fair Graphina's palm perforce, and tied
The same in hateful and despisèd band—
For I had had a baby to my bride.   6
Scarce can her infant tongue with easy voice
Her name distinguish to another's ear.
Yet, had he lived, his power (and not my choice)
Had made me solemnly the contract swear.
Have I not cause in such a change to joy?
What° though she be my niece, a princess born?
Near blood's without respect, high birth a toy,
Since love can teach [us] blood and kindred's scorn.
What booted it that he did raise my head   [25]
To be his realm's co-partner, kingdom's mate
Withal he kept Graphina from my bed
(More wished by me than thrice Judea's state)? 7
Oh, could not he be skillful judge in love
That doted so upon his Mariam's face?
He, for his passion, Doris did remove.

---

4 *imaginations*] longings;   *property*] that which is already possessed.

5 *Whose nature*] of Graphina's love;   *were in nature*] would arise from natural grief.

6 *had had a baby*] would have been assigned one of Herod's young daughters.

7 *What booted it*] What use was it.

I needed not a lawful wife displace,
It could not be but he had power to judge.
But he, that never grudged a kingdom's share,
This well-known happiness to me did grudge
And meant to be therein without compare—
Else had I been his equal in love's host.[1]
For though the diadem on Mariam's head
Corrupt the vulgar judgments, I will boast
Graphina's brow's as white, her cheek's as red.
    [*Beat.*]
Why speaks thou not, fair creature? Move thy tongue—
For silence is a sign of discontent.
It were to both our loves too great a wrong
If now this hour do find thee sadly bent.

Graphina.
Mistake me not, my lord. Too oft have I
Desired this time to come with wingèd feet—
To be enwrapped with grief when 'tis too nigh.
You know my wishes ever yours did meet.
If I be silent, 'tis no more but fear
That I should say too little when I speak.   [50]
But since you will my imperfections bear,
In spite of doubt I will my silence break.
Yet might amazement tie my moving tongue
But that I know before Pheroras' mind.[2]
I have admirèd your affection long,[3]
And cannot yet therein a reason find.
Your hand hath lifted me from lowest° state
To highest eminency, wondrous grace;
And me, your handmaid, have you made your mate,
Though all but you alone do count me base.
You have preserved me pure, at my request,
Though you so weak a vassal might constrain
To yield to your high will. Then last (not least°
In my respect) a princess you disdain;
Then need not all these favors study crave,
To be requited by a simple maid?[4]
And study still, you know, must silence have.
Then be my cause for silence justly weighed—
But study cannot boot, nor I requite,
Except your lowly handmaid's steadfast love
And fast obedience may your mind delight.[5]
I will not promise more than I can prove.

Pheroras.
That study needs not lett Graphina smile,[6]
And I desire no greater recompense.

I cannot vaunt me in a glorious style,   [75]
Nor show my love in far-fetched eloquence.
But this, believe me: never Herod's heart
Hath held his prince-born beauty-famèd wife
In nearer place than thou, fair virgin, art
To him that holds the glory of his life.
Should Herod's body leave the sepulcher
And entertain the severed ghost again,
He should not be my nuptial hinderer
Except he hind'red it with dying pain.
Come, fair Graphina, let us go in state,
This wish-endearèd time to celebrate.
    [*Exeunt.*]

ACT 2, SCENE 2°

[*Enter*] CONSTABARUS and BABA'S SONS.

Baba's First° Son.
Now, valiant friend, you have our lives redeemed—
Which lives, as saved by you, to you are due.
Command, and you shall see yourself esteemed.
Our lives and liberties belong to you.
This twice-six years, with hazard of your life,
You have concealed us from the tyrant's sword.
Though cruel Herod's sister were your wife,
You durst, in scorn of fear, this grace afford.[7]
In recompense, we know not what to say;
A poor reward were thanks for such a merit.[8]
Our truest friendship at your feet we lay,
The best requital to a noble spirit.

Constabarus.
Oh, how you wrong our friendship, valiant youth!
With friends there is not such a word as "debt."
Where amity is tied with bond of truth,
All benefits are there in common set.
Then is the golden age with them renewed;
All names of properties are banished quite.[9]
Division and distinction are eschewed;
Each hath to what belongs to other's right.[10]
And 'tis not, sure, so full a benefit
Freely to give as freely to require.
A bounteous act hath glory following it;
They cause the glory that the act desire.
All friendship should the pattern imitate   [25]
Of Jesse's son and valiant Jonathan—[11]
For neither sovereign's nor father's hate,
A friendship fixed on virtue sever can.

---

[1] *host*] army, multitude.

[2] *But that I know before*] Except that I have already known.

[3] *admired ... long*] long wondered at your affection.

[4] *study ... maid*] require meditation how I may requite your favors.

[5] *fast*] steadfast.

[6] *lett ... smile*] prevent you from smiling.

[7] *durst*] dared.

[8] *A poor ... merit*] thanks would be insufficient.

[9] *All ... properties*] all assignments of private ownership.

[10] *Each hath to*] Each hath a right to.

[11] *Jesse's son*] David. *See* I Sam. 18-20.

Too much of this! – 'tis written in the heart
And needs° no amplifying with the tongue.
Now may you from your living tomb depart,
Where Herod's life hath kept you over-long
(Too great an injury to a noble mind,
To be quick-burièd!). You had purchased fame
Some years ago, but that you were confined
While thousand meaner did advance their name. [1]
Your best of life, the prime of all your years,
Your time of action, is from you bereft.
Twelve winters have you overpassed° in fears.
Yet, if you use it well, enough is left—
And who can doubt but you will use it well?
The sons of Baba have it by descent
In all their thoughts each action to excel,
Boldly to act, and wisely to invent.

Baba's Second° Son.
Had it not like the hateful cuckoo been,
Whose riper age his infant nurse doth kill,
So long we had not kept ourselves unseen—
But Constabarus' safety° crossed our will.
For had the tyrant fixed his cruel eye
On our concealèd faces, wrath had swayed   [50]
His justice so, that he had forced us die;
And dearer price than life we should have paid—
For you, our truest friend, had fallen with us!
And we, much like a house on pillars set,
Had clean depressed our prop, and therefore, thus,
Our ready will with our concealment met.
But now that you, fair lord, are dangerless,
The sons of Baba shall their rigor show
And prove it was not baseness did oppress
Our hearts so long, but honor kept them low.

Baba's First° Son.
Yet do I fear, this tale of Herod's death
At last will prove a very "tale" indeed.
It gives me strongly in my mind, his breath
Will be preserved to make a number bleed.
I wish not therefore to be set at large—
Yet peril to myself I do not fear°.
Let us for some days longer be your charge
Till we of Herod's state the truth do hear.

Constabarus.
What, art thou turned a coward, noble youth,
That thou beginn'st to doubt undoubted truth?

Baba's First° Son.
Were it my brother's tongue that cast this doubt,
I from his heart would have the question out
With this keen falchion; but 'tis you, my lord,
Against whose head I must not lift a sword,
I am so tied in gratitude°.   [75] [2]

Constabarus.   Believe,
You have no cause [at all] to take it ill.
If any word of mine your heart did grieve,
The word dissented from the speaker's will.
I know it was not fear the doubt begun,
But rather valor and your care of me—
A coward could not be your father's son—
Yet know I doubts unnecessary be,
For who can think that, in Antonius' fall,
Herod his bosom friend should scape unbruised?
Then, Caesar, we might thee an idiot call,
If thou by him shouldst be so far abused.

Baba's Second° Son.
Lord Constabarus, let me tell you this,
Upon submission Caesar will forgive;
And therefore, though the tyrant did amiss,
It may fall out that he will let him live.   [3]
Not many years agone it is since I
(Directed thither by my father's care)
In famous Rome for twice-twelve months did lie,°
My life from Hebrews' cruelty to spare.
There, though I were but yet of boyish age,
I bent mine eye to mark, mine ears to hear—
Where I did see Octavius, then a page,
When first he did to Julius'° sight appear,
Methought I saw such mildness in his face—
And such a sweetness in his looks did grow   [100]
Withal, commixed with so majestic grace
– His physnomy° his fortune did foreshow.   [4]
For this I am indebted to mine eye;
But then mine ear received more evidence.
By that, I knew his love to clemency,
How he with hottest choler could dispense.

Constabarus.
But we have more than barely heard the news—
It hath been twice confirmed. And though some tongue
Might be so false, with false report t'abuse,
A false report hath never lasted long.
But be it so that Herod have his life,
Concealment would not then a whit avail.
For certain 'tis, that she that was my wife
Would not, to set her accusation, fail.
And therefore now, as good, the venture give,
And free ourselves from blot of cowardice
As show a pitiful desire to live—
For who can pity, but they must despise?

Baba's First Son.
I yield, but to necessity I yield.
I dare upon this doubt engage mine arm,
That Herod shall again this kingdom wield,
And prove his death to be a false alarm.

---

[2] *falchion*] short curved sword.

[3] *he ... him*] Octavius Caesar, Herod.

[4] *physnomy*] physiognomy, face.

---

[1] *quick-buried*] buried alive;   *had purchased*] would
have acquired.

Baba's Second Son.
I doubt it, too. God grant it be an error![1]
'Tis best without a cause to be in terror.
And rather had I – though my soul be mine— [125]
~~My soul should lie than prove a true divine![2]~~

Constabarus.
Come, come, let fear go seek a dastard's nest,[3]
Undaunted courage lies in a noble breast.
    [*Exeunt.*]

ACT 2, SCENE 3

[*Enter*] DORIS *and* ANTIPATER.

Doris.
You° royal buildings, bow your lofty side
And stoop° to her that is by right your queen!
Let your humility upbraid the pride
Of those in whom no due respect is seen.
Nine times have we with trumpets' haughty sound
(And banishing sour leaven from our taste)
Observed the feast that takes the fruit from ground
Since I, fair city, did behold thee last—
So long it is since Mariam's purer cheek
Did rob from mine the glory; and so long
Since I returned, my native town to seek—
And with me nothing but the sense of wrong
And thee, my boy (whose birth, though great it were,
Yet have thy after-fortunes proved but poor).
When thou wert born, how little did I fear
Thou shouldst be thrust from forth thy father's door!
Art thou not Herod's right-begotten son?
Was not the hapless Doris, Herod's wife?
Yes, ere he had the Hebrew kingdom won,
I was companion to his private life.
Was I not fair enough to be a queen?
    [*Speaking as if to Herod.*]
Why, ere thou wert to me, false monarch, tied,
My lack° of beauty might as well be seen
As after I had lived five years thy bride.[4]
Yet then thine oaths° came pouring like the rain, [25]
Which all affirmed my face without compare,
And that, if thou might'st Doris' love obtain,
For all the world besides thou didst not care.
Then was I young and rich (and nobly born),
And therefore worthy to be Herod's mate.
Yet thou, ungrateful, cast me off with scorn
When heaven's purpose raised your meaner fate.

[*To her son Antipater.*]
Oft have I begged for vengeance for this fact,[5]
And with dejected knees, aspiring hands,
Have prayed the highest power to enact
The fall of her that on my trophy stands.
Revenge I have, according to my will—
Yet, where I wished, this vengeance did not light.
I wished it should high-hearted Mariam kill,
But it against my whilom lord did fight.[6]
With thee, sweet boy, I came, and came to try
If thou before his bastards might be placed
In Herod's royal seat and dignity.
But Mariam's infants here are only graced,[7]
And now for us there doth no hope remain.
Yet we will not return till Herod's end
Be more confirmed. Perchance he is not slain—
So glorious fortunes may my boy attend
– For, if he live, he'll think it doth suffice
That he to Doris shows° such cruelty. [50][8]
(For as he did my wretched life despise,
So do I know I shall despiséd die.)
Let him but prove as natural to thee
As cruel to thy miserable mother,
His cruelty shall not upbraided be.°
But in thy fortunes,° I his faults will smother.[9]

Antipater.
Each mouth within the city loudly cries
That Herod's death is certain. Therefore we
Had best some subtle hidden plot devise
That Mariam's children might subverted be—
By poison's drink or else by murtherous knife.
So we may be advanced, it skills not how.[10]
They are but bastards! You were Herod's wife,
And foul adultery blotteth Mariam's brow.

Doris.
They are too strong to be by us removed,
Or else revenge's foulest spotted face
By our detested wrongs might be approved;
But weakness must to greater power give place.
But let us now retire to grieve alone,
For solitariness best fitteth moan.[11]
    [*Exeunt.*]

---

[1] *doubt*] suspect, fear.

[2] *divine*] diviner, prophet.

[3] *dastard's nest*] coward's lair.

[4] *thou* (lines 23-31)] Herod.

---

[5] *fact*] crime.

[6] *whilom*] former.

[7] *Mariam's...graced*] only Mariam's children are graced.

[8] *So*] If so;   *if he*] if Herod.

[9] *Let him*] If he;   *natural*] kind;   *fortunes*] good fortune; Herod's favor.

[10] *skills*] matters.

[11] *fitteth moan*] suits grief.

ACT 2, SCENE 4

[*Enter*] SILLEUS *and* CONSTABARUS.

Silleus.
Well met, Judean lord, the only wight
Silleus wished to see! I am to call
Thy tongue to strict account.

Constabarus. For what despite
I ready am to hear and answer all.
But if directly at the cause I guess
That breeds this challenge, you must pardon me,
And now some other ground of fight profess—
For I have vowed – vows must unbroken be. 1

Silleus.
What may be your exception°? Let me know.

Constabarus.
Why, aught concerning Salomé!° My sword
Shall not be wielded for a cause so low.
A blow for her my arm will scorn t'afford.

Silleus.
It is for slandering her unspotted name!—
And I will make thee, in thy vow's despite,
Suck up the breath that did my mistress blame
And swallow it again, to do her right.

Constabarus.
I prithee, give some other quarrel ground
To find beginning. Rail against my name,
Or strike me first, or let some scarlet wound
Inflame my courage; give me words of shame;
Do thou our Moses' sacred laws disgrace;
Deprave our nation; do me some despite.
I'm apt enough to fight in any case,
But yet for Salomé I will not fight.

Silleus.
Nor I for aught *but* Salomé! My sword, [25]
That owes his service to her sacred name,
Will not an edge for other cause afford;
In other fight I am not sure of fame. 2

Constabarus.
For her, I pity thee enough already. 3
For her I therefore will not mangle thee.
A woman with a heart so most unsteady
Will of herself sufficient torture be.
I cannot envy for so light a gain. 4

Her mind with such unconstancy doth run
As with a word thou didst her love obtain;
So with a word she will from thee be won.
So light as her possessions for most day
Is her affection's loss° to me! 'Tis known, 5
As good go hold the wind as make her stay.
She never loves but till she call her own. 6
She merely is a painted sepulcher
That is both fair and vilely foul at once;
Though on her outside graces garnish her,
Her mind is fil'd with worse than rotten bones. 7
And ever ready-lifted is her hand
To aim destruction at a husband's throat.
For proofs, Josephus and myself do stand,
Though once on both of us she seemed to dote.
Her mouth, though serpent-like, it never hisses;
Yet, like a serpent, poisons where it kisses. [50]

Silleus.
Well, Hebrew, well thou bark'st, but wilt not bite.

Constabarus.
I tell thee still, for her I will not fight.

Silleus.
Why then, I call thee *coward*.

Constabarus. From my heart
I give thee thanks. A coward's hateful name
Cannot to valiant minds a blot impart,
And therefore I with joy receive the same.
Thou know'st I am no "coward." Thou wert by 8
At the Arabian battle th'other day
And saw'st my sword with daring valiancy
Amongst the faint Arabians cut my way.
The blood of foes no more could let it shine—
And 'twas enameled with some of thine.
But now, have at thee! Not for Salomé
I fight, but to discharge a coward's style.
Here 'gins the fight that shall not parted be
Before a soul or two endure exile. Ay, ay!
[*They fight.* SILLEUS *is wounded.*]

Silleus.
Thy sword hath made some windows for my blood,
To show a horrid crimson physnomy. 9
To breathe, for both of us, methinks 'twere good. 10
The day will give us time enough to die.

Constabarus.
With all my heart, take breath! Thou shalt have time,
And, if thou list, a twelve-month. Let us end.   1
Into thy cheeks there doth a paleness climb.
Thou canst not from my sword thyself defend.
What needest thou for Salomé to fight?   [75]
Thou hast her and mayst keep her. None *strives* for her.
I willingly to thee resign my right,
For in my very soul I do abhor her.
Thou see'st that I am fresh, unwounded yet.
Then not for fear I do this offer make.
Thou art, with loss of blood, to fight unfit,
For here is one and there another take.   2

Silleus.
I will not leave as long as breath remains
Within my wounded body. Spare your words!
My heart, in blood's stead, courage entertains.
Salomé's love no place for fear affords.

Constabarus.
Oh, could thy soul but prophesy like mine,
I would not wonder thou shouldst long to die—
For Salomé, if I aright divine,
Will be than death a greater misery.

Silleus.
Then list, I'll breathe no longer.   3

Constabarus.   Do thy will,
I hateless fight, and charitably kill.
     [*They fight.* SILLEUS *falls.*]
Pity thyself, Silleus! Let not death
Intrude° before his time into thy heart.
(Alas, it is too late to° fear – his breath
Is from his body now about to part.)
How far'st thou, brave Arabian?

Silleus.°   Very well—
My leg is hurt. I can no longer fight.
It only grieves me that so soon I fell,
Before fair Salom's wrongs I came to right.   [100]

Constabarus.
Thy wounds are less than mortal. Never fear,
Thou shalt a safe and quick recovery find.
Come, I will thee unto my lodging bear.
I hate thy body, but I love thy mind.

Silleus.
Thanks, noble Jew. I see a courteous foe.
Stern enmity to friendship can no art.   4
Had not my heart and tongue engaged me so,
I would from thee no foe, but friend, depart.

---

¹ *list*] desire.

² *take*] blood-letting.

³ *list*] hear;   *breathe*] rest.

⁴ *can ... art*] knows no means.

My heart to Salomé is tied too° fast
To leave her love for friendship, yet my skill
Shall be employed to make your favor last,
And I will honor Constabarus still.

Constabarus.
I ope my bosom to thee, and will take
Thee in as friend, and grieve for thy complaint;
But if we do not expedition make,
Thy loss of blood, I fear, will make thee faint.
     [*Exeunt.*]

Chorus.
To hear a tale with ears prejudicate,
It spoils the judgment and corrupts the sense.
That human error, given to every state,
Is greater enemy to innocence.   5
     It makes us foolish, heady, rash, unjust;
     It makes us never try before we trust.   6
It will confound the meaning, change the words—
For it our sense of hearing much deceives.
Besides, no time to judgment it affords,   [125]
To weigh the circumstance our ear receives.
     The ground of accidents it never tries,
     But makes us take for truth ten thousand lies. 7
Our ears and hearts are apt to hold for good
That we ourselves do most desire to be,
And then we drown objections in the flood
Of partiality. 'Tis that, we see,
     That makes false rumors long, with credit passed,
     Though they (like rumors) must conclude at last. 8
The greatest part of us, prejudicate
With wishing Herod's death, do hold it true.
The being once deluded doth not bate
The credit to a better like'hood° due.   9
     Those few that wish it not, the multitude
     Do carry headlong; so they doubts conclude.   10
They not object the weak uncertain ground
Whereon they built this tale of Herod's end—
Whereof the author scarcely can be found—
And all because their wishes that way bend.   11
     They think not of the peril that ensu'th,
     If this should prove the contrary to truth.

---

⁵ *state*] estate, condition;   *error ... innocence*] the
guileless more often misconstrue than do cunning auditors.

⁶ *never ... trust*] to believe without seeking verification.

⁷ *ground of accidents*] basis of apparent phenomena.

⁸ *for good*] as true;   *That*] that which;   *with credit*]
1. with belief; 2. as currency.

⁹ *The being ... due*] having been deceived does not
abate one's belief in another, more attractive possibility.

¹⁰ *they*] those few who had doubted.

¹¹ *not object*] do not object to.

On this same doubt, on this so light a breath,
They pawn their lives and fortunes. For they all
Behave them as the news of Herod's death
They did of most undoubted credit call—   [150]
    But if their actions now do rightly hit,
    Let them commend their fortune, not their wit.[1]

ACT 3, SCENE 1

[*Enter*] PHERORAS, SALOMÉ.

Pheroras.
Urge me no more Graphina to forsake
Not twelve hours since I married her for love—
And do you think a sister's power can make°
A resolute decree so soon remove?

Salomé.
Poor minds they are, that honor not affects.°   2

Pheroras.
Who hunts for honor, happiness neglects.

Salomé.
You might have been both of felicity
And honor too in equal measure seized.

Pheroras.
It is not you can tell so well as I
What 'tis can make me happy or displeased.

Salomé.
To match for neither beauty nor respects!—   3
One mean of birth (but yet of meaner mind),
A woman full of natural defects—
I wonder what your eye in her could find.

Pheroras.
Mine eye found loveliness, mine ear found wit,
To please the one and to enchant the other.
Grace on her eye, mirth on her tongue doth sit,
In looks a child, in wisdom's house a mother.

Salomé.
But say you thought her fair (as none thinks else)—
Knows not Pheroras, beauty is a blast?—   4
Much like this flower which today excels,
But longer than a day it will not last.

Pheroras.
Her wit exceeds her beauty.°   5

Salomé.   Wit may show
The way to ill as well as good, you know.

Pheroras.
But wisdom is the porter of her head   [25]
And bars all wicked words from issuing thence.

Salomé.
But of a "porter" better were you sped
If she *against their entrance* made defense!   6

    [*Enter* ANANELL.]

Pheroras.
But wherefore comes the sacred Ananell,
That hitherward his hasty steps doth bend?
Great sacrificer, y'are arrivèd well.
Ill news from holy mouth I not attend.   7

ACT 3, SCENE 2

PHERORAS, SALOMÉ, ANANELL.

Ananell.
My lips, my son, with peaceful tidings bless'd,
Shall utter honey to your list'ning ear.
A word of death comes not from priestly breast.
I speak of life! In life there is no fear.
And for the news, I did the heavens salute
And filled the temple with my thankful voice—
For though that mourning may not me pollute,
At pleasing accidents I may rejoice.   8

Pheroras.
Is Herod then revived from certain death?

Salomé.
What? Can your news restore my brother's breath?

Ananell.
Both so, and so! The king is safe and sound,
And did such grace in royal Caesar meet
That he (with larger style than ever crowned)
Within this hour Jerusalem will greet.
I did but come to tell you, and must back
To make preparatives for sacrifice.
I knew his death your hearts, like mine, did rack—
Though to conceal it provèd° you wise.   9
    [*Exit* ANANELL.]

Salomé.
How can my joy sufficiently appear?

Pheroras.
A heavier tale did never pierce mine ear.

---

[1] *them*] themselves;   *as*] as if.

[2] *Poor ... affects*] 1. a poor mind is not influenced by
honor; 2. honor has no sympathy for a poor mind.

[3] *respects*] material considerations.

[4] *blast*] blossom.

[5] *wit*] intelligence.

[6] *better ... sped*] better off.

[7] *not attend*] do not anticipate.

[8] *though that*] even though.

[9] *conceal*] pronounce as three syllables.

Salomé.
Now Salomé of happiness may boast.

Pheroras.
But now Pheroras is in danger most.

Salomé.
I shall enjoy the comfort of my life.

Pheroras.
And I shall lose it, losing of my wife.

Salomé.
Joy, heart! for Constabarus° shall be slain.   [25]

Pheroras.
Grieve, soul, Graphina shall from me be ta'en.

Salomé.
Smile, cheeks, the fair Silleus shall be mine.

Pheroras.
Weep, eyes, for I must with a child combine.   1

Salomé.
Well, brother, cease your moans. On one condition,
I'll undertake to win the king's consent
Graphina still shall be in your tuition,
And her with you be° ne'er the less content.   2

Pheroras.
What's the condition? Let me quickly know,
That I as quickly your command may act,
Were it to see what herbs in Ophir grow
Or that the lofty Tyrus might be sacked!   3

Salomé.
'Tis not° so hard a task. It is no more
But tell the king that Constabarus° hid
The sons of Baba, doomed° to death before.
And 'tis no more than Constabarus° did.
And tell him more that I°, for Herod's sake,
Not able to endure his° brother's foe,
Did with a bill our separation make,
Though loath from Constabarus° else to go.   4

Pheroras.
Believe this tale for told! I'll go from hence,
In Herod's ear the Hebrew to deface.
And I, that never studied eloquence,
Do mean with eloquence this tale to grace.
        Exit [PHERORAS].

---

1 *combine*] be married (to Herod's daughter).

2 *consent*] consent that;   *in your tuition*] under your supervision, protection.

3 *Ophir*] a Biblical region rich in gold;   *Tyrus*] Tyre.

4 *his brother's foe*] Constabarus as Herod's foe (reflexive).

Salomé.
This will be Constabarus' quick dispatch
(Which from my mouth would lesser credit find). [50]
Yet shall he not decease without a match,
For Mariam shall not linger long behind.
First, jealousy – if that avail not, fear –
Shall be my minister to work her end.
A common error moves not Herod's ear,
Which doth so firmly to his Mariam bend.   5
She shall be chargèd with so horrid crime
As Herod's fear shall turn his love to hate:
I'll make some swear that she desires to climb
And seeks to poison him for his estate.
I scorn that she should live my birth t'upbraid,
To call me base and hungry Edomite.
With patient show her choler I betrayed—
And watched the time to be revenged, by sleight°.   6
Now tongue of mine with scandal load her name!
Turn hers to fountains, Herod's eyes to flame!
Yet first I will begin Pheroras' suit,
That he my earnest business may effect.
And I of Mariam will keep me mute,
Till first some other doth her name detect.   7
Who's there?
        [*Enter* SILLEUS' MAN.]
        Silleus' man? How fares your lord,
That your aspects do bear the badge of sorrow?   8

Silleus' man.
He hath the marks of Constabarus' sword,
And for a while desires your sight to borrow.

Salomé.
My heavy curse the hateful sword pursue!   [75]
My heavier curse on the more hateful arm
That wounded my Silleus! But renew
Your tale again. Hath he no mortal harm?

Silleus' man.
No sign of danger doth in him appear,
Nor are his wounds in place of peril seen.
He bids you be assured you need not fear.
He hopes to make you yet Arabia's queen.

Salomé.
Commend my heart to be Silleus' charge.
Tell him my brother's sudden coming now
Will give my foot no room to walk at large.
(But I will see him yet ere night, I vow.)
        [*Exeunt.*]

---

5 *common ... not*] a trivial fault angers not.

6 *With ... betrayed*] deceived her anger with my show of patience;   *sleight*] stratagem.

7 *detect*] accuse.

8 *aspects*] (accent on 2d syll.) facial features.

ACT 3, SCENE 3

[*Enter*] MARIAM *and* SOHEMUS.

Mariam.
Sohemus, tell me what the news may be
That makes your eyes so full, your cheeks so blue!

Sohemus.
I know not how to call them. Ill for me
'Tis sure they are; not so, I hope, for you.   1
Herod—

Mariam.   Oh, what of Herod?

Sohemus.   Herod lives.

Mariam.°
How! Lives? What, in some cave or forest hid?

Sohemus.
Nay, back returned with honor. Caesar gives
Him greater grace than e'er Antonius did.

Mariam.
Foretell the ruin of my family,
Tell me that I shall see our city burned,
Tell me I shall a death disgraceful die—
But tell me not that Herod is returned!

Sohemus.
Be not impatient, Madam. Be but mild,
His love to you again will soon be bred.

Mariam.
I will not to his love be reconciled!
With solemn vows I have forsworn his bed.

Sohemus.
But you must break those vows.

Mariam.   I'll rather break
The heart of Mariam. Cursèd is my fate!
But speak no more to me. In vain ye speak—°
To live with him I so profoundly hate!

Sohemus.
Great queen, you must to me your pardon give.
Sohemus cannot now your will obey.
If your command should me to silence drive,
It were not to obey, but to betray.
Reject, and slight my speeches, mock my faith,   [25]
Scorn my observance, call my counsel nought—   2
Though you regard not what Sohemus sayeth,
Yet will I ever freely speak my thought.
I fear ere long I shall fair Mariam see
In woeful state, and by herself undone.
Yet, for your issue's sake, more temp'rate be.
The heart by affability is won.

---

1 *them*] the news, or tidings.

2 *nought*] nothing, worthless.

Mariam.
And must I to my prison turn again?
Oh, now I see I was an hypocrite!
I did this morning for his death complain—
And yet do mourn, because he lives, ere night.
When I his death believed, compassion wrought
And was the stickler 'twixt my heart and him.   3
But now that curtain's drawn from off my thought,
Hate doth appear again with visage grim
And paints the face of Herod in my heart
In horrid colors, with detested look.   4
Then fear would come, but scorn doth play her part
And sayeth that scorn with fear can never brook.
I know I could enchain him with a smile
And lead him captive with a gentle word;
I scorn my look should ever man beguile,
Or other speech than *meaning* to afford—   5

Else Salomé in vain might spend her wind;
In vain might Herod's mother whet her tongue; [50]
In vain had they complotted and combined
(For I could overthrow them all, ere long).
    Oh, what a shelter is mine innocence,
To shield me from the pangs of inward grief!
'Gainst all mishaps it is my fair defense,
And to my sorrows yields a large relief.
To be commandress of the triple earth
And sit in safety from a fall secure,
To have all nations celebrate my birth,
I would not that my spirit were impure!
Let my distressèd state unpitied be.
Mine innocence is hope enough for me.
    Exit [MARIAM].

Sohemus.
Poor guiltless queen! Oh, that my wish might place
A little temper now about thy heart!
Unbridled speech is Mariam's worst disgrace,
And will endanger her without desert.   6
I am in greater hazard. O'er my head
The fatal axe doth hang unsteadily.
My disobedience, once discoverèd,
Will shake it down. Sohemus so shall die.
For when the king shall find we thought his death
Had been as certain as we see his life,
And marks withal I slighted so his breath
As to preserve alive his matchless wife—   7
Nay, more, to give to Alexandra's° hand   [75]
The regal dignity, the sovereign power

---

3 *stickler*] referee.

4 *now that curtain's*] now that that curtain is.

5 *meaning*] honest meaning.

6 *temper*] temperance, self-control;   *without desert*]
without her having deserved it.

7 *marks withal*] further observes that;   *breath*] words.

(How I had yielded up, at her command,
The strength of all the city, David's tower),
What more than common death may I expect?—
Since I too well do know his cruelty.
'Twere death, a word of Herod's to neglect
– What then to do directly contrary?
Yet, life, I quit thee with a willing spirit
And think thou couldst not better be employed.
I forfeit thee for her that more doth merit.
Ten such were better dead than she destroyed.   1
But fare thee well, chaste queen. Well may I see
The darkness palpable, and rivers part,
The Sun stand still – nay more, retorted be—
But never woman with so pure a heart!   2
Thine eyes' grave majesty keeps all in awe
And cuts the wings of every loose desire.
Thy brow is table to the modest law,
"Yet, though we dare not love, we may admire." 3
And if I die, it shall my soul content,
My breath in Mariam's service shall be spent.
        [*Exit* SOHEMUS.]

Chorus.
'Tis not enough for one that is a wife
To keep her spotless from an act of ill,
But from suspicion she should free her life
And bare her self of power as well as will. [100] 4
        'Tis not so glorious for her to be free,
        As by her proper self restrained to be.
When she hath spacious ground to walk upon,
Why on the ridge should she desire to go?
It is no glory to forbear alone
Those things that may her honor overthrow.   5
        But 'tis thankworthy if she will not take
        All lawful liberties (for honor's sake).
That wife her hand against her fame doth rear,
That (more than to her lord alone) will give
A private word to any second ear—
And though she may with reputation live,
        Yet though most chaste, she doth her glory blot
        And wounds her honor, though she kills it not.
When to their husbands they themselves do bind,
Do they not wholly give themselves away?
Or give they but their body, not their mind,
Reserving that (though best) for others, pray?
        No, sure, their thoughts no more can be their own,
        And therefore should to none but one be known. 6

Then she usurps upon another's right
That seeks to be by public language graced;
And (though her thoughts reflect with purest light)
        For in a wife it is no worse to find   [125]
        A common body than a common mind.   7
And every mind (though free from thought of ill)
That out of glory seeks a worth to show,
When any's ears but one therewith they fill,
Doth (in a sort) her pureness overthrow.   8
        Now Mariam had, but that to this she bent,
        Been free from fear, as well as innocent.   9

ACT 4, SCENE 1

Enter HEROD *and his attendants.*   10

Herod.
Hail, happy city! Happy in thy store
And happy that thy buildings such we see;
More happy in the temple where w'adore—
But most of all that Mariam lives in thee.   11
        Enter NUNTIO.
Art thou returned? How fares my Mariam, how°?

Nuntio.°
She's well, my Lord, and will anon be here
As you commanded.
        [*Exit* NUNTIO.]

Herod [*to the Sun*].   Muffle up thy brow,
Thou day's dark taper. Mariam will appear,
And where she shines we need not thy dim light.12
        [*Speaking as if to Mariam.*]
Oh, haste thy steps, rare creature! Speed thy pace,
And let thy presence make the day more bright,
And cheer the heart of Herod with thy face.
It is an *age* since I from Mariam went.
Methinks our parting was in *David's* days,
The hours are so increased by discontent!
Deep sorrow, Joshua-like, the season stays—
But when I am with Mariam, time runs on.   13

---

1 *Ten such*] Ten such as myself.

2 *retorted*] reversed in its course.

3 *table*] writing tablet.

4 *keep her*] keep herself; *bare*] 1. divest; 2. bar.

5 *alone*] only.

6 *pray?*] think you? (*with a pun on others' prey*; Q others pray);   *their thoughts*] the thoughts of married
women; *none but one*] the husband.

7 *That seeks*] who seeks; *peculiar*] private.

8 *When ... overthrow*] When a woman, with a spoken
show of her own worth, addresses but her own lord, she
overthrows her purity. (As in classical drama, the chorus here utters conventional wisdom.)

9 *but that to this she bent*] except that she was inclined
to this error of sharing her thoughts with others.

10 *Enter Herod and his attendants.* Perhaps a procession
is intended in which only Herod remains on stage. Lines
7-40 appear to be spoken solus.

11 *store*] bounty; *w'adore*] we worship.

12 *taper*] candle (*i.e.*, the sun), its light being dim when
compared to Mariam's radiance.

13 *Deep ... stay*] *i.e.*, sorrow, like Joshua, stops time.
See Josh. 10:12-27.

Her sight can make months minutes, days of weeks;
An hour is then no sooner come than gone,
When in her face mine eye for wonders seeks.

    You world-commanding city, Europe's grace,
Twice hath my curious eye your streets surveyed,
And I have seen the statue-fillèd place
That once, if not for geese°, had been betrayed. [25] [1]
I all your Roman beauties have beheld
And seen the shows your ædiles did prepare;
I saw the sum of what in you excelled,
Yet saw no miracle like Mariam rare. [2]

    The fair and famous Livia, Caesar's love,
The world's commanding mistress, did I see—
Whose beauties both the world and Rome approve.
Yet, Mariam, Livia is not like to thee.
Be patient but a little while,° mine eyes—
Within your compassed limits be contained.
That object straight shall your desires suffice
From which you were so long a while restrained.
[*Beat.*] How wisely Mariam doth the time delay,
Lest sudden joy my sense should suffocate!
[*Beat.*] I am prepared – thou need'st no longer stay.
Who's° there, my Mariam? More than happy fate!

    [*Enter* PHERORAS.]
(Oh no, it is Pheroras.) Welcome, brother!
(Now for a while, I must my passion smother.)

ACT 4, SCENE 2

HEROD, PHERORAS.

Pheroras.

All health and safety wait upon my lord!—
And may you long in prosperous fortunes live
With Rome-commanding Caesar at accord,
And have all honors that the world can give.

Herod.

Oh brother, now thou speak'st not from thy heart.
No, thou hast struck a blow at Herod's love
That cannot quickly from my memory part,
Though Salomé did me to pardon move. [3]
    [*As if to Phasaelus.*]
Valiant Phasaelus, now to thee, farewell: [4]
Thou wert my kind and honorable brother.
Oh, hapless hour, when you self-stricken fell!

Thou father's image, glory of thy mother,
Had I desired a greater suit of thee
Than to withhold thee from a harlot's bed,
Thou wouldst have granted it; but now I see
All are not like, that in a womb are bred. [5]
    [*To Pheroras.*]
Thou wouldst not, hadst thou heard of Herod's death,
Have made his burial time thy bridal hour.
Thou wouldst with clamors, not with joyful breath,
Have showed the news to be not sweet, but sour.

Pheroras.

Phasaelus' great worth, I know, did stain
Pheroras' petty valor – but they lie
(Excepting you yourself) that dare maintain
That he did honor Herod more than I:
For what I showed, love's power constrained me show–
And pardon loving faults, for Mariam's sake. [6]

Herod.

Mariam! Where is she?

Pheroras.   Nay, I do not know,
But absent use of her fair name I make.
You have forgiven greater faults than this—
For Constabarus, that against your° will
Preserved the sons of Baba, lives in bliss,
Though you commanded him the youths to kill.

Herod.

Go! Take a present order for his death,
And let those traitors feel the worst of fears.
Now Salomé will whine to beg his breath,
But I'll be deaf to prayers and blind to tears.

Pheroras.

He is, my lord, from Salomé divorced,
Though her affection did, to leave him, grieve;
Yet was she, by her love to you, enforced
To leave the man that would your foes relieve.

Herod.

Then haste them to their death.
    Exit [PHERORAS.]
                I will requite
Thee, gentle Mariam – Salomé, I mean!
(The thought of Mariam doth so steal my sprite,°
My mouth from speech of her I cannot wean.) [7]

---

[1] *city*] Rome;   *geese*] referring to the legend that Juno's sacred geese once saved Rome by squawking when the Gallic invaders approached (Livy, *The Early History of Rome*, 5.47).

[2] *ædiles*] superintendents of public buildings.

[3] *move*] pardon.

[4] *Phasaelus*] Herod's brother who, as a prisoner of the Parthians, slew himself rather than allow himself to be slain by his enemies. Herod here addresses the spirit of Phasaelus in order to shame Pheroras.

[5] *like*] alike.

[6] *loving faults*] offenses motivated by love.

[7] *sprite*] spirit.

ACT 4, SCENE 3

HEROD [*and enter*] MARIAM.

Herod.
And here she comes indeed! Happily met,
My best and dearest half! What ails my dear?
Thou dost the difference certainly forget
'Twixt dusky habits and a time so clear.   1

Mariam.
My lord, I suit my garment to my mind,
And there no cheerful colors can I find.

Herod.
Is this my welcome? Have I longed so much
To see my dearest Mariam discontent?
What is't that is the cause thy heart to touch?
Oh speak, that I thy sorrow may prevent!
Art thou not Jewry's queen, and Herod's too?
Be my commandress! Be my sovereign guide.
To be by thee directed I will woo,
For in thy pleasure lies my highest pride.
Or if thou think Judea's narrow bound
Too strict a limit for thy great command,
Thou shalt be empress of Arabia crowned,
For thou shalt rule, and I will win the land.
I'll rob the holy David's sepulcher
To give thee wealth, if thou for wealth do care.
Thou shalt have all they did with him inter,
And I for thee will make the temple bare.

Mariam.
I neither have of power nor riches want.   2
I have enough, nor do I wish for more.
Your offers to my heart no ease can grant   [25]
Except they could my brother's life restore.
No, had you wished the wretched Mariam glad,
Or had your love to her been truly tied,
Nay, had you not desired to make her sad,
My brother nor my grandsire had not died.

Herod.
Wilt thou believe no oaths to clear thy lord?
How oft have I with execration sworn
Thou art by me belov'd, by me adored—
Yet are my protestations heard with scorn.
Hyrcanus plotted to deprive my head
Of this long-settled honor that I wear;
And therefore I did justly doom him dead—
To rid the realm from peril, me from fear.
Yet I for Mariam's sake do so repent
The death of one whose blood she did inherit,
I wish I had a kingdom's treasure spent,
So I had mere expelled Hyrcanus' spirit.   3

[Let heaven but show compassion on my soul]
As I affected that same noble youth.   4
In lasting infamy my name enroll
If I not mourned his death with hearty truth.
Did I not show to him my earnest love
When I to him the priesthood did restore,
And did for him a living priest remove,
Which never had been done but once before?   [50]

Mariam.
I know that, moved by importunity,
You made him priest, and shortly after – die!   5

Herod.
I will not speak, unless to be believed.   6
This froward humor will not do you good.
It hath too much already Herod grieved
To think that you on terms of hate have stood.
Yet smile, my dearest Mariam, do but smile,
And I will all unkind conceits exile.

Mariam.
I cannot frame disguise, nor ever taught
My face a look dissenting from my thought.

Herod.
By heaven, you vex me! Build not on my love.   7

Mariam.
I will not build on so unstable ground.

Herod.
Nought is so fixed but peevishness may move.   8

Mariam.
'Tis better slightest cause than none were found.   9

Herod.
Be judge yourself if ever Herod sought,
Or would be moved, a cause of change to find.
Yet, let your look declare a milder thought,
My heart again you shall to Mariam bind.   10
How oft did I for you my mother chide,
Revile my sister, and my brother rate,
And tell them all my Mariam they belied?   11
Distrust me still if these be signs of hate!

---

1 *difference*] incongruity; *dusky habits*] dark clothing;
clear] clear of troubles, unclouded.

2 *I … want*] i.e., I have no lack of power or riches.

3 *I wish … spirit*] i.e., I wish that I had merely exiled
him, at any cost.

4 *affected*] felt affection for;   *youth*] Aristobolus,
grandson to Hyrcanus and brother to Mariam.

5 *die*] to die.

6 *froward humor*] unruly disposition.

7 *Build*] Presume.

8 *move*] 1. shake; 2. enrage.

9 *'Tis…found*] Better to be angry with slight provocation than for no reason at all (as is your custom).

10 *let*] if.

11 *rate*] berate.

ACT 4, SCENE 4

[HEROD, MARIAM, *and enter* BUTLER.]

Herod.
What hast thou here?

Butler.   A drink procuring love.
The queen desired me to deliver it.

Mariam.
Did I! Some hateful practice this will prove—
Yet can it be no worse than heavens permit.   1

Herod. [*To Butler.*]
Confess the truth, thou wicked instrument
To her outrageous will! 'Tis poison°, sure.
Tell true, and thou shalt 'scape the punishment
Which if thou do conceal thou shalt endure.

Butler.
I know not, but I doubt it be no less—
Long since the hate of you her heart did seize.°

Herod.
Know'st thou the cause thereof?

Butler.   My lord, I guess
Sohemus told the tale that did displease.

Herod.
Oh, heaven! Sohemus false? Go, let him die!
Stay not to suffer him to speak a word.
      [*Exit* BUTLER.]
Oh, damnèd villain! Did he falsify
The oath he swore, even of his own accord?
      [*To Mariam.*]
Now do I know thy falsehood, painted devil!
Thou white enchantress, oh, thou art so foul
That hyssop cannot cleanse thee! Worst of evil!   2
A beauteous body hides a loathsome soul.
Your love, Sohemus – moved by his affection,
Though he have ever heretofore been true—
Did blab forsooth that I did give direction,
If we were put to death, to slaughter you.   3
And you in black revenge attended now   [25]
To add a murther to your breach of vow.   4

Mariam.
Is this a dream?

Herod.   Oh, heaven, that 'twere no more!
I'll give my realm to who can prove it so.
I° would I were like any beggar poor,

So I for false my Mariam did not know.
Foul pith, contained in the fairest rind
That ever graced a cedar! Oh, thine eye
Is pure as heaven, but impure thy mind!—
And for impurity shall Mariam die.
Why didst thou love Sohemus?

Mariam.   They can tell
That say I loved him. Mariam says not so.

Herod [*raving*].
Oh, cannot *impudence* the coals expel
That, for thy love, in Herod's bosom glow?
It is as plain as water! —and denial
Makes of thy falsehood but a greater trial.
Hast thou beheld thyself, and couldst thou stain
So rare perfection? Even for love of thee
I do profoundly hate thee. Wert thou plain,
Thou shouldst the wonder of Judea be.   5
But oh, thou art not! Hell itself lies hid
Beneath thy heavenly show. [Yet, wert] thou chaste,
Thou mightst exalt, pull down, command, forbid,
And be above the wheel of Fortune placed.   6
Hadst thou complotted Herod's massacre
That so thy son a monarch might be styled,   [50]
Not half so grievous such an action were
As once to think that Mariam is defiled.
Bright workmanship of nature sullied o'er,
With pitchèd darkness now thine end shall be.   7
Thou shalt not live, fair fiend, to cozen more
With heavenly° semblance, as thou coz'nedst me.8
      Yet must I love thee in despite of death,
And thou shalt die in the despite of love.
For neither shall my love prolong thy breath,
Nor shall thy loss of breath my love remove.
I might have seen thy falsehood in thy face!
Where couldst thou get thy stars that served for eyes
Except by theft? – and theft is foul disgrace.
This had appeared before, were Herod wise,
But I'm a sot, a very sot, no better.
My wisdom long ago a-wand'ring fell.
Thy face, encount'ring it, my wit did fetter
And made me, for delight, my freedom sell.
Give me my heart, false creature! 'Tis a wrong
My guiltless° heart should now with thine be slain.
Thou hadst no right to lock° it up so long—
And with usurper's name I Mariam stain.
      Enter BUTLER.
Have you designed Sohemus to his end?   9

---

1 *practice*] scheme, plot.

2 *hyssop*] used for Hebraic rites of purification.

3 *we*] the royal plural.

4 *attended*] watched; intended.

5 *plain*] honest.

6 *above*] immune to the turning of fortune's wheel.

7 *pitched*] pitch-black.

8 *to cozen*] to deceive;   *thou coz'nedst me*] you cozened (cheated) me.

9 *designed*] dispatched.

Butler.
I have, my lord.

Herod.   Then call our royal guard
To do as much for Mariam—   [75]
    [*Exit* BUTLER.]
                    —They offend,   1
Leave ill unblamed, or good without reward!
    [*Enter* SOLDIERS.]
Here, take her to her death.
    [SOLDIER *seizes* MARIAM. *Exit.*]
Come back, come back!
    [*Re-enter* SOLDIER *with* MARIAM.]
What meant I to deprive the world of light?
To muffle Jewry in the foulest black,
That ever was an opposite to white!
Why, wither would you carry her?°

Soldier.   You bade
We should conduct her to her death, my lord.

Herod.
Why, sure I did not! Herod was not mad!
Why should she feel the fury of the sword?
Oh, now the grief returns into my heart,
And pulls me piecemeal. Love and hate do fight,
And now hath love° acquired the greater part—
    [*Beat.*]
Yet now hath hate affection conquered quite,
And therefore, bear her hence!
    [SOLDIER *again seizes* MARIAM.]
                    And Hebrew, why
Seize you with lion's paws the fairest lamb
Of all the flock? She must not, shall not, die.
Without her I most miserable am— [*Beat.*]
And with her, more than most! Away, away—
But bear her but to prison, not to death.
    [*Exit* MARIAM *and* SOLDIERS.]
And is she gone indeed? Stay, villains, stay!
Her looks alone preserved your sovereign's breath!
Well, let her go, but yet she shall not die.
I cannot think she meant to poison me—
But certain 'tis she lived too wantonly,
And therefore shall she never more be free.   [100]
    [*Exit* HEROD.]

ACT 4, SCENE 5
BUTLER.

Butler.
Foul villain, can thy pitchy-colored soul
Permit thine ear to hear her causeless° doom
And not enforce thy tongue that tale control
That must unjustly bring her to her tomb?
Oh, Salomé, thou hast thyself repaid

---

¹ *offend*] offend who.

For all the benefits that thou hast done!
Thou art the cause I have the queen betrayed.
Thou hast my heart to darkest falsehood won.
I am condemned! Heaven gave me not my tongue
To slander innocents, to lie, deceive,
To be the hateful instrument to wrong,
The earth of greatest glory to bereave.
My sin ascends and doth to heaven cry.
It is the blackest deed that ever was—
And there doth sit an angel notary
That doth record it down in leaves of brass.
Oh, how my heart doth quake! Achitophel,
Thou founds' a means thyself from shame to free,
And sure my soul approves. Thou didst not well–   2
All follow some, and I will follow thee.
    [*Exit.*]

ACT 4, SCENE 6

[*Enter*] CONSTABARUS, BABA'S SONS,
and their GUARD.

Constabarus.
Now here we step our last, the way to death.
We must not tread this way a second time—
Yet let us resolutely yield our breath.
Death is the only ladder, heaven to climb.

Baba's First °Son.
With willing mind I could my self resign,
But yet it grieves me, with a grief untold,
Our death should be accompanied with thine.
Our friendship we to thee have dearly sold.   3

Constabarus.
Still wilt thou wrong the sacred name of *Friend*?
Then shouldst thou never style it "friendship" more,
But "base mechanic traffic," that doth lend
Yet will be sure they shall the debt restore.
I could with needless compliment return
Thus° for thy ceremony: I could say,
"'Tis I that made the fire your house to burn,
For, but for me, she would not you betray.   4
Had not the damnèd woman sought mine end,
You had not been the subject of her hate.
You never did her hateful mind offend,
Nor could your deaths have freed our° nuptial fate.   5

---

² *Achitophel*] See 2 Sam. 15-17;   *founds'*] foundest;
a means] Achitophel hanged himself; 2 Sam. 17:23;
Thou ... thee] You, like me, were a malefactor ("didst
not well"); I, like you, will therefore hang myself.

³ *Our ... sold*] Our friendship has been costly to you.

⁴ *base mechanic traffic*] a vulgar, practical exchange of
commodities;   *they*] the borrowers;   *compliment*]
also *complement*, or outward show (as in *MFQ* 1613);
she] Salome.

⁵ *our nuptial fate*] my fated marriage with Salome.

Therefore, fair friends, though you were still unborn,
Some other subtlety devised should be
Whereby° my life, though guiltless, should be torn."
Thus have I proved, 'tis *you* that die for *me*.
And therefore should I weakly now lament?°   [25]
You have but done your duties! Friends should die
Alone their friend's disaster to prevent,
Though not compelled by strong necessity.

    But now, farewell, fair city, never more
Shall I behold your beauty shining bright.
Farewell, of Jewish men the worthy store—
But no farewell to any female wight!
You wavering crew, my curse to you I leave!   1
You had but one to give you any grace,
And you yourselves will Mariam's life bereave.
Your commonwealth doth innocency chase.   2
You creatures made to be the human curse!
You tigers, lionesses, hungry bears,
Tear-massacríng hyenas! Nay, far worse,
For they for prey do shed their feignèd tears,
But you will weep (you creatures cross to good)
For your unquenchèd thirst of human blood.   3
You were the angels cast from Heaven for pride,
And still do keep your angel's outward show,
But none of you are inly beautified—
For still your heaven-depriving pride doth grow.
Did not the sins of man° require a scourge,
Your place on earth had been by this withstood;
But since a flood no more the world must purge,
You stayed in office of a second flood.   [50] 4
You giddy creatures, sowers of debate!
You'll love today, and for no other cause
But for you yesterday did deeply hate!   5
You are the wreck of order, breach of laws.
Your° best are foolish, froward, wanton, vain;
Your worst, adulterous, murderous, cunning, proud–
And Salomé attends the latter train;
Or rather, she° their leader is allowed.
I do the sottishness of men bewail,
That do with following you enhance your pride.
'Twere better that the human race should fail
Than be by such a mischief multiplied.
Cham's servile curse to all your sex was given

Because in paradise you did offend.   6
Then do we not resist the will of Heaven
When on your wills like servants we attend?
You are to nothing constant but to ill;
You are with nought but wickedness endued;   7
Your loves are set on nothing but your will.
And thus my censure I of you conclude:
You are the least of goods, the worst of evils.
Your best are worse than men; your worst, than devils.

Baba's Second Son.
Come, let us to our death. Are we not blest?
Our death will freedom from these creatures give,
Those trouble-quiet sowers of unrest.   [75] 8
And this I vow – that, had I leave to live,
I would for ever lead a single life
And never venter on a devilish wife.   9
    [*Exeunt.*]

ACT 4, SCENE 7
[*Enter*] HEROD *and* SALOMÉ.

Herod.
Nay, she shall die. "Die," quoth you? That she shall!
But for the means – the means! Methinks 'tis hard
To find a means to murther her withal. [*Beat.*]
Therefore I am resolved she shall be spared.

Salomé.
Why, let her be beheaded!

Herod. That were well!
Think you that swords are miracles, like you?
Her skin will every curtl'axe edge refel,   10
And then your enterprise you well may rue.
What if the fierce Arabian notice take
Of this your wretched weaponless estate?   11
They answer, when we bid resistance make,
That Mariam's skin their falchions° did rebate.   12
Beware of this, you make a goodly hand
If you of weapons do deprive our land.

Salomé.
Why, drown her then!

---

1 *Farewell ... store*] *i.e.,* Farewell, you who are the treasure of Jewry; *crew*] women.

2 *Your ... chase*] The commonwealth of females drives away innocence.

3 *Tear-massacring*] the hyena was said to weep as it killed its prey; *cross*] contrary.

4 *Did not*] Were it not that; *by this withstood*] by this time successfully opposed; *flood ... purge*] *See* Gen. 9:12-17; *You ... flood*] *i.e.,* as God's scourge against mankind.

5 *But for*] than that.

6 *Cham's* [Ham's] *curse*] *See* Gen. 3:15-16, 9:28-29; Constabarus here offers a spurious biblical commentary, linking unrelated curses.

7 *endued*] endowed.

8 *trouble-quiet*] peace-wrecking.

9 *venter*] venture.

10 *like you?*] So please you? (*idiomatic*); *curtl' axe*] curtal axe, or cutlass; *refel*] repulse, repel.

11 *Arabian*] Arabian army.

12 *They*] Our own soldiers; *rebate*] to make dull or to repulse.

Herod.   Indeed, a sweet device!
Why, would not every river turn her course
Rather than do her beauty prejudice,   1
And be reverted to the proper source?—
So not a drop of water should be found
In all Judea's quondam fertile ground.   2

Salomé.
Then let the fire devour her.

Herod. 'Twill not be!
Flame is from her derived into my heart.
Thou nursest flame! Flame will not murther thee,
My fairest Mariam, fullest of desert.

Salomé.
Then let her live, for me.   3

Herod. [*Beat.*] Nay, she shall die.
But can you live without her?   [25]

Salomé.   Doubt you that?

Herod.
I'm sure *I* cannot! I beseech *you* try.
I have experience, but – I know not what.

Salomé.
How should I try?

Herod.   Why, let my love be slain—
But if we cannot live without her sight,
You'll find the means to make her breathe again,
Or else you will bereave my comfort quite.

Salomé.
Oh, ay, I° warrant you!   [*Exit* SALOMÉ.]

Herod.   What, is she gone?—
And gone to bid the world be overthrown!
What? Is her heart's composure hardest stone?
To what a pass are cruel women grown!
   [*Re-enter* SALOMÉ.]
She is returned already. Have you done?
Is't possible you can command so soon
A creature's heart to quench the flaming sun,
Or from the sky to wipe away the moon?

Salomé.
If Mariam be the sun and moon, it is—
For I already have commanded this.

Herod.
But have you seen her cheek?

Salomé.   A thousand times.

Herod. But did you mark it, too?

Salomé.   Ay,° very well.

Herod. What is't?

Salomé.   A crimson bush, that ever limes
The soul whose foresight doth not much excel.   4

Herod.
Send word she shall not die! Her cheek "a bush"!
Nay, then I see indeed you marked it not.

Salomé.
'Tis very fair – but yet will never blush,
Though foul dishonors do her forehead blot.   [50]

Herod.
Then let her die! 'Tis very true indeed,
And for this fault alone shall Mariam bleed.

Salomé.
What fault, my lord?

Herod.   What fault is't? You, that ask?
If you be ignorant, I know of none!—
To call her back from death shall be your task.
I'm *glad* that she for innocent is known.
For on the brow of Mariam hangs a fleece
Whose slend'rest twine is strong enough to bind
The hearts of kings. The pride and shame of Greece,
Troy-flaming Helen's not so fairly shined.

Salomé.
'Tis true indeed! She lays them out for nets,
To catch the hearts that do not shun a bait.
'Tis time to speak, for Herod sure forgets
That Mariam's very tresses hide deceit.   5

Herod.
Oh, do they so? Nay, then you do but well.
In sooth, I thought [indeed] it had been hair.
"Nets," call you them? Lord, how they do excel!
I never saw a net that showed so fair.
But have you heard her speak?

Salomé.   You know I have.

Herod.
And were you not amazed?

Salomé.   No, not a whit.

Hero
Then 'twas not her you heard. Her life I'll save,
For Mariam hath a world-amazing wit.

---

1 *her*] its;   *do ... prejudice*] injure.

2 *quondam*] formerly.

3 *for me*] for all I care.

4 *limes*] ensnares (birds were caught by smearing lime on branches or twigs).

5 *them*] the locks of Mariam's hair;   *tresses*] curls (but with a glance also at *tresses* as skirts).

Salomé.

She speaks a beauteous language, but within,
Her heart is false as powder; and her tongue
Doth but allure the auditors to sin,   [75]
And is the instrument to do you wrong.   1

Herod.

It may be so. Nay, 'tis so. She's unchaste.
Her mouth will ope to every stranger's ear.
Then let the executioner make haste,
Lest she enchant him if her words he hear.
Let him be deaf, lest she do him surprise
That shall to free her spirit be assigned.
Yet what boots deafness if he have his eyes?
Her murtherer must be both deaf and blind.
For if he see, he needs must see the stars
That shine on either side of Mariam's face—
Whose sweet aspect will terminate the wars
Wherewith he should a soul so precious chase.
Her eyes can speak, and in their speaking move.
Oft did my heart with reverence receive
The world's mandates. Pretty tales of love
They utter, which can human bondage weave.
But shall I let this heaven's model die
(Which for a small self-portraiture she drew)?   2
Her eyes like stars, her forehead like the sky,
She is like heaven, and must be heavenly true.

Salomé.

Your thoughts do rave with doting on the queen.
Her eyes are ebon-hued, and (you'll confess)
A sable star hath been but seldom seen.
Then speak of reason more, of Mariam less.   [100]

Herod.

Yourself are held a goodly creature here,
Yet so unlike my Mariam in your shape
That when to her you have approachèd near,
Myself hath often ta'en you for an ape.
And yet you prate of beauty. Go your ways,
You are to her a sunburnt blackamoor.   3
Your paintings cannot equal Mariam's praise,   4
Her nature is so rich, you are so poor.
Let her be stayed from death! For if she die
(We do we know-not-what to stop her breath),
A world cannot another Mariam buy. [*Beat.*]
Why stay you ling'ring? Countermand her death!

Salomé.

Then you'll no more remember what hath passed!
Sohemus' love and hers shall be forgot?
'Tis well, in truth. That fault may be her last,
And she may mend, though yet she love you not.

Herod.

Oh, God, 'tis true – Sohemus! Earth and heaven,
Why did you both conspire to make me curs'd,
In coz'ning me with shows and proofs uneven?   5
She showed the best and yet did prove the worst.
Her show was such as, had our singing king,
The holy David, Mariam's beauty seen,
The Hittite° had then felt no deadly sting,
Nor Bethsabe had never been a queen.   6
Or had his son (the wisest man of men,   [125]
Whose fond delight did most consist in change)
Beheld her face, he had been staid again.   7
No creature, having her, can wish to range.
Had Asuerus seen my Mariam's brow,
The humble Jewess° might have walked alone.   8
Her beauteous virtue should have stayed below
Whiles Mariam mounted to the Persian throne
   But what avails it all? For in the weight
She is deceitful, light as vanity.   9
Oh, she was made for nothing but a bait,
To train some hapless man to misery.   10
I am the hapless man that have been trained
To endless bondage. [*Beat.*] I will see her yet!   11
Methinks I should discern her, if she feigned.
Can human eyes be dazed by woman's wit?
Once more these eyes of mine with hers shall meet
Before the headsman do her life bereave.
Shall I for ever part from thee, my sweet,
Without the taking of my latest leave?

Salomé.

You had as good resolve to save her now!
I'll stay her death, 'tis well determinèd.
For sure she never more will break her vow—
Sohemus and Josephus both are dead.

---

1 *false as powder*] 1. as unreliable as gunpowder; 2. as deceitful as cosmetics.

2 *heaven's model*] image of heaven; *she*] heaven.

3 *blackamoor*] black African.

4 *paintings*] use of cosmetics.

5 *coz'ning*] deceiving.

6 *Hittite*] Uriah the Hittite, whom David slew by subterfuge in order to have Uriah's wife, Bathsheba; *Bethsabe*] (BET-sa-beh) *i.e.,* Bathsheba. *See* II Sam. 11-12.

7 *son*] Solomon; *staid*] constant.

8 *Asuerus*] King Ahasuerus. *See* the Book of Esther 1-11; *The humble Jewess*] Esther.

9 *weight*] scale.

10 *train*] lead.

11 *that have*] who has.

Herod.

She shall not live! Nor will I see her face—
A long-healed wound a second time doth bleed. [150]
With "Joseph" I remember her disgrace.
A shameful end ensues a shameful deed.
Oh, that I had not called to mind anew
The discontent of Mariam's wavering heart!
'Twas you! You foul-mouthed Atè, none but you,
That did the thought hereof to me impart. [1]
Hence from my sight, my black tormentor, hence!
For hadst not thou made Herod unsecure,
I had not doubted Mariam's innocence,
But still had held her in my heart for pure.

Salomé.

I'll leave you to your passion. 'Tis no time
To purge me now, though of a guiltless crime.
        Exit [SALOMÉ.]

Herod.

Destruction take thee! Thou hast made my heart
As heavy as revenge. I am so dull,
Methinks I am not sensible of smart
Though hideous horrors at my bosom pull.
My head weighs downwards. Therefore will I go
To try if I can sleep away my woe.
        [*Exit.*]

ACT 4, SCENE 8

[*Enter*] MARIAM.

Mariam.

Am I the Mariam that presumed so much
And deemed my face must needs preserve my breath?
Ay, I° it was that thought my beauty such
As° it alone could countermand my death.
Now death will teach me – he can pale as well
A cheek of roses as a cheek less bright,
And dim an eye whose shine doth most excel
As soon as one that casts a meaner light.
Had not my self against my self conspired,
No plot, no adversary from without,
Could Herod's love from Mariam have retired,
Or from his heart have thrust my semblance out.
The wanton queen that never loved for love,
False Cleopatra, wholly set on gain,
With all her sleights did prove (yet vainly prove)
For her the love of Herod to obtain. [2]

Yet her allurements, all her courtly guile,
Her smiles, her favors, and her smooth deceit,
Could not my face from Herod's mind exile,
But were with him of less than little weight:
That face and person that in Asia late
For beauty's goddess (Paphos' queen) was ta'en— [3]
That face that did captive great Julius' fate,
That very face that was Antonius' bane,
That face that to be Egypt's pride was born, [25]
That face that all the world esteemed so rare— [4]
Did Herod hate, despise, neglect, and scorn,
When with the same he Mariam's did compare.
This made that I improvidently wrought,
And on the wager even my life did pawn—
Because I thought (and yet but truly thought)
That Herod's love could not from me be drawn. [5]
But now, though out of time, I plainly see
It could be drawn (though never drawn from me). [6]
Had I but with *humility* been graced,
As well as *fair* I might have proved me *wise*.
But I did think, because I knew me *chaste*,
One virtue for a woman might suffice—
That mind for glory of our sex might stand,
Wherein humility and chastity
Doth march with equal paces, hand in hand. [7]
But one, if single seen, who setteth by?
And I had singly one (but 'tis my joy
That I was ever innocent, though sour);
And therefore can they but my life destroy;
My soul is free from adversary's power.
        Enter DORIS.
You princes great in power and high in birth,
Be great and high, I envy not your hap. [8]
Your birth must be from dust, your power on Earth:
In Heaven shall Mariam sit in Sarah's lap. [50] [9]

---

[1] *Ate*] (A-teh) the goddess of discord.

[2] *prove*] try;   *her*] herself.

[3] *person*] Cleopatra;   *Paphos' queen*] Venus, whose temple was in Paphos, Cyprus.

[4] *captive*] captivate;   *Julius'*] Julius Caesar's;   *Antonius' bane*] the ruin of Mark Antony (who succeeded Julius Caesar as Cleopatra's lover).

[5] *made ... wrought*] *i.e.*, caused me to act imprudently.

[6] *out of time*] out of season, belatedly.

[7] *that...stand*] *i.e.,* 1. that minding chastity (the feminine glory of our sex) might suffice;   *but perhaps also* 2. that intellectual power (mind) might stand for the glory of our sex;   *one*] one virtue;   *setteth by*] counts it.

[8] *hap*] lot.

[9] *on Earth*] only on Earth;   *in Sarah's lap*] the wife of Abraham; in the New Testament, the Christian dead are said to dwell "in the bosom of Abraham."

Doris.
In° Heaven! Your beauty cannot bring you thither.
Your soul is black and spotted, full of sin.
You in adultery lived nine year together,
And Heaven will never let adultery in.

Mariam.
What art thou, that dost poor Mariam pursue?
Some spirit sent to drive me to despair?
Who sees° for truth that Mariam is untrue?   1
If fair she be, she is as chaste as fair.

Doris.
I am that Doris that was once belov'd,
Belov'd by Herod – Herod's lawful wife.
'Twas you that Doris from his side removed
And robbed from me the glory of my life.   2

Mariam.
Was that adultery? Did not Moses say
That he that, being matched, did deadly hate
Might (by permission) put his wife away
And take a more belov'd to be his mate?

Doris.
What did he hate me for – for simple truth?
For bringing beauteous babes? for love to him? 3
For riches, noble birth, or tender youth?—
Or for *no* stain did Doris' honor dim?
Oh, tell me, Mariam, tell me if you know,
Which fault of these made Herod Doris' foe!
These thrice-three years have I – with hands held up
And bowèd knees fast-nailèd to the ground—
Besought for thee the dregs of that same cup,   [75]
That cup of wrath that is for sinners found.
And now thou art to drink it! Doris' curse
Upon thyself did all this while attend—
But now it shall pursue thy children worse.

Mariam.
Oh, Doris, now to thee my knees I bend!
That heart that never bowed, to thee doth bow:
Curse not mine infants! Let it thee suffice
That Heaven doth punishment to *me* allow.
Thy curse is cause that guiltless Mariam dies.

Doris.
Had I ten thousand tongues, and ev'ry tongue
Inflamed with poison's power and steeped in gall,
My curses would not answer for my wrong,
Though I in cursing thee employed them all.

[*To Heaven.*]
Hear Thou – that didst Mount Gerizim° command
To be a place whereon (with cause) to curse—   4
Stretch Thy revenging arm! Thrust forth Thy hand
And plague the mother much, the children worse!
Throw flaming fire upon the baseborn heads
That were begotten in unlawful beds—   5
But let them live till they have sense to know
What 'tis to be in miserable state.
Then be their nearest friends their overthrow!
Attended be they by suspicious hate!
     [*To Mariam.*]
And Mariam, I do hope this boy of mine
Shall one day come to be the death of thine.   [100]
     Exit [DORIS.]

Mariam.
Oh, Heaven forbid! I hope the world shall see
This curse of thine shall be returned on thee.
Now, earth, farewell – though I be yet but young,
Yet I, methinks, have known thee too too long.
     [*Exit* MARIAM.]

Chorus.
The fairest action of our human life
Is scorning° to revenge an injury.
For who forgives, without a further strife,
His adversary's heart to him doth tie.   6
     And "'Tis a firmer conquest," truly said,
     "To win the heart than overthrow the head." 7
If we a worthy enemy do find,
To yield to worth, it must be nobly done;
But if of baser metal be his mind,
In base revenge there is no honor won.   8
     Who would a worthy courage overthrow?
     And who would wrestle with a worthless foe?
We say our hearts are great and cannot yield.
Because they cannot yield, it proves them poor!
Great hearts are tasked beyond their power but seld. 9
(The weakest lion will the loudest roar.)
     Truth's school for certain doth this same allow:
     High-heartedness doth sometimes teach to bow.

---

4 *Gerizim*] According to the Hebrew scriptures, the curse was to be on Mount Ebal, and the blessing on Mount Gerizim. *See* Deut. 11.29, 27:12. Cf. the spurious exegesis of Constabarus at 4.6.63-64 above.

5 *in unlawful beds*] out of wedlock.

6 *who*] whoever.

7 *'Tis ... head*] The victory is more sure by winning love than by winning a fight (proverbial wisdom).

8 *To ... done*] It is noble to resign to a worthy foe (more noble than to seek revenge).

9 *seld*] seldom.

---

1 *sees*] possibly read: *says.*

2 *that*] who.

3 *bringing*] giving birth to.

A noble heart doth teach a virtuous scorn:
To scorn to owe a duty over-long;
To scorn to be for benefits forborne;   [125] [1]
To scorn to lie; to scorn to do a wrong;
     To scorn to bear an injury in mind;
     To scorn a free-born heart (slave-like) to bind.
But if for wrongs we needs revenge must have,
Then be our vengeance of the noblest kind.
Do we his body from our fury save,
And let our hate prevail against our mind?   [2]
     What can 'gainst him a greater vengeance be
     Than make his foe more worthy far than he? [3]
Had Mariam scorned to leave a due unpaid,
She would to Herod then have paid her love
And not have been by sullen passion swayed.
To fix her thoughts all injury above
     Is° *virtuous* pride. Had Mariam thus been
proud,°
     Long famous life to her had been allowed.

ACT 5, SCENE 1
[*Enter* NUNTIO.]

Nuntio.
When, sweetest friend, did I so far offend
Your heavenly self, that you (my fault to quit)
Have made me now relator of her end,
The end of beauty, chastity, and wit?°   [4]
Was none so hapless in the fatal place
But I, most wretched, for the queen t' choose?
'Tis certain, I have some ill-boding face
That made me culled to tell this luckless news— [5]
And yet no news to Herod! Were it new°
To him, unhappy 't had not been at all!   [6]
Yet do I long to come within his view,
That he may know his wife did guiltless fall—
And here he comes.
          Enter HEROD.
Your Mariam greets you well.

Herod.
What? Lives my Mariam? Joy, exceeding joy!
She shall not die.

---

[1] *to be...forborne*] to presume upon a debt of gratitude.

[2] *and*] yet.

[3] *more ... he*] i.e., more worthy by refusing to let hateful thoughts prevail.

[4] *sweetest friend*] spoken as if to Mariam, now slain; *her*] your (Mariam's) "heavenly self."

[5] *made me culled*] culled me out *'Tis certain... news*] re: I must have some mark on my face that caused me to be selected by fate for this unlucky task.

[6] *'t had not been*] it would not have been (*i.e.*, there is no bad news but what he already knows).

Nuntio.   Heaven doth your will repel.

Herod.
Oh, do not with thy words my life destroy!
I prithee, tell no dying-tale. Thine eye,
Without thy tongue, doth tell but too too much.
Yet, let thy tongue's addition make *me* die—
Death welcome comes to him whose grief is such.

Nuntio.
I went amongst the curious gazing troop,
To see the last of her that was the best;
To see if Death had heart to make her stoop;
To see the sun-admiring Phoenix nest.
When there I came, upon the way I saw   [25]
The stately Mariam not debased by fear.
Her look did seem to keep the world in awe,
Yet mildly did her face this fortune bear—

Herod.
Thou dost usurp my right. *My* tongue was framed
To be the instrument of Mariam's praise.
     [*Beat.*]
Yet, speak. She cannot be too often famed.
All tongues suffice not her sweet name to raise.

Nuntio.
—But as she came, she Alexandra met,
Who did her death (sweet queen!) no whit bewail.
But as if nature she did quite forget,
She did upon her daughter loudly rail.

Herod.
Why stopped you not her mouth? Where had she words
To darken° that, that Heaven made so bright?
Our sacred tongue no epithet affords
To call her other than "the world's delight."   [7]

Nuntio.
She told her that her death was too too good,
And that already she had lived too long:
She said, she shamed to have a part in blood
Of her that did the princely Herod wrong.

Herod.
Base pickthank devil! Shame? 'Twas all her *glory*,
That she to noble Mariam was the mother.   [8]
But never shall it live in any story:
Her name – except to infamy – I'll smother!
What answer did her princely daughter make?

Nuntio.
She made no answer, but she looked the while [50]
As if thereof she scarce did notice take,
Yet smiled – a dutiful, though scornful smile.

---

[7] *her*] Alexandra's; *her*] Mariam.

[8] *pickthank*] ingratiating, sycophantic.

Herod.
Sweet creature! I that look to mind do call—
Full oft hath Herod been amazed withal.   1
Go on.

Nuntio.°
    She came unmoved, with pleasant grace,
As if to triumph her arrival were,
In stately habit and with cheerful° face—
Yet every eye was moist but Mariam's there.
When justly opposite to me she came,
She picked me out from all the [sorry] crew.
She beckoned° to me, called me by my name—
For she my name, my birth, and fortune knew.

Herod.
What, did she name thee? Happy, happy man!
Wilt thou not ever love that name the better?
But what sweet tune did this fair dying swan
Afford thine ear? Tell all, omit no letter.

Nuntio.
"Tell thou my lord," said she—

Herod.   Me, meant she me?
Is't true? The more my shame! I was her lord!
Were I not mad°, her lord I still should be!
But now her name must be by me adored.
Oh say, what said she more? Each word she said
Shall be the food whereon my heart is fed.

Nuntio.
"Tell thou my lord thou saw'st me lose my breath –"

Herod.
Oh that I could that sentence now control!

Nuntio.
"—if guiltily, eternal be my death!"   [75]

Herod.
I hold her chaste even in my inmost soul.

Nuntio.
"By three days hence, if wishes could revive,
I know himself would make me oft alive."

Herod.
Three days? Three hours! Three minutes—
        not so much!
A minute in a thousand parts divide,°
My penitency for her death is such,
As in the first I wished she had not died!
—But forward in thy tale.

Nuntio.   Why, on she went—
And after she some silent prayer had said,
She died°, as if to die she were content;
And thus to Heaven her heavenly soul is fled.

Herod.
But art thou sure there doth no life remain?
Is't possible my Mariam should be dead?
Is there no trick to make her breathe again?

Nuntio.
Her body is divided from her head.

Herod.
Why yet methinks there might be found, by art,
Strange ways of cure – 'tis sure rare things are done
By an inventive head and willing heart.

Nuntio.
Let not my lord your fancies idly run.
It is as possible it should be seen
That we should make the holy Abram° live,
Though he entombed two thousand years had been,
As breath again to slaught'red Mariam give.
– But now, for more assaults prepare your ears.

Herod.
There cannot be a further cause of moan.   [100]
This accident shall shelter me from fears.
What can I fear? Already Mariam's gone.
Yet tell even what you will.

Nuntio.   As I came by
From Mariam's death, I saw upon a tree
A man that to his neck a cord did tie—
Which cord he had designed his end to be.
When me he once discerned, he downwards bowed,
And thus with fearful voice he° cried aloud:
"Go tell the king he trusted ere he tried.
I am the cause that Mariam causeless died!"

Herod.
Damnation take him! – for it was the slave
That said she meant with poison's deadly force
To end my life, that she the crown might have—
Which tale did Mariam from her self divorce.
    Oh, pardon me, thou pure unspotted ghost!
My punishment must needs sufficient be
In missing that content I valued most,
Which was thy admirable face to see.   2
I had but one inestimable jewel,
Yet one I had – no monarch had the like –
And therefore may I curse myself as cruel.
'Twas broken by a blow myself did strike.
I gazed thereon, and never thought me blest
But when on it my dazzled eye might rest;
A precious mirror, made by wondrous art,   [125]
I prized it ten times dearer than my crown
And laid it up, fast-folded, in my heart.
Yet I in sudden choler cast it down
And pashed it all to pieces! 'Twas no foe

---

1 *I ... look] i.e.,* I do call to mind that very look.

2 *content]* contentment.

That robbed me of it, no Arabian host,
Nor no Armenian guide hath used me so,
But Herod's wretched self hath Herod crossed.
She was my graceful moiety – me accurs'd,
To slay my better half and save my worst!   1
    [*Beat.*]

But sure she is not dead! You did but jest,
To put me in perplexity a while.
'Twere well indeed if I could so be dressed.
I see she is alive – methinks you smile.

Nuntio.

If sainted Abel yet deceasèd be,
'Tis certain Mariam is as dead as he.

Herod.

Why then, go call her to me! Bid her now
Put on fair habit, stately ornament,
And let no frown o'ershade her smoothest brow.
In her doth Herod place his whole content.

Nuntio.

She'll come in stately weeds to please your sense,
If now she come attired in robe of Heaven!   2
Remember you yourself did send her hence,
And now to you she can no more be given.

Herod.

She's dead. Hell take her murderers! She was fair.
Oh, what a hand she had – it was so white,   [150]
It did the whiteness of the snow impair.
I never more shall see so sweet a sight.

Nuntio.

'Tis true, her hand was rare.

Herod, [*raving*].   Her "hand"? Her hands!
She had not singly one of beauty rare,
But such a pair as here where Herod stands
He dares the world to make to both compare.
Accursèd Salomé! Hadst thou been still,
My Mariam had been breathing by my side.   3
Oh never had I – had I had my will –
Sent forth command, that Mariam should have died!4
But Salomé, thou didst with envy vex
To see thyself outmatchèd in thy sex.
Upon your sex's forehead Mariam sat,
To grace you all like an imperial crown.
But you, fond fool, have rudely pushed thereat
And proudly pulled your proper glory down.
One smile of hers – nay, not so much – a look°
Was worth a hundred thousand such as you.

Judea, how canst thou the wretches brook
That robbed from thee the fairest of the crew?
You dwellers in the now-deprivèd land
Wherein the matchless Mariam was bred,
Why grasp not each of you a sword in hand,
To aim at me your cruel sovereign's head?
Oh, when you think of Herod as your king,   [175]
And owner of the pride of Palestine,
This act to your remembrance likewise bring:
'Tis I have overthrown your royal line.
Within her purer veins the blood did run
That from her granddam Sarah she derived,
Whose beldame age the love of kings hath won.   5
O that her issue had as long been lived!
But can her eye be made, by death, obscure?   6
I cannot think but it must sparkle still.
Foul sacrilege to rob those lights, so pure,
From out a temple made by heavenly skill.
I am the villain that have done the deed,
The cruel deed, though by another's hand!
My word though not my sword made Mariam bleed.
Hyrcanus' grandchild died° at my command—
That Mariam that I once did love so dear,
The partner of my now-detested bed.
    Why shine you, Sun, with an aspèct so clear?
I tell you once again – my Mariam's *dead*!
You could but shine if some Egyptian blowze
Or Ethiopian dowdy lose her life.   7
This was (then wherefore bend you not your brows?)
The king of Jewry's fair and spotless wife!   8
Deny thy beams! And Moon, refuse thy light.
Let all the stars be dark. Let Jewry's eye   [200]
No more distinguish which is day and night—
Since her best birth did in her bosom die.   9
    Those fond idolaters, the men of Greece,
Maintain these orbs are safely governèd—
That each within themselves have gods a-piece,
By whom their steadfast course is justly led.
But were it so (as so it cannot be),
They all would put their mourning garments on.   10
Not one of them would yield a light to me,
To me that is the cause that Mariam's gone.
For though they feign° their Saturn melancholy,
Of sour behaviors and of angry mood,
They fame° him likewise to be just and holy—

---

1 *moiety*] half.

2 *weeds*] robes.

3 *still*] quiet.

4 *Oh ... will*] If I had had my own will, I never would
have.

---

5 *Sara*] Abraham's wife; *see* Gen. 12:10-20, 20:1-18;
Whose beldame age] Who even as an elderly woman.

6 *obscure*] dark.

7 *blowze*] beggar wench.

8 *then ... brows*] Then why no scowl? Why no solar
eclipse?

9 *her*] Jewry's.

10 *They*] the heavenly orbs.

And justice needs must seek revenge for blood. [1]
Their Jove – if Jove he were – would sure desire
To punish him that slew so fair a lass
(For Leda's beauty set *his* heart on fire,
Yet she not half so fair as Mariam was);
And Mars would deem his *Venus* had been slain![2]
Sol, to recover her, would never stick,
For if he want the power her life to gain,
Then physic's god is but an empiric.   [3]
The queen of love would storm for beauty's sake,
And Hermes, too, since he bestowed her wit;
The night's pale light for angry grief would shake [225]
To see chaste Mariam die in age unfit.   [4]

   But oh, I am deceived! She passed them all,
In every gift, in every property.
Her excellencies wrought her timeless fall—
And they rejoiced, not grieved, to see her die.
The Paphian goddess did repent her waste
When she to one such beauty did allow.
Mercurius thought her wit his wit surpassed,
And Cynthia envied Mariam's brighter brow.

   But these are fictions. They are void of sense.
The Greeks but dream, and dreaming falsehoods tell.
They neither can offend, nor give defense,
And not by them it was my Mariam fell.   [5]
If she had been like an Egyptian, black,
And not so fair, she had been longer lived.
Her overflow of beauty turnèd back
And drowned the spring from whence it was derived.
Her heavenly beauty 'twas that made me think
That it with chastity could never dwell—
But now I see that Heaven in her did link
A spirit and a person to excel.

   I'll muffle up myself in endless night,
And never let mine eyes behold the light.
Retire thyself, vile monster! – worse than he   [6]

---

[1] *they feign*] the Greeks (Saturn was said to be gloomy, and the planet Saturn to have a melancholy influence); *likewise ... just*] Saturn was said to have reigned over the Golden Age; his son Jove usurped the throne.

[2] *For Leda's ... Mariam was*] Leda, less beautiful than Mariam, was desired of Jove;   *Mars ... Venus*] said to have been lovers until caught in the act by Vulcan.

[3] *Sol*] the Sun, Apollo, god of medicine and the arts; *stick*] hesitate;   *For...empiric*] i.e., If Apollo cannot resurrect her, then the god of medicine is a charlatan.

[4] *storm for beauty's sake*] Venus would rage for the loss of such beauty;   *Hermes*] Mercury, god of eloquence and wit;   *her*] Mariam's;   *night's pale light*] the Moon as goddess of chastity.

[5] *They*] the Greek gods; but also, and less obliquely, "fictions" or "dreaming falsehoods."

[6] *thyself*] Herod (*speaking to himself*);   *he / That stained*] Cain, said to have committed the world's first violence by slaying his brother Abel (Gen. 4).

That stained the virgin earth with brother's blood! [250]
Still in some vault or den enclosèd be,
Where, with thy tears, thou mayst beget a flood—[7]
Which flood, in time, may drown thee. Happy day
When thou at once shalt die and find a grave.
A stone upon the vault someone shall lay,
Which monument shall an inscription have,
And these shall be the words it shall contain:
"Here Herod lies, that hath his Mariam slain."
   [*Exeunt.*]

Chorus.
Whoever hath beheld with steadfast eye
The strange events of this one only day—
How many were deceived, how many die,
That once today did grounds of safety lay—
      It will from them all certainty bereave,
      Since twice-six hours so many can deceive.
This morning: Herod, held for surely dead,
And all the Jews on Mariam did attend;
And Constabarus rose° from Salom's bed,
And neither dreamed of a divorce or end;
      Pheroras joyed that he might have his wife;
      And Baba's sons, for safety of their life.
Tonight: our Herod doth alive remain;
The guiltless Mariam is deprived of breath;
Stout Constabarus, both divorced and slain;
The valiant sons of Baba have their death;
      Pheroras, sure his love to be bereft,   [275]
      If Salomé her suit unmade had left.   [8]
Herod this morning did expect, with joy,
To see his Mariam's much-belovèd face;
And yet ere night he did her life destroy,
And surely thought she did her name disgrace.
      Yet now again (so short do humors last)
      He both repents her death and knows her chaste.
Had he with wisdom now her death delayed,
He at his pleasure might command her death;
But now he hath his power so much betrayed,
As all his woes cannot restore her breath.
      Now doth he strangely, lunaticly, rave,
      Because his Mariam's life he cannot save.
This day's events were certainly ordained
To be the warning to posterity.
So many changes are therein contained,
Such° admirably strange variety,
      This day alone, our sagest Hebrews shall,
      In after-times, the school of wisdom call.

                finis

---

[7] *Still*] Forever (*and perhaps, ironically,* Silent).

[8] *If*] even if.

Lady Mary (Sidney) Wroth (1587 - 1653)

No time, noe roome, noe thought, or writing can
Giue rest or quiett to my louing hart...
—*Pamphilia to Amphilanthus*, Folger MS V.a.104

MARY SIDNEY Wroth was the eldest daughter of Barbara (*née* Gamage) Sidney, a Welsh heiress and a first cousin to Sir Walter Ralegh. Mary's father, Robert, earl of Leicester, was the brother of Sir Philip Sidney (d. 1586) and of Mary (Sidney) Herbert, countess dowager of Pembroke. Because her father was resident governor of Flushing (in the Netherlands), Lady Mary spent most of her childhood with her mother and siblings at various family manors, chiefly Penshurst Place in Kent and at Baynards Castle in London; with frequent visits to Wiltshire to see her uncle and aunt Herbert at Wilton House, a center of literary and cultural activity, where she became acquainted with well-known musicians, poets, playwrights, clergy, and scientists. "Mall" Sidney as a child was well tutored in the arts and in academic subjects. Rowland Whyte in his dispatches to Robert Sidney in the Netherlands makes frequent mention of Lady Mary: at age eight "little Mall" is said to be "very forward in her learning, writing, and other exercises she is put to, as dancing and the virginals"; four years later, Mary and her sisters are said to be "kept at their books, they dance, they sing, they play on the lute, and are carefully kept unto it." On a visit to Penshurst by Elizabeth I in 1600, Mary, 13, danced before the Queen and her Court; again at Harefield in 1602. Robert and Barbara Sidney hoped to wed their eldest to a wealthy lord of the realm. [1]

Mary's own heart was set on her cousin, William Herbert. At the time of his father's death in January 1600/1, Herbert was in disgrace for having begotten a child by Mary Fitton, a maid of honor to Queen Elizabeth; and for stubbornly refusing to marry her. Incensed at his behavior, Elizabeth imprisoned Herbert in the Fleet from 25 March to 26 April, and banished him thereafter from her Court. Barbara Sidney viewed Fitton's disgrace as an opportunity for her own daughter's preferment as a maid of honor to the Queen. Mary in the meantime viewed Herbert's return to private life as an opportunity for romance.

Confined at home for the better part of two years, Pembroke fell in love with his young cousin and she with him. As represented in Wroth's *Urania* (and confirmed by Pembroke), the couple exchanged vows. For such a marriage to be legal, however, it would have required the consent of Mary's parents; plus a dispensation from the Archbishop permitting a union within the proscribed degrees of consanguinity; plus a publication of banns; plus cooperation from the Fittons—the absence of all which may have been what Herbert was counting on: he could bed his fourteen-year-old cousin without being obliged to marry her. But if Herbert intended not to keep his vows, he was nevertheless outraged when Mary did not keep hers: In April 1603 her parents betrothed her to another man.

Following Elizabeth's death on 24 March, the Herbert brothers joined the rush of English courtiers who left London to meet King James on his progress from Scotland, and with good success (Philip became a favorite of the King; and William, of the Queen). But within three days of Pembroke's departure, Robert and Barbara Sidney promised their daughter Mary to Robert Wroth of Loughton, a land-rich cash-poor gentleman from Essex.

When Pembroke learned of Mary's betrothal to another, he wrote a scathing verse "elegy," a farewell in which he accuses his teen cousin-fiancé of betrayal and sluttishness: [2]

Barbara Sidney and children (1597) by Marcus Gheeraerts. (Mary, second from right). Courtesy of Penshurst Place.

---

[1] *Little Mall...virginals*] R. Whyte to Robert Sidney (23 Oct. 1595), ed. DWF from *H.M.C.* De L'Isle MS C12/14; *kept at...unto it*] same to same (9 Feb. 1599/1600), *ibid.*, C12/211.

[2] *elegy*] The ensuing discussion of Herbert's "Elegy" and Wroth's "Penshurst Mount" is indebted to Garth Bond (2013); many other details are supplied by Margaret Hannay's definitive *Mary Sidney, Lady Wroth* (2010).

Elegy [to Mary Sidney]
by William Herbert, third Earl of Pembroke

WHY with unkindest swiftness dost thou turn
From me whose absence thou didst only mourn—
Of which, thou mad'st me such a seeming shew
As unbelievers would have thought it true.   [1]

   We have been private, and thou know'st of mine
(Which is even all) as much as I, of thine.
Dost thou remember? Let me call t' account
Thy pleasant garden and that leafy mount
Whose top is with an open arbor crowned
And spanned with greenest palisadès 'round,
Whereon the powers of night may oft have seen us,
And heard the contracts that have been between us.[2]

   Dost thou remember (O securest beauty)
Where – of thine own free motion, more than duty,
And unrequired – thou solemnly did'st swear
(Of which avenging Heaven can witness bear)
That from the time thou gav'st the spoils to me
Thou wouldst maintain a spotless chastity
And unprofaned by any second hand,
From sport and love's delight removèd stand,
Till I (whose absence seemingly was mourned)
Should from a foreign kingdom be returned?   [3]
Of this, thou mad'st religion and an oath—
But see the frailty of a woman's troth:
Scarce had the Sun (to many rooms assigned)   [25]
Been thrice within the changeful waves confined,
And I scarce three days' journey from thine eyes
When thou new love didst in thy heart devise
And gav'st the relics of thy virgin head
Upon the easiest prayers as could be said.

   'Tis true, I left thee to a dangerous age
Where Vice (in angel's shape!) does title wage
With ancient Virtue, both disguising so
That hardly weaker eyes can either know.
Besides, I left thee in the hour of fears
And in the covetous spring of all thy years
(What time a beauty that hath well begun
Asks other than the solace of a nun!).

But since thy wanton soul so dear did prize
The "gain" (that thou, for it, did underprize
Thy faith and all that to good fame belongs),
Couldst thou not cover it from common tongues,
But cheapest eyes must *see* thee tread amiss?   [4]
My rhymes that won thee never taught thee this!
Thou might'st have wand'red in the paths of Love
And neither leaveless hill nor shady grove
Have been unpressèd by thy wanton weight,
Yet thou thought honest, hadst thou usèd sleight.[5]
Much care and business hath the *chastest* dame
To guard herself from undeservèd blame.   [50]
What artifice and cunning then must serve
To color them that just reproof *deserve*?
'Tis not a work for every woman's wit—
And the less marvel, thou neglectedst it.

   That which amazes me the most is this:
That having never trodden *but* amiss
(And done me wrongs that do as much deny
To suffer measure as infinity),
When I approach, thou turn'st thy head awry
As if sour eyes and scorn could satisfy.
Can second wrongs the former expiate
And work them out of memory and date,
Or teach me (ill in human precepts nursed)
That second mischiefs do secure the first?

   Thou art malicious as incontinent!
—And mightst have met with such a patìent
Whose wrongèd virtue, to just rage invited,
Would have revenge and in thy dust delighted.   [6]
But I (that have no gall where once I love
And whom no great thing under Heaven can move)
Am well secured from Fortune's weak alarms
And free from apprehension as from harms.

   Thus do I leave thee to the multitude°
That on my leavings hastily intrude°.
Enjoy thou many, or rejoice in one: [75]
I was before them – and before me, none.

Wroth's earliest datable poems (1603) include "Memory be ever blest" and (on the same theme) "Penshurst Mount," a verse epistle in which she replies to Pembroke's diatribe, answering his rage with her own wistful nostalgia for their ended affair. In *Urania* (1621), Wroth resurrects "Penshurst Mount" but takes pains to obfuscate its origin, revising the text, transgendering the speaker, and coyly ascribing the poem to Dolorindus, who is said to have composed these verses "in his imagination, which after were given to Amphilanthus [*i.e.,* Pembroke] and his other companions":

---

[1] *seeming shew*] *i.e.*, of pretended grief at my absence.

[2] *pleasant garden*, etc.] Mary Wroth identifies Penshurst as the place of their budding romance.

[3] *foreign kingdom*] Scotland (April 1603), though Pembroke, upon meeting King James in progress, turned around before reaching the border.

[4] *it*] gain, money; *fame*] reputation; *it*] your betrayal.

[5] *Thou…sleight*] You could have fornicated on every hill, in every grove, and be thought chaste, with a bit of clever concealment.

[6] *a patient…delighted*] a victim who, when thus betrayed, would have gladly killed you.

Penshurst Mount

British Library MS Additional 23229, folios 91r-92r

SWEET Solitariness! (joy to those hearts
That feel the pleasure of brave Cupid's darts),
Grudge me not (though a vassal to his might
And a poor subject to curst changing's spite)
To rest in you (or rather, restless move
In your contents, to sorrow for my love).¹
A love, though living, lives as dead to me
As jewels which in richest boxes be,
Placed in a chest that overthrows° my joy
Shut up in change, which more than plagues destroy.²
This (O you solitariness) may both endure
And be a surgeon to find me a cure
For this curst corsive eating my best rest.
  Memory, sad Memory! – in it, once blest,
But now most miserable with the weight
Of that which only shows Love's strange deceit.
You are that cruel wound which inly wears
My soul; my body, wasting into tears.
You keep my eyes unclosed, my heart untied
From letting thought of my best days to slide.
  Froward Remembrance! [What] delight have you
Over my miseries to take a view?
Why do you tell me in this very place
Of Earth's best blessings, I have seen the face?
(But, masked from me, I only see the shade   [25]
Of that which once my brightest sunshine made).
You tell me that I first did here know love
And maiden passions in this room did move.
O why is this alone to bring distress
Without a salve, but tortures in excess?
A cruel steward you are, to enroll
My once blest time, of purpose to control
With eyes of sorrow, yet leave me undone
By too much confidence. My thread thus spun,
In conscience, move not such a spleen of scorn!
(Under whose swelling my despairs are born).
Are you offended (choicest Memory)
That of your perfect gift I did glory?
If I did so offend, now pardon me,
Since 'twas to set forth *your* true ex'lency!
Sufficiently, I thus do punished stand
When all which curst is, you bring to my hand.
Or is it that I no way worthy was
In so rich honor my past days to pass?
Alas, if so, and such a treason given,
Must I, for this, to hell-like "gain" be driven?

[Untitled]

From *Urania* (1621), pp. 110-11

SWEET Solitariness (joy to those hearts
That feel the pleasure of Love's sporting darts),
Grudge me not (though a vassal to his might
And a poor subject to curst changing's spite)
To rest in you (or rather, restless move
In your contents, to sorrow for my love).
A love, which living, lives as dead to me
As holy relics which in boxes be,
Placed in a chest that overthrows my joy
Shut up in change, which more than plagues destroy.
These (O you solitariness) may both endure
And be a surgeon to find me a cure
For this curst corsive eating my best rest.
  Memory, sad Memory! – in you, once blest,
But now most miserable with the weight
Of that which only shows Love's strange deceit.
You are that cruel wound that inly wears
My soul; my body, wasting into tears.
You keep mine eyes unclosed, my heart untied
From letting thought of my best days to slide.
  Froward Remembrance! What delight have you
Over my miseries to take a view?
Why do you tell me in this same-like place
Of Earth's best blessings, I have seen the face?
(But, masked from me, I only see the shade
Of that which once my brightest sunshine made).
You tell me that I then was blessed in love
When equal passions did together move.
O why is this alone to bring distress
Without a salve, but torments in excess?
A cruel steward you are, to enroll
My once-good days, of purpose to control
With eyes of sorrow, yet leave me undone
By too much confidence. My thread so spun,
In conscience, move not such a spleen of scorn!
(Under whose swellings my despairs are born).
Are you offended (choicest Memory)
That of your perfect gift I did glory?
If I did so offend, yet pardon me,
Since 'twas to set forth *your* true ex'lency!
Sufficiently, I thus do punished stand
While all that curst is, you bring to my hand.
Or is it that I no way worthy was
In so rich treasure my few days to pass?
Alas, if so, and such a treasure given,
Must I, for this, to hell-like pain be driven?

---

¹ *vassal to his might*] slave to Cupid's power;   *rest in
you*] take comfort in solitude.

² *A love*] William Herbert; my love for him.

Fully torment me now in what is best:
Together take Remembrance with the rest—
Leave not that to me (if not, for more ill,
Which punish may and millions of hearts kill). [50]
Then may I lonely sit down with my loss
Without vexation for my losses' cross,
Forgetting pleasures late embraced with love,
Linked with a faith the world could never move,
Chained in affection I hoped should not change,
Not thinking Earth had left a place to range.
But staying cruelly, you set my bliss
With deepest mourning in my sight for 'miss. [1]

    And so shall I imagine my curse more
When you I loved add to my mischief's store.
Then may I live in Niobe's sad state,
Who weeping long endured her losses' fate,
Till to a rock transformèd from her tears,
She lives to feel more drops which on her wears.
Heaven weeps on her! Then this example take
And so I'll tie myself at patient's° stake.

    If not, then Memory continue still
And torture me with your best-prizèd skill,
While you, dear Solitariness, accept
Me to your charge, whose many passions kept
In your sweet dwellings have this profit gained:
That in more delicacy, none was pained.
Your rareness now receive my rarer woe, [2]
Which change and love appoints my soul to know.

Fully torment me now, and what is best
Together take, and Memory with the rest—
Leave not that to me, since but for my ill [3]
(Which punish may, and millions of hearts kill).
Then may I lonely sit down with my loss
Without vexation for my losses' cross,
Forgetting pleasures late embraced with love,
Linked to a faith the world could never move,
Chained with affection I hoped could not change,
Not thinking Earth could yield a place to range.
But staying cruelly, you set my bliss
With deepest mourning in my sight for 'miss.
And thus must I imagine my curse more
When you I loved add to my mischief's store.

[Lines 61-66 are omitted in 1621]

    If not, then Memory continue still
And vex me with your perfectest known skill,
While you dear Solitariness, accept
Me to your charge, whose many passions kept
In your sweet dwellings have this profit gained
That in more delicacy, none was pained.
Your rareness now receive my rarer woe,
[Which] change and love appoints my soul to know.

Robert Wroth of Loughton, Pembroke's unwelcome rival, quickly became a favorite hunting companion of James I. On 8 June 1603, the King knighted him; and on 27 September 1604 the King personally wedded Sir Robert to Mary Sidney, with her parents' consent and perhaps with hers. Five weeks later, on 4 November, William Herbert wedded Mary Talbot (Arbella Stuart's cousin), not for love but for her vast fortune in real estate (he despised her); and on 27 December, Pembroke's younger brother Philip wedded Mary Wroth's best friend, Susan de Vere. All of these relationships would figure later in Wroth's fiction.

    The Wroths' marriage was unhappy from the start. Sir Robert besides his passion for hunting was a noted gambler and drinker. Lady Mary was young, beautiful, well educated, of independent mind, and still in love with her cousin. Less than two weeks after the wedding, Robert Wroth complained to his father-in-law (briefly home from the Netherlands) of "discontent": Sir Robert said he could express no "exceptions to his wife, nor [to] her carriage toward him," without friction. There was talk: Ben Jonson, a Herbert client, observed that "my Lady Wroth is unworthily married on a jealous husband." [4]

    Scuttlebutt long after his death held Sir Robert to blame for the couple's difficulties. (Sir John Leake, a former Wroth retainer, expressing sympathy for a kinswoman similarly ill-matched, describes her husband as "the foulest churl in the world: he hath only one virtue – that he seldom cometh sober to bed, a true imitation of Sir Robert Wroth.") Sir Robert's reputed alcoholism may be one reason that Mary Wroth generally lived apart from her husband and had no recorded pregnancies during her first nine years of marriage. [5]

---

[1] *staying cruelly, you*] you (Memory) by cruelly remaining with me, etc.;   *'miss*] 1. all that I now miss; 2. amiss (wrong-doing), cf. Herbert, lines 43, 56.

[2] *Your rareness*] the exquisiteness of solitude;   *rarer*] extraordinary, beyond measure.

[3] *if not, for more ill*] if Memory is not taken from me, more harm ensues;   *but for my ill*] Memory works only my harm.

[4] Robert to Barbara Sidney (10 Oct. 1604) C81/17; Jonson quoted by Drummond (1619, ed. 1842), 31.

[5] J. Leake to E. Verney (1635), Verney, *Memoirs* 1.206.

On 6 January 1604/5, at Whitehall, Lady Mary Wroth danced the part of Baryte in *The Masque of Blackness*. She is not known to have performed in any other royal entertainment. Participation in the masques was a coveted honor, but costly: the dancers were obliged to spend thousands on their costumes and costume jewelry. But even if residence at Court was beyond her means, Wroth was a frequent guest and came to be well known. Ben Jonson dedicated *The Alchemist* to her (pub. 1612); and eulogized her in a sonnet and two epigrams (*Underwood,* nos. 46, 103, 105). Composer Robert Jones made Lady Wroth the dedicatee of *The Muses Garden for Delights* (1610). Josuah Sylvester supplies her first favorable critical notice as a poet, praising her as "AL-WORTH" (LAdy WROTH) "in whom her uncle's noble vein renews," "Worthy to sing a Sidney's worthiness" (1613/4). Other printed tributes came from William Baldwin (1610), George Wither (1613/4), William Gamage (1613/4), and George Chapman (1611, 1614).

In the summer of 1608, Sir Robert became grievously ill – his physicians feared, of the plague. He was then dwelling at Loughton, and his wife at Baynards Castle (the home of her beloved though married cousin, William Herbert), where she was safely accompanied by her father, on furlough from the Netherlands. Lady Mary remained at Baynards until her husband was out of danger, then returned to Loughton, escorted by her father and by Pembroke.

In February 1613/4, Lady Mary gave birth to a son, called James, after the King. Her cousin and aunt Herbert attended the christening at Loughton, and perhaps her husband as well, though Sir Robert was not long for this world: having never regained his health, he died only a few weeks later (of "gangrene *in pudendis*," according to the Court gossip, John Chamberlain). At his death, Wroth left his widow with a jointure of £1,200 but staggering debts of some £23,000, the result his gambling addiction and profligate spending; and yet, in his will he expressed tender feeling for his "dear and loving wife," and thoughtfully excluded the content of Mary's private study and bedchamber, lest her jewels and books be seized by his creditors. [1]

It was not long after Sir Robert's death that Lady Mary wrote *Love's Victory,* a pastoral play in five acts dramatizing the vicissitudes of love: Philisses (a figure for Sir Philip Sidney [1554-1586]) is in love with Musella (Penelope Devereux [1563-1607]), and she with him; but the mother of Musella insists that she marry Rustick, a stupid churl (Sir Robert Rich [1560-1597]). Meanwhile, Philisses' sister, Simeana (Mary Sidney Herbert [1561-1621]) is fond of Lissius (Dr. Matthew Lister [1571-1656]), who has no interest. These frustrating and anachronistic affairs are complicated by Climeana (Anne Houghton Lister), who still loves Lissius after having been cast off; by Lacon, who loves Musella; and by Phillis, who loves Philisses. Forester loves Silvesta, who is devoted to chastity, having been rejected by Philisses; while easy Dalina and pleasure-seeking Arcas (rejected by Musella) will make use of anyone.

But if *Love's Victory* seems to idealize the older generation of Sidneys and Herberts while mocking the unpopular husband of Penelope Rich, the script also invites a personal reading in which Musella and Rustick represent Mary Wroth and her own boorish husband, lately deceased; while Philisses, Phillis, and Silvesta represent William Herbert, and his forsaken wife, Mary Talbot, and his rejected lover, Mary Fitton.

Engraving of Mary Sidney Wroth, n.d.
Courtesy of Viscount De L'Isle, Penshurst

[1] J. Chamberlain to D. Carleton (17 March 1613/4), *Letters* (1939), 1.519; *in pudendis*] in the privates.

Representative songs from *Love's Victory*

The action opens with a song by Philisses in which he complains of his love for coy Musella:

[1]
Philisses:
You pleasant flowery mead
Which I did once well love,
Your paths no more I'll tread,
Your pleasures no more prove,
Your beauty more admire,
Your colors more adore,
Nor grass with daintiest store
Of sweets to breed desire.

Walks (once so sought-for), now
I shun you for the dark;   [10]
Birds (to whose song did bow
My ears), your notes ne'er mark;
Brook (which so pleasing was,
Upon whose banks I lay
And on my pipe did play),
Now unregarded pass;

Meadows, paths, grass, flowers,
Walks, birds, brook, truly find
All prove but as vain showers
(Wished, welcome; else unkind).   [20]
You once I lovèd best—
But love makes me you leave.
By love, I love deceive:
Joy's lost, for life's unrest.

In a singing contest, the shepherd Lacon, who also loves Musella, complains of Cupid's deceitfulness:

[5]
Lacon:
By a pleasant river's side,
Heart and hopes on pleasure's tide,
Might I see (within a bower,
Proudly dressed with every flower
Which the spring can to us lend)
Venus, and her loving friend.

I upon her beauty gazed.
They, me seeing, were amazed,
Till at last up stepped a child
(In his face, not actions mild!):   [10]
"Fly away!" said he, "for sight
Shall both breed, and kill, delight.

"Come away, and follow me.
I will let thee beauties see."
I obeyed him. Then he stayed
Hard beside a heavenly maid
When he threw a flaming dart
And, unkindly, struck my heart.

When Philisses rejects the love of Silvesta, the forlorn shepherdess forswears love, vowing to remain chaste ever after, in service to the goddess Diana. From Musella's point of view, Silvesta's vow of chastity is a sour-grapes response to a prize that she could not obtain:

[8]
Silvesta:
Silent woods with desert's shade,
   Giving peace
Where all pleasures first are made
   To increase,
Give your favor to my moan,   [1]
Now my loving time is gone.
Chastity my pleasure is;
   Folly, fled.
From hence now I seek my bliss:
   Cross love dead.   [2] [10]
In your shadows I repose:
You then, love, I now have chose.   [3]

Musella:
Choice ill-made were better left!
   Being "cross"—
Of such "choice" to be bereft
   Were no loss!   [4]
Chastity you thus commend
Doth proceed but from love's *end.*   [5]
And if *love* the fountain was
   Of your fire,   [20]
Love must chastity surpass
   In desire.
Love, lost, bred your chastest thought:
Chastity by love is wrought.

---

[1] *moan*] grief.

[2] *From hence*] from chastity.

[3] *love*] chastity (here personified as a new beloved); *You*] chastity.

[4] *such choice*] vowing chastity now that love has ended.

[5] *chastity*] the chastity that.

In Act 5, all sorrows end as Venus intervenes to prevent the arranged marriage: Philisses and Musella will wed and live happily ever after, as will Lissius and Simeana. Forester and Silvesta will love one another chastely though unmarried; while Rustick and Dalina will go on loving so long as it feels good. Arcas will be punished for his role in the narrowly averted forced marriage of Musella to Rustick. The ending thus nudges the script toward a neoplatonic allegory that represents, not particular individuals at all, but types of love: Forester and Silvesta, chaste love; Rustic and Dalina, physical desire; Lissius and Simena, love that overcomes pride and courtly artifice; Philisses and Musella, love that transcends miscommunication and parental interference. But no matter how one reads *Love's Victory* (and it's not read very often), the text ineluctably dramatizes the playwright's desire to triumph in love, having been released by her husband's death from an unwelcome marriage arranged by her parents.

It may be that Mary Wroth in her early widowhood saw Pembroke only when accompanied by family. Pembroke's growing responsibilities – gentleman of the Privy Chamber from May 1603, Lord Lieutenant of Cornwall from 1604; Warden of the Forest of Dean from 1608; Privy Councilor from 1611; Lord Chamberlain from December 1615 – kept him at Court, or on the road. After giving birth in 1614, Mary Wroth was rarely seen at Court (her appointment as a mourner for Queen Anna in 1619, an exception, may have been her final public engagement). Losses both personal and financial kept Wroth at home: baby James, her only child, died on 5 July 1616. The widow Wroth thereby lost all of her husband's lands, houses, and rents to John Wroth, the nearest male kin. She retained the use for life of the manor house at Loughton, though with greatly diminished income. Plagued by creditors, Wroth may on occasion have found refuge in the arms of Pembroke (as seems to be implied by the dubious chronology of the Pamphilia-Amphilanthus romance in *Urania*); but if so, Herbert did little to relieve his lover of her financial distress.

It was during these melancholy years, 1614-1620, that Wroth wrote her great sonnet sequence, *Pamphilia to Amphilanthus*.

PAMPHILIA TO AMPHILANTHUS survives in two distinct versions. One is a manuscript prepared about 1619 and preserved today in the Folger Shakespeare Library, comprised of 117 poems in Wroth's own hand. A revised and shortened text of 103 songs and sonnets was printed as an appendix to *Urania* (1621). In the sonnet sequence as in the prose romance, Pamphilia (the poet's avatar, Greek for "all-loving") has lost her heart to fickle Amphilanthus (a figure for William Herbert).

In the 1621 text (selections from which appear below), the sequence is arranged in four sections. In part one, Pamphilia tells how Cupid and Venus first conquered her heart, making her a slave of love. In part two, she mocks Cupid (Eros) as infantile and self-centered. Repenting of that treason, Pamphilia in part three pays tribute to Cupid with a "Crown" of praise (fourteen interlinked sonnets), hoping that the god of love will pity her; but she ends where she began, deep in a labyrinth of desire and finding no exit. In part four, the poet rhetorically celebrates Cupid as "the god of love" and disdains Venus as the "queen of lust"; but these gendered epithets (which carry a note of self-reproach) lack conviction and provide no remedy. Pamphilia implores Cupid to let his "mother know her shame. / 'Tis time for her to leave this youthful flame." Finding only pain in love, and no solace in writing about it, Pamphilia vows to "Leave the discourse of Venus and her son / To young beginners." She trusts that her suffering, and her ideals, may yet "move some other hearts."

Title page of *The Countesse of Mountgomeries Urania*

Sonnets from *Pamphilia to Amphilanthus*

Part 1

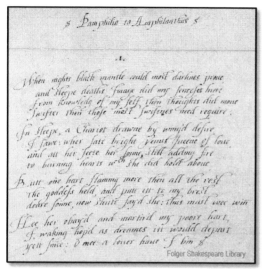

Folger Shakespeare Library

When night's black mantle could most darkness prove,
And sleep, death's image, did my senses hire
From knowledge of my self, then thoughts did move
Swifter° than those most swiftness need require.
In sleep, a chariot drawn by winged desire
I saw, where sat bright Venus, queen of love,
And, at her feet, her son, still adding fire
To burning hearts, which she did hold above—   1
But one heart flaming more than all the rest
The goddess held, and put it to my breast.
"Dear son, now shoot," said she. "Thus must we win."
He her obeyed, and martyred my poor heart.
I, waking, hoped (as dreams) it would depart,
Yet since (O me!) a lover I have been.

8.

Led by the power of grief, to wailings brought
By false conceit of change fall'n on my part,
I seek for some small ease, by lines which but°
Increase the pain. Grief is not cured by art.   2
Ah, how unkindness moves within the heart
Which still is true and free from changing thought!
What unknown woe it breeds, what endless smart,
With ceaseless tears which causelessly are wrought.³
It makes me now to shun all shining light
And seek for blackest clouds me light to give,
Which to all others only darkness drive.
They on me shine, for sun disdains my sight.
    Yet, though I dark do live, I triumph may:
    Unkindness nor this wrong shall love allay.   4

14.

Am I thus conquered? Have I lost the powers,
That to withstand which 'joys to ruin me?
Must I be still while it my strength devours,
And captive leads me prisoner, bound, unfree?
Love first shall leave° men's fant'sies to them free,
Desire shall quench Love's flames! Spring, hate
    sweet showers!
Love shall loose all his darts, have sight, and see!
His shame and wishings hinder happy hours:
Why should we *not* Love's purblind charms resist?
Must we be servile, doing what *he* list?
No! Seek some host to harbor thee! I fly
Thy babish tricks, and *freedom* do profess!
But O, my hurt makes my lost heart confess:
"I love, and must." So: farewell, liberty!

15.

Truly, poor Night, thou welcome art to me.
I love thee better in this sad attire
Than that which raiseth some men's fant'sies higher,
Like painted outsides which foul inward be.
I love thy grave and saddest looks to see,
Which seems my soul and dying heart entire,
Like to the ashes of some happy fire
That flamed in joy, but quenched in misery.   5
I love thy count'nance, and thy sober pace
Which evenly goes, and (as of loving grace)
To us and me among the rest oppressed
Gives quiet, peace to my poor self alone,
And freely grants Day leave (when thou art gone)
To give clear light: to see all ill, redressed.

20.

The Sun – which glads the Earth at his bright sight
When in the morn he shows his golden face
And takes the place from tedious drowsy night,
Making the world still happy in his grace—
Shows happiness remains not in one place.
Nor may the heavens alone to us give light,
But hide that cheerful face – though no long space,
Yet long enough for trial of their might.
But never sunset could be so obscure,
No desert ever had a shade so sad,
Nor could black darkness ever prove so bad
As pains which absence makes me now endure.
    The missing of the Sun awhile makes night,
    But absence of my joy sees never light.

---

¹ *her son*] Eros or Cupid, the god of love.

² *by false ... change*] by the mistaken belief that my love
is changeable.

³ *smart*] pain; *tears...wrought*] sorrow that is undeserved.

⁴ *Unkindness ... wrong*] Neither his unkindness, nor this
most recent injury.

---

⁵ *seems ... entire*] well befits.

21.

When last I saw thee, I did not *thee* see,
It was thine *image* – which in my thoughts lay
So lively figured, as no time's delay
Could suffer me in heart to parted be!
And sleep so favorable is to me
As not to let thy loved remembrance stray—
Lest that I, waking, might have cause to say
There was one minute found to forget thee!
Then, since my faith is such, so kind my sleep,
That gladly thee presents into my thought
(And still true lover-like thy face doth keep,
So as *some* pleasure, shadow-like, is wrought),
    Pity my loving! Nay, of conscience, give
    Reward to me in whom thy self doth live!

22.

Like to the Indians scorchèd with the Sun,
The Sun which they do as their God adore,
So am I used by Love! – for ever more
I worship him, less favors have I won.   1
Better are they who thus to blackness run
(And so can only whiteness' want deplore)
Than I, who pale and white am with *grief*'s store
(Nor can have hope, but to see hopes undone
Besides their sacrifice, received in sight
Of their chos'n saint; mine, hid as worthless rite). 2
Grant me to see where I my offerings give!
Then let me wear the mark of Cupid's might,
In *heart* (as they, in *skin*, of Phoebus' light),
Not ceasing offerings to Love, while I live.

24.

Once did I hear an aged father say
Unto his son (who with attention hears)
What age and wise experience ever clears
From doubts of fear or reason to betray: 3
"My son," said he, "behold thy father, gray.
I once had, as thou hast, fresh tender years,
And like thee sported, destitute of fears.
But my young faults made me too soon decay.
Love once I did, and like thee feared my love,
Led by the hateful thread of jealousy.
Striving to keep, I lost my liberty
And gained my grief, which still my sorrows move.
    In time, shun this. To love is no offense.
    But doubt, in youth, in age breeds penitence."

27.

Fie, tedious Hope, why do you still rebel?
Is it not yet enough you flattered me,
But cunningly you seek to use a spell
How to betray? Must *these* your trophies be?   4
I looked from you far sweeter fruit to see,
But blasted were your blossoms when they fell,
And those delights, expected from hands free,
Withered and dead (and what seemed bliss, proves hell).
No town was won by a more plotted sleight
Than I by you, who may my fortune write
In embers of that fire which ruined me.
Thus, Hope, your falsehood calls you to be tried!
You're loath, I see, the trial to abide.
Prove true at last – and gain your liberty.

30.

You blessèd Shades which give me silent rest,
Witness but this, when death hath closed mine eyes
And separated me from earthly ties,
Being from hence to higher place addressed:
How oft in you I have lain here oppressed,
And have my miseries in woeful cries
Deliv'red forth, mounting up to the skies
Yet helpless back returned to wound my breast—   5
Which wounds did strive but° how to breed more harm
To me, who can be cured by no one charm
But that of Love, which yet may me relieve.
If not, let death my former pains redeem.
My trusty friends, my faith untouched esteem,
And witness I could love, who so could grieve.

32.

How fast thou flyest, O Time, on Love's swift wings
To hopes of joy. That flatters our desire—
Which to a lover still contentment brings!
Yet, when we should *enjoy*, thou dost retire,
Thou stay'st thy pace (false Time) from our desire—
When, to our *ill*, thou hast'st with eagle's wings,
Slow only to make us see thy retire
Was for despair and harm, which sorrow brings.   6
O, slack thy pace, and milder pass to love.
Be like the bee, whose wings she doth but use
To bring home profit – masters good, to prove
Laden and weary – yet again pursues.
    So lade thyself with honey of sweet joy
    And do not me, the hive of Love, destroy.

---

1 *used by Love*] badly treated by Eros (Cupid), the god of love; *worship him*] honor Cupid.

2 *to blackness run*] tend toward dark complexion; *only whiteness' want*] have their love, though dark, lacking only whiteness; *hopes*] my hopes; *sacrifice*] sacrifice which is.

3 *ever clears ... betray*] habitually reveals, whether motivated by fearful doubts or by reason.

4 *these*] the self-flattery and ensuing betrayal of false hopes.

5 *mounting up*] so that my cries mounted up; *helpless back returned*] (prayers) fell back down upon me.

6 *still*] 1. quiet; 2. always; *stay'st ... desire*] i.e., lag your pace in order to keep us from our desire; *thou hast'st*] you do haste; *ill*] harm; *see thy retire*] see that your retiring.

35.

False Hope, which feeds but to destroy and spill
What it first breeds! unnatural to the birth
Of thine own womb, conceiving but to kill,
And plenty gives, to make the greater dearth—
So tyrants do who, falsely ruling earth,
Outwardly grace them and with profit's fill
Advance those who appointed are to death—
To make their greater fall, to please their will. [1]
Thus shadow they their wicked, vile intent,
Coloring evil with a show of good
While in fair shows their malice so is spent:
Hope kills the heart, and tyrants shed the blood.
  For Hope, deluding, brings us to the pride
  Of our desires, the farther down to slide.

38.

What pleasure can a banished creature have
In all the pastimes that invented are
By wit or learning, absence making war
Against all peace that may a *biding* crave? [2]
Can we delight but in a welcome grave
Where we may bury pains (and so be far
From loathèd company who always jar
Upon the string of mirth that pastime gave)?
The knowing part of joy is deemed the heart.
If that be gone, what joy can joy impart,
When senseless is the feeler of our mirth?
No, I am banished, and no good shall find,
But all my fortunes must with mischief bind,
Who but for misery did gain a birth. [3]

39.

If I were given to mirth, 'twould be more cross
Thus to be robbèd of my chiefest joy;
But silently I bear my greatest loss.
Who's used to sorrow, grief will not destroy.
Nor can I (as those pleasant wits) enjoy
My own framed words (which I account the dross
Of purer thoughts, or reckon them as moss)
While they, wit-sick, themselves to breath employ.
"Alas," think I, "your plenty shows your want—
For where most feeling is, words are more scant." [4]
Yet, pardon me – live, and your pleasure take!
Grudge not if I, neglected, envy show.
'Tis not to you that I dislike do owe,
But, crossed myself, wish some like me to make.

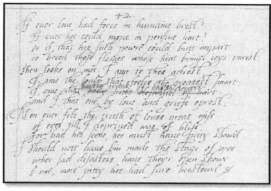

Wroth's draft (Folger Shakespeare Lib.)

42.

If ever Love had force in human breast,
If ever he could move in pensive heart
(Or if that he such power could but impart
To breed those flames, whose heat brings joy's unrest)–
Then look on me! I am, to these, addressed!
I am the soul that feels the greatest smart—
I am that heartless trunk of heart's depart—
And I that one, by Love, and grief, oppressed.
None ever felt the truth of Love's great miss
Of eyes, till I deprivèd was of bliss. [5]
For had he *seen*, he must have pity showed.
I should not have been made this stage of woe,
Where sad disasters have their open show:
O no, more pity he had sure bestowed!

45.

Good now, be still, and do not me torment
With multitude of questions. Be at rest,
And only let me quarrel with my breast,
Which still lets in new storms, my soul to rent. [6]
Fie, will you still my mischiefs more augment? [7]
You say I "answer cross" – I, that confessed
Long since! – yet must I ever be oppressed
With *your* tongue-torture, which will *ne'er* be spent? [8]
Well, then, I see no way but this will fright
That devil, speech: "Alas, I am possessed!"
(And mad folks senseless are of wisdom's right.)
The hellish spirit, Absence, doth arrest
All my poor senses to his cruel might. [9]
Spare me, then, till I am myself, and blest.

---

[1] *profit's fill*] lavish benefits (*cf.* pleasure's fill *below,* "Crown" *12.13*); *them*] themselves; *their greater fall*] the fall of "those who appointed are to death"; *their will*] the will of tyrants.

[2] *absence making*] when absence makes; *biding*] permanence.

[3] *Who*] since I; *but for*] for nothing but; *gain a birth*] was born.

[4] *your*] you "pleasant wits" (implied subject); *plenty*] abundance (of words); *want*] poverty.

---

[5] *Love's great miss of eyes*] Cupid or Eros ("Love") is figured as shooting his arrows blindfolded.

[6] *rent*] tear asunder.

[7] *still*] always; *mischiefs*] misfortunes.

[8] *cross*] in a contrary fashion; *spent*] used up.

[9] *his cruel might*] the power of your absence.

46.

Love, thou hast all! For now thou hast me made
So thine, as if for thee I were ordained.
Then take thy conquest! – nor let me be pained
More in thy sun, when I do seek thy shade.
No place for help have I left to invade,
That showed a face where least ease might be gained,
Yet found I pain increase – and but obtained
That this no way was, to have love allayed.   1
When hot and thirsty, to a well I came,
Trusting by that to quench part of my flame.°
But there I was by Love afresh embraced.
Drink I could not – but in it I did see
Myself – a living glass (as well as she)
For Love to see himself in, truly placed!   2

48.

How like a fire doth love increase in me!—
The longer that it lasts, the stronger still,
The greater, purer, brighter, and doth fill
No eye with wonder more. Then hopes still be
Bred in my breast (when fires of love are free)   3
To use that part to their best-pleasing will;
And now unpossible it is to kill
The heat so great where love his strength doth see.
Mine eyes can scarce sustain the flames! My heart
Doth trust in them my passions to impart
And languishingly strive to show my love.
My breath not able is to breathe least part
Of that increasing fuel of my smart—
Yet love I will, till I but ashes prove.

Pamphilia

Part 2

Song

I, that am of all most crossed
Having, and that had, have lost,
May with reason thus complain,
Since love breeds love, and love's pain: 4
That which I did most desire
To allay my loving fire
I may have – yet now must miss,
Since another ruler is.
Would that I no ruler had,
Or the service not so bad,
Then might I with bliss enjoy
That which now my hopes destroy—
And that wicked pleasure, got,
Brings with it the sweetest lot.
I, that must not taste the best,
Fed, must starve, and restless rest.

Sonnet 1

In night yet may we see some kind of light
Whenas the Moon doth please to show her face
And in the Sun's room yields her light and grace,
Which otherwise must suffer dullest night.   5
So are my fortunes barred from true delight,
Cold and uncertain (like to this strange place),
Decreasing, changing in an instant space
And even at full-of-joy turned to despite.
Justly on Fortune was bestowed the wheel
Whose favors, fickle and unconstant, reel,
Drunk with delight of change and sudden pain—
Where pleasure hath no settled place of stay,
But turning still for our best hope's decay
(And this, alas, we lovers often gain).

Sonnet 7.

An end, fond Jealousy! Alas, I know
Thy hiddenest and thy most secret art.
Thou canst no new invention frame, but part
I have already seen and felt with woe.
All thy dissemblings – which by feignèd show
Won my belief while Truth did rule my heart—
I with glad mind embraced, and deemed my smart
The spring of joy, whose streams with bliss should flow.
I thought excuses had been reasons true,
And that no falsehood could of thee ensue
(So soon belief in honest minds is wrought);
But now I find thy flattery and skill,
Which idly made me to observe thy will—
Thus is my learning by my bondage bought.

Song

The springtime of my first loving
Finds yet no winter of removing,
Nor frosts to make my hopes decrease,
But with the summer still increase.
The trees may teach us love's remaining,
Who suffer change with little paining;
Though winter make their leaves decrease,
Yet with the summer they increase.
As birds by silence show their mourning
In cold, yet sing at spring's returning,   [10]
So may love, nipped awhile, decrease,
But as the summer soon increase.
Those that do love but for a season
Do falsify both love and reason;
For reason wills, if love decrease,
It like the summer should increase.
Though love sometimes may be mistaken,
The truth yet ought not to be shaken;
Or though the heat awhile decrease,
It with the summer may increase.   [20]
And since the springtime of my loving
Found never winter of removing,
   Nor frosts to make my hopes decrease,
   Shall as the summer still increase.   6

---

[1] *That... gained*] In any place that seemed to offer ease; *least*] some little;   *obtained*] discovered.

[2] *as well as she*] myself and my reflection both presented a perfect image of love.

[3] *will*] (here and in line 14) possibly with a pun on *Will*, *i.e.*, William Herbert; cf. Sonnet [69] (below), line 13.

[4] *love's*] 1. love's (*possessive*); 2. love is (*pronounced as two syllables*).

---

[5] *Whenas*] when.

[6] *Shall*] my loving shall.

A Crown of Sonnets, Dedicated to Love [1]

1.

In this strange labyrinth how shall I turn?
Ways are on all sides, while the way I miss.
If to the right hand, there in love I burn.
Let me go forward, therein danger is.
If to the left, suspicion hinders bliss.
Let me turn back, shame cries I ought return,
Nor faint, though crosses with° my fortunes kiss. [2]
Stand still is harder, although sure to mourn.
Thus let me take the right- or left-hand way,
Go forward, or stand still, or back retire,
I must these doubts endure without allay
Or help, but travail find for my best hire.
  Yet that which most my troubled sense doth move
  Is to leave all and take the thread of love— [3]

2.

Is to leave all and take the thread of love,
Which line straight leads unto the soul's content,
Where choice delights with pleasure's wings do move,
And idle fant'sy never room had lent.
When chaste thoughts guide us, then our minds are bent
To take that good which ills from us remove.
Light of true love brings fruit which none repent,
But constant lovers seek, and wish to prove. [4]
Love is the shining star of blessing's light,
The fervent fire of zeal, the root of peace,
The lasting lamp fed with the oil of right,
Image of faith, and womb for joy's increase.
  Love is true virtue, and his end's delight.
  His flames are joys; his bands, true lovers' might. [5]

3.

His flames are joys, his bands true lovers' might:
No stain is there but pure as purest white,
Where no cloud can appear to dim his light,
Nor spot defile, but shame will soon requite.
Here are affections tried by love's just might,
As gold by fire and black discerned by white,
Error by truth, and darkness known by light,
Where faith is valued for love to requite.
Please him and serve him, glory in his might, [6]
And firm he'll be, as innocency white,
Clear as th' air, warm as sunbeams,° as daylight,
Just as truth, constant as fate, joyed to requite.
  Then love obey, strive to observe his might,
  And be in his brave court a glorious light.

4.

And be in his brave court a glorious light:
Shine in the eyes of faith and constancy,
Maintain the fires of love still burning bright,
Not slightly sparkling but light-flaming be,
Never to slack till earth no stars can see—
Till sun and moon do leave to us dark night
And second chaos once again do free
Us and the world from all division's spite;
Till then, affections (which his followers are)
Govern our hearts and prove his power's gain.
To taste this pleasing sting, seek with all care,
For happy smarting is it, with small pain:
  Such as, although it pierce your tender heart
  And burn, yet, burning, you will love the smart—

5.

And burn, yet, burning, you will love the smart
When you shall feel the weight of true desire
(So pleasing as you would not wish your part
Of burden should be missing from that fire),
But faithful and unfeignèd heat aspire
Which sin abolisheth and doth impart
Salves to all fear, with virtues which inspire
Souls with divine love (which shows his chaste art); [7]
And guide he is to joyings. Open eyes
He hath to happiness, and best can learn
Us means how to deserve. This he descries
Who, blind, yet doth our hiddenest thoughts discern.
  Thus we may gain, since, living in blest love,
  He may our prophet and our tutor prove.

6.

He may our prophet and our tutor prove
In whom alone we do this power find:
To join two hearts as in one frame; to move
Two bodies, but one soul to rule the mind;
Eyes which must care to one dear object bind,
Ears to each other's speech, as if above
All else they sweet and learnèd were. This kind
Content of lovers witnesseth true love.
It doth enrich the wits and make you see
That in yourself which you knew not before,
Forcing you to admire such gifts should be
Hid from your knowledge, yet in you the store. [8]
  Millions of these adorn the throne of love.
  How blest are they, then, who his favors prove!

---

[1] *Crown*] an Italian corona, with the last line of one lyric serving as the first line of the next.

[2] *ought return*] *i.e.*, that I should not go backwards either; *crosses*] frustrations; obstacles.

[3] *travail*] trouble (*with pun on* travel: *no reward but the travel itself*); *hire*] wages; *move*] urge; *thread*] path.

[4] *But*] but which.

[5] *his end's delight*] Love brings delight; *bands*] bonds.

[6] *him*] love; Cupid as god of love.

[7] *But...sin*] But aspire to that faithful and sincere passion ("heat") which abolishes sin; *his...art*] Love's (Cupid's) art.

[8] *admire*] wonder that.

7.

How blest be they, then, who his favors prove:
A life whereof the birth is just desire,
Breeding sweet flame, which hearts invite to move
In these loved eyes which kindle Cupid's fire
And nurse his longings with his thoughts entire,
Fixed on the heat of wishes formed by love.
Yet whereas fire destroys, this doth aspire,
Increase, and foster all delights above.
Love will a painter make you, such as you
Shall able be to draw your only dear
More lively, parfit, lasting, and more true
Than rarest workman, and to you more near.
    These be the least. Then all must needs confess,
    He that shuns Love doth love himself the less.

8.

He that shuns Love doth love himself the less—
And cursèd he whose spirit not admires
The worth of love, where endless blessedness
Reigns and commands, maintained by heavenly fires,
Made of virtue, joined by truth, blown by desires,
Strengthened by worth, renewed by carefulness,
Flaming in never-changing thoughts. Briars
Of jealousy shall here miss welcomeness,
Nor coldly pass in the pursuits of love
Like one long-frozen in a sea of ice.
And yet but chastely let your passions move,
No thought from virtuous love your minds entice;
    Never to other ends your fant'sies place
    But where they may return with honor's grace—

9.

But where they may return with honor's grace,
Where Venus' follies can no harbor win,
But chasèd are (as worthless of the face
Or style of love who hath lascivious been).
Our hearts are subject to her son, where sin
Never did dwell or rest one minute's space.
What faults he hath, in her did still begin;
And from her breast he sucked his fleeting pace.
If lust be counted love, 'tis falsely named,
By wickedness a fairer gloss to set
Upon that vice which else makes men ashamed—
In the own phrase to warrant (but beget)
    This child for love, who ought, like monster born,
    Be from the court of love and reason torn—

10.

Be from the court of love and reason torn,
For love in reason now doth put his trust.
Desert and liking are together born
Children of love and reason, parents just.
Reason, adviser is; love, ruler must
Be of the state (which crown he long hath worn).
Yet so as neither will in least mistrust
The government where no fear is of scorn,
Then reverence both their mights, thus made of one.
But wantonness and all those errors shun
Which wrongers be, impostures, and alone
Maintainers of all follies ill begun,
    Fruit of a sour and unwholesome ground,
    Unprofitably pleasing, and unsound—

11.

Unprofitably pleasing, and unsound,
When heaven gave liberty to frail, dull earth,
To bring forth plenty that in ills abound,
Which, ripest, yet do bring a certain dearth—
A timeless and unseasonable birth,
Planted in ill, in worse time springing found,
Which, hemlock-like, might feed a sick-wit's mirth
Where unruled vapors swim in endless round.
Then joy we not in what we ought to shun,
Where shady pleasures show, but true-born fires
Are quite quenched out or by poor ashes won
A while to keep those cool and wan desires.
    O no, let love his glory have, and might
    Be given to him who triumphs in his rite—

12.

Be given to him who triumphs in his rite,
Nor fading be, but – like those blossoms fair
Which fall for good and lose their colors bright,
Yet die not, but with fruit their loss repair –
So may love make you pale with loving care,
When sweet enjoying shall restore that light
More clear in beauty than we can compare,
If not to Venus in her chosen night°.
And who so give themselves in this dear kind,
These happinesses shall attend them still,
To be supplied with joys, enriched in mind
With treasures of content and pleasure's fill.
    Thus love to be divine doth here appear,
    Free from all fogs, but shining fair and clear—

---

[1] *this*] this "sweet flame" of true love.

[2] *parfit*] perfect.

[3] *not admires*] does not admire.

[4] *Our hearts*] the hearts of those devoted to love; *her son*] Cupid (here personified as true love) is the son of Venus (here figured as the personification of lust).

[5] *the own*] 1. its own; 2. the one; *In ... born*] by this one phrase, lust would call itself love, though lust is a monster; *this child*] lust.

[6] *might*] power; *him ... his*] the one ... Love's (*i.e.,* Cupid's).

[7] *When*] since.

[8] *who so*] those who; *in this dear kind*] in this way (*i.e.* those who love faithfully rather than lustfully).

13.
Free from all fogs, but shining fair and clear,
Wise in all good, and innocent in ill,
Where holy friendship is esteemèd dear,
With truth in love and justice in our will.
In love these titles only have their fill:
Of happy life, maintainer, and the mere
Defense of right; the punisher of skill
And fraud; from whence directions doth appear.   ¹
To thee, then – lord commander of all hearts,
Ruler of our affections kind and just,
Great king of love – my soul, from feignèd smarts
Or thought of change, I offer to your trust,
   This crown, my self, and all that I have more,
   Except my heart, which you bestowed before—   ²

14.
Except my heart, which you bestowed before,
And for a sign of conquest gave away
As worthless, to be kept in your choice store
(Yet one more spotless with you doth not stay).
The tribute which my heart doth truly pay
Is faith untouched. Pure thoughts discharge the score
Of debts for me, where constancy bears sway
And rules as lord, unharmed by envies sore.   ³
Yet other mischiefs fail not to attend:
As enemies to you, my foes must be;
Curst jealousy doth all her forces bend
To my undoing. Thus my harms I see.
   So, though in love, I fervently do burn.
   In this strange labyrinth, how shall I turn?

Part 3
1.
My heart is lost. What can I now expect?
An evening fair after a drowsy day?
Alas, fond fant'sy, this is not the way
To cure a mourning heart or salve neglect.
They who should help do me (and help) reject,
Embracing loose desires and wanton play,
While wanton base delights do bear the sway
And impudency reigns without respect.   ⁴
O Cupid, let thy° mother know her shame!
'Tis time for her to leave this youthful flame
Which doth dishonor her, is age's blame,
And takes away the greatness of *thy* name.
   Thou, "god of love"; she, only "queen of lust"
   (Yet strives, by weakening thee, to be unjust!).   ⁵

2.
Late in the forest I did Cupid see—
Cold, wet, and crying. He had lost his way
And (being blind) was farther like to stray;
Which sight, a kind compassion bred in me.
I kindly took and dried him, while that he
(Poor child!) complained he starvèd was with stay,
And pined for want of his accustomed prey
(For none, in that wild place, his host would be).
I glad was of his finding – thinking, "Sure
This service should my *freedom* still procure";
And in my arms I took him then, unharmed,
Carrying him safe unto a myrtle bower—
But in the way he made me feel his power,
Burning my heart, who had him kindly warmed.

7.
No time, no room, no thought, or writing can
Give rest or quiet to my loving heart,
Or can my memory or fant'sy scan
The measure of my still-renewing smart.   ⁶
Yet would I not, dear Love, thou shouldst depart,
But let my passions (as they first began)
Rule, wound, and please. It is thy choicest art
To give disquiet which seems ease to man.
When all alone, I think upon thy pain—
How thou dost travail, our best selves to gain.   ⁷
Then hourly thy lessons I do learn,
Think on thy glory, which shall still ascend
Until the world come to a final end—
And then shall we thy lasting power discern.

9.
My Muse, now happy, lay thyself to rest:
Sleep in the quiet of a faithful love.
Write you no more, but let these fant'sies move
Some other hearts. Wake not to new unrest—
But if you study, be those thoughts addressed
To truth which shall eternal goodness prove,
Enjoying of true joy, the most and best,
The endless gain which never will remove.
Leave the discourse of Venus and her son
To young beginners, and their brains inspire
With stories of great love – and from that fire
Get heat to write the fortunes they have won.
   And thus leave off. What's past shows you can love.
   Now let your constancy your honor prove.
                   Pamphilia.°

---

¹ *skill*] cunning; shrewd practice;   *from whence*] the
guiding light from whence.

² *thee*] Love.

³ *envies sore*] *or*, envy's sore (*Q* envyes sore).

⁴ *They...reject*] those who should help, instead reject
both me and help.

⁵ *strives*] she (Venus) strives.

---

⁶ *or*] nor; *smart*] pain.

⁷ *travail*] labor; travel; *gain*] bring forth.

Throughout the sonnet sequence, Amphilanthus remains an absent presence: his name is mentioned only in the title, not in the text; and the individual sonnets are addressed not to him, but to Cupid, Night, Fortune, Jealousy, Grief, Hope, and Time. Pamphilia wards off despair by affirming and reaffirming the worth of constancy in love; but she comes to recognize that her masculine love-object cannot be persuaded, by her person or by her writing, to share that ideal. Implicit in the sobriquet, *Amphilanthus* ("lover of both") is a paradox: he cannot love only one without ceasing to be himself. (William Herbert from 1600 to 1630 loved both Mary Wroth and Queen Elizabeth, Mary Wroth and Mary Fitton, Mary Wroth and Mary Talbot, Mary Wroth and Queen Anna, Mary Wroth and Lucy Hay – which from Pembroke's point of view may have been a kind of constancy, but it was not what Wroth had in mind.)

Seeing that she was not alone unhappy, Wroth undertook to construct a wide and universal theater in which to present more woeful pageants than her own tale of star-crossed love: *The Countess of Montgomery's Urania* – so called because she dedicated it to her best friend, Susan de Vere Herbert – is in some respects modeled on *The Countess of Pembroke's Arcadia*, by her uncle Sir Philip Sidney; which he dedicated to his sister Mary Herbert (now countess dowager, and mother of William (third Earl of Pembroke) and Philip (first Earl of Montgomery) – respectively, Wroth's lover, and Susan's husband.

Urania has a loose plot structure, comprised largely of first-person narratives. With a text populated by more than three hundred characters, Wroth had many possible permutations for star-crossed love and she explores them all. Generally speaking the unmarried women are unhappy because they cannot be united with their true loves; while the married women are unhappy for another reason.

The central heroine is not Urania (a figure for Susan Herbert), but Pamphilia, who loves Amphilanthus despite his geographical wandering and sexual philandering. Wroth here brings both Amphilanthus and her own irony into sharper focus than in the sonnets. Example: When Antissia (one of Pamphilia's many rivals) tries to seduce Amphilanthus, Wroth reports that "Kindness then betrayed them: she, showing it; he (as a kind-hearted prince to ladies) receiving it." Beholding a woman in the throes of eros, Amphilanthus "was not unexperienced; therefore soon saw remedy must be given! and *cruelty* he imagined it would be in him (who discerned he might, by his art, help her) if he refused that good, to one so fair, and so kindly loving" (1.1.51). The Amphilanthus of *Urania* is a man of strong instinctual drives who requires neither a full moon nor a pretty face but will work his magic on whatever lovesick woman is both willing and near to hand. Pamphilia loves him anyway.

From *The Countess of Montgomery's Urania*

The First Book

WHEN THE SPRING BEGAN TO APPEAR like the welcome messenger of summer, one sweet (and in that, more-sweet) morning, after Aurora had called all careful eyes to attend the day, forth came the fair shepherdess, Urania ("fair" indeed! – yet that, far too mean a title for her, who for beauty deserved the highest style could be given by best-knowing judgments). Into the mead she came, where usually she drave her flocks to feed – whose leaping and wantonness showed they were proud of such a guide. But she – whose sad thoughts led her to another manner of spending her time – made her soon leave them and follow her late-begun custom, which was (while they delighted themselves) to sit under some shade, bewailing her misfortune; while they fed, to feed upon her own sorrow and tears – which at this time she began again to summon, sitting down under the shade of a well-spread beech, the ground then blest, and the tree with full and fine-leaved branches growing proud to bear and shadow such perfections. But she, regarding nothing in comparison of her woe, thus proceeded in her grief:

"Alas, Urania," said she. "The true servant to misfortune! Of any misery that can befall woman, is not this the most and greatest, which thou art fallen into? Can there be any near the unhappiness of being ignorant – and that in the highest kind, not being certain of mine own estate or birth? Why was I not still continued in the belief I was (as I appear) a shepherdess and daughter to a shepherd? My ambition then went no higher than this estate. Now it flies unto knowledge. Then was I contented; now, perplexed. O Ignorance, can thy dullness yet procure so sharp a pain? – and that, such a thought as makes me now aspire unto knowledge! How did I joy in this poor life, being quiet, blest in the love of those I took for parents – but now, by them, I know the contrary; and by that knowledge, not to know myself! Miserable Urania, worse art thou now than these, thy lambs. For they know their dams while thou dost live unknown of any."

By this, were others come into that mead with their flocks. But she, esteeming her sorrowing thoughts her best and choicest company, left that place, taking a little path which brought her to the further side of the plain, to the foot of the rocks – speaking as she went these lines, her eyes fixed upon the ground, her very soul turned into mourning:

[U1]

Unseen, unknown, I here alone complain
To rocks, to hills, to meadows, and to springs,
Which can no help return to ease my pain,
But back my sorrows the sad Echo brings.
Thus still increasing are my woes to me,
Doubly resounded by that moanful voice
Which seems to second me in misery,
And answer gives, like friend of mine own choice. ¹
Thus only she doth my companion prove;
The others silently do offer ease.
But those that grieve, a grieving note do love;
Pleasures, to dying eyes, bring but dis-ease—
      And such am I, who (daily ending) live,
      Wailing a state which can no comfort give.

*In faraway Sicily, Limena loves Perissus, and he
loves her. Upon learning of their love, Philargus
forces Limena (his wife) to write Perissus a letter,
stating that she is to be slain and that she desires
Perissus not to avenge her death. Urania, princess of
Naples, rouses Perissus from weeping and dispatches
him to save Limena's life; or, failing to arrive in time,
to avenge her death. Pamphilia's eldest brother,
meantime (Parselius, prince of Morea), is in love
with Urania; who is in love with Steriamus, prince of
Albania. Pining away in the woods for Urania (this
is before he falls for Dalinea, at first sight), Parselius
is in the midst of a "violent fever of sorrow" when he
is suddenly distracted by a marital dispute:*

[The Tale of Limena, Wife of Philargus]

[PARSELIUS] discerned a man come from under the
rocks, […] armed at all points, leading in his hand as
beautiful a lady as Nature could frame. […] Had she
been free, how much more rare must she then of necessity appear, who in misery showed so delicate!)
The Morean Prince stayed to behold; and beholding,
did admire the exquisiteness of that sad beauty; but
more than that, did the cruelty of the armed man
seem wonderful: for leading her to a pillar which
stood on the sand (a fit place, that the sea might still
wash away the memory of such inhumanity), he tied
her to it by the hair, which was of great length, and
sun-like brightness. Then pulled he off a mantle
which she wore, leaving her from the girdle upwards
all naked. Her soft, dainty-white hands he fastened
behind her, with a cord about both wrists (in manner
of a cross, as testimony of her cruelest martyrdom). ²

When she was thus miserably bound to his unmerciful liking, with whips he was about to torment
her. But Parselius, with this sight, was quickly put out

of his admiration. Hasting to revenge her wrong,
setting spurs to his horse, he ran as swift as lightning
[…] yet sending his voice with more speed before
him, crying, "Vild traitor, hold thy hands and turn thy
spite on *me*, more fit to encounter stripes!" – hoping
thus to save her from some (which, if but one [lash],
had been too much for such delicacy to endure).

But [Philargus] (whose malice was such, as the
nearer he saw her succor, the more was his fury increased) looking up and seeing a brave knight accompany that voice – casting his hateful look again
on her and throwing away the whips – [he] drew his
sword, saying, "Nor yet shall this new champion rescue thee!" [and was] then ready to have parted that
sweet breath from that most sweet body.

Parselius came and struck down the blow with his
sword! – though not so directly but that it a little
razed her, on the left side; which she perceiving,
looking on it, and seeing how the blood did trickle (in
some, though few, drops): "Many more than these,"
said she, "have I inwardly shed for thee, my dear Perissus!" (But that last word she spake softlier than
the rest, either [so] that the strange knight [Parselius]
should not hear her, or that she could not afford that
dear name, [Perissus,] to any but her own ears.)

She being thus rescued, the knight strake fiercely
at Parselius, who met him with as much furious
strength, giving him his due in the cursted'st kind and
fullest measure; making such proof of his valor (Justice being on his side, which best guides a good
sword in a noble hand) as in short time [Parselius]
laid him at his feet, pulling off his helm, to cut off his
head. But then the lady cried unto him, beseeching
him to stay that blow.

The like did another knight, newly arrived, who
untied the lady. Whereat Parselius was offended,
thinking himself highly injured that any except himself should do her that service; telling him, he much
wondered at his boldness, which had made him offer
that wrong unto him.

"I did it," said the new knight, "but to give her
ease, and so to bring her that we *both* might
acknowledge humble thankfulness for this brave and
happy relief which hath brought her blessed safety!"

Parselius, hearing this courteous answer, was satisfied. Then, looking on the vanquished knight, he
demanded why he had used that cruelty to so perfect
a lady.

As [Philargus] was answering, the stranger knight
knew him! Casting his eye upon him, and without
any word, [Perissus] would as soon have deprived
him of his life, but Parselius stayed him – blaming
him for seeking the death of a man already dying.

---

¹ *she*] Echo, who loves Narcissus pines away until only
her voice remains (Ovid, *Metamorphoses* (III.356+).

² *Parselius*] perhaps a figure for the author's eldest
brother William, who died in 1613; *wonderful*] astonishing (not in a good way).

[Perissus], confessing his fault, asked pardon; and pulling off his helm, told [Parselius] that there he stood ready to receive punishment for twice so offending him.

Parselius, though not knowing him, yet seeing his excellent personage and princely countenance, embraced him, [...] he likewise taking off his helm.

When Limena (who was this sad tormented lady) saw her Perissus (for Perissus it was!), the Joy she conceived was just such as her Love could make her feel, seeing him her soul had only loved (after so many cruel changes and bitter passions in their crossed affection!) [...]

[*Philargus, dying, begs forgiveness of his wife and her noble lover.*] "Then, my Lord," said [Philargus], "Take her – and my heart's prayers, with best wishes to you. And my best-beloved Limena, in witness of my love to you, I bestow on you this most worthy lord (far better befitting you), and my whole estate." With that, embracing them, kissing her, and lastly lifting his eyes to Heaven, he departed; they (like true friends) closing his eyes.

Being now grown late, for that night they went into the cave which but lately had been the prison of sweet Limena. With them they carried the body, laying it in the further part of the hollowness. Then did Parselius tell them how infinitely happy he esteemed himself in having come so luckily to serve them; [...and] he desired most earnestly to hear the rest of Limena's story.

Which she thus began: "My lords, after I sent the letter, and the time expired, Philargus came for my answer, or to perform his vow [to kill me]; which with desire I attended, although he (contrary to my wishes) prolonged it. When he had what I resolved to give him for satisfaction, which was a direct denial [...] then did he command me to go with him (to my death, I hoped), when he brought me into a great wood, in the midst whereof he made a fire – the place being fit (and I think, sure had been used in former time) to offer sacrifice in, to the sylvan gods.

Then he made me undress myself, which willingly and readily I did, preparing myself to be the poor offering (but the richest that richness of faith in love could offer). When I had put off all my apparel but one little petticoat, he opened my breast, and gave me many wounds. The marks you may here yet discern" – letting the mantle fall again a little lower, to show the cruel remembrance of his cruelty; which, although they were whole, yet made they new hurts in the loving heart of Perissus, suffering more pain for them than he had done for all those himself had received in his former adventures. Therefore, softly putting the mantle up again, and gently covering them lest yet they might chance to smart, [he] besought her

to go on, longing to have an end of that tragical history, and to come again to their meeting, which was the only balm could be applied unto his [own] bleeding heart.

She, joyful to see this passion (because it was for her) and sorry it was Perissus did sorrow, proceeded:

"And after these [wounds], threatening many more, and death itself, if yet I consented not (but seeing nothing could prevail), he took my clothes, and with them wiped the blood off from me; I expecting nothing but the last act, which I thought should have been concluded with my burning. [But] his mind changed from the first resolution – so as taking me by the hair and dragging me into the wood among the bushes (whose curstness seconded their master's fury), tearing my skin and scratching my bare legs, to a tree he there tied me; but not long I continued there, for he going a little from me, returned with a pastor's coat, which he took from a poor man that was in that wood, seeking a lost beast. With this, he disguised me. And also having taken the man's horse, [he] took me behind him, putting a gag in my mouth, for fear I should speak for help – posting unused ways through the desert to the seaside, where he got a boat and so passed over to this place; where ever since, we have remained; for my part, with daily whippings and such other tortures, as pinching with irons (and many more, so terrible as for your sake – seeing your grief, my dearest lord – I will omit); declaring only this I must speak of, belonging to my story: Once every day he brought me to this pillar where you found me, and in the like manner bound me, then whipped me; after, washing the stripes and blisters with salt-water.

But this had been the last (had not you thus happily arrived); for he determined as he said, after my tormenting had been passed, instead of washing me with the sea-water, to cast me into her, and so make a final end of his tormenting and of my torments. To this end he likewise went yesterday to the town and bought this armor; arming himself to the intent that, after his purpose was accomplished, he might take his journey which way best he pleased. Thus [...] have you heard the afflicted life of poor Limena, in whom these tortures wrought no otherwise than to strengthen her love, and faith to withstand them: for could any other thought have entered into my heart, that would have been a greater affliction to my soul than the cursed strokes were to my body, subject only to his unnaturalness; but now – by your royal hand redeemed from misery – to enjoy the only blessing my heart can, or ever could, aspire to wish. And here have you now your faithful love, Limena." Perissus embraced her with that love his best love could express.

Forlorn Pamphilia, meanwhile, sighs away the night beneath an ash tree, fearing that Amphilanthus has fallen in love with Antissia. At dawn, "hastily rising from her low green bed," she resolves to write poetry, saying, "Since I find no redress, I will make others in part taste my pain and make them dumb partakers of my grief." Then, "taking a knife, she finished a sonnet which at other times she had begun to engrave in the bark of one of those fair and straight ashes, causing that sap to accompany her tears for love."

[U5]

Bear part with me, most straight and pleasant tree,
And imitate the torments of my smart
Which cruel Love doth send into my heart.
Keep, in thy skin, this testament of me
Which love engraven hath with misery,
Cutting with grief the unresisting part,
Which would with pleasure soon have learned love's art.
But wounds, still cureless, must my rulers be.
Thy sap doth weepingly bewray thy pain.   1
My heart-blood drops with storms it doth sustain. 2
Love, senseless, neither good nor mercy knows.
Pitiless I do wound thee, while that I,
Unpitied and unthought on, wounded cry.   3
Then out-live me, and testify my woes.

And on the roots whereon she had laid her head, serving (though hard) for a pillow at that time to uphold the richest world of wisdom in her sex, she writ this:

[U6]

My thoughts thou hast supported without rest.
My tired body here hath lain oppressed
With love and fear. Yet be thou ever blest:
Spring, prosper, last. I am alone unblest.

Antissia, rejected by Amphilanthus, arises early the next morning to walk in the Garden Woods. Pausing to sit "under the same ash wherein the other affectionate afflicted princess had written the sonnet, she was invited either by her own passion or [by] the imitation of that excellent lady to put some of her thoughts in some kind of measure; so as she – perplexed with love, jealousy, and loss (as she believed) – made this sonnet, looking upon the sun, which was then of a good height":

[U8]

The sun hath no long journey now to go
While I a progress have in my desires.
Disasters, dead-low-water-like, do show
The sand that overlooked my hoped-for hires.   4
Thus I remain, like one that's laid in briars,

Where turning brings new pain and certain woe;
Like one, once-burned, bids me avoid the fires—   5
But love (true fire) will not let me be slow.
Obedience, fear, and love do all conspire
A worthless conquest gained to ruin me,
Who did but feel the height of blest desire
When danger, doubt, and loss I straight did see.
    Restless I live, consulting what to do,
    And more I study, more I shall undo.

When the narrative returns to the Princess Pamphilia, we find her still sorrowing: "her passionate breast, scarce allowing her any respite from her passions, brought these verses to her mind, wherein she then imprinted them":

[U10]

Dear Love, alas, how I have wrongèd thee,   6
That ceaselessly thou still dost follow me?
My heart of diamond clear and hard I find
May yet be pierced with one of the same kind,
Which hath in it engraven a love more pure
Than spotless white, and deep still to endure,
Wrought in with tears of never-resting pain—
Carved with the sharpest point of curst disdain.
Rain oft doth wash away a slender mark;
Tears make mine firmer. And, as one small spark
In straw may make a fire, so sparks of love
Kindles incessantly in me to move—   7
While cruelest you do only pleasure take
To make me faster tied to scorn's sharp stake.
'Tis harder, and more strength must usèd be,
To shake a tree than boughs we bending see;
So, to move me, it was alone your power—
None else could e'er have found a yielding hour!
Curst be subjection! – yet blest in this sort,
That, 'gainst all but one choice, my heart a fort
Hath ever lasted; though besieged, not moved.
But by their miss, my strength the stronger proved,
Resisting, with that constant might, that win
They scarce could parley (much less foes get in!). 8
Yet worse than foes your slightings prove to be, [25]
When careless you no pity take on me.
Make good my dreams! – wherein you kind appear.
Be to mine eyes, as to my soul, most dear.
From your accustomed strangeness, at last, turn.
An ancient house, once fired, will quickly burn
And waste unhelped. My long love claims a time
To have aid granted to this height I climb:
    A diamond pure and hard, an unshaked tree,
    A burning house find help and prize – in me.

---

1 *bewray*] reveal.

2 *drops*] drips.

3 *wound thee*] (having carved her lament on the tree).

4 *hires*] wages.

5 *bids*] who bids.

6 *love*] Love, Cupid.

7 *Kindles*] kindle.

8 *their miss*] the failure of all those suitors who preceded you;   *win*] victory;   *parley*] talk; request terms for a truce.

Meeting in Cyprus, Pamphilia and Amphilanthus are brought to the Throne of Love, the birthplace of Venus and of her son Cupid, the god of love). The couple is there entertained by "the shepherds and shepherdesses of those plains, who after their manner sang and sported before them, to the greatest delight of all, especially Pamphilia, who (much loving poetry) liked their pretty expressions in their loves, some of which she caused to be twice sung."

[U12]
Dialogue: Shepherd and Shepherdess

Shepherdess.
Dear, how do thy winning eyes
My senses wholly tie?

Shepherd.
Sense of sight – wherein most lies
Change and variety!

Shepherdess.
Change in me?

Shepherd.
Choice in thee,
Some new delights to try.

Shepherdess.
When I change, or choose but thee, [1]
Then changèd be mine eyes!

Shepherd.
When you, absent, see not me, [10]
Will you not break these ties?

Shepherdess.
How can I ever fly
Where such perfection lies?

Shepherd.
Í must yet more try thy love:
How if that *I* should change?

Shepherdess.
Ín thy heart can never move
A thought so ill, so strange.

Shepherd.
Say I die?

Shepherdess.
Never I
Could from thy love estrange. [20]

Shepherd.
Dead, what canst thou love in me,
When hope, with life, is fled?

Shepherdess.
Virtue, beauty, faith in thee,
Which live will, though thou dead.

Shepherd.
Beauty dies.

Shepherdess.
Not where lies
A mind so richly sped. [2]

Shepherd.
Thou dost speak so fair, so kind,
I cannot choose but trust.

Shepherdess.
Nóne unto so chaste a mind [30]
Should ever be unjust.

Shepherd.
Then thus rest, true possessed
Of love without mistrust.

Another delicate maid (with as sweet a voice as her own lovely sweetness which was in her) in more than usual plaintfulness, sang this song, being as it seemed fallen out with Love or having some great quarrel to him:

[U13]
Love, what art thou? A vain thought,
    In our minds by fant'sy wrought!
    Idle smiles did thee beget
    While fond wishes made the net
    Which so many fools have caught.
Love, what art thou? Light, and fair,
    Fresh as morning, clear as th'air—
    But too soon thy evening change
    Makes thy worth with coldness range.
    Still thy joy is mixed with care. [10]
Love, what art thou? A sweet flower—
    Once full-blown, dead in an hour,
    Dust in wind, as stayed remains
    As thy pleasure, or our gains,
    If thy humor change to lour. [3]
Love, what art thou? Childish, vain,
    Firm as bubbles made by rain,
    Wantonness thy greatest pride.
    These foul faults thy virtues hide—
    But babes can no stayèdness gain. [20]
Love, what art thou? Causeless, curst,
    Yet, alas, these not the worst.
    Much more of thee may be said—
    But thy law I once obeyed,
    Therefore say no more at first.

This was much commended and by the ladies well liked of. Only Amphilanthus seemed to take Love's part and blame the maid for accusing him unjustly, especially for describing him with so much lightness. Then, to satisfy him, a spruce shepherd began a song, all the others keeping the burden of it, with which they did begin: [4]

---

[2] *sped*] furnished.

[3] *lour*] louring, ill humor.

[4] *him*] Cupid, god of love;   *keeping the burden of it*] singing the refrain ("Who can blame me," etc.).

---

[1] *but thee*] any one other than you.

[U14]

Who can blame me if I love,
Since Love before the world did move?
When I loved not, I despaired.
Scarce for handsomeness I cared.
Since so much I am refined,
As new-framed of state and mind,
   Who can blame me?
Some, in truth, of Love beguiled,
Have him blind and childish styled;
But let none in this persist.   [10]
Since (so judging) judgment missed,
   Who can blame me?
Love in chaos did appear.
When nothing was, yet he seemed clear;
Nor when light could be descried,
To his crown a light was tied.
   Who can blame me?
Love is truth and doth delight.
Whereas honor shines most bright,
Reason's self doth love approve—   [20]
Which makes us ourselves to love.
   Who can blame me?
Could I my passèd time begin,
I would not commit such sin
To live an hour and not to love.
Since love makes us parfit prove,[1]
   Who can blame me?

From **The Second Book**

Steriamus of Albania is in love with Pamphilia; but having been "chastely refused," he composes a verse-prayer to Diana, goddess of chastity:

[U15]

Pray thee, Diana, tell me, is it ill,
As some do say thou think'st it is, to love?
Methinks thou pleasèd art with what I prove,
Since joyful light thy dwelling still doth fill.
Thou seemst not angry, but with cheerful smiles
Beholdst my passions. Chaste indeed thy face
Doth seem, and so doth shine, with glorious grace
(For other loves, the trust of love beguiles).
Be bright then still, most chaste and clearest queen!
Shine on my torments with a pitying eye.   [10]
Thy coldness can but my despairs descry,
And my faith, by thy clearness, better seem.
Let those have heat that dally in the sun;
I scarce have known a warmer state than shade.
Yet hottest beams of zeal have purely made
Myself an offering burnt, as I was won.
Once sacrificed, but ashes can remain,
Which in an ivory box of truth enclose
The innocency whence my ruinness flows.[2]
Accept them as thine: 'tis a chaste love's gain.   [20]

Pamphilia wanders alone: "So stilly did she move as if the motion had not been in her, but that the Earth did go her course and stir, or as trees grow without sense of increase. But while this quiet outwardly appeared, her inward thoughts more busy were, and wrought, while this song came into her mind":

[U18]   **Song**

Gone is my joy while here I mourn
In pains of absence and of care.
The heavens for my sad griefs do turn
Their face to storms, and show despair.
The days are dark, the nights oppressed
With cloud'ly weeping for my pain,
Which, in their acting, seem distressed,
Sighing like grief for absent gain.
The Sun gives place and hides his face,
That day can now be hardly known;
Nor will the stars in night yield grace
To Sun-robbed heaven by woe o'erthrown.
Our light is fire in fearful flames,
The air tempestious blasts of wind;
For warmth – we have forgot the name,
Such blasts and storms are us assigned!
And still you blessèd heavens remain
Distemp'red, while this cursèd power
Of Absence rules, which brings my pain.
Let *your* care be more still to lour!
But when my sun doth back return,
Call yours again to lend his light,[3]
That they in flames of joy may burn,
Both equal-shining in our sight.

The shepherd Alanius, having learned the following song from a shepherdess, sings it to Pamphilia. When the song is ended, "Pamphilia much commended it, which pleased Urania infinitely":

[U20]

You powers divine of love-commanding eyes
(Within whose lids are kept the fires of love),
Close not yourselves to ruin me, who lies
In bands of death, while you in darkness move.
One look doth give a spark to kindle flames
To burn my heart, a martyr to your might.
Receiving one kind smile, I find new frames
For love, to build me wholly to your light.
My soul doth fix all thoughts upon your will,
Gazing unto amazement, greedy how
To see those blést lights of Love's heaven bow
Themselves on wretched me, who else they kill.[4]
   You then that rule love's god, in mercy flourish:
   Gods must not murder, but their creatures nourish.

---

[1] *parfit*] perfect.

[2] *but*] nothing but.

[3] *his*] its (the light of the Sun, now overclouded).

[4] *who else*] whom, otherwise.

Not one of the love affairs is going smoothly. Melasinda, queen of Hungary, burns a letter from her suitor, Ollorandus, the king of Bohemia, but not without "putting the ashes up in a dainty cabinet and enclosing them within these verses that she then made," as a testament to her "sorrow for the burning and the vows she made to them, burned":

[U21]

You pure and holy fire
(Which kindly now will not aspire
To hot performance of your nature), turn,
Cross to yourself, and never burn
These relics of a blessed hand,
Joined with mutual holy band
Of love and dear desire.
Blame me not, dearest lines,
That with love's flames your blackness twines.
My heart more mourning doth for you express,
But grief for sorrow is no less.
Deepest groans can cover, not change, woe.
Heart's the tomb, keeps in the show,
Which worth from ill refines.
Alas, yet as you burn,
My pity smarts, and groans to turn
Your pains away, and yet you must consume
Content in me, must bear no plume.
Dust-like despair may with me live,
Yet shall your memory out-drive
These pains wherein I mourn.
Your relics of pure love
To sacred keep with me remove,
Purged by this fire from harm and jealous fear,
To live with me both chaste and clear,   [25]
The true preserveress of pure truths,
Who to your grave gives a youth
In faith to live and move.   1
Famous bodies still in flames
Did anciently preserve their names.
Unto this funeral nobly you are come,
Honor giving you this tomb.
Tears and my love perform your rites,
To which constancy bears lights
To burn, and keep from blame.

From **The Third Book**

Bellamira, now in the company of Amphilanthus, talks of constancy in love, and of her poetry. "You did," said Amphilanthus, "in your discourse touch upon a quality rare in women, and yet I have seen some excellent things in their writings. Let me be so much bound to you as to hear some of your verses." Bellamira obliges him with a song that she wrote in a moment of hope, when it appeared that her lover might remain faithful to her:

[U29]

As these drops fall, so hope now drops on me
Sparingly, cool, yet much more than of late—
As with despair I changèd had a state,
Yet not possessed, govern but modestly.
Dearest, let these drops heavenly showers prove,
And but the sea fit to receive thy streams,
In multitudes compare but with sunbeams—   2
And make sweet mixture 'twixt them and thy love:
The sea's rich plenty, joined to our delights;
The Sun's kind warmth, unto thy pleasing smiles
(When wisest hearts thy love-make-eyes beguiles
And vassal brings to them the greatest sprites).   3
Rain on me rather than be dry! I gain
Nothing so much as by such harmless tears
Which take away the pains of loving fears
And finely wins an everlasting reign.
But if, like heat-drops, you do waste away
(Glad, as disburdened of a hot desire),
Let me be rather lost, perish in fire,
Than by those hopeful signs brought to decay.   [20]
Sweet, be a lover pure and permanent:
Cast off gay clothes of change and such false sleights.
Love is not love but where truth hath her rights –
Else like boughs from the perfect body, rent.

Pamphilia, forsaken and forlorn, still thinking that Amphilanthus has abandoned her for another woman, continues her sad pilgrimage through Arcadia. While waiting for her female companions, she finally sits to gaze into a stream and, "with many sorrowful sighs and deep groans, uttered this sonnet":

[U33]

Loss (my molester), at last patient be,
And satisfied with thy curst self – or move
Thy mournful force thus oft on perjured love,
To waste a life which lives by mischief's fee.
Who will behold true misery? View me!
And find, what wit hath feigned, I fully prove: 4
A heaven-like blessing, changed, thrown from above
Into despair, whose worst ill I do see.
Had I not happy been, I had not known
So great a loss. A king deposed feels most
The torment of a throne-like want, when lost,
And up must look to what late was his own.
  Lucifer, down-cast, his loss doth grieve.
  My paradise of joy gone, do I live?

As Pamphilia's female companions gather in a grove, they hear a nightingale sing. Recalling the tragic story of Procne and Philomela, the queen of Naples sings in reply to the nightingale:

---

1 *keep*] 1. stronghold or castle; 2. keeping.

---

2 *but*] nothing but.

3 *thy... beguiles*] Hope's love-making eyes beguile; *sprites*] spirits.

4 *Who will behold*] Whoever wishes to behold.

[U34]

O, that I might but now as senseless be
Of my felt pains, as is that pleasant tree
Of the sweet music thou, dear bird, dost make—
Who (I imagine) doth my woes partake.
Yet contrary we do our passions move,
Since in sweet notes thou dost thy sorrows prove.
I but in sighs and tears can show I grieve
(And those best spent, if worth do [some] believe).
Yet thy sweet pleasure° makes me ever find
That happiness to me (as Love is) *blind*;
And these thy wrongs, in sweetness to attire,
Throws down my hopes, to make my woes aspire.
Besides, of me th' advantage thou hast got:
Thy grief thou utterest. Mine, I utter not.
   Yet thus at last we may agree in one:
   I mourn° for what still is; thou, what is gone.

Hoping to win back her lover, but knowing many sad stories of women forsaken in love, Dorolina recites to her female companions a verse epistle. She reports having "framed these lines as my last piece, resolving, if they prevailed not, to let all go."

[U35]

Dear (though unconstant), these I send to you
As witnesses, that still my love is true.
Receive these lines as images of death
That bear the infants of my latest breath,
And to my triumph (though I die in woe),
With welcome glory (since you will it so).
Especially my ending is the less,
When I examples see of my distress:
As Dido, one whose misery was had
By love, for which she in death's robes was clad— [1]
Yet lost she less than I! for I possessed,
And love enjoyed. She liked what was professed
Most cruel (and the death-lik'st kind of ill,
To lose the blessing of contentment's will!).
Fair Ariadne never took more care
Than I did how you might in safety fare. [2]
Her thread my life was, to draw you from harm,
My study wholly how I might all charm
That dangerous were – while pleasures you obtained
(And I, the hazard with the labor gained).
Yet she thus° his life saved; he her honor lost.
That false prince Theseus, flying, left her crossed
With his abandoning her truth and love—
Leaving° her desolate, alone to prove
His love (or ended, or but given for need), [25]
Caused her with misery to gain that mead. [3]

---

[1] *Dido*] the founder and queen of Carthage. In Virgil's *Aeneid* Dido falls in love with Aeneas and, upon his departure, commits herself to the flames.

[2] *Ariadne*] In Greek myth, the daughter of the Cretan King, Minos; she helped Theseus to escape from the Labyrinth, and accompanied him to Naxos, where he deserted her.

[3] *or...or*] either...or; *that mead*] that reward (his love).

I, Ariadne, am alike oppressed,
Alike deserving, and alike distressed.
Ungrateful Demophon, to Phyllis fair,
A Thracian lady, caused [a] like despair [4]
Or greater far, for after fervent love—
In which blest time he freely still did prove
What is desired or loved – he left this queen
(And bliss) for a less kingdom which had been
Before his fathers – and by reason right,
For Theseus was his sire (that king of spite!). [5]
Thus did he both inherit state and ill,
While Phyllis' self her lovely self did kill,
Making a tree her throne, a cord the end
Of her affections, which his shame did send.
I strangled am, with your unkindness choked
While cruelty is with occasions cloaked. [6]
Medea, witch, with her enchanting skill
Did purchase what was cravèd by her will,
Yet was by Jason left at last – which shows
Love only free from all bewitching blows;
But his own witchcraft (which is worst of ills),
Never absenting till all joy it spills. [7]
Charms, it may be, withheld you now from me.
Break through them! Leave that Circes (so-oft free), [50]
The Sirens' song, Calypso's sweet delights,
And look on faith, which light is of true lights. [8]
Turn back the eyes of your changed heart – and see
How much you sought, how fondly once sought me.
What travail did you take to win my love!
How did you sue that I as kind would prove!
This is forgot, as yesterday's liked sport—
Love winning, lasting long, once won, proves short.
I, like Penelope, have all this time [9]
Of your absenting let no thought to climb
In me of change (though courted and pursued
By love, persuasions, and even fashions rude
Almost to force extending – yet still she

---

[4] *Demophon*] When Demophon is prevented from keeping his promise to marry her by the agreed time, Phyllis, a princess of Thrace, hangs herself in despair; whereupon she is changed into an almond tree. Ovid *Ars. Am.* 3.38.

[5] *less*] lesser.

[6] *occasions*] excuses.

[7] *Medea*] In Greek myth, a sorceress who married Jason, the leader of the Argonauts, after she helped him to obtain the Golden Fleece; he later deserted her, then killed himself in remorse; *Love only free*] that only love is free; *But*] nothing but.

[8] *Circes*] Circe, the sorceress who turned the companions of Odysseus into swine; *Sirens*] monsters, half woman and half bird, who enticed seamen to their death through the sweetness of their song; *Calypso*] a nymph who entertained Odysseus for seven years, but who could not overcome his longing to return home. All are used here as figures for Dorolina's female rivals.

[9] *Penelope*] the wife of Odysseus ("Ulysses") who like Dorolina resisted all suitors while awaiting his return.

Continued constant and, as I am, free).
Ten years a cause was for Ulysses' stay
While Troy besiegèd was – but then a way°
Was homeward bent by all save him, who stayed
And ten years more on foreign beauties preyed.
~~Against his will, he oft his will enjoyed,~~
And with variety at last was cloyed.   1
Change wearied him, when weary he returned
And, from his wand'ring, then to stayèdness turned.²
Come you now back! I thus invite you home
And love you as if you did never roam
(I have forgot it as if never done).   [75]
                                                                            3
And do but think me a new to be won:
I shall appear, it may be, as I did,
And all past faults shall in my breast be hid.
Try me again, and you shall truly find,
Where fairness wanteth, clearness of a mind
(Fairer and richer than the mass of all
Their persons which from me have made you fall,
If joined together!) – and from thence to frame
A mind of beauteous faith, fit for the name
Of worthy *constancy*, enriched with truth
(Which gave me to you, and so held my youth
In young desires, still growing to your love).   4
Nourish them now, and let me your love prove!
Leave the new powerful charms of strangers' tongues,
Which always truth (with their fair falsehood) wrongs.
Come back to me, who never knew the plot
To cross your mind, or to thy will a knot.°   5
Come, I say, come again, and (with Ulysses)
Enjoy the blessings of your best blisses.
Happy the comfort of a chaste love's bed!
Blessed the pillow that upholds the head
Of loyal loving! Shame's the other due:
Leave those, for me (who cannot be but true).

    Come, and give life, or in your stay send death
    To her that lives in you, else draws no breath. [100]

Many of the stories told in Urania *shadow forth love relationships of the rich, famous, or famously ill-behaved. In one thinly disguised tale, Wroth narrates the two unhappy marriages of James Hay, Viscount Doncaster (the future earl of Carlisle). In January 1607/8, Hay married Honora, the only child of Edward Lord Denny. The marriage turned quickly sour. In 1612, when Hay accused his wife of infidelity with an Italian diplomat, Denny threatened to kill her, to defend his "honor" – an incident that Wroth, taking Honora's part, satirizes. Procratus, a shepherd, tells the story to Queen Selarina.*

---

¹ *cloyed*] sated.

² *stayedness*] constancy.

³ *a new*] a new love; *also,* to be won anew.

⁴ *Where...mind*] where beauty is lacking, there is still the clearness of my mind; *clearness*] keenness, as well as cleanness; *Fairer*] of a mind (my own) that is fairer.

⁵ *knew the plot*] schemed.

[SIRELIUS] fell in love with a young lady, the only daughter of her father and mother. A great marriage she was likely to be. But the true riches he sought was her love answerable to his affections. She was very young, having so few years as her parents were loath she should hear of a husband. Yet at last his deserts (and store of friends!) brought the marriage about – and some honors were given to the father in requital of his consent.⁶

The lady grew on, and the time of marriage came, which was solemnized by the King's command at the Court – where great triumphs were, masques and banquets, and such Court delights. Never man with greater joy received a wife, nor any woman expressed more comfort in a match.⁷

But where such violence is, seldom is their love lasting: for within less than two years after the marriage – whether his fondness ran to jealousy, or her youth and love to change gave occasion, I dare not judge; but discontents grew, and dislikes of all sides spread themselves. The father took part with the son-in-law; the mother, with the daughter.

To that extremity this flew, as no fire flamed or sparkled higher. Most men's eyes were upon them, to see whither this would come, and for whom all this storm was raised. It was discovered that this stir was about a young lord who deserved, alas, not the least suspicion for any goodness that (for himself) could invite love from any above a common creature (such an one [as] he might purchase!); or she, because he was a lord, take upon trust to find more than promised. His pride was such as he would lose rather than beg; his ignorance such, as none that had understanding of worth would or could accept; his uncertainty such, as he was always making love, and his fortune such as he was still refused and his insolency requited with scorn. Yet of this fine gentleman, my noble friend [Sirelius] was mistrustful – his wife, I must confess, carrying a little too much respect to the other! (and yet, on my conscience, it was more out of her spirit that disdained to be curbed than [for] extraordinary liking of him – and that often is seen, and proves the way to make *truth* of mistrust).⁸

[Sirelius] forbade him his house, and her his company. She refused to obey "if by chance she might meet him."

---

⁶ *Sirelius*] James Hay (1580-1636);   *young lady*] Honora Hay Denny (m. 6 Jan. 1607/8; d. 16 Aug. 1614); *deserts*] deservings; *some honors*] Denny demanded and received a Barony, the grant of lands worth £1,000 p.a., the payment of £3,000 worth of debts and the waiving of rent arrears on various Crown lands.

⁷ *masques*] ""Lord Hay's Masque," written by Thomas Campion, was performed on Twelfth Night, 6 January 1607, on the eve of the Denny-Hay wedding.

⁸ *young lord*] Giulio Muscorno, secretary to the Venetian ambassador; *making love*] wooing women (who refused him, with scorn).

Her cabinets [Sirelius] broke open, threatened her servants to make them confess. Letters he found, but only such as between friends might pass in compliment – yet they appeared, to Jealousy, to be amorous.

[Sirelius] was so distempered as he used her ill. Her father, a fantastical thing, vain as courtiers, rash as madmen, and ignorant as women, would needs (out of folly, ill nature, and waywardness, which he called care of his "honor" and his friend's quiet) *kill* his daughter, and so "cut off the blame or spot" this her "offense" might lay upon his "noble blood" (as he termed it) – which ["noble blood"] by any other men must with much curiosity have been sought for – and as rarely found, as pearls in ordinary oysters. [1]

But what time chose he to execute his fury in, but before her husband! – whose love though cracked was not quite broken, nor so much crushed but that [Sirelius] held his [father-in-law's] hand, which with a dagger was giving her a cruel and untimely end. (Yet a little scratch he gave her, just on her heart, which otherwise had lain open to the disgrace of an unmerciful and unworthy father.) She cried out. The husband held his wife, who (poor lady!) was ready to fall under the weight of unkindness and danger. (It was a strange sight to behold a father incensed for a husband's sake against an only child, and that husband to be the shield of her defense, from whom – if at all! – the wrong was to rise.)

This at last with much ado was appeased, and a seeming content sprung out of these blusters among them. The lord [was] left to his pride – wherewith he puffed himself up, and was filled with it like a dropsy or a bladder blown with wind. The quarrel was taken up too between [Sirelius and his rival], and easily might it be [resolved], for my friend could not by any means provoke him to fight, [his rival] choosing rather to give satisfaction by oath, and promise never of seeing her more, and to be tied to any conditions, than drawing his sword. [2]

Matters thus pacified, God blessed [Sirelius and his wife] with a son and daughter; after which, she died, leaving them as witnesses of her love and to speak for remembrance of her after her death.

A widower he continued long, his children bred with much care and affection with the grandfather. Travel he did, both out of his own love to it and employment from the State; but all this could not root out the aptness of his disposition to *love* – so as he fell enamored of a beautiful young lady, daughter to a great duke in Romania, whose perfections and years called all eyes to admire her; and his, to be her vassals.

With much suit and means he courted her, employing all his friends to his assistance of gaining her. [...] [3]

She was not allowed the greatest liberty but affected it as much as any. She saw how brave his former wife had lived, and in what liberal fashion she might also with him continue. These were sweet motives to a great mind (and [to] a low estate of means, where "honor" called for [his] plenty to supply what she was endowed with. [4]

Her father was against it vehemently, and shut her up; but these courses prevail no more with a lover than to increase love's force in fetters (as any creature for keeping close grows the more furious when liberty comes). And so did her love grow to that heat, as whereas mild persuasions might at first have been acceptable, now nothing but marriage will content her; which so much gained in [Sirelius's] breast, as he vowed she should have what his fortune would allow her, and himself a loyal and affectionate servant and husband to her. This was agreed on, and they married with such joy as none can express but lovers who meet with equal affections – and so lived some time; but now, three years being passed, the heat reasonably cooled, other passions have crept in, like moths into good stuff. [...] [5]

The Queen smiled at this story [...and] left the shepherd, entreating him to use his best means to comfort his friend, and to carry him back to his wife (which she desired as a woman, and he promised to perform).

From **The Fourth Book**

Yet another of Pamphilia's companions, Pelarina, relates that she, too, has had ill fortune in love – but affirms that a woman has no escape from the bonds of a constant affection. "Though I came in like a giant, swollen with pride of my own power, and assurance of my conquest, the true knight, Love, came armed against me in arms of fire and truth. I yielded, and could not but (like a poor miserable poet) confess myself in rhyme, thus finding my error":

[U45]

> Did I boast of liberty?
> 'Twas an insolency vain:
> I do only look on thee,
> And I captive am again.

---

[1] *used her ill*] treated her badly; *her father*] Denny.

[2] *quarrel*] James Hay was himself a frequent quarreler who quarreled c.1618 with Wroth's brother Robert. When the dispute led to a brawl, Robert wrote a detailed account of the quarrel, in which he says he was never able to discover the cause of Hay's rage.

[3] *beautiful young lady*] Lucy Percy; *duke of Romania*] Henry Percy, 9th Earl of Northumberland.

[4] *affected it*] loved personal freedom; *brave*] lavish (James Hay, an infinite spender; for his costly lovesuit and unhappy marriage to the immortal Lucy Hay, see *Women's Works*, vol. 4.

[5] *shut her up*] Northumberland, kept his daughter Lucy with him in the Tower of London for a month, in an effort to prevent her marriage to James Hay.

*One day the dukes of Brunswick and Wurttemberg°
meet an old man and a young damsel traveling
together, he on a mule, she on a handsome palfrey.
As the couple traveled through the hills, "the manner
of their song was as odd as their adventure, [they]
singing dialogue-wise as if agreed – yet contrary to
the one's wishes."*

[U51]
Woman.
Fond agèd man, why do you on me gaze,
Knowing my answer? Resolution take!
Follow not fondly in an unused maze,
As if impossibilities to shake.
      For know I hate you still, and your poor love
      Can me as soon as rocks to pity move.

Man.
Alas, my dearest soul, too long I knew
I loved in vain. Your scorn I felt likewise,
Your hate I saw. Yet must I still pursue
Your fairest sight, though you do me despise,
      For love is blind, and (though I agèd be)
      I cannot part from it, nor it from me.

Woman.
What blame dost thou deserve, if thou wilt still
Follow my hate (who will not breathe to change)
And strive to gain (as if from scorn or ill)
Loving-disdain, as jewels rich and strange?
      Or canst thou vainly hope thy wailing cries
      Can move a pity? No, let this suffice!

Man.
Pity, alas! I ne'er could look to see
So much good hap. Yet, Dear, be not too cruel,
Though you (thus young) hate agèd love in me. [1]
My love hath youth, or you shall see love's fuel
      Deserving your reward. Then not deny!
      Let me now see those eyes kind, or I die. [2]

Woman.
These eyes of mine thou never shalt behold,   [25]
If clouds of true disdain may dim desire!
They shall as black be as thy faults are bold:
Demanding what's unfit, a poor old fire
      Wasted like triumphs. Sparkles only live,
      And, troubled, rise from embers which outlive.

Man.
I do confess a boldness 'tis in me
('Ought to resist, if your sweet self command),
Yet blind me needs you must – for, if I see,
Mine eyes must rest on you, and gazing stand. [3]
      Heaven not forbids the basest worm her way.
      Hide that dear beauty, I must needs decay.

Woman.
My beauty I will hide, mine eyes put out,
Rather than be perplexèd with thy sight!
A mischief certain worse is than a doubt.
Such is thy sight; thy absence, my delight.
      (Yet mine the ill, since now with thee I stay,
      Tired with all misfortune, cannot stray.)

Man.
Thy beauty hide? O no, still cruel live,
To me most hapless! Dim not that bright light
Which to this Earth all lights and beauties give!
Let me not cause for ever darkest night.
No, no, blest be those eyes and fairest face,
Lights of my soul, and guides to all true grace.
My sweet command'ress, shall I yet obey
And leave you here, alas, unguarded? Shall   [50]
I not then for sorrow ever stray
From quiet peace, or hope, and with curst thrall
Sit down and end? Yet if you say I must,
Here will I bide in banishment accurst
      (While you pass on as cruel, happy still),
      That none else triumph may upon mine ill.

*The old man and young damsel are followed by
Lemnia, a shepherdess passing through the woods,
"merrily and carelessly" singing a song of constancy
in love. Her song prompts the women to discuss
whether joy in love can ever be attained:*

[U55]
Love, grown proud with victory,
Seeks by sleights to conquer me.
Painted shows, he thinks, can bind
His commands in women's mind.
      Love but glories in fond caring;
      I most joy in not removing.
Love – a word, a look, a smile –
In these shapes can some beguile.
But he some new way must prove
To make me a vassal-love.
      Love but glories in fond loving;
      I most joy in not removing.
Love must all his shadows leave
Or himself he will deceive.
Who loves not the perfect sky
More than clouds that wanton fly?
      Love but glories in fond loving;
      I most joy in not removing.
      Love, yet thus thou mayest me win:
If thy stayèdness would begin,
Then like friends w'ould kindly meet.
When thou prov'st as true as sweet,
Love, then glory in thy loving,
And I'll joy in my removing. [4]

---

[1] *hap*] fortune, luck.

[2] *not*] do not (again at line 35).

[3] *Yet ... must*] Yet you have no choice but to blind me.

[4] *w'ould*] we would;   *When...removing*] If Love were
ever constant, true, and sweet, then might Cupid glory –
and I would joyfully abandon myself to love.

When Amphilanthus at last returns to Pamphilia, he finds her in the Hell of Deep Deceit. Amphilanthus attempts to rescue her, and is rebuffed; but Pamphilia awakens. The two lovers are at last happily reunited, "Amphilanthus joying worthily in her, "and she "as blessed as her thoughts, heart, and soul wished; [...] all now merry, contented, nothing amiss; grief forsaken, sadness cast off, Pamphilia is the Queen of all content.

· · ·

On the publication of Urania *in July 1621, Wroth sent presentation copies to King James and to the Marquess Buckingham. The King evidently valued the book: he responded on 21 July with the gift of a deer. But readers at Court soon realized that* The Countess of Montgomery's Urania *was not just another romantic novel: it was a juicy Jacobean gossip-sheet, with thinly disguised satire that some readers thought hilarious and others, outrageous. Among those who took offense was Edward Lord Denny, who accused Wroth of slander.*

Denny was a brutal man who prided himself on his capacity for violence. In 1601, he tried three times to murder Edward Purvey. Denny later besieged a petitioner's home with twenty armed men, thinking to starve the family into submission. And in 1612 he threatened to kill his own daughter, upon learning of her husband's suspicion that he had been cuckolded by an Italian diplomat.

Recognizing himself, his daughter, and his son-in-law James Hay in the story of Seralius, Denny complained bitterly to King James that "in her book of Urania *she doth palpably and grossly play upon him and his late daughter, the Lady Hay, besides many others she makes bold with." Denny demanded that* Urania *be recalled and burned. In the meantime, he fulminated against Wroth in a crude and libelous poem:* [1]

To Pamphilia from the Father-in-Law of Sirelius

HERMAPHRODITE in show, in deed a monster
(As by thy words and works all men may conster),
Thy wrothful° spite conceived an idle book,
Brought forth a fool which like the dam doth look—
Wherein thou strikes at some man's noble blood
(Of kin to thine if thine be counted good),
Whose vain comparison, for want of wit,
Takes up the oyster-shell to play with it.   [2]
Yet common oysters such as thine gape wide

And take in pearls (or worse) at every tide.   [3]
Both friend and foe to thee are even alike;
Thy wit runs mad, not caring who it strike.
These slanderous flying flames° rise from the pot,
For potted wits, enflamed, are raging hot.   [4]
How easy were't to pay thee with thine own,
Returning that which thou thyself hast thrown,
And write a thousand lies of thee at least
And by thy lines describe a drunken beast—
This were no more to thee than thou hast done,
A thrid but of thine own which thou hast spun,
By which thou plainly see'st in thine own glass
How easy 'tis to bring a lie to pass:
Thus hast thou made thyself a lying wonder.
Fools and their bables seldom part asunder.   [5]
   Work o' th' works: leave idle books alone,   [25]
For wise and worthier women have writ none.   [6]

· · ·

Mary Wroth replied tit-for-tat and posted her verses to Lord Denny, with a Right-back-at-ya cover letter:

My Lord,
   This day came to my hands some verses under the name of the Lord Denny's – but such vile, railing, and scandalous things as I could not believe they proceeded from any but some drunken poet (and that the° rather, because they so feelingly speak of that vice and sin); but to think my Lord Denny – who hath professed so much religion, justice, and love of *worth* – should fall into so strange a disposition as to slander and revile a woman-friend who hath ever honored him, I was loath to credit it! – especially knowing mine own innocency, which is as clear and pure as new-born, whatever such-like slanderous conceits have laid upon me.
   And much I do wonder how "nobleness" can fail so far as to let° such rudeness witness against itself – or rather, take that away, and leave base baseness in place of honor. Otherwise, before such proceedings had been, Truth and Worth would have had the matter questioned. But here is no such matter: violence and falsehood rules; whenas, had I been asked, I would have truly and constantly sworn that I no more meant harm to my Lord Denny or his house than to myself, nor did I intend ever one word of that book to his lordship's person or disgrace – and yet I will this say° to justify myself (but not in way of satisfaction, for too coarse ways are taken with me to offer or give that, but by way of justification).

---

[1] Chamberlain, *Letters* (ed. 1939), 2.427.

[2] *Hermaphrodite*] *i.e.*, a woman by writing fiction, a male prerogative, confuses her gender; *in deed*] 1. in your writing; 2. in sexual intercourse; 3. indeed; *conster*] construe; *wrothful*] wrathful (punning on Wroth's name); *dam*] mother, usually of animals; *vain*] 1. haughty; 2. futile; *want of wit*] lack of intelligence; *oyster-shell*] with reference to Wroth's remark that a drop noble blood in the veins of Sirelius's father-in-law would be as hard to find as pearls in ordinary oysters (*Urania* [1621], p. 439).

[3] *common oysters ... wide*] books (and genitals) such as thine will make room for anything (or any man).

[4] *pot*] cooking pot; *potted*] preserved in a closed pot (as was done with salted meat); *i.e.*, once you took your wit out of storage and tried to make use of it, it promptly caught fire and got over-roasted.

[5] *thrid*] 1. thread; 2. third; *lying wonder*] an amazing liar; a horizontal marvel; *bables*] 1. bauble, toy (often, a euphemism male genitalia); 2. babbles.

[6] *Work o 'th 'works*] study biblical and devotional works.

Yet, because I will not follow ill examples, I send your lordship your own lines (as they were called to me), reversed, and the first copy (as desiring your own eyes should be first witness of your reward for your poetry – if it *were* yours!). This is the course I take yet – although your lordship certainly knows I may take others and am not by this barred from any. I should have taken it as an expression of your worth, had you proceeded on just grounds. Now I shall pity your rash folly, and wish you amendment of understanding; and to take this as a morning's work.

Mary Wroth,
the 15th of February

Railing Rhymes Returned upon the Author

> by Me, Mary Wroth

HERMAPHRODITE in sense, in art a monster
(As by your railing rhymes the world may conster)
Your spiteful words against a harmless book,
Shows that an *ass* much like *the sire* doth look.   1
Men truly noble fear no touch of blood,
Nor question make of others much more good.
Can such "comparisons" seem the "want of wit"
When "oysters" have enflamed your blood with it?
(But it appears your guiltiness gaped wide
And filled with dirty doubt your brain's swollen tide.)
Both friend and foe in deed you use alike
And (your wit, mad° in sherry) equal strike.   2
These slanderous flying flames, raised from the pot,
You know are false – and raging makes you hot.   3
How easily now do you receive your own
(Turned on yourself from whence the squib was thrown),
When these few lines, not thousands writ at least,
Mainly thus prove *yourself* the drunken beast.   4
This is far less to you than you have done,
A "thrid"° but of your own (all words worse spun),
By which you lively see in your own glass
How hard it is for you to lie and pass:
Thus you have made yourself a lying wonder.   5
Fools and their pastimes should not part asunder.
  Take this, then. Now let railing rhymes alone, [25]
  For wise and worthier men have written none.

> *—Pamphilia.*

Other readers were less offended by the novel's satirical thrusts than by its erotic content. Sir Aston Cokayne wrote, "The Lady Wroth's *Urania* is replete / With elegancies, but too full of heat" – "For amo-

---

[1] *sense*] meaning; sexual desire;   *shows*] show.

[2] *in deed*] 1. indeed; 2. in your action.

[3] *These*] your own;   *flames*] burning emotions (*OED* sb. 6a);   *pot*] drinking-pot.

[4] *squib*] 1. firecracker; 2. sarcasm.

[5] *thrid*] 1. thread; 2. third;   *to lie and pass*] 1. to get away with lying; 2. to defecate (*OED* sb. 50) while lying down, drunk;   *lying wonder*] 1. an amazing liar; 2. a wonder, that you should lie in your own mess.

---

rous lines will many mischiefs raise, / And makes the cinders of affection blaze." [6]

Wroth proved the better spin-master: in December, only five months after *Urania* was printed, she wrote a letter of apology to Marquess Buckingham in which she coyly expresses astonishment that the virtuous lords and ladies of Court should see themselves reflected in her *roman á clef.* Wroth states (which may be true) that she has since directed the stationers, John Marriot and John Grismand, to withdraw *Urania* from sale and to box up unsold copies (though it is doubtful they would have done so, unless compelled by a warrant); and she expresses her willingness for purchased copies to be called in – beginning with the presentation copy that Wroth had given to Buckingham as a gift – but she doubts that anyone will forfeit so good a book without the King's warrant. Wroth closes with the usual CYA disclaimer (heard throughout the early modern period, and believed by no one) that the author played no part in the book's publication:

[Lady Mary Wroth to the Marquess Buckingham]

My Lord,

Understanding some of the strange constructions which are made of my book – contrary to my imagination and as far from my meaning as is possible for Truth to be from Conjecture; my purpose no way bent to give the least cause of offense, my thoughts free from so much as *thinking* of any such thing as I am censured for – I have with all care caused the sale of [*Urania*] to be forbidden, and the books left, to be shut up. For those that are abroad, I will likewise do my best to get them in, if it will please your lordship to procure me the King's warrant to that effect – without which, none will deliver them to me.

Besides: that your Lordship will be pleased to let me have that which I sent you – the example of which will, without question, make the others the willinger to obey.

For mine own part, I am extremely grieved that I am thus much mis-taken; but yet comforted with this: that it is an injury done to me undeservedly (although to be accused in this nature *is* a great wrong to me). I beseech your lordship therefore thus far to right me as to believe this for truth; and what I am able to do for the getting-in of books (which from the first were sold against my mind, I never purposing to have them published) I will with all care and diligence perform. So, I humbly take my leave.

From London, the 15 of December 1621,
Mary Wroth

---

[6] *The Lady Wroth's* Urania ... *blaze*] A. Cokayne, "Remedy for Love," lines 21-2, 17-18.

The exchange between Wroth and Denny continued. In his letter of 26 February Denny advises Wroth not to be so vain as to "count [her] book innocent, which all the world condemns." He sanctimoniously advises her "to follow the example of your virtuous and learned aunt, who translated so many godly books, and especially the holy Psalms of David"; and to "redeem the time with writing as large a volume [of] heavenly lays and holy love as you have of lascivious tales and amorous toys." [1]

Wroth in her reply complains that Denny has used "all ill and curst courses you could to the King against me; made these rhymes, acknowledged them against me particularly [...] with all rage and spleen." She closes her letter of 29 February with a challenge and a threat:

[...] I know how to appear equal in Truth, or near in blood to the best; therefore that is no bugbear to me. I shall with all clearness and truth witness my innocency, and not now with words (or submission, which I scorn) go about to give satisfaction, but prove and justify this I have said. If you desire truth, let me know my accusers, and you shall find me what my blood calls me to be (and what my words have said me to be). Fear not to say what you please, for my noble allies will not thank you for forbearing me, nor (when the time shall serve) spare you for what you have done.

Among those "noble allies" was William Herbert, Earl of Pembroke, Lord Chamberlain. Denny got the message. While defending his actions ("I hate to be an informer"), his final letter to Wroth is drained of the acid: "I say you are a noble lady, and for those noble allies of yours, I will ever honor and serve, when you have made the worst of me you can devise unto them." [2]

Wroth was already at work on a sequel. *The Second Part of Urania* – a holograph draft of nearly 240,000 words – is preserved today in the Newbury Library. In *The Second Part*, which commences from the final sentence of the printed book, Wroth returns to her old play, *Love's Victory*, cannibalizing its plot and characters for inclusion in her continuing epic of Love. Several illegitimate children now join the narrative, who prove their worth and noble blood despite being born out of wedlock. (The narrator equivocates about their parentage; but she is clearly quite fond of them.)

While introducing a new generation of lords, ladies, and scoundrels, the *Second Part* again features the saga of Pamphilia and Amphilanthus. Both are now married: Pamphilia is wedded to Rodomandro, King of Tartaria ("no orator," but a "plain, blunt" man who graciously indulges Pamphilia's desire to be left alone with her books). Amphilanthus (to spite Pamphilia) has married a Slavonian princess. Each feels betrayed by the other – but they do have moments of happiness. Shortly after the death of Pamphilia's husband and infant son, she is reunited with Amphilanthus on the island of Cyprus, where they reconcile and promise to be chaste Platonic lovers. But Amphilanthus must search for an illegitimate son who has gone missing, named Fair Design – at which point the manuscript ends in midsentence: "Amphilanthus was extremely." [...]

Wroth and Herbert's own relationship in the years that followed was not altogether Platonic. The poet was a frequent visitor at Baynards Castle and in 1623 gave birth to twins (a daughter, Katherine, and a son, William), fathered by Pembroke. But Herbert's support for his constant lover did not extend so far as to relieve her ongoing financial distress. In 1623 Wroth appealed to the King for one year's protection from her creditors, to avoid being arrested for debt. On 3 January 1623/4, now the mother of two infants, she wrote to Edward Conway, Secretary of State, to say that she had paid half of her debts (presumably with Pembroke's money) and hoped to pay all in a year. But it was at about this time that Pembroke discarded her. In 1629 we find him in pursuit of Lucy Hay (who figures in *Urania* as the second wife of Sirelius); it is perhaps heartbreak, rather than hostile book reviews or the quarrel with Edward Denny, that caused Wroth to abandon her Love-epic. The debts went unpaid. Year after year, Wroth applied for, and received, renewed protections from the King. But it's surprising that Pembroke, who was now one of the nation's five wealthiest men, did so little to relieve the mother of his children.

A eulogy of Pembroke written by Edward Hyde, Earl of Clarendon (a friend and great admirer) sheds light on Mary Wroth's beloved Amphilanthus:

Sure never man was planted in a Court, that was fitter for that soil or brought better qualities with him to purify that air. Yet his memory must not be flattered [...] He indulged to himself the pleasures of all kinds, almost in all excesses. To women – whether out of his natural constitution, or for want of his domestic content and delight (in which he was most unhappy, for he paid much too dear for his wife's fortune, by taking her person into the bargain) – he was immoderately given up. But therein he likewise retained such a power and jurisdiction over his very appetite that he was not so much transported with beauty and outward allurements, as with those advantages of the mind, as manifested an extraordinary wit, and spirit, and knowledge, and administered great pleasure in conversation. To these he sacrificed himself, his precious time, and much of his fortune. [°]

Living in the seventeenth century when faithfulness was demanded of women, discounted in men, and struggling along on limited means, loving the wrong man, Mary Wroth was nonetheless a woman of wit, and spirit, and knowledge. The greater sacrifice was hers. She died in obscurity in 1651 or 1653, probably in Woodford.

---

[1] H.M.C. *Salisbury* (*Cecil*) v.22 (1971) p. 161, ed. DWF.

[2] *Ibid.*

Gender, Class, and Politics

it is a naturall vertu incident to our sexe
to be pitifull of those that ar afflicted.

—Queen Elizabeth to Dr. Dale, her Ambassador to France (1 Feb. 1573/4)

KING JAMES, who showed himself to the public only when necessary, rarely missed an opportunity to exhibit his contempt for the commonalty. On migrating to England in 1603 and finding that the English people thronged to set eyes on him, he was worried for his safety and annoyed at their impudence. (As James VI of Scotland, his Majesty generally prohibited public assembly of more civilians than could be seated in a church.) Sir John Oglander reports that England's new king was neither "popular" (populist) or "plausible" (ingratiating) "to his subjects that desired to see him." When crowds gathered in the streets, King James would curse and demand of the English lords what the people wanted. When told that his subjects came out of love to see his person, "then he would cry out in Scottish, 'God's wounds! I will pull down my breeches and they shall also see my arse!'" [1]

Throughout the Jacobean period, super-rich families grasped an ever-larger portion of the nation's real estate, a trend that James not only authorized but accelerated. To reward his favorites, he gave away vast demesnes and manors. To support his spending habits, he sold off Crown lands at bargain prices to favored aristocrats. And he allowed prominent statesmen, most notably Robert Cecil, by means of their high office, to become great land-moguls.

Landed families, including provincial gentry, exploited the poor with a ruthlessness unequaled in Elizabeth's days. Rents charged to tenant-farmers soared. Those who could not afford to pay were driven off the land (many of them, families that had tilled the same field for generations). The severe plagues of 1603/4 and 1608/9 led to a shortage of workers, bringing higher wages – but the survivors found more food, better shelter, and better pay in the cities. Landowners responded by converting tillage into deer parks for hunting, and pasturage for sheep. Winters of unprecedented cold and snow, and severe summer storms and drought, contributed to the diminishing annual harvest. And as famine increased, the wealthy hoarded grain, driving up prices still further.

The poor had a customary right to forage for food or fuel and to plant vegetable gardens on public-access ground, but even that traditional right came under assault by the rapid enclosure of the common lands and wastes on which the livelihood of peasants depended. Thick hedges, fence-palings, and water-filled ditches were constructed by land-owners. Trespassers were beaten with impunity. This assault on the landless poor, which began in earnest in 1593 (thanks to relaxed prohibitions), escalated under James; in the early years of whose reign, many open-field communities were turned into rural ghettoes without means of survival, and without so much as access to the old footpaths from one place to another.

A peasants' revolt against enclosures began in Northamptonshire in April 1607. John Reynolds of Desborough rallied the poor to commit acts of creative vandalism, tearing down barriers and damming the trenches. The May Day festivities of 1607, in the vicinity of Rockingham Forest and perhaps elsewhere, were more angry than festive: protests erupted in Haselbech, Pytchley and Rushton, and soon spilled over into Leicestershire and Warwickshire.

King James on 30 May issued a Proclamation commanding his lieutenants to silence the tumult:

By the King°

WHEREAS some of the meaner sort of our people did of late assemble themselves in riotous and tumultuous manner within our county of Northampton, sometimes in the night, and sometimes in the day, under pretense of "laying open" enclosed grounds, of late years taken in ("to their damage," as they say); the repressing whereof We did first refer only to the due course of justice, and the ordinary proceedings of the Commissioners of the Peace (and other [of] our ministers in such cases); forasmuch as We have perceived since, that lenity hath bred in them rather *encouragement* than *obedience*, and that they have presumed to gather themselves in greater multitudes, as well in that county as in some others adjoining—

---

[1] *popular...arse*] Ed. DWF from Oglander (1936), 196.

We find it now very necessary to use sharper remedies. Wherefore, We will and command all lieutenants [etc....] immediately to suppress them by whatsoever means they may, be it by force of arms, if admonitions and other lawful means do not serve to reduce them to their duties. For We cannot but be justly moved to such severity against those who unjustly throw a slander upon our government, by taking that pretense for their disobedience [...] (30 May 1607).

• • •

Over the next several days, more than one thousand men and women gathered at Newton, intending to re-open lands enclosed by the hated Tresham family. The "trained bands" (the local militias) were called up to suppress the protest – but sympathetic enlisted men of Northamptonshire resisted the muster. The Treshams, Montagues, and Mildmays therefore armed their own servants.

Two of the reputed leaders were abducted and summarily executed. The vandalism continued. On 8 June, in a field near Newton, Edward Montagu and Anthony Mildmay with their private militia confronted the protesters gathered there; accused them of malicious damage to property, and of seditious libel (for being critical of James's government); and commanded the crowd to disperse. When the people refused to leave, the shooting started. Gilbert Talbot, earl of Shrewsbury, reports that "Sir Anthony Mildmay and Sir Edward Montagu repaired to Newton, Mr. Thomas Tresham's town, where 1000 of these fellows who term themselves "Levellers" were busily digging":

"These gentlemen [Mildmay, Montagu, and Tresham] (finding great backwardness in the trained bands) were constrained to use all the horse they could make, and as many foot[men] of their own servants and fellows as they could trust; and [they] first read the Proclamation twice unto [the Levellers], using all the best persuasion to them to desist that they could devise. But when nothing would prevail, they charged them with their horse and foot. [At] the first charge [the Levellers] stood and fought desperately. But at the second charge they ran away, in which were slain some forty or fifty of them, and a very great number hurt. One Sir Henry Fooks, that led the foot against them, is very sore hurt and bruised in many places of his body." [1]

Prisoners were taken and kept under guard in St. Faith's church – an unreported number of whom were then hanged and quartered by military tribunal, and their body parts hung in the villages round about as an object lesson to the peasantry that they ought not to mess with the property of others.

Anger mounted, with reports of 3,000 peasants tearing down enclosures at Hillmorton in Warwickshire, and 5,000 at Cotesbach in Leicestershire. In the city of Leicester, a new gallows was erected to hang captured protesters – and demolished by vandals the same night.

The rebels of Warwickshire, calling themselves "Diggers," circulated a proclamation of their own, a manuscript text that was presumably read aloud to the people, few of whom were literate: [2]

The Diggers of Warwickshire to All Other Diggers°

L OVING FRIENDS and subjects (all under one renowned Prince, for whom we pray long to continue in his most royal estate, to the subverting of those subjects, of what degree soever, that have or would deprive his most true-hearted commonalty both from life and living): We, as members of the whole, do feel the smart of these encroaching tyrants, which would grind our flesh upon the whetstone of poverty, and make our loyal hearts to faint with breathing – so that *they* may dwell by themselves in the midst of their herds of fat wethers.

It is not unknown unto yourselves the reason why these merciless men do resist with force against our good intents [...] They have depopulated and overthrown whole towns, and made thereof sheep pastures, nothing profitable for our commonwealth – for the common fields, being laid open, would yield us much commodity, besides the increase of corn, on which stands our life. [...]

But if you happen to show your force and might against us, we for our parts neither respect life nor living; for better it were in such case for us to manfully die (than hereafter to be pined to death for want of that which these devouring encroachers do serve their fat hogs and sheep withal). [...]

—We rest as Poor Delvers and Day-Laborers for the good of the Commonwealth, till death. [3]

---

[1] G. Talbot to Sir John Manners et al. (11 June 1607), ed. DWF from Lodge, *Illustrations* (1791): 3.320-1.

[2] *Levellers ... Diggers*] These nicknames would be remembered and adopted by democratic protesters a generation later, during the English Civil Wars. (See Mary Overton, *Women's Works*, vol. 4.)

[3] *wethers*] rams castrated for more tender mutton.

The King answered with another proclamation: in a torrent of nearly 2000 words, his Majesty condemned the Midlands rising; expressed his approval that "blood was drawn, as well by martial execution as by civil justice"; and further authorized magistrates throughout England – "merely out of love of justice" and in "Christian compassion" for law-abiding subjects, to pursue and punish the undutiful poor "with all severity for their so heinous treasons" ("By the King," 28 June 1607).

Outgunned, the peasants by mid-July were routed and subdued. No record survives of how many desperate commoners were mowed down for their heinous treasons.

A third royal proclamation offered a pardon to those protesters who came forward to their local magistrate, registered their names and habitation, and confessed to their participation in the rising— "whereof we will and command a note or entry to be made and kept" ("By the King," 24 July 1607). Among those who trusted to the King's promise of clemency was at least one woman, Winifred Turner of Stanion, who confessed her guiltiness, and signed with her mark.

(These tumults and their violent suppression registered scarcely a blip in London. But John Brinsley, who was there when it happened, was horrified by the "wickedness and impiety" of the Levellers' Insurrection: "was it not fearfully begun?" recalled Rev. Brinsley in 1622. "Did not all who lived near plainly see and dread the danger – and after, admire God's gracious deliverance? Though now it be utterly forgot" and may "seem nothing or small to them who dwelt far from it," Rev. Brinsley warns that if the rich do not soon temper "their hoarding-up" of grain and their "spoiling the poor," sinful rebellion could erupt yet again, "as a mighty stream, of a sudden.") [1]

After disbanding his first Parliament in February 1610/11, James ruled by "royal prerogative," issuing Proclamations almost as fast as his royal stationers could print them off. His decrees variously prohibited the manufacture of starch; forbade inn-holders to use large wine caskets; banned new construction within two miles of London; banned the preparation of meat during Lent; etc. Most hated by the merchant class was the King's imposition of duties payable to the Crown, above what was authorized by Parliament; and his imposed restrictions on the trade and manufacture of most commodities, with penalties for neglecting the exclusive rights of those who held patents and monopolies purchased from the Crown.

Meanwhile, landowners discovered they could increase revenue by evicting their least productive tenants and raising rents for those who remained. In a policy forged by Robert Cecil, James denied tenants' claim of entitlement to their copyhold. *A Proclamation against tenant-rights* (28 July 1620) declared that all customary rights were henceforth "extinguished and abolished," without recourse in law (a decree that has been described as "one of the most flagrant exertions of despotism to be met with in the annals of England"). This cruelty fell most heavily on families without an adult male laborer, many of whom were turned off the land, to survive by begging or prostitution until they perished by disease, hunger, or hanging. [2]

Depopulation of the villages and farmlands led to high unemployment in London, which James addressed in still another *Proclamation for the punishing of vagabonds, rogues, and idle persons*° (1616; cf. 1603). His Majesty now targeted "all persons, both men and women, that by the laws of this Realm may be taken for rogues or vagabonds, and all idle persons and masterless men not having wherewith to live, nor living by any lawful labor or occupation, and being our natural-born subjects." The King commanded "that they (and every of them) do within two days next after the publishing of this Proclamation depart and avoid themselves from the said cities of London and Westminster and the suburbs of the same, and from [...] all other towns and villages within thirty miles compass of the said cities [...] and to repair to the counties and places where they were born." The King authorized a door-to-door search, with imprisonment of all men and women who could not prove gainful employment. And if they "shall not be readily reformed," magistrates were commanded "to apprehend all such; and presently, without delay, to execute them upon the gallows, by order of martial law," without so much as a show trial.

Hunger and unemployment were finally addressed in the King's 1622 *Proclamation for Relief of the poor, and remedying the high prices of corn*°; in which James commanded "persons of quality" likewise to retire from London, to their country estates, and there to make "the poor set on work." The peers were commanded further to furnish the country markets with grain, "ratably and weekly with such quantities as reasonably they may and ought to do." Confident of this bail-out plan, the King added a threat: "his Majesty, having thus carefully provided for relief of his poor sort of subjects, doth declare and strictly

---

[1] *was it not…of a sudden*] Ed. DWF from John Brinsley, *The Third Part of the True Watch* (1622), 1v, P4v.

[2] *one of the most…annals of England*] J. Hodgson (1810), p. 189.

charge and command, that if any, under pretense of 'poverty' and 'want,' shall leave their ordinary labor, or assemble together in unfit manner, or otherwise insolently behave themselves, that they be corrected and punished."

On 28 April 1613, in the gallery at Whitehall, someone "let fall" a book called *A Vision of Balaam's Ass*. Dedicating his work to King James, "Peter Hay" (pseud.) urged ecumenism, with religious tolerance for loyal Catholics – which was the King's own policy, though it infuriated the Protestant Commons. George Cotton, the book's supposed author, was imprisoned in the Tower on 14 June, without trial. Six years later, the true author of *Balaam's Ass* was discovered to be a commoner named Williams. The King to satisfy his critics threw Williams to the wolves: the fellow was arraigned at the King's Bench on 3 May 1619 and found guilty. Two days later he was hanged, drawn, and quartered at Charing Cross.

Sensitive to criticism, King James in 1620 issued a *Proclamation against Excess of Lavish and Licentious Speech of Matters of State* – a ban on political punditry. His Majesty boasts of having permitted more "openness and liberty of discourse, even concerning matters of State (which are no themes or subjects fit for vulgar persons or common meetings) than hath been in former times used or permitted"; but while free speech in praise of his person and policies are welcome to his royal hearing, criticism is not. He will no longer endure his subjects uttering "undutiful speeches" or "speaking too freely of matters above their reach." The King's purpose in this new proclamation was

to give forewarning unto our loving subjects of this excess and presumption; and straitly to command them (and every of them, from the highest to the lowest) to take heed how they intermeddle, by pen or speech, with causes of State and secrets of empire, either at home or abroad; but contain themselves within that modest and reverent regard of matters above their reach and calling, that to good and dutiful subjects appertaineth. As also, not to give attention or any manner of applause or entertainment to such discourse, without acquainting some of our Privy Councilors or other principal officers therewithal, respective to the place where such speeches shall be used, within the space of twenty-four hours, under pain of imprisonment and our high displeasure. And let no man think, after this our warning, to pass away with impunity in respect of the multitude and generality of offenders in this kind; but know that it will light upon some of the first or forwardest of them to be severely punished, for example to others. [...]

Blaming dissent on "rashness, evil custom, or too much passion" arising "from the overflow of a worse or more corrupt fountain," James warns his critics that he will not be fooled by commentary that compliments his person only as sugar-frosting upon criticism of his policies ("By the King," 24 Dec. 1620).

His Majesty's ban on punditry proved ineffectual. Less commentary may have reached print as a result, but manuscript circulation proliferated. London satirists became more brazen, mocking the King, ridiculing the Villiers clan, and blasting government corruption. In July, James therefore reissued his Proclamation, further expressing his royal displeasure that political commentary "doth daily more and more increase" despite "the strictness of our commandment" against it ("By the King," 26 July 1621).

Further to restore civility, the King issued a *Proclamation for Suppressing Insolent Abuses committed by Base People against Persons of Quality [...] in the Streets of the City and Suburbs of London,* in which London authorities were commanded to suppress any base "gesture or countenance," "word or deed" directed by the city's poor at their betters; and "to endure these insolencies no longer" but to subdue "this wicked and devilish humor of those base people by severity of justice and punishment" ("By the King," 8 Apr. 1621). Poor women of London, though unsuspected of witchcraft, could now fear hanging just for giving a rich man the finger.

Queen Anna having died in March, she did not live to see her daughter and son-in-law crowned on 4 November 1619 as King and Queen of Bohemia. Their reign was short: only a year later, the Protestant Union was routed at White Mountain. Frederick and Elizabeth became exiles at the Hague, living on charity. The commons clamored for military aid to Continental Protestants. King James, dragging his heels, was unfairly denounced as an infidel and a coward, which was only half true.

On 16 Jan. 1620/1, James summoned Parliament, his first in seven years. The King wanted money. The Commons wanted war. The MPs might be persuaded to levy new taxes to finance their hawkish platform. By raising revenue and yet avoiding conflict, James could pocket the windfall. That was the plan – but it soon foundered. Other concerns intervened: the Commons resented the Crown's practice of raising money by selling monopolies and patents that enriched the few while afflicting hardship on everyone else. Through impeachment proceedings, the MPs went after Sir Giles Mompesson, Sir Francis Michel, and Sir Francis Bacon, the officials chiefly responsible for the abuse of patents and monopolies. Buckingham and his kin remained in the cross-hairs.

Flexing its muscles in the second session, the House of Commons in November 1621 framed a petition demanding the marriage of Charles to a Protestant; enforcement of anti-Catholic legislation at home; and a declaration of war on Spain. The King demanded a retraction. Instead, MPs of the House of Commons drafted a defiant statement affirming their rights, including the right to freedom of speech. On 8 February 1621/2, James angrily ripped those pages out of the Record Book and dissolved Parliament.

While the English nation, now in a Great Depression, dreamed of making war on Spain, Prince Charles, depressed and 22, dreamed of making love to the Spanish Infanta. King and Prince forged a plan to revive a long-dormant proposal (from the Spanish ambassador, Gondomar) for the marriage of Charles to Princess Maria Anna, with a suggested dowry of £600,000 (which was more than James had in his bankrupt treasury). James found support from the Howards and other Catholic-leaning families ("the Spanish party"), who favored ecumenism; the Protestant majority was bitterly opposed.

Among the many manuscript "libels" that circulated at Court in opposition to the Spanish match was a verse petition called "The Commons' Tears." The poem has not survived, but we have King James's irritable reply: his rebuttal makes clear that the author of "The Commons' Tears" not only denounced the planned marriage of Charles to a foreign Roman Catholic, but chastised his Majesty for not coming to the aid of Frederick and Elizabeth; went on to make unfavorable comparison between the great statesmen of Elizabeth's reign and the greedy parasites of James's regime; and complained of the King's failure to co-operate with Parliament to solve the nation's ills.

In January 1622/3, at Whitehall, King James "let fall" his unsigned reply, called "The Wiper-Away of the People's Tears." Invoking his political creed (Divine Right and the Royal Prerogative of kings), James reaffirmed his right to punish dissent with death. A surprise followed: the next anonymous poem to be discovered at Whitehall was a reply to the King "by a Lady" – presumably an aristocrat but one who took the part of the abused commons, urging the King to show some moderation and common sense, for once.

At about the same time, George Villiers (Marquess Buckingham) and Prince Charles sneaked off to Spain without an invitation, traveling incognito under the names Thomas and John Smith. Arriving in Madrid on 17 February 1622/3, they disclosed their identity to the astonished King Philip IV, and declared the purpose of their visit. The Spanish king gave his guests a gracious welcome. Never would Philip consent to the match without a repeal of England's anti-Catholic legislation and Charles's own conversion to the Roman faith, but for political advantage Philip was slow to show his hand.

As a gloomy nation awaited news from Spain, James wrote incessantly to his "dear "Baby" and "sweet Steenie," anticipating success. To lend the envoy more clout, the King on 18 May 1623 elevated Villiers to a dukedom, and dispatched to Spain a shipload of gifts and gentleman retainers. But all was for naught: Buckingham's arrogance and the Prince's goofiness made a poor impression on the Infanta, who told her father she would sooner join a nunnery than wed a stuttering English heretic.

In July, recognizing defeat, James wrote to his "sweet boys," telling them to come back home. Humiliated and bitter, Charles returned to England in October, without a bride – to the great jubilation of the Protestant majority. James was now in poor health; the domestic economy, a smoking ruins; his foreign policy, a laughingstock, and his treasury, bankrupt. Buckingham now ruled as virtual king of Britain, dictating policy, with Charles as his devoted sidekick. King James from here on out played only a ceremonial role. But he never forsook his ideal of ruling by sovereign fiat. His last decrees:

> By the King: *A Proclamation charging all Jesuits, [Roman Catholic] seminaries, etc., to depart the land* (6 May 1624) – a deportation notice for believers in the old religion, on pain of imprisonment.
>
> By the King: *A Proclamation concerning royal mines* (10 July 1624) – an advertised offer to sell long-term rights to dig for precious metals on Crown lands (a royal scam, to raise money).
>
> By the King: *A Proclamation against seditious, popish, and puritanical books and pamphlets* (15 Aug. 1624) – further censorship of nonconformists and their literature, on pain of imprisonment.
>
> By the King: *A Proclamation concerning tobacco* (29 September 1624) – a ban on the importation, snuffing, chewing, or smoking of any but Virginia-grown product.
>
> By the King: *A Proclamation for the apprehension of Edward Eakins* (14 December 1624) – a call for the arrest and execution of Eakins, a yeoman of Northamptonshire who was alleged to have poached deer from his Majesty's enclosed deer-park at Higham-Ferrers.
>
> By the King: *A Proclamation for proroguing the Parliament* (3 March 1624/5). Adjourned 15 March.

King James died on 27 March. For his wake and funeral (the most expensive ever seen in Britain), Prince Charles and the Duke of Buckingham commissioned two wax effigies of the late king; provided black robes for nine thousand official mourners; and spent upwards of £50,000 in borrowed funds. The lavish expense not only went unpaid for, but unrequited: When King Charles died twenty-four years later, he had no funeral. His beheaded corpse was coffined without ceremony, and misplaced.

The Wiper of the People's Tears, The Dryer-Up of Doubts and Fears

(*His Majesty's Answer unto a Libel* [*1623*])

O, STAY your tears, ye that complain
And cry as babes do, all in vain.
Purblind people! Why do you prate?
Too shallow for the depth of State,
You cannot judge what's truly mine
Who see no further than the ryne.   1
Kings walk the heavenly Milky Way,
But you in° bypaths go astray.
God and King do pace together,
But vulgars wander light as feather.

    I should be sorry you should see
My actions before they be
Brought to the full of my desires.
God (above all°) kings inspires.
Hold *you* the public, beaten way:
Wonder at Kings, and them obey.
For under God they are to choose
What rights, to take; and what, refuse.
Whereto, if you will not consent,
Yet hold your peace – lest you repent
And be corrected for your pride,
That kings' designs dare thus deride°
By railing rhymes and vaunting verse
(Which *your* King's breast shall never pierce!).

    Religion is the right of kings   [25]
As they best know what good it brings—
Whereto you must submit your deeds
Or be pulled up like spoiling weeds.   2

    Kings ever use their instruments
Of whom they judge by the events: 3
The good, they cherish and advance
(And many things may come by chance).
Content yourself with such as I
Shall take near me and place on° high.
The men you named served in their time
And so may mine, as clear from crime.

    All seasons have their proper vents
And bring forth several events:
Whereof the choice doth rest in kings
Who punish (and reward them brings).
O, what a calling were a king
If he might have°, nor take, no thing
But such as *you* should to him bring!
Such were a King but in a play,
If he might bear no better sway
(And then were you in worser case!).

If so to keep your ancient face,
Your° face would soon outface his° might.
Alas, fond men, play not with kings,   [50]
With lion's claws, or° serpent's stings:
They kill even by their sharp aspect.   4
The proudest mind they can deject,°
Make wretched the most mightiest man
Though he doth mutine° what he can.

    Your censures are a whurring° sound
That rise as vapors from the ground.
I know when it shall be most fit,
With whom to fill, and empty it.
The Parliament, I will appoint
When I see things more out of joint:
Then will I set all wry things straight
And not upon your pleasures wait—
Where do you speak, as *wise* men should   5
(If not, by me you shall be schooled).
Was ever King called to account,
Or ever mind so high durst mount
As for to know the cause and reason?
As to appoint the means and season
When kings should ask their subjects' aid?
Kings cannot so be made afraid!
Kings will command [and bear the sway;
Kings will inquire°] and find the way
How all of you may eas'liest pay
(Which they'll lay out as they think best   [75]
In earnest sometimes, and in jest).
What counsels would be° overthrown
If all were to the people known!
Then to no use were Council tables
If State affairs were public baubles.   6
I make no doubt all wise men know   7
This were the way to all our woe:
For ignorance of causes makes
So many gross and foul mistakes.

    The model of our princely match   8
You cannot make, but mar or patch!
Alas, how weak would prove your care!
Wish only you his best welfare,
Your reasons cannot weigh the ends,
So mixed they are 'twixt foes and friends.
Wherefore again, near-seeing people,
Strive not to see so high a steeple
Look on the ground whereon you go:

---

1 *ryne*] Scots for *regne*, or *realm*.

2 *stubborn*] "stinkinge" supra., as an alternate reading.

3 *instruments*] agents, officers.

4 *sharp aspect*] angry countenance.

5 *do you*] be sure you (imperative).

6 *Council tables*] *i.e.*, the King's Privy Council;   *baubles*] play-things; *with pun on* babbles.

7 *make no doubt*] have no doubt.

8 *princely match*] the proposed Spanish marriage.

Higher aspects will breed your woe.
Take heed your paces° be all true
And do not discontents renew.
Meddle you not with your prince's° cares
For who so doth, too much he dares.

    I do desire no more of you
But to know me, as I know you.   [100]
So shall I love; and you, obey,
And you love me in a right way.
O make me not (unwilling still)
Whom I would save, unwilling kill.
Examples in extremities
Are never the best remedies.
Thus have I pleased myself, *and*° you—
And what I say, you shall find true.
Keep every man his rank and place
And fear to fall in my disgrace.   ¹
You call [our°] children shides° of State.   ²
You claim a right unto their fate.
But know you must be pleased with what
Shall please us best, in spite of that.
Kings do make laws to bridle you
Which they may pardon (or embrue
[Their hands in the best blood you°] have
And send the greatest to his grave).

    The "Charter" which [you *great* do°] call ³
Came first from kings, to stay your fall,
From an unjust rebellion moved
By such as kingdoms little loved.
Embrace not more than you can hold°
(As often do the overbold,
As they did which your° Charter sought,   [125]
For° their own greatness – who so wrought
With kings and you, that all proved *nought*.)
The *love* your kings have to you borne
Moved° them thereto for to be sworn.

    For where small goods are to be got
We're known to them that knows us not;
But you, that know me all so well,
Why do you push me down to Hell
By making me an infidel?
'Tis true, I am a cradle king,   ⁴
Yet do remember everything
That I have heretofore put out
And yet begin not for to doubt.
[But] O, how gross your dull° device
Change to impute to kings for° *vice*.
The wise may change, yet free from fault

(Though° change to worse is ever nought).
Kings ever overreach you all
And must stay you, though that you° fall.
Kings cannot comprehended be
In common circles. Conjure ye°
All what you can by tears or terms,
Deny not what your king affirms.
He doth disdain to cast an eye
Of anger on you, lest you die   [150]
Even at the shadow of his face
(Yet gives to all that sue for grace).
I know my friends, I need no teaching;
Proud is your foolish overreaching.
Come, counsel me when I shall call.
Before? beware what may befall!
Kings will hardly take *advice*.
Of *counsel*,° they are wondrous nice—
Love and wisdom lead them still
Their Council-table up to fill.
They need no helpers in their choice.
The best "advice" is their *own* voice.
Be you assured that such are kings
As they unto their Council brings
Which always so compounded are
As some would make and some would mar.
If I once bend mine angry brow,
Your ruin comes – though not as now,
For slow I am revenge to take;
And your amendments, wrath will slake.   ⁵
Then hold your prattling, spare your pen:
Be honest and obedient men.
Urge not my justice! I am slow
To give you your deservèd woe.
If proclamations° will not serve   ⁶   [175]
I must do more, peace to preserve,
    To keep all in obedience
    And drive such busybodies hence.

             finis

The next poem to be "let fall" at Court was "An Answer to the Wiper-Away," a judicious plea for moderation penned "by a Lady." Court-watchers had only two obvious candidates for its authorship: Lucy Hay, Countess of Carlisle; and Frances Stuart, Duchess of Richmond. Following the death of Queen Anna in 1619, Lucy Hay and Frances Stuart were the only ladies of the Court who still had the confidence, wit, and opportunity to chasten his Majesty. Lucy Hay was the wife of the king's (second) favorite, James Hay, and the

---

¹ *in my disgrace*] in my withdrawing of royal grace and mercy.

² *shides*] split lumber.

³ *Charter…great*] i.e., the Magna Carta.

⁴ *cradle king*] James succeeded to the throne of Scotland when he was only a year old.

---

⁵ *amendments*] amended behavior (will ease my wrath).

⁶ *proclamations*] i.e., to suppress "Lavish and Licentious Speech of matters of State" Dec. 1620 and July 1621 (Larkin, ed., *Stuart Royal Proclamations*, 1.495-96, 1.519-520).

beloved of the king's own sweetheart, George Villiers. Though she was a Percy and a nominal Catholic, Lucy was sympathetic to the Commons. Lady Frances, though a Howard and a suspected Catholic, was a friend and supporter of Frederick and Elizabeth; and she was an accomplished poet whose 1601 "Answer" (to a tear-jerker by Sir George Rodney) resembles A Lady's 1623 "Answer" to King James in its technique of quotation-with-riposte. But "By a Lady" may be a fiction:

An Answer to the Wiper-Away of the People's Tears, by a Lady

Condemn not, gracious King, our 'plaints and tears—
We are no "babes" (the times us witness bears).
Yet, since our "father" you do represent,
To be as babes to you we are content.
'Tis true, you *can* "deject" "the proudest mind," [1]
For pride is base and soon to fall inclined.
You can "take down the mightiest man alive"
Who doth from *man* his mightiness derive. [2]
Yes, "shides of State" will chips of chance excel— [3]
Though these, in Courts, and those in dungeons, dwell,
When so you please, t' imbrue your royal hand
In blood of those that dare at bay to stand.
 But we must go in safety to our grave:
Our hearts (for ransom of our heads) you *have*.
O let not then disdain, but grace and love
Lengthen their days (whose faith, you daily prove).
 Or might we die? then kill with your "aspect,"
 Which death and life in instant doth effect. [4]

The closing lines may be read as a piety (if you kill us, our death here means instantaneous and eternal life in Heaven), or as a witticism: As king you should be focused on the common weal, not threatening to kill dissenters; but, if we must die, kill us with your scowling aspect (as you have boasted you can do), and we shall instantly recover from your impotent frown.

 On 14 February, the King announced a commission (to be led by Buckingham, of all people) that would meet weekly (when Buckingham returned from Spain) to hear complaints from the people concerning monopolies and patents, bribes,

and extortion; with a printed promise that all unjust complaints would be punished. On better advisement, the Committee of Grievances was chaired by Sir Edward Coke, Lord Chief Justice. [5]

 The ink was hardly dry on that royal proclamation when a new scandal erupted: an unidentified protester slipped into Westminster Abbey and placed in the hand of Queen Elizabeth's effigy a set of two petitions, in verse. The first, addressed to "Saint Elizabeth," has the distressed Commons of England imploring the great Queen to look down from Heaven and see what a mess King James and his favorites have made of the country. The poet then asks her Majesty to place the second petition into the hands of Almighty God, that He might take pity on Britain and throw the rascals out.

 The second petition likens events of the Jacobean era to the biblical plagues of Egypt. The poet reminds his readers that James's reign began with an outbreak of plague (an epidemic that in 1603 took 30,000 lives in London alone). He or she mentions the 1607 floods in the west counties, when waters rose above the tops of houses, destroying property and killing many. The poet reviews the catastrophic summer storms and severe winters that from 1607 damaged property and bridges and contributed to the growing food shortage. He notes the comets, eclipses, mysterious tidal movements, and prodigious births that were the stuff of printed broadsides throughout the Jacobean era. And he dwells at length on the November 1612 death of Prince Henry, the nation's last best hope.

 After this litany of sorrows, the poet turns to manmade catastrophes, with an angry indictment of a King who expended more Crown funds on his hunting dogs in any given year than for relief of the poor during his entire reign. "Justice is bought and sold": all causes at law were now determined by bribes, power, or the King's favor. Condemning "monopoly-mongers," "upstart parasites," and "base informers," the author asks the gentry to join forces with the nation's work-force to overthrow the "proud usurping Lucifers" who have made the "bold and hardy Britains" a nation of slaves.

 The King was not amused. Had the Privy Council ever learned who wrote "Saint Elizabeth," the guilty poet would have gone the way of unlucky Williams, for *Balaam's Ass*: hanged, drawn, and quartered, for the crime of speaking up, from below.

---

[1] *'Tis true*] i.e., the proudest men will fall without your threatened violence; cf. "Wiper," l. 53.

[2] *from man*] i.e., but not those who draw strength from what is right and true.

[3] *shides of State...these*] Frederick and Elizabeth; *chips of chance...those*] supporters of the Protestant cause suffering imprisonment and violence on the Continent; cf. "Wiper," line 111.

[4] *kill with your aspect*] answer to "Wiper," l. 52; *in instant doth effect*] accomplishes both, in an instant.

---

[5] *commission*] By the King: A Proclamation Declaring ... Relief against Public Grievances (14 Feb. 1622/3).

Saint Elizabeth

(Found in the hand of Queen Elizabeth's tomb at Westminster)

[I.] TO THE BLESSED SAINT ELIZABETH *of most famous memory*:

The Humble Petition of her now most wretched and most contemptible, the Commons of poor distressed England.

IF SAINTS in Heaven can either see or hear
Or help poor mortals, O then lend thine ear!
Look down, Blest Soul, and hear, O hear us now,
Whose humble hearts low as our knees do bow:
Look on our sufferings. Think but on our wrongs
That hardly can be spoke by mortal tongues.
O be not now less gracious than of old,
When each distressèd vassal might be bold
Into thine open hand to put his grief—
And thence receive timely and fair relief.
Be not less good, less gracious, than before:
In *Heaven*, the supplications of the poor
Are heard as soon as suits of greatest kings.
If our petitions, then, Blest Soul, want wings
To mount them to the Judge of judges' throne,
O help them, Mighty Sovereign, with thine own!
Carry our just complaints (since *just*, they are),
And make a tender of them at the Bar
Where no corruption, no fraud, no bribe
No gripping lawyer, avaricious scribe,
No favorite, no parasite, no minion,
Can lead or alter the opinion
Of that Great Chancellor there. O lay them down,
And merit praise in Heaven; on Earth, a crown.
  Where to begin (Deserver of All Glory)   [25]
Or how to tell our unexampled story,
Heaven knows *we* do not know; nay, which is worst,
Thy once-blest° subjects have so oft been cursed
For offering up petitions of this kind,
As see, we tremble! – till we call to mind
Thy wonted goodness. That, O that, doth cheer us.
That only, gives us hope: that thou wilt hear us!
When Heaven was pleas'd, Loved° Soul, to call thee hence
And so make wretched for some great offense
This little land, O then began° our fears!

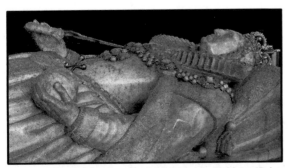

Effigy of Elizabeth in whose hand the Commons Petition to Saint Elizabeth was placed (Westminster Abbey)

And had we then the kingdom drowned with tears,
And in those floods conveyed our souls to Heaven
To wait on thine, we had not now been driven
To cry and call thee from thy fellow saints
To hear and pity these° our just complaints.
O pardon, Blest, but that (our gross omission!),[1]
And deign to further this our poor petition,
And we will make the name of blest Eliza
Equal the Avés of that great Maria!
No snuffling rascal through his hornpipe nose[2]
Shall tell thy story in his ill-tuned prose,
Nor show thy stature to each prince's groom:
The monuments *we'll* build shall make proud Rome
On pilgrimage to come, and at thy shrine
Offer their gifts as to a thing divine!   [50]
And on an altar framed of richest stones
We'll daily tender sighs, and tears°, and groans.
Eternity shall sleep and long-tongued Fame
Forget to speak, ere we forget thy name:
Read, Blest Soul! O read it, and believe us!
Then give it to His hands, that can relieve us.

—*Thy° faithful beadsmen and daily orators, the poor, the distressèd Commons of dejected England.*[3]

[II.] TO THE MOST HIGH AND MIGHTY JEHOVAH, Chief Chancellor of Heaven: The Most Humble Petition of the now most miserable, the Commons of long-afflicted England:

IF BLEEDING hearts, dejected souls, find grace,
Then, All-Disposer, turn not back thy face
From us, thy suppliants: thrice-seven suns have worn
Their summer suits since we began to mourn.[4]
Egypt's ten plagues we have endured, twice told,
Since blest Eliza was with saints enrolled.[5]
Thy messengers of wrath, their vials pour
Each day upon our heads. Nay, every hour
Plagues beget plagues, and vengeance fruitful grows
As if there were no period for our woes![6]
Have our black sins, great God, raised such a cloud
'Twixt us and Heaven, as cries (though ne'er-so-loud)
Can get no passage to Thy mercy seat?

---

[1] *our gross omission*] for years after Elizabeth's death, it was commonly noted that there were published hardly any funeral elegies or memorial poems in her honor; when Prince Henry died in November 1612, dozens of memorial poems were published.

[2] *hornpipe*] a wind instrument made from horn.

[3] *beadsmen*] almsmen who pray for benefactors.

[4] *thrice-seven suns*] 21 years (Elizabeth died 24 March 1602/3; "Saint Elizabeth" was found on 31 March or 22 June 1623 (or both).

[5] *Egypt's ten plagues*] a story from Exod. 7-12.

[6] *no period*] no endpoint.

Are our iniquities, good God, so great,
So infinite, as neither groans nor tears
Can entrance get? Remember but the years
Of our affliction! Then forget (we crave)
Our crying sins! Bury them in the grave
Of dark oblivion! Thrust them in the side
Of our Redeemer! O, let them be tied
In chains, that they may never rise again!
Let us no longer beg and sue in vain—
Let this our supplication, this complaint,
Tendered by our late Sovereign, now Thy saint,
At last find grace. Was't not (we humbly pray)   [25]
Enough that first Thou took'st that Queen away?
Was not that dove, that lamb of innocence,
Sufficient sacrifice for our offense?
Oh, no: our sins outlived her, and our crimes
Did threaten to outlast the last of times.
Thou didst remove her that she might not see
The sad beginning of our misery—
Then, like a shower of hailstones, fell Thy darts.[1]

    O angry Death, how many thousand hearts
Were wounded in one year? How many bled
And wished to die (when all they *loved*, were dead!)
Mothers left childless, children quite bereft
Of careful parents! Nay, there was not left
A pair of friends to comfort one another
Who wanted not a sister or a brother.   2
Where was the husband, where the wife, could say
"We should not be devoured this night, this day"?
Death so his rage and awful power showed
That men on Earth as corn on ground lay strowed.
The sad remembrance of it still remains.

    Then Thy stretched arm of vengeance bound in chains
The fruitful fields till birds, beasts, herbs, plants trees
Did famish, faint, dry, droop, yea, wither and freeze,
And nothing issued from the barren earth
But that lean monster and thin-faced Death.   3   [50]
    Next, inundations rose such as before
Since Noah's flood ne'er topped o'er British shore;
Where men and beasts alike engrave their bones
In the moist waves instead of marble stones.   4

How often hath the Sun withdrawn his light
And turned our day into the shape of night!
Had Egypt thicker darkness than had we
When clearest eyes at midday could not see?   5
Unwholesome mists, strange fogs, rumors of wars,
Evil-portending comets, blazing stars,
Prodigious births, unnatural sea-seasons,
Spurning philosophers beyond their reason;   6
Frighting the poor! The rich, exhorting
From their down beds, where they [lay] snorting!
    Heaven, in combustion, seemed the sky in arms:
The stars beat drums, the spheres did sound alarms.
The air did often bloody colors spread,
And all to rouse us from the puffed-up bed
Of base security. Yet nought would fright us
Till we robbed were° of that did [most] delight us:
Henry, our joy! Henry! – whose every limb
Threat'ned to conquer Death, and not Death him!
"Henry our pride," even "Henry the blest,"
In whom great Britain once set up his rest.   7
Who had not, in that one, all ample share?   [75]
What *subject* had not rather lost *his* heir?
What tender mother did not wish that dart
Had glanced from him and strook her darling's heart?
All that were virtuous, all that were good,
Turned their eyes' rivers into streams of blood.
The Egyptian waters bitter were, but know:
This, touched the very soul! (That, did not so).
O pardon, Heaven! All plagues that went before
Had lost themselves in this, and were no more
To be rememb'red! That! O, that alone
Might well have made us weep ourselves to stone.
The spawn of Pharaoh (could their blood be prized),
All the first-born that so were sacrificed,
All that base fry – compared to this, our Henry,
Deserves no mention, no thought, no memory.   8
    Lusting Sodom? Such hath Thy mercy been,
Although it did abound in crying sin,
Could not take fire until they were removed
That Thou in mercy, like in goodness, loved.   9

---

[1] *Death*] Elizabeth's death was followed in 1603-4 by the worst epidemic of bubonic plague in a decade; here compared to the Egyptian plague of hailstones, Exod. 9:18-34.

[2] *who wanted not*] who did not lose (in the epidemic of 1603-4).

[3] *barren earth*] The grain shortages of 1606-7 led to corn riots in Oxfordshire and the Midlands.

[4] *inundations*] On 30 Jan 1607, a sudden flood around the Bristol Channel killed at least 2,000 people, Britain's worst recorded natural disaster; here compared to Noah's Flood, Genesis chap. 6-9.

[5] *mists…fogs*] here compared to the Egyptian plague of darkness, Exodus 10.21-23.

[6] *evil-portending comets*] comets seen in 1607 and 1618 were thought to portend catastrophe; so, too, for birth defects ("prodigious births").

[7] *Henry*] Prince Henry died Nov. 1612 of typhoid fever, plunging the nation in grief; whereupon Charles became Prince of Wales and future king.

[8] *spawn of Pharaoh*] the story of the Passover, when Hebrew Lord YHWH sends his angel to kill all firstborn sons among the Egyptians.

[9] *Lusting Sodom*] In Genesis 18, Abraham barters with YHWH to spare the city of Sodom if there can be found in the city ten righteous citizens; but YHWH

And Thine anointed? She must leave this city   1
Before't can be destroyed! Such was Thy pity,
Such Thy goodness. O, is there yet full ten?   2
Is there, great God, a number yet of men
Whose innocence may slack Thy kindled ire
And keep this Sodom-Britain from the fire   [100]
Of Thy just anger? Is there yet a soul
Whose virtue power hath but to control
Thy heaved-up hand of Justice? If there be,
For his or her sake, rouse Thy clemency!
Awake Thy mercy! let Thy Justice slumber,
And save the greater, by the lesser, number.
For his or her sake, we do humbly pray
Respite of time: give us a longer day.
And then, enabled by Thy grace and favor,
We'll purchase pardon by our good behavior.
Plague, famine, darkness, inundations
We have endured; fear of innovations
(With expectation of the worst can follow)
Daily torments us. And we hourly swallow
Our very spirits with fear and horror.
We nightly sleep in dread; awake in terror.
 Nor are we all this while from *vermin* free:
The caterpillars hang on every tree—
Lousy projectors, monopoly-mongers,   3
A crew of upstart rascals whose hungers
Can ne'er be satisfied; a sort of slaves
More insatiable far than whores or graves;
Things without soul, bred only of the slime
Of this old age, this base decrepit time—
A crew of upstart parasites that rise   [125]
And do more mischief than the Egyptian flies: 4
These in our gardens, in our houses, swarm:
One drinks a manor; another eats a farm.
This, with a lordship, warms his lusting whore.
That, by the sale of justice, doth procure
A tenement or two; which, having got,
By violence he drowns them in a pot.   5

They enter city's corporations;
Work not, yet live by *occupations*:
They have not trade – and yet there's none are free
From paying them a tax, a fine, a fee!
 Egypt had skipping grasshoppers, I yield,
That ate the herbs and fruits of every field;
And we have skipjack courtiers, I dare say,   6
That do devour far more in one poor day
Than they in Pharaoh's age could e'er have done!
Their° bondmen were paid but from some to some;
But these, for three apprenticeships, have eat'   7
The fruit of *all* our labors, *all* our sweat.
 Have we not frogs? O yes, in every ditch!   8
Devouring *poor*, impoverishing the *rich*—
Busy intelligencers, base informers,
Like toads and frogs, lie croaking in all corners,
Promoting rascals whose envenomed tongues
Have done Thy suppliants infinite wrongs.   [150]
Where they desire to enter, there's no defense,
No ancient title, no inheritance,
Can keep them out: they wrest and stretch the law,
Keep officers and magistrates in awe.
They pluck the balance from fair Justice' hand
And make *her* minister to *their* commands.
The lawful scepter of sovereignty
Is a mercenary bawd to villainy.
There is no equity, no law, nor right.
All causes go by *favor*, or by *might*.
 O God of mercy, what can more be said?
Justice is bought and sold, become a trade—
Honors conferred on base unworthy grooms;
And clowns, for coin, may perch on highest rooms.
Poor Job had many scabs, yet none so bad   9
As we this one and twenty years have had!
Egypt had botches, murrains, sores that smarted—   10
But yet they lasted not; they soon departed.
Half forty years and more are gone and past
Since these our vexèd souls took light repast.

---

destroys the city by fire from the sky after the locals attempt a gang-rape of two angels.

1 *She must leave*] God took Elizabeth to Heaven before unleashing His anger on London and Britain.

2 *full ten*] Are we done, yet, with the Ten Plagues of God's wrath, or is worse to come?

3 *projectors*] schemers for patronage or capital investment; *monopoly mongers*] those who acquired or sold licenses monopolies on production or import of goods, a source of much economic injustice.

4 *flies*] In Exod. 8:20-31, Hebrew god YHWH sends a plague of flies upon Egypt; here figured as a plague of greedy parasites, notably George Villiers and his kin.

5 *in a pot*] having acquired rental properties by fraud, he spends the ill-gotten profits on alcohol.

---

6 *grasshoppers*] parasites and favorites of the king (such as Buckingham) who were granted monopolies that exploited the working poor; here compared to the Egyptian plague of locusts, Exodus 10:12-19; *skipjack*] shallow and foppish.

7 *three apprenticeships*] *i.e.,* twenty-one years.

8 *frogs*] political and religious informers, here compared to the Egyptian plague of frogs (Exodus 8).

9 *Poor Job*] On a wager with YHWH, the Sons of God afflict Job with boils all over his body (Job 2.7).

10 *botches*] "The LORD will smite thee with the botch of Egypt, and with the hemorrhoids, and with the scab, and with the itch, whereof thou canst not be healed" (Deut. 28:27).

Bowman, and Jowler, Ringwood and his mate,[1]
Compared to us, are in a better state:
They can be heard! they can be *rewarded*!—
When we are curst, slighted, unregarded.
Is a *people*, Heavens, fallen a degree　　　　　　[175]
Below the condition of a dog? But we!—
Was there a nation in the universe
More daring, (once) more bold, more stout, more fierce?
And is there now upon the Earth's broad face
Any that can be reckoned half so base?
Is there a people so much scorned, despised,
So laughed at°, so trod on, so vassalized?
We, that all Europe envied! We, even we,
Are slaves to those we kept in slavery!
Where is our ancient nobility become?
Alas, they are suppressed – and in their room,
Like proud usurping Lucifers, there sits
A sort of upstart fawning parasites!　　　　　　　　　　[2]
Where is the gentry? All, suppressed, disgraced!–
And arrant knights above them now are placed.
Fiddlers and fools, with dancers and with rhymers
Are now in England made the greatest climbers!
　　We had a Parliament, a salve for sores,
A Magna Carta – all, cast out of doors!　　　　　　　　[3]
The bold and hardy Britains conquered are!—
Without a drum, a sword, or sound of war.

　　If without cause, just Heaven, we do complain,
Then send our supplication back again!
More could we say, and much more could we speak—
But with the thought of this, our hearts do break.　[200]
As humble then as we began to crave
A gracious answer, O be pleased to save
The remnant of Thy people! Turn Thy face
And let us once more taste Thy saving grace!
Forsake us not, O Lord, but give
New life to those that only wish to live,
T'approve themselves. ready and faithfully,
Thy servant and beadsmen.

　　　　　　　• • •

The petition to Saint Elizabeth, and the appended Petition to God the All-Disposer, look much like the work of George Wither; but whoever the poet, the two "Saint Elizabeth" poems resonated with the rising anger of the Commons. The sheer number of surviving manuscript copies attests that these were among the most widely circulated and enduringly popular manuscript poems of the Seventeenth Century.

　　They did not go unanswered from on high. The "Saint Elizabeth" petitions provoked an angry response, written while Buckingham and Prince Charles were still in Spain, captioned, "A Gracious Answer from the Blessed Elizabeth." The poet speaks as Elizabeth but writes in support of King James (albeit with a note of mock sympathy: "For Buckingham (his spouse) is gone, / And left the widowed King alone").

　　The Jacobean era closed with famine, a Great Depression, and another epidemic of plague. On 27 March 1625, King James died in bed, amidst a fatal last blast of dysentery while cursing a painful plaster attached to his belly that failed to provide the wished benefit. And on 23 August 1628, the Duke of Buckingham was assassinated. Those events did not mark the end of an era: what followed was more of the same, only worse.

　　The "Saint Elizabeth" poems had a long afterlife. In 1642, on the eve of the Civil War, "The Humble Petition [...] of Long-Afflicted England" (part 2 of "Saint Elizabeth") was printed for the first time, in a revised text that substitutes King Charles for King James. To this was appended an abridged text of "A Gracious Answer" – not now from "the Blessed Elizabeth," but "from our Blessed Mediator," "C.I." (a clever equivocation for either "C[harles] I" or "Christ I[esus]"); who, in his "gracious answer," blasts the Commons as the same old pack of ungrateful dogs. A new ending is supplied in which C.I. warns the Commons to repent, or suffer destruction by fire.

　　The Civil Wars endured from 1642 to 1651. Crowned in 1625, King Charles was beheaded on 30 January 1648/9. On 3 September 1658, Oliver Cromwell died of septicemia, following a urinary infection, ending still another twenty years of tyranny. And on 2 February 1685, the lovable rogue, Charles II died, survived by a dozen children by seven different mistresses. His brother, James II – chased from England in 1688 for trying to restore the absolute monarchy of his father, Charles I – lived in exile in Paris until his death and anatomical dissection in 1701. None of these great potentates died greatly lamented.

　　Proved repeatedly in the Seventeenth Century was a premise that the author of "Saint Elizabeth" takes for granted: the English nation was never better off than when governed by a woman.

　　　　　　　　　　　　finis

---

[1] *Bowman, Jowler, Ringwood*] names of the king's beloved hunting dogs; with a complaint that James cares more for his hounds than for his people.

[2] *Lucifers*] George Villiers, Sir Giles Mompesson, Sir Francis Michel, Sir Francis Bacon, et al.

[3] *Magna Carta*] also called The Great Charter of the Liberties of England was signed in June 1215 between King John and his barons. The Magna Carta never actually did much to limit the arbitrary power of the monarchy but it came to be valorized in the 17th century as a statement of fundamental liberties; *Parliament*] here, James's third Parliament, Jan. 1620/1-Feb. 1621/2.

Timeline

(Asterisked dates are approximate)

1603
• 24 March, death of Elizabeth: James VI of Scotland succeeds as James I of Great Britain
• 19 July. Ralegh is arrested, and on 17 November convicted, for alleged support of the Main Plot to crown Arbella Stuart instead of Scotland's King James
• 25 July, James's coronation period (1600-1868).
• Elizabeth Melville, *Ane Godlie Dreame* (Scots)
• Mary Pannel hanged as a witch in Yorkshire

1604
• 8 Jan., *Vision of the Twelve Goddesses* performed
• Elizabeth Grymeston, *Miscellanea.*(entered in the Stationers' Register 30 Jan.; published 1606)
• English version of Melville's *Godly Dream*
• James's first Parliament, 19 Mar. 1604/5 - 9 Feb. 1610/11
• August. James ends the war with Spain
• Negotiations for union with Scotland, 1604-7

1605
• 9 Jan., the *Masque of Blackness*
• 5 Nov., Gunpowder Plot to blow up Parliament foiled

1606
• 5 Jan., masque of *Hymenaei* performed
• Charter of the Virginia Company
• 4 Aug. Joanna Harrison and her daughter hanged as witches in Hertfordshire

1607
• 6 Jan. 1607, Lord Hay's Masque performed
• April-June, Midlands rising against property owners' enclosure of non-residential land
• 1 May. Henry Hudson begins his voyage to Greenland, seeking a northerly route to the Pacific
• 14 May, Virginia Co. begins Jamestown settlement
• 7 July, death of Lady Penelope [Devereux] Rich
• September, Irish earls flee to Continent, fearing arrest

1608
• 10 Jan., *The Masque of Beauty*
• 9 Feb., masque of *The Hue and Cry after Cupid*
• 13 Feb., death of Arbella's grandmother, Bess of Hardwick, 87, England's richest woman
• 28 Feb. 1607/8, Burning of Margaret Fearnside
• *Life of Margaret Cunningham,* with divorce petition
• 9 Dec., birth of John Milton

1609
• 9 Feb., *The Masque of Queens* performed
• 4 Aug., death of Cecily Boulstred, courtesan and wit; memorialized in verse by Lucy Harington and others
• Corsairs of Barbary plunder British shipping, taking some 470 vessels between 1609 and 1616, and 27 more vessels from near Plymouth in 1625; during this period about 8,000 captive British seamen were sold into slavery, chiefly in North Africa
• English settlement of Ulster
• 25 Nov. 1609, birth of Henriette Marie, queen of Charles I
• Birth of Marie Jackson (Carey Payler), poet (vol. 4)

1610
• *Certain Old Stories* of Rose Locke Hickman
• Arbella Stuart imprisoned for her secret marriage to William Seymour
• Ravillac assassinates King Henri IV of France
• Artemisia Gentileschi, *Susanna e i Vecchioni,* her first painting
• Galileo builds a 30x telescope

1611
• 1 Jan., masque of *Oberon, the Faery Prince*
• 3 Feb., masque of *Love Freed from Ignorance and Folly*
• June Disguised as a boy, Arbella Stuart escapes from the Tower but is recaptured
• Aemilia Lanyer, *Salve Deus Rex Judaeorum* pub. (registered for printing, 2 Oct. 1610)
• Authorized version of the Bible (KJV) is published

1612
• 6 Jan., masque of *Love Restored*
• 11 April, death of Edward Wightman, Anabaptist, burned at the stake as a heretic; witch-hunting escalates
• 22 July, Mary Barber, Agnes Brown, Joan Vaughan, Helen Jenkinson, and Arthur Bill hanged as witches in Northampton
• 27 July, Jennet Preston hanged as a witch, in York.
• Birth of Anne Dudley (Bradstreet), colonial poet
• 20 August, nine hanged as witches in Lancashire; ("Old Dembdike" has died in prison); Margaret Preston pilloried for one year.
• 6 Nov. Prince Henry, 18, dies of typhoid fever

1613
• Elizabeth Cary's *Mariam* (c. 1605/6) is registered 17 Dec. 1612, printed 1613, then recalled
• Jan. First Proclamation against dueling and concealed weapons
• 14 Feb., Elizabeth Stuart weds Frederick V, Elector Palatine
• 14 Feb., *Masque of the Inner Temple and Gray's Inn*
• 15 Feb., *Memorable Masque of the Middle Temple and Lincoln's Inn*
• 30 March, Mary Sutton is hanged as a witch in Bedford; her mother is beaten unconscious and "floated."
• 29 June. Globe Theater burns down.
• 21 Nov. Death of Rose Hickman.

1614
• Pocahontas marries John Rolfe
• Birth of Margaret Askew (Fell), founder of Quakers
• Second Parliament, 5 April – 7 June, which the king dissolves when Parliament refuses to raise revenue

1615

• 19 Jan. masque of *Mercury Vindicated*
• Earl and countess of Somerset tried for the Overbuy murder; George Villiers becomes the King's new favorite
• Grey sisters' tribute to Elizabeth Grey
• Joseph Swetnam, *The Arraignment of ...Women*
• Joan Hunt hanged as a witch (Middlesex)
• Birth of Mary Tickell (Overton), civil rights activist (*Women's Works*, vol. 4)
• 25 Sep. Death of Arbella Stuart in the Tower

1616

• 1 and 6 Jan., masque of *The Golden Age Restored*
• 23 April, death of William Shakespeare
• fl. Mary Oxlie, poet (Scotland)
• Dorothy Leigh, *The Mother's Blessing* (reg. 26 Feb.)
• Elizabeth Arnold, *Against the Painting of Women*
• Anne Clifford, the Knole Diary (1616-17)
• Mary Smith and Elizabeth Rutter hanged as witches (Middlesex)
• Agnes Berry hanged as a witch (Enfield, Essex)

1617

• 6 and 19 Jan., masque of *The Vision of Delight*
• Rachel Speght, *A Mouzell for Melastomus*
• "Ester Sowernam" (Richard Brathwaite), *Ester Hath Hang'd Haman*
• "Constantia Munda" (John Stephens), *The Worming of a Mad Dogge*
• 7 Oct., death of Elizabeth Brydges

1618

• 6 Jan., masque of *Pleasure Reconciled to Virtue*
• 18 July, eight women hanged as witches in Leicestershire; another dies in custody
• 29 Oct., Sir Walter Ralegh is beheaded
• Belvoir witch trials begin. Phillip and Margaret Flower, and Ellen Green are hanged as witches; Joan Flower dies in prison (Leicestershire)
• Birth of Mary Swinhoe (Moore), author of *Wonderful News* (*Women's Works*, vol. 4)
• Beginning of the Thirty Years War, one of the most destructive conflicts in European history

1619

• 2 March. Death of Queen Anna
• 11 March, Anne Baker and Joan Willimot are hanged as witches at Lincoln Castle
• Some 30 Africans, arriving by chance in Virginia, are forced to join a workforce of about 1000 English indentured servants; the first kidnapped Africans arrive soon afterward and are forced into slavery.

1620

• 4 Mar., masque of *The World Tossed at Tennis*
• *Haec Vir* v. *Hic Mulier* controversy over gender roles
• 11 Dec., Pilgrims land at Plymouth Rock

1621

• 16 Jan., James's third Parliament opens.
• Rachel Speght, *Mortalities Memorandum*
• 19 April, Elizabeth Sawyer hanged as a witch
• July, Mary Sidney Wroth's *Urania,* published
• 3 and 5 Aug., masque of *The Gypsies Metamorphosed*
• 25 Sept., death of Lady Mary [Sidney] Herbert. countess of Pembroke, humanist, poet and translator, editor of Sir Philip Sidney's works, literary patron

1622

• 6 Jan., *The Masque of Augurs*
• Jan. "Bewitchment" of Elizabeth Jennings begins
• 8 Feb., King James disbands Parliament
• Elizabeth Clinton, *Countess of Lincolnes Nurserie*
• 21 Oct., death of Elizabeth Jocelin

1623

• 19 Jan. masque of *Time Vindicated to Himself*
• Birth of Jane Cavendish, poet and playwright (vol. 4)
• 31 March, "Saint Elizabeth" petitions at Westminster Abbey
• Birth of Margaret Lucas (Cavendish); from 1644, stepmother to Jane Cavendish; prolific author of the Restoration period.

1624

• 6 Jan., James cancels scheduled performance of *Neptune's Triumph* due to quarrel between the French and Spanish ambassadors
• Fourth Parliament, 12 Feb. 1623/4 - 27 Mar. 1625.
• March 1624. Widow Elizabeth Dale submits printed petition against the East India Company
• Infanticide statute stipulates a presumption of live birth and murder by any unmarried mother who has concealed her pregnancy and whose baby died.
• Elizabeth Jocelin's *The Mother's Legacie for her Unborne Childe* posthumously published
• 10 Aug., death of Esther Inglis, calligrapher
• A petition submitted to King James and Parliament lists 3000 citizens then in prison for debt in London alone, and proposes that a debtor whose entire estate has been seized by creditors may be released from custody rather than die in chains with an unpaid and unpayable balance (eighty debtors having died in the King's Bench prison alone, in the year previous). The petition was unsuccessful.

1625

• 9 January, masque of *The Fortunate Isles*
• Eleanor Davies, *A Warning to the Dragon and All his Angels*
• Birth of Elizabeth Cavendish (Egerton), poet (*Women's Works*, vol. 4)
• Death of Bessie Clarkson. Her *Conflict in Conscience* is published in a corrupt text (better ed., 1631)
• 27 Mar., death of King James, succeeded by Charles I
• The England colonize Barbados, and grow sugar with slave labor by men captured in West Africa

Text Notes

Words in the text placed within square brackets [thus] *are interpolations by the editor to clarify the sense. Emendations of words or phrasing in the copytext are signaled with a degree sign, like so.° Notable variants are given here where multiple texts have been consulted. To avoid footnote clutter, bibliographical information is likewise signaled by a degree sign, and supplied below.*

Introduction

Robert Anton, "Venus." Normalized text ed. DWF from *The Philosophers Satyrs* (1616), lines 253-64]

    1 at] that *Q*
    6 sate] fate *Q*
    12 Both rots] Rot both *Q*

I. LADIES OF THE COURT

ANNA of DENMARK

Prince Henry to Queen Anna (April 1603). Normalized text ed. DWF from Nichols (1828), 1.150 (Harl. MS 7007).

King James to Queen Anna (13 May 1603). Normalized text ed. DWF from Nichols, 1.153-4.

King James, Basilikon Doron. Ed. DWF fr. ed 1599, 2.98-9.

Maximilian, *Memoirs* (1603). Normalized text ed. DWF fr. Maximilian, *Memoirs*, trans. Lennox, vol. 3 (1763), 235-6.
    the King] he *1763*

Zorzi Giustinian, Venetian Ambassador [on James & Anna] (June 1607). Ed. DWF from *Cal. State Papers, Venice*, vol. 10: (1603-1607), pp. 513-5. Anon. trans.

Bentivoglio, nuncio to the Archduke [on James & Anna] (1609). Abridged trans. by Lucy Aiken (1822), 2.332-4.

Anna to King James (August 1603). Normalized text ed. DWF from Maitland Club (1835), facsimile 3.

Anna to King James (Sept. 1603). Normalized text ed. DWF from Maitland Club (1835), facsimile 2.

Anna to King James (November 1603). Normalized text ed. DWF from Maitland Club (1835), facsimile 3.

Anna to King James (n.d. Feb. 1604). Normalized text ed. DWF from Maitland Club (1835), facsimile 7.

Anna to King James (June 1604). Normalized text ed. DWF from Maitland Club (1835), facsimile 5.

John Harrington to W. Barlow (July 1606). Normalized text ed. DWF from Harington (1792), 126-9.

Enter George Villiers

Quote fr. **Abbot, *Life and Reign*** (1706), 698.
    his Majesty…Villiers…his former favorite, Robert Carr, earl of Somerset…Villiers] *DWF*; he…him…him…he *1706*.

Quote fr. **Onslow, *Life of Archbishop Abbot*** (1777), 25-6n, fr. B.L. Add. MS 72242.
    Villiers] *DWF*; him *1777*
    Villiers] *DWF* / he *1777*

Anna Regina to Sir George Villiers (June 1616). Normalized text ed. DWF from MS Harl. 6986, art. 71, f.108.

Anna to King James (August 1616). Normalized text ed. DWF from MS Harl. 6986, art. 70, f.107.

Anna Regina to George, Viscount Villiers (August 1616). Normalized text ed. DWF from MS Harl. 6986, art. 72, f.109

Anna to King James (July 1617). Ed. DWF from Nichols, ed., *Autographs* (1829), unnumbered page. MS Harl. 6986, art. 69, f.106.

Anna to George, Earl of Buckingham (Sept. 1617). Image courtesy of Bonham Auctions (sold 13 Nov 2012, now in a private collection)/

Anna to King James (June 1618). Normalized text ed. DWF from Maitland Club (1835), facsimile 5.

Anna Regina to the Marquess Buckingham (Sept. 1618). Normalized text ed. DWF from Advocates Library (Edinburgh), MS Birch 4162, art. 60.

Queen Anna's Jewels. Sources as noted.

ZSir Anthony Weldon, from **The Court and Character of King James** (*Q*). Ed. DWF from ed. 1650, pp. 124-6.
    that *Q*

ARBELLA STUART

This edition of selected letters is much indebted to the careful labors of Sara Jayne Steen. Normalized text ed. DWF from transcriptions by Steen (1994), except as noted.

Epigraph. B.L. MS Harl. 7003, f.152

To her grandmother, E. Talbot (8 Feb. 1587/8). Steen, p.119 (Huntington Lib. MS HM 803).

Abella's Adventure (Dec. 1602). Steen, p.120-2 (Hatfield House Cecil Papers 135, f. 107). Words inserted to clarify the sense of Arbella's elliptical prose style appear in square brackets:
    par. 1 [and] *DWF*; there *MS, Steen*
    para. 3 [Grey] *DWF*; there *MS, Steen*
    par. 4 [Henry]…[own]…[his acquaintance]…[information] …[secrecy]…[Good] *DWF*; there *MS, Steen*
    para. 4 the] *DWF*; there *MS, Steen*

Lady Arbella's Apology to Queen Elizabeth (<9 Jan. 1602/3). Steen, p.122 (Cecil Papers 135, f.146).

Declaration of Arbella Stuart (2 March 1602/3). Steen, pp.146-8 (Cecil Papers 135, f.142-3).

Lady Arbella to Sir Henry Brounker (7 March 1602/3). Steen, pp.158-75 (Cecil Papers 135, f.166).
    but] *DWF (for clarity)*; nor *MS, Steen*
    whom] *DWF*; which *MS, Steen*.

Lady Arbella to Sir Henry Brounker (9 March 1602/3). Steen, pp.156-7 (Cecil Papers 135, ff. 130-38).
    at Greenwich] <at Greenwich> *Steen*; *MS cancelled*
    Essex] who *DWF*; who *MS, Steen*
    to] from *MS, Steen* (i.e., favors *to*, but eclipsed *from*)

Lord of the Council to the Dowager Countess of Shrewsbury (14 March 1602/3). Norm. text ed. DWF from Smith, *Life*, 170-2 (Cecil Papers 135, f. 169-70).
    Arbella's] her *MS, Steen*
    Arbella] she *MS, Steen*
    Her Majesty] she *MS, Steen*

Lady Arbella to her uncle, Gilbert Talbot, Earl of Shrewsbury (16 Sept. 1603). From Steen, 182-4 (Lambeth Palace Library, MS 3201, ff. 124-25).

Lady Arbella to Gilbert Talbot (8 Dec. 1603). Steen, 190-3 (Talbot Papers 2, ff. 208-9).
    of] *Steen; MS om.*

Lady Arbella to Mary Talbot (8 Dec. 1603). Steen, 193-5 (Talbot Papers 2, ff. 206-7).

Sir Anthony Weldon, from **The Court and Character of King James** (*Q*). Ed. DWF from ed. 1650, pp. 28-32.

    Cecil] Salisbury *Q*

Venetian Ambassador, to the Doge and Senate (30 May 1607). Ed. DWF from *S.P. Venice*, Vol. 2, 514.

Lady Arbella to Gilbert Talbot (17 June 1609). Steen, 230-1 (Arundel Castle MSS, Autograph Letters 1585-1617, no. 167).

Lady Arbella to the Privy Council (July 1610). Steen, p.239 (B.L. Harl. MS 7003, ff. 92-3).

Lady Arbella to the Privy Council (July 1610). Steen, p.241 (B.L. Harl. MS 7003, f. 91).

Lady Arbella to King James (c. Oct. 1610). Steen, p.249 (B.L. MS Add. 32092, f. 220; Harl. 7003, ff. 87-8).

Lady Arbella to King James (c. Dec. 1610). Steen, pp.254-5 (B.L. MS Harl. 7003, f. 82; copy, f.57).

Lady Arbella to [Sir Thos. Fleming], Lord Chief Justice of England, and to Sir Edward Coke, [Lord Chief Justice of the Common Pleas] (Feb. 1610/1). Steen, pp.255-6 (B.L. Harl. MS 7003, ff. 152).

Lady Arbella to her husband, William Seymour (n.d.). Steen, pp.241-2 (B.L. Harl. MS 7003, ff. 150-1).

CECILY BOULSTRED

B. Jonson (Thomas Roe: An Elegy to Mistress Boulstred." Normalized text ed. DWF from transcript by Grierson, *Donne's Poetical Works*, 2.410-11. Copies include B.L. MSS Add. 10309, Lansdowne 704 (by "J.R."); Bodleian MS Rawl. poet. 31; Harvard, MS Norton; and Trinity College (Dublin) MS G.2.21 (by "J.R."). For collations, see Grierson.

John Roe, *To Ben Jonson, 6 [i.e., 8] Jan. 1603[/4]. Ed. DWF from Donne, ed. Grierson, 1.414. MSS copies include B.L. MSS Lansdowne 740 (anon.), f. 102; and Harl. 4064 (by "Sir J. R."), f. 247. Roe's authorship is established by Jonson's remarks in Drummond, *Conversations*, 15.

B. Jonson, *Song: To Celia*. Normalized text ed. DWF from *Volpone* (pub. 1607).

B. Jonson, *Song to Celia*. Normalized text ed. DWF from *The Forrest* (1616).

B. Jonson, *Shall I not my Celia Bring?* Normalized text ed. DWF from *Under-Wood* (1641).

John Donne, *To Sir Henry Goodyer (n.d., July 1609?)*. Normalized text ed. DWF from Donne, *Letters to Severall Persons of Honour* (1651), 216.

B. Jonson: *On the Court Pucell*. Normalized text ed. DWF from Ben Jonson, *Under-Woods* (posthumous, 1641), "An Epigram on the Court Pucelle," pp. 220-1.

    11 can at] cannot *Q*

Francis Anthony, *Part 2. Extreme Vomiting*. Normalized text ed. DWF from **Francis Anthony, *An Apology or Defense of a Medicine called Aurum Potabile*** (1616): 68-71 (I2v-I4r).

Edward Herbert, *Epitaph. Caecil. Boulser*. Normalized text ed. DWF from Herbert, *Occasional Verses* (1665): 20-1.

From J. Donne, *Elegy on Mistress Boulstred*. Norm. text ed. DWF from Donne, *Poems by J.D.* (1633), p. 69 (K3r-4r).

From J. Donne, *Elegy XI*. Norm. text ed. DWF from Donne, *Poems by J.D.* (1633), pp.296-8 (Pp4v-Qq1v).

B. Jonson: *Epitaph* (with note to George Garrard). Norm. text ed. DWF from Houghton Library (Harvard), MS Lowell (Jonson holograph). Other copies include B.L. MSS Add. 33998, f. 33; Harl. 6057, f. 33; and Harl. 4064, f. 261.

C. Boulstred: *News of My Morning Work*. Normalized text ed. DWF from Cecily Boulstred, "Newes of My Morning Work." In Overbury, *Sir Thomas Overburie his Wife*. 2d ed. (1614), sigs. H2v-3r. Reprinted in all subsequent editions.

Thomas Carew, *Ingrateful Beauty Threatened*. Normalized text ed. DWF from Carew, *Poems* (1640).

Sir Thomas Roe, *Embassy ... to the Court of the Great Mogul, 1515-1619*. Ed. DWF from ed. 1899, pp. 253-4.

LUCY RUSSELL

***Elegy on Mistress Boulstred*.** Normalized text ed. DWF from anonymous text in Donne, *Poems* (2d ed., 1635) *[1635]*, 272-3 (headed "Elegie on Mris Boulstred"). Collated with Bodleian MS Rawl. poet. 31 *[MS-R]*, f. 39r ("Elegye on the Lady Markham by C: L: of B"), and British Library MS Harl. 4064 *[MS-H]*, f. 269 ("Elegye on the lady Markham by C: L: of B."). Corrupt texts of the same poem, run together with Donne's elegy on Boulstred, appear in Beinecke Library MS Osborn b148, pp. 118-19, and British Library MS Stowe 962, ff. 94r-95r (closely related, and both more closely related to *MS-R* than to *1635* or *MS-H*; not here collated).

  2 flow] *1635*; grow/e *MS-H*, *MS-R*
  5-6 denounces ... pronounces] *1635*; denounce ... pronounce *MS-H*, *MS-R*
  6 joy] *1635*; ioyes *MS-H*, *MS-R*
  9 wherewith] *1635*; wherein *MS-R*
  12 that] *1635*; what *MS-H*, *MS-R*
  18 yet] *1635*; *MS-H* om.
  19 want or loss] *1635*; losse or want *MS-H*, *MS-R*
  20 blest] *MS-H*, *MS-R*; best *1635*
  22 souls...to...bear] *1635*; spoils...of...wear *MS-H*, *MS-R*
  23 Glory not thou thy selfe] *1635*; Glorify *MS-H*, *MS-R*
  23 these] *1635*; our *MS-H*, *MS-R*
  24 Which our face] *1635*; Our faces *MS-H*, *MS-R*
  24 her...harm...wears] *1635*; hers...harms...wear *MS-H*, *MS-R*
  26 these] *1635*; those *MS-H*, *MS-R*
  27 memory's] memories *1635*; memory *MS-H*
  28 her] *1635*; our *MS-H*
  30 those] *1635*; the *MS-H*, *MS-R*
  32 Which did i' th] *1635*; Did in the xxwhich?
  32 Spirit's] spirits *1635*; spirit *MS-H*, *MS-R*
  34 saw, heard, felt] *MS-H*, *MS-R*; saw and felt *1635*
  36 stay's] *1635*; stay ys *MS-H*; staye, is *MS-R*
  37 not by] *1635*; not wth *MS-H*, *MS-R*
  38 power] *1635*; powers *MS-H*
  39 by...rest] by which she sayles to rest] *1635*; through which yt sayle do rest *MS-H*; through wch shee sayld to rest *MS-R*
  41 teach] *1635*; preach *MS-H*, *MS-R*
  41 of her with joy and] *1635*; wch hers with ioy did *MS-H*, *MS-R* wth hirs, what ioye did *MS-R*

II. LITIGANTS

ELIZABETH BRYDGES

Frances, Lady Chandos, to John Manners, 4th Earl of Rutland. Normalized text ed. DWF from HMC, *Duke of Rutland Manuscripts* (1888) *[HMC]*, 119.
1587] HMC misdated "[1580?]"
  Sudeley] (again below) Studley *HMC*
  Elton] Etton *HMC*
  lordship's] lord *HMC* (from lord: *MS*)

Affidavit of Charles Lister before Sir Chas. Blount, Lord St. John, and Three Others. Normalized text ed. DWF from *S.P. Elizabeth* (1598-1601), pp. 131-2.

Elizabeth, Lady Russell to Robert Cecil, Viscount Cranborn (24 June 1597). Normalized text ed. DWF from H.M.C. *Salisbury (Cecil)*, Part 7, pp. 267-8.

Elizabeth, Lady Russell, to Robert Cecil, Viscount Cranborn (September 1599). Normalized text ed. DWF from H.M.C. *Salisbury (Cecil)*, Part 9, pp. 358-9.

Elizabeth, Lady Kennedy, to Robert Cecil, Viscount Cranborn (n.d., 1604). Normalized text ed. DWF from H.M.C. *Salisbury (Cecil)*, Part 16 *[HMC]*, p.255.

MARGARET CLIFFORD

Extracts from Clifford's diaries, scattered in the copytexts, are here presented in chronologically. The journals for 1603, 1616, 1617, and 1619 survive in two 18th-century transcripts of an original now lost: Portland Papers XXIII F 74-79 (1603) and F 80-119 (1616-19), and Knole/Sackville Papers U269 F48/1, ff. 1-38. The 1676 diary appears at the end of vol. three in one copy of Lady Anne's "Great Books"; and for the years 1650-75, plus the "Life of Me," in three copies of the Great Books: Cumbria Record Office, Hothfield Papers, WD/Hoth/10 and B.L. MS Harley 6177 (the latter is a transcript by Mr. Henry Fisher, Feb. 1727, from an MS diary no longer extant.). Additions and annotations by Lady Anne appearing in the margins of the manuscript copies are here quietly inserted in the main text without notice. *T.B.*

[**Introduction**]
From *The Life of Me*
 my husbands'] *TB*; their *MS*
 made] *TB*; make *MS*
A True Memorial of the Life of Me, the Lady Anne Clifford (**for the years 1603-1659).** Norm. text ed. TB, from B.L. MS Harl. 6177, ff. 49-72b. (Harl. 6177, part 1, Fisher's 1727 transcript of the "Lives" of the de Veteripont (pp. 2-16); and of the Cliffords, beg. with Walter 1st Lord Clifford (pp. 17-206), inc. "A summary of the Records, and a True Memorial of the life of me the Lady Anne Clifford" (pp. 119-206); part 2 is Fisher's transcript Clifford's funeral sermon by the bishop of Carlisle (pp. 1-32); pp. 207-222 are blank.
 1589] *TB*; one thousand five hundred and eight-nine *MS*
 1591] *TB*; one thousand five hundred ninety-one
 my father's] *TB*; his *MS*
Knole Diary. Normalized text ed. TB from Centre for Kentish Studies MS U269/F48 [*MS*], Microfilm 277 (18th C transcript).
 yet] *TB*; the *MS* (by mistaking of yet for yᵉ)
 24th] *TB*; 20th *MS*
 Robert] *TB*; R *MS*
 Burghley] *TB*; Burleigh *MS*
 Thomas] *TB*; T *MS*
 the like again] the like *MS*
 Lancilwell] *i.e.*, Lance Level
From *The Life of Me* (cont.)
 1605] *TB*; one thousand six hundred and five *MS*
 1605] *TB*; one thousand six hundred and five *MS*
 1643] *TB*; one thousand six hundred forty and three *MS*
 first] *TB*; said *MS*
 1609] *TB*; one thousand six hundred and nine *MS*
 1610] *TB*; one thousand six hundred and ten *MS*
Margaret to Anne Clifford (22 Sept. 1615). Normalized text ed. TB from Cumbria, MS WD/Hoth/Box 44.
Anne to Margaret Clifford (20 Jan. 1615/6), ed. TB from Cumbria, MS WD/Hoth/Box 44.
From **the Knole Diary**
 their] these *MS*
From *The Life of Me* (cont.)
From Anne to Margaret (26 April 1616), ed. TB from Cumbria, MS WD/Hoth/Box 44.
From **the Knole Diary** (cont.)
 That same day] *TB*; Upon the 24th *MS*
 Queen Anna] *TB*; she *MS*
 then] *TB*; that *MS*
 his Majesty] *TB*; he *MS*
 needle-working] *TB*; working *MS*
 had] *TB*; have *MS*
From **The Life of Me**. Normalized text ed. TB, from transcript by Henry Fisher, Feb. 1727, from MS diary no longer extant.
 1628] *TB*; one thousand six hundred twenty-eight
 had] *TB*; have *MS*
From **the Kendal Diary**
 1584] *TB*; one thousand five hundred and eighty-four *MS*

Mary Sidney] Mary Sidney and *MS*
My lord Philip] *TB*; he *MS*
1625] *TB*; one thousand six hundred twenty-five *MS*
Henriette Marie] *TB*; Mary *MS*
1605 *TB*; one thousand six hundred five *MS*
My second husband] *TB*; he *MS*
1630] one thousand six hundred and thirty *MS*
Philip] *TB*; him *MS*
1650] *TB*; following *MS*
Consider … crooked] *TB*; *MS om.* (Bible ref. only)

MARGARET CUNNINGHAM

A Part of the Life. Normalized text ed. E. Russell, from holograph NLS MS 906 [*MS-a*]; with collations from scribal NLS MS 874 [*MS-b*]; which in the two mss. is usually abbreviated qch in *MS-a*, and spelled quich or which in *MS-b*] which is adopted here throughout.
 Edinburgh] Edr *MS-ab* (throughout)
 Avondale] Evandale *MS-ab* (throughout)
A Part of the Life, *MS-a*, ff. 1r-8r; cf, *MS-b*, ff. 363-370r.
 destitute] *MS-a*, destituter *MS-b*
 lay bedfast six week] *MS-a*; lay abed six weeks *MS-b*
 sustain] *MS-a*; subsist sustain *MS-b*
 my lady my mother] *MS-a*; my lady mother *MS-b*
 gave fair] *MS-a*; gave her fair *MS-b*
 the day] *MS-b*; day *MS-a*
 without] *MS-b*; wᵗ [*linebreak, om.* out] *MS-a*
 come home] *MS-a*; come *MS-b*
 Martinmas] mertimess *MS-ab* (again below)
 I] *MS-a*; So I *MS-b*
 up to] *MS-a*; to *MS-b*
 good payment] *MS-a*; my paying good payment *MS-b*
 get payment] *MS-a* be-paid get payment
 again to] *MS-a*; to *MS-b*
 have had] *MS-a*; would made *MS-b*
 there before] *MS-a*; therefore there before *MS-b*
 give me nothing] *MS-a*; not give me nothing *MS-b*
 mother-in-law] *ER*; mother *MS-ab*
 marquess] *MS-a*; Margaret Marquess *MS-b*
 my husband] *MS-a*; husband] *MS-b*
 garden] gairden *MS-a*; yaird *MS-b*
 my second son] *MS-a*; my son *MS-b*
 France] *MS-a*; France and the Parson of Crawford John *MS-b*
 ever I] *MS-a*; I ever I *MS-b*
 James my husband] he *MS-ab*
 himself both holily and civilly, so that he and I dwelt together very contentedly] *MS-a*; himself contentedly *MS-b* (omitting a line)
 meantime] *MS-a*; the meantime *MS-b*
 took] *MS-a*; had took *MS-b*
 for then] *MS-a*; for *MS-b*
 all his wonted] *MS-a*; all wonted *MS-b*
 duty to me] *MS-a*; duty toward to me *MS-b*
 openly seen in all the] *MS-a*; seen in the *MS-b*
 father's sister] father sister *MS-ab*
 I was unable] *MS-a*; was unable *MS-b*
 I got] *MS-a*; got *MS-b*
 (my … John's) I] *MS-a*; and my … John I *MS-b*
 John would … furnish me no longer] *MS-a*; *om.* furnish *through* but *MS-b*
 if he took] *MS-b*; if took *MS-a*
 favors] *MS-a*; favor *MS-b*
 the hostler] *MS-a*; his hostler *MS-b*
 oldest daughter] *MS-a*; daughter *MS-b*
 requests] *ER*; request *MS-ab*
 father-n-law] *ER*; father *MS-ab*
 ate daily] eat dayly *MS-a*; dayly *MS-b*
 commanding] *MS-b*; to commanding *MS-a*
 wit] wytte *MS-a*; wrytte *MS-b*

placed] *MS-a*; pleased *MS-b*
Dunrod] Dimrod *MS-ab*
come speak] *MS-a*; come & speak *MS-b*
refused] *MS-a*; refused ~~to do~~ *MS-b*
husband's] husbands *MS-a*; husbands friends *MS-b*
showed] *ER*; shew *MS-ab*
parson] *MS-a*; Parson of Crawford John *MS-b*
show me no favor] not shew me no favour *MS-b*
pursue] *MS-a*; ~~prepare~~ persue *MS-b*
should] *MS-a*; I should *MS-b*
myself *MS-a*; himself] *MS-b*
which] qch *MS-a*; what *MS-b*
so perverse] *MS-a*; as perverse *MS-b*
I desired him ₚ^{not} to accompany with me *MS-a*
I desired not to accompany with ~~me~~ him. *MS-b*
allot] alott *MS-a*; allow *MS-b*
he was] *MS-a*; he and I was *MS-b*
precept] *MS-a*; present *MS-b*
gave but] *MS-a*; gave *MS-b*
desiring him] *MS-a*; desiring *MS-b*
baptize] *MS-a*; and baptize *MS-b*
lying-in] *MS-b*; lying *MS-a*
that I] yᵗ *MS-b*; *om. MS-b*
visiting] *MS-b*; ~~visited me~~ visiting *MS-b*
discharging] *MS-a*; discharging giving *MS-b*
my husband's] *ER*; his *MS-ab*
or] *MS-a*; either *MS-b*
answer me] *MS-a*; answer *MS-b*
he ejected] *MS-a*; ejected *MS-b*
my husband] *ER*; he *MS-ab*
remain] *ER*; remaining *MS-a*; remained *MS-b*

The true copy of a letter [to Hamilton] Norm. text ed. Emma Russell from N.L.S. MS 906 [*MS-a*], ff. 8v-11v; with comparison of MS 874 [*MS-b*], ff. 370v-375v.
  God] *MS-a*; Lord *MS-b*
  showed] shew *MS-ab*
  thereof] *MS-a*; whereof *MS-b*
  that he] *MS-b*; that he that he *MS-a*
  love] *MS-a*; loving ~~kindness~~ *MS-b*
  brings] *MS-a*; bring *MS-b*
  here who] *MS-a*; here *MS-b*
  separated] *MS-a*; sprared *MS-b*
  you – and you, ane] you and you ane; *MS-a*; you an *MS-b*
  from among] *MS-a*; from *MS-b*
  partly by] ~~whereat~~ ^{partly by} *MS-b*; partly by *MS-a*
  enticements] *MS-a*; intirements *MS-b*
  way] *MS-a*; ~~very~~ ^^{way} *MS-b*
  manfully march forward] _{manfully} march forward (manfully subscript *MS-b*)) *ER*; march forward manfully] *MS-a*
  rock] *MS-a*; rock of *MS-b*
  corrupts] *MS-a*; corrupted *MS-b*
  exceedingly] *MS-a*; exceeding *MS-b*
  forth] *MS-a*; forth of *MS-b*
  precious] *MS-a*; gracious *MS-b*
  life to us unworthy] *MS-b*; life unworthy *MS-a*
  All are] *MS-a*; are *MS-b*
  nor is in] *MS-a*; nor *MS-b*
  this land] *MS-a*: the land *MS-b*
  tuned to] *MS-a*; *turned into MS-b*
  off our head] of our head *MS-a*; of head *MS-b*
  and wicked last] *MS-a*; wicked and last *MS-b*
  I] inserted supra. *MS-b*; *ER*; *om. MS-a*
  negligent] *MS-a*; ~~neglect~~ negligent *MS-b*
  loathed of it] *MS-a*; loathed it *MS-b*
  to receive] *MS-b*; of [blot] Receive *MS-a*
  ye shall receive] *MS-a*; they shall receive *MS-b*
  graces] *MS-a*; grace *MS-b*
  others] oyʳrs *MS-a*; ours *MS-b*
  loving] *MS-a*; ~~bles~~ loving *MS-b*

hide] *MS-a*; hides *MS-b*
everlasting] *MS-a*; everlastingly *MS-b*
rather that] *MS-a*; rather *MS-b*
as red as] *MS-a*; red as *MS-b*
fearing] *MS-a*; feeling *MS-b*
write to] *MS-a*; to write to *MS-b*
thee] thē *MS-b*; thee *MS-b*
the Holy Spirit] *MS-a*; holly spirit *MS-b*
your temporal] *MS-a*; my temporal *MS-b*
banished] *MS-a*; banished ~~friends~~ *MS-b*
Lines
  go] *MS-a*; to go *MS-b*
  I shall] *MS-a*; I will *MS-b*
  thereof] *MS-a*; whereof *MS-b*
  all both citizens *MS-a*; all citizen *MS-b*
True copy of a letter to … my Lady Marquess of Hamilton (Oct. 1622). Normalized text ed. DWF from N.L.S. MS 906, ff. 15v-19v; with comparison of MS 874, pp. 32-48.
  I have] I haue also MS

ELIZABETH DALE

A Brief of the Lady Dale's Petition to the Parliament: Normalized text ed. DWF from *A Brief* (1624).
  left] *DWF*; leauing *Q*
  mistake] *DWF*; mistaken *Q*

III. ACTIVISTS
ELIZABETH ARNOLD

Against the Painting of Women. Normalized text ed. DWF from "The Invective of doctor Andreas de Laguna." In T. Tuke, ed., *A Treatise against Paintng* [sic] *and Tinctvring* (1616) [*Q*], Sigs B3r-4v.
  [1] Dr. Andreas de Laguna] *DWF (for clarity)*; he *Q*.
  [2] de Laguna] *DWF (for clarification)*; he *Q*.
  [2] 69th] *DWF*; 69 *Q*.

RACHEL SPEGHT

Women's Learning. Normalized text ed. DWF from Daniel Tuvill, *Asylum Veneris* (1616).
  the daughter] they *Q*
  the pen] it *Q*
  maidens] their *Q*
  parents] them *Q*
  women] they *Q*
  men's] their *Q*
A Muzzle for Melastomus. Normalized text ed. DWF from Speght, *A Mouzell for Melastomus* (1617) [*Q*], 3-14, 17-19 (sigs. C2r-D1r, E1v-E2r).
Epistle "to the cynical Baiter"
  roving] roaring *Q corrected in errata*
Of Woman's Excellency
Gen. 1:31] *The biblical references (printed here in parentheses within the text) appear in Muz in the outside margins. Also in the margins (here omitted) are various subheadings* "1 Obiect[ion]," "1 Obiect. answered," *etc.*
  its] it *Q*
  28] 30 *Q*
  ironia] ironica *Q corrected in errata*
  Hevah's] *DWF*; Herods *Q, corrected in errata, p.38*
  28] 30 *Q*
  Lu. 2:51] *DWF*; Luke 1:51 *Q*
Certain Queries
  Organon] Arganox *Q corrected in errata*
The Reward
  full quote of Lev. 24:14-16] *Q om.*
Mortality's Memorandum, part 1: "The Dream." Normalized text ed. DWF from R. Speght, "The Dreame." In

Mortalities Memorandum, with a Dreame Prefixed (1621) [*Q*].
Sigs. A4r-C1r.

247 outran] *DWF*; outrun *Q* (*possibly authorial*)
252 preterit tense] *DWF*; Pretertense *Q*
280 piercing] perceiuing *Q*, corrected in errata (*sig. F3r*).

ESTER SOWERNAM

Ester Hath Hanged Haman. Normalized text ed. DWF from
Ester Sowrenam, pseud., *Ester Hath Hang'd Hamam* (1617).
A second epistle, addressed "To All Worthy and Hopefull
young youths of Great-Brittaine: But respectiuely to the best
disposed and worthy Apprentices of London" (sigs. A3v-4v),
is here omitted. Also omitted is an unimaginative summary of
Sowernam's argument, in lickety-splickety end-stopped verse,
entitled "A Defence Of Women, against the Author of the
Arraignment of Women" (sigs. H1r-3r), subscribed "Joane
Sharpe." Many of the biblical citations in Q appear inconsist-
ently as marginal notations and are here run into the text.

To All Worthy and Hopeful Young Youths
  hath made] *DWF*; had made many *Q*
Chapter 1
  apostate] *DWF*; apostata *Q*
  one] *DWF*; owne *Q*
  line] *DWF*; liue *Q* (*possibly read* life)
Chapter 2
  should be] *DWF*; should not be *Q* (*the original ms. may
  have read* "should not die, but be," *with* "not die but"
  incompletely struck out by the author)
  1 Cor. 15:22] ch. 9 [*sic*] *Q*
Chapter 3
  struck] stroke *Q* (*possibly read* strook)
**What excellent blessings and graces have been bestowed
upon women in the law of grace.**] "*Chap. IIII.*" appears
here (p. 13), again on p. 17 (*sig. D1r*) for part 2 of chap. 4.
  I Sam. 15:22] I Sam. 12 [*sic*] *Q*
  Judith 13] Iudith *Q*
  Esther 7-9] Hester *Q*
  Susanna 22-44] *DWF*; Susanna *Q*
  Baptist's] *DWF*; Baptist *Q*
  9:19-22] *DWF*; 9.15. *Q*
  Luke 21] *DWF*; Luke 2.2 *Q*
Chapter 4
  Mnemosyne] *DWF*; Mnencosum *Q*
  curry] carry *Q*, corrected in Q errata (*sig. H3r*)
Chapter 5
Chapter 6
  year 1615] *DWF*; yeare &c. *Q*
Chapter 7
  scurrility] sinceritie *Q*, corrected in Q errata
  anything] something *Q*, corrected in errata
  counter] countrey *Q*, corrected in Q errata
  her off] *DWF*; her of *Q*
  contention] contempt *Q*, corrected in Q errata
  sequuntur] *DWF*; sequntur *Q*
  Chronos...Limos...Brokhos] in Greek characters, *Q*
  drown] *DWF*; drown'd *Q*
  Men...she...men...men] *DWF*; they...they...they... they *Q*

IV. SINNERS

PENDLE WITCHES

Normalized text ed. DWF from T. Potts, *A Wonderful
Discoverie* [*Q*] (1613). A few liberties have been taken:
Extracts from Potts's lengthy and disorganized publication of
the court records are here put into nearly chronological order.
Potts's "the examinate" or "the said examinate," together with
third person pronouns referencing the speaker, are here
represented by "[I]" and are not detailed below; and so
accordingly with the personal pronouns for other referents;
"said" and "the said" (adj., for *aforesaid*) are here quietly

deleted. It is not to be supposed that this reading text
accurately reproduces the original words spoken by the
depondents. Readers wishing to read the unaltered 1613 text
may consult a facsimile on *Early English Books Online.*

A particular declaration (pre. a2)

13 March 1612
The examination of ALISON DEVICE (E4r-F1v). Q at this
point introduces an error: "About about eleuen yeares agoe,
this Examinate and her mother had their firehouse broken..."
The burglary had only just happened, and was the
precipitating incident for the ensuing investigation, trial, and
hangings. "About eleven years ago" was evidently a canceled
MS phrase pertaining to John Device's death eleven years ago,
repeated in the next paragraph."
  13^(th)] thirtieth *Q*
  we] the *Q*

30 March 1612
The Examination of ABRAHAM LAW (S1r-S2r)
The Examination of ALISON DEVICE (C1r-v)
  30^(th)] xiij *Q* [*sic*], corrected in trial report to thirtieth
The Confession of ALISON DEVICE (R3v-4r)
  the] which *Q*
The examination of JAMES DEVICE (S2v)

2 April 1612
The Examination of ELIZABETH SOUTHERNS (B2v-B3v,
E1r-v, N4v-O1r)

[*Thomas Potts, Court Recorder*]
The Examination of JOHN NUTTER (O1v-O2r)
Examination ... of JAMES ROBINSON (E1v-E2v)
  Nutter] he *Q*
  these people] this people *Q*, corrected in errata
[*Thomas Potts, Court Recorder*]
  these°] this *Q*, corrected in errata (A4r)
  Redfern's] her *Q*
The Examination ... of ANNE WHITTLE (D3r-4r, B4r-v;
cf. E2v-3v)
  Fancy] the said Spirit *Q*
  Elizabeth Nutter's] whose *Q*
  methinks] she thinketh *Q*
A Charm (E2v-E3r)
  3 bitters] bitter *Q*
[*Thomas Potts, Court Recorder:*]
  she] who *Q*
  Anne Redfern] Redferne *Q*
[The Good Friday Conspiracy] (C3r-v)
  This conspiracy] This *Q*
  Elizabeth Device] her *Q*

27 April 1612
**The Examination and Evidence of JENNET DEVICE,
daughter of Elizabeth Device, late wife of John Device, of
the Forrest of Pendle, in the county of Lancaster, against
Elizabeth Device, her Mother.** (Sigs. G3v-4r)
This reported testimony is repeated verbatim on sigs. I3v-4r, as
read during the trial of her brother James, but with "Robinsons
of Barley" substituted for "Christopher Swyers of Barley" (same
person, two surnames), and repeated again during the trial of
Alice Nutter (sig. P1v), but with the statement of the dinner
menu and stolen sheep quietly elided.
  Christopher Swyer's] sig. G3v; Robinsons I3v.
  they] the persons aforesaid *Q*
Examination of JAMES DEVICE. (C2r, G2r-v, G4r-H1r,
H3r-H4r, I2v-I3v, I4v-K1r, O2v, O4r, P1r-v, P4r-v, Q3v-Q4v,
S2v)
E3v-4r
  found by us] found by them *Q*
  myself] himselfe *Q*
  mine] his *Q*

said that] that *Q*
G2r-v, H3r-v
O2v Thomas] which *Q*
H3v-4r
  buried 8 May 1608]
C2r, I2v-3r
  myself] this Examinate *Q*
  they] the aforesaid persons *Q*
Examination…of ELIZABETH DEVICE (F4r-v).

19 May 1612
The Voluntary Confession…of JAMES DEVICE (I4v-K1r)
  I answered] who answered *Q*
The Confession … of Anne Whittle (B3r-v, U4v)
  the profession] profession *Q*
  he bid us] bidde them *Q*
  our…we…we] their…they…they *Q*
  our…us…we…we] their…them…they…they Q
Examination … of JENNET BOOTH (T1r-v)
  whereupon] that the said *Q*

12 July 1612
The Examination of PETER CHADDOCK (T3r-v)
The Examination of JANE WILKINSON (T4r)
The Examination of MARGARET LYON (T4r)
The Examination of MARGARET PARR (V1r)
The Examination … of ANNE WHITTLE (S4v)
[The Hanging of Jennet Preston] (Y2v)
  it] they *Q* [sic]
Examination … of JENNET DEVICE (F4v-G1v G3v-H1r,
H4v-I1v-I2r, I3v-I4r, K1r-K2r, P1v-P2v, Q1r-v, R1r)
  They] the persons
[The Trial at Assize (16-19 August 1612)] (C3v)

[Monday, 17 August]
[Arraignment and Trial of ANNE WHITTLE] (D1v-2v)
Indictment [of ANNE WHITTLE] (D2v-3r)
  Anne Whittle] she *Q*
  lord [Bromley] lord *Q*
  Whittle] shee *Q*

[Tuesday, 18 August 1612]
The Arraignment and Trial of ELIZABETH DEVICE
(F2r-3r)
Indictment [of ELIZABETH DEVICE] (F3v-4r)
[*Thomas Potts, Court Recorder*] (F4v-G1r)
  Elizabeth Device to silence, she] her to silence *Q*
  Jennet] she *Q*
  and for] and *Q*
The Examination and Evidence of JENNET DEVICE (F4v-
G1v)
  her…her…her…her] this Examinates *Q* (x4)
[*Thomas Potts, Court Recorder*] (H1r)
  Elizabeth Device] she *Q*
The Arraignment and Trial of JAMES DEVICE (H1v-H2v)
[The Indictment of JAMES DEVICE] (H2r)
  James Device] he *Q*
  facts] with *Q*
[Third and Fourth Indictments of JAMES DEVICE] (I1r-v)
The Examination and Evidence of Jennet Device (I1v-2v)
Charm (K1v)
*James's charm as reported by Jennet Device to the court, and
by Potts to his readers, contains many obvious errors; here
imperfectly reconstructed.*
  5 Mess afore the Rood] *DWF* (*speculative*) Lord in his
  mess *Q*
  9 What in th' other hath he?] *DWF*; What hath he in his
  other hand *Q*
  11 Open, open, heaven-door] *DWF* (*speculative*); *Q om.*
  15 yond] yonder *Q*
  21 O holy bairn] And holy bairnpan *Q*

25 A cross of red, and another of blude] A cross of blue,
  and another of red *Q*
  30 Gabrielie] Gabriel *Q*
[Thomas Potts, *Court Recorder*] (K2r)
  this hellish] these hellish *Q, corrected in errata*

[Wednesday, 19 August 1612]
The Arraignment and Trial of ANNE REDFERN (N3v-Nr4)
  Anne Redfern] shee *Q*
  Anne Redfern] shee *Q*
[The Indictment of ANNE REDFERN] (N4r)
  Anne Redfern] her *Q*
The Arraignment and Trial of ALICE NUTTER (O3r-v)
  she had] had *Q*
The Indictment of ALICE NUTTER (O3v-O4r)
  Jennet] shee *Q*
  Jennet] shee *Q*
  Anne Nutter] her *Q*
  Anne Nutter] she *Q*
Arraignment and Trial of KATHERINE HEWITT (P3r-v)
  her] their *Q*
  his] this Examinates
The Arraignment and Trial of ALISON DEVICE (R2v-3r)
[The Indictment of ALISON DEVICE] (R2v-3r)
  Sir Thomas Gerard] Gerard *Q*
  wondered] wondering *Q*
The Evidence of JOHN LAW (R4v-S1r)
  have continued] continued *Q*
  John Law turned] turned *Q*
  John Law] him *Q*
  Abraham Law] he *Q*
Trial of ALISON DEVICE (R2v-R3r)
  John Law] him *Q*
  the peddler] him *Q*
**The Arraignment and Trial of Margaret Pearson of
Padiham** (S3v-4v)
… [and] … Isabel Robey [of Windle] (T2r-v)
The Verdict of Life and Death (V1r)
King James, *Daemonology*, ed. DWF.
***The Arraignment and Trial of* JENNET PRESTON *of
Gisburn*** (sigs. X4r-Z3v), ed. DWF.
  Jennet Preston] her Q
  Thomas Lister Jr.] Lister *Q*
[To the General Reader] (sigs. A2v, A3v), ed. DWF.
To…Thomas, Lord Knyvett (sigs. [a]3r-A1v), ed. DWF

THE FLOWERS OF BELVOIR CASTLE
Normalized text ed. DWF From Rev. Henry Goodcole, *The
Wonderful Discoverie of the Witchcrafts* (1619, 1621). As
with the previous, some editorial liberties have been taken:
except as noted, "[I]," "[me]" and "[my]" in the edited text
represent *she, her,* and *her* in Q; *said* and *the said* (adj.,
aforesaid) in Q1 are here quietly deleted.
  the neighbors] they *Q*.
  Margaret Flower] her *Q*
  Peake] Peate (sic) *Q*
  Lord Rutland's] so his *Q*
  the Flowers] them *Q*
  the Flowers] they *Q*
  sometimes] and sometimes *Q*
Examination of ANNE BAKER (1 March)
  Anne Baker] she *Q*
  I] and that she *Q*
  The mother…chargeth] being charged by the mother *Q*
  Elizabeth Hough] she *Q*
  I] that she *Q*
  I have] she had *Q*
  Hough's] her *Q*
Examination of Joane Willimot (28 Feb.)
  my…me] that her…her *Q*

Examination of Joane Willimot (2 Mar.)
  I] Shee further confesseth, that shee *Q*
  I could] could *Q*
Examination of JOANE WILLIMOT (17 March)
  Joane Willimot's] her *Q*
  ~~methought] shee thought~~
  lord Rutland] Lord *Q*
The examination of ELLEN GREEN (17 March)
  with me] with this Examinate
  I sent] this Examinate saith that she sent *Q*
  I removed] this examinate remoued
  Willimot] she the said Willimot
  I now dwell] she now dwelt *Q*
  Willimot called me] shee the said *Willimot* called her this Examinate
  then I sent my] then sent her said *Q*
  I saw] this examinate sayeth, that she saw the same *Q*
  myself, I gave my] herself, this examinate further sayeth, that she gave her *Q*
The examination of PHILLIP FLOWER (4 Feb.)
  given me by Master Vavasour] given her [*sic*] by Mr. Vauasour *Q*
The examination of MARGARET FLOWER (22 Jan.)
  my sister] her *Q*
The examination of PHILLIP FLOWER (25 Feb.)
The examination of MARGARET FLOWER (25 Feb.)

ELIZABETH SAWYER, *Witch of Edmonton*
Normalized text ed. DWF from Henry Goodcole, *The Wonderfull discovery of Elizabeth Sawyer a witch late of Edmonton* (1621).
  Agnes] Elizabeth *Q*
  Sawyer's] her *Q*
  Sawyer] she *Q*
  sent] send *Q*
  Elizabeth Sawyer] Who *Q*
  the three women] they *Q*
  Sawyer] she *Q*
  Elizabeth Sawyer] her *Q*
From the pulpit... Normalized text ed. DWF from Alexander Roberts, *A Treatise of Witchcraft* (1616).
  not all who...actions are strucken] *DWF* (for clarity); all who...action not strucken Q
...and the stage. Normalized text ed. DWF from Dekker et al., *The Witch of Edmonton.* (1621)

ELIZABETH JENNINGS
[The Bewitchment of Elizabeth Jennings.] Normalized text ed. DWF, from British Library MS Add. 36674, ff. 134-7.

MARGARET FEARNSIDE
Confession. etc. Normalized text ed. DWF from *The araignment & burning of Margaret Ferne-seede* (1608).
  the body] it *Q*
  beforesaid] before *Q*
  hoping] hope *Q*
  thefts] theft *Q*
  the bargemen] they *Q*
  the Fernseeds] them *Q*
  When ... she] When ... to which she *Q*

MARTHA SCAMBLER
1624 Infanticide Statute. Normalized text ed. DWF from Great Britain, Parliament. "An Acte to prevent the murthering of Bastard Children," Statutes of the Realm (Buffalo: W.S. Hein, 1993): vol. 4, pt. 2, 1234-1235.

Anon., Deeds against Nature and Monsters, sig. A3v-4v.
  contrariwise] contrariwise to *Q*
  These] which *Q*

He] who *Q*
They] which *Q*
Martha Scambler her Repentance, Sig. B2r-v.

Henri Estienne, *World of Wonders.* Ed. DWF fr. *Q* (1607).
  preachers] they *Q*

BESSIE CLARKSON

The Conflict in Conscience. Normalized text ed. DWF, from W[illiam] L[ivingston], *The Conflict in Conscience,* ed.
  visited] visit *Q*
  when] will *Q*
  wherefore] where *Q*

V. MOTHERS

ROSE HICKMAN THROCKMORTON

Michael Lok, [My Late Father.] Ed. DWF from B.L. Cotton MS Otho E.viii, f. 42 and Hakluyt, vol. 2 (1599) 2.7;

Certain Old Stories. Normalized text ed. T. Banton from British Library Add. 43827; checked against MS Add. 45027.
Anon., [*Epitaph on the Death of this Old Gentlewoman*] f. 7v, lines 1-4, 11-20.

DOROTHY (KEMPE) LEIGH
From *The Mother's Blessing.* Normalized text ed. DWF from Leigh, *The Mother's Blessing* (1616)

ELIZABETH CLINTON
The Countess of Lincoln's Nursery. Normalized text ed. DWF from *The Countesse of Lincolnes Nurserie* (Oxford, 1622) [*Q*].
  It is objected that nursing] Secondly it is obiected, that it *Q* (*sig.* C3r).

ELIZABETH (BROOKE) JOCELIN
A Mother's Legacy to her Unborn Child. Normalized text ed. DWF from Jocelin, *A Mothers Legacie* (1624).
  our child] it *Q*
  that which] that *Q*
  our child] it *Q*
  our child] it *Q*
  pride] it *Q*
  Pride] It *Q*

VI. POETS

Women's Rites: Tradition and Change
Anon, Lulla by Lully. Normalized text ed. DWF from B.L. MS Sloane 1709 (Commonplace book of Thomas Chaffyn of Meres, Wiltshire), f. 271v. (In the same manuscript are extraces from the verse of Elizabeth Grymeston).
  2 lulla] lully *MS*
  3 sleep] sleep, child *MS*

Anon.: *Love Lamenting.* Normalized text ed. DWF from Corpus Christi College (Oxford), MS 327 [*MS-C*], f. 26v. Collated with Bodleian Library MS Eng. poet. e.14 [*MS-B*], f. 29r ("A Songe"), and Beinecke Library MS Osborn b200 [*MS-O*], p. 81; *MS-B* borrows a fourth stanza from Johnson's version): "The jewell's lost, the thefe is fled / And I lye wounded in my bed / If to comeplaine I should begin / He'ele say t'was I that let him in / Weeping Ile singe [etc.]
  2 best which] what best *MS-B*
  2-3 *MS-B transposes*: For yf I sing ... / And if I weep my greife remaine [*sic*]
  6 Because that] To see, that *MS-B* (*again at 12, 18*)
  7 They ... still] the ... all *MS-B*
  9 When] Whenas *MS-B*
  11 Wherefore] weepinge *MS-B*
  13 Maidens ... ruled] Ladyes ... warned *MS-B*

14 Do ... their] Trust not to much there *MS-B*

15 While you live, live] Whilst you live, love *MS-O*; whil'st yt yee have time, liue *MS-B*

Richard Johnson, "The Maidens Complaint." Quotations ed. DWF from Johnson, *Golden Garland* (1620), G3r-v.

Anon. *XV. [Song of the Marrying Maiden.]* Normalized text ed. DWF from R. Jones, *The Muses Gardin for Delights* (1610) [*Q*], no. 15. A corrupt text in British Library MS Addit. 29409 (a 19th-century copy of an older Scotch commonplace book), ff. 267v-68r, appears to derive from the printed text of 1610 and is not here collated.

4 afeared] afraide *Q*

ELIZABETH MELVILLE

Epigraph

Elizabeth Melville to John Livingston, "Letters" (10 Dec. 1631), ed. Tweedie, p. 365.

Alexander Hume, "To...Elizabeth Melville, Lady Comrie." Normalized text ed. DWF from Hume (1599), A2r-3r.

Invocation. Normalized text ed. DWF, from the Betty Bruce papers (Beineck); photofacsimile, Jamie Reid Baxter, *Poems of Elizabeth Melville,* rear cover)

10 thy] *MS*; the [sic] *Baxter*, 25, 117.

Sonnets 3 and 4. Normalized text ed. DWF from Baxter's transcript of the Bruce MS.

Love's Lament for Christ's Absence, lines 13-24, f. 200. Ed. DWF from Baxter transcript of N.L.S. Wodrow quarto, no. 27, f. 199v ff.sta 2 (lines 13-24), identified as Melville's by Baxter.

A Godly Dream

Ed. DWF, from Elizabeth Melville, *Ane Godlie Dreame* (Scots) [Edinburgh, 1603] and *A Godlie Dreame* [Edinburgh, 1604].

1603 (Scots text)

34 Awaik] Awalk [sic] *Q 1603*

131 I ... strife] DWF (*Q1-S omits a line; in its stead, a similar line appears misplaced at the end of the stanza, following* "sair to sie"; *which reads,* I am thy Lord, that sone sall end thy race.

309 through] thocht *Q 1603*

317 I] thay *Q 1603*

353 ye mon] quhen ye mon *Q 1603; cf.* ye must *Q 1604*

386 Tirannes freat] *Q 1603; cf.* tyrants threat *Q 1604*

418 Cleave fast] Clim [sic] fast *Q 1603*

445 above] abone [sic] *Q 1603*

1604 (English text)

2 wherewith] where w^t *Q 1604*

23 o'erset] ouerset *Q 1604*

124 cast] cuist *Q 1604* (as per Scots Q 1603; prob. authorial, cf. below)

128 come] comde *Q 1604*

194 O'er] Ouer *Q 1604*

212 cast] cuist *Q 1604*

285 Ere e'er] Ere euer *Q 1604*

298 cast] *cuist Q 1604*

301 thought] though *Q 1604*

309 through] thoucht *Q 1604*

370 ye] we *Q 1604*

Letters to John Livingston. Normalized text ed. DWF from Tweedie transcripts (1845).

Lady Culross to John Livingston (n.d., about 1626), Tweedie, 352-4.

anyone] *DWF (for clarity)*; any *MS*

cannot] can [sic] *MS*

herself] *DWF (for clarity)*; her *MS*

David Dickson] *DWF*; David *MS*

Lady Culross to J. Livingston (n.d.), ed. fr. Tweedie, 355.

Lady Culross to J. Livingston (17 June 1630), ed. from Tweedie [misdated 1629], 356-7.

Lady Culross to J. Livingston (25 March 1631), ed. from Tweedie, 357-9.

Lady Culross to J. Livingston (17 June 1631), ed. from Tweedie, 359-60. Endorsed on back of MS, not in Melville's hand, probably Livingston's: "June 1631, Lady Culros."

Lady Culross to J. Livingston (10 December 1631), ed. from Tweedie, 361-5.

nor none so unworthy [as] *DWF*; none so unworthy *MS.*

Forget not] *DWF*; Forget [sic] *MS.*

MARY OXLIE of Morpeth

To William Drummond of Hawthornden. Normalized text ed. DWF from *Poems by That most Famous Wit, William Drummond of Hawthornden* (1656), sig. A8.

To the Author. Normalized text ed. *DWF* from Drummond, *Poems* (1656), p. 66, sig. F1v.

The GREY SISTERS

Normalized text ed. DWF (except "A Funeral Pyramid") from I. Casaubon, *A Letter* (1615) [*Q*]. "A Funeral Pyramid" edited from Josuah Sylvester, *Panthea* (1630), C3v.

1. **Mary Grey Drayton,** *On the Decease:* "On the Decease of my Incomparable Sister, Mistresse Elizabeth Martin," sig. D8r; *A Funeral Pyamid:* "Funerall Pyramide Erected to the Honor of ... Mrs. Elizabeth Grey," sig. C3v; ***To the Soul:*** "To the Soule," sigs. E3v-4r; signed Mary. q. G[ray]

Penelope Grey, *Parodia:* "Parodia," sigs. E1v-2r.

Anne Grey Masters, ***To Her Soul-Loved Sister:*** "To Her Soule-Loved Sister, Mris E. M," D8v.

AEMILIA LANYER

From ***Salve Deus Rex Judæorum.*** Normalized text ed. DWF from *Salve Deus Rex Iudæorum* (1611) [*Q*]; collated with Woods, ed., *The Poems of Aemilia Lanyer* (1993) [*Woods*]. Eight copies survive of *STC* 15227.5 (imprint in 5 lines), only three of which are textually complete, one copy at the Huntington Library [*Q-H1*], and two at the Folger Shakespeare Library; the Avon County Library in Bath has a copy that lacks only leaf 1. *STC* 15227 represents a variant (imprint in 4 lines), of which the Huntington library owns a unique copy [*Q-H2*], also complete. Much of the front matter is omitted from the copies of *STC* 15227.5 owned by the British Library [*Q-L*], Bodleian Library [*Q-Ox*], the Victoria and Albert Museum, and Williams College. The Bodleian Library copy [*Q-Ox*] breaks off at G4v, after line 1784 of *Salve*, omitting "The Description of Cooke-ham" and "To the Doubtful Reader." The British Library copy [*Q-L*] also lacks quire f). For a fuller description of the nine extant copies, see *Wood*, pp. xlvii-li. *Wood* follows *Q-H1* except as noted below. Rowse's 1979 text, which contains many substantive errors, is here omitted.

1. **To the Virtuous Reader** (sig. f3; *omit Q-L*)

2. **To the Queen's ... Majesty** (sigs. a3r-b1v)

3. **To the Lady Elizabeth's Grace** (sig. b2r)

4. **The Author's Dream** (sigs. c3r-d3v)

5. from **Salve Deus Rex Judæorum** (title poem)

To the Countess of Cumberland (sig. A3); *Q-L om.*

heading] *Q in margin*: The Ladie / Margaret / Countesse / Dowager of / Cumberland [A3r]

A Preamble (sig. B1); *omitted in Q-L*

[An Apology for Women] (with intro. lines, sigs. C4v-D3v)

A Brief Description of his Beauty (sig. F1v).

1297-1301 heading] *in margin Q*

To My Lady of Cumberland (sigs. F1v-G3r)
1321-23 heading] *in margin Q*
1409 Antony] Anthony *Q*
1516 free] *Wood*; ftee *Q*

7. **The Description of Cookham** (sigs. H2r-I1r)
5   Pallas] Palace *Q*
94   stem] *DWF*; steame *Q*
182 knew] know [*sic*] *Wood*

8. **To the Doubtful Reader** (sig. I1v)

ELIZABETH TANFIELD CARY

1. ***The Tragedy of Mariam, Fair Queen of Jewry.***
Normalized text ed. DWF from Elizabeth Cary, *The Tragedie of Mariam* (1613) [*Q*]; collated with suggested emendations in Greg's "List of Doubtful Readings" (ed. 1914) [*Greg*], x-xi, and with Weller and Ferguson, ed., *The Tragedy of Mariam* (1993) [*F&W*]. The copy owned by the Victoria and Albert Museum has been annotated by Alexander Dyce (author of *Specimens of British Poetesses, Selected and Chronologically Arranged* [London, 1827]); Dyce's suggested emendations are noted below only when adopted. *F&W* provide a diplomatic normalized text, following *Q* in substance except as noted below. All stage directions in brackets represent additions by the editor.

Argument
granddaughter] daughrer [*sic*] *Q*
Herod…Herod…Herod…Herod] he…he…him…he *Q*
Josephus] *Greg, F&W*; Iosophus *Q*
Herod's] his *Q*
Mariam] her *Q*
Herod…Herod] he…But he *Q*
Josephus] *Greg, F&W*; Iosophus *Q*
Herod's…Herod] his…him *Q*
Mariam…Mariam] her…she *Q*

Personæ (lacking in some copies)
son by Doris] son by Doris *Greg, F&W*; sonne by Salome *Q*
Silleus] Silleus *F&W* (*regularized throughout from inconsistent spelling in* Q); Sillius *Q*
Baba's…Baba's] *DWF* (*DF regularized throughout to* Baba; *nominative case always has* Baba, *as at* 1.4.56, 1.6.29, 2.2.42, 2.2.58, 3.2.39); Babus *Q*; Babas' *F&W* (*regularized as* Babas *F&W, throughout*); *not noted hereafter*
Butler] *F&W*; Bu. *Q*

ACT 1, SCENE 1] Actus primus. Scœna prima. *Q*
35 loveliest] *Greg, F&W*; lowlyest *Q*
47 mind] *Greg, F&W*; maide *Q*
68 admirer and my lord.] *F&W*; admirer. And my Lord, *Q*

ACT 1, SCENE 2] Actus primus: Scœna Secunda. *Q*
3 murth'rer's] *Greg*; murd'rers *F&W*; murthers *Q*
12 famed] fam'd *Greg, F&W*; fain'd *Q* (*cf. 5.1.211-13*)
44 Herod] *Greg*; Mariam *Q*
45 I know, by fits] *DWF*; I know by fits *Q*
53 Mariam.] Mar: *Greg, F&W*; Nun: *Q*
55 Of] *F&W*; In *or* Of? *Greg*; If *Q*
77 find] *Greg*; findes *Q*; finds *F&W*
104 that] *DWF*; but *Q*
104 seek] seeke *Greg*; like *F&W*; leeke *Q* (*note rhymes*)
120 And passed] *DWF*; And part *Q* (*perhaps from MS* And past *Dyce*); Apart *Greg*; cf. 5.1.227

ACT 1, SCENE 3] Actus primus. Scœna tertia. *Q*
11 discontent] *Q* (*off-rhyme*); discontents *Greg* (*to perfect the rhyme*)
12 did] doth *Greg*
36 Abram's] *DWF*; Abrahams *Q*
47 suspicion's] suspicions *Greg, F&W*; suspitious *Q*

50 Joseph's] *DWF*; Iosephs *Greg*; Josephus' *F&W*; Iosephus *Q*

ACT 1, SCENE 4] Actus primus. Scœna quarta. *Q*
16 all eyes] *Greg, F&W*; allyes *Q*
38 from] *F&W*; for *Q*;
40 Constabarus] *F&W*; Contabarus *Q*
45 men] *DWF*; man *Q*

ACT 1, SCENE 5] Actus primus. Scœna quinta. *Q*Scena *F&W*
30 oracle, / … not … will] *F&W*; oracle. / … on … will? *Greg*; oracle, / … not … will? *Q*
37 whom] *Greg, F&W*; home *Q*

ACT 1, SCENE 6] Actus primus: Scœna [*sic*] Sexta. *Q*
25 forfeited? Hapless] *DWF*; forfeited hapless *Q*; *add* to *or* by *Greg* [*not necessary*]; forfeited to *F&W*
32 makes] *DWF* (*final* -e, -ed, -s, *and* -es *endings are frequently confused on acount of MS hand*); make *Q, F&W*
51 beasts swim] beastes swim *Greg, F&W*; beastes, swine, *Q*
56 water-bearing] *DWF*;   Waters-bearing *Q* (*see t.n. 1.6.32*)
90 vow] *Greg, F&W*; vowd *Q*
127 If] *Greg, F&W*; Of *Q*
132 cheerful] *F&W*; chreefull *Qc*
133 high estate] *DWF* (*cf. dup. state at line 131 and see t.n. at 2.1.57*); higher state *Q*, F&W
136 Th' other] *F&W*; T'hother *Q*

ACT2, SCENE 1] Actus secundus. Scœna prima. *Q*
12 monarchal] *F&W*; monachall *Q*
22 What] *F&W*; What? *Q*
24 us] *Greg, F&W*; *Q omit*
50 thee] *Dyce*; the *Q, F&W*
57 lowest state] *perhaps read* low estate; *cf. t.n. at 1.6.133*
65 least] *DWF*; best *Q, F&W*; lest *Greg* (*i.e., for* least)

ACT 2, SCENE 2] Actus 2. Scœna. [*sic*] 2. *Q*
30 needs] *F&W*; need *Q*
39 overpassed] *F&W*; operpast *Q*
48 safety] *Greg*; safely *Q, F&W*
66 fear] *Greg, F&W*; leare *Q*
75 gratitude. / *Constabarus.* Believe,] *Greg, F&W*; gratitude *Const.* believe *Q*
76 at all] *DWF* (*conjectural add'n to fill short line*); *Q om.*
93 lie] *Greg, F&W*; liue *Q*
98 Julius'] *F&W*; Iulions *Q*
102 physnomy] physnomy *F&W*; Phismony *Q*

ACT 2, SCENE 3] Actus 2. Scœna 3. *Q*; Actus Secundus. Scena Tertia *F&W*
1 You] *Greg, Q*; Your *Q*
2 stoop] *Dyce, F&W*; scope *TM!* (*a possible reading*)
25 oaths] *Greg, Q*; oath *Q*
50 shows] *perhaps read* showed
55 be.] *Greg*; be *Q, F&W*
56 fortunes,] *Greg*; fortunes. *Q, F&W*

ACT 2, SCENE 4] Actus secundus. Scœna 4. *Q*, Scena Quarta *F&W*
9 exception] *Greg, F&W*; expectation *Q*
10 Salome] *Greg, F&W*; Salom *Q*
18 loss] losse *Greg*; lost *Q*
23 lack] *F&W*; lake *Q*
38 affection's loss to me!] *DWF*; affections lost, to me *Q*
92 Ay, ay! *They fight.*] *F&W*; I, I they fight *Q*
94 Intrude] *F&W*; Intru'd *Q*
95 late to] late I *Greg* (*not necessary*)
97 Arabian? / *Silleus.* Very well —] *Greg, F&W*; *Arabian? Silleus* very well, *Q*
109 too] *Greg, F&W*; so *Q*
138 like'hood] likelihood *Q*

ACT 3, SCENE 1] Actus tertius: Scœna prima. *Q*, Scena *F&W*

3 can make] *F&W*; cane mak *Q*
5 effects] *DWF*; affects *Q*
23-4 beauty. / *Salome*.] beauty, *Salo*: *Q*, *F&W*

ACT 3, SCENE 2] Actus tertius. Scœna 2. *Q*

18 proved] *DWF*; prou'd *Q*, *F&W* (*short line*)
25 Constabarus] *F&W*; *Constan*: *Q*
32 her with you be] *F&W*; *read* here with you. / *Be*? *Greg*
37 not] *F&W*; no *Q*
38 Constabarus] *F&W*; *Consta*: *Q* (*again at* 40, 44)
39 doomed] *Greg*; done (*for MS* domd?) *Q*, *F&W*
41 I] he *Q*; we *Greg* (*thereby requiring emendation of next line also*), *F&W*
42 his] our *Greg*, *F&W*
64 sleight] *F&W*; slite *Q*

ACT 3, SCENE 3] Actus 3. Scœna 3. *Q*, Tertia. Scena Tertia *F&W*

5 Herod – / *Mariam*.] *F&W*; *Herod. Mari. Q*
4 *Mariam*. How?] *F&W*; *Q* omits Mariam
19 speak –] *DWF*; speak (*no end punc.*) *Q*, *F&W*
34 hypocrite] hypcorite *Q*, *F&W*
46-47 word; / I] *perhaps read* word, / [But]
75 Alexandra's] Alexandras *Greg*; Alexanders *Q*; Alexander's *F&W*

ACT 4, SCENE 1] Actus quartus: Scœna prima. *Q*

5 Mariam, how?] *Greg*, *F&W*; Mariam? *Q*
6 *Nuntio*] *F&W*; *Nutio Q*
16 Joshua-like] *F&W*; *Iosua*like *Q*
24 geese] *Greg*; grief *Q*
33 little while, mine eyes –] *Greg*, *F&W*; little, while mine eyes *Q*
40 Who's] *F&W*; Whose *Q*

ACT 4, SCENE 2] Actus quartus. Scœna secunda. *Q*

30 your] *Greg*, *F&W*; you *Q*
37 Salome] *Greg*, *F&W*; *Salom* Q
42 *Mariam – Salome, I mean*] *F&W*; *Mariam. Salom. I meane Q*
43 sprite] *DWF*; spirit *Q*

ACT 4, SCENE 3] Actus 4. Scœna 3. *Q*, Quartus. Scena Tertia *F&W*

43 Let ... soul] *DWF* (*conjectural recons. of missing line; cf. analogous construction at 2.3.53-54*) *Q om.*

ACT 4, SCENE 4] Actus 4. Scœna 4. *Q*

1 *Butler*] *F&W*; *Bu.* Q
6 poison] *Greg*, *F&W*, *F&W*; passion *Q*
10 seize] *F&W*; cease *Q*
29 I] *Greg*, *F&W*; *Q*, copy D; other copies om. (blank space)
46 Yet, wert thou] *Greg*; Yet neuer wert thou *Q*
56 heavenly] heunly *Greg*; heav'nly *F&W*; heauy *Q*
70 guiltless] *F&W*; guliltles *Q*
71 lock] *Greg*, *F&W*; looke *Q*
81-2 her? / *Soldier*. You] *Greg*, *F&W*; her: *Sould*: you *Q*
87 love] loue *Greg*, *F&W*; boue *Q*

ACT 4, SCENE 5] Actus 4. Scœna 5 *Q*, Quartus. Scena Quinta *F&W*

5 causeless] *Greg*, *F&W*; caules *Q*

ACT 4, SCENE 6] Actus 4. Scœna 6. *Q*

14 Thus *Greg*; Tis *Q*; This *F&W*;
20 our] *Greg*; her *F&W*; your *Q*
23 Whereby] *F&W*; Were by *Q*
25 lament?] *DWF*; lament, *Q*
47 man] *Greg*, *F&W*; many *Q*
55 Your] *Greg*, *F&W*; You *Q*
58 she] *Greg*, *F&W*; he *Q* .

ACT 4, SCENE 7] Actus 4. Scœna 7 *Q*, Quartus. Scena Septima *F&W*

12 falchions] *Greg*, *F&W*; fanchions *Q*
32 Oh, ay, I] *DWF*; Oh ay: I *F&W*; Oh I: I *Q*
44 Ay, very] *DWF*; I very *Q*
66 indeed] *DWF* (*conjectural, to fill short line*); *Q om.*
123 Hittite] *F&W*; *Hittits* Q
130 Jewess] *DWF*; Iewe, she *Q*

ACT 4, SCENE 8] Actus 4. Scœna 8. *Q*, Quartus. Scena Octava *F&W*

3 Ay, I] *F&W*; I, I *Q*
4 As] *Greg. F&W*; At *Q*
51 In] *Greg*; I *Q*; Ay, *F&W*
57 sees] says *Greg* (*unecessary*)
89 Gerizim] *Greg*; Gerarim *Q*
106 scorning] *Greg*; scorniug *Q*
139 Is] In *Greg* (*not necessary*)
139 proud] *DWF*; prou'd *Q*; prov'd [*sic*] *F&W*

ACT 5, SCENE 1] Actus quintus. Scœna prima. *Q*
4 beauty, chastity, and wit?] *F&W*; beautie? Chastitie and wit, *Q*
9-10 new / To him,] *F&W*; new, / To him *Q*
38 darken] *Greg*, *F&W*; darke *Q*
54-55 withal. / Go on. / *Nuntio*. She came] *Greg*, *F&W*; withall. / *Nun.* Go on, *Q*
57 cheerful] *F&W*; cheefull *Q*
60 sorry] *DWF* (*conjectural addition to fill short line*); *Q om.*
61 beckoned] beckon'd *F&W*; beckned *Q*
69 I not livumad, her lord] *Greg*, *F&W*; I not made her lord, *Q*
80 divide] *Greg* (*note rhyme at 5.1.82*); divided *Q*
85 died] *DWF*; did *Q* (*prob. fr. MS* di'd), *F&W* (*cf. t.n. at 5.1.190*)
96 Abram] *DWF*; Abraham *Q*
108 he] *Greg*, *F&W*; she *Q*
167 hers ... look] *F&W*; hers: Nay, not so much a : looke *Q*
190 died] *Greg*, *F&W*; did *Q* (*cf. t.n. at 5.1.85*)
211 feign] *some copies read* faine, *others* fame (*cf. next, both prob. resulting from a botched correction*); feign *F&W*
213 fame] *some copies read* faine, *others* fame; feign *F&W*
267 rose] *DWF*; rise *Q*
292 Such] *DWF*; So *Q*

MARY WROTH

William Herbert, Elegy: Normalized text ed. DWF from Huntington Lib. MS HM 198, Part 2, 105 [*MS-1*]; with collations from MS HM 198, Part 2, 101r (which breaks off at line 18) [*MS-2*]; and *Poems* (1660)
2 me] *MS-1*; one *MS-2*; me, *1660*
2 only] truly 1660
3 shew] showe *MS-1*; hue *MS-2*; view, *1660*
6 to account] to accompt *MS-1*; t'account *MS-2*, *1660*
lines 10, 11, 12] *1660 om.*
15 unrequired] *MS-1*, *1660*; required *MS-2*
17 the] thy *MS-2*, *1660*
28 love...heart] loue, did'st in thy hart *MS-1*; love in thy heart didst *1660*
30 prayers as] prayer that *1660*
40 gain...did] gaine...did *MS-1*; game...didst *1660*
43 tread] *MS-1*; do *1660*
61 sour] soure *MS-1*; sore *1660*
63 nursed] nurst *MS-1*; durst *1660*
64 mischiefs to secure] mischeifs, doe secure; *MS-1*; wrongs can expiate *1660*
69 where] *MS-1*; when *1660*

73 multitude] *1660*; multitudes *MS-1*
74 leavings] *MS-1*; leaving *1660*
74 intrude] *1660*; multitudes *MS-1*

Mary Sidney Wroth, *Penshurst Mount*. Normalized text ed. DWF, on left, from B.L. MS Add. 23229, ff. 91r-92r; on right, untitled, from *Urania* (1621), pp. 110-11.

9 overthrows] or'throwes *MS*; ouerthowes *1621*
21 what] *1621*; w^t *MS*
66 patient's] patience *MS* (cf. Herbert, "Elegy," l. 66)
74 Which] *MS*; with *1621*

From *Love's Victory*: selected **Songs**. Normalized text ed. DWF from Henry E. Huntington Library MS HM 600 ("Loues Victorie"), an incomplete early draft [*MS*]. Nos. 1 (f. 1r), 5 (f. 4), 8 (f. 11r). A complete fair copy of the play in five acts survives at Penshurst, c. 1619.

1.8 desire] delight *lined out*, desire *above MS*
1.24 life's] lives *MS*

***Pamphilia to Amphilanthus*:** selected **Sonnets**. Normalized text ed. DWF fr. *Pamphilia to Amphilanthus*, in *Urania* (1621) [*Q*], sigs. Aaaa1r - Ffff4v (with irregular pagination). Collated with Folger MS V.a.104 [*MS*] (a holograph draft earlier than the revised text in *Q*). *Q* is comprised of several independently numbered sequences of songs and sonnets, for which *Rbts* supplies continuous numbering (supplied below in brackets). Roberts follows *MS*, making some emendations from *Q*.

PART 1
1.1 [*Rbts* P1], *Q* sig. Aaaa1r
  2 senses] senceses *MS*
  4 swiftness] swiftnes *MS*; switnesse [*sic*] *Q*
1.8 [*Rbts* P9] *Q* sig. Aaaa3r
  3 but] *DWF*; bought *MS, Q*
  4 Increase the] increaseth *MS*
1.14 [*Rbts* P16], *Q* sig. Aaaa4r
  5 leave] *MS*; leane *Q*
1.15 [*Rbts* P17], *Q* sig. Aaaa4r
1.20 [*Rbts* P23], *Q* sig. Bbbb2r
  4 in] by *MS*
  10 had] have *MS*
1.21 [*Rbts* P24], *Q* sig. Bbbb2r
1.22 [*Rbts* P25], *Q* sig. Bbbb2v
  9 received] receavd's *MS*
  10 *chos'n*] *DWF*; chose *MS, Q*
1.24 [*Rbts* P27], *Q* sig. Bbbb2v-3r
1.27 [*Rbts* P31], *Q* sig. Bbbb3v
  1 tedious] treacherous *MS*
  7 from hands free] late from thee *MS*
  14 gain your liberty] I will sett thee free *MS*
1.30 [*Rbts* P34], *Q* sig. Bbbb4
  9 strive but] *DWF*; but strive *Q, MS*
  13 My ... esteem] and you my, trusty freinds, my faith esteeme *MS*
1.32 [*Rbts* P37], *Q* sig. Cccc1r
  13 sweet] sought *MS*
1.35 [*Rbts* P40], *Q* sig. Cccc1v
  9 their] the *MS*
  10 a show] the mask *MS*
1.38 [*Rbts* P44], *Q* sig. Cccc2v
1.39 [*Rbts* P45], *Q* sig. Cccc3r
  5 those] thes *MS*
1.42 [*Rbts* P49], *Q* sig. Cccc3v
1.45 [*Rbts* P52], *Q* sig. Cccc4v
  2 multitude] multituds *MS*
1.46 [*Rbts* P53], *Q* sig. Cccc4v-Dddd1r
  10 flame] *MS*; paine *Q*
1.48 [*Rbts* P55], *Q* sig. Dddd1r
  5 when] wher *MS*
  7 unpossible] impossible *MS*
  10 passions] longings *MS*

PART 2
Song [*Rbts* P59], *Q* sig. Dddd2r
  13 wicked] wished *MS*
Sonnet 1 [*Rbts* P63], *Q* sig. Dddd3
  10 Whose ... reel,] Whose favors ficle, and unconstant reele; *Q*
Sonnet 7 [*Rbts* P69], *Q* sig. Dddd4v
Song [*Rbts* P73], *Q*, sig. Eeee1
  1 springtime] springing time *MS*
  3 frosts] frost *MS*
  23 frosts] frost *MS*
A Crown of Sonnets [*Rbts* P77-90], *Q* sig. Eeee2v-Ffff1r
  1.7 with] *MS*; which *Q*
  2.11 The] The *altered to* That *MS*
  3.11 sunbeams] sunn beames *MS, Rbts*; Sun's beames *Q*
  5.7 fear] feares *MS*
  5.12 thoughts] thought *MS*
  5.13 we may] may wee *MS*
  6.5 which must] with much *MS*
  6.9 make] makes *MS*
  6.14 are] be *MS*
  7.3 flame] flames *MS*
  7.4 these…kindle] those…kindles *MS*
  7.7 whereas…aspire] as wher…respire *MS*
  7.12 workman] woorkmen *MS*
  9.5 subject] subjects *MS*
  9.6 or] nor *MS*
  10.9 of] butt *MS*
  12.2 fading] vading *MS*
  12.8 night] *MS*; might *Q*
  12.12 content] contents *MS*
  13.8 directions] directnes *MS*
  14.6 Is faith untouched] faith untouch'd is *MS*

PART 3
3.1 [*Rbts* P95], *Q* sig. Ffff2v
  4 mourning heart or salve] morning hurt or soule *MS*
  7 wanton] Venus *MS*
  9 thy] *MS*; they *Q*
3.2 [*Rbts* P96], *Q* sig. Ffff3r.
3.7 [*Rbts* P101], *Q*, sig. Ffff4r
  1 or] nor *MS*
  3 Or] nor *MS*
  6 my] thy *MS*
  11 Then] when *altered to* then *MS*
  11 I do] doe I *MS*
3.9 [*Rbts* P103], *Q*, sig. Ffff4
  15 Pamphilia] *MS*; *omit Q*

The Countess of Montgomery's Urania : selections. Norm. text ed. DWF from *Urania* (1621) [*Q*]; collated with Folger MS V.a.104 [*MS*]. Numbering (U1, etc.) follows *Rbts*, with sigs. from *Q* (irreg. pagination in *Q*). Except as noted, *Rbts* follows *Q* but with *MS* orthography. Songs 12-14, 18, and 34, appearing also in *MS*, are here collated for substantive variants.

[**U1**] *Urania* [*Q*], pt. 1, bk. 1, sig. B1v.

The Tale of Limena, Wife of Philargus
  PERISSUS] *DWF* (*for clarity*); He *Q*
  Philargus] *DWF*; He *Q*
  Parselius…Parselius] *DWF*; he… He *Q*
[**U5**], *Q*, 1.1, sig. L2
[**U6**], *Q*, 1.1, sig. L2v
[**U8**], *Q*, 1.1, sig. N3v
[**U10**], *Q*, 1.1, sig. R1r
[**U12**], *Q*, 1.1, sig. T4r
  Shep] She. *Q* (*throughout*)
  5b-6 *Q as one line*
  6 delights] delight *MS*
  9 When] If *MS*
  11 ever] from thence *MS*

11-12 *Q line break after* l

17b-18 *Q as one line*

18 could] would *MS*

19 canst] could'st *MS*

20 is] were *MS*

21 Virtue, beauty] Beauty, worth, and *MS*

23b-24 *Q as one line*

29-30 *Q line break after* rest

[U13], *Q*, 1.1, sig. T4v

4 the] that *MS*

9 worth] warmth *MS*

[U14], *Q*, 1.1, sig. T4r-V1r

6 new-framed] new form'd *MS*

14 yet] *omit MS*

25 an] *omit MS*

[U15], *Q*, 1.1, sig. Vrv

[U18], *Q*, 1.1, sig. Aa1v

1 mourn] burne *MS*

3 griefs] grief *MS*

6 cloud'ly] cloudlike *MS*

12 Sun-robbed] sunn lost *MS*

15 the name] those names *MS, Rbts*

16 blasts] colde *MS*

19 brings] breeds *MS*

22 lend] give *MS*

24 equal-shining] equall shining *Q*; shining equall *MS*

[U20], *Q*, 1.1, sig. Ee2v

[U21], *Q*, 1.1, sig. Gg2

29 bodies] *DWF*; body's *Q*; bodys *Rbts*

[U29], *Q*, 1.1, sig. Tt3v-4r

[U33], *Q*, 1.1, sig. Eee4r

[U34], *Q*, 1.1, sig. Fff3v

7 sighs and tears] tears, and sighs *MS*

8 those ... some] *DWF*; those best spent, if worth doe them *Q*; best spent too, so some will *MS*

9 Yet thy sweet] butt yett (allas) thy *MS*

9 pleasure] *MS, Rbts*; pleasures *Q*

11 these] thus *MS*

12 to make my] while lasting *MS*

16 mourn] mourne *MS, Rbts*; moure *Q*;

16 still] now *MS*

[U35], 1.1, sigs. Fff4v-Ggg1v

21 thus] *DWF*; this *Q* (*alternative spelling of* thus)

24 Leaving] *Rbts*; Leaning *Q*

30 a] *DWF*; by *Q*

66 a way] *DWF*; away *Q*

92 a knot] *DWF*; an nott *Q*

[U45], *Q*, 1.1, sig. Lll2r

Tale of Sirelius. Normalized text ed. DWF from Wroth, *Urania* (1621), pp. 438-41.

Sirelius .... Sirelius...Sirelius] *DWF*; He...he...He *Q*

Sirelius] *DWF*; he *Q*

his father-in-law's] *DWF*; his *Q*

Sirelius and his rival] *DWF*; them *Q*

Sirelius and his wife] *DWF*; them *Q*

all] *DWF*; at *Q* (*sic*)

Sirelius's] *DWF*; my friends *Q*

[U51], *Q*, 1.1, sig. Ttt1

Wurttemberg] Wertenberg *Q*

[U55], *Q*, 1.1, sig. Zzz2

Sir Edward Denny. *To Pamphilia from the Father-in-Law of Serialius*. Normalized text ed. DWF from University of Nottingham Library MS Cl LM 85/3v [*MS-N*]. Pub. by permission of P. T. Clifton and the Univ. of Nottingham Lib.. Collated with (inferior texts) Beinecke Lib. MS Osborn b197 [*MS-O*], pp. 117-18; Huntington Lib. MS 198 [*MS-H*], f. 164; and B.L. MS Additional 22603 [*MS-A*], ff. 64v-65r; variant spellings not noted. *Rbts* follows *MS-N* except as noted.

tit.] *omit MS-N*; To the [*MS-H* thy] Lady Mary Wroth for writing The Countess of Mountgomery's Urania *MS-O, MS-H, MS-A*

3 wrothful] *DWF*; wrathful *MS-N, MS-O* 4 doth] did *MS-O, MS-H*

5 strikes] kick'st *MS-O, MS-H, MS-A*

5 some man's] some mens *MS-O, MS-H*, sometimes *MS-A*

6 thine] the [*i.e.,* thee] *MS-O, MS-H, MS-A*

7 whose] where *MS-O, MS-H, MS-A*

7 comparison] comparisons *MS-O, MS-H, MS-A*

8 the] an *MS-O, MS-H, MS-A*

10 in] up *MS-O, MS-H, MS-A*

12 not caring who] and cares not whom(e) *MS-O, MS-H, MS-A*

13 flying] *omit MS-O*

13 flames] *MS-O, MS-H, MS-A, Rbts*; fames *MS-N*

17 lies] lines *MS-O, MS-H, MS-A*

20 thine] thy *MS-A*

25 Work o' th' Workes; leave] Worke Lady worke, lett *MS-O, MS-H, MS-A*

26 For wise and worthier women have writ] for wisest woomen sure have written *MS-O, MS-H, MS-A*

Subscribed: To pamphilia from the father in law of Seralius *MS-N*; By the Lord Denny *MS-O*; by the L:D *MS-H*; By the Ld Denny *MS-A*.

Lady Mary Wroth to Sir Edward Denny. Norm. text ed. DWF from Univ. of Nottingham Lib. MS Cl LM 85/2 [*MS-N*]. Pub. by permission of P. T. Clifton and the Univ. of Nottingham Lib. (This is the MS noted in HMC, *Various Collections*, 7.291, formerly at Clifton Hall.) A contemporary copy is at Hatfield House, MS 130 [*MS-HH*], ff. 117-118v (corrupt transcript in *HMC*, Salisbury [Cecil] 22., p. 160). Roberts (1983) [*Rbts*] follows *MS-HH* except as noted.

the rather] *Rbts, DWF*; they rather *MS-N, MS-HH*

let] lest <*canc.*> lett *MS-N*

intend ever] *NL2*; ever intend *MS-HH*

and yet I will this say] and this I will yet say *MS-HH*

examples] example *MS-HH*

Railing Rhymes Returned. Norm. text ed. DWF from Univ. of Nottingham Lib. MS Cl LM 85/3r [*MS*]. Published by permission of P. T. Clifton and the Univ. of Nottingham. Cf. *Cal. S.P. Dom.*, 1619-23, p. 356 (9 March, 1621/2.)

12 wit, mad] *DWF*; mad wit *MS*

20 thrid] *DWF*; trid *MS*

E. Hyde: "William Herbert." Normalized text ed. DWF from Hyde (1707), 57-8.

GENDER and POLITICS

Epigraph. Normalized text ed. DWF from transcript by Francis Worship, "Copies of Two Letters of Queen Elizabeth," *Archaeologia*, vol. 28 (1840): 398.

By the King (30 May 1607): Whereas some of the meaner, etc. Ed. DWF from 1607.

Gilbert Talbot (11 June); ed. DWF from Lodge (1791) [*L*].

footmen] *DWF*; foot *L*

the Levellers] *DWF*; them *L*

At] *DWF*; But *L*

the Levellers] *DWF*; they *L*

The Diggers of Warwickshire to all other Diggers (1607), ed. DWF from B.L. MS Harl. 787, art. 11, fol. 9v (copy, in a later hand than 1607).

By the King (24 Dec. 1620): Proclamation against Excess ... Speech; ed. DWF from 1620.

By the King (8 April 1621): *Proclamation for Suppressing Insolent Abuses Committed by Base People against Persons of Quality*, ed. DWF from 1621.

King James: *The Wiper of the People's Tears* (also called The Dryer-up of Doubts and Fears). Normalized text ed. DWF from B.L. MS Lansdowne 498, ff. 32-4 (MS-L); collated with B.L. Malone 23, f. 49 (MS-M), where MS-M readings are adopted. Other extant copies include B.L. MSS Egerton 923, f. 32-33v, 37-38 (MS-E); Harl. 367, ff. 151r-152r (MS-H); Add. 28640, 123v-126 (MS-Ad.1); Add. 29303, f. 5 (MS-Ad.2); Add. 25707, f. 74r; Add. 52585, f. 4r; Add. 61481, f. 97r; and Bodleian Library MSS Ashmole 367, f. 58, Rawl. D.152, f. 11r; Rawl. D.398, f. 183r; Rawl. poet. 152, ff. 11-14 (MS-Rp); Tanner 265, f. 14, Tanner 306, ff. 242-46; Eng. Poet. c.11, ff. 15-21 (MS-E.p.); St. John's Coll. MS K.56, no. 68; and Folger MS V.b.303, p. 264.

1 ye that] *MS-L*; yow who *MS-M*
2 And cry] *MS-L*; Cry not *MS-M*
4 depth] *MS-L*;deepe *MS-M*
6 ryne] *MS-L*, *MS-M*; time, *MS-Ad.1*; rhyme *MS-R*, *MS-E* (*perhaps by Scribes unfamiliar with Scots* ryne)
8 in] by *MS-M*; go] gadd *MS-M*
14 all] *MS-M*; all men *MS-L*
22 deride *MS-L*; decide *MS-M*
28 spoiling] *MS-L*; stubborne *MS-M*; *various MSS read* stinking, stubborn, *or* evil
30 the *MS-L*; their *MS-M*
34 near me] *MS-L*; *MS-M om.* me (*sic*)
34 on high] *MS-M*; high] *MS-L* (*sic*)
38 All … vents] *MS-L*; And … intents *MS-M*
39 doth] *MS-L*; doe *MS-M*
42 have, nor take] *MS-L*; *MS-M and most other MSS read* (*less compelling*) give or take
49 his] *MS-M* this *MS-L*
51 or] *MS-M*; and] *MS-L*
53 deject] *MS-M*; correct *MS-L*; cf. "Answer," line 5.
55 mutine] *MS-L*; mutter *MS-M et al.*
56 whirring] hurring *MS-L*; hurrying *MS-M et al.*
58 it] *MS-L*; I *MS-M*
64 where do] *MS-L*; Where if *MS-M*
72-3 and…inquire] *MS-M*; *MS-L om.*
77 would be] *MS-L*; could not be *MS-L* (*sic*); should be *MS-H*, *MS-E.p.* petition; would be *MS-E.p.*
95 paces] *MS-L*; pace *MS-T2*; places *MS-H*; palyses *MS-Ad1*; playes *MS-Ad2*.
97 prince's] princes *MS-M*; princely *MS-L*
107 myself and you] *MS-L*; myself, not you *MS-M et al.*
111 our] your *MS-L*; your *MS-M et al.*
111 shides] DWF (cf. "Answer," by a Lady); Childes *MS-L* (*sic*); chicks *MS-L*; chids *MS-H*
117 Their hands in the best blood you] *MS-M et al.*; Them in the best blood they have *MS-L* (*sic*)
119 you great do call] *MS-M et al*; your Grant you call *MS-L*
123 not more than you can] not more then you can hold *MS-M*; no more than you well may *MS-L* (*sic*)
125 your *MS-L*; the *MS-M*
126 For] *MS-M*; With *MS-L*
129 Moved] *MS-M*; Moves *MS-L*
139 But O] *MS-M*; O *MS-L*
139 your dull] *MS-M*; is your dull *MS-L*
140 for] *MS-M*; as *MS-L*
142 Though] *MS-M*; The *MS-L*
144 you] *MS-M*; it *MS-L*
146 Conjure ye] *MS-M*; of coniurie *MS-L*
159 counsel] *MS-M*; counsels *MS-L*
175 proclamations] *MS-M*; proclamation *MS-L*
178 And] *MS-M*; To *MS-L*

A Lady: *An Answer to the Wiper-Away of the People's Tears.* Ed. DWF from Bodleian MS Rawl. Poet. 26, f. 20r ("by a Lady"); Other copies include Bodl. MSS MS Ashm. 36-37, f. 59r; Eng. Poet.c.50., f. 25v; Rawl. poet. 152, f. 4r.

Anon., Saint Elizabeth. Ed. DWF from Bodl. MS Malone 23 [*MS-M*] ("The Coppie of a Libell put into the hand of Queen Elizabeth's statue in Westminster by an unknown person, Anno dmn 1621 [*sic*]. Ultimo die Martii [last day of March] 1623"), pp. 32-14. Folger MS V.a. (tf. 275): "This copie was founde in the hand of Queen Elizabeths tombe at West. February [*erased*] 22 of june 1623." For a facs. of the undated Farmer-Chetham MS, see N. K. Farmer, "Poems from a 17th-century Manuscript," *Texas Q*, vol. 16 (1973): 122-85 [*MS-F*]. Other sources (not consulted) include: Bodl. MSS Ashmole 36-37, f. 303r; Eng. Poet. c.50, f. 8r; Eng. Poet.f.10, f. 107r; Rawl. D. 398, f. 222r; Rawl. Poet. 160, f. 16r; Top. Cheshire c.7, f. 3r; B.L. MSS Add. 5832, f. 202r; Add. 25707, f. 76r; Add. 34217, f. 39v; Sloane 363, f.11r; Sloane 1479, f. 6r; Brotherton MSS Lt. 28, f. 2r; Lt. q. 44, f. 2r; Nottingham MS Portland PW V 37, p. 243; St. John's MS K.56, nos. 59, 60; Beinecke MS Osborn b.197, p. 86; Folger MS V.a.275, p. 1; Huntington MS HM 198, 1.62.

To The Blessed Saint Elizabeth
28 once-blest] *MS-F*; once best *MS-M*
33 Loved Soul] Lov'd Soul *MS-F*; honour'd soule *MS-M*
35 began] *MS-F*; begunn *MS-M*
40 these] *MS-F*; those *MS-M*
45 hornpipe] *hornepipe MS-F*; Homepie [*sic*] *MS-M*
52 and tears] *MS-F*; teares *MS-M*
57 Thy° faithful beadsmen] *MS-F*; The *MS-M*

To The Most High And Mighty Jehovah (caption fr. *MS-F*)
8 Nay every hour] *MS-F*; no howre *MS-M*
64 lay] *MS-F*; lye *MS-M*
70 we robbed were of] we had worlde of *MS-M*; hee had robed us, oh
142 Their°] The *MS-M*; They *MS-F*
182 laughed at] *MS-F*; laught *MS-M*

Agnes Sampson and others accused of witchcraft receive a pre-trial beating before King James. From James Carmichael, *Newes from Scotland* (Edinburgh, 1592); in a woodcut recycled from Robert Gallis, *A Rehearsal Both Straung and True,* (STC 23267, 1579), sig. B2v.

Bibliography of Works Cited

I. Manuscripts

Advocates Library (Edinburgh), MS Birch 4162, art. 60. Queen Anna to Villiers (ns 1618).

Archives générales du département du Nord (Lille, France). MS A.D.N. (ca. 1655). (Contains [Anne] Cary, anon., "The Lady Falkland Her Life.")

Arundel Castle (West Sussex) MSS Autograph Letters 1585-1617 (Correspondence of of Arbella Stuart.)

Beinecke Library (New Haven). MS Osborn b148. (Contains J. Donne, elegy on Boulstred, pp. 118-1.)

—. MS Osborn b197. (E. Denny, "To Pamphilia," pp. 117-18.)

—. MS Osborn b200. (Anon., ["Love Lamenting,"] p. 81.)

—. MS Betty Bruce Papers, Boswell Collection, Series xv, Box 105. (Contains poems by E. Melville.)

Bodleian Library (Oxford). MS Eng. poet. e.14 ("A Songe" ["Love Lamenting,"] f. 29r).

—. MS Malone 23 (Anon., "Saint Elizabeth," pp. 32-34; (James I, ["The Wiper of the People's Tears,"] f. 49).

—. MS Rawl. poet. 31. (Contains L. Russell, ["Elegy on Mistress Bulstrode,"] " f. 39r.)

—. MS Rawl. poet. 148 (Contains an early text of Marlowe's "Passionate Shepherd," f. 96, om. lines 21-4.)

—. MS Ashmole 226 and MS Ashmole 236. (Simon Forman's Casebooks).

British Library (London). MS Additional 10309. (Contains [B. Jonson,] "An Elegy to Mistress Boulstred.")

—. MS Add. 22603. (Contains E. Denny, "To Pamphilia from the Father-in-Law of Seralius," ff. 64v-65r.)

—. MS Add. 23224. (Contains extracts from M. Wroth, *Urania*, ff. 91-92.)

—. MS Add. 23229. (Contains. M. Wroth, "Penshurst Mount," ff. 91r-92r.)

—. MS Add. 29409. (Contains. Anon., ["Song of the Marrying Maiden,"] ff. 267v-68r.)

—. MS Add. 32092, f. 220 (Letter of Arbella Stuart.)

—. MS Add. 33998. (Contains B. Jonson, "Epitaph" on C. Boulstred, f.33.)

—. MS Add. 36674, ff. 134-7. (Contains [The Bewitchment of Elizabeth Jennings].)

—. MS Add. 43827A (Rose Hickman, "Certain Old Stories," 1610).

—. MS Add. 45027 (Rose Hickman, "Certain Old Stories"; Anon., "Epitaph upon this Old Gentlewoman".)

—. MS Harley 787. (Contains "The Diggers of Warwickshire to all other Diggers" [1607], art. 11, f. 9v).

—. MS Harley 4064. (Contains B. Jonson, "Epitaph" on C. Boulstred, f. 261; L. Russell, ["Elegy on Mistress Bulstrode,"] f. 269.)

—. MS Harley 6057. (Contains B. Jonson, "Epitaph" on C. Boulstred, f. 33.)

—. MS Harley 6177 (Contains one of several 18th-C transcripts of Anne Clifford's "Great Books"; inc. "A summary of the Records, and a True Memorial of the life of me the Lady Anne Clifford..." pp. 119-206.)

—. MS Harley 6986 (Queen Anna to the king, ff. 106-107; to Villiers, 108-9).

—. MS Harley 7003 (Correspondence of of Arbella Stuart).

—. MS Harl. 7007 (Pr. Henry to Queen Anna, April 1603).

—. MS Lansdowne 498 (James I, ["The Wiper of the People's Tears,"] ff. 32-4.)

—. MS Lansdowne 704. (Contains [B. Jonson,] "An Elegy to Mistress Boulstred," "by J.R.")

—. MS Lansdowne 740. (Contains [B. Jonson,] "An Elegy to Mistress Boulstred," "by J.R.")

—. B.L. MS Sloane 1709. ("Lulla by Lullay," f. 271v).

—. MS Stowe 962. (Contains L. Russell, ["Elegy on Mistress Bulstrode,"] f. 94r; Donne, "Elegy" on Boulstred, ff. 94r-95r.)

Centre for Kentish Studies (Maidstone). MS U269/F48, Micr. 277 (A. Clifford, Knole Diary, 18th[C transcript).

Corpus Christi College (Oxford), MS 327 ("Love Lamenting," f. 26v).

Cumbria Record Office (Carlisle). MS WD/Hoth/Box 44 (Contains Clifford correspondence).

Folger Shakespeare Library (Washington, D.C.). Loseley House MS/349/52/1-11 and MS/349/59/1 (photographic copy). (Contains Ferrer-Kennedy property transactions.)

—. MS V.a.104. (M. Wroth, "Pamphilia to Amphilanthus.")

—. MS V.a. (Anon., "Saint Elizabeth," f. 275.)

Hatfield House (Hertfordshire). Cecil Papers 135 (Correspondence of Arbella Stuart.)

Henry E. Huntington Library (San Marino). MS HM 198, Part 2 (Contains W. Herbert, "Elegy" [to Mary Sidney Wroth], f. 105 and dup. of lines 1-18, f. 101r [*MS-2*]; E. Denny, "To Pamphilia," f. 164).

—. MS HM 600. (Contains an incomplete copy of M. Wroth, "Love's Victorie.")

—. MS HM 803 (Letter of Arbella Stuart).

—. MS Lowell (Contains B. Jonson, "Epitaph" on Cecily Boulstred, with note to Geo. Garrard. Holograph.)

Houghton Library (Harvard). MS Lowell (JnB102). (B. Jonson to G. Garrard, Aug. 1609. Sing. sht. holograph.)

—. MS Norton. (Contains [B. Jonson,] "An Elegy to Mistress Boulstred.")

Lambeth Palace Library (London), MS 3201 (Correspondence of of Arbella Stuart)

—. MSS Talbot Papers 2 (Letters of Arbella Stuart).

Loseley House (Guildford, Surrey). See Folger Shak. Lib.

National Library of Scotland (Edinburgh). Wodrow quarto, xxvii, f. 199v. (Contains E. Melville, "Love's Lament for Christ's Absence," no. 27, fo. 199v.)

—. MS 906. (Holograph copy of Margaret Cunningham, "A Part of the Life" ff. 1r-8r; letters to J. Maxwell, 8v-13r, and A. Cunningham, 13r-19v; and will, 15v-19v.)

—. MS 874 (Scribal copy of MS 906, "A Part of the Life," ff. 363r-370r; letters to J. Maxwell, 370v-375v, and A. Cunningham, 375v-383r; and her will, 378r-382v.)

Newberry Library (Chicago). MS Case fY 1565. W 95. 2 vols. (Contains M. Wroth, "The Secound Part of the Countesse of Montgomery's Urania.")

New College Library (Edinburgh). MS Robert Bruce (Bru.2) (Contains nineteen poems by Elizabeth Melville. For transcript, see ed. Baxter.)

Nottingham Library, University of (Nottingham). MSS Clifton C1 LM 85/1-5. (exchange between Sir Edward Denny Lady Mary Wroth" (15-27 Feb. 1621/2), 85/1-5.)

Penshurst Place (Tonbridge, Kent). MS De L'Isle. (M. Wroth, Love's Victory, c.1619).

Public Record Office (Kew). Chancery C2/James 1 L11/64.

—. P.C.C. will of Baptist Bassano. Prob. 11/58.

—. P.C.C. will of Frances (Howard) Stuart. Prob. 11/181.

Trinity College (Dublin). MS G.2.21. (Contains [B. Jonson,] "An Elegy to Mistress Boulstred," "by J.R.")

II. By Author or Editor

Abbotsford Club, *Ecclesiastical Records: Selections from the Minutes of the Presbyteries of St. Andrews.* Abbotsford Club, vol. 7. Edinburgh, 1837.

ABCDE, pseud. *Novembris monstrum.* London, 1641.

Aiken, Lucy. *Memoirs of King James I.* 2 vols. London, 1822.

Anderson, Adam, ed., *Letters and State Papers during the Reign of King James VI* [a.k.a. *The Balfour Letters*]. London: Maitland Club, 1835.

Anthony, Francis. *The Apologie, or Defence of...a Medicine called Aurum Potabile.* London, 1616.

Anton, Robert. *The Philosophers Satyrs.* London, 1616.

ARNOLD, ELIZABETH, trans. (fl. 1619). See Tuke.

Baddeley, Welbore St. Clair. *A Cotteswold Shrine... History of Hailes.* London: Kegan Paul, 1908.

Barlow, William. *The Eagle and the Body.* London, 1609.

Barrett, Charles. *The History of the Society of Apothecaries of London.* London: E. Stock, 1905.

Baxter, Jamie Reid, ed.. *Poems of Elizabeth Melville, Lady Culross.* Edinburgh: Solsequium, 2010.

Beard, Thomas. *The Theatre of Gods Judgments.* London, 1642.

Bodenham, John. *Englands Helicon.* London, 1600.

Bond, Garth. "Amphilanthus to Pamphilia: William Herbert, Mary Wroth, and Penshurst Mount." *Sidney Journal,* 31.1 (Jan. 2013): 51+.

Brathwaite, Richard (Ester Sowernam). *Ester Hath Hang'd Haman: Or an Answere to a lewd Pamphlet, entituled, The Arraignment of Women.* London, 1617.

Bretnor, Thomas, M.M., trans. and reviser. *Opiologia* (fr. a 1614 French trans. of A. Sala's Italian). London, 1618.

Bright, Timothy, M.D. *Treatise...of English Medicines.* London 1615.

Brinsley, John. *Third Part of the True Watch.* London, 1622.

Brodhead, John R. *Documents Relative to the State of New York.* Vol. 1. Albany: Weed, 1856.

Brown, Alexander. *First Republic in America.* Boston: Houghton Mifflin, 1898.

Burton, Robert. *The Anatomy of Melancholy.* London, 1621.

BULSTRODE, CECILY. "Newes of My Morning Work." In Overbury, *Wife.* 2d ed. (1614), *q.v.,* sigs. H2v-3r.

C.I. *The Commons Petition of Long Afflicted England.* London, 1642.

Campion, Thomas. *Art of English Poesy.* London, 1602.

Carew, George, and Sir Thomas Roe. *Letters,* ed. John Maclean. London: Camden Society, 1860.

Carmichael, James. *Newes from Scotland.* London, [1592].

Cary, [Anne] (in religion, Clementina), et al., anon. "The Lady Falkland Her Life." *See Women's Works,* vol. 4, and ed. Weller and Ferguson (1994).

CARY, ELIZABETH TANFIELD. *The Tragedie of Mariam, the Faire Queen of Iewry.* London 1613.

—. —. *See also* ed. Weller and Ferguson (1994).

—. *The History of the Life, Reign, and Death of Edward II ... Written by E. F[alkland].* London, 1680.

Carleton, Sir Dudley. *Letters of Dudley Carleton to John Chamberlain, 1616-1624.* Ed. Maurice Lee, New Brunswick: Rutgers Univ. Press, 1972.

Casaubon, Isaac. *A Letter of Mr. Casaubon. With a Memoriall of Mris. Elizabeth Martin, late deceased.* London, 1615.

Chamberlain, John. *Letters of John Chamberlain,* Ed. Norman E. McClure. 2 vols. Phila.: Philosophical Soc., 1939.

Chambers, Robert. *Domestic Annals of Scotland,* vol. 1. Edin.: Chambers, 1874.

Chapman, George. *The Iliads of Homer.* London, 1611.

Chester, Robert. *The anuals* [sic] *of great Brittaine.* London, 1611.

Clapham, David, trans. The Nobilitie and Excellencye of Woman Kynde. London, 1542.

CLARKSON, BESSIE (d. 1625). [Interviews.] *See* W. L[ivingston], *The Conflict in Conscience.*

Clayton, John A. *The Lancashire Witch Conspiracy.* Barrowford, England: Barrowford Pr., 2007.

Cleaver, Robert, and John Dodd. *A Godly Form of Household Government.* London, 1621.

CLIFFORD, ANNE. *See* HERBERT.

CLINTON, Lady ELIZABETH (KNYVETT). *The Countesse of Lincolnes Nurserie.* Oxford, 1622.

A Closet for Ladies and Gentlewomen; or, The Art of Preserving, Conserving, and Candying. London, 1608.

Cokayne ("Cokain"), Sir Aston, *Small Poems of Divers Sorts.* London, 1658.

Collins, Arthur. *Letters and Memorials in the Reigns of Queen Mary* [to] *Charles I* [a.k.a. the *Sidney Letters*] 2 vols. London: Osborne, 1746.

Colville, Samuel. *The Whig's Supplication* London, 1681.

Cornwallis, Jane. *The Private Correspondence of Lady Jane Cornwallis, 1613-1644.* Ed. Lord Braybrooke. London, 1842.

Costello, Louisa S. "Arbella Stuart." *Memoirs of Eminent Englishwomen.* London: Bentley, 1844. 196-333.

CUNNINGHAM, MARGARET. *A Part of the Life.* See Manuscripts, N.L.S. 874, 906.

—. Ed. C. K. Sharpe. Edinburgh: for Sharpe, 1827.

DALE, ELIZABETH, attrib. *A Brief of the Lady Dale's Petition to the Parliament.* London, 1624.

Dalrymple, Sir David, ed., *Memorials And Letters Relating to the History of Britain in the Reign of James the First.* London: Foulis, 1762.

Daniel, Samuel. *Vision of the 12. Goddesses.* London, 1604.

Darrell, John. *A True Narration of the Strange and Grievous Vexation by the Devil.* London, 1600.

Deeds against Nature and Monsters of Kind. London, 1614.

Dekker, Thomas, John Ford, and William Rowley. *The Witch of Edmonton.* London, 1621.

Denny, Lord Edward. "To Pamphilia." *See* BL MS Addl. 22603 Univ. of Nottingham MS Cl LM 81/1-5; and Wroth, *Poems,* ed. Roberts (1983).

Dickson, Thomas, and James Balfour Paul, eds. *Accounts of the Lord High Treasurer of Scotland.* Edin.: 1877-1916.

Donne, John. *Donne's Poetical Works.* Ed. H.J.C. Grierson. 2 vols. London: Oxford Univ. Press.

—. *Poems by J.D.* London, 1633.

—. *Letters to Severall Persons of Honour.* London, 1651.

—. "That Women Ought to Paint." *Juvenilia: or Certain Paradoxes.* London: 1633. Sig. B1r-2r.

Dowling, Maria, and Joy Shakespeare. "Religion and Politics in mid-Tudor England through the eyes of an English Protestant Woman." *Historical Research,* 55 (1982): 94-102.

DRAYTON, MARY GREY (fl. 1614). " A Funeral Pyramid." In J[ohn] M[artin], ed., *Panthea.* By Josuah Sylvester. London, 1630, sig. C3v.

—. "On the Decease." In Casaubon, *A Letter* (1614), *q.v.*

—. "To the Soul." In Casaubon, *A Letter* (1614), *q.v.*

Drummond, William. *Notes of Ben Jonson's Conversations with William Drummond of Hawthornden.* London: for the Shakespeare Society, 1842.

—. *Poems by that most Famous Wit, William Drummond of Hawthornden.* London, 1656.

Dunstan, A.C., and W.W. Greg, eds. *The Tragedy of Mariam*. Malone Society. London: Wittingham, 1914.

The English Reports ... in Chancery. Vol. 1. Ed. anon. London: Stevens, 1902.

FEARNSIDE, MARGARET, attrib. "Confession." In *The Araignement & Burning of Margaret Ferne-seede for the murther of her late husband*. London, 1608.

Fleming, Robert. *Fulfilling of the Scripture*. London, 1726.

Forbes, T. R. *Chronicle from Aldgate*. New Haven: Yale Univ. Press, 1971.

Forman, Simon. Casebooks. See Manuscripts. Bodleian Library. MSS Ashmole.

Gardiner, Edmund, M.D. *Phisicall and Approved Medicines*. London, 1611.

Goddard, William. *A Satirycall Dialogue...betweene Allexander the Great and...Diogynes*. London, 1616.

Goodcole, Henry. *The Wonderfull Discoverie of Elizabeth Sawyer a Witch Late of Edmonton*. London, 1621.

—. *The Wonderful Discoverie of the Witchcrafts of Margaret and Phillip Flower*. London, 1619.

Gordon, James. *History of Scots Affairs from 1637 to 1641*. 3 vols. Abberdeen: Spalding Club, 1841.

Gouge, William. *Of Domesticall Duties*. London, 1622.

Great Britain. *The English Reports*. 178 vols. London: Stevens and Sons, 1900-1932.

—. Historical Manuscripts Commission. [Cecil Papers.] *Calendar of the Manuscripts of the...Marquess of Salisbury*, 24 vols. London: HMSO, 1883-1976.

—. —. [Clifton MSS.] *Manuscripts of...Clifton Hall*, Series 55, pt. 7. London: HMSO, 1914.

—. —. [Rutland MSS.] *The Manuscripts of ... the Duke of Rutland preserved at Belvoir Castle*. 12th Report, Appendix, Part IV. Vol. 1. London: HMSO, 1888.

—. —. *Second Report*. London: HMSO, 1871.

—. —. *Seventh Report, Pt 1*. London: HMSO, 1907.

—. —. [Sidney-Whyte MSS.] *Report on the Manuscripts of Lord de l'Isle & Dudley preserved at Penshurst Place* [MSS now at the Centre for Kentish Studies]. 6 *vols*. London: HMSO, 1925-1966.

—. Parliament. House of Lords. *Journal of the House of Lords*, vol. 3 (1620-1628). London: History of Parliament Trust, 1802.

—. State Paper Office. *Acts of the Privy Council*. n.s. vol. 24. Ed. J.R. Dasent. London: Longman, 1901.

—. —. *Statutes of the Realm*. Buffalo: W.S. Hein, 1993: vol. 4, pt. 2.

—. —. *Calendar of State Papers, Colonial, America*, vol. 1. Ed. W.S. Sainsbury. London: Longman, 1860.

—. —. *Calendar of State Papers, Colonial, East Indies*, vols. 3-9. Ed. W.S. Sainsbury. London: Longman, 1870-1893.

—. —. *Calendar of State Papers, Domestic series, of the Reigns of Edward VI, Mary, and Elizabeth, James I, 1547-[1625]*. 12 vols. Ed. Mary Anne Everett Green, et al. London: Longman, 1800-1872.

—. —. *Calendar of State Papers, Domestic series, of the Reign of Charles I*. 10 vols. Ed. John Bruce, et al. London: Longman, 1858-1867.

—. —. *Calendar of State Papers, Scottish Series* (1589-1603, Vol. 2. London: Longman, 1858.

—. —. *Calendar of State Papers, Venice*. Ed. Horatio F. Brown and Allen B. Hinds. Vols. 9 (1592-1603) - 19 (1625-1626). London: Longman, 1900-1913.

Green, Mary Anne Everett. *Lives of the Princesses of England*. London: Longman, 1857.

Greer, Germaine, et al., eds. *Kissing the Rod*. New York: Farrar, Straus, Giroux, 1988.

GREY, PENELOPE (fl. 1614). "Parodia." See Casaubon.

Guillemeau, Jacques. *Childbirth or, The Happy Delivery of Women*. Anon. trans. London, 1612.

Hakluyt, Richard. *The Principal Navigations, Voyages, Traffiques and Discoueries of the English Nation*. 3 vols. London, 1598-1600.

Halli, Robert W. "Cecilia Bulstrode, 'The Court Pucell.'" *Subjects on the World's Stage: Essays*. Ed. David G. Allen and Robert A. White. Cranbury, NJ: Univ. of Delaware Press, 1995. 295-312.

Halliwell-Phillips. *Letters of the Kings of England*. London: Colburn, 1848.

Hamor, Ralph. *A True Discourse of the Present Estate of Virginia .. till the 18 of Iune. 1614*. London, 1615.

Hannay, Margaret P. *Mary Sidney, Lady Wroth*. London: Ashgate, 2010.

Harington, Sir John, et al. *Nugæ Antiquæ*. Ed.. Henry Harington and Thomas Park. 2 vols. London, 1792-1804.

Hay, Peter, pseud. (– Williams). *A Vision of Balaams Asse*. London 1619[/20].

Heale, William. *An Apologie for Women. Or An opposition to Mr. Dr. G. his assertion ... that it was lawfull for husbands to beate their wives*. Oxford, 1609.

HERBERT, ANNE (CLIFFORD). Knole Diary. Extracts, 1603-1619, 18th-C. transcript. Original not extant. Centre for Kentish Studies MS U269/ F48, Micro. 277.

Herbert, Sir Edward. *Occasional Verses*. London, 1665.

HERBERT, MARY (SIDNEY), trans. *A Discourse Of Life And Death*. By Philippe de Mornay. London, 1592; repr. 1606, 1607, 1608, et seq.

Herbert, William. *Poems, written by the Right Honorable William Earl of Pembroke*. London, 1660.

Heywood, Thomas. *Gynaikeion*. London, 1624.

HICKMAN (THROCKMORTON), ROSE (LOCKE). *See* Manuscripts, B.L. MSS Add. 43827 and Add. 45027.

Historical Manuscripts Commission. *See* Great Britain.

Hodgson, J. *A Topographical and Historical Description of Westmorland*. London, 1810.

Howell, Thomas J., et al. *A Complete Collection of State Trials...for...Treason*. Vol. 2. London: Longman, 1816.

Hume, Alexander, "To...Elizabeth Mal-vill, Ladie Cumrie." *Hymnes, or Sacred Songs*. Edinburgh, 1599.

Hyde, Edward, Earl of Clarendon. *The History of the Rebellion and Civil Wars*. Vol. 1. London, 1707.

James VI of Scotland (I of England). *Basilkon Doron*. Edin.: 1599; London: 1603.

—. *Daemonologie*. Edinburgh, 1597; repr. 1603.

—. *By the King: Whereas some of the meaner sort* [etc.] London, 30 May 1607.

—. *By the King: It is a thing notorious* [etc.] London: 28 June 1607.

—. *By the King: In calling to our princely remembrance* [etc.] London: 24 July 1607.

—. *By the King: A Proclamation for the Punishing of Vagabonds...and Idle Persons*. London: 24 July 1616.

—. *By the King: A Proclamation against Tenant-Rights*. London: 28 July 1620.

—. *By the King: Proclamation for Suppressing Insolent Abuses committed by Base People against Persons of Quality*. London: 8 April 1621.

—. *By the King: Proclamation against Excess of Lavish and Licentious Speech of Matters of State*. 2d ed., revised. London: 26 July 1621.

—. *By the King: Proclamation against Excess of Lavish ... Speech of Matters of State*. London: 24 Dec. 1620.

—. *By the King. A Proclamation for Reliefe of the Poore, and... High Prices of Corne*. London: 22 Dec. 1622.

JENKINSON, ANNE, trans. *Meditations vpon the Lamentations of Jeremy*. By G. du Vair. London, 1609.

JOCELIN, ELIZABETH (BROOOK). *A Mothers Legacie, To her Unborne Childe*. London, 1624.

Johnson, Richard. "The Maidens Complaint." *The Golden Garland of Princely Pleasures*. London, 1620. G3r-v.

Jones, Robert, composer. *The Muses Gardin for Delights, or the Fift Booke of Ayres*. London, 1610.

—. *A Musicall Dreame. or The Fourth Booke of Ayres*. London, 1609.

Jonson, Ben. *Bartholmew Fayre*. 1631.

—. "An Elegy to Mistress Boulstred" (misattrib. John Roe). See Donne, ed. Grierson; and Manuscripts, B.L. Add. 10309, Lansdowne 704; Bodleian Rawl. poet. 31; Harvard, Norton; Trinity College (Dublin) G.2.21.

—. *Epicoene, or the Silent Woman*. London, 1620.

—. —. [Anr. ed.] *The Silent Woman*. London, 1620.

—. *Epitaph* [on Cecily Boulstred]. *See* Houghton Library (Harvard), MS Lowell; B.L. MSS Add. 33998, f. 33; Harl. 6057, f. 33; and Harl. 4064, f. 261.

—. *The Forrest* [poems.] In *Works*. London, 1616 [F1].

—. *The New Inne: Or, The Light Heart*. London, 1631.

—. *The Under-wood*. [Poems.] In *Workes*, 1641 [F2]. —. *Volpone or The Foxe*. London, 1607.

—. *The Workes*. London, 1616 [F1]

—. [Anr. ed., augm.] *The Workes*. London, 1640[/1] [F2].

—. *The Works*. Ed. C.H. Hereford and Percy Simpson. 11 vols. Oxford: Clarendon, 1853-1931.

Keene, D.J., and Vanessa Harding. *Historical Gazetteer of London before the Great Fire*. London: Centre for Metropolitan History, 1987.

LANYER, AEMILIA (BASSANO). *Salve Deus Rex Judæorum*. London, 1611.

—. —. *See also* Rowse, ed. (1979); Woods, ed. (1993).

Larkin, James F. and Paul L. Hughes, ed. *Stuart Royal Proclamations*. Oxford: Clarendon, 1973.

Le Hardy, William, ed. *County of Middlesex. Calendar to the Sessions Records*, n.s., v. 2: 1614-15. London, 1936.

LEIGH, DOROTHY. *The Mothers Blessing*. London, 1616.

Leishman, Matthew, ed. *The Works of Rev. Hugh Binning*. Online, Project Gutenberg, 2008.

Leycester, Peter. *Historical Antiquities*. London, 1673.

Livingston, John. *Memorable Characteristics and Remarkable Passages* [1668]. Glasgow, 1754; repr. in *Select Biographies*, ed. W.K. Tweedie. Edinburgh: for the Wodrow Society, 1845. 1.293-348.

Livingston, William. *The Conflict in Conscience of ...Bessie Clarksone*. 2d ed. Edinburgh,1631.

Lodge, Edmund. *Illustrations of British History*, vol. 3. London: Nicol, 1791.

Lodge, Thomas, trans. *The Workes of Lucius Annæus Seneca both Morrall and naturall*. London: 1614.

Luce, Alice, ed. *The Countess of Pembroke's Antonie*. By Mary Sidney Herbert. *Litterarhistorische forschungen*, no. 3. Weimar: Felmer, 1897.

LUMLEY, Lady JOANE (FITZALAN), trans. *Iphigenia at Aulis Translated by Lady Lumley*. Ed. W.W. Greg. Malone Society. London, 1909.

Maitland Club. *Letters to King James VI from the Queen* [facsimiles.] Edinburgh: for the Maitland Club, 1835.

Malden, H.E., ed. *Victory County History*, vol. 4: *A History of the County of Surrey*. London: VCH, 1912.

Markham, Gervase, trans. *Maison rustique, or The Countrey Farme*. By Charles Estienne. London, 1616.

—. *Markhams maister-peece*. London 1610.

Martin, James, ed. *A Letter of Mr. [Isaac] Casaubon. With a Memoriall of Mris. Elizabeth Martin*. London, 1615.

—, ed. *Via Regia. The Kings Way to Heaven. With a Letter of I. Casaubon*. 2 pts. 8o. London, 1615. Pt. 2.

—, ed. *Panthea: or, Divine VVishes And Meditations: Reuised by I. M[artin]*. By Josuah Sylvester. London, 1630.

Marwick, Sir James D., ed. *Charters and Other Documents, 1175-1707*. 3 vols. in 2 Glasgow: Scottish Burgh Record Society, 1894-1906.

MASTERS, ANNE GREY (fl. 1614). "To Her Soule-loued Sister, Mris E.M." In Casaubon, *A Letter* (1614), *q.v.*

Maximilian, duke of Sully. *Memoirs of Maximilian de Bethune Duke of Sully*. 5 vols. Trans. Charlotte Lennox. London: Millar, 1761-1770. Vol. 3 (1770).

MELVILLE (COLVILLE), ELIZABETH, Lady Culross. *Ane Godlie Dreame, Complyit in Scottish Meter be M[rs]. M[elvill], Gentelvvoman in Culros*. [Scots version.] Edinburgh: R. Charteris, 1603.

—. —. [Anr. ed., revised and anglicized.] *A Godlie Dreame Compyled by Eliz. Melvill, Ladie Culros yonger*. Edinburgh: R. Charteris, [1604?].

—. "Letters from Elizabeth Daughter of Sir James Melville." In *Select Biographies*, ed. W.K. Tweedie. Edinburgh: Wodrow Society, 1845. 1.349-70.

Munda, Constantia. *See* Stephens.

Newstead, Christopher. *An Apology for Women: or, Womens Defence*. London, 1620.

Nichols, John G. *Autographs of Royal, Noble, Learned, and Remarkable Personages*. London: British Museum Dept. of Manuscripts, 1829.

—. *Progresses, Processions, and Magnificent Festivities, of King James I*. London: Society of Antiquaries, 1828.

Oglander, John. *A Royalist's Notebook: the Commonplace Book of Sir John Oglander*. Ed. Francis Bamford. London: Constable, 1936.

Onslow, Arthur. *The Life of Archbishop Abbot*. London: Russell, 1777.

Overbury, Sir Thomas. *A Wife Now the Widdow of Sir Thomas Overburye... Wherevnto are added many witty Characters, and conceited Newes*. 2nd ed., enlarged. London, 1614. Repr. London, 1614 (3d-5th eds.), 1615.

—. —. [7th ed., augm.] *Sir Thomas Overburie his Wife*. London, 1616. Repr. London, 1616 (8th-9th eds.), 1618, 1622, 1626, 1628, 1630, 1632, 1638, 1655, 1664.

OXLIE REIDHEAD, MARY, of Morpeth. "To William Drummond of Hawthornden." In Drummond, *Poems* (1656), *q.v.*, sig. A8.

—. "To the Author." In Drummond, *Poems* (1656), p. 66, sig. F1v.

Pady, Donald S. "Sir William Paddy, M.D. (1554-1634)." *Medical History*, vol. 18 (1974): 68-82.

Peacham, Henry. *The Compleat Gentleman*. London, 1622.

Peerson, Martin. *Private Musicke*. London,1620.

Perkins, Rev. William. *A Discourse of the Damned Art of Witchcraft*. London, 1610.

Peyton, Sir Edward. *The Divine Catastrophe*. London, 1652.

Pilkington, Francis. *The First Booke of Songs or Ayres*. London, 1605.

Pitcairn, Robert. *Ancient Criminal Trials in Scotland*, vol.2. Edinburgh: Bannatyne Club, 1833.

Ponet, John. *Diallacticon viri boni et literati*. London, 1688.

Potts, Thomas. *A Wonderful Discoverie of Witches in the Countie of Lancaster.* London, 1613.

Powell, Gabriel. *The Resolved Christian.* London, 1600.

Present Remedies against the Plague. "By a learned physician." London 1603.

Procter, William. *The Watchman, Warning.* London, 1625.

PROWSE, ANNE (LOK), trans. *Of the Markes of the Children of God.* By Jean Taffin. 1590, repr. 1608, 1609, 1615 et al.

Rainbow, Edward, Bishop of Carlisle. *A Sermon Preached at the Funeral of the Right Honourable Anne, Countess of Pembroke,* etc.. London, 1677.

Ravenscroft, Thomas. *A Briefe Discourse of... Measurable Musicke.* London, 1614.

Reading, John. *A Guide to the Holy City.* London, 1651.

Roberts, Alexander. *A Treatise of Witchcraft.* London, 1616.

Roberts, Josephine A., ed. *The Poems of Lady Mary Wroth.* Baton Rouge: Louisiana State Univ. Pr., 1983.

—. "An Unpublished Literary Quarrel," *N&Q* 222 (1977): 532-5.

—, ed. *The First Part of The Countess of Montgomery's Urania.* By Lady Mary Wroth. Binghamton, NY: Renaissance English Text Society, 1995.

Roe, Sir. Thomas. *The Embassy of Sir Thomas Roe to the court of the Great Mogul, 1515-1619.* Ed. Sir William Foster. London: Hakluyt Society, 1899.

Rowse, A. L. *Poems of Shakespeare's Dark Lady* [*i.e.,* of Aemilia Lanyer]. New York: Potter, 1979.

—. *Sex and Society in Shakespeare's Age.* New York: Scribner's, 1974.

RUSSELL, ELIZABETH (COOKE HOBY). *A Way of Reconciliation.* By John Ponet. London, 1605.

RUSSELL, Lady LUCY HARINGTON, countess of Bedford. ["Elegy on Mistress Bulstrode."] In John Donne, *Poems by J.D.* 2d ed. London, 1635, 272-73.

Sackville-West, Victoria, ed. *The Diary of Lady Anne Clifford.* NY: Doran, [1923].

SCAMBLER, MARTHA, attrib. "Martha Scambler's Repentance." In *Deeds against Nature and Monsters of Kind* (1614), q.v.

Scharf, George. *A Descriptive And Historical Catalogue of ... Pictures at Woburn Abbey.* London, 1877.

—. *Knole and the Sackvilles.* London: Heineman, 1922.

Sharpe, C.K. *A Pairt of the Life of Lady Margaret Cuninghame.* Edinburgh, 1827.

Sidney, Robert, and Rowland Whyte. *Letters and Memorials of State.* Ed. Arthur Collins. 2 vols. London: Osborne, 1746.

Smith, E.T. Bradley. *Life of the Lady Arbella Stuart.* London: Bentley, 1889.

SOWERNAM, ESTER. See Brathwaite.

Speght, James. *The Day-spring of Comfort.* London, 1615.

SPEGHT (PROCTER), RACHEL. *Mortalities Memorandum, with a Dreame Prefixed.* London, 1621.

—. *A Mouzell for Melastomus, the ... foule mouthed Barker against Evahs Sex.* London, 1617.

Speight, Helen. "Rachel Speght's Polemical Life." *Huntington Lib. Q.,* vol. 65, No. 3/4 (2002): 449-63.

Steen, Sara Jayne. *The Letters of Arbella Stuart.* Oxford: Oxford Univ. Press, 1994.

Stephens, John ("Constantia Munda"). *The Worming of a Mad Dogge: or, A Soppe for Cerberus.* London, 1617.

Strickland, Agnes. "Anne of Denmark." *Lives of the Queens of England,* vol. 7, 307-485. London, 1844.

STUART, ARBELLA. *See* Manuscripts, B.L. (Add. 32092, Harl. 7003); Arundel Castle (Autograph Letters);

Hatfield (Cecil Papers 135), Huntington Lib. (HM 803); Lambeth (MS 3201); Talbot Papers 2; *Letters,* ed. Steen.

Swetnam, Joseph ("Thomas Tel-troth"). *The Araignment of Lewd, Idle, Froward, and Unconstant Women.* London, 1615.

—. *The Schoole of the Noble and Worthy Science of Defense.* London, 1617.

Swetnam the Woman-Hater, Arraigned by Women: A New Comedie, Acted at the Red Bull, by the Late Queenes Seruants, 1620. Anon. London, 1620.

Thayer, G.C. *Ben Jonson, Studies in the Plays.* Norman, Oklahoma: University of Oklahoma Press, 1963.

Thrush, Andrew, and John P. Ferris, eds. *The History of Parliament: The House of Commons 1604-1629.* Cambridge: Cambridge University Press, 2010.

Tingle, Rev. Michael (vicar of Burford). *A Guide to Burford Church.* Oxford: Witney, 1989.

Topsell, Edward. *The History of Four-Footed Beasts.* London, 1607.

Tuke, Thomas. *A Treatise against Paintng* [sic] *and Tincturing of Men and Women.* London, 1616.

Turberville, George. *The Book of Falconry or Hawking.* London, 1611.

Tuvill, Daniel. *Asylum Veneris, or A Sanctuary for Ladies.* London, 1616.

Tyler, Lyon, ed. *Narratives of Early Virginia, 1606-1625.* NY: Scribners, 1907.

Vaughan, William, M.D. *Approved Directions for Health.* London, 1612.

Venner, Tobias. *Via recta ad vitam longam.* London, 1620.

Warwick, Sir Philip. *Memoirs of the Reigne of King Charles I.* Edinburgh: Balantyne, 1813.

Waters, Henry F., ed. *Genealogical Gleanings in England: Abstracts of Wills Relating to Early American Families.* 1901; repr. Baltimore: Genalogical Pub. Co., 1969.

W[eldon], Sir A[nthony]. *The Court and Character of King James.* London, 1650; repr. 1651, 1689.

Weller, Barry, and Margaret W. Ferguson, eds. *The Tragedy of Mariam the Fair Queen of Jewry with The Lady Falkland: Her Life.* Berkeley: Univ. of California Press, 1994.

Widows, Daniel, trans. *Natural Philosophy.* By Wilhelm Adolf Scribonius. London, 1621.

Williams, Ethel *Anne of Denmark.* London: Longmans, 1970.

Williams, Robert F. *The Court and Times of James the First.* 2 vols. London: Colburn, 1849.

Wilson, Arthur. *The Life and Reign of James I.* London, 1653; ed. Kennet, 1706.

Winwood, Sir Ralph. *Memorials of Affairs of State ... Elizabeth and King James I.* London: Ward, 1725.

Woods, Susanne, ed., *The Poems of Aemilia Lanyer.* Oxford: Oxford Univ. Press, 1993.

WROTH, MARY SIDNEY. *The Countesse of Mountgomeries Urania.* London, [1621]. *See also* Roberts, ed., *Poems* (1983).

—. *Love's Victory.* See Huntington Library MS HM 600; and Roberts, ed., *Poems* (1983).

—. *Pamphilia to Amphilanthus.* In *The Countesse of Mountgomeries Urania.* London, 1621. (*See also* Folger Shakespeare Lib., MS V.a.104).

—. *The Countesse of Mountgomeries Urania.* London, 1621. *See also* Roberts, ed. (1995).

First Line Index

Extracts are indexed only for the women poets.

Names Index

Acknowledgments

Women's Works, volumes 1-4, is the product of twenty-five years' labor, with travel to more than thirty libraries and private collections in England, Scotland, Wales, Ireland, France, and the United States. Along the way, the project was developed by Vassar students, many of whom have since gone on to careers in academia or publishing. Special thanks are due to Prof. Joseph Walunywa (1988), Ms. Pamela Seay Appleby (1990), Ms. Karin Cook (1990), Prof. Elizabeth Rivlin (1992), Prof. John Paul Spiro (1996), and Ms. Lexa Hillyer (2002), who helped with primary research, transcription, editing, formatting, and fact-checking. Sarah Nelson (2005), Philosophy Walker (2008), and Erica Hersh (2010) assisted with correspondence and citations. Anastasia Stevens (2015) helped with the cover design. Baynard Bailey and Blake Foster provided expert assistance with Web design. The editors are much obliged. We owe a large debt to Prof. Christine Reno, who helped extensively with last-minute proof-reading and who caught many errors we had overlooked.

We are indebted to Emma Russell for her careful transcription and collation of the two manuscripts of "A Part of the Life of Margaret Cunningham." Special thanks are owing to Laetitia Yeandle, now retired but for many years Archivist at the Folger Shakespeare Library, and a great help with the Folger's manuscript collections. Also, to Sara Jayne Steen, editor of *The Letters of Arbella Stuart* (1994); Jamie Reid Baxter, editor of the *Poems of Elizabeth Melville, Lady Culross* (2010); Susanne Woods, editor of *The Poems of Aemilia Lanyer* (1993); Margaret Ferguson and Barry Weller, editors of *The Tragedy of Mariam the Fair Queen of Jewry* (1994); and Josephine Roberts, editor of *The Poems of Lady Mary Wroth* (1983) and *The First Part of The Countess of Montgomery's Urania* (1995); whose complete, thorough, and reliable editions are invaluable resources to all who care about the early women's tradition in English.

We are grateful as well to the many institutions that have provided access to original manuscripts, printed texts, and graphics. For the selections in Volume 3, special thanks are owing to the archivists and staff of the Beinecke Library (Yale), the Folger Shakespeare Library (Washington D.C.); the Huntington Library (San Marino); the Bodleian Library (Oxford); the British Library; the Public Record Office (Kew); and county record offices throughout England and Scotland. For permission to use artwork, the editors wish to thank the Scottish National Gallery (Edinburgh); the National Portrait Gallery, the British Architectural Library, and the Victoria and Albert Museum (London); Kenwood House (North London); Woburn Abbey (Bedfordshire); Abbot Hall Art Gallery (Kendal, Cumbria); Penshurst Place (Kent); Skipton Castle (Yorkshire); La Bibliothèque nationale de France (Paris); Galleria Spada (Rome); Galleria Palatina (Florence); National Palace Museum (Taipei); Folger Shakespeare Library (Washington, D.C.); the Milwaukee Art Museum; Wikipedia Commons; and a private U.K. collection. Invaluable digital resources have included Early English Books Online (Ann Arbor), and Perdita Manuscripts (Warwick and Nottingham Trent universities).

Women's Works has been funded by grants from the Mellon Foundation, the Ford Foundation; and by research support from Vassar Colllege.

A hearty communal thanks to our colleagues at Vassar, and at academic institutions across North America and the United Kingdom, who have read drafts and made thoughtful suggestions; and to our academic collaborators in the production of Wicked Good Books.

Enjoy!

DWF and TB (2013)

Front cover: portrait of Margaret Layton,
attributed to Marcus Gheeraerts, c. 1620
© Victoria and Albert Museum, London

Women's Works would have been impossible without the prior labor of others. The scholars and writers noted here have supplied facts, ideas, and source material. Many have shared their research or assisted with fact-checking. To all, many thanks:

Elizabeth Abel, Katherine Acheson, David Adams, Mark Amodio, Bernadette Andrea, Maya Angelou, Raymond Anselment, Margaret Arnold, Kate Aughterson, David Baldwin, Ariane Balizet, Linda Bamber, Carol Barash, Irice Baron, Alexandra Barratt, Emily Bartels, Madeline Bassnett, Jamie Reid Baxter, Charles Beem, Elaine Beilin, Alexandra Bennett, Pamela Iona Bell, Joseph Benson, R. Howard Bloch, Lynda Boose, Diane Bornstein, Keith Botelho, Barbara Bowen, Emily Bowles-Smith, Virginia Brackett, Catherine Brennan, Michael Brennan, Karen Britland, Cedric Brown, Robert Bucholz, Glyn Burgess, Irene Burgess, Victoria Burke, Deborah Burks, F.D.A. Burns, Catherine Burroughs, Keith Busby, Martin Butler, Caroline Bynum, Patricia Cahill, Julie D. Campbell, Jennifer Lee Carrell, Clare Carroll, Jane Cartwright, Jocelyn Catty, Jean Cavanaugh, Sheila Cavanagh, S.P. Cerasano, Jane Chance, Danielle Clarke, Elizabeth Clarke, John Considine, Thomas Corns, Marguérite Corporaal, Julie Crawford, Patricia Crawford, Eugene Cunnar, Karen Cunningham, Peter Davidson, Norman Davis, Leanda De Lisle, Mary DeShazer, Carolyn Dinshaw, Michael Ditmore, Frances Dolan, Jane Donahue Eberwein, Michelle Dowd, Martha Driver, Peter Dronke, Heather Dubrow, Jane Dunn, Sarah Dunnigan, Mary Eagleton, Jacqueline Eales, Julie Early, John Edwards, Laurie Ellinghausen, Robert C. Evans, Margaret Ezell, Susan Felch, Margaret Ferguson, Joan Ferrante, Nona Fienberg, Iva Figes, Alison Findlay, Caitlyn Finlayson, James Fitzmaurice, Angus Fletcher, Julia Fox, Antonia Fraser, Arthur Freeman, Susan Frye, John Garrison, Margaret George, Claire Gheeraert-Graffeuille, B.J. Gibbons, Jonathan Gibson, Sandra Gilbert, Marion Glasscoe, Suzanne Gossett, Melinda Gough, Laura Gowing, Katie Gramich, Catharine Gray, Nerys Ann Howells, Amy Greenstadt, Germaine Greer, Phillipa Gregory, Erin Griffey, Marshall Grossman, Isobel Grundy, Susan Gubar, Nancy Gutierrez, Judith Haber, Heidi Brayman Hackel, Elizabeth Hageman, Anita Hagerman, Kim Hall, Pamela Hammons, Margaret Hannay, Robert Hanning, Elizabeth Hansom, Cathy Hartley, Susan Hastings, Jane Hedley, Jennifer L Heller, Diana Henderson, Katherine Usher Henderson, Margo Hendricks, Cynthia Herrup, Caroline Hibbard, Eleanor Hibbert, Jennifer Higginbotham, Susan Higginbotham, Anne Hildebrand, Elaine Hobby, Barbara Hodgdon, Stephanie Hodgson-Wright, Lisa Hopkins, Jean Howard, Cynthia Huff, Jennett Humphreys, Heidi Hutner, Lorna Hutson, Eric Ives, Frances James, Sharon Jansen, Dafydd Johnston, Michael K. Jones, Kathleen Jordan, David Scott Kastan, David Kathman, N.H. Keeble, Nely Keinanen, Sean Kelsey, Angus Kennedy, Gwynne Kennedy, Newton Key, Younkyung Kim, Arthur Kinney, Noel Kinnamon, Clare Kinney, Victoria Kirkham, Jean Klene, Rebecca Krug, Chris Kyle, Mary Ellen Lamb, Ian Lancashire, Rebecca Laroche, Katherine Larson, Jin-Ah Lee, Jongsook Lee, Barbara Kiefer Lewalski, Keith Lindley, Margaret Lloyd, Nora Lofts, Paula Loscocco, Ben Lowe, Christina Luckyj, Liz Herbert McAvoy, Kari Boyd McBride, William McCarthy, Anita McConnell, Kristen McDermott, Barbara *McManus*, Lynne Magnusson, Nadia Margolis, Zoltan Markus, Helen Marlborough, Priscilla Martin, Randall Martin, Helen Maurer, Stephen May, Elizabeth Mazzola, Heather Meakin, Carol Meale, Jeslyn Medoff, Sara Mendelson, Stephanie Merrim, G.J. Meyer, Marianne Micros, Jacqueline Miller, Naomi Miller, Nancy Weitz Miller, Jill Seal Millman, Toril Moi, William Monter, Deborah Montuori, Janel Mueller, Jessica Murphy, Anne M. Myers, J.E. Neale, Karen Nelson, Miranda Garno Nesler, David Norbrook, Marianne Novy, Michael O'Connell, Elisa Oh, Arlene Okerlund, Susan G. O'Malley, Stephen Orgel, Lena Cowen Orlin, Anita Pacheco, Helen Ostovich, John Ottenhoff, Anita Pacheco, George Parfitt, Pamela Corpron Parker, Elizabeth Patton, Helen Payne, Patricia Pender, Thomas Penn, Régine Pernoud, Patricia Phillippy, Joanna Picciotto, Meg Powers Livingston, Linda Porter, Anne Lake Prescott, Roger Prior, Diane Purkiss, Maureen Quilligan, Ayesha Ramachandran, James Ramey, Christine Reno, Judith Richards, Claire Ridgway, Anna Riehl, William Ringler, Elizabeth Rivlin, Josephine Roberts, Karen Robertson, Mark Robson, Katharine Rogers, Mary Beth Rose, Margaret Rosenthal, Laura Runge, Joanna Russ, Jesse Russell, Paul Salzman, Melissa Sanchez, Arnie Sanders, Julie Sanders, Amelia Zurcher Sandy, Melinda Sansome, Louise Schleiner, Roy Schreiber, Kimberly Schutte, Sharon Seelig, L.E. Semler, Desmond Seward, Anne Shaver, Lauren Shohet, Elaine Showalter, Elizabeth Skerpan-Wheeler, Nigel Smith, Rosalind Smith, Anne Somerset, Patrica M. Spacks, Richard Spence, Jane Spencer, Dale Spender, Harriet Spiegel, John-Paul Spiro, Liberty Stanavage, Kay Stanton, Nathan Comfort Starr, Sara Jayne Steen, Jane Stevenson, Kirilka Stavreva, Matthew Steggle, Barbara Taft, Ayanna Thompson, Audrey Tinkham, Janet Todd, Sophie Eliza Tomlinson, Valerie Traub, Betty Travitsky, Giles Tremlett, Suzanne Trill, Mary Trull, Amos Tubb, Deborah Uman, Malcolm Underwood, Steven Urkowitz, Linda Vecchi, Geraldine Wagner, Alison Wall, Wendy Wall, Gary Waller, Retha Warnicke, Joseph Walunywa, Robin Warren, Diane Watt, Valerie Wayne, Alison Weir, Barry Weller, Christopher Whitfield, Barbara Wiedemann, Anna Whitelock, Helen Wilcox, Charity Cannon Willard, Gweno Williams, Katharina Wilson, B.A. Windeatt, Brandon Withrow, Heather Wolfe, Susanne Woods, Ramona Wray, Jillian Wright, Marion Wynne-Davies, Laetitia Yeandle, Samantha Zacher, Georgianna *Ziegler*, and Judith Zinsser. *Thank you!*

New Titles from Wicked Good Books

Every retail copy sold of every WGB title supports a top-listed charity of the author or editor's choice

TRUE SHAKESPEARE

The four greatest stories ever told, edited by Alf Dotson

Othello l'Amour, by Christopher Marlowe. From the Jamestown Shakespeare Manuscripts comes the first hard-boiled detective story ever written and possibly the most thrilling. In 1588, in Venice, the daughter of a white senator eloped with the commander of the armed forces, an African, and fled to the island of Crete. Her father, Signore Brabantio, hired Christopher Marlowe (1564-1593)—poet, university wit, playwright, atheist, homosexual, and government agent—to find the doll and bring her home. Here is a tough-guy case that has it all—scandal, gold, pearls, a magic totem, a doting patriarch, a husband war-hero, a cross-dressed lover, a rosy-cheeked boy, a femme fatale, a stupid constable, ethical ambiguities, and five violent deaths in one night—all five cases being solved before breakfast. Edited for 21st century gumshoes by Alf Dotson.

ISBN-10: 0-9882820-2-X
ISBN-13: 978-0-9882820-2-5
xxii, 202 pp.

The Taming of the Pooch, by Isabella Sforza, Lady Porcigliano, is the earliest and quite possibly the greatest paperback girl-takes-charge romance of all time—witty, warm, and scrumptious. Written in 1555 by Lady Porcigliano and translated by Anne Cook Bacon, the *Taming of the Pooch* touches upon the countess's love affair with the Renaissance humorist, Hortensio Lando; but her story features the courtship of Caterina di Baptista of Padua, a romantic who teaches her husband everything that every woman ever wished her man knew about love. Recovered at last from the dustbin of patriarchalist history, Lady Porcigliano's *Taming* may be the most transformative woman's romance since Adam and Eve. Also, the funniest. Edited by Alf Dotson from the Jamestown Shakespeare Manuscripts.

ISBN-10: 0988282054
ISBN-13: 978-0-9882820-5-6
xxiv, 236 pp.

The True Mystery of Hamlet, by [Thomas] Watson. From the newly discovered Jamestown Shakespeare Manuscripts comes a 100% solution to the greatest mystery ever conceived by the mind of man: *Hamlet, Prince of Denmark.* The historical Sherlock Homes (a hero noted in Holinshed's *Chronicles*—not to be confused with Holmes, his fictional namesake) investigates the deaths of Prince Hamlet's father and uncle, the queen mother, Hamlet's school chums, his girlfriend, his girlfriend's father and brother, and of the sulky prince himself. Homes plucks the heart from Hamlet's mystery long before Sigmund Freud traced the young hero's strange fixation to an unresolved Oedipal Complex. Edited for 21st century sleuths by Alf Dotson.

ISBN-10: 0-9882820-4-6
ISBN-13: 978-0-9882820-4-9
xxii, 147 pp.

Romeo, plus Juliet, by Friar Lorenzo Frier (1503-1555): the autobiographical tale of a mad friar, a fair youth, and the dark lady who came between them. Begun in 1550 by Friar Frier (as a memoir of his sportive adolescence in Umbertide, Italy), the romance takes a dark turn as Frier seeks to justify his tragic infatuation, as a Catholic priest in his late forties, with a teenager of Verona named Romeo Montague. Edited by Alf Dotson from the Jamestown Shakespeare Manuscripts.

ISBN-10: 0988282070
ISBN-13: 978-0-9882820-7-0
xix, 183 pp.

How to Write
Not Your Usual User's Guide to the English Language
Ed. A. P. English

EVER WONDER why you get *B*s (or worse) on your classroom writing? why you get poor reviews (or none) for your blog and your published books? why your letters to the editor go unpublished? your job-applications go unrewarded? your love-letters go unrequited? Here's why: you may know how to write, but you don't know *How to Write*. At long last, from Wicked Good Books, comes a writer's guide worth reading, a book for those who need to write well compiled by those who already do. Most writing manuals are tedious and often wrong. *How to Write* compresses the wisdom and expertise of best-selling authors and educators into a single witty and indispensable volume, a book that should never be far from your nightstand or writing desk.

How to Write comes in four sections, beginning with part one, "The Ten Commandments." Memorize them. Then just follow the easy steps (also supplied) for writing original works of incredible genius.

Part two, "How do they *do* that?" unfolds the wisdom of the ages concerning the kinds of writing you are most often asked to do for others, whether in the classroom or at work or in the book industry.

Part three, "Write or Wrong," is a guide to words, thereby to prevent you from emulating the many scholars, athletes, and presidents before you who have made fritters of the English language.

Part four, "Index and Ready Reference" directs you, in a jiff, where to go, within *How to Write,* for the help you need.

ISBN-10: 0-9882820-1-1
ISBN-13: 978-0-9882820-1-8
xxi, 231 pp.

Coming soon from Wicked Good Books:

THE PLAYER'S SHAKESPEARE

Surprising but true: until The Player's Shakespeare came along—four centuries overdue—directors, actors, and drama students have had to depend on editions of Shakespeare's plays that were prepared by literary scholars for use in English classes. Each new volume, whether in cloth or paperback, has tended to repeat the mistakes made by previous editors. Entrances and exits are mismarked. Speeches are sometimes assigned to the wrong character. Bodies of the slain are left on stage with no signal given when the corpse is to be carried off. No thought is given to the relationship between the Shakespearean script and the venue in which the play may be performed. Laugh-lines are overlooked, becoming throwaway lines. The editorial "glosses"—those definitions and paraphrases at the bottom of the page—are often wrong, usually reductive, and always conservative. Dramaturgy, staging, set design, casting, doubled roles, cross-dressing, costume notes, landmark productions, receive at best a few perfunctory remarks from Shakespeare's literary editors.

The Player's Shakespeare—in the pipeline for 2017—will present Shakespeare's most popular plays in script format, in a reliable text, with notes on meter and delivery, staging, and stage history. Illustrations from past and recent productions appear on the verso (lefthand page), together with the notes. The glosses and stage directions—based on 400 years of experience in the theater—are fresh, helpful, and accurate, but never prescriptive.

The Player's Shakespeare, collaboratively edited by a team of experts—scholars, dramaturges, and actors—promises to supply the definitive acting script of Shakespeare's plays for today's theater, and for generations to come.

In the pipeline for 2015/6: *As You Like It, Macbeth, The Merchant of Venice, A Midsummer Night's Dream, Much Ado About Nothing, Henry IV Part 1, Othello, Richard III, The Tempest.*

Visit wicked-good-books.com for more information.